סדור תפילות ישראל

THE HIRSCH SIDDUR

THE ORDER OF PRAYERS FOR THE WHOLE YEAR

Translation and Commentary
by
SAMSON RAPHAEL HIRSCH

סדור תפילות ישראל

THE HIRSCH SIDDUR

THE ORDER OF PRAYERS FOR THE WHOLE YEAR

Translation and Commentary

by

SAMSON RAPHAEL HIRSCH

New, thoroughly corrected edition

THE SAMSON RAPHAEL HIRSCH PUBLICATIONS SOCIETY

FELDHEIM PUBLISHERS
Jerusalem • New York
5738   1978

ISBN 0 87306 142 x

Copyright © 1969, 1978 by

FELDHEIM PUBLISHERS, Ltd.
POB 6525 / Jerusalem, Israel

Distributed in the United States of America by

PHILIPP FELDHEIM, INC.
"THE HOUSE OF THE JEWISH BOOK"
96 East Broadway, New York 10002

ביצוע א.ג.פ. שרותים לאופסט, ירושלים

Printed in Israel

THIS NEW EDITION
OF THE HIRSCH SIDDUR WAS MADE POSSIBLE
BY A GRANT FROM

Mr. and Mrs. JACQUES SCHWALBE

IN HONOR OF

Rabbi Dr. JOSEPH BREUER

התכן

מבוא

This introduction will help the reader to gain a proper evaluation of Rabbi S. R. Hirsch's Commentary to the Prayers. There is no lack of commentaries to our תפלה, our "national treasure", which accompanied our people through the millennia of its history. What distinguishes this commentary is its central purpose of analyzing the qualities which bestow upon our "Prayers" their lofty significance.

Three times daily we are called upon to pray. This mere fact makes it impossible to identify the term תפלה as "prayer". For "prayer" is בקשה, תחנה, emanating naturally from the heart; and it would only be proper to leave it to the needs of the individual to ask for בקשה. Such בקשה must be offered in the firm knowledge that God will hear it. What gives us the right to such certainty? Is not God, Creator and Master of the universe, far too exalted to even listen to the prayer of an anxious human heart?

The right to such "prayer" must be earned. The path to this goal is paved by our תפלה. תפלה (from which derives התפלל) requires that we imbue ourselves (בלל — פלל) ever anew with the great truth and demands which must place their stamp upon our Jewish existence and consciousness. Above all, our תפלות contain תהלות : הלל, to radiate, הלל (Piel), to reflect rays. Applied from the example of the sun, this means: While God is not visible to us, we perceive the radiations of His Omnipotence in the infinite evidences of wonder which permit us to find God. To confess and proclaim this thought in words of homage — this is תהלה, the recognition of God. However, תהלה would be empty and meaningless were it not to inspire us with ברכה — dedication, the determination to "bless" God, i. e. to further the precepts of the Divine will as laid down in God's Torah, by virtue of their fulfillment.

If we are ready, permeated by יראה and אמונה and by the striving towards ever-greater sanctification of life (קדושה), to be guided through life by God (by accepting the עול מלכות שמים to which we are called upon by the daily שמע) — then we will secure for ourselves קרבת ה', the proximity of God; then God will be our גואל and we will have attained the right to the certainty that God "hears" us (שומע תפלה) when we stand before Him in שמנה עשרה three times daily. The Talmud calls the תפלה: שמנה עשרה despite the fact that it contains בקשות regarding our individual and national existence. Yet these בקשות are clothed in ברכות and this form is designed to teach us *how* to utter our בקשות: all that which we ask of God is to be dedicated to His service through ברכה; the fulfillment of our wishes we leave to His Almighty Will. Our daily תפלה aims to provide us with peace of mind and strength of life.

These basic ideas form the character of this Commentary which, for this reason, concentrates on the evaluation of קדיש, קדושה, ברכות. In the other areas of the תפלה it limits itself to the analysis of the main thoughts of the various parts of the תפלה. This Commentary was written in the assumption that the reader is familiar with the extensive research of the author's commentaries to תורה and תהלים. This is particularly true of the sections which contain the sacred order of the sacrifices. Here, the Commentary, despite its concise brevity, is in place because the עבודה in the Divine Sanctuary corresponds to the עבודה of our תפלה.

It was entirely proper to delay the (long overdue) publication of this Commentary (originally published after the death of the author) until the completion of the English editions of Hirsch's commentaries to תורה and תהלים. The latter, especially, forms a considerable part of our תפלה; the inclusion of the complete original commentary to the Psalms-passages in the תפלה would have consumed an amount of space incompatible with the concise character of this edition. This explains the brevity of this particular part of the Commentary. For a full understanding of these passages it is, therefore, highly advisable to refer to Hirsch's Psalms Commentary in the English translation.

In a veritable labor of love, Mr. Yaakov Feldheim, Jerusalem, has devoted himself to the preparation of this edition. He has earned the gratitude of a wide readership which enthusiastically welcomes this long-overdue publication of the English edition of this Commentary by the immortal teacher זצ"ל.

Rav Dr. Joseph Breuer

Rosh Chodesh Adar 5728

A SHORT BIOGRAPHY
OF SAMSON RAPHAEL HIRSCH

Under the impact of the political upheaval which followed in the wake of the French Revolution, and in the course of a profound re-evaluation of the cultural and spiritual values of the age, the early decades of the nineteenth century witnessed a gradual removal of the Jewish Ghetto walls. Until then, most of the Ghetto inhabitants had taken little part in the cultural life of the outside world. The influx of the revolutionary concepts of liberalism, individualism and humanism — which relegated religion to an equal footing with the secular life values — found many woefully unprepared. Ideas which had shaped Jewish thinking for untold centuries fell by the wayside. While some succumbed to outright baptism, others preferred to reform Judaism.

One of the chief centers of the reform movement was the German city of Hamburg where SAMSON RAPHAEL HIRSCH was born in 1808. From early youth, he was determined to join the ceaseless battle for the exposition and supremacy of Torah in Jewish life. The personality of his teacher, the great Hakham Bernays, who symbolized the new type of spiritual leader in Israel by the combination of profound Torah learning with a deep knowledge of modern philosophy and literature, left a powerful and lasting impact on his disciple.

In 1828, Hirsch left Hamburg to continue his talmudical studies at the Yeshiva of the Gaon Rabbi Jacob Ettlinger in Mannheim. His pre-eminence in Torah, Talmud and Codes was soon recognized and, after completing his secular studies at the Bonn University, he was called to fill the post of Chief Rabbi of Oldenburg left vacant by Rabbi Nathan Adler, also a disciple of Hakham Bernays. The Jewish community of Oldenburg mirrored the confusion and ignorance prevalent in the minds of the contemporary generation which substituted the idea of a wrongly conceived emancipation for the truth of historical Judaism.

Hirsch was not discouraged. He was convinced that ignorance of the precepts of Torah Judaism was the real source of the confusion which led to reformist aspirations. This, then, became the essence of his life's work: to reintroduce his generation, especially the youth, to the old, eternally new way of Torah-life, guided by a thorough understanding of the principles and details of the Jewish Law. To this end, he dedicated his epoch-making work, "HOREB, Essays on Israel's Duties in the Diaspora" (1838) addressed to "Israel's thinking young men and women". He introduced this work by publishing his famous "Nineteen Letters on Judaism" in which he raised the burning questions which confronted the younger generation. Its electrifying effect quickly paved the way for the publication of "HOREB".

In 1841 Hirsch assumed a new position in Emden where he continued his vigorous fight against the reform movement. Here, for the first time, he formulated the principle which was to become the rallying cry for Torah-true Jews everywhere : TORAH IM DEREKH ERETZ, the supremacy of Torah over whichever circumstances happen to prevail.

In 1846, having emerged as a Torah leader of world renown, Samson Raphael Hirsch accepted the post of Chief Rabbi of Moravia (part of the Austrian Empire) with Nikolsburg as central community. Here, he established a Yeshiva to which students flocked from all parts of the province. As a member of the Austrian Parliament, he became the leader in the fight for equal rights for the embattled Jews of Austria and Hungary.

Yet Hirsch was convinced that the future of his people depended not on its political status but on its spiritual power as centralized in its Kehillot and Yeshivot. With the true vision of a genius, he sensed the need of his work on other fronts. Only thus may we understand the nature of what has been called "the most heroic deed of his life" in resigning from his high and powerful office to accept a call from a tiny group of men in Frankfurt, Germany. The religious decline of this once proud Jewish community, birthplace of the Hatam Sofer, was truly apalling. In Frankfurt, the orthodox institutions were systematically undermined by the reform movement and ultimately abolished. It became a rarity to find a young man in Frankfurt who would still put on Tefillin. The sacred act of Brit Milah was attacked as a barbaric rite; public instruction in Torah was forbidden; Mikvaot were sealed up; Shekhita was prohibited.

The uprising of 1848 brought the first ray of hope to the few who still clung tenaciously to the precepts of Torah living. Eleven men received permission from the city to organize a private religious society (they were forbidden to be called "Congregation"). In a bold move, and without much hope for success, they turned to the famed Moravian Chief Rabbi, head of a network of Kehillot, member of Parliament, and offered him the obscure position of Rabbi in a tiny private religious society. Over the vigorous protests of his constituents, Hirsch accepted the offer which he envisioned as a divine call to a historic mission.

On assuming his new post in 1851, he plunged immediately into the work of building an exemplary, independent Kehilla (which he proclaimed as the rightful heir to the old Frankfurt Kehilla) which came to serve as a model and inspiration for similarly minded communities throughout the Jewish world. He established a school system which became the proto-type of the modern day school movement.

In Frankfurt, Hirsch resumed his literary work which was to continue until the end of his life. He founded "Jeschurun", a monthly in which he published hundreds of essays and articles containing his views on Torah and Judaism (subsequently gathered in six volumes of "Collected Writings"). In 1867 he began with the publication of his monumental work, "Commentary on the Pentateuch" which was followed by the famed "Commentary on the Psalms" and "Commentary on the Prayers".

In 1886, two years before his death, Hirsch founded the "Free Union for the Interests of Orthodox Judaism" which was dedicated to the fulfillment of the religious and spiritual tasks of world orthodoxy and the ultimate union of all orthodox Jews. This organization exerted an increasingly powerful influence and eventually became the blueprint for organized orthodox Jewry throughout the world.

סדור

תפלות ישראל

On entering the Synagogue:

וַאֲנִי בְּרֹב חַסְדְּךָ אָבֹא בֵיתֶךָ
אֶשְׁתַּחֲוֶה אֶל־הֵיכַל קָדְשְׁךָ בְּיִרְאָתֶךָ:

בְּבֵית אֱלֹהִים נְהַלֵּךְ בְּרָגֶשׁ:

After having entered the Synagogue:

מַה־טֹּבוּ אֹהָלֶיךָ יַעֲקֹב מִשְׁכְּנֹתֶיךָ יִשְׂרָאֵל: וַאֲנִי בְּרֹב חַסְדְּךָ
אָבֹא בֵיתֶךָ אֶשְׁתַּחֲוֶה אֶל־הֵיכַל קָדְשְׁךָ בְּיִרְאָתֶךָ: יְיָ אָהַבְתִּי
מְעוֹן בֵּיתֶךָ וּמְקוֹם מִשְׁכַּן כְּבוֹדֶךָ: וַאֲנִי אֶשְׁתַּחֲוֶה וְאֶכְרָעָה
אֶבְרְכָה לִפְנֵי־יְיָ עֹשִׂי: וַאֲנִי תְפִלָּתִי־לְךָ יְיָ עֵת רָצוֹן אֱלֹהִים
בְּרָב־חַסְדֶּךָ עֲנֵנִי בֶּאֱמֶת יִשְׁעֶךָ:

נקסה לרבי שלמה בן גבירול.

שַׁחַר אֲבַקֶּשְׁךָ · צוּרִי וּמִשְׂגַּבִּי · אֶעֱרֹךְ לְפָנֶיךָ · שַׁחֲרִי וְגַם־עַרְבִּי:
לִפְנֵי גְדֻלָּתְךָ · אֶעֱמֹד וְאֶבָּהֵל · כִּי־עֵינְךָ תִרְאֶה · כָּל־מַחְשְׁבוֹת לִבִּי:
מַה־זֶּה אֲשֶׁר יוּכַל · הַלֵּב וְהַלָּשׁוֹן לַעֲשׂוֹת, וּמַה־כֹּחִי · רוּחִי בְּתוֹךְ קִרְבִּי:
הִנֵּה לְךָ תִיטַב. זִמְרַת אֱנוֹשׁ, עַל־כֵּן אוֹדְךָ בְּעוֹד תִּהְיֶה · נִשְׁמַת אֱלוֹהַּ בִּי:

Before the morning prayer, it is customary to say the following:

אֲנִי קְרָאתִיךָ כִּי־תַעֲנֵנִי אֵל הַט־אָזְנְךָ לִי שְׁמַע אִמְרָתִי: אֲנִי
בְּצֶדֶק אֶחֱזֶה פָנֶיךָ אֶשְׂבְּעָה בְהָקִיץ תְּמוּנָתֶךָ: וַאֲנִי יְעָלֶיךָ בָטַחְתִּי
יְיָ אָמַרְתִּי אֱלֹהַי אָתָּה: שְׁמַע קוֹל תַּחֲנוּנַי בְּשַׁוְּעִי אֵלֶיךָ בְּנָשְׂאִי
יָדַי אֶל־דְּבִיר קָדְשֶׁךָ: יְיָ אֱלֹהָי שִׁוַּעְתִּי אֵלֶיךָ וַתִּרְפָּאֵנִי: אֵלֶיךָ יְיָ
אֶקְרָא וְאֶל־אֲדֹנָי אֶתְחַנָּן: הָאִירָה פָנֶיךָ עַל־עַבְדֶּךָ הוֹשִׁיעֵנִי

*)‏ אדני, כ"ה בכל כ"י וגם נמצא בהדי קל"ד וולחיין, וכן העיר הגאון בן חפני הונה
נם' אבודרהם וכן העלה המ"ש.

בְּחַסְדְּךָ׃ כִּי־לְךָ יְיָ הוֹחָלְתִּי אַתָּה תַעֲנֶה אֲדֹנָי אֱלֹהָי׃ שִׁמְעָה
תְפִלָּתִי יְיָ וְשַׁוְעָתִי הַאֲזִינָה אֶל־דִּמְעָתִי אַל־תֶּחֱרַשׁ׃ שְׁמַע־יְיָ וְחָנֵּנִי
יְיָ הֱיֵה ׀ עֹזֵר לִי ׃

שִׁיר הַמַּעֲלוֹת לְדָוִד שָׂמַחְתִּי בְּאֹמְרִים לִי בֵּית יְיָ נֵלֵךְ׃ עֹמְדוֹת
אֶנְבֵּי עַל־אֲמָרֶךָ כְּמוֹצֵא שָׁלָל רָב׃ הַקְשִׁיבָה לְקוֹל שַׁוְעִי מַלְכִּי
וֵאלֹהָי כִּי־אֵלֶיךָ אֶתְפַּלָּל׃ יְיָ בֹּקֶר תִּשְׁמַע קוֹלִי בֹּקֶר אֶעֱרָךְ־לְךָ
וַאֲצַפֶּה׃ אֲנִי קְרָאתִיךָ כִּי־תַעֲנֵנִי אֵל הַט־אָזְנְךָ לִי שְׁמַע אִמְרָתִי׃
רַגְלִי עָמְדָה בְמִישׁוֹר בְּמַקְהֵלִים אֲבָרֵךְ יְיָ׃

יִגְדַּל אֱלֹהִים חַי וְיִשְׁתַּבַּח נִמְצָא וְאֵין עֵת אֶל־מְצִיאוּתוֹ׃
אֶחָד וְאֵין יָחִיד כְּיִחוּדוֹ נֶעְלָם וְגַם אֵין סוֹף לְאַחְדּוּתוֹ׃
אֵין לוֹ דְּמוּת הַגּוּף וְאֵינוֹ גוּף לֹא נַעֲרוֹךְ אֵלָיו קְדֻשָּׁתוֹ׃
קַדְמוֹן לְכָל־דָּבָר אֲשֶׁר נִבְרָא רִאשׁוֹן וְאֵין רֵאשִׁית לְרֵאשִׁיתוֹ׃
הִנּוֹ אֲדוֹן עוֹלָם וְכָל־נוֹצָר יוֹרֶה גְּדֻלָּתוֹ וּמַלְכוּתוֹ׃
שֶׁפַע נְבוּאָתוֹ נְתָנוֹ אֶל־אַנְשֵׁי סְגֻלָּתוֹ וְתִפְאַרְתּוֹ׃
לֹא קָם בְּיִשְׂרָאֵל כְּמֹשֶׁה עוֹד נָבִיא וּמַבִּיט אֶת תְּמוּנָתוֹ׃
תּוֹרַת אֱמֶת נָתַן לְעַמּוֹ אֵל עַל־יַד נְבִיאוֹ נֶאֱמַן בֵּיתוֹ׃
לֹא יַחֲלִיף הָאֵל וְלֹא יָמִיר דָּתוֹ לְעוֹלָמִים לְזוּלָתוֹ׃
צוֹפֶה וְיוֹדֵעַ סְתָרֵינוּ מַבִּיט לְסוֹף דָּבָר בְּקַדְמָתוֹ׃
גּוֹמֵל לְאִישׁ חֶסֶד כְּמִפְעָלוֹ נוֹתֵן לְרָשָׁע רַע כְּרִשְׁעָתוֹ׃
יִשְׁלַח לְקֵץ יָמִין מְשִׁיחֵנוּ לִפְדּוֹת מְחַכֵּי קֵץ יְשׁוּעָתוֹ׃
מֵתִים יְחַיֶּה אֵל בְּרֹב חַסְדּוֹ בָּרוּךְ עֲדֵי־עַד שֵׁם תְּהִלָּתוֹ׃

אֲדוֹן עוֹלָם אֲשֶׁר מָלַךְ ‧ בְּטֶרֶם כָּל־יְצִיר נִבְרָא:
לְעֵת נַעֲשָׂה בְחֶפְצוֹ כֹּל ‧ אֲזַי מֶלֶךְ שְׁמוֹ נִקְרָא:
וְאַחֲרֵי כִּכְלוֹת הַכֹּל ‧ לְבַדּוֹ יִמְלוֹךְ נוֹרָא:
וְהוּא הָיָה וְהוּא הֹוֶה ‧ וְהוּא יִהְיֶה בְּתִפְאָרָה:
וְהוּא אֶחָד וְאֵין שֵׁנִי ‧ לְהַמְשִׁיל לוֹ לְהַחְבִּירָה:
בְּלִי רֵאשִׁית בְּלִי תַכְלִית ‧ וְלוֹ הָעֹז וְהַמִּשְׂרָה:
וְהוּא אֵלִי וְחַי גֹּאֲלִי ‧ וְצוּר חֶבְלִי בְּעֵת צָרָה:
וְהוּא נִסִּי וּמָנוֹס לִי ‧ מְנָת כּוֹסִי בְּיוֹם אֶקְרָא:
בְּיָדוֹ אַפְקִיד רוּחִי ‧ בְּעֵת אִישַׁן וְאָעִירָה:
וְעִם־רוּחִי גְּוִיָּתִי ‧ יְיָ לִי וְלֹא אִירָא:

בָּרוּךְ אַתָּה יְיָ אֱלֹהֵינוּ מֶלֶךְ הָעוֹלָם אֲשֶׁר קִדְּשָׁנוּ בְּמִצְוֹתָיו
וְצִוָּנוּ עַל נְטִילַת יָדָיִם:

אדון We recall to ourselves the independent nature of His essence and
of His greatness (Verses 1-3), His eternity, His uniqueness, His infinity
and His majesty (Verses 4-6). Remembering all this, we are confident
that this One and Unique Being, though His glory is infinite, is still so
very near, that each of us may call Him his own God, the sole source
of his life and strength. From the infinite source of His own Being, God
gives to each man a portion in life and delivers him from death and
nonentity. He sustains him in times of trouble; He is his guide and his
refuge. It is His nearness which man seeks as the only "good" when he
calls upon God to be gracious unto him. It is to the protection and guidance
of His hand that man, sleeping or awake, entrusts both his body and his
spirit, and knows no fear (Verses 7-10). מלך We can think of God as
King, with all royal power and majesty, even without the existence of a
world over which to reign. His Being gained nothing by His creation of
the world, nor would His Being lose anything if He were to allow all
that He created to recede into non-existence once again. Only His creatures,
by being alive, gain the ability to be aware of their Creator and Lord,
and are given the opportunity to worship Him. ואחרי ככלות as in אחרי כאשר יצאו

1. The Lord of the world, Who was King before any creature was formed. 2. At the time when all came into being by His will, His name was proclaimed King. 3. And even after all things shall have come to an end, He alone, awesome, will remain King. 4. And He was, and He is, and He will be in glory. 5. And He is one, and there is no second to compare with Him, to place beside Him. 6. Without beginning, without end, and His is the power and the dominion. 7. And He is my God, my living Redeemer, a Rock in my travail at the time of distress. 8. He is my Banner and my Refuge, the portion of my cup when I call. 9. To His hand I entrust my spirit, when I sleep and when I wake. 10. And with my spirit, my body also. *God* is with me; I shall not be afraid.

Blessed be You *God,* our God, King of the Universe, Who has sanctified us by His commandments, and commanded us concerning the washing of the hands.

(Joshua 2:7). נורא This thought, that God could destroy the world at any moment without any loss to His own Being, is of most awesome solemnity, and makes God the Only Being Whom all men alike must fear. להמשיל לו להחבירה Nothing is comparable to God, nor shares His dominion. חי גואלי He delivers us as חי, because He is חי and has given us a share in His own חיים, and His own immortality. צור חבלי It is from Him that we derive the strength to persevere and survive through all our sufferings. נס is the banner which serves as a guide along our way. כוס ׳is an allegorical term to describe fate (see Psalms 16:5). מנת כוסי God, the awareness of His protecting and guiding presence is the greatest favor, indeed the only truly blessed "good", which I seek.

ברוך "Blessed be You"; that is, "I pledge myself to fulfill Your will". קדשנו במצותיו It is God's will that, by fulfilling His commandments, we become ever more "holy", i.e. ever better morally, ever higher above all that is base and evil, and receptive to all that is good and sacred. וצונו The fulfillment of Rabbinical ordinances, such as this ritual washing of the hands, is also enjoined upon us by God's command. (See Commentary to Deut. 17:11). נטילת ידים The washing of hands upon awakening in the morning, in addition to its sanitary importance, also serves to "dedicate" our hands, and, through them, our whole physical being, which merely vegetated during the hours of sleep, for a life of renewed active service of God. Similarly, the priest had to consecrate himself for Divine service

בָּרוּךְ אַתָּה יְיָ אֱלֹהֵינוּ מֶלֶךְ הָעוֹלָם אֲשֶׁר יָצַר אֶת־הָאָדָם
בְּחָכְמָה וּבָרָא בוֹ נְקָבִים נְקָבִים חֲלוּלִים חֲלוּלִים גָּלוּי וְיָדוּעַ לִפְנֵי
כִסֵּא כְבוֹדֶךָ שֶׁאִם יִפָּתֵחַ אֶחָד מֵהֶם אוֹ יִסָּתֵם אֶחָד מֵהֶם אִי
אֶפְשַׁר לְהִתְקַיֵּם וְלַעֲמוֹד לְפָנֶיךָ : בָּרוּךְ אַתָּה יְיָ רוֹפֵא כָל־
בָּשָׂר וּמַפְלִיא לַעֲשׂוֹת :

בָּרוּךְ אַתָּה יְיָ אֱלֹהֵינוּ מֶלֶךְ הָעוֹלָם אֲשֶׁר קִדְּשָׁנוּ בְּמִצְוֹתָיו
וְצִוָּנוּ לַעֲסוֹק בְּדִבְרֵי תוֹרָה :

---

in the Temple by washing his hands (Exod. 30:20). Such a sanctifying "washing of the hands", is called נטילת ידים literally, a "lifting up" of the hands, from נטל, Aramaic for נשא. The hands are "lifted up", as it were, from the level of lower, purely physical nature to their higher moral purpose.

ברוך The gratification of a bodily need, so essential for the preservation of health, brings to our minds the wonderful wisdom which is manifested in the formation of the human body with its manifold orifices and cavities. Orifices, viz. the mouth, nose and excretory passages; cavities, viz. the internal organs which fulfill the functions of respiration and digestion— the trachea, the esophagus, the viscera, the intestines, etc. Should one of these openings be closed or the wall of one of these cavities be pierced, the physical existence of the person would be jeopardized and he could no longer live a life of active service in God's presence. עמד לפני always expresses a position of servitude, the master-servant relationship of an inferior to a superior. So was Joshua before Moses—Deut. 1:38, Elijah and Elisha before God—I Kings 17:1; 18:15, II Kings 3:14 et al.) This fact is well known to Divine Providence, גלוי לפני כסא כבוד, and He has taken it into account, ידוע. Hence, each time we thus satisfy one of our essential bodily needs, we renew our pledge to serve God, ברוך, the Preserver of physical health, רופא כל בשר (Cf. Exod. 15:26), Who is מפליא לעשות, Who in such a wonderful manner, has linked the non-physical, spiritual essence of the soul with the physical body, and has made the existence and the efficacy of the former dependent upon the continued good health of the latter.

ברוך This ברכה before the study of the תורה, be it the Written Torah (תשב״כ) or the Oral Torah (תשב״ם), may well be the most important of all the ברכות. As surely as the study of the תורה is the most primary and essential prerequisite for its fulfillment, so, too, the spirit in which we study it, the attitude we have toward its value and purpose, and the aim we have in mind can certainly not be a matter of indifference. Only if

Blessed be You *God,* our God, King of the Universe, Who
has formed man in wisdom and created in him manifold orifices
and cavities. It is revealed and known before the Throne of Your
glory that if one of them be opened, or one of them be closed,
it would be impossible to keep alive and to stand before Your
countenance. Blessed be You *God,* Healer of all flesh and doing
wonders.

Blessed be You *God* our God, King of the Universe, Who
has sanctified us with His commandments and commanded us to
engage in the study of the words of the Teaching.

---

we take the Torah to heart and study it as God's תורה, given to us by
God for the engendering of proper thoughts, emotions, resolutions, speech
and actions which find favor in His eyes, in order that we may arrange
our whole lives in His service, only then are we able to acquire the proper
understanding, are we able to lead a good life before God. If it is not
this proper attitude that motivates us to study the תורה, if we are not
imbued with this spirit, then Torah study may fail to achieve its true
purpose, which is the sanctification of life on the basis of the תורה. Even
worse, such misuse of the Torah may actually bring about the opposite
result. In the ברוך of ברכת התורה, we pledge, therefore, that we will
conceive of the study of the תורה as a מצוה the purpose of which is
sanctification and that we will also "bless" God through the very act
of studying. In other words, we promise to study in such a manner that,
with our study and as a result of our study, the will of God will be
fulfilled in every aspect of our lives, public and private. It can readily
be understood why our Sages (Nedarim 81a) attribute the failure of
the Torah to be transmitted to the sons of ח"ת, and our national ruin in
general, to the fact that אין מברכין בתורה תחילה, that they did not approach
the study of the Torah in the proper spirit, and that therefore their study
could not result in true salvation, but rather the reverse, (v. ר"ן ibid.). (The
fact that שלא ברכו בתורה תחלה is indicated in the statement נתתי אשר תורתי עזבם
לפניהם (Jeremiah 9:12). The Torah given *to* them for fulfillment is
indicated by אשר נתתי להם. But לפניהם indicates the Torah placed *before them,*
lying *before them* for their adoption and study. Because they did not approach this study with the proper spirit and attitude, expressed in the
ברכת התורה prior to studying, therefore their study did not lead to proper
fulfillment לעסוק בדברי תורה (ולא שמעו בקולי ולא הלכו בה) includes much more
than the mere attention to the words. It embraces also the transmitted explanations, as well as attention to the concepts, motives and inferences.

וְהַעֲרֶב־נָא יְיָ אֱלֹהֵינוּ אֶת דִּבְרֵי תוֹרָתְךָ בְּפִינוּ וּבְפִי עַמְּךָ
בֵּית יִשְׂרָאֵל וְנִהְיֶה אֲנַחְנוּ וְצֶאֱצָאֵינוּ וְצֶאֱצָאֵי עַמְּךָ בֵּית יִשְׂרָאֵל
כֻּלָּנוּ יוֹדְעֵי שְׁמֶךָ וְלוֹמְדֵי תוֹרָתֶךָ (לִשְׁמָהּ) בָּרוּךְ אַתָּה יְיָ הַמְלַמֵּד
תּוֹרָה לְעַמּוֹ יִשְׂרָאֵל: בָּרוּךְ אַתָּה יְיָ אֱלֹהֵינוּ מֶלֶךְ הָעוֹלָם אֲשֶׁר
בָּחַר־בָּנוּ מִכָּל־הָעַמִּים וְנָתַן לָנוּ אֶת תּוֹרָתוֹ בָּרוּךְ אַתָּה יְיָ
נוֹתֵן הַתּוֹרָה:

יְבָרֶכְךָ יְיָ וְיִשְׁמְרֶךָ: יָאֵר יְיָ ו פָּנָיו אֵלֶיךָ וִיחֻנֶּךָ: יִשָּׂא יְיָ ו פָּנָיו
אֵלֶיךָ וְיָשֵׂם לְךָ שָׁלוֹם: אֵלּוּ דְבָרִים שֶׁאֵין לָהֶם שִׁעוּר הַפֵּאָה
וְהַבִּכּוּרִים וְהָרָאֵיוֹן וּגְמִילוּת חֲסָדִים וְתַלְמוּד תּוֹרָה: אֵלּוּ דְבָרִים
שֶׁאָדָם אוֹכֵל פֵּרוֹתֵיהֶם בָּעוֹלָם הַזֶּה וְהַקֶּרֶן קַיֶּמֶת לוֹ לָעוֹלָם הַבָּא:
וְאֵלּוּ הֵן כִּבּוּד אָב וָאֵם וּגְמִילוּת חֲסָדִים וְהַשְׁכָּמַת בֵּית הַמִּדְרָשׁ
שַׁחֲרִית וְעַרְבִית וְהַכְנָסַת אוֹרְחִים וּבִקּוּר חוֹלִים וְהַכְנָסַת כַּלָּה
וּלְוָיַת הַמֵּת וְעִיּוּן תְּפִלָּה וַהֲבָאַת שָׁלוֹם בֵּין אָדָם לַחֲבֵרוֹ וְתַלְמוּד
תּוֹרָה כְּנֶגֶד כֻּלָּם:

והערב נא. May the heart and mind find "sweet" nourishment through
this occupation with the תורה; that is, spiritual food which will be appropriate and pleasant for the heart and mind, enlightening and ennobling
both, so that this pursuit may become for us the most loved and happiest
activity, and our enthusiasm for it be passed on to our children and
children's children. בפינו. In the Holy Scriptures Torah-study is always
related to פה, to the living, spoken word. Thus we read לא ימוש ספר התורה
הזה מפיך (Joshua 1:8). For the proper understanding depends on תשב״פ
and study itself always presupposes a gathering of a study group or of
teachers and students who discuss the material together. יודעי שמך The
knowledge of the Divine Name means the knowledge of that which God
has revealed to us concerning Himself, concerning His will which is executed
in His reign, and which we must fulfill in our lives. למוד תורה לשמה denotes
the study of the Torah in the only spirit that is pleasing to God, namely,
with the pure intention to understand and to fulfill His will ללמוד ללמד לשמור
המלמד תורה.ולעשות Even as we are in need of God's help if we are faithfully
to fulfill His Law—and we may be sure of such assistance—so must we

Cause the words of Your Teaching, *God* our God, to be sweet in our mouth and in the mouth of Your people, the House of Yisrael, so that we and our descendants, and the descendants of Your people, the House of Yisrael, may all know Your Name and study Your Teaching for its own sake. Blessed be You *God,* Who teaches His Teaching to His people Yisrael.

Blessed be You *God,* our God, King of the Universe, Who has chosen us from all the peoples and given us His Teaching. Blessed be You *God,* Giver of the Teaching.

May *God* bless you and keep you. May *God* cause His countenance to shine upon you and be gracious to you. May *God* lift His countenance to you and establish peace for you.

These are things which have no fixed limit : the corner of the field, the first-fruits, attendance in the Temple, the practice of human kindness, and Torah-study.

These are things of which man enjoys the fruits in this life, and the stock remains for him in the life to come : namely, honoring parents, the practice of human kindness, early attendance at the house of study mornings and evenings, hospitality, visiting the sick, dowering the bride, attending the dead to the grave, devotion in prayer, and making peace between man and his fellow, but the study of the Torah equals them all.

---

also have His guidance for the proper and successful study of the Torah; and here, too, we may be sure of His assistance. If we will study His Torah in the spirit of עַמּוֹ יִשְׂרָאֵל, as members of a national entity created by Him, a people shaping its entire life, private and public, in accordance with the pronouncements of His will, then He will be to us מְלַמֵּד תּוֹרָה לְעַמּוֹ יִשְׂרָאֵל. אֲשֶׁר בָּחַר בָּנוּ : from the very beginning, His purpose in electing us was to give us His Torah, to make us its bearers, students and executors (Exod. 3:12). Our entire historical significance among the nations stands and falls by the manner in which we cultivate and cherish the Torah in our midst. Should we ever cease to know the Torah, or to fulfill it, we should also cease to have a place among mankind.

יְבָרֶכְךָ This is the Priestly Blessing prescribed in Num. 6:24–26. יְבָרֶכְךָ וְיִשְׁמְרֶךָ : God's blessing and preservation of physical and material possessions. יָאֵר פָּנָיו : indicates the goals which God envisions, the aims of His providence which are to be achieved through you. He reveals these goals to you through the word of His Law and the words of His prophets. וִיחֻנֶּךָּ: and may He endow you with the spiritual capacity to recognize them and

אֱלֹהַי נְשָׁמָה שֶׁנָּתַתָּ בִּי טְהוֹרָה הִיא אַתָּה בְרָאתָהּ אַתָּה
יְצַרְתָּהּ אַתָּה נְפַחְתָּהּ בִּי וְאַתָּה מְשַׁמְּרָהּ בְּקִרְבִּי וְאַתָּה עָתִיד
לִטְּלָהּ מִמֶּנִּי וּלְהַחֲזִירָהּ בִּי לֶעָתִיד לָבֹא : כָּל־זְמַן שֶׁהַנְּשָׁמָה
בְקִרְבִּי מוֹדֶה אֲנִי לְפָנֶיךָ יְיָ אֱלֹהַי וֵאלֹהֵי אֲבוֹתַי רִבּוֹן כָּל־
הַמַּעֲשִׂים אֲדוֹן כָּל־הַנְּשָׁמוֹת בָּרוּךְ אַתָּה יְיָ הַמַּחֲזִיר נְשָׁמוֹת
לִפְגָרִים מֵתִים :

to understand them properly. יֵשָׂא: May He make you the ultimate goal
for the purposes of His providence, and may He arrange all the rest of
the world in harmonious relation to you.

אֵלּוּ דְבָרִים שֶׁאֵין לָהֶם שִׁעוּר. This is the first sentence of the first Mishnah
in Peah. פֵּאָה is that corner of the field which is to be left intact for the
poor at harvest time (Lev. 19:9). בִּכּוּרִים are the first-fruits which had
to be brought to the Temple (Exod. 23:19). רֵאָיוֹן, from יֵרָאֶה כָּל זְכוּרְךָ,
may refer either to "appearance" at the Temple on the three annual
Festivals of pilgrimage, or to the offerings to be brought at the time of
such attendance עוֹלַת רְאִיָּה וְשַׁלְמֵי חֲגִיגָה. גְּמִילוּת חֲסָדִים denotes personal acts of
lovingkindness; charity, consisting solely of the donation of money, is
called צְדָקָה. For all these aforementioned acts there is no fixed limit מִן הַתּוֹרָה.
However, מִדְּרַבָּנָן, פֵּאָה, for example, must comprise at least one sixtieth of
the produce of the field.

אֵלּוּ דְבָרִים וְכוּ', in its main theme, is the second paragraph of the above-
mentioned Mishnah. (See שׁוּ"ת מהרש"ל 64). The מִצְוֹת enumerated here,
most of which are services to be rendered to one's fellow-men, are rewarding through the joy inherent in the very act of their fulfillment, while
attendance at the houses of study and devotion at prayer constitute their
own spiritual reward because they serve to edify, purify, and exalt us.
Through their beneficial effect upon our relationships with our fellow-men
and upon our own steady progress towards personal perfection, the "interest" of such acts can be enjoyed even here below, while the "principal"
of spiritual and moral achievement which will accompany us to the hereafter will remain ours for eternity. But no other mitzvah holds such a
liberal portion of "interest" to be enjoyed on earth and of "capital"
remaining for eternity as does the genuine and industrious study of the
תּוֹרָה.

אֱלֹהַי According to our ritual and that of many other communities,
the paragraph אֱלֹהַי נְשָׁמָה immediately follows the בִּרְכַּת אֲשֶׁר יָצַר, at the end
of which there was mention of the intimate union of the soul with the

My God, the soul which You have placed within me is pure. You have created it ; You have formed it ; You have breathed it into me. You preserve it within me, and You will one day take it from me and restore it to me in the awaited future. So long as the soul is within me, I make acknowledgment before You, *God* my God and God of my fathers, Master of all works, Lord of all souls. Blessed be You *God,* Who restores the souls to dead bodies.

---

body (ד״מ to א״ח טור). This fact would explain the absence of the introductory ברוך. At any rate, אלהי נשמה makes man aware of the nature of his soul as he awakens to a new day. The most significant statement concerning the soul is : טהורה היא, it is *pure,* has never been handicapped by any inherent quality of sinfulness. It is a being which is receptive to and capable of all that is good and pure, holy and divine. The soul is endowed with these abilities here and now and has never forfeited them, for each and every soul has had these talents breathed into it by God Himself at the time of its creation. God, the One, pure and holy Being is the soul's Creator, and He has breathed that soul into us as part of His own divine essence. He will preserve it within us as long as it pleases Him to do so. Then, in His infinite wisdom, He will take it from us in death at the proper time, only to restore it to us once more at some future date. Thus, on one hand, the soul is an independent entity, completely different from the body by its very nature. On the other hand, body and soul, though they may be temporarily separated from one another by death, have been intimately bound together by Divine providence so that, jointly, they may serve Him throughout life, This thought should indeed urge upon us the moral uplifting, purification and sanctification for eternity of even the sensual aspects and physical functions of our bodies. מודה אני לפניך "I make acknowledgment before You;" that is, I have no secrets before God. That which my soul knows God knows, for the soul itself is a divine light which shines through all of our inmost being.נר ה׳ נשמת אדם חפש כל חדרי בטן (Prov. 20:27). מחזיר נשמות לפגרים מתים This refers not only to that day in the future when the dead will come to life again, but to every single morning, here and now, when the body reawakens from its nightly sleep.

בָּרוּךְ אַתָּה יְיָ אֱלֹהֵינוּ מֶלֶךְ הָעוֹלָם אֲשֶׁר נָתַן
לַשֶּׂכְוִי בִינָה לְהַבְחִין בֵּין יוֹם וּבֵין לָיְלָה:

בָּרוּךְ אַתָּה יְיָ אֱלֹהֵינוּ מֶלֶךְ הָעוֹלָם שֶׁלֹּא עָשַׂנִי נָכְרִי:

בָּרוּךְ אַתָּה יְיָ אֱלֹהֵינוּ מֶלֶךְ הָעוֹלָם שֶׁלֹּא עָשַׂנִי עָבֶד:

בָּרוּךְ אַתָּה יְיָ אֱלֹהֵינוּ מֶלֶךְ הָעוֹלָם שֶׁלֹּא עָשַׂנִי אִשָּׁה:

Women say: בָּרוּךְ אַתָּה יְיָ אֱלֹהֵינוּ מֶלֶךְ הָעוֹלָם שֶׁעָשַׂנִי כִּרְצוֹנוֹ:

נק"ק יין מוסיפין ב"א"י אלהינו מלך העולם מגביה שפלים (עיין א"ח ס"י מ"ו):

בָּרוּךְ אַתָּה יְיָ אֱלֹהֵינוּ מֶלֶךְ הָעוֹלָם פּוֹקֵחַ עִוְרִים:

בָּרוּךְ אַתָּה יְיָ אֱלֹהֵינוּ מֶלֶךְ הָעוֹלָם מַלְבִּישׁ עֲרֻמִּים:

בָּרוּךְ אַתָּה יְיָ אֱלֹהֵינוּ מֶלֶךְ הָעוֹלָם מַתִּיר אֲסוּרִים:

בָּרוּךְ אַתָּה יְיָ אֱלֹהֵינוּ מֶלֶךְ הָעוֹלָם זוֹקֵף כְּפוּפִים:

בָּרוּךְ אַתָּה יְיָ אֱלֹהֵינוּ מֶלֶךְ הָעוֹלָם רוֹקַע הָאָרֶץ עַל־הַמָּיִם:

ברוך When we first awakened, our thoughts were immediately directed upon our own body with its wondrous construction and upon our soul with its divine purity and purpose, and we were impelled to renew our pledge of loyalty (ברוך) to our God. Here we are given a number of special factors which also present themselves to us, now that we are fully awake, and which summon us once more to renew our promise as indicated by the term ברוך. First we contemplate the distinction between day and night, through which the Creator has divided all of life here below into two distinct halves, one to be devoted to the regeneration of our strength and the other to the active service of God with all the things we do each day. We are bidden to consider the unique talent of the cock, which the Creator has endowed with the ability to perceive the dawn of a new day, and to proclaim it with its loud cry to the still-sleeping world. Thus God has equipped every one of His creatures with special gifts for specific purposes. In like manner, as we are told by the ברכות which follow immediately, He also sent us out among the nations, geared and equipped for the fulfillment of a mission and purpose that is unique and all our own. When the darkness of error still enveloped the nations, the Jewish people had already been sent forth as the wakeners of dawn, and still walks among the nations as the herald of the new day which is to come for all of mankind.

Blessed be You *God,* our God, King of the Universe, Who has given the cock intelligence to distinguish between day and night.

Blessed be You *God,* our God, King of the Universe, Who has not made me a non-Jew.

Blessed be You *God,* our God, King of the Universe, Who has not made me a slave.

Blessed be You *God,* our God, King of the Universe, Who has not made me a woman.

Women say : Blessed be You *God,* our God, King of the Universe, Who has made me in accordance with His will.

Blessed be You *God,* our God, King of the Universe, Who opens the eyes of the blind.

Blessed be You *God,* our God, King of the Universe, Who clothes the naked.

Blessed be You *God,* our God, King of the Universe, Who unties those who are bound.

Blessed be You *God,* our God, King of the Universe, Who raises up those who are bowed down.

Blessed be You *God,* our God, King of the Universe, Who spreads out the earth above the waters.

ברוך שלא עשני נכרי, עבד, אשה This is not a prayer of thanks that God did not make us heathens, slaves or women. Rather, it calls upon us to contemplate the task which God has imposed upon us by making us free Jewish men, and to pledge ourselves to do justice to this mission. These three aspects of our own status impose upon us duties much more comprehensive than those required of the rest of mankind. And if our women have a smaller number of מצות to fulfill than men, they know that the tasks which they must discharge as free Jewish women are no less in accordance with the will and desire of God than are those of their brothers.

We consider the renewal of our gift of sight, our clothing, the free use of our limbs, our ability to stand upright, the ground which carries us, the footgear which protects our feet (כל צרכי), and the firmness of our gait as gifts of God, newly bestowed upon us each morning, and we pledge ourselves to utilize them all to serve Him faithfully in our daily lives. The Jew is commanded to wear a belt, or to tighten his garment at the the waist, in order to indicate the separation between the upper and lower

בָּרוּךְ אַתָּה יְיָ אֱלֹהֵינוּ מֶלֶךְ הָעוֹלָם שֶׁעָשָׂה לִי כָּל־צָרְכִּי:

בָּרוּךְ אַתָּה יְיָ אֱלֹהֵינוּ מֶלֶךְ הָעוֹלָם אֲשֶׁר הֵכִין מִצְעֲדֵי־גָבֶר:

בָּרוּךְ אַתָּה יְיָ אֱלֹהֵינוּ מֶלֶךְ הָעוֹלָם אוֹזֵר יִשְׂרָאֵל בִּגְבוּרָה:

בָּרוּךְ אַתָּה יְיָ אֱלֹהֵינוּ מֶלֶךְ הָעוֹלָם עוֹטֵר יִשְׂרָאֵל בְּתִפְאָרָה:

בָּרוּךְ אַתָּה יְיָ אֱלֹהֵינוּ מֶלֶךְ הָעוֹלָם הַנּוֹתֵן לַיָּעֵף כֹּחַ:

בָּרוּךְ אַתָּה יְיָ אֱלֹהֵינוּ מֶלֶךְ הָעוֹלָם הַמַּעֲבִיר שֵׁנָה מֵעֵינָי וּתְנוּמָה
מֵעַפְעַפָּי: וִיהִי רָצוֹן מִלְּפָנֶיךָ יְיָ אֱלֹהֵינוּ וֵאלֹהֵי אֲבוֹתֵינוּ שֶׁתַּרְגִּילֵנוּ
בְּתוֹרָתֶךָ וְדַבְּקֵנוּ בְּמִצְוֹתֶיךָ וְאַל תְּבִיאֵנוּ לֹא לִידֵי חֵטְא וְלֹא לִידֵי
עֲבֵרָה וְעָוֹן וְלֹא לִידֵי נִסָּיוֹן וְלֹא לִידֵי בִזָּיוֹן וְאַל תַּשְׁלֶט בָּנוּ יֵצֶר
הָרָע וְהַרְחִיקֵנוּ מֵאָדָם רַע וּמֵחָבֵר רַע וְדַבְּקֵנוּ בְּיֵצֶר הַטּוֹב
וּבְמַעֲשִׂים טוֹבִים וְכֹף אֶת יִצְרֵנוּ לְהִשְׁתַּעְבֶּד־לָךְ וּתְנֵנוּ הַיּוֹם
וּבְכָל־יוֹם לְחֵן וּלְחֶסֶד וּלְרַחֲמִים בְּעֵינֶיךָ וּבְעֵינֵי כָל־רוֹאֵינוּ וְתִגְמְלֵנוּ
חֲסָדִים טוֹבִים בָּרוּךְ אַתָּה יְיָ גּוֹמֵל חֲסָדִים טוֹבִים לְעַמּוֹ יִשְׂרָאֵל:

parts of his body. This is to remind us of the dual nature inherent within us: the physical and sensual, which chiefly resides in the lower half of our bodies, and the moral and spiritual, which is primarily served by the upper half. We are thus warned שלא יהא לבו רואה את הערוה that the physical, sensual aspects of our persons remain subordinate to the moral and spiritual, so that this latter part of our personality may demonstrate its "might" to dominate our physical urges. This is the might with which the Jew should be "girded". But even as the lower part of the body should be subordinate to the upper part, and the physical must bow to the spiritual, so, also, the spiritual aspect of our nature, together with the physical element under its domination, must humbly submit to God. The Jew symbolically expresses this idea by keeping his head covered, and in this subordination to God he finds his own honor (עוטר ישראל בתפארה). Finally, aware of our renewed strength and of the total disappearance of fatigue, נותן ליעף כח) and (המעביר שנה וכו' we pass over entirely to the realm of wakefulness, and pray for God's help in the faithful fulfillment of our daily tasks. The first prerequisite for the proper execution of our task is the knowledge of God's teaching. We must be so conversant with it that its commandments will accompany us and be familiar to us at every step

Blessed be You *God*, our God, King of the Universe, Who has provided me with all my needs.

Blessed be You *God*, our God, King of the Universe, Who has made firm the steps of man.

Blessed be You *God*, our God, King of the Universe, Who girds Yisrael with might.

Blessed be You *God*, our God, King of the Universe, Who crowns Yisrael with honor.

Blessed be You *God*, our God, King of the Universe, Who gives strength to the weary.

Blessed be You *God*, our God, King of the Universe, Who removes sleep from my eyes and slumber from my eyelids.

Thus may it be Your will, *God*, our God, and God of our fathers, to make us familiar with Your Teaching and to cause us to adhere to Your commandments. Lead us not into sin, transgression, iniquity, temptation or disgrace; let not evil passion have power over us. Keep us far from an evil man and a bad companion; make us cling to the good impulse and to good deeds; subdue our passion so that it may submit to You, and, today and every day, let us attain to favor, loving-kindness and compassion in Your sight and in the sight of all who behold us; and bestow loving-kindness upon us. Blessed be You *God*, our God, King of the Universe, Who bestows loving-kindness on His people Yisrael.

---

of our lives. (Therefore the prayer תרגילנו. רגיל is one who has become adept at or "familiar with" some skill through constant practice. Thus we read זקן ורגיל in Taanith 15a). Thereafter we ask for the strength to adhere firmly to God's commandments so that nothing can cause us to stray from them. We ask for Divine assistance in both of these endeavors, for we are truly in need of it at every step we take, if we are to remain free from sin, deliberate or unintentional. We need God's help if we are not to have to fear trials, shameful personal inadequacy, and the power of temptation and unbridled passion. We must have His support to grow ever more determined in our inclination to do good, to subordinate the rebellious elements within us to God's will, and to become and remain ever more worthy of the favor of God and the approval of our fellow-men. We view every such evidence of Divine assistance as another proof of God's love, and we pledge to give them proper appreciation, and put them to proper use.

יְהִי רָצוֹן מִלְּפָנֶיךָ יְיָ אֱלֹהַי וֵאלֹהֵי אֲבוֹתַי שֶׁתַּצִּילֵנִי הַיּוֹם
וּבְכָל־יוֹם מֵעַזֵּי פָנִים וּמֵעַזּוּת פָּנִים מֵאָדָם רַע וּמֵחָבֵר רַע
וּמִשָּׁכֵן רַע וּמִפֶּגַע רַע וּמִשָּׂטָן הַמַּשְׁחִית מִדִּין קָשֶׁה וּמִבַּעַל דִּין
קָשֶׁה בֵּין שֶׁהוּא בֶן־בְּרִית וּבֵין שֶׁאֵינוֹ בֶן־בְּרִית:

לְעוֹלָם יְהֵא אָדָם יְרֵא שָׁמַיִם בְּסֵתֶר וּמוֹדֶה
עַל־הָאֱמֶת וְדוֹבֵר אֱמֶת בִּלְבָבוֹ וְיַשְׁכֵּם וְיֹאמַר:

רִבּוֹן כָּל־הָעוֹלָמִים לֹא עַל־צִדְקוֹתֵינוּ אֲנַחְנוּ מַפִּילִים תַּחֲנוּנֵינוּ
לְפָנֶיךָ כִּי עַל רַחֲמֶיךָ הָרַבִּים · מָה אֲנַחְנוּ מֶה חַיֵּינוּ מֶה חַסְדֵּנוּ
מַה־צִּדְקֵנוּ מַה־יְשׁוּעָתֵנוּ מַה־כֹּחֵנוּ מַה־גְּבוּרָתֵנוּ מַה־נֹּאמַר
לְפָנֶיךָ יְיָ אֱלֹהֵינוּ וֵאלֹהֵי אֲבוֹתֵינוּ הֲלֹא כָּל־הַגִּבּוֹרִים כְּאַיִן לְפָנֶיךָ
וְאַנְשֵׁי הַשֵּׁם כְּלֹא הָיוּ וַחֲכָמִים כִּבְלִי מַדָּע וּנְבוֹנִים כִּבְלִי הַשְׂכֵּל
כִּי רֹב מַעֲשֵׂיהֶם תֹּהוּ וִימֵי חַיֵּיהֶם הֶבֶל לְפָנֶיךָ · וּמוֹתַר הָאָדָם
מִן־הַבְּהֵמָה אָיִן כִּי הַכֹּל הָבֶל:

יהי רצון This prayer affords an opportunity for every individual to insert his own requests (and supplications) in accordance with his own (personal needs and) circumstances, concerning those difficulties which meet him in his dealings and relationships with his fellow men (טור). Explicit mention is made here of dealings with עזי פנים, impudent men who deny us the consideration and respect rightly due us, and of עזות פנים, the possibility that we ourselves might sin against others through insolent lack of consideration on our own part. (We ask for Divine protection against) the wickedness of others and that of our companions, (against) unexpected mishaps and handicaps in our private lives, as well as (against) harsh judicial sentences or adversaries should our acts come within the competence of earthly courts of justice.

לעולם The following pledge of belonging to the Jewish Nation which begins with the word רבון originated at a time of persecution when it would have been dangerous to make an open avowal of the basic truths of Judaism. For this reason it is prefaced by a small introductory paragraph stating that even though these sentiments cannot be proclaimed in public, they should still be preserved in secret at all times, cherished in our hearts and avowed before God. Therefore, also, at the end, the prayer looks to the day when God will once more מקדש שמו ברבים, make it possible for us to sanctify His

May it be Your will, *God*, my God and God of my fathers, to deliver me this day, and every day, from impudent men and from insolence, from an evil man, a bad companion, and a bad neighbor, from mishap and evil hindrance, from a harsh judgment and from a hard opponent, be he a son of the Covenant or not.

Man should ever be God-fearing in private, and acknowledge the truth and speak the truth in his heart. Let him rise early and say :

Master of all times ! It is not on the basis of our merits that we pour out supplications before You, but on the basis of Your great compassion. What are we ? What is our life ? What is our loving-kindness ? What our righteousness ? What our helpfulness ? What our strength ? What our might ? What shall we say before You *God*, our God and God of our fathers ? Are not all the heroes as nothing before You, the men of renown as though they had never been, and the wise as if they were without knowledge, the intelligent as though they lacked understanding ? For the multitude of their actions are worthless; the days of their lives are as nothing before You, and the pre-eminence of man over the beast is vanished, for all is nothingness.

Name in public. The time at which this avowal originated lends it all the more significance. True, the other nations gloried in all the glitter of their power, their sagacity, their knowledge, their political skill and their historic feats, and made Israel bear the whole brunt of their contempt, oppression and persecution. But the experience and perception which Israel had gained during its wanderings through the centuries and through observation of the destinies of the nations, opened its eyes to the shallowness and nonentity of all this seeming greatness. Thus Israel, despite the outward misery of its lot, learned to appreciate the true bliss of its calling, paying no heed to all the difficulties which the faithful discharge of this mission might entail.

The people of Israel, therefore, step before the Lord of all times and declare : "We have come to know the insignificance of all those things which man derives solely from his own efforts and resources. Whatever life, love, justice, help, power and strength we may derive from our own resources and gain through our own effort are without meaning. Even the merits that might have accrued to us through our loyalty to our duty are not adequate bases for our hopes for the future. It is

אֲבָל אֲנַחְנוּ עַמְּךָ בְּנֵי בְרִיתֶךָ בְּנֵי אַבְרָהָם אֹהַבְךָ שֶׁנִּשְׁבַּעְתָּ
לוֹ בְּהַר הַמֹּרִיָּה · זֶרַע יִצְחָק יְחִידוֹ שֶׁנֶּעֱקַד עַל גַּב־הַמִּזְבֵּחַ עֲדַת
יַעֲקֹב בִּנְךָ בְּכוֹרֶךָ שֶׁמֵּאַהֲבָתְךָ שֶׁאָהַבְתָּ אֹתוֹ וּמִשִּׂמְחָתְךָ שֶׁשָּׂמַחְתָּ
בּוֹ קָרָאתָ אֶת־שְׁמוֹ יִשְׂרָאֵל וִישֻׁרוּן :

לְפִיכָךְ אֲנַחְנוּ חַיָּבִים לְהוֹדוֹת לְךָ וּלְשַׁבֵּחֲךָ וּלְפָאֶרְךָ וּלְבָרֵךְ
וּלְקַדֵּשׁ וְלָתֶת־שֶׁבַח וְהוֹדָיָה לִשְׁמֶךָ : אַשְׁרֵינוּ מַה־טּוֹב חֶלְקֵנוּ
וּמַה־נָּעִים גּוֹרָלֵנוּ וּמַה־יָּפָה יְרֻשָּׁתֵנוּ אַשְׁרֵינוּ שֶׁאֲנַחְנוּ מַשְׁכִּימִים
וּמַעֲרִיבִים עֶרֶב וָבֹקֶר וְאוֹמְרִים פַּעֲמַיִם בְּכָל־יוֹם

שְׁמַע יִשְׂרָאֵל יְיָ אֱלֹהֵינוּ יְיָ ׀ אֶחָד :

בָּרוּךְ שֵׁם כְּבוֹד מַלְכוּתוֹ לְעוֹלָם וָעֶד :

רנ"ל הי' נוהג לומר כאן כל הפרט' הראשונה של ק"ש, מנוס שלפעמים הם אומרים
קרובות מיתעכבין בקריאת שמע עד אחר זמנה ונוה הוא יולא ידי חובת ק"ש.

אַתָּה הוּא עַד שֶׁלֹּא נִבְרָא הָעוֹלָם אַתָּה הוּא מִשֶּׁנִּבְרָא
הָעוֹלָם אַתָּה הוּא בָּעוֹלָם הַזֶּה וְאַתָּה הוּא לָעוֹלָם הַבָּא קַדֵּשׁ
אֶת־שִׁמְךָ עַל מַקְדִּישֵׁי שְׁמֶךָ וְקַדֵּשׁ אֶת־שִׁמְךָ בְּעוֹלָמֶךָ וּבִישׁוּעָתְךָ
תָּרוּם וְתַגְבִּיהַּ קַרְנֵנוּ בָּרוּךְ אַתָּה יְיָ מְקַדֵּשׁ אֶת־שִׁמְךָ בָּרַבִּים :

---

solely in the boundless, inalienable Divine compassion that we may take
refuge now and ever with all our cares. And this applies not only
to our own people in our own position of impotence, historic weakness,
and helplessness, and in our own humble place among the nations.
It is true for all the rest of mankind as well. We have witnessed
the birth of all the nations and powers of world history, and we have
stood at their graves too. We have considered their origin, their existence
and their passing from the scene. We know how idle is all heroism; that
all glory passes away without a trace, all wisdom proves ignorant, and
all politics are foolish, because the sum total of their doings is worthless.
Their acts never attain their supposed aim to promote human welfare,
and all the days of their lives appear before God as an empty dream. As
long as man's ambitions and achievements are devoted to the sensuous and
the selfish, solely to fleeting goals, men will be doomed to transiency even
as the beast. Israel has no portion in the heroism and glitter of all the

But we are Your people, the sons of Your covenant, the sons of Avraham who loved You, to whom You swore on Mount Moriah, the descendants of Yitzchak, his only son, who was tied to the altar as a sacrifice, the community of Yaakov, Your first-born, whom You named Yisrael and Yeshurun because of Your love with which You loved him and the joy with which You rejoiced in him.

Therefore we are duty-bound to give thanks to You, to praise and glorify You, to bless and hallow, and to offer praise and thanksgiving to Your Name. It is we who stride forward to salvation ; how good is our portion, how pleasant our lot, how beautiful our heritage — we, who, early and late, morning and evening, twice each day, proclaim :

HEAR, YISRAEL, *GOD* OUR GOD, IS *GOD*, THE ONLY ONE!

Blessed be the Name of the glory of His Kingdom to all the future which, though veiled, is certain.

You were the same before the world was created ; You have been the same ever since the world was created ; You are the same in this world, and You will be the same in the world to come. Sanctify Your Name upon those who acknowledge the sanctity of Your Name ; sanctify Your Name in Your world. And through Your salvation let our horn rise and be exalted. Blessed be You *God,* Who causes Your Name to be sanctified publicly.

---

famous would-be powers. We cannot trace our descent to princes distinguished by earthly grandeur. But though the nations of the earth, both great and small, exclude us from their bonds of friendship, we find full compensation in the knowledge that we are the people of God and the sons of His covenant. We know that we are the sons of Abraham, whom God had found worthy to call His friend, and to whom He had given an oath affecting his own welfare, that of his descendants, and that of all the rest of mankind as well. We glory in our descent from an Isaac, whose great example of the highest type of self-sacrificing devotion to God shines before us at all times. We take pride in being the community of Jacob, whom God had called His first-born son among the entire human race returning to Him (Exod. 4:22), and to whom, as a token of His love and delight, He had given the names of "Israel" and "Yeshurun".

אַתָּה הוּא יְיָ אֱלֹהֵינוּ בַּשָּׁמַיִם וּבָאָרֶץ וּבִשְׁמֵי הַשָּׁמַיִם
הָעֶלְיוֹנִים · אֱמֶת אַתָּה הוּא רִאשׁוֹן וְאַתָּה הוּא אַחֲרוֹן וּמִבַּלְעָדֶיךָ
אֵין אֱלֹהִים · קַבֵּץ קוֹיֶךָ מֵאַרְבַּע כַּנְפוֹת הָאָרֶץ יַכִּירוּ וְיֵדְעוּ כָּל־בָּאֵי
עוֹלָם כִּי אַתָּה הוּא הָאֱלֹהִים לְבַדְּךָ לְכֹל מַמְלְכוֹת הָאָרֶץ · אַתָּה
עָשִׂיתָ אֶת־הַשָּׁמַיִם וְאֶת־הָאָרֶץ אֶת־הַיָּם וְאֶת כָּל־אֲשֶׁר בָּם ·
וּמִי בְּכָל־מַעֲשֵׂי יָדֶיךָ בָּעֶלְיוֹנִים אוֹ בַתַּחְתּוֹנִים שֶׁיֹּאמַר לְךָ מַה־
תַּעֲשֶׂה · אָבִינוּ שֶׁבַּשָּׁמַיִם עֲשֵׂה עִמָּנוּ חֶסֶד בַּעֲבוּר שִׁמְךָ הַגָּדוֹל
שֶׁנִּקְרָא עָלֵינוּ וְקַיֶּם־לָנוּ יְיָ אֱלֹהֵינוּ מַה־שֶּׁכָּתוּב בָּעֵת הַהִיא אָבִיא
אֶתְכֶם וּבָעֵת קַבְּצִי אֶתְכֶם כִּי־אֶתֵּן אֶתְכֶם לְשֵׁם וְלִתְהִלָּה בְּכֹל
עַמֵּי הָאָרֶץ בְּשׁוּבִי אֶת־שְׁבוּתֵיכֶם לְעֵינֵיכֶם אָמַר יְיָ :

וַיְדַבֵּר יְיָ אֶל מֹשֶׁה לֵּאמֹר: וְעָשִׂיתָ כִּיּוֹר נְחֹשֶׁת, וְכַנּוֹ נְחֹשֶׁת,
לְרָחְצָה. וְנָתַתָּ אֹתוֹ בֵּין אֹהֶל מוֹעֵד וּבֵין הַמִּזְבֵּחַ, וְנָתַתָּ שָׁמָּה
מָיִם. וְרָחֲצוּ אַהֲרֹן וּבָנָיו מִמֶּנּוּ אֶת יְדֵיהֶם וְאֶת רַגְלֵיהֶם. בְּבֹאָם
אֶל אֹהֶל מוֹעֵד יִרְחֲצוּ מַיִם וְלֹא יָמֻתוּ; אוֹ בְגִשְׁתָּם אֶל הַמִּזְבֵּחַ
לְשָׁרֵת, לְהַקְטִיר אִשֶּׁה לַיְיָ. וְרָחֲצוּ יְדֵיהֶם וְרַגְלֵיהֶם וְלֹא יָמֻתוּ;
וְהָיְתָה לָהֶם חָק־עוֹלָם, לוֹ וּלְזַרְעוֹ לְדֹרֹתָם.

The title of "Israel" symbolizes Jacob's wanderings through history, proclaiming the sovereignty of God, while the appellation of "Yeshurun"
indicated his task to fulfill God's will as it had been revealed to him, and
to devote his life to the execution of that which is הישר בעיני ה' "right in
the eyes of God", the One and Only God. (Deut. 12:25; 13:19). Amidst
all the miseries which we have suffered throughout history, this eternal
heritage which our fathers have handed down to us, and of which
we become aware anew each day as we avow it morn and night when
we recite the שמע, fills us with a sense of supreme bliss for which we can
never thank God enough. And, as we recite the שמע aloud, we add, in an
undertone בש"כמ"לי', thus looking into the future which, though veiled to
our eye, is sure to come, a future in which the Name of the Kingdom of
God will be glorified on earth to the fullest possible extent. We are
confident, too, that, even during our predetermined pilgrimage to His
splendid goal, God will let us also live to see a time when we will not be
compelled to keep our acknowledgement of Him in the recesses of secrecy,
hidden within our inmost being, but rather we shall be able לקדש שמו ברבים

You, *God* our God, are the same in heaven and on earth, and in the highest heaven of heavens. Truly You are the first and You are the last, and besides You there is no God. Gather those who hope for You from the four corners of the earth, so that all those who enter the world may realize and know that You alone are God over all the kingdoms of the earth. For You have made the heavens and the earth, the sea and all that is in them. Who is there among all Your works, among those above or those below, who could say to You, "What are You doing?" Our Father in heaven, deal kindly with us for the sake of Your great Name which is proclaimed over us, and fulfill for us, *God* our God, that which is written [Zephaniah 3:20]: "At that time I shall bring you home; and in time My ingathering of you will be consummated. For I will make you a name and a praise among all the peoples of the earth, when I will bring your exiles back before your eyes, says *God*."

---

to acknowledge Him openly. This hope, thank God, has actually been realized in the course of the centuries. The spelling of תרום and ותגביה would indicate that our "horn is lifted up" by the mere fact that God helps us, and we are no longer bowed down. But God then "lifts up our horn" ever higher.

אתה הוא To our prayer for the eventual universal acknowledgment of God's rule, and for a status of greater freedom in the meantime as regards the unfettered avowal of our faith, there is added the hope and the prayer that we may soon be gathered from our dispersion and brought back to the Promised Land. For God is fully independent in the execution of that which He has ordained and promised, and He has unequivocally pledged it to us that He would return us to our ancient Homeland. If we understand this quotation from Zephaniah correctly, ובעת קבצי וגו׳ means that "your ingathering will be accomplished by Me *in time*," i.e the ingathering will not come about suddenly; rather, I will bring events to pass which will prepare the way for your return and lead to it. This also explains בשובי וגו׳ לעיניכם. For this can not mean that the Return will take place before the very eyes of the returning exiles; that would be self-understood. Much rather, the thought seems to be: God will accomplish our Return after events which will prepare the way for it and lead to it. He will let us live to see these events, and even these events preliminary to our Return will cause the Jewish people to become a living testimonial to Divine sovereignty among all the peoples of the earth.

יִּ֫ד וַיְדַבֵּ֥ר יְהֹוָ֖ה אֶל־מֹשֶׁ֥ה לֵּאמֹ֑ר: צַ֚ו אֶת־בְּנֵ֣י יִשְׂרָאֵ֔ל וְאָמַרְתָּ֖ אֲלֵהֶ֑ם
אֶת־קָרְבָּנִ֨י לַחְמִ֜י לְאִשַּׁ֗י רֵ֤יחַ נִֽיחֹחִי֙ תִּשְׁמְר֔וּ לְהַקְרִ֥יב לִ֖י בְּמֹֽועֲדֹֽו:
וְאָמַרְתָּ֣ לָהֶ֗ם זֶ֤ה הָֽאִשֶּׁה֙ אֲשֶׁ֣ר תַּקְרִ֣יבוּ לַֽיהֹוָ֔ה כְּבָשִׂ֧ים בְּנֵֽי־שָׁנָ֛ה
תְמִימִ֥ם שְׁנַ֖יִם לַיֹּ֑ום עֹלָ֥ה תָמִֽיד: אֶת־הַכֶּ֥בֶשׂ אֶחָ֖ד תַּֽעֲשֶׂ֣ה בַבֹּ֑קֶר
וְאֵת֙ הַכֶּ֣בֶשׂ הַשֵּׁנִ֔י תַּֽעֲשֶׂ֖ה בֵּ֣ין הָֽעַרְבָּֽיִם: וַֽעֲשִׂירִ֧ית הָֽאֵיפָ֛ה סֹ֖לֶת
לְמִנְחָ֑ה בְּלוּלָ֛ה בְּשֶׁ֥מֶן כָּתִ֖ית רְבִיעִ֥ת הַהִֽין: עֹלַ֖ת תָּמִ֑יד הָֽעֲשֻׂיָ֔ה
בְּהַ֣ר סִינַ֔י לְרֵ֣יחַ נִיחֹ֔חַ אִשֶּׁ֖ה לַֽיהֹוָֽה: וְנִסְכֹּו֙ רְבִיעִ֣ת הַהִ֔ין לַכֶּ֖בֶשׂ
הָֽאֶחָ֑ד בַּקֹּ֗דֶשׁ הַסֵּ֛ךְ נֶ֥סֶךְ שֵׁכָ֖ר לַֽיהֹוָֽה: וְאֵת֙ הַכֶּ֣בֶשׂ הַשֵּׁנִ֔י תַּֽעֲשֶׂ֖ה
בֵּ֣ין הָֽעַרְבָּ֑יִם כְּמִנְחַ֨ת הַבֹּ֤קֶר וּכְנִסְכֹּו֙ תַּֽעֲשֶׂ֔ה אִשֵּׁ֛ה רֵ֥יחַ
נִיחֹ֖חַ לַֽיהֹוָֽה:

וידבר ‎*This chapter (Num. 28:1–9) contains the order of the תמיד,
the daily offerings. Through them, morning and night, Israel comes as a
כבש, as a "lamb", before God, the "Shepherd" of its existence, both as a
group of individuals and as a nation. Through the act of Sacrifice, Israel
expresses the dedication of its personality (דם) to the quest for the lofty
pinnacle of its destiny (זריקה על המזבח), and, by inference, the consecration
of all of its organs of perception, will-power and achievement (איברים)
as nourishment for the purifying, illuminating and life-giving fire of the
Divine Law to find favor in His eyes (לחם אשה ריח ניחח לה'). At the same
time, all Israel's wealth and sustenance (שמן and סלת) are conceived as
Divine bounty which must therefore be dedicated to God in the form of
an allegiance-gift (מנחה). We attain the supreme enjoyment of blessed
delight (יין) only in the Sanctuary of God (בקדש הסך נסך שכר לה').
קרבני, the coming near to God, the winning of His nearness ; לחמי,
through the mustering of all earthly strivings for the attainment of God's
nearness on earth; לאשי, by means of committing the personality to the

*) Here and in the notes immediately following we adhere to the explanations
given in our Commentary to the Pentateuch concerning the significance of the sacrificial
ritual. The entire order of sacrifices seems to us a means for expressing symbolically
that which we must do with all the facets of our individuality, and the work of self-
improvement which we must perform on our personalities.

God spoke to Moshe : Command the sons of Yisrael, and say unto them : My offering to be brought near as my fire-oblation, the expression of compliance with My will, you shall observe, to bring it to Me in its appointed time of assembly. And say unto them also : This is the fire-offering which you shall bring near unto *God* : Yearling lambs, in their perfection, two each day, as a perpetual elevating-offering. The lamb you shall offer, one in the morning — and the second lamb you shall offer between the two eventides. And the tenth part of an *ephah* of fine flour as an allegiance-gift thoroughly mixed with one fourth of a *hin* of pressed-out oil. A perpetual elevating-offering which is brought on Mount Sinai, as an expression of compliance, a fire-offering unto *God*. And its libation, one fourth of a *hin* for the one lamb, an oblation of strong drink to be poured to God in the Sanctuary. And the second lamb you shall offer between the two eventides, as the allegiance-gift of the morning and as its libation you shall offer a fire-offering unto *God,* an expression of compliance.

---

fiery force of God's Law, for purification and vivification, and all this only as ריח, as an indication of ניחוחי, of living a life that is pleasing to God. במועדו: God appointed מועדים, special occasions that attest to His rule and summon His people to His presence, to commemorate annually His mighty acts in Egypt, at the Red Sea, on Mount Sinai and in the wilderness. These miracles actually involved suspension by God of the natural order which He Himself had instituted, and thus bear eloquent witness to His greatness. In the same manner, God also appointed the transitions of morning and evening, which recur daily with clock-like regularity, to be מועדים too. These daily, "ordinary" natural phenomena are also to serve as messengers testifying to God's power and summoning the people to worship Him, to demonstrate to us the hand of God as it can be seen even in the present course of the world, and to call each of us to come before Him.

For the very steadiness, the regularity, of the phenomena of nature is a much clearer, more wonderful manifestation of Divine wisdom and omnipotence than the suspension of these natural laws when God's miracles were executed. In fact the purpose of these special acts of God which interrupted the regular order of nature was to point to Him as the Lawgiver of these natural laws, lest the thought of Him as Regulator, Master and Lord of the world order be lost through the steady regularity of the natural phenomena.

ויקרא
א׳ ווו׳ וְשָׁחַט אֹתוֹ עַל יֶרֶךְ הַמִּזְבֵּחַ צָפֹנָה לִפְנֵי יְהֹוָה
וְזָרְקוּ בְּנֵי אַהֲרֹן הַכֹּהֲנִים אֶת־דָּמוֹ עַל־הַמִּזְבֵּחַ סָבִיב:

אַתָּה הוּא יְיָ אֱלֹהֵינוּ שֶׁהִקְטִירוּ אֲבוֹתֵינוּ לְפָנֶיךָ אֶת־קְטֹרֶת
הַסַּמִּים בִּזְמַן שֶׁבֵּית הַמִּקְדָּשׁ קַיָּם ・ כַּאֲשֶׁר צִוִּיתָ אוֹתָם עַל יְדֵי
מֹשֶׁה נְבִיאֶךָ כַּכָּתוּב בְּתוֹרָתֶךָ:

שמות ל׳ וַיֹּאמֶר יְהֹוָה אֶל־מֹשֶׁה קַח־לְךָ סַמִּים נָטָף וּשְׁחֵלֶת וְחֶלְבְּנָה
סַמִּים וּלְבֹנָה זַכָּה בַּד בְּבַד יִהְיֶה: וְעָשִׂיתָ אֹתָהּ קְטֹרֶת רֹקַח
מַעֲשֵׂה רוֹקֵחַ מְמֻלָּח טָהוֹר קֹדֶשׁ: וְשָׁחַקְתָּ מִמֶּנָּה הָדֵק וְנָתַתָּה
מִמֶּנָּה לִפְנֵי הָעֵדֻת בְּאֹהֶל מוֹעֵד אֲשֶׁר אִוָּעֵד לְךָ שָׁמָּה קֹדֶשׁ
קָדָשִׁים תִּהְיֶה לָכֶם: וְנֶאֱמַר וְהִקְטִיר עָלָיו אַהֲרֹן קְטֹרֶת סַמִּים
בַּבֹּקֶר בַּבֹּקֶר בְּהֵיטִיבוֹ אֶת־הַנֵּרֹת יַקְטִירֶנָּה: וּבְהַעֲלֹת אַהֲרֹן אֶת־
הַנֵּרֹת בֵּין הָעַרְבַּיִם יַקְטִירֶנָּה קְטֹרֶת תָּמִיד לִפְנֵי יְהֹוָה לְדֹרֹתֵיכֶם:

תנו רבנן פטום הקטורת, הצרי והצפורן החלבנה והלבונה משקל שבעים
שבעים מנה. מור וקציעה שבולת נרד וכרכום, משקל ששה עשר ששה עשר
מנה. הקושט שנים עשר, וקלופה שלשה, וקנמון תשעה, בורית כרשינה
תשעה קבין· יין קפריסין, סאין תלתא וקבין תלתא, ואם אין לו יין קפריסין,
מביא חמר חורין עתיק, מלח סדומית רובע הקב, מעלה עשן כל שהוא· רבי
נתן אומר אף כפת הירדן כל שהוא ואם נתן בה דבש פסלה. ואם חסר אחת
מכל סמניה חייב מיתה:

אשה indicates the offering upon the fire of the altar, the concrete symbol
of the אשדת. בני שנה: In our relationship to God, we should remain forever
"young", in the full vigor of youth, and ever aware of our need for His
guidance; and we are to bring each of these offerings תמימים, in the "whole-
ness" of our being. שנים ליום: The daily offering is to consist of two כבשים,
corresponding to the "duality" of the daily phenomena of rising and setting
light. We come before the same One God, first at sunrise and again at the
time of its setting. In this manner, we visibly demonstrate that we accept
the entire alternation of the rising and setting of life's experiences as the
uniform work of the One and Only God. We recognize that it is the uniform
task of our lives, in the midst of all these vicissitudes, to walk before the
countenance of this One and Only God, and to let ourselves be led and
guided by Him.

רבן שמעון בן גמליאל אומר, הצרי אינו אלא שרף, הנוטף מעצי הקטף.
בורית כרשינה ששפין בה את הצפורן, כדי שתהא נאה. יין קפריסין ששורין
בו את הצפורן, כדי שתהא עזה. והלא מי רגלים יפין לה, אלא שאין מכניסין
מי רגלים בעזרה, מפני הכבוד:

תניא רבי נתן אומר כשהוא שוחק אומר הדק היטיב היטיב הדק מפני שהקול
יפה לבשמים. פטמה לחצאין כשרה לשליש ולרביע לא שמענו. אמר רבי
יהודה זה הכלל, אם כמדתה, כשרה לחצאין, ואם חסר אחת מכל סמניה חייב
מיתה:

תני בר קפרא אחת לששים או לשבעים שנה היתה באה של שירים
לחצאין. עוד תני בר קפרא, אלו היה נותן בה קורטוב של דבש אין אדם
יכול לעמוד מפני ריחה. ולמה אין מערבין בה דבש, מפני שהתורה אמרה כי
כל שאור וכל דבש לא תקטירו ממנו אשה ליי:

יְיָ צְבָאוֹת עִמָּנוּ מִשְׂגָּב לָנוּ אֱלֹהֵי יַעֲקֹב סֶלָה: יְיָ צְבָאוֹת
אַשְׁרֵי אָדָם בֹּטֵחַ בָּךְ: יְיָ הוֹשִׁיעָה הַמֶּלֶךְ יַעֲנֵנוּ בְיוֹם קָרְאֵנוּ:
אַתָּה סֵתֶר לִי מִצַּר תִּצְּרֵנִי רָנֵּי פַלֵּט תְּסוֹבְבֵנִי סֶלָה: וְעָרְבָה
לַיְיָ מִנְחַת יְהוּדָה וִירוּשָׁלָיִם כִּימֵי עוֹלָם וּכְשָׁנִים קַדְמֹנִיּוֹת:

תפלת רבי נחוניא בן הקנה.

אבג"יתץ	אָנָּא בְּכֹחַ גְּדֻלַּת יְמִינְךָ תַּתִּיר צְרוּרָה ·
קרע"שטן	קַבֵּל רִנַּת עַמְּךָ שַׂגְּבֵנוּ טַהֲרֵנוּ נוֹרָא ·
נגד"יכש	נָא גִבּוֹר דּוֹרְשֵׁי יִחוּדְךָ כְּבָבַת שָׁמְרֵם ·
בטר"צתג	בָּרְכֵם טַהֲרֵם רַחֲמֵי צִדְקָתְךָ תָּמִיד גָּמְלֵם ·
חקב"טנע	חֲסִין קָדוֹשׁ בְּרֹב טוּבְךָ נַהֵל עֲדָתֶךָ ·
יגל"פוק	יָחִיד גֵּאֶה לְעַמְּךָ פְּנֵה זוֹכְרֵי קְדֻשָּׁתֶךָ ·
שקו"צית	שַׁוְעָתֵנוּ קַבֵּל וּשְׁמַע צַעֲקָתֵנוּ יוֹדֵעַ תַּעֲלֻמוֹת ·

בָּרוּךְ שֵׁם כְּבוֹד מַלְכוּתוֹ לְעוֹלָם וָעֶד :

עוֹלָה, By means of our elevating-offering, we pledge our striving forward
towards the lofty heights of our destiny. בין הערבים: literally, "between the
two interminglings of day and night"; i.e. at the interval between the
moment when night already mingles with the day, and that in which day
is still mingled with the night. This means the entire afternoon. עשירית האיפה
corresponds to the עומר of the manna (Exod. 16:36), hence to the daily
nutritional requirements of one individual. The term מנחה always denotes
a gift-offering by which the giver acknowledges the receiver to be the
master of his destiny, and testifies to the giver's subservience and dependence.
So, too, when employed in connection with the sacrificial ritual, the term
indicates an allegiance-offering. בהר סיני: In Ezekiel 43:15, the upper
part of the altar is directly called הר אל, the mountain of God, and we are

On the Sabbath add:

בְּמִדְבָּר. וּבְיוֹם הַשַּׁבָּת שְׁנֵי־כְבָשִׂים בְּנֵי־שָׁנָה תְּמִימִם וּשְׁנֵי עֶשְׂרֹנִים
סֹלֶת מִנְחָה בְּלוּלָה בַשֶּׁמֶן וְנִסְכּוֹ: עֹלַת שַׁבַּת בְּשַׁבַּתּוֹ עַל־עֹלַת
הַתָּמִיד וְנִסְכָּהּ:

On Rosh Chodesh add:

בְּמִדְבָּר כֵּח. וּבְרָאשֵׁי חָדְשֵׁיכֶם תַּקְרִיבוּ עֹלָה לַיהֹוָה פָּרִים בְּנֵי־בָקָר שְׁנַיִם
וְאַיִל אֶחָד כְּבָשִׂים בְּנֵי־שָׁנָה שִׁבְעָה תְּמִימִם: וּשְׁלֹשָׁה עֶשְׂרֹנִים
סֹלֶת מִנְחָה בְּלוּלָה בַשֶּׁמֶן לַפָּר הָאֶחָד וּשְׁנֵי עֶשְׂרֹנִים סֹלֶת מִנְחָה

---

told in Psalms 68:18 that God entered into our midst when He revealed
the Law to us at Mount Sinai ה' בם סיני בקדש and that Mount Sinai
actually is *in* the Sanctuary. We, therefore, think that the term הר סיני
is used to denote the altar. The עולה and the מנחה given over to the
אש אוכלה בהר סיני symbolize our ever renewed devotion to the ריח, אש
על המזבח is a "faint intimation" of something, just as an odor makes known the
presence of an object from a distance. ניחוח is the fulfillment or satisfaction
of the will of another. The offering of sacrifices in itself does not constitute
the satisfaction of the will of God but are an intimation, a symbolic expression of that satisfaction, which, by bringing the offering, we symbolically
pledge to accomplish through the life we will lead according to God's
will. בקדש וגו', It is not sadness and sorrow, but supreme bliss and joy that
should flow forth for us from the Sanctuary. The place which receives
the offerings of Israel is also the soil with which its highest joys are
associated. ואת הכבש השני: At sunrise, and again at sunset, Israel comes
forward as the same "lamb of God's pasture", and renders homage to
Him with the same symbol of "sustenance, prosperity and joy," acknowledging the unity of its God by the unity of its life's mission and its life's joy.
וביום השבת, The Mussaph sacrifice which is to be "added" on the
Sabbath to the regular daily elevating-offering is distinguished from the *Tamid*-
offering only in that it consists of two lambs, while the law prescribes
only one lamb for the latter. Through the *Tamid*, Israel comes before God
as a single national entity. The Mussaph offering of the Sabbath however,
represents the devotion to Him in the heart of each individual member
of His people. On the Sabbath day, by refraining from all work, all
Jews humbly lay themselves and the world at the feet of God, the Creator
and Master of the world. In the same manner, by the Sabbath offering,
they come before Him as their Creator and Master, thus demonstrating
their recognition of the fact that רועה ישראל, the Shepherd of the Jewish
nation as a whole is also the personal "Shepherd" of every single Jewish

On the Sabbath add:

And on the Sabbath day two yearling lambs in their perfection; and two tenths of fine flour as an allegiance-offering thoroughly mixed with oil, and its libation. The elevating-offering of the Sabbath on its Sabbath, in addition to the continual elevating-offering and its libation.

On Rosh Chodesh add:

And at the beginnings of your months you shall bring near unto *God* an elevating-offering: two young bullocks and one ram, yearling lambs, seven in number, in their perfection. Three tenths of fine flour as an allegiance-gift thoroughly mixed with oil for

---

soul within this national entity. In this fashion they renew their pledge ever to give Him, Who is the Shepherd of all His creatures, the loyalty, obedience and devotion for the fulfillment of the goals for which He made them Jews, and for which, in His wisdom and goodness, He gave to each of them his own portion of "sustenance, prosperity and joy of life"— שני עשרונים סלת מנחה בלולה בשמן ונסכו.

ובראשי חדשיכם. Every month the renewal of the light of the New Moon calls upon us to "renew" our own selves from the darkness of moral, social and physical ills to the light of pure endeavor and of a serene life in constant striving onward toward the ideals of moral perfection and salvation which have been set for us. This ideal of the mission of Israel is expressed by the group of offerings which constitute the Mussaph sacrifice of ראש חודש. This same ideal also lies at the basis of the Mussaph offerings that must be brought on all other מועדים. This group of offerings consists of two bullocks, one ram, and seven lambs. פר, the bullock, the plough-animal which serves man, expresses the human personality working in the service of God. איל, the ram, the beast surpassing all the rest of the herd in size and strength, signifies that human personage which stands out above all the rest by virtue of wealth or nobility, while כבש, the lamb, the true beast of pasture, represents that personality which submits to the leadership and guidance of the Higher Being. The number seven, as in שבת, "the Sabbath", and שבועה "the vow", indicates the One Invisible Being Who is in close contact with the visible world and rules over it unseen. This, then, is the message of the group of sacrifices which constitute the Mussaph service: Israel is to be a nation of which every member, in eternally youthful vigor, works effectively in the service of God (פרים בני) (בקר שנים) a model nation which, in its entirety, walks ahead in blessed strength, of all the other nations of men in God's human flock (איל אחד). It is a nation whose history is nothing but a constant revelation of the

בְּלוּלָה בַשֶּׁמֶן לָאַיִל הָאֶחָד: וְעִשָּׂרֹן עִשָּׂרוֹן סֹלֶת מִנְחָה בְּלוּלָה בַשֶּׁמֶן
לַכֶּבֶשׂ הָאֶחָד עֹלָה רֵיחַ נִיחֹחַ אִשֶּׁה לַיהוָה: וְנִסְכֵּיהֶם חֲצִי הַהִין
יִהְיֶה לַפָּר וּשְׁלִישִׁת הַהִין לָאַיִל וּרְבִיעִת הַהִין לַכֶּבֶשׂ יָיִן זֹאת
עֹלַת חֹדֶשׁ בְּחָדְשׁוֹ לְחָדְשֵׁי הַשָּׁנָה: וּשְׂעִיר עִזִּים אֶחָד לְחַטָּאת
לַיהוָה עַל־עֹלַת הַתָּמִיד יֵעָשֶׂה וְנִסְכּוֹ:

אֵיזֶהוּ מְקוֹמָן הוּא נִתְקַן לְמוּד, וְכֵן בְּרַיְיתָ' דְּר' יִשְׁמָעֵאל לְכֵן צָרִיךְ לְלָמְדוּ שִׁיכִין הַפִּי'.
זבחים פ"ה.

א אֵיזֶהוּ מְקוֹמָן שֶׁל־זְבָחִים קָדְשֵׁי קָדָשִׁים שְׁחִיטָתָן בַּצָּפוֹן פַּר

hand of God through the ages through which the children of Israel move in immortal youthful vigor as the sheep of His pasture (שבעה כבשים בני שנה). Like every other עולה, this מוסף, too, is accompanied by a gift of מנחת סלת ושמן and יין נסכים, indicating that all our material possessions, our wealth, sustenance and joy of life belong to God and depend on Him. And the more profoundly we realize our position before God, the more important it is to keep in mind how very subservient we are to Him with all our possessions won in life and attained through endeavor. Therefore there is a constant increase in the measure of the *Minchah* and *Nesachim* that accompany the כבש, איל and פר. ושעיר וגו': To the symbolic expression, by means of the מוסף sacrifice, of our ideal destiny, there is always added a חטאת, a sin-offering. For, once we are reminded of this ideal, we become aware of the inadequacy of our past and present lives, and our sin-offering expresses our pledge to maintain ourselves at the high level of our sacred calling in the future.

איזהו 1. The מקדש, the Temple Sanctuary consisted of three chambers: the Holy of Holies, in the western side, also called דביר, "the Abode of the Word", in which the Ark containing the Tablets of the Law (and the original ספר תורה written by Moses himself) reposed beneath a Cherubim-cover, ארון וכפורת. East of the Holy of Holies, and separated from it by a dividing curtain, פרוכת, was the היכל, the "Abode of God's Might". At the *northern* side of this chamber there was שולחן, the "Table" with the showbread; opposite, at the *southern side*, there was מנורה, the seven-branched candelabrum, and, midway between these two, slightly forward of them in the direction of the entrance, there was the מזבח הזהב, the golden altar for incense. Before the היכל, and east thereof, was the עזרה, the antecourt which corresponded to the חצר in the משכן. In this court stood the מזבח העולה, the altar upon which the sacrifices were offered. In the *eastern* part of the עזרה, opposite the Holy of Holies, was the main

each bullock, two tenths of fine flour as an allegiance-gift thoroughly mixed with oil for the one ram, and one tenth each of fine flour as an allegiance-gift thoroughly mixed with oil, for each lamb; an elevating-offering as a hint of satisfaction to *God* by devotion to fire. And their libations : half a *hin* shall be for each bullock, one third of a *hin* for the ram, and one fourth of a *hin* for every lamb, of wine. This is the elevating-offering of the New Moon every New Moon for each month of the year. And one he-goat for a sin-offering unto *God*, in addition to the continual elevating-offering and its libation, shall it be made.

1. Which are the prescribed places of the sacrifices ? The most holy are slaughtered on the north side. The bullocks and the he-goat

---

entrance to the Sanctuary. We think that in this way the *western* side of the Sanctuary and the altar received symbolic association with the Torah (ארון), the *northern* side with the physical and material aspects of life (שולחן), the *southern* side with the spirit (מנורה) and the *eastern* side, where the entrance was located, with the nation as such. The manner in which each of the sacrifices had to be processed also had profound symbolic meaning. שחיטה symbolized the renunciation of all personal will and independence with man's personality represented by the animal on the altar; קבלת הדם signified the acceptance of man's personality, thus dedicated, into the Sanctuary; מתנות, the applications of the blood of the sacrifice through זריקה, a dashing from afar (in some cases הזיה the sprinkling of only a few drops of blood), נתינה, an act of direct "giving", and שפיכה the pouring the blood upon the ground, is a symbolic expression of constant striving to attain (הזיה, זריקה) and of the endeavor to remain on that high level (נתינה על הקרן) and of the firm implantation of the spirit in the soil of the Sanctuary of the Law (שפיכה על היסוד).

The sacrifices are classed in categories as follows :

A. קדשי קדשים Those which remind the worshipper how very far he still is from having attained the lofty level of duty. Symbolically, they demonstrate that if we are even to begin to draw near to God, we must first muster all of the physical aspects of our personalities for this purpose (This is much like the symbolic meaning of מילה). It is for this reason that their שחיטה and קבלה take place on the north (צפון) side of the altar, the side where the שולחן is situated. In this category also belong the חטאות (of Mishnayoth 1—3) which are brought to atone for transgressions of laws; the עולות (discussed in Mishnah 4) for sins of omission; and the אשמות (described in Mishnah 5) for wrongdoing. Also in this category are the שני כבשי עצרת (in Mishnah 5), the זבחי שלמי צבור which are added to the

וְשָׂעִיר שֶׁל־יוֹם הַכִּפּוּרִים שְׁחִיטָתָן בַּצָּפוֹן וְקִבּוּל דָּמָן בִּכְלִי שָׁרֵת בַּצָּפוֹן וְדָמָן טָעוּן הַזָּיָה עַל־בֵּין הַבַּדִּים וְעַל הַפָּרֹכֶת וְעַל־מִזְבַּח הַזָּהָב מַתָּנָה אַחַת מֵהֶן מְעַכָּבֶת שְׁיָרֵי הַדָּם הָיָה שׁוֹפֵךְ עַל יְסוֹד מַעֲרָבִי שֶׁלַּמִּזְבֵּחַ הַחִיצוֹן אִם־לֹא נָתַן לֹא עִכֵּב: ב פָּרִים הַנִּשְׂרָפִים וּשְׂעִירִים הַנִּשְׂרָפִים שְׁחִיטָתָן בַּצָּפוֹן וְקִבּוּל דָּמָן בִּכְלִי שָׁרֵת בַּצָּפוֹן וְדָמָן טָעוּן הַזָּיָה עַל־הַפָּרֹכֶת וְעַל־מִזְבַּח הַזָּהָב

שתי לחם on Shavuoth. These are the only "communal peace-offerings". Unlike the שלמי יחיד described in Mishnah 7, these do not derive from emotions of joy already attained. Instead, it is their purpose solely to remind Israel of the blissful contentment which each of its members is capable of attaining if only he lives in accordance with the Law which constitutes the purpose of the existence of his people. Because they symbolize a goal yet unattained, these offerings belong to the category of קדשי קדשים. Their שחיטה and קבלה take place in the צפון, thus indicating the task which we must discharge with the physical, material aspects of our lives, and the acceptance of these facets of our personalities into the Sanctuary.

B. The קדשים קלים which are described in Mishnayoth 6–8 do not signify the worshipper's failure to consecrate all of his conduct to God, and his wish to renew his dedication to this end. Like the שלמים they serve to make us aware of the sense of unclouded bliss; the תודה of joy regained, and the איל נזיר of serene happiness to be resumed. The בכור מעשר and פסח are intended to remind us that the welfare of our families and the prospering of our material possessions are dependent upon God and derived from Him alone. Therefore, the שחיטה וקבלה of these offerings are not confined to צפון, but rather בכל מקום בעזרה.

1. פר ושעיר של יה״כ, the bullock, which reminds the כהן הגדול of his calling to be the "prime worker in the *service* of the Most High", and שעיר העם, the he-goat, which serves to remind the nation as a whole of its task "faithfully to *follow* the Most High in unswerving steadfastness and constancy" are חטאות and bear an important Yom Kippur message for both priesthood and nation. They warn that the High Priest has been remiss in the performance of his calling, and that the nation has not properly discharged its mission, so that both priest and nation must redirect their entire personalities anew to the end of performing their sacred duty in the manner in which it should be fulfilled. This hallowed task of both priest and nation is nothing more and nothing less than to be the bearers and guardians of the Divine Law, even as this is expressed by the symbolic act of הזיה על בין הבדים ועל הפרוכת. They have yet to learn to accept all material wealth and spiritual talents as gifts granted us all only through and

of the Day of Atonement are slaughtered on the north side; the reception of their blood in a vessel of ministration takes place on the north side. Their blood requires sprinkling between the staves of the Ark, on the dividing curtain, and upon the golden altar. Each one of these applications is indispensable. The rest of the blood he (the Priest) poured upon the western base of the outer altar; if he failed to do so, the omission did not render the sacrifice invalid.

2. The bullocks and he-goats which are to be burned outside are slaughtered on the north side; the reception of their blood in a vessel of ministration takes place on the north side. Their blood requires sprinkling on the dividing curtain and upon the

---

for the Torah, and, to devote both entirely to the end that they be "pleasing in the sight of God." This thought is expressed in symbolic terms by the act of הזיות על מזבח הקטורת. The applications of the blood are brought על הבדים and על הפרוכת, first with the דם הפר and then with the דם השעיר, על מזבח הזהב in a mixture of both at the same time, so that priest and nation come before God side by side, as it were, united in the equal understanding of the Law and in the endeavor to fulfill the task set for them by the Torah, and to do that which is "pleasing in the sight of God." This offering is brought in forty-three מתנות at ארון, פרוכת, מזבח קטרת, and each of these מתנות is such a significant part of the thought to be expressed by the whole ceremony that not one of them must be lacking if the offering is to have validity. שירי הדם, all applications of the sacrificial blood end with the remaining blood being poured out into the base of the altar, which symbolizes the basis on which all our own conduct and relationships are rooted in the Sanctuary. The offerings mentioned here and in the Mishnah following are called חטאות פנימיות, because their מתנות דם are executed in the "inside" of the דביר or of the היכל. The priest then pours the שירים on the western base of the altar which is the first place that he passes when he leaves the היכל.

2. פרים הנשרפים. Under this heading come:

a) פר העלם דבר של צבור: The bullock which must be brought as a sin-offering separately by each tribe of the entire nation, in case an error in judgment on the part of the Highest Court, the ב״ד הגדול caused the entire nation to commit a transgression which would have been subject to the penalty of כרת (Lev. 4:13–21), if it had been committed intentionally.

b) פר כהן משיח: The bullock to be offered by the High Priest as a sin-offering if, due to an erroneous interpretation of the Law on his part, he committed a transgression which would have been subject to the penalty of כרת (Lev. 4:3—12), if it had been committed intentionally.

מַתָּנָה אַחַת מֵהֶן מְעַכֶּבֶת שְׁיָרֵי הַדָּם הָיָה שׁוֹפֵךְ עַל יְסוֹד
מַעֲרָבִי שֶׁלַּמִּזְבֵּחַ הַחִיצוֹן אִם־לֹא נָתַן לֹא־עִכֵּב אֵלּוּ וְאֵלּוּ נִשְׂרָפִין
בְּבֵית הַדָּשֶׁן: ג חַטֹּאת הַצִּבּוּר וְהַיָּחִיד אֵלּוּ הֵן חַטֹּאת הַצִּבּוּר
שְׂעִירֵי רָאשֵׁי חֳדָשִׁים וְשֶׁל־מוֹעֲדוֹת שְׁחִיטָתָן בַּצָּפוֹן וְקִבּוּל דָּמָן
בִּכְלֵי שָׁרֵת בַּצָּפוֹן וְדָמָן טָעוּן אַרְבַּע מַתָּנוֹת עַל אַרְבַּע קְרָנוֹת:
כֵּיצַד עָלָה בַכֶּבֶשׁ וּפָנָה לַסּוֹבֵב וּבָא־לוֹ לְקֶרֶן דְּרוֹמִית מִזְרָחִית.
מִזְרָחִית צְפוֹנִית. צְפוֹנִית מַעֲרָבִית. מַעֲרָבִית דְּרוֹמִית. שְׁיָרֵי
הַדָּם הָיָה שׁפֵךְ עַל יְסוֹד דְּרוֹמִי. וְנֶאֱכָלִין לִפְנִים מִן־הַקְּלָעִים
לְזִכְרֵי כְהֻנָּה בְּכָל־מַאֲכָל לְיוֹם וָלַיְלָה עַד־חֲצוֹת: ד הָעוֹלָה קֹדֶשׁ

---

c) שעירי הנשרפים are the שעירי ע״ז to be offered by the tribes of the Jewish
nation if its collective sin, resulting from an error on the part of the
Highest Court, involved ע״ז (idolatry). These פרים and שעירים are called
נשרפים, because they are burned outside the Temple-city upon the place
where the ashes are deposited. Thus they differ from the other חטאות
which are eaten by the כהנים after the offering of the אימורים, the
חלבים וכליות, the fatty parts and kidneys, which are to be burned upon the
altar. The act of removing the sacrifice from the Sanctuary and burning
it outside the environs of the Temple is symbolic of the fact that, as a
consequence of the error which the entire nation, its spiritual leaders or
the High Priest have committed, there is no priest worthy of eating the
חטאת. These פרים ושעירים הנשרפים are treated in quite the same manner
as the פר ושעיר של יה״כ mentioned in the preceding Mishnah, with the exception that none of their blood was applied על בין הבדים in the Holy of
Holies. אלו ואלו, both the sacrifices mentioned in this Mishnah and those
named in the preceding one are חטאות פנימיות.

3. חטאות הצבור. As we shall soon explain, the שעירי חטאת to be brought
together with the מוסף offerings of New Moons and Festivals, and the
חטאת יחיד, to be brought by individuals in case of transgressions committed
erroneously, which, had they been perpetrated deliberately, would have been
subject to the penalty of כרת, are חטאות חיצוניות. The term חיצוניות indicates
that the מתנות דם connected with these two offerings must be executed in the
עזרה at the מזבח העולה. Atonement for transgressions is made by the
transgressor through the solemn resolution henceforth to remain on the
lofty plane of dutiful loyalty to the Law, and to allow nothing to tempt
him away from this firm intention. Therefore, the דם מתנות of these offerings
are to be applied upon the קרנות, the high corners of the altar, upon which,
with his finger, the priest applies part of the blood received in the sacred

golden altar. Each one of these applications is indispensable. The rest of the blood he poured upon the western base of the outer altar. If he failed to do so, the omission did not render the sacrifice invalid. Both these and the preceding offerings are burned at the place where the ashes were deposited.

3. The sin offerings of the community and of the individual. — These are the communal sin offerings : the he-goats offered on the New Moon and on the Feasts appointed for Solemn Assembly. They are slaughtered on the north side, and the reception of their blood in a vessel of ministration takes place on the north side. Their blood requires four applications upon the four corners of the altar, in this manner : He (the Priest) goes up the ascent, turns to the ledge, and comes to the south-eastern, north-eastern, north-western and south-western corners. The rest of the blood he poured upon the southern base. They are eaten, prepared in any manner, within the hangings of the Temple Court, by the males of the priesthood, on the same day and evening until midnight.

---

vessel, implying that the person seeking atonement must henceforth so direct his character that he maintains it on this high level. This act is to be performed in every direction to symbolize that these efforts are to encompass every facet of the personality of both the individual and the nation. Some of the blood is to be applied first upon the south-eastern corner of the altar, which symbolizes the Jewish human and national virtues to be acquired by means of *spiritual endeavor*. Then comes the north-eastern corner of the altar, which signifies the *material and physical aspects of life* to be based upon the spirit, and the north-western corner, indicating the law-abiding life which must be made a reality with the aid of these material gifts and physical faculties. Finally, some drops of the sacrificial blood are to be applied at the south-western corner, which represents the cultivation of the spirit of the Law that constantly flows forth anew from and through such a life lived in obedience to the Law. ונאכלין. The אימורים are to be burned on the altar, symbolizing the worshipper's willingness to have all his "goals and ambitions" pervaded and dominated by the fiery force that is God's Law, so that all earthly affairs might come to be "pleasing in the sight of God," לחם אשה ריח ניחוח לה'. After that, the remaining parts of the offering are to be eaten by the כהנים within the hallowed areas, in the עזרה, (which corresponds to the חצר formed in the ancient משכן by the curtains). This is to teach us that not only our ambitions and achievements, but also our joys and pleasures, must be vested

קָדָשִׁים שְׁחִיטָתָהּ בַּצָּפוֹן וְקִבּוּל דָּמָהּ בִּכְלִי שָׁרֵת בַּצָּפוֹן וְדָמָהּ
טָעוּן שְׁתֵּי מַתָּנוֹת שֶׁהֵן אַרְבַּע וּטְעוּנָה הַפְשֵׁט וְנִתּוּחַ וְכָלִיל
לָאִשִּׁים: ה זִבְחֵי שַׁלְמֵי צִבּוּר וַאֲשָׁמוֹת· אֵלּוּ הֵן אֲשָׁמוֹת אֲשַׁם
גְּזֵלוֹת אֲשַׁם מְעִילוֹת אֲשַׁם שִׁפְחָה חֲרוּפָה אֲשַׁם נָזִיר אֲשַׁם
מְצוֹרָע אֲשַׁם תָּלוּי· שְׁחִיטָתָן בַּצָּפוֹן וְקִבּוּל דָּמָן בִּכְלִי שָׁרֵת
בַּצָּפוֹן וְדָמָן טָעוּן שְׁתֵּי מַתָּנוֹת שֶׁהֵן אַרְבַּע· וְנֶאֱכָלִין לִפְנִים מִן
הַקְּלָעִים לְזִכְרֵי כְהֻנָּה בְּכָל־מַאֲכָל לְיוֹם וָלַיְלָה עַד חֲצוֹת:
י הַתּוֹדָה וְאֵיל נָזִיר קָדָשִׁים קַלִּים שְׁחִיטָתָן בְּכָל־מָקוֹם בָּעֲזָרָה
וְדָמָן טָעוּן שְׁתֵּי מַתָּנוֹת שֶׁהֵן אַרְבַּע· וְנֶאֱכָלִין בְּכָל הָעִיר לְכָל
אָדָם בְּכָל מַאֲכָל לְיוֹם וָלַיְלָה עַד חֲצוֹת: הַמּוּרָם מֵהֶם כַּיּוֹצֵא
בָהֶם אֶלָּא שֶׁהַמּוּרָם נֶאֱכָל לַכֹּהֲנִים לִנְשֵׁיהֶם וְלִבְנֵיהֶם וּלְעַבְדֵיהֶם:

with priestly sanctity. The statement that the offering may be eaten "prepared in any manner" is meant only to distinguish these offerings from
the Pesach-offering, which could be eaten only צלי, roasted (see Mishnah
8). ליום ולילה: The parts of the offering that are to be eaten must be
consumed only in close relationship with the act of שחיטה. For this reason
they may be eaten only on the same day on which the שחיטה of the
offering had originally taken place. Physical enjoyment becomes a sacred
act only if it is based on the surrender of all selfish aims and ambitions
in favor of the Sanctuary. In the מקדש, however, days were reckoned
from morning to morning, with the night counted as part of the preceding
day. עד חצות is a Rabbinical preventive time limit.

4. עולה, the dismembered parts of which are completely consigned to
the fire of the altar, atones for sins of omission. Such atonement is made
by the solemn resolve to overcome indifference and inertia, and to strive
unceasingly towards the high standard of duty which is taught by the
Law. For this reason the offering is called עולה, an "elevating-offering".
Its blood is applied in such a manner that the blood received in the sacred
vessel is thrown from afar, בזריקה, to the lower part of the altar which
leads up to the higher part thereof. This is to indicate that the person thus
seeking atonement is still far from the path that ascends on high, and that
he must yet with all the energies of his being strive upward and onward.
שתי מתנות שהן ארבע are two four-part "applications", one to the north-eastern
corner, combining the north and east sides of the altar, and the other to
the south-western corner, combining the south and west sides. In other
words, the "north side" and what it implies should be conceived of only
in connection with the "east side" of the altar. That is, all the material
and physical aspects of life, freed from all selfishness, should be viewed

4. The elevating-offering belongs to the most holy. It is slaughtered on the north side. The reception of its blood in the vessel of ministration takes place on the north side. Its blood requires two four-part applications. The offering requires flaying, dismemberment, and is totally given over to the fire.

5. Communal peace-offerings and guilt-offerings. These are guilt-offerings: the guilt-offering for robbery, the guilt-offering for the misuse of sacred objects, the guilt-offering of a betrothed handmaid, the guilt-offering of the *nazir,* the guilt-offering of the leper, the guilt-offering of doubtful sin. They are slaughtered on the north side. The reception of their blood in a vessel of ministration takes place on the north side. Their blood requires two four-part applications. They are eaten, prepared in any manner, within the hangings of the Temple Court, by the males of the priesthood, on the same day and evening until midnight.

6. The thanksgiving-offering and the ram offered by the

---

and attained only as part and parcel of the national entity which is oriented toward the Law of God. In the same manner, the "south side" of the altar and what it symbolizes must always be paired with the "west side". That is, all spiritual life must be based upon the Law and must be nurtured through the unceasing, constant cultivation of the Teaching of the Torah. Borne by these two forces, the whole human personality, both physical and spiritual, כליל לאשים completely purified and vivified by the fire of God's Law, is transformed to please the Divine will on earth.

5. זבחי שלמי צבור: These are the two כבשי עצרת, as already noted above. אשם נזיר: Lev. 19:21; אשם שפחה חרופה: ibid. 15; אשם מעילות: Lev. 5:25; אשם גזלות Num. 6:12; אשם מצורע: ibid. 14:12; אשם תלוי: Lev. 5:18. תלוי is a "pending doubt". That is, a person is in doubt whether, either through carelessness or lack of circumspection, he has committed a sin which would have been subject to the penalty of כרת, had it been perpetrated deliberately. The מתנות in connection with these offerings are the same as those of the עולה. However, only the חלב וכליות are burned upon the altar. The rest of the offering is eaten by the כהנים even as the חטאת (see Mishnah 3).

6. תודה is the thanksgiving-offering for the restoration of a tranquil life through Divine deliverance from illness, from the perils of the sea, from distress in the wilderness or from the catastrophe of imprisonment. איל נזיר is the sacrifice offered by a Nazirite when he resumes a life without abstinence. Because they do not involve guilt or atonement, these two types of offering are קדשים קלים, of a lesser degree of sanctity. The area in which their שחיטה takes place is not limited to צפון, and those parts that may be

ז שְׁלָמִים קָדָשִׁים קַלִּים שְׁחִיטָתָן בְּכָל־מָקוֹם בָּעֲזָרָה וְדָמָן טָעוּן
שְׁתֵּי מַתָּנוֹת שֶׁהֵן אַרְבַּע וְנֶאֱכָלִין בְּכָל־הָעִיר לְכָל־אָדָם בְּכָל־
מַאֲכָל לִשְׁנֵי יָמִים וְלַיְלָה אֶחָד: הַמּוּרָם מֵהֶם כַּיּוֹצֵא בָהֶם אֶלָּא
שֶׁהַמּוּרָם נֶאֱכָל לַכֹּהֲנִים לִנְשֵׁיהֶם וְלִבְנֵיהֶם וּלְעַבְדֵיהֶם: ח הַבְּכוֹר
וְהַמַּעֲשֵׂר וְהַפֶּסַח קָדָשִׁים קַלִּים שְׁחִיטָתָן בְּכָל־מָקוֹם בָּעֲזָרָה
וְדָמָן טָעוּן מַתָּנָה אֶחָת · וּבִלְבַד שֶׁיִּתֵּן כְּנֶגֶד הַיְסֹד: שִׁנָּה
בַּאֲכִילָתָן הַבְּכוֹר נֶאֱכָל לַכֹּהֲנִים וְהַמַּעֲשֵׂר לְכָל־אָדָם וְנֶאֱכָלִין
בְּכָל־הָעִיר בְּכָל־מַאֲכָל לִשְׁנֵי יָמִים וְלַיְלָה אֶחָד · הַפֶּסַח אֵינוּ
נֶאֱכָל אֶלָּא בַלַּיְלָה וְאֵינוּ נֶאֱכָל אֶלָּא עַד־חֲצוֹת וְאֵינוֹ נֶאֱכָל אֶלָּא
לִמְנוּיָו וְאֵינוֹ נֶאֱכָל אֶלָּא צָלִי:

---

eaten may be consumed by anyone anywhere in the city which constitutes the environs of the Sanctuary. המורם מהם, the parts which are to be set aside as תרומה for the כהן, חזה ושוק etc., may also be eaten anywhere in the city, but only by the כהנים and the members of their household.

7. שלמים. The תודה and איל נזיר mentioned above are also שלמים, but they are brought only on special occasions. However, these שלמים are not occasioned by any specific event, but rather symbolize the gladsome, unclouded joy of life. These general שלמים are distinguished from the other types of offerings only in that the period during which they may be eaten is somewhat longer than that specified for the consumption of the others. תודה and איל נזיר though not explicitly involving guilt and atonement, are nevertheless not entirely free from a certain connotation of a sense of inadequacy in the performance of duty. For as a rule, danger and suffering have as their goal the purification and improvement of the personality of the one afflicted. And the vows taken by the Nazarite have as their purpose the strengthening of his moral fiber through physical abstinence. Because of the solemn significance inherent in the תודה and the איל נזיר, they may be eaten only within the same limited period as a חטאת or אשם. Ordinary שלמים may be eaten in any desired place, and thus they impart some of the holiness of the Sanctuary to the rooms of the humble home in which they are consumed. In the same manner, in figuring the time during which these sacrifices may be eaten, the ordinary day (extending from sundown to sundown) is combined with the day as reckoned in the Sanctuary (from morning to morning) to form one unit of time, thus extending the period to include two days and one night. Thus the period

nazir, were holy to a lesser degree. These are slaughtered anywhere in the Temple Court. Their blood requires two four-part applications. They are eaten, prepared in any manner, anywhere in the city, by anyone, on the same day and evening until midnight. The same rule applies to the separated share thereof, except that the separated share is eaten by the priests, their wives, their children and their slaves.

7. The peace-offerings are holy to a lesser degree. They are slaughtered anywhere in the Temple Court. Their blood requires two four-part applications, and they are eaten, prepared in any manner, anywhere in the city, by anyone, during two days and one night. The same rule applies to the separated share thereof, except that the separated share is eaten by the priests, their wives, their children and their servants.

8. The first-born animals, the tithes of cattle, and the Pesach-offering are holy to a lesser degree. They are slaughtered anywhere in the Temple Court. Their blood, requires only one application; this however, has to be above the base of the altar. They are eaten in different ways : the first-born are eaten by the priests, while the tithe is eaten by any person. They are eaten anywhere in the city, prepared in any manner, during two days and one night. The Pesach-offering is eaten only on the same evening, only until midnight, only by assigned partakers, and it is eaten only roasted.

---

during which the שלמים may be eaten includes both the "Sanctuary day" and the "day" as reckoned in Jewish life outside the Temple. The succession of day, night and the next day combines the order of the night following day and the order of the day following the night.

     8 ררור, the male first-born, and מעשר the tithe of cattle, both serve as symbolic expression of the fact that the worshipper regards the welfare and growth of his herds as the work of God, and that he therefore knows that his continued ownership of the animals is dependent upon Divine decree. To this is joined the Pesach-offering, which teaches the Jew to conceive of himself, of his home, and of his nation as creations of God. Accordingly, the blood of the sacrifice is simply poured all at one time on the base of the altar, implying that the entire personality of the worshipper, borne by Divine Providence, is rooted solely in the Law of God. בכור, which becomes the property of the כהן, and is eaten by the כהנים and the members of their household, has the character of שלמים, and may be eaten during שני ימים ולילה אחד. The same is true of the מעשר בהמה which, how-

רַבִּי יִשְׁמָעֵאל אוֹמֵר, בִּשְׁלֹשׁ עֶשְׂרֵה מִדּוֹת הַתּוֹרָה נִדְרֶשֶׁת:

מִקַּל וָחְמֶר· וּמִגְּזֵרָה שָׁוָה· מִבִּנְיַן אָב מִכָּתוּב אֶחָד וּמִבִּנְיַן אָב

מִשְּׁנֵי כְתוּבִים· מִכְּלָל וּפְרָט· וּמִפְּרָט וּכְלָל· כְּלָל וּפְרָט וּכְלָל

אִי אַתָּה דָן אֶלָּא כְּעֵין הַפְּרָט· מִכְּלָל שֶׁהוּא צָרִיךְ לִפְרָט

וּמִפְּרָט שֶׁהוּא צָרִיךְ לִכְלָל· כָּל־דָּבָר שֶׁהָיָה בִּכְלָל וְיָצָא מִן־הַכְּלָל

---

ever, unlike the בכור, remains the property of the בעלים, the ones who originally offered it as the tithe of their herd; it may be eaten by those persons or by anyone else. The Pesach-offering, on the other hand, may be eaten only during the night of the 14th, the eve of the 15th day of the month of Nisan, that is, the time of the act of Divine redemption, to the commemoration of which the offering is dedicated. ואינו נאכל אלא למנויו. The Pesach-offering symbolizes the individual Jews who, through liberating redemption have attained independence and formed independent families and households, שה לבית אבות שה לבית. Therefore, the individual partakers of the Pesach-offering had to be determined in advance of the שחיטה and the lamb could be eaten only by those who had previously agreed to express their personal independence and voluntary solidarity by partaking in that particular Pesach feast. And even as freedom and independence were handed to the people of Israel directly by God, without any human intervention, so, too, the offering commemorating that occasion may not be eaten בכל מאכל, prepared in any desired manner, but only צלי אש, roasted directly upon the fire, without the artificial additions of human hands.

רבי ישמעאל. When God, through Moses, caused that Law to be written down which He had already made known to the nation orally in full detail, He caused this Holy Writ to be composed in accordance with thirteen basic rules which made it possible to present the Written Word in such a pregnant and compact form that the detailed intention of the Lawgiver could be נדרש, investigated from the written word by means of the application of these rules which were handed down simultaneously with the Written Law. These rules are as follows:

1. קל וחומר. The subjects of the Law are classed as being קלים, lighter or חמורים, severe, depending upon the ordinances set down with regard to them. For example, the law of י"ט, which permits the preparation of אוכל נפש on holidays, and the violation of which is not subject to the penalty of כרת and סקילה, is less grave than the law governing the Sabbath, on which day אוכל נפש may not be prepared and in which case violation, unlike that of holidays, is punishable by כרת and סקילה. Hence י"ט is קל while שבת is חמור. Hence, anything explicitly permitted (קולא) by law of the Sabbath, implicitly applies also to י"ט, while any prohibition (חומרא) expressed with regard to י"ט, implicitly applies also to שבת. This conclusion

לְלַמֵּד לֹא לְלַמֵּד עַל־עַצְמוֹ יָצָא אֶלָּא לְלַמֵּד עַל־הַכְּלָל כֻּלּוֹ יָצָא.
כָּל־דָּבָר שֶׁהָיָה בִכְלָל וְיָצָא לִטְעוֹן טְעַן אֶחָד שֶׁהוּא כְעִנְיָנוֹ יָצָא
לְהָקֵל וְלֹא לְהַחֲמִיר. כָּל־דָּבָר שֶׁהָיָה בִכְלָל וְיָצָא לִטְעוֹן טְעַן אַחֵר
שֶׁלֹּא כְעִנְיָנוֹ יָצָא לְהָקֵל וּלְהַחֲמִיר. כָּל־דָּבָר שֶׁהָיָה בִכְלָל וְיָצָא
לִדּוֹן בַּדָּבָר הֶחָדָשׁ אִי אַתָּה יָכוֹל לְהַחֲזִירוֹ לִכְלָלוֹ עַד שֶׁיַּחֲזִירֶנּוּ

drawn from minor to major, and, conversely, from major to minor, is called קל וחומר.

2. גזרה שוה. When, according to tradition, two laws containing similar expressions serve to clarify each other, e.g. we find the term במועדו (Num. 9:2, 28:2) similarly used with reference to both פסח and תמיד. Thereby we are informed that both are דוחה שבת וטומאה; both must be brought even on שבת and even בטומאת מת if there is no other possibility.

3. בנין אב From the fact that, in Deut. 19:15 the word אחד is affixed to עד, to denote *one* witness, the principle is laid down זה בנה אב, that wherever the word עד is written without this affixation, it does not denote "a witness", but testimony, which must be based on at least two witnesses.

4. כלל ופרט. When a general term is followed by a specification; e.g. if the general term בהמה is followed by a specification such as בקר וצאן (see Lev. 1:2), then the law is limited to these specifications, אין בכלל אלא מה שבפרט. The law mentions the generalization and thereafter lists the specifications in order to indicate that of the whole generalization the law refers only to the species mentioned, צאן ובקר אין מידי אחרינא לא.

5. פרט וכלל. If, however, a specification is followed by a generalization, e.g. נעשה כלל מוסיף על הפרט ורבי כל מילי, (Exod. 22.9), חמור או שור או שה וכל בהמה, the generalization has the opposite effect, and is all-inclusive.

6. כלל ופרט וכלל. If, however, the generalization is followed by a specification which is followed in turn by another generalization, then the specification is raised to a generalization and includes everything that has the essential characteristics of the specification:— אי אתה דן אלא כעין הפרט. For example (Deut. 14:26) „בבל אשר תאוה נפשך‟, כלל, „בבקר ובצאן וביין ובשכר‟ פרט, „ובכל אשר תשאל נפשך‟ חזר וכלל. כלל ופרט וכלל, אי אתה דן אלא כעין הפרט, מה הפרט is an all inclu- „כל אשר תאוה נפשך‟ מפורש ולד ולדות הארץ, אף כל דבר שהוא ולד ולדות הארץ. sive generalization; בקר צאן יין ושכר are specifications, while כל אשר תשאל נפשך is again a generalization. This last generalization elevates the specification to the status of a generalization; i.e. "organic produce of the earth", which consequently includes everything that has the essential characteristics of this specification.

7. כלל הצריך לפרט. If, the generalization must be followed by the specifi- cation for the sake of clarity, then there is no limiting effect on the פרט as in a כלל ופרט (see § 4). E.g. וכסהו בעפר (Lev. 17:13), where the generali-

הַכָּתוּב לִכְלָלוֹ כְּפֵרוּשׁ · דָּבָר הַלָּמֵד מֵעִנְיָנוֹ וְדָבָר הַלָּמֵד מִסּוֹפוֹ ·
וְכֵן שְׁנֵי כְתוּבִים הַמַּכְחִישִׁים זֶה אֶת־זֶה עַד שֶׁיָּבוֹא הַכָּתוּב
הַשְּׁלִישִׁי וְיַכְרִיעַ בֵּינֵיהֶם :

---

zation וכסהו receives its clarification from the specification בעפר, to show
that what is meant is not the mere covering by means of any cover, but
the kind of covering where the object is utterly commingled with the material
covering it. In like manner. when the preceding פרט must be followed by a
כלל for clarity's sake, it does not have the all-inclusive effect of a פרט וכלל.

8. כל דבר שהיה בכלל וכו'. E.g. הבערה the lighting of a fire on שבת was
included among the prohibited מלאכות but is singled out as a separate
prohibition (Exod. 35:3). This is in order to teach, in connection with
the general law of איסור מלאכה on שבת, that the Sabbath is sanctified
by every מלאכה which is forbidden. Therefore, if someone inadvertently,
בשגגה, has performed several מלאכות on the Sabbath, he must offer up a
separate חטאת for each מלאכה. הבערה לחלק יצאה, in order to teach this חילוק
for the כלל כולו for the מלאכות.

9. נגעי שחין ומכוה the example, For .כל דבר שהיה בכלל וכו' כענינו וכו. (Lev.
13:18, 24) were included under the נגעי עור ובשר which had been discussed
before. These are given special discussion, and the קולא, the alleviation, is
applied to them to the effect that (Verses 23, 28) they are to be declared
"clean" immediately after the first week, if they remain unchanged
during that time. In the case of the other related נגעים, it was mandatory
to wait an additional week. (Verse 5) Since שחין ומכוה were thus
singled out from the others for the purpose of קולא, therefore the חומרא:
מחיה (Verse 15) which is not explicitly stated for their case, cannot be
deemed applicable to them.

10. נגעי ראש וזקן the example, For .כל דבר שהיה בכלל וכו. שלא כענינו וכו
(Lev. 13:29) differ completely from the other נגעים in that they become
טמא through שער צהוב (Verse 30), but not through שער לבן. In the case
of other נגעים (Verse 3), שער לבן effects טומאה, but שער צהוב has no
effect. Therefore, no rule [of קולא or חומרא] may be transferred from
the chapter of the other נגעים to these.

11. אשם מצורע, for example, is unlike other .דבר שהיה בכלל וכו' בדבר חדש וכו'
אשמות in that its blood, instead of being applied to the מזבח, is applied to
בהן יד ובהן רגל (Lev. 14:14). For this reason, it was necessary to state
explicity in Verse 13 ושחט את הכבש במקום וגו', that אשם מצורע is to be treated
in the same manner as the other offerings. Otherwise, it might have been
assumed that, by virtue of this דבר חדש, the offering should also be excluded
from מתן דמים ואימורים לגבי מזבח, which was required in sacrifices, other

12. לא תרצח, Because of its contextual relationship with .דבר הלמד מענינו
לא תנאף, the violation of which is subject to the penalty of death, the

May it be Your will, *God* our
God and God of our fathers,
that the Temple be soon rebuilt
in our days, and give us our
portion in Your Teaching, so
that we may serve You there
with awe as in the days of the
past and as in former years.

יְהִי רָצוֹן לְפָנֶֽיךָ יְיָ אֱלֹהֵֽינוּ
וֵאלֹהֵי אֲבוֹתֵֽינוּ שֶׁיִּבָּנֶה בֵּית
הַמִּקְדָּשׁ בִּמְהֵרָה בְיָמֵֽינוּ וְתֵן
חֶלְקֵֽנוּ בְּתוֹרָתֶֽךָ : וְשָׁם נַעֲבָדְךָ
בְּיִרְאָה כִּימֵי עוֹלָם וּכְשָׁנִים
קַדְמֹנִיּוֹת :

See page 753 for קדיש דרבנן.

---

commandment לֹא תִגְנֹב, is also referred, not to the stealing of money, but
to kidnapping, which is also punishable by death. דבר הלמד מסופו. For ex-
ample, it is inferred from the ordinance וְנָתַץ אֶת הַבַּיִת אֶת אֲבָנָיו וְאֶת עֵצָיו וְאֵת כָּל
עֲפַר וגו׳ (Lev. 14:45) that the house discussed in this chapter (Verse 34)
is to be limited to one that consists of stone, wood, and clay.

13. וְכֵן שְׁנֵי כְתוּבִים וכו׳. In Exod. 20:19, for example, we read: "You
have seen that I have spoken with you *from heaven.*" On the other hand,
Exod. 19:20 tells us: "God came down upon *Mount Sinai,* to the top of the
mountain." Deut. 4:36 harmonizes this contradiction with the words: "Out
of *heaven* He let you hear His *voice* to take you under the bond of His
discipline, and on the *earth* He let you see His great *fire,* and you heard
His words out of the fire."

יהי רצון is a wish with which we repeatedly end portions of our prayer
book. In our present Divine service, which is only a faint echo of that
originally ordained by God in the Sanctuary in Jerusalem, we express our
fervent hope that we may live to see the time when that same service will
be restored in the city of God. For the present, we pray for His help that,
now and at all times, we may attain to an understanding and fulfillment
of His Law, so that each may fulfill the Divinely-appointed purpose in life,
each according to his powers and inclinatons. Then the restoration of the
Temple becomes merely a means to a more complete discharge of our task
in the service of God. Here, at the end of the portion which introduces our
actual תפלה, this wish is all the more timely and appropriate. For immediately
after reciting the ברכת התורה, we have just completed a period of active
Torah-study devoted to the ordinances from the Written Torah concerning
the daily offerings (פרשת התמיד), and a portion of the Mishnah, the Oral
Torah, dealing with the sacrificial ritual (פרק איזהו מקומן), to which we added
a recital of a ברייתא which contains the key to חשב״פ ,י״ג מדות דר׳ ישמעאל
At this point we express our hope that the actual עבודה of the Temple may
soon be restored so that we may be enabled to discharge our Torah-task
to the fullest extent possible.

Concerning the commandment of צִיצִית, *comp.* קְרִיאַת שְׁמַע; *Horeb Ch. 39;*
Comm. Bamidbar XV, 37-41.

אַחֲרֵי אֲמִירַת בִּרְכוֹת הַשַּׁחַר קוֹדֶם בָּרוּךְ שֶׁאָמַר מִתְעַטְּפִים בְּטַלִית וְאַחַ"כ מַנִּיחִים תְּפִלִּין. וְקוֹדֶם עֲטִיפַת הַטַּלִית צָרִיךְ לִבְדּוֹק בְּלִילִית לִרְאוֹת שֶׁיִּהְיוּ כְּשֵׁרוֹת וְאַחַ"כ יֹאמַר:

Before בָּרוּךְ שֶׁאָמַר, *one dons talith and tefillin, i.e. first the talith, then the*
tefillin. Before donning the talith, one is to examine the fringes, as one does
with those of the arba kanfoth. Then the following is said:

הִנְנִי מִתְעַטֵּף בְּטַלִית שֶׁל־צִיצִת כְּדֵי לְקַיֵּם מִצְוַת בּוֹרְאִי
כַּכָּתוּב בַּתּוֹרָה וְעָשׂוּ לָהֶם צִיצִת עַל־כַּנְפֵי בִגְדֵיהֶם לְדֹרֹתָם·
וּכְשֵׁם שֶׁאֲנִי מִתְכַּסֶּה בְּטַלִית בָּעוֹלָם הַזֶּה כֵּן תִּזְכֶּה נִשְׁמָתִי
לְהִתְלַבֵּשׁ בְּטַלִית נָאֶה לָעוֹלָם הַבָּא בְּגַן עֵדֶן, אָמֵן:

The unfolded talith is held and the following is said, standing: וְאַחַ"כ יְבָרֵךְ מְעֻמָּד

בָּרוּךְ אַתָּה יְיָ אֱלֹהֵינוּ מֶלֶךְ הָעוֹלָם אֲשֶׁר
קִדְּשָׁנוּ בְּמִצְוֹתָיו וְצִוָּנוּ לְהִתְעַטֵּף בַּצִּיצִת:

וְיִתְעַטֵּף אֶת רֹאשׁוֹ וִיקַח כָּד יָמִין שֶׁל הַטַּלִית עִם שְׁתֵּי לִילִית שֶׁבּוֹ וְיַנִּיחֵם עַל כָּתֵף הַשְּׂמֹאל וִיהְיוּ
כָּל ד' לִילִית בְּצַד שְׂמֹאל וְיַעֲמוֹד כָּךְ מְעוּטָף כְּדֵי הִלּוּךְ ד' אַמּוֹת וְיֹאמַר מַה יָּקָר וְכוּ'.

Then the talith is wrapped about in such a manner that the head is completely
covered; the right part of the talith together with the two fringes is brought
across the face and above the left shoulder and the following is said:

מַה־יָּקָר חַסְדְּךָ אֱלֹהִים וּבְנֵי אָדָם בְּצֵל כְּנָפֶיךָ יֶחֱסָיוּן:
יִרְוְיֻן מִדֶּשֶׁן בֵּיתֶךָ וְנַחַל עֲדָנֶיךָ תַשְׁקֵם:
כִּי עִמְּךָ מְקוֹר חַיִּים בְּאוֹרְךָ נִרְאֶה־אוֹר:
מְשֹׁךְ חַסְדְּךָ לְיֹדְעֶיךָ וְצִדְקָתְךָ לְיִשְׁרֵי־לֵב:
יְהִי רָצוֹן מִלְּפָנֶיךָ יְיָ אֱלֹהֵינוּ וֵאלֹהֵי אֲבוֹתֵינוּ שֶׁתְּהֵי חֲשׁוּבָה
מִצְוַת צִיצַת זוֹ כְּאִלּוּ קִיַּמְתִּיהָ בְּכָל־פְּרָטֶיהָ וְדִקְדּוּקֶיהָ וְכַוָּנוֹתֶיהָ
וְתַרְיַ"ג מִצְוֹת הַתְּלוּיִם בָּהּ · אָמֵן:

לְאַחַ"כ יָסִיר הַטַּלִית מֵעַל פָּנָיו וִילַבְּשֶׁךָ סָבִיב הָרֹאשׁ וְהָגֵן וִיהְיוּ לִימִינוֹ לִילִית אַחַת לְפָנָיו וְלִילָה
אַחַת לְאַחֲרָיו וְכֵן לִשְׂמֹאלוֹ.

The talith is removed from the face and wrapped about so that on each side
one fringe is in the front and one in the back:

סדר הנחת תפלין

Concerning the commandment of תפלין, *comp.* קריאת שמע; *Horeb Ch. 38;*
Comm. Shemoth XIII, 9; Devarim VI, 8.

Before putting on the tefillin, the following is said: קודם הנחת תפלין יאמר זה

הִנְנִי מְכַוֵּן בְּהַנָּחַת תְּפִלִּין לְקַיֵּם מִצְוַת בּוֹרְאִי שֶׁצִּוָּנוּ לְהָנִיחַ תְּפִלִּין כַּכָּתוּב
בַּתּוֹרָה וּקְשַׁרְתָּם לְאוֹת עַל יָדֶךָ וְהָיוּ לְטֹטָפֹת בֵּין עֵינֶיךָ וְהֵם אַרְבַּע פָּרָשׁוֹת
אֵלּוּ, שְׁמַע, וְהָיָה אִם שָׁמֹעַ, קַדֶּשׁ, וְהָיָה כִּי יְבִאֲךָ, שֶׁיֵּשׁ בָּהֶם יִחוּדוֹ וְאַחְדּוּתוֹ
יִתְבָּרַךְ שְׁמוֹ וְשֶׁנִּזְכּוֹר נִסִּים וְנִפְלָאוֹת שֶׁעָשָׂה עִמָּנוּ בְּהוֹצִיאוּ אוֹתָנוּ מִמִּצְרַיִם
וַאֲשֶׁר לוֹ הַכֹּחַ וְהַמֶּמְשָׁלָה בָּעֶלְיוֹנִים וּבַתַּחְתּוֹנִים לַעֲשׂוֹת בָּהֶם כִּרְצוֹנוֹ,
וְצִוָּנוּ לְהָנִיחַ עַל הַיָּד לְזִכְרוֹן זְרוֹעַ הַנְּטוּיָה, וְשֶׁהִיא נֶגֶד הַלֵּב לְשַׁעְבֵּד בָּזֶה
הַתַּאֲוֹת וּמַחְשָׁבוֹת לִבֵּנוּ לַעֲבוֹדָתוֹ יִתְבָּרַךְ שְׁמוֹ, וְעַל הָרֹאשׁ נֶגֶד הַמֹּחַ
שֶׁהַנְּשָׁמָה שֶׁבְּמֹחִי עִם שְׁאָר חוּשַׁי וְכוֹחוֹתַי כֻּלָּם יִהְיוּ מְשֻׁעְבָּדִים לַעֲבוֹדָתוֹ יִתְבָּרַךְ
שְׁמוֹ. וּמִשֶּׁפַע מִצְוַת תְּפִלִּין יִתְמַשֵּׁךְ עָלַי לִהְיוֹת לִי חַיִּים אֲרוּכִים וְשֶׁפַע קֹדֶשׁ
וּמַחְשָׁבוֹת קְדוֹשׁוֹת בְּלִי הִרְהוּר חֵטְא וְעָוֹן כְּלָל וְשֶׁלֹּא יְפַתֵּנוּ וְלֹא יִתְגָּרֶה בָּנוּ יֵצֶר
הָרַע וְיַנִּיחֵנוּ לַעֲבֹד אֶת יְיָ כַּאֲשֶׁר עִם לְבָבֵנוּ · אָמֵן:

ויקח תפלה של יד ויניחנה על יד שמאל על בשר הגבוה שבזרוע, וקודם הקשירה יברך:
The תפלה של יד *is put on the left arm and this is said:*

בָּרוּךְ אַתָּה יְיָ אֱמֶ"הָ אֲשֶׁר קִדְּשָׁנוּ בְּמִצְוֹתָיו וְצִוָּנוּ לְהָנִיחַ תְּפִלִּין:

ומהדק וקושר הרטועה וכורך ז' כריכות על קנה הזרוע. ולוקח תפלה של ראש ומנ֯יחך:
Then the knot is tightened and the רצועה *wound seven times around the arm.*
The תפלה של ראש *is put on and this is said:*

בָּרוּךְ אַתָּה יְיָ אֱמֶ"הָ אֲשֶׁר קִדְּשָׁנוּ בְּמִצְוֹתָיו וְצִוָּנוּ עַל מִצְוַת תְּפִלִּין:

Immediately thereafter: בָּרוּךְ שֵׁם כְּבוֹד מַלְכוּתוֹ לְעוֹלָם וָעֶד:

ומהדקה ברח֯או, ואח"כ כורך ג' כריכות על אלבע האמלעית ויאמר:
After placing of the תפלה של ראש the רצועה של יד *is wound three times around*
the middle finger and the following verses are said:

וְאֵרַשְׂתִּיךְ לִי לְעוֹלָם · וְאֵרַשְׂתִּיךְ לִי בְּצֶדֶק וּבְמִשְׁפָּט וּבְחֶסֶד
וּבְרַחֲמִים · וְאֵרַשְׂתִּיךְ לִי בֶּאֱמוּנָה וְיָדַעַתְּ אֶת יְיָ :

יְהִי רָצוֹן מִלְּפָנֶיךָ יְיָ אֱלֹהֵינוּ וֵאלֹהֵי אֲבוֹתֵינוּ שֶׁתְּהֵי חֲשׁוּבָה
מִצְוַת הֲנָחַת תְּפִלִּין זוֹ כְּאִלּוּ קִיַּמְתִּיהָ בְּכָל פְּרָטֶיהָ וְדִקְדּוּקֶיהָ
וְכַוָּנוֹתֶיהָ וְתַרְיַ"ג מִצְוֹת הַתְּלוּיִם בָּהּ · אָמֵן:

After עלינו, *the first step is the removal of the three windings round the finger,*
followed by the taking off of the של ראש *and then of the* של יד:
On ראש חדש *the tefillin are taken off before Mussaph, on* חול המועד *before*
Hallel:

מִזְמוֹר שִׁיר חֲנֻכַּת הַבַּיִת לְדָוִד: אֲרוֹמִמְךָ יְיָ כִּי דִלִּיתָנִי, וְלֹא שִׂמַּחְתָּ אֹיְבַי
לִי: יְיָ אֱלֹהָי, שִׁוַּעְתִּי אֵלֶיךָ וַתִּרְפָּאֵנִי: יְיָ הֶעֱלִיתָ מִן שְׁאוֹל נַפְשִׁי,
חִיִּיתַנִי מִיָּרְדִי בוֹר: זַמְּרוּ לַיְיָ חֲסִידָיו, וְהוֹדוּ לְזֵכֶר קָדְשׁוֹ: כִּי רֶגַע בְּאַפּוֹ, חַיִּים
בִּרְצוֹנוֹ, בָּעֶרֶב יָלִין בֶּכִי וְלַבֹּקֶר רִנָּה: וַאֲנִי אָמַרְתִּי בְשַׁלְוִי, בַּל אֶמּוֹט לְעוֹלָם:
יְיָ בִּרְצוֹנְךָ הֶעֱמַדְתָּה לְהַרְרִי עֹז, הִסְתַּרְתָּ פָנֶיךָ הָיִיתִי נִבְהָל: אֵלֶיךָ יְיָ אֶקְרָא,
וְאֶל אֲדֹנָי אֶתְחַנָּן: מַה בֶּצַע בְּדָמִי בְּרִדְתִּי אֶל שָׁחַת, הֲיוֹדְךָ עָפָר הֲיַגִּיד
אֲמִתֶּךָ: שְׁמַע יְיָ וְחָנֵּנִי, יְיָ הֱיֵה עֹזֵר לִי: הָפַכְתָּ מִסְפְּדִי לְמָחוֹל לִי, פִּתַּחְתָּ שַׂקִּי
וַתְּאַזְּרֵנִי שִׂמְחָה: לְמַעַן יְזַמֶּרְךָ כָבוֹד וְלֹא יִדֹּם, יְיָ אֱלֹהַי, לְעוֹלָם אוֹדֶךָּ: קדיש יתום

ברוך שאמר is recited in a standing position while holding the two front fringes of the talith in the right hand (until מהולל בתשבחות). Having begun here, nothing must be allowed to interrupt the prayer until after the ש"ע (except for the responses in Kaddish with ברוך ה' המבורך with יהא שמיה. אמן at ברכו and at the קדושה with קדוש קדוש etc. and with ברוך כבוד ה'; and all this only if one has not yet reached the ש"ע; during the recital of ש"ע itself no interruption whatsoever is permitted):

If one arrives at the Synagogue in the midst of the פסוקי דזמרה one says מהולל בתשבחות until ברוך שאמר, continues with אשרי and then arranges the prayer in such a way — by adding or omitting ensuing psalms as time permits — that one begins ישתבח together with the congregation. If one arrives at a time when the congregation has already reached ישתבח, one joins with it at ברכו and continues through the ש"ע. The parts which were omitted may be said privately later on (without the introductory Bracha of ברוך שאמר and the concluding Bracha of ישתבח):

בָּרוּךְ שֶׁאָמַר וְהָיָה הָעוֹלָם. בָּרוּךְ הוּא. בָּרוּךְ
עוֹשֶׂה בְרֵאשִׁית. בָּרוּךְ אוֹמֵר וְעוֹשֶׂה. בָּרוּךְ גּוֹזֵר

ברוך שאמר is the introductory ברכה of the פסוקי דזמרה beginning with הודו, immediately following. As such it is intended to show us the proper approach to the recital of all our תהלות, and the sum total of the point of view from which we should study our Psalms is expressed for us in all-inclusive terms by the word ברוך. In their very first תהלה, the שירת הים, our ancestors proclaimed that the Lord is נורא תהלות. They declared that יראה, God-fearing obedience must be the fruit of all our תהלות, of all the songs in praise of the mighty deeds through which God revealed His greatness. All our hymns are empty if they are not employed to promote the active service of God in everyday life or to engender the fear and obedience of Him. And if lip-service should actually be deemed a substitute for such conduct, then it is nothing short of blasphemy. All these truths we now impress upon our own conscience again and again, when we prepare once more to proclaim the תהלות from our national hymnal, the collection

Blessed be He Who spoke and the world came into being. Blessed be He Who still exists today; blessed be He Who even now continues the work of the Beginning. Blessed be He Who speaks and shapes even now; blessed be He Who even now decrees and fulfills. Blessed be He Whose compassion rules over the earth; blessed be He Whose compassion rules over all creatures. Blessed be He Who well rewards those who fear Him. Blessed

---

of our hymns of praise that sing of the manifold ways in which God has revealed His glory to us through mighty deeds. ברוך, "faithful obedience to God", that is the solemn resolve which every תהלה should engender within our hearts in ever new inspiration. We are to become a "blessing" to His will and to His rule on earth. We are to render in full that contribution which He expects of us, so that all of our activities, both great and small, should further His supreme sovereignty here below, and that with our lives we may shape all things so as to be pleasing to Him, all for the hastening of the coming of His kingdom on earth, the reign of all that is good and true, of love and righteousness and of the sanctification of every aspect of human life. All this is what we mean by "blessing God", and with our pledge of ברוך we renew our promise to do these things, irrespective of what phase of the infinite greatness of His mighty deeds we may experience in our own lives. Now we meditate upon His Word by which the world was created in days of antiquity, and His sovereignty which still prevails in nature and history to this very day (ומקים — שאמר). We consider His tender mercies which He lavishes upon the world, and upon each and every one of His creatures separately (הבריות—מרחם), and the special, blessed care which He gives to all those who live out their lives in fear of Him (משלם). We reflect upon His presence which will endure forever though all else may die; upon His everlasting Being though all else round about Him may vanish (לנצח — חי). We come to realize that He can free us even from the chains of legitimate authority, even as He is ready to deliver us from the powers of wrongful violence (פודה — מציל). Finally, we contemplate His Name (שמו) through the revelation of which He has afforded us a glimpse of His rule which is so infinitely varied in form and yet one and constant in its purpose. The contemplation of these phases of His sovereignty separately, and the sum total of them in recapitulation, waken and strengthen within us the eternal resolve of our lives: to become a ברכה for the will of God with every fiber of our being and at every moment of our lives. Therefore, sustained by the knowledge that the eye of the Almighty, merciful Father is forever upon all, even upon the most unworthy of us (האל האב הרחמן), we come before Him, Whose תהלות have come down to us by the mouths of His people ever since they had first beheld "the ways of God—the ways of our God and King in holiness"

וּמָקוֹם· בָּרוּךְ מְרַחֵם עַל הָאָרֶץ· בָּרוּךְ מְרַחֵם עַל
הַבְּרִיּוֹת· בָּרוּךְ מְשַׁלֵּם שָׂכָר טוֹב לִירֵאָיו· בָּרוּךְ חַי
לָעַד וְקַיָּם לָנֶצַח· בָּרוּךְ פּוֹדֶה וּמַצִּיל בָּרוּךְ שְׁמוֹ·
בָּרוּךְ אַתָּה יְיָ אֱלֹהֵינוּ מֶלֶךְ הָעוֹלָם· הָאֵל הָאָב
הָרַחֲמָן הַמְהֻלָּל בְּפִי עַמּוֹ מְשֻׁבָּח וּמְפֹאָר בִּלְשׁוֹן
חֲסִידָיו וַעֲבָדָיו· וּבְשִׁירֵי דָוִד עַבְדֶּךָ נְהַלֶּלְךָ יְיָ
אֱלֹהֵינוּ בִּשְׁבָחוֹת וּבִזְמִירוֹת נְגַדֶּלְךָ וּנְשַׁבֵּחֲךָ וּנְפָאֶרְךָ
וְנַזְכִּיר שִׁמְךָ וְנַמְלִיכְךָ מַלְכֵּנוּ אֱלֹהֵינוּ יָחִיד חֵי
הָעוֹלָמִים· מֶלֶךְ מְשֻׁבָּח וּמְפֹאָר עֲדֵי עַד שְׁמוֹ הַגָּדוֹל·
בָּרוּךְ אַתָּה יְיָ מֶלֶךְ מְהֻלָּל בַּתִּשְׁבָּחוֹת:

הוֹדוּ לַיְיָ קִרְאוּ בִשְׁמוֹ הוֹדִיעוּ בָעַמִּים עֲלִילוֹתָיו: שִׁירוּ לוֹ

זַמְּרוּ לוֹ שִׂיחוּ בְּכָל נִפְלְאֹתָיו: הִתְהַלְלוּ בְּשֵׁם קָדְשׁוֹ יִשְׂמַח לֵב

מְבַקְשֵׁי יְיָ: דִּרְשׁוּ יְיָ וְעֻזּוֹ בַּקְּשׁוּ פָנָיו תָּמִיד: זִכְרוּ נִפְלְאֹתָיו

(Psalm 68:25) and Whose devoted servant has compiled our national
hymnal of His praise and glory (וְעֲבָדָיו — מְשַׁבֵּחַ). Now, by permitting the
hymns of David to penetrate our own souls, it is our intention to awaken
within ourselves the awareness of His greatness, praise and glory, to revive
within our minds the memory of the manifold phases of His rule that His
Name reveals to us, and to render homage to Him once more as our God
and our King, to Him, the One God, Who through all the changes of
years and days, will remain the Living Force of all the ages. He is
מֶלֶךְ מְהֻלָּל בַּתִּשְׁבָּחוֹת; every hymn of praise we sing to Him makes us recognize
and acknowledge Him as our King in ever-deepening sincerity. We pledge
to Him בָּרוּךְ אַתָּה ה׳ that we will render Him our tribute of homage by
consecrating our lives with ever growing intensity to Him and to His service.
הוֹדוּ. This portion, down to וְהַלֵּל לַה׳, is the song which, according to
I Chronicles 16:8-36, David taught the singer Assaph and his companions
as a Temple hymn to be sung on that day when he brought the Ark of the
Law into the City of David and placed it into the Tabernacle. Essentially,

be He Who lives forever and abides unto eternity. Blessed be He Who redeems and saves; blessed be His Name. Blessed be You *God,* our God, King of the Universe, Almighty God, Who is also the merciful Father Whose people laud Him for His deeds. Whose praise and glory is proclaimed by the tongue of His lovingly devoted ones and His servants. With the songs of David Your servant we shall proclaim Your praise, *God* our God, with praises and songs will we proclaim You as the great One, laud and glorify You, remember Your name and establish Your dominion our King, our God, You Sole Living One of all times, O King, Whose great Name be lauded and glorified forever. Blessed be You *God,* a King extolled with songs of praise for his deeds.

O render homage to *God,* declare His Name, make His creative acts known among the peoples. Sing praises to Him ; meditate upon all His wonders. Seek your glory in His Holy Name, so that the heart of those that seek *God* may rejoice. Seek *God* and His invincible will ; seek His face continually. Remember His wonders that He has wrought, his acts of instruction and the judgments of His mouth. O seed of Yisrael His servant,

---

however, the first half of this paragraph corresponds to the first fifteen verses of Psalm 105, and the second half to Verses 2—13 of Psalm 96 and Verses 47 and 48 of Psalm 106. According to *Seder Olam,* Chapter 14, the portion beginning with הודו and ending with אל תגעו במשיחי וגו׳ was recited each day when the morning sacrifice was offered, and the portion from שירו לד׳ to יהלל ד׳ during the evening offering, as long as the Ark reposed within the temporary Tabernacle, until the day when Solomon provided a permanent resting place for it in the Temple. The contents of this paragraph constitute a most fitting introduction to our Divine service during the centuries of our dispersion. For here we are called upon in our dispersion among the nations, to view and to prove ourselves as the heralds of God's Name and the declarers of His works and His sovereignty. We are asked to study our own history, and to look upon our patriarchs, Abraham, Isaac and Jacob, who, from the very beginning, quite like we today, had to fulfill their purpose לקרא בשם ה׳ while wandering among alien princes and nations. To them the thought of a homeland of their own existed only in the form of a Divine pledge to be fulfilled some day in the future. To that extent to which we ourselves, as dedicated

אֲשֶׁר עָשָׂה מִבְחָיו וּמִשְׁפְּטֵי־פִיהוּ: זֶרַע יִשְׂרָאֵל עַבְדּוֹ בְּנֵי יַעֲקֹב

בְּחִירָיו: הוּא יְיָ אֱלֹהֵינוּ בְּכָל־הָאָרֶץ מִשְׁפָּטָיו: זִכְרוּ לְעוֹלָם

בְּרִיתוֹ דָּבָר צִוָּה לְאֶלֶף דּוֹר: אֲשֶׁר כָּרַת אֶת־אַבְרָהָם וּשְׁבוּעָתוֹ

לְיִצְחָק: וַיַּעֲמִידֶהָ לְיַעֲקֹב לְחֹק לְיִשְׂרָאֵל בְּרִית עוֹלָם: לֵאמֹר לְךָ

אֶתֵּן אֶרֶץ־כְּנָעַן חֶבֶל נַחֲלַתְכֶם: בִּהְיוֹתְכֶם מְתֵי מִסְפָּר כִּמְעַט

וְגָרִים בָּהּ: וַיִּתְהַלְכוּ מִגּוֹי אֶל־גּוֹי וּמִמַּמְלָכָה אֶל־עַם אַחֵר: לֹא־

הִנִּיחַ לְאִישׁ לְעָשְׁקָם וַיּוֹכַח עֲלֵיהֶם מְלָכִים: אַל־תִּגְּעוּ בִּמְשִׁיחָי

וּבִנְבִיאַי אַל־תָּרֵעוּ: שִׁירוּ לַיְיָ כָּל־הָאָרֶץ בַּשְּׂרוּ מִיּוֹם־אֶל־יוֹם

יְשׁוּעָתוֹ: סַפְּרוּ בַגּוֹיִם אֶת־כְּבוֹדוֹ בְּכָל־הָעַמִּים נִפְלְאֹתָיו: כִּי

גָדוֹל יְיָ וּמְהֻלָּל מְאֹד וְנוֹרָא הוּא עַל־כָּל־אֱלֹהִים: כִּי כָּל־אֱלֹהֵי

הָעַמִּים אֱלִילִים וַיְיָ שָׁמַיִם עָשָׂה: הוֹד וְהָדָר לְפָנָיו עֹז וְחֶדְוָה

בִּמְקֹמוֹ: הָבוּ לַיְיָ מִשְׁפְּחוֹת עַמִּים הָבוּ לַיְיָ כָּבוֹד וָעֹז: הָבוּ לַיְיָ

כְּבוֹד שְׁמוֹ שְׂאוּ מִנְחָה וּבֹאוּ לְפָנָיו הִשְׁתַּחֲווּ לַיְיָ בְּהַדְרַת־קֹדֶשׁ:

חִילוּ מִלְּפָנָיו כָּל־הָאָרֶץ אַף־תִּכּוֹן תֵּבֵל בַּל־תִּמּוֹט: יִשְׂמְחוּ

הַשָּׁמַיִם וְתָגֵל הָאָרֶץ וְיֹאמְרוּ בַגּוֹיִם יְיָ מָלָךְ: יִרְעַם הַיָּם וּמְלֹאוֹ

messengers of God, will prove our loyalty through our faithful fulfillment of His Law and Covenant, we, too, will receive His protection, even as
our patriarchs did before us. Thus we, too, shall be able to complete in
safety our mission among the nations until the advent of the Kingdom of
God on earth and that glorious day when we will be gathered once again
upon the home soil of the Promised Land. יִשְׂמַח לֵב מְבַקְשֵׁי ה׳. Among the
other nations there will also be those who "seek God" and who yearn
to see evidence of His existence and sovereignty. עֹז וְעֹזוּ denotes the
Law of God as an expression of His decisive, invincible and unalterable
will (see Psalms 78:61, 132:8). אֱלִילִים are "gods that deny" or "withhold",

sons of Yaakov, His chosen ones. He still is *God* our God; His works extend over all the earth. Remember His covenant for all the future; the word which He commanded is meant still for the thousandth generation. That which He covenanted with Avraham, and which was His vow to Yitzchak, He established for Yaakov as a statute, for Yisrael as an everlasting covenant, [saying], "To you I shall give the Land of Kenaan," the portion of your inheritonce, when you were yet few in number, yea, as a little particle, and strangers in it. They wandered from nation to nation, from one kingdom to another people. He allowed no one to do them wrong, and reproved even kings for their sake. "Touch not My anointed ones, and do My prophets no harm." Sing praises to *God,* all the earth, proclaim His salvation from day to day. Relate His Honor amongst the nations, his miraculous deeds amongst all peoples. That *God* is great and most evident in mighty acts; that He is to be feared above all gods, that all the gods of the peoples are gods that deny, but that *God* has made the heavens; that glory of person and majesty of might are won before His countenance, fortitude and joy in His abode. Give to *God,* O families of nations, give to *God* honor and irresistible might. Give to *God* the honor of His Name, take up offering of homage and come before Him. Cast yourselves down before *God* in the reflected glory of the sanctuary. Called before Him, enter into the travail of rebirth, you upon all the earth, so that the world of man may also be firmly established and sway no more. Then the heavens will be glad and the earth rejoice aloud and among the nations they will say: "*God* has begun His reign." The sea roars, and the fulness thereof, the field exults

---

who in the erroneous thinking of the heathen nations, are inimical to the welfare of man. On the other hand, the very Name of ה׳ proclaims the exact opposite of "denying" or "withholding". The Lord God is not jealous of the growth and prosperity of man. Man may come before His countenance in all the full glory of his person and of his place in the world. In fact, it is only in the Sanctuary of God that man can find the joy of life and the moral strength which he needs if he is to resist evil. In the Sanctuary of God, הדרת קדש, man acquires a הדרה of God's הדר, a glory which constitutes a reflection of the glory of God Himself.

יַעֲלֹץ הַשָּׂדֶה וְכָל־אֲשֶׁר־בּוֹ ׃ אָז יְרַנְּנוּ עֲצֵי הַיָּעַר מִלִּפְנֵי יְיָ כִּי
בָא לִשְׁפֹּט אֶת־הָאָרֶץ ׃ הוֹדוּ לַיְיָ כִּי טוֹב כִּי לְעוֹלָם חַסְדּוֹ ׃ וְאִמְרוּ
הוֹשִׁיעֵנוּ אֱלֹהֵי יִשְׁעֵנוּ וְקַבְּצֵנוּ וְהַצִּילֵנוּ מִן־הַגּוֹיִם לְהֹדוֹת לְשֵׁם
קָדְשֶׁךָ לְהִשְׁתַּבֵּחַ בִּתְהִלָּתֶךָ ׃ בָּרוּךְ יְיָ אֱלֹהֵי יִשְׂרָאֵל מִן־הָעוֹלָם
וְעַד־הָעֹלָם וַיֹּאמְרוּ כָל־הָעָם אָמֵן וְהַלֵּל לַיְיָ ׃

רוֹמְמוּ יְיָ אֱלֹהֵינוּ וְהִשְׁתַּחֲווּ לַהֲדֹם רַגְלָיו קָדוֹשׁ הוּא ׃ רוֹמְמוּ
יְיָ אֱלֹהֵינוּ וְהִשְׁתַּחֲווּ לְהַר קָדְשׁוֹ כִּי קָדוֹשׁ יְיָ אֱלֹהֵינוּ ׃

ישמחו וגו׳ In every instance where the Holy Scriptures speak of mankind's eventual deliverance from sin and man's return to his own pure destiny under God, we also find mention of a flourishing rejuvenation of nature. For nature, too, suffers if man goes astray. (Gen. 3:17–19). Likewise, if man fulfills his destiny, then everything that grows and blooms for man and is used by him for his purposes will also attain its own true higher purpose and will be lifted from the fetters of physical nature to the loftier realm of the moral freedom that is man's. If, on the other hand, man should exploit all the gifts of nature only to serve his own selfish desires and profane, sensuous degeneration, then he will drag the creations of pure physical nature down with him into the morass of his degeneration and nature will mourn because it has been made a slave to such unholy, unsalubrious ends. Hence the realm of nature round about man breathes a joyous sigh of relief when man returns to his morally pure destiny under God, for then nature, which man will thus employ for better purposes, will rise with him into the sphere of his own morally noble humanity. In such Scriptural accounts the trees of the forest are given prominence among the creatures affected by the moral rise and fall of mankind. Without human intervention, the trees of the forest serve as shelter for the innocent creatures of the woods. But when they are cut down by man, they are used for the building of human habitations and other purposes of human life, both private and public, regardless of whether they are moral or otherwise. Therefore the trees, more than any other denizen of nature's sphere, will rejoice when God will take action in order to restore justice and right on earth. הודו But as for us, we recognize the merciful providence of God at all times. We know that our own people, too, will be restored to its ancient Homeland simultaneously with the moral rebirth of mankind which we will have helped to bring about through our centuries of wandering among the nations.

and all that is in it; then all the trees of the forest shall also sing for joy, for they sense themselves before the countenance of *God* Who comes to judge the earth. Avow it to *God* that He is good, that His love endures forever, and say, "Save us, O God of our salvation, and gather us and deliver us from the nations so that we may render homage to Your Name, that we may find our glory in the praise of Your mighty deeds." But blessed be *God,* the God of Yisrael, blessed from all the past that was to all the future that is yet to be, and all the people said "Amen", and they proclaimed the praise of the mighty deeds of *God.*

Extol *God* our God, and cast yourselves down before His footstool; holy is He. Extol *God* our God and cast yourselves down before His holy mountain, for the Lord our God

רוממו This paragraph, composed of verses from various Psalms, is to remind us that God, to Whom we now address ourselves in prayer, is holy, and that whatever is morally base and evil is not in accordance with the holiness of His will. Therefore, if we are to draw near to Him, we must consider His grandeur and devote every fiber of our being to the fulfillment of His Law and of the requirements placed upon us by His Sanctuary. הדום רגליו "His footstool", is the place on earth upon which He causes His reigning presence to rest. And the condition for His presence in our midst is that we loyally embrace the Sanctuary of His Law, even as He promised it to us: ועשו לי מקדש ושכנתי בתוכם (Exod. 25:8), והתהלכתי בתוככם .אם בחקתי תלכו וגו' (Lev. 26:3, 12). והוא רחום However far from perfect our past may have been, we may be certain of His atonement and merciful forgiveness if we vow Him devoted loyalty and obedience henceforth, and the more He has already done for us in the past, the more will He remember us now as the creatures and works of His creative love and He will not deny us His loving-kindness even now. תנו עז Meditate, too, upon His invincible might. See how His glory has been revealed in Israel's history even as His power is evident in the phenomena of nature. Remember also that while He must indeed be greatly feared by all those who are the foes of that which is holy in His eyes, He permits those who prove to be the bearers and loyal executors of His will to have a portion in His own invincible might. אל נקמות Of course our hearts yearn to behold the coming of God as the Champion of all injured rights and to see Him crush all spite and arrogance. But we leave the coming of our salvation in the hands of God. He alone will know when the proper time will have come and we shall not lack for His blessing as long as we remain His people. We know that He will hear us if only we call upon Him as to our King, if we are willing not only to accept His help but also to receive

וְהוּא רַחוּם יְכַפֵּר עָוֹן וְלֹא יַשְׁחִית וְהִרְבָּה לְהָשִׁיב אַפּוֹ וְלֹא יָעִיר

כָּל־חֲמָתוֹ: אַתָּה יְיָ לֹא־תִכְלָא רַחֲמֶיךָ מִמֶּנִּי חַסְדְּךָ וַאֲמִתְּךָ תָּמִיד

יִצְּרוּנִי: זְכֹר רַחֲמֶיךָ יְיָ וַחֲסָדֶיךָ כִּי מֵעוֹלָם הֵמָּה: תְּנוּ עֹז

לֵאלֹהִים עַל־יִשְׂרָאֵל גַּאֲוָתוֹ וְעֻזּוֹ בַּשְּׁחָקִים: נוֹרָא אֱלֹהִים

מִמִּקְדָּשֶׁיךָ אֵל יִשְׂרָאֵל הוּא נֹתֵן עֹז וְתַעֲצֻמוֹת לָעָם בָּרוּךְ

אֱלֹהִים: אֵל־נְקָמוֹת יְיָ אֵל נְקָמוֹת הוֹפִיעַ: הִנָּשֵׂא שֹׁפֵט הָאָרֶץ

הָשֵׁב גְּמוּל עַל־גֵּאִים: לַיְיָ הַיְשׁוּעָה עַל־עַמְּךָ בִרְכָתֶךָ סֶּלָה:

יְיָ צְבָאוֹת עִמָּנוּ מִשְׂגָּב־לָנוּ אֱלֹהֵי יַעֲקֹב סֶלָה: יְיָ צְבָאוֹת אַשְׁרֵי

אָדָם בֹּטֵחַ בָּךְ: יְיָ הוֹשִׁיעָה הַמֶּלֶךְ יַעֲנֵנוּ בְיוֹם־קָרְאֵנוּ: הוֹשִׁיעָה

אֶת־עַמֶּךָ וּבָרֵךְ אֶת־נַחֲלָתֶךָ וּרְעֵם וְנַשְּׂאֵם עַד־הָעוֹלָם: נַפְשֵׁנוּ

חִכְּתָה לַיְיָ עֶזְרֵנוּ וּמָגִנֵּנוּ הוּא: כִּי־בוֹ יִשְׂמַח לִבֵּנוּ כִּי בְשֵׁם קָדְשׁוֹ

בָטָחְנוּ: יְהִי־חַסְדְּךָ יְיָ עָלֵינוּ כַּאֲשֶׁר יִחַלְנוּ לָךְ: הַרְאֵנוּ יְיָ חַסְדֶּךָ

וְיֶשְׁעֲךָ תִּתֶּן־לָנוּ: קוּמָה עֶזְרָתָה לָּנוּ וּפְדֵנוּ לְמַעַן חַסְדֶּךָ: אָנֹכִי

יְיָ אֱלֹהֶיךָ הַמַּעַלְךָ מֵאֶרֶץ מִצְרָיִם הַרְחֶב־פִּיךָ וַאֲמַלְאֵהוּ: אַשְׁרֵי

הָעָם שֶׁכָּכָה לּוֹ אַשְׁרֵי הָעָם שֶׁיְיָ אֱלֹהָיו: וַאֲנִי בְּחַסְדְּךָ בָטַחְתִּי

יָגֵל לִבִּי בִּישׁוּעָתֶךָ אָשִׁירָה לַיְיָ כִּי גָמַל עָלָי:

His commands, and if we render Him homage in faithful obedience as the
"Lord and Master" over all our actions. הוֹשִׁיעָה Therefore we face the
future with joyous trust in God. For He Himself has given us the
assurance that we may look to Him for the fulfillment of our wishes as long
as we will consider Him "our God" and strive upward to that lofty moral
plane for the attainment of which He has led us "up" from the land of
Egypt.

is holy. But He, being merciful, also pardons sin and does not let
destruction come; He often takes back His wrath and never stirs
up all His indignation. You *God,* withhold not Your compassion
from me now; let Your mercy and Your truth continually preserve
me. Remember Your compassion, *God,* and Your acts of mercy,
as they have been of old. Ascribe invincible strength to God,
Whose majesty appears over Yisrael even as His invincible might
in the clouds. You shall be feared one day, O God, from out
of Your holy places, O God of Yisrael; it is He who grants
invincibility and power to a people, blessed be God. "O God,
Champion of Justice, *God,* Champion of Justice, shine forth!
Arise, O Judge of the earth, let that which they have wrought
return to the arrogant!" But salvation is with *God*; Your
blessing on Your people. *God* Tzevaoth is with us; the God
of Yaakov is our high tower, O *God* Tzevaoth, forward forever
strides the man who trusts in You. O *God,* grant salvation. It is
as the King that He hears us on the day on which we call. Grant
salvation to Your people and bless Your inheritance, and tend it
and bear it aloft unto eternity. Our soul has waited for *God,*
He still is our help and our shield, for only in Him will our
heart rejoice, for in His Holy Name have we put our trust. Let
Your love, O *God,* be over us, even as we have waited for You.
O *God,* let us behold Your love and Your salvation, O grant it
to us. Arise to our aid, and redeem us for the sake of Your loving-
kindness. "I, *God,* am to be your God, Who has led you out
from the land of Mitzrayim; make wide your desire, I shall fulfill
it." To salvation strides that nation with whom it is thus!
To salvation that nation whose God is *God.* And I have put
my trust in Your love, so that my heart might come to rejoice
through Your salvation; I will yet sing praises to *God,* of
how He caused all my tribulations to bear ripe fruit.

Psalm 100. מזמור לתודה. תודה can be an acknowledgement either of a
debt of gratitude or one of the awareness of guilt. In this instance it is
employed in the first interpretation. עבדו, the true service of God is
primarily and truly performed only in the process of day-to-day living. "To
serve God" means to devote all one's energy, all the means and talents
at one's disposal, and every moment of one's life to the execution of God's

On Sabbaths, Holidays, Erev Pesach, Erev Yom Kippur and
Chol Hamoed Pesach the following Psalm is not recited.

ק מִזְמוֹר לְתוֹדָה הָרִיעוּ לַיָי כָּל־הָאָרֶץ: עִבְדוּ אֶת־יְיָ בְּשִׂמְחָה בֹּאוּ לְפָנָיו
בִּרְנָנָה: דְּעוּ כִּי יְיָ הוּא אֱלֹהִים הוּא עָשָׂנוּ וְלֹא (וְלוֹ קׁ) אֲנַחְנוּ עַמּוֹ וְצֹאן מַרְעִיתוֹ:
בֹּאוּ שְׁעָרָיו ו בְּתוֹדָה חֲצֵרֹתָיו בִּתְהִלָּה הוֹדוּ לוֹ בָּרְכוּ שְׁמוֹ: כִּי־טוֹב יְיָ לְעוֹלָם
חַסְדּוֹ וְעַד־דֹּר וָדֹר אֱמוּנָתוֹ:

On שבת *and* יו"ט *the following psalms are added before* יהי כבוד

יט לַמְנַצֵּחַ מִזְמוֹר לְדָוִד: הַשָּׁמַיִם מְסַפְּרִים כְּבוֹד־אֵל וּמַעֲשֵׂה
יָדָיו מַגִּיד הָרָקִיעַ: יוֹם לְיוֹם יַבִּיעַ אֹמֶר וְלַיְלָה לְּלַיְלָה יְחַוֶּה־
דָּעַת: אֵין אֹמֶר וְאֵין דְּבָרִים בְּלִי נִשְׁמָע קוֹלָם: בְּכָל־הָאָרֶץ

---

will. Such a life, and only such a life, can give us true שמחה and it is to
this joy of life in the service of God that we are summoned, after the
preceding call of הריעו has bidden us to do solemn homage to God. באו
It is this joyous mood engendered by such active service of God that
should accompany us into His House. דעו there we should realize that the
God, Whose Law reposes in the Sanctuary, is the Creator, Lawgiver and
Regulator of the Universe, and that, by virtue of the extraordinary Revelation
given to Israel and His guidance of each and every one of us in particular
and of our community in general, He is our Creator and Master as well. To
Him we belong with every fiber of our being; we are His people, His
community; we are "the sheep of His Pasture" to be guided by Him with
regard to both our actions and the course which our lives are to take. באו,
first we come to שעריו and only then to חצרותיו. Hence תודה, the avowal
of the awareness of our debt of gratitude for what He has meant to us, must
precede תהלה, the contemplation of that which God is in general terms and
of His significance as such. הודו Render unto Him your acknowledgement
of both duty and gratitude, and spread and advance the recognition of
Him wherever you can. Spread the message that טוב ה', God is the sole
absolute Good after which men should strive, that לעולם not only rare
and extraordinary occurrences but actually every moment of our lives, constitutes a gift of His loving-kindness, and that His "guiding faithfulness"
is with us from generation to generation.

Psalm 19. למנצח. This psalm has as its theme the sources from which
one could come to recognize God and worship Him. To David these

On Sabbaths, Holidays, Erev Pesach, Erev Yom Kippur and
Chol Hamoed Pesach the following Psalm is not recited.

A Psalm of thanksgiving. Waken homage to *God*, all the earth ; serve *God*, with gladness, come before Him with exultation. Know that *God* is God ; He has made us and we are His ; [we are] His people and the sheep of His pasture. Enter into His gates with thanksgiving and into His courts with praise of His mighty deeds ; give thanks to Him [and] bless His Name. For *God* is good ; His love endures forever, and His guiding faith extends to every generation.

On weekdays begin here with יהי כבוד

To Him Who grants victory, a Psalm of David. The heavens recount the glory of God and the firmament tells the work of His hands. Day to day utters speech, and night to night speaks knowledge. There need be no speech, nor words ; their voice is heard without it. Their measuring line goes forth from them all

---

sources are the book of nature, from which he derives his knowledge of God, and the Torah, from which he has learned how to worship Him. David states that the revelation at Sinai was not essential for the recognition of the fact that there must be Someone Who is the omnipotent creator, regulator and ruler of all the world. The realization that there must be a God could come to anyone who thoughtfully contemplates nature, and the heavens in particular. The study of the heavens and earth alone, however, does not provide man with the answer to the question why he should praise God or recognize Him as his Master. The heavens and the world about us cannot answer the question of what man should do with his freedom of will and action. By merely looking at the heavens and the earth, man will never discover the Divine Law which sets a purpose for his being in this world. Whatever answer he would derive from this kind of study would only enmesh him in hopeless confusion. It is only the Word of God, the Divine Law, the Torah which was handed down to Israel and the rest of mankind on Mount Sinai, which gives him that exalting doctrine which is in harmonious accord with man's nature and which will shape man's individual and communal life in accordance with God's will. This Law of God, Who "leads mankind to its goal", tells him in an all-encompassing manner, תמימה, the significance of his entire physical and spiritual being, with its physical dependence and moral freedom of will in the kingdom of God, for the Divine kingdom of the Law which shapes and rules the world. Therefore the Torah is משיבת נפש; it leads him out of all doubt that torments

יָצָא קַוָּם וּבִקְצֵה תֵבֵל מִלֵּיהֶם לַשֶּׁמֶשׁ שָׂם־אֹהֶל בָּהֶם׃ וְהוּא

כְּחָתָן יֹצֵא מֵחֻפָּתוֹ יָשִׂישׂ כְּגִבּוֹר לָרוּץ אֹרַח׃ מִקְצֵה הַשָּׁמַיִם מוֹצָאוֹ

וּתְקוּפָתוֹ עַל־קְצוֹתָם וְאֵין נִסְתָּר מֵחַמָּתוֹ׃ תּוֹרַת יְהוָה תְּמִימָה

מְשִׁיבַת נָפֶשׁ עֵדוּת יְהוָה נֶאֱמָנָה מַחְכִּימַת פֶּתִי׃ פִּקּוּדֵי יְהוָה

יְשָׁרִים מְשַׂמְּחֵי־לֵב מִצְוַת יְהוָה בָּרָה מְאִירַת עֵינָיִם׃ יִרְאַת יְהוָה

טְהוֹרָה עוֹמֶדֶת לָעַד מִשְׁפְּטֵי־יְהוָה אֱמֶת צָדְקוּ יַחְדָּו׃ הַנֶּחֱמָדִים

מִזָּהָב וּמִפַּז רָב וּמְתוּקִים מִדְּבַשׁ וְנֹפֶת צוּפִים׃ גַּם־עַבְדְּךָ נִזְהָר

בָּהֶם בְּשָׁמְרָם עֵקֶב רָב׃ שְׁגִיאוֹת מִי־יָבִין מִנִּסְתָּרוֹת נַקֵּנִי׃ גַּם

מִזֵּדִים חֲשֹׂךְ עַבְדֶּךָ אַל־יִמְשְׁלוּ־בִי אָז אֵיתָם וְנִקֵּיתִי מִפֶּשַׁע רָב׃

יִהְיוּ לְרָצוֹן אִמְרֵי־פִי וְהֶגְיוֹן לִבִּי לְפָנֶיךָ יְהוָה צוּרִי וְגֹאֲלִי׃

לְדָוִד בְּשַׁנּוֹתוֹ אֶת־טַעְמוֹ לִפְנֵי אֲבִימֶלֶךְ וַיְגָרֲשֵׁהוּ וַיֵּלַךְ׃

אֲבָרֲכָה אֶת־יְהוָה בְּכָל־עֵת תָּמִיד תְּהִלָּתוֹ בְּפִי׃ בַּיהוָה תִּתְהַלֵּל

---

the soul. Therefore it is the sole value that is truly desirable. At first, it may seem to limit and oppose our will and our desires. But if we faithfully observe it, it will offer us a constantly growing abundance of bliss, and everyone sincerely striving to fulfill its precepts may be God's help in his endeavors. This psalm ends with the prayerful wish that this concept of the dual Divine revelation in both Law and Nature, as expressed in these words of song for man's instruction, may be in accordance with God's will and with His purposes.

תקופתו, לרוץ, יוצא. David, as do all the Holy Scriptures, talks in the language of men. דברה תורה כלשון בני אדם; he speaks the speech of men to men. His language is the same as that of Copernicus, of Keppler and Newton, and as that which we use today and which will most likely be employed by every human tongue as long as men shall be capable of speech. This language will remain the same even when the assumption that the sun is static and that the earth revolves around it—and not the sun around the

over the earth, but where the world of man ends, their words speak, "He has set a tent in them for the orb of the sun." As a bridegroom it steps forth from its chamber; it rejoices as if it had sole power to run its course. And yet, one point upon the heavens remains its origin and its orbit is within their defined bounds; and thus He is not hidden even from His sun. But the Law of *God*, all-encompassing, responds to the soul; the testimony of *God* is faithful, making wise the inexperienced. The mandates of *God* are upright, rejoicing the heart; the commandment of God is brilliant, enlightening the eyes. The fear of *God* is pure, enduring forever; the ordinances of *God* are truth, and they are universally just. They are to be desired more than gold and fine gold, and sweeter than honey and finest nectar. Thy servant also was warned by them at first; but when he kept them, he recognized the rich reward. Errors, who can discern them? Cleanse me from hidden faults. Keep back Your servant also from the wanton ones, so that they may not gain dominion over me when I am weak; thus shall I keep myself pure from great transgression. May the words of my mouth and the meditation of my heart find favor before Your countenance, O *God*, my Rock and my Redeemer.

(A Psalm) by David, when he disguised his mind before Abimelech, whereupon the latter drove him away, and he departed. I shall henceforth praise *God* at all times; let the praise [of His mighty acts] continually remain in my mouth. [Even now]

---

earth—will have been proven to be irrefutable certainty. For it is not the aim of the Holy Scriptures to teach us astronomy, cosmogony or physics, but only to guide man to the fulfillment of his life's task within the framework of the constellation of his existence. For this purpose it is quite irrelevant whether the course of the days and years is determined by the earth's revolution about the sun, or by the latter's orbit about the former.

Psalm 34. לדוד This Psalm is derived entirely from an event that took place in David's own personal life. He wishes to make known his personal experiences to all of mankind in order to show them the way to salvation. This Psalm refers to an event in David's difficult life which surely represents the nadir of all the affliction which he experienced during his sojourn on earth. David, who had shed his blood in order to insure the welfare of his people and to save its honor. David, the much-praised son-in-law of the King, now had to flee from his own father-in-law and seek refuge among

נַפְשִׁי יִשְׁמְעוּ עֲנָוִים וְיִשְׂמָחוּ: גַּדְּלוּ לַיהוָה אִתִּי וּנְרוֹמְמָה שְׁמוֹ

יַחְדָּו: דָּרַשְׁתִּי אֶת־יהוָה וְעָנָנִי וּמִכָּל־מְגוּרוֹתַי הִצִּילָנִי: הִבִּיטוּ אֵלָיו

וְנָהָרוּ וּפְנֵיהֶם אַל־יֶחְפָּרוּ: זֶה עָנִי קָרָא וַיהוָה שָׁמֵעַ וּמִכָּל־צָרוֹתָיו

הוֹשִׁיעוֹ: חֹנֶה מַלְאַךְ־יהוָה סָבִיב לִירֵאָיו וַיְחַלְּצֵם: טַעֲמוּ וּרְאוּ

כִּי־טוֹב יהוָה אַשְׁרֵי הַגֶּבֶר יֶחֱסֶה־בּוֹ: יְראוּ אֶת־יהוָה קְדֹשָׁיו כִּי

אֵין מַחְסוֹר לִירֵאָיו: כְּפִירִים רָשׁוּ וְרָעֵבוּ וְדֹרְשֵׁי יהוָה לֹא־יַחְסְרוּ

כָל־טוֹב: לְכוּ־בָנִים שִׁמְעוּ־לִי יִרְאַת יהוָה אֲלַמֶּדְכֶם: מִי־הָאִישׁ

הֶחָפֵץ חַיִּים אֹהֵב יָמִים לִרְאוֹת טוֹב: נְצֹר לְשׁוֹנְךָ מֵרָע וּשְׂפָתֶיךָ

מִדַּבֵּר מִרְמָה: סוּר מֵרָע וַעֲשֵׂה־טוֹב בַּקֵּשׁ שָׁלוֹם וְרָדְפֵהוּ: עֵינֵי

יהוָה אֶל־צַדִּיקִים וְאָזְנָיו אֶל־שַׁוְעָתָם: פְּנֵי יהוָה בְּעֹשֵׂי רָע לְהַכְרִית

(* הר' נקראת במלחמים והח' בעלם

---

the enemies of his people because there was no safe place for him in the
midst of his own nation. Then, in order to escape death at the hands of
the foes among whom he had sought safety, David had to pretend that he
was an imbecile and he had to deem it his good fortune that King Abimelech,
thinking him to be a feeble minded beggar, drove him away without harming
him. Cast down from the heights to such depths of despair, David here
proclaims those cardinal truths that contain so much practical wisdom.

מי האיש. This is not החפץ בחיים "He who *takes pleasure in* life", but
החפץ חיים "he who *desires* life", whose sole goal is life; that is, he desires
to attain such a level of existence as can truly be called "life". This is a man
of whom it can be said that he has indeed fulfilled the task for which he
was called into being. סור מרע first, and then עשה טוב; guard yourself from
a מצוה הבאה בעברה. Do not believe that the end justifies the means. And do
not seek to make up for עברות by means of מצות. Atonement for עברות
can be made only be refraining from sin henceforth, and by rendering
restitution of the damage done, if that be possible. But do not believe that
you may permit yourself to commit עברות because, or if, you also practice
מצות. Once you have done justice to your duties toward God and are in full

my soul glories in *God*; let the humble hear it and be glad.
O declare the greatness of *God* with me, and let us exalt
His Name together. I sought *God* and He answered me, and
He delivered me from all my fears. All those who ever looked
up to Him received a ray of light, and their faces never had cause
to pale. This poorest among men cried, and *God* heard, and
has saved him out of all his troubles. Thus the angel of *God*
encamps round about them that fear Him, and He has always
delivered them. Test this for yourselves, and you shall see, how
good *God* is; forward strides that man who takes refuge in
Him. O fear *God*, you who are sanctified to Him, for there
is no want to them that fear Him. Young lions have become
poor and suffered hunger, but they who seek *God* shall never want
for any good thing. Come, O sons, and hearken to me; I will
teach you the fear of *God*. Who is the man who desires life
and loves days that he may see good? Keep your tongue from
evil and your lips from deceitful speech. Keep away from evil
and do good without hesitation; seek peace and pursue it. The
eyes of *God* are toward the righteous and His ear is open to
their cry. The face of *God* is against them that do evil, to cut

---

accord with His Law by shunning evil in thought, word and deed, and by
doing good, then בקש שלום also seek to have peaceful relations with your
fellow men. Indeed, רדפהו literally "pursue" peace. Do not let it go when
it threatens to elude your grasp. If it is about to leave you, preserve it even at
the risk of personal sacrifice. Of course שלום is by no means to be the
supreme goal for which all else, even the injunction סור מרע ועשה טוב must be
cast aside. We may sacrifice, nay, we *should* sacrifice for the sake of peace
only that which is ours to give away, such as personal interests, personal
advantages, our own claims and our honor. But peaceful relations with our
fellow-men, however desirable such a state may be, can never atone for any
discord we may have with God. Whenever it is a matter of סור מרע ועשה טוב,
we must be ready, if necessary, to chance the opposition and hostility even
of an entire world and to stand alone, with God and our sense of duty as
our only allies.

מֵאֶרֶץ וְכָרָם : צֶעֲקוּ וַיהוָֹה שָׁמֵעַ וּמִכָּל־צָרוֹתָם הִצִּילָם : קָרוֹב
יְהוָֹה לְנִשְׁבְּרֵי־לֵב וְאֶת־דַּכְּאֵי־רוּחַ יוֹשִׁיעַ : רַבּוֹת רָעוֹת צַדִּיק וּמִכֻּלָּם
יַצִּילֶנּוּ יְהוָֹה : שֹׁמֵר כָּל־עַצְמוֹתָיו אַחַת מֵהֵנָּה לֹא נִשְׁבָּרָה : תְּמוֹתֵת
רָשָׁע רָעָה וְשֹׂנְאֵי צַדִּיק יֶאְשָׁמוּ : פֹּדֶה יְהוָֹה נֶפֶשׁ עֲבָדָיו וְלֹא
יֶאְשְׁמוּ כָּל־הַחֹסִים בּוֹ :

צ תְּפִלָּה לְמֹשֶׁה אִישׁ־הָאֱלֹהִים אֲדֹנָי מָעוֹן אַתָּה הָיִיתָ לָּנוּ
בְּדֹר וָדֹר : בְּטֶרֶם הָרִים יֻלָּדוּ וַתְּחוֹלֵל אֶרֶץ וְתֵבֵל וּמֵעוֹלָם עַד־
עוֹלָם אַתָּה אֵל : תָּשֵׁב אֱנוֹשׁ עַד־דַּכָּא וַתֹּאמֶר שׁוּבוּ בְנֵי־אָדָם :
כִּי אֶלֶף שָׁנִים בְּעֵינֶיךָ כְּיוֹם אֶתְמוֹל כִּי יַעֲבֹר וְאַשְׁמוּרָה בַלָּיְלָה :
זְרַמְתָּם שֵׁנָה יִהְיוּ בַּבֹּקֶר כֶּחָצִיר יַחֲלֹף : בַּבֹּקֶר יָצִיץ וְחָלָף לָעֶרֶב
יְמוֹלֵל וְיָבֵשׁ : כִּי־כָלִינוּ בְאַפֶּךָ וּבַחֲמָתְךָ נִבְהָלְנוּ : שַׁתָּ עֲוֹנֹתֵינוּ

*שתה ק'.

Psalm 90. תפלה למשה. This is a תפלה in which Moses, as איש האלקי'
the man chosen by God as the instrument of His sovereignty, reminds himself
of the significance of his historic mission in the midst of mankind. He does
so by reviewing before his mind's eye the significance of the centuries of
human development that had passed before he was entrusted with this great
calling. More than two thousand years of the history of mankind had gone
by. The world had lapsed once more into spiritual and moral תהו, chaos.
According to our sages, the election of Abraham marked the end of שני אלפי
תהו the two thousand years of chaos in man's history and the beginning of
שני אלפי תורה a new era of two millennia in which the Law of God was to
find a permanent place, to begin with, in the midst of one nation that had
been entrusted with the mission to advance the moral and spiritual rebirth
of mankind. (See Commentary to Deut. 32:36.) But it was only with the
assignment of the mission to Moses that the beginning of his new era
actually became evident. The final verse of this Psalm, ויהי נעם וגו', summarizes
the total content of the mission of Moses.

off the remembrance of them from the earth. Even such as they have cried, and *God* heard, and delivered them out of all their troubles. For *God* is near to those that are of a broken heart, and He saves such as are of a contrite spirit. Many, too, are the ills of a righteous man, but *God* delivers him out of them all. He guards all of His bones, not even one of them is broken. But evil shall kill the lawless in the end, and they that hate the righteous shall be destroyed. *God* redeems the soul of His servants and none of them who take refuge in Him shall be desolate.

A Prayer of Moshe, the Man of God. My Lord, You are the Timeless One; You have been with us in every generation. Before the mountains were brought forth, You did cause earth and the world of men to go into travail, and from all the past into all the future You are the one all-moving Power. Amoral man did You cause to sink back to contrition when You did say, "Return, O sons of man." For a thousand years in Your sight are but as yesterday when it is past; indeed, they are a watch in the night. You let them flow away; sleep they become; but in the morning it renews its vigor fresh as grass. In the morning it will grow and gain new vigor, that which, turned toward eventide, the night will cut down and it withers. For we perished by Your anger, and we were dismayed because of Your wrath. You

---

אֲדֹנָי אֵלִי in Verse 17 is either vocative; i.e. "O Thou, Who, as our God, hast called me into Thy service, may pleasantness come to us..." etc. Or, "May all that which is pleasant and which can be obtained only through א' א' be given us..." עָלֵינוּ : "may it come over us", "may it be destined for us". This supreme bliss which has been decreed by God for Israel is stated in these terms: מַעֲשֵׂה יָדֵינוּ כּוֹנְנָה עָלֵינוּ "Establish the work of our hands upon us"; that is, "make us independent, so that we alone may dispose over the work of our hands and not be beholden to any man; make us free. And מַעֲשֵׂה יָדֵינוּ כּוֹנְנֵהוּ establish Thou what it is that we must do; prescribe Thou for us what path our conduct should take; give us Thy Law." Freedom and Law, to be slave to no man but God's servant through and through, גְּאוּלָה and תּוֹרָה, these constitute Israel's blissful destiny, and they also represent the total content of the mission of Moses.

לְנֶגְדֶּךָ עֲלֻמֵנוּ לִמְאוֹר פָּנֶיךָ: כִּי כָל־יָמֵינוּ פָּנוּ בְעֶבְרָתֶךָ כִּלִּינוּ
שָׁנֵינוּ כְמוֹ־הֶגֶה: יְמֵי שְׁנוֹתֵינוּ בָּהֶם שִׁבְעִים שָׁנָה וְאִם בִּגְבוּרֹת
שְׁמוֹנִים שָׁנָה וְרָהְבָּם עָמָל וָאָוֶן כִּי גָז חִישׁ וַנָּעֻפָה: מִי־יוֹדֵעַ עֹז
אַפֶּךָ וּכְיִרְאָתְךָ עֶבְרָתֶךָ: לִמְנוֹת יָמֵינוּ כֵּן הוֹדַע וְנָבִא לְבַב חָכְמָה:
שׁוּבָה יְהוָֹה עַד־מָתָי וְהִנָּחֵם עַל־עֲבָדֶיךָ: שַׂבְּעֵנוּ בַבֹּקֶר חַסְדֶּךָ
וּנְרַנְּנָה וְנִשְׂמְחָה בְּכָל־יָמֵינוּ: שַׂמְּחֵנוּ כִּימוֹת עִנִּיתָנוּ שְׁנוֹת רָאִינוּ
רָעָה: יֵרָאֶה אֶל־עֲבָדֶיךָ פָעֳלֶךָ וַהֲדָרְךָ עַל־בְּנֵיהֶם: וִיהִי נֹעַם אֲדֹנָי
אֱלֹהֵינוּ עָלֵינוּ וּמַעֲשֵׂה יָדֵינוּ כּוֹנְנָה עָלֵינוּ וּמַעֲשֵׂה יָדֵינוּ כּוֹנְנֵהוּ:

צא יֹשֵׁב בְּסֵתֶר עֶלְיוֹן בְּצֵל שַׁדַּי יִתְלוֹנָן: אֹמַר לַיהוָֹה מַחְסִי
וּמְצוּדָתִי אֱלֹהַי אֶבְטַח־בּוֹ: כִּי הוּא יַצִּילְךָ מִפַּח יָקוּשׁ מִדֶּבֶר הַוּוֹת:

Psalm 91. ישב This psalm continues the thought expressed in Psalm
90. Moses spoke in Psalm 90 of the turning point which his mission marked
in the history of mankind, and declared that the nation which he had been
called to lead was to receive both "freedom" and "law" from the hands of
God and thus had been given the pledge that it would attain a state of
supreme bliss on earth. In Psalm 91 Moses sings of the protection and the
historic immortality which this nation would find under the direct guidance
of God.

ה', שדי, עליון denote the three stages of recognition of God through which
the Divine revelation in Israel's early history had progressively led that
nation. The ability to recognize that God is עליון, the Most High Who
surpasses all other powers on earth that men worship, that He is אלהא דאלהא
"The God of gods", as our sages put it, had not quite disappeared even
from amongst the contemporaries of Abraham. (see Commentary to Gen.
14:18). Thus the fact that there was indeed such a Being as "the Most
High" was nothing new to Abraham. But to him, this Supreme Being was
not simply the "Most High", but, in fact, the "One and Only God". Others
again viewed Him, עליון as being so exalted that He sat enthroned in
splendid isolation בסתר, in secret covert far above the world and its affairs,

have set our perverse acts before You, [and] the core dormant in us before the light of Your countenance. For all our days passed away because of Your stepping forth ; we ended our years like a thought left unspoken. Because of them the days of our years were threescore and ten and when, by reason of effort, they were fourscore years, their pride was travail and violence. For the swiftness cut off, and we flew away. But who knows the force of Your anger, and that You will step forth only according to the fear due You ? So teach us to number our days, then we shall bring home a heart of wisdom. Return, O *God* ! To what end ? Relent You concerning Your servants. Satisfy us with Your love in the morning ; then we shall exult and be glad all our days. Make us glad according to the days when You did afflict us, according to the years when we saw trouble. Let Your work become evident to Your servants and Your glory upon their children. May pleasantness come to us, O Lord our God ; establish upon us the work of our hands ; and the work of our hands, *You* establish it.

He dwelt in secret as עליון, and He wished still to dwell in the shadow as שדי. But I will say of *God*, Who is my refuge, my fortress, my God, in Whom I trust, that he will deliver you from the snare that is laid, from deadly pestilence. He will

---

and thought that the world was thus left to be ruled solely by the blind forces of nature. To Abraham and his sons, however He was revealed as שדי, as the One Who בצל, though hidden and invisible, sets His limits of די "it is sufficient to all things and Who assigns definite bounds, laws and goals to govern the development of every power and force in the universe. God revealed Himself to Abraham and his descendants as the One Who guides the natural order of things for His own purposes, and Who, through His Unity, is also די "all-sufficient" unto all the world and all of mankind. (Commentary to Gen. 17:1). But it was only to Moses that God revealed Himself in all of His free, personal essence, and showed Himself in His direct power which is not subject to the laws of the world order which He Himself had created and ordained. He demonstrated to Moses that He was near to each man as an individual as well as to mankind as such, training them all for His goal of salvation, as is borne out by His name of ה׳. (See Commentary to Exod. 6:3). Therefore Moses says, "God dwelt בסתר עליון in the covert of 'the Most High', in the shadow of שדי ; namely it was His will to keep Himself invisible *as* שדי. But as for me, I say of ה׳, Who has proven to me in my own life that He is מחסי ומצודתי and אלקי אבטח בו, that

בְּאֶבְרָתוֹ ׀ יָסֶךְ לָךְ וְתַחַת כְּנָפָיו תֶּחְסֶה צִנָּה וְסֹחֵרָה אֲמִתּוֹ: לֹא־
תִירָא מִפַּחַד לָיְלָה מֵחֵץ יָעוּף יוֹמָם: מִדֶּבֶר בָּאֹפֶל יַהֲלֹךְ מִקֶּטֶב
יָשׁוּד צָהֳרָיִם: יִפֹּל מִצִּדְּךָ ׀ אֶלֶף וּרְבָבָה מִימִינֶךָ אֵלֶיךָ לֹא יִגָּשׁ:
רַק בְּעֵינֶיךָ תַבִּיט וְשִׁלֻּמַת רְשָׁעִים תִּרְאֶה: כִּי־אַתָּה יְהֹוָה מַחְסִי
עֶלְיוֹן שַׂמְתָּ מְעוֹנֶךָ: לֹא־תְאֻנֶּה אֵלֶיךָ רָעָה וְנֶגַע לֹא־יִקְרַב בְּאָהֳלֶךָ:
כִּי מַלְאָכָיו יְצַוֶּה־לָּךְ לִשְׁמָרְךָ בְּכָל־דְּרָכֶיךָ: עַל־כַּפַּיִם יִשָּׂאוּנְךָ
פֶּן־תִּגֹּף בָּאֶבֶן רַגְלֶךָ: עַל־שַׁחַל וָפֶתֶן תִּדְרֹךְ תִּרְמֹס כְּפִיר וְתַנִּין:
כִּי בִי חָשַׁק וַאֲפַלְּטֵהוּ אֲשַׂגְּבֵהוּ כִּי־יָדַע שְׁמִי: יִקְרָאֵנִי ׀ וְאֶעֱנֵהוּ
עִמּוֹ אָנֹכִי בְצָרָה אֲחַלְּצֵהוּ וַאֲכַבְּדֵהוּ: אֹרֶךְ יָמִים אַשְׂבִּיעֵהוּ וְאַרְאֵהוּ
בִּישׁוּעָתִי: ארך ימים וכו'.

קלה הַלְלוּיָהּ ׀ הַלְלוּ אֶת־שֵׁם יְהֹוָה הַלְלוּ עַבְדֵי יְהֹוָה: שֶׁעֹמְדִים
בְּבֵית יְהֹוָה בְּחַצְרוֹת בֵּית אֱלֹהֵינוּ: הַלְלוּיָהּ כִּי־טוֹב יְהֹוָה זַמְּרוּ לִשְׁמוֹ
כִּי נָעִים: כִּי־יַעֲקֹב בָּחַר לוֹ יָהּ יִשְׂרָאֵל לִסְגֻלָּתוֹ: כִּי אֲנִי יָדַעְתִּי

הוא יצילך etc..." It is evident from Verse 2 that God is already the subject
of Verse 1, meaning that He, Who now reveals Himself to us as 'ה, is the
same One Whom even the ancient world and our forefathers had recognized
as being עליון and שדי. However, יושב, referring to עליון, and יתלונן,
referring to שדי, are in the present tense because in those circles whom the
knowledge of God in His capacity of 'ה has not yet reached, He is still
thought of, even now, as עליון and שדי dwelling in distant isolation.

Psalm 135. הללויה הללו   It is evident from Verse 14 where God's
assurance originally given to Israel through Moses (Deut. 32:36) is repeated
verbatim, that this Psalm speaks of a time when the Jewish people will
have forfeited its independence and, about to succumb to the abuses of the
nations, it will longingly await the judgment of the Lord and a change in

cover you with His pinions, and you will take refuge beneath His wings ; His truth is a barbed shield and an armor. You need not fear the terror of night, nor the arrow that flies by day, the pestilence that prowls in the darkness, nor the death that rages at noon. A thousand may fall at your left and ten thousand at your right hand ; it shall not come near to you. Only with your eyes shall you behold it, and witness the recompense of the lawless. For you have made *God*, [Who is] my refuge, the Most High, the support of your life. No trouble shall be directed to you, nor shall any finger of God come near your tent. For He will give His angels charge over you, to keep you in all your ways. They shall carry you upon their hands, lest you hurt your foot upon a stone ; you will tread upon the jackal and the asp, you will trample upon the young lion and the serpent. "For he clings to Me with yearning ; therefore I shall deliver him. I will set him on high, because he knows My Name. If he calls upon Me, then I shall answer him. I will be with him in distress, and I shall bring him to honor. I will satisfy him with length of days and let him behold My salvation."

⸴   Halaluyah! Proclaim the praise of the Name of *God*, praise Him, servants of *God* ; who still stand in the House of *God*, in the courts of the House of our God. Halaluyah! that *God* is good ; sing of His Name, how pleasant it is. For *God* has chosen Yaakov for Himself, Yisrael as His own possession. For I have recognized how great *God* is and our

---

its bitter lot. Psalm 135 is written with that time in view; it is intended to remind Israel of the greatness of God's rule, and does so by means of a contemplation of the phenomena of nature and the facts of history (Verses 5–14), and by contrasting these with a glimpse of the utter insignificance of the powers which other nations deify. Those who would worship such false gods cannot long endure. (Verses 15–18). In this connection, Israel is then urged to devote itself to the service of the Lord in accordance with the Law that has gone forth from Zion (Verses 19–21). For ברוך ה׳ מציון, that which the Lord has set down in Zion for Israel and for all the rest of mankind, that which has already gone forth thence to Israel and to all of humanity and which will yet come forth from there (Isaiah 2:4), will remain at all times and for all time, a "blessing" of the work of God on

כִּי־גָדוֹל יְהוָה וַאֲדֹנֵינוּ מִכָּל־אֱלֹהִים: כֹּל אֲשֶׁר־חָפֵץ יְהוָה עָשָׂה
בַּשָּׁמַיִם וּבָאָרֶץ בַּיַּמִּים וְכָל־תְּהוֹמוֹת: מַעֲלֶה נְשִׂאִים מִקְצֵה הָאָרֶץ
בְּרָקִים לַמָּטָר עָשָׂה מוֹצֵא רוּחַ מֵאוֹצְרוֹתָיו: שֶׁהִכָּה בְּכוֹרֵי מִצְרָיִם
מֵאָדָם עַד־בְּהֵמָה: שָׁלַח אוֹתֹת וּמֹפְתִים בְּתוֹכֵכִי מִצְרָיִם בְּפַרְעֹה
וּבְכָל־עֲבָדָיו: שֶׁהִכָּה גּוֹיִם רַבִּים וְהָרַג מְלָכִים עֲצוּמִים: לְסִיחוֹן
מֶלֶךְ הָאֱמֹרִי וּלְעוֹג מֶלֶךְ הַבָּשָׁן וּלְכֹל מַמְלְכוֹת כְּנָעַן: וְנָתַן אַרְצָם
נַחֲלָה נַחֲלָה לְיִשְׂרָאֵל עַמּוֹ: יְהוָה שִׁמְךָ לְעוֹלָם יְהוָה זִכְרְךָ לְדֹר־
וָדֹר: כִּי־יָדִין יְהוָה עַמּוֹ וְעַל־עֲבָדָיו יִתְנֶחָם: עֲצַבֵּי הַגּוֹיִם כֶּסֶף
וְזָהָב מַעֲשֵׂה יְדֵי אָדָם: פֶּה־לָהֶם וְלֹא יְדַבֵּרוּ עֵינַיִם לָהֶם וְלֹא
יִרְאוּ: אָזְנַיִם לָהֶם וְלֹא יַאֲזִינוּ אַף אֵין יֶשׁ־רוּחַ בְּפִיהֶם: כְּמוֹהֶם
יִהְיוּ עֹשֵׂיהֶם כֹּל אֲשֶׁר־בֹּטֵחַ בָּהֶם: בֵּית יִשְׂרָאֵל בָּרְכוּ אֶת־יְהוָה
בֵּית אַהֲרֹן בָּרְכוּ אֶת־יְהוָה: בֵּית הַלֵּוִי בָּרְכוּ אֶת־יְהוָה יִרְאֵי
יְהוָה בָּרְכוּ אֶת־יְהוָה: בָּרוּךְ יְהוָה מִצִּיּוֹן שֹׁכֵן יְרוּשָׁלָם
הַלְלוּיָהּ:

קְלוּ הוֹדוּ לַיהוָה כִּי־טוֹב   כִּי לְעוֹלָם חַסְדּוֹ:
הוֹדוּ לֵאלֹהֵי הָאֱלֹהִים   כִּי לְעוֹלָם חַסְדּוֹ:

---

earth. Even beyond the period of ruin and destruction, the calling of
Jerusalem to be the Abode of God's presence on earth will endure forevermore.

Lord is more than all gods. All that which *God* willed,
He has achieved in heaven and on earth, in the seas and in all
the deeps. He causes clouds to rise up from the end of the earth ;
He has made bolts of lightning for the rain when He brings forth
the wind from among His treasures. He, Who slew the first-born of
Mitzrayim, from man to beast, after He had sent signs and convincing
acts into your midst, O Mitzrayim, to Pharaoh and to all of his servants.
He, Who smote many nations and killed many kings, for Sichon,
the king of the Amorites, and for Og, the king of Bashan and
for all the kingdoms of Canaan, and gave their land as an inheritance, as an inheritance to Yisrael His people. O *God,* Your name
is forever, *God,* Your memorial is for every generation. For
God will judge His people one day and He will repent of His
counsel concerning His servants. The idols of the nations are of
silver and gold, the work of human hands ; they have mouths but
they do not speak, they have eyes but they do not see, they have
ears but they do not hear, moreover, there is no breath in their
mouths. They that make them shall become like them, indeed,
everyone who trusts in them. O House of Yisrael, bless *God* ;
O House of Aaron, bless *God.* O House of Levi, bless *God* ,
you who fear *God,* bless *God.* Blessed be *God* from out of Tzion,
Who dwells in Yerushalayim. Halaluyah!

Avow it to *God* that He is good, that His love endures forever.

Avow it to the God of gods that His love endures forever.

Psalm 136 הודו In Pesachim 118a this is called הלל הגדול "the great
praise emanating from His mighty deeds." Why? מפני שהקב״ה יושב ברומו של
עולם ומחלק מזונות לכל ברי׳ Because it portrays the Lord as enthroned in the
heights of the universe and giving sustenance to every living thing. (ibid.)
It is evident from this that the last-but-one verse of this psalm נותן לחם לכל
בשר is viewed as that sentence in which the theme of the entire psalm
culminates and to which all the preceding verses lead. Actually this verse,
[which is Verse 25,] is the only one in Psalm 136, according to grammatical

הוֹדוּ לַאֲדֹנֵי הָאֲדֹנִים   כִּי לְעוֹלָם חַסְדּוֹ:

לְעֹשֵׂה נִפְלָאוֹת גְּדֹלוֹת לְבַדּוֹ   כִּי לְעוֹלָם חַסְדּוֹ:

לְעֹשֵׂה הַשָּׁמַיִם בִּתְבוּנָה   כִּי לְעוֹלָם חַסְדּוֹ:

לְרֹקַע הָאָרֶץ עַל־הַמָּיִם   כִּי לְעוֹלָם חַסְדּוֹ:

לְעֹשֵׂה אוֹרִים גְּדֹלִים   כִּי לְעוֹלָם חַסְדּוֹ:

אֶת־הַשֶּׁמֶשׁ לְמֶמְשֶׁלֶת בַּיּוֹם   כִּי לְעוֹלָם חַסְדּוֹ:

אֶת־הַיָּרֵחַ וְכוֹכָבִים לְמֶמְשְׁלוֹת בַּלָּיְלָה   כִּי לְעוֹלָם חַסְדּוֹ:

לְמַכֵּה מִצְרַיִם בִּבְכוֹרֵיהֶם   כִּי לְעוֹלָם חַסְדּוֹ:

וַיּוֹצֵא יִשְׂרָאֵל מִתּוֹכָם   כִּי לְעוֹלָם חַסְדּוֹ:

---

form, which contains a direct statement נותן וגו׳. All the other verses are subordinate to the summons הודו and therefore begin with the preposition לעושה ל׳ וגו׳ etc. or else they continue the sentences thus begun through the addition of an object such as את השמש וגו׳ etc. or of a dependent clause such as ויוצא וגו׳ etc. In truth, all the preceding verses portray God יושב ברומו של עולם in all the greatness and majesty of His universal rule both in nature and in history. To this, then, is linked the statement נותן לחם לכל בשר thus teaching us to grasp in all its significance the great truth that every piece of bread a human being earns for himself and his dear ones through honest, conscientious toil is to be viewed only as another demonstration of all the great ways of God's rule. For the mighty acts of God in nature and history alike must interact if an honest man is to receive his daily bread in an honest manner from the loving hand of God. Therefore the statement of the sages: קשין מזונותיו של אדם כקריעת ים סוף (ibid.). דכתיב נותן לחם לכל בשר וסמיך לי׳ לגוזר ים סוף לגזרים Man does not receive his sustenance only as the result of the operation of purely physical, mechanical laws. Much rather the fact that man receives sustenance represents the effect of free, personal intervention on the part of the Lord in the course of the development of the phenomena [of nature and history]. Man owes his daily subsistence not to accident, nor even to a simple result

Avow it to the Lord of lords that His love endures forever.

To Him Who alone does great wonders, that His love endures forever.

To Him Who shapes the heavens with understanding, that His loves endures forever.

To Him Who firmly establishes the earth upon the waters, that His love endures forever.

To Him Who fashions great lights, that His love endures forever.

The sun for dominion by day, that His love endures forever.

The moon and the stars for dominion at night, that His love endures forever.

To Him Who slays Mitzrayim through its firstborn, that His love endures forever.

And led out Yisrael from their midst, that His love endures forever.

---

of an automatic interaction of natural and social conditions. Instead, he owes it to the rule of God Himself which freely commands over the forces of nature and society and leads both to fulfill His purposes. Accordingly, we can acquire the proper understanding of the ever-recurring refrain כי לעולם חסדו. This means that the same almighty mercy to which all things are possible, as demonstrated in the outstanding acts of God which are enumerated here one by one, is active לעולם always, even in the phenomena of everyday life.

In order to have us ponder this idea in all its true significance, Verses 2 and 3 proclaim God as being the sole absolute and freely commanding Force and Power that towers high above all the forces of nature which men would worship as gods, as well as above all the powers in society which men honor and fear as their overlords. God is the one true God among all the alleged gods and the one true Master among all the would-be masters. And (Verse 4) not only does He possess this power; He wields it as well. He does not simply leave the course of nature and history to the effects of the laws of nature which He had set up at the time of Creation. He intervenes even now, with His unique, free and personal will, guiding, leading and shaping all things by means of direct action. He does indeed possess this power, for (see Verses 5–9) heaven and earth and the heavenly bodies which influence the natural development of earthly things are all His work. The purpose and goal inherent in them (תבונה) as well as the arrangement of the world rendering possible the

כִּי לְעוֹלָם חַסְדּוֹ:	בְּיָד חֲזָקָה וּבִזְרוֹעַ נְטוּיָה
כִּי לְעוֹלָם חַסְדּוֹ:	לְגֹזֵר יַם־סוּף לִגְזָרִים
כִּי לְעוֹלָם חַסְדּוֹ:	וְהֶעֱבִיר יִשְׂרָאֵל בְּתוֹכוֹ
כִּי לְעוֹלָם חַסְדּוֹ:	וְנִעֵר פַּרְעֹה וְחֵילוֹ בְיַם־סוּף
כִּי לְעוֹלָם חַסְדּוֹ:	לְמוֹלִיךְ עַמּוֹ בַּמִּדְבָּר
כִּי לְעוֹלָם חַסְדּוֹ:	לְמַכֵּה מְלָכִים גְּדֹלִים
כִּי לְעוֹלָם חַסְדּוֹ:	וַיַּהֲרֹג מְלָכִים אַדִּירִים
כִּי לְעוֹלָם חַסְדּוֹ:	לְסִיחוֹן מֶלֶךְ הָאֱמֹרִי
כִּי לְעוֹלָם חַסְדּוֹ:	וּלְעוֹג מֶלֶךְ הַבָּשָׁן
כִּי לְעוֹלָם חַסְדּוֹ:	וְנָתַן אַרְצָם לְנַחֲלָה
כִּי לְעוֹלָם חַסְדּוֹ:	נַחֲלָה לְיִשְׂרָאֵל עַבְדּוֹ
כִּי לְעוֹלָם חַסְדּוֹ:	שֶׁבְּשִׁפְלֵנוּ זָכַר־לָנוּ
כִּי לְעוֹלָם חַסְדּוֹ:	וַיִּפְרְקֵנוּ מִצָּרֵינוּ

interaction of developments, are set up by Him also. And He wields this power even as He has demonstrated it in Israel's history, judging and saving, as in the יציאת מצרים, leading, protecting, nourishing, and educating as in the journey through the wilderness, overthrowing some destinies and establishing others, as in the cession of the land to Israel. And all through our history, from the time of our establishment as a nation down to the present day, we have had proof that God's love functioned not only in our past, nor did it cease with our consolidation as a nation. It survives and endures through and beyond all the ages, even through days when our fortunes are low. Even בשפלנו in our defeat, in our "lowly state", He

With a strong hand and with an outstretched arm, that His love endures forever.

To Him Who divides the Reed Sea asunder, that His love endures forever.

And led Yisrael through the midst of it, that His love endures forever.

And poured out Pharaoh and his host into the Reed Sea, that His love endures forever.

To Him Who leads His people through the wilderness, that His love endures forever.

To Him Who smites great kings, that His love endures forever.

And killed mighty kings, that his love endures forever.

For Sichon, the king of the Amorites, that His love endures forever.

And for Og, the king of Bashan, that His love endures forever.

And gave their land as an inheritance, that His love endures forever.

As an inheritance to Yisrael His servant, that His love endures forever.

Who remembered us in our lowly state, because His love endures forever.

And freed us from our oppressors, because His love endures forever.

---

has not forgotten us and has lifted from us *the yoke* of our oppressors. (That is the literal meaning of פרק). This has been demonstrated to us in all the history of our nation until this very day. But all of God's rule in which He judges and delivers, leads, protects, nourishes, disciplines, overthrows and establishes men and nations, and His constant care throughout the ages which was proven in such obvious ways in the history of the nations, is the same power which is revealed also in every moment of modest, quiet subsistence which He grants to any one person. It is to this same Divine mercy to which we owe every single crumb of our daily sustenance: נותן לחם לכל בשר כי לעולם חסדו.

נָתַן לֶחֶם לְכָל־בָּשָׂר ׃ כִּי לְעוֹלָם חַסְדּוֹ׃

הוֹדוּ לְאֵל הַשָּׁמָיִם ׃ כִּי לְעוֹלָם חַסְדּוֹ׃

לג רַנְּנוּ צַדִּיקִים בַּיהוָה לַיְשָׁרִים נָאוָה תְהִלָּה׃

הוֹדוּ לַיהוָה בְּכִנּוֹר בְּנֵבֶל עָשׂוֹר זַמְּרוּ־לוֹ׃

שִׁירוּ לוֹ שִׁיר חָדָשׁ הֵיטִיבוּ נַגֵּן בִּתְרוּעָה׃ כִּי־יָשָׁר דְּבַר־יְהוָה וְכָל־
מַעֲשֵׂהוּ בֶּאֱמוּנָה׃ אֹהֵב צְדָקָה וּמִשְׁפָּט חֶסֶד יְהוָה מָלְאָה הָאָרֶץ׃
בִּדְבַר יְהוָה שָׁמַיִם נַעֲשׂוּ וּבְרוּחַ פִּיו כָּל־צְבָאָם׃ כֹּנֵס כַּנֵּד מֵי
הַיָּם נֹתֵן בְּאֹצָרוֹת תְּהוֹמוֹת׃ יִירְאוּ מֵיְהוָה כָּל־הָאָרֶץ מִמֶּנּוּ יָגוּרוּ
כָּל־יֹשְׁבֵי תֵבֵל׃ כִּי הוּא אָמַר וַיֶּהִי הוּא צִוָּה וַיַּעֲמֹד׃ יְהוָה הֵפִיר
עֲצַת גּוֹיִם הֵנִיא מַחְשְׁבוֹת עַמִּים׃ עֲצַת יְהוָה לְעוֹלָם תַּעֲמֹד
מַחְשְׁבוֹת לִבּוֹ לְדֹר וָדֹר׃ אַשְׁרֵי הַגּוֹי אֲשֶׁר־יְהוָה אֱלֹהָיו הָעָם ׀
בָּחַר לְנַחֲלָה לוֹ׃ מִשָּׁמַיִם הִבִּיט יְהוָה רָאָה אֶת־כָּל־בְּנֵי הָאָדָם׃

Psalm 33. רננו The theme of this Psalm is one single thought; namely,
that if we contemplate the world, we should not look upon it simply as
a material creation of God. We should always remember that He Who
made the world is also the Lawgiver of all mankind, Who brought both
man and the world into being for one purpose—the fulfillment of His
moral law by man. He has not turned over the world to man unconition-
ally. Therefore, future existence and prosperity are in store only for those
who, like Israel, are God-fearing and obey His Law, and who await His
love because they fear Him. Therefore the צדיקים whose lives are guided
by loyalty to duty, are called upon here to behold the hand of God in the
development of nature and in the course of history, and to give articulate
voice to the lofty thoughts and emotions evoked by such beholding. For,
as is stated in support of this appeal, לישרים only those who fulfill their

Who gives food to all flesh, since His love endures forever.
Avow it to the God of Heaven, that His love endures
forever.

Exult, O righteous ones, in beholding God ; it behooves
the upright to sing praises of the acts that reveal His might.
Render homage to *God* with the harp, sing praises to Him
with the psaltery of ten strings. Sing to Him a new song, express
it in tones as it is seemly, with deep inner emotion. That the word
of *God* is upright and all His work is done in faithfulness.
The love of *God,* of which the earth is full, loves righteousness
and justice. It was by the word of *God* that the heavens were
created, and all the host of them by the breath of His mouth.
He Who gathers the waters of the sea as a wall also stores
up floods in treasure chambers. Therefore let all the earth
fear *God* ; let all the inhabitants of the world of men stand
back in awe of Him. For He spoke and it was ; He also commanded
and it stood still. *God* has brought to naught the counsel of
the peoples ; He has caused the thoughts of the nations to be of
no effect. The counsel of *God* stands forever ; the thoughts of
His heart shall be the heritage of all generations. Only that people
strides forward whose God is *God,* the nation which He has
chosen for His own inheritance. *God* looked down from heaven

---

purpose In life by submitting to the authority of God's Law are qualified
to recognize God in His mighty acts and, on this basis, are entitled to
proclaim His greatness. Not intelligence alone forms the essential prerequisite for the knowledge of God. One must also be possessed of a high
moral sense if he is truly to know God. He who refuses to allow
God to rule over him is prejudiced from the very beginning as regards
the recognition of God's supreme sovereignty in the world. For if he were
to recognize God's supremacy, he would inevitably have to subordinate
himself to God's will, and how could a man such as he sing God's
praises if, by his own way of life, he denies the very statements which
his lips proclaim as absolute truth?

מִמְּכוֹן־שִׁבְתּוֹ הִשְׁגִּיחַ אֶל כָּל־יֹשְׁבֵי הָאָרֶץ: הַיֹּצֵר יַחַד לִבָּם
הַמֵּבִין אֶל־כָּל־מַעֲשֵׂיהֶם: אֵין הַמֶּלֶךְ נוֹשָׁע בְּרָב־חָיִל גִּבּוֹר לֹא־
יִנָּצֵל בְּרָב־כֹּחַ: שֶׁקֶר הַסּוּס לִתְשׁוּעָה וּבְרֹב חֵילוֹ לֹא יְמַלֵּט:
הִנֵּה עֵין יְהֹוָה אֶל־יְרֵאָיו לַמְיַחֲלִים לְחַסְדּוֹ: לְהַצִּיל מִמָּוֶת נַפְשָׁם
וּלְחַיּוֹתָם בָּרָעָב: נַפְשֵׁנוּ חִכְּתָה לַיהֹוָה עֶזְרֵנוּ וּמָגִנֵּנוּ הוּא: כִּי־בוֹ
יִשְׂמַח לִבֵּנוּ כִּי בְשֵׁם קָדְשׁוֹ בָטָחְנוּ: יְהִי־חַסְדְּךָ יְהֹוָה עָלֵינוּ
כַּאֲשֶׁר יִחַלְנוּ לָךְ:

צב מִזְמוֹר שִׁיר לְיוֹם הַשַּׁבָּת: טוֹב לְהֹדוֹת לַיהֹוָה וּלְזַמֵּר לְשִׁמְךָ
עֶלְיוֹן: לְהַגִּיד בַּבֹּקֶר חַסְדֶּךָ וֶאֱמוּנָתְךָ בַּלֵּילוֹת: עֲלֵי־עָשׂוֹר וַעֲלֵי־
נָבֶל עֲלֵי הִגָּיוֹן בְּכִנּוֹר: כִּי שִׂמַּחְתַּנִי יְהֹוָה בְּפָעֳלֶךָ בְּמַעֲשֵׂי יָדֶיךָ
אֲרַנֵּן: מַה־גָּדְלוּ מַעֲשֶׂיךָ יְהֹוָה מְאֹד עָמְקוּ מַחְשְׁבֹתֶיךָ: אִישׁ בַּעַר
לֹא יֵדָע וּכְסִיל לֹא־יָבִין אֶת־זֹאת: בִּפְרֹחַ רְשָׁעִים ׀ כְּמוֹ־עֵשֶׂב

Psalm 92. מזמור This Psalm is dedicated to that institution which, is
to accompany Israel in all its wanderings through the ages like a spiritual
Well of Miriam. From it Israel should ever quaff in deep draughts the
recognition of God's Name, that is, the perception and recognition of His
providence and His will, and that serene trust and peace of mind which
it needs in order to discharge its mission. This institution is none other
than the Sabbath, "the most precious pearl", as our sages put it, which
was given to Moses to bring to his people from God, and whose message
Moses now puts into words in order to impart it to the hearts and minds
of his people. (According to tradition, Psalm 92 was also written by
Moses.) להודות: Every Sabbath day represents a twenty-four-hour period
of tribute which we pay God by actually laying our very selves and our
world at His feet. (see *Horeb*) כי שמחתני וגו׳: The Sabbath teaches us
each time anew to understand the entire world with all its manifold
phenomena as פועל ה׳, one work of the One God. This thought, even as

one day ; He beheld all the sons of men. From the place of His dwelling He looked intently upon all the inhabitants of the earth, He, Who fashions their hearts for one another ; Who considers all their doings. A king is not saved by the multitude of a host, nor is a hero delivered by great strength. A horse proves a vain thing for victory, nor can it afford escape by its great strength. But behold, the eye of *God* is toward them that fear Him, toward them that wait for His loving-kindness, to deliver their soul from death and to keep them alive in famine. It was our soul that waited for *God* ; He is still our help and our shield. For it is only in Him that our heart rejoices, because we have put our trust in His holy Name. Let Your loving-kindness, O *God,* be upon us, even as we have waited for You.

A Psalm, a Song for the Sabbath Day. It is good to pay homage to *God,* and to sing praises to Your Name, O Most High. To proclaim Your mercy in the morning and Your faithfulness in the nights, with full sound and with the plaintive tone, in meditation upon the harp ; For You have given me joy in Your work, O *God* ; I will exult in the works of Your hands. How great are Your works, O *God,* how infinitely profound Your thoughts ! A man bare of reason does not understand, nor does a conceited fool comprehend this ; when the lawless spring up as the grass

---

it is uplifting in its grandeur, also makes us joyfully aware of the harmonious unity of all the contrasting phenomena of the universe, contrasts which would rend the world asunder, were it not for the fact that they all represent the work of One Creator. Moses declares, "And therefore במעשי ידיך ארנן every single event that has occurred in the past and comes about now through the work of Thy hands, fills me with pure joy." להגיד כי ישר ה' If God has proven to be צורי the Rock Which has shaped, protected and supported Israel throught the ages, then לא עולתה בו there is no עול במשפטו, no partiality, no injustice in His providence. For it is His desire to be the same Rock of protection and support for all men, if only they will render Him homage and allow all their lives and ambitions to be guided by His Law. But the כתיב is עלתה, and this, it seems, would express both the idea of עלילה (Deut. 22:17) and that of עלה which is used in Rabbinic literature as a term for "motive" or "cause". The thought of Verse 16, then, is as follows: Not only is there no injustice in His providence; but, as a matter of fact, the 'first cause' is not even with Him. It rather rests

וַיָּצִיצוּ כָּל־פֹּעֲלֵי אָוֶן לְהִשָּׁמְדָם עֲדֵי־עַד: וְאַתָּה מָרוֹם לְעֹלָם
יְהֹוָה: כִּי הִנֵּה אֹיְבֶיךָ יְהֹוָה כִּי־הִנֵּה אֹיְבֶיךָ יֹאבֵדוּ יִתְפָּרְדוּ כָּל־
פֹּעֲלֵי אָוֶן: וַתָּרֶם כִּרְאֵים קַרְנִי בַּלֹּתִי בְּשֶׁמֶן רַעֲנָן: וַתַּבֵּט עֵינִי
בְּשׁוּרָי בַּקָּמִים עָלַי מְרֵעִים תִּשְׁמַעְנָה אָזְנָי: צַדִּיק כַּתָּמָר יִפְרָח
כְּאֶרֶז בַּלְּבָנוֹן יִשְׂגֶּה: שְׁתוּלִים בְּבֵית יְהֹוָה בְּחַצְרוֹת אֱלֹהֵינוּ יַפְרִיחוּ:
עוֹד יְנוּבוּן בְּשֵׂיבָה דְּשֵׁנִים וְרַעֲנַנִּים יִהְיוּ: לְהַגִּיד כִּי־יָשָׁר יְהֹוָה
צוּרִי וְלֹא־עַ*לָתָה בּוֹ: עֹלַתָה ק

צג יְהֹוָה מָלָךְ גֵּאוּת לָבֵשׁ לָבֵשׁ יְהֹוָה עֹז הִתְאַזָּר אַף־תִּכּוֹן תֵּבֵל
בַּל־תִּמּוֹט: נָכוֹן כִּסְאֲךָ מֵאָז מֵעוֹלָם אָתָּה: נָשְׂאוּ נְהָרוֹת יְהֹוָה
נָשְׂאוּ נְהָרוֹת קוֹלָם יִשְׂאוּ נְהָרוֹת דָּכְיָם: מִקֹּלוֹת מַיִם רַבִּים
אַדִּירִים מִשְׁבְּרֵי־יָם אַדִּיר בַּמָּרוֹם יְהֹוָה: עֵדֹתֶיךָ נֶאֶמְנוּ מְאֹד
לְבֵיתְךָ נַאֲוָה־קֹדֶשׁ יְהֹוָה לְאֹרֶךְ יָמִים:

---

with mankind itself which does not yet understand how to use this divine
gift of free will for the advancement of its own true, permanent salvation
by entering, voluntarily into the service of its God. The sages note that
this "Song and Psalm for the Sabbath Day" looks toward the perfect
Sabbath of the future יום שכלו שבת. Even as the first Sabbath day marked
the completion of physical creation, so that "perfect Sabbath of mankind"
shall mark the time when the moral moulding of man shall have reached
its goal of perfection. It will signify the culmination of a process which
had begun initially with the first Sabbath Day of Creation and which was
heralded and advanced by the institution of the Sabbath. Thus the "Sabbath
of Creation" has as its purpose and goal the attainment of the "perfect
Sabbath of mankind". (See Commentary to Gen. 2:1–3).

Psalm 93. ה מלך. This psalm is a continuation of Psalm 92. It sings
of the era when the enduring kingdom of God, which erring mankind had
opposed for so long will finally come about.

where all the abusers of might flourish, that it is [only so] that
they may be destroyed forever. But You, O *God*, will remain on
high forever. For behold, Your enemies, O *God*, lo, Your enemies
shall perish, all the abusers of might disintegrate [of] themselves,
while you did lift up my horn like [that of] the *Re'em*, and
I outlive them with ever renewed consecration. Since my eye has
seen this [come to pass] in the case of those who lie in wait for
me, therefore my ears hear it [decreed] for those that rise up
against me because they are evildoers. The righteous one shall
flourish like the palm tree; he shall grow tall like a cedar in Lebanon.
Planted in the House of *God*, they shall flourish in the courts
of our God. They shall still bear fruit even in old age, they shall
remain full of sap and vigor forever, to declare that *God* is
upright, my Rock, in Whom there is no injustice.

God has begun His reign; He has robed Himself in majesty;
God has robed Himself, He has girded Himself with strength that
none can withstand; now the world of men, too, shall be firmly established and sway no more. Your throne is henceforth established, O
You Who are from everlasting. True, the floods, O *God*, the floods
have lifted up their voices, the floods lift up their fall. The breakers
of the ocean grew mightier from the roar of many waters; *God* alone
is mighty on high. Thus Your testimonies have proven infinitely faithful; the name of "Sanctuary" truly befits Your House, O *God*, for
all the length of days.

עדתיך The universal worship of God which will be part of the coming
of God's kingdom on earth had long ago been heralded and advanced by
those institutions of Divine Law which come under the category of עדות,
"testimonies, witnesses and memorials" of Divine truths. The first and foremost of these institutions is, of course, the Sabbath. The course that
history will eventually take will attest to the veracity of these "testimonies".
And לביתך נאוה קדש the House of God which had been erected for His
Law, the House in which, as stated in שתולים בבית ה' (Psalm 92:14), the
righteous of all times have been rooted with every fiber of their moral and
spiritual being, this House shall then be truly deserving of the name קדש,
"Sanctuary". For this designation best signifies the destiny of the House
of God; namely that it should be the source of the sanctification of all
of human affairs on earth. (See Hirsch's Commentary to Exod. 29:37)

יְהִי כְבוֹד יְיָ לְעוֹלָם יִשְׂמַח יְיָ בְּמַעֲשָׂיו: יְהִי שֵׁם יְיָ
מְבֹרָךְ מֵעַתָּה וְעַד־עוֹלָם: מִמִּזְרַח־שֶׁמֶשׁ עַד־מְבוֹאוֹ
מְהֻלָּל שֵׁם יְיָ: רָם עַל־כָּל־גּוֹיִם יְיָ עַל הַשָּׁמַיִם כְּבוֹדוֹ:
יְיָ שִׁמְךָ לְעוֹלָם יְיָ זִכְרְךָ לְדֹר־וָדֹר: יְיָ בַּשָּׁמַיִם הֵכִין
כִּסְאוֹ וּמַלְכוּתוֹ בַּכֹּל מָשָׁלָה: יִשְׂמְחוּ הַשָּׁמַיִם וְתָגֵל
הָאָרֶץ וְיֹאמְרוּ בַגּוֹיִם יְיָ מָלָךְ: יְיָ מֶלֶךְ יְיָ מָלָךְ יְיָ
יִמְלֹךְ לְעוֹלָם וָעֶד: יְיָ מֶלֶךְ עוֹלָם וָעֶד אָבְדוּ גוֹיִם
מֵאַרְצוֹ: יְיָ הֵפִיר עֲצַת גּוֹיִם הֵנִיא מַחְשְׁבוֹת עַמִּים:
רַבּוֹת מַחֲשָׁבוֹת בְּלֶב־אִישׁ וַעֲצַת יְיָ הִיא תָקוּם: עֲצַת
יְיָ לְעוֹלָם תַּעֲמֹד מַחְשְׁבוֹת לִבּוֹ לְדֹר וָדֹר: כִּי הוּא
אָמַר וַיֶּהִי הוּא צִוָּה וַיַּעֲמֹד: כִּי־בָחַר יְיָ בְּצִיּוֹן אִוָּהּ
לְמוֹשָׁב לוֹ: כִּי־יַעֲקֹב בָּחַר לוֹ יָהּ יִשְׂרָאֵל לִסְגֻלָּתוֹ:
כִּי לֹא־יִטֹּשׁ יְיָ עַמּוֹ וְנַחֲלָתוֹ לֹא יַעֲזֹב: וְהוּא רַחוּם
יְכַפֵּר עָוֹן וְלֹא יַשְׁחִית וְהִרְבָּה לְהָשִׁיב אַפּוֹ וְלֹא יָעִיר
כָּל־חֲמָתוֹ: יְיָ הוֹשִׁיעָה הַמֶּלֶךְ יַעֲנֵנוּ בְיוֹם־קָרְאֵנוּ:

יהי כבוד May men at long last attain the proper understanding and
loyalty to their duty, rendering homage to God of their own free
will. **ה' שמך וגו'** all that which is expressed of God's ways by the Divine
Name of 'ה belongs to eternity in all its manifold significance, and the
full truth of it will be recognized only at the end of time. However, the
remembrance of this Name, the awareness of it, of which anyone is
capable at all times, is a guide and beacon, the comfort and stay of every
generation, for the dominion of this Name, which educates mankind and
shapes the future, will endure through all the ages. (see Commentary to
Gen. 2:4, Exod. 3:13–15).

The glory of *God* will endure forever; may *God* take delight in His creatures. Let the Name of *God* be blessed from now on unto eternity. Indeed, from sunrise to sunset the Name of *God* is proclaimed in praise of His mighty deeds; *God* is high above all peoples, His glory is above the heavens. God, Your Name is forever, God, Your memorial is for every generation. *God* has established His throne in Heaven, but His dominion extends over all things. The heavens are glad, the earth rejoices, and let it be said among the nations "*God* has begun His reign." *God* is King, *God* was King, *God* will rule as King through all eternity. *God* is King at all times, even nations are lost from His earth. *God* has brought to naught the counsel of the peoples, has denied success to the thoughts of nations. There are many thoughts in the heart of man, but it is the counsel of *God* that endures. The counsel of *God* endures for all the future, the thoughts of His heart are for every generation. For He spoke and it was; He also commanded and it stood still. For *God* has chosen Tzion; He has selected it for His dwelling place. For *God* has chosen Yaakov for Himself, Yisrael as His own possession. For *God* will not cast off His people, nor will He forsake His inheritance. And He, full of compassion, forgives sin and does not let destruction come; He often takes back His wrath and does not stir up His indignation entirely. O *God*, grant salvation. It is as the King that He hears us on the day on which we call.

ה' מלך עולם ועד וגו'   God is King at all times. He rules the world at all times. The earth is His earth, and not only the individual but all the nations residing upon it are utterly unimportant as compared to Him, and one day, when the Kingdom of God will be universally recognized, and the earth will have become ארצו *His* earth in truth, then national differences will vanish from the earth altogether. עצת ה' וגו'; the עצת גוים opposes the עצת ה', and the מחשבות עמים the מחשבות לבו. The counsels of all the nations in history, bent upon increasing national power by arrogance and tyranny, is opposed to the counsel of God which is to have the kingdom of peace and happiness rise up at long last here below beneath the all-encompassing reign of love and justice, of morality and selfless devotion to duty. This Divine counsel shall endure unalterable, until that time which, though it may still seem to us עולם, a veiled and unknown future,

אַשְׁרֵי יוֹשְׁבֵי בֵיתֶךָ עוֹד יְהַלְלוּךָ פֶּלָה:

אַשְׁרֵי הָעָם שֶׁכָּכָה לּוֹ אַשְׁרֵי הָעָם שֶׁיְיָ אֱלֹהָיו:

קִמָה תְּהִלָּה לְדָוִד

אֲרוֹמִמְךָ אֱלוֹהַי הַמֶּלֶךְ וַאֲבָרְכָה שִׁמְךָ לְעוֹלָם וָעֶד:

בְּכָל־יוֹם אֲבָרְכֶךָ וַאֲהַלְלָה שִׁמְךָ לְעוֹלָם וָעֶד:

גָּדוֹל יְהֹוָה וּמְהֻלָּל מְאֹד וְלִגְדֻלָּתוֹ אֵין חֵקֶר:

דּוֹר לְדוֹר יְשַׁבַּח מַעֲשֶׂיךָ וּגְבוּרֹתֶיךָ יַגִּידוּ:

הֲדַר כְּבוֹד הוֹדֶךָ וְדִבְרֵי נִפְלְאֹתֶיךָ אָשִׂיחָה:

וֶעֱזוּז נוֹרְאֹתֶיךָ יֹאמֵרוּ וּגְדֻלָּתְךָ אֲסַפְּרֶנָּה: וגדולתך ק׳

זֵכֶר רַב־טוּבְךָ יַבִּיעוּ וְצִדְקָתְךָ יְרַנֵּנוּ:

חַנּוּן וְרַחוּם יְהֹוָה אֶרֶךְ אַפַּיִם וּגְדָל־חָסֶד: יי״ד י׳

טוֹב־יְהֹוָה לַכֹּל וְרַחֲמָיו עַל־כָּל־מַעֲשָׂיו:

---

will nevertheless come to pass as part of God's plan. And even before then, the מחשבות לבו are constantly turned to every generation. Those who pursue only wealth and pleasures in their dealings with others, without caring for the "thoughts of God" will not be permitted to rejoice in the attainment of their selfish ends. Everywhere, the "thoughts of His heart" extend their protective care to the growth of all that which is good and true and part of His future kingdom on earth. כי הוא וגו׳ For all the acts of God at the time of the Exodus from Egypt, and particularly the miracle of קריעת ים סוף, have shown that He Who "spoke and it was", is also the One Who "commanded and it stood still". They have demonstrated that His will reigns supreme in the world which He has called into being. Only one signal from Him and all the world order, which He Himself has created, and upon whose alleged blind, masterless constancy men base their plans, comes to a standstill. כי יעקב וגו׳ For it is the weak tribe of Jacob that God has chosen for Himself in order to demonstrate His might through the

Forward forever stride those who dwell in Your house, they constantly proclaim the praise of mighty acts. To salvation strides that people with whom it is thus! To salvation that nation whose God is *God*!

Tehillah by David. I will extol You, my God, O King, and I will bless Your Name unto the future everlasting.

Every day will I bless You, and proclaim the praise of Your Name until the future everlasting.

Great is *God* and most evident in mighty acts, but His greatness is unsearchable.

Generation after generation lauds Your works, and proclaims Your almighty acts.

But I will express in meditation the beauty of the glory of Your majesty and the words of Your wonders.

And they shall speak of the invincibility of Your awesome acts, but I shall tell of the magnitude of the totality of all Your great deeds.

That they may also utter a thought of the abundance of Your goodness and exult in Your tender righteousness.

God is gracious and compassionate, slow to anger and great in devoted mercy.

God is good to all, and His compassion is over all His works.

---

fate of that small nation which, though attacked by all the other peoples, will survive them all. And He has made it the purpose of Israel, whom He has preserved victoriously, to belong to Him with all of his existence and endeavors, to become exclusively His and to remain so for all time.

אשרי. Psalm 145 actually begins with the words תהלה לדוד ארוממך. This verse, which is Verse 5 of Psalm 84, is recited by way of introduction, because we learn from it that, before we begin to pray, we must first put ourselves in the proper frame of mind for prayer by quiet meditation in the House of God. (see *Berachoth 32b*) As a matter of fact, even the quiet, contemplative sojourn in the House of God has a most beneficial effect upon mind and spirit, because the thoughts of the worshipper are then centered upon God and upon the purpose of the place where he is standing, namely, to help him come nearer to God and to purify himself before Him. However, the wording is not יושבים בביתך but ישבי ביתך; true progress on the road to salvation can be made only if, in

יוֹדוּךָ יְהֹוָה כָּל־מַעֲשֶׂיךָ וַחֲסִידֶיךָ יְבָרְכוּכָה:

כְּבוֹד מַלְכוּתְךָ יֹאמֵרוּ וּגְבוּרָתְךָ יְדַבֵּרוּ:

לְהוֹדִיעַ לִבְנֵי הָאָדָם גְּבוּרֹתָיו וּכְבוֹד הֲדַר מַלְכוּתוֹ:

מַלְכוּתְךָ מַלְכוּת כָּל־עֹלָמִים וּמֶמְשַׁלְתְּךָ בְּכָל־דּוֹר וָדֹר:

סוֹמֵךְ יְהֹוָה לְכָל־הַנֹּפְלִים וְזוֹקֵף לְכָל־הַכְּפוּפִים:

עֵינֵי כֹל אֵלֶיךָ יְשַׂבֵּרוּ וְאַתָּה נוֹתֵן־לָהֶם אֶת־אָכְלָם בְּעִתּוֹ:

פּוֹתֵחַ אֶת־יָדֶךָ וּמַשְׂבִּיעַ לְכָל־חַי רָצוֹן:

צַדִּיק יְהֹוָה בְּכָל־דְּרָכָיו וְחָסִיד בְּכָל־מַעֲשָׂיו:

קָרוֹב יְהֹוָה לְכָל־קֹרְאָיו לְכֹל אֲשֶׁר יִקְרָאֻהוּ בֶאֱמֶת:

רְצוֹן־יְרֵאָיו יַעֲשֶׂה וְאֶת־שַׁוְעָתָם יִשְׁמַע וְיוֹשִׁיעֵם:

שׁוֹמֵר יְהֹוָה אֶת־כָּל־אֹהֲבָיו וְאֵת כָּל־הָרְשָׁעִים יַשְׁמִיד:

תְּהִלַּת יְהֹוָה יְדַבֶּר פִּי וִיבָרֵךְ כָּל־בָּשָׂר שֵׁם קָדְשׁוֹ לְעוֹלָם וָעֶד:

קט״ו י״ח וַאֲנַחְנוּ נְבָרֵךְ יָהּ מֵעַתָּה וְעַד־עוֹלָם הַלְלוּיָהּ:

(*) בפסוק זה צריך לכוין בזיתר שמזכיר בו שבח השם המשגיח על בריותיו ומפרנסן.

addition to coming to the House of God at certain stated intervals, one will take the impressions gained there out into everyday life, thus spending all of one's life in the House of God, as it were, and allowing all of his days on earth to become a hymn in praise of God. To this there is added the thought in Verse 15 of Psalm 144 that all those who, in this manner, submit all of their conduct and all of their fate entirely to the guidance and leadership of God, their God, may be certain of constant progress on the road to salvation. .

All Your works shall render You homage, O *God* but Your devoted ones shall bless You.

They shall speak of the honor due Your kingdom, and they will declare Your power.

To make known to the sons of men His mighty acts, but also the glory, the beauty of His kingdom.

Your kingdom is a kingdom for all the length of days and Your rule is in every generation.

God upholds all that fall and raises up all those that are bowed down.

The eyes of all wait upon You and You give them their food in due season.

Yea, You open Your hand and satisfy the desire of every living thing.

God is just in all His ways, and full of devoted love in all His works.

God is near to all those that call upon Him, to all that call upon Him in truth.

He will fulfill the desire of them that fear Him; He also will hear their cry and give them salvation.

God will keep all those that love Him, and all the lawless will He destroy.

Let my mouth declare the praise of *God,* so that all flesh may bless His holy Name unto the future everlasting.

But we bless *God* from this moment on forever and ever, Hálaluyah!

Psalm 145. תהלה לדוד Our sages attach so much significance to this psalm that they have said concerning it: כל האומר תהלה לדוד שלשה פעמים בכל יום מובטח לו שהוא בן עולם הבא "He who thoughtfully recites this Tehillah three times each day [and takes it to heart] may be certain that he is on the path to eternal life." Its special characteristic is the alphabetical arrangement of its verses, which indicates the psalmist's intention to facilitate its recital from memory. Of further significance is the statement פותח את ידיך ומשביע לכל חי רצון contained in Verse 16 which conveys to us the main theme of the entire psalm; that is, that Divine providence cares for every living thing.

קוּמוּ הַלְלוּיָהּ הַלְלִי נַפְשִׁי אֶת־יְהֹוָה: אֲהַלְלָה יְהֹוָה בְּחַיָּי אֲזַמְּרָה

לֵאלֹהַי בְּעוֹדִי: אַל־תִּבְטְחוּ בִנְדִיבִים בְּבֶן־אָדָם ׀ שֶׁאֵין לוֹ תְשׁוּעָה:

תֵּצֵא רוּחוֹ יָשֻׁב לְאַדְמָתוֹ בַּיּוֹם הַהוּא אָבְדוּ עֶשְׁתֹּנֹתָיו: אַשְׁרֵי

שֶׁאֵל יַעֲקֹב בְּעֶזְרוֹ שִׂבְרוֹ עַל־יְהֹוָה אֱלֹהָיו: עֹשֶׂה ׀ שָׁמַיִם וָאָרֶץ

אֶת־הַיָּם וְאֶת־כָּל־אֲשֶׁר־בָּם הַשֹּׁמֵר אֱמֶת לְעוֹלָם: עֹשֶׂה מִשְׁפָּט ׀

לַעֲשׁוּקִים נֹתֵן לֶחֶם לָרְעֵבִים יְהֹוָה מַתִּיר אֲסוּרִים: יְהֹוָה ׀ פֹּקֵחַ

עִוְרִים יְהֹוָה זֹקֵף כְּפוּפִים יְהֹוָה אֹהֵב צַדִּיקִים: יְהֹוָה ׀ שֹׁמֵר אֶת־

גֵּרִים יָתוֹם וְאַלְמָנָה יְעוֹדֵד וְדֶרֶךְ רְשָׁעִים יְעַוֵּת: יִמְלֹךְ יְהֹוָה ׀

לְעוֹלָם אֱלֹהַיִךְ צִיּוֹן לְדֹר וָדֹר הַלְלוּיָהּ:

The alphabetical order in which the beginnings of these verses are arranged, omits the letter נ, because, as our sages note (*Berachoth 4b*), this letter would have had to be used for the designation of נפילה, the "fall' of man. Nevertheless, חזר דוד וסמכן ברוח הקודש שנ' סומך ה' לכל הנופלים immediately after this omission David does mention the spiritual "fall' of man, but only in connection with the Divine *support* which prevents this fall. "God upholds all that fall". Men are wont to attribute their growth and progress to their own abilities and feel that they owe their advancement and development to their own power and wisdom. It is only when they stumble and fall that they perceive the act of some Higher Power. In David's view, the opposite is true. He regards the fall

Halaluyah! Proclaim the praise of *God*, O my soul. I will proclaim the praise of *God* as long as I live; I will sing to my God as long as I have being. Put not your trust in nobles, nor in the son of man, with whom help is not. If his spirit departs, he will return to his earth. On that day all his plans are lost. Forward strides he whose help is the God of Yaakov, whose expectation is in *God* his God. He Who shapes heaven and earth, the sea and all that is in them; it is He Who keeps faith forever. He does justice to those bereft of rights; He gives bread to the hungry, *God*, Who loosens the fettered. *God* makes the blind see clearly; *God* raises up those who who are bowed down, *God*, Who loves the righteous. *God* protects strangers; He causes the orphan and the widow to endure, and He makes the way of the lawless to end in crookedness. *God* will reign in eternity; He is your God, Tzion, to every generation, Halaluyah!

---

of man as man's own doing. Men fall because of their folly and because of their disobedience toward God. But the ability to remain upright in the midst of all the vicissitudes of life, every moment of health and happiness, of spiritual and physical development and growth, every new, free and gladsome breath they draw, they owe to the mercy of God Who eternally provides for all things living and is ready at all times to grant new life. The greatness of God is revealed not in death and decay, but in growth and life. נפילה, the word designating the fall of man, belongs to the chronicles of mankind. But David's song of Divine Providence contains only that word which denotes the support and encouragement which God in His mercy grants to him who is bowed down and about to fall. (Cf. Psalm 6:6, 30:10, 115:17).

Psalm 146. הללוי׳ Psalm 145 sang of the universal character of the rule of Divine providence. In Psalm 146 the individual, that is, the individual Jew, proclaims the loving care of God as he has experienced it in the course of his own life.

קמז הַלְלוּיָהּ ׀ כִּי־טוֹב זַמְּרָה אֱלֹהֵינוּ כִּי־נָעִים נָאוָה תְהִלָּה:
בּוֹנֵה יְרוּשָׁלַ͏ִם יְהוָֹה נִדְחֵי יִשְׂרָאֵל יְכַנֵּס: הָרוֹפֵא לִשְׁבוּרֵי לֵב וּמְחַבֵּשׁ
לְעַצְּבוֹתָם: מוֹנֶה מִסְפָּר לַכּוֹכָבִים לְכֻלָּם שֵׁמוֹת יִקְרָא: גָּדוֹל
אֲדוֹנֵינוּ וְרַב־כֹּחַ לִתְבוּנָתוֹ אֵין מִסְפָּר: מְעוֹדֵד עֲנָוִים יְהוָֹה מַשְׁפִּיל
רְשָׁעִים עֲדֵי־אָרֶץ: עֱנוּ לַיהוָֹה בְּתוֹדָה זַמְּרוּ לֵאלֹהֵינוּ בְכִנּוֹר:
הַמְכַסֶּה שָׁמַיִם ׀ בְּעָבִים הַמֵּכִין לָאָרֶץ מָטָר הַמַּצְמִיחַ הָרִים חָצִיר:
נוֹתֵן לִבְהֵמָה לַחְמָהּ לִבְנֵי עֹרֵב אֲשֶׁר יִקְרָאוּ: לֹא בִגְבוּרַת הַסּוּס
יֶחְפָּץ לֹא־בְשׁוֹקֵי הָאִישׁ יִרְצֶה: רוֹצֶה יְהוָֹה אֶת־יְרֵאָיו אֶת־
הַמְיַחֲלִים לְחַסְדּוֹ: שַׁבְּחִי יְרוּשָׁלַ͏ִם אֶת־יְהוָֹה הַלְלִי אֱלֹהַיִךְ צִיּוֹן:
כִּי־חִזַּק בְּרִיחֵי שְׁעָרָיִךְ בֵּרַךְ בָּנַיִךְ בְּקִרְבֵּךְ: הַשָּׂם־גְּבוּלֵךְ שָׁלוֹם
חֵלֶב חִטִּים יַשְׂבִּיעֵךְ: הַשֹּׁלֵחַ אִמְרָתוֹ אָרֶץ עַד־מְהֵרָה יָרוּץ דְּבָרוֹ:
הַנֹּתֵן שֶׁלֶג כַּצָּמֶר כְּפוֹר כָּאֵפֶר יְפַזֵּר: מַשְׁלִיךְ קַרְחוֹ כְפִתִּים לִפְנֵי
קָרָתוֹ מִי יַעֲמֹד: יִשְׁלַח־דְּבָרוֹ וְיַמְסֵם יַשֵּׁב רוּחוֹ יִזְּלוּ־מָיִם: מַגִּיד
דְּבָרָו לְיַעֲקֹב חֻקָּיו וּמִשְׁפָּטָיו לְיִשְׂרָאֵל: לֹא עָשָׂה כֵן ׀ לְכָל־גּוֹי
וּמִשְׁפָּטִים בַּל־יְדָעוּם הַלְלוּיָהּ: *) דבריו ק.

Psalm 147. הללוי׳. This psalm means to awaken in the Jewish people
as a whole, as it endures the bitter lot of exile, the awarenes of its enduring
relationship to God which is assured for all times to come, and of its permanent position as messenger of the word of God amidst mankind which
lacks the knowledge of what is good and true. The Divine institution of
"Yerushalayim" (cf. Commentary to Psalms 76:3) did not come to an
end when we were exiled but is still developing progressively toward that

Halaluyah! For it is good to sing to our God; for it is pleasant when His praise is seemly. The Builder of Yerushalayim, *God*, He gathers together the dispersed of Yisrael. He Who heals the broken-hearted will also bind up their wounds. He Who counts the number of the stars calls all of them, too, by name. Great is our Lord and abundant in strength, and no number counts before His insight. *God* will cause the humble to endure ; He will bring down the lawless to the ground. Sing to *God* with thanksgiving ; sing to our God with the harp. He Who covers heaven with clouds, Who prepares rain for the earth, Who makes mountains bring forth grass ; Who thus gives the beast its food, to the young ravens that after which they cry ; He does not delight in the strength of the horse, and takes no pleasure in the legs of a man. *God* takes pleasure in those who fear Him, who wait upon His mercy. Laud *God*, O Yerushalayim, proclaim the praise of Your God, O Tzion. For, even as He has made fast the bars of Your gates, even as He has blessed your children within you, so it is He Who still ordains you borders for peace, and Who will satisfy you with the fat of wheat. He Who sends out His command to the earth — His word runs very swiftly — Who gives snow like flakes of wool, Who scatters hoarfrost like ashes, Who casts forth His ice like crumbs — who can stand before His cold ? Who then sends forth His word and melts them, Who causes His wind to blow, and they flow as water ; He declares His word, so varied and yet one, to Yaakov, and His statutes and ordinances to Yisrael. He has not dealt so with any nation ; and as for ordinances — they have not known them. Halaluyah!

---

future day when it will reach its perfect realization. God has prepared balm not only for the sorrow of the individual but also for the wounds of the nation. And even as every star in the heavenly host above stands under the direct guidance of God, so, too, He knows every single son of His scattered people and keeps His watchful and guiding eye upon him. True, this dispersed nation is devoid of power and brilliance and therefore is overshadowed by the other nations which are endowed with plainly obvious might and strength. But it is not such tangibles, in whose possession the nations take such pride and whose lack causes Israel such humiliation among men, that God views as the building bricks for the fulfillment

קמח הַלְלוּיָהּ ׀ הַלְלוּ אֶת־יְהֹוָה מִן־הַשָּׁמַיִם הַלְלוּהוּ בַּמְּרוֹמִים:
הַלְלוּהוּ כָל־מַלְאָכָיו הַלְלוּהוּ כָּל־צְבָאָו: הַלְלוּהוּ שֶׁמֶשׁ וְיָרֵחַ
הַלְלוּהוּ כָּל־כּוֹכְבֵי אוֹר: הַלְלוּהוּ שְׁמֵי הַשָּׁמָיִם וְהַמַּיִם אֲשֶׁר ׀ מֵעַל
הַשָּׁמָיִם: יְהַלְלוּ אֶת־שֵׁם יְהֹוָה כִּי הוּא צִוָּה וְנִבְרָאוּ: וַיַּעֲמִידֵם
לָעַד לְעוֹלָם חָק־נָתַן וְלֹא יַעֲבוֹר: הַלְלוּ אֶת־יְהֹוָה מִן־הָאָרֶץ
תַּנִּינִים וְכָל־תְּהֹמוֹת: אֵשׁ וּבָרָד שֶׁלֶג וְקִיטוֹר רוּחַ סְעָרָה עֹשָׂה
דְבָרוֹ: הֶהָרִים וְכָל־גְּבָעוֹת עֵץ פְּרִי וְכָל־אֲרָזִים: הַחַיָּה וְכָל־בְּהֵמָה
רֶמֶשׂ וְצִפּוֹר כָּנָף: מַלְכֵי־אֶרֶץ וְכָל־לְאֻמִּים שָׂרִים וְכָל־שֹׁפְטֵי אָרֶץ:
בַּחוּרִים וְגַם־בְּתוּלוֹת זְקֵנִים עִם־נְעָרִים: יְהַלְלוּ ׀ אֶת־שֵׁם יְהֹוָה
כִּי־נִשְׂגָּב שְׁמוֹ לְבַדּוֹ הוֹדוֹ עַל־אֶרֶץ וְשָׁמָיִם: וַיָּרֶם קֶרֶן ׀ לְעַמּוֹ
תְּהִלָּה לְכָל־חֲסִידָיו לִבְנֵי יִשְׂרָאֵל עַם־קְרֹבוֹ הַלְלוּיָהּ:

(*) צבאיו ק׳.

of His purposes on earth. The treasures which the Jewish people must
cherish are the moral and spiritual values. These it is to cultivate and
preserve throughout its exile. There is one treasure above all, and Jerusalem-
Zion will rise again for its sake so that it may be made a living reality,
and that is the Torah. It is the Law, whose sole guardian Israel is, and ever
shall remain, the Law by means of which the word of God, through
voluntary recognition and homage, should come to rule and shape all the
affairs of mankind on the basis of truth, justice and morality. This is
the same Law which, ever since Creation, has reigned supreme over the
phenomena of all nature at all times, and still reigns today before our
own eyes in immutable almighty power. We see God's Law at work in
every creature, in every element, substance and force. And man's high
distinction lies solely in the fact that the Law of God, which rules the
existence of all other creatures with compelling force, was communicated

Halaluyah! Proclaim the praise of *God* from the heavens, proclaim it from the high places. Proclaim it, all His messengers; proclaim it, all His hosts. Proclaim it, O sun and moon; proclaim it, all the stars of light. Proclaim it, O heavens of heavens and waters that are above the heavens. They will proclaim the praise of the Name of *God,* that He commanded, and they were created, that He has established them for all time; that he has given a statute which shall not pass away. Proclaim the praise of *God* from the earth, species of fish and all deeps, fire and hail, snow and vapor, stormy wind, fulfilling His word, mountains and all hills, fruit trees and all cedars; beasts and all cattle, creeping things and winged fowl; kings of the earth and all peoples, princes and all the judges of the earth; young men and also maidens, old men and boys together; they will all proclaim the praise of the Name of *God,* that His Name alone is exalted, His majesty is above the earth and heaven. But that He lifted up the horn for His people is a proclamation of His praise for all of His devoted ones, [but] to the sons of Yisrael [only as] the people [that had] been near to him from the beginning. Halaluyah!

---

to man, who is capable of perceiving the word of God intelligently, so that he might *accept* it out of his own free will as the law of his destiny and fulfill it in voluntary obedience. Thus man has the opportunity, with his head held high, to prove that he has *chosen* to be the servant of the Law of his Creator and Master which all other things on earth must obey instinctively and without any choice in the matter. This Psalm cites the natural phenomenon of water as an outstanding example to show us how the Law of God governs and works within the realm of nature, and to demonstrate the unconditional obedience which all things existing give to that Law simply because they are God's creatures. The swift, devoted obedience with which the water submits to the Will and Law of its Creator is illustrated by a description of the visible changes which it undergoes, ready to fulfill His behest in the form of snow, then hoarfrost, then ice, and finally again in its original liqud state. Then we are told that the One Who thus molds the forces of nature in accordance with His will is the same God Who has revealed to Jacob His Word which, despite all its apparent multiplicity, is still "one" — (כתיב: דברו, קרי: דבריו) and Who has communicated His statutes and ordinances to Israel.

Psalm 148. הללוי Psalm 147 taught us to think of God's providence

קמט הַלְלוּיָהּ ׳ שִׁירוּ לַיהוָה שִׁיר חָדָשׁ תְּהִלָּתוֹ בִּקְהַל חֲסִידִים :

יִשְׂמַח יִשְׂרָאֵל בְּעֹשָׂיו בְּנֵי־צִיּוֹן יָגִילוּ בְמַלְכָּם : יְהַלְלוּ שְׁמוֹ בְמָחוֹל

בְּתֹף וְכִנּוֹר יְזַמְּרוּ־לוֹ : כִּי־רוֹצֶה יְהוָה בְּעַמּוֹ יְפָאֵר עֲנָוִים בִּישׁוּעָה :

יַעְלְזוּ חֲסִידִים בְּכָבוֹד יְרַנְּנוּ עַל־מִשְׁכְּבוֹתָם : רוֹמְמוֹת אֵל בִּגְרוֹנָם

וְחֶרֶב פִּיפִיּוֹת בְּיָדָם : לַעֲשׂוֹת נְקָמָה בַּגּוֹיִם תּוֹכֵחוֹת בַּלְאֻמִּים :

לֶאְסֹר מַלְכֵיהֶם בְּזִקִּים וְנִכְבְּדֵיהֶם בְּכַבְלֵי בַרְזֶל : לַעֲשׂוֹת בָּהֶם ׳

מִשְׁפָּט כָּתוּב הָדָר הוּא לְכָל־חֲסִידָיו הַלְלוּיָהּ :

קנ הַלְלוּיָהּ ׳ הַלְלוּ־אֵל בְּקָדְשׁוֹ הַלְלוּהוּ בִּרְקִיעַ עֻזּוֹ : הַלְלוּהוּ

בִגְבוּרֹתָיו הַלְלוּהוּ כְּרֹב גֻּדְלוֹ : הַלְלוּהוּ בְּתֵקַע שׁוֹפָר הַלְלוּהוּ בְּנֵבֶל

וְכִנּוֹר : הַלְלוּהוּ בְתֹף וּמָחוֹל הַלְלוּהוּ בְּמִנִּים וְעֻגָב : הַלְלוּהוּ

---

and of His Law in terms of one single thought embracing both nature
and mankind, and thence to infer the future of Israel and Israel's significance for the future of all of mankind as the bearefs and preservers of
the Divine Law. Psalm 148 sings of the moment when even the non-Jewish
nations and, in short, all the world, will be imbued with that knowledge,
and all the universe, all living things from the infinite heights of heaven
above down to the depths of the earth below, will join together in one
great hymn of praise to their Creator. The psalm ends with the thought
that when at that future day, the people of Israel will rise again, this fact in
itself will guarantee to *all* men who dedicate themselves to God that
their pure lives and endeavors will eventually receive the recognition justly
due them. Then Israel will have distinction over the other nations only
by virtue of the fact that, among all the peoples of the world, it had been
the one close to God from the very beginning.

Psalm 149. הללוי Psalm 149 has the same theme as Psalm 148 but
dwells upon it in greater detail. It calls upon us to sing שיר חדש, the song
of the new future day (Cf. Psalm 33:3), when not only the Jews but
also all the others who will then come near to God with devotion,

Halaluyah! Sing to *God* a new song, His praise in the assembly of the devoted! Let Yisrael rejoice in its Creator; let the sons of Tzion rejoice in their King. Let them proclaim the praise of His Name with the dance; let them sing to Him with the timbrel and harp; for *God* takes pleasure in His people again; He adorns the humble with salvation. Let the devoted rejoice in honor; let them exult upon their beds. High praises of God are in their mouths, hence there is a two-edged sword in their hand. To exact satisfaction from the nations, to work chastisements upon the peoples, to bind their kings with chains, and their most honored ones with iron fetters, to execute upon them the judgment set down long ago: this is also due honor for all His devoted ones. Halaluyah!

Halaluyah! Proclaim the praise of God in His Sanctuary, proclaim His praise in the firmament of His invincible power. Proclaim His praise from His mighty acts. Proclaim His praise according to the abundance of His greatness. Proclaim His praise with the call of the Shofar; proclaim His praise with the psalter and harp. Proclaim His praise with the timbrel and the dance; proclaim His praise with stringed instruments and the flute.

תהלתו בקהל חסידים, will form one great assembly, and God's greatness as revealed in the praise emanating from His mighty deeds will be proclaimed in their midst. Of course it is Israel in particular that will have cause to rejoice then and to give unrestrained expression to its gladness, and this future cannot come to pass without prior execution of the Divine judgment of rulers and nations which has been announced long ago. Yet, that exultation will not be restricted to Jews alone. The חסידים of all the nations, all those, regardless of nationality, who had recognized God before and had quietly dedicated themselves to Him, and even all those who will come to know and worship God only then, will have reason to rejoice together with Isarel. For together with Israel, they, too, will come to honor. Through their sincere homage to God they will be protected from the hostility of men as well as from adverse implication in the approaching Divine judgment. Indeed, this Divine judgment will award to their pure endeavors that recognition which had been denied them on earth heretofore.

Psalm 150. הללוי׳. This psalm with which the Book of תהלות ends, recapitulates the sum total of all the תהלות that sing of the ways in which God is revealed. The Psalm does so in terms of the spheres and the ways in which we can behold God's work, and of the thoughts, emotions and

בְּצִלְצְלֵי־שָׁמַע הַלְלוּהוּ בְּצִלְצְלֵי תְרוּעָה: כָּל הַנְּשָׁמָה תְּהַלֵּל יָהּ הַלְלוּיָהּ: כְּהַתְחָיָה:

בָּרוּךְ יְיָ לְעוֹלָם אָמֵן וְאָמֵן: בָּרוּךְ יְיָ מִצִּיּוֹן שֹׁכֵן יְרוּשָׁלַיִם הַלְלוּיָהּ: בָּרוּךְ יְיָ אֱלֹהִים אֱלֹהֵי יִשְׂרָאֵל עֹשֵׂה נִפְלָאוֹת לְבַדּוֹ: וּבָרוּךְ שֵׁם כְּבוֹדוֹ לְעוֹלָם וְיִמָּלֵא כְבוֹדוֹ אֶת־כָּל־הָאָרֶץ אָמֵן וְאָמֵן:

The following through ברכו *should be recited while standing.*

ד"ה א' כ"ט:

וַיְבָרֶךְ דָּוִיד אֶת־יְיָ לְעֵינֵי כָּל־הַקָּהָל וַיֹּאמֶר דָּוִיד בָּרוּךְ אַתָּה יְיָ אֱלֹהֵי יִשְׂרָאֵל אָבִינוּ מֵעוֹלָם וְעַד־עוֹלָם: לְךָ יְיָ הַגְּדֻלָּה וְהַגְּבוּרָה וְהַתִּפְאֶרֶת וְהַנֵּצַח וְהַהוֹד כִּי־כֹל בַּשָּׁמַיִם וּבָאָרֶץ לְךָ יְיָ הַמַּמְלָכָה וְהַמִּתְנַשֵּׂא לְכֹל לְרֹאשׁ: וְהָעֹשֶׁר וְהַכָּבוֹד מִלְּפָנֶיךָ וְאַתָּה מוֹשֵׁל בַּכֹּל וּבְיָדְךָ כֹּחַ וּגְבוּרָה וּבְיָדְךָ לְגַדֵּל וּלְחַזֵּק לַכֹּל: וְעַתָּה

---

moods which such contemplation stirs up within our hearts and which are characterized by the musical instruments that serve to give them expression. Psalm 150 concludes with the declaration that every living breath is, and should be, a proclamation of God's sovereign power.

ברוך We are certain that the work and the will of God are advanced and are turned into living reality at all times; we cleave unswervingly to this truth which serves to sustain, guide and train us. לעולם: At a time which, though still veiled from our own view, is well known to God even now, שם כבודו, the Name of ה' by which God has conveyed to us a glimpse of His rule for mankind's future, will achieve its goal in the recognition, acknowledgment and worship by all of mankind. וימלא כבודו את כל הארץ and everything which fills the world will then be construed

Proclaim His praise with the loud-sounding cymbals; proclaim His praise with the stirring cymbals. Let every breath of life proclaim the praise of *God*. Halaluyah!

Blessed be *God* forever, Amen and Amen. Blessed be *God* from out of Tzion, Who causes His presence to dwell in Yerusalayim, Halaluyah. Blessed be *God,* God, the God of Yisrael, Who alone does wondrous things; blessed be the Name of His glory forever, and let His glory fill the entire earth. Amen and Amen.

The following through ברכו *should be recited while standing.*

And David blessed *God* in the presence of all the congregation, and David said, "Blessed are You, O *God*, the God of Yisrael, our father, from the most distant past to the remotest future. Yours, O *God,* is the greatness, and the power and the glory and the victory and the majesty, for all that is in heaven and on earth is Yours. Yours is the sovereignty and all that which rules over anything on earth. Wealth and honor come from You, and You rule over all. In Your hand are power and might, in Your hand it is to grant greatness and strength to all. And now,

---

as a revelation proclaiming His presence on earth (see Commentary to Exod. 16:7). אמן ואמן (see Commentary to Gen. 15:6); this is the truth of all truths to which we cleave and by which we let ourselves be guided, sustained and educated in all our wanderings through time, and which we acknowledge over and over again whenever we say יתגדל ויתקדש וגו' in our קדיש.

ויברך. ד"ה א' כ"ט. The following portion down to אתה הוא is the pledge and avowal uttered by David when he turned over to Solomon and the assembled people the funds which he had collected for the purpose of building a Temple, and after the people had added their own contributions to the original amount. David recalls our patriarch Jacob-Israel, who was the first to pronounce the concept of a "House of God" and linked with it the vow to dedicate his life to God. He recalls both to himself and to his people the extent of the glory, the power and the sovereignty which commands over all things and upon which all things depend. In this manner David makes it clear that God is not in need of a dwelling place built by our hands; it is we who need the sanctuary. The sanctuary serves the purpose of causing us to rejoice both in the fact that we have built a House of God, and in the trust thus expressed that He is indeed the God Who guides our acts and our destinies, and Who grants us the strength, the

אֱלֹהֵינוּ מוֹדִים אֲנַחְנוּ לָךְ וּמְהַלְלִים לְשֵׁם תִּפְאַרְתֶּךָ: ‏נחמ׳ ט׳

אַתָּה הוּא יְיָ לְבַדֶּךָ אַתְּ עָשִׂיתָ אֶת־הַשָּׁמַיִם שְׁמֵי הַשָּׁמַיִם וְכָל־
צְבָאָם הָאָרֶץ וְכָל־אֲשֶׁר עָלֶיהָ הַיַּמִּים וְכָל־אֲשֶׁר בָּהֶם וְאַתָּה מְחַיֶּה
אֶת־כֻּלָּם וּצְבָא הַשָּׁמַיִם לְךָ מִשְׁתַּחֲוִים: אַתָּה הוּא יְיָ הָאֱלֹהִים
אֲשֶׁר בָּחַרְתָּ בְּאַבְרָם וְהוֹצֵאתוֹ מֵאוּר כַּשְׂדִּים וְשַׂמְתָּ שְּׁמוֹ אַבְרָהָם:
וּמָצָאתָ אֶת־לְבָבוֹ נֶאֱמָן לְפָנֶיךָ וְכָרוֹת עִמּוֹ הַבְּרִית לָתֵת אֶת־
אֶרֶץ הַכְּנַעֲנִי הַחִתִּי הָאֱמֹרִי וְהַפְּרִזִּי וְהַיְבוּסִי וְהַגִּרְגָּשִׁי לָתֵת לְזַרְעוֹ
וַתָּקֶם אֶת־דְּבָרֶיךָ כִּי צַדִּיק אָתָּה: וַתֵּרֶא אֶת־עֳנִי אֲבֹתֵינוּ בְּמִצְרָיִם
וְאֶת־זַעֲקָתָם שָׁמַעְתָּ עַל־יַם־סוּף: וַתִּתֵּן אֹתֹת וּמֹפְתִים בְּפַרְעֹה
וּבְכָל־עֲבָדָיו וּבְכָל־עַם אַרְצוֹ כִּי יָדַעְתָּ כִּי הֵזִידוּ עֲלֵיהֶם וַתַּעַשׂ
לְךָ שֵׁם כְּהַיּוֹם הַזֶּה: וְהַיָּם בָּקַעְתָּ לִפְנֵיהֶם וַיַּעַבְרוּ בְתוֹךְ־הַיָּם
בַּיַּבָּשָׁה וְאֶת־רֹדְפֵיהֶם הִשְׁלַכְתָּ בִמְצוֹלֹת כְּמוֹ־אֶבֶן בְּמַיִם עַזִּים:
וַיּוֹשַׁע יְהֹוָה בַּיּוֹם הַהוּא אֶת־יִשְׂרָאֵל מִיַּד מִצְרָיִם וַיַּרְא יִשְׂרָאֵל
אֶת־מִצְרַיִם מֵת עַל־שְׂפַת הַיָּם: וַיַּרְא יִשְׂרָאֵל אֶת־הַיָּד הַגְּדֹלָה
אֲשֶׁר עָשָׂה יְהֹוָה בְּמִצְרַיִם וַיִּירְאוּ הָעָם אֶת־יְהֹוָה וַיַּאֲמִינוּ בַּיהֹוָה
וּבְמֹשֶׁה עַבְדּוֹ:

‏⁹ אתה ק׳

---

means and the position on earth which enable us to accomplish that which is
pleasing in His eyes. לְךָ וְגוֹ׳ refers to כִּי כֹל וגו׳. All kingship and
dominion on earth, and all those who occupy positions of leadership in
the affairs of men are only instruments, subordinate to God for His
purposes.

The portion beginning with אתה הוא, down to עַזִּים, originated at a
time when the Temple built already lay in ruins and the nation had returned
from Babylonian captivity only a short time before. It was necessary to
imbue the nation with a renewed consciousness of its origin and its destiny,

our God, we give thanks to You and proclaim the praise of Your mighty deeds to the Name of Your glory. You are *God* alone. You have created the heavens and the heavens of heavens and all their host, the earth and all that is upon it, the seas and all that is in them. You preserve them all, and the host of the heavens bows down before You. You are *God,* God Who chose Avram and led him out of Ur of the Kasddim and gave him the name of Avraham. You found his heart faithful in Your sight and You made a covenant with him to give to his seed the land of the Kenaanite, the Chittite, the Emorite, the Perizite, the Yevusite and the Girgashite, and You fulfilled Your words, for You are just. You did see the affliction of our fathers in Mitzrayim and You heard their cry by the Reed Sea. And You demonstrated signs and instructive acts upon Pharaoh and upon all his servants and upon all the people of his land. For You knew that they planned evil against them, and You made a name for Yourself as it is this day. You divided the sea before them so that they went through the midst of the sea on dry land, but their pursuers You cast into the shadowy deep, like a stone into mighty waters.

Thus did God save Yisrael on this day from the hand of Mitzrayim, and Yisrael saw Mitzrayim dead upon the seashore. And when Yisrael beheld the mighty hand which *God* had put forth against Mitzrayim, the people feared *God* and put their trust in *God* and in Moshe His servant.

---

and to persuade it to make sacrifices for the fulfillment of its mission. ואתה מחיה וגו' וצבא וגו'   The same almighty power which created the world, also preserves it, and all creatures and heavenly hosts, moving in the orbits which it assigned them, are its servants. In creating the people of Israel, God brought into being another such host, which serves Him and moves in the paths prescribed by His providence. This nation reveres Abram as its patriarch and is fully aware of the symbolic significance of the change of his name to Abraham with respect to his people's destiny amongst the "teeming mass of nations".

These two paragraphs form the transition to the very first hymn ever sung in praise of God's mighty deeds, the שירת הים with which we close our פסוקי דזמרה, a song which concludes on a note of confidence that God will rule forever and ever even as He reigned at the Reed Sea long ago.

שִׁירַת הַיָּם צריך לאמרה מעומד ובנגון הטעמים כמו בספר תורה.

אָז יָשִׁיר־מֹשֶׁה וּבְנֵי יִשְׂרָאֵל אֶת־הַשִּׁירָה הַזֹּאת לַיהֹוָה וַיֹּאמְרוּ

סוּס   אָשִׁירָה לַיהֹוָה כִּי־גָאֹה גָּאָה   לֵאמֹר

וְרֹכְבוֹ רָמָה בַיָּם: עָזִּי וְזִמְרָת יָהּ וַיְהִי־לִי

אֱלֹהֵי   זֶה אֵלִי וְאַנְוֵהוּ   לִישׁוּעָה

אָבִי וַאֲרֹמְמֶנְהוּ:   יְהֹוָה אִישׁ מִלְחָמָה יְהֹוָה

וּמִבְחַר   מַרְכְּבֹת פַּרְעֹה וְחֵילוֹ יָרָה בַיָּם: שְׁמוֹ:

שָׁלִשָׁיו טֻבְּעוּ בְיַם־סוּף: תְּהֹמֹת יְכַסְיֻמוּ יָרְדוּ בִמְצוֹלֹת כְּמוֹ

יְמִינְךָ   יְמִינְךָ יְהֹוָה נֶאְדָּרִי בַּכֹּחַ   אָבֶן:

יְהֹוָה תִּרְעַץ אוֹיֵב: וּבְרֹב גְּאוֹנְךָ תַּהֲרֹס

ויושע וגו׳. יראה and אמונה; the fear of God coupled with trust in Him, these are the two basic emotions which should ever fill the Jewish spirit when it turns to God. There is only One Being Whom we should fear and at the same time trust, and that is God, the One God, Who is as merciful as He is just, as just as He is merciful, and as infinitely powerful in the practice of His mercy as He is in the execution of His justice. The eternal signficance of the unique moment of deliverance when the giant hulk of Egypt lay inert at the feet of that nation of slaves which was now forever free, was simply to demonstrate and to teach these three virtues of God: His justice, which man should fear at all times, His mercy, to which we may look at all times with humble trust, and finally His power in which He may wield both justice and mercy at the same time and which freely commands over all things. This great event, however, not only served as forceful evidence of the greatness of the hand of God as it wields both justice and mercy in unlimited power, but also was ample proof of the authenticity of the mission of Moses as His servant. The hand of Moses was stretched out over the waters, and it was by means of this hand that God led Egypt to its death and paved for Israel the way to life and freedom.

עזי וגו׳. The use of the designation י׳ for the Name of God

Then Moshe and the sons of Yisrael sang this song to *God*; they said:

To *God* will I sing, how exalted, how infinitely exalted He has been;

The horse and rider He has thrown into the sea.

God is my strength and song;

And this was my salvation.

Henceforth He is my God, and to Him will I be a dwelling-place.

He was even my father's God, and I will extol Him.

God is a man of war;

"*God*" is His Name.

Pharaoh's chariots and his host

He has cast into the sea,

And the chosen of his captains

Were drowned in the Reed Sea.

The floods cover them now;

They went down to shadowy depths like a stone.

Your right hand, O *God*,

Which has proved singularly mighty in strength,

Your right hand, O *God*,

Shall henceforth dismay each foe.

In the greatness of Your majesty,

You shatter those that rise up against You.

---

always implies a demonstration of His might, a revelation of His work and His sovereignty. Hence the thought here is: "My deliverance and the very inspiration with which it has filled me, that is, both my actual fate and my inner life, constitute a revelation of God's power which has been demonstrated through what has happened to me, ויהי לי לישועה and therein lay my salvation. God delivered me because He has chosen me as a fitting instrument for the demonstration of His Providence which shapes the lives of men and nations. What won for me God's saving aid was the fact that, though my body was weak, my spirit was strong and receptive. Even as I have beheld Him here and know Him to be the sole Force that shapes my physical fate and my spiritual life, so I shall henceforth place both into His hands so that He may guide and shape them." Quite literally, "He shall become 'the force that moves me.'" It is only if a man conceives of Him in this light that he can truly call the Lord his God. ואנוהו "And in this manner I shall offer myself to Him to be His dwelling place.

קָמֶיךָ תְּשַׁלַּח חֲרֹנְךָ יֹאכְלֵמוֹ כַּקַּשׁ׃   וּבְרוּחַ

אַפֶּיךָ נֶעֶרְמוּ מַיִם   נִצְּבוּ כְמוֹ־נֵד

גֹּלִים קָפְאוּ תְהֹמֹת בְּלֶב־יָם׃   אָמַר

אוֹיֵב אֶרְדֹּף אַשִּׂיג   אֲחַלֵּק שָׁלָל תִּמְלָאֵמוֹ

נַפְשִׁי אָרִיק חַרְבִּי תּוֹרִישֵׁמוֹ יָדִי׃   נָשַׁפְתָּ

בְרוּחֲךָ כִּסָּמוֹ יָם   צָלְלוּ כַּעוֹפֶרֶת בְּמַיִם

אַדִּירִים׃   מִי

כָמֹכָה נֶאְדָּר בָּאֵלִם יְהוָה   נוֹרָא תְהִלֹּת עֹשֵׂה

פֶלֶא׃   נָטִיתָ יְמִינְךָ תִּבְלָעֵמוֹ אָרֶץ׃   נָחִיתָ

בְחַסְדְּךָ עַם־זוּ גָּאָלְתָּ   נֵהַלְתָּ בְעָזְּךָ אֶל־נְוֵה

קָדְשֶׁךָ׃   שָׁמְעוּ עַמִּים יִרְגָּזוּן   חִיל

אָחַז יֹשְׁבֵי פְּלָשֶׁת׃   אָז נִבְהֲלוּ אַלּוּפֵי

אֱדוֹם   אֵילֵי מוֹאָב יֹאחֲזֵמוֹ רָעַד   נָמֹגוּ

כֹּל יֹשְׁבֵי כְנָעַן׃   תִּפֹּל עֲלֵיהֶם אֵימָתָה

וָפַחַד   בִּגְדֹל זְרוֹעֲךָ יִדְּמוּ כָּאָבֶן   עַד־

All of my life shall henceforth be a Temple for His glorification, a sanctuary revealing His glory." This is nothing but a logical consequence of זה אלי. מי כמכה וגו׳. True, there are אלים, creative motive forces in nature, but though men may worship them as gods, their powers are limited, subject to the order which You have ordained and which binds them with all-powerful bonds. You alone, O God, are free; You are not subject to the order of nature which is Your own creation. You rule freely over Your

You would not restrain Your wrath,
Like stubble would it consume them.
And through the blast of Your command
The waters piled up,
The floods receded shyly, like a wall.
The floods were congealed in the heart of the sea.
And the enemy said :
"I will pursue, I will overtake, I will divide the spoils ;
My lust shall be sated upon them.
I will draw my sword ;
My hand shall retake them."
Then You blew with Your wind ;
The sea covered them.
They sank into the shadowy deep
Like lead in the mightily tossing waters.
Who is there like You, among the gods, O *God*,
Who is like You, singularly glorious in holiness ?
Feared in songs praising Your mighty deeds, doer of marvels ?
You stretched forth Your right hand —
The earth swallowed them.
But as for the people whom You have redeemed,
You with Your love have led it to the goal.
By Your invincible strength
You guided it to Your holy habitation.
The peoples heard it and trembled ;
Pangs gripped the inhabitants of Pelasheth.
Now the chieftains of Edom were dismayed.
Trembling seizes the mighty men of Moav,
All the inhabitants of Kenaan are melted away
Terror and dread fall upon them ;
When Your arm shows its greatness
They grow still as a stone,

---

works and over the powers and forces which men deify but which are
nothing else but part of Your creation. תהלה is the word indicating the
reflection of the brilliant rays cast by the mighty Acts of God; i.e. the
songs which proclaim the praise of God as revealed by His mighty
deeds. The attribute נורא תהלות now expresses a thought as follows: When,

יַעֲבֹר עַמְּךָ יְהֹוָה   עַד־יַעֲבֹר עַם־זוּ

תְּבִאֵמוֹ וְתִטָּעֵמוֹ בְּהַר נַחֲלָתְךָ   קָנִיתָ   מָכוֹן

לְשִׁבְתְּךָ פָּעַלְתָּ יְהֹוָה   מִקְּדָשׁ אֲדֹנָי כּוֹנְנוּ

יְהֹוָה ׀ יִמְלֹךְ לְעֹלָם וָעֶד: יָדֶיךָ   יְיָ

יִמְלֹךְ לְעוֹלָם וָעֶד:

כי בא סוס פרעה ברכבו ובפרשיו בים וישב יי עלהם
את מי הים. ובני ישראל הלכו ביבשה בתוך הים:

כִּי לַיָי הַמְּלוּכָה וּמשֵׁל בַּגּוֹיִם: וְעָלוּ מוֹשִׁעִים בְּהַר צִיּוֹן לִשְׁפֹּט
אֶת־הַר עֵשָׂו וְהָיְתָה לַיָי הַמְּלוּכָה: וְהָיָה יְיָ לְמֶלֶךְ עַל־כָּל־הָאָרֶץ
בַּיּוֹם הַהוּא יִהְיֶה יְיָ אֶחָד וּשְׁמוֹ אֶחָד: וּבְתוֹרָתְךָ כָּתוּב לֵאמֹר שְׁמַע
יִשְׂרָאֵל יְיָ אֱלֹהֵינוּ יְיָ אֶחָד:

On Sabbaths and Holidays continue here with נשמת.

See p.298

---

by inspired song, we here gather together as at a focus the rays emanating from the mighty acts of God which we ourselves have seen, we are imbued first of all with יראה. We learn to *fear* the Lord. He remains ever-present before us in His justice which is coupled with omnipresence and almighty power, and before Him, all-powerful and ever-present we must lead only such a lfe as is pervaded with loyalty and obedience to Him and therefore pleasing in His sight. This God-fearing obedience is the first fruit which nothing can replace, and which is expected to result from the recognition of God and from the expression of this recognition in words of praise. It is this fear of God, which, at the very outset, is cited as the result of the momentous event which the people had just witnessed. וייראו העם את ה׳. All hymns of praise that do not serve to instill the fear of God into the hearts of men, or those that actually are intended as substitutes for true reverence, are blasphemy pure and simple. And the term נורא תהלות shall ever be the stern standard by which to measure all

Until Your people, O *God,* has passed,
Until the people which You have acquired pass over.
You will bring them in;
You will plant them
Into the mountain of Your inheritance,
The abode prepared for Your dwelling place
Which You, O *God,* have made,
The Sanctuary, O *God,*
Which Your hands have established.
God shall reign forever and ever.
God shall reign forever and ever.

For the horse of Pharaoh with his chariots and his riders came into the sea; then *God* sent back the waters of the sea upon them, and the sons of Yisrael walked upon dry land in the midst of the sea.

For the dominion shall be *God's* and He rules over the nations. And they will go as messengers of salvation up on Mount Tzion to judge the mountain of Esav, and the dominion shall be *God's.* Then *God* will be king over all the earth; on that day *God* will be One and His Name One. (And it is written in Your Law: "Hear Yisrael, *God* our God is *God,* the Only One!")

On Sabbaths and Holidays continue here with נשמת.

---

the "hymns of praise" that will be composed subsequent to the "Song at the Sea" and which, intentionally or unintentionally, will be modelled on It. תהלות denote the objective, physical viewing of the mighty acts of the Lord, while יראה refers to the subjective, lasting effect of such occurrences.

Moses and Israel conceive of themselves as the servants and instruments of that future of salvation for which God has now laid the foundation with His almighty Providence of mercy and justice that has just been demonstrated. It is for this reason that the song ends with a vista that reaches far into the most distant future: ה׳ ימלוך לע״ו. This means "God will reign through all the future"; in other words, even as we have seen Him reign in almighty power here at the Reed Sea, so shall He reign forever and ever. But it can also be construed to mean, "One day, in a future era which, though still distant, is nevertheless sure to come, God shall be King over all of mankind."

יִשְׁתַּבַּח שִׁמְךָ לָעַד מַלְכֵּנוּ הָאֵל הַמֶּלֶךְ הַגָּדוֹל וְהַקָּדוֹשׁ בַּשָּׁמַיִם
וּבָאָרֶץ ׃ כִּי לְךָ נָאֶה יְיָ אֱלֹהֵינוּ וֵאלֹהֵי אֲבוֹתֵינוּ שִׁיר וּשְׁבָחָה הַלֵּל
וְזִמְרָה עֹז וּמֶמְשָׁלָה נֶצַח גְּדֻלָּה וּגְבוּרָה תְּהִלָּה וְתִפְאֶרֶת קְדֻשָּׁה
וּמַלְכוּת בְּרָכוֹת וְהוֹדָאוֹת מֵעַתָּה וְעַד־עוֹלָם ׃ בָּרוּךְ אַתָּה יְיָ, אֵל
מֶלֶךְ, גָּדוֹל בַּתִּשְׁבָּחוֹת, אֵל הַהוֹדָאוֹת, אֲדוֹן הַנִּפְלָאוֹת, הַבּוֹחֵר
בְּשִׁירֵי זִמְרָה, מֶלֶךְ, אֵל, חֵי הָעוֹלָמִים ׃ יֹא"ן אוֹמֵר ח"ק.

יִתְגַּדַּל וְיִתְקַדַּשׁ שְׁמֵהּ רַבָּא בְּעָלְמָא דִּי־בְרָא כִרְעוּתֵהּ וְיַמְלִיךְ
מַלְכוּתֵהּ בְּחַיֵּיכוֹן וּבְיוֹמֵיכוֹן וּבְחַיֵּי דְכָל־בֵּית יִשְׂרָאֵל בַּעֲגָלָא וּבִזְמַן
קָרִיב, וְאִמְרוּ אָמֵן ׃

יְהֵא שְׁמֵהּ רַבָּא מְבָרַךְ לְעָלַם וּלְעָלְמֵי עָלְמַיָּא ׃

יִתְבָּרַךְ וְיִשְׁתַּבַּח וְיִתְפָּאַר וְיִתְרוֹמַם וְיִתְנַשֵּׂא וְיִתְהַדָּר וְיִתְעַלֶּה
וְיִתְהַלָּל שְׁמֵהּ דְּקֻדְשָׁא בְּרִיךְ הוּא לְעֵלָּא מִן־כָּל־בִּרְכָתָא וְשִׁירָתָא
תֻּשְׁבְּחָתָא וְנֶחֱמָתָא דַּאֲמִירָן בְּעָלְמָא, וְאִמְרוּ אָמֵן ׃

ישתבח is the final *Beracha* of the פסוקי דזמרה and recapitulates the
lofty concepts that these Psalms have instilled within us concerning God
and our relationship to Him. The thought basically common to all תהלות
is that man should render homage to God in loyal obedience as the King,
and remember His greatness (which is shown by His mercy) and His glory
and holiness before which nothing base or evil can endure. Inspiration and
praise, memories of mighty deeds and expressions of deep emotion, homage
to power, glory, dominion, victory, greatness and omnipotence, praise and
sanctification, vows of obedience and avowals of thanksgiving shall all be
dedicated to God now and forever, to Him Whom we now acknowledge
as our God, as the shaper of our destinies and the guide of our conduct,
even as our fathers knew Him to be such in the past. Nor are the hymns
of praise which we have uttered to remain empty words. Their fruit
should be the vow symbolized by the word ברוך, the solemn pledge of
faithful and gladsome fulfillment of His will. This we hereby pledge to
Him Who is the fount of all power, God of all life, Whose greatness
exceeds all man's praises, to Him Whom all faiths render homage as God,
Whom every miracle proclaims anew as the Master of the world order,

Praised be Your Name, our King, forever, God, the King Who is great and holy in heaven and on earth. For to You, O *God*, our God and God of our fathers, appertain song and laud, praise and hymn, strength and dominion, victory, greatness and might, renown and glory, holiness and kingship, blessings and thanksgivings henceforth and unto eternity. Blessed be You, O *God*, God and King, great in hymns of praise, God of thanksgivings, Lord of wonders, Who takes pleasure in hymns, King, God, the Life of all times.

His great Name will be recognized in all its greatness and holiness in the world which He has created according to His pleasure. May He establish His kingdom in your lifetime and in your days and in the lifetime of all the house of Yisrael, speedily and soon, and say, Amen.

May His great Name be blessed forever and to all the eternities of eternity.

Blessed and praised, glorified, exalted and extolled, proclaimed in its majesty, grandeur and in the praise of His mighty deeds, be the Name of the Holy One, blessed be He, exalted above all the blessings, hymns, praises and consolations that are uttered in the world, and say, Amen.

---

and Who recognizes as avowals of obedience the hymns sung by men as they behold His greatness. All glory to Him, the King and God, the Life of all times.

קדיש וברכו. Any קדושה, דבר שבקדושה, קדיש and ברכו, any sanctification, any summons to sanctify the Name of God and any avowal in response to such a summons in word and action can be uttered only at an assembly of at least ten adult males that represent the body of the entire Jewish community. קדוש השם denotes the highest level of man's execution of his task on earth; through the subordination of all earthly affairs without reservation to the fulfillment of God's purposes, to demonstrate how greatly exalted He is above all things and all men, and that all else has no value and significance for us except to the extent to which it serves to carry out the will of God. Thus קידוש השם, the goal for which all of mankind is made to mature through Divine Providence, constitutes the essence of the task of the Jewish people even at the present time. It was to the Jewish community קהלת יעקב, that the Lord has entrusted as a מורשה the practical demonstration of this task, and it was the Jewish people whom He had

Those praying in private begin with ברוך יוצר.

The Congregation, in an undertone :	*Reader, aloud :*

ח' יִתְבָּרַךְ וְיִשְׁתַּבַּח וְיִתְפָּאַר וְיִתְרוֹמֵם   בָּרְכוּ אֶת־יְיָ הַמְבֹרָךְ :

קו"ח וְיִתְנַשֵּׂא שְׁמוֹ שֶׁל־מֶלֶךְ הַמְּלָכִים   בָּרוּךְ יְיָ הַמְבֹרָךְ לְעוֹלָם וָעֶד :

הַקָּדוֹשׁ בָּרוּךְ הוּא שֶׁהוּא רִאשׁוֹן וְהוּא   בָּרוּךְ אַתָּה יְיָ אֱלֹהֵינוּ

אַחֲרוֹן וּמִבַּלְעָדָיו אֵין אֱלֹהִים: סֹלוּ לָרֹכֵב   מֶלֶךְ הָעוֹלָם יוֹצֵר אוֹר

בָּעֲרָבוֹת בְּיָהּ שְׁמוֹ וְעִלְזוּ לְפָנָיו: וּשְׁמִי   וּבוֹרֵא חֹשֶׁךְ עֹשֶׂה שָׁלוֹם

קְרִיאָם עַל־כָּל־בְּרָכָה וּתְהִלָּה: וּבוֹרֵא אֶת־הַכֹּל :

בָּרוּךְ שֵׁם כְּבוֹד מַלְכוּתוֹ לְעוֹלָם וָעֶד :

יְהִי שֵׁם יְיָ מְבֹרָךְ מֵעַתָּה וְעַד עוֹלָם :

---

appointed as bearer, guardian, agent and executor of that which eventually shall be the goal of all mankind. Thus it is only from the hands of the community that any individual at any time is given his task, and it is only within the framework of his community that he can fulfill it. For the mission reaches far beyond the limited physical, moral and intellectual capacity of the short-lived individual. אין צבור עני ואין צבור מת. But a community cannot die; a community can do all things. It is only within the framework of a community that all limitations can be compensated for, that wants can be supplied, and therefore the individual can discharge his task only as part of that community. It is for this reason that only a very few of our prayers were written specifically for individuals; most of them are phrased in the plural form, and even if we recite them without a congregation, we utter them not as individuals, but only as part of the larger community. It is therefore that the sages have attached so much importance to תפלת צבור, to prayer that is said with a congregation and they recommend that, even if we should be prevented from attending a house of God, we should recite our prayers at the same time as does the congregation of which we are a part, and thus, at least, join in their worship in spirit. ברכו, קדיש and קדושה, however, can be recited only בצבור, only together with a congregation of worshippers, even as the Lord has said, ונקדשתי בתוך בני ישראל "I will be sanctified *in the midst of* the sons of Israel" (Lev. 22:32). בני ישראל, "the sons of Israel", denotes the Jewish community, the עדה which is united by and for the communal purpose and which is represented in miniature form wherever ten men meet in prayer. This congregation, in turn, delegates representative powers to the שליח צבור, the Cantor or Reader, who is chosen from among its midst.

Those praying in private begin with ברוך יוצר.

(*Reader, aloud*): Bless *God*, Who is to be blessed.

   (*Cong. & Reader*): Blessed be *God*, Who is to be blessed in all eternity.

   Blessed be You *God*, our God, King of the Universe, Who forms light and creates darkness, Who makes peace and creates all things.

(*The Congregation, in an undertone*):

   Blessed and praised, glorified, exalted and extolled be the Name of the Supreme King of Kings, the Holy One, blessed be He, for He is the First and He is the Last, and there is no God beside Him. Strive up toward Him Who guides the world through desolate places by His Name, *Yah,* and exult before His countenance. His Name is exalted far beyond all blessings and praise. Blessed be the Name of the Glory of His Kingdom to all the future which, though veiled, is sure. Be the Name of *God* blessed from this time forth and forever.

   The קדיש is an expression of that avowal of Judaism which is to be preserved at all times and wherever we may be; namely that, whatever course events may take, eventually, שמיה רבא the greatness of the Name of God in all its significance will be recognized and sanctified by all men irrefutably and without reservation, "in a world which He Himself has created כרעותיה in complete accordance with His will". As for all the deficiencies and imperfections that we see in this world, it is much more likely that they serve to advance the fulfillment of the goals of Divine providence, rather that they should obstruct them. For had God not deemed the present state of affairs to be in accordance with His purposes, he could have created this world in another fashion more suited to His will. The goal for which God made the world will surely be reached, and this goal is simply קדוש השם throughout the world, and the establishment of מלכות השם, the kingdom and supremacy of God on earth. This is the confident hope that has sustained Israel throughout the trials which were part of its wanderings through the ages, and the public avowal of this hope constitutes the very foundation upon which our entire congregational worship is based. Hence the Reader restates it on behalf of the entire congregation at the end of every major portion of our prayers, so that all the congregation may take it to heart anew each time. In this prayer, the Reader expresses the wish that this Divine goal may be attained within the life-time of his congregation, and he calls upon the worshippers to say "Amen" to indicate that they have adopted his declaration as their own and that they will permit its truth to be the "leading, guiding and sustaining support" of their lives. To this "Amen" the congregation then adds its own declaration of its desire and trust that (יהא) the great Name

הַמֵּאִיר לָאָרֶץ וְלַדָּרִים עָלֶיהָ בְּרַחֲמִים· וּבְטוּבוֹ מְחַדֵּשׁ בְּכָל־יוֹם
תָּמִיד מַעֲשֵׂה בְרֵאשִׁית: מָה רַבּוּ מַעֲשֶׂיךָ יְיָ· כֻּלָּם בְּחָכְמָה עָשִׂיתָ·
מָלְאָה הָאָרֶץ קִנְיָנֶךָ: הַמֶּלֶךְ הַמְרוֹמָם לְבַדּוֹ מֵאָז· הַמְשֻׁבָּח
וְהַמְפֹאָר וְהַמִּתְנַשֵּׂא מִימוֹת עוֹלָם: אֱלֹהֵי עוֹלָם בְּרַחֲמֶיךָ הָרַבִּים
רַחֵם עָלֵינוּ· אֲדוֹן עֻזֵּנוּ צוּר מִשְׂגַּבֵּנוּ· מָגֵן יִשְׁעֵנוּ מִשְׂגָּב בַּעֲדֵנוּ:

---

of God will be blessed; namely, that the recognition of Him should be advanced, spread and made a living reality on earth forever and ever. After the hymns of praise uttered by the congregation, praising and glorifying the greatness and majesty of the Lord, and the abundance of His mighty acts, the Reader declares that, actually, the true greatness and fullness of His glory exceed far beyond any blessings, songs, or praises that are within the power of mortal lips to proclaim, they are exalted far above any "consoling" vistas of the future, promised glory of God on earth that mortal man can express in the midst of a dark present. And again, the congregation is called upon to voice its assent to this statement also by saying "Amen".

ברכו. But that which is to become true some day in the future within the entire community of mankind shall be translated into living reality even now and at all times by the Jewish community as a whole and by every congregation which is actually a small-scale representation of that community, by every קהלה of the great קהל עדת ישראל. Therefore the Reader now calls upon his congregation, or rather, the congregation calls upon itself, through its Reader, to make a public declaration as follows: God Who is מבורך, Whose will alone is "blessed", meaning that it will eventually attain complete and irreversible fulfillment in heaven and on earth; among men in general and within the Jewish people in particular, is now also to be blessed by the members of the congregation. They, too, must dedicate themselves to the advancement and furtherance of this goal, by consecrating all of their being, and all of their strength, be it great or small, to this lofty purpose. The congregation then proclaims the pledge to do so by declaring ברוך וכו׳. Because of this concept of God as One Who is המבורך ברכו can be uttered only בצבור. ברוך אתה, the promise to bless God with the devotion of all of one's own personality, can be uttered by any individual without the presence of a congregation. But only a community which encompasses all the present and future generations in its scope can declare that God is מבורך.

He Who in compassion grants light to the earth and to them that dwell upon it, and in goodness each day renews the work of the Beginning : how manifold are Your works, O *God* ! In wisdom have You made them all ; the earth is full of Your possessions. O King Who alone has ever been exalted, praised and glorified and extolled from the days of antiquity ; O God of all times, in Your abundant compassion have mercy upon us, O Lord of our might, Rock of our stronghold, Shield of our salvation,

---

ברוך. The blessing יוצר אור pays tribute to the glory of God as demonstrated by the rays of the rising morning sun. The very first sentence of this blessing refutes one of the oldest fallacies to be devised by human thought; namely, that the contrasts found in the phenomena of nature and the world indicate the existence of more than one Deity; that is two separate and opposing divinities—a god of day, life and prosperity on one hand, and one of night, death and evil on the other. Our blessing, however, opposes this view by avowing that light and darkness were created by one and the same God, that day and night and all the other phenomena which appear to us to be antitheses of one another, actually serve, under the Providence of the One God, solely to advance one and the same purpose; the welfare of both man and nature. It is this Divine Providence which shapes this world of apparent conflicting phenomena into a unified world of perfect harmony. Therefore, when we recite this blessing in the morning we add that God Who made light is also the creator of darkness, and when we say it in the evening, we remember that the same God Who created night is also the maker of the light of day.

המאיר When we feel the beneficial effect of light, we see how God, in His fatherly benevolence and bounty, cares and provides for all His countless creatures which He has made in wisdom and preserved in His goodness. Therefore they all are *His* indeed with every ounce of their strength and with every spark of their being. We, too, sense how greatly we ourselves are in need of this eternal benevolence for our own lives and for every breath we draw on earth, and we look to Him for strength so that we may survive and grow for the preservation of salvation, and for spiritual growth in the midst of the world about us.

אֵל בָּרוּךְ גְּדוֹל דֵּעָה · הֵכִין וּפָעַל זָהֲרֵי חַמָּה · טוֹב יָצַר כָּבוֹד
לִשְׁמוֹ · מְאוֹרוֹת נָתַן סְבִיבוֹת עֻזּוֹ · פִּנּוֹת צְבָאָיו קְדוֹשִׁים רוֹמְמֵי
שַׁדַּי · תָּמִיד מְסַפְּרִים כְּבוֹד־אֵל וּקְדֻשָּׁתוֹ : תִּתְבָּרַךְ יְיָ אֱלֹהֵינוּ עַל־
שֶׁבַח מַעֲשֵׂה יָדֶיךָ · וְעַל־מְאוֹרֵי־אוֹר שֶׁעָשִׂיתָ יְפָאֲרוּךָ סֶּלָה :

תִּתְבָּרַךְ צוּרֵנוּ מַלְכֵּנוּ וְגוֹאֲלֵנוּ בּוֹרֵא קְדוֹשִׁים יִשְׁתַּבַּח שִׁמְךָ
לָעַד מַלְכֵּנוּ יוֹצֵר מְשָׁרְתִים וַאֲשֶׁר מְשָׁרְתָיו כֻּלָּם עוֹמְדִים בְּרוּם
עוֹלָם וּמַשְׁמִיעִים בְּיִרְאָה יַחַד בְּקוֹל דִּבְרֵי אֱלֹהִים חַיִּים וּמֶלֶךְ
עוֹלָם : כֻּלָּם אֲהוּבִים כֻּלָּם בְּרוּרִים כֻּלָּם גִּבּוֹרִים וְכֻלָּם עֹשִׂים
בְּאֵימָה וּבְיִרְאָה רְצוֹן קוֹנָם וְכֻלָּם פּוֹתְחִים אֶת־פִּיהֶם בִּקְדֻשָּׁה
וּבְטָהֳרָה בְּשִׁירָה וּבְזִמְרָה וּמְבָרְכִים וּמְשַׁבְּחִים וּמְפָאֲרִים וּמַעֲרִיצִים
וּמַקְדִּישִׁים וּמַמְלִיכִים

אל ברוך. The bright rays of the sun take no other direction and have
no other effect than that which the spirit of God originally fixed for them
at the time of Creation. Thus He has created "a good thing"—for was
not light the first of His works which He Himself called "good"?—in order
to reveal His existence and His will, and His invincible might is the
focal power which keeps the shining luminaries of heaven in their orbits.
Hence what the highest and most holy of the heavenly hosts at His
command proclaim is not their own greatness, but, instead, the grandeur
of their Maker as שדי, the One Who has ever determined the laws of
"sufficiency", Who has set the bounds and limits to all things. They
reveal the unattainable holiness of their Creator at every moment of the
world's existence.

תתברך The prophet Isaiah beheld Seraphim on high, round about the
throne of God, waiting upon His command, and heard from their mouths
the proclamation of His holiness. We see the same vision before us when
the rays of the morning sun once again permit us to behold the world
and thus the full glory of God's creation. The ministering hosts which the
Lord has created in His heavenly household that is the world, stand in
exalted places and proclaim that all life and growth are derived from the
creating and ruling Word of the Living God Who reigns supreme over
the world. They sense that He loves them and that they are pure; they
feel strength within themselves. In humble reverence they carry out the

You stronghold of ours! God, blessed, great in insight, has prepared and made the rays of the sun, and thus has formed a good thing to reveal His Name. He has set heavenly luminaries round about His power; the chiefs of His hosts, who in holiness exalted the All-Sufficient, continually recount the glory of God and His holiness. Be blessed, therefore, O *God* our God, for the praise of the work of Your hands and for the light-giving luminaries which You have made, so that they may glorify You forever.

Be blessed, O our Rock, our King and our Redeemer, Creator of holy beings; praised be Your Name forever, O our King, Shaper of ministering hosts. And those who serve Him all stand in the high places of the universe and proclaim aloud with reverence, in unison, the words of the Living God and King of the Universe. All of them are beloved, all of them are chosen, all of them are strong; in dread and awe they all do the bidding of their Owner, and they all open their mouth in holiness and purity with song and psalm, and they bless and praise, and glorify, and

---

will of their Owner, and they declare that obedience, praise, glorification and the acknowledgment of His might, holiness and dominion are all due to the Name of God, the great, mighty and awesome King which remains unattainable and ineffable in its sanctity. וכלם מקבלים That part of the world which is within the scope of our understanding is revealed before us as a harmonious structure of Creation. Every individual species has been assigned a specific measure of faculties and its own special sphere of activity, in order to carry out its Creator's will through another species which is dependent upon it in this particular sphere. Yet, even that creature itself is again dependent upon a higher species which also has been provided with its own specific faculties and domain for the performance of its own peculiar work in the world. Thus, while every creature is subordinate to the will of its Maker as represented by a brother being, it also has the duty to carry out simultaneously the will of God upon a dependent brother creature of its own. In the same manner, the ministering hosts around God's throne also receive the bond of the kingdom of heaven one from the other, and thus they also enable one another each to declare individually the holiness of its Creator. And in harmonious unison, they reverently proclaim: "Holy, holy, holy". However, according to the commentary of Jonathan, which we also add in the קדושה דסדרא (ובא לציון גואל) the declaration קדוש, קדוש, קדוש does not indicate degrees of heightened intensity to make us conceive of God's holiness as being at

אֶת־שֵׁם הָאֵל הַמֶּלֶךְ הַגָּדוֹל הַגִּבּוֹר וְהַנּוֹרָא קָדוֹשׁ הוּא: וְכֻלָּם
מְקַבְּלִים עֲלֵיהֶם עֹל מַלְכוּת שָׁמַיִם זֶה מִזֶּה. וְנוֹתְנִים רְשׁוּת זֶה
לָזֶה · לְהַקְדִּישׁ לְיוֹצְרָם בְּנַחַת רוּחַ בְּשָׂפָה בְרוּרָה וּבִנְעִימָה קְדֻשָּׁה
כֻּלָּם כְּאֶחָד עֹנִים וְאוֹמְרִים בְּיִרְאָה ·

קָדוֹשׁ · קָדוֹשׁ קָדוֹשׁ יְיָ צְבָאוֹת מְלֹא כָל־הָאָרֶץ כְּבוֹדוֹ:
וְהָאוֹפַנִּים וְחַיּוֹת הַקֹּדֶשׁ בְּרַעַשׁ גָּדוֹל מִתְנַשְּׂאִים לְעֻמַּת שְׂרָפִים
לְעֻמָּתָם מְשַׁבְּחִים וְאוֹמְרִים:

בָּרוּךְ כְּבוֹד־יְיָ מִמְּקוֹמוֹ:
לָאֵל בָּרוּךְ נְעִימוֹת יִתֵּנוּ · לְמֶלֶךְ אֵל חַי וְקַיָּם זְמִירוֹת יֹאמֵרוּ
וְתִשְׁבָּחוֹת יַשְׁמִיעוּ · כִּי הוּא לְבַדּוֹ פּוֹעֵל גְּבוּרוֹת עֹשֶׂה חֲדָשׁוֹת
בַּעַל מִלְחָמוֹת זוֹרֵעַ צְדָקוֹת מַצְמִיחַ יְשׁוּעוֹת בּוֹרֵא רְפוּאוֹת נוֹרָא
תְהִלּוֹת אֲדוֹן הַנִּפְלָאוֹת הַמְחַדֵּשׁ בְּטוּבוֹ בְּכָל־יוֹם תָּמִיד מַעֲשֵׂה
בְרֵאשִׁית: כָּאָמוּר לְעֹשֵׂה אוֹרִים גְּדוֹלִים כִּי לְעוֹלָם חַסְדּוֹ: אוֹר
חָדָשׁ עַל־צִיּוֹן תָּאִיר וְנִזְכֶּה כֻלָּנוּ מְהֵרָה לְאוֹרוֹ · בָּרוּךְ אַתָּה יְיָ
יוֹצֵר הַמְּאוֹרוֹת:

---

an ever more exalted distance from ourselves. Rather, it should indicate
to us that the Lord is holy not only in the highest of the high places,
but also here on earth, and that He wishes to be hallowed also in this
world which He had expressly created for the purpose of His sanctification
so that, upon it, His holy will might receive unconditional obedience and
attain supreme sovereignty. For all that which fills the earth constitutes a
revelation of His glory. ברוך כבוד Wherever the glory of God may dwell,
it always demands that it be "blessed" from the place where it dwells,
wherever that may be, and that it receive homage everywhere in the form
of the fulfillment of the Divine will.

לאל ברוך. Of Him, Who also expects man on earth to bless Him by
pledging to fulfill His will, the choir of Creation that proclaims Him
declares that it is He alone Who brings to pass all things that are mighty
and new, all forces that serve sternly to inhibit or joyously to advance in
both the phenomena of nature and the history of mankind. He Whose

declare the power and holiness and majesty of the Name of God, of the great, mighty and awesome King, holy is He. And they all take upon themselves the yoke of the kingdom of heaven, one from the other, and give leave to one another to sanctify their Creator with a serene spirit, with pure speech and sweet melody. In unison, they all proclaim holiness and declare in awe :

"Holy, holy, holy is *God Tzevaoth;* the fullness of all the earth is His glory."

And the *Ophanim* and the holy *Chayoth,* with rushing sound, rise up toward the *Seraphim;* over against them they offer laud and say:

"Blessed be the glory of *God* from its dwelling place."

To God, the blessed One, they offer sweet melodies; to the King, God, living and eternal, they utter hymns and praise, that He alone performs almighty acts, creates new things; that He is the Lord of wars, sows acts of kindness, brings forth works of salvation, and creates healing, awesome in praise, Master of wonders; that He in His goodness constantly renews each day the work of the Beginning, even as it is said, "[Avow it] to Him, Who creates great lights, that His loving-kindness endures forever" (Psalm 136). O cause a new light to shine over Tzion, so that we may all soon have a portion in its brightness. Blessed by You *God,* Shaper of the heavenly luminaries.

---

acts proclaim Him as the Exalted Being Who is to be feared, He Whose miracles reveal Him as the Supreme Sovereign of all the world order, He Whom every day heralds anew in all His creative goodness. He alone can and does grant the help and healing for which suffering mankind longs. (זורע צדקות) Man can appreciate an act of Divine kindness only once its results have become plainly discernible. But he does not perceive it as long as the Lord still prepares it, hidden in the womb of the future. Every act of Divine kindness, once performed, bears within itself the seed for future salvation.). כאמור He Who made the sun as the luminary for daytime did not stop at creating the source of light and growth for His world on earth; His loving kindness still endures at all times and for every generation. אור חדש and even as He has provided visible light for the physical world, so He has also lit a lamp in Zion, the light of His revelation for the spiritual enlightenment and the moral growth of mankind. It is the new dawning of that light which we hopefully await.

אַהֲבָה רַבָּה אֲהַבְתָּנוּ יְיָ אֱלֹהֵינוּ חֶמְלָה גְדוֹלָה וִיתֵרָה חָמַלְתָּ
עָלֵינוּ : אָבִינוּ מַלְכֵּנוּ בַּעֲבוּר אֲבוֹתֵינוּ שֶׁבָּטְחוּ בְךָ וַתְּלַמְּדֵם חֻקֵּי
חַיִּים כֵּן תְּחָנֵּנוּ וּתְלַמְּדֵנוּ : אָבִינוּ הָאָב הָרַחֲמָן הַמְרַחֵם רַחֵם
עָלֵינוּ וְתֵן בְּלִבֵּנוּ לְהָבִין וּלְהַשְׂכִּיל לִשְׁמֹעַ לִלְמֹד וּלְלַמֵּד לִשְׁמֹר
וְלַעֲשׂוֹת וּלְקַיֵּם אֶת־כָּל־דִּבְרֵי תַלְמוּד תּוֹרָתֶךָ בְּאַהֲבָה : וְהָאֵר
עֵינֵינוּ בְּתוֹרָתֶךָ וְדַבֵּק לִבֵּנוּ בְּמִצְוֹתֶיךָ וְיַחֵד לְבָבֵנוּ לְאַהֲבָה וּלְיִרְאָה
שְׁמֶךָ וְלֹא־נֵבוֹשׁ לְעוֹלָם וָעֶד : כִּי בְשֵׁם קָדְשְׁךָ הַגָּדוֹל וְהַנּוֹרָא בָּטָחְנוּ
נָגִילָה וְנִשְׂמְחָה בִּישׁוּעָתֶךָ : וַהֲבִיאֵנוּ לְשָׁלוֹם מֵאַרְבַּע כַּנְפוֹת הָאָרֶץ
וְתוֹלִיכֵנוּ קוֹמְמִיּוּת לְאַרְצֵנוּ : כִּי אֵל פּוֹעֵל יְשׁוּעוֹת אָתָּה וּבָנוּ
בָחַרְתָּ מִכָּל־עַם וְלָשׁוֹן וְקֵרַבְתָּנוּ לְשִׁמְךָ הַגָּדוֹל סֶלָה בֶּאֱמֶת ·
לְהוֹדוֹת לְךָ וּלְיַחֶדְךָ בְּאַהֲבָה : בָּרוּךְ אַתָּה יְיָ הַבּוֹחֵר בְּעַמּוֹ יִשְׂרָאֵל
בְּאַהֲבָה :   יחיד אומר אל מלך נאמן.

אהבה רבה. In the blessing immediately preceding this paragraph, our
contemplation of the physical luminaries created by God led us to consider
the spiritual and moral light of revelation which God has prepared in
Zion and as whose bearer He has appointed Israel. The blessing beginning
with אהבה רבה is a continuation of this thought. It is founded upon our
awareness of the infinite love which God has shown us by our spiritual
election, and of how utterly desolate we would be if we were to become
estranged from this spiritual heritage and if we were to fail to derive
from it the proper understanding and conviction to guide us in the fulfillment of our God-given mission in life. We therefore call upon Divine
compassion to protect us from such spiritual desolation and to guide us
to the joyous study, teaching and observance of His Law. It is only once,
with the help of God, we will have redeemed ourselves from this spiritual
desolation, that our deliverance from political misfortune will have value
for us. Hence we hopefully look forward to our return, as one united
people, to our homeland which is dedicated to the full observance of the
Law of God, and where the Abode of God at Zion, which was destined
to afford enlightenment to all of mankind, awaits our coming. חמלה
is the pity in which God redeemed us from the spiritual errors of the
rest of the nations. בעבור אבותינו Before, during and after the revelation

With love abounding have You loved us, O *God* our God. You have shown us compassion great and abundant, O our Father and our King; for the sake of our fathers who trusted in You, and whom You did teach the statutes of life, endow our spirits also and teach us. O our Father, compassionate Father, Who is ever compassionate, have mercy upon us and put it into our hearts to gain insight and understanding, to hear, to learn and to teach, to observe, to do and to fulfill with love all the words of the tradition of Your Torah. Enlighten our eyes in Your Torah, cause our heart to cleave to Your commandments, and unify our spirit to love and revere Your Name so that we may never have cause to be ashamed. For in Your great and awesome holy Name do we trust, that we shall have cause happily to exult in Your salvation. O bring us home in peace from the four corners of the earth and lead us upright into our land; for You are the God Who performs works of salvation, and You have chosen us from among all peoples and tongues, and have brought us near to Your great Name forever in truth, that we may render You homage and with love avow Your Oneness. Blessed be You, *God,* Who has chosen His people Yisrael with love.

---

of the Law of God, our fathers had to learn to trust in God and to give practical evidence of their trust, first in Egypt and then during their wanderings through the wilderness. Such trust in God is an absolute necessity if we are to overcome the many trials posed us as we strive to fulfill the requirements of God's Law חנן: חננו preponderantly denotes the granting of intellectual and spiritual powers. ללמד וכו' לשמר וכו' If our study is to prosper and achieve its true purpose, then our aim in pursuing it, from the very beginning must be to fulfill the Law of God. דברי תלמוד תורתך are the words of the transmitted explanation of the Divine Law; that is, the Talmud. באהבה Loving eagerness to understand our duty and to be faithful to it should be the attitude to guide us in both our study and our observance. בטח בשם ד' "to trust in the Name of God" means to trust in that which the Name of God reveals concerning the ways of His Providence. והביאנו לשלום It is only in our own ancient Homeland that we will find the peace which has been denied us away from it. ליחדך has reference to שמע, which follows immediately and contains the Jewish national declaration of the Oneness of God.

דברים ו׳

שְׁמַע יִשְׂרָאֵל יְהֹוָה אֱלֹהֵינוּ יְהֹוָה אֶחָד:

בלחש בָּרוּךְ שֵׁם כְּבוֹד מַלְכוּתוֹ לְעוֹלָם וָעֶד:

וְאָהַבְתָּ אֵת יְהֹוָה אֱלֹהֶיךָ בְּכָל־לְבָבְךָ וּבְכָל־נַפְשְׁךָ
וּבְכָל־מְאֹדֶךָ: וְהָיוּ הַדְּבָרִים הָאֵלֶּה אֲשֶׁר אָנֹכִי מְצַוְּךָ
הַיּוֹם עַל־לְבָבֶךָ: וְשִׁנַּנְתָּם לְבָנֶיךָ וְדִבַּרְתָּ בָּם בְּשִׁבְתְּךָ
בְּבֵיתֶךָ וּבְלֶכְתְּךָ בַדֶּרֶךְ וּבְשָׁכְבְּךָ וּבְקוּמֶךָ: וּקְשַׁרְתָּם
לְאוֹת עַל־יָדֶךָ וְהָיוּ לְטֹטָפֹת בֵּין עֵינֶיךָ:
וּכְתַבְתָּם עַל־מְזוּזֹת בֵּיתֶךָ וּבִשְׁעָרֶיךָ:

שמע. According to our sages, we have given adequate practical demonstration of our recognition of God—which we are to confirm anew each day with the שמע — if its pronunciation stirs us to render homage to His supreme sovereignty in all the universe, in heaven above and on earth below: כיון דאמליכתי׳ למעלה ולמטה ולארבע רוחות שמים תו לא צריכת (Berachoth 13:2). They teach, too, that the essence of the declaration of שמע lies in קבלת עול מלכות שמים, the subordination of all of our personality and of our entire world to the one and unique dominion of God.

In the word אחד the letter ד stands out larger than the rest, apparently in order to prevent its confusion with the letter ר which would make the word read not אחד "one" but אחר, "another". Conversely, in כי לא תשתחוה לאל אחר (Exod. 34:14), the ר in אחר is enlarged, so that the word אחר "another" may not be erroneously read אחד ("one"). The ר in אחר which stands for polytheism is pliantly rounded, while the sharp, angular ד in אחד, represents a "sharp" refutation of any alien ideology. Take away the small, sharp angle and the word אחד becomes אחר. The large ד, when joined with the prominent ע in שמע, forms the word עד, meaning "testimony" and "witness". This is quite appropriate, for the content of שמע ישראל is a "testimony" given by Israel to Israel, and everyone who utters it, by so doing appoints himself God's witness to his own person and to the world. Perhaps it would not be too far-fetched if we were to infer here that עין, "the eye", was עד "witness" to that truth which is expressed in שמע ישראל. In other words, the שמע is meant to pass on to future generations our own knowledge of God, based upon the sum

HEAR YISRAEL, *GOD* OUR GOD IS *GOD*, THE ONLY ONE!

Blessed be the Name of the glory of His kingdom in all the future which, though veiled, is certain.

And you shall love *God,* your God, with all your heart and with all your soul and with all your fortune. And these words which I command you today shall be upon your heart, And you shall teach them diligently to your sons and speak of them when you sit in your house and when you walk upon the road, when you lie down and when you rise up. And you shall bind them as a sign upon your hand, and they shall be as a head-ornament between your eyes. And you shall inscribe them upon the doorposts of your house and upon your gates.

---

total of our mental and spiritual perception of His greatness אתה הראת לדעת כי ד׳ הוא האלקי׳ אין עוד מלבדו (Deut. 4:35).

ואהבת is the direct, logical consequence of ד׳ אחד: from the Oneness of God we infer the unity of the purpose of all of life. We are to prove our love of God, our worship of Him in both thought and conviction, by mustering for this purpose every aspect of our lives, including our bodies and physical desires, and all the means at our disposal. Therefore the sages say חייב אדם לברך על הרעה כשם שמברך על הטובה שנ׳ ואהבת את ד׳ אלקיך בכל לבבך ובכל נפשך ובכל מאדך. בכל לבבך בשני יצריך ביצר טוב וביצר רע, בכל נפשך אפילו הוא נוטל את נפשך ובכל מאודך בכל ממונך. דבר אחר בכל מדה ומדה שהוא מודד לך הוי מודה לו (Berachoth 54a). Even as man vows his tribute to God in joy, so must he also pledge his homage to God in times of sorrow. For it is said, "You shall love God your God with all your heart and with all your soul and with all your fortune." "With all your heart" means "not only with your good impulses but even with your baser tendencies." "With all your soul" enjoins you to love Him "even if He should take your soul from you." "With all your might" means "with all that you possess." In other words, "Whatever the portion that He may allot to you in life, employ it to render thanks to Him in great measure." To love God בכל לבבך; i.e. both ביצר טוב וביצר רע, is the most significant and weighty consequence following from the awareness of the Unity of God. The same One God Who instilled within us the יצר הטוב, the capability to respond to the beauty of all things good and lofty and noble, also implanted within us the יצר הרע, the capacity to be tempted by the glamorous glitter of sin, baseness and vulgarity. If evil were to hold no charms for us, if the thought of sin would be contrary to our very nature and hence physically repugnant to us, while the urge to do good would draw us with irresistible magnetic force and would not involve self-discipline and self-denial, then,

דברים
י״א,י״נ וְהָיָה אִם־שָׁמֹעַ תִּשְׁמְעוּ אֶל־מִצְוֹתַי אֲשֶׁר אָנֹכִי
מְצַוֶּה אֶתְכֶם הַיּוֹם לְאַהֲבָה אֶת־יְהוָה אֱלֹהֵיכֶם וּלְעָבְדוֹ
בְּכָל־לְבַבְכֶם וּבְכָל־נַפְשְׁכֶם: וְנָתַתִּי מְטַר־אַרְצְכֶם
בְּעִתּוֹ יוֹרֶה וּמַלְקוֹשׁ וְאָסַפְתָּ דְגָנֶךָ וְתִירֹשְׁךָ וְיִצְהָרֶךָ:
וְנָתַתִּי עֵשֶׂב בְּשָׂדְךָ לִבְהֶמְתֶּךָ וְאָכַלְתָּ וְשָׂבָעְתָּ:
הִשָּׁמְרוּ לָכֶם פֶּן־יִפְתֶּה לְבַבְכֶם וְסַרְתֶּם וַעֲבַדְתֶּם
אֱלֹהִים אֲחֵרִים וְהִשְׁתַּחֲוִיתֶם לָהֶם: וְחָרָה אַף־יְהוָה
בָּכֶם וְעָצַר אֶת־הַשָּׁמַיִם וְלֹא־יִהְיֶה מָטָר וְהָאֲדָמָה לֹא
תִתֵּן אֶת־יְבוּלָהּ וַאֲבַדְתֶּם מְהֵרָה מֵעַל הָאָרֶץ הַטֹּבָה
אֲשֶׁר יְהוָה נֹתֵן לָכֶם: וְשַׂמְתֶּם אֶת־דְּבָרַי אֵלֶּה עַל־
לְבַבְכֶם וְעַל־נַפְשְׁכֶם וּקְשַׁרְתֶּם אֹתָם לְאוֹת עַל־יֶדְכֶם

---

of course, we would do no evil. But this would not make us "good",
because whatever "good" we would do would then not be of our own
free will. A good deed would then be not a human act of moral freedom,
but only a blind response to a physical urge which we would be powerless
to resist. And once there would be no more יצר הרע, we would lose all
of the moral dignity that is now ours (see Commentary to Gen. 3:1, 4:7,
6:5, 8:2). Therefore, to "love God with all your heart", with both
יצר רע and יצר טוב, means to consecrate all of our thinking, together with
all our tendencies and impulses, all of our potentialities and endeavors
without reservation to the fulfillment of God's will, and to control and use
them in His service in such a manner that will bring us nearer and nearer
to Him. Hence "loving God with our hearts" presupposes that we
should be ready at any moment to give up for that love even the most
cherished impulses and desires of our own hearts if they are not in accordance with the will of God. It means that we should cheerfully accept the
Divine denial of even our fondest wishes and dreams, content in the
knowledge that, even in withholding from us the realization of our heart's

And it shall come to pass if you will hearken with growing intentness to My commandments which I command you this day, so that you will love *God* your God and serve Him with all your heart and with all your soul, that I will give the rain of your land in its due season, the autumn rains and the spring rains, so that you may gather in your grain, your wine and your oil, and I will give grass upon your field for your cattle; you will eat thereof and you will be satiated. But take care lest your heart open itself to temptation and you turn astray and serve other gods and cast yourselves down before them. For then the wrath of *God* will blaze forth against you; He will restrain the skies and there will be no rain, and the land will not yield its produce, and you will quickly perish from the good land which *God* gives you. But even then you shall lay up these My words in your heart and in your soul, and bind them as a sign upon your hand and they

---

desire, He shows us the same love for which we would have given reverent thanks had He granted us its fulfillment.

‏אפילו נוטל את נפשו :ובכל נפשך‏, To love God with every part of our life and our being, with all the physical and spiritual facets of our personality, with every moment of our sojourn on earth, also means nothing more or less than to strive with all of our being for that Divine nearness which can be attained only through the fulfillment of His will, and to evaluate all of our life only in terms of whether or not it is worthy of that nearness. Nor must we deem the sacrifice of even physical life itself too dear a price to pay for remaining near to Him. He who loves God ‏בכל נפשו‏ draws his every breath in the loving service of his God, and will rather give up his life than break faith with his Maker. However, Jewish law itself, in another place ‏וחי בהם‏ (Lev. 18:5, see ibid.) has indicated that there are only limited circumstances under which we are expected to sacrifice our lives rather than transgress the Law of God. It is only when he must contend with forces aiming at the outright extirpation of the Law that a Jew must die, if necessary, rather than commit even the slightest violation of the Law. Under such circumstances we are told ‏יהרג ואל יעבור‏ we must die rather than transgress even if we are asked to do no more than ‏ערקתא דמסאנא‏ "change a shoelace in a manner contrary to Jewish law." Under normal conditions, however, the only laws which must never be violated even at the cost of one's very life are those concerning ‏עבודה זרה גלוי עריות ושפיכות דמים‏. As regards other precepts, however, the general principle ‏וחי בהם‏ applies. The Torah itself attaches such great importance to the preservation of human life for the fulfillment of our duty here below, that it considers it proper for a Jew

וְהָיוּ לְטוֹטָפֹת בֵּין עֵינֵיכֶם: וְלִמַּדְתֶּם אֹתָם אֶת־בְּנֵיכֶם
לְדַבֵּר בָּם בְּשִׁבְתְּךָ בְּבֵיתֶךָ וּבְלֶכְתְּךָ בַדֶּרֶךְ וּבְשָׁכְבְּךָ
וּבְקוּמֶךָ: וּכְתַבְתָּם עַל־מְזוּזוֹת בֵּיתֶךָ וּבִשְׁעָרֶיךָ: לְמַעַן
יִרְבּוּ יְמֵיכֶם וִימֵי בְנֵיכֶם עַל הָאֲדָמָה אֲשֶׁר נִשְׁבַּע
יְהֹוָה לַאֲבֹתֵיכֶם לָתֵת לָהֶם כִּימֵי הַשָּׁמַיִם עַל־הָאָרֶץ:

(יעבור ואל יהרג) to violate such laws if this action would save him from death
If a transgression of the Law might be involved in the treatment of illness,
it must be determined first whether the patient is חולה שיש בו סכנה or whether
ואין בו סכנה whether or not the patient is in immediate danger. If the
medicine prescribed should contain forbidden food, it must be established
whether the prohibition governing the consumption of that material is
דרבנן or דאוריתא, and whether the form in which it is to be taken by the
patient is כדרך הנאתו or שלא כדרך הנאתו that is, whether or not the forbidden
ingredient is to be consumed in a manner in which food is normally enjoyed.
(See י״ד 155:3). בכל ממונך : ובכל מאודך Finally, we must prove our love
of God "with all our fortune" not simply by employing all of our
money and property in the service of God, but also by renouncing any
kind of financial or material gain that can be obtained and retained only
by means of a violation of His Torah. And that Law retains inviolable
validity even in the face of financial sacrifice. We are commanded to
renounce our entire fortune even if we would have to violate just one
single prohibition in order to preserve it. The Law does not, however,
require us to make such drastic sacrifices for the fulfillment of positive
commandments. (See י״ד 157. א״ח 656).

שנן ל .ושננתם לבניך means to teach some subject matter by means of terse,
forceful and easily-to-be-remembered statements. ודברת בם means, "talk of
them", "explain them", "elucidate them". And if we combine both these
tasks, as it is written ושננתם ודברת בם, we can readily discern the procedure
we must follow in disseminating the Law. First, teach it to the student
in the form of brief, concise statements; Then impress them upon his
memory by more detailed comment and discussion. In other words, teach
him both תורה שבכתב and תורה שבעל פה as well as משנה and גמרא.

בשבתך בביתך וגו' The constant reavowal of our knowledge that
God is indeed One, (שמע) and the consequent awareness of the unity of
our life's mission (ואהבת) the subordination of all our thoughts and desires to the basic truths of our purpose, as well as to the inferences

shall be as a head-ornament between your eyes, and teach them to your sons to speak of them, when you sit in your house and when you walk upon the road, when you lie down and when you rise up. Inscribe them upon the doorposts of your house and upon your gates, so that your days and the days of your children may be prolonged upon the land which *God* swore to give to your fathers, as the days of the heavens upon the earth.

---

therefrom as revealed by God in His Laws, and our task to teach that Law to our children for their education and to pursue its study ourselves for our own spiritual growth, all this we must practice at all times and wherever we may be, whether at home or abroad, and with this, too, we are to begin both our nightly rest and our daily labors. It appears that ובשכבך ובקומך should be construed not as a continuation of the thought בשבתך וגו׳ but as referring back to the latter; that is, wherever we may be, at home or abroad, we are always to begin and to end our day with שמע and דברי תורה. בשכבך ובקומך is "at the time of your lying down and of your rising up." Hence the evening שמע may be read at any time during the night, beginning with the appearance of the stars until the hour of dawn, and the morning *Shema* may be recited at any time between the appearance of clear daylight משיראה את חברו רחוק ד׳ אמות ויכירנו until the end of the first half of the morning (that is, the completion of three-twelfths of the day). (Berachoth 2a, 8b, 9a.)

וקשרתם וגו׳ We are to bind upon our hands as a "symbol of binding duty" that sacred object which reminds us of our task to worship the One God and to dedicate our entire existence and all our endeavors to Him, the sum total of our life's task which we should take to our hearts anew each day. We are to wear it also on our heads as a "guiding symbol for our eyes." Even as it is said here, we are also told in Chap. 11:18 וקשרתם אתם לאות על ידכם והיו לטוטפת בין עיניכם, also in והי׳ לך לאות על ידך ולזכרון בין עיניך (Exod. 13:9) and והי׳ לאות על ידכה ולטוטפת בין עיניך (ibid. 16). In accordance with these statements, the Halacha teaches us to bind these four portions of the Law (Exod. 13:1—10, 11—16, Deut. 6:4—9, 11, 13—21) upon the upper arm as a symbol of consecration and upon the forepart of the head as a sign of commemoration. The phylacteries for the arm are placed not upon the hand but upon the inner biceps of the left upper arm, בגובה שביד which controls the entire grasping organ and is nearest to the heart. In like manner, the head phylacteries are actually bound not "between the eyes" but (see below) בגובה שבראש high upon the forepart of the head, the seat of thought which directs the eyes from above and receives the impressions communicated by the sense of sight. The place for the head phylacteries is on the forepart of the head, from the hairline on upward, perpendicularly above the space between the eyes. The

בַּמִּדְבָּר
ט״ו ל״ז וַיֹּ֥אמֶר יְהֹוָ֖ה אֶל־מֹשֶׁ֥ה לֵּאמֹֽר: דַּבֵּ֞ר אֶל־בְּנֵ֣י
יִשְׂרָאֵ֗ל וְאָמַרְתָּ֤ אֲלֵהֶם֙ וְעָשׂ֨וּ לָהֶ֥ם צִיצִ֛ת עַל־כַּנְפֵ֥י
בִגְדֵיהֶ֖ם לְדֹרֹתָ֑ם וְנָֽתְנ֛וּ עַל־צִיצִ֥ת הַכָּנָ֖ף פְּתִ֥יל תְּכֵֽלֶת:
וְהָיָ֣ה לָכֶם֮ לְצִיצִת֒ וּרְאִיתֶ֣ם אֹת֗וֹ וּזְכַרְתֶּם֙ אֶת־כָּל־
מִצְוֺ֣ת יְהֹוָ֔ה וַעֲשִׂיתֶ֖ם אֹתָ֑ם וְלֹֽא־תָת֜וּרוּ אַחֲרֵ֤י לְבַבְכֶם֙
וְאַחֲרֵ֣י עֵֽינֵיכֶ֔ם אֲשֶׁר־אַתֶּ֥ם זֹנִ֖ים אַחֲרֵיהֶֽם: לְמַ֣עַן

---

lower edge of the phylactery base תיתורא should not extend below the
hairline, nor should the upper edge be placed above the fontanel, that
part of the skull which is still soft in infancy. In the same manner the
term בין עיניכם in לא תשימו קרחה בין עיניכם למת (Deut. 14:1) designates a
hairy part of the forepart of the head (Menachoth 37a,b). The hand
phylacteries are put on before those for the head, but the reverse procedure
is followed at the time of their removal, for it is said, first וקשרתם לאות
על ידך and only then והיו לטטפת בין עיניך. And further, it is said, והיו לטטפת:
תפלין if one has both כל זמן שבין עיניך יהיו שנים, the head phylacteries should
not be על ידך without the hand phylacteries being בין עיניך at the same time
(Menachoth 36a). If, however, a man for some reason cannot don the hand
phylacteries, he is permitted to put on the head phylacteries alone, because
the commandments governing the phylacteries for the hand and the head
are two separate *mitzvoth* which are not mutually interdependent. (For a
detailed discussion, see Commentary to Deut. 6:4–9, *Horeb* Chap. 38.)

וכתבתם וגו' The doorposts of your homes and of your gates are to bear
the inscription of that which is to govern all your thoughts and actions.
In this manner you are to consecrate your private dwellings and places
dedicated to your public affairs to the realization of the ideals set forth
in the Law. The inscription on the *Mezuzah*, however, confines itself to
two of the four postions of the Law that are contained in the phylacteries,
namely שמע ס' and והיה אם שמע. For our homes and our cities are actually
the places where the tasks set by the Torah as they are taught us in the
שמע should be fulfilled and where the prosperity which will be the reward
of the Law's observance, or the ruin brought on by its neglect, (see
והיה אם שמע) will become visibly apparent.

And *God* spoke to Moshe, saying, "Speak to the sons of Yisrael and tell it to them so that they make for themselves fringes on the corners of their garments throughout their generations, and that they put on the fringes of the corner a thread of sky-blue wool. These shall be fringes for you so that you may look upon them and remember all the commandments of *God,* and fulfill them, and you will not cast about after your own hearts and after your own eyes, and, following them, become unfaithful

---

והיה אם שמע. The first prerequisite for all of our welfare is the continuous "hearkening unto the commandments of God" with ever growing intentness. According to *Sifri*, such absorbing interest and concern are proven above all by the diligent "study" of the Law. It is further explained that ignorance or insufficient knowledge of the Divine Law has always been at the root of every evil that has befallen our people. לעבדו ב has a two-fold meaning. First, it denotes service as performed *upon* an object; the care and shaping of that object in accordance with the will of the one served. But לעבדו ב also indicates service performed *by means* of an object; that is, the employment of an object as an instrument for the fulfillment of the purposes of the one to be served. Our sages consider that the realization of the first kind of service named here, ולעבדו בכל לבבכם the fulfillment of the will of God *as regards* our hearts, consists first of all in תפלה : איזו עבודה שהיא בלב הוי אומר זו תפלה (Taanith 2a). *Sifri* ibid. documents the conceptual identity of עבודה שבלב as expressed in תפלה with עבודת המזבח citing such Biblical verses as Psalm 141:2, Daniel 6:11,21. וכי יש פולחן בבבל הא מה ת״ל ולעבדו זו תפלה כשם שעבודת מזבח קרוי׳ עבודה כך תפלה קרוי׳ עבודה In this manner, the concept of תפלה is construed as a "project of labor *upon* one's own self" in accordance with the will of God. As is also indicated by the origin of the verb תפלה, התפלל is a means of imbuing the entire spirit with the Divine truths that enlighten the mind and ennoble the heart. The purpose of תפלה is conceived to be the elevation of thought, will and emotion which, together, comprise the human spirit, to a level worthy of God's nearness and of His favor. The purpose of every word of תפלה uttered is identical with that formerly fulfilled by the sacrificial ritual in the Temple. The act of sacrifice was intended to bring about, through a series of symbolic actions, the renunciation of all personal will and ambition, the identification of the entire personality with the guiding force of the Sanctuary of Law, the upward striving of the human personality to the lofty goals shown us by the Law and man's persistence on that high moral level. The sacrifice taught that all of man's spiritual impulses and even his baser physical urges are to be offered up to the purifying and life-restoring fire that is

תִּזְכְּרוּ וַעֲשִׂיתֶם אֶת־כָּל־מִצְוֹתָי וִהְיִיתֶם קְדֹשִׁים
לֵאלֹהֵיכֶם: אֲנִי יְהֹוָה אֱלֹהֵיכֶם אֲשֶׁר הוֹצֵאתִי אֶתְכֶם
מֵאֶרֶץ מִצְרַיִם לִהְיוֹת לָכֶם לֵאלֹהִים אֲנִי יְהֹוָה
אֱלֹהֵיכֶם: ‏ם לְבָרֵךְ אֱלֹהֵיכֶם לֶאֱמֶת.

אֱמֶת וְיַצִּיב וְנָכוֹן וְקַיָּם וְיָשָׁר וְנֶאֱמָן וְאָהוּב וְחָבִיב
וְנֶחְמָד וְנָעִים וְנוֹרָא וְאַדִּיר וּמְתֻקָּן וּמְקֻבָּל וְטוֹב וְיָפֶה
הַדָּבָר הַזֶּה עָלֵינוּ לְעוֹלָם וָעֶד: אֱמֶת אֱלֹהֵי עוֹלָם
מַלְכֵּנוּ צוּר יַעֲקֹב מָגֵן יִשְׁעֵנוּ: לְדוֹר וָדוֹר הוּא קַיָּם

---

the Law of the Lord, for the nourishment of all that is Divine on earth
and for the shaping of all earthly affairs in such a manner as to find
favor in the eyes of the Lord. Today תפלה is to fulfill that same function.

ולמדתם וגו׳ The term לימוד is more comprehensive than שנון. We
believe that it is for this reason that the Halacha bases its statement
בניכם ולא בנותיכם (Kiddushin 29b), limiting the commandment to teach
the *Torah* to the instruction of our sons exclusive of our daughters, on
the sentence ולמדתם אותם את בניכם and not on the sentence ושננתם לבניך.
The fact is that while women are not to be exposed to specialized Torah
study or theoretical knowledge of the Law, which are reserved for the
Jewish man, such understanding of our sacred literature as can teach the
fear of the Lord and the conscientious fulfillment of our duty, and all
such knowledge as is essential to the adequate execution of our tasks
should indeed form part of the mental and spiritual training not only of
our sons, but of our daughters as well. This is indicated also by the
commandment pertaining to הקהל (Deut. 31:12). See also טורי זהב to
י״ד 246:6.

ויאמר וגו׳. על כנפי בגדיהם The *Tzitzith* are to be fastened to the corners
of the garment, no further away from the hem than three thumbs'-widths,
but no nearer to the hem than קשר גודל the equivalent of the length of
the upper joint of the thumb. Only a garment actually having four corners
must be provided with *Tzitzith* on those four corners. If the garment has
only three corners, it is not subject to this law. Should the garment have
more than four corners, only four of these must be treated in accordance

to Me. That you may remember and fulfill all of My commandments and remain holy for your God. I am *God*, your God, Who brought you out of the land of Mitzrayim in order to be your God; I am *God* your God."

True and firm, established and enduring and right, believed and beloved, precious, desired and sweet, yet awesome and mighty, well-ordered and accepted through tradition, good and beautiful is this Word, and binding upon us for all eternity. True it is; the God of all time is our King; the Rock of Yaakov is the Shield of our salvation. He endures for all generations and His Name endures; His throne

---

with this precept (Menachoth 43b). The four *Tzitzith,* however, constitute one inseparable unit; hence, if *Tzitzith* should either be ritually unfit or entirely lacking on even only one of those four corners, the wearer is considered as not having fulfilled the commandment at all ארבע ציציות מעכבות זו את זו שארבעתן מצוה אחת (Menachoth 37b). תכלת is the special blue purple shade that is the basic color of the Jewish sanctuary of the Law (see Commentary to Exod. 25:4 and 28:43). No other blue dye can be employed as a substitute. When the תכלת is unobtainable, the commandment is fulfilled by the use of לבן threads (Menachoth 38a).

The injunction וראיתם אתו implies that the *Tzitzith* must be worn only during that time of day when objects can be perceived by the sense of sight. The *mitzvah* of *Tzitzith* does not explicitly state that we must wear a garment made in such a way that it must be provided with *Tzitzith.* Instead, it takes for granted the fact that we will indeed wear such garments to which this precept is applicable, and it is expected of us that we will deliberately subject ourselves to this obligation by wearing such garb. (Menachoth 41a). אני וגו' The symbol of the *Tzitzith* serves to direct our thoughts to the historic fact of יציאת מצרים. Because it made us perceive the Lord as our Redeemer and Lawgiver in our own history הוצאתי וגו' להיות וגו', this momentous event constitutes the unshakeable basis of our conviction for all times to come, and has set before us the all embracing word of God אני ד' אלקיכם as the fundamental which is to guide all of our thoughts and endeavors forevermore. (For a more detailed discussion, see Commentary to Num. 15:38—41, *Horeb* Chap. 39).

יוצר אור .אמת ויציב אהבה רבה and were the preliminary blessings which served as an introduction to the קריאת שמע. Now the portion beginning with אמת ויציב and ending with גאל ישראל comprises the concluding blessing of the קריאת שמע and the transition to the *Shemone Esrei.* Briefly, the content of the three paragraphs שמע, והיה אם שמע, ויאמר which we have just read, is as follows: 1) The avowal of the Unity of God, and hence the logical inference concerning the unity of all of Jewish life in the

וְשִׁמוֹ קַיָּם וְכִסְאוֹ נָכוֹן וּמַלְכוּתוֹ וֶאֱמוּנָתוֹ לָעַד קַיָּמֶת:
וּדְבָרָיו חָיִים וְקַיָּמִים נֶאֱמָנִים וְנֶחֱמָדִים לָעַד וּלְעוֹלְמֵי
עוֹלָמִים עַל־אֲבוֹתֵינוּ וְעָלֵינוּ וְעַל־בָּנֵינוּ וְעַל־דּוֹרוֹתֵינוּ
וְעַל כָּל־דּוֹרוֹת זֶרַע יִשְׂרָאֵל עֲבָדֶיךָ: עַל־הָרִאשׁוֹנִים
וְעַל־הָאַחֲרוֹנִים דָּבָר טוֹב וְקַיָּם לְעוֹלָם וָעֶד: אֱמֶת
וֶאֱמוּנָה חֹק וְלֹא יַעֲבוֹר: אֱמֶת שָׁאַתָּה הוּא יְיָ
אֱלֹהֵינוּ וֵאלֹהֵי אֲבוֹתֵינוּ מַלְכֵּנוּ מֶלֶךְ אֲבוֹתֵינוּ גּוֹאֲלֵנוּ
גּוֹאֵל אֲבוֹתֵינוּ · יוֹצְרֵנוּ צוּר יְשׁוּעָתֵנוּ פּוֹדֵנוּ וּמַצִּילֵנוּ
מֵעוֹלָם שְׁמֶךָ · אֵין אֱלֹהִים זוּלָתֶךָ:

עֶזְרַת אֲבוֹתֵינוּ אַתָּה הוּא מֵעוֹלָם מָגֵן וּמוֹשִׁיעַ לִבְנֵיהֶם אַחֲרֵיהֶם
בְּכָל־דּוֹר וָדוֹר: בְּרוּם עוֹלָם מוֹשָׁבֶךָ וּמִשְׁפָּטֶיךָ וְצִדְקָתְךָ עַד

---

subordination of every aspect of life and endeavor to the will of the One
God. 2) The warning that our welfare and that of our children are dependent upon the manner in which we discharge the task set us by God, and
the commandment to train and educate our children so that they may
fulfill His Law. 3) The constant warning not to permit the impressions
of our senses and the impulses of our hearts to lure us away from the
proper understanding and fulfillment of our mission, but rather to remember
at all times the facts which our miraculous redemption from Egypt has
taught us about God and about our debt to Him. The paragraph beginning
with אמת ויציב views all of the foregoing as one single Word of God
and expresses the following thoughts: This Divine Word in itself is utter
truth, and therefore firm, established, and unchangeably right and enduring.
That is, it coresponds to the true nature and purpose of things as they
are. It is incumbent upon us to accept this truth with devotion born of
conviction; we are to love it and treasure it as the bliss to be desired
above all else. At the same time we must revere in it all the awesomeness
and force of its solemn import. It was set down in the proper order in
history so that we might better be able to understand and to fulfill it,

is firmly established, and His kingdom and His guiding faith endure forever. And His words are living and enduring; they are confirmed and desirable forever and to all eternity. This stands above our fathers and ourselves, above our children and our descendants, as well as above all the descendants of Yisrael, Your servants, the first and the last alike, as a good Word, unchangeable for all eternity. It is a truth and an unchangeable conviction, a statute which shall not pass away. It is a truth that You, O *God*, are our God and the God of our fathers, our King and the King of our fathers, our Redeemer and the Redeemer of our fathers. Our Maker, the Rock of our salvation, our Redeemer and Deliverer — such has been Your Name forever. There is no God beside You.

You have ever been the Help of our fathers, a Shield and Savior to their sons after them in every generation. In the high places of the Universe is Your habitation, and Your judgments and

---

and it has been handed down to us as sacred tradition by our fathers. Therefore it can only be "good", for us, conducive to our welfare, and nothing but "beautiful"; enhancing our position in the world, if only we will view and accept it as eternally binding upon us; even as is specified in the paragraph that follows.

דבריו חיים The words of God's Law are "living". They are constantly at work, with unchanging and ennobling force, to better and to refine the spirit of every individual who will embrace them with all his heart.

עזרת This blessing dwells particularly upon the remembrance of the Exodus from Egypt to which reference had already been made at the end of the preceding פרשת ויאמר in order to comply with the injunction in Deut. 16:3 to remember daily this act of Divine deliverance. At the same time this paragraph of commemoration serves as a transition to the תפלת שמנה עשרה which follows immediately. It is סומך גאולה לתפלה and thus emphasizes that it is solely on the strength of the redemption which we have already experienced at the hands of God in the past that we now approach Him with our yearnings, prayers and hopes for our future as contained in the תפלה. Accordingly, we look back upon the instances in our past history in which God had constantly been at the side of our fathers and has ever proven to be a protector and savior of their descendants who have loyally followed in their footsteps. We recall what these acts of Divine providence have taught us; namely that, though God, exalted, is enthroned on high in the heavens, His judgments and His acts of kindness extend even to the furthest ends of the earth. We remind ourselves, too, that only he who obeys God's commandments and takes His teachings

אַפְסֵי אָרֶץ: אַשְׁרֵי אִישׁ שֶׁיִּשְׁמַע לְמִצְוֹתֶיךָ וְתוֹרָתְךָ וּדְבָרְךָ
יָשִׂים עַל־לִבּוֹ: אֱמֶת אַתָּה הוּא אָדוֹן לְעַמֶּךָ וּמֶלֶךְ גִּבּוֹר לָרִיב
רִיבָם: אֱמֶת אַתָּה הוּא רִאשׁוֹן וְאַתָּה הוּא אַחֲרוֹן וּמִבַּלְעָדֶיךָ
אֵין לָנוּ מֶלֶךְ גּוֹאֵל וּמוֹשִׁיעַ: מִמִּצְרַיִם גְּאַלְתָּנוּ יְיָ אֱלֹהֵינוּ וּמִבֵּית
עֲבָדִים פְּדִיתָנוּ · כָּל־בְּכוֹרֵיהֶם הָרַגְתָּ וּבְכוֹרְךָ גָּאָלְתָּ וְיַם־סוּף
בָּקַעְתָּ וְזֵדִים טִבַּעְתָּ וִידִידִים הֶעֱבַרְתָּ וַיְכַסּוּ מַיִם צָרֵיהֶם אֶחָד מֵהֶם

to heart can expect prosperity and salvation in the future. We acknowledge
that He has command over our lives and endeavors as our Lord even
as He champions our cause as our King, that He is unchangeable, remaining
forever that which He has been from days of old—our sole King, Redeemer
and Savior. With this avowal we begin the remembrance of our historic
deliverance from Mitzrayim; we are with our fathers in spirit as they leave
the home of bondage and as they pass through the Sea of Reeds, and we
ourselves witness with our mind's eye the sentence which God executed
upon our oppressors. Together with our fathers, we learn to fear God
and to trust in Him. Bridging the distance of time we join with them
in the song which they sang at the Sea, a hymn of thanksgiving for
deliverance which, declaring the glory of God, brought to mankind an
entirely new understanding of Him and His nature. From the mouths of
our ancestors we accept the recognition of the absolute majesty and unique
power of God, far exalted above those forces that men would deify, and
we take it to heart for our own wanderings through the ages. From their
teaching we derive the trust and certainty that He shall reign forever and
ever even as He ruled in Mitzrayim and by the shores of the Sea of Reeds.
Filled with renewed hope by this spiritual experience and sustained by this
firm conviction, we now come before God Who is Israel's eternal Rock
with our own concerns and requests, both great and small.

שְׁמֹנֶה עֶשְׂרֵה

This תְּפִלָּה the שְׁמֹנֶה עֶשְׂרֵה constitutes the culminating point of our
prayers. All that which preceded it is nothing but preparation for it, and
serves solely to imbue us with such thoughts and attitudes as are in
accordance with the spirit of this תְּפִלָּה. When the "Men of the Great
Assembly" wrote the שְׁמֹנֶה עֶשְׂרֵה they actually had in mind the daily morning and evening sacrifices, כְּנֶגֶד תְּמִידִים, that were brought in the Temple.
In fact this prayer was recited in our houses of worship outside the Temple
even during the days of the Temple, while the sacrifices were offered up

righteousness reach to the remotest ends of the earth. Forward to salvation strides that man who hearkens to Your commandments and who takes Your Torah and Your Word to his heart. True it is, You are the Lord of Your people and a mighty King to champion their cause. True it is, You are the First and You are the Last, and besides You we have no King, Redeemer and Savior. From Mitzrayim did You redeem us, O *God* our God, and have set us free from the home of slavery; all their first-born You did slay, but Your first-born You did redeem; You did divide the Sea of Reeds, You did drown the arrogant, but Your beloved ones You did lead across, and the water covered their enemies;

---

in the Sanctuary, and two of the final blessings contained in the שמנה עשרה, (ברכת כהנים) and עבודה) and (שים שלום and רצה were actually recited as part of the actual procedure of sacrifice, introduced by the paragraphs אהבה רבה (עשרת הדברות), שמע, והיה אם שמע, ויאמר, אמת ויציב (Tamid Chapter 5). In "Jeschurun" Vols. 11 and 12, we have already attempted to demonstrate that the entire order of the *Shemone Esrei* actually parallels the sacrificial procedure of the *Tamid*, and that it expresses in verbal manner the same thoughts which the עבודה connected with the *Tamid* offerings portrayed in the language of profound symbolism.

The order of the morning and evening sacrifice consists fundamentally of these three basic parts:

a. זריקת דם preceded by שחיטה, קבלה and הולכה. The blood of the sacrifice representing the נפש is given up, accepted, brought up close and then thrown up to the altar, symbolizing the endeavor of the human soul to devote itself entirely to God's will and to soar upward to the high altar of its own Divine mission.

b. הקטרת איברים preceded by הפשט וניתוח והולכת איברים לכבש, symbolizing the preparation, the offering and cession of all internal and external organs of intellectual, moral and physical activity to the fire that is the Law of God, so that, by fulfilling the tasks set by the Law, they may nourish and nurture all that is Divine on earth. This is a logical inference from the preceding act of עבודות הדם which symbolized the consecration of the soul itself.

c. מנחה ונסכים The tribute of flour, oil and wine which was part of every elevating offering. This is a symbolic demonstration of thanksgiving for sustenance, wealth and joy granted us by God.

The *Shemone Esrei* prayer, too, can be divided into three main parts as follows:

a. The *first* three blessings: אבות, גבורות and קדושה We come before Him with these three blessings in order to recall to ourselves the relation-

לֹא נוֹתָר : עַל־זֹאת שִׁבְּחוּ אֲהוּבִים וְרוֹמְמוּ אֵל וְנָתְנוּ יְדִידִים

זְמִירוֹת שִׁירוֹת וְתִשְׁבָּחוֹת בְּרָכוֹת וְהוֹדָאוֹת לְמֶלֶךְ אֵל חַי וְקַיָּם :

רָם וְנִשָּׂא גָּדוֹל וְנוֹרָא מַשְׁפִּיל גֵּאִים וּמַגְבִּיהַּ שְׁפָלִים מוֹצִיא

אֲסִירִים וּפוֹדֶה עֲנָוִים וְעוֹזֵר דַּלִּים וְעוֹנֶה לְעַמּוֹ בְּעֵת שַׁוְּעָם אֵלָיו :

תְּהִלּוֹת לְאֵל עֶלְיוֹן בָּרוּךְ הוּא וּמְבֹרָךְ · מֹשֶׁה וּבְנֵי יִשְׂרָאֵל לְךָ

עָנוּ שִׁירָה בְּשִׂמְחָה רַבָּה וְאָמְרוּ כֻלָּם :

מִי־כָמֹכָה בָּאֵלִם יְהֹוָה מִי כָּמֹכָה נֶאְדָּר בַּקֹּדֶשׁ נוֹרָא תְהִלֹּת

עֹשֵׂה פֶלֶא : שִׁירָה חֲדָשָׁה שִׁבְּחוּ גְאוּלִים לְשִׁמְךָ עַל־שְׂפַת

הַיָּם יַחַד כֻּלָּם הוֹדוּ וְהִמְלִיכוּ וְאָמְרוּ · יְהֹוָה יִמְלֹךְ לְעֹלָם וָעֶד :

צוּר יִשְׂרָאֵל קוּמָה בְּעֶזְרַת יִשְׂרָאֵל וּפְדֵה כִנְאֻמֶךָ יְהוּדָה

וְיִשְׂרָאֵל · (גֹּאֲלֵנוּ יְיָ צְבָאוֹת שְׁמוֹ קְדוֹשׁ יִשְׂרָאֵל·) בָּרוּךְ אַתָּה

יְיָ גָּאַל יִשְׂרָאֵל :

ship of our נפש our soul, our human personality (symbolized by the דם
in the sacrifice) to God, His relationship to us, and our task
evolving from these relationships. It is only then that we go on to
beseech Him for favor, and pledge that we will put to proper use all the
earthly possessions for which we look to Him alone. Whenever we recite
אבות we enter anew with our fathers into the Divine Covenant which
teaches us to view God as the Supreme Bing Who is infinitely exalted
above all things but also infinitely near to us, and to regard the pact
which He made with our ancestors as the basis of all the past and all
the future of even their most distant progeny.

In גבורות we contemplate the all-conquering omnipotence of God.
Here, too, we learn that unshakeable trust which enables us to withstand
all the vicissitudes of life and even death itself, and which enables all
those pervaded with the genuine fear of God to unlearn the fear of
human power or natural force and, in its place, to acquire the skill of
passing calmly and serenely through all the trials that are part of daily
living. קדושה then teaches us the sole condition which we must fulfill as
our part of the covenant with this Almighty Being, Who, though infinitely

not one of them was left. Therefore those who sensed that they were loved, praised and exalted God ; the beloved ones offered hymns, songs and praises, blessings and thanksgivings to the King, to the living and eternal God. He Who is high and exalted, great and awesome, brings low the haughty and raises up the lowly ; He leads captives to freedom and delivers the humble ; He helps the poor and answers His people when they cry to Him. Praise for His mighty deeds be to God the Most High, blessed be He and He is blessed ; Moshe and the sons of Yisrael sang a song to You with joy abounding and they all said :

"Who is like You among the gods, O *God* ? Who is like You, uniquely powerful in holiness? Feared in praises of His mighty deeds, performer of wonders ?"

With a new song the redeemed lauded Your Name by the shore of the sea ; they all paid homage in unison ; they acknowledged Your sovereignty, and they said :

"*God* shall reign forever and ever !"

O Rock of Yisrael arise to the help of Yisrael, and set Yehuda and Yisrael free, even as You have promised (O our Redeemer, *God* Tzevaoth, the Holy One of Yisrael is His Name). Blessed be You *God*, Who has redeemed Yisrael.

---

exalted, is also infinitely near; namely, that we must sanctify God through the moral hallowing of our own personalities.

b. The thirteen *intermediate* blessings (originally there were only twelve; see below), express in words the thought symbolized by the איברים על גבי מזבח in the daily offerings. They are pleas for Divine favor, and they pledge our dutiful, proper use of all the material possessions and of all the intellectual and spiritual values which God and God alone can grant us, such as insight (דעת) repentance (תשובה) forgiveness (סליחה) redemption (גאולה) healing (רפואה) sustenance (פרנסה). The last three of these are first sought from the standpoint of the individual, and then in behalf of the entire Jewish nation in the form of the ingathering of the dispersed (קבוץ גליות), the restoration of the supreme authority of the Law (השיבה שופטינו) and the elimination of the lawless (עדין רשעים) the preservation of those who are faithful to the Law and spread its teachings (צדיקים וסופרים), the rebuilding of Jerusalem (בנין ירושלים), the restoration of the dynasty of David (צמח דוד), and constant Divine attendance to our prayers (שומע תפלה).

אֲדֹנָי שְׂפָתַי תִּפְתָּח וּפִי יַגִּיד תְּהִלָּתֶךָ :

בָּרוּךְ אַתָּה יְיָ אֱלֹהֵינוּ וֵאלֹהֵי אֲבוֹתֵינוּ אֱלֹהֵי אַבְרָהָם
אֱלֹהֵי יִצְחָק וֵאלֹהֵי יַעֲקֹב הָאֵל הַגָּדוֹל הַגִּבּוֹר וְהַנּוֹרָא
אֵל עֶלְיוֹן גּוֹמֵל חֲסָדִים טוֹבִים וְקֹנֵה הַכֹּל וְזוֹכֵר חַסְדֵי
אָבוֹת וּמֵבִיא גוֹאֵל לִבְנֵי בְנֵיהֶם לְמַעַן שְׁמוֹ בְּאַהֲבָה ·

During the Ten Days of Repentance add:

זָכְרֵנוּ לְחַיִּים מֶלֶךְ חָפֵץ בַּחַיִּים · וְכָתְבֵנוּ בְּסֵפֶר הַחַיִּים לְמַעַנְךָ
אֱלֹהִים חַיִּים :

מֶלֶךְ עוֹזֵר וּמוֹשִׁיעַ וּמָגֵן · בָּרוּךְ אַתָּה יְיָ מָגֵן אַבְרָהָם:
אַתָּה גִבּוֹר לְעוֹלָם אֲדֹנָי מְחַיֵּה מֵתִים אַתָּה רַב
לְהוֹשִׁיעַ ·

During the winter months, add:

מַשִּׁיב הָרוּחַ וּמוֹרִיד הַגָּשֶׁם :

---

c. The three *concluding* blessings (corresponding to the thought symbolized by מנחה ונסכים in the sacrifice) constitute a plea for God's favorable acceptance at all times of our Divine service, be it in the form of prayer or sacrifice, for the return of the שכינה to the Sanctuary at Zion (עבודה) and an avowal of thanksgiving for His never-ceasing acts of kindness (הודאה). Finally, in recapitulation, we pray once more that God grant us all the material, spiritual and moral values necessary for our individual and collective welfare, combined with a pledge to employ these blessings only in accordance with His will, thus assuring ourselves of the perfect שלום which the Jewish concept of "peace" comprehends.

We shall now add a few brief explanatory notes to the individual blessings.

אדני Every individual addressing God by this Name, acknowledges Him therewith as his Lord, and views himself as God's servant. He thus pledges to employ the words of prayer to gird himself for the true service of God in everyday life.

ברוך We bow as we utter the word ברוך which is our pledge of

O *Lord,* open my lips so that my mouth may declare Your praise.

Blessed be You *God,* our God and God of our fathers, God of Avraham, God of Yitzchak and God of Yaakov, the great, mighty and awesome God, God the Most High, Who nevertheless bestows loving-kindness, Who is the Owner of all things, and remembers the fathers' acts of devotion and Who, in love, will bring a Redeemer to their children's children for His Name's sake.

During the Ten Days of Repentance add:

Remember us for life, O King Who delights in life, and inscribe us into the Book of Life for Your sake, O Living God.

O King, Helper Savior and Shield! Blessed are You *God,* the Shield of Avraham.

You, O my Lord, are all-powerful forever. You are the One Who revives the dead; You are abundantly strong to save.

In winter add

He causes the wind to blow and the rain to fall.

---

obedience, but we stand erect again when we come to say ד', for the thought of the Name of the Lord should not weigh us down but should rather sustain us at all times. For this same reason we need bow only at the beginning and at the end of the first blessing (אבות) and at the beginning and end of the הודאה (מודים). אלהינו ואלהי אבותינו "God of our Fathers"; that is, God as our ancestors knew Him, as He revealed His glory to them both by word and by means of mighty acts. This is the only way for us to conceive of God if we are to reach and to hold fast to that concept of truth which refutes all error and folly. גומל, האל etc. He thus causes us to see Him as a Being Which, though limitlessly exalted in awesome greatness and almighty power, is still so infinitely close to all of us that there is no need for the services of any intermediary between Him and ourselves. The nature of His loving Providence is such that our own lives and our own welfare, as well as those of even our remotest descendants, are assured because of the good deeds of our ancestors and theirs. It is as the sons of their fathers that they bear His Name, that they have a portion in His infinite love and that they may hopefully await the redeemer to be sent by Him. He is their King, Help, Savior and Shield even as He was that of their fathers. Let us, then, emulate our father Abraham. When God calls upon us to set us new tasks or to test us with new trials, let us respond with the simple answer that Abraham taught

מְכַלְכֵּל חַיִּים בְּחֶסֶד מְחַיֶּה מֵתִים בְּרַחֲמִים רַבִּים
סוֹמֵךְ נוֹפְלִים וְרוֹפֵא חוֹלִים וּמַתִּיר אֲסוּרִים וּמְקַיֵּם
אֱמוּנָתוֹ לִישֵׁנֵי עָפָר · מִי כָמוֹךָ בַּעַל גְּבוּרוֹת וּמִי דּוֹמֶה
לָּךְ מֶלֶךְ מֵמִית וּמְחַיֶּה וּמַצְמִיחַ יְשׁוּעָה ·

During the Ten Days of Repentance add:

מִי כָמוֹךָ אַב הָרַחֲמִים זוֹכֵר יְצוּרָיו לְחַיִּים בְּרַחֲמִים ·

וְנֶאֱמָן אַתָּה לְהַחֲיוֹת מֵתִים · בָּרוּךְ אַתָּה יְיָ מְחַיֵּה
הַמֵּתִים:

קְדוּשָׁה לַשַּׁ"ץ בַּחֲזָרַת הַתְּפִלָּה.

אַתָּה קָדוֹשׁ נְקַדֵּשׁ אֶת שִׁמְךָ בָּעוֹלָם כְּשֵׁם שֶׁמַּקְדִּישִׁים
אוֹתוֹ בִּשְׁמֵי מָרוֹם כַּכָּתוּב עַל יַד נְבִיאֶךָ וְקָרָא

---

us to give: הנני "I am ready," "Here I am." If we will choose to follow
this path, then God will prove to be our own Shield today even as He was
the Shield of Avraham long ago. (For Notes on the additional paragraphs
to be recited during the days of Repentance see p. 159).

אתה גבור If God is our shield, then we need fear nothing, not
even death. For God is mightier than death; He can reawaken even the
dead to renewed life. Thus He is abundantly powerful להושיע to grant
new יש, new, vigorous and true "being" and life at any moment. This
He demonstrates by His gracious gifts of wind and rain which determine
the course of all the earth's physical development, and also in the high
and low periods that are part of the lives of men. Everywhere it is His
almighty power that acts to preserve the living, to bring new life to the
dying and the dead, to support those who stumble, to heal the sick, and
to unchain the prisoner. ומקים אמונתו etc. could be construed as indicating
any one, or perhaps all, of these three thoughts: 1) "Even if the person
himself should die without receiving the salvation for which he had
looked to God, God will still keep faith with him even in the world
to come, and with his children who will live after him." 2) "God
is sure to fulfill the promise which He made to those who would
be loyal to Him, namely, the pledge that He will reward the children

He sustains the living with loving-kindness, revives the dead with great compassion, supports the falling, heals the sick, unchains the bound, and keeps His faith with the slumberers in the dust. Who is like You, O Master of Mighty acts, and who, like You, is a King Who kills and restores life and causes salvation to grow?

During the Ten Days of Repentance add:

Who, like You, is a Father of compassion, Who in compassion remembers His creatures for life.

And You are faithful to revive the dead. Blessed be You *God*, Who revives the dead.

When the Reader repeats the Shemone Esre, the following is said:

(*Reader*) We will sanctify Your Name in this world, even as they sanctify it in the heavens above, even as it is written by

---

and even grandchidren for the good deeds of their parents, even though the parents themselves might long since have joined the slumberers in the dust." 3) "God, in unchanging faithfulness, will fulfill the promise He had given the slumberers in the dust that He will one day awaken them and cause them to rise again to a new life." ברוך וכו׳ מחיה המתים There can hardly be another thought that can so inspire man firmly to resolve to live a life so vigorous, unwavering, fearless and unswervingly dutiful than the belief in תחית המתים. This is the firm conviction that to God not even the dead are lost forever, and that, even for the physical body, death is not the end but only a transition period from one life to the next.

וקדושים — אתה קדוש. There is one truth which must pervade all of our lives and all our endeavors before God, a truth the practical application of which will set the tone for our conduct and thus for our entire relationship with Him. We refer to the truth taught in Lev. 19:2 that God is "holy" and that we will be His only if we, too, are holy. This means that we must overcome whatever is in conflict with the element of holiness within us, that we must be "ready" to do whatever is holy and pleasing in the sight of God if we are to strive with unstinting devotion to sanctify all our being and all our behavior as long as we live. (ibid. 20:7, 26). קדושים יהללוך; only those who themselves are "holy" or who at least "aspire to holiness" may praise God and have תהלות ה׳ upon their lips. To praise God while leading a life that is at variance with His holy and sanctifying will would be gross blasphemy. He is נאמר בקדש and therefore נורא תהלות, even as our fathers declared it when the first תהלת ה׳ ever to be uttered came forth from their lips. (Exod. 15:11.)

קדושה. See above in *Yotzer*. There it is intended to show the manner in which God is sanctified by the chorus of His holy heavenly hosts. Here, how-

וְשִׁמָּךְ קָדוֹשׁ זֶה אֶל זֶה וְאָמַר: ח"י קָדוֹשׁ, קָדוֹשׁ, קָדוֹשׁ יְיָ צְבָאוֹת
מְלֹא כָל הָאָרֶץ כְּבוֹדוֹ: ח' לְעֻמָּתָם בָּרוּךְ יֹאמֵרוּ.

וּקְדוֹשִׁים קֹ"ח בָּרוּךְ כְּבוֹד יְיָ מִמְּקוֹמוֹ: ח' וּבְדִבְרֵי קָדְשָׁךְ
כָּתוּב לֵאמֹר • קֹ"ח יִמְלֹךְ יְיָ לְעוֹלָם אֱלֹהַיִךְ צִיּוֹן

בְּכָל-יוֹם לְדֹר וָדֹר הַלְלוּיָהּ:

ח' לְדוֹר וָדוֹר נַגִּיד גָּדְלֶךָ וּלְנֵצַח נְצָחִים קְדֻשָּׁתְךָ
וְהַלְלוּךְ סֶּלָה: נַקְדִּישׁ וְשִׁבְחֲךָ אֱלֹהֵינוּ מִפִּינוּ לֹא יָמוּשׁ לְעוֹלָם
וָעֶד כִּי אֵל מֶלֶךְ גָּדוֹל וְקָדוֹשׁ אָתָּה •

בָּרוּךְ אַתָּה יְיָ הָאֵל (בעשרת ימי תשובה אומרים: הַמֶּלֶךְ) הַקָּדוֹשׁ:

אַתָּה חוֹנֵן לְאָדָם דַּעַת וּמְלַמֵּד לֶאֱנוֹשׁ בִּינָה • חָנֵּנוּ
מֵאִתְּךָ דֵּעָה בִּינָה וְהַשְׂכֵּל • בָּרוּךְ אַתָּה יְיָ חוֹנֵן
הַדָּעַת:

הֲשִׁיבֵנוּ אָבִינוּ לְתוֹרָתֶךָ וְקָרְבֵנוּ מַלְכֵּנוּ לַעֲבוֹדָתֶךָ
וְהַחֲזִירֵנוּ בִּתְשׁוּבָה שְׁלֵמָה לְפָנֶיךָ • בָּרוּךְ אַתָּה יְיָ
הָרוֹצֶה בִּתְשׁוּבָה:

---

ever, the *kedushah* is meant to serve as a model upon which to pattern our own
Kiddush Hashem, the sanctification of God on earth, the supreme goal of the
Jewish mission which can be attained only jointly and within the community as
a whole. For this reason this paragraph of *kedushah* can be recited only together
with a congregation numbering at least ten adult males. (See above, before לריש
ובובכו) קדוש וגו'. See above (p. 103). לעמתם ברוך יאמרו They declare it one to
another that whatever they do and accomplish serves solely to fulfill the will
of the Lord. דברי קדשך וגו' See above (p. 109). ברוך כבוד וגו' refers to the
books of the *Kethuvim,* as distinguished from the words of the *Neviim*
mentioned before. ימלך וגו' To sanctify God on earth means that we are to
render homage to His rule by subordinating every aspect of our lives to His
will and to His Providence as indicated in the Law which He revealed to us
and which reposed in Zion.

דעה ,דעת, אתה חונן denotes the true perception of the real nature of
things and conditions. בינה is the insight into the interrelationships of things,
to be gained by logical judgment. השכל, practical wisdom, is the proper application of what has thus been learned. The prayer for such mental ability

Your prophet: "And one of them calls to the other and says:

(*Cong. & Reader*) 'Holy, holy, holy is *God Tzevaoth*, the fulness of all the earth is His glory.'

(*Reader*) "Facing one another, they say, 'Blessed —

(*Cong. & Reader*) 'Blessed be the glory of *God* from its abode.' "

(*Reader*) And in Your holy words it is written:

(*Cong. & Reader*) "*God* shall reign forever, your God, O Tzion, from generation to generation, Halaluyah!"

(*Reader*) From generation to generation shall we declare Your greatness and to all eternity will we proclaim Your holiness, and Your praise, O our God, shall never depart from our mouth, for You, O God, are a great and holy King. Blessed be You *God*, the holy God (*in the Ten Days of Repentance say:* "the holy King").

You are holy, and Your Name is holy, and the holy ones proclaim the praise of Your mighty deeds each day. Blessed be You *God*, the holy God (*in the Ten Days of Repentance say:* "the holy King").

You favor man with perception and teach mortal man insight. O favor us with perception, insight and wisdom from You. Blessed be You *God*, gracious Giver of perception.

Lead us back, our Father, to Your Torah, and draw us near, our King, to Your service, and cause us to return in perfect repentance to Your presence. Blessed be You *God*, Who takes pleasure in a repentant return.

---

represents the foremost concern of the Jewish person, taking precedence over all his other wishes. For the virtues of morality and loyal fulfillment of duty are very much dependent upon proper understanding. If man lacks wisdom and insight, his conduct cannot remain free of fault and error. Da'ath, to a great extent, is a talent given to man which develops by itself in and through experience. But he cannot acquire *binah* without an effort on his own part. Therefore the term מלמד is employed with reference to *binah* instead of *chonen* which is used in the case of *da'ath*. לאדם דעת: without *da'ath*, man can never be truly human. לאנוש בינה: The acquisition of *binah* requires strenuous effort to which man may not be equal and for which which he may well lack the strength; for this reason he cannot attain *binah* without the help of God.

השיבנו. No one is immune to sin or error. Therefore it is incumbent upon us to stop repeatedly each day to examine carefully all what we have said or

סְלַח־לָנוּ אָבִינוּ כִּי חָטָאנוּ מְחַל־לָנוּ מַלְכֵּנוּ כִּי
פָשָׁעְנוּ בתענית לצבּר אומרין כאן סליחות כִּי מוֹחֵל וְסוֹלֵחַ אָתָּה ׃
בָּרוּךְ אַתָּה יְיָ חַנּוּן הַמַּרְבֶּה לִסְלוֹחַ ׃

רְאֵה בְעָנְיֵנוּ וְרִיבָה רִיבֵנוּ וּגְאָלֵנוּ מְהֵרָה לְמַעַן שְׁמֶךָ
כִּי גוֹאֵל חָזָק אָתָּה ׃ בָּרוּךְ אַתָּה יְיָ גּוֹאֵל יִשְׂרָאֵל ׃

(נ"ל מוסיף הש"ץ כאן עננו ומסיים בָּרוּךְ אַתָּה יְיָ הָעוֹנֶה בְּעֵת צָרָה׃)

רְפָאֵנוּ יְיָ וְנֵרָפֵא הוֹשִׁיעֵנוּ וְנִוָּשֵׁעָה כִּי תְהִלָּתֵנוּ
אָתָּה ׃ וְהַעֲלֵה רְפוּאָה שְׁלֵמָה לְכָל־מַכּוֹתֵינוּ כִּי אֵל
מֶלֶךְ רוֹפֵא נֶאֱמָן וְרַחֲמָן אָתָּה ׃ בָּרוּךְ אַתָּה יְיָ רוֹפֵא
חוֹלֵי עַמּוֹ יִשְׂרָאֵל ׃

בָּרֵךְ עָלֵינוּ יְיָ אֱלֹהֵינוּ אֶת־הַשָּׁנָה הַזֹּאת וְאֶת־כָּל־
מִינֵי תְבוּאָתָהּ לְטוֹבָה וְתֵן *) (טַל וּמָטָר לְ) בְּרָכָה עַל
פְּנֵי הָאֲדָמָה וְשַׂבְּעֵנוּ מִטּוּבֶךָ וּבָרֵךְ שְׁנָתֵנוּ כַּשָּׁנִים
הַטּוֹבוֹת ׃ בָּרוּךְ אַתָּה יְיָ מְבָרֵךְ הַשָּׁנִים ׃

* Starting from the night of the 59th day after the תקופת תשרי until Pessach
ותן טל ומטר לברכה is added here:

---

done. And if we should find that we have strayed from the right path by trans-
gressing God's Law, or that through omission or neglect, we have failed to
progress in perfecting ourselves for the fulfillment of our duty to God, then
we must seek out again the path of the Law and return to it, and resume
our progress on the road leading to ever more faithful service. Therefore we
seek Divine aid for both our return to God and our progress toward Him.

סליחה, סלח is personal forgiveness granted so that the transgression that
was committed may not permanently blight the relationship of the transgressor
to the one against whom he has sinned. מחילה is objective pardon, the waiver

Forgive us, our Father, for we have sinned; pardon us, our King, for we have transgressed, for You pardon and forgive. Blessed be You *God,* Who is gracious and Who forgives abundantly.

Look upon our affliction, and fight our fight, and redeem us speedily for Your Name's sake, for You are a mighty Redeemer. Blessed be You *God,* the Redeemer of Yisrael.

Heal us, O *God,* and we shall be healed; save us and we shall be saved, for You are our praise. And let perfect healing come to all our ills, for You, O *God* Who reigns as King, are a faithful and compassionate Healer. Blessed be You *God,* Who heals the sick among His people, Yisrael.

Bless for us, O *God* our God, this year, and all the varieties of its produce for the best, and bestow (*dew and rain for) a blessing upon the face of the earth. Satisfy us from Your bounty and bless our year like [other] good years. Blessed be You *God,* Who blesses the years.

---

of the punishment which the transgressor would have deserved. There can be hope for such "forgiveness" or "pardon" only after the transgressor has demonstrated his *teshuvah;* that is, only after he has made amends (as far as possible)' and has solemnly resolved to be more attentive to his duty in the future. Therefore the prayer for *selichah* follows our plea for Divine aid in *teshuvah.*

עַנֵּנוּ. רְאֵה affliction which is not caused by the hostility of others. רִיבֵנוּ the trouble that befalls us as a result of the unjustified conduct of our fellow-men. לְמַעַן שְׁמָךְ; "If our own merits should not be sufficient to justify such deliverance, then, *God,* deliver us for the sake of the loving-kindness and compassion which Your Name assures us."

רְפָאֵנוּ. רְפוּאָה is the restoration to health of the disturbed or handicapped organism, יְשׁוּעָה essentially denotes the granting of new, refreshed and vigorous "being" (יֵשׁ). Either can be obtained only from God. To Him alone praise is due for whatever human skill and knowledge have achieved in the art of healing, for it is He Who endows man with insight and talent to labor in His service and Who determines whether or not man's efforts are to succeed.

בָּרֵךְ עָלֵינוּ. Stress is placed here on both עָלֵינוּ and לְטוֹבָה, for a year may be "blessed" and still not afford blessings to us. Such a year cannot then be a blessed one as far as we are concerned. It is quite possible for the soil to yield abundant produce and the fields to flourish without man benefitting therefrom. As our Sages have put it: הַגֶּפֶן תִּתֵּן פִּרְיָהּ וְהַיַּיִן בְּיוֹקֶר : "the vine may give of its fruit and still the wine may be expensive." Field and pasture may abound with luscious fruit and yet, because of human folly and because of

תְּקַע בְּשׁוֹפָר גָּדוֹל לְחֵרוּתֵנוּ וְשָׂא נֵס לְקַבֵּץ
גָּלְיוֹתֵינוּ וְקַבְּצֵנוּ יַחַד מֵאַרְבַּע כַּנְפוֹת הָאָרֶץ. בָּרוּךְ
אַתָּה יְיָ מְקַבֵּץ נִדְחֵי עַמּוֹ יִשְׂרָאֵל:

הָשִׁיבָה שׁוֹפְטֵינוּ כְּבָרִאשׁוֹנָה וְיוֹעֲצֵינוּ כְּבַתְּחִלָּה
וְהָסֵר מִמֶּנּוּ יָגוֹן וַאֲנָחָה וּמְלֹךְ עָלֵינוּ אַתָּה יְיָ לְבַדְּךָ
בְּחֶסֶד וּבְרַחֲמִים וְצַדְּקֵנוּ בַּמִּשְׁפָּט. בָּרוּךְ אַתָּה יְיָ
מֶלֶךְ אוֹהֵב צְדָקָה וּמִשְׁפָּט:

During the Ten Days of Repentance, say:

הַמֶּלֶךְ הַמִּשְׁפָּט וְאִם לֹא אָמְרוֹ, דַּעַת רוֹב הַפּוֹסְקִים שָׁאֵין צָרִיךְ לַחֲזוֹר.

וְלַמַּלְשִׁינִים אַל־תְּהִי תִקְוָה וְכָל־עוֹשֵׂי רִשְׁעָה
כְּרֶגַע יֹאבֵדוּ וְכֻלָּם מְהֵרָה יִכָּרֵתוּ. וְהַזֵּדִים מְהֵרָה
תְעַקֵּר וּתְשַׁבֵּר וּתְמַגֵּר וְתַכְנִיעַ בִּמְהֵרָה בְיָמֵינוּ.
בָּרוּךְ אַתָּה יְיָ שׁוֹבֵר אֹיְבִים וּמַכְנִיעַ זֵדִים:

---

crookedness and perversity in human relationships, dearth and famine will hold sway and spoil our lives. Therefore we ask God not only to "bless" the fields, but also to arrange circumstances in such a manner that the "blesssed" year may prove a blessing to mankind also, and that the abundant harvest of field and pasture may thus bring happiness and prosperity to the homes of men.

תקע. This is the plea for the גאולה of the entire Jewish community, for whom there can be no חרות while it is in galuth. Its redemption will begin only once all of its members will be gathered together out of this dispersion in order to be reunited. But such a reunion cannot be brought about by human action or even only through the intermediary of human effort; we must wait for God Himself to sound the Shofar. Even as the individual can hope for גאולה, (ראה בעניינו) only after he has first passed through the stages of *da'ath, teshuvah* and *selichah,* so our people can expect collective *geulah* only after all of us have re-acquired for ourselves the only true perspective of things, and after we all will have returned to His Law and to His faithful service so as to be deserving of forgiveness and pardon. Any allegation that deliverance can be obtained by other means than those is nothing but dangerous folly.

Sound the great *Shofar* for our freedom and lift up the banner to gather our exiles, and gather us in from the four ends of the earth. Blessed be You *God*, Who gathers in the dispersed of Your people Yisrael.

Restore our judges as before and our counsellors as at the beginning; remove from us sorrow and sighing, and reign alone over us, O *God*, in lovingkindness and compassion, and justify us in judgment. Blessed be You *God*, King Who loves righteousness and justice. (*During the Ten Days of Repentance, say:* Blessed be You *God*, King, Judge).

And for slanderers let there be no hope, and may all those who do evil perish instantly and may they all speedily cease to be. May You speedily uproot, break, destroy and humble those who do wrong with evil intent, speedily and in our days. Blessed be You *God*, Who breaks enemies and humbles those who do wrong with evil intent.

השיבה and ולמלשינים. These prayers represent the plea for the entire Jewish community. As long as the Jewish national organism is dispersed in exile it is sick. If the Divine Law that is to constitute its very life blood is to be translated into living reality, our people needs leaders, men who will champion the truth and right of God in its midst and who will have the true welfare of their people at heart in all their deliberations. As long as the Jewish people is in exile, it will lack the benefit of the leadership to be provided by such judges and counsellors. Its members, scattered throughout the world, are exposed to corrosive influences which lead them to stray from the paths of Jewish truth and Jewish salvation. This results in a state of affairs which cannot be justified before God's judgment seat and which fills every Jewish heart with sorrow and sadness. We therefore yearn for the time which has been promised us (Isa. 1:26) when, after having reunited us, God will also restore to us the leaders who had originally been ordained to serve as our judges and counsellors. It is under their guidance that we will regain our health as a nation and will unstintingly subordinate every aspect of our communal existence and endeavors to the sovereignty of God. Then it will be possible for Him to reign over us with love and mercy and He will no longer have cause to condemn us when He judges us. The paragraph beginning with *velamalshinim*, which is a prayer for the suppression and elimination of pernicious elements within our people was added at Yavneh during the administration of Rabban Gamaliel at a time when certain elements within the Jewish comunity, who had become estranged from true Judaism, sought by means of crafty calumny and inveiglement to wield such a dangerous influence among

עַל־הַצַּדִּיקִים וְעַל־הַחֲסִידִים וְעַל־זִקְנֵי עַמְּךָ בֵּית
יִשְׂרָאֵל וְעַל־פְּלֵיטַת סוֹפְרֵיהֶם וְעַל גֵּרֵי הַצֶּדֶק וְעָלֵינוּ
יֶהֱמוּ רַחֲמֶיךָ יְיָ אֱלֹהֵינוּ וְתֵן שָׂכָר טוֹב לְכָל הַבּוֹטְחִים
בְּשִׁמְךָ בֶּאֱמֶת וְשִׂים חֶלְקֵנוּ עִמָּהֶם לְעוֹלָם וְלֹא נֵבוֹשׁ
כִּי־בְךָ בָּטָחְנוּ · בָּרוּךְ אַתָּה יְיָ מִשְׁעָן וּמִבְטָח
לַצַּדִּיקִים :

וְלִירוּשָׁלַיִם עִירְךָ בְּרַחֲמִים תָּשׁוּב וְתִשְׁכּוֹן בְּתוֹכָהּ
כַּאֲשֶׁר דִּבַּרְתָּ וּבְנֵה אוֹתָהּ בְּקָרוֹב בְּיָמֵינוּ בִּנְיַן עוֹלָם
וְכִסֵּא דָוִד מְהֵרָה לְתוֹכָהּ תָּכִין · נחם לט״ב. (* בָּרוּךְ
אַתָּה יְיָ בּוֹנֵה יְרוּשָׁלָיִם :

*) בתשעה באב במנחה אומרים זה :

נַחֵם יְיָ אֱלֹהֵינוּ אֶת־אֲבֵלֵי צִיּוֹן · וְאֶת־אֲבֵלֵי יְרוּשָׁלַיִם · וְאֶת־
הָעִיר הָאֲבֵלָה וְהַחֲרֵבָה וְהַבְּזוּיָה וְהַשּׁוֹמֵמָה · הָאֲבֵלָה מִבְּלִי בָנֶיהָ ·
וְהֶחָרֵבָה מִמְּעוֹנוֹתֶיהָ · וְהַבְּזוּיָה מִכְּבוֹדָהּ · וְהַשּׁוֹמֵמָה מֵאֵין
יוֹשֵׁב · וְהִיא יוֹשֶׁבֶת וְרֹאשָׁהּ חָפוּי כְּאִשָּׁה עֲקָרָה שֶׁלֹּא יָלָדָה ·
וַיְבַלְּעוּהָ לִגְיוֹנוֹת · וַיִּירָשׁוּהָ עוֹבְדֵי פְסִילִים · וַיָּטִילוּ אֶת־עַמְּךָ
יִשְׂרָאֵל לֶחָרֶב · וַיַּהַרְגוּ בְזָדוֹן חֲסִידֵי עֶלְיוֹן · עַל־כֵּן צִיּוֹן בְּמַר
תִּבְכֶּה · וִירוּשָׁלַיִם תִּתֵּן קוֹלָהּ · לִבִּי לִבִּי עַל חַלְלֵיהֶם מֵעַי מֵעַי עַל

---

their people that they represented a real threat to the survival of traditional,
Torah-true Judaism. As a result of the addition of this prayer to the petition
for the restoration of the original leadership of the Law, the *Tefillah* today
actually has nineteen blessings instead of eighteen, from which original number
it had derived the title of *Shemone Esrei*.

    עַל הצדיקיםThis is a prayer that corresponds to the individual's entreaty
for *parnassah*. It is voiced by the nation as a whole, beseeching the Lord to

Toward the righteous and toward the devoted, toward the elders of Your people, toward the surviving remnant of their scholars, toward righteous proselytes and toward ourselves, may Your compassion be moved, O *God* our God. Grant a good reward to all those who put their trust in Your Name in truth. Set our portion with them forever, and let us not be deceived when we put our trust in You. Blessed be You *God,* the stay and trust of the righteous.

And to Yerushalayim, Your city, return in compassion, and let Your presence dwell within it, as You have promised. And rebuild it soon, in our days, as an everlasting structure, and speedily establish in it the throne of David. *) Blessed be You *God,* the Builder of Yerushalayim.

---

*)   *During Mincha services on the Ninth of Av, say:*

Comfort, O *God* our God, those who mourn for Tzion and those who mourn for Yerushalayim, and the City, mourning, ruined, despised and desolate—mourning because she is bereft of her children, ruined in her dwellings, despised as contrasted to her former glory, desolate without her inhabitants. And she sits there with her head covered like a barren woman who has not borne children. Legions have devoured her; idolators have deprived her of her inheritance and have put Your people Yisrael to the sword, and have wantonly slain those whose devotion was to the Most High. Therefore Tzion weeps bitterly, and Yerushalayim raises her voice, "O my heart, my

---

preserve and strengthen those elements that constitute the spiritual and moral sustenance of the Jewish national organism: namely, the צדיקים, חסידים, זקנים and סופרים, the learned men who guard and preserve the Holy Writ. It is only after we have prayed for the welfare of these sages that we commend to the sustaining compassion of God the גרי צדק, those proselytes who have embraced Judaism in truth and sincerity, and finally ourselves. ושים חלקנו עמהם: May we ourselves seek and find our own portion in life only in conjunction with those on whom the spiritual and moral survival of Judaism is founded.

ולירושלים Jerusalem is the permanent dwelling-place for the national *geulah* which will be accomplished through קבוץ גליות.

אבלי ציון (נחם:) are those who mourn the destruction of the spiritual sanctuary. אבלי ירושלים are those who grieve at the downfall of the Jewish Commonwealth which was to flourish round about Zion and in which the Law of God that reposed in Zion should have become a living reality.)

אֶת־צֶמַח דָּוִד עַבְדְּךָ מְהֵרָה תַצְמִיחַ וְקַרְנוֹ תָּרוּם
בִּישׁוּעָתֶךָ כִּי לִישׁוּעָתְךָ קִוִּינוּ כָּל־הַיּוֹם ּ בָּרוּךְ אַתָּה
יְיָ מַצְמִיחַ קֶרֶן יְשׁוּעָה:

שְׁמַע קוֹלֵנוּ יְיָ אֱלֹהֵינוּ חוּס וְרַחֵם עָלֵינוּ וְקַבֵּל
בְּרַחֲמִים וּבְרָצוֹן אֶת־תְּפִלָּתֵנוּ כִּי אֵל שׁוֹמֵעַ תְּפִלּוֹת
וְתַחֲנוּנִים אָתָּה ּ וּמִלְּפָנֶיךָ מַלְכֵּנוּ רֵיקָם אַל תְּשִׁיבֵנוּ ּ
(*

אֲלֵיהֶם ּ כִּי אַתָּה יְיָ בָּאֵשׁ הִצַּתָּה ּ וּבָאֵשׁ אַתָּה עָתִיד לִבְנוֹתָהּ
כָּאָמוּר וַאֲנִי אֶהְיֶה־לָּהּ נְאֻם־יְיָ חוֹמַת אֵשׁ סָבִיב ּ וּלְכָבוֹד אֶהְיֶה
בְתוֹכָהּ ּ בָּרוּךְ אַתָּה יְיָ מְנַחֵם צִיּוֹן וּבוֹנֵה יְרוּשָׁלָם: את צמח וכו'

) בתענית צבור במנחה אומרים זה והש״ץ בחזרת התפלה גם בתפלת שחרית קודם ברכת רפאנו:

עֲנֵנוּ יְיָ עֲנֵנוּ ּ בְּיוֹם צוֹם תַּעֲנִיתֵנוּ ּ כִּי בְצָרָה גְדוֹלָה אֲנָחְנוּ ּ
אַל־תֵּפֶן אֶל־רִשְׁעֵנוּ ּ וְאַל־תַּסְתֵּר פָּנֶיךָ מִמֶּנּוּ ּ וְאַל־תִּתְעַלַּם
מִתְּחִנָּתֵנוּ ּ הֱיֵה נָא קָרוֹב לְשַׁוְעָתֵנוּ ּ יְהִי נָא חַסְדְּךָ לְנַחֲמֵנוּ ּ
טֶרֶם נִקְרָא אֵלֶיךָ עֲנֵנוּ ּ כַּדָּבָר שֶׁנֶּאֱמַר וְהָיָה טֶרֶם יִקְרָאוּ וַאֲנִי
אֶעֱנֶה ּ עוֹד הֵם מְדַבְּרִים וַאֲנִי אֶשְׁמָע: כִּי אַתָּה יְיָ הָעוֹנֶה בְּעֵת
צָרָה ּ ּ פּוֹדֶה וּמַצִּיל בְּכָל עֵת צָרָה וְצוּקָה: כי אתה וכו'

את צמח דוד The scion of David will be the permanent standard bearer
of the spiritual and moral *refuah* of the nation which will be brought about by
the restoration of the *shofetim veyo'atzim*, the leaders who will act as judges
and counsellors, in accordance with the promise given in Chapter 11 of the
Book of Isaiah. מצמיח קרן ישועה the "horn" of salvation, which is God's to
give, grows slowly and almost imperceptibly, but all the more constantly
and with ever more enduring strength. For God has said of this son of David
כי הנני מביא את עבדי צמח (Zech. 3:8).

Speedily cause the offspring of David, Your servant, to sprout, so that his horn may be lifted up by Your salvation, for we hope for Your salvation each day. Blessed be You *God,,* Who causes the horn of salvation to grow.

Hear our voice, O *God* our God, spare us and have compassion on us, and accept our prayer in compassion and favor, for You, O God, hear prayers and supplications, and let us not return empty from your, presence our King,*) for You hear the prayer of Your people Yisrael in compassion.Blessed be You *God,* Who hears prayer.

heart, [how it grieves] for their slain; my soul, my soul, [how it yearns] for their slain!" For You, O *God,* did consume her with fire, and with fire will You rebuild her one day, as it is said, "I will be to her, says *God,* a wall of fire round about, and I shall be a glory in her midst." Blessed be You *God,* Comforter of Tzion and Builder of Yerushalayim.

*)   *On Fast Days, during Mincha services, add the following:*

Answer us, O *God,* answer us on this day of renunciation, when we are fasting, for we are in great distress. Turn not to our lawlessness, hide not Your countenance from us, and remove Yourself not from our supplication. O, be near to our cry; let Your loving-kindness be a comfort to us, answer us even before we call to You, as it is said, "It shall come to pass that I will answer before they will call; while they are yet speaking I will hear," for You, O *God,* are He Who answers in time of distress, the Deliverer and Rescuer at all times of distress and woe.

שמע קולנו The essential spiritual and moral "sustenance" of both the individual Jew and the entire Jewish national organism still is, and shall always be *tefillah,* that inner self-refinement, which is accomplished before God through recognition of the truth and through the resolve to do good. We are told that, even after we will be reunited in Zion-Yerushalayim and when the dynasty of David will flourish once more, והביאותים אל הר קדשי ושמחתים בבית תפלתי (Isa. 56:7). It is for this reason that *tefillah* "prayer", constitutes the theme of this final blessing in which we beseech God for favor and, simultaneously, pledge that we will loyally put to the proper use whatever He will grant us. We pray that God may see fit to accept our *tefillah* with *rachamim* and *ratzon*—with *rachamim* as regards our fate and in *ratzon* as regards our endeavors. Whether our prayer takes the form of pure *tefillah,*

כִּי אַתָּה שׁוֹמֵעַ תְּפִלַּת עַמְּךָ יִשְׂרָאֵל בְּרַחֲמִים . בָּרוּךְ
אַתָּה יְיָ שׁוֹמֵעַ תְּפִלָּה:

רְצֵה יְיָ אֱלֹהֵינוּ בְּעַמְּךָ יִשְׂרָאֵל וּבִתְפִלָּתָם . וְהָשֵׁב
אֶת־הָעֲבוֹדָה לִדְבִיר בֵּיתֶךָ וְאִשֵּׁי יִשְׂרָאֵל וּתְפִלָּתָם
בְּאַהֲבָה תְקַבֵּל בְּרָצוֹן וּתְהִי לְרָצוֹן תָּמִיד עֲבוֹדַת
יִשְׂרָאֵל עַמֶּךָ ·

*) יש מתודים וידוי זו קודם כי אתה שומע ·

אָנָּא יְיָ חָטָאתִי עָוִיתִי וּפָשַׁעְתִּי לְפָנֶיךָ מִיּוֹם הֱיוֹתִי עַל הָאֲדָמָה עַד הַיּוֹם
הַזֶּה (וּבִפְרָט בְּחֵטְא. .) אָנָּא יְיָ עֲשֵׂה לְמַעַן שִׁמְךָ הַגָּדוֹל וְתִכְפֹּר לִי עֲוֹנוֹתַי וַחֲטָאַי
וּפְשָׁעַי שֶׁחָטָאתִי וְשֶׁעָוִיתִי וְשֶׁפָּשַׁעְתִּי לְפָנֶיךָ מִנְּעוּרַי עַד הַיּוֹם הַזֶּה וְתַעַזְרֵנִי לָשׁוּב
בִּתְשׁוּבָה שְׁלֵמָה לְפָנֶיךָ: כי אתה שומע וכו'

ויש מתפללים תפלה זו על הפרנסה.

אַתָּה הוּא יְיָ הָאֱלֹהִים הַזָּן וּמְפַרְנֵס וּמְכַלְכֵּל מִקַּרְנֵי רְאֵמִים עַד בֵּיצֵי כִנִּים
הַטְרִיפֵנִי לֶחֶם חֻקִּי וְהַמְצִיא לִי וּלְכָל בְּנֵי בֵיתִי מְזוֹנוֹתַי קֹדֶם שֶׁאֶצְטָרֵךְ לָהֶם
בְּנַחַת וְלֹא בְצַעַר בְּהֶתֵּר וְלֹא בְאִסּוּר לְחַיִּים וּלְשָׁלוֹם מִשֶּׁפַע בְּרָכָה עֶלְיוֹנָה כְּדֵי
שֶׁאוּכַל לַעֲשׂוֹת רְצוֹנֶךָ וְלַעֲסוֹק בְּתוֹרָתֶךָ וּלְקַיֵּם מִצְוֹתֶיךָ וְאַל תַּצְרִיכֵנִי לִידֵי מַתְּנַת
בָּשָׂר וָדָם וִיקֻיַּם בִּי מִקְרָא שֶׁכָּתוּב פּוֹתֵחַ אֶת יָדֶךָ וּמַשְׂבִּיעַ לְכָל חַי רָצוֹן: כי וכו'.

the correction and ennoblement of our souls for its own sake, or that of pertinent *tachanunim*, the correction and ennoblement of our souls in order thus
to make ourselves worthy of having God regard our requests with favor, may
our entreaties not remain "empty" (ריקם) and ineffectual before Him.

(וענני). The original meaning of צום is a kind of gathering that is limited,
hence the term denotes not only fasting, but also a gathering. מדה may also
denote liberation from a confining constraint that is actually justified. הציל
denotes rescue from danger caused by enemies.)

Take pleasure, O *God*, our God in Your people Yisrael and in their prayer. Restore the sacrificial service to the Abode of Your Word in Your House, and accept Yisrael's fire offerings and their prayer with love and favor, and may the service of Your people Yisrael ever be pleasing to You.

רצה The three concluding blessings of the *Shemone Esrei, retzeh, modim, shalom* also form one unit. At the heart of this group of blessings is *hodaah, modim* the avowal of thanksgiving, which, even as the *minchath nesachim* that was added to the daily sacrifice in the Temple, expresses our awareness of the debt of gratitude which we owe God for all our life that He has granted us, with all the wealth, strength and joy that we may acquire while we live. The blessings beginning with רצה and שים שלום were also part of the daily sacrificial service in the Temple. This *Hodaah* is preceded by *retzeh (Avodah)*. There we pray that God be pleased with our devotion to His "service" which should take the form of the fulfillment of our duty in everyday life, a high resolve symbolized in acts of sacrifice and expressed in words of prayer. The *Hodaah* is followed by the prayer for *shalom*, peace, which, as the Sages put it, is the "vessel that gathers and preserves within itself all of life's blessings." The order in which these three concluding blessings are arranged expresses a most profound thought: The prayer for *shalom* does not come first, but last of all; even as there can be no *hodaah* without *avodah*, so, too, without both *hodaah* and *avodah* there can be no *shalom*. Our *shalom* can have value for our people only if it is attained through united thanksgiving and united devotion to the service of the Law of God, and any kind of thanksgiving that is not preceded by a pledge of devotion to that service is nothing but blasphemy.

בעמך ישראל ובתפלתם. רצה God is entreated to take pleasure *first* in עמך ישראל and only *then* in תפלתם. This is to teach us that we may hope for God's acceptance of our prayers only if our own lives and endeavors are not unworthy of His favor, or if, at least, we make a sincere effort to have our lives and our endeavors become worthy of Him. But the hoped-for effect of our prayers as regards the sanctification of our personalities and of our aspirations can be attained in full only once our Divine service will be restored to the Abode of God's Word in Zion, and when verbal prayer will serve only as an accompaniment for the symbolic acts of sacrificial offering upon the fire of God's altar which symbolizes the Law of God. Our eyes are turned in prayer to the place in Zion where the *Shechinah* dwelt once long ago, where the Law of God reposed beneath the wings of Cherubim, the place to which God promised that He would one day cause His *Shechinah* to return. This site in Zion, though now desolate, remains the rallying point, invisible but yet sufficiently strong and mighty to draw to itself the hearts of all the

On Rosh Chodesh and the Intermediate Days of Festivals say:

אֱלֹהֵינוּ וֵאלֹהֵי אֲבוֹתֵינוּ · יַעֲלֶה וְיָבֹא וְיַגִּיעַ וְיֵרָאֶה וְיֵרָצֶה וְיִשָּׁמַע
וְיִפָּקֵד וְיִזָּכֵר זִכְרוֹנֵנוּ וּפִקְדוֹנֵנוּ וְזִכְרוֹן אֲבוֹתֵינוּ · וְזִכְרוֹן מָשִׁיחַ בֶּן
דָּוִד עַבְדֶּךָ · וְזִכְרוֹן יְרוּשָׁלַיִם עִיר קָדְשֶׁךָ · וְזִכְרוֹן כָּל עַמְּךָ בֵּית
יִשְׂרָאֵל לְפָנֶיךָ · לִפְלֵיטָה וּלְטוֹבָה וּלְחֵן וּלְחֶסֶד וּלְרַחֲמִים וּלְחַיִּים
וּלְשָׁלוֹם בְּיוֹם לר״ח רֹאשׁ הַחֹדֶשׁ לפסח חַג הַמַּצּוֹת · לסכות חַג הַסֻּכּוֹת
הַזֶּה · זָכְרֵנוּ יְיָ אֱלֹהֵינוּ בּוֹ לְטוֹבָה וּפָקְדֵנוּ בוֹ לִבְרָכָה וְהוֹשִׁיעֵנוּ בוֹ
לְחַיִּים · וּבִדְבַר יְשׁוּעָה וְרַחֲמִים · חוּס וְחָנֵּנוּ וְרַחֵם עָלֵינוּ
וְהוֹשִׁיעֵנוּ · כִּי אֵלֶיךָ עֵינֵינוּ · כִּי אֵל מֶלֶךְ חַנּוּן וְרַחוּם אָתָּה:
וְתֶחֱזֶינָה עֵינֵינוּ בְּשׁוּבְךָ לְצִיּוֹן בְּרַחֲמִים · בָּרוּךְ
אַתָּה יְיָ הַמַּחֲזִיר שְׁכִינָתוֹ לְצִיּוֹן:

dispersed sons and daughters of our people who have remained loyal to God
and to His Law. This is the place which will remain the eternal fount of
inspired homage to God and His Law for all our future generations. "Even
the desolate site of our Sanctuary remains a throne of glory, of a grandeur
and might much greater than that of the original Temple" (Jer. 17:12). Now
we solemnly pledge to demonstrate our confidence in the eternal significance
of Zion and our constant expectation of its resurrection by living a life borne
by the spirit of Zion and devoted to the service of the Lord.

אוי״א יעלה Our *Mo'adim* commemorate the extraordinary events in our
history which demonstrated the particular concern of Divine Providence in
the establishment and survival of our nation. Our days of Rosh Chodesh regularly come to remind us that God is also constantly near, even in the course
of ordinary day-to-day living. On these Festivals, then, we insert into the
regular order of *Birkath Avodah* a prayer that our fate as a nation may be
of immediate concern to the loving and compassionate insight of Divine Providence on those "days of commemoration, appointed for communion with
God." According to the account in the Book of Numbers (10:10) all the
temidim and *musafim* were accompanied by the sounding of the *chatzotzeroth*
which, according to Verse 9 ibid. were meant to be a symbolic expression of
our cry to God for help. Accordingly, we are told in Verse 10 with reference
to the *chatzotzeroth* which accompanied the communal offerings: והיו לכם
לזכרון לפני אלקים. Our present prayer beginning with *Ya'aleh veyavo* utters

On Rosh Chodesh and the Intermediate Days of Festivals say:

Our God and God of our fathers, may our remembrance and the consideration of us and the remembrance of our fathers, the remembrance of Messiah the son of David Your servant, the remembrance of Yerushalayim, Your holy City, and the remembrance of all Your people, the House of Yisrael, rise and come, reach You and be seen, be accepted and heard, considered and remembered for deliverance and for well-being, for favor and loving-kindness, for compassion, for life and for peace on this day of —The New Moon —The Festival of Unleavened Bread —the Festival of Tabernacles. Remember us this day, O *God* our God, for good, be mindful of us for blessing, and save us for life; and in the promise of salvation and compassion spare us and favor us, for our eyes look up to You; for You, O God, are a gracious and compassionate King.

And may our eyes behold Your return to Tzion in compassion. Blessed be You *God*, Who restores Your Presence to Tzion.

---

in words that same thought which was symbolized by the sound of the *chatzotzeroth* in the Temple, with the one difference, however, that while the *chatzotzeroth* were sounded each day, *Ya'aleh veyavo* is recited only on Rosh Chodesh and on Festivals. זכר is "to remember", while פקד means "to consider", or "to be mindful". זכרון denotes personal remembrance, the remembrance of a person and the relationship of that person to him who remembers. פקדון, on the other hand, is the mindfulness and the consideration of the fate which is to be visited upon, or decreed for another. We now pray as follows, "May both our personal life and our fate *be raised beyond* the ordinary course of earthly things (יעלה); may they *come* to be matters of your special concern (ויבא). ויגיע May that which may stand in the way of their special acceptance not hinder them from *reaching* You. ויראה: May they be *viewed* favorably for what they are in themselves, and וירצה: may they not be found entirely unworthy of God's *favor*. May the course of our life and fate also be evaluated in accordance with the impact that they have upon our souls. וישמע: May God *hear* the thoughts and emotions which they stir up within us, and, accordingly, may He remember us and be mindful of our prayers to give them favorable consideration." זכרון אבותינו denotes the past, from which we derive the covenant made by God with our ancestors; זכרון משיח indicates the future linked with the promise of the restoration of the dynasty of David. זכרון ירושלים refers to our own present day, in which Yerushalayim and its ruins hopefully await the time when they can truly fulfill their destiny as the Holy City of God.

מודים דרבנן

מוֹדִים אֲנַחְנוּ לָךְ שָׁאַתָּה הוּא יְיָ
אֱלֹהֵינוּ וֵאלֹהֵי אֲבוֹתֵינוּ לְעוֹלָם
וָעֶד· צוּר חַיֵּינוּ
מָגֵן יִשְׁעֵנוּ אַתָּה
הוּא לְדוֹר וָדוֹר·
נוֹדֶה לְךָ וּנְסַפֵּר
תְּהִלָּתֶךָ·

מוֹדִים אֲנַחְנוּ לָךְ שָׁאַתָּה הוּא יְיָ
אֱלֹהֵינוּ וֵאלֹהֵי אֲבוֹתֵינוּ אֱלֹהֵי כָל בָּשָׂר
יוֹצְרֵנוּ יוֹצֵר בְּרֵאשִׁית· בְּרָכוֹת וְהוֹדָאוֹת
לְשִׁמְךָ הַגָּדוֹל וְהַקָּדוֹשׁ עַל שֶׁהֶחֱיִיתָנוּ
וְקִיַּמְתָּנוּ· כֵּן תְּחַיֵּנוּ וּתְקַיְּמֵנוּ וְתֶאֱסוֹף
גָּלֻיּוֹתֵינוּ לְחַצְרוֹת קָדְשֶׁךָ לִשְׁמוֹר חֻקֶּיךָ
וְלַעֲשׂוֹת רְצוֹנֶךָ וּלְעָבְדְּךָ בְּלֵבָב שָׁלֵם· עַל
שֶׁאֲנַחְנוּ מוֹדִים לָךְ· בָּרוּךְ אֵל הַהוֹדָאוֹת:

עַל חַיֵּינוּ הַמְּסוּרִים בְּיָדֶךָ וְעַל נִשְׁמוֹתֵינוּ הַפְּקוּדוֹת לָךְ
וְעַל נִסֶּיךָ שֶׁבְּכָל־יוֹם עִמָּנוּ וְעַל נִפְלְאוֹתֶיךָ וְטוֹבוֹתֶיךָ
שֶׁבְּכָל־עֵת· עֶרֶב וָבֹקֶר וְצָהֳרָיִם· הַטּוֹב כִּי לֹא־כָלוּ
רַחֲמֶיךָ וְהַמְרַחֵם כִּי לֹא־תַמּוּ חֲסָדֶיךָ מֵעוֹלָם
קִוִּינוּ לָךְ:

מודים   The blessings that went before look to the future. They are prayers for the bestowal of the many gifts and favors that will serve to sustain and further our lives both as individuals and as members of the Jewish people. The *birkath hodaah*, beginning with *modim*, reminds us of the great debt of gratitude which we owe to our Maker even now for all the things which He has given us in the past and for all the favors that we still receive at every moment of the present. תודה, הודאה is not mere verbal thanksgiving. Derived from the ידה, from which is also derived יד, the Hebrew for "hand", it actually means "to give God one's hand"; that is, to devote all the activities of our lives to the fulfillment of His will. It is homage deriving from our awareness of what we owe him, an acknowledgment of our debt of gratitude. In fact, our "hand" *belongs* to God for it is from Him alone that we have whatever strength and ability we possess. To be part of Israel means to "sign our hand over to God" יכתב ידו לה' ובשם ישראל יכנה (Isa. 44:5). Hence we avow it to Him that He is our God now even as He was the God of our fathers in the past, and that He proves Himself as such to us at all times. He is צור, the Creator, the Shaper and the firm Support of our lives, and the

We gratefully avow to You that You, O *God,* are our God and the God of our fathers in all eternity. You are the Rock of our life, the Shield of our salvation from generation to generation. We avow our thanks to You and recount Your praise, for our lives, which are committed to Your hand, and for our souls which are in Your care, and for Your miracles which are with us each day, and for Your wondrous deeds and favors that are performed at all times, evening, morning and noon. You are the Beneficient One, for Your compassion has never ceased, the Compassionate One, for Your kindnesses have never ended. Ever have we placed our hopes in You.

מודים דרבנן

We gratefully avow to You, that You, O *God,* are our God and the God of our fathers, the God of all flesh, our Creator and the Creator of the Beginning. Blessings and thanks to Your great and holy Name because You have kept us alive and have preserved us. So may You continue to keep us in life and preserve us, and gather our dispersed to the Courts of Your Sanctuary, to keep Your statutes, to do Your will and to serve You wholeheartedly. For our very act of avowal to You, be You blessed, God of thanksgivings.

Protector of whatever ישע true, genuine "being" we may have. The phrase ערב ובקר וצהרים refers not to God's "wondrous deeds and favors" but to נודה לך. Whether the day is on the wane, whether it is on the rise or whether it shines at bright noontide, we make our avowal to Him, proclaiming that His creation, His work and His rule (תהלתי) are revealed in all things that happen, that our lives are committed to His hand, that our souls are secure in His care and that we ourselves experience נסים ונפלאות and טובות from Him each day and at every moment. Every breath we take is a gift of His special care, His *hashgachah peratith.* Everything that happens to us, even though we may consider it to be a calamity at the time is actually *tovah,* "goodness". He is always the Beneficient One, for His *rachamim,* His fatherly compassion toward us has no limits; He sets no bounds to His רחמים, and He practices it at all times, because His חסדים, His kindnessses are inexhaustible He bestows them upon us at all times, even when we are not actually aware of them. It is for this reason that we have always reposed our hopes and our trust in Him from the very beginning.

On Chanukkah and Purim add:

עַל הַנִּסִּים וְעַל הַפֻּרְקָן וְעַל הַגְּבוּרוֹת וְעַל הַתְּשׁוּעוֹת וְעַל
הַמִּלְחָמוֹת שֶׁעָשִׂיתָ לַאֲבוֹתֵינוּ בַּיָּמִים הָהֵם בַּזְּמַן הַזֶּה :

לחנוכה.

בִּימֵי מַתִּתְיָהוּ בֶן יוֹחָנָן כֹּהֵן גָּדוֹל
חַשְׁמוֹנַאי וּבָנָיו · כְּשֶׁעָמְדָה מַלְכוּת
יָוָן הָרְשָׁעָה עַל-עַמְּךָ יִשְׂרָאֵל לְהַשְׁכִּיחָם
תּוֹרָתֶךָ וּלְהַעֲבִירָם מֵחֻקֵּי רְצוֹנֶךָ :
וְאַתָּה בְּרַחֲמֶיךָ הָרַבִּים עָמַדְתָּ לָהֶם
בְּעֵת צָרָתָם, רַבְתָּ אֶת-רִיבָם דַּנְתָּ אֶת-
דִּינָם נָקַמְתָּ אֶת-נִקְמָתָם מָסַרְתָּ
גִבּוֹרִים בְּיַד חַלָּשִׁים וְרַבִּים בְּיַד מְעַטִּים
וּטְמֵאִים בְּיַד טְהוֹרִים וּרְשָׁעִים בְּיַד

לפורים.

בִּימֵי מָרְדְּכַי וְאֶסְתֵּר
בְּשׁוּשַׁן הַבִּירָה כְּשֶׁעָמַד
עֲלֵיהֶם הָמָן הָרָשָׁע ·
בִּקֵּשׁ לְהַשְׁמִיד לַהֲרֹג
וּלְאַבֵּד אֶת-כָּל-
הַיְּהוּדִים מִנַּעַר וְעַד-
זָקֵן טַף וְנָשִׁים בְּיוֹם
אֶחָד בִּשְׁלוֹשָׁה עָשָׂר
לְחֹדֶשׁ שְׁנֵים-עָשָׂר

מודים דרבנן. הודאה, the avowal of thanksgiving constitutes so basic a principle in our relationship to God that the compilers of our prayer book did not deem it sufficient merely to have the congregation signify its assent by saying "Amen" at the end of the *Hodaah* recited aloud by the Reader. Instead they ordained that while the Reader bows and begins to recite the *Hodaah*, the congregation, too, should bow and recite its own *Modim* jointly with the Reader's *Hodaah*. מודים אנחנו לך וגו' על שאנחנו מודים לך: "We thank You for the very fact that we make this avowal of gratitude to You." We sense the infinite debt of gratitude which we owe our God for having caused us to become aware of how very much we are beholden to Him. That על שאנחנו מודים לך and מודים אנחנו לך should be construed as one sentence is indicated to us in Sota 40a. For this *modim* is a composite of the texts used by the various *chachamim* for their avowals of thanksgiving. (It is for this reason that it is called מודים דרבנן.) But the basic device of all these avowals of gratitude is the same; namely *modim*, etc. על שאנחנו מודים לך.

על הנסים There are in the Jewish year two festivals which serve to commemorate the miraculous manner in which God intervened in behalf of our people even after it had lost its political independence. These are Chanukka, in memory of God's miraculous action in behalf of the preservation

On Chanukkah and Purim add:

For the miracles, for the deliverance, for the mighty acts, for the victories and for the battles which You performed for our fathers in those days at this season.

<table>
<tr><td>

On Chanukkah:

In the days of Matithyahu, the son of Yochanan the High Priest, the Hasmonean and his sons, when the despotic kingdom of Greece rose up against Your people Yisrael to make them forget Your Law and to lead them astray from the statutes of Your will. But You in Your great compassion stood by them at the time of their distress. You championed their cause, defended their rights and avenged their wrong. You delivered the strong into the hands of the weak, the many into the hands of the few, the lawless into the hands of the just, the

</td><td>

On Purim:

In the days of Mordechai and Esther, in the capital city of Shushan, when Haman the tyrant rose up against them, and sought to exterminate, slaughter and destroy all the Jews, young and old, infants and women, in one day, on the thirteenth of the twelfth month which is the month of Adar, and to take their wealth as booty. But You in Your abundant compassion thwarted his plan and frustrated his intention, and caused that which he sought to do to recoil on his own head; and they hanged him and his sons upon the gallows.

</td></tr>
</table>

---

of our spiritual values, and Purim, on which we celebrate His intervention which ensured our physical survival. On these two holidays, we add to our regular *Hodaah* the portion beginning with *al hanisim* to express our special gratitude for the direct action of God in behalf of our survival, both physical and spiritual, which we have experienced in our history. In full awareness of what we owe Him, we here give thanks to God על הנסים for the obvious acts of intervention of His Divine Providence, ועל הפרקן, for our liberation from every other power in general, and from the yoke of human tyranny in particular, which was the immediate result of our miraculous rescue each time, ועל הגבורות ועל התשועות for the mighty acts and the victories, but particularly על המלחמות for the battles from which He has allowed us to emerge victorious. For it was through these battles which we had to fight for their preservation that we have truly come to appreciate and treasure the values which had been in such grave danger. Our Sages say מצוה שמסרו ישראל עצמן עליהן למיתה בשעת גזירות המלכות that every *mitzvah* for the fulfillment of which the Jews have

הוּא־חֹדֶשׁ אֲדָר וְשָׁלַל	צַדִּיקִים וְזֵדִים בְּיַד עוֹסְקֵי תוֹרָתֶךָ:
לְבוֹז: וְאַתָּה בְּרַחֲמֶיךָ	וּלְךָ עָשִׂיתָ שֵׁם גָּדוֹל וְקָדוֹשׁ בְּעוֹלָמֶךָ
הָרַבִּים הֵפַרְתָּ אֶת־עֲצָתוֹ	וּלְעַמְּךָ יִשְׂרָאֵל עָשִׂיתָ תְּשׁוּעָה גְדוֹלָה
וְקִלְקַלְתָּ אֶת־מַחֲשַׁבְתּוֹ	וּפֻרְקָן כְּהַיּוֹם הַזֶּה: וְאַחַר כֵּן בָּאוּ
וַהֲשֵׁבוֹתָ גְּמוּלוֹ בְּרֹאשׁוֹ	בָנֶיךָ לִדְבִיר בֵּיתֶךָ וּפִנּוּ אֶת־הֵיכָלֶךָ
וְתָלוּ אֹתוֹ וְאֶת־בָּנָיו עַל	וְטִהֲרוּ אֶת־מִקְדָּשֶׁךָ וְהִדְלִיקוּ נֵרוֹת
הָעֵץ:	בְּחַצְרוֹת קָדְשֶׁךָ וְקָבְעוּ שְׁמוֹנַת יְמֵי
	חֲנֻכָּה אֵלּוּ לְהוֹדוֹת וּלְהַלֵּל לְשִׁמְךָ
	הַגָּדוֹל:

---

had to pay with their heart's blood in times of persecution עדיין היא מוחזקת בידן becomes firmly entrenched within their hearts for all time to come. (Sabbath 130a). It was only as a result of the persecution we have suffered that we have come to appreciate even our physical survival as a gracious gift of that special Divine Providence which has understood how to help us survive all the fanatical excesses of the mobs of the nations as the one immortal nation in world history.

בימי מתתיהו. חנוכה, One hundred and fifty years prior to the destruction of the Second Temple. מלכות יון refers to the Graeco-Syrian empire of Antiochus Epiphanes. להשכיחם תורתך ולהעבירם מחקי רצונך The knowledge of the Torah which contains God's Law is the first prerequisite for the fulfillment of that Law. This the enemies of Torah-true Judaism have known at all times, and for this reason their chief efforts were aimed at the exclusion of the teaching of Torah from the training of the young and at the suppression of its study by the old, for they knew that once the Law would no longer be taught or studied in Yisrael, it would be an easy thing for them to induce the Jews to transgress it. But the Greeks attempted to use force as well to compel the Jews to abandon their Law. ריבם refers to the justified resistance offered by the Jews to the unjustified demands of the enemy. דינם denotes their sacred right to freedom of conscience. נקמתם refers to the vengeance exacted from their adversaries for the violation of their human rights.

The terms: זדים, and רשעים, טמאים refer to Jews who had forsaken the Law and had taken the side of the Greeks. They preferred טומאה, the immorality which titillated their senses to the moral purity required by Judaism, and they chose רשעה lawless unrestraint in preference to the path of loyalty to duty which requires the Jew to stop at every step to examine his actions in

wanton sinners into the hands of the diligent pursuers of Your Law. And for Yourself You made a great and holy Name in Your world, and for Your people Yisrael You worked a great victory and liberation even as this day. Thereafter Your sons came to the Abode of Your Word in Your House, they cleansed the Abode of Your Power, purified Your Sanctuary and kindled lights in Your holy Courts and instituted these eight days of Chanukkah for avowing thanks and rendering praise to Your great Name.

---

the light of the standards set by the Law. They consciously and deliberately (בזדון) sought to bring about the cessation of the study and observance of Jewish Law (the term עשק התורה includes both study and observance in its meaning). They therefore not only viewed the actions of the Greeks with favor but actually aided and abetted them. ואחר כן, "thereafter." It was only after they had wrested from the foe the right to reestablish their undisturbed, dutiful observance of the Law which was to govern both their family and communal life outside the Temple walls, that the sons of Yisrael began the work of cleansing and reconsecrating the Temple itself. For if the Law which reposes in the דביר, the Holy of Holies, and from which the entire Sanctuary derives its true sanctity, should have no place within the hearts and lives of the people outside, then the whole Temple with all its consecration would serve no purpose whatever. בחצרות קדשך ; in the environs of the Temple, in the houses of the city which were grouped around the Temple that was their focal point. The true Chanukkah lights are not the lamps which flicker in the Menorah in the היכל nor even those that are to be kindled in every Jewish home. The lights that burned in the Temple had been either extinguished or desecrated by Greek violence. It was only in one home, in the house of Matith-yahu, that the light of true Judaism remained pure and bright, and strong enough to kindle the same light also within the hearts of his brethren and to make it shine again in all their homes. It was only thanks to this one light that it was possible to rekindle the Divine light, pure and permanent, also in the Temple. This was a truth to be remembered forever, a truth which God ultimately confirmed for all subsequent generations through His miraculous might as evidenced by the miracle of the one remaining cruse of pure oil. להודות ולהלל The chief observance of Chanukkah that is required of us is thanksgiving. But first the value which the miracle of Chanukkah preserved for us, namely the possibility to study and to fulfill the Law, must become so dear to us that our avowal of gratitude to God for its preservation must come from the very depths of our hearts. It is only once we have attained this stage that we may, and should, praise the greatness of God as demonstrated by His mighty acts. But if these spiritual treasures should ever cease to have

וְעַל־כֻּלָּם יִתְבָּרֵךְ וְיִתְרוֹמֵם שִׁמְךָ מַלְכֵּנוּ תָּמִיד לְעוֹלָם וָעֶד:

During the Ten Days of Repentance, say:

וּכְתוֹב לְחַיִּים טוֹבִים כָּל־בְּנֵי בְרִיתֶךָ:

וְכֹל הַחַיִּים יוֹדוּךָ סֶּלָה וִיהַלְלוּ אֶת־שִׁמְךָ בֶּאֱמֶת הָאֵל יְשׁוּעָתֵנוּ וְעֶזְרָתֵנוּ סֶלָה · בָּרוּךְ אַתָּה יְיָ הַטּוֹב שִׁמְךָ וּלְךָ נָאֶה לְהוֹדוֹת:

בשחרית ומוסף, ובתענית צבור אף במנחה אומר הש״ץ א׳׳א ברכנו, וא׳׳א בבית אבל.

אֱלֹהֵינוּ וֵאלֹהֵי אֲבוֹתֵינוּ בָּרְכֵנוּ בַּבְּרָכָה הַמְשֻׁלֶּשֶׁת בַּתּוֹרָה הַכְּתוּבָה עַל־יְדֵי מֹשֶׁה עַבְדֶּךָ הָאֲמוּרָה מִפִּי אַהֲרֹן וּבָנָיו כֹּהֲנִים עַם קְדוֹשֶׁךָ כָּאָמוּר: יְבָרֶכְךָ יְיָ וְיִשְׁמְרֶךָ: יָאֵר יְיָ פָּנָיו אֵלֶיךָ וִיחֻנֶּךָּ: יִשָּׂא יְיָ פָּנָיו אֵלֶיךָ וְיָשֵׂם לְךָ שָׁלוֹם:

בשחרית שים שלום (ובתענית צבור אף במנחה).   במנחה ובערבית שלום רב.

שָׁלוֹם רָב עַל־	שִׂים שָׁלוֹם טוֹבָה וּבְרָכָה חֵן
יִשְׂרָאֵל עַמְּךָ תָּשִׂים	וָחֶסֶד וְרַחֲמִים עָלֵינוּ וְעַל כָּל
לְעוֹלָם כִּי אַתָּה	יִשְׂרָאֵל עַמֶּךָ בָּרְכֵנוּ אָבִינוּ
הוּא מֶלֶךְ אָדוֹן	כֻּלָּנוּ כְּאֶחָד בְּאוֹר פָּנֶיךָ כִּי
לְכָל־הַשָּׁלוֹם · וְטוֹב	בְאוֹר פָּנֶיךָ נָתַתָּ לָּנוּ יְיָ אֱלֹהֵינוּ
בְּעֵינֶיךָ לְבָרֵךְ	תּוֹרַת חַיִּים וְאַהֲבַת חֶסֶד
	וּצְדָקָה וּבְרָכָה וְרַחֲמִים וְחַיִּים
	וְשָׁלוֹם · וְטוֹב בְּעֵינֶיךָ לְבָרֵךְ

אֶת־עַמְּךָ יִשְׂרָאֵל בְּכָל־עֵת וּבְכָל־שָׁעָה בִּשְׁלוֹמֶךָ:

meaning for us, then the songs of praise we sing on Chanukkah would also be utterly meaningless. It is for this reason that we add *Al hanisim* to the *Hodaah* in the *Shemone Esrei* as well as in the Grace after Meals. And the national refrain that has served as our guiding motto throughout the centuries is not הודו לה׳ כי טוב but הללו את ה׳ כי טוב.

For all this, Our King, may Your Name be continually blessed and exalted for all eternity.

During the Ten Days of Repentance add:

And inscribe all the sons of Your covenant for a good life.

And everything that lives shall avow thanks to You and render praise to Your Name in truth as the God of our salvation and our help forever. Blessed be You *God,* the Beneficent One is Your Name, and to You thanksgiving is due.

When the Shemone Esrei is repeated, the Reader recites the following:

Our God and God of our fathers, bless us with the threefold blessing in the Torah, which was written by the hand of Moshe Your servant and spoken through the mouth of Aharon and his sons, the priests, Your holy people, as it is said: "May *God* bless you and keep you. May *God* light up His countenance for you and favor you. May *God* turn His countenance toward you and establish peace for you."

During Morning Prayers say:

Establish peace, well-being and blessing, favor, loving-kindness and compassion upon us and upon all of Yisrael, Your people. Bless us, O our Father, all of us together, with the light of Your countenance. For by the light of Your countenance

At Mincha and Evening Services say:

Establish p e a c e abundant upon Your people Yisrael forever, for You, O King, are the Lord of all peace, and may it be good in Your sight to bless Your people Yisrael at all times and at every hour with Your peace.

You have given us, O *God* our God, the Torah of life and the love of devotion and loyalty to duty, blessing and compassion, life and peace. May it be good in Your sight to bless Your people Yisrael at all times and at every hour with Your peace.

פורים. בימי מרדכי, The paragraph commemorating the event that is celebrated by Purim is much briefer than the one recited on Chanukkah, for its subject matter, too, is brief and simple. The danger which threatened the Jewish people at this time was obvious; it was the physical extermination of all Jews together with their wives and children. A full account of this historic episode has been preserved for us in the Book of Esther so that further elaboration is not needed. המן הרשע It is interesting to note that this prototype of all future planned anti-Semitic campaigns, too, had originated not within the

During the Days of Repentance add :

בְּסֵפֶר חַיִּים בְּרָכָה וְשָׁלוֹם וּפַרְנָסָה טוֹבָה נִזָּכֵר וְנִכָּתֵב לְפָנֶיךָ אֲנַחְנוּ וְכָל עַמְּךָ בֵּית יִשְׂרָאֵל לְחַיִּים טוֹבִים וּלְשָׁלוֹם · בָּרוּךְ אַתָּה יְיָ עוֹשֵׂה הַשָּׁלוֹם :

בָּרוּךְ אַתָּה יְיָ הַמְבָרֵךְ אֶת־עַמּוֹ יִשְׂרָאֵל בַּשָּׁלוֹם :

אֱלֹהַי · נְצוֹר לְשׁוֹנִי מֵרָע וּשְׂפָתַי מִדַּבֵּר מִרְמָה וְלִמְקַלְלַי נַפְשִׁי תִדּוֹם וְנַפְשִׁי כֶּעָפָר לַכֹּל תִּהְיֶה : פְּתַח לִבִּי בְּתוֹרָתֶךָ וּבְמִצְוֹתֶיךָ תִּרְדּוֹף נַפְשִׁי וְכָל הַחוֹשְׁבִים עָלַי רָעָה מְהֵרָה הָפֵר עֲצָתָם וְקַלְקֵל מַחֲשַׁבְתָּם · עֲשֵׂה לְמַעַן שְׁמֶךָ · עֲשֵׂה לְמַעַן יְמִינֶךָ · עֲשֵׂה לְמַעַן קְדֻשָּׁתֶךָ · עֲשֵׂה לְמַעַן תּוֹרָתֶךָ · לְמַעַן יֵחָלְצוּן יְדִידֶיךָ הוֹשִׁיעָה יְמִינְךָ וַעֲנֵנִי : יִהְיוּ לְרָצוֹן אִמְרֵי־פִי וְהֶגְיוֹן לִבִּי לְפָנֶיךָ יְיָ צוּרִי וְגוֹאֲלִי : עֹשֶׂה שָׁלוֹם בִּמְרוֹמָיו הוּא יַעֲשֶׂה שָׁלוֹם עָלֵינוּ וְעַל כָּל יִשְׂרָאֵל וְאִמְרוּ אָמֵן :

Gentile populace itself but had been put into motion by the influence of one evil individual. It has ever been thus. Throughout our history, the mobs that have atacked us never did so spontaneously but turned upon us only after they had been incited by evil men who knew how to stir up base animal passions in the hearts of the masses.

וכל החיים And even as we ourselves have come to know our God and to thank Him, so may our own persevering acknowledgement of Him and the demonstrations of His power in all the events which come to pass with His help and His salvation in our own history, teach all the rest of mankind too, to give thanks to Him and to recognize Him in truth.

שים שלום In Lev. 9:22 we read that, after having completed the *Avodah*, Aharon lifted up his hands and blessed the people. In like manner, his descendants, the *Kohanim*, uttered the ברכת כהנים prescribed in Num. 6:23–26 after having performed the *Avodah* in the Temple. In our own day, whenever the ceremony of נשיאת כפים takes place, it is performed just before *Sim shalom*, and immediately following the *Avodah* which had been completed by the *Hodaah*. If the ceremony cannot be performed, the pertinent precept is mentioned by the Reader in אוא ברכנו. The *Birkath kohanim* concludes with the phrase וישם לך שלום. This blessing, which looks to the eventual establishment of universal, permanent peace is then given in detail in *Sim shalom*. There

(During the Days of Repentance add): May we be remembered and in-scribed before You in the Book of life, blessing, peace and good sus-tenance, we and all Your people, the House of Yisrael, for a good life and for peace. Blessed be You *God*, the Creator of Peace.

Blessed be You *God*, Who blesses Your people Yisrael with peace.

My God, guard my tongue from evil and my lips from speaking falsehood. Let my soul be silent to those who curse me, and let my soul be as the dust to all things. Open my heart to Your Torah, and may my soul earnestly strive after Your commandments. But as for all those who plot evil against me, thwart their counsel and frustrate their intentions. Do it for the sake of Your Name, do it for the sake of Your right hand, do it for the sake of Your Torah; therefore set free those whom You have found worthy of Your love. Let Your right hand be seen in salvation and answer me! May the words of my mouth and the meditation of my heart be pleasing before Your countenance, O *God*, my Rock and my Redeemer.

May He Who makes peace in His high places make peace for us and for all of Yisrael, and say, Amen.

---

we pray that, in addition to all the gifts and favors for which we implored Him and which, if granted, we pledge to employ for good purposes, God may establish peace in our midst. Many and varied are the conflicts with our fellow-men in which we may be involved through the gifts and favors granted us by God and in our efforts to use them in a manner that is in accordance with our duty. At times it is incumbent upon us to demonstrate our desire for peace by voluntarily renouncing certain rights and possessions. But there are some rights and values which it is not within our power to relinquish, and for this reason we must look to the blessed help of God to enable us to enjoy peace even while fulfilling with unswerving steadfastness the requirements of His Law of life. We pray, therefore, that God may "establish peace for us"; that is, that He may grant us peace, and firmly establish and preserve it in our midst. "Bless all of us together," we pray, באור פניך "so that we may see Your countenance, recognize Your rule, and come to know the goals of Your Providence and the ends which it is Your wish that we fulfill."

כאחד Once this light will enlighten us all *equally*, once we will all be of one mind in the recognition of God and of what is pleasing in His sight, then the peaceful harmony of life will be a natural outgrowth of this unity of conviction and endeavor. For through this enlightenment all of us are given

יְהִי רָצוֹן לְפָנֶיךָ יְיָ אֱלֹהֵינוּ וֵאלֹהֵי אֲבוֹתֵינוּ שֶׁיִּבָּנֶה

בֵּית הַמִּקְדָּשׁ בִּמְהֵרָה בְיָמֵינוּ וְתֵן חֶלְקֵנוּ בְּתוֹרָתֶךָ:

וְשָׁם נַעֲבָדְךָ בְּיִרְאָה כִּימֵי עוֹלָם וּכְשָׁנִים קַדְמוֹנִיּוֹת:

וְעָרְבָה לַיָי מִנְחַת יְהוּדָה וִירוּשָׁלָם כִּימֵי עוֹלָם וּכְשָׁנִים קַדְמוֹנִיּוֹת:

הש״ץ חוזר התפלה בקול ואומר מתחלה אדני שפתי תפתח בלחש.

*On Rosh Chodesh, Chanukkah and on the Intermediate Days of Festivals,
the Hallel is recited here. During the Ten Days of Repentance*
אבינו מלכנו *is said here.* (p. 628)

Whoever takes a fastday upon himself on the following day says this at מנחה
before יהיו לרצון:

רִבּוֹן הָעוֹלָמִים · הֲרֵי אֲנִי לְפָנֶיךָ בְּתַעֲנִית נְדָבָה לְמָחָר · יְהִי

רָצוֹן לְפָנֶיךָ יְיָ אֱלֹהַי וֵאלֹהֵי אֲבוֹתַי · שֶׁתְּקַבְּלֵנִי בְּאַהֲבָה וּבְרָצוֹן ·

וְתָבֹא לְפָנֶיךָ תְּפִלָּתִי · וְתַעֲנֶה עֲתִירָתִי בְּרַחֲמֶיךָ הָרַבִּים · כִּי אַתָּה

שׁוֹמֵעַ תְּפִלַּת כָּל־פֶּה: יהיו לרצון וכו׳.

---

the Divine Law of life to aid us in the acquisition of understanding, the love of selfless devotion to shape our conviction, and loyalty to duty as the character trait to motivate our conduct. In this manner blessing, compassion, life and peace will come to all men.

שלום רב During the hours of *Mincha* and *Maariv*, which come when night is about to begin, we are inclined to view peace in terms of protection from all physical attack by foes. Therefore *Shalom rav*, which we recite in our *Mincha* and *Maariv* services in place of *Sim shalom* is much briefer than the latter.

אלהי נצור All the prayers and supplications contained in the *Shemone Esrei*, even those that directly concern the life of the individual only, are always recited by the worshipper not as an individual but as a member of the community, and viewed as the collective concern of all the individuals comprising the congregation of Israel. אלהי נצור, however, is the personal petition of the individual. It comprises the prayers which it was the custom of Mar bereh deRavina (see Berachoth 17a) to recite after he had completed his *Tefillah*. He prays that his mouth, his tongue and his lips, which have just served as the instruments for his communion with God, now will not forfeit any of their moral purity through his dealings with his fellow-men (Yaavetz). He implores God to be at his side so that his lips and tongue may not become soiled with evil or enter the employ of falsehood and deceit. He needs the

May it be Your will, O *God,* our God and God of our fathers, that the Temple be speedily rebuilt in our days, and give us our portion in Your Torah, so that we may serve You there with awe as in the days of old and as in former years. Then the tribute of homage of Yehuda and Yerushalayim will be pleasing to *God* as in the days of the past and as in former years.

On Rosh Chodesh, Chanukkah and on the Intermediate Days of Festivals, the Hallel is recited here. During the Ten Days of Repentance אבינו מלכנו *is said here.* (p. 628)

---

aid of God if he is to remain in control of himself, if he is to permit no insult to provoke his wrath and if he is to be able to remain calm and silent even in the face of a curse. He must have this Divine support if, even as he will not allow himself to be swayed to take verbal revenge, he is not to give way to the temptation to work physical vengeance, and if he is to remain patient, humble, selfless and as unassuming as the dust of the earth in the face of whatever may befall him. But when it comes to תורתך "Your Torah", he prays פתח לבי, "open my heart." "May I have an open, receptive and understanding mind and spirit in all matters pertaining to Your Law. When it comes to תרדף נפשי ,מצותך, let my soul know no indifference, indolence or passivity. Let me demonstrate zealous and vigorous endeavor in all things pertinent to Your *mitzvoth.* וכל החושבים To You I leave the task of thwarting the hostile plans of my foes. עשה Do as is seemly to Your Name, to Your right hand which is ready at all times to render help, to Your holiness and to Your Law. למען Therefore for the sake of all of these, let those whom You have deemed worthy of Your love יחלצון experience a sense of release from every form of bondage." אמרי פי, "that which I have said"; והגיון לבי refers to "that which has remained unspoken within my heart." יעשה שלום. The high places of heaven, where every one of God's creatures completes the course set for it by its Creator, without disturbing or inhibiting any other creation of God in the completion of its own Divinely-assigned orbit, represent the ideal of peace. May that same undisturbed peace reign supreme also on earth beneath the supreme sovereignty of the Kingdom of God.

During the Ten Days of *Teshuvah* this prayer is recited with certain changes and additions in keeping with the solemn significance of these days. These are the days of the Divine judgment which inquires into all our past lives and from whose sentence we await the dealing of all our future fate. This period summons us to *Teshuvah,* to introspection, and to a "return" to the path of our duty before God, the sole Master Who has command over us and over all the world, so that, through renewed homage to our "King and Master" which can be performed only by loyal obedience, henceforth, we may be deemed worthy anew of "life", the right which we had forfeited

On the day of the fastday, in the evening at מנחה, the following is said before
יהיו לרצון:

רִבּוֹן הָעוֹלָמִים · גָּלוּי וְיָדוּעַ לְפָנֶיךָ · בִּזְמַן שֶׁבֵּית הַמִּקְדָּשׁ קַיָּם
אָדָם חוֹטֵא מַקְרִיב קָרְבָּן , וְאֵין מַקְרִיבִים מִמֶּנּוּ אֶלָּא חֶלְבּוֹ
וְדָמוֹ , וְאַתָּה בְּרַחֲמֶיךָ הָרַבִּים מְכַפֵּר · וְעַכְשָׁו יָשַׁבְתִּי בְּתַעֲנִית
וְנִתְמַעַט חֶלְבִּי וְדָמִי : יְהִי רָצוֹן לְפָנֶיךָ שֶׁיְּהֵא חֶלְבִּי וְדָמִי
שֶׁנִּתְמַעֵט הַיּוֹם כְּאִלּוּ הִקְרַבְתִּיו לְפָנֶיךָ עַל־גַּב הַמִּזְבֵּחַ
וְתִרְצֵנִי :   יהיו לרצון וכו' ·

Daily after ש"ע of שחרית and מנחה the רחום וחנון is said. On Mondays and
Thursdays the והוא רחום below is added in the morning. The exceptions are the
following days on which no תחנון is said: ערב שבת and ערב יו"ט at מנחה;
ראש חדש; during the whole month of Nissan; ל"ג בעמר; from ר"ח סיון until
after אסרו חג שבועות; on ערב ר"ה and ט' באב; (According to the Frankfurt Minhag until atfer ט"ו בשבט, פורים קטן וגדול, חנוכה, on (ר"ח חשון); and
ט"ו בשבט, ט"ו באב, ל"ג בעמר (according to the Frankfurt Minhag on ט"ו באב,
the תחנון is omitted only at שחרית).

וְהוּא רַחוּם יְכַפֵּר עָוֹן וְלֹא יַשְׁחִית וְהִרְבָּה לְהָשִׁיב אַפּוֹ וְלֹא
יָעִיר כָּל־חֲמָתוֹ : אַתָּה יְיָ לֹא־תִכְלָא רַחֲמֶיךָ מִמֶּנּוּ חַסְדְּךָ וַאֲמִתְּךָ
תָּמִיד יִצְּרוּנוּ : הוֹשִׁיעֵנוּ יְיָ אֱלֹהֵינוּ וְקַבְּצֵנוּ מִן־הַגּוֹיִם לְהוֹדוֹת לְשֵׁם
קָדְשֶׁךָ לְהִשְׁתַּבֵּחַ בִּתְהִלָּתֶךָ : אִם־עֲוֹנוֹת תִּשְׁמָר־יָהּ אֲדֹנָי מִי
יַעֲמֹד : כִּי־עִמְּךָ הַסְּלִיחָה לְמַעַן תִּוָּרֵא : לֹא כַחֲטָאֵינוּ
תַּעֲשֶׂה־לָּנוּ וְלֹא כַעֲוֹנֹתֵינוּ תִּגְמֹל עָלֵינוּ : אִם־עֲוֹנֵינוּ עָנוּ בָנוּ יְיָ

by reason of the inadequacy of our past conduct. During the Days of Teshuvah, we learn to think of malchuth, the supremacy of God in terms of a
relationship of our Maker with ourselves which we must take to heart with
renewed earnestness of purpose by way of teshuvah. We learn to conceive of
life as a gift of God's grace which, too, can be attained only by means of
teshuvah. These are the thoughts which are woven into the warp and woof
of our regular prayers during the days of Penitence. In the Avoth portion
of the Shemone Esrei, in which we base our own hopes for the future upon
God and upon His remembrance of our fathers, and in Gevuroth where we
remember God's almighty power which can defeat even death on our behalf,
the paragraphs זכרנו and מי כמוך respectively, which are added during the
Ten Days of Teshuvah, stress the thought of חיים, the life for which we are

And He, being merciful, forgives sin and does not destroy; many a time He turns away His anger, and never stirs up all His wrath. Withhold not Your compassion from us, O *God,* let Your loving-kindness and Your truth continually protect us. Save us, O *God,* and gather us from among the nations, to render grateful homage to Your holy Name and to glory in Your praise. If You should mark iniquities, O *God,* who could stand? But Yours is forgiveness, so that You may be feared henceforth. Therefore deal with us not according to our sins; let not our fate come to pass according to our iniquities. If our iniquities testify against us, then, O *God,* act for Your Name's sake.

---

dependent upon the grace of God. This same idea is predominant also in וכתוב which is added to the *Hodaah,* and in even greater detail in בספר חיים which is added to the prayer for *shalom.* In keeping with the concept of מלכות, we say המלך הקדוש instead of האל הקדוש in the *Kedushah,* and substitute the appellation המלך המשפט for מלך אוהב צדקה ומשפט in השיבה שופטינו Since the text reads המלך המשפט and not מלך המשפט, the word *melech* is not a construct form. Hence *mishpat* is not justice, nor does it denote judgment in terms of the enforcement of justice. Instead, it indicates judgment in terms of the persons taking part in a trial at a court of law, even as it does in ונגשו אל המשפט (Deut. 25:1). In His Person God incorporates all the function-aries of the court of justice; He is not only the Judge, but also the Prosecutor and the Witness for the Prosecution. In the concluding blessing, the words עושה השלום are substituted for המברך את עמו ישראל בשלום. Any transgression or any neglect of duty of which we may be guilty, banishes peace and brings discord into our physical and spiritual lives. But God, in His wondrous might, is ready at all times to cancel the ills that would ordinarily be the inevitable consequence of our transgressions. He is ready to return to our souls the purity and serenity we have forfeited and to restore to our relationship with Him and with the world about us the harmony we have lost, if only we will make ourselves worthy of it through genuine *teshuvah* and Yom Kippur. It is this merciful God Who is the true "Creator of Peace."

והוא רחום It was on the fifth day of the week that, for the first time since the incident of the Golden Calf, Moshe left his people once more for a period of forty days in order to ascend Mount Sinai and once again to receive there the original Law, now re-written by God upon new tablets. And it was on the second day of the week that Moshe came down again from the moun-tain and returned to the people, bringing to them the new tablets as a security for the Divine covenant which, thus renewed on the strength of the original Law, served as atonement for their transgression. Ever since, the second and

עֲשֵׂה לְמַעַן שְׁמֶךָ: זְכֹר רַחֲמֶיךָ יְיָ וַחֲסָדֶיךָ כִּי מֵעוֹלָם הֵמָּה:

יַעֲנֵנוּ יְיָ בְּיוֹם צָרָה יְשַׂגְּבֵנוּ שֵׁם אֱלֹהֵי יַעֲקֹב: יְיָ הוֹשִׁיעָה, הַמֶּלֶךְ

יַעֲנֵנוּ בְיוֹם־קָרְאֵנוּ: אָבִינוּ מַלְכֵּנוּ חָנֵּנוּ וַעֲנֵנוּ כִּי אֵין בָּנוּ מַעֲשִׂים,

צְדָקָה עֲשֵׂה עִמָּנוּ לְמַעַן שְׁמֶךָ: אֲדוֹנֵנוּ אֱלֹהֵינוּ שְׁמַע קוֹל

תַּחֲנוּנֵינוּ וּזְכָר־לָנוּ אֶת־בְּרִית אֲבוֹתֵינוּ וְהוֹשִׁיעֵנוּ לְמַעַן שְׁמֶךָ:

וְעַתָּה אֲדֹנָי אֱלֹהֵינוּ אֲשֶׁר הוֹצֵאתָ אֶת־עַמְּךָ מֵאֶרֶץ מִצְרַיִם בְּיָד

חֲזָקָה וַתַּעַשׂ־לְךָ שֵׁם כַּיּוֹם הַזֶּה חָטָאנוּ רָשָׁעְנוּ: אֲדֹנָי כְּכָל־

צִדְקֹתֶךָ יָשָׁב־נָא אַפְּךָ וַחֲמָתְךָ מֵעִירְךָ יְרוּשָׁלַיִם הַר קָדְשֶׁךָ כִּי

בַחֲטָאֵינוּ וּבַעֲוֹנוֹת אֲבוֹתֵינוּ יְרוּשָׁלַיִם וְעַמְּךָ לְחֶרְפָּה לְכָל־סְבִיבֹתֵינוּ:

וְעַתָּה שְׁמַע אֱלֹהֵינוּ אֶל־תְּפִלַּת עַבְדְּךָ וְאֶל־תַּחֲנוּנָיו וְהָאֵר פָּנֶיךָ

עַל־מִקְדָּשְׁךָ הַשָּׁמֵם לְמַעַן אֲדֹנָי:

הַטֵּה אֱלֹהַי אָזְנְךָ וּשֲׁמָע פְּקַח עֵינֶיךָ וּרְאֵה שֹׁמְמֹתֵינוּ וְהָעִיר

אֲשֶׁר־נִקְרָא שִׁמְךָ עָלֶיהָ כִּי לֹא עַל־צִדְקֹתֵינוּ אֲנַחְנוּ מַפִּילִים

תַּחֲנוּנֵינוּ לְפָנֶיךָ כִּי עַל־רַחֲמֶיךָ הָרַבִּים: אֲדֹנָי שְׁמָעָה אֲדֹנָי

סְלָחָה אֲדֹנָי הַקְשִׁיבָה וַעֲשֵׂה אַל־תְּאַחַר לְמַעַנְךָ אֱלֹהַי כִּי־שִׁמְךָ

---

the fifth day of each week, every Monday and Thursday, have been a summons to the Jewish people to assemble anew before God, reawakening within their hearts the firm confidence that they could obtain atonement for all past sin through constant re-affirmation of their sincere "return" to the ancient Law of God. In keeping with the historic significance of those days, our regular order of prayer is augmented on Mondays and Thursdays by additional supplications (*tachanunim*). Designed to aid us in searching our souls and then, in seeking God again, these special prayers help us become worthy of Divine grace and favor. Mondays and Thursdays were later appointed for the public reading of the Law of God and eventually came to be the days on which sessions of the Court of Justice were regularly held. (See Baba Kama 82a, Tosaphoth ibid.)

Remember, O *God,* that Your compassion and Your kindnesses are eternal. *God* will hear us on the day of distress, the Name of the God of Yisrael will set us up on high. O *God,* grant salvation; it is as the King that He will hear us on the day on which we call. Our Father, Our King, favor us and answer us, for we have no merits to show; deal kindly with us for Your Name's sake. Our Lord, our God, hear the voice of our supplications; remember for us the covenant of our fathers and save us for Your Name's sake. And now, my Lord, our God, Who has brought out Your people from the land of Mitzrayim with a mighty hand, and has established for Yourself a Name even to this day: we have sinned and acted contrary to Your Law. O my Lord, according to all Your acts of kindness, pray let Your anger and Your indignation be turned away from Yerushalayim Your City, Your holy mountain, for because of our sins and because of the iniquities of our fathers, Yerushalayim and Your people have become an object of scorn all those who surround us. Now therefore hearken to the prayer of Your servant and to his supplications, and let Your countenance shine again upon Your desolate Sanctuary, as is seemly to my Lord.

Incline Your ear, O my God, and hear; open Your eyes and behold our desolate places and the city upon which Your Name is proclaimed, for it is not because of proven merit that we pour out our supplications before You, but because of Your great compassion. My Lord, pray hear, O my Lord, pray forgive, my Lord, pray hearken and take action. Do not delay! For Your sake, O my God, for Your

---

אם עוונות וגו' כי עמך וגו' Were it not for the grace of God, any sin of which we may be guilty would deprive us of the right to continued existence. However, through the grace of Divine forgiveness, God makes it possible for us to atone for past sin by future God-fearing conduct. למען שמך, in keeping with מדת הרחמים, the quality of compassion inherent in Your rule which You have revealed to us in Your Name. זכר וגו' כי מעולם המה All of our existence is a work of that love and compassion with which You have always dealt with us, and it is because we are the work and the creation of Your infinite mercy, that we continue to hope for Your love. For does not the human heart, too, cherish with special devotion that treasure for whose creation and preservation it has made the greatest sacrifice? שם אלהי יעקב : Because of the trials and tribulations that marked the course of his life, Yaakov has become the model personality for the people which is descended from him. This people, which

נִקְרָא עַל-עִירָךְ וְעַל-עַמָּךְ: אָבִינוּ הָאָב הָרַחֲמָן הַרְאֵנוּ אוֹת
לְטוֹבָה וְקַבֵּץ נְפוּצוֹתֵינוּ מֵאַרְבַּע כַּנְפוֹת הָאָרֶץ יַכִּירוּ וְיֵדְעוּ כָּל-
הַגּוֹיִם כִּי אַתָּה יְיָ אֱלֹהֵינוּ: וְעַתָּה יְיָ אָבִינוּ אָתָּה אֲנַחְנוּ הַחֹמֶר
וְאַתָּה יֹצְרֵנוּ וּמַעֲשֵׂה יָדְךָ כֻּלָּנוּ: הוֹשִׁיעֵנוּ לְמַעַן שְׁמֶךָ צוּרֵנוּ
מַלְכֵּנוּ וְגוֹאֲלֵנוּ: חוּסָה יְיָ עַל-עַמֶּךָ וְאַל-תִּתֵּן נַחֲלָתְךָ לְחֶרְפָּה
לִמְשָׁל-בָּם גּוֹיִם לָמָּה יֹאמְרוּ בָעַמִּים אַיֵּה אֱלֹהֵיהֶם: יָדַעְנוּ כִּי
חָטָאנוּ וְאֵין מִי יַעֲמֹד בַּעֲדֵנוּ, שִׁמְךָ הַגָּדוֹל יַעֲמָד-לָנוּ בְּעֵת צָרָה:
יָדַעְנוּ כִּי אֵין בָּנוּ מַעֲשִׂים, צְדָקָה עֲשֵׂה עִמָּנוּ לְמַעַן שְׁמֶךָ: כְּרַחֵם
אָב עַל-בָּנִים תְּרַחֵם יְיָ עָלֵינוּ וְהוֹשִׁיעֵנוּ לְמַעַן שְׁמֶךָ: חֲמוֹל עַל-
עַמֶּךָ רַחֵם עַל-נַחֲלָתֶךָ חוּסָה-נָא כְּרֹב רַחֲמֶיךָ חָנֵּנוּ וַעֲנֵנוּ כִּי
לְךָ יְיָ הַצְּדָקָה עֹשֵׂה נִפְלָאוֹת בְּכָל-עֵת:

הַבֶּט-נָא רַחֶם-נָא עַל-עַמְּךָ מְהֵרָה לְמַעַן שְׁמֶךָ בְּרַחֲמֶיךָ
הָרַבִּים יְיָ אֱלֹהֵינוּ חוּס וְרַחֵם וְהוֹשִׁיעָה צֹאן מַרְעִיתֶךָ וְאַל-יִמְשָׁל-
בָּנוּ קֶצֶף כִּי לְךָ עֵינֵינוּ תְלוּיוֹת הוֹשִׁיעֵנוּ לְמַעַן שְׁמֶךָ: רַחֵם עָלֵינוּ

carries on his name, is to preserve its trust in God through all the bitter blows
that may befall it, and is to be sustained by this trust even as Yaakov was,
confident that God will be mindful of it even as He remembered its ancestor
Yaakov long ago and eventually led him to a pinnacle of joy and happiness.
המלך יענו It is by pledging Him our obedience "as our King" that we hope
that He will answer us. כיום הזה A name "even as it still exists to this very
day" and has come to be recognized to an ever-growing extent among men.
This fact which God has demonstrated in our own history and has thus revealed to all the rest of mankind as well should have served first and foremost
to make us acknowledge God at all times out of conviction and in loyalty.
But we have violated this loyalty by our levity and our forgetfulness of the
Law. בחטאינו ובעונות אבתינו Through sincere atonement and the earnest resolve
to do our duty, we could have restored that which has been lost because of
the wanton conduct of our ancestors. But instead, we ourselves have left
much to be desired in this respect (Yaavetz). למען אדני "as is seemly to my
Lord"; i.e. "to the extent to which I render homage to You as my Lord."

Name is proclaimed over Your city and Your people. Our Father, compassionate Father, show us a sign for good and gather our dispersed from the four ends of the earth, so that all the nations may realize and know that You, O *God,* are our God. And now. O *God* You are our Father; we are the clay and You are our Moulder, and we are entirely the work of Your hands. Save us for Your Name's sake, O Rock, our King and our Redeemer. Spare Your people, O *God,* and let not Your heritage be an object of contempt, so that nations should not hold sway over it. Why should they say among the nations, "Where is their God?" We know that we have sinned and that there is none to stand up for us. Let Your great Name, then, stand for us at the time of distress. We know that we have no merits; deal kindly with us for Your Name's sake. Even as a father has compassion on his children, so do You have compassion upon us, O *God,* and save us for Your Name's sake. Have pity upon Your people, have compassion on Your inheritance, spare, we pray You, in keeping with the abundance of Your compassion. Favor us, and answer us, for Yours is the righteousness, O You Who does wondrous things at all times.

Look, we beseech You, and speedily have compassion upon Your people for Your Name's sake. In Your great compassion, O *God* our God, spare us and have pity, and save the sheep of Your

---

הטה "Hear that which others say and think about us" or "hear our cry for help." פקח "behold our situation." אדני, "Our Lord, Who has called us to Your service, and in Whose service we stand." כי שמך "If the city which You have founded should fall, and the people whom You have chosen should perish, the cause of the universal acknowledgment of You would suffer. But if both this city and this people should survive and rise again, then the recognition of You and of Your Providence would also grow in the hearts of men." אבינו etc. "And we hope for the restoration of our original destiny from You not only because You are our Master, but because You are also our Father, for are we not Your work through and through?" נחלתך, עמך "Our unity as Your people is based upon our common obligation, both as individuals and as members of the community, to do Your will. It is this guiding principle that unites us as Your nation. And at a time when all the rest of mankind was lost to the knowledge and recognition of Thee, we alone became Your inheritance."

לְמַעַן בְּרִיתֶךָ הַבִּיטָה וַעֲנֵנוּ בְּעֵת צָרָה כִּי לְךָ יְיָ הַיְשׁוּעָה בְּךָ
תוֹחַלְתֵּנוּ אֱלוֹהַּ סְלִיחוֹת אָנָּא סְלַח־נָא אֵל טוֹב וְסַלָּח כִּי אֵל מֶלֶךְ
חַנּוּן וְרַחוּם אָתָּה:

אָנָּא מֶלֶךְ חַנּוּן וְרַחוּם זְכוֹר וְהַבֵּט לִבְרִית בֵּין הַבְּתָרִים וְתֵרָאֶה
לְפָנֶיךָ עֲקֵדַת יָחִיד לְמַעַן יִשְׂרָאֵל: אָבִינוּ מַלְכֵּנוּ חָנֵּנוּ וַעֲנֵנוּ כִּי שִׁמְךָ
הַגָּדוֹל נִקְרָא עָלֵינוּ עֹשֵׂה נִפְלָאוֹת בְּכָל־עֵת עֲשֵׂה עִמָּנוּ כְּחַסְדֶּךָ
חַנּוּן וְרַחוּם הַבִּיטָה וַעֲנֵנוּ בְּעֵת צָרָה כִּי לְךָ יְיָ הַיְשׁוּעָה: אָבִינוּ
מַלְכֵּנוּ מַחֲסֵנוּ אַל־תַּעַשׂ עִמָּנוּ כִּרֹעַ מַעֲלָלֵינוּ זְכֹר רַחֲמֶיךָ יְיָ
וַחֲסָדֶיךָ וְכֹרַב טוּבְךָ הוֹשִׁיעֵנוּ וַהֲמָל־נָא עָלֵינוּ כִּי אֵין לָנוּ אֱלוֹהַּ
אַחֵר מִבַּלְעָדֶיךָ צוּרֵנוּ: אַל־תַּעַזְבֵנוּ יְיָ אֱלֹהֵינוּ אַל־תִּרְחַק מִמֶּנּוּ ·
כִּי נַפְשֵׁנוּ קָצְרָה מֵחֶרֶב וּמִשֶּׁבִי וּמִדֶּבֶר וּמִמַּגֵּפָה וּמִכָּל־צָרָה וְיָגוֹן
הַצִּילֵנוּ כִּי לְךָ קִוִּינוּ וְאַל־תַּכְלִימֵנוּ יְיָ אֱלֹהֵינוּ וְהָאֵר פָּנֶיךָ בָּנוּ

הבט נא This, our cry for help appeals to the compassionate ways for which the Name of God stands, and to the promise that is part of the Divine covenant. We expect that God will answer the pleas of the "sheep of His pasture," the people led and guided by His Providence.

אנא. ברית בין הבתרים (Gen. Chap. 15) is the covenant in which God pledged eternal protection and infinite reward to Abraham, and in which He also promised our patriarch that his descendants would enjoy direct Divine guidance even as the stars above, and that they would receive the land of Canaan as a permanent possession. Abraham was assured, too, that, even if there should be times when his descendants, like dismembered carcasses, would appear as welcome fodder for birds of prey, the strength of the covenant of Abraham would fend off the vultures and the promise of that covenant would be unerringly fulfilled. עקדת יחיד refers to Abraham's willingness to sacrifice Yitzchak, the sole person who could fulfill for posterity the promise given to his father. This attempted sacrifice symbolized the readiness which would be demonstrated by all the future descendants of Abraham to await and accept with self-sacrificing devotion whatever fate Divine Providence might have decreed for them. It was on the strength of the partiarch's willingness to offer up his only son that God once again repeated His promise, this time with a blessing that was far broader in scope that the first, and included the future prosperity of all the other nations as well. למען ישראל, finally, for the sake

pasture; let not wrath hold sway over us, for our eyes are bent upon You; save us for Your Name's sake. Have compassion upon us for the sake of Your covenant; look, we beseech You, and answer us at the time of distress, for Yours, O *God,* is salvation. Our hope rests with You, O God of forgiveness. Forgive, we beseech You, O good and forgiving God, for You, O God, are a gracious and compassionate King.

We beseech You, O gracious and compassionate King, remember, and look upon the covenant made between the pieces [with Abraham] and let the readiness [of Abraham] to offer up his only son appear before You, for Yisrael's sake. Our Father, our King, favor us and answer us, You Who does wonders at all times, deal with us according to Your loving-kindness, gracious and full of compassion, look, and answer us in the time of distress. For Yours, O *God,* is salvation. Deal with us not according to the evil of our doings; remember, O *God,* Your compassion and Your loving-kindness in keeping with Your abundant goodness save us, and have pity upon us, for we have no God beside You, O our Rock. Forsake us not, O *God,* our God; be not far from us. For our soul is spent from the sword and captivity, from pestilence and plague. Deliver us from every trouble and sorrow, for we hope in You; put us not to shame, O *God* our God; cause Your countenance that was turned from us to shine upon us once

---

of Yisrael, under which name Yaakov, the third of our patriarchs, was assigned the destiny which he was to pass on to his descendants as their inheritance. Despite his weak outer appearance, or perhaps even because of it, Yaakov was to become the living testimony of the "supreme power of God" in world history. אבינו מלכנו This dual appellation includes every aspect of our relationship to God. אבינו He is "our Father", for we owe Him our very existence and our survival. It is He Who cares for our physical, spiritual and moral welfare, and it is He Who trains, guides and disciplines us and Who has shown us where our duty lies. For this reason we give Him our love, our veneration and render Him filial obedience. מלכנו He is "our King", but infinitely more so than any ruler of flesh and blood could be, for His power is also infinitely broader in scope than that of any man. He has command over all our lives, our endeavors and achievements, and over our thoughts and emotions as well. His Will is our Law and all our life lies in the performance of His service. He is the Master of our destiny, and all our woe and weal waits upon His command. We fear Him and we obey Him, we trust in Him

וְזָכָר־לָנוּ אֶת־בְּרִית אֲבוֹתֵינוּ וְהוֹשִׁיעֵנוּ לְמַעַן שְׁמֶךָ · רְאֵה בְצָרוֹתֵינוּ
וּשְׁמַע קוֹל תְּפִלָּתֵנוּ כִּי אַתָּה שׁוֹמֵעַ תְּפִלַּת כָּל־פֶּה:

אֵל רַחוּם וְחַנּוּן רַחֵם עָלֵינוּ וְעַל כָּל־מַעֲשֶׂיךָ כִּי אֵין כָּמוֹךָ יְיָ
אֱלֹהֵינוּ · אָנָּא שָׂא נָא פְּשָׁעֵינוּ אָבִינוּ מַלְכֵּנוּ צוּרֵנוּ וְגֹאֲלֵנוּ אֵל חַי
וְקַיָּם הַחֲסִין בַּכֹּחַ חָסִיד וְטוֹב עַל כָּל־מַעֲשֶׂיךָ כִּי אַתָּה הוּא יְיָ
אֱלֹהֵינוּ: אֵל אֶרֶךְ אַפַּיִם וּמָלֵא רַחֲמִים עֲשֵׂה עִמָּנוּ כְּרוֹב רַחֲמֶיךָ
וְהוֹשִׁיעֵנוּ לְמַעַן שְׁמֶךָ: שְׁמַע מַלְכֵּנוּ תְּפִלָּתֵנוּ וּמִיַּד אוֹיְבֵינוּ הַצִּילֵנוּ
שְׁמַע מַלְכֵּנוּ תְּפִלָּתֵנוּ וּמִכָּל־צָרָה וְיָגוֹן הַצִּילֵנוּ: אָבִינוּ מַלְכֵּנוּ
אַתָּה וְשִׁמְךָ עָלֵינוּ נִקְרָא אַל־תַּנִּיחֵנוּ: אַל־תַּעַזְבֵנוּ אָבִינוּ וְאַל־
תִּטְּשֵׁנוּ בּוֹרְאֵנוּ וְאַל־תִּשְׁכָּחֵנוּ יוֹצְרֵנוּ כִּי אֵל מֶלֶךְ חַנּוּן וְרַחוּם
אָתָּה:

אֵין כָּמוֹךָ חַנּוּן וְרַחוּם יְיָ אֱלֹהֵינוּ אֵין כָּמוֹךָ אֵל אֶרֶךְ אַפַּיִם
וְרַב־חֶסֶד וֶאֱמֶת הוֹשִׁיעֵנוּ כְּרַחֲמֶיךָ הָרַבִּים הָרַעַשׁ וּמִרְגְּזוֹ הַצִּילֵנוּ:
זְכוֹר לַעֲבָדֶיךָ לְאַבְרָהָם לְיִצְחָק וּלְיַעֲקֹב אַל־תֵּפֶן אֶל־קַשְׁיֵנוּ וְאֶל־

---

and dedicate ourselves to Him entirely. הָאֵר פָּנֶיךָ בָּנוּ The word *banu* is an
attribute referring not to *haer* but to *panecha*, indicating "the countenance that
is now turned *against us* in anger."

אֵל רחום ,וְעַל כל מעשיך, even in a world that is turned against us in hostility, we beseech God's compassion not for ourselves alone, but for all of
His creatures. אל תניחנו. The literal meaning of הניח is "to put something
aside"; that is, "no longer to care." "This You would not do," we pray,
"because Your Name is proclaimed upon us; the nations know Your Providence by our fate." עזב .אל תעזבנו, "to abandon", means, "to leave a person
to his own devices." "You know that our own strength and intelligence are
not adequate for us to care for ourselves, and therefore You will not cease
to give us Your fatherly care." בוראנו; We are Your ואל תטשנו "You are
creation in world history. In the ordinary course of events we would never
have become a people. But it is obvious that You have deemed our existence
as a nation in history as so essential for the fulfillment of Your purposes

more; remember for us the covenant of our fathers, and save us for Your Name's sake. Look into our troubles and hear the voice of our prayer, for You hear the prayer of every mouth.

O compassionate and gracious God, have compassion upon us and upon all Your works, for there is none like You, O *God* our God. We beseech You, forgive our transgressions, our Father, our King, our Rock and our Redeemer. Living and everlasting God, mighty in strength, Who is kind and good to all Your works, for You, O *God,* are our God. O God, Who is slow to anger and full of compassion, deal with us in keeping with the abundance of Your compassion, and save us for Your Name's sake. Hear our prayer, O our King, and deliver us from the hand of our enemies; hear our prayer, O our King, and deliver us from all trouble and sorrow. You are our Father, our King, and Your Name is proclaimed over us; desert us not. Abandon us not, O our Father, cast us not off, O our Creator, and forget us not, O our Molder, for You, O God, are a gracious and compassionate King.

There is none like You, O gracious and compassionate *God,* our God; There is none like You. O God, slow to anger and abundant in loving-kindness and truth, help us in Your great compassion and deliver us from storm and rage. Remember Your servants, Abraham, Yitzchak and Yaakov; look not upon our stubbornness, our lawlessness

---

that You placed us among the nations as a direct work of Your hands, a phenomenon quite at variance with normal historic conditions. And now should this work of Your hands indeed have become so utterly worthless that You would cast it off and cease to be concerned with its survival? Lastly, You are יוצרנו. You did not merely make us at one time by one single act of creation; You have labored upon us ever since, as it were, to mold and to shape us in order to make us better suited to carry out Your purposes which You would have us fulfill. Therefore we are confident that You will not forget us; You will not cease to make us the object of Your guiding care in which You mold and shape us for Your purposes."

הצליחה. הושיעה. אין כמוך "Help us to achieve *teshuvah* and let our effort at *teshuvah* meet with success (Yaavetz)."

נאמו. They declare it as a verdict of their gods. They forget, however, that the future belongs only to Your dominion and the universal recognition of You, and that every knee which now is still bent to another god, and every

רְשַׁעְנוּ וְאַל־חַטָּאתֵנוּ: שׁוּב מֵחֲרוֹן אַפֶּךָ וְהִנָּחֵם עַל־הָרָעָה לְעַמֶּךָ ·
וְהָסֵר מִמֶּנּוּ מַכַּת הַמָּוֶת כִּי רַחוּם אָתָּה כִּי כֵן דַּרְכֶּךָ עֲשֵׂה חֶסֶד
חִנָּם בְּכָל־דּוֹר וָדוֹר : חוּסָה יְיָ עַל־עַמֶּךָ וְהַצִּילֵנוּ מִזַּעְמֶךָ וְהָסֵר
מִמֶּנּוּ מַכַּת הַמַּגֵּפָה וּגְזֵרָה קָשָׁה כִּי אַתָּה שׁוֹמֵר יִשְׂרָאֵל : לְךָ
אֲדֹנָי הַצְּדָקָה וְלָנוּ בְּשֶׁת הַפָּנִים : מַה־נִּתְאוֹנֵן מַה־נֹּאמַר מַה־
נְּדַבֵּר וּמַה־נִּצְטַדָּק: נַחְפְּשָׂה דְרָכֵינוּ וְנַחְקֹרָה וְנָשׁוּבָה אֵלֶיךָ כִּי
יְמִינְךָ פְּשׁוּטָה לְקַבֵּל שָׁבִים : אָנָּא יְיָ הוֹשִׁיעָה נָּא אָנָּא יְיָ
הַצְלִיחָה נָא : אָנָּא יְיָ עֲנֵנוּ בְּיוֹם קָרְאֵנוּ: לְךָ יְיָ חִכִּינוּ לְךָ יְיָ קִוִּינוּ
לְךָ יְיָ נְיַחֵל אַל־תֶּחֱשֶׁה וּתְעַנֵּנוּ כִּי נָאֲמוּ גוֹיִם אָבְדָה תִקְוָתָם
בְּכָל־בֶּרֶךְ וְכָל־קוֹמָה לְךָ לְבַד תִּשְׁתַּחֲוֶה :

הַפּוֹתֵחַ יָד בִּתְשׁוּבָה לְקַבֵּל פּוֹשְׁעִים וְחַטָּאִים נִבְהֲלָה נַפְשֵׁנוּ
מֵרוֹב עִצְּבוֹנֵנוּ אַל־תִּשְׁכָּחֵנוּ נֶצַח קוּמָה וְהוֹשִׁיעֵנוּ כִּי חָסִינוּ בָךְ :
אָבִינוּ מַלְכֵּנוּ אִם אֵין בָּנוּ צְדָקָה וּמַעֲשִׂים טוֹבִים זְכָר־לָנוּ אֶת־
בְּרִית אֲבוֹתֵינוּ וְעֵדוֹתֵינוּ בְּכָל־יוֹם יְיָ אֶחָד: הַבִּיטָה בְעָנְיֵנוּ כִּי רַבּוּ
מַכְאוֹבֵינוּ וְצָרוֹת לְבָבֵנוּ: חוּסָה יְיָ עָלֵינוּ בְּאֶרֶץ שִׁבְיֵנוּ וְאַל־
תִּשְׁפּוֹךְ חֲרוֹנְךָ עָלֵינוּ כִּי אֲנַחְנוּ עַמֶּךָ בְּנֵי בְרִיתֶךָ : אֶל הַבִּיטָה

---

earthly power which now still rears its proud and arrogant head will eventually bow down before You and before You only.

הפותח may mean either "You open Your hand with the summons to do
teshuvah" or "The teshuvah which men do moves You to open Your hand
to receive them." עד מתי : In Psalm 78:61 we read concerning the Ark of the
Covenant which had fallen into the hands of the Philistines: ויתן לשבי עזו
ותפארתו ביד צר. עזו refers to Torah as the manifestation of the will of God
which none can withstand. The term תפארתו refers to the Ark which symbolizes the glorification of God through the fulfillment of His Law. As long
as Yisrael is in Galuth, the Torah too, will be in exile, since it can be fulfilled
freely and in its entirety in daily living only upon our own home soil. ה' אחד

and our levity. Turn back from the blazing of Your anger and let Your mind be changed concerning the evil intended for Your people; turn from us the stroke of death, for You are compassionate, for such is Your way, showing undeserved kindness to every generation. Spare Your people, O *God,* deliver us from Your wrath and turn aside from us the scourge of pestilence and harsh decree, for You are the Guardian of Yisrael. Yours, O my Lord, is tender righteousness, while ours is the shame that covers the face. How can we complain? What can we say, what can we speak, or how can we justify ourselves? Let us search into our ways and examine them and return to You, for Your right hand is stretched out to receive all those who return, O *God,* grant new life, we beseech You! O *God,* grant success, we beseech You; answer us on the day when we call. For You, O *God,* we wait; for You, O *God,* we hope; upon You, O *God,* we shall wait; be not silent and leave us not to torment, for the nations have already predicted: "Their hope is lost." But every knee and all that stands erect shall bow before You alone.

O You Who opens Your hand by reason of repentant return, to receive transgressors and sinners, our soul is dismayed by the fullness of our grief. Forget us not forever; arise and save us, for in You do we trust. Our Father, our King, though we be without righteousness and good deeds, remember for us the covenant of our fathers and our daily testimony: "O *God,* You only God." Look into our affliction, for many are our sufferings and the sorrows of our hearts. Spare us, O *God,* in the land of our captivity, and pour not out Your wrath upon us, because we are Your people, the sons of Your covenant. O God, look, our glory has sunk low among the nations and

---

may be either a vocative, an appeal to God, or it may be an accusative referring to עֵדוּתֵינוּ, as in יִרְאָתָם אֹתִי (Isa. 29:13), denoting that our worship belongs to the One Only God.

תחנון The תַּחֲנוּנִים, (וְהוּא רַחוּם) with which the *Tachanun* is augmented on Mondays and Thursdays have reference to the dire need of the entire nation for Divine aid. They thus quite aptly follow the *Shemone Esrei,* for in that portion of the service, too, it is only as members of the larger community and on behalf of all our brethren that we address to God the petitions pertinent to our lives as individuals. The daily *Tachanun* on the other hand,

דַּל כְּבוֹדֵנוּ בַּגּוֹיִם וְשִׁקְּצֽוּנוּ כְּטֻמְאַת הַנִּדָּה: עַד־מָתַי עֻזֶּֽךָ בַּשֶּׁבִי
וְתִפְאַרְתְּךָ בְּיַד־צָר: עֽוֹרְרָה גְבוּרָתְךָ וְקִנְאָתְךָ עַל־אוֹיְבֶֽיךָ הֵם
יֵבֽוֹשׁוּ וְיֵחַֽתּוּ מִגְּבוּרָתָם וְאַל־יִמְעֲטוּ לְפָנֶֽיךָ תְּלָאוֹתֵֽינוּ: מַהֵר
יְקַדְּמֽוּנוּ רַחֲמֶֽיךָ בְּיוֹם צָרָתֵֽנוּ וְאִם־לֹא לְמַעֲנֵֽנוּ לְמַעַנְךָ פְּעַל וְאַל־
תַּשְׁחֵית זֵֽכֶר שְׁאֵרִיתֵֽנוּ: וְחָנֵּֽנוּ הַמְיַחֲדִים שִׁמְךָ פַּעֲמַֽיִם בְּכָל־
יוֹם תָּמִיד בְּאַהֲבָה וְאוֹמְרִים שְׁמַע יִשְׂרָאֵל יְיָ אֱלֹהֵֽינוּ יְיָ, אֶחָד:

וַיֹּֽאמֶר דָּוִד אֶל־גָּד צַר־לִי מְאֹד נִפְּלָה־נָּא בְיַד־
יְהֹוָה כִּי־רַבִּים רַחֲמָיו וּבְיַד אָדָם אַל־אֶפֹּֽלָה:

רַחוּם וְחַנּוּן חָטָֽאתִי לְפָנֶֽיךָ יְיָ מָלֵא רַחֲמִים רַחֵם עָלַי וְקַבֵּל
תַּחֲנוּנַי: יְיָ אַל־בְּאַפְּךָ תוֹכִיחֵֽנִי וְאַל־בַּחֲמָתְךָ תְיַסְּרֵֽנִי: חָנֵּֽנִי יְיָ
כִּי־אֻמְלַל אָֽנִי רְפָאֵֽנִי יְיָ כִּי נִבְהֲלוּ עֲצָמָי: וְנַפְשִׁי נִבְהֲלָה מְאֹד

makes the individual aware of his separate identity and of his own need for help if he is to examine himself and turn heavenward to God. These are words which, originally uttered by David, guarantee even to one burdened by guilt and rejected by men the possibility of regaining God's favor and help.

ויאמר דוד (II Sam. 24:14) David had gravely sinned, and his heart was still crushed with remorse when Gad the prophet, at God's command, placed before him a choice of three punishments from which he, David, was told to select one; three years of famine, or three months of defeat in war, or three days of pestilence. David chose the last of these three alternatives explaining his choice in these words which give expression to his trust in God's compassion. His hopes were fulfilled. The pestilence lasted only half a day instead of three, and we should note here that many years later the Temple was erected at the very place where the dying was arrested.

they abominate us as the impurity of the unclean. How long shall Your invincible one be delivered into captivity; the one that glorifies You to the hand of the foe? Arouse Your almighty power and Your zeal over Your enemies, so that they may be deceived and collapse from their power, and may our sufferings not seem to trifling in Your sight. May Your compassion soon come to meet us on the day of our distress, and if not for our sake, do it for Your sake, and let the remembrance of our remnant not be destroyed. O favor the nation which proclaims the Unity of Your Name in constant love twice every day, saying "Hear Yisrael, *God*, our God, is *God* the Only *One*."

And David said to Gad, "I am greatly distressed; let us fall into the hand of *God*, for His compassion is great, but let me not fall into the hand of man." O You who are compassionate and gracious, I have sinned before You; O *God*, full of compassion, have compassion upon me and accept my supplications.

(Psalm 6) O *God*, rebuke me not in Your anger, and chastise me not in Your wrath. Favor me, O *God*, for I am bowed down. Heal me, O *God*, for my bones are afflicted. And my soul, above all,

---

If there is a *Sefer Torah* in the room where the prayer is recited, the worshippers bow their heads and cover their faces when reciting the *Tachanun*. נפילת אפים bowing before the Lord is tantamount to bowing before His Law (in accordance with Josh. 7:6).

ה׳ אל באפך May God not find it necessary to give outward expression of His anger in order to bring man to realize that he has erred, and may He not, in His righteous wrath, condemn him to suffer continued pain so that he might mend his ways. David is already filled with this awareness, but he lacks the strength to do anything about it; particularly, does he lack the strength of soul which has been crushed by his sufferings. ואתה ה׳ "And yet You are *God* ready at all times to grant new life and strength." אין במות זכרך Death is not the concept that is representative of God's being and of His sovereignty. The death of a human being is only a consequence of the law of nature handed down by God when the world began, and thus is merely a

וְאַתָּ יְיָ עַד־מָתָי׃ שׁוּבָה יְיָ חַלְּצָה נַפְשִׁי הוֹשִׁיעֵנִי לְמַעַן חַסְדֶּךָ׃

כִּי אֵין בַּמָּוֶת זִכְרֶךָ בִּשְׁאוֹל מִי יוֹדֶה־לָּךְ׃ יָגַעְתִּי

בְּאַנְחָתִי אַשְׂחֶה בְכָל־לַיְלָה מִטָּתִי בְּדִמְעָתִי עַרְשִׂי אַמְסֶה׃

עָשְׁשָׁה מִכַּעַס עֵינִי עָתְקָה בְּכָל־צוֹרְרָי׃ סוּרוּ מִמֶּנִּי כָּל־פֹּעֲלֵי

אָוֶן כִּי־שָׁמַע יְיָ קוֹל בִּכְיִי׃ שָׁמַע יְיָ תְּחִנָּתִי יְיָ תְּפִלָּתִי יִקָּח׃

יֵבֹשׁוּ וְיִבָּהֲלוּ מְאֹד כָּל־אֹיְבָי יָשֻׁבוּ יֵבֹשׁוּ רָגַע׃

On Monday and Thursday morning the following is added:

חי״ק יְיָ אֱלֹהֵי יִשְׂרָאֵל שׁוּב מֵחֲרוֹן אַפֶּךָ וְהִנָּחֵם עַל־הָרָעָה
לְעַמֶּךָ׃

ק׳ הַבֵּט מִשָּׁמַיִם וּרְאֵה כִּי הָיִינוּ לַעַג וָקֶלֶס בַּגּוֹיִם נֶחְשַׁבְנוּ כְּצֹאן
לַטֶּבַח יוּבָל לַהֲרוֹג וּלְאַבֵּד וּלְמַכָּה וּלְחֶרְפָּה׃

קו״ח וּבְכָל־זֹאת שִׁמְךָ לֹא שָׁכָחְנוּ נָא אַל־תִּשְׁכָּחֵנוּ׃ יי

ק׳ זָרִים אוֹמְרִים אֵין תּוֹחֶלֶת וְתִקְוָה, חוֹן אוֹם לְשִׁמְךָ מְקַוֶּה,

---

manifestation of the existence of that order of nature, the power of which no man can escape. But life, and resurrection in particular, the regaining of a life once lost—that is the force which truly reveals God in His power. It shows His standing above the forces of nature which He Himself had ordained, and proves that He is ready at all times to grant renewed life and vigor to man for all his future loyal endeavors in his service to God on earth. This is the basic difference between the heathen idea of idolatry on one hand and Jewish Divine truth on the other. To the heathen mind the power of its idols is demonstrated when these deities overthrow the strongest of human forces in the dreaded lethal force to which all living things succumb. This is so, because the heathen deities are in reality the forces of nature ordained by God. Jewish truth, however, tells us this: "As truly as I live," says *God,* "I do not take pleasure in the death of the wicked but in the repentance of the sinner from his path so that he may attain new life." It is not premature death,

is stricken, and You are *God*. How long, then? Return, O *God*, free my soul; help me for the sake of your loving-kindness. For in death there is no remembrance of You; in the grave, who will do homage to You? I am weary with sighing; I make my bed swim every night, I melt away my couch with my tears. My eye has rotted because of care; it has moved from its socket because of all that which oppresses me; yet depart from me, all you workers of violence, for *God* has heard the voice of my weeping. *God* has heard my supplication; *God* will also accept my prayer. My enemies all shall find themselves deceived and be greatly dismayed; they will return, and they shall suddenly find themselves deceived.

(Reader and Cong.) O *God*, God of Israel, turn back from the blazing of Your anger and let Your mind be changed concerning the evil intended for Your people.

(Cong.) Look down from heaven and see how we have become an object of scorn and derision among the nations; we are counted as sheep led to the slaughter, to be slain and destroyed, to be smitten and shamed.

(Cong. & Reader) And yet, despite all this, we have not forgotten Your Name; we beseech You, forget us not, O *God*, God of Yisrael turn back from the blazing of Your anger and let Your mind be changed concerning the evil intended for Your people.

(Cong.) Strangers say, "There is no more prospect and no hope." O favor the nation which places its hope in Your Name, O pure One!

---

but persevering life, paying due tribute to God, that is in accordance with His will. It is from this conviction that David, even when he seems to be at the end of his strength, draws his faith from the wondrous loving-kindness of God as confirmed by His very Name. תחנתי is the prayer entreating God for help; "supplications". תפלתי is the prayer seeking spiritual purification and proper understanding. רגע His recovery came suddenly. His life was restored from within as soon as his heart turned to God and his spirit attained the proper understanding.

ה׳ אלקי ישראל On Mondays and Thursdays, the days on which the nation is to look into itself and gather its thoughts before God (see above p. 161), we add supplications for help arising from our state of distress as a nation.

טָהוֹר יְשׁוּעָתֵנוּ קָרְבָה, יָגַעְנוּ וְלֹא הוּנַח־לָנוּ, רַחֲמֶיךָ יִכְבְּשׁוּ אֶת־כַּעַסְךָ מֵעָלֵינוּ:

קו"ח אָנָּא שׁוּב מֵחֲרוֹנָךְ וְרַחֵם סְגֻלָּה אֲשֶׁר בָּחָרְתָּ: יי

ק' חוּסָה יְיָ עָלֵינוּ בְּרַחֲמֶיךָ וְאַל־תִּתְּנֵנוּ בִּידֵי אַכְזָרִים, לָמָּה יֹאמְרוּ הַגּוֹיִם אַיֵּה נָא אֱלֹהֵיהֶם לְמַעַנְךָ עֲשֵׂה עִמָּנוּ חֶסֶד וְאַל־תְּאַחַר:

קו"ח אָנָּא שׁוּב מֵחֲרוֹנָךְ וְרַחֵם סְגֻלָּה אֲשֶׁר בָּחָרְתָּ: יי

ק' קוֹלֵנוּ תִשְׁמַע וְתָחֹן וְאַל־תִּטְּשֵׁנוּ בְּיַד אוֹיְבֵינוּ לִמְחוֹת אֶת־שְׁמֵנוּ, זְכוֹר אֲשֶׁר נִשְׁבַּעְתָּ לַאֲבוֹתֵינוּ כְּכוֹכְבֵי הַשָּׁמַיִם אַרְבֶּה אֶת־זַרְעֲכֶם, וְעַתָּה נִשְׁאַרְנוּ מְעַט מֵהַרְבֵּה:

קו"ח וּבְכָל־זֹאת שִׁמְךָ לֹא שָׁכָחְנוּ נָא אַל־תִּשְׁכָּחֵנוּ: יי

ק' עָזְרֵנוּ אֱלֹהֵי יִשְׁעֵנוּ עַל־דְּבַר כְּבוֹד־שְׁמֶךָ וְהַצִּילֵנוּ וְכַפֵּר עַל־חַטֹּאתֵינוּ לְמַעַן שְׁמֶךָ:

קו"ח יְיָ אֱלֹהֵי יִשְׂרָאֵל שׁוּב מֵחֲרוֹן אַפֶּךָ וְהִנָּחֵם עַל־הָרָעָה לְעַמֶּךָ:

On a public fastday (in many congregations every day) שומר ישראל *is added here:*

שׁוֹמֵר יִשְׂרָאֵל שְׁמוֹר שְׁאֵרִית יִשְׂרָאֵל וְאַל־יֹאבַד יִשְׂרָאֵל הָאוֹמְרִים שְׁמַע יִשְׂרָאֵל:

שוב וגו' are the words of Moshe with which he prayed for atonement for the transgression involving the *egel*. His prayer was answered.

Here is a description of our nation's abject state of destitution. We are despised by the other nations; they view us as a people having no right to demand that it not be exterminated (הבט), The nations of the world claim that we have neither hope nor prospects of deliverance (זרים). The hostile masses treat us with callous cruelty (חוסה). In the face of all this, we point out that, despite all this misery, we have never forgotten the Name of God

Bring Your salvation soon; we have worn ourselves out without finding rest; may Your compassion subdue and turn Your anger from us.

(Cong. & Reader) O turn back from Your wrath and have compassion upon the people whom You have chosen for Your own. O *God,* God of Yisrael, turn back from the blazing of Your anger and let Your mind be changed concerning the evil intended for Your people.

(Cong.) Spare us, O *God,* in Your compassion, and deliver us not into the hands of the cruel foes. Why should the nations say, "Where is their God now?" For Your own sake, deal kindly with us and do not delay.

(Cong. & Reader) O turn back from Your wrath and have compassion upon the people whom You have chosen for Your own. O *God,* God of Israel, turn back from the blazing of Your anger and let Your mind be changed concerning the evil intended for Your people.

(Cong.) Hear our voice and be gracious, and leave us not in the hand of our enemies to blot out our name. Remember what You have sworn to our fathers: "I will make your seed as numerous as the stars in heaven," and now we are left only a few out of many.

(Cong. & Reader) And yet, despite all this, we have not forgotten Your Name; we beseech You, forget us not. O *God,* God of Yisrael, turn back from the blazing of Your anger and let Your mind be changed concerning the evil intended for Your people.

(Cong.) Help us, O God of our salvation, for the sake of the glory of Your Name; deliver us, and pardon our sins according to Your Name.

(Cong. & Reader) O *God,* God of Yisrael, turn back from the blazing of Your anger and let Your mind be changed concerning the evil intended for Your people.

---

for the sake of Whose revelation we have had to bear all this suffering (וּבְכָל זֹאת) and now we appeal to the compassion of God (רַחֲמֶיךָ). We remind Him that it is through our survival that the nations of the world will recognise Him (לָמָּה יֹאמְרוּ), and we recall to Him the promise which He Himself had given to our ancestors, זְכוֹר אֲשֶׁר נִשְׁבַּעְתָּ.

שׁוֹמֵר גּוֹי אֶחָד שְׁמוֹר שְׁאֵרִית עַם אֶחָד וְאַל־יֹאבַד גּוֹי אֶחָד
הַמְיַחֲדִים שִׁמְךָ יְיָ אֱלֹהֵינוּ יְיָ אֶחָד :

שׁוֹמֵר גּוֹי קָדוֹשׁ שְׁמוֹר שְׁאֵרִית עַם קָדוֹשׁ וְאַל־יֹאבַד גּוֹי קָדוֹשׁ
הַמְשַׁלְּשִׁים בְּשָׁלֹשׁ קְדֻשּׁוֹת לְקָדוֹשׁ :

מִתְרַצֶּה בְּרַחֲמִים וּמִתְפַּיֵּם בְּתַחֲנוּנִים הִתְרַצֵּה וְהִתְפַּיֵּם לְדוֹר
עָנִי כִּי אֵין עוֹזֵר :

אָבִינוּ מַלְכֵּנוּ חָנֵּנוּ וַעֲנֵנוּ כִּי אֵין בָּנוּ מַעֲשִׂים עֲשֵׂה עִמָּנוּ
צְדָקָה וָחֶסֶד וְהוֹשִׁיעֵנוּ :

וַאֲנַחְנוּ לֹא נֵדַע מַה־נַּעֲשֶׂה כִּי עָלֶיךָ עֵינֵינוּ : זְכֹר רַחֲמֶיךָ יְיָ
וַחֲסָדֶיךָ כִּי מֵעוֹלָם הֵמָּה : יְהִי־חַסְדְּךָ יְיָ עָלֵינוּ כַּאֲשֶׁר יִחַלְנוּ
לָךְ : אַל־תִּזְכָּר־לָנוּ עֲוֹנוֹת רִאשׁוֹנִים מַהֵר יְקַדְּמוּנוּ רַחֲמֶיךָ כִּי
דַלּוֹנוּ מְאֹד : חָנֵּנוּ יְיָ חָנֵּנוּ כִּי־רַב שָׂבַעְנוּ בוּז : בְּרֹגֶז רַחֵם
תִּזְכּוֹר : כִּי הוּא יָדַע יִצְרֵנוּ זָכוּר כִּי־עָפָר אֲנָחְנוּ : עָזְרֵנוּ אֱלֹהֵי
יִשְׁעֵנוּ עַל־דְּבַר כְּבוֹד־שְׁמֶךָ וְהַצִּילֵנוּ וְכַפֵּר עַל־חַטֹּאתֵינוּ לְמַעַן
שְׁמֶךָ :

שומר ישראל This is an appeal to God in which we plead with Him to
guard the shattered remnant of Yisrael which, as "Yisrael", should serve as
a memorial of the dominion of God over man, a nation which, through the
declaration of *Shema*, constantly reminds itself of the task which, as the nation of God's sovereignty, it must fulfill. We beseech Him to preserve the
remnant of that people which is united in the unity and uniqueness of its purpose, the people which still bears through the world the avowal of the One
God. We beg Him to preserve that people which must guard its moral sanctity, both as גוי, a nation among other nations, and as עם, a people in its own
inner life. This is the people which recites the three-fold call of sanctification
that was originally voiced by the angel hosts, as a constant reminder that the
Lord expects to be hallowed not only by angels in the heavens but also by
the men on earth by unstinting devotion to the fulfillment of His will. (See
notes above to קדושת יוצר.)

O Guardian of Yisrael, guard the remnant of Yisrael, and let not Yisrael perish, who say, "Hear Yisrael."

O Guardian of the one people, guard the remnant of the one people and let not the one people perish, who proclaim the Oneness of Your Name, saying, "*God* our God, is *God* the Only *One.*"

O Guardian of the holy people, guard the remnant of the holy people, and let not the holy people perish who repeat the three-fold hallowing of the Holy One.

O You Who are moved by compassion and conciliated by supplications, be moved and reconciled to the afflicted generation, for there is none else to help.

Our Father, our King, favor us and answer us; if we have no merits, then You show us righteousness and loving-kindness and save us.

As for us, we know not what to do, for our eyes are upon You. Remember Your compassion and Your kindnesses O *God,* as they have been of old. Let Your loving-kindness O *God* be upon us, even as we have waited for You. Remember not the sins of those who came before us; let Your compassion come to meet us, for we are brought very low. Favor us, O *God,* favor us, for we are exceedingly sated with contempt; even while we tremble, remember to have compassion. For He Who knows our form remembers that we are dust. Help us, O God of our salvation, for the sake of the glory of Your Name; deliver us and pardon our sins according to Your Name.

ואנחנו לא נדע This is the sentence with which King Yehoshaphat (II Chron. 20:12) concluded his prayer for Divine aid in his struggle against the hostile nations that were united against him. His prayer was answered. As we rise once more after having taken stock of ourselves and gathered our thoughts before God, we, too, know that we still have one refuge for all times to come and regardless of what the years may bring—God, to Whom we turn our eyes with trusting hope. For even while we are still trembling, He already remembers His compassion in judging us, taking into account the weaknesses of the earthly element within us to which the spiritual and Divine spark in our souls is wed while our bodies live here below. He will grant us help, deliverance, and atonement for our sins for the sake of the ways of His Providence as implied in His Name, and so that His Name may be glorified.

The following paragraph is added on Mondays and Thursdays (and in many communities also on every Fast Day), except on Rosh Chodesh, Passover Eve, the Intermediate Days of Festivals, Chanukkah and Purim.

מנהג פולין גדול.   מנהג אשכנז וביהם ופולין קטן.

אֵל אֶרֶךְ אַפַּיִם וְרַב־חֶסֶד וֶאֱמֶת | אֵל אֶרֶךְ אַפַּיִם וְרַב־חֶסֶד

אַל־תַּסְתֵּר פָּנֶיךָ מִמֶּנּוּ : חוּסָה יְיָ | וֶאֱמֶת צַ־בְּאַפְּךָ תוֹכִיחֵנוּ : חוּסָה

עַל־יִשְׂרָאֵל עַמֶּךָ וְהַצִּילֵנוּ מִכָּל־ | יְיָ עַל־עַמֶּךָ וְהוֹשִׁיעֵנוּ מִכָּל־

רָע : חָטָאנוּ לְךָ אָדוֹן סְלַח־נָא כְּרוֹב רַחֲמֶיךָ אֵל :

סדר קריאת התורה

When the Torah is taken from the Ark, the following is said:

וַיְהִי בִּנְסֹעַ הָאָרֹן וַיֹּאמֶר מֹשֶׁה קוּמָה יְיָ וְיָפֻצוּ אֹיְבֶיךָ וְיָנֻסוּ

מְשַׂנְאֶיךָ מִפָּנֶיךָ : כִּי מִצִּיּוֹן תֵּצֵא תוֹרָה וּדְבַר־יְיָ מִירוּשָׁלָםִ :

בָּרוּךְ שֶׁנָּתַן תּוֹרָה לְעַמּוֹ יִשְׂרָאֵל בִּקְדֻשָּׁתוֹ :

ויש שאומרים עוד בריך שמה וכו'

בְּרִיךְ שְׁמֵהּ דְּמָרֵא עָלְמָא בְּרִיךְ כִּתְרָךְ וְאַתְרָךְ · יְהֵא רְעוּתָךְ

עִם עַמָּךְ יִשְׂרָאֵל לְעָלַם · וּפֻרְקַן יְמִינָךְ אַחֲזֵי לְעַמָּךְ בְּבֵית

אל ארך אפים. Moshe and the associates who stood by his side ordained that portions from the Torah be read at public congregational assemblies on Sabbaths, Mondays and Thursdays. Later, Ezra instituted the practice of reading the Law at Mincha services on the Sabbath, and fixed the number of persons to be called upon to read, as well as the size of the portions to be read on Mondays and Thursdays. Mondays, Thursdays, and also Fast Days, were designated as times when the entire nation was to take stock of itself and assemble before the Lord. When, on those days, we ascend to the Ark to bring down into our midst the Book of God's Law for public reading, we realize that if we measure our worth by the standard of God's will as set down in this Book, we must admit that we are wanting, and that we are unworthy even to take the Torah into our hands. Indeed, we cannot help sensing that we are hardly even worthy to live on as its bearers. Thus aware of our inadequacy and unworthiness we utter the words אל ארך אפים with which, before we go up to open the Ark of the Law on those days of particular self-examination, we appeal to the grace of God, Who is slow to anger and ready at all times to grant forgiveness.

The following paragraph is added on Mondays and Thursdays (and in many communities also on every Fast Day), except on Rosh Chodesh, Passover Eve, the Intermediate Days of Festivals, Chanukkah and Purim.

O God, slow to anger and full of loving-kindness and truth, hide not Your face from us. Spare Your people Yisrael, O God, and deliver us from all evil. We have sinned against You, O Lord. forgive, we beseech You, according to the abundance of Your compassion, O God.

O *God,* slow to anger and full of loving-kindness and truth, rebuke us not in Your anger. Spare Your people Yisrael, O God, and save us from all

When the Torah is taken from the Ark, the following is said:

And it came to pass, whenever the Ark went forth, that Moshe would say, "Rise up, O *God,* so that Your enemies be scattered and that those who hate You may flee before Your countenance." For out of Tzion shall go forth the Torah, and the Word of *God* from Yerushalayim: Blessed be He Who in His holiness gave the Torah to His people Yisrael.

In some communities the following is added:

Blessed be the Name of the Master of the Universe. Blessed be Your dominion and Your abode. May Your good will abide forever with Your people Yisrael, and may Your people behold the salvation

---

ויהי בנסע When the Law of *God* goes forth from the Ark to enter into our midst to do its blessed work, we repeat the words which Moshe said whenever the Ark of the Covenant went forth from its resting-place. (Num. 10:35). In this manner do we remind ourselves of the invincibility of the Word of God which none can withstand and which in the end will emerge victorious over all its enemies, and by so doing, even before we read from His Law, we endeavor to prepare for Him within our own hearts that throne from which we shall let His Word reign over every phase of our lives. For wherever the Torah enters, there God enters also, and those who hate this Divine Law are also the foes of God. כי מציון For the word of God is to go forth from our midst far beyond the confines of Yisrael and to enter into the hearts and minds of all the rest of mankind; but if it is to achieve this end, it must first succeed in hallowing the lives and personalities of the members of our own people. Hence we pledge to do the will of Him (ברוך) Who has chosen us as His people, Who has given us the Law in order that we may discharge our task to be "Yisrael", the messenger of His dominion, and Who has said to us concerning His sanctity, "Be holy, for I, your God, am holy" (Lev. 19:1).

מִקְדְּשָׁךְ וּלְאַמְטוֹיֵא לָנָא מְטוֹב נְהוֹרָךְ וּלְקַבֵּל צְלוֹתָנָא בְּרַחֲמִין׃
יְהֵא רַעֲוָא קֳדָמָךְ דְּתוֹרִיךְ לָן חַיִּין בְּטִיבוּתָא וְלֶהֱוֵא אֲנָא פְקִידָא
בְּגוֹ צַדִּיקַיָּא לְמִרְחַם עֲלַי וּלְמִנְטַר יָתִי וְיָת כָּל־דִּי לִי וְדִי לְעַמָּךְ
יִשְׂרָאֵל׃ אַנְתְּ הוּא זָן לְכֹלָּא וּמְפַרְנֵס לְכֹלָּא׃ אַנְתְּ הוּא שַׁלִּיט עַל
כֹּלָּא׃ אַנְתְּ הוּא דְּשַׁלִּיט עַל־מַלְכַיָּא וּמַלְכוּתָא דִּילָךְ הִיא׃ אֲנָא עַבְדָּא
דְקֻדְשָׁא בְּרִיךְ הוּא דְּסָגִדְנָא קַמֵּהּ וּמִקַּמָּא דִּיקַר אוֹרַיְתֵהּ בְּכָל־
עִדָּן וְעִדָּן׃ לָא עַל אֱנָשׁ רָחִיצְנָא וְלָא עַל־בַּר־אֱלָהִין סָמִיכְנָא׃
אֶלָּא בֵּאלָהָא דִשְׁמַיָּא׃ דְּהוּא אֱלָהָא קְשׁוֹט׃ וְאוֹרַיְתֵהּ קְשׁוֹט׃
וּנְבִיאוֹהִי קְשׁוֹט׃ וּמַסְגֵּא לְמֶעְבַּד טַבְוָן וּקְשׁוֹט׃ בֵּהּ אֲנָא רָחִיץ׃
וְלִשְׁמֵהּ קַדִּישָׁא יַקִּירָא אֲנָא אֲמַר תּוּשְׁבְּחָן׃ יְהֵא רַעֲוָא קֳדָמָךְ
דְּתִפְתַּח לִבִּי בְּאוֹרַיְתָא וְתַשְׁלִם מִשְׁאֲלִין דְּלִבִּי׃ וְלִבָּא דְכָל־עַמָּךְ
יִשְׂרָאֵל׃ לְטָב וּלְחַיִּין וְלִשְׁלָם׃

The חזן *receives the* ספר תורה *and intones:*

גַּדְּלוּ לַיְיָ אִתִּי׃ וּנְרוֹמְמָה שְׁמוֹ יַחְדָּו׃

קהל׃ לְךָ יְיָ הַגְּדֻלָּה וְהַגְּבוּרָה וְהַתִּפְאֶרֶת וְהַנֵּצַח וְהַהוֹד כִּי

גדלו When the Reader takes up the Scroll of the Law to bring it into the midst of the congregation, he calls upon the assembly to picture the greatness of God and to pay Him the tribute due His exalted majesty. The congregation then responds with לך וגו׳, proclaiming the greatness, power, glory and all-conquering majesty of God to Whom belong all things, individually and collectively, in Heaven and on earth, and declaring that all persons occupying positions of leadership among men and all forces wielding power in nature are merely servants and instruments of God's own sovereignty. And if we thus acknowledge the supreme grandeur and majesty of God, it follows quite naturally that we must dedicate ourselves entirely to Him and subordinate all our conduct and every facet of our personalities to His rule. But our

of Your right hand in Your Sanctuary, to give us of the good of Your light and to accept our prayer in compassion. May it be Your will to prolong our life in happiness, so that I may be remembered along with the righteous, so that You may have compassion upon me and protect me and mine and all that belongs to Your people Yisrael. You are the One Who grants sustenance and preservation to all; You are the One Who reigns over all things; You are the One Who reigns over kings, and the kingship is Yours. I am the servant of the Holy One, blessed be He. I bow at all times before the majesty of His Torah. I trust in no man nor do I rely on any angel* but only in the God of Heaven Who is the true God, Whose Torah is truth, Whose prophets are true and Who performs many deeds of goodness and truth. In Him do I put my trust, and to His holy honored Name do I utter praises. May it be Your will to open my heart to Your Torah and to fulfill the wishes of my heart and of the hearts of all Your people Yisrael for the good, for life and for peace.

(*Reader*) O declare the greatness of *God* with me, and let us exalt His Name together.

(*Cong.*) Yours, O *God,* is the greatness and the power and the glory and the victory and the majesty, for all that is in Heaven and on

---

* בר אלהין is the term used for "angels" in Daniel 3:25.

---

dedication to God is simply devotion to His Law, the abode of which He has called His Sanctuary and His "footstool"; that is, the place of His presence on earth. And if we cause our lives on earth to strive upward to set up this Divine Law and its Sanctuary as the lofty pinnacle of all endeavors, the Law in its turn will transfigure all our lives into a "mountain of the Lord" which participates in the consecration of His holiness. Hence the command to cast ourselves down at His footstool and His holy mountain, that is, to dedicate ourselves wholly and unstintingly to His Law and to the endeavor to raise all earthly things to the lofty level of the Law, would be a logical consequence of our acknowledgement of the majesty and grandeur of God. For our God is holy, and the tribute which He demands of us is nothing more and nothing less than the hallowing of all of our own being, in accordance with His will as it is set forth in His Law.

כל בַּשָּׁמַיִם וּבָאָרֶץ לְךָ יְיָ הַמַּמְלָכָה וְהַמִּתְנַשֵּׂא לְכָל לְרֹאשׁ
רוֹמְמוּ יְיָ אֱלֹהֵינוּ וְהִשְׁתַּחֲווּ לַהֲדֹם רַגְלָיו קָדוֹשׁ הוּא: רוֹמְמוּ יְיָ
אֱלֹהֵינוּ וְהִשְׁתַּחֲווּ לְהַר קָדְשׁוֹ כִּי קָדוֹשׁ יְיָ אֱלֹהֵינוּ:

אַב הָרַחֲמִים הוּא יְרַחֵם עַם עֲמוּסִים וְיִזְכֹּר בְּרִית אֵיתָנִים
וְיַצִּיל נַפְשׁוֹתֵינוּ מִן הַשָּׁעוֹת הָרָעוֹת וְיִגְעַר בְּיֵצֶר הָרַע מִן הַנְּשׂוּאִים
וְיָחֹן אוֹתָנוּ לִפְלֵיטַת עוֹלָמִים וִימַלֵּא מִשְׁאֲלוֹתֵינוּ בְּמִדָּה טוֹבָה
יְשׁוּעָה וְרַחֲמִים:

וְתִגָּלֶה וְתֵרָאֶה מַלְכוּתוֹ עָלֵינוּ בִּזְמַן קָרוֹב וְיָחֹן פְּלֵיטָתֵנוּ וּפְלֵיטַת
עַמּוֹ בֵּית יִשְׂרָאֵל לְחֵן וּלְחֶסֶד וּלְרַחֲמִים וּלְרָצוֹן וְנֹאמַר אָמֵן:

אב הרחמים This task of ours to sanctify our personalities and our lives carries with it the call to fight against the evil inclination of lust, a struggle in which we need Divine assistance if we are to emerge as the victors. Therefore we now pray for help, for deliverance and protection during the evil hours of temptation. In Isaiah 46:3,4 we are called העמוסים מני בטן הנשואים מני רחם the people which, from the very outset of its history, has been chosen to bear the burden of difficult tasks and grievous sufferings, but which, at the same time, has been upheld by God Himself for this purpose from the very beginning. These prophetic words assure us of God's help for all times to come so that we may shoulder our burdens and successfully discharge our tasks. The terms עמוסים and נשואים as employed in this paragraph refer to this our destiny and to this Divine promise. פליטה denotes escape from a dangerous situation. עולמים may imply "for both worlds"; that is, for both this world and the world to come.

ותגלה is a continuation and conclusion of the paragraph beginning with Av harachamim. The thought expressed here is that once, with the help of God, we will have won the victory over our baser urges, the time of deliverance, which will demonstrate God's reign over us to all of mankind, will be close at hand.

earth is Yours. Yours is the sovereignty and all that which rules over anything on earth. Exalt *God* our God and cast yourselves down at His footstool, holy is He. Exalt *God* our God and cast yourselves down at His holy mountain, for *God,* our God, is holy.

May the Father of compassion have compassion upon the people of the heavy laden. May he remember the covenant with the Patriarchs; may He deliver our souls from evil hours; may He frighten away the evil inclination from those who have been upheld, and may He favor us with deliverance for all eternity and fulfill our petitions in accordance with the measure of good, of salvation and of compassion.

When the Torah is unrolled, the Reader says:

So that His kingdom may soon be revealed and become visible to us, and that He may favor our rescued remnants and the rescued remnants of His people the House of Yisrael with grace, loving-kindness, compassion and good will. And let us say, Amen.

הבו גדל לאלהינו, הכל It was with these words that Moshe, in his valedictory ode to his assembled people (Deut. 32:3) began the proclamation by which he put before us the ways of God's rule and set down for his contemporaries and for all future generations the nature of our relationship to God and our obligation toward Him. From this call to recognize the word of God Himself in the words of Moshe and to pay Him the tribute due His greatness, the Sages inferred that a blessing had to be said before the reading of the Torah and that the congregation should join in this blessing, doing homage to God and to His word. Therefore we have here again the same summons, addressed this time to הכל "all of them", signifying that not only the person called to read from the Scroll, but the entire congregation with him, should participate in both the blessing and the reading, doing homage to God and paying honor to His Word. In accordance with the injunction *vekidashto* (Lev. 21:8) that priority should be given to descendants of the priestly family of Aharon at any occasion where their sacred office can be honored, the first person to be called to the Torah is a *Kohen,* if there is one present in the congregation. It is only after him that a Levite is so honored, and the ordinary "Israelite" comes third. Before the person called to the Torah recites his own blessing, the entire congregation is reminded that the Law of God, the Holy

הַכֹּל הָבוּ גֹדֶל לֵאלֹהֵינוּ וּתְנוּ כָבוֹד לַתּוֹרָה: כֹּהֵן קְרַב יַעֲמֹד
(ר"פ ב"פ הכהן): בָּרוּךְ שֶׁנָּתַן תּוֹרָה לְעַמּוֹ יִשְׂרָאֵל בִּקְדֻשָּׁתוֹ:
תּוֹרַת יְיָ תְּמִימָה מְשִׁיבַת נָפֶשׁ: עֵדוּת יְיָ נֶאֱמָנָה מַחְכִּימַת פֶּתִי:
פִּקּוּדֵי יְיָ יְשָׁרִים מְשַׂמְּחֵי־לֵב מִצְוַת יְיָ בָּרָה מְאִירַת עֵינָיִם: יְיָ עֹז
לְעַמּוֹ יִתֵּן יְיָ יְבָרֵךְ אֶת־עַמּוֹ בַשָּׁלוֹם: הָאֵל תָּמִים דַּרְכּוֹ אִמְרַת
יְיָ צְרוּפָה. מָגֵן הוּא לְכֹל הַחוֹסִים בּוֹ:

קהל ויחן וְאַתֶּם הַדְּבֵקִים בַּיְיָ אֱלֹהֵיכֶם חַיִּים כֻּלְּכֶם הַיּוֹם:

The person called to read from the Law recites the following blessing:

בָּרְכוּ אֶת־יְיָ הַמְבֹרָךְ:

קהל : בָּרוּךְ יְיָ הַמְבֹרָךְ לְעוֹלָם וָעֶד:

The person called to read from the Law repeats this response and continues:

בָּרוּךְ אַתָּה יְיָ, אֱלֹהֵינוּ מֶלֶךְ הָעוֹלָם, אֲשֶׁר בָּחַר־בָּנוּ מִכָּל־הָעַמִּים,
וְנָתַן־לָנוּ אֶת־תּוֹרָתוֹ. בָּרוּךְ אַתָּה יְיָ, נוֹתֵן הַתּוֹרָה:

After the reading of the Portion of the Law, he recites the following blessing:

בָּרוּךְ אַתָּה יְיָ, אֱלֹהֵינוּ מֶלֶךְ הָעוֹלָם, אֲשֶׁר נָתַן־לָנוּ תּוֹרַת אֱמֶת,
וְחַיֵּי עוֹלָם נָטַע בְּתוֹכֵנוּ. בָּרוּךְ אַתָּה יְיָ, נוֹתֵן הַתּוֹרָה:

One, was given us in order that we, too, may become holy, that it affords us instruction, wisdom, serenity and enlightenment for all the concerns and desires of our souls, that it seeks to inure us against all temptation and that it is designed to cause us to dwell together in peace by teaching all of us to live in harmony with our God. תמים דרכו His Providence is constantly and unalterably lovingkindness and justice, and whatever He may decree for us is meant to purify and to refine us, so that we may better be able to discharge the task set us by His Law. And whoever, trusting in God, walks in the path shown by this Law and holds fast to Him, is assured of life and Divine protection. ואתם הדבקים is what Moshe told all those (Deut. 4:4) who steadfastly resisted the lure to forsake their God for the cult of the *Baal Pe'or*.

Let all magnify our God and give honor to the Law. Let a *Kohen* come forward. Arise, ... the *Kohen*. Blessed be He Who in His holiness gave the Law to His people Yisrael. But the Law of *God*, all-encompassing, responds to the soul; the testimony of *God* is faithful, making wise the inexperienced. The mandates of *God* are upright, rejoicing the heart; the commandment of *God* is brilliant, enlightening the eyes. To His people, *God* will grant power to be victorious over all; *God* will bless His people with peace. God, His way is perfect, purification is the word of *God*; He is a shield to all who put their trust in Him.

(Cong. & Reader)

And you who have held fast to *God* your God are all alive today.

> *The person called to read from the Law recites the following blessing:*
> Bless *God* Who is to be blessed.

(Cong.) Blessed be *God*, Who is to be blessed, in all eternity.

> *The person called to read from the Law repeats this response and continues:*

Blessed be You *God* our God, King of the Universe, Who has chosen us from among all the peoples and given us Your Torah. Blessed be You *God*, Giver of the Torah.

> *After the reading of the Portion of the Law, he recites the following blessing:*

Blessed be You *God* our God, King of the Universe, Who has given us the Torah of truth and has planted life eternal in our midst. Blessed be You *God*, Giver of the Torah.

ברכו, See above p. 106.

ברוך אשר בחר, See above p. 8.

ברוך או"נ Before we read the portion from the Torah we take to our hearts the thought that the sole purpose of our election as a "chosen people" was and still is the Torah; in other words, that we recognize and fulfill the Law of God. Now, after the portion from the Law has been read, we declare what the Torah is and what it should mean to us. The Law is truly *torath emeth;* it is eternally unchangeable because it is that truth which is subject to neither change nor evolution. It is we who, through study and observance of the Law, should constantly endeavor to alter and to readjust our personalities in accordance with the requirements of this Law, and thus gain eternal life. It is for this purpose that God has planted the Torah *within us* or *in our midst* (בתוכנו can mean either) as the עץ החיים, the Tree of Life.

*Persons who have recovered from a serious illness, who have safely come
through a journey by sea or some dangerous experience, now recite the
following prayer:*

בָּרוּךְ אַתָּה יְיָ, אֱלֹהֵינוּ מֶלֶךְ הָעוֹלָם, הַגּוֹמֵל לְחַיָּבִים

(כ"ח לרעים) טוֹבוֹת, שֶׁגְּמָלַנִי כָּל־טוֹב:

דיא געאיינדע: מִי שֶׁגְּמָלְךָ כָּל־טוֹב הוּא יִגְמָלְךָ כָּל־טוֹב סֶלָה:

When the Torah is raised, the Congregation says:

וְזֹאת הַתּוֹרָה אֲשֶׁר־שָׂם מֹשֶׁה לִפְנֵי בְּנֵי יִשְׂרָאֵל עַל־פִּי יְיָ
בְּיַד־מֹשֶׁה: עֵץ־חַיִּים הִיא לַמַּחֲזִיקִים בָּהּ וְתֹמְכֶיהָ מְאֻשָּׁר:
דְּרָכֶיהָ דַרְכֵי־נֹעַם וְכָל־נְתִיבֹתֶיהָ שָׁלוֹם: אֹרֶךְ יָמִים בִּימִינָהּ
בִּשְׂמֹאלָהּ עֹשֶׁר וְכָבוֹד: יְיָ חָפֵץ לְמַעַן צִדְקוֹ יַגְדִּיל תּוֹרָה
וְיַאְדִּיר:

ברוך הגומל Psalm 107 bids all those who have been delivered from mortal
danger to avow their gratitude to God before an assembled congregation. Accordingly the person making his avowal of thanksgiving publicly declares that
God deals kindly even with *chayavim* those who not only are undeserving of
favor but who, in fact, might have been deserving of the very opposite of
kindness. Therefore, if God has rendered him "every kindness" he must view
this act of Divine favor not as a reward for any past merits of his own, but
as a binding obligation for the future. Then the entire congregation in unison
voices the wish that God may continue to deal kindly with him.

וזאת The *Sefer Torah* is raised aloft, high above the heads of the assembled congregation and, unrolled, is held up for all to see. For the Torah
is the treasure which rules supreme over the congregation and which the congregation must uphold and raise on high. (Cf. Ramban to Deut. 27:26.) To
this very day we recognize it as the same Law which Moshe placed before
the Children of Yisrael for them to keep and to fulfill. However, it is by no
means "The Law of *Moshe*". It was by the mouth of God Himself that it
was first pronounced. The hand of Moshe served solely as an instrument to
write it down and to bring it to the people. עץ חיים The soil gives of its strength
and substance to the tree that is planted in it. In this manner the soil ennobles
its own wealth by having it absorbed into the life and growth of the tree so
that the latter blossoms and bears fruit. And what is true of the soil, is true

Persons who have recovered from a serious illness, who have safely come through a journey by sea or some dangerous experience, now recite the following prayer:

Blessed be You *God* our God, King of the Universe, Who does good to the undeserving and Who has rendered every kindness to me.

(Cong.) May He Who rendered you every kindness continue to do good to you forever.

When the Torah is raised, the Congregation says:

And this is the Torah which Moshe placed before the sons of Yisrael, at *God's* command, through Moshe. It is a tree of life to those who cleave to it, and a happy group are those who support it. Its ways are ways of pleasantness and all its paths are peace. Long life is in its right hand; in its left hand are riches and honor. *God* was pleased, because of His righteousness, to render the Torah increasingly great and glorious.

---

also of those men who cleave to the Law of the Lord and let it be their guide. Because they thus dedicate all their energies and substance to the spirit of this Law and to the power of the will of God as revealed in its words, their own wealth grows and their talents unfold, they are ennobled and refined and bear ripe fruit, and this fruit is none other than חיים "life", for only the Divine ideal, thus translated into living reality, can be true life. תומכיה is in the plural, while מאושר is in the singular. This indicates that if it is for the sake of the preservation and upholding of the Torah that the many pool their energies, these many will be welded into one united group through their common striving in behalf of the Torah. דרכיה, the goals after which the Torah teaches us to strive, and the paths which it shows us to these goals are in keeping with the true nature of man and of human society, therefore even the very effort involved in this striving should make man happy. נתיבתיה (נתב related to נדב) the "paths" which are not explicitly indicated in the Torah but are to be chosen freely by each individual according to his own personality. They must, however, be in the spirit of the Law. הטוב והישר By virtue of the Torah spirit which engenders them, they are free of all selfish motives and hence will bring about universal peace. ארך ימים is "length of days", "long life", liberation from the bonds of all that is transitory, a gift of God which weds all the thoughts, endeavors and achievements even of physical life here below to the eternity of all things Godly and makes them endure beyond the brief span of fleeting transiency. *Orech Yamim* is the actual gift which the Torah offers

הגולל! המפה בספר תורה יאמר פסוק לך יי הגדולה וגו' גם יאמר יהי רצון
מלפניך יי אלהי ואלהי אביתי שיתגוללו רחמיך על מדותיך ותתנהג
עם בניך במדת טובך ותכנס להם לפנים משורת הדין.

On those Mondays and Thursdays on which תחנון *is said, the Reader recites*
the following before returning the Torah to the Ark:

יְהִי רָצוֹן מִלִּפְנֵי אָבִינוּ שֶׁבַּשָּׁמַיִם · לְכוֹנֵן אֶת־בֵּית חַיֵּינוּ וּלְהָשִׁיב

אֶת־שְׁכִינָתוֹ בְּתוֹכֵנוּ בִּמְהֵרָה בְיָמֵינוּ · וְנֹאמַר אָמֵן :

יְהִי רָצוֹן מִלִּפְנֵי אָבִינוּ שֶׁבַּשָּׁמַיִם · לְרַחֵם עָלֵינוּ וְעַל פְּלֵיטָתֵנוּ

וְלִמְנוֹעַ מַשְׁחִית וּמַגֵּפָה מֵעָלֵינוּ וּמֵעַל כָּל־עַמּוֹ בֵּית יִשְׂרָאֵל ·

וְנֹאמַר אָמֵן :

יְהִי רָצוֹן מִלִּפְנֵי אָבִינוּ שֶׁבַּשָּׁמַיִם · לְקַיֶּם־בָּנוּ חַכְמֵי יִשְׂרָאֵל ·

הֵם וּנְשֵׁיהֶם וּבְנֵיהֶם וּבְנוֹתֵיהֶם וְתַלְמִידֵיהֶם וְתַלְמִידֵי תַלְמִידֵיהֶם

בְּכָל־מְקוֹמוֹת מוֹשְׁבוֹתֵיהֶם · וְנֹאמַר אָמֵן :

יְהִי רָצוֹן מִלִּפְנֵי אָבִינוּ שֶׁבַּשָּׁמַיִם · שֶׁנִּשְׁמַע וְנִתְבַּשֵּׂר בְּשׂוֹרוֹת

טוֹבוֹת יְשׁוּעוֹת וְנֶחָמוֹת · וִיקַבֵּץ נִדָּחֵינוּ מֵאַרְבַּע כַּנְפוֹת הָאָרֶץ ·

וְנֹאמַר אָמֵן :

אַחֵינוּ כָּל־בֵּית־יִשְׂרָאֵל הַנְּתוּנִים בְּצָרָה וּבְשִׁבְיָה · הָעוֹמְדִים

בֵּין בַּיָּם וּבֵין בַּיַּבָּשָׁה · הַמָּקוֹם יְרַחֵם עֲלֵיהֶם וְיוֹצִיאֵם מִצָּרָה

לִרְוָחָה · וּמֵאֲפֵלָה לְאוֹרָה · וּמִשִּׁעְבּוּד לִגְאֻלָּה · הַשְׁתָּא בַּעֲגָלָא

וּבִזְמַן קָרִיב · וְנֹאמַר אָמֵן :

---

as a reward with its "right hand" to those who cleave to it. But riches and
honor which the Torah holds out in its left hand as a supplement to its gift
of life, also follow in its wake. This additional gift belongs to the loyal adherents of the Torah even if the short-sighted, superficial gaze should fail
to see it. And it is only the Torah that can transform this superficial material
wealth and glory also into true, genuine "riches and honor."

ה' חפץ. The term צדק is always employed in Prophetic literature to denote
the ideal of Divine righteousness which one day, by His Providence, will reign

On those Mondays and Thursdays on which תחנון *is said, the Reader recites the following before returning the Torah to the Ark:*

May it be the will of our Father in Heaven to establish the House of our life and to cause His presence to dwell in our midst once more, speedily in our days, and let us say, Amen.

May it be the will of our Father in Heaven to have compassion upon us and upon our rescued remnant, and to ward off destruction and plague from us and from all of His people, the House of Yisrael, and let us say, Amen.

May it be the will of our Father in Heaven to preserve in our midst the wise men of Yisrael, them, their wives, their sons and daughters, their disciples and the disciples of their disciples, in all their dwelling places, and let us say, Amen.

May it be the will of our Father in Heaven that we may hear and receive good tidings of salvation and consolation, and that He may gather our dispersed from all the four ends of the earth, and let us say, Amen.

As for our brethren, the entire house of Yisrael, who still remain in distress and captivity, whether they be on the sea or on dry land, may the Omnipresent have compassion upon them and lead them from [the straits of] oppression to the breadth [of relief], from darkness to light, from slavery to redemption, now, speedily, and at a near time, and let us say, Amen.

---

supreme upon all the earth. It is in the service of such a future that the Torah stands, and it is for the sake of this goal that it is pleasing in the sight of God to have the Torah grow increasingly in greatness and glory.

יהי רצון Now we plead for the fulfillment of the yearnings and desires common to us all: for the restoration of the Temple, for the protection and preservation of the remnant of our people that has escaped destruction, for the life and welfare of the teachers of the Torah together with their families and disciples, and finally for the coming of the promised tidings of salvation and consolation and the ingathering of our dispersed. בית חיינו is the Temple whose Holy of Holies was the Abode of God's Law, which is the source and support of our lives.

אחינו This is a prayer for all our brethren, near and far away, who, enmeshed in oppression and distress, patiently await their deliverance. We pray that God, in keeping with His good will, redeem them; if not now, then speedily or at least in the not too-distant future.

The Reader takes the Torah back to the Ark and says:

יְהַלְלוּ אֶת־שֵׁם יְהֹוָה כִּי־נִשְׂגָּב שְׁמוֹ לְבַדּוֹ:

קהל · הוֹדוֹ עַל־אֶרֶץ וְשָׁמָיִם · וַיָּרֶם קֶרֶן לְעַמּוֹ תְּהִלָּה לְכָל־
חֲסִידָיו לִבְנֵי יִשְׂרָאֵל עַם קְרֹבוֹ הַלְלוּיָהּ:

כד לְדָוִד מִזְמוֹר · לַיהֹוָה הָאָרֶץ וּמְלוֹאָהּ תֵּבֵל וְיֹשְׁבֵי
בָהּ: כִּי־הוּא עַל־יַמִּים יְסָדָהּ וְעַל־נְהָרוֹת יְכוֹנְנֶהָ:
מִי־יַעֲלֶה בְהַר יְהֹוָה וּמִי־יָקוּם בִּמְקוֹם קָדְשׁוֹ: נְקִי
כַפַּיִם וּבַר לֵבָב אֲשֶׁר לֹא־נָשָׂא לַשָּׁוְא נַפְשִׁי וְלֹא נִשְׁבַּע
לְמִרְמָה: יִשָּׂא בְרָכָה מֵאֵת יְהֹוָה וּצְדָקָה מֵאֱלֹהֵי יִשְׁעוֹ: זֶה דּוֹר
דֹּרְשָׁיו מְבַקְשֵׁי פָנֶיךָ יַעֲקֹב סֶלָה: שְׂאוּ שְׁעָרִים רָאשֵׁיכֶם וְהִנָּשְׂאוּ
פִּתְחֵי עוֹלָם וְיָבוֹא מֶלֶךְ הַכָּבוֹד: מִי זֶה מֶלֶךְ הַכָּבוֹד · יְהֹוָה עִזּוּז
וְגִבּוֹר יְהֹוָה גִּבּוֹר מִלְחָמָה: שְׂאוּ שְׁעָרִים רָאשֵׁיכֶם וּשְׂאוּ פִּתְחֵי

יהללו As the Reader takes the Book of the Torah into his hands to return it to the Ark, he declares that God's glory, as revealed in His mighty acts, should be recognized and praised far beyond the confines of the Jewish people, wherever the heavens are spread out over the earth. When the Lord will lead Yisrael to honor and salvation, it will also be a sign of praise and appreciation for all those, regardless of nationality, who dedicate themselves to Him. And the only distinction that Yisrael will then have among all the others is that it will be acknowledged as the one people which had been near to God from the very beginning.

לדוד מזמור (Psalm 24). This Psalm extols that eventual gathering of all of mankind when it will return to God and to His moral law. This will be the entry of God into the portals of human affairs which mankind will then open wide for Him even as we now symbolically open the portals of the Ark so that His Law may come to rest in our midst. The terrestrial sphere of nature belongs לה', to God, Who trains mankind for the purposes of His moral law. Therefore the world of man which is rooted in the earth and derives from it all the things it needs in order to live and prosper, is His also. Hence all the earth is a holy mountain striving upward toward God, on which only those people and things that live and exist in accordance with His moral law, can grow and endure. נקי is superficial cleanliness, freedom from dirt. כפים denotes the hands, taking hold of a possession. בר לבב connotes purity of heart and mind. Both together imply the duty of each man to his fellow-men.

The Reader takes the Torah back to the Ark and says:

Let them proclaim the praise of the Name of *God,* that His Name alone is exalted.

(Cong.): His majesty is above the earth and Heaven. When He lifted up the horn for His people, it is a praise of His mighty acts for all of His devoted ones, but to the sons of Yisrael [only because they have been] the people near to Him from the beginning. Halaluyah!

By David, a Psalm. The earth is *God's* and the fullness thereof, the world of men and they that dwell therein. For He has founded it upon the seas and, guiding it, constantly establishes it upon the floods. Who shall ascend to the mountain of *God,* and who shall stand in the place of His Sanctuary? "He that is clean of hands and pure of heart, who has not lifted up his soul, which is Mine, unto vanity, and has not sworn deceitfully. He shall receive a blessing from *God* and kindness from the God of his salvation." This is the generation of them that seek after Him, that seek your face, O Yaakov! Lift up your heads, O gates, be lifted up to become portals of the future, so that the King of Glory may come in. "Who is this King of Glory?" "*God,* invincible and strong, *God,* the Mighty One in battle." Lift up your heads again,

---

אשר לא נשא לשוא נפשי : The *kethiv* is נפשו but *keri* is נפשי ; in other words, the phrase speaks of him who "will not lift up his soul, which, in fact, is Mine (God's) to transitory things and vanities which will alienate it from God" and who will keep every טומאה ,שקץ and תועבה far away from his soul. This characterizes the duty of man to his God. ולא נשבע למרמה : He whose piety is genuine and who will not use the name of God to deceive others. דרשיו : those who seek both help and instruction from God. It is quite obvious that we can expect help from God only if we live and act in accordance with His will. דרש, *kethiv* singular; *keri* plural. By rendering homage to one and the same Divine Law, mankind, with all its variety of cultures and civilizations, will become truly united, and מבקשי וגו' they will attain this goal by following the lead of that people which, thus far has had to stand back, powerless, even as Yaakov long ago. שאו וגו' והנשאו וגו' : At first the portals of human society do not open of their own accord to admit God into the midst of men; they are lifted up by force as God subdues all evil which stands opposed to His will. But in the end שאו וגו' ושאו וגו' the portals of human society will indeed open of their own accord. At that time God will enter into them not as an invincible Force but as ה' צבאות as the God of mankind. Then it will be under His banner that all the many groups comprising mankind will gather to be led and guided by Him forevermore.

עוֹלָם וְיָבֹא מֶלֶךְ הַכָּבוֹד: מִי הוּא זֶה מֶלֶךְ הַכָּבוֹד · יְהֹוָה צְבָאוֹת
הוּא מֶלֶךְ הַכָּבוֹד סֶלָה:

As the Torah is returned to the Ark, the Reader says:

וּבְנֻחֹה יֹאמַר שׁוּבָה יְהֹוָה רִבְבוֹת אַלְפֵי יִשְׂרָאֵל: קוּמָה יְהֹוָה
לִמְנוּחָתֶךָ אַתָּה וַאֲרוֹן עֻזֶּךָ: כֹּהֲנֶיךָ יִלְבְּשׁוּ־צֶדֶק וַחֲסִידֶיךָ יְרַנֵּנוּ:
בַּעֲבוּר דָּוִד עַבְדֶּךָ אַל־תָּשֵׁב פְּנֵי מְשִׁיחֶךָ: כִּי לֶקַח טוֹב נָתַתִּי
לָכֶם תּוֹרָתִי אַל־תַּעֲזֹבוּ: עֵץ־חַיִּים הִיא לַמַּחֲזִיקִים בָּהּ וְתֹמְכֶיהָ
מְאֻשָּׁר: דְּרָכֶיהָ דַרְכֵי־נֹעַם וְכָל־נְתִיבוֹתֶיהָ שָׁלוֹם: הֲשִׁיבֵנוּ יְהֹוָה
אֵלֶיךָ וְנָשׁוּבָה חַדֵּשׁ יָמֵינוּ כְּקֶדֶם:

ובנוחה is a continuation of ויהי בנסע הארון, which was chanted when the
Scroll was taken from the Ark. Those were the words uttered by Moshe when
the Ark decamped. Now we read the prayer which he recited when the Ark
came to rest once more. In *vayehi bineso'a* and *uvnucho yomar* Moshe had
already declared that which much later, the Psalmist proclaimed in the psalm
which we have just read with reference to the struggle and the victory of the
word of God over any force which might resist His entry into human affairs, and
of God's peaceful entrance into the portals of mankind which will then open
of their own accord to receive Him. First the Word of God goes about among
men, subduing the enemies and haters of the Divine and causing them to withdraw. Then, with victory won, the Word of God "gently" takes up its permanent abode in the midst of mankind (the ה in בנחה is a feminine ending),
and the thousands of the people of Israel will grow into myriads through natural increase from within and accessions from without. קומה was the call voiced
in Psalm 132 to the Ark of the Law of the Covenant to cease traveling from
one temporary abode to another and to enter, instead, into its permanent home
in the Sanctuary. כהניך It is only when the Law of the Lord enters the Holy
of Holies and takes its place there that the raiment which sets the Priests apart
from other men will truly become garments consecrated to the service of the
Law. Only then will these priestly vestments symbolize the dedication of their
wearers to the service of the Law whose total content is simply צדק, the Divine
ideal of righteousness for both the individual and society on earth. The same
holds true even today in our own houses of worship, those inadequate imitations
of the ancient Sanctuary. Once the Scrolls of God's Law enter and come to

O gates, lift them up to become portals of the future, so that the King of Glory may come in. "Who, then, is this King of Glory?" "*God Tzevaoth,* He is the King of Glory!"

As the Torah is returned to the Ark, the Reader says:

And when it gently came to rest, Moshe would say, "Return, O *God,* to the myriads of the thousands of Yisrael." Arise, O *God,* to Your resting place, You and the Ark of Your invincible might, that Your priests may clothe themselves in righteousness and that Your devoted ones may shout for joy. For the sake of David Your servant, turn not away the face of Your anointed. For I have given you an instruction that will be for your good if you will but take it up; forsake not My Torah. It is a tree of life for those who cleave to it, and a happy group are those who support it. Its ways are ways of pleasantness and all its paths are peace. Lead us back to You, O *God,* and we shall find the way back; renew our days as of old.

---

rest in our own Holy of Holies, our present-day houses of God also become abodes of His Law and all our own consecration and dedication to God becomes consecration and dedication to His Torah. וחסידיך denotes that people which, in gladsome faithfulness to duty, devotes itself to God fulfilling His Law. God Himself promised that He would give visible proof of His presence, bestowing His blessing, wherever an abode would be prepared for His Law in truth and sincerity. It is at the thought of this visible demonstration of God's presence that the people will "shout for joy." וירא כל העם וירנו (Lev. 9:20). May the nation of God, then, even in dispersion, be made joyously aware of the visible blessing of God wherever in exile it will prepare room for the Law of God in truth and sincerity. בעבור Even Shelomo, the "Anointed of God" waited for such a proof of God's presence, but not as a reward for any merits of his own or for the splendid Temple edifice which he had reared. He expected it solely for the sake of the merits which his father, the "servant" of God, had accumulated through his achievements in behalf of both Yisrael and the rest of mankind for all times to come. לקח denotes the Law from the standpoint of him who is studying it, "*taking* it up". תורה ("Teaching"), indicates the Law from the standpoint of the instructor. דרכיה, עץ חיים, see above p. 188.

השיבנו "Help us so that we may return to You with true *teshuvah,* and then we shall also find the road back to political independence in the land of our fathers. This return, however, can be effected only by the hand of God, Who had originally been the sole Creator of our former position as a nation."

אַשְׁרֵי יוֹשְׁבֵי בֵיתֶךָ עוֹד יְהַלְלוּךָ סֶּלָה:

אַשְׁרֵי הָעָם שֶׁכָּכָה לּוֹ אַשְׁרֵי הָעָם שֶׁיְיָ אֱלֹהָיו:

קמה תְּהִלָּה לְדָוִד

אֲרוֹמִמְךָ אֱלוֹהַי הַמֶּלֶךְ וַאֲבָרְכָה שִׁמְךָ לְעוֹלָם וָעֶד:

בְּכָל־יוֹם אֲבָרְכֶךָּ וַאֲהַלְלָה שִׁמְךָ לְעוֹלָם וָעֶד:

גָּדוֹל יְהוָה וּמְהֻלָּל מְאֹד וְלִגְדֻלָּתוֹ אֵין חֵקֶר:

דּוֹר לְדוֹר יְשַׁבַּח מַעֲשֶׂיךָ וּגְבוּרֹתֶיךָ יַגִּידוּ:

הֲדַר כְּבוֹד הוֹדֶךָ וְדִבְרֵי נִפְלְאֹתֶיךָ אָשִׂיחָה:

וֶעֱזוּז נוֹרְאֹתֶיךָ יֹאמֵרוּ וּגְדֻלָּתְךָ אֲסַפְּרֶנָּה: ‏ יגדולתך ק׳

זֵכֶר רַב־טוּבְךָ יַבִּיעוּ וְצִדְקָתְךָ יְרַנֵּנוּ:

חַנּוּן וְרַחוּם יְהוָה אֶרֶךְ אַפַּיִם וּגְדָל־חָסֶד: ‏ יתיר י׳

טוֹב־יְהוָה לַכֹּל וְרַחֲמָיו עַל־כָּל־מַעֲשָׂיו:

אשרי See above, p. 81. As we have stated elsewhere, the Sages attach a great deal of significance to Psalm 145. תהלה לדוד This Psalm, in praise of God's merciful Providence, recurs three times in our daily prayers. It is with this psalm that we begin the *Pesukei Dezimrah,* the psalms in our prayer book which sing the praises of the Lord as revealed by His mighty acts. And it is with this same psalm that we begin the third portion of our Morning Service which is to serve as a transition from the prayerful gathering of our thoughts before God back to the activities of everyday life in His service. Here אשרי is followed by ובא לציון גואל, of which the Aramaic translation of the *Kedushah* by Yonathan constitutes the focal point. At the end of Sota this *Kedushah* is called *Kedushah Desidra,* and we are told that the world, which otherwise would have perished long ago, has been preserved solely by virtue of this *Kedushah* and by virtue of the אמן יהא שמיה רבה which is part of the *Kaddish* to be recited after the study of the *Aggadah.* We would believe that the expression *Kedusha Desidra* (and not *Seder Kedushah* as we might have ex-

Forward forever stride those that dwell in Your house: continually they utter the praise of Your mighty acts!—Forward to salvation strides that people with whom it is so. Forward strides that nation whose God is *God*.

Tehillah by David. I will extol You, my God, O King, and I will bless Your Name unto the future everlasting.

Every day will I bless You, and proclaim the praise of Your Name until the future everlasting.

Great is *God* and most evident in mighty acts, but His greatness is unsearchable.

Generation after generation will laud Your works, and shall proclaim Your mighty acts.

But I will express in meditation the beauty of the glory of Your majesty and the words of Your wonders.

And they shall speak of the invincibility of Your awesome acts, but I shall tell of the uniform greatness of all Your great deeds.

That they may also utter a thought of the abundance of Your goodness and exult in Your tender righteousness.

God is gracious and compassionate, slow to anger and great in devoted loving-kindness.

God is good to all, and His compassion is over all His works.

---

pected to read here) indicates the significance of this *Kedushah* as a *Kedushah* introduced into the "everyday order of things." (As a matter of fact, Tosaphot in Berachoth 3a indicates that it should be read *sidra dikedushatha,* but in Sota 49 we read *Kedusha Desidra.*) First, in *Yotzer* and in the *Shemone Esrei,* we hallowed the Name of God in words of prayer as we composed our thoughts before Him. Now we are to take the "sanctification of God" with us out into the ordinary activities of day-to-day living so that we may remember and heed what it implies in whatever we may do. Nor should the behest to "sanctify God" be interpreted as a command to dwell in splendid isolation, remote from all earthly affairs. Instead, we are meant to understand our task as one to be performed in the very midst of all the activities, the common trials and temptations that are part of ordinary, everyday living. This is the thought which is at the root of Yonathan's interpretation of the *Kedushah.* According to his view, the "thrice holy" in the *Kedushah* does not indicate three ascending degrees of sanctification. Instead, it implies a declaration that He Who is holy in the loftiest of the lofty regions of His heavenly abode is holy not only there but also on earth, in the creation of His almighty

יוֹדוּךָ יְהֹוָה כָּל־מַעֲשֶׂיךָ וַחֲסִידֶיךָ יְבָרְכוּכָה:

כְּבוֹד מַלְכוּתְךָ יֹאמֵרוּ וּגְבוּרָתְךָ יְדַבֵּרוּ:

לְהוֹדִיעַ לִבְנֵי הָאָדָם גְּבוּרֹתָיו וּכְבוֹד הֲדַר מַלְכוּתוֹ:

מַלְכוּתְךָ מַלְכוּת כָּל־עֹלָמִים וּמֶמְשַׁלְתְּךָ בְּכָל־דּוֹר וָדֹר:

סוֹמֵךְ יְהֹוָה לְכָל־הַנֹּפְלִים וְזוֹקֵף לְכָל־הַכְּפוּפִים:

עֵינֵי כָל־אֵלֶיךָ יְשַׂבֵּרוּ וְאַתָּה נוֹתֵן־לָהֶם אֶת־אָכְלָם בְּעִתּוֹ:

פּוֹתֵחַ אֶת־יָדֶךָ וּמַשְׂבִּיעַ לְכָל־חַי רָצוֹן:

צַדִּיק יְהֹוָה בְּכָל־דְּרָכָיו וְחָסִיד בְּכָל־מַעֲשָׂיו:

קָרוֹב יְהֹוָה לְכָל־קֹרְאָיו לְכֹל אֲשֶׁר יִקְרָאֻהוּ בֶאֱמֶת:

רְצוֹן־יְרֵאָיו יַעֲשֶׂה וְאֶת־שַׁוְעָתָם יִשְׁמַע וְיוֹשִׁיעֵם:

שׁוֹמֵר יְהֹוָה אֶת־כָּל־אֹהֲבָיו וְאֵת כָּל־הָרְשָׁעִים יַשְׁמִיד:

תְּהִלַּת יְהֹוָה יְדַבֶּר פִּי וִיבָרֵךְ כָּל־בָּשָׂר שֵׁם קָדְשׁוֹ לְעוֹלָם וָעֶד:

קט״ו י״ח וַאֲנַחְנוּ ׀ נְבָרֵךְ יָהּ מֵעַתָּה וְעַד־עוֹלָם הַלְלוּיָהּ:

power, and that He was not only holy in the past, but that He is holy even now and will ever be so throughout all the ages to come. For the final phrase of that paragraph explicitly states that "the entire earth" is full of His glory. We read in Isaiah 6:4 that the very foundation pillars of the Temple trembled before this proclamation of God's holiness from the mouth of the angels, and it seemed as if the Temple were about to vanish in smoke. But what caused the Temple to be shaken to its very foundations was not the proclamation of the grandeur of God in the heavenly regions. What the Temple, which had already been estranged in part from its true purpose and function, was unable to withstand was the realization of God's infinite nearness on earth. For the

All Your works shall render You homage, O *God*, but Your devoted ones shall bless You.

They shall speak of the honor due Your kingdom, and they will declare Your power.

To make known to the sons of men His mighty acts, but also the glory, the beauty of His kingdom.

Your kingdom is a kingdom for all distant times and Your rule is in every generation.

God upholds all that fall and raises up all those that are bowed down.

The eyes of all wait upon You and You give them their food in due season.

Yea, You open Your hand and satisfy the desire of every living thing.

God is just in all His ways, and full of devoted loving-kindness in all His works.

God is near to all those that call upon Him, to all that call upon Him in truth.

He will fulfill the desire of them that fear Him; He also will hear their cry and give them salvation.

God will keep all those that love Him, and all the lawless He will let perish.

Let my mouth declare the praise of *God*, so that all flesh may bless His holy Name unto the future everlasting.

As for us, we will bless God from this time forth and forever. Halaluyah!

---

sinner cannot be moved by the thought of the supreme grandeur of God in itself. But the awareness of God's immediate nearness can cause him to be shaken to the very core of his being. In truth, the realization that it is God's will to dwell in our midst on earth and to be hallowed by us there with every breath of our lives and with our every endeavor requires that we make drastic changes in our way of life. If we heed this summons, it will not shatter us but, instead, fill us with serene bliss which nothing can disturb or destroy. It is this truth that the *Kedushah Desidra* gives us to take with us as we go forth into the "order" of daily living. It is preceded by *vaani, veata kadosh* in *Uva letzion,* the testimony of the eternal duration of the covenant that God

למנצח *is not said on Rosh Chodesh, Chol Hamoed, Chanukkah, Purim
and Purim Katan, Tisha B'Av, Erev Yom Kippur and Erev Pesach. In many
congregations it is also omitted on Erev Rosh Hashanah, the day after Yom
Kippur, Erev Sukkoth, Erev Shavuoth and Isru Chag.*

כ לַמְנַצֵּחַ מִזְמוֹר לְדָוִד: יַעַנְךָ יְהֹוָה בְּיוֹם צָרָה יְשַׂגֶּבְךָ שֵׁם ׀

אֱלֹהֵי יַעֲקֹב: יִשְׁלַח־עֶזְרְךָ מִקֹּדֶשׁ וּמִצִּיּוֹן יִסְעָדֶךָּ: יִזְכֹּר כָּל־

מִנְחֹתֶךָ וְעוֹלָתְךָ יְדַשְּׁנֶה־סֶּלָה: יִתֶּן־לְךָ כִלְבָבֶךָ וְכָל־עֲצָתְךָ

יְמַלֵּא: נְרַנְּנָה ׀ בִּישׁוּעָתֶךָ וּבְשֵׁם־אֱלֹהֵינוּ נִדְגֹּל יְמַלֵּא יְהֹוָה כָּל־

מִשְׁאֲלוֹתֶיךָ: עַתָּה יָדַעְתִּי כִּי הוֹשִׁיעַ יְהֹוָה מְשִׁיחוֹ יַעֲנֵהוּ מִשְּׁמֵי

קָדְשׁוֹ בִּגְבֻרוֹת יֵשַׁע יְמִינוֹ: אֵלֶּה בָרֶכֶב וְאֵלֶּה בַסּוּסִים וַאֲנַחְנוּ ׀

בְּשֵׁם־יְהֹוָה אֱלֹהֵינוּ נַזְכִּיר: הֵמָּה כָּרְעוּ וְנָפָלוּ וַאֲנַחְנוּ קַּמְנוּ

וַנִּתְעוֹדָד: יְהֹוָה הוֹשִׁיעָה הַמֶּלֶךְ יַעֲנֵנוּ בְיוֹם־קָרְאֵנוּ:

made with us through the Torah. It is followed by ה' אלקי אברהם down to
המלך יעננו the expression of prayerful confidence that God will train us at all
times to enable us to ascend to the lofty ideal represented by this truth, and
it ends on a vote of that exultation which comes from the knowledge that we
have fulfilled our destiny, and the pledge that we will endeavor so to fulfill it
at all times, ברוך הוא אלקינו etc.

למנצח מזמור לדוד (Psalm 20) On those days that bear no special festive
or commemorative character, this psalm is recited. It is inserted between *Tehillah leDavid* which is a hymn of praise of God's rule as such, and *Uva letzion* which pictures to us the spiritual grandeur and magnitude of our task
and destiny. Psalm 20 is addressed to David by the people of Israel. It is a
testimonial of the trust that the people have in him, the Divinely-anointed
King who is accustomed to victory and triumph. At the same time it proclaims
the eternal truth that the victories which our King won for our people are
to be attributed not to his bravery, nor to his sword, nor to his soldiers but
solely to his relationship to God and to the Sanctuary of God's Law. It is a
voice from our past as an independent nation, a message most apt to inspire
Israel, wandering through centuries of exile deprived of all political autonomy
and might, with that trust and confidence in God and in His Law which were

למנצח *is not said on Rosh Chodesh, Chol Hamoed, Chanukkah, Purim and Purim Katan, Tisha B'Av, Erev Yom Kippur and Erev Pesach. In many congregations it is also omitted on Erev Rosh Hashanah, the day after Yom Kippur, Erev Sukkoth, Erev Shavuoth and Isru Chag.*

To Him Who grants victory. A Psalm to David. *God* will answer you in the day of trouble; the Name of the God of Yaakov will raise you on high. He will send forth your help from the Sanctuary and will strengthen you from Tzion. He will accept the memorial of all your offerings of homage and will ever free your ascent offering from its ashes for constant repetition!—May He grant you according to your own heart and may He fulfill all your counsel. We shall shout for joy at your victory and rally round your banner in the name of our God; may *God* fulfill all your desires. For now I have come to know that *God* has granted happiness to His anointed; He will always hear him from the heaven of His Sanctuary with the omnipotent acts of salvation of His right hand. Some see God in chariots, and others in horses, but as for us, we remember our God by the name of *"God"*. When they knelt they fell down; but we have always risen again and have constantly kept ourselves upright. May *God* grant salvation. As the King, He will answer us on the day on which we call upon Him.

---

also the sole true pillars of its power when it was still a great independent nation. לדוד : *"to* David." יַעֲנְךָ ה' בְּיוֹם צָרָה "in the day of trouble." According to the Sages, this is the time of dire need, when all circumstances seem to point to inevitable disaster. שֵׁם אֱלֹקֵי יַעֲקֹב The understanding and the confident clinging to God, as He was revealed to Yaakov in the trial-filled course of his life. For the name of Yaakov has become the cognomen for his people for all the periods of exile in its history. יִשְׁלַח עֶזְרְךָ מִקֹּדֶשׁ : God will help you because of your attitude to His Sanctuary, because all of your existence is consecrated to it and your deliverance will therefore advance the sacred cause of His Law. וּמִצִּיּוֹן יִסְעָדֶךָ : He will let spiritual refreshment and strength come to you from the spiritual fount that flows forth from Zion. יִזְכֹּר כָּל מִנְחֹתֶיךָ : מנחה, is that sacrifice which symbolizes the worshipper's "meal, oil and incense," his food, his prosperity, his joy of life, and thus symbolically his entire fate, which is humbly placed at the feet of God. A handful of this offering, *kometz*, is taken away and burned at the alter as an *azkarah*. The *azkarah* expresses the plea that God, on Whom we depend for our food, our prosperity and our happiness, may "remember" us and bless all the material goods which constitute our material happiness in life. עוֹלָה is the "elevating-offering." By means of this sacrifice the worshipper pledges himself to "ascend" steadily to

וּבָא לְצִיּוֹן גּוֹאֵל וּלְשָׁבֵי פֶשַׁע בְּיַעֲקֹב נְאֻם יְיָ: וַאֲנִי זֹאת בְּרִיתִי
אֹתָם אָמַר יְיָ רוּחִי אֲשֶׁר עָלֶיךָ וּדְבָרַי אֲשֶׁר־שַׂמְתִּי בְּפִיךָ לֹא
יָמוּשׁוּ מִפִּיךָ וּמִפִּי זַרְעֲךָ וּמִפִּי זֶרַע זַרְעֲךָ אָמַר יְיָ מֵעַתָּה וְעַד
עוֹלָם: וְאַתָּה קָדוֹשׁ יוֹשֵׁב תְּהִלּוֹת יִשְׂרָאֵל: וְקָרָא זֶה אֶל־זֶה
וְאָמַר קָדוֹשׁ · קָדוֹשׁ קָדוֹשׁ יְיָ צְבָאוֹת מְלֹא כָל־הָאָרֶץ כְּבוֹדוֹ:
וּמְקַבְּלִין דֵּין מִן דֵּין וְאָמְרִין קַדִּישׁ בִּשְׁמֵי מְרוֹמָא עִלָּאָה בֵּית
שְׁכִינְתֵּהּ, קַדִּישׁ עַל אַרְעָא עוֹבַד גְּבוּרְתֵּהּ, קַדִּישׁ לְעָלַם וּלְעָלְמֵי
עָלְמַיָּא· יְיָ צְבָאוֹת מַלְיָא כָל־אַרְעָא זִיו יְקָרֵהּ: וַתִּשָּׂאֵנִי רוּחַ
וָאֶשְׁמַע אַחֲרַי קוֹל רַעַשׁ גָּדוֹל בָּרוּךְ כְּבוֹד־יְיָ מִמְּקוֹמוֹ: וּנְטָלַתְנִי
רוּחָא וְשִׁמְעֵת בַּתְרַי קָל זִיעַ סַגִּיא דִּמְשַׁבְּחִין וְאָמְרִין בְּרִיךְ
יְקָרָא דַיְיָ מֵאֲתַר בֵּית שְׁכִינְתֵּהּ: יְיָ יִמְלֹךְ לְעוֹלָם וָעֶד: יְיָ

---

that height shown us by the symbol of the Divine altar of the Sanctuary of the Law. This sacrifice symbolizes the consecration of his דם, his entire "personality" and the dedication of all of this physical faculties (איברים) to the flaming power of God's law, for the fulfillment of God's will. (לריח ניחוח לה'). דשן means "to free (an object) from ashes" (see Num. 4:13). The *Kohen* opened the series of daily offerings with תרומת הדשן, taking one *Kometz*, a handful of the residue of ashes on the altar from the previous day's sacrifices, and placing it near the altar as an everlasting memorial thus symbolically linking the task of the day with that of the day before, so that the task of yesterday has its continuation in our activities today. ידשנה is an unusual form. It seems to be a combination of ידשן and ישנה, and would thus mean: "God has approved your work, your progress of the day just past, and He will encourage you to carry on in the same spirit on every new day."

אנחנו נזכיר אלהינו בשם ה' but אלה יזכירו אלהיהם ברכב ואלה בסוסים i.e. אלה המה כרעו ונפלו They always succumbed and fell. But as for us, while we may indeed reel under the impact of blows dealt us, have always managed to rise again and have always kept ourselves erect. ה' הושיעה see above p. 164.

ובא לציון The first message with which our *tefillah* seeks to send us forth into the strife and struggle of day-to-day living is the firm trust in the sure coming of redemption which can be ours if only we return to God and to our

The Redeemer shall come to Tzion and to those in Yaakov who turn back from defection, says *God*. "As for Me," said *God*, "this My covenant shall remain their very being; My spirit, which rests upon you, and My words which I have put in your mouth shall not depart from your mouth nor from the mouths of your children, nor from the mouths of your children's children," said *God*, "from now on to all eternity." And You O holy One, are still enthroned upon Yisrael's songs of praise. And one calls to the other and says, "Holy, holy, holy is *God Tzevaoth*, the fullness of all the earth is His glory." They receive it from one another and say, "Holy in the highest heights of Heaven, the Abode of His Presence, holy on earth, the creation of His almighty power, holy forever and for all the eternities of eternity, is *God Tzevaoth*; the whole earth is filled with the radiance of His glory." When the spirit lifted me up, I heard behind me the voice of a great rushing, "Blessed be the glory of *God* from His Abode." And the spirit lifted me up, and I heard behind me the noise of a great movement of those who praised and spoke, "Blessed be the glory of *God* from the Abode of His Presence." "*God* shall reign forever and ever."

---

duty, since it was only due to our defection that we have become *Yaakov*, an exiled nation. בריתי אותם indicates more than would בריתי אתם. The covenant was made not simply *with* us; it constitutes our very being and this covenant implies the eternity of the Torah, that the spirit emanating from the Torah and the Word of God which was put into our mouths by the Torah should never depart from our mouths and from the mouths of our children's children, that all our generations should come to know this eternal Word through study, champion and proclaim it, and finally teach it to their descendants.

ואתה and God is holy; His nature and His purposes are constant and unchanging, and even as He was יושב הכרובים once long ago, so is He now יושב תהלות ישראל. תהלות ישראל, the Psalms of Yisrael, serve as the spiritual "Cherubim" in exile, as it were. For Yisrael is the sole bearer of the recognition of God for all the rest of mankind, and *Tehilloth Yisrael*, the psalms of Yisrael, have served to carry this great message into every home and into every heart, and have tended and nurtured it there until this very day. ויקרא (See above, p. 109). But the most sublime revelation of God ever to have come to Yisrael is the sanctification that was proclaimed by the mouths of the angels on high. This heavenly proclamation of the holiness of God tells us that it is the task and purpose of every living thing on earth wholly to subordinate and dedicate its life and all of its endeavors to the will of God, so that every

מַלְכוּתֵהּ קָאֵם לְעָלַם וּלְעָלְמֵי עָלְמַיָּא: יְיָ אֱלֹהֵי אַבְרָהָם יִצְחָק
וְיִשְׂרָאֵל אֲבֹתֵינוּ שָׁמְרָה־זֹּאת לְעוֹלָם לְיֵצֶר מַחְשְׁבוֹת לְבַב עַמֶּךָ
וְהָכֵן לְבָבָם אֵלֶיךָ: וְהוּא רַחוּם יְכַפֵּר עָוֹן וְלֹא יַשְׁחִית וְהִרְבָּה
לְהָשִׁיב אַפּוֹ וְלֹא יָעִיר כָּל־חֲמָתוֹ: כִּי־אַתָּה אֲדֹנָי טוֹב וְסַלָּח וְרַב־
חֶסֶד לְכָל־קֹרְאֶיךָ: צִדְקָתְךָ צֶדֶק לְעוֹלָם וְתוֹרָתְךָ אֱמֶת: תִּתֵּן
אֱמֶת לְיַעֲקֹב חֶסֶד לְאַבְרָהָם אֲשֶׁר־נִשְׁבַּעְתָּ לַאֲבֹתֵינוּ מִימֵי קֶדֶם:
בָּרוּךְ אֲדֹנָי יוֹם יוֹם יַעֲמָס־לָנוּ הָאֵל יְשׁוּעָתֵנוּ סֶלָה: יְיָ צְבָאוֹת
עִמָּנוּ מִשְׂגָּב לָנוּ אֱלֹהֵי יַעֲקֹב סֶלָה: יְיָ צְבָאוֹת אַשְׁרֵי אָדָם
בֹּטֵחַ בָּךְ: יְיָ הוֹשִׁיעָה · הַמֶּלֶךְ יַעֲנֵנוּ בְיוֹם־קָרְאֵנוּ: בָּרוּךְ הוּא
אֱלֹהֵינוּ שֶׁבְּרָאָנוּ לִכְבוֹדוֹ וְהִבְדִּילָנוּ מִן־הַתּוֹעִים וְנָתַן לָנוּ תּוֹרַת
אֱמֶת וְחַיֵּי עוֹלָם נָטַע בְּתוֹכֵנוּ · הוּא יִפְתַּח לִבֵּנוּ בְּתוֹרָתוֹ וְיָשֵׂם
בְּלִבֵּנוּ אַהֲבָתוֹ וְיִרְאָתוֹ וְלַעֲשׂוֹת רְצוֹנוֹ וּלְעָבְדוֹ בְּלֵבָב שָׁלֵם לְמַעַן
לֹא נִיגַע לָרִיק וְלֹא נֵלֵד לַבֶּהָלָה: יְהִי רָצוֹן מִלְפָנֶיךָ יְיָ אֱלֹהֵינוּ
וֵאלֹהֵי אֲבוֹתֵינוּ שֶׁנִּשְׁמוֹר חֻקֶּיךָ בָּעוֹלָם הַזֶּה וְנִזְכֶּה וְנִחְיֶה וְנִרְאֶה
וְנִירַשׁ טוֹבָה וּבְרָכָה לִשְׁנֵי יְמוֹת הַמָּשִׁיחַ וּלְחַיֵּי הָעוֹלָם הַבָּא:
לְמַעַן יְזַמֶּרְךָ כָבוֹד וְלֹא יִדֹּם · יְיָ אֱלֹהַי לְעוֹלָם אוֹדֶךָ: בָּרוּךְ

---

spot on earth may become a place where He is glorified. ותשאני רוח (Ezek.
3:12) "When the spirit lifted me up above the earth, I heard behind me,
rising up from the earth, the voice of the benediction and glorification of God
as it is performed on earth below." שמרה זאת May God ever keep before us
this ideal of His sanctification by the entire universe which is His own creation;
may He keep it in the thoughts and emotions of our hearts as the eternal ideal
which it is our task to translate into living reality, so that it may never be far
from our thoughts, and may He ever keep our hearts turned toward Him.
(יצר see Commentary to Gen. 6:5.) Regardless of the inadequacies and failings
with which our own conscience would charge us if we would but measure our
own worth against the standard set by this ideal, והוא רחום etc. אמת ליעקב
denotes the promise which God made to Yaakov (Gen. 29:15) that He would

God, His kingship remains forever and for all eternities of eternity. O *God,* God of Abraham, Yitzchak, and Yisrael, our fathers, keep this forever as the purpose in the thoughts of the hearts of Your people and turn their minds to You. But He being full of compassion forgives iniquity and does not destroy, and many a time repents of His anger and never stirs up all His wrath. For You, O my Lord, are good and forgiving and great in loving kindness for all those that call upon You. The righteousness You have taught is eternal righteousness and your teaching is truth. Grant to Yaakov the truth and to Abraham the loving-kindness which You have sworn to our fathers from the days of old. Blessed be my Lord day by day; may He give us [a burden] to bear. Even the same God is also our salvation! *God Tzevaoth* is with us; the God of Yaakov is our high tower!— *God Tzevaoth,* forward forever strides the man that trusts in You!—May *God* grant salvation. As the King will He answer us on the day on which we call upon Him. Blessed be He, our God, Who created us for His glory and set us apart from those who go astray and Who has given us the Torah of truth and implanted life eternal into us. May He open our heart to His Torah, and put the love and fear of Him into our hearts, to do His will and to serve Him with a whole heart, so that we may not labor in vain nor bring forth for dismay. May it be Your will, O *God* our God and God of our fathers, that we may keep Your statutes in this world and thus become worthy of living, of seeing and inheriting happiness and blessings in the years of the days of the Messiah and in the life of the world to come. So that all that is glorious shall ceaselessly sing to You. O *God,* my God, I will do You homage forever. Blessed is the

---

not forsake him. This is a promise to which we, the descendants of Yaakov who have become "humble, exiled Yaakovs" ourselves, are to look with confidence at all times. And if we prove to be true sons of Abraham and properly carry out the testament left us by Abraham לשמור דרך ה' לעשית צדקה ומשפט then we may expect to receive also the blessings which were promised to Abraham in Genesis 12:2,3. 22:17,18. עמס ,יעמס is "to impose a burden." The God Who gives us burdens to bear and tasks to fulfill each day, also will grant us the help we need in order to be equal to the duties He thus imposes upon us. יפתח לבנו בתורתו, so that we may have an open heart as regards His Law, so that we may have a heart capable of accepting His teachings and embracing them as its own. יזמרך כבוד everything great and glorious that declares the existence of a Higher Power—that is the literal import of the word

הַגֶּבֶר אֲשֶׁר יִבְטַח בַּיָי וְהָיָה יְיָ מִבְטַחוֹ: בִּטְחוּ בַיָי עֲדֵי־עַד כִּי
בְּיָה יְיָ צוּר עוֹלָמִים: וְיִבְטְחוּ בְךָ יוֹדְעֵי שְׁמֶךָ כִּי לֹא־עָזַבְתָּ דֹרְשֶׁיךָ
יְיָ: יְיָ חָפֵץ לְמַעַן צִדְקוֹ יַגְדִּיל תּוֹרָה וְיַאְדִּיר: ק"ת

וְעַתָּה יִגְדַּל־נָא כֹּחַ אֲדֹנָי כַּאֲשֶׁר דִּבַּרְתָּ לֵאמֹר:

זְכֹר רַחֲמֶיךָ יְיָ וַחֲסָדֶיךָ כִּי מֵעוֹלָם הֵמָּה:

יִתְגַּדַּל וְיִתְקַדַּשׁ שְׁמֵהּ רַבָּא בְּעָלְמָא דִּי־בְרָא כִרְעוּתֵהּ וְיַמְלִיךְ
מַלְכוּתֵהּ בְּחַיֵּיכוֹן וּבְיוֹמֵיכוֹן וּבְחַיֵּי דְכָל־בֵּית יִשְׂרָאֵל בַּעֲגָלָא וּבִזְמַן
קָרִיב, וְאִמְרוּ אָמֵן ·

יְהֵא שְׁמֵהּ רַבָּא מְבָרַךְ לְעָלַם וּלְעָלְמֵי עָלְמַיָּא:

יִתְבָּרַךְ וְיִשְׁתַּבַּח וְיִתְפָּאַר וְיִתְרוֹמַם וְיִתְנַשֵּׂא וְיִתְהַדָּר וְיִתְעַלֶּה
וְיִתְהַלָּל שְׁמֵהּ דְּקֻדְשָׁא בְּרִיךְ הוּא לְעֵלָּא מִן־כָּל־בִּרְכָתָא וְשִׁירָתָא
תֻּשְׁבְּחָתָא וְנֶחֱמָתָא דַּאֲמִירָן בְּעָלְמָא, וְאִמְרוּ אָמֵן:

ז' קַבֵּל בְּרַחֲמִים וּבְרָצוֹן אֶת תְּפִלָּתֵנוּ:

כבוד — should proclaim You as the One Possessor of all this might and as
the One Source of all this glory, and should never cease thus proclaiming You.
When the good and beautiful things of life abide with us for long, let us
never come to take them for granted and to permit the remembrance of God
gradually to fade from our hearts. As our life's joys and blessings increase,
let us also increase and deepen our grateful homage to God. והיה ה' מבטחו.
He does not just put his trust in God while relying, in addition, upon a great
many other factors which he considers the essential supports of his life and
happiness; no, God alone is the source of his trust; he relies in none other
than God. עדי עד Persevere patiently עדי עד (literally "until that time to which
we refer by 'until' shall have come to pass"), that is, until the goal set by
God shall have come to pass. Wait for it patiently even though it seems to
tarry. For "The Rock of All Times" rests not only in the rule of discipline
that is implied by God's full Name, but also in that aspect of His reign which
demonstrates His all-conquering might as indicated by the designation יה.

man who trusts in *God,* and to whom *God* is also the the source of His trust. Trust in *God* until the end of days, for in God, *God,* rests the Rock of All Time. And those who know Your Name shall trust in You, for You have never forsaken those who seek You, O *God.* God was pleased, because of His righteousness, to render the Torah increasingly great and glorious.

His great Name will be recognized in all its greatness and holiness in the world which He has created according to His will. May He establish His kingdom in your lifetime and in your days and in the lifetime of all the House of Yisrael, speedily and soon, and say, Amen.

May His great Name be blessed forever and to all the eternities of eternity.

Blessed and praised, glorified, exalted and extolled, proclaimed in its majesty, grandeur and in the praise of His mighty acts, be the Name of the Holy One, blessed be He, high above all the blessings, hymns, praises and consolations that are uttered in the world, and say, Amen.

The rock of all times rests in both of them together; the show of force as symbolized by the Name of *Yah* must precede, before the loving-kindness implied by the Name ה' can unfold its full power. יודעי שמך "those who know the ways of Your reign as taught us by Your Name." דורשיך "those who seek both help and instruction from You." צדקו is the Divine ideal of the moral law whose final fulfillment is the goal of all the course of Divine Providence. יגדיל תורה It is the will of God that His Torah constantly grow in strength and become a powerful influence in all the life unfolding round about us, and particularly in our own lives.

יתגדל See above, p. 105. In this concluding Kaddish (called קדיש שלם or קדיש תתקבל) there is added a petition for the favorable acceptance by God of our prayers and supplications together with those of all of Yisrael, and then the all-encompassing prayer for the "peace and life" which we hope to enjoy together with all the rest of our people. By thus viewing our own welfare as closely interrelated with that of the entire community of which we are a part, we eliminate all self-centered narrowness from our own prayers.

תִּתְקַבַּל צְלוֹתְהוֹן וּבָעוּתְהוֹן דְּכָל־יִשְׂרָאֵל קֳדָם אֲבוּהוֹן דִּי בִשְׁמַיָּא. וְאִמְרוּ אָמֵן: ק' יְהִי שֵׁם יְיָ מְבֹרָךְ מֵעַתָּה וְעַד עוֹלָם:

יְהֵא שְׁלָמָא רַבָּא מִן־שְׁמַיָּא וְחַיִּים עָלֵינוּ וְעַל־כָּל־יִשְׂרָאֵל, וְאִמְרוּ אָמֵן: ק' עֶזְרִי מֵעִם יְיָ עֹשֵׂה שָׁמַיִם וָאָרֶץ:

עֹשֶׂה שָׁלוֹם בִּמְרוֹמָיו הוּא יַעֲשֶׂה שָׁלוֹם עָלֵינוּ וְעַל־כָּל־יִשְׂרָאֵל, וְאִמְרוּ אָמֵן:

עָלֵינוּ לְשַׁבֵּחַ לַאֲדוֹן הַכֹּל. לָתֵת גְּדֻלָּה לְיוֹצֵר בְּרֵאשִׁית, שֶׁלֹּא עָשָׂנוּ כְּגוֹיֵי הָאֲרָצוֹת, וְלֹא שָׂמָנוּ כְּמִשְׁפְּחוֹת הָאֲדָמָה, שֶׁלֹּא שָׂם חֶלְקֵנוּ כָּהֶם וְגוֹרָלֵנוּ כְּכָל־הֲמוֹנָם* וַאֲנַחְנוּ כּוֹרְעִים וּמִשְׁתַּחֲוִים וּמוֹדִים לִפְנֵי מֶלֶךְ מַלְכֵי הַמְּלָכִים הַקָּדוֹשׁ בָּרוּךְ הוּא, שֶׁהוּא נוֹטֶה שָׁמַיִם וְיוֹסֵד אָרֶץ, וּמוֹשַׁב יְקָרוֹ בַּשָּׁמַיִם מִמַּעַל וּשְׁכִינַת עֻזּוֹ בְּגָבְהֵי מְרוֹמִים: הוּא אֱלֹהֵינוּ אֵין עוֹד. אֱמֶת מַלְכֵּנוּ אֶפֶס זוּלָתוֹ. כַּכָּתוּב בְּתוֹרָתוֹ וְיָדַעְתָּ הַיּוֹם וַהֲשֵׁבֹתָ אֶל־לְבָבֶךָ כִּי יְהוָה הוּא הָאֱלֹהִים בַּשָּׁמַיִם מִמַּעַל וְעַל־הָאָרֶץ מִתָּחַת אֵין עוֹד:

* שֶׁהֵם מִשְׁתַּחֲוִים לְהֶבֶל וָרִיק וּמִתְפַּלְלִים אֶל אֵל לֹא יוֹשִׁיעַ.
°(נ"א וְכִסֵּא כְבוֹדוֹ)   * (נ"א אֵין אַחֵר)

עלינו is one of the most significant portions of our order of prayers. In its first part it proclaims the sharp contrast between our own concept of God and of our relationship to Him, and that of the other nations of mankind. But in the second part of this prayer beginning with על כן etc., we cite our own concept of God as the basis of our firm confidence that one day all the rest of mankind, too, will return and dedicate itself wholly and without reservations to the exclusive service of God, the One Sole God, and we express the fervent hope that this day may come to pass soon and that we may see it with our own eyes. According to the teachings of Judaism, however, such a hoped-for "return" is not meant to be identical with a mass conversion of all men to Judaism; it will be no more than the conversion of all mankind to

May the prayers and supplications of all Yisrael be accepted before their Father in Heaven, and say, Amen.

May there be abundant peace from heaven and life for us and for all of Yisrael, and say, Amen.

May He Who makes peace in His high places, make peace for us and for all of Yisrael, and say, Amen.

It is incumbent upon us to praise the Lord of All Things, to ascribe greatness to Him Who still continues to shape the work of the Beginning, Who has not made us like the peoples of the lands, and not given us a position like the families of the earth, since He did not let our portion be like theirs, nor our lot like that of all their multitudes. For we bend the knee and cast ourselves down and avow it before the Supreme King of Kings, the Holy One, blessed be He, that it is He Who stretches forth the heavens and establishes the earth, that the seat of His glory is in Heaven above, and the presence of His invincible might is in the loftiest heights. He is our God, none beside Him. He is our King in truth; there is none beside Him, even as it is written in His Torah: "You shall know it this day, and repeatedly lay it upon your heart, that *God* alone is God, in Heaven above and on earth below; there is none beside Him."

---

true humanity. It merely means that all men will then recognize God, the One Sole God, as the only God in Heaven above and on earth below, and do Him homage forever by living a life of loyal obedience in accordance with the universal moral law which has been handed down in the Torah of Judaism for all the rest of mankind as well to follow.

שלא עשנו It was in a very unusual manner that God made us into a nation, ולא שמנו and He gave us a unique position among the families of mankind. חלקנו Our unique portion on earth is rooted in our unique relationship to God and to His Law, and it is for this reason that גורלנו our fate, too, is unique. כורעים implies subordination, and משתחוים the complete dedication to the fulfillment of the will of God. ומודים; the object of *modim* is שהוא, etc. מלך מלכי המלכים Terrestrial empires are divided into first-rate powers and second-rate powers, so that even the mightiest of kings have at least one other equal in both rank and power. But God, the One Sole God, stands high above them all; it is upon Him that their very kingship depends, and He rules over them all in power and majesty. He is truly the "King over all the kings." הקדוש ברוך הוא this, the most commonly used term among Jews with reference

עַל־כֵּן נְקַוֶּה לְּךָ יְיָ אֱלֹהֵינוּ לִרְאוֹת מְהֵרָה בְּתִפְאֶרֶת עֻזֶּךָ
לְהַעֲבִיר גִּלּוּלִים מִן הָאָרֶץ וְהָאֱלִילִים כָּרוֹת יִכָּרֵתוּן · לְתַקֵּן עוֹלָם
בְּמַלְכוּת שַׁדַּי · וְכָל־בְּנֵי בָשָׂר יִקְרְאוּ בִשְׁמֶךָ · לְהַפְנוֹת אֵלֶיךָ כָּל־
רִשְׁעֵי אָרֶץ · יַכִּירוּ וְיֵדְעוּ כָּל־יוֹשְׁבֵי תֵבֵל כִּי לְךָ תִּכְרַע כָּל־בֶּרֶךְ
תִּשָּׁבַע כָּל־לָשׁוֹן : לְפָנֶיךָ יְיָ אֱלֹהֵינוּ יִכְרְעוּ וְיִפֹּלוּ · וְלִכְבוֹד שִׁמְךָ
יְקָר יִתֵּנוּ · וִיקַבְּלוּ כֻלָּם אֶת־עֹל מַלְכוּתֶךָ · וְתִמְלוֹךְ עֲלֵיהֶם
מְהֵרָה לְעוֹלָם וָעֶד · כִּי הַמַּלְכוּת שֶׁלְּךָ הִיא · וּלְעוֹלְמֵי עַד תִּמְלוֹךְ
בְּכָבוֹד · כַּכָּתוּב בְּתוֹרָתֶךָ יְהֹוָה יִמְלֹךְ לְעֹלָם וָעֶד : וְנֶאֱמַר וְהָיָה
יְיָ לְמֶלֶךְ עַל־כָּל־הָאָרֶץ בַּיּוֹם הַהוּא יִהְיֶה יְיָ אֶחָד וּשְׁמוֹ
אֶחָד : קדיש יתום

אַל תִּירָא מִפַּחַד פִּתְאֹם וּמִשֹּׁאַת רְשָׁעִים כִּי תָבֹא : עֻצוּ
עֵצָה וְתֻפָר דַּבְּרוּ דָבָר וְלֹא יָקוּם כִּי עִמָּנוּ אֵל : וְעַד זִקְנָה אֲנִי
הוּא וְעַד שֵׂיבָה אֲנִי אֶסְבֹּל אֲנִי עָשִׂיתִי וַאֲנִי אֶשָּׂא וַאֲנִי אֶסְבֹּל
וַאֲמַלֵּט :

---

to God expresses His infinitely exalted majesty and at the same time His infinite and immediate nearness to all. He is *Kadosh* infinitely exalted above
all things, and yet He is also *Baruch;* He expects that every breath of ours
should serve to advance the fulfillment of His purposes and symbolize our
dedication to the realization of His will. שהוא נוטה שמים ויוסד ארץ Long ago
heaven and earth came into being through Him. But this was not the end of
Creation, for it is only because of Him that heaven and earth still exist today;

We therefore put our hope in You, O *God* our God, that we may soon behold the glorification of Your invincible might, to banish the idols from the earth so that the [false] gods will vanish entirely, that the world will be perfected through the reign of the All-Sufficient, so that all mortals will call upon Your Name, to turn all the lawless of the earth to You, so that all the inhabitants of the world of men may realize and know that to You every knee must bend, every tongue must swear allegiance. Before You, O *God,* our God, they will bend the knee and cast themselves down; they will give honor to the glory of Your Name and they will all accept the yoke of Your kingdom. Thus may You soon reign over them forever, for the kingdom is Yours, and to all eternity will You reign in glory, even as is written in Your Torah: "*God* shall reign in all eternity," and it is said: "Then *God* will be King over all the earth; on that day shall *God* be One and His Name One."

---

it is His will that preserves them in their original form and nature. אפס זולתו All things living, from the greatest to the smallest, exist only because of Him, even when the hand of God appears to us only indirectly evident in their birth and survival. והשבת אל לבבך and if the awareness of this fact should ever grow faint, or fade within your mind, if it should ever seem to be about to depart from you, then keep "bringing it back to your soul" and let it rule with renewed power over your soul and spirit.

עַל כֵּן It is on the basis of this our conviction of the Unity, the majesty and might of the will of God that rules over all things that we cleave with equal firmness to the trust that we shall not forever hold a monopoly on the acknowledgement and homage of God. We know that God, true to His promise, will bring to pass that happy time when everything that may stand in the way of His recognition and homage will vanish from the earth, and all of mankind will stand united in the acknowledgement and worship of God as the One Sole God. What we pray for here is not that God may truly make this come to pass; for we are firmly convinced that it will indeed be so. What we express here is solely our fervent hope and prayer that it may happen מהרה "speedily and soon."

After the Morning Service the following psalms are recited:

On Sundays: היום יום ראשון בשבת שבו הלויים היו אומרים במקדש

כד לְדָוִד מִזְמוֹר ・ לַיהֹוָה הָאָרֶץ וּמְלוֹאָהּ תֵּבֵל וְיֹשְׁבֵי
בָהּ: כִּי־הוּא עַל־יַמִּים יְסָדָהּ וְעַל־נְהָרוֹת יְכוֹנְנֶהָ:
מִי־יַעֲלֶה בְהַר יְהֹוָה וּמִי־יָקוּם בִּמְקוֹם קָדְשׁוֹ: נְקִי
כַפַּיִם וּבַר לֵבָב אֲשֶׁר לֹא־נָשָׂא לַשָּׁוְא נַפְשִׁי וְלֹא נִשְׁבַּע
לְמִרְמָה: יִשָּׂא בְרָכָה מֵאֵת יְהֹוָה וּצְדָקָה מֵאֱלֹהֵי יִשְׁעוֹ: זֶה דּוֹר
דֹּרְשָׁיו מְבַקְשֵׁי פָנֶיךָ יַעֲקֹב סֶלָה: שְׂאוּ שְׁעָרִים רָאשֵׁיכֶם וְהִנָּשְׂאוּ
פִּתְחֵי עוֹלָם וְיָבוֹא מֶלֶךְ הַכָּבוֹד: מִי זֶה מֶלֶךְ הַכָּבוֹד ・ יְהֹוָה עִזּוּז
וְגִבּוֹר יְהֹוָה גִּבּוֹר מִלְחָמָה: שְׂאוּ שְׁעָרִים רָאשֵׁיכֶם וּשְׂאוּ פִּתְחֵי
עוֹלָם וְיָבֹא מֶלֶךְ הַכָּבוֹד: מִי הוּא זֶה מֶלֶךְ הַכָּבוֹד ・ יְהֹוָה צְבָאוֹת
הוּא מֶלֶךְ הַכָּבוֹד סֶלָה: *) נפשי קרי

On Mondays: היום יום שני בשבת שבו הלויים היו אומרים במקדש

מח שִׁיר מִזְמוֹר לִבְנֵי־קֹרַח: גָּדוֹל יְהֹוָה וּמְהֻלָּל מְאֹד בְּעִיר
אֱלֹהֵינוּ הַר־קָדְשׁוֹ: יְפֵה נוֹף מְשׂוֹשׂ כָּל־הָאָרֶץ הַר־צִיּוֹן יַרְכְּתֵי

Psalm 24. לדוד מזמור See above p. 192.

Psalm 48. שיר מזמור This psalm shows us the manner in which God reveals His greatness also to the other nations through Yisrael. God selected Jerusalem, our City of God, as the place where He would make known His greatness and His mighty acts. And Jerusalem is merely הר קדש, Zion, the mountain of His Sanctuary serving as a symbol of that which the Law reposing there has set down as being God's will with regard to the way of life, both private and communal, that He expects man to follow. The function of Jerusalem is to set the example for all the rest of Yisrael to follow, even as

After the Morning Service the following psalms are recited:

On Sundays:

By David. A Psalm. The earth is *God's* and the fullness therof, the world of men and they that dwell therein. For He has founded it upon the seas and, guiding it, constantly establishes it upon the floods. Who shall ascend to the mountain of *God,* and who shall stand in the place of His Sanctuary? "He that is clean of hands and pure of heart, who has not lifted up his soul, which is Mine, unto vanity and has not sworn deceitfully. He shall receive a blessing from *God* and kindness from the God of his salvation." This is the generation of them that seek after Him, that seek your face, O Yaakov!—Lift up your heads, O gates, be lifted up to become portals of the future, so that the King of Glory may come in. "Who is this King of Glory?" *God,* invincible and strong, *God,* the Mighty One in battle." Lift up your heads again, O gates, lift them up to become portals of the future, so that the King of Glory may come in. "Who, then, is this King of Glory?" "*God Tzevaoth,* He is the King of Glory!"

On Mondays:

A Song, A Psalm by the sons of Korach. Great is *God* and clearly revealed by His mighty acts in the city of our God, the mountain of His Sanctuary. Fair in situation, the joy of all the land, the mountain

---

Yisrael is the nation set up as a model for all the other peoples of the world to emulate. Because it fulfills God's will, this city shall attain *shalom,* the state of supreme, harmonious and blissful perfection, and in this *shalom* the will of God and His blessed presence יראה shall become manifest. Therefore the name Jerusalem. ציון is a "monument," a memorial for someone who has departed this life. Spelled ציון, it is the name for the site of the Jewish sanctuary, which is to serve as a memorial for the preservation of truth in the midst of mankind, a virtue which, as God demands, must not disappear from the memory of man.

צָפוֹן קִרְיַת מֶלֶךְ רָב: אֱלֹהִים בְּאַרְמְנוֹתֶיהָ נוֹדַע לְמִשְׂגָּב: כִּי־
הִנֵּה הַמְּלָכִים נוֹעֲדוּ עָבְרוּ יַחְדָּו: הֵמָּה רָאוּ כֵּן תָּמָהוּ נִבְהֲלוּ
נֶחְפָּזוּ: רְעָדָה אֲחָזָתַם שָׁם חִיל כַּיּוֹלֵדָה: בְּרוּחַ קָדִים תְּשַׁבֵּר
אֳנִיּוֹת תַּרְשִׁישׁ: כַּאֲשֶׁר שָׁמַעְנוּ ׀ כֵּן רָאִינוּ בְּעִיר יְהֹוָה־צְבָאוֹת
בְּעִיר אֱלֹהֵינוּ אֱלֹהִים יְכוֹנְנֶהָ עַד־עוֹלָם סֶלָה: דִּמִּינוּ אֱלֹהִים
חַסְדֶּךָ בְּקֶרֶב הֵיכָלֶךָ: כְּשִׁמְךָ אֱלֹהִים כֵּן תְּהִלָּתְךָ עַל־קַצְוֵי־אֶרֶץ
צֶדֶק מָלְאָה יְמִינֶךָ: יִשְׂמַח ׀ הַר־צִיּוֹן תָּגֵלְנָה בְּנוֹת יְהוּדָה לְמַעַן
מִשְׁפָּטֶיךָ: סֹבּוּ צִיּוֹן וְהַקִּיפוּהָ סִפְרוּ מִגְדָּלֶיהָ: שִׁיתוּ לִבְּכֶם ׀
לְחֵילָה פַּסְּגוּ אַרְמְנוֹתֶיהָ לְמַעַן תְּסַפְּרוּ לְדוֹר אַחֲרוֹן: כִּי זֶה ׀
אֱלֹהִים אֱלֹהֵינוּ עוֹלָם וָעֶד הוּא יְנַהֲגֵנוּ עַל־מוּת:

On Tuesdays: הַיּוֹם יוֹם שְׁלִישִׁי בְּשַׁבָּת שֶׁבּוֹ הַלְוִיִּם הָיוּ אוֹמְרִים בַּמִּקְדָּשׁ

פב מִזְמוֹר לְאָסָף אֱלֹהִים נִצָּב בַּעֲדַת־אֵל בְּקֶרֶב אֱלֹהִים יִשְׁפֹּט:
עַד־מָתַי תִּשְׁפְּטוּ־עָוֶל וּפְנֵי רְשָׁעִים תִּשְׂאוּ־סֶלָה: שִׁפְטוּ־דָל
וְיָתוֹם עָנִי וָרָשׁ הַצְדִּיקוּ: פַּלְּטוּ־דַל וְאֶבְיוֹן מִיַּד רְשָׁעִים הַצִּילוּ:
לֹא יָדְעוּ ׀ וְלֹא יָבִינוּ בַּחֲשֵׁכָה יִתְהַלָּכוּ יִמּוֹטוּ כָּל־מוֹסְדֵי אָרֶץ:
אֲנִי אָמַרְתִּי אֱלֹהִים אַתֶּם וּבְנֵי עֶלְיוֹן כֻּלְּכֶם: אָכֵן כְּאָדָם תְּמוּתוּן

Psalm 92. מזמור לאסף It is evident from the concluding verse of this Psalm
that Asaph does not think here only of the Jewish people, but also pleads the
cause of the salvation of all mankind on earth, all of whose existence and welfare is dependent, first of all, upon the proper enforcement of justice and

of Tzion, the goal of the North, is the great city of a mighty King. In its palaces, God has been recognized as a stronghold. For behold, the kings had assembled, and they also came away together. They saw and straightway they were startled; they were terrified and they hastened away. Trembling seized them there, pangs, as of a woman in travail. With a wind from the east You break the ships of Tarshish. Even as we have heard it in the past, so have we seen it now in the City of *God Tzevaoth,* in the City of our God, that God will establish it forever!—We had heretofore conceived of Your loving-kindness, O God, as being in the midst of Your Temple. As is Your Name, O God, so is now the praise of Your mighty acts unto the ends of the earth; Your right hand is full of righteousness. The mountain of Tzion is glad, the daughters of Yehudah rejoice because of Your judgments. Rally around Tzion, gather about her closely, count her towers. Mark well her circular wall, raise aloft her palaces, so that you may tell of it to all future generations, that this God is our God forever; He leads us beyond mortality.

On Tuesdays:

A Psalm of Assaph. God stands in every tribunal of God; He judges in the midst of the judges. "How much longer will you enforce violence in your judgment, and respect the persons of the lawless?—Help also him who has been brought low, and an orphan, to obtain their rightful due, and proclaim the right of those bereft of wealth and station. Rescue him who has been brought low, and the defenseless; save them out of the hand of the lawless. This they have never known nor shall they ever understand it; they will walk on in darkness, therefore all pillars of the earth totter. I had thought you were gods, and all of you the sons of the Most High. But you will die

---

right. There is nothing that reveals God to the straight-thinking man more clearly as the Founder and Maintainer of human society than the sense of justice which was ingrained into the spirit and conscience of each man at the time of his creation. It is this sense of justice and right which should be enforced by the judges among men and should become the correct and rightful order in all interpersonal relationships as well as in the dealings of the individual with the community and those of the community with the individual.

וּכְאַחַד הַשָּׂרִים תִּפֹּלוּ: קוּמָה אֱלֹהִים שָׁפְטָה הָאָרֶץ כִּי־אַתָּה
תִנְחַל בְּכָל־הַגּוֹיִם:

On Wednesdays: הַיּוֹם יוֹם רְבִיעִי בְּשַׁבָּת שֶׁבּוֹ הָלְוִיִּם הָיוּ אוֹמְרִים בַּמִּקְדָּשׁ

אֵל־נְקָמוֹת יְהֹוָה אֵל נְקָמוֹת הוֹפִיעַ: הִנָּשֵׂא שֹׁפֵט הָאָרֶץ
הָשֵׁב גְּמוּל עַל־גֵּאִים: עַד־מָתַי רְשָׁעִים יְהֹוָה עַד־מָתַי רְשָׁעִים
יַעֲלֹזוּ: יַבִּיעוּ יְדַבְּרוּ עָתָק יִתְאַמְּרוּ כָּל־פֹּעֲלֵי אָוֶן: עַמְּךָ יְהֹוָה
יְדַכְּאוּ וְנַחֲלָתְךָ יְעַנּוּ: אַלְמָנָה וְגֵר יַהֲרֹגוּ וִיתוֹמִים יְרַצֵּחוּ: וַיֹּאמְרוּ
לֹא יִרְאֶה־יָּהּ וְלֹא יָבִין אֱלֹהֵי יַעֲקֹב: בִּינוּ בֹּעֲרִים בָּעָם וּכְסִילִים
מָתַי תַּשְׂכִּילוּ: הֲנֹטַע אֹזֶן הֲלֹא יִשְׁמָע אִם־יֹצֵר עַיִן הֲלֹא יַבִּיט:
הֲיֹסֵר גּוֹיִם הֲלֹא יוֹכִיחַ הַמְלַמֵּד אָדָם דָּעַת: יְהֹוָה יֹדֵעַ מַחְשְׁבוֹת
אָדָם כִּי הֵמָּה הָבֶל: אַשְׁרֵי הַגֶּבֶר אֲשֶׁר־תְּיַסְּרֶנּוּ יָּהּ וּמִתּוֹרָתְךָ
תְלַמְּדֶנּוּ: לְהַשְׁקִיט לוֹ מִימֵי רָע עַד יִכָּרֶה לָרָשָׁע שָׁחַת: כִּי־
לֹא־יִטֹּשׁ יְהֹוָה עַמּוֹ וְנַחֲלָתוֹ לֹא יַעֲזֹב: כִּי־עַד־צֶדֶק יָשׁוּב מִשְׁפָּט
וְאַחֲרָיו כָּל־יִשְׁרֵי־לֵב: מִי־יָקוּם לִי עִם־מְרֵעִים מִי־יִתְיַצֵּב לִי עִם־
פֹּעֲלֵי אָוֶן: לוּלֵי יְהֹוָה עֶזְרָתָה לִּי כִּמְעַט שָׁכְנָה דוּמָה נַפְשִׁי:
אִם־אָמַרְתִּי מָטָה רַגְלִי חַסְדְּךָ יְהֹוָה יִסְעָדֵנִי: בְּרֹב שַׂרְעַפַּי בְּקִרְבִּי:

Psalm 94. אל נקמות. This psalm attempts to check the despondency which
takes hold of many as they behold the apparent success of evil and which
causes them to doubt God's Providence. אל נקמות ה׳ is an appeal rising up to
God from the midst of Yisrael during a time fraught with the sufferings of

like men, and fall like one of the princes. Therefore arise, O God, judge the earth; for You desire to assume inheritance among all the nations.

On Wednesdays:

O God, Champion of Justice, *God,* God, Champion of Justice, shine forth! Arise, O Judge of the earth, let that which they have wrought return to the arrogant ."How long shall the lawless, O *God,* how long shall the lawless exult?" They gush out, they openly utter unseemly things, they speak their minds, all the workers of abuse. They crush Your people, O *God,* and they afflict Your inheritance; they slay the widow and the stranger, and they murder the orphans. And they have already said it, "The Almighty will not see, nor will the God of Yaakov notice." Consider, you [who are] devoid of sense in the midst of the people; and you conceited ones, when will you put your reason to good use? He that implants the ear, should He not hear? He that shapes the eye, should He not see? He that restrains the nations, should He not correct, He that teaches man knowledge? *God* knows the thoughts of men, that they are vanity. For forward strides that man whom You, O God, train by discipline and whom You teach out of Your Law the while, to let rest come for him from the days of evil, while the pit is dug for the lawless. For *God* will not cast off His people, nor will He forsake His inheritance, for the world order shall revert to justice, and he who is upright in heart strives after it. Who will rise up for me against evildoers?' Who will stand up for me against workers of abuse? Had *God* not been my help, but for a little and my soul would long ago have been imbedded in silence. Whenever I said, "My foot has slipped," Your loving-kindness, O *God,* upheld me. When my thoughts were at war within me, Your

---

Galuth, when it seems as if God had indeed forsaken His people. Even when He acts as אֵל נְקָמוֹת, He still remains ה'. Indeed, the call is addressed to Him as ה', denoting His merciful Providence. He is urged to reveal Himself as אֵל נְקָמוֹת. For נָקָם essentially denotes a restitution of rights that have been infringed upon. (See Commentary to Gen. 4:15). It is expected that God, because He is ה', namely, for the sake of mankind's future salvation, will reveal Himself as the champion of injured right by casting down all evil.

תַּנְחוּמֶֽיךָ יְשַׁעַשְׁעוּ נַפְשִׁי: הַיְחָבְרְךָ כִּסֵּא הַוּוֹת יֹצֵר עָמָל עֲלֵי־
חֹק: יָגֽוֹדּוּ עַל־נֶֽפֶשׁ צַדִּיק וְדָם נָקִי יַרְשִׁיעוּ: וַיְהִי יְהוָֹה לִי לְמִשְׂגָּב
וֵאלֹהַי לְצוּר מַחְסִי: וַיָּֽשֶׁב עֲלֵיהֶם אֶת־אוֹנָם וּבְרָעָתָם יַצְמִיתֵם
יַצְמִיתֵם יְהוָֹה אֱלֹהֵֽינוּ:

ה' ידע וגו' Why, then, at times, does God fail to act to check wrongdoing?
There are two reasons why this should be so. First, we must remember that
it is only to our limited insight that evil appears to be making constant progress in the attainment of its goal. God in His infinite wisdom, however, knows
that it will all end in הבל, in vanity. And it is this eventual demonstration
of the worthlessness of any ambition based upon wrong and violence that will
be the sole saving and penetrating *tochachah* which will lead all of mankind
at long last to render sincere homage to that which is good and true. אשרי
Secondly, the evil which God at times seems to tolerate actually serves to discipline man by helping to increase his moral strength and to ennoble him. The
wrong which a man must endure is part of that training course of suffering
which will refine him through discipline, a discipline to which God subjects
only those of His children who are capable of improvement and ennoblement.
(Cf. Commentary to Deut. 8:5.) Alas for the man whom God no longer deems
worthy of the experience of suffering, for he is the one whom God has ceased
to attempt to better and to refine. In order to be worthy of being accepted
into this Divine training course, a man must fulfill two basic requirements:
first, he must be גבר, he must not be a weakling who can be utterly crushed
by suffering, nor may he be one whose moral energies have been completely
dissipated and debauchery. Instead, he must still bear within himself a reserve of moral energy and fortitude which is to be activated by the
suffering he must undergo and which will enable him to wield the reins of
self-control so that he may guide himself along the path of what is good and
right. Secondly, ומתורתך תלמדנו his attitude toward the teaching of God must
still be such that he will view any sufferings that will come his way simply
as an admonition to delve more deeply into that Law in order to derive from
it the standard of what a life filled with duty and loyalty to God should be,
and then to measure his own past existence against that standard. When suffering strikes us, we are not to grope for superficial remedies which have no
bearing on our moral improvement. Instead, our Sages teach us אם רואה אדם
שיסורין באין עליו יפשפש במעשיו. פשפש ולא מצא יתלה בביטול תורה שני אשרי הגבר אשר
תיסרנו יה ומתורתך תלמדנו ". "Should we see that troubles overcome us, this should
be an admonition to us to examine the life we have led heretofore, to see whe-

comforts soothed my soul; "Can a throne of evil have fellowship with You, which frames mischief into statute? That masses shall gather against the righteous one and condemn innocent blood? Then *God* became my High Tower, and my God the Rock, of my refuge. And He turned back upon them their own might. He stunned them in their own evil; they are stunned because *God* is our God.

---

ther we have not done wrong, or neglected to do our duty, or whether we would not have been able to be better than we actually have been. If we have subjected ourselves to this test and can find no specific wrong that we might have done, and that might be the cause of our sorrows, then we must ascribe our present troubles to the fact that we have neglected to occupy ourselves sufficiently with the study of God's Law" (Berachoth 8a). For it is through such a serious omission that the awareness of what God requires of us as regards a Jewish life led in accordance with our duty may have faded from our minds. Therefore let our sufferings serve as an admonition to us to return to the Torah, to this wellspring from which we can derive the recognition of where our duty lies in accordance with the will of God. Trouble should remind us that the Torah alone should serve as the standard by which we should revise our own notions of right and wrong, duty and sin, and of the life-mission set us by God. And when, as a consequence, we muster all the moral energy within us to expunge the blots upon the pages of our past life and to become truly human beings in accordance with the standards set by the Torah, in accordance with the will of God as revealed to us, then we will truly come to understand the truth inherent in Verse 12 אשרי וגו׳.He whom God trains and disciplines through suffering and thus leads to seek instruction from God's Torah is the very one who will steadily stride forward to salvation. Thus we see that suffering is not reserved for the most wicked on earth, and, for that matter, that the very wickedness of evil men, unknown to themselves, actually serves to advance the perfect salvation of those better than they, who are made to suffer at their hands — כל פעל ה׳ למענהו וגם רשע ליום רעה "God has created all things for His purposes, and He has made even the lawless man for the day of trouble" (Prov. 16:4). כל לא יטש And even as God trains the individual in this manner, so He also disciplines His entire people through suffering (Deut. 8:5). Verse 4 states עמך ה׳ ידכאו. This is not meant to say that God permits this to happen *even though* Yisrael is His people, but *for the very reason* that Yisrael is indeed His nation, because He will not abandon it or cease in His efforts to train it even when it has strayed. And even though *nachalatho ye'anu,* this does not mean that God has forsaken His inheritance; He will not allow it to succumb to its troubles; for He has set a definite goal and purpose for Yisrael's sufferings.

On Thursdays: היום יום חמישי בשבת שבו הלויים היו אומרים במקדש

פא לַמְנַצֵּחַ עַל־הַגִּתִּית לְאָסָף: הַרְנִינוּ לֵאלֹהִים עוּזֵּנוּ הָרִיעוּ

לֵאלֹהֵי יַעֲקֹב: שְׂאוּ־זִמְרָה וּתְנוּ־תֹף כִּנּוֹר נָעִים עִם־נָבֶל: תִּקְעוּ

בַחֹדֶשׁ שׁוֹפָר בַּכֶּסֶה לְיוֹם חַגֵּנוּ: כִּי חֹק לְיִשְׂרָאֵל הוּא מִשְׁפָּט

לֵאלֹהֵי יַעֲקֹב: עֵדוּת בִּיהוֹסֵף שָׂמוֹ בְּצֵאתוֹ עַל־אֶרֶץ מִצְרָיִם

שְׂפַת לֹא־יָדַעְתִּי אֶשְׁמָע: הֲסִירוֹתִי מִסֵּבֶל שִׁכְמוֹ כַּפָּיו מִדּוּד

תַּעֲבֹרְנָה: בַּצָּרָה קָרָאתָ וָאֲחַלְּצֶךָּ אֶעֶנְךָ בְּסֵתֶר רַעַם אֶבְחָנְךָ עַל־

מֵי מְרִיבָה סֶלָה: שְׁמַע עַמִּי וְאָעִידָה בָּךְ יִשְׂרָאֵל אִם־תִּשְׁמַע־

Psalm 81 למנצח על הגתית The phrase על הגתית in the superscription of
a psalm indicates that the Psalm thus prefaced meditates either upon the ennobling power of the discipline of suffering decreed by God, or upon the
spiritual refinement itself brought about by God in man through the means
of suffering (Cf. Midrash Tehillim). Psalm 80 portrayed Yisrael as a "vine"
and depicted the sad fate that awaits this plant of God. Now Psalm 81 is
meant to describe the splendor which this fruit may be sure of attaining if
it does not shrink from undergoing the ennobling process of the "wine pressing." כי חק לישראל "For Yisrael has a statute"; the happiness and joy of life
in which "Yisrael" as such should rejoice cannot be found by sheer caprice.
They are primarily dependent upon whether or not Yisrael fulfills the "statute"
which it has been given in order that it may discharge its "mission as Yisrael."
And משפט לאלקי יעקב, before He will raise us up from our humble "Yaakov-
like" state to the status of "Yisrael in flower," the God of Yaakov will first
sit in judgment to evaluate the manner in which we have fulfilled this Law.
הסירותי וגו' It was in God's power to grant us physical freedom and to rid
our shoulder of the burden, and He did so. However, no one else but we ourselves can make us free morally and spiritually as well and liberate us from
the power of lust, and this is what God expects us to do. כפיו מדוד תעברנה
"Let his hands stay away from the kettle." Yisrael shall never again say
בצרה קראת וגו' זכרנו את הדגה (Num. 11:5), בשבתנו על סיר הבשר (Exod. 16:3).
The same God Who was so obviously near us to deliver us from trouble also
was near us when He disciplined us. He was near us even at those times when

On Thursdays:

To Him Who grants victory over the "wine pressing". By Asaph. Stir up jubilation to God of our strength; waken homage to the God of Yaakov; take up the melody, sound the timbrel, the sweet harp with the psaltery. But blow the Shofar on the New Moon, on the day of the veiling of the moon for our feast-day. For there is a statute for Yisrael, and the God of Yaakov sits in judgment. He had appointed it in Yoseph as a testimony, when He went forth over the land of Mitzrayim; I shall henceforth hear the speech of One Whom I had not perceived before. "I have removed his shoulder from burden, now let his hands stay away from the kettle. You called in trouble, and I made you free, so I shall answer you even hidden in thunder; I shall test you at the waters of contention.—Hear, O My people, I shall testify against you, O Yisrael, if you would only hearken to Me. There shall

---

it seemed as if He had withdrawn His countenance from us behind a thundercloud, as it were, and tried and trained us by denying us the fulfillment of our heart's desires. These two verses refer to Yisrael's journey through the wilderness. In Deut. 8:1–5 Moshe, in retrospect, discusses the significance of this journey as a period of training in Yisrael's history. Here, however, this reminiscence serves only as an introduction to the verses that follow, telling us that God has freed us from slavery only in order to train us to achieve spiritual and moral greatness both as individuals and as a nation. שמע וגו׳ This, and the verses that follow until the end of the psalm constitute the content of the עדות which the blast of the Shofar proclaims in our midst on the day of Rosh Hashanah. God speaks to Yisrael as follows: "When I redeemed you, I said שמע עמי : ולקחתי אתכם לי לעם; you were to become a group of men that belongs to Me and must therefore subordinate all your affairs to Me. Hence I have the right to demand that you hearken to Me, and that you heed the testimony which I shall demonstrate upon you as well as that which I must make against you" ישראל אם וגו׳ "You will be 'Yisrael'—your entire history will demonstrate the all-surpassing supremacy of God —ישר אל— only if you will bring the influence of His reign to bear upon every aspect of your lives both as individuals and as a nation. Only if תשמע לי will you be Yisrael," says God. לא יהיה וגו׳ "There shall be no alien god within you." לא יהיה בך אל זר איזהו אל זר שיש בגופו של אדם הוי אומר זה יצר הרע (Sabbath 105 b). "Do not cede divine power over your spiritual lives to your sensual urges, drives and passions."

לִי: לֹא־יִהְיֶה בְךָ אֵל זָר וְלֹא תִשְׁתַּחֲוֶה לְאֵל נֵכָר: אָנֹכִי ׀

יְהֹוָה אֱלֹהֶיךָ הַמַּעַלְךָ מֵאֶרֶץ מִצְרָיִם הַרְחֶב־פִּיךָ וַאֲמַלְאֵהוּ: וְלֹא־

שָׁמַע עַמִּי לְקוֹלִי וְיִשְׂרָאֵל לֹא־אָבָה לִי: וָאֲשַׁלְּחֵהוּ בִּשְׁרִירוּת

לִבָּם יֵלְכוּ בְּמוֹעֲצוֹתֵיהֶם: לוּ עַמִּי שֹׁמֵעַ לִי יִשְׂרָאֵל בִּדְרָכַי יְהַלֵּכוּ:

כִּמְעַט אוֹיְבֵיהֶם אַכְנִיעַ וְעַל־צָרֵיהֶם אָשִׁיב יָדִי: מְשַׂנְאֵי יְהֹוָה

יְכַחֲשׁוּ־לוֹ וִיהִי עִתָּם לְעוֹלָם: וַיַּאֲכִילֵהוּ מֵחֵלֶב חִטָּה וּמִצּוּר

דְּבַשׁ אַשְׂבִּיעֶךָ:

On Fridays: היום יום ששי בשבת שבו הלויים היו אומרים במקדש

צג יְהֹוָה מָלָךְ גֵּאוּת לָבֵשׁ לָבֵשׁ יְהֹוָה עֹז הִתְאַזָּר אַף־תִּכּוֹן תֵּבֵל

בַּל־תִּמּוֹט: נָכוֹן כִּסְאֲךָ מֵאָז מֵעוֹלָם אָתָּה: נָשְׂאוּ נְהָרוֹת ׀ יְהֹוָה

נָשְׂאוּ נְהָרוֹת קוֹלָם יִשְׂאוּ נְהָרוֹת דָּכְיָם: מִקֹּלוֹת ׀ מַיִם רַבִּים

אַדִּירִים מִשְׁבְּרֵי־יָם אַדִּיר בַּמָּרוֹם יְהֹוָה: עֵדֹתֶיךָ ׀ נֶאֶמְנוּ מְאֹד

לְבֵיתְךָ נַאֲוָה־קֹדֶשׁ יְהֹוָה לְאֹרֶךְ יָמִים:

בימים שאומרים תחנון נוהגי' בהרבה קהלות לומר בכל יום אחר שיר של יום מזמור פ"ג,
ואומרין אותו חפילו בחנוכה ויפורים וט"ב באמחה, ויא"א אותו בבית אבל רל.

פג שִׁיר מִזְמוֹר לְאָסָף: אֱלֹהִים אַל־דֳּמִי־לָךְ אַל־תֶּחֱרַשׁ וְאַל־

תִּשְׁקֹט אֵל: כִּי־הִנֵּה אוֹיְבֶיךָ יֶהֱמָיוּן וּמְשַׂנְאֶיךָ נָשְׂאוּ רֹאשׁ: עַל־

Psalm 93 ה' מלך See above p. 76.

Psalm 83 שיר מזמור לאסף This psalm has the characteristic features of a
שיר. First, it "looks back" upon the mighty acts which God has perpetrated

be no alien god within you, nor shall you cast yourselves down before
a foreign deity. I, *God,* shall be your God, Who has brought you up
from the land of Mitzrayim; spread wide your desire, I shall fulfill
it. But My people did not hearken to My voice, and Yisrael would
not submit to Me.. Then I let it go after the stubbornness of their
heart; let them walk in their own counsels. O that My people would
hearken to Me, that Yisrael would earnestly walk in My ways; I would
speedily subdue their enemies and turn My hand back against their
oppressors. The haters of *God* would feign [homage] to Him so that
their fate, too, should endure forever. And while He would feed it
with the fat of wheat I would satisfy you with honey out of the rock."

On Fridays:

God has begun His reign; He has girded Himself with majesty;
God has clothed Himself; He has girded Himself with strength that
none can withstand; now the world of men, too, shall be firmly established and sway no more. Your throne is henceforth established,
O You Who are from everlasting. True, the floods O *God,* the floods
have lifted up their voice, the floods lift up their fall. The breakers
of the ocean grew mightier from the roar of many waters; *God* alone
is mighty on high. Thus Your testimonies have proven infinitely faithful; the name of "Sanctuary" truly befits Your House, O *God,* for
all the length of days.

*Then the following מזמור is recited. In many congregations, however, it is said
only on days when Tachanun is recited.*

A Song, a Psalm of Asaph. O God Who sits in judgment, You
cannot keep silence; You cannot hold Your peace and be still, O Almighty One. For lo, it is Your enemies that are in an uproar and that
spread hatred of You; they have lifted up their head. It is against Your

---

upon Yisrael's oppressors who, even in those days long ago, had meant to
fight God by attacking Yisrael. Secondly, the Psalmist voices his confident
expectation that God will intervene in the same manner even now in order
to chastise the nations that are presently fighting against Him. כי הנה וגו'.
Judaism, with its concept of an invisible God and its idealistic views of the
world and of life as a whole, has always been the butt of the hatred of those
who capitalize upon the degeneracy and corruptibility of man.

עָמְךָ יַעֲרִימוּ סוֹד וְיִתְיָעֲצוּ עַל־צְפוּנֶיךָ: אָמְרוּ לְכוּ וְנַכְחִידֵם

מִגּוֹי וְלֹא־יִזָּכֵר שֵׁם־יִשְׂרָאֵל עוֹד: כִּי נוֹעֲצוּ לֵב יַחְדָּו עָלֶיךָ בְּרִית

יִכְרֹתוּ: אָהֳלֵי אֱדוֹם וְיִשְׁמְעֵאלִים מוֹאָב וְהַגְרִים: גְּבָל וְעַמּוֹן

וַעֲמָלֵק פְּלֶשֶׁת עִם־יֹשְׁבֵי צוֹר: גַּם־אַשּׁוּר נִלְוָה עִמָּם הָיוּ זְרוֹעַ

לִבְנֵי־לוֹט סֶלָה: עֲשֵׂה־לָהֶם כְּמִדְיָן כְּסִיסְרָא כְיָבִין בְּנַחַל קִישׁוֹן:

נִשְׁמְדוּ בְעֵין־דֹּאר הָיוּ דֹּמֶן לָאֲדָמָה: שִׁיתֵמוֹ נְדִיבֵמוֹ כְּעֹרֵב

וְכִזְאֵב וּכְזֶבַח וּכְצַלְמֻנָּע כָּל־נְסִיכֵמוֹ: אֲשֶׁר אָמְרוּ נִירְשָׁה לָּנוּ אֵת

נְאוֹת אֱלֹהִים: אֱלֹהַי שִׁיתֵמוֹ כַגַּלְגַּל כְּקַשׁ לִפְנֵי־רוּחַ: כְּאֵשׁ

תִּבְעַר־יָעַר וּכְלֶהָבָה תְּלַהֵט הָרִים: כֵּן תִּרְדְּפֵם בְּסַעֲרֶךָ וּבְסוּפָתְךָ

תְבַהֲלֵם: מַלֵּא פְנֵיהֶם קָלוֹן וִיבַקְשׁוּ שִׁמְךָ יְהֹוָה: יֵבֹשׁוּ וְיִבָּהֲלוּ

עֲדֵי־עַד וְיַחְפְּרוּ וְיֹאבֵדוּ: וְיֵדְעוּ כִּי־אַתָּה שִׁמְךָ יְהֹוָה לְבַדֶּךָ עֶלְיוֹן

עַל־כָּל־הָאָרֶץ:

From the second day of Rosh Chodesh Ellul *till* Shemini Atzereth *the following Psalm is said.*

מן ר"ח אלול עד אסר י"כ צבוקר וגעכב בכל יוס אומריס זה [ומנהגינו לאמרינו עד אסר הוש"כ]:

כז לְדָוִד יְיָ אוֹרִי וְיִשְׁעִי מִמִּי אִירָא יְיָ מָעוֹז חַיַּי מִמִּי אֶפְחָד: בִּקְרֹב עָלַי מְרֵעִים

לֶאֱכֹל אֶת־בְּשָׂרִי צָרַי וְאֹיְבַי לִי הֵמָּה כָּשְׁלוּ וְנָפָלוּ: אִם־תַּחֲנֶה עָלַי מַחֲנֶה לֹא

יִירָא לִבִּי אִם־תָּקוּם עָלַי מִלְחָמָה בְּזֹאת אֲנִי בוֹטֵחַ: אַחַת שָׁאַלְתִּי מֵאֵת יְיָ אוֹתָהּ

אֲבַקֵּשׁ שִׁבְתִּי בְּבֵית יְיָ כָּל־יְמֵי־חַיַּי לַחֲזוֹת בְּנֹעַם יְיָ וּלְבַקֵּר בְּהֵיכָלוֹ: כִּי יִצְפְּנֵנִי

בְּסֻכֹּה בְּיוֹם רָעָה יַסְתִּירֵנִי בְּסֵתֶר אָהֳלוֹ בְּצוּר יְרוֹמְמֵנִי: וְעַתָּה יָרוּם רֹאשִׁי עַל

אֹיְבַי סְבִיבוֹתַי וְאֶזְבְּחָה בְאָהֳלוֹ זִבְחֵי תְרוּעָה אָשִׁירָה וַאֲזַמְּרָה לַיְיָ: שְׁמַע יְיָ קוֹלִי

אֶקְרָא וְחָנֵּנִי וַעֲנֵנִי: לְךָ אָמַר לִבִּי בַּקְּשׁוּ פָנָי אֶת־פָּנֶיךָ יְיָ אֲבַקֵּשׁ: אַל־תַּסְתֵּר

פָּנֶיךָ מִמֶּנִּי אַל תַּט בְּאַף עַבְדֶּךָ עֶזְרָתִי הָיִיתָ אַל תִּטְּשֵׁנִי וְאַל תַּעַזְבֵנִי אֱלֹהֵי

יִשְׁעִי: כִּי אָבִי וְאִמִּי עֲזָבוּנִי וַיְיָ יַאַסְפֵנִי: הוֹרֵנִי יְיָ דַּרְכֶּךָ וּנְחֵנִי בְּאֹרַח מִישׁוֹר

לְמַעַן שׁוֹרְרָי: אַל תִּתְּנֵנִי בְּנֶפֶשׁ צָרָי כִּי קָמוּ בִי עֵדֵי שֶׁקֶר וִיפֵחַ חָמָס: לוּלֵא ‌

הֶאֱמַנְתִּי לִרְאוֹת בְּטוּב יְיָ בְּאֶרֶץ חַיִּים: קַוֵּה אֶל־יְיָ חֲזַק וְיַאֲמֵץ לִבֶּךָ וְקַוֵּה אֶל־יְיָ:

people that they plot craftily and they take counsel against those sheltered by You. They say, "Come, let us destroy them as a nation; the name of 'Yisrael' shall be remembered no more." For when they consult together with a unanimous heart, then it is against You that they make a covenant. The tents of Edom and the Yishmaelites, Moab and the Hagrites, Gebal, Amon and Amalek, Philistia with the inhabitants of Tyre. Ashur, also, has joined them; they have become the arm of the sons of Lot!—Do to them as to Midian, as to Sisera, as to Yabin in the valley of Kishon. They were destroyed at En Dor, they became dung for the soil. Make them, their nobles, like Oreb and Zeeb, and like Zebach and Zalmuna all their princes, who have also said, "We shall conquer for ourselves the pleasant habitations of God." O my God, make them as whirling dust, as stubble before the wind, as the fire that burns the forest, as the flame that sets the mountains ablaze. So pursue them with Your tempest, and terrify them with Your storm. Fill their faces with shame, so that they may seek Your Name at last, O *God*. Let them be deceived and dismayed forever, let them be unmasked and sense that they are about to perish, and know that You alone, Whose Name is *God,* are the Most High over all the earth.

In the house of a mourner the following Psalm is said.

צאית הצבל אומרים זה בנווקר וענערב :

מט לַמְנַצֵּחַ לִבְנֵי קֹרַח מִזְמוֹר: שִׁמְעוּ זֹאת כָּל־הָעַמִּים הַאֲזִינוּ כָּל יֹשְׁבֵי חָלֶד:
גַּם־בְּנֵי אָדָם גַּם־בְּנֵי־אִישׁ יַחַד עָשִׁיר וְאֶבְיוֹן: פִּי יְדַבֵּר חָכְמוֹת וְהָגוּת לִבִּי
תְבוּנוֹת: אַטֶּה לְמָשָׁל אָזְנִי אֶפְתַּח בְּכִנּוֹר חִידָתִי: לָמָּה אִירָא בִּימֵי רָע עֲוֹן עֲקֵבַי
יְסֻבֵּנִי: הַבֹּטְחִים עַל־חֵילָם וּבְרֹב עָשְׁרָם יִתְהַלָּלוּ: אָח לֹא פָדֹה יִפְדֶּה אִישׁ לֹא
יִתֵּן לֵאלֹהִים כָּפְרוֹ: וְיֵקַר פִּדְיוֹן נַפְשָׁם וְחָדַל לְעוֹלָם: וִיחִי עוֹד לָנֶצַח לֹא יִרְאֶה
הַשָּׁחַת: כִּי יִרְאֶה חֲכָמִים יָמוּתוּ יַחַד כְּסִיל וָבַעַר יֹאבֵדוּ וְעָזְבוּ לַאֲחֵרִים חֵילָם:
קִרְבָּם בָּתֵּימוֹ לְעוֹלָם מִשְׁכְּנֹתָם לְדֹר וָדֹר קָרְאוּ בִשְׁמוֹתָם עֲלֵי־אֲדָמוֹת: וְאָדָם
בִּיקָר בַּל יָלִין נִמְשַׁל כַּבְּהֵמוֹת נִדְמוּ: זֶה־דַרְכָּם כֵּסֶל לָמוֹ וְאַחֲרֵיהֶם בְּפִיהֶם יִרְצוּ
סֶלָה: כַּצֹּאן לִשְׁאוֹל שַׁתּוּ מָוֶת יִרְעֵם וַיִּרְדּוּ בָם יְשָׁרִים לַבֹּקֶר וְצוּרָם לְבַלּוֹת
שְׁאוֹל מִזְּבֻל־לוֹ: אַךְ אֱלֹהִים יִפְדֶּה נַפְשִׁי מִיַּד שְׁאוֹל כִּי יִקָּחֵנִי סֶלָה: אַל־תִּירָא
כִּי יַעֲשִׁר אִישׁ כִּי יִרְבֶּה כְּבוֹד בֵּיתוֹ: כִּי לֹא בְמוֹתוֹ יִקַּח הַכֹּל לֹא יֵרֵד אַחֲרָיו
כְּבוֹדוֹ: כִּי נַפְשׁוֹ בְּחַיָּיו יְבָרֵךְ וְיוֹדֻךָ כִּי תֵיטִיב לָךְ: תָּבוֹא עַד דּוֹר אֲבוֹתָיו עַד־
נֵצַח לֹא יִרְאוּ אוֹר: אָדָם בִּיקָר וְלֹא יָבִין נִמְשַׁל כַּבְּהֵמוֹת נִדְמוּ:

נכון ליזהר בכל יום ד' זכירות אלו:

לְמַעַן תִּזְכֹּר אֶת יוֹם צֵאתְךָ מֵאֶרֶץ מִצְרַיִם כֹּל יְמֵי חַיֶּיךָ:

זָכוֹר אֶת יוֹם אֲשֶׁר עָמַדְתָּ לִפְנֵי יְיָ אֱלֹהֶיךָ בְּחֹרֵב

פֶּן תִּשְׁכַּח אֶת הַדְּבָרִים אֲשֶׁר רָאוּ עֵינֶיךָ:

זָכוֹר אֵת אֲשֶׁר־עָשָׂה לְךָ עֲמָלֵק בַּדֶּרֶךְ בְּצֵאתְכֶם מִמִּצְרָיִם:

אֲשֶׁר קָרְךָ בַּדֶּרֶךְ וַיְזַנֵּב בְּךָ כָּל־הַנֶּחֱשָׁלִים אַחֲרֶיךָ וְאַתָּה עָיֵף

וְיָגֵעַ וְלֹא יָרֵא אֱלֹהִים: וְהָיָה בְּהָנִיחַ יְיָ אֱלֹהֶיךָ לְךָ מִכָּל־אֹיְבֶיךָ

מִסָּבִיב בָּאָרֶץ אֲשֶׁר־יְיָ אֱלֹהֶיךָ נֹתֵן לְךָ נַחֲלָה לְרִשְׁתָּהּ תִּמְחֶה

אֶת־זֵכֶר עֲמָלֵק מִתַּחַת הַשָּׁמָיִם לֹא תִּשְׁכָּח:

זָכוֹר אֵת אֲשֶׁר־עָשָׂה יְיָ אֱלֹהֶיךָ לְמִרְיָם בַּדֶּרֶךְ בְּצֵאתְכֶם

מִמִּצְרָיִם:

In the mornings and evenings, at the conclusion of all תפלות, *the following is said:*

יְהִי יְיָ אֱלֹהֵינוּ עִמָּנוּ כַּאֲשֶׁר הָיָה עִם־אֲבֹתֵינוּ אַל־יַעַזְבֵנוּ וְאַל־

יִטְּשֵׁנוּ: לְהַטּוֹת לְבָבֵנוּ אֵלָיו לָלֶכֶת בְּכָל־דְּרָכָיו וְלִשְׁמֹר מִצְוֹתָיו

וְחֻקָּיו וּמִשְׁפָּטָיו אֲשֶׁר צִוָּה אֶת־אֲבֹתֵינוּ: וְיִהְיוּ דְבָרַי אֵלֶּה אֲשֶׁר

הִתְחַנַּנְתִּי לִפְנֵי יְיָ קְרֹבִים אֶל־יְיָ אֱלֹהֵינוּ יוֹמָם וָלָיְלָה לַעֲשׂוֹת

מִשְׁפַּט עַבְדּוֹ וּמִשְׁפַּט עַמּוֹ יִשְׂרָאֵל דְּבַר־יוֹם בְּיוֹמוֹ: לְמַעַן דַּעַת

כָּל־עַמֵּי הָאָרֶץ כִּי יְיָ הוּא הָאֱלֹהִים אֵין עוֹד: יְיָ נְחֵנִי בְצִדְקָתֶךָ

לְמַעַן שׁוֹרְרָי הַיְשַׁר לְפָנַי דַּרְכֶּךָ: וַאֲנִי בְּתֻמִּי אֵלֵךְ פְּדֵנִי וְחָנֵּנִי,

כִּי־יָחִיד וְעָנִי אָנִי: רַגְלִי עָמְדָה בְמִישׁוֹר בְּמַקְהֵלִים אֲבָרֵךְ יְיָ: יְיָ

שָׁמְרִי יְיָ צִלְּךָ עַל־יַד יְמִינִי: עֶזְרִי מֵעִם יְיָ עֹשֵׂה שָׁמַיִם וָאָרֶץ: יְיָ

יִשְׁמָר־צֵאתְךָ וּבוֹאֶךָ לְחַיִּים וּלְשָׁלוֹם מֵעַתָּה וְעַד־עוֹלָם: הַשְׁקִיפָה

מִמְּעוֹן קָדְשְׁךָ מִן־הַשָּׁמַיִם וּבָרֵךְ אֶת־עַמְּךָ אֶת־יִשְׂרָאֵל וְאֵת

הָאֲדָמָה אֲשֶׁר נָתַתָּה לָנוּ כַּאֲשֶׁר נִשְׁבַּעְתָּ לַאֲבֹתֵינוּ אֶרֶץ זָבַת

חָלָב וּדְבָשׁ: אֵל הַכָּבוֹד אֶתֵּן לְךָ שִׁיר וָהַלֵּל · וְאֶעֱבָד־לְךָ יוֹם

וָלָיְל: בָּרוּךְ יָחִיד וּמְיֻחָד · הָיָה הֹוֶה וְיִהְיֶה: יְיָ אֱלֹהֵי

יִשְׂרָאֵל מֶלֶךְ מַלְכֵי הַמְּלָכִים הַקָּדוֹשׁ בָּרוּךְ הוּא · הוּא אֱלֹהִים

חַיִּים, מֶלֶךְ חַי וְקַיָּם לָעַד וּלְעוֹלְמֵי עוֹלָמִים: בָּרוּךְ שֵׁם כְּבוֹד

מַלְכוּתוֹ לְעוֹלָם וָעֶד: לִישׁוּעָתְךָ קִוִּיתִי יְיָ:

כשיולא מבה"כ יעב מעט ויאמר:

אַךְ צַדִּיקִים יוֹדוּ לִשְׁמֶךָ יֵשְׁבוּ יְשָׁרִים אֶת־פָּנֶיךָ:

ואח"כ יעמוד וישתחוה מול ארון הקודם ויאמר פסוקים אלו:

כִּי כָל־הָעַמִּים יֵלְכוּ אִישׁ בְּשֵׁם אֱלֹהָיו ּ וַאֲנַחְנוּ נֵלֵךְ בְּשֵׁם־יְיָ
אֱלֹהֵינוּ לְעוֹלָם וָעֶד: עוּרִי מֵעַם יְיָ עֹשֵׂה שָׁמַיִם וָאָרֶץ: יְיָ יִמְלֹךְ
לְעֹלָם וָעֶד:

ואח"כ ילך אל הפתח לאחריו וישתחוה אל ארון הקודם ויאמר:

יְיָ נְחֵנִי בְצִדְקָתֶךָ לְמַעַן שׁוֹרְרָי הַיְשַׁר לְפָנַי דַּרְכֶּךָ:

ואח"כ כשהולך לו יאמר אלו ג' פסוקים:

גָּד גְּדוּד יְגוּדֶנּוּ וְהוּא יָגֻד עָקֵב: וַיְהִי דָוִד לְכָל־דְּרָכָיו מַשְׂכִּיל
וַיְיָ עִמּוֹ: וְנֹחַ מָצָא חֵן בְּעֵינֵי יְיָ:

אם בדעתו לעסוק בעסק במשא ומתן יוסיף לומר אלו הפסוקים:

עוּרִי מֵעַם יְיָ עֹשֵׂה שָׁמַיִם וָאָרֶץ: הַשְׁלֵךְ עַל־יְיָ יְהָבְךָ וְהוּא
יְכַלְכְּלֶךָ: שָׁמְרָתָם וּרְאֵה יָשָׁר כִּי־אַחֲרִית לְאִישׁ שָׁלוֹם: בְּטַח
בַּיְיָ וַעֲשֵׂה טוֹב שְׁכָן־אֶרֶץ וּרְעֵה אֱמוּנָה: הִנֵּה אֵל יְשׁוּעָתִי אֶבְטַח
וְלֹא אֶפְחָד ּ כִּי עָזִּי וְזִמְרָת יָהּ יְיָ וַיְהִי־לִי לִישׁוּעָה: רִבּוֹנוֹ שֶׁל־
עוֹלָם, בְּדִבְרֵי קָדְשֶׁךָ כָּתוּב לֵאמֹר הַבּוֹטֵחַ בַּיְיָ חֶסֶד יְסוֹבְבֶנּוּ,
וְכָתוּב וְאַתָּה מְחַיֶּה אֶת־כֻּלָּם ּ יְיָ אֱלֹהִים אֱמֶת תֵּן בְּרָכָה וְהַצְלָחָה
בְּכָל־מַעֲשֵׂי יָדַי ּ כִּי בָטַחְתִּי בָךְ שֶׁעַל יְדֵי מַשָּׂא וּמַתָּן וַעֲסָקִים
שֶׁלִּי תִּשְׁלַח לִי בְּרָכָה כְּדֵי שֶׁאוּכַל לְפַרְנֵס אֶת־עַצְמִי וּבְנֵי בֵיתִי
בְּנַחַת וְלֹא בְצַעַר בְּהֶתֵּר וְלֹא בְאִסוּר לְחַיִּים וּלְשָׁלוֹם וִיקֻיַּם בִּי
מִקְרָא שֶׁכָּתוּב הַשְׁלֵךְ עַל־יְיָ יְהָבְךָ וְהוּא יְכַלְכְּלֶךָ ּ אָמֵן ּ

ראוי לאמר בכל יום פרשת עקדה ופרשת המן ועשרת הדברות׃

בראשית כ"ב א'. **פָּרָשַׁת עֲקֵדָה**

וַיְהִי אַחַר הַדְּבָרִים הָאֵלֶּה וְהָאֱלֹהִים נִסָּה אֶת־אַבְרָהָם וַיֹּאמֶר
אֵלָיו אַבְרָהָם וַיֹּאמֶר הִנֵּנִי: וַיֹּאמֶר קַח־נָא אֶת־בִּנְךָ אֶת־יְחִידְךָ

אֲשֶׁר־אָהַבְתָּ אֶת־יִצְחָק וְלֶךְ־לְךָ אֶל־אֶרֶץ הַמֹּרִיָּה וְהַעֲלֵהוּ שָׁם לְעֹלָה עַל אַחַד הֶהָרִים אֲשֶׁר אֹמַר אֵלֶיךָ: וַיַּשְׁכֵּם אַבְרָהָם בַּבֹּקֶר וַיַּחֲבֹשׁ אֶת־חֲמֹרוֹ וַיִּקַּח אֶת־שְׁנֵי נְעָרָיו אִתּוֹ וְאֵת יִצְחָק בְּנוֹ וַיְבַקַּע עֲצֵי עֹלָה וַיָּקָם וַיֵּלֶךְ אֶל־הַמָּקוֹם אֲשֶׁר־אָמַר־לוֹ הָאֱלֹהִים: בַּיּוֹם הַשְּׁלִישִׁי וַיִּשָּׂא אַבְרָהָם אֶת־עֵינָיו וַיַּרְא אֶת־הַמָּקוֹם מֵרָחֹק: וַיֹּאמֶר אַבְרָהָם אֶל־נְעָרָיו שְׁבוּ־לָכֶם פֹּה עִם־הַחֲמוֹר וַאֲנִי וְהַנַּעַר נֵלְכָה עַד־כֹּה וְנִשְׁתַּחֲוֶה וְנָשׁוּבָה אֲלֵיכֶם: וַיִּקַּח אַבְרָהָם אֶת־עֲצֵי הָעֹלָה וַיָּשֶׂם עַל־יִצְחָק בְּנוֹ וַיִּקַּח בְּיָדוֹ אֶת־הָאֵשׁ וְאֶת־הַמַּאֲכֶלֶת וַיֵּלְכוּ שְׁנֵיהֶם יַחְדָּו: וַיֹּאמֶר יִצְחָק אֶל־אַבְרָהָם אָבִיו וַיֹּאמֶר אָבִי וַיֹּאמֶר הִנֶּנִּי בְנִי וַיֹּאמֶר הִנֵּה הָאֵשׁ וְהָעֵצִים וְאַיֵּה הַשֶּׂה לְעֹלָה: וַיֹּאמֶר אַבְרָהָם אֱלֹהִים יִרְאֶה־לּוֹ הַשֶּׂה לְעֹלָה בְּנִי וַיֵּלְכוּ שְׁנֵיהֶם יַחְדָּו: וַיָּבֹאוּ אֶל־הַמָּקוֹם אֲשֶׁר אָמַר־לוֹ הָאֱלֹהִים וַיִּבֶן שָׁם אַבְרָהָם אֶת־הַמִּזְבֵּחַ וַיַּעֲרֹךְ אֶת־הָעֵצִים וַיַּעֲקֹד אֶת־יִצְחָק בְּנוֹ וַיָּשֶׂם אֹתוֹ עַל־הַמִּזְבֵּחַ מִמַּעַל לָעֵצִים: וַיִּשְׁלַח אַבְרָהָם אֶת־יָדוֹ וַיִּקַּח אֶת־הַמַּאֲכֶלֶת לִשְׁחֹט אֶת־בְּנוֹ: וַיִּקְרָא אֵלָיו מַלְאַךְ יְהוָֹה מִן־הַשָּׁמַיִם וַיֹּאמֶר אַבְרָהָם ׀ אַבְרָהָם וַיֹּאמֶר הִנֵּנִי: וַיֹּאמֶר אַל־תִּשְׁלַח יָדְךָ אֶל־הַנַּעַר וְאַל־תַּעַשׂ לוֹ מְאוּמָה כִּי ׀ עַתָּה יָדַעְתִּי כִּי־יְרֵא אֱלֹהִים אַתָּה וְלֹא חָשַׂכְתָּ

אֶת־בִּנְךָ אֶת־יְחִידְךָ מִמֶּנִּי: וַיִּשָּׂא אַבְרָהָם אֶת־עֵינָיו וַיַּרְא וְהִנֵּה־
אַיִל אַחַר נֶאֱחַז בַּסְּבַךְ בְּקַרְנָיו וַיֵּלֶךְ אַבְרָהָם וַיִּקַּח אֶת־הָאַיִל
וַיַּעֲלֵהוּ לְעֹלָה תַּחַת בְּנוֹ: וַיִּקְרָא אַבְרָהָם שֵׁם־הַמָּקוֹם הַהוּא
יְהֹוָה יִרְאֶה אֲשֶׁר יֵאָמֵר הַיּוֹם בְּהַר יְהֹוָה יֵרָאֶה: וַיִּקְרָא מַלְאַךְ
יְהֹוָה אֶל־אַבְרָהָם שֵׁנִית מִן־הַשָּׁמָיִם: וַיֹּאמֶר בִּי נִשְׁבַּעְתִּי נְאֻם־
יְהֹוָה כִּי יַעַן אֲשֶׁר עָשִׂיתָ אֶת־הַדָּבָר הַזֶּה וְלֹא חָשַׂכְתָּ אֶת־בִּנְךָ
אֶת־יְחִידֶךָ: כִּי־בָרֵךְ אֲבָרֶכְךָ וְהַרְבָּה אַרְבֶּה אֶת־זַרְעֲךָ כְּכוֹכְבֵי
הַשָּׁמַיִם וְכַחוֹל אֲשֶׁר עַל־שְׂפַת הַיָּם וְיִרַשׁ זַרְעֲךָ אֵת שַׁעַר אֹיְבָיו:
וְהִתְבָּרֲכוּ בְזַרְעֲךָ כֹּל גּוֹיֵי הָאָרֶץ עֵקֶב אֲשֶׁר שָׁמַעְתָּ בְּקֹלִי: וַיָּשָׁב
אַבְרָהָם אֶל־נְעָרָיו וַיָּקֻמוּ וַיֵּלְכוּ יַחְדָּו אֶל־בְּאֵר שָׁבַע וַיֵּשֶׁב אַבְרָהָם
בִּבְאֵר שָׁבַע:

אֱלֹהֵינוּ וֵאלֹהֵי אֲבוֹתֵינוּ זָכְרֵנוּ בְּזִכָּרוֹן טוֹב לְפָנֶיךָ וּפָקְדֵנוּ
בִּפְקֻדַּת יְשׁוּעָה וְרַחֲמִים מִשְּׁמֵי שְׁמֵי קֶדֶם וּזְכָר לָנוּ יְיָ אֱלֹהֵינוּ
אֶת הַבְּרִית וְאֶת הַחֶסֶד וְאֶת הַשְּׁבוּעָה אֲשֶׁר נִשְׁבַּעְתָּ לְאַבְרָהָם
אָבִינוּ בְּהַר הַמּוֹרִיָּה וְתֵרָאֶה לְפָנֶיךָ עֲקֵדָה שֶׁעָקַד אַבְרָהָם אָבִינוּ
אֶת יִצְחָק בְּנוֹ עַל גַּב הַמִּזְבֵּחַ וְכָבַשׁ רַחֲמָיו לַעֲשׂוֹת רְצוֹנְךָ בְּלֵבָב
שָׁלֵם כֵּן יִכְבְּשׁוּ רַחֲמֶיךָ אֶת כַּעַסְךָ מֵעָלֵינוּ וּמֵעַל כָּל יִשְׂרָאֵל עַמֶּךְ ·
וְיִגֹּלוּ רַחֲמֶיךָ עַל מִדּוֹתֶיךָ · וְהִתְנַהֵג עִמָּנוּ בְּמִדַּת הַחֶסֶד וְהָרַחֲמִים
וּבְטוּבְךָ הַגָּדוֹל יָשׁוּב חֲרוֹן אַפְּךָ מֵעַמְּךָ וּמֵעִירְךָ וּמִנַּחֲלָתֶךָ · וְקַיֶּם
לָנוּ יְיָ אֱלֹהֵינוּ מַה שֶּׁהִבְטַחְתָּנוּ עַל יְדֵי מֹשֶׁה עַבְדֶּךָ וְזָכַרְתִּי אֶת

בְּרִיתִי יַעֲקוֹב וְאַף אֶת בְּרִיתִי יִצְחָק וְאַף אֶת בְּרִיתִי אַבְרָהָם
אֶזְכֹּר וְהָאָרֶץ אֶזְכֹּר · וְעָזְרֵנוּ אֱלֹהֵי יִשְׁעֵנוּ עַל דְּבַר כְּבוֹד שְׁמֶךָ
לְהַכְנִיעַ אֶת עָרְפֵּנוּ וְלָכֹף אֶת יִצְרֵנוּ הָרַע לְהִשְׁתַּעְבֶּד לָךְ וְלַעֲשׂוֹת
אֶת כָּל רְצוֹנְךָ בְּאַהֲבָה וּבְיִרְאָה וּלְעָבְדְּךָ בְּלֵבָב שָׁלֵם כָּל יָמֵינוּ
לְעוֹלָם :

פ ר ש ת ה מ ן

שמות י"ו ל'

וַיֹּאמֶר יְהֹוָה אֶל־מֹשֶׁה הִנְנִי מַמְטִיר לָכֶם לֶחֶם מִן־הַשָּׁמָיִם
וְיָצָא הָעָם וְלָקְטוּ דְּבַר־יוֹם בְּיוֹמוֹ לְמַעַן אֲנַסֶּנּוּ הֲיֵלֵךְ בְּתוֹרָתִי
אִם־לֹא : וְהָיָה בַּיּוֹם הַשִּׁשִּׁי וְהֵכִינוּ אֵת אֲשֶׁר־יָבִיאוּ וְהָיָה מִשְׁנֶה
עַל אֲשֶׁר־יִלְקְטוּ יוֹם יוֹם : וַיֹּאמֶר מֹשֶׁה וְאַהֲרֹן אֶל־כָּל־בְּנֵי
יִשְׂרָאֵל עֶרֶב וִידַעְתֶּם כִּי יְהֹוָה הוֹצִיא אֶתְכֶם מֵאֶרֶץ מִצְרָיִם :
וּבֹקֶר וּרְאִיתֶם אֶת־כְּבוֹד יְהֹוָה בְּשָׁמְעוֹ אֶת־תְּלֻנֹּתֵיכֶם עַל־יְהֹוָה
וְנַחְנוּ מָה כִּי תַלִּינוּ* עָלֵינוּ : וַיֹּאמֶר מֹשֶׁה בְּתֵת יְהֹוָה לָכֶם בָּעֶרֶב
בָּשָׂר לֶאֱכֹל וְלֶחֶם בַּבֹּקֶר לִשְׂבֹּעַ בִּשְׁמֹעַ יְהֹוָה אֶת־תְּלֻנֹּתֵיכֶם
אֲשֶׁר־אַתֶּם מַלִּינִם עָלָיו וְנַחְנוּ מָה לֹא־עָלֵינוּ תְלֻנֹּתֵיכֶם כִּי עַל־
יְהֹוָה : וַיֹּאמֶר מֹשֶׁה אֶל־אַהֲרֹן אֱמֹר אֶל־כָּל־עֲדַת בְּנֵי יִשְׂרָאֵל
קִרְבוּ לִפְנֵי יְהֹוָה כִּי שָׁמַע אֵת תְּלֻנֹּתֵיכֶם : וַיְהִי כְּדַבֵּר אַהֲרֹן אֶל־
כָּל־עֲדַת בְּנֵי־יִשְׂרָאֵל וַיִּפְנוּ אֶל־הַמִּדְבָּר וְהִנֵּה כְּבוֹד יְהֹוָה נִרְאָה
בֶּעָנָן : וַיְדַבֵּר יְהֹוָה אֶל־מֹשֶׁה לֵּאמֹר : שָׁמַעְתִּי אֶת־תְּלוּנֹת בְּנֵי

_____

יִשְׂרָאֵל דַּבֵּר אֲלֵהֶם לֵאמֹר בֵּין הָעַרְבַּיִם תֹּאכְלוּ בָשָׂר וּבַבֹּקֶר
תִּשְׂבְּעוּ־לָחֶם וִידַעְתֶּם כִּי אֲנִי יְהֹוָה אֱלֹהֵיכֶם: וַיְהִי בָעֶרֶב וַתַּעַל
הַשְּׂלָו וַתְּכַס אֶת־הַמַּחֲנֶה וּבַבֹּקֶר הָיְתָה שִׁכְבַת הַטָּל סָבִיב
לַמַּחֲנֶה: וַתַּעַל שִׁכְבַת הַטָּל וְהִנֵּה עַל־פְּנֵי הַמִּדְבָּר דַּק מְחֻסְפָּס
דַּק כַּכְּפֹר עַל־הָאָרֶץ: וַיִּרְאוּ בְנֵי־יִשְׂרָאֵל וַיֹּאמְרוּ אִישׁ אֶל־אָחִיו
מָן הוּא כִּי לֹא יָדְעוּ מַה־הוּא וַיֹּאמֶר מֹשֶׁה אֲלֵהֶם הוּא הַלֶּחֶם
אֲשֶׁר נָתַן יְהֹוָה לָכֶם לְאָכְלָה: זֶה הַדָּבָר אֲשֶׁר צִוָּה יְהֹוָה לִקְטוּ
מִמֶּנּוּ אִישׁ לְפִי אָכְלוֹ עֹמֶר לַגֻּלְגֹּלֶת מִסְפַּר נַפְשֹׁתֵיכֶם אִישׁ
לַאֲשֶׁר בְּאָהֳלוֹ תִּקָּחוּ: וַיַּעֲשׂוּ־כֵן בְּנֵי יִשְׂרָאֵל וַיִּלְקְטוּ הַמַּרְבֶּה
וְהַמַּמְעִיט: וַיָּמֹדּוּ בָעֹמֶר וְלֹא הֶעְדִּיף הַמַּרְבֶּה וְהַמַּמְעִיט לֹא
הֶחְסִיר אִישׁ לְפִי־אָכְלוֹ לָקָטוּ: וַיֹּאמֶר מֹשֶׁה אֲלֵהֶם אִישׁ אַל־
יוֹתֵר מִמֶּנּוּ עַד־בֹּקֶר: וְלֹא־שָׁמְעוּ אֶל־מֹשֶׁה וַיּוֹתִרוּ אֲנָשִׁים
מִמֶּנּוּ עַד־בֹּקֶר וַיָּרֻם תּוֹלָעִים וַיִּבְאַשׁ וַיִּקְצֹף עֲלֵהֶם מֹשֶׁה: וַיִּלְקְטוּ
אֹתוֹ בַּבֹּקֶר בַּבֹּקֶר אִישׁ כְּפִי אָכְלוֹ וְחַם הַשֶּׁמֶשׁ וְנָמָס: וַיְהִי
בַּיּוֹם הַשִּׁשִּׁי לָקְטוּ לֶחֶם מִשְׁנֶה שְׁנֵי הָעֹמֶר לָאֶחָד וַיָּבֹאוּ כָּל־
נְשִׂיאֵי הָעֵדָה וַיַּגִּידוּ לְמֹשֶׁה: וַיֹּאמֶר אֲלֵהֶם הוּא אֲשֶׁר דִּבֶּר
יְהֹוָה שַׁבָּתוֹן שַׁבַּת־קֹדֶשׁ לַיהֹוָה מָחָר אֵת אֲשֶׁר־תֹּאפוּ אֵפוּ וְאֵת
אֲשֶׁר־תְּבַשְּׁלוּ בַּשֵּׁלוּ וְאֵת כָּל־הָעֹדֵף הַנִּיחוּ לָכֶם לְמִשְׁמֶרֶת עַד־
הַבֹּקֶר: וַיַּנִּיחוּ אֹתוֹ עַד־הַבֹּקֶר כַּאֲשֶׁר צִוָּה מֹשֶׁה וְלֹא הִבְאִישׁ

וְרָמָה לֹא־הֶיְתָה־בּוֹ: וַיֹּאמֶר מֹשֶׁה אִכְלֻהוּ הַיּוֹם כִּי־שַׁבָּת הַיּוֹם
לַיהוָה הַיּוֹם לֹא תִמְצָאֻהוּ בַּשָּׂדֶה: שֵׁשֶׁת יָמִים תִּלְקְטֻהוּ וּבַיּוֹם
הַשְּׁבִיעִי שַׁבָּת לֹא יִהְיֶה־בּוֹ: וַיְהִי בַּיּוֹם הַשְּׁבִיעִי יָצְאוּ מִן־הָעָם
לִלְקֹט וְלֹא מָצָאוּ: וַיֹּאמֶר יְהוָה אֶל־מֹשֶׁה עַד־אָנָה מֵאַנְתֶּם
לִשְׁמֹר מִצְוֹתַי וְתוֹרֹתָי: רְאוּ כִּי־יְהוָה נָתַן לָכֶם הַשַּׁבָּת עַל־כֵּן
הוּא נֹתֵן לָכֶם בַּיּוֹם הַשִּׁשִּׁי לֶחֶם יוֹמָיִם שְׁבוּ · אִישׁ תַּחְתָּיו אַל־
יֵצֵא אִישׁ מִמְּקֹמוֹ בַּיּוֹם הַשְּׁבִיעִי: וַיִּשְׁבְּתוּ הָעָם בַּיּוֹם הַשְּׁבִעִי:
וַיִּקְרְאוּ בֵית־יִשְׂרָאֵל אֶת־שְׁמוֹ מָן וְהוּא כְּזֶרַע גַּד לָבָן וְטַעְמוֹ
כְּצַפִּיחִת בִּדְבָשׁ: וַיֹּאמֶר מֹשֶׁה זֶה הַדָּבָר אֲשֶׁר צִוָּה יְהוָה מְלֹא
הָעֹמֶר מִמֶּנּוּ לְמִשְׁמֶרֶת לְדֹרֹתֵיכֶם לְמַעַן · יִרְאוּ אֶת־הַלֶּחֶם אֲשֶׁר
הֶאֱכַלְתִּי אֶתְכֶם בַּמִּדְבָּר בְּהוֹצִיאִי אֶתְכֶם מֵאֶרֶץ מִצְרָיִם: וַיֹּאמֶר
מֹשֶׁה אֶל־אַהֲרֹן קַח צִנְצֶנֶת אַחַת וְתֶן־שָׁמָּה מְלֹא־הָעֹמֶר מָן
וְהַנַּח אֹתוֹ לִפְנֵי יְהוָה לְמִשְׁמֶרֶת לְדֹרֹתֵיכֶם: כַּאֲשֶׁר צִוָּה יְהוָה
אֶל־מֹשֶׁה וַיַּנִּיחֵהוּ אַהֲרֹן לִפְנֵי הָעֵדֻת לְמִשְׁמָרֶת: וּבְנֵי יִשְׂרָאֵל
אָכְלוּ אֶת־הַמָּן אַרְבָּעִים שָׁנָה עַד־בֹּאָם אֶל־אֶרֶץ נוֹשָׁבֶת אֶת־הַמָּן
אָכְלוּ עַד־בֹּאָם אֶל־קְצֵה אֶרֶץ כְּנָעַן: וְהָעֹמֶר עֲשִׂרִית
הָאֵיפָה הוּא:

אָנָּא הָאֵל הַמֵּכִין פַּרְנָסָה לְכָל־בְּרִיָּה וּמַזְמִין מַלְבּוּשׁ לְכָל־
נִבְרָא וְשׁוֹלֵחַ לָהֶם מִחְיָה תֶּן־לִי אֶת־מִחְיָתִי וְתַכְלְכְּלֵנִי וּתְפַרְנְסֵנִי
אוֹתִי וְאֶת־כָּל אַנְשֵׁי בֵיתִי וְאֶת־כָּל־יִשְׂרָאֵל פַּרְנָסָה טוֹבָה בְּנַחַת

וְלֹא בְצַעַר בְּחֶתֶּר וְלֹא בְאִסּוּר פַּרְנָסָה שֶׁאֵין בָּהּ שׁוּם בּוּשָׁה
וּכְלִמָּה פַּרְנָסָה שֶׁלֹּא תַצְרִיכֵנִי בָהּ לִידֵי מַתְּנַת בָּשָׂר וָדָם כִּי
אִם־מִיָּדְךָ הַמְּלֵאָה וְהָרְחָבָה פַּרְנָסָה שֶׁאוּכַל לַעֲסוֹק בְּתוֹרָתְךָ
הַקְּדוֹשָׁה וְהַטְּהוֹרָה וְהַתְּמִימָה וּלְקַיֵּם אֶת־מִצְוֹתֶיךָ בְּלִי טָרְדָּה
וְאֵשֵׁב בְּשָׁלוֹם עַל שֻׁלְחָנִי וּבְכָבוֹד עִם כָּל־בְּנֵי בֵיתִי וְלֹא יְהִי
עָלַי שׁוּם עֹל בָּשָׂר וָדָם כִּי אִם עֹל מַלְכוּתֶךָ לְעָבְדְּךָ בְּלֵבָב שָׁלֵם
וְאֶזְכֶּה לְהַכְנִיס אוֹרְחִים וְלִגְמוֹל חֶסֶד אֶת־כָּל־אָדָם וְלַעֲשׂוֹת
צְדָקָה לְהָרְאוּיִם לָהּ וְלֹא אֲבַשֵּׁל בִּבְנֵי אָדָם שֶׁאֵינָם
הֲגוּנִים · אָמֵן :

עשרת הדברות

שמות כ' א'

וַיְדַבֵּר אֱלֹהִים אֵת כָּל־הַדְּבָרִים הָאֵלֶּה לֵאמֹר : אָנֹכִי יְהֹוָה
אֱלֹהֶיךָ אֲשֶׁר הוֹצֵאתִיךָ מֵאֶרֶץ מִצְרַיִם מִבֵּית עֲבָדִים : לֹא־יִהְיֶה
לְךָ אֱלֹהִים אֲחֵרִים עַל־פָּנָי : לֹא־תַעֲשֶׂה לְךָ פֶסֶל וְכָל־תְּמוּנָה
אֲשֶׁר בַּשָּׁמַיִם מִמַּעַל וַאֲשֶׁר בָּאָרֶץ מִתָּחַת וַאֲשֶׁר בַּמַּיִם מִתַּחַת
לָאָרֶץ : לֹא־תִשְׁתַּחֲוֶה לָהֶם וְלֹא תָעָבְדֵם כִּי אָנֹכִי יְהֹוָה אֱלֹהֶיךָ
אֵל קַנָּא פֹּקֵד עֲוֹן אָבֹת עַל־בָּנִים עַל־שִׁלֵּשִׁים וְעַל־רִבֵּעִים לְשֹׂנְאָי :
וְעֹשֶׂה חֶסֶד לַאֲלָפִים לְאֹהֲבַי וּלְשֹׁמְרֵי מִצְוֹתָי : לֹא תִשָּׂא אֶת־
שֵׁם־יְהֹוָה אֱלֹהֶיךָ לַשָּׁוְא כִּי לֹא יְנַקֶּה יְהֹוָה אֵת אֲשֶׁר־יִשָּׂא אֶת־
שְׁמוֹ לַשָּׁוְא : זָכוֹר אֶת־יוֹם הַשַּׁבָּת לְקַדְּשׁוֹ : שֵׁשֶׁת יָמִים תַּעֲבֹד
וְעָשִׂיתָ כָּל־מְלַאכְתֶּךָ : וְיוֹם הַשְּׁבִיעִי שַׁבָּת לַיהֹוָה אֱלֹהֶיךָ לֹא־
תַעֲשֶׂה כָל־מְלָאכָה אַתָּה וּבִנְךָ וּבִתֶּךָ עַבְדְּךָ וַאֲמָתְךָ וּבְהֶמְתֶּךָ
וְגֵרְךָ אֲשֶׁר בִּשְׁעָרֶיךָ : כִּי שֵׁשֶׁת־יָמִים עָשָׂה יְהֹוָה אֶת־הַשָּׁמַיִם

וְאֶת־הָאָרֶץ אֶת־הַיָּם וְאֶת־כָּל־אֲשֶׁר־בָּם וַיָּנַח בַּיּוֹם הַשְּׁבִיעִי עַל
כֵּן בֵּרַךְ יְהוָה אֶת־יוֹם הַשַּׁבָּת וַיְקַדְּשֵׁהוּ: כַּבֵּד אֶת־אָבִיךָ וְאֶת־
אִמֶּךָ לְמַעַן יַאֲרִכוּן יָמֶיךָ עַל הָאֲדָמָה אֲשֶׁר־יְהוָה אֱלֹהֶיךָ נֹתֵן
לָךְ: לֹא תִרְצַח לֹא תִנְאָף לֹא תִגְנֹב לֹא־תַעֲנֶה בְרֵעֲךָ עֵד שָׁקֶר:
לֹא תַחְמֹד בֵּית רֵעֶךָ לֹא־תַחְמֹד אֵשֶׁת רֵעֶךָ וְעַבְדּוֹ וַאֲמָתוֹ
וְשׁוֹרוֹ וַחֲמֹרוֹ וְכֹל אֲשֶׁר לְרֵעֶךָ:

שלשה עשר עקרים

א   אֲנִי מַאֲמִין בֶּאֱמוּנָה שְׁלֵמָה שֶׁהַבּוֹרֵא יִתְבָּרַךְ שְׁמוֹ הוּא בּוֹרֵא
וּמַנְהִיג לְכָל־הַבְּרוּאִים וְהוּא לְבַדּוֹ עָשָׂה וְעוֹשֶׂה וְיַעֲשֶׂה לְכָל־
הַמַּעֲשִׂים:

ב   אֲנִי מַאֲמִין בֶּאֱמוּנָה שְׁלֵמָה שֶׁהַבּוֹרֵא יִתְבָּרַךְ שְׁמוֹ הוּא יָחִיד
וְאֵין יְחִידוּת כָּמוֹהוּ בְּשׁוּם פָּנִים וְהוּא לְבַדּוֹ אֱלֹהֵינוּ הָיָה הֹוֶה
וְיִהְיֶה:

ג   אֲנִי מַאֲמִין בֶּאֱמוּנָה שְׁלֵמָה שֶׁהַבּוֹרֵא יִתְבָּרַךְ שְׁמוֹ אֵינוֹ גוּף ·
וְלֹא יַשִּׂיגוּהוּ מַשִּׂיגֵי הַגּוּף · וְאֵין לוֹ שׁוּם דִּמְיוֹן כְּלָל:

ד   אֲנִי מַאֲמִין בֶּאֱמוּנָה שְׁלֵמָה שֶׁהַבּוֹרֵא יִתְבָּרַךְ שְׁמוֹ הוּא
רִאשׁוֹן וְהוּא אַחֲרוֹן:

ה   אֲנִי מַאֲמִין בֶּאֱמוּנָה שְׁלֵמָה שֶׁהַבּוֹרֵא יִתְבָּרַךְ שְׁמוֹ לוֹ לְבַדּוֹ
רָאוּי לְהִתְפַּלֵּל וְאֵין רָאוּי לְהִתְפַּלֵּל לְזוּלָתוֹ:

י   אֲנִי מַאֲמִין בֶּאֱמוּנָה שְׁלֵמָה שֶׁכָּל־דִּבְרֵי נְבִיאִים אֱמֶת:

ז אֲנִי מַאֲמִין בֶּאֱמוּנָה שְׁלֵמָה שֶׁנְּבוּאַת מֹשֶׁה רַבֵּנוּ עָלָיו הַשָּׁלוֹם
הָיְתָה אֲמִתִּית· וְשֶׁהוּא הָיָה אָב לַנְּבִיאִים לַקּוֹדְמִים לְפָנָיו וְלַבָּאִים
אַחֲרָיו:

ח אֲנִי מַאֲמִין בֶּאֱמוּנָה שְׁלֵמָה שֶׁכָּל־הַתּוֹרָה הַמְּצוּיָה עַתָּה בְיָדֵינוּ
הִיא הַנְּתוּנָה לְמֹשֶׁה רַבֵּנוּ עָלָיו הַשָּׁלוֹם:

ט אֲנִי מַאֲמִין בֶּאֱמוּנָה שְׁלֵמָה שֶׁזֹּאת הַתּוֹרָה לֹא תְהִי מָחֲלֶפֶת
וְלֹא תְהִי תוֹרָה אַחֶרֶת מֵאֵת הַבּוֹרֵא יִתְבָּרַךְ שְׁמוֹ:

י אֲנִי מַאֲמִין בֶּאֱמוּנָה שְׁלֵמָה שֶׁהַבּוֹרֵא יִתְבָּרַךְ שְׁמוֹ יוֹדֵעַ כָּל־
מַעֲשֵׂה בְּנֵי אָדָם וְכָל־מַחְשְׁבוֹתָם· שֶׁנֶּאֱמַר הַיּוֹצֵר יַחַד לִבָּם
הַמֵּבִין אֶל־כָּל־מַעֲשֵׂיהֶם:

יא אֲנִי מַאֲמִין בֶּאֱמוּנָה שְׁלֵמָה שֶׁהַבּוֹרֵא יִתְבָּרַךְ שְׁמוֹ גּוֹמֵל
טוֹב לְשׁוֹמְרֵי מִצְוֹתָיו וּמַעֲנִישׁ לְעוֹבְרֵי מִצְוֹתָיו:

יב אֲנִי מַאֲמִין בֶּאֱמוּנָה שְׁלֵמָה בְּבִיאַת הַמָּשִׁיחַ וְאַף עַל־פִּי
שֶׁיִּתְמַהְמֵהַּ עִם כָּל־זֶה אֲחַכֶּה־לּוֹ בְּכָל־יוֹם שֶׁיָּבֹא:

יג אֲנִי מַאֲמִין בֶּאֱמוּנָה שְׁלֵמָה שֶׁתִּהְיֶה תְּחִיַּת הַמֵּתִים בְּעֵת
שֶׁתַּעֲלֶה רָצוֹן מֵאֵת הַבּוֹרֵא יִתְבָּרַךְ שְׁמוֹ וְיִתְעַלֶּה זִכְרוֹ לָעַד וּלְנֵצַח
נְצָחִים:

לִישׁוּעָתְךָ קִוִּיתִי יְיָ· קִוִּיתִי יְיָ לִישׁוּעָתְךָ· יְיָ לִישׁוּעָתְךָ קִוִּיתִי:
לְפֻרְקָנָךְ סַבְּרִית יְיָ· סַבְּרִית יְיָ לְפֻרְקָנָךְ· יְיָ לְפֻרְקָנָךְ סַבְּרִית:

AFTERNOON PRAYER FOR WEEKDAYS

The Afternoon *or* Mincha *service begins with* Ashrei *(page 80). Thereafter the Reader recites the* Half-Kaddish. *(On Fast Days the Scroll of the Law is taken from the Ark and* Vayechal *is read.) Then the congregation silently recites the* Shemone Esrei *(page 130), substituting* Shalom Rav *for* Sim Shalom *except on Fast Days. The Reader then repeats the* Shemone Esrei *aloud, and recites* Kedushath Nekadesh *as part of it. He does not, however, recite* Elokeinu Velokei Avoteinu Barcheinu *except on Fast Days. After the* Shemone Esrei, Tachanun *(p. 172) is recited, followed by* Kaddish Tithkabel *(p. 753) and* Aleinu Leshabei'ach *(p. 208). If, however, the Afternoon Service is immediately followed by* Evening *Prayers* (Maariv), Aleinu *is not said until the end of the Evening Service.*

EVENING PRAYER FOR WEEKDAYS

See Evening Prayer at the Conclusion of the Sabbath (page 532).

הדלקת נר שבת

WELCOMING THE SABBATH

Before the beginning of the Sabbath the lady of the house kindles the Sabbath lights. (If there is no woman in the household, the duty devolves upon the master of the house.) She then spreads out her hands between her eyes and the lights and recites the following blessing:

בָּרוּךְ אַתָּה יְיָ, אֱלֹהֵינוּ מֶלֶךְ הָעוֹלָם, אֲשֶׁר קִדְּשָׁנוּ
בְּמִצְוֹתָיו, וְצִוָּנוּ לְהַדְלִיק נֵר שֶׁל־שַׁבָּת:

Blessed be You, *God* our God, King of the Universe, Who has sanctified us by Your commandments and commanded us to kindle the Sabbath light.

סדר תפלת מנחה בערב שבת וקבלת שבת

After מנחה (without תחנון) the following psalms are said at קבלת שבת:

צה חי לְכוּ נְרַנְּנָה לַיְיָ נָרִיעָה לְצוּר יִשְׁעֵנוּ:

ק' נְקַדְּמָה פָנָיו בְּתוֹדָה בִּזְמִרוֹת נָרִיעַ לוֹ:

ח' כִּי אֵל גָּדוֹל יְיָ וּמֶלֶךְ גָּדוֹל עַל־כָּל־אֱלֹהִים:

ז' אֲשֶׁר בְּיָדוֹ מֶחְקְרֵי־אָרֶץ וְתוֹעֲפוֹת הָרִים לוֹ:

ח' אֲשֶׁר־לוֹ הַיָּם וְהוּא עָשָׂהוּ וְיַבֶּשֶׁת יָדָיו יָצָרוּ:

ק' בֹּאוּ נִשְׁתַּחֲוֶה וְנִכְרָעָה נִבְרְכָה לִפְנֵי־יְיָ עֹשֵׂנוּ:

ח' כִּי הוּא אֱלֹהֵינוּ וַאֲנַחְנוּ עַם מַרְעִיתוֹ וְצֹאן יָדוֹ הַיּוֹם אִם־בְּקֹלוֹ תִשְׁמָעוּ: י אַל־תַּקְשׁוּ לְבַבְכֶם כִּמְרִיבָה

O go forth, let us sing in exultation to *God,* stir up homage to the Rock of our salvation. Let us come before His countenance with thanksgiving; with songs let us stir up homage to Him. For *God* is a great God and a great King above all gods, in Whose hands are the foundations of the earth, and the high places after which the mountains strive are His also. The sea is His, and He has made it, and His hands fashioned the dry land. Come, let us cast ourselves down and kneel, let us bend the knee before *God* our creator, for He is our God and we are the people of His pasture and the flock of His hand, even today, if you will but hearken to His voice. Harden not your heart. as at Meribah, as on the day of testing in the wilderness, when your

---

Psalm 95. לכו נרננה This Psalm diverts us from the sad thoughts of our outward suffering by portraying our exile to us as a second "journey through the wilderness" to which we ourselves can put an end at any time through our own good conduct. This psalm appeals to us to complete that pilgrimage

כְּיוֹם מַסָּה בַּמִּדְבָּר: ‏ט‎ אֲשֶׁר נִסּוּנִי אֲבוֹתֵיכֶם בְּחָנוּנִי

גַּם־רָאוּ פָעֳלִי: ‏י‎ אַרְבָּעִים שָׁנָה ׀ אָקוּט בְּדוֹר וָאֹמַר

עַם תֹּעֵי לֵבָב הֵם וְהֵם לֹא־יָדְעוּ דְרָכָי: ‏קי‎ אֲשֶׁר־

נִשְׁבַּעְתִּי בְאַפִּי אִם־יְבֹאוּן אֶל־מְנוּחָתִי:

‏צו‎ ‏ח‎ שִׁירוּ לַיָי שִׁיר חָדָשׁ שִׁירוּ לַיָי כָּל־הָאָרֶץ:

‏ק‎ שִׁירוּ לַיָי בָּרְכוּ שְׁמוֹ בַּשְּׂרוּ מִיּוֹם־לְיוֹם יְשׁוּעָתוֹ:

‏ח‎ סַפְּרוּ בַגּוֹיִם כְּבוֹדוֹ בְּכָל־הָעַמִּים נִפְלְאוֹתָיו: ‏ק‎ כִּי

גָדוֹל יְיָ וּמְהֻלָּל מְאֹד נוֹרָא הוּא עַל־כָּל־אֱלֹהִים:

‏ק‎ כִּי ׀ כָּל־אֱלֹהֵי הָעַמִּים אֱלִילִים וַיָי שָׁמַיִם עָשָׂה:

‏ק‎ הוֹד־וְהָדָר לְפָנָיו עֹז וְתִפְאֶרֶת בְּמִקְדָּשׁוֹ: ‏ח‎ הָבוּ

לַיָי מִשְׁפְּחוֹת עַמִּים הָבוּ לַיָי כָּבוֹד וָעֹז: ‏ק‎ הָבוּ לַיָי

כְּבוֹד שְׁמוֹ שְׂאוּ מִנְחָה וּבֹאוּ לְחַצְרוֹתָיו: ‏ח‎ הִשְׁתַּחֲווּ

---

through the ages with gladness, and thereby pave the way for the universal worship of God on earth. כי הוא וגו׳ "For He is still our God, with every act of ours we are still the people whom He guides, and we are the flock of His almighty hand with every turn our destinies shall take. All this is true and fully valid היום even today, if only we will hearken to His voice." Obedience is the only condition necessary for *geulah*. The Holy Scriptures and our Sages state no other stipulation for our deliverance than *teshuvah*, a "return" to perfect obedience to God. היום אם בקולו תשמעו.

אל תקשו וגו׳. The voice of the prophet whose task it was to usher in our Galuth wanderings through the ages toward final redemption called us במדבר "into the wilderness" (Isa. 40:3). "I shall bring you into the wilderness of

fathers put Me to the test, though they had tried Me, and had also seen My work. For forty years I quarreled with one generation, and I thought they are a people of erring heart, and they, they still did not recognize My ways, so that I swore in My wrath, "They shall not enter into My rest."

Sing to *God* a new song; sing praises to *God* upon all the earth. Sing praises to *God,* bless His Name, proclaim His salvation from day to day. Declare His honor among the nations, His wondrous works among the peoples, that *God* is great and most evident in mighty acts; that He is to be feared above all gods; that all the gods of the peoples are gods that deny, but *God* has made the heavens; that glory of being and majesty of power are before His countenance; fortitude and beauty of development in His Sanctuary. Give to *God,* O families of nations, give to *God* honor and might. Give to *God* the honor of His Name, take up offering of homage and come into His courts. Cast yourselves

---

the nations and I shall judge you there face to face, even as I have judged your fathers in the wilderness of Egypt," Ezekiel told us. (Ezek. 20:35). Thus our wanderings through exile simply constitute a second journey through the wilderness toward the promised land of independence and freedom regained. Ezekiel goes on to state that this second journey, like the original one, should also end in purification, in the sifting out and the elimination of all those elements which demonstrate by their defection and disloyalty that they are incapable and unworthy of having a part in our foreordained future. This corresponds to the final verses of this psalm, which hold up to us the warning example of our first Exodus and the tragic errors of which Yisrael had then been guilty.

Psalm 96. שירו לה׳ At the end of Psalm 95 we were told of a negative aspect of our task while in Galuth, namely, of the errors from which we must guard ourselves during our long wanderings through exile. This Psalm, on the other hand, has as its theme the fulfillment of the great and blissful purpose of our journeys among the nations, namely, the "wakening of awe" of God throughout the world, of which mention was already made in Verse 1 of Psalm 95. It is Yisrael's task to enter into the midst of the nations with a "new song" that is to "behold" God's greatness, and the "newness" of this song lies in the fact that in it, we read the call שירו לה׳ כל הארץ, summoning all of mankind to unite in "beholding" the greatness of the One God.

לְיָ בְּהַדְרַת־קֹדֶשׁ חִילוּ מִפָּנָיו כָּל־הָאָרֶץ: זְ אִמְרוּ
בַגּוֹיִם יְיָ מָלָךְ אַף־תִּכּוֹן תֵּבֵל בַּל־תִּמּוֹט יָדִין עַמִּים
בְּמֵישָׁרִים: יִ יִשְׂמְחוּ הַשָּׁמַיִם וְתָגֵל הָאָרֶץ יִרְעַם
הַיָּם וּמְלֹאוֹ: יֹ יַעֲלֹז שָׂדַי וְכָל־אֲשֶׁר־בּוֹ אָז יְרַנְּנוּ
כָּל־עֲצֵי־יָעַר: קיֹא לִפְנֵי יְיָ כִּי בָא כִּי בָא לִשְׁפֹּט
הָאָרֶץ יִשְׁפֹּט־תֵּבֵל בְּצֶדֶק וְעַמִּים בֶּאֱמוּנָתוֹ:

צֹ יֹ יְיָ מָלָךְ תָּגֵל הָאָרֶץ יִשְׂמְחוּ אִיִּים רַבִּים: יֹ עָנָן
וַעֲרָפֶל סְבִיבָיו צֶדֶק וּמִשְׁפָּט מְכוֹן כִּסְאוֹ: יֹ אֵשׁ
לְפָנָיו תֵּלֵךְ וּתְלַהֵט סָבִיב צָרָיו: יֹ הֵאִירוּ בְרָקָיו תֵּבֵל
רָאֲתָה וַתָּחֵל הָאָרֶץ: יֹ הָרִים כַּדּוֹנַג נָמַסּוּ מִלִּפְנֵי יְיָ
מִלִּפְנֵי אֲדוֹן כָּל־הָאָרֶץ: יֹ הִגִּידוּ הַשָּׁמַיִם צִדְקוֹ וְרָאוּ
כָל־הָעַמִּים כְּבוֹדוֹ: יֹ יֵבֹשׁוּ כָּל־עֹבְדֵי פֶסֶל
הַמִּתְהַלְלִים בָּאֱלִילִים הִשְׁתַּחֲווּ־לוֹ כָּל־אֱלֹהִים:
יֹ שָׁמְעָה וַתִּשְׂמַח צִיּוֹן וַתָּגֵלְנָה בְּנוֹת יְהוּדָה לְמַעַן
מִשְׁפָּטֶיךָ יְיָ: יֹ כִּי־אַתָּה יְיָ עֶלְיוֹן עַל־כָּל־הָאָרֶץ
מְאֹד נַעֲלֵיתָ עַל־כָּל־אֱלֹהִים: יֹ אֹהֲבֵי יְיָ שִׂנְאוּ רָע

<hr>

*) שנאו רע הר׳ בקקן בם״ח וכ״י וכמשפט העול׳ ויור׳ שים לו כח לשטת הנקוד כמו
האתנח וס״ם.

down before *God* in the reflected glory of the Sanctuary; go before Him in the travail of rebirth, you upon all the earth. Tell it among the nations; once *God* reigns, the world of men will also be firmly established and sway no more. He will judge the peoples with straightness. The heavens are glad and the earth rejoices—but the sea roars, and the fulness thereof. The field exults and all that is in it, then all the trees of the forest shall also sing for joy, before *God,* for He comes, He comes to judge the earth; He will judge the world of man with justice, and the peoples in His faithfulness.

Once *God* will reign, the earth will rejoice, and the multitudes of islands will be glad. But now clouds and darkness are still round about Him; justice and lawful order are the foundation of His throne. A fire goes before Him, and burns round about His adversaries. But once His bolts of lightning have lit up the world of man, when the earth has gained insight and gone into travail, when the mountains will have melted like wax before the countenance of *God,* before the countenance of the Lord of all the earth, then the heavens have declared His justice and all the nations see His glory. Then deceived, ashamed shall be all those who now serve graven images, who boast of gods that deny; for then all the gods will have cast themselves down before Him. But Tzion has heard it and is glad, then the daughters of Yehudah will rejoice because of Your judgements, O *God;* that You, O *God,* are now most high over all the earth, exalted far above all gods. Therefore you who love *God,* hate evil; He preserves the souls

---

Psalm 97. ‏ה׳ מלך‎ This psalm continues the theme of the preceding one and speaks of the solemn events which must precede the happy advent of God's kingdom. Only the downfall of all the enemies of God's kingdom and of all the powers and forces that men mistakenly worship can pave the way for a time when all the world will be truly aware of the existence of God and of His sovereign power. Then we are told of the impact which the beginning of this new day will have upon Zion and upon the cities of Yehudah which had been relegated to the background for so long. This psalm ends with a discussion of the conclusion that all the honest and righteous men on earth should draw even now through their confidence that this future is sure to come.

שֹׁמֵר נַפְשׁוֹת חֲסִידָיו מִיַּד רְשָׁעִים יַצִּילֵם: ⁱⁱ אוֹר־

זָרֻעַ לַצַּדִּיק וּלְיִשְׁרֵי־לֵב שִׂמְחָה: ⁱⁱⁱ שִׂמְחוּ צַדִּיקִים

בַּיֻ וְהוֹדוּ לְזֵכֶר קָדְשׁוֹ:

צⁱ מִזְמוֹר שִׁירוּ לַיֻ ⁱ שִׁיר חָדָשׁ כִּי־נִפְלָאוֹת

עָשָׂה הוֹשִׁיעָה־לּוֹ יְמִינוֹ וּזְרוֹעַ קָדְשׁוֹ: ⁱⁱ הוֹדִיעַ יֻ

יְשׁוּעָתוֹ לְעֵינֵי הַגּוֹיִם גִּלָּה צִדְקָתוֹ: ⁱⁱⁱ זָכַר חַסְדּוֹ

וֶאֱמוּנָתוֹ לְבֵית יִשְׂרָאֵל רָאוּ כָל־אַפְסֵי־אָרֶץ אֵת

יְשׁוּעַת אֱלֹהֵינוּ: ⁱ הָרִיעוּ לַיֻ כָּל־הָאָרֶץ פִּצְחוּ וְרַנְּנוּ

וְזַמֵּרוּ: ⁱⁱ זַמְּרוּ לַיֻ בְּכִנּוֹר בְּכִנּוֹר וְקוֹל זִמְרָה:

ⁱ בַּחֲצֹצְרוֹת וְקוֹל שׁוֹפָר הָרִיעוּ לִפְנֵי ⁱ הַמֶּלֶךְ יֻ:

ⁱⁱ יִרְעַם הַיָּם וּמְלֹאוֹ תֵּבֵל וְיֹשְׁבֵי בָהּ: ⁱ נְהָרוֹת

יִמְחֲאוּ־כָף יַחַד הָרִים יְרַנֵּנוּ: ⁱⁱⁱ לִפְנֵי יֻ כִּי בָא

לִשְׁפֹּט הָאָרֶץ יִשְׁפֹּט־תֵּבֵל בְּצֶדֶק וְעַמִּים בְּמֵישָׁרִים:

צⁱ יֻ מָלָךְ יִרְגְּזוּ עַמִּים יֹשֵׁב כְּרוּבִים תָּנוּט הָאָרֶץ:

ⁱ יֻ בְּצִיּוֹן גָּדוֹל וְרָם הוּא עַל־כָּל־הָעַמִּים: ⁱⁱ יוֹדוּ

שִׁמְךָ גָּדוֹל וְנוֹרָא קָדוֹשׁ הוּא: ⁱ וְעֹז מֶלֶךְ מִשְׁפָּט

אָהֵב אַתָּה כּוֹנַנְתָּ מֵישָׁרִים מִשְׁפָּט וּצְדָקָה בְּיַעֲקֹב

אַתָּה עָשִׂיתָ: ⁱ רוֹמְמוּ יֻ אֱלֹהֵינוּ וְהִשְׁתַּחֲווּ לַהֲדֹם

of His devoted ones; He delivers them out of the hand of the lawless. There is sown light for the righteous, and gladness for the upright in heart. Be glad in *God*, you who are righteous, and gratefully render homage to His holy memorial.

A Psalm. Sing to *God* a new song, for He has done marvelous things; His saving right hand and His holy arm alone have assisted Him. *God* has made known His salvation; He has revealed His merciful justice before the eyes of the nations. He has remembered His loving-kindness and His guiding faithfulness toward the house of Yisrael; all the ends of the earth have seen the salvation of our God. Therefore waken the homage of *God,* all you [who dwell] on earth, give voice to your gladness and rejoice and sing; Sing to *God* with the harp, with the harp and loud song. But with trumpets and the sound of the Shofar waken homage before *God,* the King. The sea will roar and its fulness, the world of men and they who dwell in it; the rivers will clap their hands, and the mountains will exult together with them, before *God,* when He will come to set the earth aright; He will judge the world of men with justice and societies with uprightness.

God has begun His reign; the nations tremble. He has established Himself upon Cherubim; the earth gives way. *God,* great in Tzion, is now high above all the nations. They shall render homage to Your Name; great and awesome, holy is He. The strength of the king loves lawful order; You have established uprightness; You have fashioned lawful order and righteousness in Yaakov. Therefore exalt *God* our

---

Psalm 98. מזמור שירו This psalm and the one following deal with the impact that the resurrection of Yisrael as such is to have upon the nations which will now awaken and acquire better understanding. This impact is discussed in terms of two aspects: first, God's sovereignty which becomes so shiningly evident through Yisrael's restoration and therefore will lead man to acquire a better *knowledge* of God, and secondly, the instruction that Yisrael can give the rest of the world concerning the true *worship* of Him.

Psalm 99. ה' מלך In Psalm 98 we are told that when we call upon God we should not so much stress what we hope to receive from Him, but, above all, bear in mind what God expects of us. Psalm 99 is devoted primarily to those requirements which God imposes upon all the nations of the earth. No one can be in doubt concerning the content of these requirements. The Law

רַגְלָיו קָדוֹשׁ הוּא : ° מֹשֶׁה וְאַהֲרֹן · בְּכֹהֲנָיו וּשְׁמוּאֵל
בְּקֹרְאֵי שְׁמוֹ קֹרְאִים אֶל־יְיָ וְהוּא יַעֲנֵם : ° בְּעַמּוּד
עָנָן יְדַבֵּר אֲלֵיהֶם שָׁמְרוּ עֵדֹתָיו וְחֹק נָתַן־לָמוֹ :
° יְיָ אֱלֹהֵינוּ אַתָּה עֲנִיתָם אֵל נֹשֵׂא הָיִיתָ לָהֶם וְנֹקֵם
עַל־עֲלִילוֹתָם : °° רוֹמְמוּ יְיָ אֱלֹהֵינוּ וְהִשְׁתַּחֲווּ לְהַר
קָדְשׁוֹ כִּי קָדוֹשׁ יְיָ אֱלֹהֵינוּ :

כט °° מִזְמוֹר לְדָוִד הָבוּ לַיהוָה בְּנֵי אֵלִים הָבוּ לַיהוָה
כָּבוֹד וָעֹז : ° הָבוּ לַיהוָה כְּבוֹד שְׁמוֹ הִשְׁתַּחֲווּ לַיהוָה
בְּהַדְרַת־קֹדֶשׁ : ° קוֹל יְהוָה עַל־הַמָּיִם אֵל־הַכָּבוֹד
הִרְעִים יְהוָה עַל־מַיִם רַבִּים : ° קוֹל־יְהוָה בַּכֹּחַ קוֹל
יְהוָה בֶּהָדָר : ° קוֹל יְהוָה שֹׁבֵר אֲרָזִים וַיְשַׁבֵּר יְהוָה
אֶת־אַרְזֵי הַלְּבָנוֹן : ° וַיַּרְקִידֵם כְּמוֹ־עֵגֶל לְבָנוֹן וְשִׂרְיוֹן
כְּמוֹ בֶן־רְאֵמִים : ° קוֹל־יְהוָה חֹצֵב לַהֲבוֹת אֵשׁ :

_____

* האלף נעלם

_____

upon which God has chosen to establish His throne for mankind's new future
is the same Law that has long reposed beneath the pinions of the Cherubim.
To render homage to God means to regard as binding His Law and its social
legislation concerning justice, duty and humane conduct. This is the Law which
God has realized and implemented in the nation of Yaakov, a nation which
had hitherto been held in contempt. It is the Law which is now to be adopted
by all of mankind. All of humanity, therefore, is repeatedly summoned to

God, and cast yourselves down at His footstool; holy is He. Moshe
and Aharon, [who were] prominent among His priests, and Shemuel
among them that declare His Name, called upon *God* and He heard
them. He spoke to them in a pillar of clouds; they were the keepers of
His testimonies and He gave them the statute. O *God* our God, You
heard them; You were a forgiving God for their sake, though You did
exact justice for their own deeds. Therefore exalt *God* our God and
cast yourselves down at His holy mountain; for *God,* our God, is holy.

A Psalm of David. Ascribe to *God,* O you who are endowed with
strength, ascribe to *God* glory and might. Ascribe to *God* the glory
due His Name, cast yourselves down before *God* in the beauty of
holiness. The voice of *God* was upon those waters then; thus, if the
omnipotence of creation's glory still thunders, then it is *God* Who
rules over the many waters. The voice of *God* is within every force;
the voice of *God* is in all things beautiful. The voice of *God* also
breaks cedars, as *God* also broke the cedars of Lebanon. As He made
them skip like calves, Lebanon and Sirion like young *Re'emim.* The
voice of *God* also strikes flames of fire; the voice of *God* lets the

---

recognize and to acknowledge God not only as the One Who is exalted far
above all things, but also as the "Holy One" Who, because He is holy, accepts
only one form of worship as true Divine service; namely, the sanctification
of human life on both the individual and the communal level. And men and
nations alike may come near to Him only by way of holy endeavors; meaning,
endeavors that are morally pure.

Psalm 29. מזמור לדוד This psalm has as its purpose to waken within us
the feeling of devoted obedience to God's voice, which speaks to us through
the medium of His Law. This purpose is served in Psalm 29 by a portrayal
of the glory and invincibility in which both this voice and God Himself, Who
speaks to us through His Law, reveal themselves in both nature and history.
Those who, by their loyal obedience to the voice of His Law, shall demonstrate
that they are indeed members of God's nation shall also partake of the blessing
of that peace which can be found with Him alone, and nowhere without Him.

קול ה' יחיל מדבר. According to Sabbath 98a, Tosaphoth ibid., the entire
Sinai desert bears the name of קדש, as well as the name of Paran, Zin, etc.
Any of these names, which are primarily used to designate definite localities
within that desert, is also employed to refer to the entire wilderness which
comprises the regions of Kedemoth, Paran, Zin, Sinai, Kadesh. Kadesh was

יּ קוֹל יְהוָֹה יָחִיל מִדְבָּר יָחִיל יְהוָֹה מִדְבַּר קָדֵשׁ:

יּ קוֹל יְהוָֹה יְחוֹלֵל אַיָּלוֹת וַיֶּחֱשֹׂף יְעָרוֹת וּבְהֵיכָלוֹ

כֻּלּוֹ אֹמֵר כָּבוֹד: יּ יְהוָֹה לַמַּבּוּל יָשָׁב וַיֵּשֶׁב יְהוָֹה

מֶלֶךְ לְעוֹלָם: יּ יְהוָֹה עֹז לְעַמּוֹ יִתֵּן יְהוָֹה יְבָרֵךְ אֶת־

עַמּוֹ בַשָּׁלוֹם:

אָנָּא בְּכֹחַ גְּדֻלַּת יְמִינְךָ תַּתִּיר צְרוּרָה ·

קַבֵּל רִנַּת עַמְּךָ שַׂגְּבֵנוּ טַהֲרֵנוּ נוֹרָא ·

נָא גִבּוֹר דּוֹרְשֵׁי יְחוּדְךָ כְּבָבַת שָׁמְרֵם ·

בָּרְכֵם טַהֲרֵם רַחֲמֵם צִדְקָתְךָ תָּמִיד גָּמְלֵם ·

חֲסִין קָדוֹשׁ בְּרֹב טוּבְךָ נַהֵל עֲדָתֶךָ ·

יָחִיד גֵּאֶה לְעַמְּךָ פְּנֵה זוֹכְרֵי קְדֻשָּׁתֶךָ ·

שַׁוְעָתֵנוּ קַבֵּל וּשְׁמַע צַעֲקָתֵנוּ יוֹדֵעַ תַּעֲלוּמוֹת ·

בָּרוּךְ שֵׁם כְּבוֹד מַלְכוּתוֹ לְעוֹלָם וָעֶד :

the border outpost of the wilderness from which the scouts were sent into
the land of Canaan and from which the people of Yisrael could have entered
the Promised Land immediately, had the sin of these emissaries not caused
the entire nation to be condemned to forty years of wandering in the wilderness. Since the journey of the Children of Yisrael from Egypt up to that point
accounted for two years of wandering, they still had to spend thirty-eight
years in the wilderness before they could enter the land. Kadesh was the place
where Yisrael had sinned, and there they sojourned for a period of nineteen
years within sight of the Holy Land which that generation had forfeited by
its transgression. (See Commentary to Deut. 1:46, 2:1.) At no other place

wilderness go into travail, even as *God* makes the wilderness of Kadesh go into travail. The voice of *God* makes hinds to calve, even while it strips the forests bare, and in His Temple all that is His says, "Glory." *God* remained calmly upon His throne even at the flood, and thus *God* set Himself up as King forever. To His people, however, *God* will grant power to be victorious over all; *God* will bless His people with peace.

---

in the wilderness did they remain for so long a period of time, and thus Kadesh was the place in which the penitent parents raised and trained a new generation which was to be worthy of a better future and of the Divinely-ordained inheritance of the Promised Land. Midbar Kadesh, therefore, is the name which most vividly calls to mind the memories of the wilderness and their significance for Yisrael's moral training and maturing for its destiny. The significance of the Midbar Kadesh extends even to our day and far into the future. Our own period of exile and wandering in the *midbar ha'amim* "wilderness of the nations," as the prophet calls it, was ordained when God decided, at Kadesh, that the particular generation then alive had forfeited its inheritance of the Holy Land. Its children must be raised to maturity in the wilderness so that they might be fit to take possession of the Land once the older, unworthy generation would have passed on. (See Psalm 106:24–27. Commentary to Num. 14:23.) Despite the disobedience of His people, which caused Him to decree their punishment at Kadesh, God neither changed nor abandoned the goals and plans He had originally set for Yisrael. Instead, He caused that entire generation of sinners to perish and waited calmly for the rise of a new generation that would better serve His purposes. In the same manner, God had previously sat unchanged and unshaken upon the throne of His Sovereignty even in the face of the corruption of all mankind at the time of the Flood. ה׳ למבול ישב. The degenerate have perished, but God and the goals of His rule have endured. God showed עוז, the invincible and changeless power and might of His will and His standards to all of mankind at the time of the Flood, and to Yisrael in the wilderness of Kadesh. In both these instances He demonstrated His *oz* by causing those generations who opposed His will to perish from the earth. But the same God who uproots the wicked allows those who obey His will as revealed to them, to partake in His eternal, invincible strength and majesty. Those who with their obedience demonstrate that they are indeed עמו, and who serve the only goals that are sure to win the final victory over all opposing forces, will themselves have a part in the fruits of this victorious perseverance. Those men who submit to the will of God will alone receive the true blessing of peace for all their desires and achievements; even if a whole world should stand against them, ה׳ יברך את עמו בשלום.

הכ"ן מכנן בעציסה.   רחבי החרייא שלמה הלוי.

לְכָה דוֹדִי לִקְרַאת כַּלָה· פְּנֵי שַׁבָּת נְקַבְּלָה: לכה

שָׁמוֹר וְזָכוֹר בְּדִבּוּר אֶחָד· הִשְׁמִיעָנוּ אֵל הַמְיֻחָד· יְיָ אֶחָד וּשְׁמוֹ

אֶחָד· לְשֵׁם וּלְתִפְאֶרֶת וְלִתְהִלָּה: לכה

לִקְרַאת שַׁבָּת לְכוּ וְנֵלְכָה· כִּי הִיא מְקוֹר הַבְּרָכָה· מֵרֹאשׁ מִקֶּדֶם

נְסוּכָה· סוֹף מַעֲשֶׂה בְּמַחֲשָׁבָה תְּחִלָּה: לכה

מִקְדַּשׁ מֶלֶךְ עִיר מְלוּכָה· קוּמִי צְאִי מִתּוֹךְ הַהֲפֵכָה· רַב לָךְ

שֶׁבֶת בְּעֵמֶק הַבָּכָא· וְהוּא יַחֲמוֹל עָלַיִךְ חֶמְלָה: לכה

הִתְנַעֲרִי מֵעָפָר, קוּמִי· לִבְשִׁי בִּגְדֵי תִפְאַרְתֵּךְ עַמִּי· עַל־יַד בֶּן־

יִשַׁי בֵּית הַלַּחְמִי· קָרְבָה אֶל־נַפְשִׁי גְאָלָהּ:   לכה

לכה דודי This is a hymn to welcome the Sabbath in which the Sabbath is portrayed as the Bride of Yisrael. The Sages recount that when God first introduced the Sabbath Day into Creation, the Sabbath bitterly complained to God saying: "To every other day of the week You have given a mate; the creation of the First Day was sustained and completed by that of the Second Day; the creation of the Third Day by that of the Fourth, and that of the Fifth Day by the Sixth, but me, the Seventh Day, You have left alone without a companion." Thereupon God replied, "I still have one more work of Creation to bring forth, and that will be the people of Yisrael, and Yisrael shall be your betrothed. ישראל יהא בן זוגך." Thus, when He gave His Law to Yisrael on Mount Sinai, God said to His people, "Behold, the Sabbath stands there alone and forgotten; remember her and hallow her unto yourselves even as a bridegroom sanctifies his bride unto himself on his wedding day." זכור את יום השבת לקדשו ! (Bereshith Rabba 11). Ever since that day, every week the people of Yisrael has celebrated its eternal betrothal to the Sabbath, and Yisrael supports, protects, loves and cherishes the Sabbath even as a faithful husband cherishes his beloved wife. Every week the people of Yisrael welcomes the Sabbath and leads her into its midst as the true, blessed friend and companion that has been betrothed to Yisrael, its bridegroom, forever, gladdening and sustaining him. Without Yisrael to keep it, the Sabbath would have vanished entirely from among mankind long ago. On the other hand, were it not for the Sabbath, the people of Yisrael would have succumbed long ago to the misery and affliction that have accompanied it upon its wanderings through history.

Come, my Friend, to meet the Bride; let us welcome the Sabbath.
Come, my Friend, to meet the Bride; let us welcome the Sabbath.

"Observe" and "Remember", the One God caused us to hear in one single utterance; *God* is One and His Name is One, for renown, for glory and for praise.

Come, my Friend, to meet the Bride; let us welcome the Sabbath.

Let us go forth together to meet the Sabbath, for it is a source of blessing, from the very beginning, of old, it was ordained, the end of Creation, the first in thought.

Come, my Friend, to meet the Bride; let us welcome the Sabbath.

O Sanctuary of the King, O royal city, arise, come forth from your ruins, too long have you dwelt in the vale of tears. He will have compassion upon you.

Come, my Friend, to meet the Bride; let us welcome the Sabbath.

Shake off your dust, arise, clothe yourself with My people as with your garments of glory, through the son of Yishai, the Bethlehemite, draw near to my soul, O redeem it.

Come, my Friend, to meet the Bride; let us welcome the Sabbath.

דודי, "my Friend" is none other than God Himself, (cf. Isa. 5:1 and Song of Songs). Together, God and Yisrael go forth to welcome the Sabbath Day.

שמור The Sabbath commandment as stated in Exodus 20:8 reads זכור את יום השבת לקדשו. In Deuteronomy 5:12, on the other hand, we are told שמור את יום השבת לקדשו. *Zachor* implies that we are to "remember" the Sabbath in our thoughts and to give *verbal expression* to the importance of the Sabbath as a memorial of God's Creation and of the homage which it behooves us to render Him as the Creator and Master of the Universe. *Shamor*, on the other hand, refers to the *physical demonstration* of this remembrance of the Sabbath and our homage to the Lord, which entails the cessation of all workday activities, of all *melachah*. The Sages teach that both *zachor* and *shamor* were uttered simultaneously in one single pronouncement, and from this we infer that these two different aspects of Sabbath observance are actually one and inseparable. *Zachor* without *shamor*, a mere spiritual "remembrance" of the "ideals symbolized by the Sabbath," would render the entire Sabbath invalid, for that day of rest derives its very name of שבת from שביתת מלאכה, "the cessation of all workday activities." Such mere "theoretical" observance of the Sabbath would actually be a denial in practice of the very homage to God which that person would wish to render in theory and by lip service.

הִתְעוֹרְרִי הִתְעוֹרְרִי · כִּי בָא אוֹרֵךְ קוּמִי אוֹרִי · עוּרִי עוּרִי שִׁיר
דַבֵּרִי · כְּבוֹד יְיָ עָלַיִךְ נִגְלָה: לכה

לֹא תֵבֽשִׁי וְלֹא תִכָּלְמִי · מַה תִּשְׁתּוֹחֲחִי וּמַה תֶּהֱמִי · בָּךְ יֶחֱסוּ
עֲנִיֵּי עַמִּי · וְנִבְנְתָה עִיר עַל־תִּלָּהּ:   לכה

But neither does *shamor* without *zachor* represent the proper observance of the Sabbath, for that would imply nothing more than a visible acting out of *shevithath melachah* while the concept of which *shevithath melachah* is a symbolic demonstration would neither be taken to heart nor accepted by the spirit. This intimate connection between the concepts of *shamor* and *zachor,* the physical demonstration and the spiritual adoption of one and the same truth, not only in the case of the institution of Sabbath observance but also in the case of all the other Mitzvoth contained in the Law of God, clearly reveals to us the requirement that is basic to all of our vocation as Jews. We are to allow every aspect of our lives and endeavors, physical and spiritual alike, to be subordinate to one and the same truth and to be permeated with one and the same sanctificaton. Hence the spurious concept of a so-called "adoration of God in spirit and in truth" in which the spirit is supposed to soar heavenward while the body is free to wallow far away from God in the cesspool of animal lust should be foreign to Judaism. The intimate union and common destiny of both the physical and the spiritual elements in human life and endeavor is the first and most immediate inference to be drawn from הָאֵל הַמְּיֻחָד the acknowledgement that God is indeed One. This same inference is also obvious in *Shema Yisrael* where the statement recognizing God as ה' אֶחָד is immediately followed by the commandment וְאָהַבְתָּ וגו' בְּכָל לְבָבְךָ וּבְכָל נַפְשְׁךָ וּבְכָל מְאֹדֶךָ. In other words, the unity of the sum total of all the phases of human life and personality is a logical inference, derived directly from the Unity of God Himself. This truth, ה' אֶחָד וּשְׁמוֹ אֶחָד, should be proclaimed by שֵׁם, by the Name of God which itself implies our spiritual perception of Him, by תִּפְאֶרֶת, our life of dutiful obedience which should serve to glorify Him עַבְדִּי אַתָּה יִשְׂרָאֵל אֲשֶׁר בְּךָ אֶתְפָּאָר (Isa. 49:3) and תְּהִלָּה by songs recounting the manner in which God has revealed Himself through mighty acts.

לִקְרַאת The Sabbath is *mekor haberachah* "a source of blessing." When God first instituted it as a memorial to His Creation, He blessed it with the power, by means of the truth it symbolizes and communicates to Yisrael to recognize and to take to its heart, to train man for his spiritual and moral destiny and to strengthen and ennoble him so that he may be able to fulfill his destiny, מֵרֹאשׁ וגו' · וַיְבָרֶךְ וַיְקַדֵּשׁ אוֹתוֹ. The Sabbath is as old as Creation itself. In fact, it is even older; it is not only *rosh*, but *kedem*, for סוֹף מַעֲשֶׂה וכו'. Man represents the ultimate goal of physical Creation. It was at man's feet

Arouse yourself, arouse yourself, for your light has come; arise and shine. Awake, awake, utter a song; the glory of *God* is revealed upon you.

Come, my Friend, to meet the Bride; let us welcome the Sabbath.

Be not deceived, nor blush with shame; why are you downcast and why are you disquieted? The poor of my people trust in you, that the city shall be rebuilt upon its ruins.

Come, my Friend, to meet the Bride; let us welcome the Sabbath.

---

that the Creator willed to lay His completed work so that man might administer it in a Godly manner and in obedient service rendered of his own free choice. But if man is to discharge this mission faithfully, he is in need of constant guidance and discipline, and it was the Sabbath that was charged with the task of supplying this guidance and spiritual training and thus providing an assurance that the goal originally envisioned in Creation would truly be fulfilled. Hence the Sabbath represents the ultimate purpose of Creation and, even as thought and intention always precede the planning of what is to be created, so, too, the Sabbath Day existed as part of the Divine plan even before the actual work of creation was begun.

לקראת וכו׳ is the call upon all the members of the Jewish community to welcome and receive the Sabbath as the source of all blessings. Truly, even as the Sages have said it, the Sabbath is the "most precious pearl" that God could give His people from His treasure chamber. Happy is he who, in keeping with the purpose of the Sabbath, welcomes that day by placing himself and his whole world, together with all of his endeavors and ambitions, his successes and failures, his gains and his losses at the feet of God. Our Sages have taught that a person who follows this course, knowing that he has either fulfilled his duty entirely or, at least, made atonement for past error, and who, for the twenty-four hours of the Sabbath that follow, does not permit himself even to think of his ordinary weekday pursuits, with each Sabbath receives *me'en olam habbah* a glimpse of the bliss of the world to come. All of terrestrial life, with its misery and woe, with its care and distress, retreats before the serene majesty of the Sabbath, and the eyes of man, reflecting his contented smile, sense the nearness of the grace of his Father in Heaven Who, with a tender look of approval rewards him for having delivered up to his Maker, for a period of twenty-four hours, the struggle and strife of the week. But even as all the pain and sorrow of the individual recede before the holy Sabbath, which brings comfort and hope to every wounded heart, so the Sabbath also transforms the sad and sorrowful outlook as regards Yisrael's collective fate as a nation into glorious vistas of hope and consolation. Yerushalayim is once more מקדש מלך עיר מלוכה, the Sanctuary and the City of God, of that God Whom the Sabbath proclaims as the King of the Universe in all

וְהָיוּ לִמְשִׁסָּה שֹׁאסָיִךְ · וְרָחֲקוּ כָּל־מְבַלְּעָיִךְ · יָשִׂישׂ עָלַיִךְ אֱלֹהָיִךְ ·
כִּמְשׂוֹשׂ חָתָן עַל־כַּלָּה :

לך

יָמִין וּשְׂמֹאל תִּפְרֹצִי · וְאֶת־יְיָ תַּעֲרִיצִי · עַל יַד־אִישׁ בֶּן פַּרְצִי ·
וְנִשְׂמְחָה וְנָגִילָה :

לך

בּוֹאִי בְשָׁלוֹם עֲטֶרֶת בַּעְלָהּ · גַּם בְּשִׂמְחָה וּבְצָהֳלָה · תּוֹךְ אֱמוּנֵי
עַם סְגֻלָּה · בּוֹאִי כַלָּה · בּוֹאִי כַלָּה :

לך

צב מִזְמוֹר שִׁיר לְיוֹם הַשַּׁבָּת: טוֹב לְהֹדוֹת לַיהוָה וּלְזַמֵּר לְשִׁמְךָ
עֶלְיוֹן: לְהַגִּיד בַּבֹּקֶר חַסְדֶּךָ וֶאֱמוּנָתְךָ בַּלֵּילוֹת: עֲלֵי עָשׂוֹר וַעֲלֵי
נָבֶל עֲלֵי הִגָּיוֹן בְּכִנּוֹר: כִּי שִׂמַּחְתַּנִי יְהוָה בְּפָעֳלֶךָ בְּמַעֲשֵׂי יָדֶיךָ
אֲרַנֵּן: מַה־גָּדְלוּ מַעֲשֶׂיךָ יְהוָה מְאֹד עָמְקוּ מַחְשְׁבֹתֶיךָ: אִישׁ בַּעַר
לֹא יֵדָע וּכְסִיל לֹא־יָבִין אֶת־זֹאת: בִּפְרֹחַ רְשָׁעִים ׀ כְּמוֹ־עֵשֶׂב

His supreme sovereignty. Once again He gathers His people about Him like a garment of glory, so that the sons of His nation will all serve to glorify Him. (Cf. Isa. 49:18 כבלה וכו׳. כי כלם כעדי תלבשי ותקשרים ככלה .כלם נקבצו באו־לך .קרבה וכו׳) then joins to the *Lechah Dodi* which follows, in which the "Friend" addressed is none other than God. התעוררי וכו׳, Zion will cause the light and word of God's glory that had been entrusted to it, to shine and sound forth through the dawn of the morning of its rebirth.

This is the confident hope which each Sabbath awakens within us anew. לא תבושי וכו׳. Zion will not be deceived in its trust, nor will she be found unworthy of the fulfillment of the hopes thus fostered. Even now that she is in ruins, Zion still remains the mother of her people, consoling and comforting its remnants. In vain והיו וכו׳ do ruthless tyrants seek to destroy her;

Those that despoiled you shall themselves become a spoil, and they who would swallow you up shall be far away. But your God will rejoice in you, even as a bridegroom rejoices in his bride.

Come, my Friend, to meet the Bride; let us welcome the Sabbath.

You shall spread out to the right and to the left, and you shall reveal *God* as the One mighty in strength. Through the offspring of the house of Peretz we shall be glad and exult.

Come, my Friend, to meet the Bride; let us welcome the Sabbath.

Come in peace, O crown of your Husband, come with joy and good cheer, into the midst of God's own chosen people, come, O Bride, come, O Bride!

Come, my Friend, to meet the Bride; let us welcome the Sabbath.

A Psalm, a Song for the Sabbath Day. It is good to pay homage to *God,* and to sing praises to Your Name, O Most High; to proclaim Your loving-kindness in the morning and Your faithfulness in the nights, with full sound and with the plaintive tone, in meditation upon the harp. For You have given me joy in Your work, O *God;* I will exult in the works of Your hands. How great are Your works, O *God,* how infinitely profound Your thoughts! A man bare of reason does not understand, nor does a conceited fool comprehend this; when the lawless spring up as the grass where all the abusers of might flourish,

---

they will all perish, but Zion and Yisrael will live on. In due time the attacks of the nations against her will cease and the ancient covenant which God made with Zion long ago will come into view once more serenely and in all its glory. All the rest of mankind to the left and to the right of Zion shall then join her, and, once the sovereign power of God will be revealed through Zion's resurrection for all to see, joy and serenity will hold triumphant entry on earth.

בואי May the Sabbath, then, thus enter into our midst and find harmonious response in every heart and spirit; may it be welcomed as the crowning glory of the nation that is wed to it forever. And even as we delight in the Sabbath, so may the Sabbath, too, have cause to rejoice in us and may it find a secure place in the midst of God's own chosen nation.

וַיִּצְּיְצוּ כָּל־פֹּעֲלֵי אָוֶן לְהִשָּׁמְדָם עֲדֵי־עַד: וְאַתָּה מָרוֹם לְעֹלָם

יְהוָֹה: כִּי הִנֵּה אֹיְבֶיךָ יְהוָֹה כִּי־הִנֵּה אֹיְבֶיךָ יֹאבֵדוּ יִתְפָּרְדוּ כָּל־

פֹּעֲלֵי אָוֶן: וַתָּרֶם כִּרְאֵים קַרְנִי בַּלֹּתִי בְּשֶׁמֶן רַעֲנָן: וַתַּבֵּט עֵינִי

בְּשׁוּרָי בַּקָּמִים עָלַי מְרֵעִים תִּשְׁמַעְנָה אָזְנָי: צַדִּיק כַּתָּמָר יִפְרָח

כְּאֶרֶז בַּלְּבָנוֹן יִשְׂגֶּה: שְׁתוּלִים בְּבֵית יְהוָֹה בְּחַצְרוֹת אֱלֹהֵינוּ יַפְרִיחוּ:

עוֹד יְנוּבוּן בְּשֵׂיבָה דְּשֵׁנִים וְרַעֲנַנִּים יִהְיוּ: לְהַגִּיד כִּי־יָשָׁר יְהוָֹה

צוּרִי וְלֹא־עַוְלָתָה בּוֹ:

צג יְהוָֹה מָלָךְ גֵּאוּת לָבֵשׁ לָבֵשׁ יְהוָֹה עֹז הִתְאַזָּר אַף־תִּכּוֹן תֵּבֵל

בַּל־תִּמּוֹט: נָכוֹן כִּסְאֲךָ מֵאָז מֵעוֹלָם אָתָּה: נָשְׂאוּ נְהָרוֹת יְהוָֹה

נָשְׂאוּ נְהָרוֹת קוֹלָם יִשְׂאוּ נְהָרוֹת דָּכְיָם: מִקֹּלוֹת מַיִם רַבִּים

אַדִּירִים מִשְׁבְּרֵי־יָם אַדִּיר בַּמָּרוֹם יְהוָֹה: עֵדֹתֶיךָ נֶאֶמְנוּ מְאֹד

לְבֵיתְךָ נָאֲוָה־קֹּדֶשׁ יְהוָֹה לְאֹרֶךְ יָמִים: קדיש יתום.

that it is [only so] that they may be destroyed forever. But You, O *God*, will remain on high forever. For behold, Your enemies, O *God*, lo, Your enemies shall perish, all the abusers of might disintegrate [of] themselves, while You lifted up my horn like that of the *Re'em*, and I outlive them with ever renewed consecration. Since my eye has seen this [come to pass] in the case of those who lie in wait for me, therefore my ears hear it [decreed] for those that rise up against me because they are evildoers. The righteous shall flourish like the palm tree; he shall grow tall like a cedar in Lebanon. Planted in the House of *God*, they shall flourish in the courts of our God. They will still bear fruit even in old age, they will remain full of sap and vigor forever, to declare that *God* is upright, my Rock, in Whom there is no injustice.

God has begun His reign; He has robed Himself in majesty; *God* has robed Himself, He has girded Himself with strength that none can withstand; now the world of men, too, shall be firmly established and sway no more. Your throne is henceforth established, O You Who are from everlasting. True, the floods, O *God*, the floods have lifted up their voices, the floods lift up their fall. The breakers of the ocean grew mightier from the roar of many waters; *God* alone is mighty on high. Thus Your testimonies have proven infinitely faithful; the name of "Sanctuary" truly befits Your House, O *God*, for all the length of days.

Psalm 92—93 See p. 74 above.

בשעה שהחזן אומר ברכו אומרים הקהל יתברך:

ק׳ יִתְבָּרַךְ וְיִשְׁתַּבַּח וְיִתְפָּאַר וְיִתְרוֹמַם
וְיִתְנַשֵּׂא שְׁמוֹ שֶׁל־מֶלֶךְ מַלְכֵי הַמְּלָכִים
הַקָּדוֹשׁ בָּרוּךְ הוּא שֶׁהוּא רִאשׁוֹן וְהוּא
אַחֲרוֹן וּמִבַּלְעָדָיו אֵין אֱלֹהִים: סֹלּוּ לָרֹכֵב
בָּעֲרָבוֹת בְּיָהּ שְׁמוֹ וְעִלְזוּ לְפָנָיו: וּשְׁמוֹ
מְרוֹמַם עַל־כָּל־בְּרָכָה וּתְהִלָּה:
בָּרוּךְ שֵׁם כְּבוֹד מַלְכוּתוֹ לְעוֹלָם וָעֶד:
יְהִי שֵׁם יְיָ מְבֹרָךְ מֵעַתָּה וְעַד עוֹלָם:

ח׳ **בָּרְכוּ אֶת־יְיָ הַמְבֹרָךְ:**
קו״ח

בָּרוּךְ יְיָ הַמְבֹרָךְ לְעוֹלָם וָעֶד:

בָּרוּךְ אַתָּה יְיָ אֱלֹהֵינוּ מֶלֶךְ
הָעוֹלָם אֲשֶׁר בִּדְבָרוֹ מַעֲרִיב
עֲרָבִים בְּחָכְמָה פּוֹתֵחַ שְׁעָרִים
וּבִתְבוּנָה מְשַׁנֶּה עִתִּים
וּמַחֲלִיף אֶת־הַזְּמַנִּים וּמְסַדֵּר אֶת־הַכּוֹכָבִים בְּמִשְׁמְרוֹתֵיהֶם בָּרָקִיעַ
כִּרְצוֹנוֹ בּוֹרֵא יוֹם וָלָיְלָה גּוֹלֵל אוֹר מִפְּנֵי־חֹשֶׁךְ וְחֹשֶׁךְ מִפְּנֵי־
אוֹר· וּמַעֲבִיר יוֹם וּמֵבִיא לָיְלָה וּמַבְדִּיל בֵּין יוֹם וּבֵין לָיְלָה
יְיָ צְבָאוֹת שְׁמוֹ· אֵל חַי וְקַיָּם תָּמִיד יִמְלוֹךְ עָלֵינוּ לְעוֹלָם וָעֶד·
בָּרוּךְ אַתָּה יְיָ הַמַּעֲרִיב עֲרָבִים:

ברכו, See p. 103 above.

בדברו. ברוך The same command of the Creator which appointed the light to serve as "day" and the darkness to be "night" is still valid even now, every day when night begins to fall. שערים denotes the gates of sunrise and sunset, phenomena through the regular alternation of which the Creator, in His infinite wisdom, has divided all of life on earth into two complementary halves. In Ecclesiastes 3:1 we read לכל זמן ועת לכל חפץ "All things need time and each endeavor has its own season." This maxim indicates to us that while the Hebrew term זמן denotes "time" as such, עת signifies a specific season, hour or moment of that time. The division of time into day and night is such that even the individual moments of day or night are not alike. Each minute is part of a gradual, steady change either from day to night or from night to day. However, the phenomena of daytime on one hand and nighttime on the other do represent two definitely opposing concepts. So that the transition from one to the other should not be too abrupt, God, in His loving care and insight, causes day and night to alternate not suddenly but by means of slow and very gradual changes that take place with every passing minute. He is

(Reader) Bless *God,* Who is to be blessed.

(יתברך for trans. see p. 105)

(Congregation) Blessed be *God,* Who is to be blessed, in all eternity.

Blessed be You *God,* our God, King of the Universe, Who with His Word brings on the evenings. with wisdom opens the gates, and with insight changes the minutes and varies the seasons, and arranges the stars in their watches in the firmament according to His will. He creates day and night. He causes the light to recede from darkness and darkness from light; He causes the day to pass away and the night to come, and sets apart the day from night; *God Tzevaoth* is His Name. He, the living and changeless God, will ever reign over us to all eternity. Blessed be You *God,* Who brings on the evenings.

ומסדר. מחליף את הזמנים and thus משנה עתים The stars appear as the watchmen appointed by God to stand guard over the sleeping world below, as it were, and it is He, too, that has assigned them their places in definite orbits כרצונו in accordance with His purposes that are known to Him alone. Man can behold the stars and plot their course, but their true nature and purpose lie beyond his range of comprehension. He is בורא יום ולילה in the evening even as He is יוצר אור ובורא חשך at dawn. This is repeated testimony of the truth of the Oneness and unique nature of God in his world full of contrasts and opposites. Day and night are created by one and the same Almighty Power, and day and night alike serve the unified, harmonious purposes of the One God. He requires the services of both light and darkness, of day as well as of night, and He gives to each of these phenomena the sphere it needs in order to function in accordance with His will. גולל, the light of day is literally "rolled back" as the lengthening shadows of night advance; even as darkness retreats as the light of day grows stronger. ומעביר יום, and when day has done its appointed task, God relieves it from duty and assigns night to begin its work. ומבדיל He arranges this alternation in such a manner that neither one of these contrasting phenomena interferes with the function of the other. Therefore His Name is ה' צבאות, He Who takes all the infinite variety of hosts of creatures and unites them so as to act and interact as parts of one single unified Universe. אל חי: He is the one eternally living Power among all the mortal forces of the Universe; He is the One Who will remain when all else will have departed, and He reigns *tamid* constantly over us *le'olam va'ed* in all eternity, and therefore we are all subject to His sovereignty and to His guidance not only during the days, but also during all the nights which we spend on earth.

אַהֲבַת עוֹלָם בֵּית יִשְׂרָאֵל עַמְּךָ אָהָבְתָּ, תּוֹרָה וּמִצְוֹת חֻקִּים
וּמִשְׁפָּטִים אוֹתָנוּ לִמַּדְתָּ. עַל־כֵּן יְיָ אֱלֹהֵינוּ בְּשָׁכְבֵנוּ וּבְקוּמֵנוּ
נָשִׂיחַ בְּחֻקֶּיךָ, וְנִשְׂמַח בְּדִבְרֵי תוֹרָתֶךָ וּבְמִצְוֹתֶיךָ לְעוֹלָם וָעֶד, כִּי
הֵם חַיֵּינוּ וְאֹרֶךְ יָמֵינוּ וּבָהֶם נֶהְגֶּה יוֹמָם וָלָיְלָה · וְאַהֲבָתְךָ אַל־
תָּסִיר מִמֶּנּוּ לְעוֹלָמִים · בָּרוּךְ אַתָּה יְיָ, אוֹהֵב עַמּוֹ יִשְׂרָאֵל:

יָחִיד אוֹמֵר אֵל מֶלֶךְ נֶאֱמָן.

דברים ו׳

שְׁמַע יִשְׂרָאֵל יְהֹוָה אֱלֹהֵינוּ יְהֹוָה ׀ אֶחָד:

בלחש   בָּרוּךְ   שֵׁם   כְּבוֹד   מַלְכוּתוֹ   לְעוֹלָם   וָעֶד:

וְאָהַבְתָּ אֵת יְהֹוָה אֱלֹהֶיךָ בְּכָל־לְבָבְךָ וּבְכָל־נַפְשְׁךָ
וּבְכָל־מְאֹדֶךָ: וְהָיוּ הַדְּבָרִים הָאֵלֶּה אֲשֶׁר אָנֹכִי מְצַוְּךָ
הַיּוֹם עַל־לְבָבֶךָ: וְשִׁנַּנְתָּם לְבָנֶיךָ וְדִבַּרְתָּ בָּם בְּשִׁבְתְּךָ
בְּבֵיתֶךָ וּבְלֶכְתְּךָ בַדֶּרֶךְ וּבְשָׁכְבְּךָ וּבְקוּמֶךָ: וּקְשַׁרְתָּם
לְאוֹת עַל־יָדֶךָ וְהָיוּ לְטֹטָפֹת בֵּין עֵינֶיךָ:
וּכְתַבְתָּם עַל־מְזֻזוֹת בֵּיתֶךָ וּבִשְׁעָרֶיךָ:

אהבת עולם All the other possessions which God may bestow upon a nation
or an individual are not of permanent duration. But the Torah with its teachings to instruct us and its laws by which we are to abide, is our most precious
possession, an eternal gift of God's everlasting love. It remains with us even
through the darkest moments of our lives as individuals and through the
blackest centuries of our history as a nation. The Torah and the teachings and
commandments it contains are the inalienable, blessed heritage not simply of
עמך, our nation as such, but of בית ישראל each and every individual member

With love everlasting have You loved the House of Yisrael Your people; the Torah and commandments, statutes and ordinances You have taught us. Therefore, O *God* our God, when we lie down and when we rise up, we will meditate upon Your statutes and rejoice in the words of Your Torah and in Your commandments forever, for they are our life and the length of our days and upon them we will meditate day and night. May You never remove Your love from us. Blessed be You *God*, Who loves Your people Yisrael.

HEAR ISRAEL, *GOD* OUR GOD, IS *GOD* THE ONLY ONE! Blessed be the Name of the glory of His kingdom to all the future which, though veiled, is certain.

And you shall love *God,* your God, with all your heart and with all your soul and with all your fortune. And these words which I command you today shall be upon your heart, and you shall teach them diligently to your sons and speak of them when you sit in your house and when you walk upon the road, when you lie down and when you rise up. And you shall bind them as a sign upon your hand, and they shall be as a head ornament between your eyes. And you shall inscribe them upon the doorposts of your house and upon your gates.

---

of this entity which comprises the "House of Yisrael", of all those who have been born, reared and trained for the purpose and calling to be "Yisrael", a mission the discharge of which alone can lend true content and meaning to their lives. בדברי תורתך — in the theoretical study of the Torah, ובמצותיך, and in the practical fulfillment of the commandments given therein.

שמע See p. 114 above.

דברים
י"א. וְהָיָה אִם־שָׁמֹעַ תִּשְׁמְעוּ אֶל־מִצְוֹתַי אֲשֶׁר אָנֹכִי
מְצַוֶּה אֶתְכֶם הַיּוֹם לְאַהֲבָה אֶת־יְהֹוָה אֱלֹהֵיכֶם וּלְעָבְדוֹ
בְּכָל־לְבַבְכֶם וּבְכָל־נַפְשְׁכֶם: וְנָתַתִּי מְטַר־אַרְצְכֶם
בְּעִתּוֹ יוֹרֶה וּמַלְקוֹשׁ וְאָסַפְתָּ דְגָנֶךָ וְתִירֹשְׁךָ וְיִצְהָרֶךָ:
וְנָתַתִּי עֵשֶׂב בְּשָׂדְךָ לִבְהֶמְתֶּךָ וְאָכַלְתָּ וְשָׂבָעְתָּ:
הִשָּׁמְרוּ לָכֶם פֶּן־יִפְתֶּה לְבַבְכֶם וְסַרְתֶּם וַעֲבַדְתֶּם
אֱלֹהִים אֲחֵרִים וְהִשְׁתַּחֲוִיתֶם לָהֶם: וְחָרָה אַף־יְהֹוָה
בָּכֶם וְעָצַר אֶת־הַשָּׁמַיִם וְלֹא־יִהְיֶה מָטָר וְהָאֲדָמָה לֹא
תִתֵּן אֶת־יְבוּלָהּ וַאֲבַדְתֶּם מְהֵרָה מֵעַל הָאָרֶץ הַטֹּבָה
אֲשֶׁר יְהֹוָה נֹתֵן לָכֶם: וְשַׂמְתֶּם אֶת־דְּבָרַי אֵלֶּה עַל־
לְבַבְכֶם וְעַל־נַפְשְׁכֶם וּקְשַׁרְתֶּם אֹתָם לְאוֹת עַל־יֶדְכֶם
וְהָיוּ לְטוֹטָפֹת בֵּין עֵינֵיכֶם: וְלִמַּדְתֶּם אֹתָם אֶת־בְּנֵיכֶם
לְדַבֵּר בָּם בְּשִׁבְתְּךָ בְּבֵיתֶךָ וּבְלֶכְתְּךָ בַדֶּרֶךְ וּבְשָׁכְבְּךָ
וּבְקוּמֶךָ: וּכְתַבְתָּם עַל־מְזוּזוֹת בֵּיתֶךָ וּבִשְׁעָרֶיךָ: לְמַעַן
יִרְבּוּ יְמֵיכֶם וִימֵי בְנֵיכֶם עַל הָאֲדָמָה אֲשֶׁר נִשְׁבַּע
יְהֹוָה לַאֲבֹתֵיכֶם לָתֵת לָהֶם כִּימֵי הַשָּׁמַיִם עַל־הָאָרֶץ:

במדבר
ט"ו ל"ז. וַיֹּאמֶר יְהֹוָה אֶל־מֹשֶׁה לֵּאמֹר: דַּבֵּר אֶל־בְּנֵי
יִשְׂרָאֵל וְאָמַרְתָּ אֲלֵהֶם וְעָשׂוּ לָהֶם צִיצִת עַל־כַּנְפֵי
בִגְדֵיהֶם לְדֹרֹתָם וְנָתְנוּ עַל־צִיצִת הַכָּנָף פְּתִיל תְּכֵלֶת:

And it shall come to pass if you will hearken with growing intentness to My commandments which I command you this day, so that you will love *God* your God and serve Him will all your heart and with all your soul, then I will give the rain of your land in its due season, the autumn rains and the spring rains, so that you may gather in your grain, your wine and your oil, and I will give grass upon your field for your cattle; you will eat thereof and you will be satiated. But take care lest your heart open itself to temptation and you turn astray and serve other gods and cast yourselves down before them. For then the wrath of *God* will blaze forth against you; He will restrain the skies and there will be no rain, and the land will not yield its produce, and you will quickly perish from the good land which *God* gives you. But even then you shall lay up these My words in your heart and in your soul, and bind them as a sign upon your hand and they shall be as a head-ornament between your eyes, and teach them to your sons to speak of them, when you sit in your house and when you walk upon the way, when you lie down and when you rise up. Inscribe them upon the doorposts of your house and upon your gates, so that your days and the days of your children may be prolonged upon the land which *God* swore to give to your fathers, as the days of the heavens upon the earth.

And *God* spoke to Moshe, saying, "Speak to the sons of Yisrael and tell it to them so that they make for themselves fringes upon the corners of their garments through all their generations, and that they put upon the fringe of each corner a thread of sky-blue wool. These

וְהָיָה לָכֶם לְצִיצִת וּרְאִיתֶם אֹתוֹ וּזְכַרְתֶּם אֶת־כָּל־
מִצְוֺת יְהֹוָה וַעֲשִׂיתֶם אֹתָם וְלֹא תָתוּרוּ אַחֲרֵי לְבַבְכֶם
וְאַחֲרֵי עֵינֵיכֶם אֲשֶׁר־אַתֶּם זֹנִים אַחֲרֵיהֶם: לְמַעַן
תִּזְכְּרוּ וַעֲשִׂיתֶם אֶת־כָּל־מִצְוֺתָי וִהְיִיתֶם קְדֹשִׁים
לֵאלֹהֵיכֶם: אֲנִי יְהֹוָה אֱלֹהֵיכֶם אֲשֶׁר הוֹצֵאתִי אֶתְכֶם
מֵאֶרֶץ מִצְרַיִם לִהְיוֹת לָכֶם לֵאלֹהִים אֲנִי יְהֹוָה
אֱלֹהֵיכֶם: ‏יֹם לוֹמַר אֱלֹהֵיכֶם לֶאֱמֶת.

אֱמֶת וֶאֱמוּנָה כָּל־זֹאת וְקַיָּם עָלֵינוּ. כִּי הוּא יְיָ אֱלֹהֵינוּ וְאֵין

אמת In the Morning Service the paragraph beginning with אמת ויציב
is the concluding blessing of the *Keriath Shema,* recapitulating the three
preceding portions that comprise the *Keriath Shema* in terms of the fundamentals laid down in them for our lives and our conduct. In keeping with
its significance as a preliminary as it were, to the practical business of daily
living, that paragraph puts particular stress upon the function of the laws
set forth in the *Keriath Shema* as a standard, "given and firmly established"
for us by which to measure our own lives and endeavors. אמת ואמונה which
concludes the *Keriath Shema* of the evening service, on the other hand, has
a purpose quite different from that of the corresponding portion in the morning prayers. In keeping with the thoughts and emotions engendered by the
coming of night, emphasis is put here upon the two-fold lesson taught us
by the miracle of *Yetziath Mitzrayim* which was recalled in the preceding
portion. We are reminded that our many deliverances in the past should be
to us a source of trust in God through all the dark moments that the future
may bring. At the same time we must remember that the many instances of
Divine redemption and deliverance from those forces that have threatened

shall be fringes for you so that you may look upon them and remember all the commandments of *God*, and fulfill them, and you will not cast about after your own hearts and after your own eyes, and, following them, become unfaithful to Me. That you may remember and fulfill all of My commandments and remain holy for your God. I am *God*, your God, Who brought you out of the land of Mitzrayim in order to be your God; I am *God* your God."

True and trustworthy is all this and steadfast for us that He, *God*, is our God and there is none beside Him, and that we are Yisrael,

---

to destroy us as a nation, beginning with our miraculous liberation at the time of *Yetziath Mitzrayim*, should be to us also a basis for קבלת עול מלכות שמים our particular subjection and subordination to the will of God as the will of our Sovereign King. Two *berachoth; Emeth Ve'emunah* and *Hashkivenu*, are devoted to this dual lesson deriving from *Yetziath Mitzrayim*. אמת ואמונה has reference to the subordination of our lives to God's sovereignty, to the *Malchuth Shamayim* which must willingly be borne by each and every one of us forever, while *Hashkivenu* has as its theme our complete trust and confidence in His help and in the *shemirah* which God grants to us at all times. Whereas the *Keriath Shema* of the Morning Service concludes with only one *beracha*, the *Geulah* of the Evening Service is divided into two *berachoth*. Actually, however, these two blessings should be construed as only one *berachah*, כגאולה אריכתא דמיא (Berachoth 4b), for both of them deal with the inferences to be drawn from the historic event of the *Yetziath Mitzrayim*. השם נפשנו בחיים Without Him, Yisrael would have vanished long ago from among the living. המדריכנו על במות אויבינו He allows us to arrive at those high places which our foes have tried to reach in vain.

זוּלָתוֹ וַאֲנַחְנוּ יִשְׂרָאֵל עַמּוֹ הַפְּדֵנוּ מִיַּד מְלָכִים מַלְכֵּנוּ הַגּוֹאֲלֵנוּ

מִכַּף כָּל־הֶעָרִיצִים הָאֵל הַנִּפְרָע לָנוּ מִצָּרֵינוּ וְהַמְשַׁלֵּם גְּמוּל

לְכָל־אֹיְבֵי נַפְשֵׁנוּ הָעֹשֶׂה גְדֹלוֹת עַד אֵין חֵקֶר וְנִפְלָאוֹת עַד אֵין

מִסְפָּר · הַשָּׂם נַפְשֵׁנוּ בַּחַיִּים וְלֹא־נָתַן לַמּוֹט רַגְלֵנוּ הַמַּדְרִיכֵנוּ

עַל־בָּמוֹת אוֹיְבֵינוּ וַיָּרֶם קַרְנֵנוּ עַל כָּל־שֹׂנְאֵינוּ · הָעֹשֶׂה לָנוּ

נִסִּים וּנְקָמָה בְּפַרְעֹה אוֹתֹת וּמוֹפְתִים בְּאַדְמַת בְּנֵי חָם · הַמַּכֶּה

בְּעֶבְרָתוֹ כָּל־בְּכוֹרֵי מִצְרָיִם וַיּוֹצֵא אֶת־עַמּוֹ יִשְׂרָאֵל מִתּוֹכָם

לְחֵרוּת עוֹלָם · הַמַּעֲבִיר בָּנָיו בֵּין גִּזְרֵי יַם־סוּף אֶת־רוֹדְפֵיהֶם

וְאֶת־שׂוֹנְאֵיהֶם בִּתְהֹמוֹת טִבַּע : וְרָאוּ בָנָיו גְּבוּרָתוֹ שִׁבְּחוּ וְהוֹדוּ

לִשְׁמוֹ וּמַלְכוּתוֹ בְּרָצוֹן קִבְּלוּ עֲלֵיהֶם. מֹשֶׁה וּבְנֵי יִשְׂרָאֵל לְךָ עָנוּ

שִׁירָה בְּשִׂמְחָה רַבָּה וְאָמְרוּ כֻלָּם :

מִי־כָמֹכָה בָּאֵלִם יְהֹוָה מִי כָּמֹכָה נֶאְדָּר בַּקֹּדֶשׁ נוֹרָא תְהִלֹּת

עֹשֵׂה פֶלֶא : מַלְכוּתְךָ רָאוּ בָנֶיךָ בּוֹקֵעַ יָם לִפְנֵי מֹשֶׁה זֶה אֵלִי עָנוּ

וְאָמְרוּ ·

יְהֹוָה · יִמְלֹךְ לְעֹלָם וָעֶד :

וְנֶאֱמַר כִּי־פָדָה יְיָ אֶת־יַעֲקֹב וּגְאָלוֹ מִיַּד חָזָק מִמֶּנּוּ · בָּרוּךְ

אַתָּה יְיָ גָּאַל יִשְׂרָאֵל :

מי כמכה Two thoughts stand out in this hymn contemplating the mighty
miracle which God wrought at the Sea of Reeds: מי כמכה and ה' ימלוך לעולם
ועד.

His people. It is He Who has freed us from the hand of kings, our King, Who has delivered us from the grasp of all the tyrants; [He is] the God Who on our behalf exacts atonement from our oppressors, Who requites all the enemies of the soul, Who does great things beyond [our] understanding, and wonders without number. Who sustains our soul in life and did not allow our foot to be moved, Who leads us to the high places of our enemies and lifted up our horn above all those that hated us, Who wrought miracles for us and retribution upon Pharaoh, signs and convincing acts in the land of the sons of Cham; Who in His wrath as it went forth slew all the firstborn of Mitzrayim when He led forth His people Yisrael from their midst to freedom everlasting, Who led His sons through the cleft parts of the Sea of Reeds, and caused their pursuers and those who hated them to sink into its depths. His sons saw His almighty power; they praised and rendered homage to His Name and willingly accepted His kingdom. Moshe and the sons of Yisrael song a song to You with great rejoicing and they all said:

"Who is like You among the gods, O *God*! Who is like You, uniquely exalted in holiness, revered in songs of praise, doing wonders?"

Your sons beheld Your sovereign power, when You parted the sea before Moshe: "This is my God," they exclaimed, and said:

"*God* will reign forever and ever."

And it is said; "For *God* has set Yaakov free and redeemed him from the hand of him who was stronger than he."

Blessed be You *God*, Who has redeemed Yisrael.

מי כמוכה expresses the conviction, gained on the occasion of the miraculous event that took place at the Sea of Reeds, of God's absolute majesty and power that is exalted high above all those elements and forces which human folly would worship as divine. *Yirah,* obedience to God born of awe is an indispensable component of this conviction, the first and basic fruit of all the songs in praise of God's greatness and almighty power.

ה׳ ימלוך לע״ו, on the other hand, gives expression to the confidence that God, even as He reigned at the Sea of Reeds long ago, delivering His people. and punishing its foes, will also continue to reign through the ages, doing justice and practicing mercy. It is in a similar spirit, too, that Jeremiah (31:10)

הַשְׁכִּיבֵנוּ יְיָ אֱלֹהֵינוּ לְשָׁלוֹם וְהַעֲמִידֵנוּ מַלְכֵּנוּ לְחַיִּים וּפְרֹשׂ

עָלֵינוּ סֻכַּת שְׁלוֹמֶךָ וְתַקְּנֵנוּ בְּעֵצָה טוֹבָה מִלְּפָנֶיךָ וְהוֹשִׁיעֵנוּ

לְמַעַן שְׁמֶךָ וְהָגֵן בַּעֲדֵנוּ וְהָסֵר מֵעָלֵינוּ אוֹיֵב דֶּבֶר וְחֶרֶב וְרָעָב

וְיָגוֹן וְהָסֵר שָׂטָן מִלְּפָנֵינוּ וּמֵאַחֲרֵינוּ וּבְצֵל כְּנָפֶיךָ תַּסְתִּירֵנוּ כִּי

אֵל שׁוֹמְרֵנוּ וּמַצִּילֵנוּ אָתָּה כִּי אֵל מֶלֶךְ חַנּוּן וְרַחוּם אָתָּה וּשְׁמוֹר

צֵאתֵנוּ וּבוֹאֵנוּ לְחַיִּים וּלְשָׁלוֹם מֵעַתָּה וְעַד עוֹלָם · וּפְרֹשׂ עָלֵינוּ

סֻכַּת שְׁלוֹמֶךָ · בָּרוּךְ אַתָּה יְיָ הַפּוֹרֵשׂ סֻכַּת שָׁלוֹם עָלֵינוּ וְעַל כָּל־

עַמּוֹ יִשְׂרָאֵל וְעַל־יְרוּשָׁלָיִם :

לשבת. (שמות לא טו.)

וְשָׁמְרוּ בְנֵי־יִשְׂרָאֵל אֶת־הַשַּׁבָּת לַעֲשׂוֹת אֶת־הַשַּׁבָּת לְדֹרֹתָם

בְּרִית עוֹלָם : בֵּינִי וּבֵין בְּנֵי יִשְׂרָאֵל אוֹת הִיא לְעֹלָם

כִּי־שֵׁשֶׁת יָמִים עָשָׂה יְהֹוָה אֶת־הַשָּׁמַיִם וְאֶת־הָאָרֶץ וּבַיּוֹם

הַשְּׁבִיעִי שָׁבַת וַיִּנָּפַשׁ :

---

calls out to the generations of even the remotest future in which God will
fulfill His ultimate, final *geulah* that it was only through God that the people
of Yaakov, the exiled nation which stood utterly defenseless in the face of
all the powers of the world, could, and did, attain redemption and freedom.

שלום .השכיבנו undisturbed peace, and *chayim*, new strength for a new
day of vigorous living—these are gifts that night brings and for which
we trustingly pray to God. But particularly we ask of Him תקננו בעצה טובה
מלפניך, and this is the most important request of all. Daytime is the time for
achievement, but the rest that comes with night is made for man to compose
his thoughts and to frame the best and most fitting resolutions for his future
life. In fact, simply by virtue of the complete relaxation it affords, even

Cause us, O *God* our God, to lie down in peace, and cause us, O *God,* to rise up again to life. Spread over us the shelter of Your peace, direct us aright with good resolve, save us for Your Name's sake, protect us and keep far from us foe and pestilence, sword, famine and sorrow; remove also the adversary from before us and behind us, and shelter us in the shadow of Your wing. For You, O God, are our Protector and Deliverer, even as You, O God, are a gracious and compassionate King. Guard our going out and our coming in to life and peace from this time forth and forever, and spread over us the shelter of Your peace. Blessed be You *God,* Who spreads the shelter of peace over us, over all Your people Yisrael and over Yerushalayim.

(On Sabbaths):   And the sons of Yisrael shall keep the Sabbath, in order to fulfill the Sabbath for their descendants as an everlasting covenant. It is a sign between Me and the sons of Yisrael forever, that in six days *God* made heaven and earth, and with the Seventh Day He ceased from work, and withdrew into His own Essence.

---

sleep endows the mind and spirit with renewed vigor so that we may obtain a clearer perspective of things as they are and acquire the ability to evaluate them correctly. Hence we pray here for Divine aid so that our nightly rest may help us take wise counsel and frame worthy resolutions. מלפנינו is that which may be on the path that is yet before us; מאחרינו that which might result from past achievement. ופרוש Up to this point this nightly prayer is identical with the one recited at evening services throughout the week. But since, on Friday nights, this is the point of transition to the actual *Tefillah* of the Sabbath, the concluding phrase is changed on the Sabbath eve from שומר עמו ישראל to הפורש סוכת שלום עלינו. For the Sabbath by its very nature causes every thought of grief and danger to fade away. It mitigates and soothes all sadness, sorrow and pain. In place of the awareness of our particular need for protection, it affords us the blissful sense of peace, free of all discord, into which our Father in Heaven receives all of His own beneath the wings of His loving-kindness.

ושמרו On the Sabbath there is joined to the concept of פרישת סוכת שלום the utterance of the Word of God characterizing the Sabbath as ברית עולם and אות בין ה' ובין בני ישראל, and therefore asking us to keep and observe it as such. If we observe the commandment of *Shemirath Shabbath,* that is, if we "fulfill" it by refraining from all creative labor on that day, we make of the Sabbath a reality, an eternally unbreakable bond linking us and our

מֶן דְעֶן שׁלֹשׁ רְגָלִים וַיְדַבֵּר מֹשֶׁה אֶת־מֹעֲדֵי יְהֹוָה אֶל־בְּנֵי יִשְׂרָאֵל:
(ויקרא כג מד)

מֶן רֹאשׁ הַשָׁנָה תִּקְעוּ בַחֹדֶשׁ שׁוֹפָר בַּכֵּסֶה לְיוֹם חַגֵּנוּ: כִּי חֹק
(תהלים פא ד)
לְיִשְׂרָאֵל הוּא מִשְׁפָּט לֵאלֹהֵי יַעֲקֹב:

מֶן יוֹם כִּפוּר כִּי־בַיּוֹם הַזֶּה יְכַפֵּר עֲלֵיכֶם לְטַהֵר אֶתְכֶם מִכֹּל
(ויקרא טז ל)
חַטֹּאתֵיכֶם לִפְנֵי יְהֹוָה תִּטְהָרוּ:

הש"ץ אומר ח"ק ואח"כ מתפללין תפלה בלחש.

descendants with God forever, This, our cessation of all labor, by which we demonstrate our Sabbath observance, is the visible "sign" between God and ourselves. ביני ובין וגו׳ It is with this "sign" that we avow our homage to God as the God and Creator of the world, and it is by this "sign", too, that God can recognize us as being His dedicated servants who have consecrated their lives to His service. This *berith* and *oth* constitute the key which gives us access to the wings of peace beneath which God shelters all His own.

וידבר. The Sabbath, being a permanent Divinely-established institution, recurring every seventh day, is the instrument of our eternal link with God as that of the creature with its Creator. In the same manner the days commemorating the extraordinary acts of God which Yisrael has experienced as His Nation have been appointed as seasons at which God expects us to "meet with Him," days which were to be publicly proclaimed as such by the leaders of our community. Like the weekly Sabbath, the Mo'adei Hashem, these meetings with our "Redeemer", "Lawgiver" and "Preserver" also let us sense the bliss that comes with the knowledge that we are covered by the wing of peace beneath which God shelters all of His own.

תקעו. Rosh Hashanah, too, is a *Mo'ed,* which leads to the festival of חג הסוכות זמן שמחתנו, the most joyous *Mo'ed* of them all, which has the same relationship to Rosh Hashanah as the Full Moon to the New Moon. On Rosh Hashanah the solemn sound of the Shofar summons us to come forth from the depths of darkness and from the alienation from God into which we may have drifted, to return to God and to a pure life so that we may become worthy of the rejoicing before His Presence which beckons to us in the form of the approaching festival of Succoth. By thus calling upon us to return to God, the Shofar represents the guarantee that God is ready even now to receive us once more beneath the wings of His loving care.

(On Passover, Shavuoth and Succoth): And Moshe declared *God's* appointed times of meeting to the sons of Yisrael.

(On Rosh-Hashanah): But blow the Shofar on the New Moon, on the day of the veiling of the moon for our feast day. For there is a statute for Yisrael and the God of Yaakov sits in judgment.

(On Yom Kippur): For on this day He shall make atonement for you, to cleanse you; you shall become cleansed of all your sins before *God.*

כי ביום. Rosh Hashanah is the beginning of the path to *teshuvah,* to the "return" to God and to a life of loyalty to our duty before Him. Succoth keeps before us the goal of the pure joy of life before God which it is within our own power to regain. But upon the path between the beginning and the end there is the solemn Yom Kippur, the day which is designed to afford us the opportunity to rise up to a new life. It is Yom Kippur that can deliver us from the consequences of our errors that might spell disaster to our lives us such (כפרה) and cleanse the soul from the remnants of past sin that might disturb its inner serenity (טהרה). Yom Kippur frees us from the calamities which would be the fruit of our every sin if it were not for God's all-powerful and wondrous goodness in which He intervenes, protecting and cleansing us. It is God alone Who, by suspending the operation of the law of cause and effect which He Himself has instituted in His world order, can make whatever happened to be as if it had never come to pass. This Divine cancellation of what, in the ordinary course of events, would have been the inevitable consequences of sin has been promised to all those who will make themselves worthy of this favor by means of *teshuvah* and Yom Kippur. It is only before God Himself that we can attain such rebirth. However, our Sages remind us that, if our sin has been a crime not only against God but also against our fellow-man, we can come before God to ask for atonement only if we have previously done everything within our power to appease also the person we have injured and to secure his forgiveness. Once we have been thus reborn, every conflict that may stir within us will vanish. Hence that gift of God of which we hope to make ourselves worthy on Yom Kippur reveals Him truly as *ose hashalom* the Creator of Peace Who makes it possible for all of us to be received in the peaceful shelter of His wing.

Thus the paragraphs *Veshameru, Vayedabber, Tik'u, Ki Vayom* are quite a logical conclusion to the הפורש סוכת שלום etc. at the end of *geulah.* It is obvious, then, that they are to be construed only as a גאולה אריכתא and not as an interruption of the desired סמיכת גאולה לתפלה.

אֲדֹנָי שְׂפָתַי תִּפְתָּח וּפִי יַגִּיד תְּהִלָּתֶךָ:

בָּרוּךְ אַתָּה יְיָ אֱלֹהֵינוּ וֵאלֹהֵי אֲבוֹתֵינוּ אֱלֹהֵי אַבְרָהָם
אֱלֹהֵי יִצְחָק וֵאלֹהֵי יַעֲקֹב הָאֵל הַגָּדוֹל הַגִּבּוֹר וְהַנּוֹרָא
אֵל עֶלְיוֹן גּוֹמֵל חֲסָדִים טוֹבִים וְקֹנֵה הַכֹּל וְזוֹכֵר חַסְדֵי
אָבוֹת וּמֵבִיא גוֹאֵל לִבְנֵי בְנֵיהֶם לְמַעַן שְׁמוֹ בְּאַהֲבָה.

On שבת שובה, say:

זָכְרֵנוּ לְחַיִּים מֶלֶךְ חָפֵץ בַּחַיִּים · וְכָתְבֵנוּ בְּסֵפֶר הַחַיִּים לְמַעַנְךָ
אֱלֹהִים חַיִּים:

מֶלֶךְ עוֹזֵר וּמוֹשִׁיעַ וּמָגֵן · בָּרוּךְ אַתָּה יְיָ מָגֵן אַבְרָהָם:

אַתָּה גִּבּוֹר לְעוֹלָם אֲדֹנָי מְחַיֵּה מֵתִים אַתָּה רַב
לְהוֹשִׁיעַ·

During the winter months add:

מַשִּׁיב הָרוּחַ וּמוֹרִיד הַגֶּשֶׁם:

מְכַלְכֵּל חַיִּים בְּחֶסֶד מְחַיֵּה מֵתִים בְּרַחֲמִים רַבִּים
סוֹמֵךְ נוֹפְלִים וְרוֹפֵא חוֹלִים וּמַתִּיר אֲסוּרִים וּמְקַיֵּם
אֱמוּנָתוֹ לִישֵׁנֵי עָפָר · מִי כָמוֹךָ בַּעַל גְּבוּרוֹת וּמִי דּוֹמֶה
לָּךְ מֶלֶךְ מֵמִית וּמְחַיֶּה וּמַצְמִיחַ יְשׁוּעָה·

On שבת שובה add:

מִי כָמוֹךָ אַב הָרַחֲמִים זוֹכֵר יְצוּרָיו לְחַיִּים בְּרַחֲמִים·

וְנֶאֱמָן אַתָּה לְהַחֲיוֹת מֵתִים · בָּרוּךְ אַתָּה יְיָ מְחַיֵּה
הַמֵּתִים:

אַתָּה קָדוֹשׁ וְשִׁמְךָ קָדוֹשׁ וּקְדוֹשִׁים בְּכָל יוֹם
יְהַלְלוּךָ סֶּלָה · בָּרוּךְ אַתָּה יְיָ הָאֵל (בשבת שובה הַמֶּלֶךְ) הַקָּדוֹשׁ:

O *Lord,* open my lips so that my mouth may declare the praise of Your mighty deeds.

Blessed be You, *God,* our God and God of our fathers, God of **Avraham,** God of **Yitzchak** and God of **Yaakov,** the great, mighty **and** awesome God, God the Most High, Who nevertheless bestows lovingkindness, Who is the Owner of all things, and remembers the fathers' acts of devotion, and Who, in love, will bring a redeemer to their children's children for His Name's sake.

(On שבת שובה, *say:*

Remember us for life, O King Who delights in life, and inscribe us into the Book of Life for Your sake, O Living God.)

O King, Helper, Savior and Shield! Blessed be You *God,* the Shield of Avraham.

You, O my Lord, are all-powerful forever. You are the One Who revives the dead; You are abundantly powerful to save.

(During the winter months add: He causes the wind to blow and the rain to fall.)

He sustains the living with loving-kindness, revives the dead with great compassion, supports the falling, heals the sick, unchains the bound, and keeps His faith with the slumberers in the dust. Who is like You, Master of mighty acts, and who, like You, is a King Who kills and restores life and causes salvation to grow?

(On שבת שובה *add:* Who, like You, is a Father of compassion, Who in compassion remembers His creatures for life?)

And You are faithful to revive the dead. Blessed be You *God,* Who revives the dead.

You are holy, and Your Name is holy, and the holy ones proclaim Your praise each day. Blessed be You *God,* the Holy God. *(On* שבת שובה: the holy King).

ברוך. See p. 130 above.

אתה קדשת The first three and the last three blessings of the *Shemone Esrei* for Sabbaths and Yom Tov are identical with those recited on week-days. But the intermediate blessings of the weekday *Shemoneh Esrei* which concern weekday activities and endeavors are replaced on Sabbaths by one single *berachah,* which expresses the sacred significance of that day so that we may take it to heart, and which, therefore, is referred to as *kedushath ha-yom.* Thus, on Sabbaths and holidays we actually have only שבע ברכות instead

אַתָּה קִדַּשְׁתָּ אֶת־יוֹם הַשְּׁבִיעִי לִשְׁמֶךָ · תַּכְלִית
מַעֲשֵׂה שָׁמַיִם וָאָרֶץ · וּבֵרַכְתּוֹ מִכָּל־הַיָּמִים וְקִדַּשְׁתּוֹ
מִכָּל־הַזְּמַנִּים · וְכֵן כָּתוּב בְּתוֹרָתֶךָ:

וַיְכֻלּוּ הַשָּׁמַיִם וְהָאָרֶץ וְכָל־צְבָאָם: וַיְכַל אֱלֹהִים
בַּיּוֹם הַשְּׁבִיעִי מְלַאכְתּוֹ אֲשֶׁר עָשָׂה וַיִּשְׁבֹּת בַּיּוֹם
הַשְּׁבִיעִי מִכָּל־מְלַאכְתּוֹ אֲשֶׁר עָשָׂה: וַיְבָרֶךְ אֱלֹהִים
אֶת־יוֹם הַשְּׁבִיעִי וַיְקַדֵּשׁ אֹתוֹ כִּי בוֹ שָׁבַת מִכָּל־
מְלַאכְתּוֹ אֲשֶׁר־בָּרָא אֱלֹהִים לַעֲשׂוֹת:

אֱלֹהֵינוּ וֵאלֹהֵי אֲבוֹתֵינוּ רְצֵה בִמְנוּחָתֵנוּ קַדְּשֵׁנוּ
בְּמִצְוֹתֶךָ וְתֵן חֶלְקֵנוּ בְּתוֹרָתֶךָ שַׂבְּעֵנוּ מִטּוּבֶךָ
וְשַׂמְּחֵנוּ בִּישׁוּעָתֶךָ וְטַהֵר לִבֵּנוּ לְעָבְדְּךָ בֶּאֱמֶת
וְהַנְחִילֵנוּ יְיָ אֱלֹהֵינוּ בְּאַהֲבָה וּבְרָצוֹן שַׁבַּת קָדְשֶׁךָ
וְיָנוּחוּ בָהּ יִשְׂרָאֵל מְקַדְּשֵׁי שְׁמֶךָ · בָּרוּךְ אַתָּה יְיָ
מְקַדֵּשׁ הַשַּׁבָּת:

רְצֵה יְיָ אֱלֹהֵינוּ בְּעַמְּךָ יִשְׂרָאֵל וּבִתְפִלָּתָם · וְהָשֵׁב אֶת־הָעֲבוֹדָה

of *Shemone Esrei*. This intermediate *berachah* takes a different form in each of the four *Tefilloth* that are recited on the Sabbath Day. In the Maariv, which ushers in the Sabbath on Friday night, the prayer is *Attah Kiddashta*, declaring the sacred purpose and significance of the Sabbath. In the Shacharith service, it is *Yismach Moshe*, expressing the exalting that stems from the gladsome blessings inherent in the Sabbath. In the Musaph service, the intermediate blessing begins with *Tikkanta Shabbath*, commemorating the special Sabbath sacrifices that were offered in the Temple and the ideas which these sacrifices were meant to symbolize. In the Mincha service, when the end of the Sabbath draws near, a portion beginning with *Attah echad* views the Sabbath in retrospect as a day of rest and recalls to us the true nature of perfect Sabbath peace.

אתה קדשת The Jewish Sabbath is not a day of rest arbitrarily appointed by men. It is God Himself Who sanctified it "לשמך" for *His Name*, that is, to

You have sanctified the Seventh Day for Your Name, the goal of the creation of Heaven and earth; You blessed it above all the days and sanctified it above all seasons and thus it is written in Your Torah:

And Heaven and earth and all their host were completed; then, with the Seventh Day, God completed His work which He had made, and with the Seventh Day He ceased from all of His work which He had made. And God blessed the Seventh Day and made it holy, for with it He had ceased from all of His work which He, God, had brought into existence in order to continue the work of creation upon it.

Our God and God of our fathers, take pleasure in our rest, hallow us by Your commandments and grant our portion in Your Torah. Satisfy us from Your good, gladden us with Your salvation, purify our hearts to serve You in truth, and in Your love and favor, O *God* our God, let Your holy Sabbath remain our inheritance, and may Yisrael, who sanctify Your Name, rest on it. Blessed be You *God,* Who hallows the Sabbath.

---

the end that He be recognized and that homage be rendered Him. תכלית וכו׳ "The goal of Creation" is the kind of man who will acknowledge God as his God and serve Him; hence the Sabbath, through which such homage and service are assured, plays an essential part in the fulfillment of God's purpose. ברכתו מכל הימים, of all the days of the week, the Sabbath is the one that is most blessed and the day that can bring the greatest blessing to man. וקדשתו מכל הזמנים it is also the holiest of all the festivals. Even Yom Kippur is only secondary to the Sabbath in importance, for a desecration of Yom Kippur is punished only by *kareth,* but the violation of the Sabbath is subject to the death penalty by *sekilah,* and a public profanation of the Sabbath day is the only breach of religious observance that Jewish law considers tantamount to עובד עבודה זרה, idol worship.

ויכלו This statement concerning Heaven and earth embodies within itself all of the Jewish concept of God and the world. Heaven and earth were brought into being without their will by the might of a Higher Power Who is above them and to Whose command they are still subject to this very day. And (*vayechulu*) their present form was envisioned as תכלית, an "end" or "goal" long before they even came to exist. Thus they represent a plan mapped out by that Higher Power Who created them. Hence we can see that even long before Heaven and earth first came to be, there existed a thinking, almighty Will, sure of its purposes and capable of attaining them, a Will

לִדְבִיר בֵּיתֶךָ וְאִשֵׁי יִשְׂרָאֵל וּתְפִלָּתָם בְּאַהֲבָה תְקַבֵּל בְּרָצוֹן וּתְהִי
לְרָצוֹן תָּמִיד עֲבוֹדַת יִשְׂרָאֵל עַמֶּךָ ·

On Rosh Chodesh and the Intermediate Days of Festivals:

אֱלֹהֵינוּ וֵאלֹהֵי אֲבוֹתֵינוּ · יַעֲלֶה וְיָבֹא וְיַגִּיעַ וְיֵרָאֶה וְיֵרָצֶה וְיִשָּׁמַע
וְיִפָּקֵד וְיִזָּכֵר זִכְרוֹנֵנוּ וּפִקְדוֹנֵנוּ וְזִכְרוֹן אֲבוֹתֵינוּ · וְזִכְרוֹן מָשִׁיחַ בֶּן
דָּוִד עַבְדֶּךָ · וְזִכְרוֹן יְרוּשָׁלַיִם עִיר קָדְשֶׁךָ · וְזִכְרוֹן כָּל עַמְּךָ בֵּית
יִשְׂרָאֵל לְפָנֶיךָ · לִפְלֵיטָה וּלְטוֹבָה וּלְחֵן וּלְחֶסֶד וּלְרַחֲמִים וּלְחַיִּים
וּלְשָׁלוֹם בְּיוֹם לר"ח רֹאשׁ הַחֹדֶשׁ לפסח חַג הַמַּצוֹת לסכות חַג הַסֻּכּוֹת
הַזֶּה · זָכְרֵנוּ יְיָ אֱלֹהֵינוּ בּוֹ לְטוֹבָה וּפָקְדֵנוּ בוֹ לִבְרָכָה וְהוֹשִׁיעֵנוּ בוֹ
לְחַיִּים · וּבִדְבַר יְשׁוּעָה וְרַחֲמִים · חוּס וְחָנֵּנוּ וְרַחֵם עָלֵינוּ
וְהוֹשִׁיעֵנוּ · כִּי אֵלֶיךָ עֵינֵינוּ · כִּי אֵל מֶלֶךְ חַנּוּן וְרַחוּם אָתָּה :
וְתֶחֱזֶינָה עֵינֵינוּ בְּשׁוּבְךָ לְצִיּוֹן בְּרַחֲמִים · בָּרוּךְ אַתָּה יְיָ
הַמַּחֲזִיר שְׁכִינָתוֹ לְצִיּוֹן :

to which Heaven and earth are subject to this very day. וכל צבאם All the infinite variety of hosts in Heaven above and on earth below is one single צבא, one united host subject to the command of the One Sole Lord. And all of His Creation is מלאכתו. The Hebrew term מלאכה, is derived from מלאך, "messenger". In other words, all the individuals in the host that constitutes the Universe, singly and collectively, have been sent by God on an "errand" which they must discharge. Every creature is a "messenger" of God, serving to carry out His plan. ויכל To this visible world which He had completed in six days of creation, God added a Seventh Day as a seal of completion and as surety for the fulfillment of His purposes. This Seventh Day was to be a memorial to God Himself, to the invisible Sole Creator and Master of the world. וישבת: It was only with the coming of the Seventh Day that God ceased from all His work. Everything that God created must serve the advancement of the moral goal the realization of which God has entrusted to man. Only in order that man might fulfill this mission did God lay the world at his feet and institute the Sabbath as a memorial to teach and train man for his purpose in the world of God. ויברך: It was for this educational task that God endowed the Sabbath with the power to inspire and ennoble man, ויקדש and appointed it as an inviolable sanctity, and as an inexhaustible source of sanctity for mankind. כי בו; for it was with the Sabbath, this instrument for the training of humanity for its sacred, moral, spiritual calling that God concluded His labor of *creation* and started upon His endeavor at *training* man for the purpose of which He had created all His world.

Take pleasure, O *God* our God, in Your people Yisrael and in their prayer. Restore the sacrificial service to the Abode of Your Word in Your House, and accept Yisrael's fire offerings and their prayer with love and favor, and may the service of Your people Yisrael ever be pleasing to You.

On Rosh Chodesh and the Intermediate Days of Festivals:

Our God and God of our fathers, may our remembrance and the consideration of us, and the remembrance of our fathers, the remembrance of the anointed, the son of David Your servant, the remembrance of Yerushalayim, Your holy City, and the remembrance of all Your people, the House of Yisrael, rise and come, reach You and be seen, accepted and heard, considered and remembered for deliverance and for well-being, for favor and loving-kindness, for compassion, for life and for peace on this day of:

The New Moon — The Festival of Unleavened Bread —
The Festival of Tabernacles.

Remember us this day, O *God* our God, for good; be mindful of us for blessing, and save us for life, and in the promise of salvation and compassion spare us and favor us, for our eyes look up to You; for You, O God, are a gracious and compassionate King.

And may our eyes behold Your return to Tzion in compassion. Blessed be You *God,* Who restores Your presence to Tzion.

אלהינו ואלהי אבותינו is the prayer that God may enable the Sabbath to fulfill its purpose in our lives. רצה במנוחתנו: May our Sabbath rest be one that is in accordance with God's will; may His commandments truly serve their purpose which is our own moral hallowing, ותן חלקנו בתורתך and may we thus receive our full portion of the blessings that are inherent in the Torah of God. שבענו מטובך (Cf. Psalm 65:5 נשבעה בטוב ביתך) We pray, "May we be satisfied with that which You deem 'good', for it is only then that we may hope to be found worthy of Your salvation and that we may express the prayerful wish שמחנו בישועתך." טהר לבנו We ask God to "enable us to attain such purity of heart and attitude that we will do Your bidding without any other motive in mind than the performance of Your will," even as it is said in Psalm 103:20 of the servants round about the Heavenly Throne עושי דברו לשמוע בקול דברו. והנחילנו: The Sabbath is the spiritual heritage which originally was intended for all mankind. But when the rest of mankind

מוֹדִים אֲנַחְנוּ לָךְ שָׁאַתָּה הוּא יְיָ אֱלֹהֵינוּ וֵאלֹהֵי אֲבוֹתֵינוּ
לְעוֹלָם וָעֶד צוּר חַיֵּינוּ מָגֵן יִשְׁעֵנוּ אַתָּה הוּא לְדוֹר וָדוֹר· נוֹדֶה
לְךָ וּנְסַפֵּר תְּהִלָּתֶךָ עַל חַיֵּינוּ הַמְּסוּרִים בְּיָדֶךָ וְעַל נִשְׁמוֹתֵינוּ
הַפְּקוּדוֹת לָךְ וְעַל נִסֶּיךָ שֶׁבְּכָל יוֹם עִמָּנוּ וְעַל נִפְלְאוֹתֶיךָ וְטוֹבוֹתֶיךָ
שֶׁבְּכָל עֵת, עֶרֶב וָבֹקֶר וְצָהֳרָיִם· הַטּוֹב כִּי לֹא כָלוּ רַחֲמֶיךָ
וְהַמְרַחֵם כִּי לֹא תַמּוּ חֲסָדֶיךָ מֵעוֹלָם קִוִּינוּ לָךְ: נחנוכה על הנסים·

וְעַל־כֻּלָּם יִתְבָּרַךְ וְיִתְרוֹמַם שִׁמְךָ מַלְכֵּנוּ תָּמִיד
לְעוֹלָם וָעֶד:

On שבת שובה, add:

וּכְתוֹב לְחַיִּים טוֹבִים כָּל־בְּנֵי בְרִיתֶךָ:

וְכֹל הַחַיִּים יוֹדוּךָ סֶּלָה וִיהַלְלוּ אֶת־שִׁמְךָ בֶּאֱמֶת
הָאֵל יְשׁוּעָתֵנוּ וְעֶזְרָתֵנוּ סֶלָה· בָּרוּךְ אַתָּה יְיָ הַטּוֹב
שִׁמְךָ וּלְךָ נָאֶה לְהוֹדוֹת:

שָׁלוֹם רָב עַל־יִשְׂרָאֵל עַמְּךָ תָּשִׂים לְעוֹלָם כִּי אַתָּה הוּא מֶלֶךְ
אָדוֹן לְכָל הַשָּׁלוֹם· וְטוֹב בְּעֵינֶיךָ לְבָרֵךְ אֶת־עַמְּךָ יִשְׂרָאֵל בְּכָל־
עֵת וּבְכָל שָׁעָה בִּשְׁלוֹמֶךָ·

On שבת שובה, add:

בְּסֵפֶר חַיִּים בְּרָכָה וְשָׁלוֹם וּפַרְנָסָה טוֹבָה נִזָּכֵר וְנִכָּתֵב לְפָנֶיךָ
אֲנַחְנוּ וְכָל עַמְּךָ בֵּית יִשְׂרָאֵל לְחַיִּים טוֹבִים וּלְשָׁלוֹם· בָּרוּךְ אַתָּה
יְיָ עוֹשֶׂה הַשָּׁלוֹם:

---

scorned and neglected it, it became the portion of Israel. As the prophet puts
it (Isa. 58:14), the Sabbath is נחלת יעקב אביגו, the heritage which, according
to our Sages, is "unlimited" and which the descendants of Yaakov serenely
bear with them as a blessing in their wanderings through the world even in
the face of the harshest blows of fate, of humiliation such as is symbolized
by the very name of their ancestor Yaakov. באהבה וברצון. The statement *beahavah* is in keeping with the nature of the Sabbath, so that the word *beahavah*
is repeatedly inserted in various portions of the Yom Tov services when that
Yom Tov should coincide with the Sabbath. For the Sabbath is that day on

We gratefully avow to You that You, O *God,* are our God and the God of our fathers in all eternity. You are the Rock of our life, the Shield of our salvation, from generation to generation. We avow our thanks to You and recount Your praise, for our lives, which are committed to Your hand, and for our souls which are in Your care, and for Your miracles which are with us each day, and for Your wondrous deeds and favors that are performed at all times, evening, morning and noon. You are the Beneficent One, for Your compassion has never ceased; the Compassionate One, for Your kindnesses have never ended. Ever have we placed our hopes in You.

(על הנסים : חנוכה *On*)

For all this, O our King, may Your Name be continually blessed and exalted for all eternity. (*On* שבת שובה, *add:* and inscribe all the sons of Your covenant for a good life).

And everything that lives shall avow thanks to You and render praise to Your Name in truth as the God of our salvation and our help forever. Blessed be You *God,* "The Beneficent One" is Your Name, and to You thanksgiving is due.

Establish peace abundant upon Your people Yisrael forever, for You, O King, are the Lord of all peace, and may it be good in Your sight to bless Your people Yisrael at all times and at every hour with Your peace.

(*On* שבת שובה, *add:* May we be remembered and inscribed before You in the Book of Life, blessing, peace and good sustenance, we and all Your people, the House of Yisrael, for a good life and for peace. Blessed be You *God,* the Creator of Peace).

---

which the creature is reunited with its Creator in purity; it is the day appointed by the Creator so that His creature will not forget Him. Thus the basic characteristic of the Sabbath is *love,* the love of the creature for its Maker, and the love of the Maker, in turn, for His creation. וינוחו בה וכו'. The cessation of all business and work on the Sabbath is a *Kiddush Hashem,* a "hallowing of the Name of God," a testimonial to His creation of the world and to His supreme sovereignty over it, and a demonstration of our own obedience to Him as His creatures and His subjects.

כל המתפלל בערב שבת ואומר ויכלו מעלה עליו In Sabbath 110a we read ויכלו הכתוב כאלו נעשה שותף להקדוש ברוך הוא במעשה בראשית "He who, in his prayers that usher in the Sabbath, recites ויכלו, this original decree for the institution

בָּרוּךְ אַתָּה יְיָ הַמְבָרֵךְ אֶת־עַמּוֹ יִשְׂרָאֵל בַּשָּׁלוֹם:

אֱלֹהַי · נְצוֹר לְשׁוֹנִי מֵרָע וּשְׂפָתַי מִדַּבֵּר מִרְמָה וְלִמְקַלְלַי נַפְשִׁי
תִדּוֹם וְנַפְשִׁי כֶּעָפָר לַכֹּל תִּהְיֶה: פְּתַח לִבִּי בְּתוֹרָתֶךָ וּבְמִצְוֹתֶיךָ
תִּרְדּוֹף נַפְשִׁי וְכָל הַחוֹשְׁבִים עָלַי רָעָה מְהֵרָה הָפֵר עֲצָתָם וְקַלְקֵל
מַחֲשַׁבְתָּם · עֲשֵׂה לְמַעַן שְׁמֶךָ · עֲשֵׂה לְמַעַן יְמִינֶךָ · עֲשֵׂה לְמַעַן
קְדֻשָּׁתֶךָ · עֲשֵׂה לְמַעַן תּוֹרָתֶךָ · לְמַעַן יֵחָלְצוּן יְדִידֶיךָ הוֹשִׁיעָה
יְמִינְךָ וַעֲנֵנִי: יִהְיוּ לְרָצוֹן אִמְרֵי־פִי וְהֶגְיוֹן לִבִּי לְפָנֶיךָ יְיָ צוּרִי
וְגוֹאֲלִי: עֹשֶׂה שָׁלוֹם בִּמְרוֹמָיו הוּא יַעֲשֶׂה שָׁלוֹם עָלֵינוּ וְעַל כָּל־
יִשְׂרָאֵל וְאִמְרוּ אָמֵן :

יְהִי רָצוֹן לְפָנֶיךָ יְיָ אֱלֹהֵינוּ וֵאלֹהֵי אֲבוֹתֵינוּ שֶׁיִּבָּנֶה
בֵּית הַמִּקְדָּשׁ בִּמְהֵרָה בְיָמֵינוּ וְתֵן חֶלְקֵנוּ בְּתוֹרָתֶךָ :

אֵין הַחַזָּן מַחֲזִיר הַתְּפִלָּה אֲבָל אוֹמֵר בִּרְכַּת מֵעֵין שֶׁבַע וְאֵינוֹ אוֹמֵר תְּחִלָּה וִיכַלּוּ וְהִקְהַל עוֹנִין
עִמּוֹ. בִּרְכַּת מֵעֵין ז' אוֹמְרִין גַּם בְּשַׁבָּת שֶׁאַחַר י"ט וְכֵן בְּי"ט שֶׁחָל לִהְיוֹת בְּשַׁבָּת (חוּץ
מִלֵּיל רִאשׁוֹן דְּפֶסַח)

The Reader repeats וִיכַלּוּ [p. 272] *together with the congregation.*
Then he continues as follows:

יח בָּרוּךְ אַתָּה יְיָ אֱלֹהֵינוּ וֵאלֹהֵי אֲבוֹתֵינוּ אֱלֹהֵי
אַבְרָהָם אֱלֹהֵי יִצְחָק וֵאלֹהֵי יַעֲקֹב הָאֵל הַגָּדוֹל
הַגִּבּוֹר וְהַנּוֹרָא אֵל עֶלְיוֹן קֹנֵה שָׁמַיִם וָאָרֶץ:

of the Sabbath, is regarded by God as a co-worker, as it were, in His work
of creation." The works that were brought forth on the other six days were
completed by virtue of the very act of their creation. But the Divinely-given
Seventh Day, the spiritual memorial to God's creation and majesty, has true

Blessed be You *God,* Who blesses Your people Yisrael with peace.

My God, guard my tongue from evil and my lips from speaking falsehood. Let my soul be silent to those who curse me, and let my soul be as the dust to all things. Open my heart to Your Torah, and may my soul earnestly strive after Your commandments. But as for all those who plot evil against me, thwart their counsel and frustrate their intentions. Do it for the sake of Your Name; do it for the sake of Your right hand; do it for the sake of Your holiness; do it for the sake of Your Torah; therefore set free those whom You have found worthy of Your love. Let Your right hand be seen in salvation and answer me! May the words of my mouth and the meditation of my heart be pleasing before Your countenance, O *God,* my Rock and my Redeemer. May He Who makes peace in His high places, make peace for us and for all of Yisrael, and say: Amen.

The Reader repeats ויכלו *[p. 272] together with the congregation.*
Then he continues as follows:

(*Reader*): Blessed be You *God,* our God and God of our fathers, God of Avraham, God of Yitzchak and God of Yaakov, the great, mighty and awesome God, God the Most High, the Owner of Heaven and Earth.

---

being only once it enters and is received into the hearts and minds of men. Forgotten and neglected by the human spirit, the Sabbath would be as good as non-existent. The weekly reading of the Divine decree ordaining the Sabbath is thus an act of collaboration, as it were, in behalf of the preservation of the Sabbath on earth, a שותפות להקדוש ברוך הוא במעשה בראשית. For this reason *Vayechulu* is repeated aloud by Reader and Congregation in unison after the completion of the *Tefillah* of the Sabbath.

ברוך Our House of God is not only a *beth tefillah* but also a *beth knes-seth.* We are not only to meet God there, but, also to join with our community in His presence in the spirit of brotherhood. This cultivation of a sense of oneness with our community is so essential a part of the purpose of our prayers that, in fact, most of our prayers are not written for personal use by the individual but are meant to be recited by the individual in his capactiy as a member of the larger community. We are to seek the fulfillment of all our personal yearnings and prayers only in conjunction with the welfare of the entire community. Through this cultivation of a sense of brotherhood with

ק׳ מָגֵן אָבוֹת בִּדְבָרוֹ מְחַיֵּה מֵתִים בְּמַאֲמָרוֹ הָאֵל (נט״ז הַמֶּלֶךְ)
הַקָּדוֹשׁ שֶׁאֵין כָּמוֹהוּ הַמֵּנִיחַ לְעַמּוֹ בְּיוֹם שַׁבַּת קָדְשׁוֹ כִּי בָם
רָצָה לְהָנִיחַ לָהֶם · לְפָנָיו נַעֲבוֹד בְּיִרְאָה וָפַחַד וְנוֹדֶה לִשְׁמוֹ בְּכָל-
יוֹם תָּמִיד מֵעֵין הַבְּרָכוֹת · אֵל הַהוֹדָאוֹת אֲדוֹן הַשָּׁלוֹם מְקַדֵּשׁ
הַשַּׁבָּת וּמְבָרֵךְ שְׁבִיעִי וּמֵנִיחַ בִּקְדֻשָּׁה לְעַם מְדֻשְּׁנֵי עֹנֶג זֵכֶר
לְמַעֲשֵׂה בְרֵאשִׁית :

ח׳ אֱלֹהֵינוּ וֵאלֹהֵי אֲבוֹתֵינוּ רְצֵה בִמְנוּחָתֵנוּ קַדְּשֵׁנוּ בְּמִצְוֹתֶיךָ
וְתֵן חֶלְקֵנוּ בְּתוֹרָתֶךָ שַׂבְּעֵנוּ מִטּוּבֶךָ וְשַׂמְּחֵנוּ בִּישׁוּעָתֶךָ וְטַהֵר
לִבֵּנוּ לְעָבְדְּךָ בֶּאֱמֶת וְהַנְחִילֵנוּ יְיָ אֱלֹהֵינוּ בְּאַהֲבָה וּבְרָצוֹן שַׁבַּת
קָדְשֶׁךָ וְיָנוּחוּ בָהּ יִשְׂרָאֵל מְקַדְּשֵׁי שְׁמֶךָ · בָּרוּךְ אַתָּה יְיָ מְקַדֵּשׁ
הַשַּׁבָּת : ק״ת.

On יו״ט, שבת חול המועד as well as on שבת or ערב שבת which coincides with במה מדליקין is not said:

בַּמֶּה מַדְלִיקִין וּבַמָּה אֵין מַדְלִיקִין, אֵין מַדְלִיקִין לֹא בְלֶכֶשׁ
וְלֹא בְחֹסֶן וְלֹא בְכַלָּךְ, וְלֹא בִפְתִילַת הָאִידָן וְלֹא בִפְתִילַת
הַמִּדְבָּר, וְלֹא בִירוֹקָה שֶׁעַל פְּנֵי הַמָּיִם, וְלֹא בְזֶפֶת וְלֹא בְשַׁעֲוָה,
וְלֹא בְשֶׁמֶן קִיק וְלֹא בְשֶׁמֶן שְׂרֵפָה, וְלֹא בְאַלְיָה וְלֹא בְחֵלֶב· נַחוּם
הַמָּדִי אוֹמֵר מַדְלִיקִין בְּחֵלֶב מְבֻשָּׁל, וַחֲכָמִים אוֹמְרִים אֶחָד

the larger group, the individual worshipper comes to feel respect and consideration for his fellow-congregants. We are told in Berachoth 5b that if
two men enter a house of prayer, the one finishing his prayers first must
not leave the synagogue until his fellow-worshipper has completed the order
of service. If he does not observe this courtesy, his prayer will be rejected as
worthless, because he has acted as if he had thought he was the only person
worthy of consideration by God. It is because of this reason that, together

(Congregation) The Shield of our Fathers with His Word, Who revives the dead with His promise, the holy God *(on* שבת שובה: holy King), to Whom none can compare; Who gives rest to His people on His holy Sabbath Day because He has found them worthy of His favor to grant them rest. Him will we serve with reverence and awe and daily avow thanks to His Name in accordance with the blessings appropriate for each day. O God of [utterances of] thanksgiving, Lord of peace, Who sanctifies the Sabbath and blesses the Seventh Day and grants rest in holiness to the people which draws blissful delight from the memorial to the work of Creation.

(Reader): Our God and God of our fathers, take pleasure in our rest, hallow us by Your commandments and grant our portion in Your Torah. Satisfy us from Your good, gladden us with Your salvation, purify our hearts to serve You in truth, and in Your love and favor, O *God* our God, let Your holy Sabbath remain our inheritance, and may Yisrael, who sanctify Your Name, rest on it. Blessed be You *God,* Who hallows the Sabbath.

---

with the Reader, we repeat in abridged form the contents of *sheva berachoth,* ברכה אחת מעין שבע (and, according to Tosaphoth ibid. 4b, also the ברוך ה' לעולם וכו' יראו עינינו וכו' at the conclusion of the weekday evening service), in order thus to allow time for latecomers to finish their prayers. מעין הברכות in accordance with the specific blessings that are in keeping with the character of the day. (See Berachoth 40a.)

במה מדליקין Through the truths which it teaches us and which it has us express by our cessation from all our labors for twenty-four hours, the Sabbath seeks to bring serene brightness and light into our hearts and minds. For this reason as the Sabbath enters, the rooms of our physical habitations should also create an impression of shining brightness in keeping with the spirit of this holy day. Hence the kindling of lights to welcome the Sabbath is part of the commandment of Sabbath observance; it is a duty which, as is explained in this excerpt from the Mishna, is incumbent particularly upon our women, the priestesses of our homes. There should be light in every room of our homes that we are likely to enter on the Sabbath Eve, and it is particularly important that there be lights on the table at which we eat our Sabbath dinner. For it is not in the synagogues but in our homes, where our family life unfolds, that the Sabbath is truly meant to enter and to be observed. It is customary to have at least two lights burning at our Sabbath table to symbolize the dual aspect of Sabbath observance, *zachor* and *shamor,* that is emphasized in the

מְבַשֵּׁל וְאֶחָד שֶׁאֵינוּ מְבַשֵּׁל אֵין מַדְלִיקִין בּוֹ: (ב) אֵין מַדְלִיקִין
בְּשֶׁמֶן שְׂרֵפָה בְּיוֹם טוֹב · רַבִּי יִשְׁמָעֵאל אוֹמֵר אֵין מַדְלִיקִין
בְּעִטְרָן מִפְּנֵי כְּבוֹד הַשַּׁבָּת · וַחֲכָמִים מַתִּירִין בְּכָל הַשְּׁמָנִים
בְּשֶׁמֶן שֻׁמְשְׁמִין בְּשֶׁמֶן אֱגוֹזִים בְּשֶׁמֶן צְנוֹנוֹת בְּשֶׁמֶן דָּגִים בְּשֶׁמֶן
פַּקּוּעוֹת בְּעִטְרָן וּבְנִפְט · רַבִּי טַרְפוֹן אוֹמֵר אֵין מַדְלִיקִין אֶלָּא
בְּשֶׁמֶן זַיִת בִּלְבָד: (ג) כָּל הַיּוֹצֵא מִן הָעֵץ אֵין מַדְלִיקִין בּוֹ אֶלָּא
פִשְׁתָּן · וְכָל הַיּוֹצֵא מִן הָעֵץ אֵינוֹ מְטַמֵּא טֻמְאַת אֹהָלִים אֶלָּא
פִשְׁתָּן · פְּתִילַת הַבֶּגֶד שֶׁקִּפְּלָהּ וְלֹא הִבְהֲבָהּ, רַבִּי אֱלִיעֶזֶר אוֹמֵר
טְמֵאָה הִיא וְאֵין מַדְלִיקִין בָּהּ, רַבִּי עֲקִיבָא אוֹמֵר טְהוֹרָה הִיא
וּמַדְלִיקִין בָּהּ: (ד) לֹא יִקּוֹב אָדָם שְׁפוֹפֶרֶת שֶׁל בֵּיצָה וִימַלְאֶנָּה
שֶׁמֶן וְיִתְּנֶנָּה עַל פִּי הַנֵּר בִּשְׁבִיל שֶׁתְּהֵא מְנַטֶּפֶת וַאֲפִילּוּ הִיא
שֶׁל חֶרֶס, וְרַבִּי יְהוּדָה מַתִּיר · אֲבָל אִם חִבְּרָהּ הַיּוֹצֵר מִתְּחִלָּה

Sabbath hymn with which we usher in this holy day on Friday night, so
that the precepts *shamor* and *zachor* may combine to be for us one source of
serenity and good cheer. But it is only the cessation of all workday activity,
the *shemirah* of the Sabbath by *isur melachah* that lends the Sabbath its true,
genuine character. This is the kind of Sabbath observance which God explicitly
appointed as *oth,* a "sign between Him and ourselves," a sign by which He
will know that we truly render Him homage as our Lord and Maker. Thus
every single act of work in violation of the Sabbath would be an actual denial
of such homage, a sin for which atonement cannot be made by any word of
song or prayer, a transgression which degrades to the level of base blasphemy
every word of homage mouthed by the lips of him who is guilty of it. For
this reason it behooves us to take great care, above all, that the arrangements
which we make to celebrate and beautify the Sabbath should not lead to the
performance of such work as is forbidden on that day, and it is our duty

מָתָר מִפְּנֵי שֶׁהוּא כְלִי אֶחָד· לֹא יְמַלֵּא אָדָם קְעָרָה שֶׁמֶן וְיִתְּנֶנָּה
בְּצַד הַנֵּר וְיִתֵּן רֹאשׁ הַפְּתִילָה בְּתוֹכָהּ בִּשְׁבִיל שֶׁתְּהֵא שׁוֹאֶבֶת,
וְרַבִּי יְהוּדָה מַתִּיר: (ה) הַמְכַבֶּה אֶת הַנֵּר מִפְּנֵי שֶׁהוּא מִתְיָרֵא
מִפְּנֵי גוֹיִם מִפְּנֵי לִסְטִים מִפְּנֵי רוּחַ רָעָה אוֹ בִּשְׁבִיל הַחוֹלֶה
שֶׁיִּישָׁן, פָּטוּר· כְּחָס עַל הַנֵּר כְּחָס עַל הַשֶּׁמֶן כְּחָס עַל הַפְּתִילָה,
חַיָּב· רַבִּי יוֹסֵי פּוֹטֵר בְּכֻלָּן חוּץ מִן הַפְּתִילָה מִפְּנֵי שֶׁהוּא עוֹשָׂה
פֶּחָם : (ו) עַל שָׁלֹשׁ עֲבֵרוֹת נָשִׁים מֵתוֹת בִּשְׁעַת לֵדָתָן, עַל שֶׁאֵינָן
זְהִירוֹת בְּנִדָּה בְּחַלָּה וּבְהַדְלָקַת הַנֵּר: (ז) שְׁלֹשָׁה דְבָרִים צָרִיךְ
אָדָם לוֹמַר בְּתוֹךְ בֵּיתוֹ עֶרֶב שַׁבָּת עִם חֲשֵׁכָה· עִשַּׂרְתֶּם עֵרַבְתֶּם
הַדְלִיקוּ אֶת הַנֵּר· סָפֵק חֲשֵׁכָה סָפֵק אֵינָהּ חֲשֵׁכָה, אֵין מְעַשְּׂרִין
אֶת הַוַּדַּאי, וְאֵין מַטְבִּילִין אֶת הַכֵּלִים, וְאֵין מַדְלִיקִין אֶת הַנֵּרוֹת,
אֲבָל מְעַשְּׂרִין אֶת הַדְּמַאי וּמְעָרְבִין וְטוֹמְנִין אֶת הַחַמִּין:

to take every precaution in advance in order to avoid any violation of the
Sabbath. Such precautionary measures are particularly imperative in connection with the kindling of the Sabbath lights which has been commanded
us as part of our Sabbath observance. The excerpt from the Mishna beginning
with *Bameh madlikin* which we read before we bring the Sabbath into our
homes is an ordinance of profound significance. It deals primarily with the
care that should be taken to select only such wicks and oils for the Sabbath
lights as will burn properly so that we will not perchance be brought to
violate the Sabbath by adding other fuel to the flame. The cessation of all
labor is basic to our Sabbath observance which takes precedence over all other
festivals. Therefore, the importance of this reminder should never be under-
estimated, not only in connection with the kindling of the Sabbath lights, but
also in connection with every other aspect of Sabbath celebration, as the
Sabbath day enters into our homes.

אָמַר רַבִּי אֶלְעָזָר אָמַר רַבִּי חֲנִינָא · תַּלְמִידֵי חֲכָמִים מַרְבִּים
שָׁלוֹם בָּעוֹלָם : שֶׁנֶּאֱמַר וְכָל בָּנַיִךְ לִמּוּדֵי יְיָ וְרַב שְׁלוֹם בָּנָיִךְ :
אַל תִּקְרָא בָּנָיִךְ אֶלָּא בּוֹנָיִךְ : שָׁלוֹם רָב לְאֹהֲבֵי תוֹרָתֶךָ וְאֵין
לָמוֹ מִכְשׁוֹל : יְהִי־שָׁלוֹם בְּחֵילֵךְ שַׁלְוָה בְּאַרְמְנוֹתָיִךְ : לְמַעַן אַחַי
וְרֵעָי אֲדַבְּרָה־נָּא שָׁלוֹם בָּךְ : לְמַעַן בֵּית־יְיָ אֱלֹהֵינוּ אֲבַקְשָׁה
טוֹב לָךְ : יְיָ עֹז לְעַמּוֹ יִתֵּן יְיָ יְבָרֵךְ אֶת־עַמּוֹ בַשָּׁלוֹם : קדיש דרבנן

הַמַ"ן מקדש נבי"ה"כ בשבתית וי"ט חון עלי"ל חֹ' וכ' של פסח. ואימרין עלינו ,קַ"י ,יגדל.

ספירת העומר—page 749

On שבת *and* יו"ט *the children are blessed by pronouncing:*

לבנים : יְשִׂמְךָ אֱלֹהִים כְּאֶפְרַיִם וְכִמְנַשֶּׁה :

לבנות : יְשִׂמֵךְ אֱלֹהִים כְּשָׂרָה רִבְקָה רָחֵל וְלֵאָה :

After returning home from the Synagogue, the following is said:

שָׁלוֹם עֲלֵיכֶם מַלְאֲכֵי הַשָּׁרֵת מַלְאֲכֵי עֶלְיוֹן

מִמֶּלֶךְ מַלְכֵי הַמְּלָכִים הַקָּדוֹשׁ בָּרוּךְ הוּא : ג"פ

בּוֹאֲכֶם לְשָׁלוֹם מַלְאֲכֵי הַשָּׁלוֹם מַלְאֲכֵי עֶלְיוֹן

אמר ר' אלעזר Several tractates of the Talmud; namely Berachoth, Yeba-
moth, Nazir, and Kerithoth, end with these sentences. The thought expressed
here is the following: The Rabbis regarded themselves not as *chachamim*,
as creators and possessors of wisdom, but only as *talmidei chachamim*, as
the *"disciples* of the wise" from whom they had received the traditions of
wisdom. The spiritual achievements of these great teachers not only benefitted
our relationship with God but had a most beneficial effect also upon the
relationship of man to man, creating and multiplying the blessings of peace.
Our Rabbis have taught us how to subordinate all of the relationships of our
lives to God and to God alone, and how to let our lives be regulated and
arranged by Him. By so guiding us, the teachings of our Sages have cleansed

Rabbi Eleazar said, "Rabbi Chanina said, 'The disciples of the wise increase peace in the world, for it is said, "... and [if] all your sons are disciples of *God,* then the peace of your sons shall be abundant" (Isa. 54:13). Do not read this *banayich* (your sons), but *bonayich* (your builders). Peace abundant will be theirs who love Your Torah and no ill fortune shall befall them. Let there be peace in your precincts, serenity within your palaces. For the sake of my brethren and companions I will wish that peace be yours. For the sake of the House of *God,* our God, I will pray for your good. To His people, however, *God* will grant power to be victorious over all, *God* will bless His people with peace.

---

our attitudes and beliefs of that egotism which regards one's own selfish wants and desires as the sole point of departure and standard for every endeavor and achievement. Such egotism, if allowed to continue, eventually will pit plan against plan and will against will and may well cause human society to be crushed in the struggle of man against man. It is true that the use of force may put a temporary halt to the havoc wrought by such a universal search for the gratification of selfish desire. But it is only through the voluntary and happy subordination of all things to the one counsel and the one will of the One God, as taught by the traditions of Jewish wisdom, that the struggle of greed against greed can be truly resolved—and universal, permanent peace brought about. If our sons will become disciples of the Torah of God, then our בנים, our "sons" will become our בונים, our "builders". In fact, the very derivation of the word בנים, בן from בנה "to build" is in keeping with the true purpose of our children to be both builders and building blocks participating in the completion of the eternal edifice of mankind as orginally envisioned by God, the בנין עדי עד as it is called in our ברכות נישואין, which it is God's will that man should erect. It is for this reason that our *talmidei chachamim* are called also *banaim,* "builders" who see to it that all human relationships be built up in accordance with the blueprint of God, the one true and supreme Architect of all our lives and achievements on earth. These sentences alluding to the blessings of peace as the fruit of all true homage to God are the message with which we go forth from our Sabbath services, evening and morning, to return to our homes, to our families and to our communities.

נ"פ : מִמֶּלֶךְ מַלְכֵי הַמְּלָכִים הַקָּדוֹשׁ בָּרוּךְ הוּא

בָּרְכוּנִי לְשָׁלוֹם מַלְאֲכֵי הַשָּׁלוֹם מַלְאֲכֵי עֶלְיוֹן

נ"פ : מִמֶּלֶךְ מַלְכֵי הַמְּלָכִים הַקָּדוֹשׁ בָּרוּךְ הוּא

צֵאתְכֶם לְשָׁלוֹם מַלְאֲכֵי הַשָּׁלוֹם מַלְאֲכֵי עֶלְיוֹן

נ"פ : מִמֶּלֶךְ מַלְכֵי הַמְּלָכִים הַקָּדוֹשׁ בָּרוּךְ הוּא

כִּי מַלְאָכָיו יְצַוֶּה־לָּךְ לִשְׁמָרְךָ בְּכָל־דְּרָכֶיךָ :

יְיָ יִשְׁמָר־צֵאתְךָ וּבוֹאֶךָ מֵעַתָּה וְעַד־עוֹלָם :

Then the following is said:

משלי ל"א י'
אֵשֶׁת־חַיִל מִי יִמְצָא וְרָחֹק מִפְּנִינִים מִכְרָהּ : בָּטַח בָּהּ לֵב

בַּעְלָהּ וְשָׁלָל לֹא יֶחְסָר : גְּמָלַתְהוּ טוֹב וְלֹא־רָע כֹּל יְמֵי חַיֶּיהָ :

דָּרְשָׁה צֶמֶר וּפִשְׁתִּים וַתַּעַשׂ בְּחֵפֶץ כַּפֶּיהָ : הָיְתָה כָּאֳנִיּוֹת סוֹחֵר

מִמֶּרְחָק תָּבִיא לַחְמָהּ : וַתָּקָם בְּעוֹד לַיְלָה וַתִּתֵּן טֶרֶף־לְבֵיתָהּ

וְחֹק לְנַעֲרֹתֶיהָ : זָמְמָה שָׂדֶה וַתִּקָּחֵהוּ מִפְּרִי כַפֶּיהָ נָטְעָ* כָּרֶם :

_____

*) נטעה ק'

1. שלל The literal meaning of שלל is "booty"; hence it implies a gain to which one had no claim and which one had never expected. Thus והיתה לך נפשו לשלל. The trust of her husband was not only justified at all times, but actually surpassed by her actions.

He who finds a valiant wife—her price is far more than that of pearls.

The heart of her husband trusted in her and he never lacked gain.[1]

She did him good and never evil all the days of her life.[2]

She sought out wool and flax and worked it with the willingness of her hands;[3]

She was like a merchant ship; she brought her bread from afar[4],

It was still night when she arose and gave food to her household and work to her maids.

She saved for [the purchase of] a field[5] and bought it, and she planted a vineyard from the fruit of [the work of] her hands.

---

2. A person can do much good to another, and still cause him moments of chagrin and hurt by personal whims and caprices, and by the manner in which he acts toward him. But the woman to whom this hymn is dedicated gave her husband nothing but happiness and never even a moment of grief all the days of her life.

3. She was industriousness and assiduity incarnate. She sought out material in order to process it "with the willingness of her hands." It is significant that the term used here is not חפץ ידיה as we might have expected, but חפץ כפיה. The term כפים denotes not the hand as a working, creative organ, but actually the "palm of the hand," the hand as an instrument for grasping or enclosing an object. In other words, chefetz kapehah implies that her hands could not bear to be idle, and even if her palms were folded at rest, they were "willing" and anxious to work.

4. She was always busy and because of her providential planning for even the remotest contingencies she managed to provide all manner of advantages for her household.

חָגְרָה בְעוֹז מָתְנֶיהָ וַתְּאַמֵּץ זְרוֹעֹתֶיהָ: טָעֲמָה כִּי־טוֹב סַחְרָהּ לֹא־
יִכְבֶּה בַלַּיְלָ נֵרָהּ: יָדֶיהָ שִׁלְּחָה בַכִּישׁוֹר וְכַפֶּיהָ תָּמְכוּ פָלֶךְ:
כַּפָּהּ פָּרְשָׂה לֶעָנִי וְיָדֶיהָ שִׁלְּחָה לָאֶבְיוֹן: לֹא־תִירָא לְבֵיתָהּ מִשָּׁלֶג
כִּי כָל־בֵּיתָהּ לָבֻשׁ שָׁנִים: מַרְבַדִּים עָשְׂתָה־לָּהּ שֵׁשׁ וְאַרְגָּמָן
לְבוּשָׁהּ: נוֹדָע בַּשְּׁעָרִים בַּעְלָהּ בְּשִׁבְתּוֹ עִם־זִקְנֵי־אָרֶץ: סָדִין
עָשְׂתָה וַתִּמְכֹּר וַחֲגוֹר נָתְנָה לַכְּנַעֲנִי: עֹז וְהָדָר לְבוּשָׁהּ וַתִּשְׂחַק
לְיוֹם אַחֲרוֹן: פִּיהָ פָּתְחָה בְחָכְמָה וְתוֹרַת־חֶסֶד עַל־לְשׁוֹנָהּ:

בלילה כ' (°

---

5. The literal meaning of זמם is "to produce great and far-reaching achievements from small and seemingly humble beginnings." Here it implies that the woman, through constant thrift, managed to accumulate savings sufficient to purchase a field.

6. She was not robust or strong by nature; she "made herself" strong. It was her zeal and her sense of duty that gave her strength and might.

7. During the winter all the members of her household were dressed in wool, but she needed warm coverings only at night when she rested. During the day when she was busily at work no one ever saw her dressed in anything but linen. Whatever woolen garments she wore served only as ornaments. Her constant activity kept her from feeling the cold.

8. When her husband sat in the councils of the city or of the nation, he was pointed out as the husband of the valiant woman whose moral and spiritual influence was discernible in the words and actions of the man in public life. Thus through the voice of her husband, the fine example she set and her prudent, wise counsel became a beneficial force in the affairs of the community.

9. If this verse were meant only to laud her profitable endeavors to provide for the welfare of her household, it would not fit into the context of

She girded herself with might and made her arms strong.[6]

She found that her endeavor was good; now her lamp did not go out at night.

Now she put her hands to the spindle and her hand held the distaff,

But she also opened her hand to the poor and stretched out her hands to the needy.

She did not fear frost for her household; all her household was clothed in fine wool;

She prepared beds for herself, but her clothing was of linen and purple.[7]

Her husband was known in the public gatherings when he sat with the elders of the land.[8]

She made a cloth and sold it, and she gave a belt to the peddler.[9]

Strength and beauty were her garb, and smiling she faced the last day.[10]

She opened her mouth with wisdom and the teaching of loving-kindness was upon her tongue.

---

the hymn which extols the woman's moral and spiritual influence and it would then have been more appropriate at the very beginning where the thrifty manner in which she managed her household is described. Fortunately the statement וחגור נתנה לכנעני indicates the necessity for a different interpretation of this verse. נתן does not mean "to sell", but denotes the very opposite of "selling". (Cf. לגר תתגנה או מכור לנכרי) Accordingly, this sentence seems intended to explain how she managed to procure the means for the charity she practiced. She wanted to help her fellow men with her own strength and with the fruit of her own labors. She would spin thread and use it to weave a cloth. As for the thread which was left over, the product of the work of her own hands through which she raised the value of the original raw material, she did not simply give it away in its natural state. Instead, she fashioned it into a belt which she gave as a gift to the poor peddler, who stood to profit by it much more than had she given him the proceeds of the sale or if she had simply given the belt to a beggar. Thus she was conscientious and

צוֹפִיָּה הֲלִיכוֹת בֵּיתָהּ וְלֶחֶם עַצְלוּת לֹא תֹאכֵל: קָמוּ בָנֶיהָ וַיְאַשְּׁרוּהָ
בַּעְלָהּ וַיְהַלְלָהּ: רַבּוֹת בָּנוֹת עָשׂוּ חָיִל וְאַתְּ עָלִית עַל־כֻּלָּנָה:
שֶׁקֶר הַחֵן וְהֶבֶל הַיֹּפִי אִשָּׁה יִרְאַת־יְהֹוָה הִיא תִתְהַלָּל: תְּנוּ־
לָהּ מִפְּרִי־יָדֶיהָ וִיהַלְלוּהָ בַשְּׁעָרִים מַעֲשֶׂיהָ:

(* הליכות ק'.

---

charitable at the same time, and knew how to make use of the fruits of her labor in such a manner as to give the greatest possible benefit to her fellow-men. Hence the purpose of this verse is to give only one example of how the "valiant woman's" work, her fear of God coupled with prudence, proved to be of practical value and provided a shining example for her husband who was to apply the same principles in his deliberations in the councils of his community.

10. The conscientiousness and kindness which shine forth from the example just given were basic to her entire personality. These qualities made up the strength (actually the resoluteness) and the beauty עז והדר which constituted her character, and that is the reason why she could face even the last day of her life with a smile.

This is a splendid picture indeed of the life and the work of a Jewish homemaker. Even if from all the past history of our womanhood, the word of the Sacred Scriptures would have preserved for us nothing else but this one glorious testimonial, this one hymn in itself would be a most forceful refutation of the fable fabricated by inconceivable thoughtlessness that the Jewish woman of ancient history had been enslaved and degraded after the fashion of Oriental women. Where is there a European woman of the present century who would not look upon this portrayal from the remote past of Jewish history as a shining ideal which it would be the greatest bliss even only to approximate in her own life?

She kept constant watch over the ways of her household, and would never eat the bread of idleness.

Therefore now her sons rise up and laud her, her husband, and he praises her:

"Many women have done valiantly,
But you have excelled them all.
Charm is deceit and beauty is vain;
A woman who fears *God* brings praise upon herself.
Give her of the fruit of her hands,
So that her works may praise her in the gates."

What, then, is the position of the Jewish woman? She is her husband's trusted friend and she makes him happy. His heart is secure in his trust in her and she is the inspiration behind his greatest achievements.

She enjoys full independence as the manager and director of her household. But she wants to be more than that. She is not content simply to take her husband's earnings and to use them for her home and for the maintenance and comfort of her household. Instead, she makes her own economic contribution to the prosperity of her home, and so, of her own free will, she becomes an active partner in her husband's toil and labor.

Constant activity is her element, doing good her delight; wisdom dwells upon her lips and her every word and action is a lesson in selfless love and devotion.

She is the ever-alert watchman over her own household and at the same time the quiet wise counselor of her husband in matters affecting the welfare of her entire community.

The memory of what she has been will live on forever in the hearts of her husband and her children who, throughout their lives, will respectfully rise at the remembrance of her and will never tire of praising her. Her memory will live on, too, even outside her immediate family, in the hearts of all her community as an eternal praise and a valiant example to be followed by future generations.

Happy and immortal is the people which can boast of having produced wives and mothers such as these.

הִנְנִי מוּכָן וּמְזֻמָּן לְקַיֵּם מִצְוַת עֲשֵׂה לְקַדֵּשׁ
עַל הַיַּיִן כַּכָּתוּב זָכוֹר וְשָׁמוֹר זָכְרֵהוּ עַל הַיָּיִן :

בלחש וַיְהִי־עֶרֶב וַיְהִי־בֹקֶר נקול יוֹם הַשִּׁשִּׁי : וַיְכֻלּוּ הַשָּׁמַיִם
וְהָאָרֶץ וְכָל־צְבָאָם : וַיְכַל אֱלֹהִים בַּיּוֹם הַשְּׁבִיעִי מְלַאכְתּוֹ אֲשֶׁר
עָשָׂה וַיִּשְׁבֹּת בַּיּוֹם הַשְּׁבִיעִי מִכָּל־מְלַאכְתּוֹ אֲשֶׁר עָשָׂה : וַיְבָרֶךְ
אֱלֹהִים אֶת־יוֹם הַשְּׁבִיעִי וַיְקַדֵּשׁ אֹתוֹ כִּי בוֹ שָׁבַת מִכָּל־מְלַאכְתּוֹ
אֲשֶׁר־בָּרָא אֱלֹהִים לַעֲשׂוֹת :

קידוש "Remember the Sabbath day to keep it holy." It was with these words (Exod. 20:8) that God commanded us to remember the Sabbath when He gave us His Law. Whenever the Sabbath, the day which had been forgotten and thus forfeited by the rest of mankind, enters into our midst, we are to recall to ourselves and to our families the purpose of the Seventh Day, to be holy in our midst. But even though we have already declared in words of prayer this holy purpose of the Sabbath and the Divine decree which originally ordained it in our midst, the true observance and celebration of the Sabbath should take place not in our synagogues but in our homes. For it is not in our houses of worship and at our Divine services, but in the rooms where our family lives unfold and where our everyday business activities go on that, by refraining from all weekday pursuits, we must demonstrate that we are indeed serious about doing homage to the Sabbath, and that we will gladly and conscientiously pay it that tribute which is due it as a sacred institution appointed by God. Remember: this homage should be performed not only conscientiously, but gladly. If this entails the complete cessation on our part of every activity of gainful occupation, we should not feel crushed and saddened as if this constituted a sacrifice of our independence and an abdication of our power. Instead, this total submission of all our being, of our desires and our possessions to the will of God, the merger of all our little transitory endeavors and achievements into the one great Will of God, should sustain us, uplift our spirits beyond all our own little troubles, fill us with

And it was evening and it was morning; the Sixth Day. And Heaven and earth and all their host were completed; then, with the Seventh Day, God completed His work which He had made, and with the Seventh Day He ceased from all of His work which He had made. And God blessed the Seventh Day and made it holy, for with it He had ceased from all of His work which He, God, had brought into existence in order to continue the work of creation upon it.

---

the purest joy of life and impel us on to new creative acivity. In fact, it is only such dedication on our part to the will of God that can give us true joy of living and the blissful knowledge that we are living our lives in the presence of God. To the Jew the Sabbath does not represent a loss; instead, he views it as the sole true, genuine and sure gain that he can draw from the urn of life. Long ago, the Prophet Isaiah said, "If, because of the Sabbath, you will restrain your foot from pursuing your odinary endeavors on My holy day, and if you will call the Sabbath a delight, if you have honored the day that was sanctified by God, and if you honor it by refraining from the completion of your errands, by desisting from your weekday pursuits even in your speech, then you will feel delight in God; I shall cause you to ascend to the high places of the earth and enjoy the inheritance of your father Yaakov for the mouth of God has spoken it" (58:13, 14). This עוֹנֶג, this sense of "delight" with which the Sabbath is to bless us, finds its visible expression in the extraordinary pleasure with which we partake of our Sabbath meal, a feast which must therefore be opened by the *Kiddush,* the recital of the original ordinance that sanctified the Sabbath. It is this קידוש במקום סעודה, this Kiddush which is recited at the place where we partake of the Sabbath meal, that is the true *Kiddush* of the Sabbath. The Kiddush which we recite in the synagogue originated in ancient times when transients were served their Sabbath meals by the community in a room adjoining the synagogue. It was for the benefit of those guests of the community that the Reader read the Kiddush. May the fact that we have retained this Kiddush as part of our synagogue service to this very day serve as a reminder to us of the hospitality which it has been the duty of the Jewish community at all times to extend to the stranger and the transient.

The word כוס, "cup", is employed in our Scriptures to symbolize every measure and decree appointed for us by God. Thus, too, the Kiddush, the declaration of the sanctity of the purpose of the Sabbath, which is also a Divine decree and which we are to accept and take to our hearts, must be pronounced over a *kos shel yayin,* a "cup" of wine.

סַבְרִי מָרָנָן וְרַבָּנָן וְרַבּוֹתַי

בָּרוּךְ אַתָּה יְיָ אֱלֹהֵינוּ מֶלֶךְ הָעוֹלָם בּוֹרֵא פְּרִי הַגָּפֶן :

בָּרוּךְ אַתָּה יְיָ אֱלֹהֵינוּ מֶלֶךְ הָעוֹלָם אֲשֶׁר קִדְּשָׁנוּ בְּמִצְוֹתָיו

וְרָצָה בָנוּ וְשַׁבַּת קָדְשׁוֹ בְּאַהֲבָה וּבְרָצוֹן הִנְחִילָנוּ זִכָּרוֹן לְמַעֲשֵׂה

בְרֵאשִׁית · כִּי הוּא יוֹם תְּחִלָּה לְמִקְרָאֵי קֹדֶשׁ זֵכֶר לִיצִיאַת

מִצְרָיִם · כִּי־בָנוּ בָחַרְתָּ וְאוֹתָנוּ קִדַּשְׁתָּ מִכָּל־הָעַמִּים וְשַׁבַּת קָדְשְׁךָ

בְּאַהֲבָה וּבְרָצוֹן הִנְחַלְתָּנוּ · בָּרוּךְ אַתָּה יְיָ מְקַדֵּשׁ הַשַּׁבָּת :

וּשְׁתָה מְיוּשָׁב כִּמְלֹא לֻגְמָיו, וְיִתֵּן גַּם לְכָל הַמְסוּבִּין מִכּוֹס שֶׁל בְּרָכָה

וְאַחַ"כ יִבְרֵךְ עַל לֶחֶם מִשְׁנֶה.

בָּרוּךְ אַתָּה יְיָ אֱלֹהֵינוּ מֶלֶךְ הָעוֹלָם הַמּוֹצִיא לֶחֶם מִן־הָאָרֶץ:

ויכלו see p. 273 above. Before we begin with Kiddush, we recite the last
two words of the Biblical description of the six previous days of Creation,
יום הששי; the initial letters of the words יום הששי, together with the initials
of ויכלו השמים spell out the ineffable Name of God. The Sabbath is an immediate and essential part of Creation itself. It is the seventh great work of
Creation, the seal of the Name of the Invisible Creator upon the visible world
of His making.

קדשנו במצותיו By giving us His commandments, He lifted us up to a
higher, holy purpose for His ends, and each of His commandments is designed
to lead us on to a higher level of moral perfection. ורצה בנו Our appointment
to be the bearers of the Sabbath is not a stern command; it is actually a sign
of God's love and favor. ושבת קדשו וכו' The Sabbath is a gift of love and
favor originally intended for all of mankind (See Commentary to Exod. 16:23,
20:8). The Sabbath was given by God to us as our inheritance which we
in turn are to pass on to our own descendants forever. The Sabbath is
תחלה למקראי קדש. In Leviticus 23:2 the Festival Seasons are called *Mikraei*
Kodesh "convocations to the Sanctuary," or, rather "convocations to the Holy
One," "holy convocations." Every *Kodesh* is a *mikra kodesh*. Each individual
Kodesh, through the strength of the truth which it is to symbolize and proclaim,
calls to us to come out and to ascend to the lofty moral level of readiness to

Blessed be You *God,* our God, King of the Universe, Who creates the fruit of the vine.

Blessed be You *God,* our God, King of the Universe, Who has sanctified us by His commandments and taken pleasure in us, and, in love and favor, has given us His holy Sabbath as an inheritance, the memorial, of the work of the world's beginning. For it is this day which is first among all the days of holy convocation, a remembrance of the Exodus from Mitzrayim. For You have chosen us; You have sanctified us from among all peoples, and in love and favor have You given us Your holy Sabbath as an inheritance, Blessed be You *God,* Who sanctifies the Sabbath.

Blessed be You *God,* our God, King of the Universe, Who causes the bread to grow forth from the earth.

---

do our duty with devotion and without reservations. The *Mo'adei Hashem,* the days of remembrance that summon us to communion with God, commemorating as they do the demonstrations of His might both in the realm of nature and in the history of man, must first be proclaimed to the nation אשר תקראו אתם מקראי קדש to call us to this *kodesh.* The Sabbath, on the other hand (ibid. Verse 3) is the one day that was fixed and sanctified by God forever, a day which need not first be set by the nation. Its sanctification does not come from the people, and there is no need for the nation to proclaim it as a "day of convocation to the Holy One." As opposed to all the other *Mo'adei Hashem,* the Sabbath is *mikra kodesh* by the very fact of its coming and thus we see it as the only day firmly fixed for all times as the starting point and climax of all the hallowed seasons. Since it is זכר למעשה בראשית, it is both first and fundamental among all the days that summon us forth from the ordinary pursuits of weekday life to the Sanctuary of God. At the same time, the Sabbath is זכר ליציאת מצרים, the memorial to a historic event which we ourselves have witnessed, a proof of the truths which the Sabbath teaches us concerning God, the Creator, Lord, Master and Ruler of the Universe. כי בנו בחרת The Sabbath is so much the basis of all of Judaism that one can truly say that by redeeming us from Mitzrayim, God had appointed our people to be the bearers of the Sabbath.

יוֹם זֶה לְיִשְׂרָאֵל אוֹרָה וְשִׂמְחָה · שַׁבַּת מְנוּחָה: יוֹם זֶה

צִוִּיתָ פִּקּוּדִים. בְּמַעֲמַד סִינַי · שַׁבָּת וּמוֹעֲדִים, לִשְׁמוֹר בְּכָל־שָׁנַי ·

לַעֲרוֹךְ לְפָנַי מַשְׂאֵת וַאֲרוּחָה · שַׁבַּת מְנוּחָה: יוֹם זֶה

חֶמְדַּת הַלְּבָבוֹת, לְאֻמָּה שְׁבוּרָה. לִנְפָשׁוֹת נִכְאָבוֹת, נְשָׁמָה יְתֵרָה ·

לְנֶפֶשׁ מְצֵרָה, יָסִיר אֲנָחָה · שַׁבַּת מְנוּחָה: יוֹם זֶה

קִדַּשְׁתָּ בֵּרַכְתָּ, אוֹתוֹ מִכָּל־יָמִים · בְּשֵׁשֶׁת כִּלִּיתָ, מְלֶאכֶת עוֹלָמִים ·

בּוֹ מָצְאוּ עֲנוּמִים, הַשְׁקֵט וּבִטְחָה · שַׁבַּת מְנוּחָה: יוֹם זֶה

לְאִסוּר מְלָאכָה, צִוִּיתָנוּ נוֹרָא · אֶזְכֶּה הוֹד מְלוּכָה, אִם שַׁבָּת

אֶשְׁמוֹרָה · אַקְרִיב שַׁי לַמֹּרָא, מִנְחָה מֶרְקָחָה · שַׁבַּת

מְנוּחָה:　　　　　　יוֹם זֶה

חַדֵּשׁ מִקְדָּשֵׁנוּ, זָכְרָה נֶחֱרֶבֶת · טוּבְךָ מוֹשִׁיעֵנוּ, תְּנָה לַנֶּעֱצֶבֶת ·

בְּשַׁבָּת יוֹשֶׁבֶת בְּזָמִיר וּשְׁבָחָה · שַׁבַּת מְנוּחָה: יוֹם זֶה

מְנוּחָה וְשִׂמְחָה אוֹר לַיְּהוּדִים. יוֹם שַׁבָּתוֹן יוֹם מַחֲמַדִּים. שׁוֹמְרָיו
וְזוֹכְרָיו הֵמָּה מְעִידִים. כִּי לְשִׁשָּׁה כֹּל בְּרוּאִים וְעוֹמְדִים: שְׁמֵי שָׁמַיִם
אֶרֶץ וְיַמִּים. כָּל־צְבָא מָרוֹם גְּבֹהִים וְרָמִים. תַּנִּין וְאָדָם וְחַיַּת רְאֵמִים.
כִּי בְּיָהּ יְיָ צוּר עוֹלָמִים: הוּא אֲשֶׁר דִּבֶּר לְעַם סְגֻלָּתוֹ. שָׁמוֹר לְקַדְּשׁוֹ
מִבֹּאוֹ עַד צֵאתוֹ. שַׁבַּת־קֹדֶשׁ יוֹם חֶמְדָּתוֹ. כִּי בוֹ שָׁבַת מִכָּל־מְלַאכְתּוֹ:
בְּמִצְוַת שַׁבָּת אֵל יַחֲלִיצָךְ. קוּם קְרָא אֵלָיו יָחִישׁ לְאַמְּצָךְ. נִשְׁמַת
כָּל־חַי וְגַם נַעֲרִיצָךְ. אֱכֹל בְּשִׂמְחָה כִּי כְבָר רָצָךְ: כְּמִשְׁנֶה לֶחֶם
וְקִדּוּשׁ רַבָּה. בְּרֹב מַטְעַמִּים וְרוּחַ נְדִיבָה. יִזְכּוּ לְרַב־טוּב הַמִּתְעַנְּגִים
בָּהּ. בְּבִיאַת גּוֹאֵל לְחַיֵּי עוֹלָם הַבָּא:

יָהּ רִבּוֹן עָלַם וְעָלְמַיָּא · אַנְתְּ הוּא מַלְכָּא מֶלֶךְ
מַלְכַיָּא: עוֹבַד גְּבוּרְתֵּךְ וְתִמְהַיָּא שְׁפַּר קֳדָמָךְ
לְהַחֲוַיָּא:
יה רבון

שְׁבָחִין אֲסַדֵּר צַפְרָא וְרַמְשָׁא · לָךְ אֱלָהָא קַדִּישָׁא דִּי בְרָא כָל־
נַפְשָׁא · עִירִין קַדִּישִׁין וּבְנֵי אֱנָשָׁא · חֵיוַת בָּרָא וְעוֹפֵי שְׁמַיָּא:
יה רבון

רַבְרְבִין עוֹבְדָךְ וְתַקִּיפִין · מָכֵךְ רָמַיָּא זָקֵף כְּפִיפִין · לוּ יְחֵי
גְבַר שְׁנִין אַלְפִין · לָא יֵעַל גְּבוּרְתֵּךְ בְּחֻשְׁבְּנַיָּא:
יה רבון

אֱלָהָא דִּי לֵהּ יְקָר וּרְבוּתָא · פְּרֹק יָת עָנָךְ מִפֻּם אַרְיָוָתָא ·
וְאַפֵּק יָת עַמֵּךְ מִגּוֹ גָלוּתָא · עַמָּךְ דִּי בְחַרְתְּ מִכָּל־אֻמַּיָּא:
יה רבון

לְמִקְדְּשָׁךְ תּוּב וּלְקֹדֶשׁ קֻדְשִׁין · אֲתַר דִּי בֵהּ יֶחֱדוּן רוּחִין
וְנַפְשִׁין · וִיזַמְּרוּן לָךְ שִׁירִין וְרַחֲשִׁין · בִּירוּשְׁלֵם קַרְתָּא דְשֻׁפְרַיָּא:
יה רבון

צוּר מִשֶּׁלּוֹ אָכַלְנוּ בָּרְכוּ אֱמוּנַי ·
שָׂבַעְנוּ וְהוֹתַרְנוּ, כִּדְבַר יְיָ:

הַזָּן אֶת־עוֹלָמוֹ, רוֹעֵנוּ אָבִינוּ · אָכַלְנוּ אֶת־לַחְמוֹ, וְיֵינוֹ שָׁתִינוּ ·
עַל־כֵּן נוֹדֶה לִשְׁמוֹ, וּנְהַלְלוֹ בְּפִינוּ · אָמַרְנוּ וְעָנִינוּ, אֵין־קָדוֹשׁ
כַּיְיָ:
צור

בְּשִׁיר וְקוֹל תּוֹדָה, נְבָרֵךְ לֵאלֹהֵינוּ · עַל אֶרֶץ חֶמְדָּה טוֹבָה,
שֶׁהִנְחִיל לַאֲבוֹתֵינוּ · מָזוֹן וְצֵידָה, הִשְׂבִּיעַ לְנַפְשֵׁנוּ · חַסְדּוֹ גָּבַר
עָלֵינוּ, וֶאֱמֶת יְיָ:
צור

רַחֵם בְּחַסְדֶּךָ, עַל עַמְּךָ צוּרֵנוּ · עַל צִיּוֹן מִשְׁכַּן כְּבוֹדֶךָ, וְבוּל בֵּית תִּפְאַרְתֵּנוּ · בֶּן דָּוִד עַבְדֶּךָ, יָבֹא וְיִגְאָלֵנוּ · רוּחַ אַפֵּינוּ, מְשִׁיחַ יְיָ:

צור

יִבָּנֶה הַמִּקְדָּשׁ, עִיר צִיּוֹן תְּמַלֵּא · וְשָׁם נָשִׁיר שִׁיר חָדָשׁ, וּבִרְנָנָה נַעֲלֶה · הָרַחֲמָן הַנִּקְדָּשׁ, יִתְבָּרַךְ וְיִתְעַלֶּה · עַל כּוֹס יַיִן מָלֵא, כְּבִרְכַּת יְיָ:

צור

סדר תפלת שחרית לשבת וי"ט

בשחר כשנכנסין לבה"כ ואומרין כל סדר הברכות ופ' הקרבנות כיו ביומי החול אלא שמוסיכין וביום השבת. שבת וי"ט לאו זמן תפילין היא, אבל מתעטפין בטלית. ויתחילין ברוך שאמר בנועם קול זמר, ואומרין פסוקי דזמרה ויכלוג מזמור לתודה ויוסיפין למנצח מזמור לדוד ושארי החזורים החונרים מעטי בראשית שכלו בשבת יחתן תורה שהי' נ. ואחירין ידי כבוד ואשרי והללויה וכו' עד ישתבח ויתחילין כאן נשמת.

After reciting the Morning Prayers until Yishtabách, continue as follows:

נִשְׁמַת כָּל חַי תְּבָרֵךְ אֶת שִׁמְךָ יְיָ אֱלֹהֵינוּ · וְרוּחַ כָּל בָּשָׂר תְּפָאֵר וּתְרוֹמֵם זִכְרְךָ מַלְכֵּנוּ תָּמִיד · מִן הָעוֹלָם וְעַד הָעוֹלָם אַתָּה אֵל · וּמִבַּלְעָדֶיךָ אֵין לָנוּ מֶלֶךְ גּוֹאֵל וּמוֹשִׁיעַ פּוֹדֶה וּמַצִּיל וּמְפַרְנֵס וּמְרַחֵם בְּכָל עֵת צָרָה וְצוּקָה אֵין לָנוּ מֶלֶךְ אֶלָּא אַתָּה: אֱלֹהֵי

MORNING PRAYER FOR SABBATHS AND FESTIVALS

After reciting the Weekday Morning Prayers until ישתבח, *continue as follows:*

The soul of every living thing shall bless Your Name, O *God* our God, and the spirit of all flesh shall ever glorify and exalt Your remembrance, O our King. From the remotest past to the most distant future, You are God, and beside You we have no King, Who redeems, and saves, delivers and rescues, sustains and has compassion; in all times of trouble and distress we have no King but You. God of the

---

נשמת On Sabbaths and also on Yom Tov when the soul becomes aware in an increased measure of its place in the presence of God, we recite the paragraph beginning with נשמת at the end of the *Pesukei Dezimrah*. This prayer declares that every soul, every breath and every thought, conscious or unconscious, in all the things that have life and feeling, joins with the chorus of all other creatures in one hymn of praise, glorifying God and paying the tribute of obedience to the Name and the concept of God that dwells within the heart of man. בכל עת צרה "Even in times of trouble and distress, when it appears as if You were far away, we still know of no other guiding Force in the world and in our own destiny but You." אלהי הראשנים Even as God reigned over all the generations of the past, so will He rule over the genera- tions of even the most distant future. His loving and merciful rule and guid- ance is extended not only to us, but also to the entire world, to all of His creatures and to all that they beget and produce. וה׳ לא ינום Even as He Himself is ever-alert, eternally strong in His power and His reign, so He also causes new strength and vigor to flow into the weakened and handicapped among men. לך לבדך Therefore it is incumbent upon us to avow our gratitude to Him and Him alone with all that is ours, whether we have obtained it directly from God, or indirectly through the world order which is led and guided by Him. אלו פינו But this is not a debt that can be paid by words alone. In order properly to discharge our debt to Him, we must enlist our mouths, our eyes, our hands, our feet, all our speech, perception and know- ledge, all our endeavors, pursuits and achievements in the service of God. But even if we were to possess all these abilities and faculties to an infinitely greater degree than we actually do, we would still not be able to do justice to the debt which we owe God for even one of the countless acts of kindness

הָרִאשׁוֹנִים וְהָאַחֲרוֹנִים· אֱלוֹהַּ כָּל־בְּרִיּוֹת אֲדוֹן כָּל־
תּוֹלָדוֹת הַמְהֻלָּל בְּרֹב הַתִּשְׁבָּחוֹת הַמְנַהֵג עוֹלָמוֹ
בְּחֶסֶד וּבְרִיּוֹתָיו בְּרַחֲמִים· וַיְיָ לֹא־יָנוּם וְלֹא־יִישָׁן·
הַמְעוֹרֵר יְשֵׁנִים וְהַמֵּקִיץ נִרְדָּמִים· וְהַמֵּשִׂיחַ אִלְּמִים·
וְהַמַּתִּיר אֲסוּרִים וְהַסּוֹמֵךְ נוֹפְלִים וְהַזּוֹקֵף כְּפוּפִים·
לְךָ לְבַדְּךָ אֲנַחְנוּ מוֹדִים· אִלּוּ פִינוּ מָלֵא שִׁירָה כַּיָּם
וּלְשׁוֹנֵנוּ רִנָּה כַּהֲמוֹן גַּלָּיו וְשִׂפְתוֹתֵינוּ שֶׁבַח כְּמֶרְחֲבֵי
רָקִיעַ· וְעֵינֵינוּ מְאִירוֹת כַּשֶּׁמֶשׁ וְכַיָּרֵחַ· וְיָדֵינוּ פְרוּשׂוֹת
כְּנִשְׁרֵי שָׁמָיִם· וְרַגְלֵינוּ קַלּוֹת כָּאַיָּלוֹת: אֵין אֲנַחְנוּ
מַסְפִּיקִים לְהוֹדוֹת לְךָ יְיָ אֱלֹהֵינוּ וֵאלֹהֵי אֲבוֹתֵינוּ·
וּלְבָרֵךְ אֶת־שְׁמֶךָ· עַל־אַחַת מֵאָלֶף אֶלֶף אַלְפֵי
אֲלָפִים וְרִבֵּי רְבָבוֹת פְּעָמִים הַטּוֹבוֹת שֶׁעָשִׂיתָ עִם־
אֲבוֹתֵינוּ וְעִמָּנוּ: מִמִּצְרַיִם גְּאַלְתָּנוּ יְיָ אֱלֹהֵינוּ וּמִבֵּית
עֲבָדִים פְּדִיתָנוּ בְּרָעָב זַנְתָּנוּ וּבְשָׂבָע כִּלְכַּלְתָּנוּ
מֵחֶרֶב הִצַּלְתָּנוּ· וּמִדֶּבֶר מִלַּטְתָּנוּ וּמֵחֳלָיִם רָעִים
וְנֶאֱמָנִים דִּלִּיתָנוּ: עַד־הֵנָּה עֲזָרוּנוּ רַחֲמֶיךָ· וְלֹא־

---

which He extended to our fathers and thus, directly and indirectly, to us
as well. ובשבע כלכלתנו. "When we were so amply satisfied in times of plenty,

first and of the last, God of all creatures, Lord of all that is begotten, proclaimed in an abundance of praises, Who guides His world with loving-kindness and His creatures with compassion. And *God* neither slumbers nor sleeps; it is He, rather Who awakens those who sleep, Who rouses those that are stunned, Who gives speech to the mute, Who sets free those that are bound, supports the falling and raises up those that are bowed down. To You and to You alone do we avow thanks. Though our mouths were filled with song as the sea, and our tongues with joy's outpouring as the swell of its waves, and our lips with praise as the expanse of Heaven, and though our eyes were brilliant like the sun and moon, our hands spread out like the eagles of the heavens, and our feet as light as the deer—we would still be unable to thank You, *God* our God and God of our fathers, and to bless Your Name for even one thousandth of the countless millions of favors which You have bestowed upon our fathers and upon us. You have redeemed us from Mitzrayim, O *God* our God, and freed us from the house of slavery, You have fed us in famine and satisfied us in plenty. You have delivered us from the sword, freed us from pestilence and relieved us from severe and lasting diseases. Until now Your compassion has helped us, and Your kindnesses have not forsaken

---

it was to You that we owed these prosperous years and it was due to Your goodness that we could partake of all this good and enjoy it." For it would be quite possible to starve even in the midst of plenty. ברכי נפשי. The soul, the immortal part of man's person, has a close relationship with God from Whom it originated and to Whom it is closely akin by virtue of its nature.

עֲזָבוּנוּ חֲסָדֶיךָ ׃ וְאַל־תִּטְּשֵׁנוּ יְיָ אֱלֹהֵינוּ לָנֶצַח ׃ עַל־
כֵּן אֵבָרִים שֶׁפִּלַּגְתָּ בָּנוּ ׃ וְרוּחַ וּנְשָׁמָה שֶׁנָּפַחְתָּ
בְּאַפֵּינוּ וְלָשׁוֹן אֲשֶׁר שַׂמְתָּ בְּפִינוּ ׃ הֵן הֵם יוֹדוּ וִיבָרְכוּ
וִישַׁבְּחוּ וִיפָאֲרוּ וִירוֹמְמוּ וְיַעֲרִיצוּ וְיַקְדִּישׁוּ וְיַמְלִיכוּ
אֶת־שִׁמְךָ מַלְכֵּנוּ ׃ כִּי כָל־פֶּה לְךָ יוֹדֶה ׃ וְכָל־לָשׁוֹן
לְךָ תִשָּׁבַע ׃ וְכָל־בֶּרֶךְ לְךָ תִכְרַע ׃ וְכָל־קוֹמָה לְפָנֶיךָ
תִשְׁתַּחֲוֶה ׃ וְכָל־לְבָבוֹת יִירָאוּךָ ׃ וְכָל־קֶרֶב וּכְלָיוֹת
יְזַמְּרוּ לִשְׁמֶךָ ׃ כַּדָּבָר שֶׁכָּתוּב כָּל עַצְמוֹתַי תֹּאמַרְנָה
יְיָ מִי כָמוֹךָ מַצִּיל עָנִי מֵחָזָק מִמֶּנּוּ וְעָנִי וְאֶבְיוֹן
מִגֹּזְלוֹ ׃ מִי יִדְמֶה־לָּךְ וּמִי יִשְׁוֶה־לָּךְ וּמִי יַעֲרָךְ־לָךְ ׃
הָאֵל הַגָּדוֹל הַגִּבּוֹר וְהַנּוֹרָא אֵל עֶלְיוֹן קֹנֵה שָׁמַיִם
וָאָרֶץ ׃ נְהַלֶּלְךָ וּנְשַׁבֵּחֲךָ וּנְפָאֶרְךָ וּנְבָרֵךְ אֶת־שֵׁם
קָדְשֶׁךָ ׃ כָּאָמוּר לְדָוִד בָּרְכִי נַפְשִׁי אֶת־יְיָ וְכָל־קְרָבַי
אֶת־שֵׁם קָדְשׁוֹ ׃ הָאֵל בְּתַעֲצֻמוֹת עֻזֶּךָ ׃ הַגָּדוֹל
בִּכְבוֹד שְׁמֶךָ ׃ הַגִּבּוֹר לָנֶצַח וְהַנּוֹרָא בְּנוֹרְאוֹתֶיךָ ׃
הַמֶּלֶךְ הַיּוֹשֵׁב עַל כִּסֵּא רָם וְנִשָּׂא ׃

Therefore it is the soul that is now called upon to come near to Him by
endeavoring to do His will. קרבי are the physical organs which serve the soul
as instruments of perception, thought and willpower while it dwells on earth.
These organs are to consecrate themselves to שם קדש, His holy Name, to the
ideals of that which He has revealed to us concerning Himself, as a guiding
light for our lives here below.

us, so *God* our God, forsake us never. Therefore the limbs which You have apportioned for us, the spirit and soul which You have breathed into our nostrils and the tongue which You have put into our mouth, shall all render homage, bless, praise, glorify, exalt and declare the power, the holiness and dominion of Your Name, O our King. For every mouth shall render You homage, every tongue shall swear You allegiance, every knee shall bend before You and all that stands upright shall fall down before You; all hearts shall fear You, and all the inmost passions shall sing praises to Your Name, even as it is written, "All my limbs shall say, Who is like You, O *God* Who delivers the poor from one that is too strong for him, the poor and the defenseless from one who would rob him." Who is like You, who is equal to You, and who can be compared to You, O great, strong and awesome God, God the Most High, the Owner of Heaven and Earth? We shall proclaim Your praise, laud You, glorify You and bless Your Holy Name, even as it is said: "By David. Bless *God,* O my soul, and all that is within me, bless His holy Name. O God, in the abundance of Your might, great in the glory of Your Name, almighty in eternity and feared for Your awesome acts, the King Who, exalted, are seated upon a throne on high.

שוכן עד God is near at all times to the world which is His Creation, and He makes it the abode of His Presence, even though, מרום וקדוש שמו, we must ever be mindful of the all-surpassing, sacred and unapproachable character of His majesty. רננו צדיקים Only those who live for the loyal fulfillment of their duty are capable of beholding God as He is revealed in the development of nature and in the course of history. Only ישרים, those who themselves will do only what is pleasing to God, and Who will permit Him to rule over all their lives will be fit and qualified to declare the praise of His rule and of His ways in the world. (*Rannenu* Cf. וירא כל העם וירנו Lev. 9:24). It seems that קלס as employed in *Tanach* always bears the connotation of disparagement and derision, as in לעג וקלס (Psalm 44:14) *et al.* In the language of our prayer-book, however, the term very definitely denotes praise and exaltation. Hence, and in the Tanach, too, the term קלס may well also have a connotation of "one exalting himself above all others." For this reason it is preponderantly used in the התפעל with ב preceding the object; e.g. במלכים יתקלס (Hab. 1:10), יתקלסו בך (Ezek. 22:5 ff).

שׁוֹכֵן עַד, מָרוֹם וְקָדוֹשׁ שְׁמוֹ . וְכָתוּב
רַנְּנוּ צַדִּיקִים בַּיָי לַיְשָׁרִים נָאוָה תְהִלָּה:

בְּפִי יְשָׁרִים תִּתְהַלָּל . וּבְדִבְרֵי צַדִּיקִים תִּתְבָּרַךְ .

וּבִלְשׁוֹן חֲסִידִים תִּתְרוֹמָם . וּבְקֶרֶב קְדוֹשִׁים תִּתְקַדָּשׁ:

וּבְמַקְהֲלוֹת רִבְבוֹת עַמְּךָ בֵּית יִשְׂרָאֵל בְּרִנָּה . יִתְפָּאַר שִׁמְךָ
מַלְכֵּנוּ בְּכָל־דּוֹר וָדוֹר . שֶׁכֵּן חוֹבַת כָּל־הַיְצוּרִים לְפָנֶיךָ יְיָ
אֱלֹהֵינוּ וֵאלֹהֵי אֲבוֹתֵינוּ לְהוֹדוֹת לְהַלֵּל לְשַׁבֵּחַ לְפָאֵר לְרוֹמֵם
לְהַדֵּר לְבָרֵךְ לְעַלֵּה וּלְקַלֵּס עַל כָּל־דִּבְרֵי שִׁירוֹת וְתִשְׁבְּחוֹת דָּוִד
בֶּן־יִשַׁי עַבְדְּךָ מְשִׁיחֶךָ:

יִשְׁתַּבַּח שִׁמְךָ לָעַד מַלְכֵּנוּ הָאֵל הַמֶּלֶךְ הַגָּדוֹל וְהַקָּדוֹשׁ בַּשָּׁמַיִם
וּבָאָרֶץ . כִּי לְךָ נָאֶה יְיָ אֱלֹהֵינוּ וֵאלֹהֵי אֲבוֹתֵינוּ שִׁיר וּשְׁבָחָה הַלֵּל
וְזִמְרָה עֹז וּמֶמְשָׁלָה נֶצַח גְּדֻלָּה וּגְבוּרָה תְּהִלָּה וְתִפְאֶרֶת קְדֻשָּׁה
וּמַלְכוּת בְּרָכוֹת וְהוֹדָאוֹת מֵעַתָּה וְעַד־עוֹלָם: בָּרוּךְ אַתָּה יְיָ, אֵל
מֶלֶךְ, גָּדוֹל בַּתִּשְׁבָּחוֹת, אֵל הַהוֹדָאוֹת, אֲדוֹן הַנִּפְלָאוֹת, הַבּוֹחֵר
בְּשִׁירֵי זִמְרָה, מֶלֶךְ, אֵל, חֵי הָעוֹלָמִים: יכ"ן אומ' ח"ק.

Reader, aloud:	The Congregation, in an undertone:
בָּרְכוּ אֶת־יְיָ הַמְבֹרָךְ:	ח' יִתְבָּרַךְ וְיִשְׁתַּבַּח וְיִתְפָּאַר וְיִתְרוֹמַם ק' וְיִתְנַשֵּׂא שְׁמוֹ שֶׁל־מֶלֶךְ מַלְכֵי הַמְּלָכִים
קו"ח בָּרוּךְ יְיָ הַמְבֹרָךְ לְעוֹלָם וָעֶד:	הַקָּדוֹשׁ בָּרוּךְ הוּא שֶׁהוּא רִאשׁוֹן וְהוּא
בָּרוּךְ אַתָּה יְיָ אֱלֹהֵינוּ	אַחֲרוֹן וּמִבַּלְעָדָיו אֵין אֱלֹהִים: סֹלּוּ לָרֹכֵב בָּעֲרָבוֹת בְּיָהּ שְׁמוֹ וְעִלְזוּ לְפָנָיו: וּשְׁמוֹ
מֶלֶךְ הָעוֹלָם יוֹצֵר אוֹר	מְרוֹמָם עַל־כָּל־בְּרָכָה וּתְהִלָּה:
וּבוֹרֵא חֹשֶׁךְ עֹשֶׂה שָׁלוֹם	בָּרוּךְ שֵׁם כְּבוֹד מַלְכוּתוֹ לְעוֹלָם וָעֶד:
וּבוֹרֵא אֶת־הַכֹּל:	יְהִי שֵׁם יְיָ מְבֹרָךְ מֵעַתָּה וְעַד עוֹלָם:

Dwelling in eternity, His Name is exalted and holy. And it is written: "Exult, O righteous ones, in beholding *God;* it behooves the upright to sing praises of the acts that reveal His might." By the mouth of the upright there is song in Your praise, by the words of the righteous You are blessed, by the tongue of Your devoted ones You are extolled, and in the midst of the holy You are sanctified.

And in the assemblies of the tens of thousands of Your people Yisrael, Your Name, O our King, is glorified in every generation with fervent emotion. For it is the duty of all creatures to avow thanks before You, O *God* our God and God of our fathers, and to praise Your mighty acts, to laud, glorify, exalt and proclaim Your might, to extol You and to glorify You in keeping with all the words and songs of praise by Your servant David, the son of Yishai, Your anointed.

Praised be Your Name forever, O our King, God, the King Who is great and holy in Heaven and on earth. For to You, O *God* our God and God of our fathers, pertain song and laud, praise and hymn, strength and dominion, victory, greatness and might, renown and glory, holiness and kingship, blessings and [utterances of] thanksgiving henceforth and unto eternity. Blessed be You *God,* God and King, great in hymns of praise, God of thangsgivings, Lord of wonders, Who takes pleasure in hymns, King, God, the Life of all times.

(Reader, aloud): Bless *God,* Who is to be blessed.

(Cong. & Reader):   Blessed be *God,* Who is to be blessed in all eternity.

Blessed be You *God,* our God, King of the Universe, Who forms light and creates darkness, Who makes peace and creates all things.

(The Congregation, in an undertone):

Blessed and praised, glorified, exalted and extolled be the Name of the Supreme King of Kings, the Holy One, blessed be He, fur He is the First and He is the Last, and there is no God beside Him. Strive up toward Him Who guides the world through desolate places by His Name, *Yah,* and exult before His countenance. His Name is exalted far beyond all blessings and praise. Blessed be the Name of the Glory of His Kingdom to all the future which, though veiled, is sure. Be the Name of *God* blessed from this time forth and forever.

כשאומרין יוצר מוסיפין זה: אוֹר עוֹלָם בְּאוֹצַר חַיִּים אוֹרוֹת מֵאֹפֶל אָמַר וַיֶּהִי:

On Holidays which do not fall on a Sabbath, say הַמֵּאִיר לָאָרֶץ [p. 106]
instead of הַכֹּל יוֹדוּךָ

הַכֹּל יוֹדוּךָ וְהַכֹּל יְשַׁבְּחוּךָ · וְהַכֹּל יֹאמְרוּ אֵין
קָדוֹשׁ כַּיְיָ: הַכֹּל יְרוֹמְמוּךָ סֶּלָה יוֹצֵר הַכֹּל · הָאֵל
הַפּוֹתֵחַ בְּכָל־יוֹם דַּלְתוֹת שַׁעֲרֵי מִזְרָח: וּבוֹקֵעַ חַלּוֹנֵי
רָקִיעַ · מוֹצִיא חַמָּה מִמְּקוֹמָהּ וּלְבָנָה מִמְּכוֹן שִׁבְתָּהּ:
וּמֵאִיר לְעוֹלָם כֻּלּוֹ וּלְיוֹשְׁבָיו שֶׁבָּרָא בְּמִדַּת
רַחֲמִים: הַמֵּאִיר לָאָרֶץ וְלַדָּרִים עָלֶיהָ בְּרַחֲמִים ·
וּבְטוּבוֹ מְחַדֵּשׁ בְּכָל־יוֹם תָּמִיד מַעֲשֵׂה בְרֵאשִׁית:
הַמֶּלֶךְ הַמְרוֹמָם לְבַדּוֹ מֵאָז · הַמְשֻׁבָּח וְהַמְפֹאָר
וְהַמִּתְנַשֵּׂא מִימוֹת עוֹלָם: אֱלֹהֵי עוֹלָם בְּרַחֲמֶיךָ
הָרַבִּים רַחֵם עָלֵינוּ · אֲדוֹן עֻזֵּנוּ צוּר מִשְׂגַּבֵּנוּ · מָגֵן
יִשְׁעֵנוּ מִשְׂגָּב בַּעֲדֵנוּ: אֵין כְּעֶרְכֶּךָ וְאֵין זוּלָתֶךָ · אֶפֶס
בִּלְתֶּךָ וּמִי דוֹמֶה־לָּךְ: אֵין כְּעֶרְכְּךָ יְיָ אֱלֹהֵינוּ בָּעוֹלָם
הַזֶּה · וְאֵין זוּלָתְךָ מַלְכֵּנוּ לְחַיֵּי הָעוֹלָם הַבָּא: אֶפֶס

הַכֹּל יוֹדוּךָ In keeping with the significance of the Sabbath as the day
commemorating Creation, יוֹצֵר אוֹר, the first preliminary blessing of the Keriath
Shema is augmented by special prayers in praise of Creation in general and
of the creation of light in particular. Since הַכֹּל in הַכֹּל יוֹדוּךָ simply takes up
and continues the thought of הַכֹּל in בּוֹרֵא אֶת הַכֹּל, it is obvious that *hakol* here
is meant to refer not only to all of mankind, but to all of Creation as such,
to every living thing. יוֹדוּךָ, etc., denotes not verbal expressions of praise and
gratitude, but, like *hashamayim mesapperim*, it signifies the emotions that
well up in our hearts as we contemplate any one of the works of God. All
creatures owe the gladsome blessing of life to God and hence by virtue of
their very existence they are forms of praise to the greatness and wisdom of
their Creator. They all declare אֵין קָדוֹשׁ כה׳, there is nothing so "holy", so

On Holidays which do not fall on a Sabbath, say המאיר לארץ[p. 106]

instead of הכל יודוך

All shall thank You, all shall laud You, all shall say, "There is none holy like *God.*" All shall extol You, the Creator of all, God, Who each day opens the doors of the portals of sunrise, Who uncloses the windows of Heaven, Who causes the sun to come forth from its place, and the moon from its abode, and Who gives light to the whole world and its inhabitants whom He has created with the attribute of compassion. He Who in compassion grants light to the earth and to them that dwell upon it, and in His goodness each day renews the work of the beginning, He is the King Who alone has ever been exalted, praised, glorified and extolled from the days of antiquity. O God of all times, in Your abundant compassion have mercy upon us, O Lord of our Might, Rock of our Stronghold, Shield of our Salvation, You stronghold of ours! There is none to be compared to You, and none beside You; there is nothing without You, and Who is like You? There is none to be compared to You, O *God* our God, in this world, there is none beside You, O our King, for life in the world to come; there is nothing without You, O our Redeemer, in the days of the Messiah, and none is like You, O our Savior, in the revival of the dead.

---

unchanging and unalterable as the goodness of God which remains the same forever. פתיחת דלתי שערי מזרח refers to the dawn of morning which diffuses the light of the sun's rays over the whole eastern sky long before the sun has actually risen on the heavens. חלוני רקיע denotes the places on the eastern sky at which the sun rises, locations that vary to the north or to the south depending upon the season of the year. In like manner, the moon, too, can rise only within the confines of a specifically defined space in the sky. ומאיר וכו' He has established the orbits of the heavenly bodies in such a manner that the blessings of light eventually reach all the far flung regions of the world and the inhabitants thereof. שברא; probably refers to עולם and יושביו, and במדת הרחמים is adverbial to ומאיר. In His infinite compassion, God causes the sun to shine upon all of His creatures, and every ray of the sun serves both as a reminder and a guarantee to righteous and sinners alike that God still awaits the return of them all to the path of duty. המאיר לארץ וכו' המלך וכו'. He, Whom we praise today as the Giver of the blessing of light, is the same Almighty God Who has reigned over us from days of old and of Whom every day, ever since antiquity, has been a form of praise. אין כערכך. While thus claiming for ourselves the benefits of God's fatherly grace which

בִּלְתֶּךָ גּוֹאֲלֵנוּ לִימוֹת הַמָּשִׁיחַ׳ וְאֵין דּוֹמֶה־לָּךְ מוֹשִׁיעֵנוּ לִתְחִיַּת הַמֵּתִים:

הָאֵל יָרְדוֹן עַל כָּל־הַמַּעֲשִׂים׳ בָּרוּךְ וּמְבֹרָךְ בְּפִי כָל־נְשָׁמָה: גָּדְלוֹ וְטוּבוֹ מָלֵא עוֹלָם׳ דַּעַת וּתְבוּנָה סֹבְבִים אוֹתוֹ: הַמִּתְגָּאֶה עַל־חַיּוֹת הַקֹּדֶשׁ׳ וְנֶהְדָּר בְּכָבוֹד עַל־הַמֶּרְכָּבָה: זְכוּת וּמִישׁוֹר לִפְנֵי כִסְאוֹ׳ חֶסֶד וְרַחֲמִים לִפְנֵי כְבוֹדוֹ: טוֹבִים מְאוֹרוֹת שֶׁבָּרָא אֱלֹהֵינוּ׳ יְצָרָם בְּדַעַת בְּבִינָה וּבְהַשְׂכֵּל: כֹּחַ וּגְבוּרָה נָתַן בָּהֶם׳ לִהְיוֹת מוֹשְׁלִים בְּקֶרֶב תֵּבֵל: מְלֵאִים זִיו וּמְפִיקִים נֹגַהּ׳ נָאֶה זִיוָם בְּכָל־הָעוֹלָם: שְׂמֵחִים בְּצֵאתָם וְשָׂשִׂים בְּבוֹאָם׳ עוֹשִׂים בְּאֵימָה רְצוֹן קוֹנָם:

פְּאֵר וְכָבוֹד נוֹתְנִים לִשְׁמוֹ׳ צָהֳלָה וְרִנָּה לְזֵכֶר מַלְכוּתוֹ: קָרָא לַשֶּׁמֶשׁ וַיִּזְרַח־אוֹר׳ רָאָה וְהִתְקִין צוּרַת הַלְּבָנָה: שֶׁבַח נוֹתְנִים־לוֹ כָּל־צְבָא מָרוֹם׳ תִּפְאֶרֶת וּגְדֻלָּה שְׂרָפִים וְאוֹפַנִּים וְחַיּוֹת הַקֹּדֶשׁ:

---

*) צהלה, הה׳ בק״ח כי הוא שם זנר כחנרו ורכב, וכמוהו בקדושה ובטהרה הה׳ בק״ח.

He extends to all the world, we remind ourselves that, even though there are many forces and beings on earth that determine and affect our welfare, none of these can be compared even remotely to God and to His acts of kindness. Whatever they may do to affect our lives, they do unwittingly and without any will of their own. For whatever action they may take in our behalf was originally envisioned and desired not by them but by none other than God Himself, Whose servants and instruments they all are. The favors we receive from our fellow-men, too, either stem from motives of personal advantage, in which case we owe them no thanks at all, or else they are acts of obedience to a command from God, done with His aid and in compliance with His decree. Thus, actually, it always is none other than God

God, Lord of all creatures, Who is blessed and to be blessed
by the mouth of every soul! His greatness and goodness fill the Universe; knowledge and insight surround Him, Who rises on high
above the holy *Chayoth* and, surrounded by majesty, dwells in glory
above the *Merkabah*. Merit and uprightness stand before His throne;
loving-kindness and compassion before His glory. Good are the luminaries which our God created; He has formed them with knowledge,
insight and reason. Strength and power has He placed into them so
that they may rule in the midst of man's world. Full of luster and
radiating brightness, their luster brings joy to all the world, joyous
at their rising and exultant at their setting, they reverently fulfill the
will of their Owner. They give glory and honor to His Name, jubilation and exultation at the remembrance of His kingdom. He called
to the sun and light began to shine; He looked and He regulated the
form of the moon. All the hosts on high, laud him. The *Seraphim*
and *Ophanim* and the holy *Chayoth* render glory and greatness.

Who is our only true Benefactor; there is none beside Him and none can
help us without Him, and thus He remains the One Beyond Compare forevermore. Nothing which supports and advances our welfare בעולם הזה, in this
world, can reach even distantly to the good which comes to us from the hands
of God, and לחיי עולם הבא, in the world to come, to which we can not take
with us any of the things of this world, we shall again have none beside
Him. Finally, the bliss that will be ours with the advent of redemption in
the days of the Messiah, too, cannot come to pass without the aid of God.
It all happens only at God's behest, so that, even in the days of the Messiah,
it will still be only God, and none beside Him, Who will be our true Redeemer.
But there is nothing that so reveals God in all His incomparable, all-conquering majesty as the תחית המתים, which we await, secure in the trust that even
death which overpowers all other things, will itself be defeated by God and
that, to Him, not even the dead are lost forever.

אל אדון All creatures serve God as their Lord, but only man can pledge
Him a vow of faithful obedience out of his own free will. Only man can
bless Him and say *baruch,* and it is also by men that God is *mevorach,* that
this free-will pledge will be truly and genuinely fulfilled. גדלו וטובו By virtue
of its very form, every creature attests to God's greatness and, because of
the provisions that have been made for its continued existence, every living
thing is tesimony also to the goodness of its Creator. דעת, the *knowledge* of
things as they are, and תבונה the understanding of the interrelationships of
things, the *"insight"* into the relation בין "between" things, these constitute

לָאֵל אֲשֶׁר שָׁבַת מִכָּל־הַמַּעֲשִׂים בַּיּוֹם הַשְּׁבִיעִי הִתְעַלָּה
וְיָשַׁב עַל־כִּסֵּא כְבוֹדוֹ · תִּפְאֶרֶת עָטָה לְיוֹם הַמְּנוּחָה עֹנֶג קָרָא
לְיוֹם הַשַּׁבָּת: זֶה שֶׁבַח שֶׁל־יוֹם הַשְּׁבִיעִי שֶׁבּוֹ שָׁבַת אֵל מִכָּל־
מְלַאכְתּוֹ: וְיוֹם הַשְּׁבִיעִי מְשַׁבֵּחַ וְאוֹמֵר מִזְמוֹר שִׁיר לְיוֹם הַשַּׁבָּת
טוֹב לְהוֹדוֹת לַיָי: לְפִיכָךְ יְפָאֲרוּ וִיבָרְכוּ לָאֵל כָּל־יְצוּרָיו · שֶׁבַח
יְקָר וּגְדֻלָּה יִתְּנוּ לָאֵל מֶלֶךְ יוֹצֵר כֹּל הַמַּנְחִיל מְנוּחָה לְעַמּוֹ
יִשְׂרָאֵל בִּקְדֻשָּׁתוֹ בְּיוֹם שַׁבַּת קֹדֶשׁ: שִׁמְךָ יְיָ אֱלֹהֵינוּ יִתְקַדַּשׁ,
וְזִכְרְךָ מַלְכֵּנוּ יִתְפָּאַר, בַּשָּׁמַיִם מִמַּעַל וְעַל־הָאָרֶץ מִתָּחַת:
תִּתְבָּרַךְ מוֹשִׁיעֵנוּ עַל־שֶׁבַח מַעֲשֵׂה יָדֶיךָ · וְעַל־מְאוֹרֵי־אוֹר
שֶׁעָשִׂיתָ יְפָאֲרוּךָ סֶּלָה:

המתנאה His Court. They stand in His service, as it were, ready to do His will.
Chayoth and *Merkabah* refer to the visions of God's presence and rule which
the prophet Ezekiel beheld. But the actual majesty of God's glory is exalted
high above these visions of Divine might. זכות, the acknowledgement of innocence and merit, and מישור the uprightness which renders each man his
just due, stand before His throne; they represent both the tools and the goals
of God's sovereign rule of the Universe. חסד ורחמים: Loving-kindness and
compassion, on the other hand, are the defenders that plead before His Presence
in our behalf. טובים: The pagan world trembles with fear at the thought of
the heavenly bodies; it dreads the effect they may have on its destiny, but
to the Jewish mind these luminaries are not independent, mighty forces, only
nothing else than works of God even as we ourselves, and we know that God
has made them solely for the purpose of doing "good". יצרם, their entire
structure, their form and substance, their position and orbit are all the work
of His wisdom, the result of His infinite understanding of every single thing
in the Universe as well as of the interrelationships of all things, and of His
haskel, the active demonstration of His wisdom, ordaining His purposes and
fulfilling His aims. כח, the strength and power which the luminaries possess
were given them solely as part of the role that has been assigned them by
God. שמחים וכו׳, מלאים וכו׳ Shining and radiant though they may be, bringing
joy and delight to all from their rising to their setting, all these heavenly
bodies are still merely servants of God, punctiliously doing the bidding of
their Lord. פאר: It is not to themselves, but to Him that they dedicate their
radiant crowns of glory, and thus they cause the concept of His sovereignty
to impart joy and exultation to all. קרא, In obedience to His command to

To God Who rested from all His works, Who on the Seventh Day ascended to sit upon the throne of His honor. He enveloped Himself in glory for the Day of Rest; He called the Sabbath a delight. Such is the praise of the Seventh Day: that on it, God rested from all of His work, and the Seventh Day offers laud and utters the Psalm, the Song for the Sabbath Day, "It is good to render homage to *God*." Therefore let all of His creatures glorify and bless God, let them render laud, honor and greatness to God, the King, Who fashions all things and Who in His holiness has given rest to His people Yisrael on the holy Sabbath. Hallowed be Your Name, O *God* our God, and be Your remembrance, O our King, glorified in Heaven above and on earth below. Be You blessed our Savior, for the excellence of Your handiwork and for the bright luminaries which You have created so that they may glorify You forever.

---

the sun, the light began to shine and it was in accordance with His insight that He shaped the phases of the moon. שבח. And even as the heavenly luminaries in the visible world laud God, so too, the heavenly servants standing round about His throne in the high places unseen by mortal man glorify their Lord.

לאל This paragraph is a continuation of the thoughts expressed in the preceding *shevach nothenim lo* etc. "They render praise *to God Who...*" The Seventh Day marked the advent of the Sabbath of Creation. Since then, no new form of creation has been fashioned. Instead, God now ascended above the visible world which He had created, up to His invisible abode in the high places, where He took His seat upon the throne of His sovereignty in order to guide and to rule over the world which He had made. The world, now completed, became His glory. It hides its Creator from the physical organ of sight, but it clearly reveals His greatness to the eye of the perceptive mind. God ordained the Sabbath to be a delight also for man. Even as man should have spent his six working days in the faithful service of God in moral and spiritual Godliness, so he should refrain from all labor on the Seventh Day, to contemplate in retrospect that which he has accomplished for God, to rejoice in his achievements of the week just past and to find in them the glorification of His Maker. זה שבח For "such is the true praise of the Sabbath.' Contrary to the myth devised by some minds which would divest the Sabbath of its true, blessed nature, the Sabbath was not ordained simply so that man should have a day of rest and recreation. The true purpose of the Sabbath is ever to remind man anew of the fact that the present world-wide Sabbath was preceded by a work of Creation which the Creator completed on the

תִּתְבָּרַךְ צוּרֵנוּ מַלְכֵּנוּ וְגֹאֲלֵנוּ בּוֹרֵא קְדוֹשִׁים יִשְׁתַּבַּח שִׁמְךָ
לָעַד מַלְכֵּנוּ יוֹצֵר מְשָׁרְתִים. וַאֲשֶׁר מְשָׁרְתָיו כֻּלָּם עוֹמְדִים בְּרוּם
עוֹלָם וּמַשְׁמִיעִים בְּיִרְאָה יַחַד בְּקוֹל דִּבְרֵי אֱלֹהִים חַיִּים וּמֶלֶךְ
עוֹלָם : כֻּלָּם אֲהוּבִים כֻּלָּם בְּרוּרִים כֻּלָּם גִּבּוֹרִים וְכֻלָּם עֹשִׂים
בְּאֵימָה וּבְיִרְאָה רְצוֹן קוֹנָם וְכֻלָּם פּוֹתְחִים אֶת־פִּיהֶם בִּקְדֻשָׁה
וּבְטָהֳרָה בְּשִׁירָה וּבְזִמְרָה וּמְבָרְכִים וּמְשַׁבְּחִים וּמְפָאֲרִים וּמַעֲרִיצִים
וּמַקְדִּישִׁים וּמַמְלִיכִים

אֶת־שֵׁם הָאֵל הַמֶּלֶךְ הַגָּדוֹל הַגִּבּוֹר וְהַנּוֹרָא קָדוֹשׁ הוּא : וְכֻלָּם
מְקַבְּלִים עֲלֵיהֶם עוֹל מַלְכוּת שָׁמַיִם זֶה מִזֶּה. וְנוֹתְנִים רְשׁוּת זֶה
לָזֶה. לְהַקְדִּישׁ לְיוֹצְרָם בְּנַחַת רוּחַ בְּשָׂפָה בְרוּרָה וּבִנְעִימָה. קְדֻשָׁה
כֻּלָּם כְּאֶחָד עוֹנִים וְאוֹמְרִים בְּיִרְאָה ·

קָדוֹשׁ · קָדוֹשׁ קָדוֹשׁ יְיָ צְבָאוֹת מְלֹא כָל־הָאָרֶץ כְּבוֹדוֹ :
וְהָאוֹפַנִּים וְחַיּוֹת הַקֹּדֶשׁ בְּרַעַשׁ גָּדוֹל מִתְנַשְּׂאִים לְעֻמַּת שְׂרָפִים
לְעֻמָּתָם מְשַׁבְּחִים וְאוֹמְרִים :

(כשאומרין אופן חוזרין וְהַחַיּוֹת יְשׁוֹרֵרוּ וּכְרוּבִים יְפָאֲרוּ וּשְׂרָפִים יָרֹנּוּ
במקום והאופנים :
וְאֶרְאֵלִים יְבָרֵכוּ פְּנֵי כָל־חַיָּה וְאוֹפָן וּכְרוּב לְעֻמַּת שְׂרָפִים לְעֻמָּתָם
מְשַׁבְּחִים וְאוֹמְרִים :)

בָּרוּךְ כְּבוֹד־יְיָ מִמְּקוֹמוֹ :

לָאֵל בָּרוּךְ נְעִימוֹת יִתֵּנוּ · לְמֶלֶךְ אֵל חַי וְקַיָּם זְמִירוֹת יֹאמֵרוּ
וְתִשְׁבָּחוֹת יַשְׁמִיעוּ · כִּי הוּא לְבַדּוֹ פּוֹעֵל גְּבוּרוֹת עֹשֶׂה חֲדָשׁוֹת
בַּעַל מִלְחָמוֹת זוֹרֵעַ צְדָקוֹת מַצְמִיחַ יְשׁוּעוֹת בּוֹרֵא רְפוּאוֹת נוֹרָא
תְהִלּוֹת אֲדוֹן הַנִּפְלָאוֹת הַמְחַדֵּשׁ בְּטוּבוֹ בְּכָל־יוֹם תָּמִיד מַעֲשֵׂה
בְרֵאשִׁית : כָּאָמוּר לְעֹשֵׂה אוֹרִים גְּדֹלִים כִּי לְעוֹלָם חַסְדּוֹ : אוֹר
חָדָשׁ עַל־צִיּוֹן תָּאִיר וְנִזְכֶּה כֻלָּנוּ מְהֵרָה לְאוֹרוֹ · בָּרוּךְ אַתָּה יְיָ
יוֹצֵר הַמְּאוֹרוֹת :

אַהֲבָה רַבָּה אֲהַבְתָּנוּ יְיָ אֱלֹהֵינוּ חֶמְלָה גְדוֹלָה וִיתֵרָה חָמַלְתָּ

Be You blessed, O our Rock, our King and our Redeemer, Creator of holy beings; praised be Your Name forever, O our King, Shaper of ministering hosts. And those who serve Him all stand in the high places of the Universe and with reverence they proclaim, aloud, in unison, the words of the Living God and King of the Universe. All of them are beloved, all of them are chosen, all of them are strong; in dread and awe they all do the bidding of their Owner, and they all open their mouths in holiness and purity with song and psalm, and they bless and praise and glorify, and declare the power and holiness and majesty of the Name of God, of the great, mighty and awesome King, holy is He. And they all take upon themselves the yoke of the kingdom of Heaven, one from the other, and give leave to one another to sanctify their Creator with a serene spirit, with pure speech and sweet melody. In unison, they all proclaim holiness and declare in awe:

"Holy, holy, holy is *God Tzevaoth;* the fullness of all the earth is His glory."

And the *Ophanim* and the holy *Chayoth,* with rushing sound, rise up toward the *Seraphim;* over against them they offer laud and say:

"Blessed be the glory of *God* from its dwelling place."

To God, the blessed One, they offer sweet melodies; to the King, God, living and eternal, they utter hymns and praise, that He alone performs almighty acts, creates new things; that He is the Lord of wars, sows acts of kindness, brings forth works of salvation, and creates healing, awesome in praise, Master of wonders; that He in His goodness constantly renews each day the work of the Beginning, even as it is said, "[Avow it] to Him, Who creates great lights, that His loving-kindness endures forever" (Psalm 136). O cause a new light to shine over Tzion, so that we may all soon have a portion in its brightness. Blessed by You *God,* Shaper of the heavenly luminaries.

With love abounding have You loved us, O *God* our God. You

Seventh Day, so that man may not forget Him Who is the Lord and Creator of himself and of the world in which he lives. The Sabbath is to help him perceive and take to heart the truth that is declared in the Psalms; namely, that there is only one "good thing" which constitutes the root of all good things, and that is—to render homage to God. לפיכך All creatures rejoice in

עָלֵינוּ : אָבִינוּ מַלְכֵּנוּ בַּעֲבוּר אֲבוֹתֵינוּ שֶׁבָּטְחוּ בְךָ וַתְּלַמְּדֵם חֻקֵּי
חַיִּים כֵּן תְּחָנֵּנוּ וּתְלַמְּדֵנוּ : אָבִינוּ הָאָב הָרַחֲמָן הַמְרַחֵם רַחֵם
עָלֵינוּ וְתֵן בְּלִבֵּנוּ לְהָבִין וּלְהַשְׂכִּיל לִשְׁמֹעַ לִלְמֹד וּלְלַמֵּד לִשְׁמֹר
וְלַעֲשׂוֹת וּלְקַיֵּם אֶת־כָּל־דִּבְרֵי תַלְמוּד תּוֹרָתֶךָ בְּאַהֲבָה : וְהָאֵר
עֵינֵינוּ בְּתוֹרָתֶךָ וְדַבֵּק לִבֵּנוּ בְּמִצְוֹתֶיךָ וְיַחֵד לְבָבֵנוּ לְאַהֲבָה וּלְיִרְאָה
שְׁמֶךָ וְלֹא־נֵבוֹשׁ לְעוֹלָם וָעֶד : כִּי בְשֵׁם קָדְשְׁךָ הַגָּדוֹל וְהַנּוֹרָא בָּטָחְנוּ
נָגִילָה וְנִשְׂמְחָה בִּישׁוּעָתֶךָ : וַהֲבִיאֵנוּ לְשָׁלוֹם מֵאַרְבַּע כַּנְפוֹת הָאָרֶץ
וְתוֹלִיכֵנוּ קוֹמְמִיּוּת לְאַרְצֵנוּ : כִּי אֵל פּוֹעֵל יְשׁוּעוֹת אָתָּה וּבָנוּ
בָחַרְתָּ מִכָּל־עַם וְלָשׁוֹן וְקֵרַבְתָּנוּ לְשִׁמְךָ הַגָּדוֹל סֶלָה בֶּאֱמֶת .
לְהוֹדוֹת לְךָ וּלְיַחֶדְךָ בְּאַהֲבָה : בָּרוּךְ אַתָּה יְיָ הַבּוֹחֵר בְּעַמּוֹ יִשְׂרָאֵל
בְּאַהֲבָה : יחיד אומר אל מלך נאמן
דברים ו'

שְׁמַע יִשְׂרָאֵל יְהֹוָה אֱלֹהֵינוּ יְהֹוָה ׀ אֶחָד :

בלחש בָּרוּךְ שֵׁם כְּבוֹד מַלְכוּתוֹ לְעוֹלָם וָעֶד :

וְאָהַבְתָּ אֵת יְהֹוָה אֱלֹהֶיךָ בְּכָל־לְבָבְךָ וּבְכָל־נַפְשְׁךָ
וּבְכָל־מְאֹדֶךָ : וְהָיוּ הַדְּבָרִים הָאֵלֶּה אֲשֶׁר אָנֹכִי מְצַוְּךָ
הַיּוֹם עַל־לְבָבֶךָ : וְשִׁנַּנְתָּם לְבָנֶיךָ וְדִבַּרְתָּ בָּם בְּשִׁבְתְּךָ
בְּבֵיתֶךָ וּבְלֶכְתְּךָ בַדֶּרֶךְ וּבְשָׁכְבְּךָ וּבְקוּמֶךָ : וּקְשַׁרְתָּם
לְאוֹת עַל־יָדֶךָ וְהָיוּ לְטֹטָפֹת בֵּין עֵינֶיךָ :
וּכְתַבְתָּם עַל־מְזֻזוֹת בֵּיתֶךָ וּבִשְׁעָרֶיךָ :

---

the knowledge that in Yisrael the Sabbath has regained its true and real
nature. For it is the Sabbath that affords to the entire physical world the
spiritual and moral goal of its purpose. Without the Sabbath the world would
run the danger of being buried alive through the folly and sin of man, of

have shown us compassion great and abundant, O our Father and our King; for the sake of our fathers who trusted in You, and whom You did teach the statutes of life, endow our spirits also and teach us. O our Father, compassionate Father, Who is ever compassionate, have mercy upon us and put it into our hearts to gain insight and understanding, to hear, to learn and to teach, to observe, to do and to fulfill with love all the words of the tradition of Your Torah. Enlighten our eyes in Your Torah, cause our heart to cleave to Your commandments, and unify our spirit to love and reverence Your Name so that we may never have cause to be ashamed. For in Your great and awesome holy Name do we trust, that we shall have cause happily to exult in Your salvation. O bring us home in peace from the four ends of the earth and lead us upright into our land; for You are the God Who performs works of salvation, and You have chosen us from among all peoples and tongues, and have brought us near to Your great Name forever in truth, that we may render You homage and with love avow Your Oneness. Blessed be You *God,* Who has chosen His people Yisrael with love.

HEAR YISRAEL, *GOD* OUR GOD, IS *GOD,* THE ONLY *ONE*!

Blessed be the Name of the glory of His kingdom
to all the future which, though veiled, is certain.

And you shall love *God,* your God, with all your heart and with all your soul and with all your fortune. And these words which I command you today shall be upon your heart. And you shall teach them diligently to your sons and speak of them when you sit in your house and when you walk upon the road, when you lie down and when you rise up. And you shall bind them as a sign upon your hand, and they shall be as a head-ornament between your eyes. And you shall inscribe them upon the doorposts of your house and upon your gates.

---

the very being to whom God had originally entrusted the world so that he might manage it sanely and wisely.

(For the Commentary to those prayers which are part also of the Weekday Morning Service, see the appropriate pages ibid.)

דברים
י"א י"ג. וְהָיָה אִם־שָׁמֹעַ תִּשְׁמְעוּ אֶל־מִצְוֹתַי אֲשֶׁר אָנֹכִי
מְצַוֶּה אֶתְכֶם הַיּוֹם לְאַהֲבָה אֶת־יְהֹוָה אֱלֹהֵיכֶם וּלְעָבְדוֹ
בְּכָל־לְבַבְכֶם וּבְכָל־נַפְשְׁכֶם: וְנָתַתִּי מְטַר־אַרְצְכֶם
בְּעִתּוֹ יוֹרֶה וּמַלְקוֹשׁ וְאָסַפְתָּ דְגָנֶךָ וְתִירֹשְׁךָ וְיִצְהָרֶךָ:
וְנָתַתִּי עֵשֶׂב בְּשָׂדְךָ לִבְהֶמְתֶּךָ וְאָכַלְתָּ וְשָׂבָעְתָּ:
הִשָּׁמְרוּ לָכֶם פֶּן־יִפְתֶּה לְבַבְכֶם וְסַרְתֶּם וַעֲבַדְתֶּם
אֱלֹהִים אֲחֵרִים וְהִשְׁתַּחֲוִיתֶם לָהֶם: וְחָרָה אַף־יְהֹוָה
בָּכֶם וְעָצַר אֶת־הַשָּׁמַיִם וְלֹא־יִהְיֶה מָטָר וְהָאֲדָמָה לֹא
תִתֵּן אֶת־יְבוּלָהּ וַאֲבַדְתֶּם מְהֵרָה מֵעַל הָאָרֶץ הַטֹּבָה
אֲשֶׁר יְהֹוָה נֹתֵן לָכֶם: וְשַׂמְתֶּם אֶת־דְּבָרַי אֵלֶּה עַל־
לְבַבְכֶם וְעַל־נַפְשְׁכֶם וּקְשַׁרְתֶּם אֹתָם לְאוֹת עַל־יֶדְכֶם
וְהָיוּ לְטוֹטָפֹת בֵּין עֵינֵיכֶם: וְלִמַּדְתֶּם אֹתָם אֶת־בְּנֵיכֶם
לְדַבֵּר בָּם בְּשִׁבְתְּךָ בְּבֵיתֶךָ וּבְלֶכְתְּךָ בַדֶּרֶךְ וּבְשָׁכְבְּךָ
וּבְקוּמֶךָ: וּכְתַבְתָּם עַל־מְזוּזוֹת בֵּיתֶךָ וּבִשְׁעָרֶיךָ: לְמַעַן
יִרְבּוּ יְמֵיכֶם וִימֵי בְנֵיכֶם עַל הָאֲדָמָה אֲשֶׁר נִשְׁבַּע
יְהֹוָה לַאֲבֹתֵיכֶם לָתֵת לָהֶם כִּימֵי הַשָּׁמַיִם עַל־הָאָרֶץ:

במדבר
ט"ו ל"ז. וַיֹּאמֶר יְהֹוָה אֶל־מֹשֶׁה לֵּאמֹר: דַּבֵּר אֶל־בְּנֵי
יִשְׂרָאֵל וְאָמַרְתָּ אֲלֵהֶם וְעָשׂוּ לָהֶם צִיצִת עַל־כַּנְפֵי
בִגְדֵיהֶם לְדֹרֹתָם וְנָתְנוּ עַל־צִיצִת הַכָּנָף פְּתִיל תְּכֵלֶת:

And it shall come to pass if you will hearken with growing intentness to My commandments which I command you this day, so that you will love *God* your God and serve Him with all your heart and with all your soul, that I will give the rain of your land in its season, the autumn rains and the spring rains, so that you may gather in your grain, your wine and your oil, and I will give grass upon your field for your cattle; you will eat thereof and you will be satiated. But take care lest your heart open itself to temptation and you turn astray and serve other gods and cast yourselves down before them. For then the wrath of *God* will blaze forth against you; He will restrain the skies and there will be no rain, and the land will not yield its produce, and you will quickly perish from the good land which *God* gives you. But even then you shall lay up these My words in your heart and in your soul, and bind them as a sign upon your hand and they shall be as a head-ornament between your eyes, and teach them to your sons to speak of them, when you sit in your house and when you walk upon the road, when you lie down and when you rise up. Inscribe them upon the doorpost of your house and upon your gates, so that your days and the days of your children may be prolonged upon the land which *God* swore to give to your fathers, as the days of the heavens upon the earth.

And *God* spoke to Moshe, saying, "Speak to the sons of Yisrael and tell it to them so that they make for themselves fringes upon the corners of their garments throughout their generations, and that they put upon the fringes of the corner a thread of sky-blue wool.

וְהָיָה לָכֶם לְצִיצִת וּרְאִיתֶם אֹתוֹ וּזְכַרְתֶּם אֶת־כָּל־
מִצְוֹת יְהוָֹה וַעֲשִׂיתֶם אֹתָם וְלֹא תָתוּרוּ אַחֲרֵי לְבַבְכֶם
וְאַחֲרֵי עֵינֵיכֶם אֲשֶׁר־אַתֶּם זֹנִים אַחֲרֵיהֶם: לְמַעַן
תִּזְכְּרוּ וַעֲשִׂיתֶם אֶת־כָּל־מִצְוֹתָי וִהְיִיתֶם קְדֹשִׁים
לֵאלֹהֵיכֶם: אֲנִי יְהוָֹה אֱלֹהֵיכֶם אֲשֶׁר הוֹצֵאתִי אֶתְכֶם
מֵאֶרֶץ מִצְרַיִם לִהְיוֹת לָכֶם לֵאלֹהִים אֲנִי יְהוָֹה
אֱלֹהֵיכֶם:

יֵּ לְצִיף אֱלֹהֵיכֶם לֶאֱמֶת.

אֱמֶת וְיַצִּיב וְנָכוֹן וְקַיָּם וְיָשָׁר וְנֶאֱמָן
וְאָהוּב וְחָבִיב וְנֶחְמָד וְנָעִים וְנוֹרָא
וְאַדִּיר וּמְתֻקָּן וּמְקֻבָּל וְטוֹב וְיָפֶה הַדָּבָר
הַזֶּה עָלֵינוּ לְעוֹלָם וָעֶד אֱמֶת אֱלֹהֵי
עוֹלָם מַלְכֵּנוּ צוּר יַעֲקֹב מָגֵן יִשְׁעֵנוּ:
לְדֹר וָדוֹר הוּא קַיָּם וּשְׁמוֹ קַיָּם וְכִסְאוֹ
נָכוֹן וּמַלְכוּתוֹ וֶאֱמוּנָתוֹ לָעַד קַיֶּמֶת
וּדְבָרָיו חָיִים וְקַיָּמִים נֶאֱמָנִים וְנֶחֱמָדִים
לָעַד וּלְעוֹלְמֵי עוֹלָמִים עַל־אֲבוֹתֵינוּ
וְעָלֵינוּ עַל־בָּנֵינוּ וְעַל־דּוֹרוֹתֵינוּ וְעַל כָּל־
דּוֹרוֹת זֶרַע יִשְׂרָאֵל עֲבָדֶיךָ: עַל־
הָרִאשׁוֹנִים וְאֶל־הָאַחֲרוֹנִים דָּבָר טוֹב
וְקַיָּם לְעוֹלָם וָעֶד: אֱמֶת וֶאֱמוּנָה חֹק
וְלֹא יַעֲבוֹר: אֱמֶת שָׁאַתָּה הוּא יְיָ

כְּשֶׁאוֹמְרִים זֹאֵלֶת אוֹמְרִין בְּלַחֲשׁ
אֱמֶת וְיַצִּיב זֶה עַד אֵין אֱלֹהִים
זוּלָתֶךָ אֲבָל בְּפוֹלִין מַחֲלִיפִין רַק עַל
הָרִאשׁוֹנִים.

אֱמֶת וְיַצִּיב וְנָכוֹן וְקַיָּם וְיָשָׁר
וְנֶאֱמָן וְטוֹב וְיָפֶה הַדָּבָר
הַזֶּה עַל אֲבוֹתֵינוּ וְעָלֵינוּ
עַל בָּנֵינוּ וְעַל דּוֹרוֹתֵינוּ וְעַל כָּל־
דּוֹרוֹת זֶרַע יִשְׂרָאֵל עֲבָדֶיךָ:
עַל הָרִאשׁוֹנִים וְעַל הָאַחֲרוֹנִים
לְעוֹלָם וָעֶד חֹק וְלֹא יַעֲבוֹר ·
אֱמֶת שָׁאַתָּה הוּא יְיָ אֱלֹהֵינוּ
וֵאלֹהֵי אֲבוֹתֵינוּ לְעוֹלָם וָעֶד:
אַתָּה הוּא מַלְכֵּנוּ מֶלֶךְ אֲבוֹתֵינוּ
אָפֶה. לְמַעַן שִׁמְךָ מַהֵר לִגְאָלֵנוּ
כַּאֲשֶׁר נָאַלְתָּ אֶת אֲבוֹתֵינוּ:
אֱמֶת מֵעוֹלָם שִׁמְךָ הַגָּדוֹל עָלֵינוּ

These shall be fringes for you so that you may look upon them and remember all the commandments of *God,* and fulfill them, and you shall not cast about after your own hearts and after your own eyes, and following them, become unfaithful to Me. That you may remember and fulfill all of My commandments and remain holy for your God. I am *God,* your God, Who brought you out from the land of Mitzrayim in order to be your God; I am *God* your God."

True and firm, established and enduring and right, believed and beloved, precious, desired and sweet, yet awesome and mighty, well-ordered and accepted through tradition, good and beautiful is this Word, and binding upon us for all eternity. True it is; the God of all time is our King; the Rock of Yaakov is the Shield of our salvation. He endures for all generations and His Name endures; His Throne is firmly established, and His kingdom and His guiding faithfulness endure forever. And His words are living and enduring; they are confirmed and desirable forever and to all eternity. This stands above our fathers and ourselves, above our children and our descendants, as well as above all the descendants of Yisrael, Your servants, the first and the last alike, as a good Word, unchangeable for all eternity. It is a truth and a trustworthy fundamental, a statute which shall not pass away. True it is that You, O *God,* are our God and the God of our fathers, our King and the King of our fathers, our Redeemer and the Redeemer of our fathers. Our Maker, the Rock of our salvation, our Redeemer and Deliverer—such has been Your Name forever. There is no God beside You.

אֱלֹהֵינוּ וֵאלֹהֵי אֲבוֹתֵינוּ מַלְכֵּנוּ מֶלֶךְ   נִקְרָא בְּאַהֲבָה אֵין אֱלֹהִים

אֲבוֹתֵינוּ גּוֹאֲלֵנוּ גּוֹאֵל אֲבוֹתֵינוּ יוֹצְרֵנוּ   זוּלָתֶךָ :

צוּר יְשׁוּעָתֵנוּ פּוֹדֵנוּ וּמַצִּילֵנוּ מֵעוֹלָם   *) לְגָאֳלֵנוּ הֵא׳ נק״ח כמשפט לֹא יִחְפֹּץ לְגָאֳלֵךְ (רות ג׳

שְׁמֶךָ · אֵין אֱלֹהִים זוּלָתֶךָ :   י׳).

עֶזְרַת אֲבוֹתֵינוּ אַתָּה הוּא מֵעוֹלָם מָגֵן וּמוֹשִׁיעַ לִבְנֵיהֶם אַחֲרֵיהֶם
בְּכָל־דּוֹר וָדוֹר : בְּרוּם עוֹלָם מוֹשָׁבֶךָ וּמִשְׁפָּטֶיךָ וְצִדְקָתְךָ עַד־
אַפְסֵי אָרֶץ : אַשְׁרֵי אִישׁ שֶׁיִּשְׁמַע לְמִצְוֹתֶיךָ וְתוֹרָתְךָ וּדְבָרְךָ
יָשִׂים עַל־לִבּוֹ : אֱמֶת אַתָּה הוּא אָדוֹן לְעַמֶּךָ וּמֶלֶךְ גִּבּוֹר לָרִיב
רִיבָם : אֱמֶת אַתָּה הוּא רִאשׁוֹן וְאַתָּה הוּא אַחֲרוֹן וּמִבַּלְעָדֶיךָ
אֵין לָנוּ מֶלֶךְ גּוֹאֵל וּמוֹשִׁיעַ : מִמִּצְרַיִם גְּאַלְתָּנוּ יְיָ אֱלֹהֵינוּ וּמִבֵּית
עֲבָדִים פְּדִיתָנוּ : כָּל־בְּכוֹרֵיהֶם הָרָגְתָּ וּבְכוֹרְךָ גָּאָלְתָּ וְיַם־סוּף
בָּקַעְתָּ וְזֵדִים טִבַּעְתָּ וִידִידִים הֶעֱבַרְתָּ וַיְכַסּוּ מַיִם צָרֵיהֶם אֶחָד מֵהֶם
לֹא נוֹתָר : עַל־זֹאת שִׁבְּחוּ אֲהוּבִים וְרוֹמְמוּ אֵל וְנָתְנוּ יְדִידִים
זְמִירוֹת שִׁירוֹת וְתִשְׁבָּחוֹת בְּרָכוֹת וְהוֹדָאוֹת לְמֶלֶךְ אֵל חַי וְקַיָּם :
רָם וְנִשָּׂא גָּדוֹל וְנוֹרָא מַשְׁפִּיל גֵּאִים וּמַגְבִּיהַּ שְׁפָלִים מוֹצִיא
אֲסִירִים וּפוֹדֶה עֲנָוִים וְעוֹזֵר דַּלִּים וְעוֹנֶה לְעַמּוֹ בְּעֵת שַׁוְּעָם אֵלָיו :
תְּהִלּוֹת לְאֵל עֶלְיוֹן בָּרוּךְ הוּא וּמְבֹרָךְ · מֹשֶׁה וּבְנֵי יִשְׂרָאֵל לְךָ
עָנוּ שִׁירָה בְּשִׂמְחָה רַבָּה וְאָמְרוּ כֻלָּם :

מִי־כָמֹכָה בָּאֵלִם יְהוָֹה מִי כָּמֹכָה נֶאְדָּר בַּקֹּדֶשׁ נוֹרָא תְהִלֹּת
עֹשֵׂה פֶלֶא : שִׁירָה חֲדָשָׁה שִׁבְּחוּ גְאוּלִים לְשִׁמְךָ עַל־שְׂפַת
הַיָּם יַחַד כֻּלָּם הוֹדוּ וְהִמְלִיכוּ וְאָמְרוּ · יְהוָֹה יִמְלֹךְ לְעֹלָם וָעֶד :

צוּר יִשְׂרָאֵל קוּמָה בְּעֶזְרַת יִשְׂרָאֵל וּפְדֵה כִנְאֻמֶךָ יְהוּדָה
וְיִשְׂרָאֵל · (גֹּאֲלֵנוּ יְיָ צְבָאוֹת שְׁמוֹ קְדוֹשׁ יִשְׂרָאֵל·) בָּרוּךְ אַתָּה
יְיָ גָּאַל יִשְׂרָאֵל :

You have ever been the Help of our fathers, a Shield and Savior to their sons after them in every generation. In the high places of the Universe is Your habitation, and Your judgments and righteousness reach to the remotest ends of the earth. Forward to salvation strides that man who hearkens to Your commandments and who takes Your Torah and Your Word to his heart. True it is, You are the Lord of Your people and a mighty King to champion their cause. True it is, You are the First and You are the Last, and besides You we have no King, Redeemer and Savior. From Mitzrayim did You redeem us, O *God* our God, and have set us free from the home of slavery; all their first-born You did slay, but Your first-born You did redeem; You did divide the Sea of Reeds, You did drown the arrogant, but Your beloved ones You did lead across, and the water covered their enemies; not one of them was left. Therefore those who sensed that they were loved, praised and exalted God; the beloved ones offered hymns, songs and praises, blessings and thanksgivings to the King, to the living and eternal God. He Who is high and exalted, great and awesome, brings low the haughty and raises up the lowly; He leads captives to freedom and delivers the humble; He helps the poor and answers His people when they cry to Him. Praise for His mighty deeds be to God the Most High, blessed be He and He is blessed; Moshe and the sons of Yisrael sang a song to You with joy abounding and they all said:

"Who is like You among the gods, O *God*? Who is like You, uniquely powerful in holiness? Feared in praises of His mighty deeds, performer of wonders?"

With a new song the redeemed lauded Your Name by the shore of the sea; they all paid homage in unison; they acknowledged Your sovereignty, and they said:

"*God* shall reign forever and ever!"

O Rock of Yisrael arise to the help of Yisrael, and set Yehuda and Yisrael free, even as You have promised (O our Redeemer, *God* Tzevaoth, the Holy One of Yisrael is His Name). Blessed be You *God*, Who has redeemed Yisrael.

אֲדֹנָי שְׂפָתַי תִּפְתָּח וּפִי יַגִּיד תְּהִלָּתֶךָ:

בָּרוּךְ אַתָּה יְיָ אֱלֹהֵינוּ וֵאלֹהֵי אֲבוֹתֵינוּ אֱלֹהֵי אַבְרָהָם
אֱלֹהֵי יִצְחָק וֵאלֹהֵי יַעֲקֹב הָאֵל הַגָּדוֹל הַגִּבּוֹר וְהַנּוֹרָא
אֵל עֶלְיוֹן גּוֹמֵל חֲסָדִים טוֹבִים וְקֹנֵה הַכֹּל וְזוֹכֵר חַסְדֵי
אָבוֹת וּמֵבִיא גוֹאֵל לִבְנֵי בְנֵיהֶם לְמַעַן שְׁמוֹ בְּאַהֲבָה·

On שבת שובה add:

זָכְרֵנוּ לְחַיִּים מֶלֶךְ חָפֵץ בַּחַיִּים · וְכָתְבֵנוּ בְּסֵפֶר הַחַיִּים לְמַעַנְךָ
אֱלֹהִים חַיִּים:

מֶלֶךְ עוֹזֵר וּמוֹשִׁיעַ וּמָגֵן · בָּרוּךְ אַתָּה יְיָ מָגֵן אַבְרָהָם:

אַתָּה גִבּוֹר לְעוֹלָם אֲדֹנָי מְחַיֵּה מֵתִים אַתָּה רַב
לְהוֹשִׁיעַ·

During the winter months, add:

מַשִּׁיב הָרוּחַ וּמוֹרִיד הַגָּשֶׁם:

מְכַלְכֵּל חַיִּים בְּחֶסֶד מְחַיֵּה מֵתִים בְּרַחֲמִים רַבִּים
סוֹמֵךְ נוֹפְלִים וְרוֹפֵא חוֹלִים וּמַתִּיר אֲסוּרִים וּמְקַיֵּם
אֱמוּנָתוֹ לִישֵׁנֵי עָפָר · מִי כָמוֹךָ בַּעַל גְּבוּרוֹת וּמִי דוֹמֶה
לָּךְ מֶלֶךְ מֵמִית וּמְחַיֶּה וּמַצְמִיחַ יְשׁוּעָה·

On שבת שובה add:

מִי כָמוֹךָ אַב הָרַחֲמִים זוֹכֵר יְצוּרָיו לְחַיִּים בְּרַחֲמִים·

וְנֶאֱמָן אַתָּה לְהַחֲיוֹת מֵתִים · בָּרוּךְ אַתָּה יְיָ מְחַיֵּה
הַמֵּתִים:

O *Lord,* open my lips so that my mouth may declare Your praise.

Blessed be You *God,* our God and God of our fathers, God of Avraham, God of Yitzchak and God of Yaakov, the great, mighty and awesome God, God the Most High, Who nevertheless bestows loving-kindness, Who is the Owner of all things, and remembers the fathers' acts of devotion and Who, in love, will bring a Redeemer to their children's children for His Name's sake.

(On שבת שובה *add:*   Remember us for life, O King Who delights in life, and inscribe us into the Book of Life for Your sake, O living God.)

O King, Helper, Savior and Shield! Blessed be You,*God,* the Shield of Avraham.

You, O my Lord, are all-powerful forever. You are the One Who revives the dead; You are abundantly powerful to save.

(During the winter months, add: He causes the wind to blow and the rain to fall.)

He sustains the living with loving-kindness, revives the dead with great compassion, supports the falling, heals the sick, unchains the bound, and keeps His faith with the slumberers in the dust. Who is like You, O Master of Mighty acts, and who, like You, is a King Who kills and restores life and causes salvation to grow?

(On שבת שובה *add:*   Who, like You, is a father of compassion, Who in compassion remembers His creatures for life?)

And You are faithful to revive the dead. Blessed be You *God,* Who revives the dead.

You are holy, and Your Name is holy, and the holy ones proclaim Your praise each day. Blessed be You *God,* the holy God *(On* שבת שובה *say:* the holy King).

אַתָּה קָדוֹשׁ וְשִׁמְךָ קדושה לש"ן נחזרת התפלה.
קָדוֹשׁ וּקְדוֹשִׁים בְּכָל יוֹם נְקַדֵּשׁ אֶת שִׁמְךָ בָּעוֹלָם כְּשֵׁם
יְהַלְלוּךָ סֶּלָה• בָּרוּךְ א"י שֶׁמַּקְדִּישִׁים אוֹתוֹ בִּשְׁמֵי מָרוֹם
הָאֵל (נט"ש הַמֶּלֶךְ) הַקָּדוֹשׁ: כַּכָּתוּב עַל יַד נְבִיאֶךָ וְקָרָא זֶה אֶל
יְיָ צְבָאוֹת מְלֹא כָל הָאָרֶץ זֶה וְאָמַר: קו"ח קָדוֹשׁ קָדוֹשׁ קָדוֹשׁ
וְחָזָק מַשְׁמִיעִים קוֹל כְּבוֹדוֹ: י' אָז בְּקוֹל רַעַשׁ גָּדוֹל אַדִּיר
יֹאמֵרוּ קו"ח בָּרוּךְ מִתְנַשְּׂאִים לְעֻמַּת שְׂרָפִים לְעֻמָּתָם בָּרוּךְ
וְתִמְלוֹךְ עָלֵינוּ כִּי כְּבוֹד יְיָ מִמְּקוֹמוֹ: י' מִמְּקוֹמְךָ מַלְכֵּנוּ תוֹפִיעַ
בְּיָמֵינוּ לְעוֹלָם וָעֶד תִּשְׁכּוֹן: מְחַכִּים אֲנַחְנוּ לָךְ מָתַי תִּמְלֹךְ בְּצִיּוֹן בְּקָרוֹב
עִירְךָ לְדוֹר וָדוֹר וּלְנֵצַח נְצָחִים: תִּתְגַּדַּל וְתִתְקַדַּשׁ בְּתוֹךְ יְרוּשָׁלַיִם
הָאָמוּר בְּשִׁירֵי עֻזֶּךָ עַל יְדֵי דָּוִד מְשִׁיחַ צִדְקֶךָ: וְעֵינֵינוּ תִרְאֶינָה מַלְכוּתֶךָ כַּדָּבָר
לְעוֹלָם אֱלֹהַיִךְ צִיּוֹן לְדוֹר וָדוֹר הַלְלוּיָהּ: קו"ח יִמְלֹךְ יְיָ

י' לְדוֹר וָדוֹר נַגִּיד גָּדְלֶךָ וּלְנֵצַח נְצָחִים קְדֻשָּׁתְךָ נַקְדִּישׁ
וְשִׁבְחֲךָ אֱלֹהֵינוּ מִפִּינוּ לֹא יָמוּשׁ לְעוֹלָם וָעֶד כִּי אֵל מֶלֶךְ גָּדוֹל
וְקָדוֹשׁ אָתָּה• בָּרוּךְ אַתָּה יְיָ הָאֵל (נט"ש הַמֶּלֶךְ) הַקָּדוֹשׁ:

נקדש See Weekday Morning Prayer, p. 133. When on the Sabbath, the
day commemorating Creation, we recall how God is hallowed in the high
places of Heaven, there comes to us with full force the realization that while,
originally, God had desired to have His glory dwell on earth, among men
(עיקר שכינה בתחתונים, as our Sages put it) He had withdrawn it from the
earth because of man's errors. Yisrael's election and the establishment of
Zion were intended to herald the return of the glory of God to earth, but
due to Yisrael's wrongdoing, this return, too, was not permanent. And yet
the thought that the world and all that is in it was created by God does not
admit of any doubt that one day Yisrael and all of mankind, and thus the
entire world, will be truly and permanently reclaimed and return forever to
their original destiny which is to be near to God. We hear the call that shakes
the world and conquers it, summoning all the earth to fulfill its true destiny,

(The Reader, when he repeats the Shemone Esrei): We will sanctify Your Name in this world, even as they sanctify it in the heavens above, as it is written by Your prophet, "And one of them calls to the other and says:

(Cong. & Reader) 'Holy, holy, holy, is *God Tzevaoth,* the fullness of all the earth is His glory.'

(Reader) "Then with a loud sound, mighty and strong, they make their voices heard, raising themselves up toward the *Seraphim,* facing one another, they say: 'Blessed—

(Cong. & Reader) 'Blessed be the glory of *God* from its abode.' "

(Reader) From Your abode, O our King, appear, and reign over us, for we wait for You. When will You reign in Tzion? Speedily, in our days, abide there forever. Reveal Yourself in greatness and holiness in Yerushalayim, Your city, for all the generations and to all eternity. May our eyes behold Your kingdom as it is said in the songs of Your might by David, the anointed of Your righteousness:

(Cong. & Reader) "*God* shall reign forever, your God, O Tzion, from generation to generation. Halaluyah!"

(Reader) From generation to generation shall we declare Your greatness and to all eternity will we proclaim Your holiness, and Your praise, O our God, shall never depart from our mouth, for You O God, are a great and holy King. Blessed be You *God,* the holy God. *(On* שבת שובה *say:* "the holy King").

---

in its position of dwelling-place for His glory, to "bless" God. In other words, God seeks, and will receive, the tribute of obedience in the form of the fulfillment of His will, and we look confidently and longingly to that day when God will return to Zion, this time forever, and when, from out of Zion, He will make the sovereignty of His Kingdom on earth become a living reality. בשירי עזו The chief purpose of the Psalms of David is to sing of *oz,* of the ultimate victory of God's kingdom on earth, and to pave the way for the coming of that kingdom by moving men to render homage to that which is good and right in accordance with the will of their God. It is for this reason that David is called משיח צדקו. צדק is that ideal of righteousness in the shaping of all earthly affairs which will become a living reality with the coming of the kingdom of God to earth. It was this ideal future that David served to advance and it was for the purpose of thus bringing nearer the fulfillment of this vision that David was anointed King. Hence David is called *meshiach tzidko.*

יִשְׂמַח מֹשֶׁה בְּמַתְּנַת חֶלְקוֹ כִּי עֶבֶד נֶאֱמָן קָרָאתָ
לּוֹ · כְּלִיל תִּפְאֶרֶת בְּרֹאשׁוֹ נָתָתָּ · בְּעָמְדוֹ לְפָנֶיךָ עַל
הַר־סִינַי · וּשְׁנֵי לֻחֹת אֲבָנִים הוֹרִיד בְּיָדוֹ · וְכָתוּב
בָּהֶם שְׁמִירַת שַׁבָּת · וְכֵן כָּתוּב בְּתוֹרָתֶךָ: וְשָׁמְרוּ
בְנֵי־יִשְׂרָאֵל אֶת־הַשַּׁבָּת לַעֲשׂוֹת אֶת־הַשַּׁבָּת לְדֹרֹתָם
בְּרִית עוֹלָם: בֵּינִי וּבֵין בְּנֵי יִשְׂרָאֵל אוֹת הִיא לְעֹלָם
כִּי־שֵׁשֶׁת יָמִים עָשָׂה יְהוָֹה אֶת־הַשָּׁמַיִם וְאֶת־הָאָרֶץ
וּבַיּוֹם הַשְּׁבִיעִי שָׁבַת וַיִּנָּפַשׁ:

יִשׂמח Moshe told his people ראו כי ה' נתן לכם השבת "Behold, *God* gave
you the Sabbath as a gift." The Sabbath is called not a burden but *mattanah
tovah* a "good gift". The prohibition of work on that day is not meant to be
a restrictive burden. The Sabbath is God's most precious and blessed gift of
which Moshe was privileged to be the bearer, to implant and nurture in the
hearts of his people the gladdening understanding and fulfillment of the
Sabbath. How greatly, indeed, must Moshe rejoice if his spirit should look
upon the abundance of blessings that the Divine Sabbath which he brought
to his people and nurtured in its midst, has given to Yisrael through all the
centuries of the millennia that have elapsed since his passing, blessings which
increase with each and every Sabbath that enters into the living presence of
his people. כי עבד נאמן For God has called Moshe a faithful servant in the
cause of His purposes and Moshe had indeed proven to be such by the faithful
manner in which he successfully and permanently implanted the Sabbath into
the hearts and minds of his people. It was not in vain that the radiant crown
was set upon his head when he stood before God on Mount Sinai and brought
down with him the Tablets of the Law upon which the commandment of
Sabbath observance was engraved as the mainstay and bearer of the entire
Torah.

ושמרו It is written in the Torah that this prohibition of work on the
Sabbath, by the observance of which we give expression to the true meaning
of the Day of Rest, is to be guarded by all of our descendants as well, as a
berith olam, as a Divine institution that is changeless and inalienable forever.

Let Moshe rejoice in the gift of his portion, for You called him
a faithful servant. A crown of glory have You placed upon his head
when he stood before You on Mount Sinai and brought down in his
hand two tablets of stone upon which [the command of] Sabbath
observance was inscribed. And thus it is written in Your Torah: "And
the sons of Yisrael shall keep the Sabbath, in order to fulfill the
Sabbath for their descendants as an everlasting covenant. It is a sign
between Me and the sons of Yisrael forever, that in six days *God*
made heaven and earth, and with the Seventh Day He ceased from
work, and withdrew into His own Essence."

Our fulfillment of this covenant is the "sign" set up by God between Him
and ourselves, to know that we recognize Him to be the Creator of Heaven
and earth, and that we acknowledge Him as such by subordinating to Him
all of our own lives, our ambitions and our achievements. ולא נתחו There are
thoughtless men who would like to view the Sabbath simply as a day of respite
from physical labor and effort which man, working by the sweat of his brow,
needs in order to survive. If this were true, and the Sabbath were nothing
else but a day of respite from bodily toil instead of a token of homage to
God, conviction, attitude, and moral observance or non-observance would be
a matter of indifference. Every man would then have a Sabbath of his own,
for everyone who works must have rest at some time. Indeed, it would then
be difficult to understand the need for a Divine commandment or for the
establishment of the Sabbath for a specific day of the week. The day of rest
would then be a natural outgrowth of man's need for relaxation and recreation
and the day on which that rest would take place would be immaterial. But
this is not the purpose of the cessation of all work on the Sabbath; the Sabbath
was meant to be much more than just a day for physical respite. As opposed
to creative labor which entails the subordination of the world to the strength
and power of man, the observance of the Sabbath is meant to be an expression
of the obedience of man, of man's subordination of himself and of the world
about him to God, an act of homage by man to God as his Lord and Creator.
Hence the proper observance of the Sabbath requires a complete change from
the views, attitudes and moral relationships that commonly prevail. It is for
this reason that God did not give the Sabbath, which is to be marked by the
cessation of all work (see Commentary to Exod. 20:8) to גויי הארצות those
nations whose existence is rooted in their "land" which they have won and
maintain by power and force. He did not permit the Sabbath to become the
inheritance of those who view the world as a territory peopled by a multitude

וְלֹא נְתַתּוֹ יְיָ אֱלֹהֵינוּ לְגוֹיֵי הָאֲרָצוֹת· וְלֹא הִנְחַלְתּוֹ
מַלְכֵּנוּ לְעוֹבְדֵי פְסִילִים· וְגַם בִּמְנוּחָתוֹ לֹא יִשְׁכְּנוּ
עֲרֵלִים· כִּי לְיִשְׂרָאֵל עַמְּךָ נְתַתּוֹ בְּאַהֲבָה· לְזֶרַע
יַעֲקֹב אֲשֶׁר בָּם בָּחָרְתָּ· עַם מְקַדְּשֵׁי שְׁבִיעִי כֻּלָּם
יִשְׂבְּעוּ וְיִתְעַנְּגוּ מִטּוּבֶךָ· וְהַשְּׁבִיעִי רָצִיתָ בּוֹ וְקִדַּשְׁתּוֹ
חֶמְדַּת יָמִים אוֹתוֹ קָרָאתָ זֵכֶר לְמַעֲשֵׂה בְרֵאשִׁית:

אֱלֹהֵינוּ וֵאלֹהֵי אֲבוֹתֵינוּ רְצֵה בִמְנוּחָתֵנוּ קַדְּשֵׁנוּ
בְּמִצְוֹתֶיךָ וְתֵן חֶלְקֵנוּ בְּתוֹרָתֶךָ שַׂבְּעֵנוּ מִטּוּבֶךָ
וְשַׂמְּחֵנוּ בִּישׁוּעָתֶךָ וְטַהֵר לִבֵּנוּ לְעָבְדְּךָ בֶּאֱמֶת
וְהַנְחִילֵנוּ יְיָ אֱלֹהֵינוּ בְּאַהֲבָה וּבְרָצוֹן שַׁבַּת קָדְשֶׁךָ
וְיָנוּחוּ בָה יִשְׂרָאֵל מְקַדְּשֵׁי שְׁמֶךָ· בָּרוּךְ אַתָּה יְיָ
מְקַדֵּשׁ הַשַּׁבָּת:

of powerful forces which they worship as gods. Nor can the true peace that
is to be won through genuine Sabbath rest be attained by those who do not
begin their homage to God with subordination of their own physical appetites.
In view of all these considerations it was to Yisrael and not to the others
that God gave the Sabbath, for Yisrael is a people which owes its very existence as a nation to Him alone. He gave the Sabbath to the descendants of
Yaakov, who had become heir to the recognition of God and to the covenant
of Abraham and thus had become worthy of being chosen for His purposes.
Moreover, it was with "love" that He had given the Sabbath to Yisrael. The
Sabbath is not a burden; instead, it is the most gladsome and blessed gift
of love that God could bestow upon men. It is for this reason that the apposition *beahavah* constantly recurs in the prayerbook with every mention of
the Sabbath. He who submits to God for review all of his earthly activities
with all their successes and failures (as is symbolized by the *lechem hapanim*

And You did not give it, O *God* our God, to the peoples of the lands, nor did You, O our King, give it as an inheritance to the idol worshippers; it is not the uncircumcised that dwell in its rest, but it is to Yisrael, Your people, that You gave it in love, to the seed of Yaakov, whom You had chosen. The people that sanctify the Seventh Day—they all shall be satisfied and delight in Your good. In the Seventh Day You took pleasure and You hallowed it. You proclaimed it—the most desirable of days—as a memorial to the work of the World's Beginning.

Our God and God of our fathers, take pleasure in our rest, hallow us by Your commandments and grant our portion in Your Torah. Satisfy us from Your good, gladden us with Your salvation, purify our hearts to serve You in truth, and in Your love and favor, O *God* our God, let Your holy Sabbath remain our inheritance, and may Yisrael, who sanctify Your Name, rest on it. Blessed be You *God*, Who hallows the Sabbath.

---

in the Temple), who submits to the examining eye of God all the work he has completed during the week, and is happy at the thought of having labored beneath the eye of God and worked in His service before His Presence, will be satisfied and contented with whatever portion life may allot him. He who knows that, though his strength may be feeble and his tangible achievments therefore small, he still has made a contribution to the fulfillment of God's will on earth, a contribution which however small, God will not despise, if only it has been made in the spirit of faith and loyalty, will have a share in the delight, in the good granted by God and in the Divine goodness which are the inheritance of our father Yaakov. (Isa. 58:14). The Sabbath is חמדת ימים; it is through the Sabbath that the preceding six days of Creation and our own six days of work that have just passed, receive their true purpose, worth and meaning. אותו קראת All the other festivals are dependent upon proclamation and appointment by the nation and its constituted authorities; it is only by virtue of their proclamation in this manner that they become *mikraei kodesh* "convocations" to the Sanctuary. Of all these sacred seasons, the Sabbath is the only holiday that has been proclaimed and established by God Himself for all times to come; thus the Sabbath is the only *Mikra Kodesh* that was determined by God Himself.

אלהינו see above p. 273.

רְצֵה יְיָ אֱלֹהֵינוּ בְּעַמְּךָ יִשְׂרָאֵל וּבִתְפִלָּתָם. וְהָשֵׁב
אֶת־הָעֲבוֹדָה לִדְבִיר בֵּיתֶךָ וְאִשֵׁי יִשְׂרָאֵל וּתְפִלָּתָם
בְּאַהֲבָה תְקַבֵּל בְּרָצוֹן וּתְהִי לְרָצוֹן תָּמִיד עֲבוֹדַת
יִשְׂרָאֵל עַמֶּךָ.

On Rosh Chodesh and the Intermediate Days of Festivals say:

אֱלֹהֵינוּ וֵאלֹהֵי אֲבוֹתֵינוּ. יַעֲלֶה וְיָבֹא וְיַגִּיעַ וְיֵרָאֶה וְיֵרָצֶה וְיִשָּׁמַע
וְיִפָּקֵד וְיִזָּכֵר זִכְרוֹנֵנוּ וּפִקְדוֹנֵנוּ וְזִכְרוֹן אֲבוֹתֵינוּ. וְזִכְרוֹן מָשִׁיחַ בֶּן
דָּוִד עַבְדֶּךָ. וְזִכְרוֹן יְרוּשָׁלַיִם עִיר קָדְשֶׁךָ. וְזִכְרוֹן כָּל עַמְּךָ בֵּית
יִשְׂרָאֵל לְפָנֶיךָ. לִפְלֵיטָה וּלְטוֹבָה וּלְחֵן וּלְחֶסֶד וּלְרַחֲמִים וּלְחַיִּים
וּלְשָׁלוֹם בְּיוֹם לר"ח רֹאשׁ הַחֹדֶשׁ ן לפסח חַג הַמַּצוֹת ן לסכות חַג הַסֻּכּוֹת
הַזֶּה. זָכְרֵנוּ יְיָ אֱלֹהֵינוּ בּוֹ לְטוֹבָה וּפָקְדֵנוּ בוֹ לִבְרָכָה וְהוֹשִׁיעֵנוּ בוֹ
לְחַיִּים. וּבִדְבַר יְשׁוּעָה וְרַחֲמִים. חוּס וְחָנֵּנוּ וְרַחֵם עָלֵינוּ
וְהוֹשִׁיעֵנוּ. כִּי אֵלֶיךָ עֵינֵינוּ. כִּי אֵל מֶלֶךְ חַנּוּן וְרַחוּם אָתָּה:

וְתֶחֱזֶינָה עֵינֵינוּ בְּשׁוּבְךָ לְצִיוֹן בְּרַחֲמִים. בָּרוּךְ אַתָּה
יְיָ הַמַּחֲזִיר שְׁכִינָתוֹ לְצִיוֹן:

מודים דרבנן.

מוֹדִים אֲנַחְנוּ לָךְ שָׁאַתָּה הוּא יְיָ	מוֹדִים אֲנַחְנוּ
אֱלֹהֵינוּ וֵאלֹהֵי אֲבוֹתֵינוּ אֱלֹהֵי כָל בָּשָׂר	לָךְ שָׁאַתָּה הוּא
יוֹצְרֵנוּ יוֹצֵר בְּרֵאשִׁית. בְּרָכוֹת וְהוֹדָאוֹת	יְיָ אֱלֹהֵינוּ וֵאלֹהֵי
לְשִׁמְךָ הַגָּדוֹל וְהַקָּדוֹשׁ עַל שֶׁהֶחֱיִיתָנוּ	אֲבוֹתֵינוּ לְעוֹלָם
וְקִיַּמְתָּנוּ. כֵּן תְּחַיֵּנוּ וּתְקַיְּמֵנוּ וְתֶאֱסוֹף	וָעֶד. צוּר חַיֵּינוּ
גָּלֻיּוֹתֵינוּ לְחַצְרוֹת קָדְשֶׁךָ לִשְׁמוֹר חֻקֶּיךָ	מָגֵן יִשְׁעֵנוּ אַתָּה
	הוּא לְדוֹר וָדוֹר.

Take pleasure, O *God* our God, in Your people Yisrael and in their prayer. Restore the sacrificial service to the Abode of Your Word in Your House, and accept Yisrael's fire offerings and their prayer with love and favor, and may the service of Your people Yisrael ever be pleasing to You.

On Rosh Chodesh and the Intermediate Days of Festivals say:

Our God and God of our fathers, may our remembrance and the consideration of us and the remembrance of our fathers, the remembrance of Messiah the son of David Your servant, the remembrance of Yerushalayim, Your holy City, and the remembrance of all Your people, the House of Yisrael, rise and come, reach You and be seen, be accepted and heard, considered and remembered for deliverance and for well-being, for favor and loving-kindness, for compassion, for life and for peace on this day of —The New Moon — The Festival of Unleavened Bread — The Festival of Tabernacles. Remember us this day, O *God* our God, for good, be mindful of us for blessing, and save us for life; and in the promise of salvation and compassion spare us and favor us, for our eyes look up to You; for You, O God, are a gracious and compassionate King.

And may our eyes behold Your return to Tzion in compassion. Blessed be You *God,* Who restores Your Presence to Tzion.

We gratefully avow to You that You, O *God,* are our God and the God of our fathers in all eternity. You are the Rock of our life, the Shield of our salvation from generation to generation. We avow our thanks to You and recount Your praise, for our lives, which are committed to Your hand, and for our souls which are in Your care, and for Your miracles which are with us each day, and

מודים דרבנן

We gratefully avow to You, that You, O *God,* are our God and the God of our fathers, the God of all flesh, our Creator and the Creator of the Beginning. Blessings and thanks to Your great and holy Name because You have kept us alive and have preserved us. So may You continue to keep us in life and preserve us, and gather our dispersed to the Courts of Your

נוֹדֶה לְךָ וּנְסַפֵּר וְלַעֲשׂוֹת רְצוֹנֶךָ וּלְעָבְדְּךָ בְּלֵבָב שָׁלֵם· עַל
תְּהִלָּתֶךָ · עַל שֶׁאֲנַחְנוּ מוֹדִים לָךְ· בָּרוּךְ אֵל הַהוֹדָאוֹת:
חַיֵּינוּ הַמְּסוּרִים בְּיָדֶךָ וְעַל נִשְׁמוֹתֵינוּ הַפְּקוּדוֹת לָךְ
וְעַל נִסֶּיךָ שֶׁבְּכָל־יוֹם עִמָּנוּ. וְעַל נִפְלְאוֹתֶיךָ וְטוֹבוֹתֶיךָ
שֶׁבְּכָל־עֵת· עֶרֶב וָבֹקֶר וְצָהֳרָיִם· הַטּוֹב כִּי לֹא־כָלוּ
רַחֲמֶיךָ וְהַמְרַחֵם כִּי לֹא־תַמּוּ חֲסָדֶיךָ מֵעוֹלָם
קִוִּינוּ לָךְ:

On Chanukkah add על הנסים p. 150

וְעַל־כֻּלָּם יִתְבָּרַךְ וְיִתְרוֹמַם שִׁמְךָ מַלְכֵּנוּ תָּמִיד
לְעוֹלָם וָעֶד:

During the Ten Days of Repentance add:

וּכְתוֹב לְחַיִּים טוֹבִים כָּל־בְּנֵי בְרִיתֶךָ:

וְכֹל הַחַיִּים יוֹדוּךָ סֶּלָה וִיהַלְלוּ אֶת־שִׁמְךָ בֶּאֱמֶת
הָאֵל יְשׁוּעָתֵנוּ וְעֶזְרָתֵנוּ סֶלָה· בָּרוּךְ אַתָּה יְיָ הַטּוֹב
שִׁמְךָ וּלְךָ נָאֶה לְהוֹדוֹת:

א״ן אֱלֹהֵינוּ וֵאלֹהֵי אֲבוֹתֵינוּ בָּרְכֵנוּ בַּבְּרָכָה הַמְשֻׁלֶּשֶׁת בַּתּוֹרָה
הַכְּתוּבָה עַל־יְדֵי מֹשֶׁה עַבְדֶּךָ הָאֲמוּרָה מִפִּי אַהֲרֹן וּבָנָיו כֹּהֲנִים
עַם קְדוֹשֶׁךָ כָּאָמוּר: יְבָרֶכְךָ יְיָ וְיִשְׁמְרֶךָ: יָאֵר יְיָ· פָּנָיו אֵלֶיךָ
וִיחֻנֶּךָ: יִשָּׂא יְיָ· פָּנָיו אֵלֶיךָ וְיָשֵׂם לְךָ שָׁלוֹם:

שִׂים שָׁלוֹם טוֹבָה וּבְרָכָה חֵן וָחֶסֶד וְרַחֲמִים עָלֵינוּ
וְעַל כָּל יִשְׂרָאֵל עַמֶּךָ בָּרְכֵנוּ אָבִינוּ כֻּלָּנוּ כְּאֶחָד בְּאוֹר
פָּנֶיךָ כִּי בְאוֹר פָּנֶיךָ נָתַתָּ לָּנוּ יְיָ אֱלֹהֵינוּ תּוֹרַת חַיִּים
וְאַהֲבַת חֶסֶד וּצְדָקָה וּבְרָכָה וְרַחֲמִים וְחַיִּים וְשָׁלוֹם·

for Your wondrous deeds and favors that are performed at all times, evening, morning and noon. You are the Beneficient One, for Your compassion has never ceased, the Compassionate Sanctuary, to keep Your statutes, to do Your will and to serve You wholeheartedly. For our very act of avowal to You, be You blessed, God of thanksgivings.

One, for Your kindnesses have never ended. Ever have we placed our hopes in You.

On Chanukkah add עַל הַנִּסִים *p.* 151

For all this, Our King, may Your Name be continually blessed and exalted for all eternity.

During the Ten Days of Repentance add:

And inscribe all the sons of Your covenant for a good life.

And everything that lives shall avow thanks to You and render praise to Your Name in truth as the God of our salvation and our help forever. Blessed be You *God,* the Beneficent One is Your Name, and to You thanksgiving is due.

When the Shemone Esrei is repeated, the Reader recites the following:

Our God and God of our fathers, bless us with the threefold blessing in the Torah, which was written by the hand of Moshe Your servant and spoken through the mouth of Aharon and his sons, the priests, Your holy people, as it is said: "May *God* bless you and keep you. May *God* light up His countenance for you and favor you. May *God* turn His countenance toward you and establish peace for you."

Establish peace, well-being and blessing, favor, loving-kindness and compassion upon us and upon all of Yisrael, Your people. Bless us, O our Father, all of us together, with the light of Your countenance. For by the light of Your countenance You have given us, O *God* our God, the Torah of life and the love of devotion and loyalty to duty, blessing and compassion, life and peace. May it be good in

וְטוֹב בְּעֵינֶיךָ לְבָרֵךְ אֶת־עַמְּךָ יִשְׂרָאֵל בְּכָל־עֵת וּבְכָל־שָׁעָה בִּשְׁלוֹמֶךָ:

add: **שבת שובה** On

בְּסֵפֶר חַיִּים בְּרָכָה וְשָׁלוֹם וּפַרְנָסָה טוֹבָה נִזָּכֵר וְנִכָּתֵב לְפָנֶיךָ אֲנַחְנוּ וְכָל עַמְּךָ בֵּית יִשְׂרָאֵל לְחַיִּים טוֹבִים וּלְשָׁלוֹם · בָּרוּךְ אַתָּה יְיָ עוֹשֵׂה הַשָּׁלוֹם:

בָּרוּךְ אַתָּה יְיָ הַמְבָרֵךְ אֶת־עַמּוֹ יִשְׂרָאֵל בַּשָּׁלוֹם:

אֱלֹהַי · נְצוֹר לְשׁוֹנִי מֵרָע וּשְׂפָתַי מִדַּבֵּר מִרְמָה וְלִמְקַלְלַי נַפְשִׁי תִדּוֹם וְנַפְשִׁי כֶּעָפָר לַכֹּל תִּהְיֶה: פְּתַח לִבִּי בְּתוֹרָתֶךָ וּבְמִצְוֹתֶיךָ תִּרְדּוֹף נַפְשִׁי וְכֹל הַחוֹשְׁבִים עָלַי רָעָה מְהֵרָה הָפֵר עֲצָתָם וְקַלְקֵל מַחֲשַׁבְתָּם · עֲשֵׂה לְמַעַן שְׁמֶךָ · עֲשֵׂה לְמַעַן יְמִינֶךָ · עֲשֵׂה לְמַעַן קְדֻשָּׁתֶךָ · עֲשֵׂה לְמַעַן תּוֹרָתֶךָ · לְמַעַן יֵחָלְצוּן יְדִידֶיךָ הוֹשִׁיעָה יְמִינְךָ וַעֲנֵנִי: יִהְיוּ לְרָצוֹן אִמְרֵי־פִי וְהֶגְיוֹן לִבִּי לְפָנֶיךָ יְיָ צוּרִי וְגֹאֲלִי: עֹשֶׂה שָׁלוֹם בִּמְרוֹמָיו הוּא יַעֲשֶׂה שָׁלוֹם עָלֵינוּ וְעַל כָּל יִשְׂרָאֵל וְאִמְרוּ אָמֵן :

יְהִי רָצוֹן לְפָנֶיךָ יְיָ אֱלֹהֵינוּ וֵאלֹהֵי אֲבוֹתֵינוּ שֶׁיִּבָּנֶה בֵּית הַמִּקְדָּשׁ בִּמְהֵרָה בְיָמֵינוּ וְתֵן חֶלְקֵנוּ בְּתוֹרָתֶךָ: וְשָׁם נַעֲבָדְךָ בְּיִרְאָה כִּימֵי עוֹלָם וּכְשָׁנִים קַדְמוֹנִיּוֹת: וְעָרְבָה לַיְיָ מִנְחַת יְהוּדָה וִירוּשָׁלָםִ כִּימֵי עוֹלָם וּכְשָׁנִים קַדְמוֹנִיּוֹת:

הש"ץ חוזר התפלה בקולות נקרוש ואח"כ אומר קדיש תתקבל: בר"ח וחנוכה וח"הם אומרין הלל אחר חזרת גמר התפלה קודם קדיש:

Before taking out the תורה, *the following is said in some congregations:*

אֵין כָּמוֹךָ בָאֱלֹהִים אֲדֹנָי וְאֵין כְּמַעֲשֶׂיךָ: מַלְכוּתְךָ מַלְכוּת כָּל עוֹלָמִים וּמֶמְשַׁלְתְּךָ בְּכָל דּוֹר וָדֹר: יְיָ מֶלֶךְ יְיָ מָלָךְ יְיָ יִמְלֹךְ לְעוֹלָם וָעֶד: יְיָ עֹז לְעַמּוֹ יִתֵּן יְיָ יְבָרֵךְ אֶת עַמּוֹ בַשָּׁלוֹם:

אַב הָרַחֲמִים הֵיטִיבָה בִרְצוֹנְךָ אֶת צִיּוֹן תִּבְנֶה חוֹמוֹת יְרוּשָׁלָםִ: כִּי בְךָ לְבַד בָּטָחְנוּ מֶלֶךְ אֵל רָם וְנִשָּׂא אֲדוֹן עוֹלָמִים:

Your sight to bless Your people Yisrael at all times and at every hour with Your peace.

(On שבת שובה add: May we be remembered and inscribed before You in the book of life, blessing, peace and good sustenance, we and all Your people, the House of Yisrael, for a good life and for peace. Blessed be You *God,* the Creator of Peace.)

Blessed be You *God,* Who blesses Your people Yisrael with peace.

My God, guard my tongue from evil and my lips from speaking falsehood. Let my soul be silent to those who curse me, and let my soul be as the dust to all things. Open my heart to Your Torah, and may my soul earnestly strive after Your commandments. But as for all those who plot evil against me, thwart their counsel and frustrate their intentions. Do it for the sake of Your Name, do it for the sake of Your right hand, do it for the sake of Your Torah; therefore set free those whom You have found worthy of Your love. Let Your right hand be seen in salvation and answer me! May the words of my mouth and the meditation of my heart be pleasing before Your countenance, O *God,* my Rock and my Redeemer. May He Who makes peace in His high places, make peace for us and for all Yisrael, and say: Amen.

May it be Your will, O *God* our God and God of our fathers, that the Temple be speedily rebuilt in our days, and give us our portion in Your Torah, so that we may serve You there with awe as in the days of old and as in former years. Then the tribute of homage of Yehudah and Yerushalayim will be pleasing to *God* as in the days of the past and as in former years.

On Rosh Chodesh, Chanukkah and on the Intermediate
Days of Festivals, the Hallel is recited here.

When the Torah is taken from the Ark, the following is said:

וַיְהִי בִּנְסֹעַ הָאָרֹן וַיֹּאמֶר מֹשֶׁה קוּמָה יְיָ וְיָפֻצוּ אֹיְבֶיךָ וְיָנֻסוּ
מְשַׂנְאֶיךָ מִפָּנֶיךָ : כִּי מִצִּיּוֹן תֵּצֵא תוֹרָה וּדְבַר־יְיָ מִירוּשָׁלָם :
בָּרוּךְ שֶׁנָּתַן תּוֹרָה לְעַמּוֹ יִשְׂרָאֵל בִּקְדֻשָּׁתוֹ :

בְּרִיךְ שְׁמֵיהּ. *See p.* 180

Upon receiving the ספר תורה, *the* חזן *says:*

טי״ק אוֹמֵר בְּקוֹל רָם שְׁמַע יִשְׂרָאֵל יְיָ אֱלֹהֵינוּ יְיָ אֶחָד :
אֶחָד אֱלֹהֵינוּ גָּדוֹל אֲדוֹנֵנוּ קָדוֹשׁ [וְנוֹרָא] שְׁמוֹ :

גַּדְּלוּ לַיְיָ אִתִּי . וּנְרוֹמְמָה שְׁמוֹ יַחְדָּו :

הקהל עונין : לְךָ יְיָ הַגְּדֻלָּה וְהַגְּבוּרָה וְהַתִּפְאֶרֶת וְהַנֵּצַח וְהַהוֹד כִּי
כֹל בַּשָּׁמַיִם וּבָאָרֶץ לְךָ יְיָ הַמַּמְלָכָה וְהַמִּתְנַשֵּׂא לְכֹל לְרֹאשׁ :
רוֹמְמוּ יְיָ אֱלֹהֵינוּ וְהִשְׁתַּחֲווּ לַהֲדֹם רַגְלָיו קָדוֹשׁ הוּא : רוֹמְמוּ יְיָ
אֱלֹהֵינוּ וְהִשְׁתַּחֲווּ לְהַר קָדְשׁוֹ כִּי קָדוֹשׁ יְיָ אֱלֹהֵינוּ :

עַל הַכֹּל יִתְגַּדַּל וְיִתְקַדַּשׁ וְיִשְׁתַּבַּח וְיִתְפָּאַר וְיִתְרוֹמַם וְיִתְנַשֵּׂא
שְׁמוֹ שֶׁל־מֶלֶךְ מַלְכֵי הַמְּלָכִים הַקָּדוֹשׁ בָּרוּךְ הוּא : בָּעוֹלָמוֹת
שֶׁבָּרָא הָעוֹלָם הַזֶּה וְהָעוֹלָם הַבָּא : כִּרְצוֹנוֹ וְכִרְצוֹן יְרֵאָיו וְכִרְצוֹן
כָּל־בֵּית יִשְׂרָאֵל : צוּר הָעוֹלָמִים אֲדוֹן כָּל־הַבְּרִיּוֹת אֱלוֹהַּ כָּל־

ויהי בנסע see above p. 181.

על הכל The paragraph beginning with *al hakol* dwells upon the thought
of the holiness and majesty of God which was brought to us so profoundly
a few moments ago when we carried His Torah into our midst in order to
read from it. In this manner we are to become aware of all the splendor and
greatness of the task which has been imposed upon us by the Torah of so exalted
and holy a God. We are reminded that, even as He is sanctified through
all His world-wide sovereignty and through the heavenly servants and messengers who are part of this rule and who bear His glory, so should He
be hallowed also through our own lives and conduct for all mankind to behold

When the Torah is taken from the Ark, the following is said:

And it came to pass, whenever the Ark went forth, that Moshe would say, "Rise up, O *God*, so that Your enemies be scattered and that those who hate You may flee before Your countenance." For out of Tzion shall go forth the Torah, and the Word of *God* from Yerushalayim. Blessed be He Who in His holiness gave the Torah to His people Yisrael.

בריך שמיה. *See p.* 181

(Reader) O declare the greatness of *God* with me, and let us exalt His Name together.

(Cong.) Yours, O *God*, is the greatness and the power and the glory and the victory and the majesty, for all that is in Heaven and on earth is Yours. Yours is the sovereignty and all that which rules over anything on earth. Exalt *God* our God and cast yourselves down at His footstool, holy is He. Exalt *God* our God and cast yourselves down at His holy mountain, for *God*, our God, is holy.

May the Name of the Supreme King of Kings, the Holy One, blessed be He, be recognized in all its greatness and holiness, praised, glorified, exalted and extolled above all things, in the worlds which He created, both in this world and in the world to come, in accordance with His desire and with the desire of all those Who fear Him and with the desire of all the House of Yisrael. Rock of all times, Lord of all creatures, God of all souls, He, Who dwells in the wide ex-

---

and to know. We pray that this our sanctification of Him may be revealed visibly by God through what He will do on our behalf, and demonstrated through us by virtue of what we will do in faithful obedience to Him. The term שיר חדש is always employed to denote a hymn which sings of the full redemption to come after we have passed through all the tests and trials that have been appointed for us. The term רכב, derived from the terminology of the management of horses and chariots, is used to denote God's management and guidance of the world. ערבות, derived from ערבה, "devastated places" is an allegorical term for hopeless situations from which there seems to be no prospect of relief for man. יה, related to כה, and כח always implies a show of force and might on the part of God, a visible demonstration of His work and of His will. In other words, the thought here is, "Soar up in song to Him Who guides us on, even through situations which seem utterly hopeless, to the gladsome goals of His universal sovereignty."

הַנְּפָשׁוֹת: הַיּוֹשֵׁב בְּמֶרְחַבֵּי מָרוֹם הַשּׁוֹכֵן בִּשְׁמֵי שְׁמֵי קֶדֶם: קְדָשָׁתוֹ עַל־הַחַיּוֹת וּקְדֻשָּׁתוֹ עַל־כִּסֵּא הַכָּבוֹד: וּבְכֵן יִתְקַדַּשׁ שִׁמְךָ בָּנוּ יְיָ אֱלֹהֵינוּ לְעֵינֵי כָּל־חָי: וְנֹאמַר לְפָנָיו שִׁיר חָדָשׁ כַּכָּתוּב: שִׁירוּ לֵאלֹהִים זַמְּרוּ שְׁמוֹ סֹלּוּ לָרֹכֵב בָּעֲרָבוֹת בְּיָהּ שְׁמוֹ וְעִלְזוּ לְפָנָיו: וְנִרְאֵהוּ עַיִן בְּעַיִן בְּשׁוּבוֹ אֶל־נָוֵהוּ כַּכָּתוּב: כִּי עַיִן בְּעַיִן יִרְאוּ בְּשׁוּב יְיָ צִיּוֹן: וְנֶאֱמַר וְנִגְלָה כְּבוֹד יְיָ וְרָאוּ כָל־בָּשָׂר יַחְדָּו כִּי פִּי יְיָ דִּבֵּר:

נדרך הליכתו אומרין אב הרחמים.

אַב הָרַחֲמִים הוּא יְרַחֵם עַם עֲמוּסִים וְיִזְכֹּר בְּרִית אֵיתָנִים וְיַצִּיל נַפְשׁוֹתֵינוּ מִן־הַשָּׁעוֹת הָרָעוֹת וְיִגְעַר בְּיֵצֶר הָרַע מִן הַנְּשׂוּאִים וְיָחֹן אוֹתָנוּ לִפְלֵיטַת עוֹלָמִים וִימַלֵּא מִשְׁאֲלוֹתֵינוּ בְּמִדָּה טוֹבָה יְשׁוּעָה וְרַחֲמִים:

כשמגיע הש"ץ על הבימה מכיח הס"ת על השולחן ופיתח יאומר :

וְיַעֲזֹר וְיָגֵן וְיוֹשִׁיעַ לְכָל הַחוֹסִים בּוֹ וְנֹאמַר אָמֵן: הָבוּ גֹדֶל לֵאלֹהֵינוּ וּתְנוּ כָבוֹד לַתּוֹרָה כֹּהֵן קְרָב· יַעֲמֹד (פְּלוֹנִי בַר פְּלוֹנִי הכהן): בָּרוּךְ שֶׁנָּתַן תּוֹרָה לְעַמּוֹ יִשְׂרָאֵל בִּקְדֻשָּׁתוֹ: תּוֹרַת יְיָ תְּמִימָה מְשִׁיבַת נָפֶשׁ עֵדוּת יְיָ נֶאֱמָנָה מַחְכִּימַת פֶּתִי: פִּקּוּדֵי יְיָ יְשָׁרִים מְשַׂמְּחֵי לֵב מִצְוַת יְיָ בָּרָה מְאִירַת עֵינָיִם: יְיָ עֹז לְעַמּוֹ יִתֵּן יְיָ יְבָרֵךְ אֶת עַמּוֹ בַשָּׁלוֹם: הָאֵל תָּמִים דַּרְכּוֹ אִמְרַת יְיָ צְרוּפָה מָגֵן הוּא לְכֹל הַחֹסִים בּוֹ:

קי"ח וְאַתֶּם הַדְּבֵקִים בַּיְיָ אֱלֹהֵיכֶם חַיִּים כֻּלְּכֶם הַיּוֹם:

דיא פֿאָר־ אונד נאך־גריסט מיבער דיא ספר תורה זיעהע זייטע 186.
בײַ'ם עאָפֿענעהבען דער ספר תורה:

וְזֹאת הַתּוֹרָה אֲשֶׁר־שָׂם מֹשֶׁה לִפְנֵי בְּנֵי יִשְׂרָאֵל עַל־פִּי יְיָ בְּיַד־מֹשֶׁה: עֵץ־חַיִּים הִיא לַמַּחֲזִיקִים בָּהּ וְתֹמְכֶיהָ מְאֻשָּׁר: דְּרָכֶיהָ דַרְכֵי־נֹעַם וְכָל־נְתִיבֹתֶיהָ שָׁלוֹם: אֹרֶךְ יָמִים בִּימִינָהּ בִּשְׂמֹאלָהּ עֹשֶׁר וְכָבוֹד: יְיָ חָפֵץ לְמַעַן צִדְקוֹ יַגְדִּיל תּוֹרָה וְיַאְדִּיר:

tended high places, Who inhabits the high heavens of antiquity, Whose holiness is above the *Chayoth* and Whose holiness is above the Throne of Glory. So shall Your Name, O *God* our God, be sanctified also by us in the sight of all things living and we shall utter a new song before His countenance even as it is said: Sing to God, sing praises to His Name, soar up to Him Who guides worlds through barrennesses by His Name, *Yah,* and exult greatly before His countenance. May we see Him eye to eye when He returns to His abode even as it is said, "For they shall see eye to eye when *God* returns to Tzion," and it is said, "And the glory of *God* will be revealed, and all flesh will see it together that it is the mouth of *God* that has spoken."

May the Father of Compassion have compassion upon the people of the heavy-laden. May He remember the covenant with the Patriarchs; may He deliver our souls from evil hours; may He frighten away the evil inclination from those who have been upheld, and may He favor us with deliverance for the eternities and fulfill our petitions in accordance with the measure of good, of salvation and of compassion.

קריאת התורה See above p. 181 ff.

The term Haftarah, derived from פטר, "to dismiss" is the designation used closely related in content to the portion from the Torah for that particular reading from the Torah. It is the concluding portion of the Shacharith service, and marks the "dismissal" of the congregation from the first part of the service, as it were. The selections from Prophetic literature that are read are closely related in content to the portion from the Torah for that particular Sabbath or holiday. It is a precept of profound meaning that no one who has not read from the Torah directly before may read the *Haftarah* before the congregation. This practice serves as a constant reminder of the position of precedence due the Torah. It is a constantly-repeated proclamation of the truth that prophecy and the vocation of the prophet are deeply rooted in the Torah, and in the Torah only. We must always remember that the Prophets were called for no other purpose but to spread among the people the realization of the Law of God as set down in its complete form in the Torah. The Prophets were to serve as intermediaries, warning and cautioning their brethren. It was their function to interpret to their people the Word of God and to offer them consolation, to teach them the true meaning of the joy which had been predicted long before in the Torah as the consequence of Israel's obedience, and

קודם קריאת ההפטרה ואחר שגמר הגולל יברך המפטיר ברכה זו.

בָּרוּךְ אַתָּה יְיָ אֱלֹהֵינוּ מֶלֶךְ הָעוֹלָם אֲשֶׁר בָּחַר בִּנְבִיאִים

טוֹבִים וְרָצָה בְדִבְרֵיהֶם הַנֶּאֱמָרִים בֶּאֱמֶת בָּרוּךְ אַתָּה יְיָ הַבּוֹחֵר

בַּתּוֹרָה וּבְמֹשֶׁה עַבְדּוֹ וּבְיִשְׂרָאֵל עַמּוֹ וּבִנְבִיאֵי הָאֱמֶת וָצֶדֶק :

אחר ההפטרה יברך הברכות האלה.

בָּרוּךְ אַתָּה יְיָ אֱלֹהֵינוּ מֶלֶךְ הָעוֹלָם צוּר כָּל־הָעוֹלָמִים צַדִּיק

בְּכָל־הַדּוֹרוֹת הָאֵל הַנֶּאֱמָן הָאוֹמֵר וְעוֹשֶׂה הַמְדַבֵּר וּמְקַיֵּם שֶׁכָּל־

דְּבָרָיו אֱמֶת וָצֶדֶק : נֶאֱמָן אַתָּה הוּא יְיָ אֱלֹהֵינוּ וְנֶאֱמָנִים דְּבָרֶיךָ

וְדָבָר אֶחָד מִדְּבָרֶיךָ אָחוֹר לֹא־יָשׁוּב רֵיקָם כִּי אֵל מֶלֶךְ נֶאֱמָן

וְרַחֲמָן אָתָּה : בָּרוּךְ אַתָּה יְיָ הָאֵל הַנֶּאֱמָן בְּכָל־דְּבָרָיו :

רַחֵם עַל־צִיּוֹן כִּי הִיא בֵּית חַיֵּינוּ וְלַעֲלוּבַת נֶפֶשׁ תּוֹשִׁיעַ בִּמְהֵרָה

בְיָמֵינוּ • בָּרוּךְ אַתָּה יְיָ מְשַׂמֵּחַ צִיּוֹן בְּבָנֶיהָ :

---

the significance of the misfortune which comes as the result of disobedience. Hence the procedure prescribed in connection with the reading of the *Haftarah* serves to refute, once and for all, the spurious idea that there were two separate forms of Judaism, the "Mosaic" on one hand and the "Prophetic" on the other.

אשר בחר בנביאים טובים God chooses as His prophets only *tovim,* "good" men who are "good" or "fit" to serve in this capacity. To Judaism the mere fact that a man who, only yesterday, was known for no other qualities but simple-mindedness, ignorance, rudeness and lack of education suddenly utters clever words that kindle the enthusiasm of those that hear him does not indicate at all that this man was in truth Divinely inspired and entrusted with a higher mission. The man whom Judaism is to acknowledge as a true prophet must have been distinguished as a *chacham*, a *gibbor* and an *ashir* long before he was called by God. He must have absorbed the knowledge and wisdom which may be found in the Torah and in the Torah alone. He must be healthy and strong in both body and character so that his spirit will not be tainted either by lust or by the irascibility that comes with physical weakness. He must be "rich"; that is, he must be completely content with his portion in life. Not wanting or desiring any advantage for himself, he must be capable

Blessing to be recited before the Reading of the Haftarah:

Blessed be You *God* our God, King of the Universe, Who has chosen good prophets and taken pleasure in their words which were spoken in truth. Blessed be You *God*, Who has chosen the Torah, His servant Moses, His people Yisrael, and the prophets of truth and right.

Blessing to be recited after the Reading of the Haftarah:

Blessed be You *God*, our God, King of the Universe, Rock of all ages, just in all generations, faithful God, Who promises and performs, speaks and fulfills, Whose words are all truth and right. Faithful are You, O *God* our God, and faithful are Your words, and not one of Your words shall return void, for You are a faithful and compassionate God and King. Blessed be You *God*, Who is a faithful God in all His words.

Have compassion upon Tzion, for it is the home of our life and save the saddened of soul speedily in our days. Blessed be You *God*, Who causes Tzion to rejoice in her sons.

---

of the most selfless devotion to his task of judging and evaluating the world about him with regard to its conduct and its fate. Finally, the true prophet must be genuinely *tov* "good" and a friend to all men both in his attitude and in his conduct. Unlike the heart of Bileam (see Commentary to Num. 22:8) the heart of a true prophet in Yisrael must be capable of genuine rejoicing when individuals and mankind flourish, and of sincere sorrow when they go into decline. The Jewish prophet stands in the service of *tov*, of the kingdom of the absolute good whose messenger he is meant to be. When he is משמיע שלום משמיע ישועה, he is מבשר טוב. To him *shalom* and *yeshu'ah* are identical with *tov;* he knows that, without *tov* there can be neither *shalom* nor *yeshu'ah*, and there is no *tov* that does not, in fact, beget *shalom* and *yeshu'ah*. It is for this reason, too, that the *ruach hakodesh* which emanates from God is called *ruach tovah* (Psalm 143:10, Neh. 9:20), and God chooses only *tovim* to be the messengers of that *tov*. ורצה בדבריהם All that the prophet has been given as a basic premise is the content of the ideals which he is to proclaim. The words in which he expresses the theme communicated to him are his own, and, according to the Sages אין שני נביאים מתנבאין בסגנון אחד (Sanhedrin 89a), each prophet has a style, peculiar to him alone, for setting forth the truths which he has been commanded to proclaim. Hence a prophet needs not only certain personal and mental qualifications, but also the gift of eloquence, and God chooses as His prophets only such men whose words

שִׂמְּחֵנוּ יְיָ אֱלֹהֵינוּ בְּאֵלִיָּהוּ הַנָּבִיא עַבְדֶּךָ וּבְמַלְכוּת בֵּית דָּוִד

מְשִׁיחֶךָ בִּמְהֵרָה יָבֹא וְיָגֵל לִבֵּנוּ · עַל־כִּסְאוֹ לֹא־יֵשֶׁב זָר וְלֹא־

יִנְחֲלוּ עוֹד אֲחֵרִים אֶת־כְּבוֹדוֹ · כִּי בְשֵׁם קָדְשְׁךָ נִשְׁבַּעְתָּ לּוֹ

שֶׁלֹּא־יִכְבֶּה נֵרוֹ לְעוֹלָם וָעֶד · בָּרוּךְ אַתָּה יְיָ מָגֵן דָּוִד:

בְּכָל שַׁבְּתוֹת הַשָּׁנָה גַם בְּשַׁבָּת חה"מ פֶּסַח אוֹמְרִים זֶה.

עַל־הַתּוֹרָה וְעַל־הָעֲבוֹדָה וְעַל־הַנְּבִיאִים וְעַל־יוֹם הַשַּׁבָּת הַזֶּה

שֶׁנָּתַתָּ לָּנוּ יְיָ אֱלֹהֵינוּ לִקְדֻשָּׁה וְלִמְנוּחָה לְכָבוֹד וּלְתִפְאָרֶת · עַל־

הַכֹּל יְיָ אֱלֹהֵינוּ אֲנַחְנוּ מוֹדִים לָךְ וּמְבָרְכִים אוֹתָךְ ·

יִתְבָּרַךְ שִׁמְךָ בְּפִי כָּל־חַי תָּמִיד לְעוֹלָם וָעֶד · בָּרוּךְ אַתָּה יְיָ

מְקַדֵּשׁ הַשַּׁבָּת:

בְּשָׁלֹשׁ רְגָלִים גַם בְּשַׁבָּת חה"מ סוֹכּוֹת אוֹמְרִים זֶה.

עַל־הַתּוֹרָה וְעַל־הָעֲבוֹדָה וְעַל־הַנְּבִיאִים וְעַל־יוֹם השבת הזה

וְעַל־יוֹם לכסח חַג הַמַּצּוֹת הַזֶּה לשטעות חַג הַשָּׁבֻעוֹת הַזֶּה לסוכות חַג

הַסֻּכּוֹת הַזֶּה לש"ע ויה"ש הַשְּׁמִינִי חַג הָעֲצֶרֶת הַזֶּה שֶׁנָּתַתָּ לָּנוּ יְיָ

אֱלֹהֵינוּ לקדשה ולמנוחה לְשָׂשׂוֹן וּלְשִׂמְחָה לְכָבוֹד וּלְתִפְאָרֶת · עַל־

הַכֹּל יְיָ אֱלֹהֵינוּ אֲנַחְנוּ מוֹדִים לָךְ וּמְבָרְכִים אוֹתָךְ · יִתְבָּרַךְ שִׁמְךָ

בְּפִי כָּל־חַי תָּמִיד לְעוֹלָם וָעֶד · בָּרוּךְ אַתָּה יְיָ מְקַדֵּשׁ השבת

וְיִשְׂרָאֵל וְהַזְּמַנִּים:

נאמרים באמת ; qualified to be the faithful, true expression of the thoughts and ideals which He wishes to have the prophet proclaim on earth. הבוחר בתורה וכו' In order to expound the Torah which Moshe brought down in his capacity as the servant of God, and which Yisrael received as the people of God, God chose prophets who had to enlist their gift of eloquence in the cause of the universal acknowledgement of the truths set down in the Torah and for the fulfillment of the righteous ordinances contained therein.

It is in this spirit that we approach the words of the Prophets. After the reading is completed, we recapitulate the truths which shine forth for us from every page of Prophetic literature concerning God, His relationship

Cause us to rejoice, O *God* our God, in Elijah the Prophet, Your servant, and in the kingdom of the house of David, Your anointed. May he soon come and cause our heart to exult. Let no stranger sit upon his throne and let others no longer partake in his glory. For by Your holy Name have You sworn to him that his light shall not be quenched forever. Blessed be You *God,* the Shield of David.

For the Torah and for the Divine service, for the Prophets and for this Sabbath day, which You, O *God* our God, have given us for sanctification and rest, for honor and glory, for all these things, O *God* our God, do we avow You grateful homage and bless You. May Your Name be blessed forever, in eternity, by the mouth of every living thing. Blessed be You *God,* Who hallows the Sabbath.

(On שלש רגלים say): For the Torah and for the Divine service, for the Prophets (and for this Sabbath Day) and for the day of:

This Festival of Unleavened Bread — This Festival of Weeks
— This Festival of Tabernacles — This Eighth Day,
the Festival of *Atzereth*

Which You, O *God* our God, have given us (for sanctification and rest) for bliss and joy, for honor and glory, for all these things, O *God* our God, do we avow You grateful homage and bless You. May Your Name be blessed forever, in eternity, by the mouth of every living thing. Blessed be You *God,* Who hallows (the Sabbath), Yisrael and the [festive] seasons.

---

with the world and to history, and concerning our hopes and our convictions, which we take with us on our way through the ages. God is צור, the Rock of All Times Who fashions the ages, Who champions the cause of the right in every era of history, the faithful God Who performs what He has promised, Who does as He has spoken, and Whose words are all identical with truth and right. In the words of His prophets we put our trust, for not one of the words which they have uttered at God's command concerning the course of the future will return "void", without having fulfilled its mission. Therefore we adhere with firm conviction to all His promises concerning Zion and its sons, the Prophet Elijah as a Divine messenger, and the advent of the Messianic Kingdom of David. And when we read the words of the Prophets on Sabbaths and Holidays we become gratefully aware, with ever-growing exaltation, of the bliss inherent in the lofty ideals of the Torah, in the Divine service, in the words of the Prophets and in the Sabbath days and Festival seasons that have been given to us as our own.

בר׳ה אומרים זה

עַל־הַתּוֹרָה וְעַל־הָעֲבוֹדָה וְעַל־הַנְּבִיאִים וְעַל־יוֹם השבת הזה

וְיוֹם הַזִּכָּרוֹן הַזֶּה שֶׁנָּתַתָּ לָּנוּ יְיָ אֱלֹהֵינוּ לקדשה ולמנוחה לְכָבוֹד

וּלְתִפְאָרֶת · עַל־הַכֹּל יְיָ אֱלֹהֵינוּ אֲנַחְנוּ מוֹדִים לָךְ וּמְבָרְכִים

אוֹתָךְ יִתְבָּרַךְ שִׁמְךָ בְּפִי כָּל־חַי תָּמִיד לְעוֹלָם וָעֶד וּדְבָרְךָ אֱמֶת

וְקַיָּם לָעַד : בָּרוּךְ אַתָּה יְיָ מֶלֶךְ עַל כָּל הָאָרֶץ מְקַדֵּשׁ השבת

וְיִשְׂרָאֵל וְיוֹם הַזִּכָּרוֹן :

בר׳הכ אומרים זה

עַל־הַתּוֹרָה וְעַל־הָעֲבוֹדָה וְעַל־הַנְּבִיאִים וְעַל־יוֹם השבת הזה

וְיוֹם הַכִּפֻּרִים הַזֶּה שֶׁנָּתַתָּ לָּנוּ יְיָ אֱלֹהֵינוּ לקדשה ולמנוחה לִמְחִילָה

וְלִסְלִיחָה וּלְכַפָּרָה לְכָבוֹד וּלְתִפְאָרֶת · עַל־הַכֹּל יְיָ אֱלֹהֵינוּ אֲנַחְנוּ

מוֹדִים לָךְ וּמְבָרְכִים אוֹתָךְ יִתְבָּרַךְ שִׁמְךָ בְּפִי כָּל־חַי תָּמִיד

לְעוֹלָם וָעֶד · וּדְבָרְךָ אֱמֶת וְקַיָּם לָעַד · בָּרוּךְ אַתָּה יְיָ, מֶלֶךְ מוֹחֵל

וְסוֹלֵחַ לַעֲוֹנוֹתֵינוּ וְלַעֲוֹנוֹת עַמּוֹ בֵּית יִשְׂרָאֵל · וּמַעֲבִיר אַשְׁמוֹתֵינוּ בְּכָל שָׁנָה וְשָׁנָה

מֶלֶךְ עַל־כָּל־הָאָרֶץ מְקַדֵּשׁ השבת וְיִשְׂרָאֵל וְיוֹם הַכִּפֻּרִים :

On Sabbaths the following paragraph is said
after the Reading of the Haftarah:

יְקוּם פּוּרְקָן מִן שְׁמַיָּא חִנָּא וְחִסְדָּא וְרַחֲמֵי וְחַיֵּי אֲרִיכֵי וּמְזוֹנֵי

רְוִיחֵי וְסִיַּעְתָּא דִשְׁמַיָּא וּבַרְיוּת גּוּפָא וּנְהוֹרָא מַעַלְיָא · זַרְעָא חַיָּא

וְקַיָּמָא · זַרְעָא דִי לָא יִפְסוֹק וְדִי לָא יִבְטוֹל מִפִּתְגָּמֵי אוֹרַיְתָא ·

לְמָרָנָן וְרַבָּנָן חֲבוּרָתָא קַדִּישָׁתָא דִּי בְּאַרְעָא דְיִשְׂרָאֵל וְדִי בְּבָבֶל ·

לְרֵישֵׁי כַלֵּי וּלְרֵישֵׁי גַלְוָתָא וּלְרֵישֵׁי מְתִיבָתָא וּלְדַיָּנֵי דִי בָבָא ·

יקום פורקן The readings from the Torah and from the Nevi'im, the
Divine laws and teachings that were handed down to us in writing, are followed by the recital of prayers for the welfare, survival and strengthening of
all those men and institutions that work for the realization of these teachings
and precepts of God. First and foremost among these servants of God's law
are the *maranan verabbanan*, the men to whom we are to look up as leading

(On ראש השנה *say):* For the Torah and for the Divine service, for the Prophets (and for this Sabbath Day) and for this Day of Remembrance, which You, O *God* our God, have given us (for sanctification and rest), for honor and glory; for all these things, O *God,* our God, do we avow You grateful homage and bless You. May Your Name be blessed forever, in all eternity, by the mouth of every living thing, and Your word is truth and endures forever. Blessed be You *God,* King over all the earth, Who hallows (the Sabbath), Yisrael and the Day of Remembrance.

(On יום כפור *say):* For the Torah and for the Divine service, for the Prophets (and for this Sabbath Day) and for this Day of Atonement which You, O *God* our God, have given us (for sanctification and rest), for pardon, forgiveness and atonement, for honor and glory; for all these things, O *God,* our God do we avow You grateful homage and bless You. May Your Name be blessed forever, in all eternity, by the mouth of every living thing, and Your word is truth and endures forever. Blessed be You *God,* King over all the earth, Who hallows (the Sabbath), Yisrael and the Day of Atonement.

*On Sabbaths the following paragraph is said
after the Reading of the Haftarah:*

May redemption from Heaven, favor, loving-kindness, compassion, long life, ample sustenance, heavenly aid, bodily health, a higher enlightenment and vigorous and abiding offspring, offspring that will not cease or neglect the study of the words of the Torah, come to our masters and teachers, to the holy associations, to those that are in the land of Yisrael and those that are in Babylonia, to the heads of the academies and to the heads of the exiled communities, to the heads of the Yeshivoth and to the judges at the gates, to all their disciples and

---

authorities because of their extensive knowledge of the Law and their loyalty to it, men who, aided by the commentaries of the Oral Tradition which are no less Divine than the Written Law, teach and promote the understanding of God's laws and doctrines in our midst. חברותא קדישתא are the associations, great and small, which, in the form of congregations, brotherhoods, societies, and so forth, dedicate their combined efforts in behalf of the sacred spiritual and moral purposes of God's law. כלא, רישי כלי is the Chaldean term for "calling out aloud", or "proclaiming", as in אכלי בגרונך : קרא בגרון אל תחשוך (Isa. 58:1). From this was derived the term כלה, plural כלי, which is employed

לְכָל־תַּלְמִידֵיהוֹן וּלְכָל־תַּלְמִידֵי תַלְמִידֵיהוֹן וּלְכָל מָן־דְּעָסְקִין
בְּאוֹרַיְתָא · מַלְכָּא דְעָלְמָא יְבָרֵךְ יָתְהוֹן יַפִּישׁ חַיֵּיהוֹן וְיַסְגֵּא יוֹמֵיהוֹן
וְיִתֵּן אַרְכָה לִשְׁנֵיהוֹן · וְיִתְפָּרְקוּן וְיִשְׁתֵּיזְבוּן מִן כָּל עָקָא וּמִן כָּל־
מַרְעִין בִּישִׁין מָרָן דִּי בִשְׁמַיָּא יְהֵא בְּסַעְדְּהוֹן כָּל־זְמַן וְעִדָּן וְנֹאמַר
אָמֵן :

Those saying their prayers at home omit the following:

יְקוּם פּוּרְקָן מִן שְׁמַיָּא חִנָּא וְחִסְדָּא וְרַחֲמֵי וְחַיֵּי אֲרִיכֵי וּמְזוֹנֵי
רְוִיחֵי וְסִיַּעְתָּא דִשְׁמַיָּא וּבַרְיוּת גּוּפָא וּנְהוֹרָא מַעַלְיָא · זַרְעָא חַיָּא
וְקַיָּמָא זַרְעָא דִי לָא יִפְסוֹק וְדִי לָא יִבְטוֹל מִפִּתְגָמֵי אוֹרַיְתָא ·
לְכָל קְהָלָא קַדִּישָׁא הָדֵין · רַבְרְבַיָּא עִם זְעֵרַיָּא טַפְלָא וּנְשַׁיָּא·
מַלְכָּא דְעָלְמָא יְבָרֵךְ יָתְכוֹן יַפִּישׁ חַיֵּיכוֹן וְיַסְגֵּא יוֹמֵיכוֹן וְיִתֵּן
אַרְכָה לִשְׁנֵיכוֹן · וְתִתְפָּרְקוּן וְתִשְׁתֵּיזְבוּן מִן כָּל־עָקָא וּמִן כָּל־
מַרְעִין בִּישִׁין · מָרָן דִּי בִשְׁמַיָּא יְהֵא בְּסַעְדְּכוֹן · כָּל זְמַן וְעִדָּן
וְנֹאמַר אָמֵן :

Reader :

מִי שֶׁבֵּרַךְ אֲבוֹתֵינוּ אַבְרָהָם יִצְחָק וְיַעֲקֹב הוּא יְבָרֵךְ אֶת־כָּל־
הַקָּהָל הַקָּדוֹשׁ הַזֶּה עִם כָּל־קְהִלּוֹת הַקֹּדֶשׁ, הֵם וּנְשֵׁיהֶם וּבְנֵיהֶם

---

to denote public lectures, particularly the great assemblies of study that took place during the months of Elul and Adar. The leaders of those "academies" were called רֵישֵׁי כַלֵי (Chulin 49a). רֵישֵׁי גָלוּתָא; the Exilarch who administered the affairs of the exiled nation and whose residence was in the City of Babylon, was called רֵישׁ גָלוּתָא, However, the term is employed in the plural here; i.e. *reshei galutha.* Now by right only one person at a time could hold the exalted office of Exilarch. It may be that, at the time this prayer was written, the institution of the *resh galuthah,* the Exilarch, might still have been extant. But the fact that the term is used here in the plural should indicate to us that reference is made here not to that one official, but rather to all the men who assumed position of leadership in the communities in exile; in other words, the officers and leaders of the communities and congregations. רֵישֵׁי מְתִיבְתָא are the heads of the faculties of the Yeshivoth, the "Talmudical

to all the disciples of their disciples, and to all those who occupy themselves with the Torah. May the King of the Universe bless them; may He prolong their lives, may He increase their days and lengthen their years. May they be redeemed and set free from all distress and evil suffering. May our Lord in Heaven be at their side at all times and at every hour, and let us say, Amen.

Those saying their prayers at home omit the following:

May redemption from Heaven, favor, loving-kindness, compassion, long life, ample sustenance, heavenly aid, bodily health, a higher enlightenment and vigorous and abiding offspring, offspring that will not cease or neglect the study of the words of the Torah, come to all of this holy congregation, to the great and to the small, to the children and to the women. May the King of the Universe bless you; may He prolong your lives,, may He increase your days and lengthen your years. May you be redeemed and set free from all distress and evil sufferings. May our Lord in Heaven be at your side at all times and at every hour, and let us say, Amen.

(Reader): May He Who blessed our fathers, Avraham, Yitzchak and Yaakov, bless all this holy congregation, together with all other holy congregations, them, their wives, their sons and daughters, and

---

academies". דיני די בבא : בבא is the Chaldean for שער meaning the "gate" or "portal" of the city which in ancient times served as the site at which the Court of Justice sat; hence we read והציגו בשער משפט (Amos 5:15). Therefore *dayanei di baba* are what we would call today "municipal judges", the judges of the city.

יקום פורקן This is the same prayer for blessing, preservation and strength, now recited for the congregation in general. This is followed by מי שברך, the prayer for God's blessing upon the entire congregation, together with all other congregations. We ask that the same blessing be bestowed also upon all those who further the purposes of the community by not only establishing houses of worship but also attending services there, and by donating what is required for the religious and philanthropic needs of the community. Finally, we ask God's blessing also for all those who faithfully administer the affairs of our religious communities.

הנותן תשועה Here, in keeping with the precept first mentioned in Jeremiah 29:7 and reiterated by our Sages in the Ethics of the Fathers (Chap. 3, Verse 2) we now recite a prayer for the welfare of the government of the country in which we reside. הנותן בים דרך (Isa. 43:16). This refers to "God Who, at the shore of the Sea of Reeds, taught us to know how He intervenes to

וּבְנוֹתֵיהֶם וְכָל אֲשֶׁר לָהֶם · וּמִי שֶׁמְּיַחֲדִים בָּתֵּי כְנֵסִיּוֹת לִתְפִלָּה ·
וּמִי שֶׁבָּאִים בְּתוֹכָם לְהִתְפַּלֵּל · וּמִי שֶׁנּוֹתְנִים נֵר לַמָּאוֹר וְיַיִן
לְקִדּוּשׁ וּלְהַבְדָּלָה וּפַת לָאוֹרְחִים וּצְדָקָה לָעֲנִיִּים · וְכָל־מִי
שֶׁעוֹסְקִים בְּצָרְכֵי צִבּוּר בֶּאֱמוּנָה · הַקָּדוֹשׁ בָּרוּךְ הוּא יְשַׁלֵּם
שְׂכָרָם וְיָסִיר מֵהֶם כָּל־מַחֲלָה וְיִרְפָּא לְכָל־גּוּפָם וְיִסְלַח לְכָל־
עֲוֹנָם וְיִשְׁלַח בְּרָכָה וְהַצְלָחָה בְּכָל־מַעֲשֵׂה יְדֵיהֶם עִם כָּל־יִשְׂרָאֵל
אֲחֵיהֶם · וְנֹאמַר אָמֵן :

Prayer for the Government

הַנּוֹתֵן תְּשׁוּעָה לַמְּלָכִים וּמֶמְשָׁלָה לַנְּסִיכִים · מַלְכוּתוֹ מַלְכוּת
כָּל־עוֹלָמִים · הַפּוֹצֶה אֶת־דָּוִד עַבְדּוֹ מֵחֶרֶב רָעָה · הַנּוֹתֵן בַּיָּם
דֶּרֶךְ וּבְמַיִם עַזִּים נְתִיבָה · הוּא יְבָרֵךְ וְיִשְׁמֹר וְיִנְצֹר וְיַעֲזֹר
וִירוֹמֵם וִיגַדֵּל וִינַשֵּׂא לְמַעְלָה אֶת ‏ יָרוּם הוֹדוֹ : מֶלֶךְ
מַלְכֵי הַמְּלָכִים בְּרַחֲמָיו יְחַיֵּהוּ וְיִשְׁמְרֵהוּ וּמִכָּל־צָרָה וְיָגוֹן וָנֶזֶק
יַצִּילֵהוּ · וְיַדְבֵּר עַמִּים תַּחַת רַגְלָיו וְיַפִּיל שׂוֹנְאָיו לְפָנָיו וּבְכָל
אֲשֶׁר־יִפְנֶה יַצְלִיחַ · מֶלֶךְ מַלְכֵי הַמְּלָכִים בְּרַחֲמָיו יִתֵּן בְּלִבּוֹ וּבְלֵב
כָּל־יוֹעֲצָיו וְשָׂרָיו רַחֲמָנוּת לַעֲשׂוֹת טוֹבָה עִמָּנוּ וְעִם כָּל־יִשְׂרָאֵל ·
בְּיָמָיו וּבְיָמֵינוּ תִּוָּשַׁע יְהוּדָה וְיִשְׂרָאֵל יִשְׁכֹּן לָבֶטַח וּבָא לְצִיּוֹן גּוֹאֵל ·
וְכֵן יְהִי רָצוֹן · וְנֹאמַר אָמֵן :

On the Sabbath preceding Rosh Chodesh the following is said:

יְהִי רָצוֹן מִלְּפָנֶיךָ יְיָ אֱלֹהֵינוּ וֵאלֹהֵי אֲבוֹתֵינוּ שֶׁתְּחַדֵּשׁ עָלֵינוּ
אֶת־הַחֹדֶשׁ הַזֶּה לְטוֹבָה וְלִבְרָכָה וְתִתֶּן־לָנוּ חַיִּים אֲרֻכִּים חַיִּים

fashion the fate of the nations." בימיו ובימינו: The universal salvation of all
of mankind for which we all hope is so closely linked with the yearned for
redemption of our own Tzion that when we pray for the welfare of the government of the country in which we now reside we also add a prayer for the
deliverance of Yehudah and Tzion.

all that belong to them, those who unite to form synagogues for prayer, and those who enter therein to pray, those who donate lamps for lighting, and wine for Kiddush and Havdalah, those who give bread to the wanderer and alms to the poor, and all those who faithfully occupy themselves with the affairs of the community. May the Holy One, blessed be He, pay them their reward; may He keep far from them all sickness, heal all their body, forgive all their iniquity and send blessing and prosperity to all the work of their hands, together with all of Yisrael, their brethren, and let us say, Amen.

Prayer for the Government

He Who gives victory to kings and dominion to princes, Whose reign is a reign spanning all the ages, Who freed David, His servant, from the evil sword, Who opened a way through the sea and a path through mighty waters, may He bless, guard, protect, help, exalt, make great and raise on high...............

May the Supreme King of Kings in His compassion preserve him in life and guard him and deliver him from all distress, from all grief and trouble; may he lead nations to come to his feet; may He cause those who hate him to fall down before him, and grant him success wherever his efforts may turn. May the Supreme King of Kings in His compassion instill compassion into his heart and into the hearts of all his counselors and ministers so that he may deal kindly with us and with all of Yisrael. In his days and in ours may Yehudah be saved and Yisrael dwell securely, and may the Redeemer come to Tzion; may this be His will, and let us say, Amen.

מִי שֶׁעָשָׂה The very first institution that God established for us immediately preceding our redemption from Egypt was that of the "New Moon." We were still slaves in every respect when God appointed for us the New Moon, which was intended to be a symbol of the "renewal" to deliver us from every "darkness and cloud" that may mar our lives, physical, spiritual or moral, both as individuals and as members of the larger community. This is a favor for which we can strive again and again and which we may hopefully await at any time. Therefore, whenever we hear the proclamation of a New Moon to come during the week to follow, our spirits hopefully look to the redemption and renewal which we, too, may expect, and we pray that, with the "renewal" of the Moon, God may bring about a rebirth of prosperity and salvation for us as well.

שֶׁל־שָׁלוֹם חַיִּים שֶׁל־טוֹבָה חַיִּים שֶׁל־בְּרָכָה חַיִּים שֶׁל־פַּרְנָסָה
חַיִּים שֶׁל־חִלּוּץ עֲצָמוֹת חַיִּים שֶׁיֵּשׁ בָּהֶם יִרְאַת שָׁמַיִם וְיִרְאַת חֵטְא
חַיִּים שֶׁאֵין בָּהֶם בּוּשָׁה וּכְלִמָּה חַיִּים שֶׁל־עֹשֶׁר וְכָבוֹד חַיִּים
שֶׁתְּהִי בָנוּ אַהֲבַת תּוֹרָה וְיִרְאַת שָׁמַיִם חַיִּים שֶׁיִּמָּלְאוּ מִשְׁאֲלוֹת
לִבֵּנוּ לְטוֹבָה אָמֵן סֶלָה:

וְאוֹמֵר הַשַּׁ"ץ מִי שֶׁעָשָׂה וְכוּ'.

ח' מִי שֶׁעָשָׂה נִסִּים לַאֲבוֹתֵינוּ וְגָאַל אוֹתָם מֵעַבְדוּת לְחֵרוּת·
הוּא יִגְאַל אוֹתָנוּ בְּקָרוֹב וִיקַבֵּץ נִדָּחֵינוּ מֵאַרְבַּע כַּנְפוֹת
הָאָרֶץ · חֲבֵרִים כָּל־יִשְׂרָאֵל · וְנֹאמַר אָמֵן ·

הַשַּׁ"ן לוֹקֵחַ סֵ"ת בְּיָדוֹ וְאוֹמֵר ר"ח פְלוֹנִי יְהִי' בְּיוֹם פְלוֹנִי (הַבָּא עָלֵינוּ וְעַל כָּל יִשְׂרָאֵל לְטוֹבָה).

קי"ח יְחַדְּשֵׁהוּ הַקָּדוֹשׁ בָּרוּךְ הוּא עָלֵינוּ וְעַל כָּל־עַמּוֹ
בֵּית יִשְׂרָאֵל · לְחַיִּים וּלְשָׁלוֹם · לְשָׂשׂוֹן וּלְשִׂמְחָה ·
לִישׁוּעָה וּלְנֶחָמָה: וְנֹאמַר אָמֵן:

וְאוֹמְרִים אָב הָרַחֲמִים, וְאֵין אוֹמְרִים אוֹתוֹ בְּיָמִים שֶׁאֵין אוֹמְרִים בָּהֶם תַּחֲנוּן בְּחוֹל, וְלֹא בְשַׁבָּת
שֶׁיֵּשׁ בָּהּ חָתָן אוֹ מִילָה, וְלֹא בְשַׁבָּת שֶׁמְּבָרְכִין בָּהּ אֶת הַחֹדֶשׁ (חוּץ מִימֵי הַסְּפִירָה).

אַב הָרַחֲמִים שׁוֹכֵן מְרוֹמִים · בְּרַחֲמָיו הָעֲצוּמִים · הוּא יִפְקֹד
בְּרַחֲמִים · הַחֲסִידִים וְהַיְשָׁרִים וְהַתְּמִימִים · קְהִלּוֹת הַקֹּדֶשׁ שֶׁמָּסְרוּ
נַפְשָׁם עַל קְדֻשַּׁת הַשֵּׁם: הַנֶּאֱהָבִים וְהַנְּעִימִים בְּחַיֵּיהֶם וּבְמוֹתָם
לֹא נִפְרָדוּ · מִנְּשָׁרִים קַלּוּ וּמֵאֲרָיוֹת גָּבֵרוּ · לַעֲשׂוֹת רְצוֹן קוֹנָם
וְחֵפֶץ צוּרָם: יִזְכְּרֵם אֱלֹהֵינוּ לְטוֹבָה · עִם שְׁאָר צַדִּיקֵי עוֹלָם ·

אב הרחמים Though God dwells on high, far above the hubbub of earthly
affairs, His compassion is here below with every one of His works and He,
too, feels the pain which affects any one of His creatures on earth. But His
compassion is most of all with those whose troubles are caused by abuses
from the hands of men who have gone astray, and particularly with those
who have been made to suffer because of their steadfast loyalty to Him. Thus
may He, then, remember those who have persevered in their devotion to Him

*On the Sabbath preceding Rosh Chodesh the Reader announces
the coming of the New Moon as follows:*

(Reader): May He Who performed miracles for our fathers and
redeemed them from slavery to freedom, speedily redeem us and
gather our dispersed people from the four ends of the earth, all of
Yisrael united, and let us say, Amen.

The Reader takes the Torah and recites:

The New Moon of . . . . will be on . . . . May it come
to us and to all of Yisrael for good.

(Cong. and Reader): May the Holy One, blessed be He, renew
it for us and for His people, all the House of Yisrael, for life and
for peace, for bliss and for joy, for salvation and consolation, and
let us say, Amen.

May the Father of Compassion Who dwells on high, in His
profound compassion, be mindful of the devoted, the upright and
blameless, the holy congregations, who gave their lives for the sanctification of the Divine Name, who were beloved and pleasant in their
lives and even in death refused to let themselves be parted from Him.
Swifter than eagles they were, and stronger than lions to do the will
of their Owner and the desire of their Rock. May our God remember
them for good together with the other righteous of all the ages, and

---

and who have remained steadfast in their uprightness and have kept their
moral integrity intact. We pray that He may remember them all, individuals
and congregations alike, who have thus remained true to their sacred purpose,
who have demonstrated their loyalty by their willingness to die for it, and
who have paid with their lives for having sanctified the Name of God.
During their lifetime, and by virtue of the life they lived, they made themselves worthy of God's love and approval, and even in death they remained
close to Him. They recognized God as קונם, as their "Owner" to Whom they
belonged with every fiber of their being and with every ounce of their strength,
and Who alone could command over them. They acknowledged, too, that He
was צורם, the sole Rock, Creator and Support of their destiny, and they knew
that they were in His hands not only in life but even in death. It was this knowledge that gave them power to soar up with ease, like the eagle, beyond all the
earthly scruples and temptations that might have tended to make them swerve
from the straight track which had been plotted for them by the will of their

וְיִנְקוֹם לְעֵינֵינוּ נִקְמַת דַּם עֲבָדָיו הַשָּׁפוּךְ: כַּכָּתוּב בְּתוֹרַת מֹשֶׁה
אִישׁ הָאֱלֹהִים · הַרְנִינוּ גוֹיִם עַמּוֹ כִּי דַם עֲבָדָיו יִקּוֹם · וְנָקָם יָשִׁיב
לְצָרָיו וְכִפֶּר אַדְמָתוֹ עַמּוֹ : וְעַל יְדֵי עֲבָדֶיךָ הַנְּבִיאִים כָּתוּב לֵאמֹר ·
וְנִקֵּיתִי דָמָם לֹא נִקֵּיתִי · וַיְיָ שֹׁכֵן בְּצִיּוֹן · וּבְכִתְבֵי הַקֹּדֶשׁ נֶאֱמַר ·
לָמָה יֹאמְרוּ הַגּוֹיִם אַיֵּה אֱלֹהֵיהֶם : יִוָּדַע בַּגּוֹיִם לְעֵינֵינוּ · נִקְמַת
דַּם עֲבָדֶיךָ הַשָּׁפוּךְ : וְאוֹמֵר כִּי דֹרֵשׁ דָּמִים אוֹתָם זָכָר לֹא שָׁכַח
צַעֲקַת עֲנָוִים : וְאוֹמֵר יָדִין בַּגּוֹיִם מָלֵא גְוִיּוֹת מָחַץ רֹאשׁ עַל אֶרֶץ
רַבָּה: מִנַּחַל בַּדֶּרֶךְ יִשְׁתֶּה עַל כֵּן יָרִים רֹאשׁ:

Here אשרי (*page 80*) *is said.*

Owner. It caused them to be stronger than lions in surmounting difficulties
and in fighting all resistance in order to fulfill the desire of their Rock. יזכרם
etc. וינקום etc. They knew that God would never forget the blood of innocent
men that had been shed, particularly if it was spilled in the cause of His
service and for the sake of loyalty to Him. Knowing this, and given new
confidence by this allusion to God's promise, our people throughout the ages
have committed to God and to God alone the task of avenging the blood of
their murdered fathers and mothers, wives and children. This promise sustained them and kept them free of bitter and burning lust for vengeance
against their oppressors and murderers, and it made them strong enough to
suppress every impulse of vengefulness and thus, even as the most persecuted
of peoples, to remain the meekest nation on earth. They left vengeance to
God and never lifted up their own hands to avenge themselves or their own.
Such is the fruit yielded by these prayers in which the worshipper views God
as the Avenger of the innocent. הרנינו. This appeal to the nation stresses three
prominent considerations which should motivate them to ·deal more kindly
with the Jewish people. First, the Children of Yisrael are *avadav;* they bear
the Name of God among the nations, and this same God will avenge any
innocent blood shed from that people, נקם ישיב לצריו. Secondly, the nations are
reminded that those who would deny the validity of the duty to practice
justice and humanity, actually deny the Rulership of God. Thus they are צריו,
the enemies of His kingdom, and the Lord causes every violation of the laws
of justice and humanity to recoil upon those guilty of it. וכפר אדמתו עמו.
Finally, it is by dealing more kindly with the people of God that the nations
should express their subordination to God's moral law and their homage, at
long last, to His rule on earth. Only in this manner will they be able to atone
for the crimes they had committed against the kingdom of God Who demands
justice and humanity of all men. ונקיתי "Even though I forgive much iniquity

avenge the blood of His servants that has been shed, even as it is
written in the Torah of Moshe, the man of God: "O Nations, make
joyous the lot of His people, for He will avenge the blood of His
servants, and He will wreak vengeance upon His enemies, and His
earth will atone for His people." And it is written by the hand of
Your servants, the Prophets: "Whatever [else] I may have forgiven,
I have not forgiven [the shedding of] their blood, and *God* still
dwells in Tzion." And it is said in the Holy Writings : "Wherefore
should the nations say, 'Where is their God?' Let Him be recognized
among the nations before our eyes, as vengeance for the blood of Your
servants that has been shed." And he says: "For He Who avenges
blood has remembered them; He has not forgotten the cry of the
humble." And he says : "He shall one day judge the cadaverous
among the nations, after He will have cleft the head that commands
over the mighty land. Who proudly lifts up his head because he drinks
from the river that flows for him along the way."

---

and allow many misdeeds to go unpunished," says God, "I shall not permit
their blood which has been shed to go unavenged." It may seem as if God
had forgotten His people so that any tyrant may violate it with impunity,
but this is only an illusion. For the destiny of Zion to be the abode of God's
Presence in the midst of His people has still not been annulled. God dwells
in Zion even now. If יודע were to refer to נקמת, the text would not read   יודע
at all, but תודע ; hence, as employed here, it refers to אלהיהם, the God Whose
existence they deny because they fail to see His work. The thought here is:
"If the descendants of those who failed to recognize the God of Jewish truth
and who slaughtered His servants will be made to witness the survival and
the eventual deliverance of the succeeding generations of Yisrael whom the
martyrs had inspired by their own glorious example to remain faithful and
of good courage, that will be atonement for the blood of Your servants. If,
witnessing Yisrael's survival and redemption, the nations will acquire a better
understanding and eventually recognize Jewish truth, then those who were
innocently slaughtered will not have died in vain." ידין, גויות מלא is the
object of ידין, referring to the people which will be the first to be affected
by God's judgment, a people whose wealth was built up by murder, whose
riches stem from death and are therefore built of corpses, as it were.
ראש על ארץ רבה is one who rules over a great, wealthy and powerful nation.
This ruler has not built up his position of power by dint of his own strength;
he has merely exploited the favorable opportunities which God had sent his
way. The river of prosperity and power flowed upon his path, and all he did
was draw water from it, and yet he is arrogant.

The Reader takes the Torah back to the Ark and says:

יְהַלְלוּ אֶת־שֵׁם יְהֹוָה כִּי־נִשְׂנָּב שְׁמוֹ לְבַדּוֹ:

congregation : הוֹדוֹ עַל־אֶרֶץ וְשָׁמָיִם · וַיָּרֶם קֶרֶן לְעַמּוֹ תְּהִלָּה לְכָל־
חֲסִידָיו לִבְנֵי יִשְׂרָאֵל עַם קְרוֹבוֹ הַלְלוּיָהּ:

On Sabbaths, say:

כט מִזְמוֹר לְדָוִד · הָבוּ לַיהֹוָה בְּנֵי אֵלִים הָבוּ לַיהֹוָה כָּבוֹד וָעֹז: הָבוּ
לַיהֹוָה כְּבוֹד שְׁמוֹ הִשְׁתַּחֲווּ לַיהֹוָה בְּהַדְרַת־קֹדֶשׁ: קוֹל יְהֹוָה עַל־
הַמָּיִם אֵל־הַכָּבוֹד הִרְעִים יְהֹוָה עַל־מַיִם רַבִּים: קוֹל־יְהֹוָה בַּכֹּחַ
קוֹל יְהֹוָה בֶּהָדָר: קוֹל יְהֹוָה שֹׁבֵר אֲרָזִים וַיְשַׁבֵּר יְהֹוָה אֶת־אַרְזֵי
הַלְּבָנוֹן: וַיַּרְקִידֵם כְּמוֹ־עֵגֶל לְבָנוֹן וְשִׂרְיוֹן כְּמוֹ בֶן־רְאֵמִים: קוֹל־
יְהֹוָה חֹצֵב לַהֲבוֹת אֵשׁ: קוֹל יְהֹוָה יָחִיל מִדְבָּר יָחִיל יְהֹוָה מִדְבַּר
קָדֵשׁ: קוֹל יְהֹוָה יְחוֹלֵל אַיָּלוֹת וַיֶּחֱשֹׂף יְעָרוֹת וּבְהֵיכָלוֹ כֻּלּוֹ אֹמֵר
כָּבוֹד: יְהֹוָה לַמַּבּוּל יָשָׁב וַיֵּשֶׁב יְהֹוָה מֶלֶךְ לְעוֹלָם: יְהֹוָה עֹז לְעַמּוֹ
יִתֵּן, יְהֹוָה יְבָרֵךְ אֶת־עַמּוֹ בַשָּׁלוֹם:

On Festivals occurring on Weekdays say:

כד לְדָוִד מִזְמוֹר · לַיהֹוָה הָאָרֶץ וּמְלוֹאָהּ תֵּבֵל וְיֹשְׁבֵי
בָהּ: כִּי־הוּא עַל־יַמִּים יְסָדָהּ וְעַל־נְהָרוֹת יְכוֹנְנֶהָ:
מִי־יַעֲלֶה בְהַר יְהֹוָה וּמִי־יָקוּם בִּמְקוֹם קָדְשׁוֹ: נְקִי
כַפַּיִם וּבַר לֵבָב אֲשֶׁר לֹא־נָשָׂא לַשָּׁוְא נַפְשׁוֹ וְלֹא נִשְׁבַּע

Psalm 29 מזמור לדוד See above p. 244. This psalm is sung when the Torah is returned to the Ark on the Sabbath, the day commemorating the creation of the world. The theme of this psalm is a contemplation and praise of the truth that the same God and the same Voice which speaks to us from His Law to shape our lives and which with overpowering might exacts obedience from man, also reigns supreme in the course and creation of the world

The Reader takes the Torah back to the Ark and says:

Let them proclaim the praise of the Name of *God*, that His Name alone is exalted.

(Cong.): His majesty is above the earth and heaven. When He lifted up the horn for His people, it is a praise of His mighty acts for all of His devoted ones, but to the sons of Yisrael [only because they have been] the people near to Him from the beginning. Halaluyah!

On Sabbaths, say:

A Psalm of David. Ascribe to *God*, O you who are endowed with strength, ascribe to *God* glory and might. Ascribe to *God* the glory due His Name, cast yourselves down before *God* in the beauty of holiness. The voice of *God* was upon those waters then; thus, if the omnipotence of creation's glory still thunders, then it is *God* Who rules over the many waters. The voice of *God* is within every force; the voice of *God* is in all things beautiful. The voice of *God* also breaks cedars, as *God* also broke the cedars of Lebanon. As He made them skip like calves, Lebanon and Sirion like young *Re'emim*. The voice of *God* also strikes flames of fire; the voice of *God* lets the wilderness go into travail, even as *God* makes the wilderness of Kadesh go into travail. The voice of *God* makes hinds to calve, even while it strips the forests bare, and in His Temple all that is His says, "Glory." *God* remained calmly upon His throne even at the flood, and thus *God* set Himself up as King forever. To His people, however, *God* will grant power to be victorious over all; *God* will bless His people with peace.

On Festivals occurring on Weekdays say:

By David, a Psalm. The earth is *God*'s and the fullness thereof, the world of men and they that dwell therein. For He has founded it upon the seas and, guiding it, constantly establishes it upon the floods. Who shall ascend to the mountain of *God*, and who shall stand in the place of His Sanctuary? "He that is clean of hands and pure of heart, who has not lifted up his soul, which is Mine, unto

---

about us, all-powerful, shaping both the phenomena of nature and the history of man.

לְמִרְמָה: יִשָּׂא בְרָכָה מֵאֵת יְהוָה וּצְדָקָה מֵאֱלֹהֵי יִשְׁעוֹ: זֶה דּוֹר
דֹּרְשָׁיו מְבַקְשֵׁי פָנֶיךָ יַעֲקֹב סֶלָה: שְׂאוּ שְׁעָרִים רָאשֵׁיכֶם וְהִנָּשְׂאוּ
פִּתְחֵי עוֹלָם וְיָבוֹא מֶלֶךְ הַכָּבוֹד: מִי זֶה מֶלֶךְ הַכָּבוֹד · יְהוָה עִזּוּז
וְגִבּוֹר יְהוָה גִּבּוֹר מִלְחָמָה: שְׂאוּ שְׁעָרִים רָאשֵׁיכֶם וּשְׂאוּ פִּתְחֵי
עוֹלָם וְיָבֹא מֶלֶךְ הַכָּבוֹד: מִי הוּא זֶה מֶלֶךְ הַכָּבוֹד · יְהוָה צְבָאוֹת
הוּא מֶלֶךְ הַכָּבוֹד סֶלָה:

As the Torah is returned to the Ark, the Reader says:

וּבְנֻחֹה יֹאמַר שׁוּבָה יְהוָה רִבְבוֹת אַלְפֵי יִשְׂרָאֵל: קוּמָה יְהוָה
לִמְנוּחָתֶךָ אַתָּה וַאֲרוֹן עֻזֶּךָ: כֹּהֲנֶיךָ יִלְבְּשׁוּ־צֶדֶק וַחֲסִידֶיךָ יְרַנֵּנוּ:
בַּעֲבוּר דָּוִד עַבְדֶּךָ אַל־תָּשֵׁב פְּנֵי מְשִׁיחֶךָ: כִּי לֶקַח טוֹב נָתַתִּי
לָכֶם תּוֹרָתִי אַל־תַּעֲזֹבוּ: עֵץ־חַיִּים הִיא לַמַּחֲזִיקִים בָּהּ וְתֹמְכֶיהָ
מְאֻשָּׁר: דְּרָכֶיהָ דַרְכֵי־נֹעַם וְכָל־נְתִיבוֹתֶיהָ שָׁלוֹם: הֲשִׁיבֵנוּ יְהוָה
אֵלֶיךָ וְנָשׁוּבָה חַדֵּשׁ יָמֵינוּ כְּקֶדֶם:

סדר תפלת מוסף

On שבת חול המועד the מוסף of יו״ט is said. ק״ש אומר הש״ן

אֲדֹנָי שְׂפָתַי תִּפְתָּח וּפִי יַגִּיד תְּהִלָּתֶךָ:

בָּרוּךְ אַתָּה יְיָ אֱלֹהֵינוּ וֵאלֹהֵי אֲבוֹתֵינוּ אֱלֹהֵי אַבְרָהָם
אֱלֹהֵי יִצְחָק וֵאלֹהֵי יַעֲקֹב הָאֵל הַגָּדוֹל הַגִּבּוֹר וְהַנּוֹרָא
אֵל עֶלְיוֹן גּוֹמֵל חֲסָדִים טוֹבִים וְקֹנֵה הַכֹּל וְזוֹכֵר חַסְדֵי
אָבוֹת וּמֵבִיא גוֹאֵל לִבְנֵי בְנֵיהֶם לְמַעַן שְׁמוֹ בְּאַהֲבָה·

vanity, and has not sworn deceitfully. He shall receive a blessing from
God and kindness from the God of his salvation." This is the generation of them that seek after Him, that seek your face, O Yaakov!—
Lift up your heads, O gates, be lifted up to become portals of the
future, so that the King of Glory may come in. "Who is this King
of Glory?" "*God,* invincible and strong, *God,* the mighty One in
battle." Lift up your heads again, O gates, lift them up to become
portals of the future, so that the King of Glory may come in. "Who,
then, is this King of Glory?" "*God* of Hosts, He is the King of
Glory!"—

As the Torah is returned to the Ark, the Reader says:

And when it gently came to rest, Moshe would say, "Return, O
God, to the myriads of the thousands of Yisrael." Arise, O *God,* to
Your resting place, You and the Ark of Your invincible might, that
Your priests may clothe themselves in righteousness and that Your
devoted ones may shout for joy. For the sake of David Your servant,
turn not away the face of Your anointed. For I have given you an
instruction that will be for your good if you will but take it up; forsake
not My Torah. It is a tree of life for those who cleave to it, and a
happy group are those who support it. Its ways are ways of pleasantness and all its paths are peace. Lead us back to You, O *God,* and we
shall find the way back; renew our days as of old.

MUSAF PRAYER FOR SABBATHS

O *Lord,* open my lips so that my mouth may declare the praise
of Your mighty deeds.

Blessèd be You, *God,* our God and God of our fathers, God of
Avraham, God of Yitzchak and God of Yaakov, the great, mighty
and awesome God, God the Most High, Who nevertheless bestows
lovingkindness, Who is the Owner of all things, and remembers the
fathers' acts of devotion, and Who, in love, will bring a redeemer to
their children's children for His Name's sake.

On שבת שובה, say:

זָכְרֵנוּ לְחַיִּים מֶלֶךְ חָפֵץ בַּחַיִּים · וְכָתְבֵנוּ בְּסֵפֶר הַחַיִּים לְמַעַנְךָ אֱלֹהִים חַיִּים :

מֶלֶךְ עוֹזֵר וּמוֹשִׁיעַ וּמָגֵן · בָּרוּךְ אַתָּה יְיָ מָגֵן אַבְרָהָם :

אַתָּה גִבּוֹר לְעוֹלָם אֲדֹנָי מְחַיֵּה מֵתִים אַתָּה רַב לְהוֹשִׁיעַ ·

During the winter months add:

מַשִּׁיב הָרוּחַ וּמוֹרִיד הַגָּשֶׁם :

מְכַלְכֵּל חַיִּים בְּחֶסֶד מְחַיֵּה מֵתִים בְּרַחֲמִים רַבִּים סוֹמֵךְ נוֹפְלִים וְרוֹפֵא חוֹלִים וּמַתִּיר אֲסוּרִים וּמְקַיֵּם אֱמוּנָתוֹ לִישֵׁנֵי עָפָר · מִי כָמוֹךָ בַּעַל גְּבוּרוֹת וּמִי דוֹמֶה לָּךְ מֶלֶךְ מֵמִית וּמְחַיֵּה וּמַצְמִיחַ יְשׁוּעָה ·

On שבת שובה add:

מִי כָמוֹךָ אַב הָרַחֲמִים זוֹכֵר יְצוּרָיו לְחַיִּים בְּרַחֲמִים :

וְנֶאֱמָן אַתָּה לְהַחֲיוֹת מֵתִים · בָּרוּךְ אַתָּה יְיָ מְחַיֵּה הַמֵּתִים :

קדושה לס״ן נחזרת התפלה.

אַתָּה קָדוֹשׁ וְשִׁמְךָ נַעֲרִיצְךָ וְנַקְדִּישְׁךָ כְּסוֹד שִׂיחַ קָדוֹשׁ וּקְדוֹשִׁים בְּכָל־יוֹם שַׂרְפֵי קֹדֶשׁ הַמַּקְדִּישִׁים שְׁמֶךָ יְהַלְלוּךָ סֶּלָה · בָּרוּךְ בַּקֹּדֶשׁ · כַּכָּתוּב עַל־יַד נְבִיאֶךָ אַתָּה יְיָ הָאֵל (נס״ו הַמֶּלֶךְ) וְקָרָא זֶה אֶל־זֶה וְאָמַר · קי״ס קָדוֹשׁ הַקָּדוֹשׁ : קָדוֹשׁ קָדוֹשׁ יְיָ צְבָאוֹת מְלֹא כָל־

(On שבת שובה, *say:*

Remember us for life, O King Who delights in life, and inscribe us into the Book of Life for Your sake, O Living God.)

O King, Helper, Savior and Shield! Blessed be You *God,* the Shield of Avraham.

You, O my Lord, are all-powerful forever. You are the One Who revives the dead; You are abundantly powerful to save.

(During the winter months add: He causes the wind to blow and the rain to fall.)

He sustains the living with loving-kindness, revives the dead with great compassion, supports the falling, heals the sick, unchains the bound, and keeps His faith with the slumberers in the dust. Who is like You, Master of mighty acts, and who, like You, is a King Who kills and restores life and causes salvation to grow?

(On שבת שובה *add:* Who, like You, is a Father of compassion, Who in compassion remembers His creatures for life?)

And You are faithful to revive the dead. Blessed be You *God,* Who revives the dead.

You are holy, and Your Name is holy, and the holy ones proclaim Your praise each day. Blessed be You *God,* the holy God. *(On* שבת שובה;the holy King).

נעריצך It is in the Musaph service, which corresponds to the *korban musaph,* the special offering brought in the Temple on each Festival, that special emphasis is placed upon the spirit of the holiday. In the case of the Sabbath, the paragraph beginning with *yismechu bemalchuthecha* lays stress on the truth of the supreme sovereignty of God in the Universe, a truth derived directly from the fact that God was the world's Creator. It emphasizes our readiness gladly to submit to His rule. In keeping with this spirit, the *Kedushah,* too, stresses the true significance of the mission of Yisrael under God and on behalf of His sovereignty. Here, together with קדוש קדוש קדוש, the proclamation of God as uttered by the celestial hosts in the heavenly spheres, we have *Shema Yisrael,* the declaration of His supremacy as pronounced by the people of Yisrael in the midst of mankind. בקדש may denote the heavenly Abode of God's Presence, or it may mean not "the Sanctuary" but "in holiness" as it does in Psalms 68:25 and 77:14. משרתיו The place of His glory is hidden even from the hosts of His heavenly servants, but they are content to forego this insight which they, like ourselves, are incapable of attaining, and, facing one another, they declare: ברוך; "Let His will be

הָאָרֶץ כְּבוֹדוֹ: יְ׳ כְּבוֹדוֹ מָלֵא עוֹלָם · מְשָׁרְתָיו שׁוֹאֲלִים זֶה

לָזֶה אַיֵּה מְקוֹם כְּבוֹדוֹ · לְעֻמָּתָם בָּרוּךְ יֹאמֵרוּ · קֹי׳׳ בָּרוּךְ כְּבוֹד־יְיָ

מִמְּקוֹמוֹ: יְ׳ מִמְּקוֹמוֹ הוּא יִפֶן בְּרַחֲמִים וְיָחֹן עַם הַמְיַחֲדִים שְׁמוֹ

עֶרֶב וָבֹקֶר בְּכָל־יוֹם תָּמִיד פַּעֲמַיִם בְּאַהֲבָה שְׁמַע אוֹמְרִים

קֹי׳׳ שְׁמַע יִשְׂרָאֵל יְיָ אֱלֹהֵינוּ יְיָ אֶחָד: יְ׳ אֶחָד הוּא אֱלֹהֵינוּ הוּא

אָבִינוּ הוּא מַלְכֵּנוּ הוּא מוֹשִׁיעֵנוּ · וְהוּא יַשְׁמִיעֵנוּ בְּרַחֲמָיו שֵׁנִית

לְעֵינֵי כָּל־חַי לִהְיוֹת לָכֶם לֵאלֹהִים · קֹי׳׳ אֲנִי יְיָ אֱלֹהֵיכֶם:

On Holidays, add:

(אַדִּיר אַדִּירֵנוּ יְיָ אֲדֹנֵנוּ מָה־אַדִּיר מָהַדאַדִּיר שִׁמְךָ בְּכָל־הָאָרֶץ: וְהָיָה

יְיָ לְמֶלֶךְ עַל־כָּל־הָאָרֶץ בַּיּוֹם הַהוּא יִהְיֶה יְיָ אֶחָד וּשְׁמוֹ אֶחָד:)

יְ׳ וּבְדִבְרֵי קָדְשְׁךָ כָּתוּב לֵאמֹר · קֹי׳׳ יִמְלֹךְ יְיָ לְעוֹלָם אֱלֹהַיִךְ צִיּוֹן

לְדֹר וָדֹר, הַלְלוּיָהּ:

יְ׳ לְדוֹר וָדוֹר נַגִּיד גָּדְלֶךָ וּלְנֵצַח נְצָחִים קְדֻשָּׁתְךָ נַקְדִּישׁ

וְשִׁבְחֲךָ אֱלֹהֵינוּ מִפִּינוּ לֹא יָמוּשׁ לְעוֹלָם וָעֶד כִּי אֵל מֶלֶךְ גָּדוֹל

וְקָדוֹשׁ אָתָּה · בָּרוּךְ אַתָּה יְיָ הָאֵל (נט״ם הַמֶּלֶךְ) הַקָּדוֹשׁ:

---

done everywhere, regardless of the place which we might deem the Abode of
His glory", for they themselves have acknowledged that the entire world is
filled with His glory. ממקומו Compassion, רחמים, is an attribute of God that
is near to every living thing, for it is the feeling of a father for his child,
and of a creator for his work, and Yisrael is indeed a creature of God as
regards not only its physical existence but also its survival in history as a
nation in the midst of mankind. For this reason the Children of Yisrael may
hope at all times that God, though He is exalted far beyond the earthly world,
may still turn to them with compassion. They may indeed trust that יחון
He will favor them with all the necessary skills and abilities which will enable
them to remain the heralds of His Oneness and Uniqueness. For the Jewish
people is the nation which, not only at the rising and the setting of the sun,
but also at both the rise and the decline of its fortunes, will constantly and
unswervingly declare its recognition of God's Oneness and avow that He
alone is its God, its Father, its King and its Savior. Yisrael confidently looks

The following is said when the Reader repeats the Shemone Esrei :

(Reader): We will proclaim Your might and Your holiness in accordance with the mystic speech of the holy *Seraphim,* who sanctify Your Name in the Sanctuary, even as it is written by Your prophet: "And one of them calls to the other and says:

(Cong. & Reader): 'Holy, holy, holy is *God Tzevaoth,* the fullness of all the earth is His glory.' "

(Reader): The Universe is filled with His glory; His servants ask of one another: "Where is the abode of His glory?" Facing one another, they say: 'Blessed—

(Cong. & Reader): "Blessed be the glory of *God* from its Abode."

(Reader): From His Abode may He turn with compassion; and favor the people who, evening and morning, twice each day, proclaim with constancy the Oneness of His Name, saying, with love: "Hear—

(Cong. & Reader): "Hear Yisrael, *God* our God, is *God,* the Only One!"

(Reader): One is our God, He is our Father, He is our King, He is our Savior, and in His compassion, He will let us hear, a second time, in the presence of all things living, "To be to you a God."

(Cong. & Reader): "I, *God,* am your God."

(On Holidays, add): O You most glorious One, Whom we recognize in Your glory, O *God* our Lord, how glorious is Your Name over all the earth! And *God* will be king over all the earth; on that day shall *God* be one and His Name One.

(Reader): And in Your holy words it is written:

(Cong. & Reader): "*God* shall reign forever, your God, O Tzion, from generation to generation, Halaluyah!"

(Reader): From generation to generation shall we declare Your greatness and to all eternity will we proclaim Your holiness; and Your praise, O our God, shall never depart from our mouth, for You, O God, are a great and holy King. Blessed be You *God,* the holy God. *(On* שבת שובה *say:* "the holy King").

---

to the time when God will reveal and show Himself as our God before the eye of all, even as He did in days of old. And on that day, all the rest of mankind, too, will at long last acknowledge and recognize *God* as the Only *One.*

On Sabbath Rosh Chodesh:

תִּכַּנְתָּ שַׁבָּת רָצִיתָ
קָרְבְּנוֹתֶיהָ · צִוִּיתָ
פֵּרוּשֶׁיהָ עִם סִדּוּרֵי
נְסָכֶיהָ · מְעַנְּגֶיהָ לְעוֹלָם
כָּבוֹד יִנְחָלוּ · טוֹעֲמֶיהָ
חַיִּים זָכוּ · וְגַם הָאוֹהֲבִים
דְּבָרֶיהָ גְּדֻלָּה בָּחָרוּ ·
אָז מִסִּינַי נִצְטַוּוּ עָלֶיהָ ·
וַתְּצַוֵּנוּ יְיָ אֱלֹהֵינוּ לְהַקְרִיב
בָּהּ קָרְבַּן מוּסַף שַׁבָּת
כָּרָאוּי · יְהִי רָצוֹן מִלְּפָנֶיךָ
יְיָ אֱלֹהֵינוּ וֵאלֹהֵי אֲבוֹתֵינוּ
שֶׁתַּעֲלֵנוּ בְשִׂמְחָה
לְאַרְצֵנוּ וְתִטָּעֵנוּ
בִּגְבוּלֵנוּ · וְשָׁם נַעֲשֶׂה
לְפָנֶיךָ אֶת־קָרְבְּנוֹת
חוֹבוֹתֵינוּ · תְּמִידִים
כְּסִדְרָם וּמוּסָפִים

אַתָּה יָצַרְתָּ עוֹלָמְךָ מִקֶּדֶם
כִּלִּיתָ מְלַאכְתְּךָ בַּיּוֹם הַשְּׁבִיעִי ·
אָהַבְתָּ אוֹתָנוּ וְרָצִיתָ בָּנוּ וְרוֹמַמְתָּנוּ
מִכָּל־הַלְּשׁוֹנוֹת וְקִדַּשְׁתָּנוּ
בְּמִצְוֹתֶיךָ וְקֵרַבְתָּנוּ מַלְכֵּנוּ
לַעֲבוֹדָתֶךָ וְשִׁמְךָ הַגָּדוֹל
וְהַקָּדוֹשׁ עָלֵינוּ קָרָאתָ · וַתִּתֶּן
לָנוּ יְיָ אֱלֹהֵינוּ בְּאַהֲבָה שַׁבָּתוֹת
לִמְנוּחָה וְרָאשֵׁי חֳדָשִׁים לְכַפָּרָה ·
וּלְפִי שֶׁחָטָאנוּ לְפָנֶיךָ אֲנַחְנוּ
וַאֲבוֹתֵינוּ חָרְבָה עִירֵנוּ וְשָׁמֵם
בֵּית מִקְדָּשֵׁנוּ וְגָלָה יְקָרֵנוּ וְנִטַּל
כָּבוֹד מִבֵּית חַיֵּינוּ · וְאֵין אֲנַחְנוּ
יְכוֹלִים לַעֲשׂוֹת חוֹבוֹתֵינוּ בְּבֵית
בְּחִירָתֶךָ בַּבַּיִת הַגָּדוֹל וְהַקָּדוֹשׁ
שֶׁנִּקְרָא שִׁמְךָ עָלָיו מִפְּנֵי הַיָּד
שֶׁנִּשְׁתַּלְּחָה בְּמִקְדָּשֶׁךָ : יְהִי רָצוֹן
מִלְּפָנֶיךָ יְיָ אֱלֹהֵינוּ וֵאלֹהֵי אֲבוֹתֵינוּ
שֶׁתַּעֲלֵנוּ בְשִׂמְחָה, לְאַרְצֵנוּ
וְתִטָּעֵנוּ בִּגְבוּלֵנוּ · וְשָׁם נַעֲשֶׂה
לְפָנֶיךָ אֶת־קָרְבְּנוֹת חוֹבוֹתֵינוּ
תְּמִידִים כְּסִדְרָם וּמוּסָפִים
כְּהִלְכָתָם · וְאֶת־מוּסְפֵי יוֹם הַשַּׁבָּת

You instituted the Sabbath and took pleasure in its offerings, You commanded the commentaries pertaining to it together with the order of its drink offerings. Those who observe it with delight will partake of honor everlasting and those who enjoy it have become worthy of life even now, and even those who love its teachings have chosen greatness. It was from Mount Sinai that they were commanded concerning it, and You commanded us, O *God* our God, to bring upon it the Musaf offering of the Sabbath as is seemly. May it be Your will, O *God* our God and God of our fathers, to lead us up to our land in joy and to plant us within our borders so that, there, we may bring before You our obligatory offerings, the regular offerings according to their order, and the additional offerings according to their rule. There we shall also prepare and bring near to You the additional offering of this Sabbath Day with love in accordance with

On Sabbath Rosh Chodesh:

You formed Your world from of old; You completed Your work on the Seventh Day. You loved us and took pleasure in us; You have exalted us above all tongues and sanctified us by Your commandments; and You, O our King, have brought us near to Your service. And You have proclaimed Your great and holy Name over us, and You O *God* our God, gave us in love Sabbaths for rest and New Moons for atonement. And because we have sinned before You, we and our fathers, our city was destroyed and the house of our Sanctuary was laid waste, our honor has vanished and the glory was removed from the House of our life. We cannot perform the offerings which it is our duty to bring in Your chosen House, in the great and holy House over which Your Name is called, because of the violence that was done to Your sanctuary. May it be Your will, O *God* our God and God of our fathers, to lead us up to our

---

תכנת The Sabbath is a Divinely-appointed institution. The offerings prescribed in connection with it are in accordance with the will of God, and not only is the basic law that established the Sabbath the Law of God, but even פירושיה the pertinent commentaries that have been handed down to us and that give us directions for Sabbath observance are no less part of the Divine command. נסכיה may be a derivative from נסך which, in Num.

בְּהִלְכָתָם• וְאֶת־מוּסַף
יוֹם הַשַּׁבָּת הַזֶּה נַעֲשֶׂה
וְנַקְרִיב לְפָנֶיךָ בְּאַהֲבָה
כְּמִצְוַת רְצוֹנֶךָ כְּמוֹ
שֶׁכָּתַבְתָּ עָלֵינוּ בְּתוֹרָתֶךָ
עַל־יְדֵי מֹשֶׁה עַבְדֶּךָ מִפִּי
כְבוֹדֶךָ כָּאָמוּר: וּבְיוֹם
הַשַּׁבָּת שְׁנֵי־כְבָשִׂים בְּנֵי־
שָׁנָה תְּמִימִם וּשְׁנֵי
עֶשְׂרֹנִים סֹלֶת מִנְחָה
בְּלוּלָה בַשֶּׁמֶן וְנִסְכּוֹ:
עֹלַת שַׁבַּת בְּשַׁבַּתּוֹ עַל־
עֹלַת הַתָּמִיד וְנִסְכָּהּ:
יִשְׂמְחוּ בְמַלְכוּתְךָ
שׁוֹמְרֵי שַׁבָּת וְקוֹרְאֵי
עֹנֶג עַם מְקַדְּשֵׁי שְׁבִיעִי•
כֻּלָּם יִשְׂבְּעוּ וְיִתְעַנְּגוּ
מִטּוּבֶךָ• וּבַשְּׁבִיעִי רָצִיתָ

הַזֶּה וְיוֹם רֹאשׁ הַחֹדֶשׁ הַזֶּה
נַעֲשֶׂה וְנַקְרִיב לְפָנֶיךָ בְּאַהֲבָה
כְּמִצְוַת רְצוֹנֶךָ כְּמוֹ שֶׁכָּתַבְתָּ
עָלֵינוּ בְּתוֹרָתֶךָ עַל־יְדֵי מֹשֶׁה
עַבְדֶּךָ מִפִּי כְבוֹדֶךָ כָּאָמוּר:
וּבְיוֹם הַשַּׁבָּת שְׁנֵי־כְבָשִׂים
בְּנֵי־שָׁנָה תְּמִימִם וּשְׁנֵי
עֶשְׂרֹנִים סֹלֶת מִנְחָה בְּלוּלָה
בַשֶּׁמֶן וְנִסְכּוֹ: עֹלַת שַׁבַּת
בְּשַׁבַּתּוֹ עַל־עֹלַת הַתָּמִיד וְנִסְכָּהּ:
וּבְרָאשֵׁי חָדְשֵׁיכֶם תַּקְרִיבוּ
עֹלָה לַיָי פָּרִים בְּנֵי־בָקָר שְׁנַיִם
וְאַיִל אֶחָד כְּבָשִׂים בְּנֵי־שָׁנָה
שִׁבְעָה תְּמִימִם: וּמִנְחָתָם
וְנִסְכֵּיהֶם כִּמְדֻבָּר שְׁלֹשָׁה
עֶשְׂרֹנִים לַפָּר וּשְׁנֵי עֶשְׂרֹנִים
לָאַיִל וְעִשָּׂרוֹן לַכֶּבֶשׂ וְיַיִן כְּנִסְכּוֹ
וְשָׂעִיר לְכַפֵּר וּשְׁנֵי תְמִידִים
כְּהִלְכָתָם: יִשְׂמְחוּ בְמַלְכוּתְךָ שׁוֹמְרֵי

4:7, is employed to refer to the "preparing" of the altar in the Sanctuary
upon which the *lechem hapanim*, "the Bread of the Countenance" was set out
each Sabbath Day. Or else the term may have been used here in its customary
connotation of "drink offering", referring to the "drinking offerings" which,

the commandment of Your will, even as You have prescribed it as incumbent upon us in Your Torah through Moshe Your servant, by the sentence of Your glory, as it is said,

"But on the Sabbath day two yearling lambs without blemish; two tenths parts of fine flour as a gift of tribute mixed with oil, along with its drink offering. This is the elevating-offering of the Sabbath on every Sabbath, in addition to the regular ascent offering and the drink offering thereof."

Those who keep the Sabbath and call it a delight shall rejoice in Your kingdom; the nation which sanctifies the Seventh Day shall all be satisfied and shall delight in Your good. You took pleasure in the Seventh Day and hallowed it; the [most] desirable of days You proclaimed as the memorial to the work of the world's beginning.

Our God and God of our fathers, take pleasure in our rest, hallow us by Your commandments and grant our portion in Your Torah. Satisfy us from Your good, gladden us with Your salvation, purify our hearts to serve You in truth, and in Your love and favor, O *God*

land in joy and to plant us within our borders so that, there, we may bring before You our obligatory offerings, the regular offerings according to their order, and the additional offerings according to their rule. There we shall also prepare and bring near to You the additional offerings of this Sabbath Day and of this New Moon with love in accordance with the commandment of Your will, even as You have prescribed it as incumbent upon us in Your Torah through Moshe Your servant, by the sentence of Your glory, as it is said,

"But on the Sabbath Day two yearling lambs without blemish; two tenth parts of fine flour as a gift of tribute mixed with oil, along with its drink offering. This is the elevating-offering of the Sabbath on every Sabbath, in addition to the regular elevating-offering and the drink offering thereof."

"And at the beginnings of your months you shall offer to *God* an elevating-offering: two young bullocks and one ram, yearling lambs seven in number, without blemish. And their gift of tribute and their drink offerings as declared: three tenths for each bullock, two tenths for

בּוֹ וְקִדַּשְׁתּוֹ חֶמְדַּת יָמִים
אוֹתוֹ קָרָאתָ זֵכֶר
לְמַעֲשֵׂה בְרֵאשִׁית:
אֱלֹהֵינוּ וֵאלֹהֵי אֲבוֹתֵינוּ.
רְצֵה בִמְנוּחָתֵנוּ. קַדְּשֵׁנוּ
בְּמִצְוֹתֶיךָ וְתֵן חֶלְקֵנוּ
בְתוֹרָתֶךָ, שַׂבְּעֵנוּ מִטּוּבֶךָ
וְשַׂמְּחֵנוּ בִּישׁוּעָתֶךָ וְטַהֵר
לִבֵּנוּ לְעָבְדְּךָ בֶּאֱמֶת,
וְהַנְחִילֵנוּ יְיָ אֱלֹהֵינוּ
בְּאַהֲבָה וּבְרָצוֹן שַׁבַּת
קָדְשֶׁךָ, וְיָנוּחוּ בָהּ יִשְׂרָאֵל
מְקַדְּשֵׁי שְׁמֶךָ. בָּרוּךְ
אַתָּה יְיָ, מְקַדֵּשׁ הַשַּׁבָּת:

לשבת ור"ח

שַׁבָּת וְקוֹרְאֵי עֹנֶג עַם מְקַדְּשֵׁי
שְׁבִיעִי כֻּלָּם יִשְׂבְּעוּ וְיִתְעַנְּגוּ
מִטּוּבֶךָ · וּבַשְּׁבִיעִי רָצִיתָ בּוֹ
וְקִדַּשְׁתּוֹ חֶמְדַּת יָמִים אוֹתוֹ קָרָאתָ
זֵכֶר לְמַעֲשֵׂה בְרֵאשִׁית:
אֱלֹהֵינוּ וֵאלֹהֵי אֲבוֹתֵינוּ.
רְצֵה בִמְנוּחָתֵנוּ וְחַדֵּשׁ עָלֵינוּ
בְּיוֹם הַשַּׁבָּת הַזֶּה אֶת הַחֹדֶשׁ
הַזֶּה לְטוֹבָה וְלִבְרָכָה · לְשָׂשׂוֹן
וּלְשִׂמְחָה · לִישׁוּעָה וּלְנֶחָמָה ·
לְפַרְנָסָה וּלְכַלְכָּלָה · לְחַיִּים
וּלְשָׁלוֹם · לִמְחִילַת חֵטְא
וְלִסְלִיחַת עָוֹן (בשנת העבור
וּלְכַפָּרַת פָּשַׁע): כִּי בְעַמְּךָ יִשְׂרָאֵל
בָּחַרְתָּ מִכָּל הָאֻמּוֹת · וְשַׁבַּת
קָדְשְׁךָ לָהֶם הוֹדָעְתָּ וְחֻקֵּי רָאשֵׁי
חֳדָשִׁים לָהֶם קָבָעְתָּ: בָּרוּךְ אַתָּה
יְיָ מְקַדֵּשׁ הַשַּׁבָּת וְיִשְׂרָאֵל וְרָאשֵׁי
חֳדָשִׁים:

---

according to precept, were to accompany the other sacrifices named above. In either case the thought expressed in this paragraph would be the same. God commanded the observance of the Sabbath as well as the pertinent offerings which should symbolize our homage to Him as the Ruler and Creator of the Universe. Even, the commentaries to the Sabbath Law, by the proper observance of which we lay at God's feet all of our creative efforts and endeavors, are of Divine origin. But over and beyond all this, God has given us the commandment pertaining to the *lechem hapanim* which must be performed anew each Sabbath Day, and with this commandment He instilled into us the confidence that impels us to submit also the "bread" which symbolizes our sustenance and the "incense" which represents the gratification of our needs, before the kindly countenance of Him to Whose kingdom we

our God, let Your holy Sabbath remain our inheritance, and may Yisrael, who sanctify Your Name, rest on it. Blessed be You *God*, Who hallows the Sabbath.

the ram, and one tenth for each lamb, and wine like its drink offering and one he-goat for atonement and two regular offerings according to their rule.

Those who keep the Sabbath and call it a delight shall rejoice in Your kingdom; the nation which sanctifies the Seventh Day shall all be satisfied and shall delight in Your good. You took pleasure in the Seventh Day and hallowed it; the [most] desirable of days You proclaimed as the memorial to the work of the world's beginning.

Our God and God of our fathers, take pleasure in our rest, and on this Sabbath day renew for us this month for good and for blessing, for bliss and for joy, for salvation and consolation, for sustenance and maintenance, for life and for peace, for the pardon of sin and the forgiveness of iniquity (and for the atonement of transgression). For You have chosen Your people Yisrael from all nations, and made known to them the statutes pertaining to the beginnings of the months. Blessed be You *God*, Who hallows the Sabbath, Yisrael and the beginnings of the months.

---

render homage by loyally performing our duty. Then, God also gave us precepts concerning *nesachim* (including *minchat nesachim* and *nesachim* in the broader sense of its meaning). These drink offerings which are to serve as accompaniments to the elevating-offering of each Sabbath as well as to every other elevating-offering, symbolize our willingness to offer up for consecration, to God, to Whom we must dedicate our every deed, also the material goods of our life and prosperity, represented by the flour and the oil, and of our highest earthly happiness as symbolized by the wine.

This is followed immediately by מעוגיה etc. Here we speak of those who equate their subordination to God as expressed in the observance of the Sabbath by the cessation of all labor not with loss or handicap, but with actual gain and true delight. Those who have this attitude to Sabbath observance will receive honor that is truly everlasting. Those who know how to appreciate and savor the spiritual values symbolized by the Sabbath will partake of the bliss of eternal life even in this world. The mere knowledge gathered by him who studies the Sabbath laws represents a great gain in itself. קרבן מוסף שבת etc. Concerning the meaning of the Sabbath offering which is added to the *tomid,* see p. 24 above.

ישמחו במלכותך How utterly miserable would we be, and how cheerless all

רְצֵה יְיָ אֱלֹהֵינוּ בְּעַמְּךָ יִשְׂרָאֵל וּבִתְפִלָּתָם · וְהָשֵׁב אֶת־הָעֲבוֹדָה
לִדְבִיר בֵּיתֶךָ וְאִשֵּׁי יִשְׂרָאֵל וּתְפִלָּתָם בְּאַהֲבָה תְקַבֵּל בְּרָצוֹן וּתְהִי
לְרָצוֹן תָּמִיד עֲבוֹדַת יִשְׂרָאֵל עַמֶּךָ ·

וְתֶחֱזֶינָה עֵינֵינוּ בְּשׁוּבְךָ לְצִיּוֹן בְּרַחֲמִים · בָּרוּךְ אַתָּה יְיָ הַמַּחֲזִיר
שְׁכִינָתוֹ לְצִיּוֹן :

מודים דרבנן.

מוֹדִים אֲנַחְנוּ לָךְ שָׁאַתָּה הוּא יְיָ	מוֹדִים אֲנַחְנוּ
אֱלֹהֵינוּ וֵאלֹהֵי אֲבוֹתֵינוּ אֱלֹהֵי כָל בָּשָׂר	לָךְ שָׁאַתָּה הוּא
יוֹצְרֵנוּ יוֹצֵר בְּרֵאשִׁית· בְּרָכוֹת וְהוֹדָאוֹת	יְיָ אֱלֹהֵינוּ וֵאלֹהֵי
לְשִׁמְךָ הַגָּדוֹל וְהַקָּדוֹשׁ עַל שֶׁהֶחֱיִיתָנוּ	אֲבוֹתֵינוּ לְעוֹלָם
וְקִיַּמְתָּנוּ· כֵּן תְּחַיֵּנוּ וּתְקַיְּמֵנוּ וְתֶאֱסוֹף	וָעֶד· צוּר חַיֵּינוּ
גָּלֻיּוֹתֵינוּ לְחַצְרוֹת קָדְשֶׁךָ לִשְׁמוֹר חֻקֶּיךָ	מָגֵן יִשְׁעֵנוּ אַתָּה
וְלַעֲשׂוֹת רְצוֹנֶךָ וּלְעָבְדְּךָ בְּלֵבָב שָׁלֵם· עַל	הוּא לְדוֹר וָדוֹר ·
שֶׁאֲנַחְנוּ מוֹדִים לָךְ · בָּרוּךְ אֵל הַהוֹדָאוֹת:	נוֹדֶה לְּךָ וּנְסַפֵּר
	תְּהִלָּתֶךָ · עַל

חַיֵּינוּ הַמְּסוּרִים בְּיָדֶךָ וְעַל נִשְׁמוֹתֵינוּ הַפְּקוּדוֹת לָךְ
וְעַל נִסֶּיךָ שֶׁבְּכָל־יוֹם עִמָּנוּ וְעַל נִפְלְאוֹתֶיךָ וְטוֹבוֹתֶיךָ
שֶׁבְּכָל־עֵת· עֶרֶב וָבֹקֶר וְצָהֳרָיִם· הַטּוֹב כִּי לֹא־כָלוּ
רַחֲמֶיךָ וְהַמְרַחֵם כִּי לֹא־תַמּוּ חֲסָדֶיךָ מֵעוֹלָם
קִוִּינוּ לָךְ:

On חנוכה : על הנסים

וְעַל כֻּלָּם יִתְבָּרַךְ וְיִתְרוֹמַם שִׁמְךָ מַלְכֵּנוּ תָּמִיד לְעוֹלָם וָעֶד:

add: שבת שובה On

וּכְתוֹב לְחַיִּים טוֹבִים כָּל־בְּנֵי בְרִיתֶךָ:

וְכֹל הַחַיִּים יוֹדוּךָ סֶּלָה וִיהַלְלוּ אֶת שִׁמְךָ בֶּאֱמֶת הָאֵל יְשׁוּעָתֵנוּ
וְעֶזְרָתֵנוּ סֶלָה· בָּרוּךְ אַתָּה יְיָ הַטּוֹב שִׁמְךָ וּלְךָ נָאֶה לְהוֹדוֹת:

Take pleasure, O *God* our God, in Your people Yisrael and in their prayer. Restore the sacrificial service to the Abode of Your Word in Your House, and accept Yisrael's fire-offerings and their prayer with love and favor, and may the service of Your people Yisrael ever be pleasing to You.

And may our eyes behold Your return to Tzion in compassion. Blessed be You *God,* Who restores Your presence to Tzion.

We gratefully avow to You that You, O *God,* are our God and the God of our fathers in all eternity. You are the Rock of our life, the Shield of our salvation from generation to generation. We avow our thanks to You and recount Your praise, for our lives, which are committed to Your hand, and for our souls which are in Your care, and for Your miracles which are with us each day, and for Your wondrous deeds and favors that are performed at all times, evening, morning and noon. You are the Beneficient One, for Your compassion has never ceased, the Compassionate

מודים דרבנן

We gratefully avow to You, that You, O *God,* are our God and the God of our fathers, the God of all flesh, our Creator and the Creator of the Beginning. Blessings and thanks to Your great and holy Name because You have kept us alive and have preserved us. So may You continue to keep us in life and preserve us, and gather our dispersed to the Courts of Your Sanctuary, to keep Your statutes, to do Your will and to serve You wholeheartedly. For our very act of avowal to You, be You blessed, God of thanksgivings.

One, for Your kindnesses have never ended. Ever have we placed our hopes in You.

On Chanukkah add על הנסים *p.* 151

our endeavors, were we not aware at all times of God's sovereignty, were we not to remember throughout our lives that whatever we do and achieve unfolds beneath the supreme reign of God's will and in accordance with the dictates of His approval. This awareness of God above us is the lesson taught us by each Sabbath day and impresses upon even the very least of our activities the stamp of permanent value. To live and to work, to endeavor and to strive beneath the sovereignty of God is the sole foundation of the genuine joy of living.

אֱלֹהֵ֫ינוּ וֵאלֹהֵי אֲבוֹתֵ֫ינוּ בָּרְכֵ֫נוּ בַבְּרָכָה הַמְשֻׁלֶּ֫שֶׁת בַּתּוֹרָה
הַכְּתוּבָה עַל־יְדֵי מֹשֶׁה עַבְדֶּ֫ךָ הָאֲמוּרָה מִפִּי אַהֲרֹן וּבָנָיו כֹּהֲנִים
עַם קְדוֹשֶׁ֫ךָ כָּאָמוּר : יְבָרֶכְךָ יְיָ וְיִשְׁמְרֶ֫ךָ : יָאֵר יְיָ ׀ פָּנָיו אֵלֶ֫יךָ
וִֽיחֻנֶּ֫ךָּ : יִשָּׂא יְיָ ׀ פָּנָיו אֵלֶ֫יךָ וְיָשֵׂם לְךָ שָׁלוֹם :

שִׂים שָׁלוֹם טוֹבָה וּבְרָכָה חֵן וָחֶ֫סֶד וְרַחֲמִים עָלֵ֫ינוּ
וְעַל כָּל יִשְׂרָאֵל עַמֶּ֫ךָ בָּרְכֵ֫נוּ אָבִ֫ינוּ כֻּלָּ֫נוּ כְּאֶחָד בְּאוֹר
פָּנֶ֫יךָ כִּי בְאוֹר פָּנֶ֫יךָ נָתַ֫תָּ לָּ֫נוּ יְיָ אֱלֹהֵ֫ינוּ תּוֹרַת חַיִּים
וְאַ֫הֲבַת חֶ֫סֶד וּצְדָקָה וּבְרָכָה וְרַחֲמִים וְחַיִּים וְשָׁלוֹם.
וְטוֹב בְּעֵינֶ֫יךָ לְבָרֵךְ אֶת־עַמְּךָ יִשְׂרָאֵל בְּכָל־עֵת וּבְכָל־
שָׁעָה בִּשְׁלוֹמֶ֫ךָ :

During the Ten Days of Repentance add:

בְּסֵ֫פֶר חַיִּים בְּרָכָה וְשָׁלוֹם וּפַרְנָסָה טוֹבָה נִזָּכֵר וְנִכָּתֵב לְפָנֶ֫יךָ
אֲנַ֫חְנוּ וְכָל עַמְּךָ בֵּית יִשְׂרָאֵל לְחַיִּים טוֹבִים וּלְשָׁלוֹם ׃ בָּרוּךְ אַתָּה
יְיָ עוֹשֵׂה הַשָּׁלוֹם :

בָּרוּךְ אַתָּה יְיָ הַמְבָרֵךְ אֶת־עַמּוֹ יִשְׂרָאֵל בַּשָּׁלוֹם:

אֱלֹהַי · נְצוֹר לְשׁוֹנִי מֵרָע וּשְׂפָתַי מִדַּבֵּר מִרְמָה וְלִמְקַלְלַי נַפְשִׁי
תִדּוֹם וְנַפְשִׁי כֶּעָפָר לַכֹּל תִּהְיֶה׃ פְּתַח לִבִּי בְּתוֹרָתֶ֫ךָ וּבְמִצְוֹתֶ֫יךָ
תִּרְדּוֹף נַפְשִׁי וְכָל הַחוֹשְׁבִים עָלַי רָעָה מְהֵרָה הָפֵר עֲצָתָם וְקַלְקֵל
מַחֲשַׁבְתָּם · עֲשֵׂה לְמַ֫עַן שְׁמֶ֫ךָ · עֲשֵׂה לְמַ֫עַן יְמִינֶ֫ךָ · עֲשֵׂה לְמַ֫עַן
קְדֻשָּׁתֶ֫ךָ · עֲשֵׂה לְמַ֫עַן תּוֹרָתֶ֫ךָ · לְמַ֫עַן יֵחָלְצוּן יְדִידֶ֫יךָ הוֹשִׁ֫יעָה
יְמִינְךָ וַעֲנֵ֫נִי · יִהְיוּ לְרָצוֹן אִמְרֵי־פִי וְהֶגְיוֹן לִבִּי לְפָנֶ֫יךָ יְיָ צוּרִי
וְגֹאֲלִי׃ עֹשֶׂה שָׁלוֹם בִּמְרוֹמָיו הוּא יַעֲשֶׂה שָׁלוֹם עָלֵ֫ינוּ וְעַל כָּל
יִשְׂרָאֵל וְאִמְרוּ אָמֵן :

יְהִי רָצוֹן מִלְּפָנֶ֫יךָ יְיָ אֱלֹהֵ֫ינוּ וֵאלֹהֵי אֲבוֹתֵ֫ינוּ שֶׁיִּבָּנֶה
בֵּית הַמִּקְדָּשׁ בִּמְהֵרָה בְיָמֵ֫ינוּ וְתֵן חֶלְקֵ֫נוּ בְּתוֹרָתֶ֫ךָ :
וְשָׁם נַעֲבָדְךָ בְּיִרְאָה כִּימֵי עוֹלָם וּכְשָׁנִים קַדְמוֹנִיּוֹת :
וְעָֽרְבָה לַיָי מִנְחַת יְהוּדָה וִירוּשָׁלָ֫יִם כִּימֵי עוֹלָם וּכְשָׁנִים קַדְמוֹנִיּוֹת:

For all this, Our King, may Your Name be continually blessed and exalted for all eternity.

During the Ten Days of Repentance add:

And inscribe all the sons of Your covenant for a good life.

And everything that lives shall avow thanks to You and render praise to Your Name in truth as the God of our salvation and our help forever. Blessed be You *God,* the Beneficent One is Your Name, and to You thanksgiving is due.

When the Shemone Esrei is repeated, the Reader recites the following:

Our God and God of our fathers, bless us with the threefold blessing in the Torah, which was written by the hand of Moshe Your servant and spoken through the mouth of Aharon and his sons, the priests, Your holy people, as it is said: "May *God* bless you and keep you. May *God* light up His countenance for you and favor you. May *God* turn His countenance toward you and establish peace for you."

Establish peace, well-being and blessing, favor, loving-kindness and compassion upon us and upon all of Yisrael, Your people. Bless us, O our Father, all of us together, with the light of Your countenance. For by the light of Your countenance You have given us, O *God* our God, the Torah of life and the love of devotion and loyalty to duty, blessing and compassion, life and peace. May it be good in Your sight to bless Your people Yisrael at all times and at every hour with Your peace.

(On שבת שובה *add:* May we be remembered and inscribed before You in the book of life, blessing, peace and good sustenance, we and all Your people, the House of Yisrael, for a good life and for peace. Blessed be You *God,* the Creator of Peace.)

Blessed be You *God,* Who blesses Your people Yisrael with peace.

see p. 335 for translation of אלקי נצור

נשבת שיג אופן אחורין נחאכב אלהיכם נסוף הקדושה.

לשבת שובה חתוב שם המחבר שמואל חזק

אֱלֹהֵיכֶם שׁוֹפֵט צֶדֶק וּבְמִישׁוֹר לְאֻמִּים · מִדַּת הַדִּין יַהֲפוֹךְ לְרַחֲמִים · וִיכַפֵּר זְדוֹנוֹת וּשְׁגָגוֹת עֲוֹנוֹת וַאֲשָׁמִים · אָדוֹן חֲטָאִים הַצַּחַר וְהַלְבֵּן כְּתָמִים · לְכַפָּרָה מְקוֹם לֵילוֹת וְיָמִים · חֲזֵה עַמְּךָ מִתְעַנִּים וְצָמִים · זְכוֹר בְּרִית רִאשׁוֹנִים הַיְּשָׁרִים וְהַתְּמִימִים · קַיֵּם לִבְנֵיהֶם שְׁבֻעָה קְדוּמִים · וְיִמְלוֹךְ מַלְכָּם לְעוֹלְמֵי עוֹלָמִים :
י' וּבְדִבְרֵי קָדְשְׁךָ כָּתוּב לֵאמוֹר :

לשבת חול המועד סוכות. חתוס שם המחבר יהודה.

אֱלֹהֵיכֶם יָשִׁיב בְּשָׁלֵם סֻכּוֹ וּמְעוֹנָתוֹ · הָקֵם יָקוּם דְּבִירוֹ וַחֲדַר מִטָּתוֹ · וְעַד סֶלָה יִשְׁכֹּן שָׁם הוֹד שְׁכִינָתוֹ · דִּירַת סֻכָּה תִּהְיֶה לְצֵל לְשׁוֹמְרֵי סֻכָּתוֹ · הָעֵת יַעֲמִיד עַל אֶרֶץ אֲגֻדָּתוֹ · יִמְלוֹךְ עַל־כָּל־הָאָרֶץ הַבּוֹנֶה בַּשָּׁמַיִם מַעֲלָתוֹ : וּבְדִבְרֵי קָדְשְׁךָ.

לשבת ראש חדש. חתום שם המחבר יהודה חזק.

אֱלֹהֵיכֶם יַזְרִיחַ שִׁמְשׁוֹ · שִׁבְעָתַיִם בִּגְבוּרָתוֹ · הַיָּרֵחַ בְּהִתְחַדְּשׁוֹ · כַּשֶּׁמֶשׁ זְרִיחָתוֹ · וְהַחֹדֶשׁ בְּהִתְקַדְּשׁוֹ · לְחַדֵּשׁ כַּפָּרָתוֹ · דַּת הַיּוֹם לְשַׁמְּשׁוֹ · חֲזוֹת קָדְשַׁת שְׁכִינָתוֹ · מְדֵי חֹדֶשׁ בְּחָדְשׁוֹ · וּמְדֵי שַׁבָּת בְּשַׁבַּתּוֹ : וּבְדִבְרֵי קָדְשְׁךָ.

לשבת בראשית. חתום שם המחבר יהודה חזק.

אֱלֹהֵיכֶם יַשְׂכִּיל עַבְדּוֹ יָכוֹן כִּסְאוֹ כְּמֵרֵאשִׁירֵת · הָעִיר עַל תִּלָּהּ יִבָּנֶה וְאַרְמוֹן נָשִׁית · וּמִזְבְּחוֹ יֵרָפֵא וּמָקוֹם נָסוּךְ לַחֲשִׁית · דְּרוֹר יִקְרָא לַעֲבָרָיו הֱיוֹתָהּ חָפְשִׁית · הִנֵּה חָזָק זְעַמּוֹ קָמָיו יָפִיץ חֲרִישִׁית · יִמְלוֹךְ עַל עַם שׁוֹמֵר שַׁבָּת בְּרֵאשִׁית : וּבְדִבְרֵי קָדְשְׁךָ.

לשבת חוה״מ סוכות *Shalem* is the ancient name for Jerusalem by which that city was known long before it became Yerushalayim, the dwelling place of God's revelation to Yisrael. סובו : the protection which the Sanctuary of God affords us. מעונתו : the abode of God's presence that dwells in our midst. See Psalm 76:3. דביר , derived from דבר , is the Holy of Holies in which the Word of God rested and from which it went forth to us. דירת סוכה תהיה לצל (Exod. 25:21, 22). Thus we read in *the Pesikta*: וסוכה תהיה לצל אמר לשומרי סוכתו ר' לוי כל מי שמקים מצות סוכה בעולם הזה אומר הקדוש ברוך הוא, הוא קיים מצות סוכה אני מסיך עליו מחמתו של יום הבא He who fulfills the commandments concerning the sojourn in Tabernacles during Succoth in the proper spirit, by so doing

*Additional prayers to be recited on Special Sabbaths after
"...I am God Your God", at the end of Kedushah.*

On Shabbath Shuvah, say: May your God, Who judges nations righteously and with uprightness turn the attribute of justice to compassion and grant atonement for both wanton transgressions and [unwitting] errors, sins and wrongs. O Lord, cleanse iniquities and make stains white; day and night they wait for atonement. Behold Your people mortifying themselves and fasting; remember the covenant of the forefathers, of the upright and the perfect; keep for their children the vow of the forebears, and let their King reign in all eternity. *(Reader):* And in Your holy words it is written...

On the Intermediate Shabbath of Sukkoth say: Your God will restore His Tabernacle and His Dwelling-place to Shalem; He will rebuild the Abode of His Word and the Place of His residence, and He will then cause the majesty of His Presence to rest there in all eternity. Dwelling in Tabernacles will afford protection to those who keep His commandment concerning the Tabernacles, at the time when He will establish His society of mankind on earth. Then He will reign on earth, He Who builds His high places of ascending order in Heaven. *(Reader):* And in Your holy words it is written...

On Shabbath Rosh Chodesh say: Your God will cause the sun to glow in sevenfold brilliance, and the moon to shine in its renewal like the sun, and He will cause the New Moon, by its hallowing, to renew [its] atonement, to fulfill the purpose of the day, that man may behold the holiness of His Presence, to observe the New Moon on its New Moon Day and the Sabbath on its Sabbath Day. *(Reader):* And in Your holy words it is written...

On Shabbath Bereshith say: Your God will endow His servant with understanding, so that His throne will be established as it was in the beginning. He will rebuild the city upon its ruins and prepare the palace and heal its altar in order to prepare the place of the drink offerings. He will proclaim that the Hebrew Woman has come home, that she is free at last. Behold, the might of His fury will scatter His enemies, and He will reign over the nation that keeps the Sabbath of the world's beginning. *(Reader):* And in Your holy words it is written...

לשבת חנוכה. <small>חתום שם המחבר יהודה חזק.</small>

אֱלֹהֵיכֶם יִשְׁלַח מְשִׁיחוֹ אֵזוֹר צֶדֶק וְהָאֱמוּנָה יַרְבִּיד · הָרָשָׁע יָמִית בְּשֵׁבֶט
פִּיו אוֹיֵב יַאֲבִיד · וְעַל הַנִּסִּים הַלֵּל לִגְמוֹר צָעִיר מְהֻעֲבִיד · הֵעָה חֲדָשָׁה יְחַדֵּשׁ
הַטּוּ אֹזֶן מַהַכְבִּיד · הֲדַר חֶמְדַּת זְבוּל קֹדֶשׁ יְקוֹמֵם וַיַּזְבִּיד · וְנָשִׁיר מִזְמוֹר שִׁיר
חֲנֻכַּת הַבַּיִת לְדָוִד : ‏ וּבדברי קדשך

לשבת נחמו. <small>חתום שם המחבר יהודה חזק.</small>

אֱלֹהֵיכֶם יוֹסִיף יָדוֹ לְקַבֵּץ נְפוּצוֹתֵיכֶם · הָעֵת יָחִישׁ לֵאמֹר צְאוּ מֵאֲסוּרֵיכֶם ·
וּמַלְאַךְ בְּרִיתוֹ יִשְׁלַח לְהָשִׁיב לְבַבְכֶם · דַּרְכּוּ פַנּוּ וְהָיָה הֶעָקֹב לְמִישׁוֹר וְלָעִירוּ
יַקְבְּצְכֶם · הַשּׁוֹמְרִים שַׁבָּת בְּרִית הִיא בֵּינוֹ וּבֵינֵיכֶם · בָּרְכוּ שְׁמוֹ וְאַל תִּתְּנוּ
דֳמִי לָכֶם · חַי זֵכֶר קָדְשׁוֹ נַחֲמוּ נַחֲמוּ יֹאמַר אֱלֹהֵיכֶם · כִּי אֲנִי הוּא מַלְכְּכֶם וְאֶמְלוֹךְ
עֲלֵיכֶם : ‏ וּבדברי קדשך

---

has already divested himself, even here in this materialistic world, of the
worship of wealth and the cult of vainglorious pride. Therefore he will not
need the raging fire of the coming Day of Judgment on earth to teach him
how insignificant and fleeting all human greatness and splendor really are
unless they are oriented toward God. This is the Day of Judgment
which must come to pass before God will establish the society of mankind round about Him and begin the reign of His kingdom in their
midst. מעלתו, אגדתו Amos 9:6. The heavenly hosts above arrange themselves
in degrees of ascending order, but men on earth should form one united band,
with one supplementing and perfecting the other.

לשבת ראש חדש When man succumbed to error, nature, which surrounded
and sustained him, went down with him. But, in the same manner once man
will return to God and to moral perfection, nature, too, will rise again to
renewed glory. Then God will create a new Heaven and a new earth (Isa.
66:23); On the day when God will bind up the bruises of His people and
heal the wound that He Himself has inflicted, the light of the moon will be
like the brilliance of the sun, and the sun's brightness will be seven times that
of the light of the seven days. (Ibid. 30:26). It is the purpose of the Day
of the New Moon to act as the herald proclaiming this physical and moral
rebirth, and it will fulfill its function of atonement with which it has been
entrusted by Divine decree. Then the presence of God, dwelling in His
Sanctuary, will be beheld on earth and the teaching of the New Moon will
be properly observed on every Rosh Chodesh, and that of the Sabbath Law
on every Sabbath Day (Isa. 66:23).

לשבת בראשית Each year on this Sabbath we read anew the Biblical account
of the world's beginning and we are told that the beginning of the world was

On Shabbath Chanukkah say: Your God will send His Anointed, who will adorn himself with the girdle of truth and right. He will slay the lawless with the staff of his mouth; he will cause the foe to perish, so that the entire *Hallel* may be recited because of the miracles, for the younger son has now ceased to be a slave. Then He will renew knowledge restored so that every ear may be inclined in pliant obedience. He will restore the glory of the Holy Place of [our] desire, and He shall give it as a portion everlasting, and then we shall sing the Psalm, the Song for the Consecration of the Temple, by David. *(Reader):* And in Your holy words it is written...

On Shabbath Nachamu say: Your God will raise His hand once more to gather in your dispersed. He will hasten the time when He will say, "Go forth from your chains." He will send the messenger of His covenant, to turn back your heart. Clear the way for Him, so that the crooked may become straight and He may gather you into His city. For you, who keep the Sabbath, it is a covenant between Him and yourselves. Bless His Name and give yourselves no rest. His holy memorial lives on. "Comfort ye," your God will say, "for I am your King and will reign over you forever. *(Reader):* And in Your holy words it is written...

---

a free, voluntary act of creation by an Almighty God. This fact should be a guarantee for us also that redemption, the ultimate goal promised us by Him, is certain to come, for even as God created the world by acts of free, almighty power, so He also continues to lead and guide it for His purposes in unrestricted omnipotence.

ירביד לשבת חנוכה. derived from ירבד, "adornment", as in רבד הזהב (Gen. 41:42).

לשבת נשואין In some communities it is customary at the Sabbath service for the entire congregation publicly to demonstrate its rejoicing in the marriage of one of its members by adding to the *Haftarah* for that day the selection from Prophetic literature beginning with שוש אשיש (Isa. 61:10–62) and by inserting this paragraph in the *kedushah*. The theme of this additional prayer *Elokeichem* is in keeping with the spirit prevailing at all Jewish weddings because it deals with the remembrance of Jerusalem. According to Psalm 137:5–6, Yisrael must never forget Yerushalayim, and the expression of hope for the speedy rebuilding of the holy city should have first place at every joyous occasion.

לשבת נשיאין. חתום שם המחבר שמואל חזק.

אֱלֹהֵיכֶם שָׁכְנוּ שָׁם בָּם עֵילָמוֹ. מַלְאָכָיו רוּחוֹת רָז לֹא לָמוֹ. וְאַיֵּה מְקוֹם

כְּבוֹדוֹ דוֹלְמוֹ. אוֹמְרִים בָּרוּךְ כְּבוֹד יְיָ מִמְּקוֹמוֹ. לְעֵת יִמְלֹךְ לְיוֹם קוּמוֹ. חֲזֵה

צִיּוֹן גָּנוֹן בִּמְקוֹמוֹ. זֶה יִרְאוּ וְיֵדְעוּ כָּל־יְקוּמוֹ. קָרוֹא לִירוּשָׁלַיִם כִּסֵּא מְקוֹמוֹ:

ובדברי קדשך:

לשבת ברית מילה.

אֱלֹהֵיכֶם אֲנִי זוֹכֵר הַבְּרִית. הִנֵּה שׁוֹלֵחַ לִשְׁאֵרִית. אֶת נִסְתָּר בְּנַחַל כְּרִית.

מְבַשֵּׂר טוֹב וְשָׁלוֹם בְּאַחֲרִית. יְדַע זֹאת כָּל כְּרוּתֵי בְרִית. אָמַר לְצִיּוֹן מָלַךְ אֱלֹהַיִךְ

זָהוֹרִית: ובדברי קדשך:

אֵין כֵּאלֹהֵינוּ· אֵין כַּאדוֹנֵינוּ· אֵין כְּמַלְכֵּנוּ· אֵין כְּמוֹשִׁיעֵנוּ: מִי כֵאלֹהֵינוּ· מִי כַאדוֹנֵינוּ· מִי כְמַלְכֵּנוּ· מִי כְמוֹשִׁיעֵנוּ: נוֹדֶה לֵאלֹהֵינוּ· נוֹדֶה לַאדוֹנֵינוּ· נוֹדֶה לְמַלְכֵּנוּ· נוֹדֶה לְמוֹשִׁיעֵנוּ: בָּרוּךְ אֱלֹהֵינוּ· בָּרוּךְ אֲדוֹנֵינוּ· בָּרוּךְ מַלְכֵּנוּ· בָּרוּךְ מוֹשִׁיעֵנוּ: אַתָּה הוּא אֱלֹהֵינוּ· אַתָּה הוּא אֲדוֹנֵינוּ· אַתָּה הוּא מַלְכֵּנוּ· אַתָּה הוּא מוֹשִׁיעֵנוּ: אַתָּה הוּא שֶׁהִקְטִירוּ אֲבוֹתֵינוּ לְפָנֶיךָ אֶת קְטֹרֶת הַסַּמִּים:

את נסתר בנחל כרית .לשבת ברית מילה i.e. the Prophet Elijah (I Kings 17:5).
Elijah should be remembered particularly on the occasion of a ברית מילה,
because of his outcry כי עזבו בריתך בני ישראל (ibid. 19:10) which, according
to Pirkei deRabbi Eliezer implies that Yisrael had forsaken the *brith* of the
milah. As a reward for his zeal, the prophet was thereupon reassured that,
wherever in the future a *milah* should be performed in a home in Yisrael in
the spirit of true loyalty to the covenant, he, Elijah, would be privileged to
be a witness at this demonstration of faithfulness. Hence the *kisei shel Eliyahu*
which is prepared for him at every *milah* ceremony. For this reason, too,
Elijah is called the *malach habrith* whom we await (Mal. 3:1) and who will
come to us as the herald of the great day of Divine judgment and deliverance
(ibid. 23).

אין כאלהינו The burning, on the golden altar in the Sanctuary, of the
incense of explicitly specified content was intimately linked with the tending

On the Sabbath after a wedding say: Your God has appointed His unseen Throne as the Abode of His Presence for you. Even His angels, the [heavenly] spirits, know not the secret where the place of His glory is: "Blessed be the glory of *God* from its Abode," they say. When He will come forth as the King, on that day will He arise; let Tzion behold Him, guarding, in His Abode. Then all His creatures will see and know that He calls Yerushalayim the Throne of His Abode. *(Reader):* And in Your holy words it is written...

On the Sabbath of a Brith Milah say: I, your God, remember the covenant; I shall send to the remnant him who is hidden in the valley of Kerith. He brings good news and peace in the end—let all those marked by the covenant know this: He says to Tzion, "Your God has begun His reign in shining glory." *(Reader):* And in Your holy words it is written...

There is none like our God; there is none like our Lord; there is none like our King; there is none like our Savior. Who is like our God? Who is like our Lord? Who is like our King? Who is like our Savior? We render grateful homage to our God; we render grateful homage to our Lord; we render grateful homage to our King; we render grateful homage to our Savior. You are our God; You are our Lord; You are our King; You are our Savior. You are He before Whose countenance our fathers burned the incense of spices.

---

of the lamp in the Sanctuary, a rite which had to be performed every day, morning and evening. (See Exod. 30:1–9, 34–38). The offerings that were brought upon the copper altar as elevating-offerings (the corresponding altar in the Temple was made of stone) symbolized the ultimate goal to have every aspect of man's life, every facet of his personality and all of his endeavors and possessions purified in the fire of the Law of God so that man in his entirety may become אשה ריח ניחוח לה׳. an expression of obedience to God to be fashioned by an offering of fire." The *reach nichoach*, on the other hand, which we behold before us in the Temple court where it symbolizes the goal to be attained by such purification, is seen in the *heichal* (which has the same relationship to the Temple court as gold has to copper) as *ketoreth*, an independent *reach nichoach*, a complete dedication, to the pleasure of God. *Menorah* and *ketoreth* together constitute the visible expression of the ideal of moral and spiritual perfection. But the essential prerequisite for such complete and perfect dedication of all our affairs to the pleasure of God is the unshakeable conviction of His absolute Oneness as our Lord and Creator.

פִּטוּם הַקְּטֹרֶת הַצֳּרִי וְהַצִּפֹּרֶן וְהַחֶלְבְּנָה וְהַלְּבוֹנָה· מִשְׁקַל שִׁבְעִים שִׁבְעִים מָנֶה: מוֹר וּקְצִיעָה שִׁבֹּלֶת נֵרְדְּ וְכַרְכֹּם מִשְׁקַל שִׁשָּׁה עָשָׂר שִׁשָּׁה עָשָׂר מָנֶה· הַקֹּשְׁטְ שְׁנֵים עָשָׂר· וְקִלּוּפָה שְׁלֹשָׁה· וְקִנָּמוֹן תִּשְׁעָה· בֹּרִית כַּרְשִׁינָה תִּשְׁעָה קַבִּין· יֵין קַפְרִיסִין סְאִין תְּלָתָא וְקַבִּין תְּלָתָא· וְאִם אֵין לוֹ יֵין קַפְרִיסִין מֵבִיא חֲמַר חִוַּרְיָן עַתִּיק· מֶלַח סְדוֹמִית רֹבַע (הַקַּב)· מַעֲלֶה עָשָׁן כָּל שֶׁהוּא· רַבִּי נָתָן אוֹמֵר אַף כִּפַּת הַיַּרְדֵּן כָּל שֶׁהוּא וְאִם נָתַן בָּהּ דְּבַשׁ פְּסָלָהּ· אִם חִסַּר אַחַת מִכָּל סַמְמָנֶיהָ חַיָּב מִיתָה: רַבָּן שִׁמְעוֹן בֶּן גַּמְלִיאֵל אוֹמֵר· הַצֳּרִי אֵינוֹ אֶלָּא שְׂרָף הַנּוֹטֵף מֵעֲצֵי הַקְּטָף· בֹּרִית כַּרְשִׁינָה שֶׁשָּׁפִין בָּהּ אֶת הַצִּפֹּרֶן· כְּדֵי שֶׁתְּהֵא נָאָה· יֵין קַפְרִיסִין שֶׁשּׁוֹרִין בּוֹ אֶת הַצִּפֹּרֶן· כְּדֵי שֶׁתְּהֵא עַזָּה: וַהֲלֹא מֵי רַגְלַיִם יָפִין לָהּ אֶלָּא שֶׁאֵין מַכְנִיסִין מֵי רַגְלַיִם בָּעֲזָרָה מִפְּנֵי הַכָּבוֹד:

משנה סוף מס' תמיד, וסופרים פי"ח·

הַשִּׁיר שֶׁהַלְוִיִּם הָיוּ אוֹמְרִים בְּבֵית הַמִּקְדָּשׁ:

בַּיּוֹם הָרִאשׁוֹן הָיוּ אוֹמְרִים· לַיְיָ הָאָרֶץ וּמְלוֹאָהּ תֵּבֵל וְיֹשְׁבֵי בָהּ: (כ"ד)

We must be convinced that He alone established and perfected every phase of our lives, individual and communal alike, so that it should be inconceivable for us to subordinate any of our affairs to any other factor. For this reason the reading of the excerpt from the Talmud dealing with *ketoreth* is preceded by *Ein Kelohenu*, the chanting of the avowal that God is indeed the one Sole and Unique God. The terms *Elohenu* and *Adonenu*, the former naming God as the Creator and Preserver of our lives, and the latter showing Him as the Bearer and Ordainer of all our conduct, refer to the place which He occupies in our lives as individuals. The designations *Malkenu* and *Moshienu* imply God's role in the life of our community as such, as the Guiding Force determining our destinies and causing them to culminate in our collective salvation.

The Song which the Levites used to recite in the Sanctuary: On the *First Day* [of the week] they used to recite Psalm 24: "The earth is *God*'s and the fullness thereof, the world of men and they that dwell therein." On the *Second Day* they used to recite Psalm 48: "Great is *God* and clearly revealed by His mighty acts in the city of

---

First, we declare the Unity of God in positive terms: *Ein Kelohenu*. Only thereafter do we elaborate on this simple declaration; we invite inquiry as it were, as to whether there could possibly be any limitation or restriction to God's Oneness: *Mi Kelohenu*. Then we turn to Him as our Sole God and Rock, (*Atah hu*), and vow to Him our homage as a logical consequence, dedicating to Him all of our being which not only belongs to Him but is also forever in His debt (*Nodeh*). This homage is expressed symbolically by the various prescribed spices that constitute the ingredients of the *ketoreth*. One of the essential ingredients of the *ketoreth* was a foul-smelling substance called חלבנה. This symbolized those aspects of our individual and communal lives which are imperfect and repugnant but which are nevertheless essential for the fulfillment of our task. For it is only if evil is also present that perfection can prove its power before God by overcoming that which is imperfect and by accomplishing the transformation of that which is most unpleasant in ourselves and in our lives into the gladsome, rewarding awareness of duty faithfully performed.

פטום הקטרת This paragraph deals with the composition of the incense; i.e. balsamic resin, onycha, galbanum, frankincense, etc. We have not attempted to translate this paragraph, because we still are not entirely sure of the exact and proper rendering for all the spice names mentioned in the Hebrew text.

השיר The final ceremony of the *Tamid,* of the regular daily offering, as well as that of the *Musaph* offering on the Sabbath, was ניסוך היין, the wine offering which accompanied both the *Tamid* and the *Musaph*. This served to express in symbolic terms that our greatest joys even here below are rooted as it were, in the base of the altar of the Sanctuary. The songs of the Levites שיר שהיו הלויים אומרים במקדש were part of this ceremony of *nisuch hayayin,* with the hymns accompanying the *Musaph* differing from those that were sung at the performance of the *Tamid*.

In Rosh Ha-Shanah 31a we have the following explanations concerning the meaning of each of these psalms in connection with the seven days of the week as days of creation. On the First Day, the Levites chanted Psalm 24: על שם שקנה והקנה ושליט בעולמו because this Psalm is in keeping with the significance of the First Day of Creation, since it praises God as the Owner of all the Universe, and hence of Earth as well by virtue of having created it all, God Who therefore is the Owner also of that part of the physical

בַּשֵּׁנִי הָיוּ אוֹמְרִים,

גָּדוֹל יְיָ וּמְהֻלָּל מְאֹד בְּעִיר אֱלֹהֵינוּ הַר־קָדְשׁוֹ: (מ״ח)

בַּשְּׁלִישִׁי הָיוּ אוֹמְרִים,

אֱלֹהִים נִצָּב בַּעֲדַת־אֵל בְּקֶרֶב אֱלֹהִים יִשְׁפֹּט: (פ״ב)

בָּרְבִיעִי הָיוּ אוֹמְרִים,

אֵל־נְקָמוֹת יְיָ אֵל נְקָמוֹת הוֹפִיעַ: (צ״ד)

בַּחֲמִישִׁי הָיוּ אוֹמְרִים,

הַרְנִינוּ לֵאלֹהִים עוּזֵּנוּ הָרִיעוּ לֵאלֹהֵי יַעֲקֹב: (פ״א)

בַּשִּׁשִּׁי הָיוּ אוֹמְרִים,

יְיָ מָלָךְ גֵּאוּת לָבֵשׁ, לָבֵשׁ יְיָ עֹז הִתְאַזָּר אַף־תִּכּוֹן תֵּבֵל בַּל־

תִּמּוֹט: (צ״ג)

בַּשַּׁבָּת הָיוּ אוֹמְרִים,

מִזְמוֹר שִׁיר לְיוֹם הַשַּׁבָּת: (צ״ב)

מִזְמוֹר שִׁיר לֶעָתִיד לָבֹא · לְיוֹם שֶׁכֻּלּוֹ שַׁבָּת וּמְנוּחָה לְחַיֵּי הָעוֹלָמִים:

אָמַר רַבִּי אֶלְעָזָר אָמַר רַבִּי חֲנִינָא · תַּלְמִידֵי חֲכָמִים מַרְבִּים
שָׁלוֹם בָּעוֹלָם · שֶׁנֶּאֱמַר וְכָל־בָּנַיִךְ לִמּוּדֵי יְיָ וְרַב שְׁלוֹם בָּנָיִךְ:
אַל תִּקְרָא בָּנָיִךְ אֶלָּא בּוֹנָיִךְ: שָׁלוֹם רָב לְאֹהֲבֵי תוֹרָתֶךָ וְאֵין
לָמוֹ מִכְשׁוֹל: יְהִי־שָׁלוֹם בְּחֵילֵךְ שַׁלְוָה בְּאַרְמְנוֹתָיִךְ: לְמַעַן
אַחַי וְרֵעָי אֲדַבְּרָה־נָּא שָׁלוֹם בָּךְ: לְמַעַן בֵּית־יְיָ אֱלֹהֵינוּ אֲבַקְשָׁה
טוֹב לָךְ: יְיָ עֹז לְעַמּוֹ יִתֵּן, יְיָ יְבָרֵךְ אֶת־עַמּוֹ בַשָּׁלוֹם קדיש דרבנן

עָלֵינוּ. page 208. כאן אומרים: היום שבת קודש שבו הלוים היו אומרים
במקדש, מזמור שיר ליום השבת page 252. קדיש יתום.
שיר היחוד—page 742 שיר הכבוד—page 744

world which He has assigned to man as his sphere. In this world God makes
salvation possible only for him who, in that world of God and by his use
of the resources of that world, acknowledges the supreme sovereignty of his
Maker and lives in accordance with God's will. This is the ideal recognition
of His sovereignty, to which God guides mankind victoriously past all the

our God, the mountain of His Sanctuary. On the *Third Day* they
used to recite Psalm 82: "God stands in every congregation of God;
He judges in the midst of the judges." On the *Fourth Day* they used
to recite Psalm 94: "O *God* Who champions justice; O *God* Who
champions justice shine forth." On the *Fifth Day* they used to recite
Psalm 81: "Waken rejoicing to God, our strength, stir up homage to
the God of Yaakov." On the *Sixth Day* they used to recite Psalm 93:
"*God* has begun His reign; He has clothed Himself with majesty;
He has girded Himself with invincibility. Now the world of men, too,
will be firmly established and be moved no more." On the *Sabbath*
they used to recite Psalm 92: "A Psalm, a Song for the Sabbath Day."
A Song, a Psalm for the future that is destined to come, for that day
which will be all Sabbath and rest for life everlasting.

אמר רבי אלעזר See p. 284 for Trans. and Comm.

---

forces that would withstand His might. לה׳ הארץ וגו׳ תבל וגו׳ מי יעלה וגו׳ נקי כפים
וגו׳ ישא ברכה וגו׳ שאו שערים וגו׳ ה׳ עזוז וגבור וגו׳ שאו שערים וגו׳ ה׳ צבאות וגו׳.
On the **Second Day**, Psalm 48: על שם שחילק מעשיו ומלך עליהן On the
Second Day of Creation there came to pass the great separation of the world
of nature into two contrasting spheres, terrestrial and extra-terrestrial, both
of which, under the rule and management of God, by concerted action and
mutual interaction, together serve to bring the world nearer to its ultimate
goal of salvation. In the same manner, God has divided the world of mankind
also into two contrasting elements, the Jewish world on one hand and the
non-Jewish world on the other, and He leads them both, under His almighty
rule, over and above the struggling of the foes who attempt to stop Him,
toward one constant, eternal goal. Hence, because it sings of God's all-powerful reign, Psalm 48 was chosen as the hymn for the Second Day of the week.
On the **Third Day**, Psalm 82: על שם שגלה ארץ בחכמתו והכין תבל לעדתו
On the Third Day of Creation, God raised the masses of land above the
waters to serve as the soil upon which human life was to develop. Mankind,
which was to dwell on the continents of the earth, was to form a society
dedicated to the fulfillment of the will of God which was to be revealed
on earth as the governing order that shapes all things and rules over them.
It is of this supreme world order for which both the earth and mankind
were created that Psalm 82 sings.
On the **Fourth Day**, Psalm 94: על שם שברא חמה ולבנה ועתיד ליפרע מעובדיהן
On the Fourth Day of Creation, God formed the great heavenly luminaries,
the sun and the moon. Men, in their foolish error, worshipped these as Divine
forces because they seemed subject to no restraint. It was on this erroneous
view that they patterned their own conduct of equally uncontrolled violence.

אסור להתענות בשבת על שם שעות, ולשם תענית אפילו שעה אסור. יהא שולחנו ערוך כמו
בסעודת לילה. ומקדשין על היין, ובמקום שאין יין מטי יכל לקדש על כל שאר המשקין שהם
חמר מדינה, (ואם אין לו שום משקין בולע מיד על הפת). ולוקח הכוס מלא יין בידו ואומר
ושמרו וכו'

וְשָׁמְרוּ בְנֵי־יִשְׂרָאֵל אֶת־הַשַּׁבָּת לַעֲשׂוֹת אֶת־
הַשַּׁבָּת לְדֹרֹתָם בְּרִית עוֹלָם: בֵּינִי וּבֵין בְּנֵי יִשְׂרָאֵל
אוֹת הִוא לְעוֹלָם כִּי־שֵׁשֶׁת יָמִים עָשָׂה יְהֹוָה אֶת־
הַשָּׁמַיִם וְאֶת־הָאָרֶץ וּבַיּוֹם הַשְּׁבִיעִי שָׁבַת וַיִּנָּפַשׁ:

They lacked the gift of spiritual perception to rise to the moral level of the
conviction that there is a God Who can see and hear far beyond all physical
forces, Who formed the eye and ear of man, and Who causes men, wallowing
in excesses of unbridled self-adoration, to become aware of His majesty which
strikes them numb and paralyzed so that they must stop short in their path
of violence. This is the theme also of Psalm 94.

On the Fifth Day, Psalm 81: על שם שברא עופות ודגים לשבח לשמו On the
Fifth Day of Creation, God made the birds and the fish which disport themselves happily and contentedly each in their own habitat. Psalm 81 reminds
us that such happiness and contentment could be ours as well, if only we
would resolve to forego the ways of wilfulness and conceit and, instead,
direct our endeavors upon the paths that God has shown us.

On the Sixth Day, Psalm 93: על שם שגמר מלאכתו ומלך עליהם On the Sixth
Day God completed His work of creation by creating man. He now began
His rule which had as its purpose to bring about the universal homage of all
mankind to Him. In this manner the same unswerving and changeless order
that was arbitrarily imposed upon the rest of the world was to be accepted
and established also in humanity which had been given the ennobling privilege
of freedom of choice. This is the thought that is the basic theme also of Psalm
93.

On the Seventh Day, Psalm 92: מזמור שיר לעום השבת ליום שכולו שבת
This Psalm, intended for the Sabbath Day, does not praise the work of God
in Creation that culminated in the Sabbath. Rather, it sings of the work of
God's sovereign rule *after* the completion of Creation, a process of rearing
and training which has extended down to this very day and will continue
even to the most distant future. It sings of the Sabbath, which was appointed
as the hallowed and hallowing bearer and instrument of this Divine work
among men. Thus, from the vantage point of the Sabbath of Creation, the
Psalm looks into the future to view that universal Sabbath when all evil will

זָכוֹר אֶת־יוֹם הַשַּׁבָּת לְקַדְּשׁוֹ: שֵׁשֶׁת יָמִים תַּעֲבֹד

וְעָשִׂיתָ כָּל־מְלַאכְתֶּךָ: וְיוֹם הַשְּׁבִיעִי שַׁבָּת לַיהוָה

אֱלֹהֶיךָ לֹא־תַעֲשֶׂה כָל־מְלָאכָה אַתָּה וּבִנְךָ וּבִתֶּךָ

עַבְדְּךָ וַאֲמָתְךָ וּבְהֶמְתֶּךָ וְגֵרְךָ אֲשֶׁר בִּשְׁעָרֶיךָ: כִּי

שֵׁשֶׁת־יָמִים עָשָׂה יְהוָה אֶת־הַשָּׁמַיִם וְאֶת־הָאָרֶץ אֶת־

הַיָּם וְאֶת־כָּל־אֲשֶׁר־בָּם וַיָּנַח בַּיּוֹם הַשְּׁבִיעִי עַל־כֵּן בֵּרַךְ

יְהוָה אֶת־יוֹם הַשַּׁבָּת וַיְקַדְּשֵׁהוּ:   סַבְרִי מָרָנָן וְרַבָּנָן וְרַבּוֹתַי

בָּרוּךְ אַתָּה יְיָ אֱלֹהֵינוּ מֶלֶךְ הָעוֹלָם בּוֹרֵא פְּרִי הַגָּפֶן:

יִשְׁתֶּה מְיוּשָׁב כְּדֵי רְבִיעִית וְכוֹתֵן גַּם לַמְסוּבִּין לִשְׁתּוֹת מִכּוֹס שֶׁל בְּרָכָה. וְאַחַ"כ מְבָרֵךְ עַל לֶחֶם מִשְׁנֶה.

בָּרוּךְ אַתָּה יְיָ אֱלֹהֵינוּ מֶלֶךְ הָעוֹלָם הַמּוֹצִיא לֶחֶם מִן־הָאָרֶץ:

וּבוֹצֵעַ עַל לֶחֶם הָעֶלְיוֹן וְיֹאכַל וְיִתֵּן לַמְסוּבִּין פְּרוּסָה לְכָל אֶחָד וְאֶחָד.

When visiting a sick person, the following is said upon leaving:

שַׁבָּת הִיא מִלִּזְעֹק וּרְפוּאָה קְרוֹבָה לָבוֹא וְשִׁבְתּוּ בְּשָׁלוֹם:

When one meets with a mourner on שבת, *the following is said:*

שַׁבָּת הִיא מִלְּנַחֵם וְנֶחָמָה קְרוֹבָה לָבוֹא וְשִׁבְתִּי בְּשָׁלוֹם:

---

have vanished and the good will flourish on earth. Then the Sabbath will
have attained its ultimate goal, and a time will begin שֶׁכֻּלּוֹ שַׁבָּת וּמְנוּחָה לְחַיֵּי הָעוֹלָם
הַבָּא.

נמנחה נכנסין לנ"ה ואומרין אשרי וגו' ,והנ"ן צריך להתעטף נטלית חפני וצוד קה"ת.

אַשְׁרֵי יוֹשְׁבֵי בֵיתֶךָ עוֹד יְהַלְלוּךָ סֶּלָה:

אַשְׁרֵי הָעָם שֶׁכָּכָה לּוֹ אַשְׁרֵי הָעָם שֶׁיְיָ אֱלֹהָיו:

קְמַה תְּהִלָּה לְדָוִד

אֲרוֹמִמְךָ אֱלוֹהַי הַמֶּלֶךְ וַאֲבָרְכָה שִׁמְךָ לְעוֹלָם וָעֶד:

בְּכָל־יוֹם אֲבָרְכֶךָּ וַאֲהַלְלָה שִׁמְךָ לְעוֹלָם וָעֶד:

נָּדוֹל יְהוָה וּמְהֻלָּל מְאֹד וְלִגְדֻלָּתוֹ אֵין חֵקֶר:

דּוֹר לְדוֹר יְשַׁבַּח מַעֲשֶׂיךָ וּגְבוּרֹתֶיךָ יַגִּידוּ:

הֲדַר כְּבוֹד הוֹדֶךָ וְדִבְרֵי נִפְלְאֹתֶיךָ אָשִׂיחָה:

וֶעֱזוּז נוֹרְאֹתֶיךָ יֹאמֵרוּ וּגְדֻלָּתְךָ אֲסַפְּרֶנָּה: ינדולתך ק'

זֵכֶר רַב־טוּבְךָ יַבִּיעוּ וְצִדְקָתְךָ יְרַנֵּנוּ:

חַנּוּן וְרַחוּם יְהוָה אֶרֶךְ אַפַּיִם וּגְדָל־חָסֶד: יהיך י'

טוֹב־יְהוָה לַכֹּל וְרַחֲמָיו עַל־כָּל־מַעֲשָׂיו:

יוֹדוּךָ יְהוָה כָּל־מַעֲשֶׂיךָ וַחֲסִידֶיךָ יְבָרְכוּכָה:

כְּבוֹד מַלְכוּתְךָ יֹאמֵרוּ וּגְבוּרָתְךָ יְדַבֵּרוּ:

לְהוֹדִיעַ לִבְנֵי הָאָדָם גְּבוּרֹתָיו וּכְבוֹד הֲדַר מַלְכוּתוֹ:

קדושה דסדרא .אשרי ובא לציון proclaims the presence of God on earth which
we are to hallow, as well as the Divine covenant founded upon the spirit
of Torah which we are to pass on to our descendants for all time. In the

Forward forever stride those that dwell in Your house: continually they utter the praise of Your mighty acts!—Forward to salvation strides that people with whom it is so. Forward strides that nation whose God is *God*.

Tehillah by David. I will extol You, my God, O King, and I will bless Your Name unto the future everlasting.

Every day will I bless You, and proclaim the praise of Your Name until the future everlasting.

Great is *God* and most evident in mighty acts, but His greatness is unsearchable.

Generation after generation will laud Your works, and shall proclaim Your mighty acts.

But I will express in meditation the beauty of the glory of Your majesty and the words of Your wonders.

And they shall speak of the invincibility of Your awesome acts, but I shall tell of the uniform greatness of all Your great deeds.

That they may also utter a thought of the abundance of Your goodness and exult in Your tender righteousness.

God is gracious and compassionate, slow to anger and great in devoted loving-kindness.

God is good to all, and His compassion is over all His works.

All Your works shall render You homage, O *God,* but Your devoted ones shall bless You.

They shall speak of the honor due Your kingdom, and they will declare Your power.

To make known to the sons of men His mighty acts, but also the glory, the beauty of His kingdom.

---

weekday service this portion is part of our transition from worship to our daily activities. On the Sabbath we find it in the *Mincha* service, for it is the purpose of the Sabbath afternoon service to have us look back upon the Sabbath day as it gradually nears its close, and to cause us to gather all the truths that we have learned anew on the Sabbath as a blissful keepsake to take with us as we pass from Sabbath rest to creative weekday living. Hence we now take the Book of the Word of God once more from its Ark into our midst, and we continue the *Keriath haTorah*, the reading from the Torah, continuing from the place where we left off in the morning. For the Torah is our support and our destiny. All our hopes for the future are founded

מַלְכוּתְךָ מַלְכוּת כָּל־עֹלָמִים וּמֶמְשַׁלְתְּךָ בְּכָל־דּוֹר וָדֹר׃

סוֹמֵךְ יְהֹוָה לְכָל־הַנֹּפְלִים וְזוֹקֵף לְכָל־הַכְּפוּפִים׃

עֵינֵי כֹל אֵלֶיךָ יְשַׂבֵּרוּ וְאַתָּה נוֹתֵן־לָהֶם אֶת־אָכְלָם בְּעִתּוֹ׃

פּוֹתֵחַ אֶת־יָדֶךָ וּמַשְׂבִּיעַ לְכָל־חַי רָצוֹן׃

צַדִּיק יְהֹוָה בְּכָל־דְּרָכָיו וְחָסִיד בְּכָל־מַעֲשָׂיו׃

קָרוֹב יְהֹוָה לְכָל־קֹרְאָיו לְכֹל אֲשֶׁר יִקְרָאֻהוּ בֶאֱמֶת׃

רְצוֹן־יְרֵאָיו יַעֲשֶׂה וְאֶת־שַׁוְעָתָם יִשְׁמַע וְיוֹשִׁיעֵם׃

שׁוֹמֵר יְהֹוָה אֶת־כָּל־אֹהֲבָיו וְאֵת כָּל־הָרְשָׁעִים יַשְׁמִיד׃

תְּהִלַּת יְהֹוָה יְדַבֶּר־פִּי וִיבָרֵךְ כָּל־בָּשָׂר שֵׁם קָדְשׁוֹ לְעוֹלָם וָעֶד׃

קטי״ח וַאֲנַחְנוּ נְבָרֵךְ יָהּ מֵעַתָּה וְעַד־עוֹלָם הַלְלוּיָהּ׃

וּבָא לְצִיּוֹן גּוֹאֵל וּלְשָׁבֵי פֶשַׁע בְּיַעֲקֹב נְאֻם יְיָ׃ וַאֲנִי זֹאת בְּרִיתִי אוֹתָם אָמַר יְיָ רוּחִי אֲשֶׁר עָלֶיךָ וּדְבָרַי אֲשֶׁר־שַׂמְתִּי בְּפִיךָ לֹא יָמוּשׁוּ מִפִּיךָ וּמִפִּי זַרְעֲךָ וּמִפִּי זֶרַע זַרְעֲךָ אָמַר יְיָ מֵעַתָּה וְעַד־עוֹלָם׃ וְאַתָּה קָדוֹשׁ יוֹשֵׁב תְּהִלּוֹת יִשְׂרָאֵל׃ וְקָרָא זֶה אֶל־זֶה וְאָמַר קָדוֹשׁ קָדוֹשׁ קָדוֹשׁ יְיָ צְבָאוֹת מְלֹא כָל־הָאָרֶץ כְּבוֹדוֹ׃ וּמְקַבְּלִין דֵּין מִן דֵּין וְאָמְרִין קַדִּישׁ בִּשְׁמֵי מְרוֹמָא עִלָּאָה בֵּית שְׁכִינְתֵּהּ, קַדִּישׁ עַל אַרְעָא עוֹבַד גְּבוּרְתֵּהּ, קַדִּישׁ לְעָלַם וּלְעָלְמֵי עָלְמַיָּא· יְיָ צְבָאוֹת מַלְיָא כָל־אַרְעָא זִיו יְקָרֵהּ׃ וַתִּשָּׂאֵנִי רוּחַ וָאֶשְׁמַע אַחֲרַי קוֹל רַעַשׁ גָּדוֹל בָּרוּךְ כְּבוֹד־יְיָ מִמְּקוֹמוֹ׃ וּנְטָלַתְנִי

upon the constant growth of the power of the Torah so that it may rule and flourish everywhere on earth, but particularly in our own midst, even as

Your kingdom is a kingdom for all distant times and Your rule is in every generation.

God upholds all that fall and raises up all those that are bowed down.

The eyes of all wait upon You and You give them their food in due season.

Yea, You open Your hand and satisfy the desire of every living thing.

God is just in all His ways, and full of devoted loving-kindness in all His works.

God is near to all those that call upon Him, to all that call upon Him in truth.

He will fulfill the desire of them that fear Him; He also will hear their cry and give them salvation.

God will keep all those that love Him, and all the lawless He will let perish.

Let my mouth declare the praise of *God,* so that all flesh may bless His holy Name unto the future everlasting.

As for us, we will bless God from this time forth and forever. Halaluyah!

The Redeemer shall come to Tzion and to those in Yaakov who turn back from defection, says *God.* "As for Me," said *God,* "this My covenant shall remain their very being; My spirit, which rests upon you, and My words which I have put in your mouth shall not depart from your mouth nor from the mouths of your children, nor from the mouths of your children's children," said *God,* "from now on to all eternity." And You O holy One, are still enthroned upon Yisrael's songs of praise. And one calls to the other and says, "Holy, holy, holy is *God Tzevaoth,* the fullness of all the earth is His glory." They receive it from one another and say, "Holy in the highest heights of Heaven, the Abode of His Presence, holy on earth, the creation of His almighty power, holy forever and for all the eternities of eternity, is *God Tzevaoth;* the whole earth is filled with the radiance of His glory." When the spirit lifted me up, I heard behind me the voice of a

---

this hope is expressed in ה׳ חפץ למען צדקו וגו׳, the concluding sentence of *Uva Letzion.*

רוּחָא וְשָׁמְעֵת בַּתְרַי קָל זְיעַ סַגִּיא דִּמְשַׁבְּחִין וְאָמְרִין בְּרִיךְ יְקָרָא דַיְיָ מֵאֲתַר בֵּית שְׁכִינְתֵּהּ: יְיָ יִמְלֹךְ לְעֹלָם וָעֶד: יְיָ מַלְכוּתֵהּ קָאֵם לְעָלַם וּלְעָלְמֵי עָלְמַיָּא: יְיָ אֱלֹהֵי אַבְרָהָם יִצְחָק וְיִשְׂרָאֵל אֲבוֹתֵינוּ שָׁמְרָה־זֹּאת לְעוֹלָם לְיֵצֶר מַחְשְׁבוֹת לְבַב עַמֶּךָ וְהָכֵן לְבָבָם אֵלֶיךָ: וְהוּא רַחוּם יְכַפֵּר עָוֹן וְלֹא יַשְׁחִית וְהִרְבָּה לְהָשִׁיב אַפּוֹ וְלֹא יָעִיר כָּל־חֲמָתוֹ: כִּי־אַתָּה אֲדֹנָי טוֹב וְסַלָּח וְרַב חֶסֶד לְכָל־קֹרְאֶיךָ: צִדְקָתְךָ צֶדֶק לְעוֹלָם וְתוֹרָתְךָ אֱמֶת: תִּתֵּן אֱמֶת לְיַעֲקֹב חֶסֶד לְאַבְרָהָם אֲשֶׁר־נִשְׁבַּעְתָּ לַאֲבֹתֵינוּ מִימֵי קֶדֶם: בָּרוּךְ אֲדֹנָי יוֹם יוֹם יַעֲמָס־לָנוּ הָאֵל יְשׁוּעָתֵנוּ סֶלָה: יְיָ צְבָאוֹת עִמָּנוּ מִשְׂגָּב לָנוּ אֱלֹהֵי יַעֲקֹב סֶלָה: יְיָ צְבָאוֹת אַשְׁרֵי אָדָם בֹּטֵחַ בָּךְ: יְיָ הוֹשִׁיעָה הַמֶּלֶךְ יַעֲנֵנוּ בְיוֹם־קָרְאֵנוּ: בָּרוּךְ הוּא אֱלֹהֵינוּ שֶׁבְּרָאָנוּ לִכְבוֹדוֹ וְהִבְדִּילָנוּ מִן־הַתּוֹעִים וְנָתַן לָנוּ תּוֹרַת אֱמֶת וְחַיֵּי עוֹלָם נָטַע בְּתוֹכֵנוּ הוּא יִפְתַּח לִבֵּנוּ בְּתוֹרָתוֹ וְיָשֵׂם בְּלִבֵּנוּ אַהֲבָתוֹ וְיִרְאָתוֹ וְלַעֲשׂוֹת רְצוֹנוֹ וּלְעָבְדוֹ בְּלֵבָב שָׁלֵם לְמַעַן לֹא נִיגַע לָרִיק וְלֹא נֵלֵד לַבֶּהָלָה: יְהִי רָצוֹן מִלְּפָנֶיךָ יְיָ אֱלֹהֵינוּ וֵאלֹהֵי אֲבוֹתֵינוּ שֶׁנִּשְׁמוֹר חֻקֶּיךָ בָּעוֹלָם הַזֶּה וְנִזְכֶּה וְנִחְיֶה וְנִרְאֶה וְנִירַשׁ טוֹבָה וּבְרָכָה לִשְׁנֵי יְמוֹת הַמָּשִׁיחַ וּלְחַיֵּי הָעוֹלָם הַבָּא: לְמַעַן יְזַמֶּרְךָ כָבוֹד וְלֹא יִדֹּם יְיָ אֱלֹהַי לְעוֹלָם אוֹדֶךָּ: בָּרוּךְ הַגֶּבֶר אֲשֶׁר יִבְטַח בַּיְיָ וְהָיָה יְיָ מִבְטַחוֹ: בִּטְחוּ בַיְיָ עֲדֵי־עַד כִּי

great rushing, "Blessed be the glory of *God* from His Abode." And
the spirit lifted me up, and I heard behind me the noise of a great movement of those who praised and spoke, "Blessed be the glory of *God*
from the Abode of His Presence." "*God* shall reign forever and ever."
God, His kingship remains forever and for all eternities of eternity.
O *God*, God of Abraham, Yitzchak, and Yisrael, our fathers, keep
this forever as the purpose in the thoughts of the hearts of Your people
and turn their minds to You. But He being full of compassion forgives
iniquity and does not destroy, and many a time repents of His anger
and never stirs up all His wrath. For You, O my Lord, are good and
forgiving and great in loving kindness for all those that call upon You.
The righteousness You have taught is eternal righteousness and your
teaching is truth. Grant to Yaakov the truth and to Abraham the loving-kindness which You have sworn to our fathers from the days of
old. Blessed be my Lord day by day; may He give us [a burden] to
bear. Even the same God is also our salvation! *God Tzevaoth* is with
us; the God of Yaakov is our high tower!— *God Tzevaoth*, forward
forever strides the man that trusts in You!—May *God* grant salvation.
As the King will He answer us on the day on which we call upon Him.
Blessed be He, our God, Who created us for His glory and set us apart
from those who go astray and Who has given us the Torah of truth
and implanted life eternal into us. May He open our heart to His Torah, and put the love and fear of Him into our hearts, to do His will
and to serve Him with a whole heart, so that we may not labor in vain
nor bring forth for dismay. May it be Your will, O *God* our God and
God of our fathers, that we may keep Your statutes in this world and
thus become worthy of living, of seeing and inheriting happiness and
blessings in the years of the days of the Messiah and in the life of the
world to come. So that all that is glorious shall ceaselessly sing to
You. O *God*, my God, I will do You homage forever. Blessed is the
man who trusts in *God*, and to whom *God* is also the the source of
His trust. Trust in *God* until the end of days, for in God, *God*, rests

בְּךָ יְיָ צוּר עוֹלָמִים: וְיִבְטְחוּ בְךָ יוֹדְעֵי שְׁמֶךָ כִּי לֹא־עָזַבְתָּ דֹרְשֶׁיךָ

יְיָ: יְיָ חָפֵץ לְמַעַן צִדְקוֹ יַגְדִּיל תּוֹרָה וְיַאְדִּיר: חזק

The Reader recites וַאֲנִי תְפִלָּתִי *and the Congregation repeats it.*

וַאֲנִי תְפִלָּתִי לְךָ יְיָ עֵת רָצוֹן אֱלֹהִים בְּרָב חַסְדֶּךָ עֲנֵנִי בֶּאֱמֶת יִשְׁעֶךָ:

חולין ס"ת וקורין ג' אנשים נראה הסדרה של שבת הבאה, ואין מפטירין ואין אומרין
קדיש אחר קה"ת על הנימה אלא אחר שהבליעו ס"ת שומד הט"ן ואומר ח"ק ח"ז עולה לקריאה
שקראו ולתפלה הסמוכה, לפי שלעולם אין עומדין הלבור בתפלה אלא אחר קדיש וסומכין איתו
לה כל מה דאפשר.

אֲדֹנָי שְׂפָתַי תִּפְתָּח וּפִי יַגִּיד תְּהִלָּתֶךָ:

בָּרוּךְ אַתָּה יְיָ אֱלֹהֵינוּ וֵאלֹהֵי אֲבוֹתֵינוּ אֱלֹהֵי אַבְרָהָם
אֱלֹהֵי יִצְחָק וֵאלֹהֵי יַעֲקֹב הָאֵל הַגָּדוֹל הַגִּבּוֹר וְהַנּוֹרָא
אֵל עֶלְיוֹן גּוֹמֵל חֲסָדִים טוֹבִים וְקֹנֵה הַכֹּל וְזוֹכֵר חַסְדֵי
אָבוֹת וּמֵבִיא גוֹאֵל לִבְנֵי בְנֵיהֶם לְמַעַן שְׁמוֹ בְּאַהֲבָה.

On שבת שובה *say:*

זָכְרֵנוּ לְחַיִּים מֶלֶךְ חָפֵץ בַּחַיִּים · וְכָתְבֵנוּ בְּסֵפֶר הַחַיִּים
לְמַעַנְךָ אֱלֹהִים חַיִּים:

מֶלֶךְ עוֹזֵר וּמוֹשִׁיעַ וּמָגֵן · בָּרוּךְ אַתָּה יְיָ מָגֵן אַבְרָהָם:
אַתָּה גִבּוֹר לְעוֹלָם אֲדֹנָי מְחַיֵּה מֵתִים אַתָּה רַב
לְהוֹשִׁיעַ ·

During the winter months add:

מַשִּׁיב הָרוּחַ וּמוֹרִיד הַגָּשֶׁם:

מְכַלְכֵּל חַיִּים בְּחֶסֶד מְחַיֵּה מֵתִים בְּרַחֲמִים רַבִּים
סוֹמֵךְ נוֹפְלִים וְרוֹפֵא חוֹלִים וּמַתִּיר אֲסוּרִים וּמְקַיֵּם

the Rock of All Time. And those who know Your Name shall trust in You, for You have never forsaken those who seek You, O *God*. *God* was pleased, because of His righteousness, to render the Torah increasingly great and glorious.

But as for me, my prayer shall be to You, O *God,* for but [one] instant of favor; O God Who even while judging remains in the abundance of Your loving-kindness, answer me in the truth of Your salvation.

O *Lord*, open my lips so that my mouth may declare Your praise.

Blessed be You, O *God,* our God and God of our fathers, God of Abraham, God of Yitzchak and God of Yaakov, the great, mighty and awesome God, God the Most High, Who nevertheless bestows lovingkindness, Who is the Owner of all things, and remembers the fathers' acts of devotion, and Who, in love, will bring a redeemer to their children's children for His Name's sake.

(On שבת שובה *say:* Remember us for life, O King Who delights in life, and inscribe us into the Book of Life for Your sake, O Living God.)

O King, Helper, Savior and Shield! Blessed be You *God,* the Shield of Abraham.

You, O my Lord, are all-powerful forever. You are the One Who revives the dead; You are abundantly powerful to save.

(During the winter months add: He causes the wind to blow and the rain to fall).

He sustains the living with loving-kindness, revives the dead with great compassion, supports the falling, heals the sick, unchains the bound, and keeps His faith with the slumberers in the dust. Who

---

ואני תפלתי In Psalm 69, Verse 14, Israel declared that it can always take refuge with God even in the midst of all the persecution, ridicule and oppression with which it is hounded by the hostility of evil men. Even one moment of Divine pleasure affords His people ample compensation for all the ills which it has had to bear. Only that salvation which can be sought from God and found with Him is true salvation; all else is nothing but empty deceit and falsehood. Thus it is these words that we repeat also in the Sabbath Afternoon Service, and before we continue our prayer we first gather once more around the Torah, that source of all truth, so that we may

אֱמוּנָתוֹ לִישֵׁנֵי עָפָר · מִי כָמְוֹךָ בַּעַל גְּבוּרוֹת וּמִי דְוֹמֶה
לָךְ מֶלֶךְ מֵמִית וּמְחַיֶּה וּמַצְמִיחַ יְשׁוּעָה ·

On שבת שובה add:

מִי כָמְוֹךָ אַב הָרַחֲמִים זוֹכֵר יְצוּרָיו לְחַיִּים בְּרַחֲמִים:

וְנֶאֱמָן אַתָּה לְהַחֲיוֹת מֵתִים · בָּרוּךְ אַתָּה יְיָ מְחַיֵּה
הַמֵּתִים:

קדושה לש"ץ בחזרת התפלה.

אַתָּה קָדוֹשׁ   נְקַדֵּשׁ אֶת שִׁמְךָ בָּעוֹלָם כְּשֵׁם שֶׁמַּקְדִּישִׁים
אוֹתוֹ בִּשְׁמֵי מָרוֹם כַּכָּתוּב עַל יַד נְבִיאֶךָ וְקָרָא

וְשִׁמְךָ קָדוֹשׁ   זֶה אֶל זֶה וְאָמַר:קו"ח קָדוֹשׁ קָדוֹשׁ קָדוֹשׁ יְיָ צְבָאוֹת
מְלֹא כָל הָאָרֶץ כְּבוֹדוֹ : ח' לְעֻמָּתָם בָּרוּךְ יֹאמֵרוּ·

וּקְדוֹשִׁים   קו"ח בָּרוּךְ כְּבוֹד יְיָ מִמְּקוֹמוֹ: ח' וּבְדִבְרֵי קָדְשְׁךָ
כָּתוּב לֵאמֹר · קו"ח יִמְלֹךְ יְיָ לְעוֹלָם אֱלֹהַיִךְ צִיּוֹן

בְּכָל–יוֹם   לְדֹר וָדֹר הַלְלוּיָהּ:

ח' לְדוֹר וָדוֹר נַגִּיד גָּדְלֶךָ וּלְנֵצַח נְצָחִים קְדֻשָּׁתְךָ

יְהַלְלוּךָ סֶּלָה: נַקְדִּישׁ וְשִׁבְחֲךָ אֱלֹהֵינוּ מִפִּינוּ לֹא יָמוּשׁ לְעוֹלָם
וָעֶד כִּי אֵל מֶלֶךְ גָּדוֹל וְקָדוֹשׁ אָתָּה·

בָּרוּךְ אַתָּה יְיָ הָאֵל (מ"ץ שבת שובה: הַמֶּלֶךְ) הַקָּדוֹשׁ:

אַתָּה אֶחָד וְשִׁמְךָ אֶחָד · וּמִי כְּעַמְּךָ יִשְׂרָאֵל גּוֹי
אֶחָד בָּאָרֶץ · תִּפְאֶרֶת גְּדֻלָּה · וַעֲטֶרֶת יְשׁוּעָה · יוֹם

draw from it once again a spark from that truth through which alone God
will give us of His salvation.

אתה אחד "Even as You are One, so that which Your Name implies concerning Your ways is unique also and cannot be attributed to any other
being. Your people Yisrael, too, is unique on earth and distinguished as such
particularly by the Sabbath which, as a day of both rest and sanctification,

is like You, O Master of mighty acts, and who, like You, is a King
Who kills and restores life and causes salvation to grow?

(On שבת שובה add: Who, like You, is a Father of compassion,
Who in compassion remembers His creatures for life.)

And You are faithful to revive the dead. Blessed be You, *God*,
Who revives the dead.

You are holy, and Your
Name is holy, and the holy ones
proclaim Your praise each day.
Blessed be You *God*, the holy
God. (On שבת שובה   the holy
King).

*(The Reader, when he repeats
the Shemone Esrei):* W e   w i l l
sanctify Your Name in this
world, even as they sanctify it
in the heavens above, as it is
written by Your prophet: "And
one of them calls to the other

and says:

(Cong. & Reader): 'Holy, holy, holy, is *God Tzevaoth*, the fulness
of all the earth is His glory'.

(Reader): "Facing one another, they say, 'Blessed—

(Cong. & Reader): 'Blessed be the glory of *God* from its Abode.' "

(Reader): And in Your holy words it is written:

(Cong. & Reader): "*God* shall reign forever, your God, O Tzion,
from generation to generation. Halaluyah!"

(Reader): From generation to generation shall we declare Your
greatness and to all eternity will we proclaim Your holiness, and
Your praise, O our God, shall never depart from our mouth, for
You, O God, are a great and holy King. Blessed be You, O *God*,
the holy God. (On שבת שובה *say:* the holy King)

You are One and Your Name is One, and who is like Your people
Yisrael, a people unique on earth? As a glorification of greatness and as

reveals this nation in all its greatness and crowns it with salvation." A Sabbath
truly observed by the renunciation of even the most tempting opportunity for
gain betokens a spiritual and moral greatness characterized by trust in God
and by regard only for values far greater than tangible, material treasures.
Moreover, the Sabbath sanctifies all of our energies so that we may faithfully
employ them in the service of our God even during the workday week. Even
by virtue of its influence, making us more worthy of Divine aid and support,
the Sabbath already crowns us with a sense of Divinely-given salvation. According to our Sages (Mechilta to Exod. 20:9) he who truly keeps the Seventh
Day, has already completed his work on earth with the beginning of every

מְנוּחָה וּקְדֻשָׁה לְעַמְּךָ נָתָתָּ: אַבְרָהָם יָגֵל· יִצְחָק
יְרַנֵּן· יַעֲקֹב וּבָנָיו יָנוּחוּ בוֹ: מְנוּחַת אַהֲבָה וּנְדָבָה·
מְנוּחַת אֱמֶת וֶאֱמוּנָה· מְנוּחַת שָׁלוֹם וְשַׁלְוָה וְהַשְׁקֵט
וָבֶטַח· מְנוּחָה שְׁלֵמָה שָׁאַתָּה רוֹצֶה בָהּ· יַכִּירוּ בָנֶיךָ
וְיֵדְעוּ כִּי מֵאִתְּךָ הִיא מְנוּחָתָם וְעַל מְנוּחָתָם יַקְדִּישׁוּ
אֶת שְׁמֶךָ:

אֱלֹהֵינוּ וֵאלֹהֵי אֲבוֹתֵינוּ· רְצֵה בִמְנוּחָתֵנוּ· קַדְּשֵׁנוּ
בְּמִצְוֹתֶיךָ וְתֵן חֶלְקֵנוּ בְּתוֹרָתֶךָ, שַׂבְּעֵנוּ מִטּוּבֶךָ
וְשַׂמְּחֵנוּ בִּישׁוּעָתֶךָ וְטַהֵר לִבֵּנוּ לְעָבְדְּךָ בֶּאֱמֶת,
וְהַנְחִילֵנוּ יְיָ אֱלֹהֵינוּ בְּאַהֲבָה וּבְרָצוֹן שַׁבַּת
קָדְשֶׁךָ, וְיָנוּחוּ בָהּ יִשְׂרָאֵל מְקַדְּשֵׁי שְׁמֶךָ· בָּרוּךְ
אַתָּה יְיָ, מְקַדֵּשׁ הַשַּׁבָּת:

רְצֵה יְיָ אֱלֹהֵינוּ בְּעַמְּךָ יִשְׂרָאֵל וּבִתְפִלָּתָם· וְהָשֵׁב
אֶת־הָעֲבוֹדָה לִדְבִיר בֵּיתֶךָ וְאִשֵּׁי יִשְׂרָאֵל וּתְפִלָּתָם
בְּאַהֲבָה תְקַבֵּל בְּרָצוֹן וּתְהִי לְרָצוֹן תָּמִיד עֲבוֹדַת
יִשְׂרָאֵל עַמֶּךָ·

Sabbath. If, with the coming of each Sabbath, he takes all that he has created
in the loyal service of God during the workday week, having done his share,
regardless of whether or not he has attained his goals, and humbly lays it
all at God's feet, submitting it to His examining eye, has already made his
contribution in full. He has then achieved his goal, for he needs and wants
nothing else but the gladdening realization that he has faithfully performed
his service before the countenance of God. Every Sabbath will make him happy.
אברהם יגל : Avraham, Yitzchak and Yaakov are named here to illustrate a

a crown of salvation You have given to Your people a day of rest and sanctification. Abraham exults in it; Yitzchak jubilates, Yaakov and his sons find rest through it. A rest of love and devotion, a rest of truth and trust, a rest of peace and well-being, of quiet and confidence, a perfect rest with which You are pleased. Your children will realize it and they will know that such rest is theirs from You, and for their rest they will hallow Your Name.

Our God and God of our fathers, take pleasure in our rest, hallow us by Your commandments and grant our portion in Your Torah. Satisfy us from Your good, gladden us with Your salvation, purify our hearts to serve You in truth, and in Your love and favor, O *God* our God, let Your holy Sabbath remain our inheritance, and may Yisrael, who sanctify Your Name, rest on it. Blessed be You, *God,* Who hallows the Sabbath.

Take pleasure, O *God* our God, in Your people Yisrael and in their prayer. Restore the sacrificial service to the Abode of Your Word in Your House, and accept Yisrael's fire offerings and their prayer with love and favor, and may the service of Your people Yisrael ever be pleasing to You.

---

decline in the fortunes of a family. Abraham was a נשיא אלהים, a great personality among men, gladdened by God and ennobled by His nearness. But his son Yitzchak was forced to fight against the rebuffs of envy and the hostility of jealousy. The lot of Yaakov was harsher still; it was his fate to have to eke out a living for himself and his family by hard and servile labor in the household of a crafty master. This account has profound meaning for us today. Regardless of what our own life's portion may be at the time the Day of Rest enters into our midst, the Sabbath always brings us joy. An "Abraham", blessed with happiness, will find the pinnacle of his blessings, the true rejoicing in his gladness only in that awareness of God which the Sabbath gives him, reminding him that all the good that is his has come from God alone. To a "Yitzchak", thrown back upon his own resources and upon his family, the Sabbath affords ample compensation for the friendship of his fellow-man, for the Sabbath makes him and the small circle about him aware that God is near and present in their midst. On the Sabbath, even a family of a "Yaakov", laboring under the weight of distress and oppression, finds both physical rest and spiritual calm and serenity. (גיל related to קול, is the loud expression of joy. רנן is a rejoicing evoked by the awareness of the presence of God. See Ps. 33:1, Lev. 9:24).

On Rosh Chodesh and the Intermediate Days of Festivals :

אֱלֹהֵינוּ וֵאלֹהֵי אֲבוֹתֵינוּ · יַעֲלֶה וְיָבֹא וְיַגִּיעַ וְיֵרָאֶה וְיֵרָצֶה וְיִשָּׁמַע
וְיִפָּקֵד וְיִזָּכֵר זִכְרוֹנֵנוּ וּפִקְדוֹנֵנוּ וְזִכְרוֹן אֲבוֹתֵינוּ · וְזִכְרוֹן מָשִׁיחַ בֶּן
דָּוִד עַבְדֶּךָ · וְזִכְרוֹן יְרוּשָׁלַיִם עִיר קָדְשֶׁךָ · וְזִכְרוֹן כָּל עַמְּךָ בֵּית
יִשְׂרָאֵל לְפָנֶיךָ · לִפְלֵיטָה וּלְטוֹבָה וּלְחֵן וּלְחֶסֶד וּלְרַחֲמִים וּלְחַיִּים
וּלְשָׁלוֹם בְּיוֹם צ״ל ראשׁ הַחֹדֶשׁ לפסח חַג הַמַּצּוֹת. לסכות חַג הַסֻּכּוֹת
הַזֶּה · זָכְרֵנוּ יְיָ אֱלֹהֵינוּ בּוֹ לְטוֹבָה וּפָקְדֵנוּ בוֹ לִבְרָכָה וְהוֹשִׁיעֵנוּ בוֹ
לְחַיִּים · וּבִדְבַר יְשׁוּעָה וְרַחֲמִים · חוּס וְחָנֵּנוּ וְרַחֵם עָלֵינוּ
וְהוֹשִׁיעֵנוּ · כִּי אֵלֶיךָ עֵינֵינוּ · כִּי אֵל מֶלֶךְ חַנּוּן וְרַחוּם אָתָּה :

וְתֶחֱזֶינָה עֵינֵינוּ בְּשׁוּבְךָ לְצִיּוֹן בְּרַחֲמִים · בָּרוּךְ
אַתָּה יְיָ הַמַּחֲזִיר שְׁכִינָתוֹ לְצִיּוֹן :

מוֹדִים אֲנַחְנוּ לָךְ שָׁאַתָּה הוּא יְיָ אֱלֹהֵינוּ וֵאלֹהֵי אֲבוֹתֵינוּ
לְעוֹלָם וָעֶד צוּר חַיֵּינוּ מָגֵן יִשְׁעֵנוּ אַתָּה הוּא לְדוֹר וָדוֹר · נוֹדֶה
לְּךָ וּנְסַפֵּר תְּהִלָּתֶךָ עַל חַיֵּינוּ הַמְּסוּרִים בְּיָדֶךָ וְעַל נִשְׁמוֹתֵינוּ
הַפְּקוּדוֹת לָךְ וְעַל נִסֶּיךָ שֶׁבְּכָל יוֹם עִמָּנוּ וְעַל נִפְלְאוֹתֶיךָ וְטוֹבוֹתֶיךָ
שֶׁבְּכָל עֵת · עֶרֶב וָבֹקֶר וְצָהֳרָיִם · הַטּוֹב כִּי לֹא כָלוּ רַחֲמֶיךָ
וְהַמְרַחֵם כִּי לֹא תַמּוּ חֲסָדֶיךָ מֵעוֹלָם קִוִּינוּ לָךְ: בחנוכה על הנסים: page 150

(מודים דרבנן ייעהע וייטע 368.)

וְעַל כֻּלָּם יִתְבָּרַךְ וְיִתְרוֹמַם שִׁמְךָ מַלְכֵּנוּ תָּמִיד
לְעוֹלָם וָעֶד :

On שבת שובה add:

וּכְתֹב לְחַיִּים טוֹבִים כָּל בְּנֵי בְרִיתֶךָ :

מנוחת אהבה The commandment of Sabbath rest is not a respite forced
upon us by stern decree against our will. It is fulfilled with love and devotion,
of our free will; our Sabbath observance is based upon true perception, and
on selfless devotion to the truths which we have thus come to know and un-

(On Rosh Chodesh and the Intermediate Days of Festivals):

Our God and God of our Fathers, may our remembrance and the consideration of us, and the remembrance of our fathers, the remembrance of Messiah the son of David Your servant, the remembrance of Yerushalayim, Your holy city, and the remembrance of all Your people, the House of Yisrael, rise and come, reach You and be seen, accepted and heard, considered and remembered for deliverance and for well-being, for favor and loving kindness, for compassion, for life and for peace on this day of

The New Moon — The Festival of Unleavened Bread—
The Festival of Tabernacles

Remember us this day, O *God* our God, for the good; be mindful of us for blessing, and save us for life, and in the promise of salvation and compassion spare us and favor us, for our eyes look up to You; for You, O God, are a gracious and compassionate King.

And may our eyes behold Your return to Tzion in compassion. Blessed be You, O *God,* Who restores Your presence to Tzion.

We gratefully avow to You that You, O *God* are our God and the God of our fathers in all eternity. You are the Rock of our life, the Shield of our Salvation, from generation to generation. We avow our thanks to You and recount Your praise, for our lives, which are committed to Your hand, and for our souls which are in Your care, and for Your miracles which are with us each day, and for Your wondrous deeds and favors that are performed at all times, evening, morning and noon. You are the Beneficent One, for Your compassion has never ceased; the Compassionate One, for Your kindnesses have never ended. Ever have we placed our hopes in You.

(*On* חנוכה: על הנסים)

For all this, O our King, may Your Name be continually blessed and exalted for all eternity. *(On* שבת שובה *add:* and inscribe all the sons of Your covenant for a good life.)

---

derstand. Therefore our Sabbath is a rest which affords peace and a sense of well-being, tranquility and confidence to him who truly keeps it. It is a perfect rest for the whole man, such as can be obtained only from a rest which is pleasing to God. (It is only by the command of God that man *may* and *can*

וְכָל הַחַיִּים יוֹדוּךָ סֶּלָה וִיהַלְלוּ אֶת־שִׁמְךָ בֶּאֱמֶת
הָאֵל יְשׁוּעָתֵנוּ וְעֶזְרָתֵנוּ סֶלָה · בָּרוּךְ אַתָּה יְיָ הַטּוֹב
שִׁמְךָ וּלְךָ נָאֶה לְהוֹדוֹת:

בפולין אומרים זה: באשכנז אומרין זה:

שָׁלוֹם רָב עַל־
יִשְׂרָאֵל עַמְּךָ תָּשִׂים
לְעוֹלָם כִּי אַתָּה
הוּא מֶלֶךְ אָדוֹן
לְכָל־הַשָּׁלוֹם · וְטוֹב
בְּעֵינֶיךָ   לְבָרֵךְ

שִׂים שָׁלוֹם טוֹבָה וּבְרָכָה חֵן
וָחֶסֶד וְרַחֲמִים עָלֵינוּ וְעַל כָּל
יִשְׂרָאֵל עַמֶּךָ בָּרְכֵנוּ אָבִינוּ
כֻּלָּנוּ כְּאֶחָד בְּאוֹר פָּנֶיךָ כִּי
בְאוֹר פָּנֶיךָ נָתַתָּ לָּנוּ יְיָ אֱלֹהֵינוּ
תּוֹרַת חַיִּים וְאַהֲבַת חֶסֶד
וּצְדָקָה וּבְרָכָה וְרַחֲמִים וְחַיִּים
וְשָׁלוֹם · וְטוֹב בְּעֵינֶיךָ לְבָרֵךְ

אֶת־עַמְּךָ יִשְׂרָאֵל בְּכָל־עֵת וּבְכָל־שָׁעָה בִּשְׁלוֹמֶךָ:

During the Days of Repentance add):

בְּסֵפֶר חַיִּים בְּרָכָה וְשָׁלוֹם וּפַרְנָסָה טוֹבָה נִזָּכֵר וְנִכָּתֵב לְפָנֶיךָ
אֲנַחְנוּ וְכָל עַמְּךָ בֵּית יִשְׂרָאֵל לְחַיִּים טוֹבִים וּלְשָׁלוֹם · בָּרוּךְ אַתָּה
יְיָ עוֹשֶׂה הַשָּׁלוֹם:

בָּרוּךְ אַתָּה יְיָ הַמְבָרֵךְ אֶת־עַמּוֹ יִשְׂרָאֵל בַּשָּׁלוֹם:

אֱלֹהַי · נְצוֹר לְשׁוֹנִי מֵרָע וּשְׂפָתַי מִדַּבֵּר מִרְמָה וְלִמְקַלְלַי נַפְשִׁי
תִדּוֹם וְנַפְשִׁי כֶּעָפָר לַכֹּל תִּהְיֶה · פְּתַח לִבִּי בְּתוֹרָתֶךָ וּבְמִצְוֹתֶיךָ
תִּרְדּוֹף נַפְשִׁי וְכָל הַחוֹשְׁבִים עָלַי רָעָה מְהֵרָה הָפֵר עֲצָתָם וְקַלְקֵל

indeed find peace in the midst of life's struggle, that he may rest and be at
rest. The arbitrary fixing of an additional Sabbath by man may actually be

And everything that lives shall avow thanks to You and render praise to Your Name in truth as the God of our salvation and our help forever. Blessed be You *God*, "The Beneficent One" is Your Name, and to You thanksgiving is due.

In congregations following the German ritual:	*In congregations following the Polish ritual the following is now said:*
Establish peace, well-being and blessing, favor, loving-kindness and compassion upon us and upon all of Yisrael, Your people. Bless us, O our Father, all of us together, with the light of Your countenance. For by the light of Your countenance	Establish p e a c e abundant upon Your people Yisrael forever, for You, O King, are the Lord of all peace, and may it be good in Your sight to bless Your people Yisrael at all times and at every hour with Your peace.

You have given us, O *God* our God, the Torah of life and the love of devotion and loyalty to duty, blessing and compassion, life and peace. May it be good in Your sight to bless Your people Yisrael at all times and at every hour with Your peace.

(During the Days of Repentance add): May we be remembered and inscribed before You in the Book of life, blessing, peace and good sustenance, we and all Your people, the House of Yisrael, for a good life and for peace. Blessed be You *God*, the Creator of Peace.

Blessed be You *God*, Who blesses Your people Yisrael with peace.

My God, guard my tongue from evil and my lips from speaking falsehood. Let my soul be silent to those who curse me, and let my soul be as the dust to all things. Open my heart to Your Torah, and may my soul earnestly strive after Your commandments. But as for all those who plot evil against me, thwart their counsel and frustrate

---

a sin.) Those who keep the Sabbath know that they can obtain a true Sabbath only from God, and they gratefully render homage to His Name for the Sabbath rest which He has given them.

מִחַשְּׁבוֹתָם: עֲשֵׂה לְמַעַן שְׁמֶךָ עֲשֵׂה לְמַעַן יְמִינֶךָ עֲשֵׂה לְמַעַן

קְדֻשָּׁתֶךָ עֲשֵׂה לְמַעַן תּוֹרָתֶךָ· לְמַעַן יֵחָלְצוּן יְדִידֶיךָ הוֹשִׁיעָה

יְמִינְךָ וַעֲנֵנִי: יִהְיוּ לְרָצוֹן אִמְרֵי פִי וְהֶגְיוֹן לִבִּי לְפָנֶיךָ יְיָ צוּרִי וְגוֹאֲלִי:

עֹשֶׂה שָׁלוֹם בִּמְרוֹמָיו הוּא יַעֲשֶׂה שָׁלוֹם עָלֵינוּ וְעַל כָּל יִשְׂרָאֵל

וְאִמְרוּ אָמֵן: יְהִי רָצוֹן לְפָנֶיךָ יְיָ אֱלֹהֵינוּ וֵאלֹהֵי אֲבוֹתֵינוּ שֶׁיִּבָּנֶה

בֵּית הַמִּקְדָּשׁ בִּמְהֵרָה בְיָמֵינוּ וְתֵן חֶלְקֵנוּ בְּתוֹרָתֶךָ:

וְשָׁם נַעֲבָדְךָ בְּיִרְאָה כִּימֵי עוֹלָם וּכְשָׁנִים קַדְמֹנִיּוֹת:

וְעָרְבָה לַיְיָ מִנְחַת יְהוּדָה וִירוּשָׁלָיִם כִּימֵי עוֹלָם וּכְשָׁנִים קַדְמֹנִיּוֹת:

הש"ץ חוזר התפלה בקול ואומר קדושה נקרא וגומר התפל'וצח"כ אומר' צדקתך וכו' ובימים
שא"א תחנון בחול אין אומר' צדקתך, ולא בנית חתן בו'יה"מ ולא בבית האבל.

On a שבת during the time of the year when no תחנון is said (see p. 160) the צדקתך
below is not said:

צִדְקָתְךָ צֶדֶק לְעוֹלָם וְתוֹרָתְךָ אֱמֶת: וְצִדְקָתְךָ אֱלֹהִים עַד

מָרוֹם אֲשֶׁר עָשִׂיתָ גְדֹלוֹת אֱלֹהִים מִי כָמוֹךָ: צִדְקָתְךָ כְּהַרְרֵי־אֵל

מִשְׁפָּטֶיךָ תְּהוֹם רַבָּה אָדָם וּבְהֵמָה תוֹשִׁיעַ יְיָ: ק"ת

טעה ולא התפלל מנחה בשבת מתפלל במ"ש שתים של חול ומבדיל בראשונה ואינו
מבדיל בשני', ואם לא הבדיל בראשונה והבדיל בשני', שני' עלתה לו וצריך לחזור
ולהתפלל לתשלומין, ואם הבדיל בשתיהן או לא הבדיל בשתיהן ילא.

צדקתך By the time the Sabbath Mincha service is done, the day is on
the decline, the Sabbath is drawing to a close and thoughts of our life's
task, of the striving and creating, the struggling and suffering of the coming
week gradually seep back into our consciousness. On those Sabbaths which
do not bear a festive character in addition to the holiness of the ordinary
Sabbath, no attempt is made to repress these workday thoughts. But these
brief verses from the Psalms offer us some truths which we should take to
heart and which should serve to give the proper direction to our thinking as

their intentions. Do it for the sake of Your Name, do it for the sake of Your right hand, do it for the sake of Your Torah; therefore set free those whom You have found worthy of Your love. Let Your right hand be seen in salvation and answer me! May the words of my mouth and the meditation of my heart be pleasing before Your countenance, O *God,* my Rock and my Redeemer.

May He Who makes peace in His high places make peace for us and for all of Yisrael, and say, Amen.

May it be Your will, O *God,* our God and God of our fathers, that the Temple be speedily rebuilt in our days, and give us our portion in Your Torah, so that we may serve You there with awe as in the days of old and as in former years. Then the tribute of homage of Yehuda and Yerushalayim will be pleasing to *God* as in the days of the past and as in former years.

The righteousness You have taught was eternal justice to men, and Your Teaching was truth. And Your merciful justice reaches unto high heaven, O You Who have done great things, O God, Who is like You? Your righteousness is like the mighty mountains, Your judgments are like the great deep, man and beast You will preserve, O *God.*

---

we approach the beginning of a new week. First we are given basic certainties concerning the unchanging truth and righteousness which are unshakeable pillars of our duty and of our understanding, the wondrous ways of the loving righteousness of God in which He trains mankind, and the Divine judgment which is as essential for human salvation as is His clemency. (The term צדקה when employed in connection with God, has a connotation quite different from either צדק or משפט. It is not stern righteousness, but clemency; it denotes God's rule as it combines mercy with justice, rendering to man not that which he would have deserved in accordance with his past life but that which should help guide him to future conduct more in keeping with his destiny. When used with reference to persons, *tzedakah* indicates "righteousness" implying the loyalty to duty with which the person "does justice" to his task. (See Commentary to Gen. 18:19.) Since, in this instance, *Tzidkath Hashem* occurs together with *tzedek,* we believe that this should be interpreted not as the *tzedakah practiced* by God Himself, but as the *tzedakah* which He *taught* man, as in Psalm 5:9. The second half of the sentence, ותורתך אמת, would bear out the correctness of this interpretation.) These three convictions should be the basic guiding and sustaining forces in our lives.

From עלינו; שבת בראשית *until* שבת הגדול *the following psalms are said before*
beginning from the שבת *after* פסח, פרקי אבות *are said:*

קי בָּרְכִי נַפְשִׁי אֶת־יְיָ: יְיָ אֱלֹהַי גָּדַלְתָּ מְאֹד, הוֹד וְהָדָר לָבָשְׁתָּ:
עֹטֶה אוֹר כַּשַּׂלְמָה נוֹטֶה שָׁמַיִם כַּיְרִיעָה: הַמְקָרֶה בַמַּיִם
עֲלִיּוֹתָיו · הַשָּׂם־עָבִים רְכוּבוֹ הַמְהַלֵּךְ עַל־כַּנְפֵי־רוּחַ: עֹשֶׂה
מַלְאָכָיו רוּחוֹת מְשָׁרְתָיו אֵשׁ לֹהֵט: יָסַד אֶרֶץ עַל־מְכוֹנֶיהָ בַּל־
תִּמּוֹט עוֹלָם וָעֶד: תְּהוֹם כַּלְּבוּשׁ כִּסִּיתוֹ, עַל־הָרִים יַעַמְדוּ מָיִם:
מִן־גַּעֲרָתְךָ יְנוּסוּן מִן־קוֹל רַעַמְךָ יֵחָפֵזוּן: יַעֲלוּ הָרִים יֵרְדוּ
בְקָעוֹת אֶל־מְקוֹם זֶה יָסַדְתָּ לָהֶם: גְּבוּל־שַׂמְתָּ בַּל־יַעֲבֹרוּן
בַּל־יְשׁוּבוּן לְכַסּוֹת הָאָרֶץ: הַמְשַׁלֵּחַ מַעְיָנִים בַּנְּחָלִים בֵּין הָרִים
יְהַלֵּכוּן: יַשְׁקוּ כָּל־חַיְתוֹ שָׂדָי יִשְׁבְּרוּ פְרָאִים צְמָאָם: עֲלֵיהֶם
עוֹף־הַשָּׁמַיִם יִשְׁכּוֹן מִבֵּין עֳפָאיִם יִתְּנוּ־קוֹל: מַשְׁקֶה הָרִים

First: The precepts concerning our duty and the contents of what we should
know have been set down for us by God unalterably and permanently in the
teachings on truth and duty contained in His Torah. Second: It is certain
that any deviation from this path of duty and every denial on our part of
any one of these truths should deprive us of our right to continue existing
before God. However, God does not cause us to perish immediately as a consequence of our errors, but, instead, permits His loving-kindness to prevail
in His judgment and is ready at all times to perform the greatest miracle of
His wondrous might on our behalf; that is, to cancel the dire consequences
of our iniquities and to open for us the gates to a new and better future.
We are told here that God causes His loving righteousness to supersede the
order of cause and effect which He Himself has instituted upon earth. It is
through this loving righteousness, transforming a forfeited life into new and
better being, that He has always revealed Himself in all His unique and
matchless grandeur.

Third: However, the משפטי ה', the "decrees" or "righteous ordinances"
that ordain trouble and sorrow are no less a part of His loving-kindness in
which He provides for our salvation. Even as the earth consists of continents
and of the deep oceans that surround them, and life on earth can flourish
only through their reciprocal action upon one another (for it is the ocean
that gives birth to the clouds of the sky, without which earth would shrivel

Bless *God*, O my soul, O *God*, my God, You are very great; You have clothed Yourself with majesty and glory. You cover with light as with a garment; You stretch out the heavens like a carpet. You are He Who fashions the beams of His upper chambers from water; Who makes clouds His team, Who walks upon the wings of the Wind. Who makes winds His messengers, the flamingfire His ministers; Who has established the earth upon its foundations that it shall not be moved forever and ever. The billowy deep, You have spread it like a garment; the waters stood upon the mountains. At Your rebuke they flee, they hasten away at the voice of Your thunder. They ascend mountains, they descend to valleys, to the one place which You had appointed for them. You set a bound which they should not transgress, and not return to cover the earth. You are the One Who sends forth springs into brooks, that they may run between the mountains, to give drink to every beast of the fields; the creatures of the forest quench their thirst. Beside them dwell the fowl of the heavens; they lift up their voices from out among the clefts. You are He Who waters the

---

to a mass of barren rocks), the interaction of צדקת ה' and משפטי ה', is essential to the moral growth and development of man. Like צדקת ה', הררי אל supplies a firm foundation to man's moral growth containing all the resources conditioning its work. *Mishpetei Hashem,* on the other hand, with their sufferings which penetrate and shake the souls of those affected, constitute the ותהום רבה without which man would become corrupt in the midst of plenty and pleasure and would allow the mental and moral faculties with which he has been endowed to go to waste. אדם ובהמה If the earth were meant to be the dwelling-place of the animal kingdom only, then God's pure *chesed* could reign there alone, just as it does among the heavenly bodies. But man, unlike the beast, does have the choice to deviate from God's Law and hence is in need of discipline. The earth must supply him with a foundation from which he, too, may reach his Divinely ordained destiny. Therefore, in order best to serve also the welfare of man, God must modify His *chesed* to *tzedakah,* and, in addition to *tzedakah,* which grants favors, the *mispetei Hashem* which at times deny man's desires and limit his aspirations, must come into play. According to a view dating back to the days of the *Geonim,* Moshe is supposed to have died on the Sabbath at the Mincha hour; hence the solemn thoughts of God's "righteous ordinances" would be a most fitting memorial to his passing much as the צדוק הדין is recited today on the occasion of any death. However, the data contained in the Talmud is not in agreement with this assumption. According to information available in Talmudic sources, Moshe died on a Friday.

מֵעֲלִיּוֹתָיו, מִפְּרִי מַעֲשֶׂיךָ תִּשְׂבַּע הָאָרֶץ: מַצְמִיחַ חָצִיר לַבְּהֵמָה וְעֵשֶׂב לַעֲבֹדַת הָאָדָם לְהוֹצִיא לֶחֶם מִן־הָאָרֶץ: וְיַיִן יְשַׂמַּח לְבַב־אֱנוֹשׁ לְהַצְהִיל פָּנִים מִשָּׁמֶן, וְלֶחֶם לְבַב־אֱנוֹשׁ יִסְעָד: יִשְׂבְּעוּ עֲצֵי יְיָ אַרְזֵי לְבָנוֹן אֲשֶׁר נָטָע: אֲשֶׁר־שָׁם צִפֳּרִים יְקַנֵּנוּ חֲסִידָה בְּרוֹשִׁים בֵּיתָהּ: הָרִים הַגְּבֹהִים לַיְּעֵלִים, סְלָעִים מַחְסֶה לַשְׁפַנִּים: עָשָׂה יָרֵחַ לְמוֹעֲדִים, שֶׁמֶשׁ יָדַע מְבוֹאוֹ: תָּשֶׁת חֹשֶׁךְ וִיהִי לָיְלָה בּוֹ תִרְמֹשׂ כָּל־חַיְתוֹ־יָעַר: הַכְּפִירִים שֹׁאֲגִים לַטָּרֶף וּלְבַקֵּשׁ מֵאֵל אָכְלָם: תִּזְרַח הַשֶּׁמֶשׁ יֵאָסֵפוּן וְאֶל־מְעוֹנֹתָם יִרְבָּצוּן: יֵצֵא אָדָם לְפָעֳלוֹ וְלַעֲבֹדָתוֹ עֲדֵי־עָרֶב: מָה־רַבּוּ מַעֲשֶׂיךָ יְיָ, כֻּלָּם בְּחָכְמָה עָשִׂיתָ, מָלְאָה הָאָרֶץ קִנְיָנֶךָ: זֶה הַיָּם גָּדוֹל וּרְחַב יָדָיִם· שָׁם רֶמֶשׂ וְאֵין מִסְפָּר חַיּוֹת קְטַנּוֹת עִם־גְּדֹלוֹת: שָׁם אֳנִיּוֹת יְהַלֵּכוּן, לִוְיָתָן זֶה יָצַרְתָּ לְשַׂחֶק־בּוֹ: כֻּלָּם אֵלֶיךָ יְשַׂבֵּרוּן לָתֵת אָכְלָם בְּעִתּוֹ: תִּתֵּן לָהֶם יִלְקֹטוּן, תִּפְתַּח יָדְךָ יִשְׂבְּעוּן טוֹב: תַּסְתִּיר פָּנֶיךָ יִבָּהֵלוּן· תֹּסֵף רוּחָם יִגְוָעוּן וְאֶל־עֲפָרָם יְשׁוּבוּן: תְּשַׁלַּח רוּחֲךָ יִבָּרֵאוּן, וּתְחַדֵּשׁ פְּנֵי אֲדָמָה: יְהִי כְבוֹד יְיָ לְעוֹלָם, יִשְׂמַח יְיָ בְּמַעֲשָׂיו: הַמַּבִּיט לָאָרֶץ וַתִּרְעָד יִגַּע בֶּהָרִים וְיֶעֱשָׁנוּ: אָשִׁירָה לַיְיָ בְּחַיָּי, אֲזַמְּרָה לֵאלֹהַי בְּעוֹדִי: יֶעֱרַב עָלָיו שִׂיחִי, אָנֹכִי אֶשְׂמַח בַּיְיָ: יִתַּמּוּ חַטָּאִים· מִן־הָאָרֶץ וּרְשָׁעִים עוֹד אֵינָם· בָּרְכִי נַפְשִׁי אֶת־יְיָ· הַלְלוּיָהּ:

קכ שִׁיר הַמַּעֲלוֹת· אֶל־יְיָ בַּצָּרָתָה לִּי קָרָאתִי וַיַּעֲנֵנִי: יְיָ הַצִּילָה נַפְשִׁי מִשְּׂפַת־שֶׁקֶר מִלָּשׁוֹן רְמִיָּה: מַה־יִּתֵּן לְךָ וּמַה־יֹּסִיף לָךְ

mountains from His upper chambers; the earth is satisfied by the fruit of Your works. You are He Who causes the grass to spring up for the cattle, and herb for the service of man, to bring forth bread from out of the earth, and wine that makes glad the heart of man, to make the face to be bright from oil, and bread that refreshes the heart of man. The trees of *God* also have their fill; the cedars of Lebanon which He has planted, where the birds make their nests; as for the stork, he builds his nest upon fir trees. The high mountains are for the wild goats, the rocks are a refuge for the conies. He has appointed the moon to set the seasons, the sun knows [the time of] its going down. You make darkness, and it is night, when all the beasts of the forest stir; the young lions roar after prey and to seek their food also from God. When the sun rises they slink away and crouch in their dens. Then man goes forth to his work and to his employment until the evening. How manifold are Your works, O *God*! In wisdom have You made them all, the earth is full of Your property. Yonder sea, great and wide, there are creeping things innumerable, living creatures both small and great. There go the ships, but You have made the multitude of animals to disport themselves therein. They all wait for You, that You may give them their food in due time. When You give it to them, they gather it in; when You open Your hand, they are satisfied with good. When You hide Your face, they are dismayed; when You take back their spirit, they perish and return to their dust. You send Your spirit again, they will be created anew, and You renew the surface of the earth. The glory of *God* will endure forever; may *God* take delight in His creatures. [He] Who looks to earth, and it has trembled; He touches the mountains and they vanish in smoke. I will sing to *God* as long as I live; I will sing praise to my God while I have being. Sweet is my musing upon Him, [even] *I* will rejoice in *God*. Then sinners will at last cease to be from the earth, and the lawless will be no more. Bless *God*, O my soul. Halaluyah!

A Song of Ascents. I have called to *God* in the past in such distress as is mine [now] and He answered me, "O *God*, deliver my soul from the lip of falsehood, from a deceitful tongue." What will it give to You, and what increase will it bring you, O deceitful tongue?

לָשׁוֹן רְמִיָּה: חִצֵּי גִבּוֹר שְׁנוּנִים עִם גַּחֲלֵי רְתָמִים: אוֹיָה לִי כִּי־
גַרְתִּי מֶשֶׁךְ שָׁכַנְתִּי עִם־אׇהֳלֵי קֵדָר רַבַּת שָׁכְנָה־לָּהּ נַפְשִׁי עִם
שׂוֹנֵא שָׁלוֹם: אֲנִי שָׁלוֹם וְכִי אֲדַבֵּר, הֵמָּה לַמִּלְחָמָה:

קכא שִׁיר לַמַּעֲלוֹת · אֶשָּׂא עֵינַי אֶל־הֶהָרִים, מֵאַיִן יָבֹא עֶזְרִי:
עֶזְרִי מֵעִם יְיָ עֹשֵׂה שָׁמַיִם וָאָרֶץ: אַל־יִתֵּן לַמּוֹט רַגְלֶךָ אַל־יָנוּם
שֹׁמְרֶךָ: הִנֵּה לֹא יָנוּם וְלֹא יִישָׁן שׁוֹמֵר יִשְׂרָאֵל: יְיָ שֹׁמְרֶךָ יְיָ
צִלְּךָ עַל־יַד יְמִינֶךָ: יוֹמָם הַשֶּׁמֶשׁ לֹא־יַכֶּכָּה וְיָרֵחַ בַּלָּיְלָה: יְיָ
יִשְׁמׇרְךָ מִכׇּל־רָע יִשְׁמֹר אֶת־נַפְשֶׁךָ: יְיָ יִשְׁמׇר־צֵאתְךָ וּבוֹאֶךָ
מֵעַתָּה וְעַד־עוֹלָם:

קכב שִׁיר הַמַּעֲלוֹת לְדָוִד · שָׂמַחְתִּי בְּאֹמְרִים לִי בֵּית יְיָ נֵלֵךְ:
עֹמְדוֹת הָיוּ רַגְלֵינוּ בִּשְׁעָרַיִךְ יְרוּשָׁלָ͏ִם: יְרוּשָׁלַ͏ִם הַבְּנוּיָה כְּעִיר
שֶׁחֻבְּרָה־לָּהּ יַחְדָּו: שֶׁשָּׁם עָלוּ שְׁבָטִים שִׁבְטֵי־יָהּ עֵדוּת לְיִשְׂרָאֵל
לְהֹדוֹת לְשֵׁם יְיָ: כִּי שָׁמָּה יָשְׁבוּ כִסְאוֹת לְמִשְׁפָּט כִּסְאוֹת לְבֵית
דָּוִד: שַׁאֲלוּ שְׁלוֹם יְרוּשָׁלָ͏ִם, יִשְׁלָיוּ אֹהֲבָיִךְ: יְהִי־שָׁלוֹם בְּחֵילֵךְ
שַׁלְוָה בְּאַרְמְנוֹתָיִךְ: לְמַעַן־אַחַי וְרֵעָי אֲדַבְּרָה־נָּא שָׁלוֹם בָּךְ؛
לְמַעַן בֵּית־יְיָ אֱלֹהֵינוּ אֲבַקְשָׁה טוֹב לָךְ:

קכג שִׁיר הַמַּעֲלוֹת · אֵלֶיךָ נָשָׂאתִי אֶת־עֵינַי הַיֹּשְׁבִי בַּשָּׁמָיִם: הִנֵּה
כְעֵינֵי עֲבָדִים אֶל־יַד אֲדוֹנֵיהֶם כְּעֵינֵי שִׁפְחָה אֶל־יַד גְּבִרְתָּהּ, כֵּן
עֵינֵינוּ אֶל־יְיָ אֱלֹהֵינוּ עַד שֶׁיְּחׇנֵּנוּ: חׇנֵּנוּ יְיָ חׇנֵּנוּ כִּי־רַב שָׂבַעְנוּ
בוּז: רַבַּת שָׂבְעָה־לָּהּ נַפְשֵׁנוּ הַלַּעַג הַשַּׁאֲנַנִּים הַבּוּז לִגְאֵיוֹנִים:

The arrows of a mighty one are sharp even now, with ever-glimmering coals. O would that I had sojourned among Meshech, that I had dwelt beside the tents of Kedar. My soul has had its fill of dwelling with those who hate peace. I represent peace even when I speak. But they are for war.

A Song for the Ascents. Shall I lift up my eyes to the hills [to see] from where my help will come? Let my help come from *God* Who shapes heaven and earth. May He not permit your foot to waver; may your Keeper not slumber. Behold, the Keeper of Yisrael neither slumbers nor sleeps. If *God* is your Keeper, if *God* is your shade at your right hand, the sun will not harm you by day and there will be a moon at night. *God* will keep you from all evil; He will keep your soul. *God* will preserve your going out and your home-coming from this time forth and for all the future.

A Song of Ascents by David. Once I [Yisrael] had the joy that they said to me, "Let us go to the House of *God.*" Our feet stood still within your gates, Yerushalayim. Yerushalayim that is built like a city which is compact together! For there tribes went up, tribes of *God,* up to the testimony for Yisrael to render homage to the Name of *God.* For thither were set chairs for the judgment, chairs for the house of David. Inquire after the peace of Yerushalayim; those who love you view the future unafraid. Peace be within your precincts, serenity within Your palaces. For the sake of my brethren and companions I will wish that peace be yours. For the sake of the House of *God,* our God, I will pray for your good.

A Song of Ascents. To You have I lifted my eyes, O You Who are enthroned in the heavens for me. Behold, as the eyes of servants to the hand of their master, as the eyes of the maid to the hand of her mistress, so our eyes look to *God* our God until He will favor us. Favor us, O *God,* favor us, for we are fully sated with contempt. Our soul is fully sated with the scorn of the fortunate, and with the contempt given the proud among the weak.

קכד שִׁיר הַמַּעֲלוֹת לְדָוִד · לוּלֵי יְיָ שֶׁהָיָה לָנוּ יֹאמַר־נָא יִשְׂרָאֵל: לוּלֵי יְיָ שֶׁהָיָה לָנוּ בְּקוּם עָלֵינוּ אָדָם: אֲזַי חַיִּים בְּלָעוּנוּ בַּחֲרוֹת אַפָּם בָּנוּ: אֲזַי הַמַּיִם שְׁטָפוּנוּ נַחְלָה עָבַר עַל־נַפְשֵׁנוּ: אֲזַי עָבַר עַל־נַפְשֵׁנוּ הַמַּיִם הַזֵּידוֹנִים: בָּרוּךְ יְיָ שֶׁלֹּא נְתָנָנוּ טֶרֶף לְשִׁנֵּיהֶם נַפְשֵׁנוּ כְּצִפּוֹר נִמְלְטָה מִפַּח יוֹקְשִׁים, הַפַּח נִשְׁבָּר וַאֲנַחְנוּ נִמְלָטְנוּ: עֶזְרֵנוּ בְּשֵׁם יְיָ עֹשֵׂה שָׁמַיִם וָאָרֶץ:

קכה שִׁיר הַמַּעֲלוֹת· הַבֹּטְחִים בַּיְיָ כְּהַר־צִיּוֹן לֹא־יִמּוֹט לְעוֹלָם יֵשֵׁב: יְרוּשָׁלַםִ הָרִים סָבִיב לָהּ, וַיְיָ סָבִיב לְעַמּוֹ מֵעַתָּה וְעַד־עוֹלָם: כִּי לֹא יָנוּחַ שֵׁבֶט הָרֶשַׁע עַל גּוֹרַל הַצַּדִּיקִים, לְמַעַן לֹא־יִשְׁלְחוּ הַצַּדִּיקִים בְּעַוְלָתָה יְדֵיהֶם: הֵיטִיבָה יְיָ לַטּוֹבִים וְלִישָׁרִים בְּלִבּוֹתָם: וְהַמַּטִּים עֲקַלְקַלּוֹתָם יוֹלִיכֵם יְיָ אֶת־פֹּעֲלֵי הָאָוֶן · שָׁלוֹם עַל־יִשְׂרָאֵל:

קכו שִׁיר הַמַּעֲלוֹת · בְּשׁוּב יְיָ אֶת־שִׁיבַת צִיּוֹן הָיִינוּ כְּחוֹלְמִים: אָז יִמָּלֵא שְׂחוֹק פִּינוּ וּלְשׁוֹנֵנוּ רִנָּה, אָז יֹאמְרוּ בַגּוֹיִם הִגְדִּיל יְיָ לַעֲשׂוֹת עִם־אֵלֶּה: הִגְדִּיל יְיָ לַעֲשׂוֹת עִמָּנוּ הָיִינוּ שְׂמֵחִים: שׁוּבָה יְיָ אֶת־שְׁבִיתֵנוּ כַּאֲפִיקִים בַּנֶּגֶב: הַזֹּרְעִים בְּדִמְעָה, בְּרִנָּה יִקְצֹרוּ: הָלוֹךְ יֵלֵךְ וּבָכֹה נֹשֵׂא מֶשֶׁךְ־הַזָּרַע, בֹּא־יָבֹא בְרִנָּה נֹשֵׂא אֲלֻמֹּתָיו:

קכז שִׁיר הַמַּעֲלוֹת לִשְׁלֹמֹה · אִם־יְיָ לֹא־יִבְנֶה בַיִת שָׁוְא עָמְלוּ בוֹנָיו בּוֹ, אִם־יְיָ לֹא־יִשְׁמָר־עִיר שָׁוְא שָׁקַד שׁוֹמֵר: שָׁוְא לָכֶם מַשְׁכִּימֵי קוּם מְאַחֲרֵי־שֶׁבֶת אֹכְלֵי לֶחֶם הָעֲצָבִים · כֵּן יִתֵּן לִידִידוֹ שֵׁנָא: הִנֵּה נַחֲלַת יְיָ בָּנִים שָׂכָר פְּרִי הַבָּטֶן: כְּחִצִּים בְּיַד־גִּבּוֹר

A Song of Ascents by David. Had it not been *God* Who was for us—let Yisrael declare it now! Had it not been *God* Who was for us when men rose up over us, then they would have swallowed us alive when their wrath was kindled against us. Then the waters would have washed us away when it had gone over our soul as if toward a riverbed. Then it would have gone over our soul in the raging waters. Blessed be *God* Who did not leave us as prey for their teeth. Our soul escaped like a bird out of the snare of the fowlers; the snare broke and we were free. Our help is in the Name of *God,* Who shapes heaven and earth.

A Song of Ascents. Those who trust in *God* are as Mount Tzion which cannot be moved but abides forever. Yerushalayim has mountains round about it, but *God* is round about His people from this time forth and forever. For the rod of wickedness shall never come to rest upon the lot of the righteous; therefore the righteous need not lay their hands upon violence. Do good, O *God,* to the good and to those who remain upright in their hearts. But as for those that turn their crooked ways ever further from the straight path, may *God* let them go with the workers of violence—peace be upon Yisrael.

A Song of Ascents. When *God* will turn once more to the return of Tzion, we will have been like those who dream. Then our mouth will fill with laughter and our tongue with exultation; then they will say among the nations, "*God* has done great things with these." *God* has done great things with us at all times; we have remained glad. Turn, O *God,* to our captivity once more, as the springs in the south. Those who sow in tears will reap in exultation. Though he who bears the measure of seed goes on his way weeping, he shall surely come home with exultation, bearing his sheaves.

A Song of Ascents by Shelomo. If *God* does not build on a house, then its builders have labored in vain upon it; if *God* will not keep a city, the watchman has watched in vain. It is in vain for you that you rise early, that you sit up late; therefore you eat the bread of troubles [but] it is thus that He gives His beloved ones sleep. Behold, children are an inheritance of *God;* the fruit of the womb is a reward. As arrows in the hand of a mighty man, so are the children of youth. Forward strides the man who has his quiver full of

בֶּן בְּנֵי הַנְּעוּרִים: אַשְׁרֵי הַגֶּבֶר אֲשֶׁר מִלֵּא אֶת־אַשְׁפָּתוֹ מֵהֶם ·
לֹא יֵבֹשׁוּ כִּי־יְדַבְּרוּ אֶת־אוֹיְבִים בַּשָּׁעַר:

קכח שִׁיר הַמַּעֲלוֹת · אַשְׁרֵי כָּל־יְרֵא יְיָ הַהֹלֵךְ בִּדְרָכָיו: יְגִיעַ כַּפֶּיךָ
כִּי תֹאכֵל אַשְׁרֶיךָ וְטוֹב לָךְ: אֶשְׁתְּךָ כְּגֶפֶן פֹּרִיָּה בְּיַרְכְּתֵי בֵיתֶךָ,
בָּנֶיךָ כִּשְׁתִלֵי זֵיתִים סָבִיב לְשֻׁלְחָנֶךָ: הִנֵּה כִי־כֵן יְבֹרַךְ גָּבֶר יְרֵא
יְיָ: יְבָרֶכְךָ יְיָ מִצִּיּוֹן, וּרְאֵה בְּטוּב יְרוּשָׁלָםִ כֹּל יְמֵי חַיֶּיךָ: וּרְאֵה־
בָנִים לְבָנֶיךָ · שָׁלוֹם עַל יִשְׂרָאֵל:

קכט שִׁיר הַמַּעֲלוֹת · רַבַּת צְרָרוּנִי מִנְּעוּרַי יֹאמַר נָא יִשְׂרָאֵל:
רַבַּת צְרָרוּנִי מִנְּעוּרָי, גַּם לֹא יָכְלוּ־לִי: עַל־גַּבִּי חָרְשׁוּ חֹרְשִׁים
הֶאֱרִיכוּ לְמַעֲנִיתָם: יְיָ צַדִּיק, קִצֵּץ עֲבוֹת רְשָׁעִים: יֵבֹשׁוּ וְיִסֹּגוּ
אָחוֹר כֹּל שֹׂנְאֵי צִיּוֹן: יִהְיוּ כַּחֲצִיר גַּגּוֹת שֶׁקַּדְמַת שָׁלַף יָבֵשׁ:
שֶׁלֹּא מִלֵּא כַפּוֹ קוֹצֵר וְחִצְנוֹ מְעַמֵּר: וְלֹא אָמְרוּ הָעֹבְרִים בִּרְכַּת
יְיָ אֲלֵיכֶם, בֵּרַכְנוּ אֶתְכֶם בְּשֵׁם יְיָ:

קל שִׁיר הַמַּעֲלוֹת · מִמַּעֲמַקִּים קְרָאתִיךָ יְיָ: אֲדֹנָי שִׁמְעָה בְקוֹלִי
תִּהְיֶינָה אָזְנֶיךָ קַשֻּׁבוֹת לְקוֹל תַּחֲנוּנָי: אִם־עֲוֹנוֹת תִּשְׁמָר־יָהּ אֲדֹנָי
מִי יַעֲמֹד: כִּי־עִמְּךָ הַסְּלִיחָה לְמַעַן תִּוָּרֵא: קִוִּיתִי יְיָ קִוְּתָה נַפְשִׁי
וְלִדְבָרוֹ הוֹחָלְתִּי: נַפְשִׁי לַאדֹנָי מִשֹּׁמְרִים לַבֹּקֶר שֹׁמְרִים לַבֹּקֶר:
יַחֵל יִשְׂרָאֵל אֶל־יְיָ כִּי־עִם־יְיָ הַחֶסֶד וְהַרְבֵּה עִמּוֹ פְדוּת: וְהוּא
יִפְדֶּה אֶת־יִשְׂרָאֵל מִכֹּל עֲוֹנוֹתָיו:

them; they will not be deceived when they speak with enemies ir
public places.

A Song of Ascents. Forward strides each one who fears *God,*
Who walks in His ways. The labor of your hands, when you eat oi
it, then you will stride forward and the good will be yours. Your
wife is a fruitful vine in the innermost parts of your house, your
children are like olive shoots around your table. Behold, if this is so,
then the man who fears *God* is blessed. May *God* bless you out of
Tzion, and [may you] look upon the good of Yerushalayim all the
days of your life, and [may you] see children of your children. Peace
upon Yisrael.

A Song of Ascents. Much have they persecuted me from my
youth on; let Yisrael declare it now. "Much have they persecuted me
from my youth on," but also, "they have not prevailed against me.
The plowmen plowed upon my back; they wished to make their fur-
row long. But *God* is just; He cut the cords of the lawless asunder."
They shall be deceived and turned back, all the haters of Tzion. They
shall be as grass upon the rooftops which withers before one plucks
it, wherewith the reaper has never filled his hand, nor the sheaf-
binder his arm, and the passers-by have never said, "The blessing of
God be upon you; we bless you in the Name of *God.*"

A Song of Ascents. Out of the depths have I called You, O *God.*
O my Lord, hear my voice; let Your ears remain alert to the voice of
my supplications. If You, O *God,* should always mark iniquities in
Your world dominion—O my Lord, who could stand before You?
For with You there is forgiveness so that You may be feared. Therefore it was for *God* that I hoped when my soul hoped, and I waited
upon His word. My soul is my Lord's, more so than they that hope
for the morning, watch for the coming of dawn. Therefore, O Yisrael,
wait upon *God;* for with *God* there is mercy and with Him there is
redemption in infinite abundance. He will redeem Yisrael from all
of its iniquities.

קלא שִׁיר הַמַּעֲלוֹת לְדָוִד ׀ יְיָ לֹא־גָבַהּ לִבִּי וְלֹא־רָמוּ עֵינַי וְלֹא־
הִלַּכְתִּי בִּגְדֹלוֹת וּבְנִפְלָאוֹת מִמֶּנִּי: אִם־לֹא שִׁוִּיתִי וְדוֹמַמְתִּי נַפְשִׁי
כְּגָמֻל עֲלֵי אִמּוֹ כַּגָּמֻל עָלַי נַפְשִׁי: יַחֵל יִשְׂרָאֵל אֶל־יְיָ מֵעַתָּה
וְעַד־עוֹלָם:

קלב שִׁיר הַמַּעֲלוֹת ׀ זְכוֹר יְיָ לְדָוִד אֵת כָּל־עֻנּוֹתוֹ: אֲשֶׁר־נִשְׁבַּע
לַיְיָ נָדַר לַאֲבִיר יַעֲקֹב: אִם־אָבֹא בְּאֹהֶל בֵּיתִי אִם־אֶעֱלֶה עַל־
עֶרֶשׂ יְצוּעָי: אִם־אֶתֵּן שְׁנַת לְעֵינָי לְעַפְעַפַּי תְּנוּמָה: עַד־אֶמְצָא
מָקוֹם לַיְיָ מִשְׁכָּנוֹת לַאֲבִיר יַעֲקֹב: הִנֵּה־שְׁמַעֲנוּהָ בְאֶפְרָתָה
מְצָאנוּהָ בִּשְׂדֵי־יָעַר: נָבוֹאָה לְמִשְׁכְּנוֹתָיו נִשְׁתַּחֲוֶה לַהֲדֹם רַגְלָיו:
קוּמָה יְיָ לִמְנוּחָתֶךָ אַתָּה וַאֲרוֹן עֻזֶּךָ: כֹּהֲנֶיךָ יִלְבְּשׁוּ־צֶדֶק
וַחֲסִידֶיךָ יְרַנֵּנוּ: בַּעֲבוּר דָּוִד עַבְדֶּךָ אַל־תָּשֵׁב פְּנֵי מְשִׁיחֶךָ: נִשְׁבַּע
יְיָ לְדָוִד אֱמֶת לֹא־יָשׁוּב מִמֶּנָּה מִפְּרִי בִטְנְךָ אָשִׁית לְכִסֵּא־לָךְ:
אִם־יִשְׁמְרוּ בָנֶיךָ ׀ בְּרִיתִי וְעֵדֹתִי זוֹ אֲלַמְּדֵם גַּם־בְּנֵיהֶם עֲדֵי־עַד
יֵשְׁבוּ לְכִסֵּא־לָךְ: כִּי־בָחַר יְיָ בְּצִיּוֹן אִוָּהּ לְמוֹשָׁב לוֹ: זֹאת־מְנוּחָתִי
עֲדֵי־עַד, פֹּה אֵשֵׁב כִּי אִוִּתִיהָ: צֵידָהּ בָּרֵךְ אֲבָרֵךְ אֶבְיוֹנֶיהָ
אַשְׂבִּיעַ לָחֶם: וְכֹהֲנֶיהָ אַלְבִּישׁ יֶשַׁע וַחֲסִידֶיהָ רַנֵּן יְרַנֵּנוּ: שָׁם
אַצְמִיחַ קֶרֶן לְדָוִד עָרַכְתִּי נֵר לִמְשִׁיחִי: אוֹיְבָיו אַלְבִּישׁ בֹּשֶׁת,
וְעָלָיו יָצִיץ נִזְרוֹ:

קלג שִׁיר הַמַּעֲלוֹת לְדָוִד ׀ הִנֵּה מַה־טּוֹב וּמַה־נָּעִים שֶׁבֶת אַחִים
גַּם־יָחַד: כַּשֶּׁמֶן הַטּוֹב עַל־הָרֹאשׁ יֹרֵד עַל־הַזָּקָן, זְקַן אַהֲרֹן
שֶׁיֹּרֵד עַל־פִּי מִדּוֹתָיו: כְּטַל־חֶרְמוֹן שֶׁיֹּרֵד עַל־הַרְרֵי צִיּוֹן כִּי־שָׁם
צִוָּה יְיָ אֶת־הַבְּרָכָה, חַיִּים עַד־הָעוֹלָם:

· A Song of Ascents, by David. O *God*, my spirit was not proud, my eyes did not look haughty; I did not exercise myself in things that were too great and too remote for me. For I had put my soul at peace and soothed it like a weaned child with its mother. Like a weaned child was my soul with me. But let Yisrael hope in *God* from this time forth and forever.

A Song of Ascents. O *God*, remember unto David all his renunciation. How he swore to *God*, to the Source of Yaakov's strength, I will not enter into the tent of my house; I will not go up into the bed that is spread for me. I will not give sleep to my eyes, nor slumber to my eyelids, until I shall have found the place for *God*, dwelling places for the Source of Yaakov's strength. Lo, we heard of it in the province of Ephraim; we found it in the field of the forest. Now we come to His dwelling-place; we cast ourselves down at His footstool. Arise, O *God*, to Your resting place, You and the Ark of Your might; that Your priests may clothe themselves in righteousness, and that Your devoted ones may shout for joy. For the sake of David Your servant, turn not away the face of Your anointed. For *God* has sworn to David a truth from which He will never turn back: "Of the fruit of your body will I set for you upon the throne; If your sons will keep My covenant and this the entirety of My testimony which I shall teach them, then their sons, too, shall be on hand for the throne for you until the end of time." For *God* has chosen Tzion; He has desired it for His habitation: "This is My resting place to the end of time. Here will I dwell, for I have desired it. I will abundantly bless its sustenance; I will satisfy its needy with bread. I will clothe its priests with salvation, and the devoted ones within it shall ever shout for joy. There I shall cause David's horn to spring up; there I have readied a lamp for My anointed. His enemies will I clothe with shame, but upon him his crown will blossom."

A Song of Ascents, by David. Behold, how good and how pleasant [it is] when brethren also dwell together. Like the precious oil upon the head coming down upon the beard, even as it is the beard of Aharon which comes down as far as his garments reach, so is the dew of Hermon which comes down upon the mountains of Tzion, for there *God* has commanded the blessing, life unto eternity.

קלד שִׁיר הַמַּעֲלוֹת ׃ הִנֵּה בָּרֲכוּ אֶת־יְיָ כָּל־עַבְדֵי יְיָ הָעֹמְדִים
בְּבֵית יְיָ בַּלֵּילוֹת ׃ שְׂאוּ־יְדֵכֶם קֹדֶשׁ וּבָרֲכוּ אֶת־יְיָ ׃ יְבָרֶכְךָ יְיָ
מִצִּיּוֹן עֹשֵׂה שָׁמַיִם וָאָרֶץ ׃

עָלֵינוּ, קדיש יתום.

פרקי אבות

From Pesach *till* Rosh Hashanah *a chapter of* Pirkei Avoth *is read each
Sabbath after* Minchah.

כָּל יִשְׂרָאֵל יֵשׁ לָהֶם חֵלֶק לְעוֹלָם הַבָּא, שֶׁנֶּאֱמַר וְעַמֵּךְ כֻּלָּם
צַדִּיקִים לְעוֹלָם יִירְשׁוּ אָרֶץ נֵצֶר מַטָּעַי מַעֲשֵׂה יָדַי לְהִתְפָּאֵר ׃

עולם הבא. כל ישראל denotes a two-fold future; one in the world to come,
and one in this world. The future in the world to come is that bliss into which
the soul of man enters when, immediately after the death of the body, it
departs from earth. The future in this world is the coming of the kingdom
of felicity, perfection and peace which God will establish on earth; it is the
final purpose of all human progress and development. כל ישראל Any individual
who remains worthy of the name of *Yisrael* and who has not utterly divorced
himself from Israel's lofty spiritual and ethical destiny and task has a portion
in both of these—in the future of the world to come as well as in that of the
world here below. His portion may vary depending on his degree of loyalty
to Israel's task and destiny, but as long as he will remain *Yisrael* he will never
lose it entirely. Whatever good we achieve in loyal obedience to God here
below becomes a spiritual accomplishment which will accompany us into the
world to come and into the presence of our Father in Heaven. At the same
time it serves as still another seedling sown into the field of mankind's future
with which we add to the total of the harvest of what is good and pleasing in
the sight of God, a sowing which will ripen one day into salvation for mankind on earth and through which we attain immortality even here below.

The expression ירש ארץ appears in the Psalms and in Prophetic literature
to denote that two-fold future which may be inherited by virtue of a life of

A Song of Ascents . Behold: bless *God*, all you servants of *God* who stand in the House of *God* in the nights. Lift up your hands, as one, to the Sanctuary, and bless *God*. *God* will bless you out of Tzion; He still shapes heaven and earth.

SAYINGS OF THE FATHERS

All Israel have a portion in the world to come, as it is said, "Thy people, all of them righteous, shall inherit the earth forever, the flower of My repeated plantings, the work of My hands, to glorify Me."

---

loyal obedience on earth, and which becomes the inheritance of the righteous since the unfaithful have forfeited it by their disregard of their duty. (See Comm. Psalms Notes to Psalm 25:13, 37:22 et al.) שנאמר: (Isaiah 60:21), נצר מטעי, the goal of universal moral perfection and bliss proclaimed in these verses will not materialize all at once. God will plant and replant His people over and over again, as it were, until it will finally be ripe for that future salvation, at which time it will stand confirmed as the uniform work of God made for His glorification.

Actually, the verse beginning with כל ישראל is not part of Pirkei Avoth but is taken from the Mishnah (Sanhedrin 90a) where it serves to introduce the final portion of the Tractate. It is placed here as an introduction to Pirkei Avoth because it outlines the great goal for which the maxims contained in these *Perakim* are intended to strengthen and train us and because, at the same time, it furnishes added incentive to all to apply themselves vigorously to the pursuit of that goal which is within the reach of all. It is most appropriate, then, that the sages of our Law should be referred to in these passages as *Avoth*, for with these sayings they truly act as our "fathers", providing us, in their discerning wisdom, with the ethical guidance we need to attain the state of perfection ordained for us by God.

א מֹשֶׁה קִבֵּל תּוֹרָה מִסִּינַי, וּמְסָרָהּ לִיהוֹשֻׁעַ וִיהוֹשֻׁעַ לִזְקֵנִים
וּזְקֵנִים לִנְבִיאִים וּנְבִיאִים מְסָרוּהָ לְאַנְשֵׁי כְנֶסֶת הַגְּדוֹלָה. הֵם
אָמְרוּ שְׁלֹשָׁה דְבָרִים, הֱווּ מְתוּנִים בַּדִּין וְהַעֲמִידוּ תַלְמִידִים
הַרְבֵּה וַעֲשׂוּ סְיָג לַתּוֹרָה:

---

1. מִסִּינַי. As Wessely explains in יין לבנון, his commentary to *Pirkei Avoth*, "Sinai" is the historic event of the Giving of the Law which took place in the sight and hearing of the entire Jewish people. In this manner, the Divine origin of the Law that came to us through Moses was established as a certainty through personal experience which permanently rules out all doubt and is not part of belief but of actual knowledge. "Behold, I am coming to you," God told Moses (Exod. 19:9) "in a thick cloud so that the people may hear when I speak with you, and then they will also believe you forever." You yourselves have seen," we read in Exod. 20:22, "that I have spoken with you from Heaven." "These words", we further read in Deut. 5:19–24, "God spoke to all your assembly on the mountain out of the midst of the fire, of the cloud and of the thick darkness...and you came near to me, all the heads of your tribes and your elders, and you said, 'Behold, God, our God, has let us see His glory and His greatness and we have heard His voice out of the midst of the fire; we have seen this day that God spoke to man and he remained alive. And now why should we die that this great fire should consume us...You go near and hear all that God, our God, may say to you;...we will hear it and do it.'" "Only take heed to yourself and guard your soul exceedingly, lest you forget the facts which your eyes have seen, and lest they depart from your heart all the days of your life; and make them known to your children and your children's children; the day when you stood before God, your God, in Horeb, when God said to me: 'Assemble Me the people and I will make them hear My words that they may learn to fear Me all the days that they live upon the earth and that they may teach their children.'" (Deut. 4:9–10) "To you it was shown that you might know, הראת לדעת, that God is God alone; there is none else beside Him. Out of Heaven He made you hear His voice in order to discipline you..." (Deut. 4:35–36)

It is the direct character of this Divine revelation that the term *Misinai* is intended to recall, for it should bring to mind the Divine origin of the Law and its preservation by way of a process of transmission carried on from age to age and through the leaders of each generation. משה קבל. Moses received the Law from the Lord on Mount Sinai in the full view of all the people and expounded it to the people during the forty years of their wanderings through the wilderness. But then, before he died, *mosar*—he "handed it over" to

CHAPTER I

1. Moshe received the Torah from Sinai and handed it down to Yehoshua; Yehoshua to the Elders; the Elders to the Prophets; the Prophets handed it down to the Men of the Great Assembly. The latter said three things: Be cautious in judgment, raise up many disciples and make a fence for the Law.

Joshua to ensure its perpetuation through study and observance. With the same purpose in mind, Joshua, in turn, handed over the Law to the Elders who survived and succeeded him. (Joshua 24:31) From these the Prophets took over the task of guarding and protecting the Torah. Eventually, when the Jewish exiles returned from Babylonian captivity and the building of the Second Temple was begun in Jerusalem, the place of the Prophets was taken by "The Men of the Great Assembly", a body of one hundred and twenty members. Haggai, Zechariah and Malachi, the last of the Prophets, were among the members of this group. According to the Sages, (Yoma 69b) this "great" Assembly proved its "greatness" primarily by its ability to comprehend the greatness of the sovereignty of God which they saw revealed no less gloriously in the miraculous survival of the Jewish people despite its state of dependence, weakness, and dispersion among hostile peoples than in Israel's original establishment as an independent nation. It was for this reason that, in the prayers which it composed, the Assembly restored to the liturgy of its brethren the characterization of God as האל הגדול הגבור והנורא. This designation for God was first used by Moses (Deut. 10:17). Later, however, Jeremiah and Daniel had deleted the adjectives *gibor* and *nora* in view of the tragic era of national disaster that had befallen our people. Eventually, the Men of the Great Assembly restored them; as the Sages put it, (ibid.) החזירו העטרה ליושנה "they restored the crown of glorification to its former splendor." They were convinced that all the centuries of *Galuth* that were to come would be no less significant in our history than their own era, that of the Second Temple, which they felt was merely an introductory period to what was to follow. They manifested this conviction by composing prayers and establishing that order of worship which have served to this day constantly to improve, enrich and strengthen our spiritual and emotional life with the treasures of the truths of Judaism. But beyond that they gave practical expression to their thinking in the manner in which they accomplished the task which had fallen to them to provide for the continued study and observance of the Law. The precepts and the institutions which they established have prompted and preserved the study and the observance of the Law to this very day. It is in this passage that they set down the three principles which guided them in their own successful endeavors and which they recommended to their successors for adoption.

ב שִׁמְעוֹן הַצַּדִּיק הָיָה מִשְׁיָרֵי כְנֶסֶת הַגְּדוֹלָה. הוּא הָיָה אוֹמֵר,
עַל־שְׁלֹשָׁה דְבָרִים הָעוֹלָם עוֹמֵד עַל הַתּוֹרָה וְעַל הָעֲבוֹדָה וְעַל
גְּמִילוּת חֲסָדִים:

הוו מתונים בדין. We believe that the term *din* does not only refer to
judgments in the narrower meaning of property rights, *dinei memonoth* and
dinei nefashoth, but also includes all those decisions that deal with the application of law, such as דן את הדין, זיכה את החייב וכו', טימא את הטהור וכו', דן את
הדין, זיכה וחייב, טימא וטיהר, אסר והתיר (Bechoroth 28b, Chullin 44b); in these
passages the term *dan eth hadin* seems to connote the general, and the passages *zika* etc. which follow apparently denote the particulars under these
headings. הוו מתונים בדין is an admonition counseling the expounder of the
Law and the judge to consider each case on its own merits and from every
possible angle and not to render decisions in routine fashion.

העמידו תלמידים הרבה The Torah is *"morasha kehilath Yaakov";* it is
meant to be the common possession of the entire community, and the
maximum dissemination of the knowledge of the Law is viewed as our
supreme task and our most sacred concern. The prayerful wish מי יתן
כל עם ה' נביאים was not an idle phrase in the mouth of Moses; it spelled
out what he and his loyal successors viewed as their supreme task in
life. In this way every Jew was to be rendered capable of consulting
the original sources of the Law by himself to find guidance for his
daily life. At the same time, this means that the decisions handed down
by the judges and by the expounders of the Law would be subject to control
by the largest possible number among the general Jewish public. In all likelihood the sages of Jewish religious doctrine are now and have always been
the only teachers in any religion on earth to regard it as the supreme goal of
their endeavors to render their own services superfluous.

עשו משמרת למשמרתי (Lev. 18:30) ושמרתם את משמרתי. ועשו סיג לתורה Keep
the charge which I have placed into your keeping; make provisions to guard
the Law against transgression and to promote its observance. This task had
been entrusted to the authorities of the Law from the very outset, when the
Law was given; as a matter of fact we have *takanoth* and *gezeroth,* provisions
and precepts to promote and preserve the observance of the Law, that date
back to Moses and King Solomon. Likewise, the wording of the law: לא תסור מן
הדבר אשר יגידו לך ימין ושמאל (Deut. 17:11) imposes upon us the obligation not
to deviate, either to the right or to the left, from any ordinances that may be
enacted by future expounders of the Torah. However, despite the fact that,
according to the Law, these authorities actually had the power to declare as
universally binding any provision they might make to safeguard the observance
of the Law, they did not, as a rule, make use of these broad powers but

2.   Shimon the Just was one of the last survivors of the Great Assembly. He used to say: The world is based on three things; the Torah, Serving God and active loving-kindness.

---

endowed their provisions with full legal force only once these enactments had received a final stamp of approval in the form of acceptance, in practice, by a majority of the people פשט איסורו ברוב ישראה גזרו וקבלו (*Avod. Zar. 36*). It is quite clear, of course, that maximum dissemination of the knowledge of the Law could act as a powerful agent to predispose the people for the acceptance and observance of such enactments. Moreover, such maximum dissemination and preservation of Torah knowledge, as well as the provisions designed to safeguard observance, were of commanding importance particularly in those times which the Men of the Great Assembly in their wisdom foresaw as eras of increasing dispersion when the people would be moved physically further and further away from the spiritual center of the nation where teaching and guidance could be obtained and at the same time where they would be exposed to an infinite number of temptations to deviate from the path of scrupulous observance.

2.   At the end of this Chapter there is a verse reading על שלשה דברים העולם קים. The difference in meaning between the term *omed* as used in this verse and *kayam*, in Mishna 18 seems to be as follows: *omed*, lit. "stands": that on which something "stands" or "is based" constitutes its foundation; if it loses that base or foundation it will fall. *Kayam*, on the other hand, denotes a "standing up" or "enduring" through time; i.e. stability or permanence. If a thing loses that on which it depends for stability or permanence it may continue to exist but it will not endure. תורה implies the *knowledge* of the *truth* and the *will of God* with regard to every aspect of our lives, personal and public, individual and social. עבודה denotes *dutiful obedience,* serving God by fulfilling His will in every phase of our lives, personal and public, individual and social. גמילות חסדים signifies selfless, active loving-kindness to promote the welfare of our fellow-men. These are the three things which shape and perfect the world of man and all that pertains to it in accordance with the measure and way of its destiny. Whenever and wherever any of these three are inadequate or altogether lacking there is a gap which cannot be filled and there is no manifest destiny. Without *Torah* the human spirit lacks the wellsprings of true knowledge; it will be blind to that basic, indispensable element which makes man a human being and it will be receptive to everything except truth and right. Without *Avodah* man cannot have the proper attitude toward God, his Master and Creaor, and toward the world into which God put him in order to develop and protect it in accordance with God's will. Instead of serving God he will think he is the master when, as a matter of fact, he will be the slave of his passions and his lust. He will pander to anything that he feels can serve or prejudice his interests, and instead of being exalted

ג אַנְטִיגְנוֹס אִישׁ סוֹכוֹ קִבֵּל מִשִּׁמְעוֹן הַצַּדִּיק · הוּא הָיָה אוֹמֵר,
אַל־תִּהְיוּ כַּעֲבָדִים הַמְשַׁמְּשִׁין אֶת־הָרַב עַל־מְנָת לְקַבֵּל פְּרָס.
אֶלָּא הֱווּ כַּעֲבָדִים הַמְשַׁמְּשִׁין אֶת־הָרַב שֶׁלֹּא עַל־מְנָת לְקַבֵּל
פְּרָס וִיהִי מוֹרָא שָׁמַיִם עֲלֵיכֶם:

ד יוֹסֵי בֶּן־יוֹעֶזֶר אִישׁ צְרֵדָה וְיוֹסֵי בֶּן־יוֹחָנָן אִישׁ יְרוּשָׁלַיִם קִבְּלוּ
מֵהֶם · יוֹסֵי בֶּן־יוֹעֶזֶר אִישׁ צְרֵדָה אוֹמֵר, יְהִי בֵיתְךָ בֵּית וַעַד
לַחֲכָמִים וֶהֱוֵה מִתְאַבֵּק בַּעֲפַר רַגְלֵיהֶם וֶהֱוֵה שׁוֹתֶה בַצָּמָא אֶת־
דִּבְרֵיהֶם:

and ennobled by him in accordance with God's purpose, everything he touches will receive the impress of his depravity and error. If he omits *Gemiluth Chasadim* he will be without that characteristic which is the very first trait of godliness. Instead of being God-like in acting as a creator of happiness and prosperity for his fellow-men, he will harden his heart in callous selfishness, and mankind will lack that bond of brotherhood and loving-kindness within which alone all happiness and joy of life can prosper. *Torah* enables man to do justice to himself; by way of *Avodah* he will meet the requirements of God; and through *Gemiluth Chasadim* he performs his duty toward his fellowmen. In all likelihood this is the reason why *Gemiluth Chasadim* is enumerated as a separate concept even though, in fact, it is also part of *Avodah*, which is practical, active obedience in the service of God.

3. In Mishna 1 we read that Moses *mesoroh*, "handed down" the Law to Joshua from whom it passed to the Elders, then from the Elders to the Prophets and eventually from the Prophets to the Men of the Great Assembly. In each instance we are told that the Law was "handed down" (or "handed over") as a precious heritage to be preserved. In each instance the receivers had become the guardians of the Law by explicit appointment of their elders. As distinguished from these, Antigonus and all those who followed him were just members of a group of disciples who studied at the feet of the masters and "received" the Oral Tradition verbally as they listened to the learned discourses. Since they were acknowledged to be the most capable and proficient scholars in the group, these men were eventually chosen not by their elders but by their contemporaries to be teachers and leaders of the nation after the elders had passed on.

המשמשין: While an *eved* as such does not necessarily have personal contact with his employer, the term *shamash*, like the Hebrew *sharat*, implies

3. Antigonus of Socho received [the tradition] from Shimon the Just. He used to say: Be not like servants who minister to their master for the sake of receiving a reward, but be like servants who minister to their master not for the sake of a reward, and let the fear of Heaven be upon you.

4. Yosé ben Yo'ezer of Tzeredah and Yosé ben Yochanan of Jerusalem received [the tradition] from them. Yosé ben Yo'ezer of Tzeredah says: Let your house be a meeting place for sages, cover yourself with the dust of their feet and drink in their words thirstily.

---

personal ministrations to a master. It can be readily presumed that there do exist *avadim* who, if they have the good fortune to be called upon to render personal services to their employer, derive so much pleasure from this personal contact with their master that they regard it sufficient reward in itself and have no thought of any other compensation. Such, Antigonus declares, should be our relationship with God in our life's service to Him. The fulfillment of His commandments should not be treated as an activity apart or remote from Him. Rather, every commandment should serve to call us into His presence, before His countenance, in order to perform, within His sight, a service pleasing to Him. Every such act should bring us nearer to Him and should so enrich us with His approval that the realization of His nearness and approval may render the true human being so happy that he will find his "service to God" to be his richest reward and it will not even occur to him to seek additional compensation. This is that attitude which our Sages characterize elsewhere by the terms לשמה, לשם שמים.

ויהי מורא שמים עליכם. In human relationships, the greater intimacy of contact involved in personal ministrations to a master usually tends to lessen the servant's respect for his employer. But the Lord says, (Lev. 10:3) בקרבי אקדש: The nearer a man is to Me, the more do I expect to be sanctified by him, so that My nearness may preserve him from even the slightest transgression; hence the passage משמשין שלא על מנת לקבל פרס is followed by the admonition ויהי מורא שמים עליכם.

4. ביתך. Be such a friend to learning and show such kindness and hospitality to its guardians and teachers that they will feel drawn to your home and will be happy to gather there. Accord them a place of honor in your house, sit at their feet and listen intently to their conversation, for, as the Sages state elsewhere אפילו שיחת חולין של תלמידי חכמים צריכה למוד (Succah 21b): Even the ordinary conversation of sages [is instructive and] should be studied.

ה יוֹסֵי בֶּן־יוֹחָנָן אִישׁ יְרוּשָׁלַיִם אוֹמֵר, יְהִי בֵיתְךָ פָּתוּחַ לָרְוָחָה
וְיִהְיוּ עֲנִיִּים בְּנֵי בֵיתֶךָ וְאַל־תַּרְבֶּה שִׂיחָה עִם הָאִשָּׁה, בְּאִשְׁתּוֹ
אָמְרוּ קַל וָחֹמֶר בְּאֵשֶׁת חֲבֵרוֹ· מִכַּאן אָמְרוּ חֲכָמִים כָּל־הַמַּרְבֶּה
שִׂיחָה עִם הָאִשָּׁה גּוֹרֵם רָעָה לְעַצְמוֹ וּבוֹטֵל מִדִּבְרֵי תוֹרָה וְסוֹפוֹ
יוֹרֵשׁ גֵּיהִנָּם:

י יְהוֹשֻׁעַ בֶּן־פְּרַחְיָה וְנִתַּאי הָאַרְבֵּלִי קִבְּלוּ מֵהֶם· יְהוֹשֻׁעַ בֶּן־פְּרַחְיָה
אוֹמֵר, עֲשֵׂה לְךָ רַב וּקְנֵה לְךָ חָבֵר וֶהֱוֵי דָן אֶת־כָּל־הָאָדָם
לְכַף זְכוּת:

---

5. לרוחה. In Exod. 8:11 the term *revacha* is used to denote "relief", literally
a "widening" or "loosening" of the bonds of want and distress. Said Rabbi
Yosé: Let your home be open always to those who suffer and seek relief, and
even if you are not able to eliminate all want and distress, be ready at all
all times to ease and relieve suffering to the best of your ability. Let the
poor be members of your household; regard them as children in your home.
Consider your house as established not only for yourself and your immediate
family; let the homeless poor share in the pleasures of your home whenever
and to whatever extent you can, and when you extend your hospitality to the
poor, treat them as you do the members of your own household.

אל תרבה שיחה עם האשה, We are not told אל תדבר הרבה or תרבה דברים, "Do not
talk too much with your wife." As a matter of fact, the sayings of the Sages are
replete with maxims stressing the high esteem in which womanhood should
be held, the respect and honor due one's wife and particularly the great importance that a husband should attach to the views, opinions and counsel of
his wife. And especially in this context, where we have just read about the
virtues of helpfulness, charity, kindness and hospitality which should emanate
from the home and hence are so greatly dependent on the work and coop-
eration of the wife, the statement immediately following certainly should not
be construed in a way derogatory to her. In fact, this very statement may
well be founded on genuine appreciation of the vital role played by both
husband and wife in the discharge of the task to be fulfilled by the home.
Sichah does not mean serious conversation but merely idle talk and gossip.
Cf. *sichat yeladim* (3:14) and *mi'ut sichah* (6:6). A man who truly respects
his wife will have more to offer her than just trivial talk and idle chatter
for her amusement. He will want to discuss with her the serious concerns of
life and will derive enjoyment from the resulting exchange of views and
counsel. Moreover, engaging in trifling talk with other women and other

5. Yosé ben Yochanan of Jerusalem says: Let your house be open for relief and let the poor be members of your household. Do not engage in too much idle talk with women. This has been said even with regard to one's own wife; how much more does it apply to the wife of one's neighbor. Accordingly, the Sages said: He who engages in too much idle talk with women brings trouble upon himself; he neglects the study of the Torah and will in the end inherit *Gehinnom*.

6. Yehoshua ben Perachyah and Nittai the Arbelite received [the tradition] from them. Yehoshua ben Perachyah says: Provide yourself with a teacher, get yourself a companion and judge all men favorably.

---

men's wives may imperil moral purity. מכאן: From these passages was derived this maxim, according to which indulgence in more idle chatter than is seemly even within one's own household may gravely jeopardize the spirit of earnest duty and study to which life should be consecrated.

The tenet of Antigonus is meant to promote *Avodah,* that of Yosé of Tzeredah is aimed at the cultivation of *Torah* and that of Yosé of Jerusalem at the promotion of *Gemiluth Chasadim.* We may well look with admiring envy upon a society in which it is expected even of ordinary citizens to make their homes the dwelling places of learning (see Mishna 4) and of active lovingkindness (Mishna 5).

6. The injunction עשה לך רב corresponds to *Torah;* וקנה לך חבר to *Avodah* and הוי דן וכו' to *Gemiluth Chasadim.* "Provide yourself" with a teacher; bring it to pass that a capable man accepts you as his disciple and thus affords you an opportunity to attain spiritual perfection through his wisdom and knowledge. We are not told to "get" ourselves a teacher, for in accordance with Judaism, the Torah, and particularly the תורה שבעל פה, the Talmud, should be taught without financial reward; indeed, it is a *mitzvah* incumbent on everyone to impart to qualified disciples whatever teachings of God one may have acquired. A *chaver,* a friend and companion in life, on the other hand, who is a helper and counselor at our side in our work and our endeavors must be "got" or "acquired"; this means that we must win him by way of accommodation, association and empathy; hence we are told קנה לך חבר. "Teacher" and "friend"—these appelations represent the highest level on which we can cherish another human being and as a rule there are only a few whom we are able to designate as such. But even if there are only a few people chosen for and by us to whom we can feel so close and who will feel so close to us in return, we must be careful not to be too harsh in our judgment of others and certainly we must not be so arrogant as to seek to keep aloof from them. Rather, it should be our endeavor to keep the best possible opinion of all men, and even in instances where their conduct seems to us of dubious and questionable character, we should be as charitable as we can in our judgment of them.

ז נִתַּאי הָאַרְבֵּלִי אוֹמֵר הַרְחֵק מִשָּׁכֵן רָע וְאַל־תִּתְחַבֵּר לָרָשָׁע
וְאַל־תִּתְיָאֵשׁ מִן־הַפּוּרְעָנוּת:

ח יְהוּדָה בֶּן טַבַּאי וְשִׁמְעוֹן בֶּן שָׁטַח קִבְּלוּ מֵהֶם · יְהוּדָה בֶּן־טַבַּאי
אוֹמֵר, אַל־תַּעַשׂ עַצְמְךָ כְּעוֹרְכֵי הַדַּיָּנִין וּכְשֶׁיִּהְיוּ בַּעֲלֵי הַדִּין
עוֹמְדִים לְפָנֶיךָ יִהְיוּ בְעֵינֶיךָ כִּרְשָׁעִים וּכְשֶׁנִּפְטָרִים מִלְּפָנֶיךָ יִהְיוּ
בְעֵינֶיךָ כְזַכָּאִין   כְּשֶׁקִּבְּלוּ עֲלֵיהֶם אֶת־הַדִּין:

ט שִׁמְעוֹן בֶּן־שָׁטַח אוֹמֵר, הֱוֵי מַרְבֶּה לַחֲקוֹר אֶת־הָעֵדִים
וֶהֱוֵי זָהִיר בִּדְבָרֶיךָ שֶׁמָּא מִתּוֹכָם יִלְמְדוּ לְשַׁקֵּר:

י שְׁמַעְיָה וְאַבְטַלְיוֹן קִבְּלוּ מֵהֶם · שְׁמַעְיָה אוֹמֵר, אֱהַב אֶת־
הַמְּלָאכָה וּשְׂנָא אֶת־הָרַבָּנוּת וְאַל־תִּתְוַדַּע לָרָשׁוּת:

---

7. We can remove ourselves physically, by changing our residence, from a neighbor who could have a harmful and detrimental effect on us by reason of his quarrelsome, underhanded character and downright wickedness. Therefore we are told הרחק משכן רע. In or daily dealings with others, however, we cannot avoid contact with individuals who have thrown God's Law aside. But we neither need nor should enter into close relations with them. "Do not associate with them," do not make common cause with them and particularly—and this is the literal meaning of *hithchaber le*— do not become a member in communities in which *reshaim* dominate. In the end there is a penalty to pay for all these things, for remaining near an evil neighbor as well as for association with evil men. Even if you have maintained such associations over a long period of time without feeling any adverse effects, it is inevitable that your thoughtlessness and indifference must result in harm to you in the long run.

8. Should you be called upon to function as a judge, do not be like the legal advisors who offer to place their juridicial knowledge at the service of the litigating parties. Do not instruct them how to testify and how to counter arguments in court. In your office of judge you must remain silent and abstain from interference in the arguments brought before you. Do not by even so much as a gesture seek to influence either prosecution or defense. (As distinct from this injunction we have a legal maxim פתח פיך לאלם in Gittin 37b, Kethuvoth 36a, Choshen Mishpat 17:9, according to which, in extraordinary cases only, of course, it is the right and at times even the duty of the judge to call attention to or elaborate upon particulars that were not stressed in

7. Nittai the Arbelite says: Keep away from an evil neighbor and do not associate with a lawless man, and do not give up the belief in retribution.

8. Yehudah ben Tabbai and Shimon ben Shetach received [the tradition] from them. Yehudah ben Tabbai says: In the office of judge, do not act the counsel, and as long as the parties [in the lawsuit] stand before you, let them be as guilty in your eyes, but when they depart from you, once they have submitted to the judgment, regard them [both] as innocent.

9. Shimon ben Shetach says: Examine the witnesses thoroughly and be careful with your words lest they learn through them to falsify.

10. Shemayah and Avtalyon received [the tradition] from them. Shemayah says: Love work, hate the holding of high office and do not seek to become intimate with the authorities.

---

the evidence due to obvious ignorance or awkwardness on the part of one of the litigating parties.). וכשיהיו וכו׳, As long as the parties are before you, you must view them both as equally unreliable and must interpret and evaluate their allegations objectively, dispassionately, without regard to personalities, and solely on the merit of their testimony. For there are disputes in which even the best man may be in the wrong and the worst man in the right. On the other hand, once the parties have accepted your judgment and the case has been closed, do not carry with you into your life outside of court any adverse impression you may have obtained, without realizing it, of one or the other party during the hearing. Once their dispute has been settled you must regard them both as equally free of guilt.

9. חקירה The purpose of the examination and questioning of witnesses is, by probing into the particulars in the case, to uncover inconsistencies between the testimonies of two or more of the witnesses. In this process, unguarded statements or ill-considered phrasing of questions on the part of the judge can easily reveal to the witnesses the sort of testimony that may be beneficial or detrimental to either side and cause them to deviate from the truth.

10. It seems that the purpose of these three maxims of Shemayah is to counsel us to preserve our personal independence. We are told: Love work, for it is your assurance of economic independence. Hate the holding of high office, for the office-holder quickly becomes a slave to his position. He will do things—or he will believe that, for the sake of his position, he must do certain things—which actually are contrary to his own views and inclinations and which he would never do if he were free to follow his own principles and his personal philosophies of life. Finally, do not seek to become intimate with the ruling authorities; for this is the literal meaning of רשות. Such relationships may impair your independence and may make you do many

יא אַבְטַלְיוֹן אוֹמֵר, חֲכָמִים הִזָּהֲרוּ בְּדִבְרֵיכֶם שֶׁמָּא תָחוּבוּ חוֹבַת
גָּלוּת וְתִגְלוּ לִמְקוֹם מַיִם הָרָעִים וְיִשְׁתּוּ הַתַּלְמִידִים הַבָּאִים
אַחֲרֵיכֶם וְיָמוּתוּ וְנִמְצָא שֵׁם שָׁמַיִם מִתְחַלֵּל:

יב הִלֵּל וְשַׁמַּאי קִבְּלוּ מֵהֶם. הִלֵּל אוֹמֵר, הֱוֵה מִתַּלְמִידָיו שֶׁל־
אַהֲרֹן אוֹהֵב שָׁלוֹם וְרוֹדֵף שָׁלוֹם אוֹהֵב אֶת־הַבְּרִיּוֹת וּמְקָרְבָן
לַתּוֹרָה:

יג הוּא הָיָה אוֹמֵר, נְגִיד שְׁמָא אֲבַד שְׁמֵהּ וּדְלָא מוֹסִיף יָסֵף
וּדְלָא יַלִּיף קְטָלָא חַיָּב וּדְאִשְׁתַּמַּשׁ בְּתַגָּא חָלָף:

---

things that may coincide with the will, the inclinations, wishes and views of
your powerful friends whom you do not want to alienate but that may be
quite contrary to your own wishes, views and inclinations. Only one who is
content to live unobtrusively, to remain in a humble position and to sustain himself by dint of his own labors can be truly free.

11. According to the Torah the penalty for accidental manslaughter was
Galuth, exile in the form of enforced relocation to one of the Cities of Refuge.
In this Mishna the "penalty of *Galuth*" is used with reference also to moral
manslaughter, Scholars are warned against making rash or careless statements
in their discourses that might cause the moral downfall of their disciples.
They are cautioned against delivering themselves of utterances that are inac-
curate, vague or ambiguous and that may inspire erroneous views and result
in spiritual and moral deviations from goodness and truth. A pernicious process of this type, started by a learned discourse, is portrayed here in allegoric
terms as follows: The lecturer "comes upon a place of perilous waters,"
meaning that he presents to his audience teachings and views which may
endanger moral life if they are misinterpreted, without cautioning his listeners
against such misinterpretation. As a result, his disciples will follow the material presented in the lecture; they will accept the erroneous interpretation as if
it were taught by their master and thereby they will fall victim to moral
disintegration. Such an error on the part of a lecturer is also referred to by
the Hebrew term *galah.* He "departs" or "emigrates" from the sheltered abode
of truth and strays into perilous places which it would have been better had
they remained unknown to him. Or perhaps יתגלו is derived not from *galah*
but from its homonym, *galah* meaning "to uncover". For in the *Kal* inflection,
too, *galah* means "to uncover". In this case, the interpretation would be that
the lecturer "uncovers" wells of poisoned water and leaves them exposed
instead of re-covering them with a lid to protect the passer-by.

11. Avtalyon says: Scholars, be careful with your words, for you may incur the penalty of *Galuth* and come upon a place of evil waters, and the disciples who follow you may drink from them and die, and the Name of Heaven would be profaned.

12. Hillel and Shammai received [the tradition] from them. Hillel says: Be of the disciples of Aaron, loving peace and pursuing peace, loving [your fellow] creatures and bringing them nearer to the Torah.

13. He used to say: He who seeks a name loses his name; he who does not increase [his knowledge] decreases [it]; he who does not study is deserving of death he who makes [improper] use of the crown [of the Torah] will pass away.

---

12. In the Book of Malachi (2:6) it is said of Aaron that בשלום ובמישור הלך אתי ורבים השיב מעון "He walked with Me in peace and uprightness and brought many back from sin", a description to which the characterization given in this Mishna corresponds. רודף שלום is more than אוהב שלום The "lover of peace" merely avoids whatever may endanger peace, but the *rodef shalom* actively does whatever he can to restore peace that has already fled, and will be ready to make whatever sacrifice he can for the sake of peace except that, of course, he must not under any circumstances compromise the loyalty he owes to God and to his duty.

בריות, lit. "creatures" is a term embracing all of mankind without distinction. He loves all men because they are the creatures of God.

13. A good name that endures must come unsought; it will come only to him who performs good and commendable deeds and acts of helpfulness for no other motive but out of his sense of duty without caring what others may think. As for him who is greedy for honor and fame, who is motivated in his actions solely by the ambition to acquire a name for himself, his fellowmen will soon discover that he is prompted by selfish motives alone. Besides, his gluttony for fame and honors will quickly lead him also to reprehensible conduct, and then whatever good reputation he may have gained at the outset will vanish apace. There is, however, one field in which no one should ever feel that he has done enough, and that is study and practical observance. He who stands still in these paths is actually regressing. He who does not study is not worthy of life because he neglects to acquaint himself with the tasks for which he was given life and to acquire the skills and knowledge necessary for their fulfillment. This statement seems harsh but it was never more justified than it was in those past days in the history of our people when all schooling was free of charge and everyone possessed of knowledge deemed it his duty to give freely of his wisdom to anyone seeking it. Certainly there has never been one more fully within his rights to make such a statement than was Hillel. According to the account in Yoma 35b, Hillel was

יד הוּא הָיָה אוֹמֵר, אִם אֵין אֲנִי לִי מִי לִי וּכְשֶׁאֲנִי לְעַצְמִי מָה אֲנִי וְאִם לֹא עַכְשָׁו אֵימָתַי:

טו שַׁמַּאי אוֹמֵר, עֲשֵׂה תוֹרָתְךָ קֶבַע אֱמוֹר מְעַט וַעֲשֵׂה הַרְבֵּה וֶהֱוֵה מְקַבֵּל אֶת־כָּל־הָאָדָם בְּסֵבֶר פָּנִים יָפוֹת:

טז רַבָּן גַּמְלִיאֵל אוֹמֵר, עֲשֵׂה לְךָ רַב וְהִסְתַּלֵּק מִן הַסָּפֵק וְאַל־תַּרְבֶּה לְעַשֵּׂר אֹמָדוֹת:

---

so poor in his youth that he earned no more than one *tarpek* a day by his labors. Of this he had to give half to the doorkeeper of the House of Study as an admission fee; the other half had to do for his wants and the needs of his family. It came to pass one day that he could find no work and hence could not pay the doorkeeper. Therefore he lay down atop the skylight on the roof of the House of Study and from that position he listened to the learned discourses of Shemayah and Abtalyon, his teachers, all night long. The next morning it still seemed to be unusually dark in the House of Study. When some men investigated the cause, they came upon Hillel buried under a foot of snow that had fallen during the night. Therefore it is said הלל מחייב עניים. If a man pleads poverty and economic worries as an excuse for not studying, let him be reminded of the example set by Hillel.

תגא : ודאשתמש בתגא, "the crown", refers to the *Kether Torah*, the crown of knowledge of the Torah. He who would debase this "crown" to serve as a common tool for the acquisition of honor or personal advantage, חלף; he will not acquire either of these on a basis of permanence. This sentence may be interpreted as a justification for the statement that precedes it. If no one will exploit his knowledge of the Torah for financial gain and everyone will give instruction without payment, there will be no excuse for anyone not to study.

14. It is only through his own efforts that a man can attain spiritual fitness and moral worth, which are the most essential attributes to which he can aspire. Similarly, it is primarily upon himself, his own diligence, his own efforts and his own good sense that man must depend in the process of acquiring and certainly of preserving the worldly goods he needs. True, others can help him in these endeavors, but without earnest effort on his own part he will not be able to acquire, much less keep whatever there is to be gained. But even though he may have become who and what he is solely by dint of his own efforts, a man must never say: "Since it is solely by my own efforts that I have become what I am, I will use my attainments for myself alone." For it is only when, in selfless devotion, he actively works to create, to establish and to increase the happiness and prosperity of his fellowmen that a man

14.   He used to say: If I am nothing to myself, who will be for me?
And if I am for myself only, what am I? And if not now, when?

15.   Shammai says: Make your study of the Torah a regular
activity, promise little but do much, and receive all men with a kindly
countenance.

16.   Rabban Gamliel says: Provide yourself with a teacher and free
yourself of doubt, for you must not give an excess tithe through
guesswork.

---

begins to become truly human in the image of his God. If he exists for
himself alone, of what value is he? And never put off accomplishing this
human calling either for yourself, or, through you, for others, for to this task
every moment of your life should be devoted. Do you know whether, indeed,
you still will have another moment in which to do the work?

15.   The study of Torah is our first and most important task because it
determines the extent to which we will understand and fulfill our life's duties.
Therefore, regardless of any other pursuit to which we may give of our time,
we must not leave the study of the Torah to chance but should establish a
regular daily time and schedule for study and adhere to it, for otherwise we
might allow other pursuits to keep us from study and as a result we would
drift away more and more from this source of our spiritual sustenance. But
while we are told to establish a definite schedule for our studies in advance,
we must not make the same inflexible plans as regards our actions. When it
comes to action, we should promise little but do all the more. However,
even though our spoken word should not promise too much or too easily, our
conduct and approach to every human being should be so friendly in character
that all will be convinced that we are kindly disposed toward them and that
we are ready at all times to the best of our abilities to fulfill whatever good
and reasonable request another may make of us.

16.   It is only through study with a reliable and scrupulous teacher whom
you can consult in cases of doubt that you can establish with certainty what
your duty is and how you should conduct yourself. Therefore see that you
provide yourself with a teacher who has these qualifications. You must not
think that you can manage without instruction by simply following the stricter
precept in cases of doubt, by refraining from what may even be permissible
and by doing more than is actually required of you. To be sure, if you have
no possibility to obtain such instruction, you have no other choice but to
follow this course. On the other hand, you must not believe that this alternative will safeguard you from error in *every* instance. The illustration given
in this Mishna has reference, as an example, to *maaser,* the mandatory tithe
of grain. If, instead of measuring out the amount of grain from which the
tithe is to be taken, a man takes the tithe by guesswork, he would be remiss
in his duty not only if he should thereby make his tithe too little but also if

יי שִׁמְעוֹן בְּנוֹ אוֹמֵר, כָּל־יָמַי גָּדַלְתִּי בֵּין הַחֲכָמִים וְלֹא מָצָאתִי
לַגּוּף טוֹב מִשְּׁתִיקָה וְלֹא הַמִּדְרָשׁ עִקָּר אֶלָּא הַמַּעֲשֶׂה, וְכָל־הַמַּרְבֶּה
דְּבָרִים מֵבִיא חֵטְא:

יח רַבָּן שִׁמְעוֹן בֶּן־גַּמְלִיאֵל אוֹמֵר, עַל־שְׁלשָׁה דְבָרִים הָעוֹלָם
קַיָּם עַל־הָאֱמֶת וְעַל־הַדִּין וְעַל־הַשָּׁלוֹם שֶׁנֶּאֱמַר אֱמֶת וּמִשְׁפַּט
שָׁלוֹם שִׁפְטוּ בְּשַׁעֲרֵיכֶם:

רַבִּי חֲנַנְיָא בֶּן־עֲקַשְׁיָא אוֹמֵר, רָצָה הַקָּדוֹשׁ בָּרוּךְ הוּא לְזַכּוֹת אֶת־יִשְׂרָאֵל
לְפִיכָךְ הִרְבָּה לָהֶם תּוֹרָה וּמִצְוֹת. שֶׁנֶּאֱמַר יְיָ חָפֵץ לְמַעַן צִדְקוֹ יַגְדִּיל תּוֹרָה
וְיַאְדִּיר: קדיש.

---

he should make it too much. For instance, if a man determines his tithe by
taking one out of every five instead of one of ten, the tithe itself would
contain an unredeemed part which would be *tevel* and therefore *assur*.
המרבה במעשרות פירותיו מתוקנים ומעשרותיו מקולקלין (Eruvin 50a).

17. The של״ה interprets this Mishna as follows: I have spent all my time in
the company of sages and from them, who wield their influence through the
spoken word, I have learned the true significance of speech. But as regards
the physical aspects of life and the personal affairs of men, I have found
silence to be the best policy. One is duty-bound to make provision for these
things but one must not talk much about them. Let the speech of men and
their discussions center on spiritual and moral concerns. Indeed, there is
nothing more offensive than the pompous gusto with which men converse
about the merits of food and drink. As a matter of fact, there are limits to
the usefulness of speech even in the teaching and inquiry associated with
things moral and spiritual; deeds and accomplishments count the most. *Too
much* talk is always bad. Clarity and conciseness always are conducive to the
desired ends. Needless effusions of words weaken even the best-taken point
and verbosity invites error and wrong. As the Sages point out, in most of
the "lamentations" that deplore error, the letter *Pe* (mouth) comes before the
letter *Ayin* (eye); the mouth utters what the eye has not seen and the mind

17. Shimon his son says: All my life I have grown up amongst sages and have found nothing better for the physical welfare of man than silence; study is not the most important thing but practice, and too much talk brings sin.

18. Rabban Shimon ben Gamliel said: By virtue of three things does the world endure: truth, justice, and peace, as it is said: You shall administer truth and the justice of peace in your gates.

Rabbi Chananya ben Akashyah said: The Holy One, blessed be He, desired to bestow great favor on Israel; hence He gave them Torah and laws in abundant measure. For it is said: God was pleased for the sake of His righteousness to render the Torah increasingly great and glorious.

---

has not tested. One of the worst consequences of profuse talk, however, is that people who have spoken long and much and zealously of and in behalf of a cause may persuade themselves that this alone constitutes action, and should a voice within them accuse them of being remiss in their concrete efforts for the cause, they will calm their conscience by recalling the enthusiasm and the brilliance with which they had carried on the discussion of the matter at hand!

18. If *truth* should be removed from human speech and understanding so that truth could no longer be known, uttered and taught, and speech would serve man only to conceal his thoughts and to spread error, falsehood and deceit; if *justice* should be eliminated from the deeds and the affairs of men so that men would no longer honor right as the most sacred of inalienable values before which all selfishness, violence and personal interest must bow and there would be no supreme authority to defend the rights of all with steadfast determination and against every act of aggression and usurpation; if *peace* should be banished from the sentiments and the esteem of men so that there would be no one who of his own free will would waive for the sake of peace whatever is his to sacrifice—save, of course, his conscience and his duty; if truth and justice and peace should vanish from the earth; then, no matter what else the world might have in which to glory, the affairs of men will attain neither stability nor permanent value.

פֶּרֶק שֵׁנִי

כל ישראל וכו'

א רַבִּי אוֹמֵר, אֵיזוֹ הִיא דֶרֶךְ יְשָׁרָה שֶׁיָּבוֹר לוֹ הָאָדָם כָּל־שֶׁהִיא
תִּפְאֶרֶת לְעוֹשֶׂהָ וְתִפְאֶרֶת לוֹ מִן הָאָדָם, וֶהֱוֵי זָהִיר בְּמִצְוָה קַלָּה
כְּבַחֲמוּרָה שֶׁאֵין אַתָּה יוֹדֵעַ מַתַּן שְׂכָרָן שֶׁל־מִצְוֹת, וֶהֱוֵי מְחַשֵּׁב
הֶפְסֵד מִצְוָה כְּנֶגֶד שְׂכָרָהּ וּשְׂכַר עֲבֵרָה כְּנֶגֶד הֶפְסֵדָהּ. הִסְתַּכֵּל
בִּשְׁלשָׁה דְבָרִים וְאֵין אַתָּה בָא לִידֵי עֲבֵרָה, דַּע מַה־לְמַעְלָה
מִמְּךָ עַיִן רוֹאָה וְאֹזֶן שׁוֹמַעַת וְכָל־מַעֲשֶׂיךָ בַּסֵּפֶר נִכְתָּבִים:

---

1. When we are faced with a choice of action, there are two things which
we must consider; first, whether the action would be in accord with the will
and the ordinances of God so that its performance as such will be to our
credit, and secondly, whether there is a chance that it may be misinterpreted
by others. This is the same principle that is set forth elsewhere in the command
ויהיתם נקיים מה' ומישראל. When it comes to the performance of a Divine commandment, be as careful and as scrupulous in the execution of one which
is easy to fulfill, or seems easy to you, as you would be with one that appears
more difficult to fulfill, for you do not know the standard by which God
apportions the reward for our good deeds. We are here told מתן שכרן, as distinct from שכר מצוה ועברה which follows. For good deeds and sins alike carry
a two-fold recompense. First, there is the objective reward or punishment;
this comes to us sooner or later, whichever may be ordained in God's decree,
either in this world or in the world to come, it is to this form of recompense
that מתן שכרן refers. The other recompense is spiritual in character and it comes
to us immediately; it is inherent in the good deed or in the sin itself. The immediate reward of any Divine command scrupulously performed is a sense
of moral elevation, an increase in our moral strength, and the awareness, most
blissful of all, that we are worthy of the nearness of God because we have
faithfully carried out our duty toward Him. The recompense for any evil
act is also instantaneous; it takes the form of a sense of loss of moral purity,
a weakening of moral fiber, a greater propensity to additional sin, and most
crushing of all, the realization which renders us unable to look up calmly to
our God; namely, that we have failed to fulfill our purpose, sinned against
our destiny and hence forfeited the approval of God and, indeed, the right
to be satisfied with ourselves. Such reward and such punishment are easy
enough to comprehend; it is to these that the terms שכר מצוה and הפסד עברה
in this Mishna refer. We are admonished to balance any sacrifice of pleasures
and possessions that may be involved in the fulfillment of a Divine command
over against the gain, surpassing all else, embodied in the sense of happiness
with which faithful perseverance in our duty and its performance fills us.

1. Rabbi [Yehudah Ha-Nasi] said: Which is the right course that a man should choose? Any one which in itself does credit to him who adopts it and which also brings him honor from men; and be careful of a light precept even as of a grave one, for you do not know the reward for the commandments; balance the loss incurred in the performance of a commandment against its reward and the gain gotten from a sin against the loss it entails. Consider three things and you will not fall into the grip of sin. Know what is above you: a seeing eye and a hearing ear, and that all your deeds are recorded in the The Book.

Indeed, the greater the sacrifices we have to make to duty, the greater the happiness inherent in duty done. On the other hand, balance any promise of unlawful gain and impious pleasures by which iniquitous temptation might seek to lure us away from the path of duty over against the irreplaceable loss of inner purity and peace and the persistent, crushing torture inherent in that sense of guilt which compels us to condemn ourselves and to be denied the approval of our God. But then we know of nothing that makes it easier for us gladly to do good and steadfastly to avoid all evil than to keep before us at all times the three things mentioned in this Mishna; namely, the "seeing eye" and the "hearing ear" which are directed upon us from on high, and the fact that all our deeds will be recorded in "The Book". The knowledge that whatever we say and do is seen and heard by a Supreme Being Who rules over us and over all else as well certainly provides us with the most powerful incentive for being both careful [to avoid evil] and joyously ready [to do good] in all our words and actions. However, these attitudes of prudence and willingness are enhanced still further by the knowledge that whatever we do will be recorded בספר in "The Book". It is not *besefer* but *basefer*. As we have noted in our Commentary to Exodus (32:32) all the many phases of the world's development under the guidance of God are regarded as one uniform whole, "one book", as it were, in which there is room to record everything of significance in this process of continuous growth. "Never forget," we are told here, "that the consequences and repercussions of everything you do reach far beyond the fleeting time span in which your act occurred. God is mindful even of the least conspicuous of your actions, and they all will be recalled to you when your life will pass in review at the end of your days; and what is more, they will continue to be operative, for good or for evil, through all the days to come. This should be sufficient reason for you to do nothing of which you might have to be ashamed in the presence of God and of your own self-respect; it should be sufficient reason to be careful, with all your deeds, to plant nothing but seeds of goodness into the soil of the future yet unborn."

ב רַבָּן גַּמְלִיאֵל בְּנוֹ שֶׁל־רַבִּי יְהוּדָה הַנָּשִׂיא אוֹמֵר, יָפֶה תַלְמוּד
תּוֹרָה עִם דֶּרֶךְ אֶרֶץ שֶׁיְּגִיעַת שְׁנֵיהֶם מַשְׁכַּחַת עָוֹן וְכָל־תּוֹרָה
שֶׁאֵין עִמָּהּ מְלָאכָה סוֹפָהּ בְּטֵלָה וְגוֹרֶרֶת עָוֹן וְכָל־הָעוֹסְקִים עִם־
הַצִּבּוּר יִהְיוּ עוֹסְקִים עִמָּהֶם לְשֵׁם שָׁמַיִם שֶׁזְּכוּת אֲבוֹתָם מְסַיַּעְתָּם
וְצִדְקָתָם עוֹמֶדֶת לָעַד וְאַתֶּם מַעֲלֶה אֲנִי עֲלֵיכֶם שָׂכָר הַרְבֵּה
כְּאִלּוּ עֲשִׂיתֶם:

ג הֱווּ זְהִירִין בִּרְשׁוּת שֶׁאֵין מְקָרְבִין לוֹ לְאָדָם אֶלָּא לְצֹרֶךְ

---

2. The term דרך ארץ includes all the situations arising from and dependent
upon the circumstance that the earth is the place where the individual must
live, fulfill his destiny and dwell together with others and that he must utilize
resources and conditions provided on earth in order to live and to accomplish
his purpose. Accordingly, the term *derech eretz* is used primarily to refer to
ways of earning a living, to the social order that prevails on earth, as well
as to the mores and considerations of courtesy and propriety arising from
social living and also to things pertinent to good breeding and general education. We believe that the explanation שיגיעת שניהם וכו׳ implies that the term
derech eretz as used here denotes, above all, the business and occupational
activities carried on for purposes of earning a living. We are not told that
שיגיעת שניהם "keeps away sin" but משכחת that it causes sin to be forgotten,
that it "keeps sinful thoughts from arising." By this, we believe, is meant
that only a way of life devoted to the pursuit of study as well as of economic
independence can take up our time to such a degree that there will be no
unoccupied hours during which we could indulge in thoughts that are far
from good and that could make us drift away from the path of goodness.
Nay, more, וכל תורה וכו׳, he who does not pursue some gainful employment
alongside the study of the Torah runs the risk of being forced to stop his
studies because of poverty and of being driven to wrongdoing by destitution
and misery. It is difficult to find the logical connection between the foregoing
statements and the next sentence which begins with the words וכל העוסקים.
We believe that there is a connection as follows: After Rabbi Yehudah Ha-
Nasi, the compiler of the Mishna, died and had been succeeded by his
son, there began in Babylonia an era when academies of Jewish learning
and Jewish communal life were in full flower. At the same time there was a
steady increase in the number of Jewish settlements outside of Palestine. It
was probably this trend that impelled the son of Rabbenu Yehudah Ha-Nasi
to put stress on those elements that are basic to the maintenance and continu-

2. Rabban Gamliel, the son of Rabbi Yehudah Ha-Nasi, said: The study of Torah together with an occupation is an excellent thing, for the pursuit of both of these [together] keeps sinful thoughts from arising, while any study of Torah without some kind of work must fail in the end and is conducive to sin. Let all those who occupy themselves with the [affairs of the] community do so only for the sake of Heaven, for the merit of their fathers will sustain them and their devotion to duty, too, will endure forever. "But as for you," [says God,] I credit you with great reward, as if you had accomplished it."

3. Be cautious with the ruling authorities, for they befriend a man

---

ation of our existence both as individuals and as a people. These elements are; דרך ארץ, תורה, and מלאכה in the case of the *individual,* and conscientious attention to communal affairs in the case of *communities.* In regard to the latter he tells us that all those who occupy themselves with communal affairs should do so only לשם שמים. לשם שמים is a concept typical of the Jewish philosophy of life. It denotes action prompted solely by a sense of duty, without any ulterior motives. In this manner our attention is directed to the great and eternal role of the *community* in Jewish life. The community embodies that which is truly eternal in Jewry. In every age there still survive in the community the merits and the good deeds of generations past, acting as the foundation on and by means of which the present is built. Likewise, all the good and righteous deeds that are performed by that present generation will live on in the community through the generations to come. ואתם, As for you, who attend honestly and faithfully to the affairs of the community, who know how to inspire the members of the community to care for the institutions which they are duty-bound to maintain, and who, with scrupulous honesty and wisdom, make use, to this end, of the resources that have been entrusted to you for this purpose, you will be given great reward just as if you had done it all with your own resources. For, as the Sages state elsewhere גדול המעשה יותר מן העושה (Bava Bathra 9a) he who inspires and causes others to do good deeds and to fulfill their duty has even greater merit than he who does the same good with his own resources. Such devotion to communal affairs demands far more self-denial and sustained faithfulness and devotion than is required for one individual who happens to possess the needed means to decide to use these resources in behalf of the good cause.

3. If our interpretation of the preceding passage is not in error, it may be assumed that this statement was intended to be a supplement to what was said in Mishna 2 regarding the new challenges our people had to face as they dispersed and settled in increasing numbers in lands where alien rulers held

עַצְמָן נִרְאִין כְּאוֹהֲבִין בִּשְׁעַת הֲנָאָתָן וְאֵין עוֹמְדִין לוֹ לְאָדָם
בִּשְׁעַת דָּחֳקוֹ:

ד הוּא הָיָה אוֹמֵר, עֲשֵׂה רְצוֹנוֹ כִּרְצוֹנֶךָ כְּדֵי שֶׁיַּעֲשֶׂה רְצוֹנְךָ
כִּרְצוֹנוֹ· בַּטֵּל רְצוֹנְךָ מִפְּנֵי רְצוֹנוֹ כְּדֵי שֶׁיְּבַטֵּל רְצוֹן אֲחֵרִים מִפְּנֵי
רְצוֹנֶךָ:

ה הִלֵּל אוֹמֵר, אַל־תִּפְרֹשׁ מִן־הַצִּבּוּר וְאַל־תַּאֲמִין בְּעַצְמְךָ עַד
יוֹם מוֹתְךָ וְאַל־תָּדִין אֶת־חֲבֵרְךָ עַד שֶׁתַּגִּיעַ לִמְקוֹמוֹ וְאַל־תֹּאמַר
דָּבָר שֶׁאִי אֶפְשָׁר לִשְׁמוֹעַ שֶׁסּוֹפוֹ לְהִשָּׁמַע וְאַל־תֹּאמַר לִכְשֶׁאֶפָּנֶה
אֶשְׁנֶה שֶׁמָּא לֹא תִפָּנֶה:

---

sway. רשות is almost synonymous with רשות "permission", "power", and
hence denotes any "authority" in whom power is vested.

4. With these words we are asked to identify our will entirely with the will
of God, so that we may perform joyously and willingly whatever is pleasing
to God as being fully in accord with our own wishes, and give no place in
our aspirations to any endeavor that is not in accordance with the will of
God. If we ourselves have no other wishes but those identical with the wishes
of God Himself, we will have a greater right than anyone else to hope that
our own wishes will be fulfilled and we will have less cause than others to
fear such wishes as may be inimical to our welfare.

5. It is not to the individual, but to the community, מורשה קהלת יעקב, that
God entrusted His Torah as an inheritance for all the generations to come.
For this reason every individual is duty-bound to join forces with his community in thought, in word and in deed and loyally to share in its tasks and
obligations, so long as that community proves to be a faithful guardian and
supporter of the Torah. Indeed, it is essential in the discharge of his own
life's task that the individual be part of a larger community. For whatever he
may be able to do on his own is inadequate and short-lived; it is only in
conjunction with the achievements of others that his own actions can have
importance. Moreover, his good principles and convictions will gain considerable strength and support from the fact that he holds them in common with
the whole of a genuinely Jewish community. Let no one, Hillel hastens to
add, be so presumptuous as to believe that he is morally perfect and therefore
think that he will never need the support of a community to guard him against
weakness and error, for man is not immune to error and moral frailty as long
as he breathes on earth. Likewise, let no one presume to pass judgment on

only for their own interests; they appear as friends when it is to their advantage but they do not stand by a man in times of distress.

4. He used to say: Do His will as you would do your own will, so that He may do your will just as He does His will. Set aside your will for the sake of His will, so that He may set aside the will of others before your will.

5. Hillel said: Do not set yourself apart from the community; do not be sure of yourself until the day of your death. Do not judge your fellow man until you have been in his position; do not say of any word that it cannot possibly be heard, for in the end it will be heard. And do not say: "When I shall have leisure I shall study" for you may never have leisure.

---

others, for does he know the circumstances of his erring brother and the temptations that led him astray, and how can he know whether, in similar circumstances and exposed to the same temptations, he would have been more steadfast in his devotion to duty?

ואל תאמר. This sentence has been the object of many different interpretations. In our opinion it should be understood in association with the statement preceding it. Accordingly, we would submit the following interpretation. Hillel said: Even if you should be the only person in your community to hold a given view, do not say that you will never be able to gain a hearing from the other members of the community. As long as the view you represent is truly right and aims only at what is good and true, do not refrain from expressing it. Continue your fight, tirelessly and undaunted, for what is good and right, for years, if need be; in the end—provided, of course, that you have fought for your cause solely for its own sake, without ulterior, selfish motives   you will be heard.

And even as you must always maintain close ties with your community, so, too, you must remain in constant touch with the study of the Torah, that source of all truth for individual and community alike. However great the pressures of your other affairs may be, you must set aside a definite period each day for study, as has already been indicated previously, and never postpone your study for a period of leisure that seems more convenient. For it may be that you will never have leisure time "more convenient" for study, and as a result you will drift further and further away from the one source at which you may enrich and set aright your knowledge and your attitude as regards what is good and true.

י הוּא הָיָה אוֹמֵר, אֵין בּוּר יְרֵא חֵטְא וְלֹא עַם הָאָרֶץ חָסִיד
וְלֹא הַבַּיְשָׁן לָמֵד וְלֹא הַקַּפְּדָן מְלַמֵּד וְלֹא כָּל־הַמַּרְבֶּה בִסְחוֹרָה
מַחְכִּים וּבַמָּקוֹם שֶׁאֵין אֲנָשִׁים הִשְׁתַּדֵּל לִהְיוֹת אִישׁ:

ז אַף הוּא רָאָה גֻּלְגֹּלֶת אַחַת שֶׁצָּפָה עַל־פְּנֵי הַמָּיִם. אָמַר לָהּ,
עַל דַּאֲטֵיפְתְּ אַטִיפוּךְ וְסוֹף מְטַיְפָיִךְ יְטוּפוּן:

ח הוּא הָיָה אוֹמֵר, מַרְבֶּה בָשָׂר מַרְבֶּה רִמָּה מַרְבֶּה נְכָסִים
מַרְבֶּה דְאָגָה מַרְבֶּה נָשִׁים מַרְבֶּה כְשָׁפִים מַרְבֶּה שְׁפָחוֹת מַרְבֶּה

---

6. In the preceding Mishna we were admonished to keep in constant touch with the Teaching of the Law. By way of continuation we are now told that ignorance is never the mother of virtue. בור : A man who is totally ignorant has no idea of the conditions that prevail around him and of the duties which he must fulfill; he will sin without even being aware that he is doing wrong. עם הארץ : It is true that one who, through his upbringing and personal experience, has come to know the conditions in which he moves and the duties he must discharge will take care not to do wrong. But if he has received no instruction in the Teachings of the Law, he cannot be a חסיד. If, as the Sages are careful to point out, he has not had the benefit of personal association with, and the personal example of true sages to teach him how properly to fulfill life's duties in actual practice (this is the type of person to whom the term *am ha-aretz* refers), he cannot know genuine *chasiduth*, true Jewish virtuousness. He may attach significance to things which are actually without value; on the other hand, he may regard as unimportant matters which, in fact, should be viewed as most significant, and, more often than not, he will fail to put his pious intentions into proper practice. לא הבישן למד וכו' : He who is too timid to ask questions for fear of betraying his ignorance to his fellow-students and will rather go without instruction will never acquire knowledge. A pedantic person, lacking patience with beginners whose learning capacity is still largely undeveloped, will not be successful as a teacher. He will frighten his disciples away and they will learn nothing from him. ובמקום : In circumstances where the affairs of the community receive proper attention and the good and the right are adequately represented, do not push yourself forward. Under these conditions modesty is a virtue, and any forwardness on your part may be presumptuous and may tend to push aside men who are better qualified than you to do the work. But in situations where true men are lacking, where the interests of the community suffer for lack of proper leader-

6. He used to say: An ignorant man cannot be sin-fearing, a man lacking instruction cannot be pious, nor can a timid man learn; a man without patience cannot teach, and one who is too deeply involved in business will not grow in wisdom, and in a place where there are no men, strive to be a man.

7. Moreover, he saw a skull floating on the surface of the water, and he said to it: Even if they have drowned you because you drowned [others], those who drowned you will themselves be drowned.

8. He used to say: The more flesh, the more decay; the more property, the more worry; the more women, the more superstition; the more maid-servants, the more lewdness; the more men-servants, the

---

ship, and where, in default of adequate support, goodness and truth remain unrecognized and unrealized—it is your duty to strive to become a man qualified to act as a leader and spokesman, and once you have acquired these skills, endeavor to take part in affairs where articulate leadership is needed, for under such conditions reticence would not be modest but downright criminal.

7. It was obvious to Hillel that the man whose skull was floating on the water had not died by accident but as the result of violence. The head of a corpse floating on the water will not come off; therefore Hillel had to assume that the person had died by violence, and that the murderers had severed the head from the body and then thrown it into the water. Hence the "drowning of another and being drowned" should be interpreted as an allegory rather than as an actual description of the way in which the murder was committed. (As it is, the literal meaning of אטיף is not "to drown another" but "to wash away" or "to allow to float".) As others, too, have pointed out, it is hardly likely that Hillel's intent had been to postulate that every murder victim must have been a murderer himself and that his murderer will be murdered in turn, for such an assumption would not be borne out by fact. Many an innocent man has been a murder victim and not every murderer dies by the hand of another killer. Rather, the thought Hillel wanted to express must have been as follows: Even though a murder may be, in fact, an execution of a Divinely-ordained death sentence, the murderer is still subject to God's judgment for his crime. "The great Master of the Universe has all things at His service, even folly and crime" (Prov. 26:10).

8. This is an enumeration of things which may seem eminently desirable to many but which can have an adverse effect on those who possess them. Next, by way of contrast, there are listed a number of values which are all associated with Torah and which bring happiness in direct proportion to the extent to which they are present.

מרבה בשר refers to obesity resulting from rich foods.

זְמָה מַרְבֶּה עֲבָדִים מַרְבֶּה גָזֵל. מַרְבֶּה תוֹרָה מַרְבֶּה חַיִּים מַרְבֶּה יְשִׁיבָה מַרְבֶּה חָכְמָה מַרְבֶּה עֵצָה מַרְבֶּה תְבוּנָה מַרְבֶּה צְדָקָה מַרְבֶּה שָׁלוֹם קָנָה שֵׁם טוֹב קָנָה לְעַצְמוֹ קָנָה לוֹ דִבְרֵי תוֹרָה קָנָה לוֹ חַיֵּי הָעוֹלָם הַבָּא:

י רַבָּן יוֹחָנָן בֶּן־זַבַּאי קִבֵּל מֵהִלֵּל וּמִשַּׁמַּאי. הוּא הָיָה אוֹמֵר, אִם לָמַדְתָּ תוֹרָה הַרְבֵּה אַל־תַּחֲזִיק טוֹבָה לְעַצְמֶךָ כִּי לְכָךְ נוֹצַרְתָּ: · חֲמִשָּׁה תַלְמִידִים הָיוּ לוֹ לְרַבָּן יוֹחָנָן בֶּן־זַבַּאי · וְאֵלּוּ הֵן (רַבִּי) אֱלִיעֶזֶר בֶּן־הוֹרְקָנוֹם (רַבִּי) יְהוֹשֻׁעַ בֶּן־חֲנַנְיָא (רַבִּי) יוֹסֵי הַכֹּהֵן רַבִּי שִׁמְעוֹן בֶּן־נְתַנְאֵל (וְרַבִּי) אֶלְעָזָר בֶּן־עֲרָךְ:

יא הוּא הָיָה מוֹנֶה שִׁבְחָם· (רַבִּי) אֱלִיעֶזֶר בֶּן־הוֹרְקָנוֹם בּוֹר סוּד שֶׁאֵינוֹ מְאַבֵּד טִפָּה (רַבִּי) יְהוֹשֻׁעַ בֶּן־חֲנַנְיָא אַשְׁרֵי יוֹלַדְתּוֹ (רַבִּי) יוֹסֵי הַכֹּהֵן חָסִיד (רַבִּי) שִׁמְעוֹן בֶּן־נְתַנְאֵל יְרֵא חֵטְא (רַבִּי) אֶלְעָזָר בֶּן־עֲרָךְ כְּמַעְיָן הַמִּתְגַּבֵּר:

יב הוּא הָיָה אוֹמֵר, אִם יִהְיוּ כָּל־חַכְמֵי יִשְׂרָאֵל בְּכַף מֹאזְנַיִם וֶאֱלִיעֶזֶר בֶּן־הוֹרְקָנוֹם בְּכַף שְׁנִיָּה מַכְרִיעַ אֶת־כֻּלָּם: אַבָּא שָׁאוּל אוֹמֵר מִשְּׁמוֹ, אִם יִהְיוּ כָּל־חַכְמֵי יִשְׂרָאֵל בְּכַף מֹאזְנַיִם וֶאֱלִיעֶזֶר בֶּן־הוֹרְקָנוֹם אַף עִמָּהֶם וְאֶלְעָזָר בֶּן־עֲרָךְ בְּכַף שְׁנִיָּה מַכְרִיעַ אֶת־כֻּלָּם:

מרבה תורה: The more the Torah will be acquired in theory and observed in practice, the more will human existence become life in the true, genuine sense of the word.

מרבה ישיבה may be applicable to teacher and disciple alike, for not only the disciple but also the teacher will profit in the process of teaching. As he teaches, the instructor finds that his ideas grow clearer and more logical in their formulation and expression, and the questions and comments of alert disciples add to his knowledge. As one of our Sages put it, "It is from my

more larceny; the more Torah, the more life; the more study, the more wisdom; the more counsel, the more understanding; the more devotion to duty, the more peace. One who has acquired a good name has made an acquisition for himself; one who has acquired the words of Torah for himself has acquired Eternal Life for himself.

9. Rabbi Yochanan ben Zakkai received [the tradition] from Hillel and Shammai. He used to say: If you have learned much Torah, do not pride yourself in it, for this is the purpose for which you were created.

10. Rabbi Yochanan ben Zakkai had five disciples; namely, Rabbi Eliezer ben Horkenos, Rabbi Yehoshua ben Chananyah, Rabbi Yosé the Priest, Rabbi Shimon ben Nethanel and Rabbi Elazar ben Arach.

11. He used to enumerate their merits: Rabbi Eliezer ben Horkenos is a whitewashed cistern which loses not a drop. Rabbi Yehoshua ben Chananyah: happy is she who bore him. Rabbi Yosé the Priest is truly pious; Rabbi Shimon ben Nethanel is sin-fearing; Rabbi Elazar ben Arach is like a spring which steadily increases its flow.

12. He used to say: If all the sages of Israel were in one scale of the balance and Eliezer ben Horkenos in the other, he would outweigh them all. Abba Shaul said in his name: If all the sages of Israel, including Eliezer ben Horkenos, were in one scale of the balance, and Elazar ben Arach in the other, he would outweigh them all.

---

disciples that I have learned the most" אמר ר׳ חנינא הרבה למדתי מרבותי ומחברי יותר

מרבותי ומתלמידי יותר מכולם "Much have I learned from my teachers, still more from my colleagues, but most of all from my disciples" (Taanith 7a).

קנה לו שם טוב: Any other personal attainments, including ethical and spiritual values, will also benefit others to a great extent. But the profit inherent in a good name is of benefit chiefly, indeed almost exclusively, to him who has acquired it and will remain his on earth even after he himself has departed.

קנה לו דברי תורה implies that the individual has absorbed the words of the Torah to such a degree that they have become part and parcel of his thoughts and emotions and that he has learned how to apply them in study and in his personal development. According to the Sages, once the individual has reached this stage, the words of the Torah become "his own".

9–12. In many cases the moral merit of one with less mental ability who has acquired only a modest amount of learning is greater by far than that of a superior intellect who has succeeded in gathering a great amount of knowledge. For the man of less mental ability can acquire his modest amount of knowledge only by dint of extraordinary effort and devotion. To the brilliant

יג אָמַר לָהֶם, צְאוּ וּרְאוּ אֵיזוֹ הִיא דֶרֶךְ טוֹבָה שֶׁיִּדְבַּק בָּהּ הָאָדָם,
רַבִּי אֱלִיעֶזֶר אוֹמֵר עַיִן טוֹבָה רַבִּי יְהוֹשֻׁעַ אוֹמֵר חָבֵר טוֹב רַבִּי
יוֹסֵי אוֹמֵר שָׁכֵן טוֹב רַבִּי שִׁמְעוֹן אוֹמֵר הָרוֹאֶה אֶת־הַנּוֹלָד רַבִּי
אֶלְעָזָר אוֹמֵר לֵב טוֹב: אָמַר לָהֶם רוֹאֶה אֲנִי אֶת־דִּבְרֵי אֶלְעָזָר
בֶּן־עֲרָךְ מִדִּבְרֵיכֶם שֶׁבִּכְלַל דְּבָרָיו דִּבְרֵיכֶם:

---

mind, on the other hand, learning comes very easily and his vast knowledge
is due primarily to his innate aptitude for learning. His sole merit is one which
he shares with the man of less ability whose store of knowledge is much
smaller than his; namely, that he has not wasted the talents with which his
Creator has endowed him but has used them in accordance with their purpose.
Coming from Yochanan ben Zakkai, who himself was a prototype of vast
erudition, who had many disciples and who, as a matter of fact, was the
bearer and preserver of the Torah after the collapse of the Jewish State, this
assertion is all the more significant. It was an admonition even to the most
proficient of his disciples to remain humble and to make the proper use of
their aptitudes, and at the same time a challenge to lesser talents to continue
their efforts undismayed. The five men described here in terms of their dom-
inant character traits were his most outstanding disciples. The posthumous
praise אשרי יולדתו which Yochanan ben Zakkai bestowed upon the mother of
Rabbi Yehoshua implies that Yehoshua was a man of moral and spiritual
excellence. It appears as if tradition was divided as to the relative merits
of Rabbi Eliezer ben Horkenos and Rabbi Elazar ben Arach, but this indecision
is only an apparent one. Actually, each has been accorded a position of equal
pre-eminence, equally justified, in his own field of knowledge. Rabbi Eliezer
ben Horkenos was superior in the faithful, loyal and accurate manner in
which he preserved the treasure of learning that had been handed down to
him. Rabbi Elazar ben Arach excelled in the ability to make broad application
of the Law and to draw from it a wealth of inferences for the shaping of
human affairs in accordance with the will of God as revealed to us. To be
sure, the qualities of ירא חטא and חסיד are demonstrated primarily in the
moral sphere, but they may be valid also in the area of scholarship. One who
is ירא חטא will be careful, above all, not to deliver himself of erroneous as-
sertions; conceit will not impel him to expound as a newly-discovered truth
an idea concerning which he himself still has secret doubts. When he realizes
the erroneous or even the doubtful character of a view he has propounded
he will not persist in it just because he once happened to set it forth. He will
never obstinately insist on his own views, but will be glad to be instructed by
others. One who is a perfect *chasid* will demonstrate his utter selflessness

13. He said to them: Go forth and see which is the good way to which a man should adhere. Rabbi Eliezer said: A good eye. Rabbi Yehoshua said: A good friend. Rabbi Yosé said: A good neighbor. Rabbi Shimon said: One who considers the consequences. Rabbi Elazar said: A good heart. He said to them: I prefer the words of Rabbi Elazar ben Arach to yours, because in his words yours are included.

---

also in the realm of scholarship. His sole concern will be the knowledge and the teaching of goodness and truth, regardless of whether the credit for its discovery will go to him or to some other man. Indeed, he will be glad to look into the view advanced by another, to test it, and to improve upon it; he will endeavor to find evidence and arguments in its support and will adopt it himself if it seems to him better than his own. We find innumerable instances of this character in the debates recorded in the Talmud.

13. Go forth into the realm of everyday life and search for a "way", a guiding principle to which a man should be able to adhere come what may in order to remain on the path that leads to the good. עין טובה, a "good eye" designates an attitude of kindness and good will toward all others, toward their concerns, their aspirations, their achievements and their possessions. A man with this attitude will rejoice when his fellow-man prospers; he will wish everyone well, and envy, jealousy, ill-will and rivalry will be utterly alien to him. "A good eye" should certainly keep us from placing obstacles into the path of the happiness and prosperity of our neighbor and should impel us gladly to do whatever may promote his welfare. It is self-evident that association with חבר טוב, a friend who desires only what is good, and—perhaps even more so because his proximity permits more frequent contact—with שכן טוב, a neighbor who desires only what is good, can provide us with a mighty bulwark against error and act as a potent help and support in our good endeavors. הרואה את הנולד : One who considers and foresees the consequences in whatever he may do will never become guilty of frivolous, irresponsible behavior. Fleeting attractions will not lead him astray, nor will immediate difficulties deter him from doing good. He will be able to foresee the bitter long-range consequences of sweet but fleeting pleasures; he will be mindful of the sense of bliss which can be purchased with every act of self-sacrificing devotion willingly performed, and therefore he will remain strong in the struggle against evil and mighty in doing good. The term לב טוב actually complies infinitely more than what is ordinarily thought of as a "good heart"; it involves much more that just kindness, readiness to perform good deeds and reluctance to turn down another's request. The term *lev* denotes a typically Jewish concept, the wellspring of *every* emotion, *every* aspiration, *every* endeavor, the source of *every* moral and spiritual impulse and tendency, even of all thought and character. Hence *lev* denotes the root and source of every

יד אָמַר לָהֶם, צְאוּ וּרְאוּ אֵיזוֹ הִיא דֶּרֶךְ רָעָה שֶׁיִּתְרַחֵק
מִמֶּנָּה הָאָדָם, רַבִּי אֱלִיעֶזֶר אוֹמֵר עַיִן רָעָה רַבִּי יְהוֹשֻׁעַ אוֹמֵר
חָבֵר רָע רַבִּי יוֹסֵי אוֹמֵר שָׁכֵן רָע רַבִּי שִׁמְעוֹן אוֹמֵר הַלֹּוֶה
וְאֵינוֹ מְשַׁלֵּם, אֶחָד הַלֹּוֶה מִן הָאָדָם כְּלֹוֶה מִן הַמָּקוֹם שֶׁנֶּאֱמַר
לֹוֶה רָשָׁע וְלֹא יְשַׁלֵּם וְצַדִּיק חוֹנֵן וְנוֹתֵן, רַבִּי אֶלְעָזָר אוֹמֵר
לֵב רָע: אָמַר לָהֶם, רוֹאֶה אֲנִי אֶת דִּבְרֵי אֶלְעָזָר בֶּן עֲרָךְ
מִדִּבְרֵיכֶם שֶׁבִּכְלָל דְּבָרָיו דִּבְרֵיכֶם:

טו הֵם אָמְרוּ שְׁלֹשָׁה דְבָרִים. רַבִּי אֱלִיעֶזֶר אוֹמֵר, יְהִי כְבוֹד
חֲבֵרָךְ חָבִיב עָלֶיךָ כְּשֶׁלָּךְ וְאַל תְּהִי נוֹחַ לִכְעֹס וְשׁוּב יוֹם אֶחָד
לִפְנֵי מִיתָתָךְ וֶהֱוֵה מִתְחַמֵּם כְּנֶגֶד אוּרָן שֶׁל חֲכָמִים וֶהֱוֵה זָהִיר
בְּגַחַלְתָּן שֶׁלֹּא תִכָּוֶה שֶׁנְּשִׁיכָתָן נְשִׁיכַת שׁוּעָל וַעֲקִיצָתָן עֲקִיצַת
עַקְרָב וּלְחִישָׁתָן לְחִישַׁת שָׂרָף וְכָל דִּבְרֵיהֶם כְּגַחֲלֵי אֵשׁ:

---

endeavor and every achievement. If, therefore, the "heart" is "good"; if the "heart" is receptive only to the good and directed to the good alone, the *whole* man will be under the rule of the good; he will not be *capable* of desiring evil and will be ready for every good endeavor. Thus the characterization *lev tov* truly defines all the paths and devices that lead toward the good.

14. עין רעה, "an evil eye", denotes the opposite attitude. A man with "an evil eye" will not only feel no joy but experience actual distress when others prosper, and will rejoice when others suffer loss and sorrow, grief and misery. A person of this character, as well as לב רע, שכן רע, חבר רע represent so great a danger to our own moral purity that we are not just forbidden to associate with them but are told יתרחק ממנה, to keep far away from them. We must avoid any influence that may tarnish the character of our own "eye" and heart and bring us closer to evil friends and evil neighbors. הלוה ואינו משלם. This characterization implies the antithesis of the thoughtful attitude which leads a man to weigh the consequences of whatever he is about to do. It refers to the attitude of irresponsible thoughtlessness of him who never stops to consider the heavy burden of debt which any neglect of duty places upon our shoulders. Whatever we receive from this world—and indeed, the entire Universe makes countless contributions to every breath we take on earth—is only a loan granted us to help us strive for and bring about those goals by means of which we advance the welfare of God's world in accordance with His will as revealed to us in His Law. No one exists solely for himself, and

14.   He said to them: Go and see which is the evil way from which a man should stand apart. Rabbi Eliezer said: An evil eye. Rabbi Yehoshua said: A bad friend. Rabbi Yosé said: A bad neighbor. Rabbi Shimon said: One who borrows and does not repay, regardless of whether he borrows from the Omnipresent or from men, for it is said, "A lawless man borrows and never repays his debt but a righteous man deals generously and is a giver." (Psalms 37:21). Rabbi Elazar said: An evil heart. Thereupon he said to them: I prefer the words of Rabbi Elazar ben Arakh to yours, because in his words yours are included.

15.   They said three things: Rabbi Eliezer said: Let the honor of your friend be as dear to you as your own and be not easily moved to anger and repent one day before your death. Warm yourself by the fire of the sages but beware of their glowing coals lest you burn yourself, for the proscription in force as regards any injury done them is [like] the bite of the fox, the sting of the scorpion and the hiss of the serpent, and all their words are like coals of fire.

---

the greater the loan he has been granted, the greater his obligation and the sum total of achievement that may be expected of him in return. Therefore he who idles away his time in this world, who pays no regard to law or duty, who lives only for *himself* and for the satisfaction of his own needs, desires and caprices and is content to build his happiness at the expense of his fellowmen without ever thinking of the return which he is expected to make and for which God has created him, borrows from the world without repaying his debt. With every breath he takes he becomes more deeply indebted to the world, and the greater the wealth and pleasures he has borrowed, the greater and the more crushing will be the bankruptcy of his life which will be charged against him by God and by the world. There is hardly a better metaphor than לוה ואינו משלם to denote thoughtlessness as opposed to צדיק חונן. רואה את הנולד ונוחן. The righteous man is not so. Because he places his duty above all else and devotes his whole life to its fulfillment, striving solely to "do justice" to God and to His world, it is the world that owes him a debt of gratitude. And the fewer the goods and pleasures he has received from the world, the more does the world owe him, and it is usually as a major "creditor" that the *tzadik* departs from the earth.

15.   Let the honor of your fellow man be as dear to you as your own. Therefore do not be quick to anger, lest your outburst of temper violate his honor. Rather than feeling anger at your friend's conduct, think of your own shortcomings and work unceasingly at the improvement of your own character. "Repent one day before your death;" regard every day as if it were your last, and mend your ways today because you have no way of knowing whether

טו רַבִּי יְהוֹשֻׁעַ אוֹמֵר, עַיִן הָרַע וְיֵצֶר הָרַע וְשִׂנְאַת הַבְּרִיּוֹת מוֹצִיאִין אֶת־הָאָדָם מִן־הָעוֹלָם:

טז רַבִּי יוֹסֵי אוֹמֵר, יְהִי מָמוֹן חֲבֵרְךָ חָבִיב עָלֶיךָ כְּשֶׁלָּךְ וְהַתְקֵן עַצְמְךָ לִלְמוֹד תּוֹרָה שֶׁאֵינָהּ יְרֻשָּׁה־לָךְ וְכָל־מַעֲשֶׂיךָ יִהְיוּ לְשֵׁם שָׁמָיִם:

---

you will still be alive tomorrow. You can hardly do more for the improvement of your character than make yourself familiar with teachings of the Sages and with the example they have set and follow their precepts. For their words give you not only light but warmth, supplying you with vigorous life and strength for every good endeavor. But beware of their "glowing coals!" Many a word they have uttered and many a precept they have ordained may seem to you outworn, extinct, "burned out", as it were, because the "fire" seems to have gone from it, and you may lay your hand irreverently upon it and toy with it at your pleasure. But it behooves you to look out, for not a word or precept of the Sages can ever become obsolete or lose its fiery force. That which seems burned out to you still holds within it an eternal flame and will burn the hand that would dare touch it with irreverence. The power of the pro-scription in force with regard to the words and precepts of the Sages is fre-quently portrayed in our sacred literature by the metaphor of the "bite" or "sting" that will afflict him who would dare wilfully to violate it. וכל דבריהם כגחלי אש they never turn into *gechalim* but remain *gachale esh* forever.

16. Any one of these three things is sufficient to cause a man to lose that position which he would be qualified to fill in the world: An evil eye which can never rejoice as long as it sees others prosper; an evil passion or vice which a man has permitted to gain ascendancy over him; and misanthropy which makes him scorn his fellowmen, making him aware only of the evil in others and causing him to overlook the good which is never entirely absent in any human being. The Sages use a beautiful expression to describe men in their admonitions to us to love mankind and to shun malice. They call our fellow-men בריות, "creatures" of God, and they employ this term to include all men, without exception, thus stressing the motive which is at the basis of the behest to love all men. We are to respect in a human being, whoever and whatever he may be, the "creature of God" and we must not deny this love to any fellowman, seeing that we were all made by the same Creator.

17. These three maxims are teachings that should guide us and keep us in the paths of goodness and truth in our relations with other human beings, in our attitude toward the Torah and, indeed, in every other aspect of our lives as well. Even as we take care to preserve our own wealth and to increase

16.   Rabbi Yehoshua said: An evil eye, evil passion and misanthropy put a man out of the world.

17.   Rabbi Yosé said: Let the property of your friend be as dear to you as your own; charge yourself to study the Torah, for it does not come to you by inheritence, and let everything you do be done to honor God.

---

it, so, too, it is not enough merely not to be envious of the wealth of our fellow-man or to view it with unconcern; we should be happy when he prospers, we must not stand by idly if we can guard him from injury and we should rejoice at any opportunity we may have to help him improve his lot.

We may have had the good fortune to have been born and reared by parents and in an environment that have not allowed us to remain strangers to the knowledge of the Torah and to the way of life that it demands. Indeed, the importance of the teaching and example set by the home in the acquisition of Torah in both theory and practice cannot be overestimated. However, we must always remember that the mere circumstance that the Torah has thus become our "inheritance" does not spell the completion of our own work in behalf of the Torah. In the case of wealth inherited from our parents we may indeed be satisfied with our inheritance as it stands, and while we will be careful to keep it intact, we are under no obligation to increase it by our own efforts. But in the case of Torah knowledge inherited by way of the training and guidance we have received from our parents, we must never be content to stand still. Rather, it is incumbent upon us, throughout our lives, to make continuous advances in the limitless realm of Torah wisdom, and the greater the fundamental inheritance of Torah knowledge that we have been privileged to take with us from the home of our parents into our own independent lives, the greater will be our obligation to continue building upon these foundations and by dint of our own efforts and the application of all our mental powers; to increase our portion in the everlasting spiritual treasure that the Torah is. It is self-understood, of course, that this admonition applies also, and indeed all the more so, to one who has not been so fortunate as to receive much Torah wisdom—or even any Torah knowledge at all—from the hands of his parents. התקן עצמך ללמוד תורה: discipline and train yourself, charge yourself to study the Torah. For the Torah is the spiritual treasure that belongs to the entire Jewish nation, a treasure in which every Jew is meant and required to assume an active share in accordance with his abilities. One who was not fortunate enough to receive training to this end in childhood is obligated to make up for this deficiency on his own accord in adolescence and adulthood, שאינה ירושה לך for the extent to which we fulfill our destiny for Torah must not be made merely dependent on the size of the Torah inheritance we have received from our parents. וכל מעשיך יהיו לשם שמים What-

יח רַבִּי שִׁמְעוֹן אוֹמֵר, הֱוֵי זָהִיר בִּקְרִיאַת שְׁמַע וּבִתְפִלָּה וּכְשֶׁאַתָּה מִתְפַּלֵּל אַל־תַּעַשׂ תְּפִלָּתְךָ קֶבַע אֶלָּא רַחֲמִים וְתַחֲנוּנִים לִפְנֵי הַמָּקוֹם שֶׁנֶּאֱמַר כִּי־חַנּוּן וְרַחוּם הוּא אֶרֶךְ אַפַּיִם וְרַב־חֶסֶד וְנִחָם עַל־הָרָעָה · וְאַל־תְּהִי רָשָׁע בִּפְנֵי עַצְמֶךָ :

יט רַבִּי אֶלְעָזָר אוֹמֵר, הֱוֵי שָׁקוּד לִלְמוֹד תּוֹרָה וְדַע מַה־שֶּׁתָּשִׁיב לְאֶפִּיקוֹרוֹס וְדַע לִפְנֵי מִי אַתָּה עָמֵל וּמִי הוּא בַּעַל מְלַאכְתְּךָ שֶׁיְּשַׁלֶּם־לָךְ שְׂכַר פְּעֻלָּתֶךָ :

כ רַבִּי טַרְפוֹן אוֹמֵר, הַיּוֹם קָצֵר וְהַמְּלָאכָה מְרֻבָּה וְהַפּוֹעֲלִים עֲצֵלִים וְהַשָּׂכָר הַרְבֵּה וּבַעַל הַבַּיִת דּוֹחֵק :

---

ever we do, we are to do *leshem shamayim*. Even the good that we do loses much of its value if we do not do it from a pure and God-oriented sense of duty, or if we are motivated in our action by expectations of personal advantage or honor. Indeed, the motive implied by the term *leshem shamayim* should dominate every aspect of our lives, even that phase which is devoted primarily to personal maintenance and to the care of our physical selves so that this side of our lives, too, may be lifted, as it should be, beyond the borders of the physical and the selfish into the realm of moral achievement and duty fulfilled in the service of God. In this manner all the phases of our lives will be preserved for the ways of goodness and purity that are in accord with our duty. As is stated in Prov. 3:6: בכל דרכיך דעהו והוא יישר ארחתיך "Have your mind directed to God in all your ways, and He will direct your path."

18. The שמע is addressed to you and therefore is clearly meant for you to take to your heart as you read it in prayerful reverence. In the same manner the words of prayer, though formally addressed directly to God, are designed to be taken to the heart of the worshipper so that their content may become part of his heart and mind and that the confessions, petitions and high resolutions expressed in them may become his own. It is only if he permits prayer thus to affect him that he can expect his prayer to be effective before God; he cannot expect that his prayer should perform that service for him if he performs it as קבע as an appointed routine act which was imposed upon him from some outside source and which can be properly discharged by rote recitation. ואל תהי רשע וכו' Do not allow yourself to be taken in by the erroneous idea advanced by alien philosophies that man on his own must of necessity be crushed by the weight of his guilt and that it is solely through the gracious

18. Rabbi Shimon said; Be careful in reading the *Shema* and in prayer, and when you pray, do not regard your prayer as an appointed routine but as an appeal for mercy and favor before the Omnipresent, as it is said: "For He is gracious and full of mercy, slow to anger and abundant in loving-kindness, and relenting of the evil decree"; and do not consider yourself as wicked when left to depend on your own efforts.

19. Rabbi Elazar said: Be diligent to study the Torah and know what to answer him who treats the Law with scorn. Know, too, before Whose countenance you are laboring and who your Employer is, who will pay you the reward for your labor.

20. Rabbi Tarphon said: The day is short, the task is great, the workmen are sluggish, the reward is great, and the Employer is insistent.

---

intercession of another that he can gain control over evil and be delivered from the burden of his sin. The one person able to free you from sin and to raise you to the level of pure and free devotion to duty in the service of God is none other than you yourself, and prayer uttered in the proper spirit will be that source from which you will derive the strength and Divine aid that you need in all your efforts at self-liberation from evil.

19. Only one who is not thoroughly familiar with the Torah will be afraid of the arguments advanced by אפיקורסים. One who has studied and continues to study the law adequately and thoroughly and delves into it with devotion will clearly see the speciousness and the invalidity of their allegations and will know that their arguments are founded on ignorance and distortion of facts. Know, too, under Whose supervision it is that you complete your life's task in study and practice alike and that He in Whose service you are laboring will not let your faithful toil go unrewarded.

20. Life is short and the task that each individual must complete on earth is great, yet men are slow to complete their work. They race in hot pursuit of pleasure as if they had only one day left to live but they are as slow in fulfilling their duty as if they had an eternity at their disposal for this purpose. Yet the reward we may expect is great and rich; it is a sense of God's approval and of His blessed nearness, the happy knowledge of duty loyally discharged, Divine aid in this ·life and bliss in the world to come. And if all this should not be sufficient incentive to conquer our laziness, then certainly the thought of the service we owe our Supreme Employer should spur us to vigorous action. For our Employer, Who is none other than God Himself, will not permit the work which He wants to see done to remain uncompleted because of our sluggishness. That which his workmen will refuse to do with

כא הוּא הָיָה אוֹמֵר, לֹא עָלֶיךָ הַמְּלָאכָה לִגְמוֹר וְלֹא־אַתָּה בֶן־
חוֹרִין לְהִבָּטֵל מִמֶּנָּה אִם לָמַדְתָּ תּוֹרָה הַרְבֵּה נוֹתְנִין לְךָ שָׂכָר
הַרְבֵּה וְנֶאֱמָן הוּא בַּעַל מְלַאכְתְּךָ שֶׁיְּשַׁלֵּם לְךָ שְׂכַר פְּעֻלָּתֶךָ וְדַע
שֶׁמַּתַּן שְׂכָרָן שֶׁל־צַדִּיקִים לֶעָתִיד לָבוֹא: רבי חנניא בן עקשיה וכו׳

פרק שלישי
כל ישראל וכו׳.

א עֲקַבְיָא בֶּן־מַהֲלַלְאֵל אוֹמֵר הִסְתַּכֵּל בִּשְׁלשָׁה דְבָרִים וְאֵין
אַתָּה בָא לִידֵי עֲבֵרָה דַּע מֵאַיִן בָּאתָ וּלְאָן אַתָּה הוֹלֵךְ וְלִפְנֵי מִי
אַתָּה עָתִיד לִתֵּן דִּין וְחֶשְׁבּוֹן · מֵאַיִן בָּאתָ מִטִּפָּה סְרוּחָה, וּלְאָן
אַתָּה הוֹלֵךְ לִמְקוֹם עָפָר רִמָּה וְתוֹלֵעָה, וְלִפְנֵי מִי אַתָּה עָתִיד
לִתֵּן דִּין וְחֶשְׁבּוֹן לִפְנֵי מֶלֶךְ מַלְכֵי הַמְּלָכִים הַקָּדוֹשׁ בָּרוּךְ הוּא·

---

loyalty and dispatch, He will know how to force through despite their aversion
for effort. The way of His world-wide rule is such that He is amply supplied
with industrious servants and willing workers for His world order.

21.   The good that God wants to see accomplished on earth is not all meant
for one individual to complete. Any human being can contribute only one
fraction to the whole, and it is only through the united efforts of all that
the salvation to come into flower on earth can be brought about. But even
though no one individual is capable of doing all the work by himself, each
and every man is obligated to make his contribution to the full extent of his
abilities. No one has a right to argue, "What I can do is but so little," and
sit back idly. True, your contribution may not amount to much when measured against the task at hand, but as far as you are concerned it is very great;
indeed, it represents the total content of your life. Even if you should remain
alone in your good endeavors, continue to perform your round of duty faithfully and painstakingly, and leave it to your Employer to add your loyal and
honest contribution to all the other resources which He employs to accomplish
the work of salvation ordained through His will. If you accomplish a great
deal, be it in study or in practice, you will receive your reward. Even if the
greatest of your contributions is still not in excess of what was expected of
you in accordance with the abilities and resources with which you have been
endowed, and even if the utmost in devotion on your part yields only a fraction of the whole to be accomplished, your reward will be great nevertheless

21.   He used to say: It is not up to you to complete the work, yet you are not free to desist from it. If you have studied much Torah, much reward will be given you, and your Employer is faithful to pay you the reward for your work; but know that the reward of the righteous will be in the world to come.

CHAPTER III

1.   Akavyah ben Mahalalel said: Reflect upon three things, and you will not come into the grip of sin: Know whence you came, where you are going, and before Whom you will have to render account and reckoning. *Whence you came*—from a putrid drop. *Where are you going*—to a place of dust, of decay and vermin. *Before whom you will have to render account and reckoning*—Before the Supreme King of Kings, the Holy One, blessed be He.

---

in terms of the measure of your contribution. But do not seek to measure the reward for good deeds by what man receives in this world. The true compensation is in store for him only in the world to come.

CHAPTER III

1.   Most of our sins are outgrowths of an over-emphasis of the sensuous physical aspects of our being and of their demands, and of a disregard or at least, of insufficient regard for the spiritual and moral facets of our personality and its purpose. We must bear in mind at all times that, someday, we will be called upon to render strict accounting for the manner in which we fulfilled, or failed to fulfill, this our purpose. We are reminded, too, that our whole sensuous bodily being is doomed to decay from the very beginning. It is only the spiritual and moral element within us, that part of us which is conscious of its destiny and is capable of decision and judgment over our actions, that will survive the decay of the purely physical and will enter into eternity. There it will render accounting as to the extent to which it has achieved its destiny on earth, and as to the manner in which it has husbanded the resources and the faculties with which it had been endowed for this purpose. And the One before Whom this accounting is to be made is none other than He Who is the absolute Ruler over all things and Who is fully able to ensure for Himself the ultimate total obedience of all things and all men.

ב רַבִּי חֲנִינָא סְגַן הַכֹּהֲנִים אוֹמֵר, הֱוֵה מִתְפַּלֵּל בִּשְׁלוֹמָהּ שֶׁל־
מַלְכוּת שֶׁאִלְמָלֵא מוֹרָאָהּ אִישׁ אֶת־רֵעֵהוּ חַיִּים בְּלָעוֹ:

ג רַבִּי חֲנַנְיָא בֶּן־תְּרַדְיוֹן אוֹמֵר, שְׁנַיִם שֶׁיּוֹשְׁבִין וְאֵין בֵּינֵיהֶם
דִּבְרֵי תוֹרָה הֲרֵי זֶה מוֹשַׁב לֵצִים שֶׁנֶּאֱמַר וּבְמוֹשַׁב לֵצִים לֹא יָשָׁב ·
אֲבָל שְׁנַיִם שֶׁיּוֹשְׁבִין וְיֵשׁ בֵּינֵיהֶם דִּבְרֵי תוֹרָה שְׁכִינָה שְׁרוּיָה
בֵּינֵיהֶם שֶׁנֶּאֱמַר אָז נִדְבְּרוּ יִרְאֵי יְיָ אִישׁ אֶל־רֵעֵהוּ וַיַּקְשֵׁב יְיָ וַיִּשְׁמָע
וַיִּכָּתֵב סֵפֶר זִכָּרוֹן לְפָנָיו לְיִרְאֵי יְיָ וּלְחֹשְׁבֵי שְׁמוֹ · אֵין לִי אֶלָּא
שְׁנַיִם, מִנַּיִן אֲפִלּוּ אֶחָד שֶׁיּוֹשֵׁב וְעוֹסֵק בַּתּוֹרָה שֶׁהַקָּדוֹשׁ בָּרוּךְ
הוּא קוֹבֵעַ לוֹ שָׂכָר שֶׁנֶּאֱמַר יֵשֵׁב בָּדָד וְיִדֹּם כִּי נָטַל עָלָיו:

---

2. Actually, the three considerations given in the Mishna immediately preceding should be sufficient deterrents from all sin and excesses, even without
the intervention of a human authority and, in fact, they are sufficient for him
who has remained pure. But human society is still in that state of moral im-
perfection where it fears even the lowliest visible human authority more than
the unseen omnipotence of the King of Kings. Hence the orderly, undisturbed
development towards that happiness to which all men are entitled is dependent
upon the preservation of the authority of earthly powers and officials. Therefore, respect the authorities of the place and of the country in which you
reside, and pray for their welfare. This duty was enjoined upon the Jew when
he first left his homeland to dwell in the midst of the many nations of the
world (see Jeremiah 29:7). We are obliged not only לדרוש, to do everything
to promote the welfare of the countries in which we live, but actually להתפלל,
to pray, before God and as good citizens, with sincere devotion known and
recognized as such by Him alone, to beseech Him for the welfare of the government. For if the government could not exercise its authority, the hand of
everyone would be lifted up against all the others and all of society would
disintegrate

3. לצים are the foes of God's Law who, by glibness of speech, undermine
the respect and reverence in which the Torah should be held. Now it is evident
from the words אז נדברו which is quoted and ליראי ה' ולחשבי שמו in the sentence
explained here, that the term *divrei Torah* should be construed in a broader
sense than just the "words" of Torah, the study and explanation of God's
Law. For the verse speaks not of למודי ה', but of יראי ה' and חושבי שמו, and

2. Rabbi Chaninah, the Assistant of the High-Priests, said: Pray for the welfare of the government, for were it not for the fear of it, men would swallow each other alive.

3. Rabbi Chananyah, ben Teradyon, said: If two sit together and words of Torah are not exchanged between them, this is a "seat of the scornful", as it is said, "And he never sat there where the scornful sit." But if two sit together and interchange words of Torah, the Presence of God abides with them, for it is said, "They that feared *God* spoke with one another, and *God* noted and heard, and a book of remembrance was written before Him for those who fear *God* and think upon His Name." This verse refers to two people. How, then, can we know that even if one person sits and occupies himself with the Torah, the Holy One, blessed be He, will determine a reward for him? Because it is said: "Though he may sit alone, let his mind be at rest, for he has received that which was appointed for him."

---

these are designations denoting practical fulfillment rather than mere theoretical study. According to the Sages, too (see Berachoth 6a), the חושבי שמו are those whose intentions are upon the fulfillment of a mitzvah. On this they base the teaching that חשב אדם לעשות מצוה ונאנס ולא עשאה מעלה עליו הכתוב כאילו עשאה, if a person had in mind to perform a mitzvah, then, even if he would be prevented from carrying out his good intention, it would be counted as if he had actually succeeded in fulfilling his high resolve. Or, as we read in Kiddushin 40a, מחשבה טובה מצרפה למעשה, any good thought that, through unavoidable circumstances, could not be translated into action, is nevertheless counted by God as part of the good deed. Besides, the term *divrei Torah* cannot properly be interpreted here in its narrow sense. The place where people deliberate on how best to perform a mitzvah is certainly not a *moshav letzim*. As a matter of fact, Yaavetz notes in connection with this Mishna that even a discussion of anything necessary for human life cannot possibly be classed as a *moshav letzim*. Rather, our Mishna refers to people who, instead of occupying themselves with *divrei Torah*, talk דברים בטלים, of such things as are of absolutely no use and no value. We believe therefore, that the meaning of *divrei Torah* would include not only the actual teaching contained in the Torah itself, but also everything else that derives from the Torah for the fashioning of human affairs, as well as anything that is shaped in accordance with the Torah's teachings and is fulfilled in accordance with the spirit of the Law of God. But those who, instead of turning their thoughts to the serious things of life, in the broadest sense, waste their leisure time on frivolity and worthless trifles, their assembly is indeed classed by the Mishna as *moshav letzim* even

ד רַבִּי שִׁמְעוֹן אוֹמֵר, שְׁלֹשָׁה שֶׁאָכְלוּ עַל שֻׁלְחָן אֶחָד וְלֹא
אָמְרוּ עָלָיו דִּבְרֵי תוֹרָה כְּאִלּוּ אָכְלוּ מִזִּבְחֵי מֵתִים שֶׁנֶּאֱמַר כִּי
כָל־שֻׁלְחָנוֹת מָלְאוּ קִיא צוֹאָה בְּלִי מָקוֹם · אֲבָל שְׁלֹשָׁה שֶׁאָכְלוּ
עַל שֻׁלְחָן אֶחָד וְאָמְרוּ עָלָיו דִּבְרֵי תוֹרָה כְּאִלּוּ אָכְלוּ מִשֻּׁלְחָנוֹ
שֶׁל־מָקוֹם · שֶׁנֶּאֱמַר וַיְדַבֵּר אֵלַי זֶה הַשֻּׁלְחָן אֲשֶׁר לִפְנֵי יְיָ׃

ה רַבִּי חֲנִינָא בֶּן־חֲכִינַאי אוֹמֵר, הַנֵּעוֹר בַּלַּיְלָה וְהַמְהַלֵּךְ בַּדֶּרֶךְ
יְחִידִי וּמְפַנֶּה לִבּוֹ לְבַטָּלָה הֲרֵי זֶה מִתְחַיֵּב בְּנַפְשׁוֹ׃

---

if, in fact, their words are not, strictly taken, in contempt of the Torah. For
the failure as such to discuss *divrei Torah* is in itself an indication of disregard
for the Torah, since it is said: 'במושב לצים לא ישב כי אם בתורת ה' חפצו וגו, "He
never sat in the seat of the letzim, because, instead, he strove after the teaching
of the Lord, and all his thoughts moved within His teachings both day and
night." We read in Sanhedrin 99a that כל שאפשר לו לעסוק בתורה ואינו עוסק,
"He who could occupy himself with the Torah but does not do so is counted
among those of whom it is said: כי דבר ה' בזה".

4. Sanhedrin 3a presumes the knowledge of the Law among our people to
be so widespread that any three adult Jewish males are deemed capable and
qualified to act as a judicial tribunal to decide on matters of property, for
אי אפשר דלית בהו חד דגמיר it is taken for granted that surely at least one of these
three must have adequate knowledge of what is right and wrong according
to the Law. Therefore, if three eat together at a table, it is presumed that
at least one of them will not be entirely ignorant of the Teaching of God. If
nevertheless, their meal will not be enhanced with even one word of Torah,
of things of the spirit, then that meal was not worthy of a human being. In
such a case, the meal, instead of being a part of the spiritual and moral aspects
of living, is only an act of animal gratification in which the purely human
element is not seen. זבחי מתים are sacrificial meals that were offered to the
idols representing that lack of freedom which the heathens worshipped. It is
the term employed in the Psalms (Psalm 106:28) to denote the ceremonial
meals dedicated to *Peor*, the god of degenerate shamelessness. זה השולחן אשר לפני ה'
(Ezechiel 41:22) refers to the *mizbe'ach* which had been named and described
previously. From this, Berachoth 55a derives the teaching that "As long as
the Temple still stood, the altar wrought atonement for Israel." Indeed, we
may rightly say that the prime feature distinguishing man from the beast and
rendering him civilized is the table at which men eat together. When the

4.   Rabbi Shimon said: If three ate at a table and did not utter one word of Torah there, it is as if they had partaken of meal offerings made to the dead, for it is said, "All the tables are filled with execrable things without room [for aught else]." But if three have eaten at a table and uttered words of Torah there, it is as if they had eaten at the table of God, for it is said, "He said to me: This is the table which is before the countenance of *God*."

5.   Rabbi Chanina ben Chachinai, said: He who keeps awake at night, and he who goes on his way alone, and makes room in his heart for idleness, sins against his own soul.

---

animal eats, it thinks only of itself and views any other animal that eats with it as a rival. Man is not so; he will not even enjoy his meal if he must eat it alone. He feels a real need to eat together with others. And the act of sharing a meal with his fellow-man reminds him at once that even the physical aspects of his body were not created for his own pleasure. This warning takes on even greater meaning and solemnity by virtue of the ברכת הזמון, the joint grace after meals to which our sages have attached so much significance. If then, as is presumed in this passage of Tractate Berachoth, this sense of brotherhood finds expression in the fact that the master of the house prepares the table not only for himself and the members of his household but also for the poor and needy, and if, as our Mishna likewise presupposes, the physical enjoyment of food is accompanied by spiritual nourishment from the Word of God, that table is truly one consecrated to the cultivation of human virtues and Divine teachings of which it can be rightly said זה השולחן אשר לפני ה'. Those who dined at this table have, in fact, eaten from God's own board, as it were, since they have partaken not only of the physical food but also of the moral and spiritual nourishment which God has apportioned for man who serves Him. In like manner it is written concerning the priests who received for their sustenance the portions of the sacrifices consecrated by the altar: משולחן גבוה קזכו.

5.   A man who keeps awake at night because he cannot sleep, or one who walks on his way alone, has perfect, undisturbed leisure during those lone and wakeful hours. He who, instead of utilizing those quiet moments for serious meditation and reflection, wastes them on frivolous and idle thoughts, sins against his own soul. For in this manner he has cheated his soul of spiritual and moral gains which it would have had the opportunity thus to acquire, and, at the same time, he has exposed it to all the perils which idle thoughts so easily engender.

י רַבִּי נְחוּנְיָא בֶּן־הַקָּנָה אוֹמֵר, כָּל־הַמְקַבֵּל עָלָיו עוֹל תּוֹרָה
מַעֲבִירִין מִמֶּנּוּ עוֹל מַלְכוּת וְעוֹל דֶּרֶךְ אֶרֶץ וְכָל־הַפּוֹרֵק מִמֶּנּוּ
עוֹל תּוֹרָה נוֹתְנִין עָלָיו עוֹל מַלְכוּת וְעוֹל דֶּרֶךְ אֶרֶץ:

י רַבִּי חֲלַפְתָּא בֶּן־דּוֹסָא אִישׁ כְּפַר חֲנַנְיָא אוֹמֵר, עֲשָׂרָה
שֶׁיּוֹשְׁבִין וְעוֹסְקִין בַּתּוֹרָה שְׁכִינָה שְׁרוּיָה בֵּינֵיהֶם שֶׁנֶּאֱמַר
אֱלֹהִים נִצָּב בַּעֲדַת־אֵל · וּמִנַּיִן אֲפִילוּ חֲמִשָּׁה שֶׁנֶּאֱמַר וַאֲגֻדָּתוֹ
עַל־אֶרֶץ יְסָדָהּ · וּמִנַּיִן אֲפִילוּ שְׁלֹשָׁה שֶׁנֶּאֱמַר בְּקֶרֶב אֱלֹהִים
יִשְׁפֹּט · וּמִנַּיִן אֲפִילוּ שְׁנַיִם שֶׁנֶּאֱמַר אָז נִדְבְּרוּ יִרְאֵי יְיָ אִישׁ אֶל־
רֵעֵהוּ וַיַּקְשֵׁב יְיָ וַיִּשְׁמָע · וּמִנַּיִן אֲפִילוּ אֶחָד שֶׁנֶּאֱמַר בְּכָל־הַמָּקוֹם
אֲשֶׁר אַזְכִּיר אֶת־שְׁמִי אָבֹא אֵלֶיךָ וּבֵרַכְתִּיךָ:

ה רַבִּי אֶלְעָזָר אִישׁ בַּרְתּוֹתָא אוֹמֵר, תֶּן־לוֹ מִשֶּׁלּוֹ שֶׁאַתָּה

---

6. The Jew has a dual burden to bear. First, there is that additional burden, which the government of the country in which he resides imposes upon him because it treats him as a stranger within its territory. Secondly, along with all others, he bears the burden which day-to-day secular living entails. He who freely submits to the yoke of the Torah, who will put all of his thoughts and actions in the service of the Torah, will not feel oppressed by these burdens. In fact, he will accept and bear them cheerfully as part of the purpose ordained for him by God Himself. He who shrugs off the Torah service which he owes his God, even as he would cast off a yoke imposed upon him, may indeed imagine that he has freed himself. However, he fails to see that it is precisely under these circumstances that all the other cares of his life as a citizen and as a member of society will weigh upon him as crushing burdens. For once he has cast off the yoke of the Law, he will lack the staying power which can be derived only from serving the Torah; he will lack that serene contentment and vitality which can be gained only through service of the Torah.

7. Any group of ten men united in accordance with the spirit of· Judaism for truly Jewish causes constitutes a "congregation" and represents, on a small scale, the entire Jewish community. When such men occupy themselves jointly with the study of the Torah and the endeavor to understand the tasks it has set them, they are an עדת אל, a "congregation of the Almighty." God is present in their midst, for, according to the verse from the Psalms quoted here, God נצב "stands ready" to intervene in behalf of "His own" congrega-

6. Rabbi Nechunyah ben Hakanah, said: He who takes upon himself the yoke of the Torah, from him the yoke of the government and the yoke of secular life will be removed. But he who casts off the yoke of the Torah, upon him will be laid the yoke of the government and the yoke of secular life.

7. Rabbi Chalaftah ben Dosa, of the village of Chananyah, said: When ten people sit together and occupy themselves with the Torah, the Presence of God dwells among them, for it is said, "God stands in a congregation of the Almighty." And whence can it be shown that the same applies also to five? Because it is said: "He has founded His band upon earth." And whence can it be shown that the same applies even to three? Because it is said: "He judges in the midst of judges." And whence can it be shown that it applies even to two? Because it is said, "Then those who feared *God* spoke one with the other and *God* listened and heard." And whence can it be shown that it applies even to one? Because it is said: "In any place where I shall cause My Name to be remembered, I will come to you and bless you."

8. Rabbi Elazar of Barthotha said: Give Him what is His, because

---

tion, protecting and reigning, furthering and aiding, even as it is written of *Yaakov*, who lives on in every *kehilath Yaakov* to this very day: והנה ה' נצב עליו. Even five people who have banded together in this spirit for these purposes represent אגדתו, a "godly band". It is God, His word and His will, that has united them , and על ארץ יסדה it is He that gives their union a firm foundation and endurance, support and soundness on earth. And even if it is only three that have joined in the effort to glean from the Torah the standard of truth and right for the orderly development of human affairs and to enforce that standard by righteous sentence, God will abide with them and guide their study and their understanding so that their pronouncements will be in accordance with His own word. In fact, even when there are only two God-fearing men who occupy themselves with the word of God and who discuss its contents and the tasks that it poses, God will listen and will not allow even one of their words that genuinely seeks after truth to pass in vain. Indeed even the one person who sits alone and occupies himself with the Torah, is told: "In every place where I, God, cause My Name to be mentioned, wherever you are impelled to declare My Name not out of delusion, caprice or folly, but for My own sake, for the sake of My word, My teaching and the fulfillment of My command, I will come to you and bless you. I shall bless your study, your endeavors and your achievements."

8. All that you are and all that you have belongs to God, for whatever you

וְשֶׁלְּךָ שֶׁלּוֹ וְכֵן בְּדָוִד הוּא אוֹמֵר כִּי־מִמְּךָ הַכֹּל וּמִיָּדְךָ נָתַנּוּ לָךְ:

ט רַבִּי יַעֲקֹב אוֹמֵר, הַמְהַלֵּךְ בַּדֶּרֶךְ וְשׁוֹנֶה, וּמַפְסִיק מִמִּשְׁנָתוֹ וְאוֹמֵר מַה־נָּאֶה אִילָן זֶה מַה־נָּאֶה נִיר זֶה מַעֲלֶה עָלָיו הַכָּתוּב כְּאִלּוּ מִתְחַיֵּב בְּנַפְשׁוֹ:

י רַבִּי דוֹסְתַּאי בַּר יַנַּאי מִשּׁוּם רַבִּי מֵאִיר אוֹמֵר, כָּל־הַשּׁוֹכֵחַ דָּבָר אֶחָד מִמִּשְׁנָתוֹ מַעֲלֶה עָלָיו הַכָּתוּב כְּאִלּוּ מִתְחַיֵּב בְּנַפְשׁוֹ שֶׁנֶּאֱמַר רַק הִשָּׁמֶר לְךָ וּשְׁמֹר נַפְשְׁךָ מְאֹד פֶּן־תִּשְׁכַּח אֶת־הַדְּבָרִים אֲשֶׁר רָאוּ עֵינֶיךָ· יָכוֹל אֲפִילוּ תָּקְפָה עָלָיו מִשְׁנָתוֹ תַּלְמוּד לוֹמַר וּפֶן־ יָסוּרוּ מִלְּבָבְךָ כָּל יְמֵי חַיֶּיךָ, הָא אֵינוֹ מִתְחַיֵּב בְּנַפְשׁוֹ עַד־שֶׁיֵּשֵׁב וִיסִירֵם מִלִּבּוֹ:

יא רַבִּי חֲנִינָא בֶּן־דוֹסָא אוֹמֵר, כָּל שֶׁיִּרְאַת חֶטְאוֹ קוֹדֶמֶת לְחָכְמָתוֹ חָכְמָתוֹ מִתְקַיֶּמֶת וְכֹל שֶׁחָכְמָתוֹ קוֹדֶמֶת לְיִרְאַת חֶטְאוֹ אֵין חָכְמָתוֹ מִתְקַיֶּמֶת:

---

may be and whatever you may possess you have received from Him alone. If you will keep this thought before you at all times, then you will be ready, gladly and at any time, to muster all your physical and spiritual faculties and resources in the service of the fulfillment of His will. Then you will never find it within your heart to pride yourself on what you have given or on what you have achieved, for you will know that you could have neither given nor achieved without having received the strength and the means from Him, and that whatever has been given you, you have received only for the purpose of employing it to do the will of God.

9. משנתו, "his" teaching, that teaching which deals with man's voluntary shaping of his own life and of his own affairs in accordane with the will of his Creator and Master, a teaching which lends to human life and development a harmony, perfection and moral splendor before which the physical beauties of nature all recede into the shadows. For what does this teaching do but build the most intimate unity out of the most diverse variety of human life experiences through the free permeation of the latter with the Divine spirit in accordance with the will of God, a harmony which realizes the concept of beauty in the most sublime sense of the word. This Mishna teaches us the

you and all that you have are His. Thus it is said by David: "All things come from You and of Your own we have given You."

9. Rabbi Yaakov said: He who is walking by the way and studies and breaks off his study and exclaims: "How beautiful is this tree!" "How fine is that field!" is regarded as if he had sinned against his own soul.

10. Rabbi Dostai bar Yannai, said, in the name of Rabbi Meir: Whosoever forgets [even] one word of his study, him the Scripture regards as if he had sinned against his soul; for it is said: "Only take heed of yourself and guard your soul diligently that you may not forget the facts which your eyes have beheld." Now one might suppose that the same result would follow even if the retention of what he has studied has been too hard for him. To guard against such an inference, the Torah adds "And lest they depart from your heart all the days of your life." Accordingly, he is guilty of sinning against his soul only if he sits down idly and deliberately removes [these teachings] from his heart.

11. Rabbi Chanina ben Dosa, said: He in whom the fear of sin goes before his wisdom, his wisdom shall endure; but he in whom wisdom precedes the fear of sin, his wisdom will not endure.

---

following great lesson: He who, while studying, does not become aware of this higher beauty of God's teaching, so that he will break off his sacred work to exclaim over the beauty of nature, is as if he had sinned against his own soul, or, rather, as if he had forfeited his soul. For, despite his study, he thus shows that he has not come to understand the dignity and beauty of a human soul that is guided and enlightened by the spirit of God; a beauty and dignity that surpasses all earthly beauty by far.

10. That which is said primarily concerning the historical fact of the Revelation of the Law, an event which we ourselves have experienced, and which we are bidden to keep before us always and never to allow to depart from our minds, is applied here also to the actual contents of that revealed Law. With solemn rigor we are held responsible for every word of the contents of the Law which we might indeed have studied but then forgotten due to negligence, indolence or indifference.

11. The "fear of sin", the fear of committing some act that would not be in accordance with the will of God, is a direct outgrowth and practical demonstration of the "fear of God". The fear of God and the fear of sin are character qualities which are not dependent upon wisdom and erudition, but which, in fact, must come before these intellectual gifts if the wisdom and erudition

יב הוּא הָיָה אוֹמֵר, כֹּל שֶׁמַּעֲשָׂיו מְרֻבִּים מֵחָכְמָתוֹ חָכְמָתוֹ
מִתְקַיֶּמֶת וְכֹל שֶׁחָכְמָתוֹ מְרֻבָּה מִמַּעֲשָׂיו אֵין חָכְמָתוֹ
מִתְקַיֶּמֶת:

יג הוּא הָיָה אוֹמֵר, כֹּל שֶׁרוּחַ הַבְּרִיּוֹת נוֹחָה הֵימֶנּוּ רוּחַ הַמָּקוֹם
נוֹחָה הֵימֶנּוּ וְכֹל שֶׁאֵין רוּחַ הַבְּרִיּוֹת נוֹחָה הֵימֶנּוּ אֵין רוּחַ הַמָּקוֹם
נוֹחָה הֵימֶנּוּ:

יד רַבִּי דוֹסָא בֶּן־הַרְכִּינַס אוֹמֵר, שֵׁנָה שֶׁל־שַׁחֲרִית וְיַיִן שֶׁל־
צָהֳרַיִם וְשִׂיחַת הַיְלָדִים וִישִׁיבַת בָּתֵּי כְנֵסִיּוֹת שֶׁל־עַמֵּי הָאָרֶץ
מוֹצִיאִין אֶת־הָאָדָם מִן־הָעוֹלָם:

---

are to be true and of the right kind. Particularly the wisdom of the Torah
to which the term חכמה primarily refers here, can be properly grasped only
by him who regards it as the God-given source of truth and duty. It can be
truly understood only by him who approaches its study with the desire and
the high resolve to derive from it guidance for understanding and a standard
for his conduct, and protection against error and sin in theory or practice. As
such a person walks on the road of life, his wisdom will gain in clarity with
every step he takes; it will grow in the power to guide and to discipline, and
to afford his soul blissful satisfaction, and it will walk beside him as his most
faithful companion until the very end of his days. But he whose approach to
wisdom and knowledge is devoid of the fear of God and the fear of sin, to
whom the fear of God and the fear of sin are only to proceed from his wisdom, he will neither gain true wisdom nor acquire the genuine fear of God.
He will regard every word of the Torah's wisdom only as a hindrance and
impediment to the imagined freedom that he has enjoyed heretofore. He will
distort its contents for his own purposes, changing and perverting them to
suit his own view of life which is estranged from God—to what extent is
immaterial—and finally he will discard it altogether as useless ballast and
ignore it as an inconvenient intruder upon his freedom.

12. This verse is a continuation and a supplement of what has gone before.
Here we are told: There are also persons who, though having adopted the
right approach to the study of the Torah, nevertheless shall never attain true
and enduring wisdom. Such a person may indeed have sought help in enriching
and improving his understanding, and guidance for his life's duty from the
Torah, but, if in practical life he lacks the strength to translate the knowledge
of what is right into proper conduct, his wisdom cannot endure. Such a man
may know what his duty is, but if he does not perform it in practice, or at

12. He used to say: He whose deeds exceed his wisdom, his wisdom shall endure, but he whose wisdom exceeds his deeds, his wisdom will not endure.

13. He used to say: He who is pleasing to his fellow-men is pleasing also to God; and he who is not pleasing to men is also displeasing to God.

14. Rabbi Dosa ben Harkinas, said: Morning sleep and midday wine, children's talk and sitting in the assembly houses of the ignorant put a man out of the world.

---

least not to the extent to which he knows he should be doing it, and thus is rich in wisdom but poor in deeds, his wisdom has no permanence. It is stunted because it does not reach that stage of bloom and fruition in which it must be proven and in which alone it can attain its true worth and value. Accordingly, the sages have also said elsewhere: לימוד גדול שהלימוד מביא לידי מעשה "Study is great, for study leads to deeds," and לא המדרש עיקר אלא המעשה "The main thing is not inquiry, but deeds."

13. The designation of מקום for God implies the universal relationship of God to the world. God is מקומו של עולם; He supports the world; it is through Him that the world endures. The designation for "man", which embraces all of mankind, regardless of individual differences, is בריות, literally, "creations". God created men for a universal union. Even as all men, being the creatures of God, enjoy the same relationship to Him Who is their sole Creator and are united through Him, so despite all the many ways in which individuals differ from one another, men should draw closer to one another and each one should accept all the good found in the others so that, eventually, they will all form one single union of human beings beneath the reign of the Father of all Mankind. Therefore it is not in keeping with God's will that any one person should separate himself from all the others. True we may differ from one another with regard to principles and inalienable convictions which each of us must steadfastly keep and follow for himself, and as a consequence, also with regard to the way of life we must adopt. Yet there is possible a way of living together that all of us can accept, so that no one may become unpleasant and burdensome, hostile or unkind to the other, but that, instead, each of us may find pleasure in the company of the other and feel drawn to him. Unkind and hostile conduct toward other men is displeasing also to God and is in direct contradiction to the goals intended by God to be attained through mankind's life together. If you are really wiser, better and nobler than the others, then strive also to be more pleasant and amiable, so that people will like to be near you and absorb into their own personalities some of your wisdom, goodness and moral nobility.

14. It is obvious that he who sleeps away the morning hours, who at noon

טו רַבִּי אֶלְעָזָר הַמּוֹדָעִי אוֹמֵר, הַמְחַלֵּל אֶת־הַקֳּדָשִׁים וְהַמְבַזֶּה
אֶת־הַמּוֹעֲדוֹת וְהַמַּלְבִּין פְּנֵי חֲבֵרוֹ בָּרַבִּים וְהַמֵּפֵר בְּרִיתוֹ שֶׁל־
אַבְרָהָם אָבִינוּ וְהַמְגַלֶּה פָנִים בַּתּוֹרָה שֶׁלֹּא כַהֲלָכָה, אַף עַל פִּי
שֶׁיֵּשׁ בְּיָדוֹ תּוֹרָה וּמַעֲשִׂים טוֹבִים, אֵין לוֹ חֵלֶק לָעוֹלָם הַבָּא:

dulls his mental clarity and alertness by indulging in strong drink, and who
wastes his evenings with childish trifles or at the tavern, will not have much
time left to devote to the earnest endeavor to fulfill the purpose for which
he has been put into the world. It is not unlikely that the Mishna frowns upon
each of these four idle pursuits separately as a thoughtless squandering of
time—that most precious gift that has been given man; time granted him for
the dutiful and faithful completion of life's task.

15. In Sanhedrin 99a this Mishna is quoted as follows: המחלל את הקדשים והמבזה
את המועדות והמפר בריתו של אברהם אבינו והמגלה פנים בתורה וכו' והמלבין פני חברו ברבים
The holy objects in the Temple, the Festivals and the rite of circumcision are
Divinely-established institutions through which the awareness of the holy
purpose of the individual and the community, and convictions and resolves for
its loyal and dutiful realization, are to be held fast, maintained and protected
from any misinterpretation and distortion not only for the present but for all
the generations to come. They are named here in the reverse chronological
order of their creation. All mo'adim, which are based on yetziat Mitzrayim,
preceded the erection of the mishkan. בריתו של אברהם אבינו marked the beginning
of our very existence as a nation. The bedrock and source of this knowledge
is the Torah. Before the election of Abraham, the awareness of man's moral
destiny was derived from man's consciousness of his general dignity as the
creature made in the image of God. Now this Mishna deems it possible that
one might think that a person might attain a certain degree of Torah wisdom
and also perform good deeds even though he disregards קדשים, מועדות and
מילה, and actually has a negative attitude to these sacred institutions, and has
no understanding at all of the inalienable higher Godly dignity of man. Yet
the Mishna tells us that notwithstanding his knowledge and good deeds a
person such as this has forfeited his portion in the world to come. For the
great basic Jewish institutions, the holy objects in the Temple, the Festivals,
the rite of circumcision, the revealed Word of God and the teaching that man
was made in God's image were all given to each one of us not simply as a
means for our own personal moral and spiritual advancement. They are much
more important than that; they represent the great Divine treasure entrusted
to us for the spiritual and moral improvement of our Jewish community and of

15.   Rabbi Elazar Ha-Mudai, said: He who profanes sacred things, who neglects the festivals, who humiliates his fellow-man in public and violates the covenant of Avraham, our father, and who interprets the Torah in a manner contradictory to the Halachah—though he may have the knowledge of Torah and good deeds—has no share in the world to come.

---

the larger community of mankind. We, as messengers, instruments and priests of the Kingdom of God that is to come upon earth, are to defend this treasure with our heart's blood and we are to put all of our thoughts, our ambitions and achievements into the endeavor to promote the ever-increasing recognition and acknowledgment of it. Therefore he who neglects any one of these Divinely-appointed institutions is guilty of contributing to the undermining of the future of God's kingdom on earth. Hence, regardless of any spiritual or moral qualities he might possess, he has forfeited his share in the eternity of the world to come.

In Sanhedrin 99a all these five transgressions are included in the pronouncement כי דבר ה' בזה ; they are viewed as a show of disdain for the word of God. For, since they serve the perpetuation and realization of the Word of God on earth, the five sacred institutions to which reference is made and against which these sins have been committed, are emanations of the Word of God. מלבין פני חברו ברבים is the gravest of all sins against the dignity and nobleness inherent in every human being by virtue of the fact that he was made in the image of God. According to Sanhedrin 99b the term מגלה פנים בתורה may also have an interpretation other than that offered here. According to that source, *panim* would not indicate the *interpretation* of the Torah as it does in many instances; e.g. in the sentence מ״ט פנים לתורה. Instead, *panim* would be construed in its literal meaning of "countenance", and thus the term גלוי פנים would indicate the opposite of הסתרת פנים (hiding one's face, an expression of modesty)—in other words, it would denote "impudence" or "impertinence". (Targum to Exod. 14:8 and Num. 15:30 renders ביד רמה by the term בריש גלי which means "with head uncovered"). Thusly interpreted, מגלה פנים בתורה would mean to treat the Torah with impudence and impertinence. One example of such behavior would be מבזה תלמידי חכמים the insulting and slighting of teachers of the Torah. This would include even מבזה חברו בפני תלמיד חכם, an instance where a person has so little respect for a תלמיד חכם, that, he would deliberately humiliate a fellow-man even in the presence of such a sage. If we accept this interpretation, the explanation of שלא כהלכה would present some difficulty. Apparently, the Talmud, according to this interpretation, generally omits these two words.

טז רַבִּי יִשְׁמָעֵאל אוֹמֵר, הֱוֵה קַל לְרֹאשׁ וְנוֹחַ לְתִשְׁחֹרֶת וֶהֱוֵה
מְקַבֵּל אֶת־כָּל־הָאָדָם בְּשִׂמְחָה:

יז רַבִּי עֲקִיבָה אוֹמֵר, שְׂחוֹק וְקַלּוּת רֹאשׁ מַרְגִּילִין אֶת־הָאָדָם
לְעֶרְוָה: מַסֹּרֶת סְיָג לַתּוֹרָה, מַעְשְׂרוֹת סְיָג לָעֹשֶׁר, נְדָרִים סְיָג
לַפְּרִישׁוּת. סְיָג לַחָכְמָה שְׁתִיקָה:

---

16. ראש here denotes a person who occupies the position of "head", of leadership, in an organization or in any endeavor. קל, literally, "easy to be led",
"amenable". נוח is "quiet", "cautious". תשחרת is "youth", the "morning" of
life, as in מרחם משחר (Psalm 110:31), and הילדות והשחרות (Eccl. 11:10). When
dealing with a person entrusted with the leadership of an assembly, a group
or a community to which you belong, be amenable. Do not be difficult, submit to his direction, and do not regard this submission as a loss of face. But
when you deal with the inexperienced young, be cautious. Give ample thought
to the matter at hand before making your decision. However once you find
that what they seek to achieve is good, then join them in their endeavors even
though they are younger than you. When other men offer you their help in
your own endeavors, accept them cheerfully. Do not be led by pride to seek to
do everything by yourself. Do not reject anyone from the outset; instead, receive
everyone gladly, and then consider whether or not he is suitable for you and
your endeavors. All these three verses urge that you selflessly ignore personal
factors in favor of pure devotion to the cause you seek to serve.

17. In moments of jest and levity we may permit ourselves to treat lightly
those things which are normally taken as seriously as they should be. By the
light treatment we give them at such moments we run the risk of having
sacred and solemn things lose their lofty and inviolable character for us and
thus, in fact, of drawing close to lewdness and unchastity, first in thought and
word and then, gradually, even in deed. —מסרת, the traditional text of the
Written Word of God guards the Scriptures against falsification; and the
traditional interpretation of the content of the Law protects the latter from
distortion. —מעשרות: The three tithes, מעשר ראשון, מעשר שני and מעשר עני,
guard our riches against perverted use by teaching us the proper uses for
them and guiding us to the practical implementation of these teachings. The
maaser rishon, the tithe to be given to the Levites, teaches and accustoms us
to attend to the spiritual needs of our Torah knowledge and to the maintenance

16. Rabbi Yishmael said: Be amenable with a superior, cautious with the young, and receive all men with cheerfulness.

17. Rabbi Akiva said: Jesting and levity accustom a man to lewdness. The transmission is a protective fence about the Torah, the tithes are a fence for riches, vows are a fence for abstinence; a fence for wisdom is silence.

---

of the bearers and teachers of the Torah before seeking to gratify our own physical needs. The *maaser sheni,* the second tithe, which must be eaten in the environs of the Sanctuary in Jerusalem, teaches and accustoms us to make even our act of physical enjoyment so sacred that, thus elevated to the sphere of duty in the service of God, it need not shun even the presence of God and the environs of His sanctuary. The *maaser ani,* the tithe for the poor teaches and accustoms us to view the possessions given us by God as having been given us not only for ourselves, not only for our own physical nourishment and sustenance, but also as a means for giving aid and support to our less fortunate brethren. Thus we learn to regard ourselves as Divinely-appointed instruments and messengers of God's own bounty. But our sages teach us that while the *maaseroth* are thus fences guarding our riches against misuse, they serve, at the same time, to protect our wealth against decline. They teach us that עשר תעשר, עשר בשביל שתתעשר, tithing will make you rich; and in Malachi 3:10 we are told הביאו את כל המעשר וגו' "Bring all your tithes, etc.," ובחנוני נא בזאת וגו', "and thus put me to the test, to see whether I will not open the heavens for you and pour upon you blessings without an end." (Taanith 9a). — נדרים: God does not view the making of vows with favor; it is expected that we do good without first having to resort to vows to re solve to do so. Nevertheless, the vow is commended as a means for the exercise and the strengthening of our resolve to abstain from sin in the struggle against evil impulses. — סיג לחכמה שתיקה: Surely this does not mean "absolute silence". What is meant is that art of remaining silent practiced by him who would rather say nothing at all than deliver himself of a rash ill-considered statement, who listens quietly to the views of others in order to learn from them, and who does not have the urge to shine forth with his own opinions and to refuse to let others get in a word edgewise. Such a person will devote more time to thought than to speech and will therefore never run the danger of making any statement that is thoughtless or ill-considered.

יה הוּא הָיָה אוֹמֵר, חָבִיב אָדָם שֶׁנִּבְרָא בְּצֶלֶם · חִבָּה יְתֵרָה
נוֹדַעַת לוֹ שֶׁנִּבְרָא בְּצֶלֶם (אֱלֹהִים) שֶׁנֶּאֱמַר כִּי בְּצֶלֶם אֱלֹהִים
עָשָׂה אֶת־הָאָדָם: חֲבִיבִין יִשְׂרָאֵל שֶׁנִּקְרְאוּ בָנִים (לַמָּקוֹם)· חִבָּה
יְתֵרָה נוֹדַעַת לָהֶם שֶׁנִּקְרְאוּ בָנִים לַמָּקוֹם שֶׁנֶּאֱמַר בָּנִים אַתֶּם
לַיָי אֱלֹהֵיכֶם: חֲבִיבִין יִשְׂרָאֵל שֶׁנִּתַּן לָהֶם כְּלִי חֶמְדָּה· חִבָּה
יְתֵרָה נוֹדַעַת לָהֶם שֶׁנִּתַּן לָהֶם כְּלִי חֶמְדָּה שֶׁבּוֹ נִבְרָא הָעוֹלָם
שֶׁנֶּאֱמַר כִּי לֶקַח טוֹב נָתַתִּי לָכֶם תּוֹרָתִי אַל־תַּעֲזֹבוּ:

18. The Mishna here enumerates the privileges of which man was found worthy as distinguished from other creatures, and the special signs of Divine love by which Israel, in turn, was singled out from the rest of mankind. The fact that these distinctions were not given without the recipients' being made aware of them, is construed as an additional mark of Divine favor. Man was favored by having been created in the image of God. This in itself would be a wondrous gift, even if man would not be aware of it at all. For by virtue of the godly qualities with which he was thus endowed at the time of his creation he would do much that is morally and spiritually good, even though he would not be aware that by so conducting himself he was merely demonstrating his resemblance to God. But this special divine favor attained its full worth only by virtue of the fact that man was taught explicitly that his dignity and nobleness which raises him above all other creatures, and his destiny which guides him toward God in moral and spiritual perfection are based upon his having been created in the image of the Lord.—The divine favor accorded Israel as distinguished from all other men is that the relationship it enjoys with God is much closer than that of the rest of mankind. The tie which links God with Israel is like that which binds a father to his child. Even if God would simply have given Israel this special fatherly love, guidance and training, without Israel ever becoming aware of its special position and relationship to God, it would have been no mean favor. But actually, this token of God's love, too, shines forth in its true worth only by virtue of the fact that Israel was told of it and thus spurred on to hallowing self-respect and to childlike, loving obedience and childlike trust in God. Accompanying this favor of being called "the children of God", and, in fact, its true purpose and goal, is the other great privilege accorded Israel—its

18. He used to say: Privileged is man, for he was created in His image. But it was an act of special favor that it was made known to him that he was created in His image, as it is said: "For in the image of God did He create man." Privileged are Yisrael, for they are called children. But it was an act of special favor that it was made known to them that they are called the children of God; for it is said: "You are children to *God* your God." Privileged are Yisrael, for a precious instrument was given them through which the world was created, for it is said: "I have given you a teaching that is suited to the good; forsake not My Torah."

---

appointment as bearer of the Torah. Even if Israel were merely to accept the contents of the Torah as a God-given guide to moral and spiritual perfection and the fulfillment of its life's task, if it were to live for its realization with the unreserved devotion of all its being, its thoughts, and its efforts, all without having been told of the unique and sacred significance of the Torah for the whole world, this Divine appointment would have been a priceless privilege. But God explicitly made His people aware of the fact that the Torah was a כלי חמדה, literally "an instrument with which to strive after the goal" through which and for the sake of which the whole world was made. The laws of the Torah are those laws by which all the creatures, phenomena, and developments of all the rest of creation continue and endure, transposed into a smaller scale to be a law for the shaping of the lives of individuals and nations. At the same time the Torah is the instrument for the fulfillment of that goal for which the Lord created the whole world to begin with. The purpose and the goal of the physical world is טוב, the realization of all that is morally good; the verdict of *tov* was pronounced over the work of every single day of creation and finally over the sum total of the Universe that was thus brought into being. But this "good", the goal for which the entire world was made and which it is man's task to achieve, can be attained only through the Torah. The Torah is לקח טוב; it is a teaching through which the good can be won. Therefore God warns us: תורתי אל תעזבו. Thus our awareness of the unique and lofty significance of the Torah should help us view the Torah as that inalienable good for whose preservation, realization and ever-increasing acknowledgement we should live, offering up to its fulfillment all that we are and all that we have, and, if need be, even life itself.

יט הַכֹּל צָפוּי וְהָרְשׁוּת נְתוּנָה· וּבְטוֹב הָעוֹלָם נָדוֹן· וְהַכֹּל לְפִי
רֹב הַמַּעֲשֶׂה:

כ הוּא הָיָה אוֹמֵר· הַכֹּל נָתוּן בָּעֵרָבוֹן· וּמְצוּדָה פְרוּשָׁה עַל־כָּל־
הַחַיִּים· הֶחָנוּת פְּתוּחָה וְהַחֶנְוָנִי מַקִּיף· וְהַפִּנְקֶס פָּתוּחַ וְהַיָּד כּוֹתֶבֶת·
וְכָל הָרוֹצֶה לִלְווֹת יָבֹא וְיִלְוֶה · וְהַגַּבָּאִין מַחֲזִירִין תָּדִיר בְּכָל־יוֹם·
וְנִפְרָעִין מִן־הָאָדָם מִדַּעְתּוֹ וְשֶׁלֹּא מִדַּעְתּוֹ וְיֵשׁ לָהֶם עַל מַה
שֶּׁיִּסְמֹכוּ· וְהַדִּין דִּין אֱמֶת וְהַכֹּל מְתֻקָּן לִסְעוּדָה:

כא רַבִּי אֶלְעָזָר בֶּן־עֲזַרְיָה אוֹמֵר· אִם אֵין תּוֹרָה אֵין דֶּרֶךְ אֶרֶץ,
אִם אֵין דֶּרֶךְ אֶרֶץ אֵין תּוֹרָה· אִם אֵין חָכְמָה אֵין יִרְאָה, אִם אֵין
יִרְאָה אֵין חָכְמָה· אִם אֵין דַּעַת אֵין בִּינָה, אִם אֵין בִּינָה אֵין דַּעַת·
אִם אֵין קֶמַח אֵין תּוֹרָה, אִם אֵין תּוֹרָה אֵין קֶמַח:

---

19. When God first made the world and put man into it, He foresaw that man could do both good and evil. Therefore He ordered the world in such a manner that the evil done by man would not thwart the goal of His world sovereignty but that, instead, even the evil that would be done by man would prove an instrument for the good in the end, although those who did it would never know and never have intended that this should be so. Man has been given the freedom of choice. In fact, if it were not within man's power to do evil, were sin to hold no charms for him, indeed, man would then not be human at all. His virtue would be no virtue, and all of his actions would be on a level no higher than animal instinct. And the world is judged in accordance with the good that is done in it. In His reign over the world God sees to it that the good, of which we have seen a beginning even now among men, is not suppressed or choked off by the weed of evil. And He so guides the course of time that the good which exists will not be lost but, instead, gain ground and spread steadily, and in the end spring into full bloom as a kingdom of the good on earth. But the gauge with which any one period of time will be measured, and by which its fate will be determined, will be the nature, good or bad, of the majority of that which has come to pass and still comes to pass through the deeds of men.

20. Everything that has been given us by God imposes an obligation upon us, and whatever we are and whatever we possess constitutes the pledge for the discharge of our debt. No man can escape either this obligation or the attachment of this pledge. We all have the freedom to choose whether to

19. Everything is foreseen, yet freedom [of choice] is given, and the world is judged according to the good, and the judgment of all is according to the nature of the majority of the events that have come to pass.

20. He used to say: Everything is given on pledge and a net is spread out over all the living. The shop is open, the merchant extends credit, the ledger is open and the hand records [therein]. Whosoever wishes to borrow—let him come and borrow. The collectors make their appointed round each day and take payment from man whether he knows it or not. It is on hand, that on which they can rely; the legal procedure is right. But all is ready for the festive banquet.

21. Rabbi Elazar ben Azariah, said: Where there is no Torah, there is no civic society; if there is no civic society, there is no Torah. Where there is no wisdom, there is no fear of God; where there is no fear of God, there is no wisdom. Where there is no knowledge, there is no understanding; where there is no understanding there is no knowledge. Where there is no sustenance there is no Torah; where there is no Torah there is no sustenance.

---

limit our debt by a life of moderation, or whether to increase it by lack of restraint. But we must remember at all times that no unpaid debt is ever cancelled. Even if we should forget about it, God will exact payment in His own way, whether we know of it or not. No one is pressed for payment, for the pledges are valid security, available at all times, and the procedure of redemption is in strict accordance with truth and justice. But even as payment is exacted for every neglect of duty, so rich reward await those who have remained steadfastly loyal to their task.

21. Without the Torah, without the spiritual guidance and moral ennoblement communicated by the Teaching of God, any endeavor to establish, maintain and advance a civilized society on earth will be in vain. Conversely, without דרך ארץ, if an orderly way of life is not fostered, then the guidance and ennoblement inherent in the Torah lack a foundation on earth. In that case the understanding for a great many situations covered by the Torah's teachings will be lost, as will be just as great a part of its practical application to daily living. Without חכמה, without the spiritual enlightenment to be derived from the Torah of God, the fear of God will not be properly realized or applied without error. Conversely, without יראה, without the fear of God, the endeavor to gather wisdom from the Torah is deprived of its basic prerequisite and motivation. Without דעת, without the knowledge of the nature and reality of things and circumstances, בינה, understanding, the good sense

כב הוּא הָיָה אוֹמֵר, כָּל שֶׁחָכְמָתוֹ מְרֻבָּה מִמַּעֲשָׂיו לְמָה הוּא
דּוֹמֶה, לְאִילָן שֶׁעֲנָפָיו מְרֻבִּין וְשָׁרָשָׁיו מֻעָטִין וְהָרוּחַ בָּאָה
וְעוֹקַרְתּוֹ וְהוֹפַכְתּוֹ עַל פָּנָיו· שֶׁנֶּאֱמַר וְהָיָה כְּעַרְעָר בָּעֲרָבָה וְלֹא
יִרְאֶה כִּי־יָבוֹא טוֹב וְשָׁכַן חֲרֵרִים בַּמִּדְבָּר אֶרֶץ מְלֵחָה וְלֹא תֵשֵׁב·
אֲבָל כָּל שֶׁמַּעֲשָׂיו מְרֻבִּים מֵחָכְמָתוֹ לְמָה הוּא דוֹמֶה, לְאִילָן
שֶׁעֲנָפָיו מֻעָטִין וְשָׁרָשָׁיו מְרֻבִּין שֶׁאֲפִילוּ כָּל־הָרוּחוֹת שֶׁבָּעוֹלָם
בָּאוֹת וְנוֹשְׁבוֹת בּוֹ אֵין מְזִיזִין אוֹתוֹ מִמְּקוֹמוֹ, שֶׁנֶּאֱמַר וְהָיָה כְּעֵץ
שָׁתוּל עַל־מַיִם וְעַל־יוּבַל יְשַׁלַּח שָׁרָשָׁיו וְלֹא יִרְאֶה כִּי־יָבֹא חֹם
וְהָיָה עָלֵהוּ רַעֲנָן וּבִשְׁנַת בַּצֹּרֶת לֹא יִדְאָג וְלֹא יָמִישׁ מֵעֲשׂוֹת
פֶּרִי:

כג רַבִּי אֶלְעָזָר (בֶּן־) הִסְמָא אוֹמֵר, קִנִּין וּפִתְחֵי נִדָּה הֵן הֵן
גּוּפֵי הֲלָכוֹת·תְּקוּפוֹת·וְגִמַטְרִיָּאוֹת פַּרְפְּרָאוֹת לַחָכְמָה:

רבי חנניא וכו' קדיש·
—

---

to be employed in making judgments, and in drawing inferences and conclusions, lacks a factual basis and will dissipate itself in false and unreal imaginings. But conversely, without that "good sense" with which to test, evaluate,
and draw conclusions, *Daath,* that part of intelligence which constitutes knowledge, may go astray; it will take appearance for reality and will have no
protection against error and deception. Without *kemach,* without sustenance,
neither the study nor the dissemination of the Torah can be promoted. Conversely, without the Torah, without earnest attention to the moral and spiritual
"sustenance" to be derived through the Torah, the search after purely physical
sustenance not only loses all true worth and significance but actually is
destroyed by the outgrowths of crude materialism.

22. He used to say: He whose wisdom exceeds his deeds is like a tree whose branches are many but whose roots are few. The wind comes and uproots it and overturns it upon its top. Of such a man it is said: "He shall be like a lonely man in the wasteland and shall not see when good comes; he shall dwell upon the parched soil in the wilderness, a salt-saturated land which is uninhabitable." But he whose deeds exceed his wisdom is like a tree whose branches are few but whose roots are many. Even if all the winds of the world come and blow upon it, they cannot move it from its place. Of such a man it is said: "He shall be like a tree planted by the waters, which spreads out its roots to the stream of water; he shall not perceive it when the heat comes, but his leaf shall remain fresh; he will not be troubled in the year of drought, neither will he cease to bear fruit."

23. Rabbi Elazar ben Chisma, said: The chapters pertinent to the bird sacrifices and to the beginnings of woman's unclean period are important ordinances of the Law. Astronomy and geometry are condiments to wisdom.

---

22. Only such wisdom as is proven in practical action can endure and will in turn sustain him who is blessed with it. It is not extensive knowledge but only the knowledge that he has done good deeds in abundance that will steel a man against all trials and temptations, and will gain for him the protection and aid inherent in Divine approval.

23. קנין (Tractate Kinin in *Seder Kodshim*) and פתחי נדה (Arachin 8a) are stressed here solely as illustrations of treatises that serve to advance the conscientious fulfillment of our duty and bear resemblance to תקופות and גמטריות only insofar as they, too, involve calculations. פרפראות are "condiments" or "auxiliary sciences". Rabbi Eleazar Chisma was himself a mathematician of such renown that it was hyperbolically said of him that he knew how to determine the number of drops of water contained in the ocean. (Horioth 10a).

פֶּרֶק רְבִיעִי

כל ישראל וכו'.

א בֶּן־זוֹמָא אוֹמֵר, אֵיזֶהוּ חָכָם, הַלּוֹמֵד מִכָּל־אָדָם שֶׁנֶּאֱמַר
מִכָּל־מְלַמְּדַי הִשְׂכַּלְתִּי (כִּי עֵדְוֹתֶיךָ שִׂיחָה לִי): אֵיזֶהוּ גִבּוֹר,
הַכּוֹבֵשׁ אֶת־יִצְרוֹ שֶׁנֶּאֱמַר טוֹב אֶרֶךְ אַפַּיִם מִגִּבּוֹר וּמשֵׁל בְּרוּחוֹ
מִלֹּכֵד עִיר: אֵיזֶהוּ עָשִׁיר, הַשָּׂמֵחַ בְּחֶלְקוֹ שֶׁנֶּאֱמַר יְגִיעַ כַּפֶּיךָ כִּי
תֹאכֵל אַשְׁרֶיךָ וְטוֹב לָךְ · אַשְׁרֶיךָ בָּעוֹלָם הַזֶּה וְטוֹב לָךְ לָעוֹלָם
הַבָּא: אֵיזֶהוּ מְכֻבָּד, הַמְכַבֵּד אֶת־הַבְּרִיּוֹת שֶׁנֶּאֱמַר כִּי מְכַבְּדַי
אֲכַבֵּד וּבֹזַי יֵקָלּוּ:

---

1. According to these "Ethics of the Fathers" it is primarily the knowledge of the Torah that stamps a person as a חכם. This Godly teaching contains nothing that is supernatural or other-worldly. Indeed, it is the purpose of the Torah of God to shape and regulate in every detail every single one of the manifold aspects and relationships of practical life on earth. It therefore deals in exhaustive detail with all the immediate things of the here and now. The basic prerequisite for the proper fulfillment of the laws of God is knowledge, as extensive as possible, of the realities of all earthly, human relationships; a vast and varied store of wisdom such as has been amassed and left to us by our sages in sciences such as agriculture, cattle breeding, industry, commerce, pharmacology, and nutrition, to name but a few. In view of the foregoing, the true *talmid chacham* will find that he can learn something from every person with whom he speaks, for any person can be more expert than he in at least one calling or pursuit and thus can give him valuable practical information which he may then utilize for his study of the Law of God. For the laws of the Torah are not simply עדות, "testimonies" of God; they are also עדות, "ornaments" designed to impress upon all human affairs the stamp of the morally good and beautiful.

איזהו גבור. Even the mightiest hero may fall victim to the pull of his passion. Therefore he who can subdue his passions is mightier than the bravest of warriors.

The greed for physical pleasure is circumscribed by gratification and satiation. But the striving after money, the *means* for pleasure, has no limit for though money in itself does not give pleasure, it makes possible all future enjoyment. Therefore the lust for money can never be satisfied. And a man's craving for more and more wealth may well grow to such excess that the

1. Ben Zoma said: Who is wise? He who learns from all men. For it is said: "From all those who have taught me I have gotten understanding, for Your ennobling testimonies are my pursuits." Who is strong? He who subdues his passions. For it is said: "He who is slow to anger is better than a hero, and he who has control over his will is better than he who conquers a city." Who is rich? He who rejoices in his portion. For it is said: "When you enjoy the work of your hands, then you shall stride forward and it shall be well with you." Progress in this world and good in the world to come. Who is honored? He who honors others. For it is said: "For those who honor Me I will honor and those who despise Me shall be held in contempt."

---

lack of what he does not now possess may actually mar his joy in whatever he does have at present. Yet it is precisely this joy in what one possesses, this contentment with one's portion that constitutes the only genuine treasure and the sole true happiness in life; without it, even the richest of men will remain poor in the midst of all his wealth. Hence the surest way not only to become rich but also to remain so is to limit one's wishes to the modest measure of that which is necessary and within reach, and above all, to learn to view חלקו, whatever God has given one, with rejoicing, as the "portion" granted him by Heaven to be utilized for the discharge of his task on earth. This awareness of where one's duty lies can endow any God-given "portion" with irreplaceable, infinitely blissful worth.* Desire no more than you have— and you are indeed rich.

איזהו מכובד. It is the most common thing that people who seek honor for themselves behave toward others with reserve bordering on arrogance, and that they make very much of themselves but very little of others. Such conduct, they think, is the surest way to secure the respect and esteem of others. But this Mishna knows otherwise. Honor, genuine honor, is just another one of the gifts deriving from God, and it has a way of going to him who covets it least. He who does not despise any of his fellowmen, but respects them all as בריות, as "creations" of God, giving them due honor for the sake of Him Who created them, actually honors God, the Creator of them all. And of such a man, God says, "Him who honors Me, I shall honor." Conversely, he who despises his fellow-men God will let sink into oblivion.

---

* The German term "reich" is appropriate: Rich ("reich") is he who has achieved ("erreicht") what he wants.

ב בֶּן־עַזַּאי אוֹמֵר, הֱוֵי רָץ לְמִצְוָה קַלָּה וּבוֹרֵחַ מִן־הָעֲבֵרָה,
שֶׁמִּצְוָה גּוֹרֶרֶת מִצְוָה וַעֲבֵרָה גּוֹרֶרֶת עֲבֵרָה שֶׁשְּׂכַר מִצְוָה מִצְוָה
וּשְׂכַר עֲבֵרָה עֲבֵרָה:

ג הוּא הָיָה אוֹמֵר, אַל־תְּהִי בָז לְכָל־אָדָם וְאַל־תְּהִי מַפְלִיג
לְכָל־דָּבָר שֶׁאֵין לְךָ אָדָם שֶׁאֵין לוֹ שָׁעָה וְאֵין לְךָ דָּבָר שֶׁאֵין
לוֹ מָקוֹם:

ד רַבִּי לְוִיטַס אִישׁ יַבְנֶה אוֹמֵר, מְאֹד מְאֹד הֱוֵי שְׁפַל רוּחַ
שֶׁתִּקְוַת אֱנוֹשׁ רִמָּה:

ה רַבִּי יוֹחָנָן בֶּן־בְּרוֹקָה אוֹמֵר, כָּל־הַמְחַלֵּל שֵׁם שָׁמַיִם בְּסֵתֶר
נִפְרָעִין מִמֶּנּוּ בַּגָּלוּי· אֶחָד שׁוֹגֵג וְאֶחָד מֵזִיד בְּחִלּוּל הַשֵּׁם:

---

2. Should you have an opportunity to perform a *Mitzvah*, do not let it pass
by; perhaps the *Mitzvah* seems so easy that you might think there would be
ample opportunity to do it at other times; or perhaps, since it appears to
be so simple, it may seem to you so trifling as to make you think that even
failure to perform it would not hurt your conscience overmuch. Yet, let
nothing deter you from fulfilling it, for you cannot afford to overlook the
consequences, both seen and unseen, of any *Mitzvah*. The good that you do
will lead to more good, and every act of duty done bears its own reward.
The knowledge that you have done the will of your Father in Heaven will
bring you closer to Him; it will enrich your spirit with the happy awareness
of having done the right thing, and reinforce your moral capacity for doing
good. The reverse is true of sin. Do not underestimate the consequences of
even the most trivial wrong. It is not enough merely not to sin in action; Flee
far from evil and shun anything that might lead to it. For you can foresee
neither the effect nor sequel of a sin. Evil leads to more evil, and every sin
bears within itself the seeds of its own punishment. It removes you from the
pure and loving Presence of your Father in Heaven; it will awaken within
you the torturing pangs of conscience, it will dull the keen edge of your moral
judgement and weaken your resistance to future evil.

3. There is no such person or thing that cannot be of serious harm or,
conversely, of great profit to you at some future time. Therefore it behooves
you never to despise any person or any thing.

4. It would seem probable that this statement derives from the view that
all arrogance and all prideful presumption are rooted in the sensuous physical
aspects of the human personality. The purely spiritual and moral forces within

2.   Ben Azzai said: Hasten to do even the slightest *Mitzvah* and flee
from all sin, for one *Mitzvah* will lead to another *Mitzvah,* and one
sin to another sin, for the recompense of a *Mitzvah* is inherent in the
Mitzvah, while the recompense of sin is the sin.

3.   He used to say: Despise not any man and do not deem anything
unworthy of consideration, for there is no man that does not have
his hour and no thing that does not have its place.

4.   Rabbi Levitas of Yavneh said: Be exceedingly humble in spirit,
for the hope of earthly man is but decay.

5.   Rabbi Yochanan bên Berokah, said: He who profanes the Name
of God in secret will suffer the penalty of being unmasked in public.
This is true regardless of whether the *Chillul Hashem* is perpetrated
in error or intentionally.

---

us make for modesty as a matter of course, for they are so deeply imbued with
the magnitude of the task at hand that whatever we may have achieved or accomplished needs must fade ino utter insignificance when compared to the vast-
ness of the task to be fulfilled. Therefore it is appropriate to admonish the
proud and the arrogant to remember that all those aspirations that depend
on the realm of the physical and sensual can end only in decay.

5. חלול השם is deemed the most serious of all transgressions. It is that sin
which is perpetrated when a person who is qualified, by virtue of his calling
or station, to teach and, both by word and by personal example, to champion
and promote among men the hallowing of God's Name and the conscientious
fulfillment of His Law, publicly shows contempt for the Name of God and
openly transgresses the command of His will. We are told here that, even if
such a man feigns dutiful loyalty in public and leads a sinful life in private
only, he will suffer the punishment of being exposed in public for what he
really is so that all may behold his unworthiness. — אחד שוגג any error in
the sphere of the fulfillment of life's duty betokens a lack of understanding,
caution and circumspection in this aspect of living, and also a certain degree
of indifference to the concept of loyalty properly due to the Law of God.
Therefore, any error committed in this connection by one to whom men look
up in admiration as an example for themselves to emulate, has an adverse
influence upon the attitude that should by right be adopted by his fellow men.
This is true even if it was obvious to all that the act committed had been an
error. And the fact is that, all too often, such acts are not always or by all
recognized as errors and thus one error may persist in memory as a dangerous
example set by a man whom others seek to emulate. For this reason it is not
enough that a person to whom others look as a model by which to guide their
own conduct should take more than ordinary care to keep from sinning on

י רַבִּי יִשְׁמָעֵאל בַּר רַבִּי יוֹסֵי אוֹמֵר, הַלּוֹמֵד עַל־מְנָת לְלַמֵּד מַסְפִּיקִים בְּיָדוֹ לִלְמוֹד וּלְלַמֵּד וְהַלּוֹמֵד עַל־מְנָת לַעֲשׂוֹת מַסְפִּיקִים בְּיָדוֹ לִלְמוֹד וּלְלַמֵּד לִשְׁמוֹר וְלַעֲשׂוֹת:

י רַבִּי צָדוֹק אוֹמֵר, אַל־(תִּפְרוֹשׁ מִן־הַצִּבּוּר וְאַל־הַעַשׂ עַצְמְךָ כְּעוֹרְכֵי הַדַּיָּנִין וְאַל־)תַּעֲשֶׂהָ עֲטָרָה לְהִתְגַּדֶּל־בָּהּ, וְלֹא קַרְדּוֹם לַחְפָּר־בָּהּ. וְכַךְ הָיָה הִלֵּל אוֹמֵר וּדְאִשְׁתַּמֵּשׁ בְּתַגָּא חֲלָף, הָא לָמַדְתָּ כָּל־הַנֶּהֱנֶה מִדִּבְרֵי תוֹרָה נוֹטֵל חַיָּיו מִן־הָעוֹלָם:

ה רַבִּי יוֹסֵי אוֹמֵר, כָּל־הַמְכַבֵּד אֶת־הַתּוֹרָה גּוּפוֹ מְכֻבָּד עַל־הַבְּרִיּוֹת וְכָל־הַמְחַלֵּל אֶת־הַתּוֹרָה גּוּפוֹ מְחֻלָּל עַל־הַבְּרִיּוֹת:

purpose; it is required of him that he must be carefully on his guard to avoid doing such wrongs even unwittingly or in error.

6. Quite aside from its predominant *Mitzvah* value, the intention to pass on, by means of instruction, that which one has learned, is itself conducive to study, for the one who studies for this purpose is thus compelled to delve even more thoroughly into the material to be learned and to seek greater clarity of thought than he might otherwise. But the supreme purpose of learning Torah is to translate the teaching of the Word of God into practical deeds in loyal fulfillment thereof. This purpose embraces not only the duty to act in this manner, but also that of teaching the Word of God to everyone who is needful of such instruction and capable of grasping it. Quite aside from the all-important *Mitzvah* value inherent in this act, the very intention and resolve to fulfill that which is to be learned is at the same time that attitude which is most conducive to proper study. To discern, from the Word of the Law, the will of God as regards the arrangement of our own lives requires the clearest, broadest and most profound penetration and understanding of the Torah. But over and beyond even this, that laudable intention is in itself inimical to any erroneous view, be it ever so ingenious, that may corrupt the mind with its wit and casuistry; and it will ever keep before us the reminder that "any error in theoretical study will lead to wrongdoing in practice."— שגגת תלמוד עולה זדון.

7. It is not through the individual, but through the community and through the congregation which represent that community on a smaller scale, that Judaism lives on forever. Besides, it was not the Jewish individual but the *Kehilath Yaakov*, the Jewish community that God appointed as the bearer

6. Rabbi Yishmael ben Rabbi Yosé said: To him who learns in order to teach, Heaven will grant the opportunity both to learn and to teach; but to him who learns in order to practice, Heaven will grant the opportunity to learn and to teach, to guard and to practice.

7. Rabbi Tzadok said: Do not set yourself apart from the community and act not as the counsel of the judges. Make not of it [the Torah] a crown with which to aggrandize yourself, nor an axe with which to strike. Thus said Hillel: "He who makes use of the crown [of the Torah] shall pass away." Thence you may learn that he who derives selfish gain from the words of the Torah thereby takes his own life away from this world.

8. Rabbi Yosé said: He who honors the Torah will himself be honored by mankind, but he who dishonors the Torah will himself be disdained by mankind.

---

of His sacred cause. Therefore the Jewish individual can fulfill his true purpose only in communion with the congregation, and accordingly he is earnestly admonished not to separate himself from the congregation, but to cleave to it in both joy and sorrow, to share its burdens and to help it discharge its tasks. However, it is self-understood that this duty exists only so long as the congregation, in its turn, will not forsake the inalienable eternal destiny of the Jewish community and thus, in fact, cease to be Jewish. Once that should happen, then the course to be taken by the individual is equally clear and unequivocal. He must then abide by the ruling: לא תהיה אחרי רבים לרעות which tells us not to follow the majority on the path of evil. — אל תעש וכו' (see Chap. 1:8). — אל תעשה וכו'. Do not debase the wisdom of the Word of God to use it as a tool for self-aggrandizement or selfish gain. The sacred wisdom is a crown of which it is written כי הוא חייכם "The Word of God is your very life." He who debases the Torah violates it and therefore brings about his own destruction. — וכך היה הלל אומר (see Chap. 1:13).

8. He who accepts the Torah as the sole, supreme source of truth and of guiding human purpose will receive from the Torah in turn that spiritual stature and moral ennoblement which will earn him the honor and respect of his fellow-men without his having to seek such recognition. But he who will deny the Torah the honor and respect due it and will not permit the Torah to bring its spiritual and moral influence to bear upon his thoughts and endeavors will descend to a level of base worthlessness and will have to forego all hope of ever receiving the esteem and respect of others.

ט רַבִּי יִשְׁמָעֵאל בְּנוֹ אוֹמֵר, הַחוֹשֵׂךְ עַצְמוֹ מִן־הַדִּין פּוֹרֵק מִמֶּנּוּ אֵיבָה וְגָזֵל וּשְׁבוּעַת שָׁוְא, וְהַגַּס לִבּוֹ בְּהוֹרָאָה שׁוֹטֶה רָשָׁע וְגַס רוּחַ:

י הוּא הָיָה אוֹמֵר, אַל־תְּהִי דָן יְחִידִי שֶׁאֵין דָּן יְחִידִי אֶלָּא אֶחָד, וְאַל־תֹּאמַר קַבְּלוּ דַעְתִּי שֶׁהֵם רַשָּׁאִים וְלֹא אָתָּה:

יא רַבִּי יוֹנָתָן אוֹמֵר, כָּל־הַמְקַיֵּם אֶת־הַתּוֹרָה מֵעֹנִי סוֹפוֹ לְקַיְּמָהּ מֵעשֶׁר, וְכָל־הַמְבַטֵּל אֶת־הַתּוֹרָה מֵעשֶׁר סוֹפוֹ לְבַטְּלָהּ מֵעֹנִי:

יב רַבִּי מֵאִיר אוֹמֵר, הֱוֵי מְמַעֵט בְּעֵסֶק וַעֲסֹק בַּתּוֹרָה וֶהֱוֵה שְׁפַל־רוּחַ בִּפְנֵי כָל־אָדָם וְאִם־בָּטַלְתָּ מִן־הַתּוֹרָה יֶשׁ־לְךָ בְּטֵלִים הַרְבֵּה כְּנֶגְדֶּךָ וְאִם־עָמַלְתָּ בַתּוֹרָה יֶשׁ־לוֹ שָׂכָר הַרְבֵּה לִתֶּן־לָךְ:

---

9. If there is another properly qualified person available to administer justice, it is the part of wisdom to decline the function of judge or arbitrator. For, though he may have made his decision in strict accordance with the dictates of his conscience, the judge as a rule incurs the hostility of the losing party. Besides, even with best of intentions and after the most conscientious deliberation, a judge is still not immune to error and may thus, albeit unintentionally, perpetrate a miscarriage of justice and wrongfully deprive one party of its just due. Finally, most of the cases where sworn testimony is required, involve either שבועת שקר, outright perjury, or else, in instances where he against whom the testimony is made, is convinced of the truth of that testimony even without a sworn deposition, שבועת שוא, an oath taken in vain. It is true that, in cases where he is the only one fit to administer justice, the person filling the function of judge has carried out a most important duty. In fact, in the Hebrew language a conscientious judge is called by the name of God Himself, אלקים, implying that he acts as a representative of God on earth. But by the same token he who is not compelled to act in this capacity is spared a responsibility that is certainly not to be taken lightly. Of course he who impudently seeks to force his own decision upon others only exposes thereby his deficiency in wisdom and scruples, as well as his foolish conceit.

10. Even though any man of recognized faithfulness to the law (מומחה לרבים) is permitted to act as a judge without associates, it is advisable that he refrain from doing so. For only God, the sole Judge with Whom error is impossible, should judge alone. If you should be a member of a tribunal of judges, do not insist on your own views. For in any tribunal it is only the majority of the judges, rather than any single one among them, that has the authority to make the decision.

9. Rabbi Yishmael, his son, said: He who shuns judicial office rids himself of hatred, robbery and perjury. But he who presumptuously lays down decisions on the law is foolish, lawless and arrogant.

10. He used to say: Judge not alone, for there is only One Who may judge alone. And say not, "Accept my view," for it is they and not you that have the authority.

11. Rabbi Yonathan says: He who fulfills the Torah out of poverty shall also fulfill it out of wealth; he who neglects the Torah out of wealth shall also neglect it out of poverty.

12. Rabbi Meir says: Limit your business activities and occupy yourself with the Torah instead, and be of humble spirit before all men. If you should neglect the Torah you will have to compete with many [others] who neglect the Torah, but if you toil in the Torah, God has abundant recompense to give you.

---

11. He whom the lack of material wealth, joys and pleasures will bring only nearer to the Torah, to that eternally inalienable, ever-present source of all moral and spiritual riches, bliss, and joy, and who finds in the Torah ample compensation for the things he must do without,—he will observe the Torah even if his circumstances should improve. Even if his material wealth should increase, he will still proudly cleave to the faithful study and observance of the Torah which alone endows earthly wealth with true and genuine worth. The greater the treasures he may acquire, the more will he devote them to the effort the better to discharge his God-given task. Not so he whom the superabundance of material possessions and pleasures makes insensitive and impervious to those moral and spiritual values that can be derived only from the faithful study and observance of the Torah. If his wealth in earthly goods should ever crumble, he will be so utterly absorbed in desperate attempts to recoup his lost fortune that he will have neither the wish, nor, he thinks, the time, to seek the way to that wealth and to that happiness which changes on earth cannot affect, and which can be found only in the study and observance of the Laws of the Torah.

12. Do a little less business so that you may gain additional time to engage in the study of the Torah. The financial sacrifice involved will be easier for you if you will accustom yourself to a more modest standard of living in the social circles in which you move. Remember that if, in order not to lag behind in other endeavors, you deprive the Torah of its rightful place in your life, you will have chosen a path upon which you will have many competitors to contend with, men who, like you, have neglected the Torah in order to devote their energies to the race for selfish gain. At the same time, bear in mind that the Lord has ample recompense in store for him who foregoes all other gain in order to toil upon the field of the Torah.

יג רַבִּי אֱלִיעֶזֶר בֶּן־יַעֲקֹב אוֹמֵר, הָעוֹשֶׂה מִצְוָה אַחַת קוֹנֶה
לוֹ פְּרַקְלִיט אֶחָד וְהָעוֹבֵר עֲבֵרָה אַחַת קוֹנֶה לוֹ קַטֵּגוֹר אֶחָד,
תְּשׁוּבָה וּמַעֲשִׂים טוֹבִים כִּתְרִיס בִּפְנֵי הַפֻּרְעָנוּת:

יד רַבִּי יוֹחָנָן הַסַּנְדְּלָר אוֹמֵר, כָּל־כְּנֵסִיָּה שֶׁהִיא לְשֵׁם שָׁמַיִם
סוֹפָהּ לְהִתְקַיֵּם וְשֶׁאֵינָהּ לְשֵׁם שָׁמַיִם אֵין סוֹפָהּ לְהִתְקַיֵּם:

טו רַבִּי אֶלְעָזָר בֶּן שַׁמּוּעַ אוֹמֵר, יְהִי כְבוֹד תַּלְמִידְךָ חָבִיב עָלֶיךָ
כְּשֶׁלָּךְ וּכְבוֹד חֲבֵרְךָ כְּמוֹרָא רַבָּךְ וּמוֹרָא רַבָּךְ כְּמוֹרָא
שָׁמָיִם:

טז רַבִּי יְהוּדָה אוֹמֵר, הֱוֵה זָהִיר בְּתַלְמוּד שֶׁשִּׁגְגַת תַּלְמוּד
עוֹלָה זָדוֹן:

יז רַבִּי שִׁמְעוֹן אוֹמֵר, שְׁלֹשָׁה כְתָרִים הֵן· כֶּתֶר תּוֹרָה וְכֶתֶר
כְּהֻנָּה וְכֶתֶר מַלְכוּת· וְכֶתֶר שֵׁם טוֹב עוֹלֶה עַל גַּבֵּיהֶן:

---

13. Our happiness in both this world and the next depends upon our conduct as regards our duty. Every *Mitzvah* we fulfill will be one more advocate before God to speak in our behalf, while every sin we commit will stand as one more accuser to testify against us before Him who guides our destinies. Constant endeavor to become better and good deeds serve as protective armors against any calamity.

14. The term לשם שמים describes any endeavor for the promotion of a good thing for its own sake, without any ulterior motive. As Abrabanel notes in connection with this Mishna, any organization so conceived bears within itself the prerequisite for permanent endurance by virtue of the fact that its members all bear allegiance to its good cause and will subordinate all personal interests to this their common goal. But in an organization based on ignoble motives the members will soon be led to dicker with one another over personal interests, and such rivalry bears within it the seed of sure disintegration which will then be only a matter of time.

15. The subject of discussion here is not the extent to which the honor of one's student should be protected, nor the degree of reverence due to a teacher or to God Himself. What is brought out here is simply the fact that honor is due even to our pupils and disciples and that we are duty bound to protect it; and that we are not to violate the reverence due our teachers and our God. When teaching our students and in our dealings with them we must never

13. Rabbi Eliezer ben Yaakov, said: He who fulfills one commandment gains for himself one advocate; and he who commits one sin acquires for himself one accuser [thereby]. Repentance and good deeds are a shield against calamity.

14. Rabbi Yochanan Ha-Sandlar said: Every assembly out of pure motives for the promotion of noble purposes will in the end endure, but that which is not out of pure motives and for noble purposes will in the end not endure.

15. Rabbi Elazar ben Shamua, said: Let the honor of your student be as dear to you as your own; let the honor of your friend be as dear to you as the reverence due your teacher; and let the reverence due your teacher be as dear to you as the reverence due to Heaven.

16. Rabbi Yehuda said: Be cautious in study, for an error in study amounts to intentional sin.

17. Rabbi Shimon said: There are three crowns; the crown of the Torah, the crown of priesthood and the crown of kingship. But the crown of a good name excels them all.

---

allow ourselves, in our zeal to teach and discipline, to degrade or injure the dignity of a disciple. When associating with our equals on a more familiar footing, we must not let intimacy lead us to forget for one moment the deference with which we must treat their honor. Finally, any violation on our part of the reverence we owe to our teachers should weigh upon our conscience as heavily as would any act of irreverence against God Himself.

16. The neglect, or the improper or superficial study of our Torah in theory will give rise to error and sin in practice. Our sin may be due to error only, but if that error results from indifference to the knowledge of our duty, and from intentional failure to seek better guidance by studying our Torah, then, in view of the indifference and intentional neglect that is at its cause, the error, though unintentional in itself, becomes a sin subject to punishment. Thus we read in Lev. 17:21 פשעיהם לכל חטאתם (see Commentary ibid.).

17. The "crown of a good name" excels the other three, first by virtue of the fact that it is within the reach of all, without exception, and secondly because all the other three are without value unless they are linked with the crown of a good name. Any of these three crowns can be truly "crowns" only if he who wears them is deserving also of the crown of a good name because he shines forth both as a human being and as a Jew, distinguished in moral purity and devotion to duty, and particularly in the exemplary fulfillment of those duties and those opportunities to do good that are connected with the station of honor and privilege he occupies. It may also be that עולה על גביהן means [that the "crown of a good name]...must be linked with them all."

יח רַבִּי נְהוֹרַאי אוֹמֵר, הֱוֵי גוֹלֶה לִמְקוֹם תּוֹרָה וְאַל־תֹּאמַר
שֶׁהִיא תָבוֹא אַחֲרֶיךָ שֶׁחֲבֵרֶיךָ יְקַיְּמוּהָ בְיָדֶךָ וְאֶל־בִּינָתְךָ אַל־
תִּשָּׁעֵן:

יט רַבִּי יַנַּאי אוֹמֵר, אֵין בְּיָדֵינוּ לֹא מִשַּׁלְוַת הָרְשָׁעִים וְאַף לֹא
מִיִּסּוּרֵי הַצַּדִּיקִים:

כ רַבִּי מַתְיָא בֶּן־חָרָשׁ אוֹמֵר, הֱוֵי מַקְדִּים בִּשְׁלוֹם כָּל־אָדָם
וֶהֱוֵי זָנָב לָאֲרָיוֹת וְאַל־תְּהִי רֹאשׁ לַשּׁוּעָלִים:

כא רַבִּי יַעֲקֹב אוֹמֵר, הָעוֹלָם הַזֶּה דּוֹמֶה לִפְרוֹזְדוֹר בִּפְנֵי הָעוֹלָם
הַבָּא· הַתְקֵן עַצְמְךָ בַּפְּרוֹזְדוֹר כְּדֵי שֶׁתִּכָּנֵס לַטְּרַקְלִין:

כב הוּא הָיָה אוֹמֵר, יָפָה שָׁעָה אַחַת בִּתְשׁוּבָה וּמַעֲשִׂים טוֹבִים
בָּעוֹלָם הַזֶּה מִכָּל חַיֵּי הָעוֹלָם הַבָּא וְיָפָה שָׁעָה אַחַת שֶׁל־קוֹרַת
רוּחַ בָּעוֹלָם הַבָּא מִכָּל־חַיֵּי הָעוֹלָם הַזֶּה:

---

18. Seek out a place where the Torah is diligently studied, even if it means leaving your home that you love. Do not say that the wisdom of the Torah will be at your beck and call wherever you may be. For whatever skill you have will grow and survive only if you associate with people of similar interests. If you lack such companionship your talent—in this instance the knowledge of the Torah—will eventually atrophy.

19. To determine the relationship between the visible fate of a man and his moral worthiness or lack thereof is utterly beyond our power. It is not only the prosperity of the wicked that so frequently confronts us with an enigma. The fact that honest men should suffer seems just as perplexing, even though we believe that it is easier to assert that actually a person thus afflicted is wicked than to concede that he is good. The evil that a man does is never done under false pretenses, but the good he does may well be motivated by any number of considerations unknown to us, which are ignoble and thus cancel whatever value the supposed good deed might otherwise have had. However, we do not have sufficient insight either to determine a person's moral worth or worthlessness, or to judge whether that which befalls him is indeed a blessing or a calamity. Therefore it behooves us to abstain from passing judgment in either case, and not to permit our own short-sighted view of the events we witness to influence our own decisions.

18. Rabbi Nehorai said: Emigrate to a place where there is Torah wisdom, and say not that it will follow you, for it is your associates who will keep it ever in your hand and do not rely upon your own understanding.

19. Rabbi Yannai said: Nothing is in our hands; [we can explain] neither the prosperity of the lawless nor the sufferings of the righteous.

20. Rabbi Mathyah ben Charash, said: Anticipate every man's salutation; be rather a tail among lions than a head among foxes.

21. Rabbi Yaakov said: This world is like the vestibule before the world to come; prepare yourself in the vestibule so that you may [be able to] enter the banquet hall.

22. He used to say: One hour of repentance and good deeds in this world is worth more than the whole life of the world to come; and one hour of spiritual bliss in the world to come is worth more than the whole life of this world.

---

20. Do not expect others, as a sign of respect, to salute you first, but be the one to offer the first salute. Above all, seek the company of men who are superior to you both spiritually and morally, even though you would occupy an inferior position in their midst and would have to submit to their guidance. Conversely, shun any association with your moral and spiritual inferiors, even if you would stand out as a leader in their midst.

21. All of us have been invited to the banquet of the King of Kings, but only he who has made himself worthy of this invitation will be admitted to the banquet hall. This world is the vestibule in which to prepare yourselves. Make use of your sojourn in the vestibule to make yourself worthy of entering the great hall itself.

22. Each of these two worlds has its own purpose and thus a value peculiarly its own which the other cannot afford us. This world is the place where you may prepare yourself by self-ennoblement through the discharge of your physical, moral and spiritual tasks. You cannot make up in the world to come for any of the moral and spiritual refinement that you have not attained in this world by such faithful performance of your tasks. Hence even one hour of repentance and good deeds here on earth is more important for the improvement of your soul than all the life of the next; for that which you have failed to do in one hour of life's task here below you cannot retrieve even in all the eternity of the world to come. The world to come, on the other hand, is one of blissful happiness, and all the joys and pleasures which even the longest lifetime on earth could afford, cannot outweigh even one single hour of spiritual satisfaction such as is found in the world to come.

כג רַבִּי שִׁמְעוֹן בֶּן־אֶלְעָזָר אוֹמֵר, אַל־תְּרַצֶּה אֶת־חֲבֵרְךָ בִּשְׁעַת
כַּעֲסוֹ וְאַל־תְּנַחֲמֵהוּ בְּשָׁעָה שֶׁמֵּתוֹ מֻטָּל לְפָנָיו · וְאַל־תִּשְׁאַל לוֹ
בִּשְׁעַת נִדְרוֹ · וְאַל־תִּשְׁתַּדֵּל לִרְאוֹתוֹ בִּשְׁעַת קַלְקָלָתוֹ:

כד שְׁמוּאֵל הַקָּטָן אוֹמֵר, בִּנְפֹל אוֹיִבְךָ אַל־תִּשְׂמָח וּבִכָּשְׁלוֹ אַל־
יָגֵל לִבֶּךָ · פֶּן־יִרְאֶה יְיָ וְרַע בְּעֵינָיו וְהֵשִׁיב מֵעָלָיו אַפּוֹ:

כה אֱלִישָׁע בֶּן־אֲבוּיָה אוֹמֵר, הַלּוֹמֵד יֶלֶד לְמָה הוּא דוֹמֶה לִדְיוֹ
כְתוּבָה עַל־נְיָר חָדָשׁ וְהַלּוֹמֵד זָקֵן לְמָה הוּא דוֹמֶה לִדְיוֹ כְתוּבָה
עַל־נְיָר מָחוּק:

כו רַבִּי יוֹסֵי בַּר יְהוּדָה אִישׁ כְּפַר הַבַּבְלִי אוֹמֵר, הַלּוֹמֵד מִן
הַקְּטַנִּים לְמָה הוּא דוֹמֶה לְאוֹכֵל עֲנָבִים קֵהוֹת וְשׁוֹתֶה יַיִן מִגִּתּוֹ
וְהַלּוֹמֵד מִן־הַזְּקֵנִים לְמָה הוּא דוֹמֶה לְאוֹכֵל עֲנָבִים בְּשׁוּלוֹת
וְשׁוֹתֶה יַיִן יָשָׁן:

כז רַבִּי (מֵאִיר) אוֹמֵר, אַל־תִּסְתַּכֵּל בְּקַנְקָן אֶלָּא בְּמָה שֶׁיֶּשׁ־בּוֹ ·

---

23. When you seek to help your neighbor—wait for an appropriate time to
do it. Do not think that good intentions alone are sufficient excuse and justification for all things. If you wish to influence your neighbor's mood, do not
attempt to do so at the time when he is shaken and agitated, but wait until
he has grown calmer and hence more amenable to reasonable suggestion. This
rule holds true in whatever it is you seek to accomplish; whether it be to
appease your fellow-man, or to comfort him, to spur him on to dissolve the
vow he has made, or else to offer him your sympathy. — אל תשתדל Do not
go out of your way to visit someone who suffered something unpleasant if
you know that he would rather remain alone and unseen in his distress.

24. If your enemy who has pursued you should fall, do not rejoice, and if
he commits a moral blunder do not exult in the knowledge that, at long last,
the whole world will see how wicked he is. For if you were thus to gloat at
another's misfortune, you would commit a grievous sin against God. It may
very well be that God has tolerated your foe's pursuit of you only as a means
to bring about your moral betterment. Your malicious joy at his downfall
would then indicate to God that you have still not attained moral maturity;

23. Rabbi Shimon ben Elazar, said: Seek not to appease your fellow-man at the time of his anger; nor to comfort him when his dead
lies before him; nor suggest ways to reconsider his vow at the time
he took it; and strive not to see him at the time of his humiliation.

24. Shemuel Ha-Katan said: Rejoice not when your enemy falls, and
let not your heart exult when he stumbles; lest the Lord see it and
be displeased and He turn away his wrath from him.

25. Elisha ben Abuyah, said: That which one learns in his youth is
like ink written on clean paper; that which one learns in his old age
is like ink written on blotted paper.

26. Rabbi Yosé bar Yehudah, from Kfar Ha-Bavli, said: He who
learns from young men is like one who eats unripe grapes and drinks
wine from the wine press. He who learns from old men is like one
who eats ripe grapes and drinks old wine.

27. Rabbi Meir says: Look not at the vessel but at what it contains.

---

as a consequence, it may be that He will let your pursuer rise again in order
to complete the process of your moral betterment. Shemuel Ha-Katan quotes
this admonition from Prov. 24:17, 18 to remind himself and others, too, how
closely we must guard at all times against entertaining any feeling of malice
toward any of our fellow-men. It is not enough merely not to do evil to our
foe and not to wish him ill. Even malicious joy at misfortune that came to
him without any act on our part is a grievous sin indeed before the Lord.

25. That which man learns in his youth he absorbs with an intellect still
clear of other images and concepts; therefore that material which he then
studies can leave a clear and lasting impression. But by the time a man is
old, his mind is already prejudiced by much extraneous matter which must
be pushed aside before the new can be accepted. Hence what he learns in
his old age will not impress itself so easily upon his mind, nor deeply enough
to remain with him permanently.

26. While the most desirable students are young students, men of more
mature age should be sought as teachers. Even as unripe grapes lack the ripe-
ness acquired with time from the sun, so the knowledge which young men
have absorbed and are able to communicate, lacks the mellowness that only
years of experience and repeated reflection can afford. And even as wine
newly taken from the press is still cloudy and unsettled, so the ideas which
the young develop from the learning they have acquired and which they
would pass on as truths based on solid knowledge still lack that calm and
clear prudence by which the mature can sift the true from the false.

27. Rabbi Meir points out, however, that the general statement set forth
in Mishna 26 is not universally applicable. One should consider not so much

יֵשׁ קַנְקַן חָדָשׁ מָלֵא יָשָׁן·וְיָשָׁן שֶׁאֲפִילוּ חָדָשׁ אֵין בּוֹ:

כח רַבִּי אֶלְעָזָר הַקַּפָּר אוֹמֵר, הַקִּנְאָה וְהַתַּאֲוָה וְהַכָּבוֹד מוֹצִיאִים אֶת־הָאָדָם מִן הָעוֹלָם:

כט הוּא הָיָה אוֹמֵר, הַיִּלּוֹדִים לָמוּת וְהַמֵּתִים לִהְיוֹת וְהַחַיִּים לָדוֹן, לֵידַע וּלְהוֹדִיעַ וּלְהִוָּדַע, שֶׁהוּא אֵל הוּא הַיּוֹצֵר הוּא הַבּוֹרֵא הוּא הַמֵּבִין הוּא הַדַּיָּן הוּא הָעֵד הוּא בַּעַל דִּין הוּא עָתִיד לָדוֹן בָּרוּךְ הוּא שֶׁאֵין לְפָנָיו לֹא עַוְלָה וְלֹא שִׁכְחָה וְלֹא מַשּׂוֹא פָנִים וְלֹא מִקַּח שֹׁחַד, שֶׁהַכֹּל שֶׁלּוֹ·וְדַע שֶׁהַכֹּל לְפִי הַחֶשְׁבּוֹן וְאַל־יַבְטִיחֲךָ יִצְרְךָ, שֶׁהַשְּׁאוֹל בֵּית מָנוֹס לָךְ, שֶׁעַל כָּרְחֲךָ אַתָּה נוֹצָר וְעַל כָּרְחֲךָ אַתָּה נוֹלָד וְעַל כָּרְחֲךָ אַתָּה חַי וְעַל כָּרְחֲךָ אַתָּה מֵת וְעַל כָּרְחֲךָ אַתָּה עָתִיד לִתֵּן דִּין וְחֶשְׁבּוֹן לִפְנֵי מֶלֶךְ מַלְכֵי הַמְּלָכִים הַקָּדוֹשׁ בָּרוּךְ הוּא:

רבי חנניא וכו׳ קדיש:

---

the age of the teacher as the content of the teaching that he has to offer. There are many young men whose minds are mature, while there are old men who do not possess even the knowledge of the young.

28. God caused man to live in the world and made him fit for it. It is only in connection with this world and through the endeavor to utilize his energies in the service of the world and its welfare that man fulfills his purpose. The vices listed here, however, make selfish interest the sole purpose of him whom they dominate and so they cause him to clash with the rest of the world, for under such circumstances the world has value to him only as long as it will cater to his desires. Thus he forfeits the destiny for which God made him.

29. Birth, death, resurrection and reckoning,—these are the preordained periods into which our lives are divided and of which we are to be aware at all times. We are to remember, always, that our life here below is bounded by death, but that death, too, is only a transient phase, leading to a new and different form of existence. Not only the soul is untouched by death but the body, too, is destined to live again. However with all of this we shall have to pass before the presence of the Lord in order to render accounting as to

There may be a new vessel full of old wine and an old vessel that has not even new wine in it.

28. Rabbi Elazar Ha-Kapar said: Envy, greed and thirst for honor take a man out from the world.

29. He used to say: Those who are born are destined to die, and the dead to rise again; the living, to be judged; to know, to teach and to make it known that God is the Maker, He the Creator, He the Discerner, He the Judge, He the Witness, He the Complainant. It is He that will in the future judge, blessed be He; in Whose presence there is no wrong, no forgetfulness, nor partiality, nor taking of bribes. Know also that everything comes to pass according to reckoning. And let not your fancy give you hope that the grave will be a place of refuge for you, for it was perforce that you were formed, perforce you were born, perforce you live, perforce you shall die, and perforce you will have to give account and reckoning before the Supreme King of Kings, the Holy One, blessed be He.

---

how and for what we have employed the life and existence granted us. — לידע ולהודיע ולהודע We ourselves are to know it, and to make others aware of it by teaching it to them, and, without explicit proclamation, we must let this truth become evident through everything we do, that God is not only the originator of our existence, but also that it was He Who shaped and fashioned us for our special purpose, and He carefully watches over our every step to discern whether or not we do justice to this our destiny. Therefore, if our behavior should not be in keeping with our Divinely-ordained destiny, God will also act as the Judge, Witness and Prosecutor and call us to account for our actions. In a court of justice over which a human judge presides, some human weakness on the part of the judge might save us, but in the Heavenly Tribunal there is no such chance. — הכל לפי החשבון The sentence does not depend upon the general impression left by the defendant; instead, it is determined by the accurate sum total of all our individual acts, both good and evil. Therefore let not even the smallest good that you accomplish, or even the least evil that you do, be a matter of indifference to you. For your every good deed adds to your merits before God, while every evil act of yours adds to the burden of your guilt. And there is no way for you to escape from this cycle that was preordained for you long before you were born; you have no choice with regard to either your creation or your birth, your life or your death, or with regard to your appearance before the Tribunal of God to render accounting for your past.

פרק חמישי

א בַּעֲשָׂרָה מַאֲמָרוֹת נִבְרָא הָעוֹלָם. וּמַה תַּלְמוּד לוֹמַר וַהֲלֹא בְּמַאֲמָר אֶחָד יָכוֹל לְהִבָּרְאוֹת. אֶלָּא לְהִפָּרַע מִן הָרְשָׁעִים שֶׁמְּאַבְּדִים אֶת הָעוֹלָם שֶׁנִּבְרָא בַּעֲשָׂרָה מַאֲמָרוֹת וְלִתֵּן שָׂכָר טוֹב לַצַּדִּיקִים שֶׁמְּקַיְּמִין אֶת הָעוֹלָם שֶׁנִּבְרָא בַּעֲשָׂרָה מַאֲמָרוֹת:

ב עֲשָׂרָה דוֹרוֹת מֵאָדָם וְעַד נֹחַ לְהוֹדִיעַ כַּמָּה אֶרֶךְ אַפַּיִם לְפָנָיו שֶׁכָּל הַדּוֹרוֹת הָיוּ מַכְעִיסִים לְפָנָיו עַד שֶׁהֵבִיא עֲלֵיהֶם אֶת מֵי הַמַּבּוּל:

ג עֲשָׂרָה דוֹרוֹת מִנֹּחַ וְעַד אַבְרָהָם, לְהוֹדִיעַ כַּמָּה אֶרֶךְ אַפַּיִם לְפָנָיו, שֶׁכָּל הַדּוֹרוֹת הָיוּ מַכְעִיסִים לְפָנָיו עַד שֶׁבָּא אַבְרָהָם אָבִינוּ וְקִבֵּל (עָלָיו) שְׂכַר כֻּלָּם:

ד עֲשָׂרָה נִסְיוֹנוֹת נִתְנַסָּה אַבְרָהָם אָבִינוּ וְעָמַד בְּכֻלָּם לְהוֹדִיעַ כַּמָּה חִבָּתוֹ שֶׁל אַבְרָהָם אָבִינוּ:

---

1. Had the entire process of Creation been completed by one single Divine utterance, and had it been thus recorded for us in the Torah also, then all things, the whole and all the parts thereof, would have appeared to be immediately caused by God's command of Creation only, and the position of man in the scheme of things would have been fixed on one plane with that of all the other works of creation. However, in this world, which was led to greater perfection by ten different utterances of Creation, one following the other, all the things that were made first were contributing factors in the creation of what came after them, and were, in fact, completed by the latter. Hence all that which came into being at a later time represents the completion of what has gone before and, in fact, is dependent upon the latter. All things sustain and are sustained in their turn. Man is the final work of creation, the goal and summit of the whole, in whom all of creation culminates. But his existence and his efficacy, too, are dependent upon the existence and the efficacy of all the rest of the world. If man fulfills his great task, then all the world of creation will attain through him the prerequisite for its survival. Hence, with the care that man extends to even the most minute fraction of the world entity in line with his task and duty, he makes a contribution not only

1. By ten utterances was the world created. What does this teach us? Could it not [all] have been created by one utterance? It is only to call to account the lawless who destroy the world that was created by ten utterances, and to give good reward to the righteous who preserve the world that was created by ten utterances.

2. There were ten generations from Adam to Noach, to show how long-suffering He is, seeing that all these generations acted contrary to His will, until He brought upon them the waters of lifelessness.

3. There were ten generations from Noach to Avraham, to show how long-suffering He is, seeing that all these generations acted contrary to His will, until our Father Avraham came and earned for himself the merit of them all.

4. With ten trials was our Father Avraham tried and he stood firm through them all, to show how great was the love of our Father Avraham for God.

---

to his own survival but also to that of the whole. But if man, in criminal lawlessness, should cast away his great destiny, he will only help prejudice the survival of the whole of creation, and by his unlawful destruction or neglect of even one fraction of the whole, he destroys and neglects that upon which depends not only his own salvation, but that of all the rest of creation as well.

2. היו מכעיסים: They stirred up, or evoked, His wrath; they were fully deserving of His anger. But God, being slow to anger, allowed them time to repent until the days of Noah.

3. קבל שכר כולם Every single member of the generations preceding Abraham should have felt himself called upon to counteract the steadily spreading evil and to pave the way for a better future. But it was only Abraham who earned the merit and was found worthy of being chosen as the instrument for bringing about that better future.

4. חבתו של אברהם אבינו. According to the context, it would seem that חבתו של אברהם אבינו has an active connotation, denoting Abraham's love for God. If, however, one should wish to construe this phrase in the more customary manner, that is, as denoting the love of God for Abraham, then the repeated trials should be taken as evidence in themselves of the high regard in which God held Abraham. As the Mishna has it: "The potter will strike only those pots that are good and whole to test them, because he knows that they will withstand even repeated blows."

ה. עֲשָׂרָה נִסִּים נַעֲשׂוּ לַאֲבוֹתֵינוּ בְמִצְרַיִם וַעֲשָׂרָה עַל הַיָּם:

י. עֶשֶׂר מַכּוֹת הֵבִיא הַקָּדוֹשׁ בָּרוּךְ הוּא עַל הַמִּצְרִיִּים בְּמִצְרַיִם וְעֶשֶׂר עַל הַיָּם:

ז. עֲשָׂרָה נִסְיוֹנוֹת נִסּוּ אֲבוֹתֵינוּ אֶת־הַקָּדוֹשׁ בָּרוּךְ הוּא בַּמִּדְבָּר שֶׁנֶּאֱמַר וַיְנַסּוּ אֹתִי זֶה עֶשֶׂר פְּעָמִים וְלֹא שָׁמְעוּ בְּקוֹלִי:

ח. עֲשָׂרָה נִסִּים נַעֲשׂוּ לַאֲבוֹתֵינוּ בְּבֵית הַמִּקְדָּשׁ · לֹא הִפִּילָה אִשָּׁה מֵרֵיחַ בְּשַׂר הַקֹּדֶשׁ, וְלֹא הִסְרִיחַ בְּשַׂר הַקֹּדֶשׁ מֵעוֹלָם, וְלֹא נִרְאָה זְבוּב בְּבֵית הַמַּטְבָּחַיִם, וְלֹא אֵרַע קֶרִי לְכֹהֵן גָּדוֹל בְּיוֹם הַכִּפּוּרִים, וְלֹא כִבּוּ הַגְּשָׁמִים אֵשׁ שֶׁל־עֲצֵי הַמַּעֲרָכָה, וְלֹא נִצְחָה הָרוּחַ אֶת־עַמּוּד הֶעָשָׁן, וְלֹא נִמְצָא פְּסוּל בָּעֹמֶר וּבִשְׁתֵּי הַלֶּחֶם וּבְלֶחֶם הַפָּנִים, עוֹמְדִים צְפוּפִים וּמִשְׁתַּחֲוִים רְוָחִים וְלֹא הִזִּיק נָחָשׁ וְעַקְרָב בִּירוּשָׁלַיִם מֵעוֹלָם, וְלֹא אָמַר אָדָם לַחֲבֵרוֹ צַר לִי הַמָּקוֹם שֶׁאָלִין בִּירוּשָׁלָיִם:

ט. עֲשָׂרָה דְבָרִים נִבְרְאוּ בְּעֶרֶב שַׁבָּת בֵּין הַשְּׁמָשׁוֹת וְאֵלּוּ הֵן.

---

6. We have but scant knowledge of these עשר מכות which struck the Egyptians at the Reed Sea. The miracles which our fathers experienced both in Mitzrayim and at the Reed Sea consisted primarily in the fact that they remained untouched by the plagues with which the Egyptians were stricken.

7. These repeated incidents of doubt and mutiny against the Will of God which marked the wanderings of our fathers in the wilderness are certainly ample proof for him who desires it that, contrary to what many would like to have themselves and others believe, the Torah did not originate with the Jewish people. Unlike all other codes of religious law, the Jewish "religion" and the Jewish law did *not* originate and emanate from *within* the people but were handed to it from *without,* thus of metaphysical origin, and proceeded to establish its Divine power in the ultimate conquest of the people. This people was to undergo an unparalleled martyrdom of many centuries for the very law against which it had resisted so stubbornly in the beginning. Similarly, the repeated instances of doubt are, in fact, a truly valid guarantee

5. Ten miracles were wrought for our fathers in *Mitzrayim* and ten at the Sea.

6. Ten plagues did the Holy One, blessed be He, bring upon the Egyptians in Egypt and ten at the Sea.

7. Ten times did our fathers try the Holy One, blessed be He, in the wilderness, as it is said, "Now they have tried me ten times and have not listened to My voice."

8. Ten miracles were wrought for our fathers in the Temple Sanctuary: No woman miscarried from the scent of the sacrificial meat; the sacrificial meat never became putrid; no fly was ever seen in the slaughter house of the Temple; no unclean accident ever befell the High Priest on the Day of Atonement; the rain never extinguished the fire on the wood pile on the altar; the wind did not prevail over the column of smoke that rose from the altar; no disqualifying defect was ever found in the Omer, in the two Shevuoth loaves or in the show-breads. [The people] stood closely pressed together and yet found ample space to prostrate themselves; no snake or scorpion ever did injury in Jerusalem, and no man ever said to his fellow: "There is too little room for me to lodge overnight in Jerusalem."

9. Ten things were created on the [first] Sabbath Eve at twilight:

---

for the factual truth of the Divine Revelation and the Divine miracles which accompanied the creation of our people and which we proclaimed to mankind. They demonstrate that the generation which partook of this Divine revelation and guidance was not composed of naive and credulous men who were ready to subscribe unconditionally to these new and unprecedented phenomena and events. This was—as they are described by our Sages—a דור דעה, a "sophisticated" generation which recognized and acknowledged the revealed demonstrations of Divinity only after repeated trials. Thus, in the end, it was not on the basis of "convenient belief" but with the "conviction of knowledge" based on the truth that they were ready to fight for and defend that which they had recognized to be the essence of their very existence.

8. These miraculous occurrences bore testimony to the constant presence of God both in the Holy City and in the Sanctuary, safeguarding the sacred rites performed in these holy places.

9. The creative process that took place during the Six Days of Creation embraces all the visible world. The Seventh Day, the Sabbath, is the memorial to the unseen Creator and Master of the world; it serves to train man to recognize and render homage to this his unseen Lord and Maker. In keeping

פִּי הָאָרֶץ פִּי הַבְּאֵר פִּי הָאָתוֹן הַקֶּשֶׁת וְהַמָּן וְהַמַּטֶּה וְהַשָּׁמִיר
הַכְּתָב וְהַמִּכְתָּב וְהַלֻּחוֹת · וְיֵשׁ אוֹמְרִים אַף הַמַּזִּיקִין וּקְבוּרָתוֹ
שֶׁל־מֹשֶׁה וְאֵילוֹ שֶׁל־אַבְרָהָם אָבִינוּ וְיֵשׁ אוֹמְרִים אַף צְבָת
בִּצְבָת עֲשׂוּיָה :

י שִׁבְעָה דְבָרִים בַּגֹּלֶם וְשִׁבְעָה בֶּחָכָם · חָכָם אֵינוֹ מְדַבֵּר
לִפְנֵי מִי שֶׁגָּדוֹל מִמֶּנּוּ בְּחָכְמָה וּבְמִנְיָן, וְאֵינוֹ נִכְנָס לְתוֹךְ דִּבְרֵי
חֲבֵרוֹ, וְאֵינוֹ נִבְהָל לְהָשִׁיב, שׁוֹאֵל כָּעִנְיָן וּמֵשִׁיב כַּהֲלָכָה,

with their nature, the things enumerated here are part of the physical world which was made during the first days of Creation. But their purpose is more in keeping with that of the Seventh Day, because, like the Sabbath, they, too, have the function of training man for his moral destiny. Thus they stand midway, as it were, between the works of the Six Days, and the Sabbath, forming a transition from the one to the other. — פי הארץ refers to the gaping hole that opened up to swallow Korah and his kin to demonstrate that Moses had indeed been sent by God and that therefore any mutiny against him or denial of his mission was a criminal act. — פי הבאר denotes the Well of Miriam which accompanied our fathers in the wilderness and thus made their every drink of water a testimony to the presence of Divine Providence. — פי האתון alludes to the faculty of speech that was temporarily given the she-ass to humble Bileam, to teach a lesson to that man of brilliant speech at the moment when, led by base passion and impudent conceit, he sought to misuse his human gift of speech to curse a whole nation. — קשת refers to the rainbow which God caused to appear after the Flood as an eternal symbol of His patience with human error. — מן is the heavenly Mannah which, like no other act of Divine sovereignty, bore testimony to the care with which God remembers every living thing, and which was to teach men to trust in God and cheerfully to obey Him not only then, but throughout all the generations to come. — המטה is the staff of Moses which served as the visible symbol of God's intervention in His own world order to train man and to chastise him for his disobedience and his pusillanimity. — שמיר was the worm which was employed in the erection of the Sanctuary to cut stones when the use of ordinary metal cutting or cleaving tools was forbidden. — הכתב: In the case of the first Tablets of the Law not only the writing as such, but the Tablets as well were the work of God Himself, as it is written והלוחות מעשה אלקים המה והמכתב מכתב אלקים (Exod. 32:16). But as for the second set of Ten Commandments, though once again God Himself had written the words, it was Moses who had hewed out the stone tablets as it is written פסל לך שני לחות

the Mouth of the Earth, the Mouth of the Well, the Mouth of the She-ass, the Rainbow, the Mannah, the Staff, the Shamir, the Written Characters, the Writing, and the Tablets. Some say: the *Mazikin* also, and the grave of Moshe, and the ram of our Father Avraham. Others say: Also the tongs made by means of tongs.

10.   There are seven marks of a boor and seven of a wise man. The wise man does not speak before him who is greater than he is in wisdom and experience; he does not interrupt the speech of his companion. He is not hasty to answer; he asks questions in keeping with the subject and answers to the point. He speaks of the first thing first

---

אבנים ... וכתבתי על הלחות את הדברים וגו' (Exod. 34:1). In view of the foregoing, the word הכתב would refer to the second set of Tablets, while והמכתב would allude to the first. — מזיקין: It is difficult to determine with any degree of certainty what is meant by this term. At any rate, as the term itself implies and as is indicated in Berachoth 6a, it alludes to those influences which are detrimental or "damaging" to continued human welfare. According to this view, the Mazikin, too, belonged to those factors which, while in themselves part of the physical world, served the advancement of man's moral and spiritual salvation.—Because no one knows where it may be found, (Deut. 34:6) the grave of Moses, too, helps advance our spiritual and moral salvation. For were its site known, ceaseless pilgrimages would have given rise to a cult of quasi-idolatry which would have been most detrimental to our spiritual welfare. — אילו של א״א:This is the ram which presented itself to Abraham for sacrifice after God had told him to spare Isaac, his son. Thus the ram became the symbol of all future sacrifices by which man selflessly pledges all of his being, his skills, his endeavors and his achievement to the fulfillment of God's will for all the times to come. — צבת: This statement is based on the premise that even the original pair of tongs was made with a special pair of tongs produced by Divine providence to handle the red-hot metal out of which this, the first tool, was then formed. In other words, even as it was God Himself Who gave man his first garment (Gen. 3:21), so, too, man received his first tool directly from the hands of God, thus implying that industry, like clothing, should also be dedicated to fulfill a higher moral purpose.

10. אינו מדבר לפני וכו': He does not speak before the others do, and he allows those who are wiser and more experienced than he to voice their opinions first. ובמנין: i.e. greater experience either in terms of the number of years lived or in terms of the number of disciples taught. Both of these factors make for experience, and we have made our translation convey this thought. ואומר על ראשון:His speech is logical; he mentions and discusses the subjects in their logical sequence. מודה על האמת:He does not stubbornly insist upon the validity of a statement which he has made once. If he sees, or learns, that he has

וְאוֹמֵר עַל־רִאשׁוֹן רִאשׁוֹן וְעַל־אַחֲרוֹן אַחֲרוֹן, וְעַל מַה־שֶּׁלֹּא
שָׁמַע אוֹמֵר לֹא שָׁמַעְתִּי, וּמוֹדֶה עַל־הָאֱמֶת, וְחִלּוּפֵיהֶן בְּגֹלֶם:

יא שִׁבְעָה מִינֵי פֻרְעָנִיּוֹת בָּאִין לָעוֹלָם עַל־שִׁבְעָה גוּפֵי עֲבֵרָה:
מִקְצָתָן מְעַשְּׂרִין וּמִקְצָתָן אֵינָן מְעַשְּׂרִין רָעָב שֶׁל־בַּצֹּרֶת
בָּא מִקְצָתָן רְעֵבִים וּמִקְצָתָן שְׂבֵעִים: נָמְרוּ שֶׁלֹּא לְעַשֵּׂר רָעָב
שֶׁל מְהוּמָה וְשֶׁל־בַּצֹּרֶת בָּא: וְשֶׁלֹּא לִטּוֹל אֶת־הַחַלָּה רָעָב
שֶׁל־כְּלָיָה בָּא: הֶבֶר בָּא לָעוֹלָם עַל־מִיתוֹת הָאֲמוּרוֹת בַּתּוֹרָה
שֶׁלֹּא נִמְסְרוּ לְבֵית דִּין וְעַל פֵּרוֹת שְׁבִיעִית: חֶרֶב בָּאָה לָעוֹלָם

---

made an error, he will be ready and willing to concede that he has been wrong.

11. The laws pertaining to מעשר ; that is, the מעשר ראשון, "the Levite's tithe"; מעשר שני, the tithe to be eaten in the Holy City; and מעשר עני, the tithe to be set aside for the poor, symbolize claims made upon the blessed harvest for things of the spirit, for the hallowing of physical enjoyment and for the practical demonstration of altruism. The law concerning the חלה, the separation of the bread dough, teaches every individual to view his own share in the general harvest as a special demonstration of God's care and providence, and to consider the devoted study and fulfillment of the Law of God an obligation incumbent upon each and every man to discharge in return for that Divine care. If these laws which pertain to the fruits of the soil are neglected or ignored in any manner, then the spiritual elements of life, its moral consecration, the love of man and the fear of God that should be part of the life which the harvest was meant to preserve, will give way to desecration, profanation, selfishness and godlessness And to the extent that godlessness is on the rise, God will cause the blessings of the harvest to decrease and finally to be absent altogether.

מיתות וגו׳ שלא נמסרו לב״ד: The capital transgression which the criminal cannot expiate by way of the intervention of an earthly court of justice. פרות שביעית All those fruits that grow untended during the Sabbatical year are to be consecrated as a tribute to God, the original Owner and Master of the soil. Therefore our right to make use of them is circumscribed by law and any transgression of those limitations would constitute an act of contempt and mutiny against the sovereignty of God. He who is guilty of a capital transgression and has not expiated for it thus forfeits the right to existence, and he who mutinies against the sovereignty of God thereby forfeits the right to remain on the earth which is the Lord's. In such cases it is a fate of death decreed by God that acts as the executioner.

and of the last last. Regarding that which he has not learned, he says, "I have not learned this" and he acknowledges the truth. The reverse of all this is to be found in the boor.

11.   Seven kinds of punishment come into the world for seven kinds of transgressions: If some give their tithes and others do not, there will be famine from dearth and some will suffer hunger while others will have plenty. If they have all ceased to give tithes there will be a famine caused by panic and dearth. If they have all ceased to take *Hallah* from their dough there will be a famine of extermination. Pestilence comes into the world to execute those death penalties enumerated in the Torah which are not within the purview of the Court of Justice, and for the violations involving the fruits of the Seventh Year. The sword comes into the world for the delay of justice, for

---

חרב : The Lord conferred statehood upon His people so that they might defend the enforcement of justice and preserve the truth contained in our Law as handed down by transmission. If the Jewish State will carry out this mission, it can be sure of Divine support against all enemy powers, and no other nation will dare attack it. But if the Jewish State should cast off its task and destiny or put it to wrongful use, it will thereby become a nation at the mercy of fate just like all the other states of the world, and God will withdraw His protection from it. As a human power, the Jewish State has always been at a disadvantage when set off against the other nations; therefore, once Divine protection is denied the Jewish State, hostile powers will not hesitate to wield the sword against it.

חיה רעה : As long as man will submit to God and remain erect by virtue of his obedience, the beast will retreat before him in awe. But if, by indifference to the sacred nature of a vow, he will deny his allegiance to God or actually contravene it, so that as a result of his conduct the homage of others to God will be lessened, too, the beast will no longer view him as its superior, as the master before whom it must timidly keep its distance, and will attack him. גלות : שפיכות דמים and גלוי עריות, עבודה זרה are the capital transgressions against the fundamentals of that Law for the sake of which God had originally promised and given us the Holy Land. These deadly sins constitute violations of the reverence due God, of the respect due oneself and of the regard we owe to our neighbors. שמטה. The law commanding us to let our land lie fallow during the Sabbatical year is the great public proclamation that God is the Ruler and Owner of the land which He turned over to us with the explicit stipulation that we acknowledge His sovereignty and carry out his will as laid down in His Law. Hence, if the inhabitants of God's land so far forget their God and their duty to Him that they commit any of the

עַל־עִנּוּי הַדִּין וְעַל־עִוּוּת הַדִּין וְעַל־הַמּוֹרִים בַּתּוֹרָה, שֶׁלֹּא
כַהֲלָכָה: חַיָּה רָעָה בָּאָה לָעוֹלָם עַל־שְׁבוּעַת שָׁוְא וְעַל־חִלּוּל
הַשֵּׁם: גָּלוּת בָּאָה לָעוֹלָם עַל־עוֹבְדֵי אֱלִילִים וְעַל־גִּלּוּי עֲרָיוֹת
וְעַל־שְׁפִיכוּת דָּמִים וְעַל־שְׁמִטַּת הָאָרֶץ:

יא בְּאַרְבָּעָה פְרָקִים הַדֶּבֶר מִתְרַבֶּה, בָּרְבִיעִית וּבַשְּׁבִיעִית
וּבְמוֹצָאֵי שְׁבִיעִית וּבְמוֹצָאֵי הֶחָג שֶׁבְּכָל־שָׁנָה וְשָׁנָה: בָּרְבִיעִית
מִפְּנֵי מַעֲשַׂר עָנִי שֶׁבַּשְּׁלִישִׁית בַּשְּׁבִיעִית מִפְּנֵי מַעֲשַׂר עָנִי
שֶׁבַּשִּׁשִּׁית, בְּמוֹצָאֵי שְׁבִיעִית מִפְּנֵי פֵּרוֹת שְׁבִיעִית, בְּמוֹצָאֵי הֶחָג
שֶׁבְּכָל־שָׁנָה וְשָׁנָה מִפְּנֵי גֶּזֶל מַתְּנוֹת עֲנִיִּים:

יג אַרְבַּע מִדּוֹת בָּאָדָם · הָאוֹמֵר שֶׁלִּי שֶׁלִּי וְשֶׁלְּךָ שֶׁלָּךְ זוֹ
מִדָּה בֵּינוֹנִית וְיֵשׁ אוֹמְרִים זוֹ מִדַּת סְדוֹם, שֶׁלִּי שֶׁלָּךְ וְשֶׁלְּךָ
שֶׁלִּי עַם הָאָרֶץ, שֶׁלִּי (שֶׁלָּךְ) וְשֶׁלְּךָ שֶׁלָּךְ חָסִיד, שֶׁלָּךְ (שֶׁלִּי)
וְשֶׁלִּי שֶׁלִּי רָשָׁע:

---

first three transgressions named here, or else that they publicly deny His
supreme sovereignty by violating the *Shemittah* law, these criminal acts in
themselves will serve to condemn them to expulsion and banishment from
their homeland.

12. If, even in times of general calamity such as pestilence, the people should
deprive the poor of the gifts lawfully due them, this alone would be sufficient
reason for a worsening of the epidemic. During the third and sixth of the
seven-year *Shemittah* cycle the second tithe, which during other years had to
be eaten in Jerusalem, would be turned over to the poor. Those fruits and
vegetables that grew untended during the Sabbatical year were regarded as
ownerless and the poor were permitted to benefit from them.—The מתנות עניים
are the gifts set aside for the poor from the harvest each year, such as לקט,
שכחה, פאה, etc.

13. It would seem that the view that every person should keep that which
is his and that no one else should derive benefit from the property of another
is midway between good and evil. Some, however, feel that it is a most reprehensible attitude because it would expunge from the human heart and mind
that guiding principle of loving-kindness without which man would lose his

the perversion of justice and on those who do not teach the Law in accordance with the transmitted interpretation. Wild beasts come into the world because of perjury and the profanation of the Divine Name. Exile comes into the world because of idolatry, immorality, murder, and the non-observance of the year of rest for the soil.

12. At four periods does pestilence increase: in the fourth year, in the seventh, and at the conclusion of the seventh year, and at the conclusion of the Feast of Tabernacles in every year. In the fourth year for failure to give the tithe to the poor in the third year; in the seventh year for failure to give the tithe to the poor in the sixth year; at the conclusion of the seventh year for transgressions involving the fruits of the Seventh Year; at the conclusion of the Feast of Tabernacles in every year for depriving the poor of the gifts lawfully due them.

13. There are four character types among men: He who says: "What is mine is mine, and what is yours is yours" is an average character; some say that this is the character of Sodom. He who says: "What is mine is yours and what is yours is mine" is an ignoramus. [He who says] "What is mine is yours and what is yours is yours" is godly; [He who says] "What is yours is mine and what is mine is mine," is a lawless man.

Divinely-given nobility, and human society would be deprived of the goal ordained for it as its destiny. The second alternative, שלי שלך ושלך שלי to abolish all private ownership and institute the common holding of property, is likewise based on deplorable ignorance. For its practical implementation would not only cancel the sanctity of the individual's right to own property and thus his one possibility for true independence, but it would also deprive man of the opportunity to practice mercy of his own free will. For I practice mercy, only if, of my own free will and sense of duty, I give to another that which it would be my right to keep for myself and which he has no legal right to demand from me. If I were to give to my fellow-man only that which he would be entitled to take by himself even without my consent, there will certainly be no love between us. It is only where justice is recognized that there is room also for loving-kindness, and conversely it is only where mercy, too, is a motivating power that justice can attain its goal which is to advance the general welfare. Justice is the foundation of society, and mercy is its finishing touch. He who has the virtue of חסידות, who shows practical piety by acts of loving-kindness will say: "I shall give to all others of that which is mine, and I will make no claims upon them in return: שלי שלך and שלך שלך."

יד אַרְבַּע מִדּוֹת בְּדֵעוֹת · נוֹחַ לִכְעוֹס וְנוֹחַ לִרְצוֹת יָצָא הֶפְסֵדוֹ
בִּשְׂכָרוֹ, קָשֶׁה לִכְעוֹס וְקָשֶׁה לִרְצוֹת יָצָא שְׂכָרוֹ בְּהֶפְסֵדוֹ, קָשֶׁה
לִכְעוֹס וְנוֹחַ לִרְצוֹת חָסִיד, נוֹחַ לִכְעוֹס וְקָשֶׁה לִרְצוֹת רָשָׁע:

טו אַרְבַּע מִדּוֹת בְּתַלְמִידִים · מָהִיר לִשְׁמוֹעַ וּמָהִיר לְאַבֵּד יָצָא
שְׂכָרוֹ בְּהֶפְסֵדוֹ, קָשֶׁה לִשְׁמוֹעַ וְקָשֶׁה לְאַבֵּד יָצָא הֶפְסֵדוֹ בִּשְׂכָרוֹ,
מָהִיר לִשְׁמוֹעַ וְקָשֶׁה לְאַבֵּד זוֹ חֵלֶק טוֹב, קָשֶׁה לִשְׁמוֹעַ וּמָהִיר
לְאַבֵּד זוֹ חֵלֶק רָע:

טז אַרְבַּע מִדּוֹת בְּנוֹתְנֵי צְדָקָה · הָרוֹצֶה שֶׁיִּתֵּן וְלֹא יִתְּנוּ אֲחֵרִים
עֵינוֹ רָעָה בְּשֶׁל-אֲחֵרִים, יִתְּנוּ אֲחֵרִים וְהוּא לֹא יִתֵּן עֵינוֹ רָעָה
בְּשֶׁלּוֹ, יִתֵּן וְיִתְּנוּ אֲחֵרִים חָסִיד, לֹא יִתֵּן וְלֹא יִתְּנוּ אֲחֵרִים רָשָׁע:

---

14. נוח לרצות The person who is ready not only להתרצות "to let himself be
pacified" but who, once he was angry or has been provoked to wrath, will
calm down by himself (לרצות) without the persuasion of others, is blessed
with a good disposition. It is so deeply rooted in basic goodness of the heart
that it will outweigh even the weakness of נוח לכעוס of being easy to anger,
for which, of course, we hold no brief. Even if he should become angry, a
person of such disposition will quickly repent of his wrath and will show that
he regrets his conduct. He will be kindly disposed toward all his fellow-men
and his innate kindness will enable him to maintain at all times that type
of disposition which will make him a joy both to himself and to those about
him. Not so the person who, though slow to anger, is most difficult to appease once he has been provoked and nurses his resentment, bearing a smol-
dering grudge in his heart long after the untoward incident has passed. That
type of person, as a rule, holds too high an estimate of himself and of what
others owe to him. His heart lacks that goodness which makes man noble
and more like His God Who is נושא עון ועובר על פשע. And since in this world
there is no lack of just cause for wrath, the weakness of being קשה לרצות
will readily give rise to a disposition that can make a man remain permanently
at odds with those about him; hence יצא שכרו בהפסדו.

15. Frequently quick forgetting is a result of too great speed and ease in
learning. Because the student of that type need not exert himself to under-

14.   There are four kinds of disposition: He who is easy to provoke and easy to pacify—his loss disappears in his gain. He who is hard to provoke and hard to pacify—his gain disappears in his loss. He who is hard to provoke and easy to pacify is a godly man. He who is easy to provoke and hard to pacify is a lawless man.

15.   There are four types of students: Quick to learn and quick to forget—his gain disappears in his loss. Slow to learn and slow to forget—his loss disappears in his gain. Quick to learn and slow to forget is the best portion. Slow to learn and quick to forget is the worst portion.

16.   There are four types of donors to charity. He who desires to give but not that others should give, begrudges the privilege of others. He who desires that others should give but will not give himself is grudging of his own. He who desires that both he and others should give is pious. He who will not give and does not want others to give is lawless.

---

stand the lecture material, he will learn it only superficially, and he will make no great effort to retain it, for he will say to himself that, if he should forget it, he will have no trouble re-learning it whenever he should so desire. A student who has more difficulty in learning has an advantage over him, for by virtue of the effort and repeated study in which he must engage in order to learn, he has better impressed the material upon his memory. Thus, while in the first instance, the weakness of forgetfulness cancels out the talent of ease in learning, so the virtue of better retention here cancels out the handicap of difficulty in learning.

16.   It is somewhat difficult to determine the manner in which to construe בשלו and עינו רעה בשל אחרים and הרוצה וכו' ולא יתנו אחרים. It appears that these statements are severe criticisms of the view according to which it is a meritorious deed to refrain from persuading others to give charity or even actually to prevent them from doing so, in the erroneous opinion that one does them a service by thus helping them keep their fortune intact. People with an erroneous attitude such as this neither know nor understand that, in fact, it is primarily that wealth which is spent on good works that truly becomes the permanent possession of its giver, benefitting him by advancing his eternal salvation. Thus to restrain oneself or others from giving charity is not an act of kindness at all, but actually a disservice both to oneself and one's fellows.

יז אַרְבַּע מִדּוֹת בְּהוֹלְכֵי בֵית הַמִּדְרָשׁ · הוֹלֵךְ וְאֵינוּ עֹשֶׂה שְׂכַר
הֲלִיכָה בְּיָדוֹ. עֹשֶׂה וְאֵינוּ הוֹלֵךְ שְׂכַר מַעֲשֶׂה בְּיָדוֹ, הוֹלֵךְ וְעֹשֶׂה
חָסִיד, לֹא הוֹלֵךְ וְלֹא עֹשֶׂה רָשָׁע:

יח אַרְבַּע מִדּוֹת בְּיוֹשְׁבִים לִפְנֵי חֲכָמִים, סְפוֹג, וּמַשְׁפֵּךְ מְשַׁמֶּרֶת
וְנָפָה · סְפוֹג שֶׁהוּא סוֹפֵג אֶת־הַכֹּל, וּמַשְׁפֵּךְ שֶׁמַּכְנִיס בְּזוֹ וּמוֹצִיא
בְזוֹ, מְשַׁמֶּרֶת שֶׁמּוֹצִיאָה אֶת־הַיַּיִן וְקוֹלֶטֶת אֶת־הַשְּׁמָרִים.
וְנָפָה שֶׁמּוֹצִיאָה אֶת־הַקֶּמַח וְקוֹלֶטֶת אֶת־הַסֹּלֶת:

יט כָּל־אַהֲבָה שֶׁהִיא־תְלוּיָה בְדָבָר בָּטֵל דָּבָר בְּטֵלָה אַהֲבָה,
וְשֶׁאֵינָהּ תְּלוּיָה בְדָבָר אֵינָהּ בְּטֵלָה לְעוֹלָם · אֵיזוֹ הִיא אַהֲבָה
שֶׁהִיא־תְלוּיָה בְדָבָר זוֹ אַהֲבַת אַמְנוֹן וְתָמָר, וְשֶׁאֵינָהּ תְּלוּיָה בְדָבָר
זוֹ אַהֲבַת דָּוִד וִיהוֹנָתָן:

---

17. In the days of the Mishna one had to attend lectures at the house of
study if one desired to "learn" because the Oral Teaching had not yet been
put down in writing. Thus attendance at the house of study was synonymous
with what we know today as "learning". By virtue of the fact that the Tradition was thus taught by direct communication through the living world and
studied in communion with many others, such "learning" in the house of study
was, in fact, made all the more fruitful. We are told in this Mishna that
even he who, though regularly attending the house of study, does not put
into practice what he has learned there has reaped at least some benefit from
his attendance at the classes. It is inevitable that his mind and spirit should
absorb at least a part of what he has heard there, and we know that repeated
study eventually leads to observance in practice. Conversely, even he who
does not neglect to keep the Law in practice, but on the other hand does not
make the effort continuously to amend, enrich and perfect his knowledge of the

17. There are four types among those who attend the house of study. He who attends the house of study but does not practice [its teachings] still secures the reward for attending. He who practices [its teachings] but does not attend the house of study secures the reward for practicing. He who attends [there] and practices is godly; he who neither attends nor practices is lawless.

18. There are four types of those who sit before the Sages; a sponge, a funnel, a strainer and a sieve. A sponge which absorbs everything; a funnel, which lets in at one end and out at the other; a strainer which lets the wine pass out and retains the sediment; and a sieve which lets out the bran-dust and retains the fine flour.

19. All such love as depends on a [physical] cause will pass away once the cause is no longer there, but that love which is not dependent on a [physical] cause will never pass away. Which love was dependent on a [physical] cause? The love of Amnon and Tamar. And which love depended on no such cause? The love of David and Yonathan.

Law's requirements through regular "learning" at the house of study will not fail to reap some profit through his law-abiding conduct. Yet his gain would be infinitely greater and constantly growing if, in addition, he were to increase his knowledge and ennoble his character by means of faithful, regular study.

18. נפה   As we learn from Menachoth 76b, the grains of wheat, after separation from the chaff, were repeatedly shaken in a sieve to eliminate the קמח, the inferior flour dust which forms the outer layer. Then only the סולת, the fine inner kernel would be retained in the sieve. This should explain the simile employed in the above Mishna.

19. Wherever love is rooted in the spiritual and moral worth of the beloved person, there the love will be as abiding as the values on which it is founded. But a love based on physical attraction will not outlast those fleeting charms.

כ כָּל־מַחֲלֹקֶת שֶׁהִיא לְשֵׁם שָׁמַיִם סוֹפָהּ לְהִתְקַיֵּם וְשֶׁאֵינָהּ
לְשֵׁם שָׁמַיִם אֵין סוֹפָהּ לְהִתְקַיֵּם · אֵיזוֹ הִיא מַחֲלֹקֶת שֶׁהִיא לְשֵׁם
שָׁמַיִם זוֹ מַחֲלֹקֶת הִלֵּל וְשַׁמַּאי, וְשֶׁאֵינָהּ לְשֵׁם שָׁמַיִם זוֹ מַחֲלֹקֶת
קֹרַח וְכָל־עֲדָתוֹ :

כא כָּל־הַמְזַכֶּה אֶת־הָרַבִּים אֵין חֵטְא בָּא עַל־יָדוֹ וְכָל־הַמַּחֲטִיא
אֶת־הָרַבִּים אֵין־מַסְפִּיקִין בְּיָדוֹ לַעֲשׂוֹת תְּשׁוּבָה · מֹשֶׁה זָכָה
וְזִכָּה אֶת־הָרַבִּים זְכוּת הָרַבִּים תָּלוּי בּוֹ שֶׁנֶּאֱמַר צִדְקַת יְיָ עָשָׂה
וּמִשְׁפָּטָיו עִם־יִשְׂרָאֵל. יָרָבְעָם בֶּן־נְבָט חָטָא וְהֶחֱטִיא אֶת־הָרַבִּים
חֵטְא הָרַבִּים תָּלוּי בּוֹ שֶׁנֶּאֱמַר עַל־חַטֹּאות יָרָבְעָם אֲשֶׁר חָטָא
וַאֲשֶׁר הֶחֱטִיא אֶת־יִשְׂרָאֵל :

20. When in a controversy both parties are guided solely by pure motives and seek noble ends (such is the implication of the term לשם שמים), and when both parties seek solely to find the truth, then, of course, only one view will constitute the truth and only one of the two opposing views can and will prevail in practice. But actually, both views will have permanent value because, through the arguments each side has presented, both parties will have served to shed new light on the issue under debate, and will have contributed to the attainment of the proper understanding of the question discussed. They shall be remembered as long as there are men sincerely interested both in the subject of the debate and in the finding of the truth. For such men, retaining an abiding memory of the differences and the attempts on both sides to prove the validity of their views, will study the arguments of both sides thoroughly and repeatedly, thus advancing the cause of the genuine knowledge of truth. Thus, controversies such as those between Hillel and Shammai and between the other *Tannaim* and *Amoraim* have remained a permanent and important component of our Torah and its study.

20. Any controversy with a noble purpose will result in abiding value, but any controversy that has no noble purpose shall not have abiding value. Which controversy was one that had a noble purpose? The controversy between Hillel and Shammai. And which controversy had no noble purpose? The controversy of Korach and his company.

21. He who leads the multitude to righteousness shall have no sin come into his hand, but he who leads the multitude to sin shall not get the opportunity to succeed in his repentance. Moshe was righteous and led the multitude to righteousness. The righteousness of the multitude was ascribed to him forever, as it is said, "He performed the righteousness of *God* and his righteous ordinances remained with Yisrael." Yaravam, the son of Nevat, sinned and led the multitude to sin. The sin of the multitude was ascribed to him forever, as it is said, "Because of the sin of Yaravam who sinned and caused Yisrael to sin."

---

21. He who leads his people to righteousness will be guarded from sin by the grace of God. This could mean that no wrong will be done *through him*, and could also mean that no wrong will be perpetrated *by him*, so that he will always remain a shining example for that community which he himself guided to a life of purity. Thus by virtue of the righteousness which he practiced himself and also enjoined upon Israel to practice, Moses, for instance, remains associated forever with all the acts of righteousness that his people will carry out through all the generations to come. But he who induces a multitude to lead a life of sin will never succeed even in genuinely repenting of his own misdeeds and in seeking to do better. For the first prerequisite for his own genuine repentance is that he must lead back to the good life all those whom he has led astray, and that is certainly impossible. Indeed, the criminal act of inducement to sin goes on and on and continues to fester as a pernicious growth in the midst even of all the generations that come after the one which was originally led astray. We are told in Kings I, 15:30 that the entire dynasty of Jeroboam perished by reason of the criminal seduction perpetrated by its ancestor. All the accounts in the Book of Kings of the transgressions perpetrated by the rulers of the Kingdom of Israel stress that it was the evil example of their ancestor that caused them to sin, and at the very outset (Kings I, 14:15, 16) it is asserted that the seduction committed by Jeroboam will result in the banishment of his people.

כב כָּל־מִי שֶׁיֶּשׁ־בּוֹ שְׁלשָׁה דְבָרִים הַלָּלוּ הוּא מִתַּלְמִידָיו שֶׁל־
אַבְרָהָם אָבִינוּ, וּשְׁלשָׁה דְבָרִים אֲחֵרִים הוּא מִתַּלְמִידָיו שֶׁל־
בִּלְעָם הָרָשָׁע · עַיִן טוֹבָה וְרוּחַ נְמוּכָה וְנֶפֶשׁ שְׁפָלָה מִתַּלְמִידָיו
שֶׁל־אַבְרָהָם אָבִינוּ. עַיִן רָעָה וְרוּחַ גְּבוֹהָה וְנֶפֶשׁ רְחָבָה מִתַּלְמִידָיו
שֶׁל־בִּלְעָם הָרָשָׁע · מַה בֵּין תַּלְמִידָיו שֶׁל־אַבְרָהָם אָבִינוּ
לְתַלְמִידָיו שֶׁל־בִּלְעָם הָרָשָׁע · תַּלְמִידָיו שֶׁל־אַבְרָהָם אָבִינוּ
אוֹכְלִין בָּעוֹלָם הַזֶּה וְנוֹחֲלִין הָעוֹלָם הַבָּא שֶׁנֶּאֱמַר לְהַנְחִיל
אֹהֲבַי יֵשׁ וְאוֹצְרֹתֵיהֶם אֲמַלֵּא · תַּלְמִידָיו שֶׁל־בִּלְעָם הָרָשָׁע יוֹרְשִׁין
גֵּי־הִנֹּם וְיוֹרְדִין לִבְאֵר שַׁחַת שֶׁנֶּאֱמַר וְאַתָּה אֱלֹהִים תּוֹרִדֵם
לִבְאֵר שַׁחַת אַנְשֵׁי דָמִים וּמִרְמָה לֹא־יֶחֱצוּ יְמֵיהֶם וַאֲנִי אֶבְטַח־בָּךְ:
כג יְהוּדָה בֶּן־תֵּימָא אוֹמֵר, הֱוֵה עַז כַּנָּמֵר וְקַל כַּנֶּשֶׁר רָץ
כַּצְּבִי וְגִבּוֹר כָּאֲרִי לַעֲשׂוֹת רְצוֹן אָבִיךָ שֶׁבַּשָּׁמָיִם:

---

22. The life of Abraham was characterized by these virtues: עַיִן טוֹבָה:
he truly loved his fellow-men and therefore he could rejoice without envy or
reserve in their every good fortune; he was modest and he was undemanding.
These qualities immediately came to the fore, when Abraham left his father's
house, and gave up all the pleasures, riches, comforts, and honors of home to
go out into the strange and inhospitable unknown; all in order to advance the
welfare of his fellow-men. They were proven, too, by Abraham's conduct
toward his nephew and his wife, by the practical mercy he showed to wan-
derers whom he did not know, by the battle he waged to aid his ungrateful
nephew, long estranged from him, and by his unselfishness after he had won
the victory. The picture of his long and trial-laden life shows no trace whatever of conduct at variance with these noble traits. In striking contrast to
this, we behold the arrogance, the insatiable ambition and the greed of the
malicious Bileam who was ready to pronounce a curse over an entire people.
We cannot find in Bileam's character sketch even one stroke that might mitigate this unsavory picture in the gallery of history. The disciples of Abraham
love their fellow-men, they are modest, humble, utterly untainted by envy.
These sterling qualities not only open for them the portals of bliss in the
world to come, but give them serenity and happiness even here on earth regardless of the lack of material wealth and pleasures and the burden of
trials and privation that life may bring. Their measure of calamities seems

22. He who has these three attributes is among the disciples of Father Avraham, and three other attributes mark the disciples of the lawless Bileam. A good eye, a humble mind and an undemanding soul are the characteristics of the disciples of our Father Avraham. An evil eye, a haughty mind and a demanding soul are the characteristics of the disciples of the lawless Bileam. What difference is there between the lot of the disciples of our Father Avraham and that of the disciples of the lawless Bileam? The disciples of our Father Avraham enjoy this world and inherit the world to come, as it is said, "That I may cause those who love Me to inherit substance, and I shall fill their treasuries." The disciples of the lawless Bileam, on the other hand, inherit Gehinnom and descend into the pit of destruction; for it is said: "You, O *God,* will bring them down into the pit; men of murder and deceit shall not live out [even] half their days, but I will trust in You."

23. Yehudah the son of Tema, said: Be strong as a leopard, light as an eagle, swift as a stag and mighty as a lion to do the will of your Father in Heaven.

---

small in their eyes, and the happiness of others which they create, promote, and observe affords them a source of joy which the disciples of Bileam cannot possibly surmise. As for the disciples of Bileam, their malice, their arrogance and their insatiable greed and ambition not only make it impossible for them to walk upon the road to salvation in the world to come, but also keep them from finding one moment's true contentment, even in the midst of an abundance of riches and pleasures. Any joy, honor or prosperity that comes to others is a bitter drop in their cup of joy and whatever they may already have achieved loses all value in their eyes when they contemplate those of their desires that are still unfulfilled. Hence לא יחצו ימיהם they do not receive a portion in either of the two worlds originally appointed for them, even as they had been for all other men. The world to come is closed to them and the happiness possible in this world is truly lost to them as well.

23. עז — "strong as a leopard" to resist any attempt to lure you away from good and to induce you to do evil. קל—"light as an eagle" so that, leaving all earthly impediments behind you, you may soar up to God. רץ— "swift as a hart" so that you will know neither procrastination nor hesitation in matters of the performance of your duty. גבור "mighty as a lion" to overcome all obstacles, both within and without.

כד הוּא הָיָה אוֹמֵר, עַז פָּנִים לְגֵיהִנֹם וּבֹשֶׁת פָּנִים לְגַן עֵדֶן:

יְהִי רָצוֹן מִלְּפָנֶיךָ יְיָ אֱלֹהֵינוּ וֵאלֹהֵי אֲבוֹתֵינוּ שֶׁיִּבָּנֶה בֵּית הַמִּקְדָּשׁ בִּמְהֵרָה בְיָמֵינוּ וְתֵן חֶלְקֵנוּ בְּתוֹרָתֶךָ:

כה הוּא הָיָה אָמַר, בֶּן חָמֵשׁ שָׁנִים לַמִּקְרָא בֶּן עֶשֶׂר שָׁנִים לַמִּשְׁנָה בֶּן שְׁלֹשׁ עֶשְׂרֵה לַמִּצְוֹת בֶּן חֲמֵשׁ עֶשְׂרֵה לַתַּלְמוּד בֶּן שְׁמוֹנֶה עֶשְׂרֵה לַחֻפָּה בֶּן עֶשְׂרִים לִרְדּוֹף בֶּן שְׁלֹשִׁים לַכֹּחַ בֶּן אַרְבָּעִים לַבִּינָה בֶּן חֲמִשִּׁים לְעֵצָה בֶּן שִׁשִּׁים לְזִקְנָה בֶּן שִׁבְעִים לְשֵׂיבָה בֶּן שְׁמוֹנִים לִגְבוּרָה בֶּן תִּשְׁעִים לָשׁוּחַ בֶּן מֵאָה כְּאִלּוּ מֵת וְעָבַר וּבָטֵל מִן הָעוֹלָם:

כו בֶּן בַּג בַּג אוֹמֵר, הֲפָךְ בָּהּ וַהֲפָךְ בָּהּ דְּכֹלָּא בָהּ וּבָהּ תֶּחֱזֵא וְסִיב וּבְלֵה בָהּ וּמִנָּהּ לָא תָזוּעַ שֶׁאֵין לְךָ מִדָּה טוֹבָה הֵימֶנָּה:

כז בֶּן הֵא הֵא אוֹמֵר, לְפֻם צַעֲרָא אַגְרָא:

רבי חנניא וכו׳. קדיש.

---

24. We have read in the Mishna immediately preceding that firmness and defiance against obstacles is praiseworthy when it comes to fulfilling the will of God. But such conduct is not necessarily beneficial in our relationships with our fellowmen and in the attainment of objectives placed at man's own discretion. Here boldness without consideration may easily lead to such impudence, utterly devoid of scruples, as will be conducive only to sure ruin. A certain degree of timidity, on the other hand, will guard a man from many errors and will give rise to prudence, the deliberate weighing of every step to be taken, a virtue that will support and raise the moral value of life in terms of duty fulfilled. יהי רצון: The connection of this prayer with the verses that precede is not quite clear. It may be based on a thought as follows: We have just learned that under the guidance of the Word of God and employed in the service of His Torah even the most differing and mutually contradictory talents and potentialities can be utilized for good, whereas without such guidance, and subordinated to alien endeavors these same qualities would lead to utter ruin. Therefore we now pray that, speedily and soon, we may be permitted to rejoice in the rebuilding of the Sanctuary of the Law and thus in God's complete guidance and that then, every man, each according to his own talents and abilities, may find "his own portion" in the fulfillment of God's Law on earth.

24. He used to say: The impudent is destined for Gehinnom; the shamefaced for the Garden of Eden. May it be Your will, *God* our God, that the Sanctuary be rebuilt speedily in our days and give us our portion in Your Teaching.

25. He used to say: At five years [the age is reached] for [the study of] the Scriptures, at ten for [the study of] the Mishna, at thirteen for the Mitzvoth, at fifteen for [the study of] the Gemarah, at eighteen for marriage, at twenty for the pursuit of the aim [in life], at thirty for strength, at forty for insight, at fifty for counsel; at sixty man attains old age, at seventy, the hoary head; at eighty, extreme old age, at ninety, decline, and at one hundred he is as if he were already dead and gone and departed from this world.

26. Ben Bagbag said: Occupy yourself with it over and over again, for everything is contained in it, and it is through it that your view will attain clarity; grow old and gray with it and depart not from it, for there is no better pursuit for you than the Torah.

27. Ben He-he said: According to the effort is the reward.

---

25. If, as specified in this passage, a boy, by the time he has reached the age of fifteen, has behind him ten years of מקרא, of Bible study, and five of Mishna, he should have become so familiar with the basic truths of Judaism and with the fundamental concepts and requirements of our Law that it should be an easy thing for him to make the transition to the commentaries, reasonings and inferences contained in the Gemarah, the work that "completes" the Torah. After five years spent in the study of the Mishna, no subject contained in the Gemarah should be foreign to the young scholar; by this time he should be able to follow all the debates in the Gemarah with full comprehension and grasp their conclusions with ease. Ah, when shall we see the day when our young people will once again tread the path to spiritual and mental development in accordance with the teaching left us by our wise "fathers"!

It is probable that the term לרדוף, as in צדק תרדוף and רודף שלום, connotes serious, intent *pursuit*, in this case the pursuit of one's daily bread and the concern that should be devoted to the loyal fulfillment of duty. כח denotes the mature strength and energy for toil and labor; בינה refers to the maturing of intellectual powers; עצה implies the mature judgement of things and situations, based on long experience in living, and of the course to be followed in accordance with the dictates of such mature judgement.

26 & 27. Both these verses are in keeping with the way of life outlined in the preceding Mishna, Verse 26 seeks to preclude a possible misinterpretation

כָּל יִשְׂרָאֵל וכו'

שָׁנוּ חֲכָמִים בִּלְשׁוֹן הַמִּשְׁנָה בָּרוּךְ שֶׁבָּחַר בָּהֶם וּבְמִשְׁנָתָם:

א רַבִּי מֵאִיר אוֹמֵר, כָּל־הָעוֹסֵק בַּתּוֹרָה לִשְׁמָהּ זוֹכֶה לִדְבָרִים הַרְבֵּה וְלֹא עוֹד אֶלָּא שֶׁכָּל־הָעוֹלָם כֻּלּוֹ כְּדַי הוּא לוֹ, נִקְרָא רֵעַ אָהוּב אוֹהֵב אֶת־הַמָּקוֹם אוֹהֵב אֶת־הַבְּרִיּוֹת מְשַׂמֵּחַ אֶת הַמָּקוֹם מְשַׂמֵּחַ אֶת הַבְּרִיּוֹת וּמַלְבַּשְׁתּוֹ עֲנָוָה וְיִרְאָה וּמַכְשַׁרְתּוֹ לִהְיוֹת צַדִּיק חָסִיד יָשָׁר וְנֶאֱמָן וּמְרַחַקְתּוֹ מִן הַחֵטְא וּמְקָרַבְתּוֹ לִידֵי זְכוּת וְנֶהֱנִין מִמֶּנּוּ עֵצָה וְתוּשִׁיָּה בִּינָה וּגְבוּרָה שֶׁנֶּאֱמַר לִי עֵצָה וְתוּשִׁיָּה אֲנִי בִינָה לִי גְבוּרָה וְנוֹתֶנֶת לוֹ מַלְכוּת וּמֶמְשָׁלָה וְחִקּוּר דִּין וּמְגַלִּין לוֹ רָזֵי תוֹרָה וְנַעֲשֶׂה כְּמַעְיָן שֶׁאֵינוֹ פוֹסֵק וּכְנָהָר הַמִּתְגַּבֵּר וְהוֹלֵךְ וְהֹוֶה צָנוּעַ וְאֶרֶךְ רוּחַ וּמוֹחֵל עַל־עֶלְבּוֹנוֹ וּמְגַדַּלְתּוֹ וּמְרוֹמַמְתּוֹ עַל־כָּל־הַמַּעֲשִׂים:

---

of the course of study indicated in Verse 25. When it is said that בֶּן חָמֵשׁ לַמִּקְרָא, בֶּן עֶשֶׂר לַמִּשְׁנָה וכו', we are taught that this does not mean that a boy need study the Scriptures only until he is ten years old, the Mishna only until he is fifteen, that he need study the Gemarah no longer than until his eighteenth or twentieth year, and that thereafter the study of the Torah must yield place to other pursuits. Quite the contrary—it is pointed out here that it is incumbent upon us to occupy ourselves with the Scriptures, as well as with the Mishnah and the Gemarah throughout our lives. We are bidden to return to this sacred pursuit over and over again, for the Torah is the one inexhaustible source of all the knowledge of what is good and true and worthwhile, and the longer and the more faithfully we occupy ourselves with it, the broader and stronger will our power of spiritual vision grow. Therefore let the Torah remain at your side even when you are old and when your energies for all other pursuits have declined, and do not depart from it as long as you live, for you can acquire no greater consecration for your endeavors. Ben He He adds to this overview of the plan for our life's course: It is not the quantitative measure of the moral and spiritual and social goals you have actually achieved that constitutes the true worth of a life's course. It is צַעֲרָא, the measure of earnest striving, of devoted endeavor, of sacrifices made and privation endured, all for the realization of good purposes such as meet with God's approval that determines the true worth of both a man and his life. For actual success can only come from the hands of God Himself.

The sages taught the following in the style of the Mishna; blessed be He Who chose them and their teaching.

1. Rabbi Meir said: He who occupies himself with the Torah with a pure purpose acquires many things; nay more, he alone would be sufficient for the continued existence of the whole world. He is called friend, beloved; he loves God, he loves [His] creatures, he gladdens God and he gladdens [God's] creatures, and it clothes him in meekness and the fear of God; it enables him to be just, merciful, upright and faithful; it keeps him far from error and will bring him to virtue. Through him men benefit from counsel and sound wisdom, insight and strength, for it is said: "Counsel is mine and sound wisdom; I am insight, mine is strength." It gives him sovereignty and dominion and discerning judgement; the secrets of the Torah are revealed to him, and he becomes like a fountain that never fails, and like a river which constantly gains in vigor, and he remains modest, patient and forgiving of insults, and it makes him great and exalted over all creatures.

CHAPTER VI

The verses contained in this portion do not constitute Mishna but ברייתות, verses which have been preserved "outside" or "apart from" the actual Mishna code; they are written in the style of the Mishna and constitute explanations and supplements to the Mishna passages. ברוך, blessed be "He", God, Who chose the Sages and their teaching to labor in His service.

1. To "occupy oneself with תורה לשמה" means to study it thoroughly and for one purpose only; that is, to discern from it the will of God, and to do God's will by fulfilling it oneself and teaching it to others. The study of the Torah in this spirit, free of all baser motives and founded on the purest of purposes, will render life, thus guided by the Word of God, rich in blessed attainment and will enable man and his endeavors to reach so high a plane that the entire world will derive satisfaction from him. If in all the course of its development, there will come forth upon earth even only one single person of this type, then the world will not have existed in vain. Such a person is "כדאי" of this world.

But particularly and especially it is spiritual and moral character attainments that the pure study of the Torah affords. — נקרא רע: The Torah describes men in their relationship to each other in pure conformity with its Law as רע, implying that in this ideal situation each man offers himself to

נ אָמַר רַבִּי יְהוֹשֻעַ בֶּן־לֵוִי, בְּכָל־יוֹם וָיוֹם בַּת־קוֹל יוֹצֵאת
מֵהַר חוֹרֵב וּמַכְרֶזֶת וְאוֹמֶרֶת אוֹי לָהֶם לַבְּרִיּוֹת מֵעֶלְבּוֹנָהּ שֶׁל־
תּוֹרָה, שֶׁכָּל־מִי שֶׁאֵינוֹ עוֹסֵק בַּתּוֹרָה נִקְרָא נָזוּף שֶׁנֶּאֱמַר נֶזֶם
זָהָב בְּאַף חֲזִיר אִשָּׁה יָפָה וְסָרַת טָעַם: וְאוֹמֵר, וְהַלֻּחֹת מַעֲשֵׂה
אֱלֹהִים הֵמָּה וְהַמִּכְתָּב מִכְתַּב אֱלֹהִים הוּא חָרוּת עַל־הַלֻּחֹת, אַל־
תִּקְרָא חָרוּת אֶלָּא חֵרוּת שֶׁאֵין לְךָ בֶּן־חוֹרִין אֶלָּא מִי שֶׁעוֹסֵק
בְּתַלְמוּד תּוֹרָה וְכָל־מִי שֶׁעוֹסֵק בְּתַלְמוּד תּוֹרָה הֲרֵי זֶה מִתְעַלֶּה
שֶׁנֶּאֱמַר וּמִמַּתָּנָה נַחֲלִיאֵל וּמִנַּחֲלִיאֵל בָּמוֹת:

the other as a "pasture", devoting himself to the "satisfaction" of the other's needs and finding the satisfaction of his own in the welfare and prosperity of the others. Only the pure understanding and fulfillment of the Torah can endow man with such an attitude to his brothers. ומלבשתו : it invests him with ענוה and יראה that is, it makes ענוה and יראה ; be those qualities which, like a garment, cling to his personality as inalienable companions. צדיק וחסיד ישר. His נאמן and נאמן complement the character of the צדיק and חסיד. His צדקות and his חסידות are not dependent on vague, unstable moods that can easily transgress the boundary of what is right. The חסידות and צדקות that are based upon the clear conceptual truths of the Torah are נאמן ; and ישר they do not deviate from the straight path and remain steadfast forever. Since they will be no different tomorrow from what they were today they will guard man from error and bring him closer to moral perfection. ונהנין His fellow-men, too, will benefit from his spiritual and moral qualities; therefore they will entrust him with the guidance, the fashioning and the leadership of their affairs even as they would a king, and they will obtain their decisions in matters of justice from his insight and his conscientiousness. ומגלין It is only through such practical activation and application of his Torah knowledge in real-life situations that the inner meaning of God's Law will truly lie revealed before him, and the fountain and the stream of his mental and spiritual talents will grow in vigor to dominate ever-widening territory. והוה (this is the version of our Mishna according to יעב"ץ) and nevertheless he remains צנוע. He prefers to remain modestly retiring; he does not strut about, nor does he glory in the wealth of his accomplishments, and it is on account of this modesty and humility that the Torah will make him great and raise him above all of his fellow-creatures.

2. The Revelation on Mount Horeb has not as yet attained its ultimate goal among men. As long as there are still men who will not recognize the true

2. Rabbi Yehoshua ben Levi, said: Day after day a daughter-voice goes forth from Mount Horeb proclaiming these words: "Woe to them, to mankind, for their disregard of the Torah" for whoever does not labor in the Torah is called "rebuked"; for it is said: "A golden ring in a swine's snout; a beautiful woman and yet foolish." And it is said, "The Tablets are the works of God and the writing is the writing of God, *charut*, engraved, upon the Tablets." Read not *charut* (engraved) but *cherut* (meaning "freedom"), for man is never more free than when he occupies himself with the study of the Torah, and he who occupies himself with the study of the Torah will be exalted, for it is said: "From *Mattanah* (meaning "gift of God") to *Nachaliel* (meaning "inheritance of God"), and from Nachaliel to *Bamoth* (meaning "the high place").

---

worth of the Teaching and Law thus revealed, and who will not employ it for the spiritual and moral perfection and sanctification of both the inner life and their outward actions, Mount Sinai will stand as a silent rebuke, as it were, before mankind, and without cease a call resounds from Horeb, saying, "It is not the Torah but only man that will suffer loss and distress because he has despised and insulted the Torah." נזיפה denotes the first degree of "banishment" such as occurs when a man of high spiritual and moral plane dismisses from his presence as unworthy a person guilty of reprehensible conduct. In quite the same manner a person who, though he has received the revealed Word of God, has not allowed it to influence his physical and spiritual life for his ennoblement and betterment is unworthy of being near God and is therefore sent away from His presence. Because it is so contrary to the ideal set forth in the Divine Teaching he has received, his crude and ignoble character, unchanged by the Word of God, is unworthy of God's holy Presence. It is as offensive as a woman whose body is beautiful but whose mind and morals are ugly and whose spiritual crudity and moral turpitude are all the more repulsive and obnoxious because of her physical beauty. For physical beauty is a gift which should serve as constant admonition to its possessor, of the spiritual and moral beauty and harmony after which he should strive with all his soul and spirit. Since physical beauty thus suggests spiritual and moral grace and hence holds attraction for those who look upon it, the lack of such spiritual and moral qualities is all the more repugnant. And all who behold this creature will say: "Alas for the beautiful body, even as for the golden ring which adorns a swine and which the beast heedlessly buries in the filth."

Even as the Torah ennobles us, so a truly devoted study of it also makes us free, free from error, free from the temptations of physical lusts and

ג הַלּוֹמֵד מֵחֲבֵרוֹ פֶּרֶק אֶחָד אוֹ הֲלָכָה אַחַת אוֹ פָּסוּק אֶחָד אוֹ
דִּבּוּר אֶחָד אוֹ אֲפִילוּ אוֹת אַחַת צָרִיךְ לִנְהוֹג בּוֹ כָבוֹד, שֶׁכֵּן
מָצִינוּ בְּדָוִד מֶלֶךְ יִשְׂרָאֵל שֶׁלֹּא לָמַד מֵאֲחִיתֹפֶל אֶלָּא שְׁנֵי
דְבָרִים בִּלְבַד קְרָאוֹ רַבּוֹ אַלּוּפוֹ וּמְיֻדָּעוֹ שֶׁנֶּאֱמַר וְאַתָּה אֱנוֹשׁ
כְּעֶרְכִּי אַלּוּפִי וּמְיֻדָּעִי: וַהֲלֹא דְבָרִים קַל וָחֹמֶר, וּמַה דָּוִד מֶלֶךְ
יִשְׂרָאֵל שֶׁלֹּא לָמַד מֵאֲחִיתֹפֶל אֶלָּא שְׁנֵי דְבָרִים בִּלְבַד קְרָאוֹ
רַבּוֹ אַלּוּפוֹ וּמְיֻדָּעוֹ, הַלּוֹמֵד מֵחֲבֵרוֹ פֶּרֶק אֶחָד אוֹ הֲלָכָה אַחַת
אוֹ פָּסוּק אֶחָד אוֹ דִבּוּר אֶחָד אוֹ אֲפִילוּ אוֹת אַחַת עַל־אַחַת
כַּמָּה וְכַמָּה שֶׁצָּרִיךְ לִנְהוֹג בּוֹ כָבוֹד · וְאֵין כָּבוֹד אֶלָּא תוֹרָה
שֶׁנֶּאֱמַר כָּבוֹד חֲכָמִים יִנְחָלוּ, וּתְמִימִים יִנְחֲלוּ טוֹב · וְאֵין טוֹב
אֶלָּא תוֹרָה שֶׁנֶּאֱמַר כִּי לֶקַח טוֹב נָתַתִּי לָכֶם תּוֹרָתִי אַל־תַּעֲזֹבוּ:
ד כָּךְ הִיא דַּרְכָּהּ שֶׁל־תּוֹרָה, פַּת בְּמֶלַח תֹּאכֵל וּמַיִם בִּמְשׂוּרָה

---

desires and free from the crushing and degrading power of the multitude of
worries and troubles of daily living. The Sages derived this truth from the
etymological reinterpretation of חרות to imply חרות, the more so since, according to tradition, the writing engraved through the stone Tablets itself, as in
the (character of the suspension of the inner parts of the letters ם, ס,) and the
exemplified support of earthly lives that is free of all external bands and is
borne only by the power of God (ם וסמך שבלוחות בנס הם עומדין). The place names
מתנה, נחליאל, במות are taken from the song which Israel sang of the Well
(Num. 21:19) and allude to the stations of Miriam's Well which accompanied our forefathers on their journey through the wilderness. These place
names are apt allegorical designations for the stations of learning and development through which we will pass if we will let ourselves be guided by the
Well of God's Torah on our earthly pilgrimage and if we will draw from it the
life-giving waters of spiritual and moral ennoblement. We are to accept the
Torah as מתנה "the gift of God". Then, once we allow it to penetrate our
inmost being through and through, it will become our inalienable "Godly
inheritance" and will lead us on to those "high places" toward which all on
earth may aspire.

3. The proper understanding of the Word of God is of such great importance; upon it depends to such great extent whether or not we can give proper
direction to our thoughts, our endeavors and our achievements; that we must

3. He who learns from his fellow-man even one chapter, one rule,
one verse, one expression or even one single letter, must pay him
honor. Thus we find in the case of David, the King of Israel, who
learned only two things from Achitophel and yet he called him his
master, his guide and his confidant. For it is said: "You are a man
equal to me; you are my guide and my confidant." Now we may infer
[as follows]: If David, the King of Israel, who had learned only two
things from Achitophel, called him his teacher, his guide and his
familiar friend, how much more ought one who learns from his
fellow one chapter, one rule, one verse, one expression or even only
one single letter, to pay him honor? And honor is inherent only in
the Torah, for it is said, "The wise ones will inherit honor and that
which is good will be inherited by those who are observant [of the
Torah]." Only the Torah is truly good, for it is said, "I have given
you a good Teaching, forsake not My Torah."

4. This is the way of the Torah: To eat bread with salt, to drink
water by measure, to sleep upon the ground and live a life of hardship,

---

honor as our greatest benefactor any man who has contributed to our better
understanding of the Torah, regardless of how small his contribution may
seem. The nature of our Hebrew language is such that the manner in which
we interpret even one single letter can be of decisive importance in our understanding of the whole. In Hebrew, particles, prepositions and conjunctions
are represented by one single letter; likewise, tense and mood, number, gender
of the object, and so forth, are indicated by changes in individual letters.
Thus the connotation of such words in a sentence and its context can often
be determined only by the correct interpretation of one specific letter. We are
told that Achitophel taught David just two things—the importance of studying
the Torah with a group, and the importance of worshipping as a congregation. This is indicated in Psalm 55:15 where David says of Achitophel:
אשר יחדו נמתיק סוד בבית אלהים נהלך ברגש "Together we savored the sweetness of
delving into the inmost meaning of the Torah, and we walked in the House
of God in the midst of the teeming multitude." It is the Torah that holds
our true human dignity and our true salvation. Therefore אין כבוד ואין טוב אלא
תורה.
4. Verse 3 told of the honor and the happiness which can be won through
constant diligent toil in the Torah. This verse is added by way of amendment,
lest you should come to believe that the kind of honor and happiness that
can be gained upon the path of Torah must always be visible and tangible.

תִּשְׁתֶּה וְעַל הָאָרֶץ תִּישָׁן וְחַיֵּי צַעַר תִּחְיֶה וּבַתּוֹרָה אַתָּה עָמֵל
אִם־אַתָּה עֹשֶׂה כֵּן אַשְׁרֶיךָ וְטוֹב לָךְ אַשְׁרֶיךָ בָּעוֹלָם הַזֶּה וְטוֹב
לָךְ לָעוֹלָם הַבָּא:

ה אַל־תְּבַקֵּשׁ גְּדֻלָּה לְעַצְמֶךָ וְאַל־תַּחְמוֹד כָּבוֹד· יוֹתֵר מִלִּמּוּדֶךָ
עֲשֵׂה וְאַל־תִּתְאַוֶּה לְשֻׁלְחָנָם שֶׁל־מְלָכִים שֶׁשֻּׁלְחָנְךָ גָּדוֹל
מִשֻּׁלְחָנָם וְכִתְרְךָ גָּדוֹל מִכִּתְרָם וְנֶאֱמָן הוּא בַּעַל מְלַאכְתְּךָ
שֶׁיְּשַׁלֵּם לְךָ שְׂכַר פְּעֻלָּתֶךָ:

י גְּדוֹלָה תּוֹרָה יוֹתֵר מִן־הַכְּהֻנָּה וּמִן־הַמַּלְכוּת· שֶׁהַמַּלְכוּת
נִקְנֵית בִּשְׁלשִׁים מַעֲלוֹת וְהַכְּהֻנָּה בְּעֶשְׂרִים וְאַרְבַּע, וְהַתּוֹרָה
נִקְנֵית בְּאַרְבָּעִים וּשְׁמוֹנָה דְבָרִים· וְאֵלּוּ הֵן, בְּתַלְמוּד, בִּשְׁמִיעַת
הָאֹזֶן, בַּעֲרִיכַת שְׂפָתָיִם, בְּבִינַת הַלֵּב, בְּשִׂכּוּל הַלֵּב, בְּאֵימָה,
בְּיִרְאָה, בַּעֲנָוָה, בְּשִׂמְחָה, (בטהרה) בְּשִׁמּוּשׁ חֲכָמִים, בְּדִבּוּק

The true power inherent in the Torah lies in the very fact that it can teach its true disciples readily and serenely to forego all outward honor and prosperity and that it permits them to find and enjoy in day-to-day living such happiness and bliss which, in the midst of privation and renunciation, can turn life on earth into a wellspring of the purest joy and imbue them with confidence in the future bliss of the world to come.

5. Seek recognition not for your own person but solely for the sacred cause for which you live and strive. Do not allow yourself to become envious when others are honored while you stand aside unnoticed. Do not devote yourself only to theoretical study, but do and accomplish more than you have learned. If you so live, then your "table"—that which life offers you and with which you gird yourself for service to your life's duty—will be far more opulent than even the festive boards of kings. Then your study and your deeds will have influence and dignity far greater even than the sovereign power of kings, and the Employer in Whose service you study and labor will let you find the reward for your selfless loyalty.

6. In Chapter 4, Verse 13 we are told that there are three crowns; the crown of Torah, that of priesthood and that of kingship. In this passage these three crowns are compared with one another with respect to דברים שנקנין בם.

and to study the Torah diligently all the while. If you do this, then you will be happy and it shall be well with you; you will be happy in this life and it shall be well with you in the world to come.

5. Seek not greatness for yourself and strive not after honor; let your works exceed your learning and crave not after the tables of kings; for your table is greater than theirs and your crown is greater than their crowns, and your Employer is faithful to pay you the reward for your work.

6. The Torah is greater than priesthood and kingship, for while kingship is acquired by thirty prerogatives, and the priesthood by twenty-four, the Torah is acquired by forty-eight qualifications. And these are they: by study, by proper listening, by ordered speech, by understanding, by pondering over what one has understood, by earnestness, by reverence, by modesty, by joy, (by purity), by association with wise men, by communion with colleagues, by discussion

---

Now שנקנין בם cannot be given the same interpretation in connection with all the three crowns. Priesthood, for example, can never be "acquired"; it is a title which can be inherited by birth only. Kingship, too, is generally hereditary; if only the son will fill his father's place in the genuine, conscientious fear of God, ממלא מקומו ביראה, the majesty of kingship will automatically pass from father to son. Actually, the thirty and twenty-four מעלות which are mentioned here in connection with מלכות and כהונה respectively, (for an enumeration of those of kingship see Chapter 9 of the First Book of Samuel, and Sanhedrin 18; for those of priesthood, Chapter 18 of the Book of Numbers) are not moral or spiritual virtues, but *prerogatives* that are part of the office of kingship and priesthood. They are not מעלות by means of which these titles can be acquired, but qualities which are associated with them and which are acquired together with the office. The forty-eight דברים enumerated here in connection with the תורה, however, are not prerogatives associated with the "crown" which Torah affords, but "qualifications", moral and spiritual talents and virtues, which he who strives after the crown of the Torah must acquire and employ through diligent labor upon his own personality before he can attain to the goal of the Torah. These forty-eight attributes are not *gifts* which are acquired together with the Torah, but *means* through which alone it is possible to acquire the crown of the Torah. If one wishes one may also logically say that all the moral and spiritual attributes named here are indeed acquired simultaneously with the Torah because, in fact, it is possible to acquire the Torah only if one also possesses these virtues. — בלימוד: by *teaching*. Personal guidance and instruction by a teacher are essential for

חֲבֵרִים, בְּפִלְפּוּל הַתַּלְמִידִים, בְּיִשּׁוּב, בְּמִקְרָא, בְּמִשְׁנָה. וּבְמַעוּט
סְחוֹרָה, בְּמַעוּט דֶּרֶךְ אֶרֶץ, בְּמַעוּט תַּעֲנוּג, בְּמַעוּט שֵׁנָה, בְּמַעוּט
שִׂיחָה, בְּמַעוּט שְׂחוֹק, בְּאֶרֶךְ אַפַּיִם, בְּלֶב־טוֹב, בֶּאֱמוּנַת חֲכָמִים,
בְּקַבָּלַת הַיִּסּוּרִין, הַמַּכִּיר אֶת־מְקוֹמוֹ, וְהַשָּׂמֵחַ בְּחֶלְקוֹ, וְהָעוֹשֶׂה
סְיָג לִדְבָרָיו, וְאֵינוֹ מַחֲזִיק טוֹבָה לְעַצְמוֹ, אָהוּב, אוֹהֵב אֶת־

---

knowledge and understanding of the Torah. Even though the Oral Tradition has been put down in writing, it still cannot be passed on properly without also being taught by the spoken word. בשמיעת אזן: Proper, accurate and thorough *listening* is the first demand made on the learner. Such intent and accurate listening precludes any carelessness, inattention or distraction by other things. בעריכת שפתים: The importance of the proper, accurate and logical *enunciation* and *verbalization* of what has been learned cannot be overestimated, for such verbalization serves not only as a test of the thought but also as a means for impressing and retaining in the mind the subject matter thus thought over. That which we cannot put into words clearly and distinctly we cannot possibly know with any degree of clarity; verbalization will clarify our thinking and help to fix permanently in our minds the subject of our thinking. בכונת הלב: by *attention;* literally, "by the *intention* of the heart". The student must be anxious truly to learn that which he must study; he must apply all of his mental power to both the learning and the retention of the material to be studied. בבינת הלב: However, he must not be content merely to absorb the knowledge exactly as it was presented to him; he must make himself comprehend and understand that which the teacher has told him; and digest it mentally. באימה ביראה: At the same time, though, he must ever be aware of the sacred meaning of the subject and also of the medium through which he acquires his knowledge. The source from which he is to draw nourishment for his mind so that he may arrange all of the thoughts, desires and achievements of his life in accordance with the will of God, is Divine revelation, and the Written and Oral Tradition which open to him the wellsprings of wisdom, are Divinely appointed media for this purpose. Once he realizes all this, he will be constantly and anxiously on guard lest, by overestimating his mental capacities and by impertinent disregard of his inadequacies, he should violate the dignity of the sacred subject and its bearers and thus block his own path to true wisdom. As he advances in his studies, he will be imbued with ever growing awe and reverence for both the Torah and its teachers. Thus, even while studying, he will acquire ענוה, modesty, that loftiest of virtues which will remain his most faithful guard and protection against any misstep and error on the path to wisdom and practical observance. בשמחה: According to the teaching of our Sages there is no greater

with students, by prudence, by knowledge of the Scriptures and of the Mishna; by moderation in business activity, in civic affairs, in physical pleasure, in sleep, in conversation, and in jest; by patience, by good-naturedness, by trust in the Sages, and by acceptance of sufferings. [A person such as] he knows his place, he rejoices in his portion, he puts a fence to his words, he does not claim merit for

---

means for spiritual progress and elevation than that serenity and joy of the spirit which will cause a man to rejoice in life with all its tasks and burdens. It is that שמחה של מצוה which will make him resolve all of life with its manifold aspects and changing situations into the one thought of מצוה, and thus acquire that joyful vitality which nothing can quench or subdue. The Sages teach us that the mood that makes man worthy and capable of attaining the nearness of the Divine Spirit is not: עצלות עצבות שחוק קלות ראש ודברים בטלים, neither apathy nor sadness; nor jest, levity or aimless talk, but שמחה, שמחה של מצוה (Pesachim 117a). Thus a disciple of Torah wisdom must have not only אימה, יראה וענוה but also שמחה which will make him rejoice in his every spiritual advance in his understanding of the Word of God and which will keep his spirit alert and quick for the arduous climb upon the steep road to wisdom. בשמוש חכמים בדבוק חברים בפלפל תלמידים: Isolation is incompatible with Jewish knowledge; it is only by association with living sages, in close communion with associates, and the by clarity of thought and judgment that can be attained by teaching it to disciples that the knowledge of Torah can be nurtured and promoted. בישוב, by calm and prudence. The joy in spiritual perception must not lead the student to quick, premature grasping, and to rash thoughts and conclusions, without first having taken the time to study every aspect of the subject and prudently testing the premises. Calm and prudent learning is the mother of true and thorough knowledge. במקרא במשנה: It would seem that the quality of ישוב was intentionally placed just before the knowledge of מקרא and משנה; מקרא and משנה both precede the Talmud and constitute its basis. Now ישוב, such prudent, methodical study as will lead to the desired goal will not simply guard against omitting these preliminary disciplines but will, in fact, constantly pursue the cultivation of these preliminaries even as it advances to more complex subject matter. במיעוט שנה: In order to gain time for his studies, he who is desirous of acquiring Torah wisdom must limit his hours of sleep to the minimum that is necessary for the preservation of his health. במיעוט שיחה: Nor must he waste his time on idle, superfluous chatter; generally speaking, the great Masters of our wisdom deem excessive talk detrimental to the needed earnestness and spiritual composure essential for study. (see Chapter 1, Verse 17). במיעוט סחורה The Mishna presumes that anyone who is anxious to acquire Torah wisdom does not engage in this high pursuit for material gain, but has another source of livelihood to which he

הַמָּקוֹם, אוֹהֵב אֶת־הַבְּרִיּוֹת, אוֹהֵב אֶת־הַצְּדָקוֹת, אוֹהֵב אֶת־
הַמֵּישָׁרִים, אוֹהֵב אֶת הַתּוֹכָחוֹת, וּמִתְרַחֵק מִן־הַכָּבוֹד, וְלֹא־מֵגִיס
לִבּוֹ בְּתַלְמוּדוֹ, וְאֵינוֹ שָׂמֵחַ בְּהוֹרָאָה, נוֹשֵׂא בְעוֹל עִם־חֲבֵרוֹ,
וּמַכְרִיעוֹ לְכַף זְכוּת, וּמַעֲמִידוֹ עַל־הָאֱמֶת, וּמַעֲמִידוֹ עַל־הַשָּׁלוֹם

must of necessity devote a certain amount of time and activity. But if he is to attain the prize of knowledge then he must restrict his business activities, too, to a minimum. This limitation should teach him, in the first place, gladly to forego שחוק and תענוג, sport and luxury. במיעוט דרך ארץ : All of the earthly life, both individual and communal, constitutes the subject of the Torah's wisdom, and the Torah seeks to teach us to view and arrange all human affairs on earth in the light of the Teaching of God. Therefore active participation in civic and communal endeavors is not only a duty which must not be neglected but actually is a contribution of no mean significance to the practical knowledge required for this wisdom. Nevertheless, moderation is essential even in this aspect of living if time, mental clarity and emotional calm are to be preserved for the cultivation of the Torah's wisdom. באורך אפים : He who is quick to anger will find that, in his inevitable dealings with others, he will lose the calm and composure which he should bring to his studies. ארך אפים calm, persevering patience not only in our approach to the subject matter itself but also in our relationships with our teachers, with our companions in the search for knowledge, and with the disciples whom we, in turn, teach—is a virtue not to be understimated in our Torah living and in the pursuit of Torah knowledge. לב טוב : a "good" heart, one to which envy, jealousy and hate can gain no access, leaves both mind and spirit free for one's own complete immersion in the task of seeking knowledge, and is beneficial in no small measure also to our associations with our fellow-students. He who has a "good" heart will rejoice in the spiritual achievements of his companions in the search for knowledge; he will gladly and appreciatively add them to his own store of learning and will not allow carping envy to obscure for him the knowledge and acknowledgement of those facts of truth and right that were discovered and uttered by others. באמונת חכמים. Original, creative activity is most enticing for a mentally gifted and eager disciple of any science, but it may well lead him to depart from the path of truth. For all that, a wisdom such as ours which has been handed down by transmission does indeed offer extensive opportunities and an inexhaustible source for creative mental activity, both for retrospective research into the motives behind the given facts and for the development of deductions to elaborate upon this basic data. However, our wisdom has at its side most effective and corrective safeguards against all error in these endeavors. These are the actual content

his achievements, he is loved, he loves God, loves men, loves kindness, loves rectitude, and loves reproof; he keeps himself far from
honor, he does not feel arrogantly of his learning, he does not delight
in handing down decisions, he shares the burden of his fellow-man
and tends to judge him favorably; he teaches him the viewpoint of
truth and teaches him the position of peace; he engages in mature

---

of the Torah as handed down by transmission, the transmitted canons governing
inquiry, the exemplary precedents established by the bearers and communi-
cators of our tradition, and אמונת חכמים; faithful adherence to the tradition,
the teaching and the example left us by those men whom we rightly call our
חכמים. The measuring and testing of the results of our own thinking against
the standard of the truths they have taught and championed will keep our
own thinking also in the paths of truth. בקבלת יסורין: According to our
Sages, suffering is part of the course by means of which God trains both
mind and spirit for the knowledge and fulfillment of His Teaching. Acceptance and utilization for our spiritual and moral enlightenment of those sufferings that are inseparably a part of our Jewish living, as well as of those
which are specifically ordained by Divine Providence is an important part of
the Torah student's task. Instead of allowing those sufferings to alienate him
from the study of the Torah, it is his duty in the midst of distress to devote
himself all the more fervently to it. המכיר את מקומו: יעב״ץ believes that this
change in construction (we read here not בשמחה בחלקו, בהכרת מקומו but
השמח בחלקו, המכיר את מקומו etc.) indicates that the traits named here and
thereafter are those qualities which will be acquired through the cultivation
of all those virtues enumerated before. המכיר את מקומו: He knows his place
in the field of knowledge; he neither overestimates his abilities nor boasts of
them. He knows the spiritual and moral demands which knowledge makes of
him; he knows the inadequacy of what he has achieved thus far; he does not
push himself forward but remains humble and modest. והשמח בחלקו: Even as
he is content with that portion of earthly goods that has been given him, so
it is in the field of striving for knowledge; he rejoices in the modest measure
of intellectual talent that has been granted him. Though he is fully aware that
he must stand back in favor of others who are far more gifted than he is,
he derives satisfaction from the knowledge that he has faithfully employed
his modest abilities for the advancement of his skills and learning, for he
knows that his Father in Heaven evaluates the achievements of His children
solely in terms of the extent to which they have made good use of the faculties with which He has endowed them. והעושה סיג לדבריו: This modest self-
comprehension shows also in his speech. He will not force his own views
on others; and while he does not restrain himself from voicing his convictions
when outspokenness is fitting and proper, he will qualify all his utterances

וּמִתְיַשֵּׁב לִבּוֹ בְּתַלְמוּדוֹ שׁוֹאֵל וּמֵשִׁיב שׁוֹמֵעַ וּמוֹסִיף, הַלּוֹמֵד עַל
מְנָת לְלַמֵּד, וְהַלּוֹמֵד עַל־מְנָת לַעֲשׂוֹת, הַמַּחְכִּים אֶת־רַבּוֹ, וְהַמְכַוֵּן
אֶת־שְׁמוּעָתוֹ, וְהָאוֹמֵר דָּבָר בְּשֵׁם אוֹמְרוֹ · הָא לָמַדְתָּ כָּל־הָאוֹמֵר
דָּבָר בְּשֵׁם אוֹמְרוֹ מֵבִיא גְאֻלָּה לָעוֹלָם שֶׁנֶּאֱמַר וַתֹּאמֶר אֶסְתֵּר
לַמֶּלֶךְ בְּשֵׁם מָרְדֳּכָי:

---

with the reservation that they are true only to the best of his knowledge. יאינו מחזיק טובה לעצמו. Nor will such good as he may have achieved in the field of knowledge and of life fill him with self-praise. He knows how much of his attainments he owes to favorable circumstances and influences which were not of his own making but had been placed into his path by the love of Divine providence. He knows how dependent he has ever been upon God's help in everything he has ever done and that therefore he can take credit for nothing more than, at best, his good intention. Knowing all this, he will view whatever he may have achieved in his life with no other emotion but humility.

אהוב אוהב את המקום אוהב את הבריות: Nothing is more suited to endear a man to both God and his fellows and to fill him, in turn, with love for God and mankind, than the study of Jewish wisdom. A true disciple of the knowledge of Torah will first apply and realize in his own person the tasks and requirements with which his studies deal and to the profound understanding of which he devotes his soul and spirit. In this manner his own personality will be ennobled to such an extent that he will gain the love of his fellow-men without ever seeking it. Moreover, since his wisdom leads him to view all of life on earth and all the human affairs and relationships taking place there from the one vantage point of nearness to God and of Divine approval, his heart will go out, unbidden, to God. And in this great love of God he will include all men as well, for after all, he knows that mankind is included in God's purpose and is one of the creations in which God delights. אוהב את הצדקות אוהב את המישרים These are two principal concepts within whose framework all his knowledge moves: Firstly, the concept of that which is due both men and circumstances in accordance with the claims inherent in them, or that which is claimed for them by the will of God. These demands are all included in the definitions of צדקה in the broadest sense of the word. Secondly, there is that which, aside from the men and circumstances which it affects, befits us and is therefore in keeping with the nature and purpose of him who discharges the obligation. These attitudes and obligations are defined by the term מישרים.

A true disciple of Torah study loves right, duty and fairness and will defend them wherever he may go. אוהב את התוכחות Since his ultimate goal is his own personal moral ennoblement and improvement—which is nothing

reflection when studying; he asks and answers, he listens and adds to his learning. He studies in order to teach and he studies in order to practice; he promotes the wisdom of his teacher; he grasps and retains accurately what has been handed down to him by transmission, and what he has heard of others he will quote in the name of him of whom he has heard it. For so you have learned: He who quotes something in the name of the person who said it brings deliverance to the world. For it is said: "And Esther said to the King in the name of Mordechai."

---

else but the practical fulfillment of the ideals taught him by his studies—he will not be angry with him who will point out to him his errors and faults but will instead thank him with all his heart and view him as his greatest benefactor. ומתרחק מן הכבוד His inner life is so profound, he knows so well how far he still is from true perfection in every respect, he knows the dangerous pitfalls, hindering all advancement, that are inherent in honor and public recognition; therefore he will seek to keep outward honor and recognition as far from himself as he can ולא מגיס לבו בתלמודו ואינו שמח בהוראה This modest opinion of his own mental and spiritual worth will keep him from conceit with regard to his wisdom, and it will guard him, too, from seeking the opportunity to propound his own views and opinions by way of a decision unless it is necessary and required by duty that he do so. נושא בעול עם חברו ומכריעו לכף זכות ומעמידו על האמת ומעמידו על השלום : Even as he seeks to ease his neighbor's burdens in daily living, so, too, he will seek to render assistance to every fellow-seeker of knowledge. He will help ease for him the task of learning and the ways of study; he will seek to give direction to the other's tentative questing so that he will choose the good path, and to strengthen his resolve so that he may champion the cause of truth and peace. ומתישב לבי בתלמודו שואל ומשיב שומע ומוסיף Even once he has attained mastery in his studies, he will preserve for the rest of his life those virtues which he had acquired in his early student days. He will remain prudent and will continue to strive after accuracy in his knowledge; he will remain in close touch with teachers and fellow students, exchanging questions and answers in order to clarify and consolidate his own understanding; he endeavors at all times to enrich his own knowledge by listening to the opinions of others. הלומד על מנת ללמד והלומד על מנת לעשות המחכים את רבו והמכון את שמועתו והאומר דבר בשם אומרו : Even now that he himself is a master, he continues to study with a view to both teaching and practice; he seeks knowledge from others and those who supply it gain knowledge from him in turn. He is careful to absorb and repeat accurately whatever he has heard from others and he will never pass off as his own that which others have told him.

ז גְּדוֹלָה תוֹרָה שֶׁהִיא נוֹתֶנֶת חַיִּים לְעוֹשֶׂיהָ בָּעוֹלָם הַזֶּה
וּבָעוֹלָם הַבָּא, שֶׁנֶּאֱמַר כִּי־חַיִּים הֵם לְמוֹצְאֵיהֶם וּלְכָל־בְּשָׂרוֹ
מַרְפֵּא: וְאוֹמֵר רִפְאוּת תְּהִי לְשָׁרֶּךָ וְשִׁקּוּי לְעַצְמוֹתֶיךָ:
וְאוֹמֵר עֵץ־חַיִּים הִיא לַמַּחֲזִיקִים בָּהּ וְתֹמְכֶיהָ מְאֻשָּׁר: וְאוֹמֵר
כִּי לִוְיַת חֵן הֵם לְרֹאשֶׁךָ וַעֲנָקִים לְגַרְגְּרֹתֶיךָ: וְאוֹמֵר תִּתֵּן לְרֹאשְׁךָ
לִוְיַת־חֵן עֲטֶרֶת תִּפְאֶרֶת תְּמַגְּנֶךָּ: וְאוֹמֵר כִּי בִי יִרְבּוּ יָמֶיךָ
וְיוֹסִיפוּ לְךָ שְׁנוֹת חַיִּים: וְאוֹמֵר אֹרֶךְ יָמִים בִּימִינָהּ בִּשְׂמֹאולָה
עֹשֶׁר וְכָבוֹד: וְאוֹמֵר כִּי אֹרֶךְ יָמִים וּשְׁנוֹת חַיִּים וְשָׁלוֹם יוֹסִיפוּ לָךְ:

ח רַבִּי שִׁמְעוֹן בֶּן־יְהוּדָה מִשֵּׁם רַבִּי שִׁמְעוֹן בֶּן־יוֹחַאי אוֹמֵר,
הַנּוֹי וְהַכֹּחַ וְהָעֹשֶׁר וְהַכָּבוֹד וְהַחָכְמָה וְהַזִּקְנָה וְהַשֵּׂיבָה וְהַבָּנִים
נָאֶה לַצַּדִּיקִים וְנָאֶה לָעוֹלָם, שֶׁנֶּאֱמַר עֲטֶרֶת תִּפְאֶרֶת שֵׂיבָה

---

7. The fulfillment of the precepts of the Torah—and this includes both study in theory and fulfillment in practice—affords life in this world as well as in the next. Its mandates enable every aspect of man's nature to achieve that growth and activation which is their destiny. In this manner every moment of his existence here below achieves its full value and thus becomes true living, and even the most fleeting moment will acquire permanent and eternal significance. Such is the greatness of the Teaching of God. הם "They", the words themselves and not just the consequences of their fulfillment, are life itself to all those whom they can reach. Every human spirit which reflects upon the Word of God and thinks it through with care, will come alive, and every human body that musters its strength for this purpose will become healthy. רפאות תהי The fulfillment of the precepts of the Teaching of God will guard man's physical organs from physical decline and will keep the marrow in his bones strong and sound. עץ חיים : By giving us the Torah, the Lord has given us once again a "Tree of Life"; wherever we will plant and nurture it, it will transform our surroundings, wherever they may be, into a new Paradise. In the original Garden of Eden, the "Tree of Life" and the "Tree of Knowledge" were two separate plants; therefore we lost the "Tree of Life" because of the fruits of the "Tree of Knowledge". But in the Torah the "Tree of Life" and the "Tree of Knowledge" are one and the same, and hence both, inseparable, are the inalienable possession of him who will plant and nurture the Torah even as he would a tree and who will devote all of his life, both physical and spiritual, to serve as its soil. ותומכיה And if a

7. Great is the Torah, for to those who find it it gives life in this world and in the world to come, as it is said: "For they are life to them that find them and health to all his flesh." And it is said: "It shall be health to your body and give marrow to your bones." And it is said: "It is a tree of life to those who maintain it, and those who lean upon it are a community that stride forward to salvation." And it is said: "They shall be a graceful garland about your head and necklaces around your neck." And it is said: "They give to your head a graceful garland and will allow you to forego a crown of glory." And it is said: "For by Me your days shall grow many, and the years of your life shall be increased." And it is said: "Length of days is in its right hand; in its left hand are riches and honor." And it is further said: "They shall add to you length of days and years of life and peace."

8. Rabbi Shimon ben Yehudah said in the name of Rabbi Shimon ben Yochai: Beauty, strength, riches, honor, wisdom, old age, a hoary head, and children are comely to the righteous and thus also for the world; as it is said: "The hoary head is a crown of glory; it is found

---

great many people will cleave to it, the Torah will form a bond, unifying the many into one single unit, prosperous and striding ever forward to salvation. לוית חן: It is through the Torah that your head, your mind and your understanding will gain the gift of Divine approval such as causes man's spiritual life to flourish. Then וענקים לגרגרותיך all your physical body, culminating in the neck that bears your head, will be so ennobled that the whole man shall come to honor. Once you have this Divine approval which rests upon your head and accompanies all of your spiritual endeavors, you will gladly forego any other crown of human glory. (תמגנך): "it will enable you to forego any other crown of glory") כי בי ירבו-ימיך: Through תורה your days will last beyond the transient span of this life and even the years during which you dwell on earth will be turned for you into years of true living. אורך ימים בימינה: And if you seek nothing from the תורה but life eternal, as its gift to you from its "right hand", then it will endow you also with riches and honors with its "left hand" without your asking for it. It will render you rich by teaching you contentment, and it will bring you to honor by securing for you recognition from your fellow-men.

8. All the things enumerated here, which indeed comprise all that a man may desire, will be an ornament not only to him who possesses them but also to the entire world, if only the person having them will make use of them solely in the path of duty. עטרת תפארת שיבה: a "hoary head", the acquisition

בְּדֶרֶךְ צְדָקָה תִּמָּצֵא: וְאוֹמֵר תִּפְאֶרֶת בַּחוּרִים כֹּחָם וַהֲדַר
זְקֵנִים שֵׂיבָה: וְאוֹמֵר עֲטֶרֶת חֲכָמִים עָשְׁרָם: וְאוֹמֵר עֲטֶרֶת
זְקֵנִים בְּנֵי בָנִים וְתִפְאֶרֶת בָּנִים אֲבוֹתָם: וְאוֹמֵר וְחָפְרָה הַלְּבָנָה
וּבוֹשָׁה הַחַמָּה כִּי־מָלַךְ יְיָ צְבָאוֹת בְּהַר צִיּוֹן וּבִירוּשָׁלַיִם וְנֶגֶד
זְקֵנָיו כָּבוֹד: רַבִּי שִׁמְעוֹן בֶּן־מְנַסְיָא אוֹמֵר, אֵלּוּ שֶׁבַע מִדּוֹת
שֶׁמָּנוּ חֲכָמִים לַצַּדִּיקִים כֻּלָּם נִתְקַיְּמוּ בְרַבִּי וּבְבָנָיו :

ט אָמַר רַבִּי יוֹסֵי בֶּן־קִסְמָא, פַּעַם אַחַת הָיִיתִי מְהַלֵּךְ בַּדֶּרֶךְ
וּפָגַע בִּי אָדָם אֶחָד וְנָתַן־לִי שָׁלוֹם וְהֶחֱזַרְתִּי לוֹ שָׁלוֹם· אָמַר
לִי, רַבִּי מֵאֵיזֶה מָקוֹם אַתָּה, אָמַרְתִּי לוֹ מֵעִיר גְּדוֹלָה שֶׁל
חֲכָמִים וְשֶׁל־סוֹפְרִים אָנִי· אָמַר לִי, רַבִּי רְצוֹנְךָ שֶׁתָּדוּר עִמָּנוּ
בִּמְקוֹמֵנוּ וַאֲנִי אֶתֵּן לְךָ אֶלֶף אַלְפִים דִּינְרֵי זָהָב וַאֲבָנִים טוֹבוֹת
וּמַרְגָּלִיּוֹת, אָמַרְתִּי לוֹ אִם אַתָּה נוֹתֵן לִי כָּל־כֶּסֶף וְזָהָב וַאֲבָנִים
טוֹבוֹת וּמַרְגָּלִיּוֹת שֶׁבָּעוֹלָם אֵינִי דָר אֶלָּא בִּמְקוֹם תּוֹרָה, וְכֵן
כָּתוּב בְּסֵפֶר תְּהִלִּים עַל יְדֵי־דָוִד מֶלֶךְ יִשְׂרָאֵל טוֹב לִי תּוֹרַת
פִּיךָ מֵאַלְפֵי זָהָב וָכָסֶף· וְלֹא עוֹד שֶׁבִּשְׁעַת פְּטִירָתוֹ שֶׁל אָדָם
אֵין מְלַוִּין לוֹ לְאָדָם לֹא כֶסֶף וְלֹא זָהָב וְלֹא אֲבָנִים טוֹבוֹת
וּמַרְגָּלִיּוֹת אֶלָּא תּוֹרָה וּמַעֲשִׂים טוֹבִים בִּלְבָד, שֶׁנֶּאֱמַר בְּהִתְהַלֶּכְךָ

---

of long years of living, marks the old man as a person to whom honor is
due. But a hoary head as such is a mark of distinction only if the life of the
man has been a good and righteous one. Even as the hoary head lends dignity
to the old, so strength, not squandered in excesses, is an ornament to youth.
עטרת חכמים: Riches, too, are a crown, provided that it is a wise man whom
they adorn. עטרת זקנים: Grandchildren will be the crown of the old, if the
parents have been the pride of their children. If children have made it a matter
of pride to raise their offspring in the image of their own parents, then honest,
decent grandchildren will be the rewarding climax of their grandparents' lives.
וחפרה הלבנה: When the Kingdom of God will go forth from Jerusalem and
Zion, then His elders, who were the teachers and heralds of His Kingdom,

in the path of righteousness." And it is said: "The ornament of young men is their strength and the adornment of old men is a hoary head." And it is said: "The crown of the wise is their riches." And it is said: "Children's children are the crown of the old, and the adornment of children are their parents." And it is said: "The moon shall grow pale and the sun ashamed, for ה׳ צבאות has begun His reign in Mount Tzion and in Yerushalayim, and honor shall meet His elders." Rabbi Shimon ben Menasya, said: "These seven qualifications which the Sages enumerated as pertaining to the righteous were all realized in Rabbi [Judah the Prince] and in his sons.

9. Rabbi Yosé ben Kisma, said: I was once walking by the way when a man met me and greeted me. I returned the greeting. He said to me: "Rabbi, from what place are you?" I replied: "I come from a great city of sages and scholars." Thereupon he said to me: "Rabbi, if you would be willing to dwell with us in our place I would give you a million golden dinars and precious stones and pearls." I replied: "Were you to give me all the silver and gold and precious stones and pearls in the world, I would still not live anywhere except in a place of Torah." For thus it is also written in the Book of Psalms by David, the King of Israel, that "The teaching of Your mouth is worth more to me than thousands in gold and silver." Furthermore, when a man dies, neither silver nor gold nor precious stones nor pearls accompany him, but only the Torah and good works, for it

---

will shine forth in a splendor of spirit that will eclipse the physical light emanating from both sun and moon.

9. An explanation is still needed why Rabbi Yosé should have taken this inquiry as to his place of residence as a request to describe its nature. One might tend to think that מאיזה מקום אתה means "from what manner of place are you?". However, אי זה מקום denotes only the simple question "From what place...?" Cf. Sanhedrin 40a: עמנו במקומנו. באיזה שעה באיזה מקום —"my townsmen are all all simple people like myself; they are not חכמים or סופרים. "טוב לי etc. ולא עוד etc. The possession of the תורה is worth more and is more blissful than that of riches; it is immortal and thus remains with man even beyond the threshold of the grave where he has to leave behind all his other possessions. והקיצות : When you regain consciousness in the world to come, you will become conscious of such thoughts as you had originally derived from your study of the Torah while you were on earth.

תֵּנְחֶה אֹתָךְ בְּשָׁכְבְּךָ תִּשְׁמֹר עָלֶיךָ וַהֲקִיצֹוֹתָ הִיא תְשִׂיחֶךָ׃ בְּהִתְהַלֶּכְךָ תַּנְחֶה אֹתָךְ בָּעֹולָם הַזֶּה בְּשָׁכְבְּךָ תִּשְׁמֹר עָלֶיךָ בַּקֶּבֶר וַהֲקִיצֹוֹתָ הִיא תְשִׂיחֶךָ לָעֹולָם הַבָּא׃ וְאֹמֵר לִי הַכֶּסֶף וְלִי הַזָּהָב נְאֻם יְיָ צְבָאֹות׃

, חֲמִשָּׁה קִנְיָנִים קָנָה (לֹו) הַקָּדֹושׁ בָּרוּךְ הוּא בְּעֹולָמֹו וְאֵלּוּ הֵן. תֹּורָה קִנְיָן אֶחָד שָׁמַיִם וָאָרֶץ קִנְיָן אֶחָד אַבְרָהָם קִנְיָן אֶחָד יִשְׂרָאֵל קִנְיָן אֶחָד בֵּית הַמִּקְדָּשׁ קִנְיָן אֶחָד׃ תֹּורָה מִנַּיִן, דִּכְתִיב יְיָ קָנָנִי רֵאשִׁית דַּרְכֹּו קֶדֶם מִפְעָלָיו מֵאָז׃ שָׁמַיִם וָאָרֶץ מִנַּיִן דִּכְתִיב כֹּה אָמַר יְיָ הַשָּׁמַיִם כִּסְאִי וְהָאָרֶץ הֲדֹום רַגְלָי אֵי־זֶה בַיִת אֲשֶׁר תִּבְנוּ־לִי וְאֵי־זֶה מָקֹום מְנוּחָתִי׃ וְאֹומֵר מָה רַבּוּ מַעֲשֶׂיךָ יְיָ כֻּלָּם בְּחָכְמָה עָשִׂיתָ מָלְאָה הָאָרֶץ קִנְיָנֶךָ׃ אַבְרָהָם מִנַּיִן, דִּכְתִיב וַיְבָרְכֵהוּ וַיֹּאמַר בָּרוּךְ אַבְרָם לְאֵל עֶלְיֹון קֹנֵה שָׁמַיִם וָאָרֶץ׃ יִשְׂרָאֵל מִנַּיִן, דִּכְתִיב עַד־יַעֲבֹר עַמְּךָ יְיָ עַד־יַעֲבֹר עַם־ זוּ קָנִיתָ׃ וְאֹומֵר לִקְדֹושִׁים אֲשֶׁר בָּאָרֶץ הֵמָּה וְאַדִּירֵי כָּל־חֶפְצִי־בָם׃

לי הכסף וגו׳: To the extent that the possession of material riches is good and useful, and indeed, necessary for the fulfillment of the tasks set us by the Torah, God Himself will grant us whatever in His wisdom He deems necessary and desirable for us, without our having to pursue it ourselves at the cost of the eternal values that the Torah affords.

10. Of all the Universe which is עולמו "His world" as a whole and in all its parts, created and ruled by Him alone, the Lord has singled out five things as His special possessions because they perform a special service to advance the purposes of His Creation and His sovereignty. First there is the Torah, the essence and the revelation of the purpose of His Kingdom on earth which it is man's task to translate into reality. Then come heaven and earth as the soil and the domain upon which the Torah is to be fulfilled. Then, Abraham, as the cornerstone for the winning of mankind for the Kingdom of God; Israel, as the messenger for the extension of the Covenant of Abraham to all of mankind; and finally the מקדש, the Sanctuary of God and of His Law which is to serve the preservation and advancement of Israel for this holy

is said: "When you walk it shall lead you; when you lie down it shall watch over you, and when you awaken it shall address you." "When you walk, it shall lead you"—in this world. "When you lie down it shall watch over you"—in the grave. "And when you awaken it shall address you"—in the world to come. And it is also said: "Mine is the silver and Mine is the gold, says ה' צבאות."

10. Five possessions has the Holy One, blessed be He, declared His own in this world: The Torah is a special possession; Heaven and earth are a special possession; Abraham is a special possession; Yisrael is a special possession; the Temple is a special possession. The Torah: Because it is written: *"God* possessed me as the beginning of His way before all His works, from of old." Heaven and earth: Because it is written: "Thus says *God*: The Heaven is My throne, the earth is my footstool; what manner of house will you build for Me, and what manner of place for My rest?" And it is written: "How manifold are Your works, O *God;* in wisdom have You made them all; the earth is full of Your possessions." Abraham: Because it is written: "Blessed be Avram to the Most High God, the Possessor of heaven and earth." Yisrael: Because it is written: "Until Your people pass over, O *God,* until the people whom You have acquired pass over." And it is written: "The holy ones that are on

---

purpose. ה' קנני ראשית דרכו Since it was the actual end for which the world was brought into being, the concept of the Torah preceded Creation and was employed by the Creator as the guiding standard for the Universe He made. השמים כסאי וגו' But it was not only at one time, at their Creation, that Heaven and earth were directly related to God, their Creator. Even now and forevermore they are the throne of His dominion and the soil of His sovereignty. Heaven is His throne from which, leading and guiding, He fashions the events and phenomena of earth. The earth, in turn, is His footstool; all changes in nature and history are but footprints of His progress through the ages. Temples and houses of worship are all only rooms used by men to gather to worship the presence and sovereignty of God in heaven and on earth. ברוך אברם לאל עליון Abraham is blessed not *by* God, but *to* God. The blessing that is Abraham's serves to advance those purposes which God has set as the goal of His sovereignty and which He seeks to bring about through His guidance of Heaven and earth.

עם זו קנית : Israel had lost all those qualifications upon which its survival,

בֵּית הַמִּקְדָּשׁ מִנַּיִן, דִּכְתִיב מָכוֹן לְשִׁבְתְּךָ פָּעַלְתָּ יְיָ מִקְדָּשׁ אֲדֹנָי
כּוֹנְנוּ יָדֶיךָ: וְאוֹמֵר וַיְבִיאֵם אֶל־גְּבוּל קָדְשׁוֹ הַר זֶה קָנְתָה יְמִינוֹ:

יא כָּל מַה־שֶּׁבָּרָא הַקָּדוֹשׁ בָּרוּךְ הוּא בְּעוֹלָמוֹ לֹא בְרָאוֹ אֶלָּא
לִכְבוֹדוֹ, שֶׁנֶּאֱמַר כֹּל הַנִּקְרָא בִשְׁמִי וְלִכְבוֹדִי בְּרָאתִיו יְצַרְתִּיו אַף
עֲשִׂיתִיו: וְאוֹמֵר, יְיָ יִמְלֹךְ לְעֹלָם וָעֶד:

רַבִּי חֲנַנְיָא בֶּן־עֲקַשְׁיָא אוֹמֵר, רָצָה הַקָּדוֹשׁ בָּרוּךְ הוּא לְזַכּוֹת אֶת־יִשְׂרָאֵל
לְפִיכָךְ הִרְבָּה לָהֶם תּוֹרָה וּמִצְוֹת. שֶׁנֶּאֱמַר, יְיָ חָפֵץ לְמַעַן צִדְקוֹ יַגְדִּיל תּוֹרָה וְיַאְדִּיר:
קדיש.

---

both individual and national, depended, and it was only through direct Divine
intervention in the course of history that the children of Israel became free
as individuals and politically independent as a nation. By virtue of this act
of God the people of Israel, both as individuals and as a group, became
God's own possession forever, to serve to do His will and to advance His
purpose on earth. All those who, with pure and complete devotion, live on
earth for the realization of this their destiny are called by God, "His holy ones
on earth." They do not shine forth in their own power and glory, but glory
solely in the fact that God regards them as instruments for the fulfillment of
His will. מכון לשבתך When the Lord apportioned the regions of earth among
men, He retained for Himself, for a special purpose, one land ארץ ישראל,
the Land of the Jews, which was to serve as the soil for His Law and of
His people which was to live for the fulfillment of His Law. And within
this one land He reserved for a special purpose one place, the Holy Mountain,
to serve as the abode for the Sanctuary of His Law. From this place He would
proclaim His presence and it was from this place, too, that the Law with its
hallowing force was to win over, first Israel and then all the other nations of
the world for God and for His Law. כי מציון תצא תורה ודבר ה' מירושלים.

earth, who are splendid by virtue of the fact that all My will is done through them." The Temple: Because it is written: "The place, O *God*, prepared for You to dwell in, which You, O *God*, have attained; the Sanctuary, O *God*, which Your hands have established." And it is written. "He brought them to the region of His Sanctuary, to this mountain, which His right hand had acquired."

11.   Whatever the Holy One, blessed be He, created in His world, He created solely for His glory, as it is said: "Everything that is called after My Name and that I have created for My glory I have formed and I have fashioned it." And it is said: "*God* shall reign for all eternity."

---

11.   The teachings of wisdom of our "fathers" end with the thought that not only the Jewish people but, in fact, everything else that as a creation of God bears the Name of God, has no other purpose but to serve the Glorification of God, its Creator, Lord and Master. It is inevitable that all things should fulfill this destiny, for God has created each one of them especially for this purpose, and fashioned and guided it accordingly. The nature with which every creature is endowed at the time of its birth and all the influences that affect him under God's own guidance both have the ultimate goal to guide all things and all men along that path which will lead to the glorification of God alone on earth. ה' ימלוך לעולם ועד This thought appears already at the close of the שירת הים, the Song at the Reed Sea which beholds God in His workings. As we have indicated in the Commentary to Exodus 15:18, this may mean not only "*God* will reign throughout all the future to come," but also, and particularly in this context: "Some day in the future which may still be distant but is no less sure to come, God will reign as King over all mankind." (ibid.)

ערבית למוצאי שבת

On מוצאי שבת *the evening service is introduced with the following two psalms:*

קמד לְדָוִד · בָּרוּךְ יְהֹוָה · צוּרִי הַמְלַמֵּד יָדַי לַקְרָב אֶצְבְּעוֹתַי
לַמִּלְחָמָה: חַסְדִּי וּמְצוּדָתִי מִשְׂגַּבִּי וּמְפַלְטִי־לִי מָגִנִּי וּבוֹ חָסִיתִי
הָרוֹדֵד עַמִּי תַחְתָּי: יְהֹוָה מָה־אָדָם וַתֵּדָעֵהוּ בֶּן־אֱנוֹשׁ וַתְּחַשְּׁבֵהוּ:
אָדָם לַהֶבֶל דָּמָה יָמָיו כְּצֵל עוֹבֵר: יְהֹוָה הַט־שָׁמֶיךָ וְתֵרֵד גַּע
בֶּהָרִים וְיֶעֱשָׁנוּ: בְּרוֹק בָּרָק וּתְפִיצֵם שְׁלַח חִצֶּיךָ וּתְהֻמֵּם: שְׁלַח
יָדֶיךָ מִמָּרוֹם פְּצֵנִי וְהַצִּילֵנִי מִמַּיִם רַבִּים מִיַּד בְּנֵי־נֵכָר: אֲשֶׁר־
פִּיהֶם דִּבֶּר־שָׁוְא וִימִינָם יְמִין שָׁקֶר: אֱלֹהִים שִׁיר חָדָשׁ אָשִׁירָה

ערבית למוצאי שבת

לדוד ברוך We accompany our re-entry into weekday life with its strife
and struggle, its endeavors and achievements, its successes and failures, with
two psalms which are well qualified to gird us, both as individuals and as
a community, with vigorous courage and calm confidence. Optimism such
as this can be derived only from the certainty that God is the support of all
human life and endeavor and the Guiding force in all the course of earth's
development, and that He will grant man a future of salvation. In Psalm 144,
David, the most victorious of all the Kings of the Jewish people, quite frankly
acknowledges that he owes all of his strength, all of his prowess in battles

PRAYERS FOR THE CONCLUSION OF THE SABBATH

By David. Blessed be *God,* my Rock, Who trains my hands for battle and my fingers for war. My Loving-kindness and my Fortress, my High Tower and my Deliverer, for me, my Shield in Whom I put my trust; it is He who makes my people submit to me. But *God,* what is man that You have recognized him, the son of fallen mankind that You are mindful of him? Man is like a breath; his days are like a passing shadow. O *God* bend Your heavens and descend; touch the mountains and they will vanish as vapor. Send forth one flash of lightning and You will scatter them; send out your arrows and You will confound them. Stretch forth Your hands from on high, rescue me and deliver me out of many waters, from the tyranny of the sons of the stranger, whose mouth utters deceit and whose right hand is a right hand of falsehood. O God I will declare a new song

---

and all his victories to God alone. At the same time he sincerely deplores the sad necessity for having wars at all, and he declares that he will bless the day when we will be able to leave the "evil" sword in its sheath forever and to rejoice in the realization of the sole Jewish ideal of national prosperity and welfare; that is, the flourishing of our youth to spiritual and moral nobility, modesty and humility preserved and proven even in wealth and prosperity under the protection and guidance of God. Psalm 67, למנצח בנגינות, reminds us that, under God's Providence and leadership, all the rest of humanity, too, moves forward to this same future of salvation, and assures us that God will permit His Providence among all the nations on earth to complete its path to that goal.

לָךְ בְּגֵל עָשׂוֹר אֲמֵרָה־לָּךְ: הַנּוֹתֵן תְּשׁוּעָה לַמְּלָכִים הַפּוֹצֶה אֶת־דָּוִד עַבְדּוֹ מֵחֶרֶב רָעָה: פְּצֵנִי וְהַצִּילֵנִי מִיַּד בְּנֵי־נֵכָר אֲשֶׁר פִּיהֶם דִּבֶּר־שָׁוְא וִימִינָם יְמִין שָׁקֶר: אֲשֶׁר בָּנֵינוּ כִּנְטִעִים מְגֻדָּלִים בִּנְעוּרֵיהֶם בְּנוֹתֵינוּ כְזָוִיּוֹת מְחֻטָּבוֹת תַּבְנִית הֵיכָל: מְזָוֵינוּ מְלֵאִים מְפִיקִים מִזַּן אֶל זַן צֹאונֵנוּ מַאֲלִיפוֹת מְרֻבָּבוֹת בְּחוּצוֹתֵינוּ: אַלּוּפֵינוּ מְסֻבָּלִים אֵין פֶּרֶץ וְאֵין יוֹצֵאת וְאֵין צְוָחָה בִּרְחֹבֹתֵינוּ: אַשְׁרֵי הָעָם שֶׁכָּכָה לּוֹ אַשְׁרֵי הָעָם שֶׁיֲהוָה אֱלֹהָיו: *) יתיר ו׳.

סו לַמְנַצֵּחַ בִּנְגִינֹת מִזְמוֹר שִׁיר: אֱלֹהִים יְחָנֵּנוּ וִיבָרְכֵנוּ יָאֵר פָּנָיו אִתָּנוּ סֶלָה: לָדַעַת בָּאָרֶץ דַּרְכֶּךָ בְּכָל־גּוֹיִם יְשׁוּעָתֶךָ: יוֹדוּךָ עַמִּים ׀ אֱלֹהִים יוֹדוּךָ עַמִּים כֻּלָּם: יִשְׂמְחוּ וִירַנְּנוּ לְאֻמִּים כִּי־תִשְׁפֹּט עַמִּים מִישֹׁר וּלְאֻמִּים ׀ בָּאָרֶץ תַּנְחֵם סֶלָה: יוֹדוּךָ עַמִּים ׀ אֱלֹהִים יוֹדוּךָ עַמִּים כֻּלָּם: אֶרֶץ נָתְנָה יְבוּלָהּ יְבָרְכֵנוּ אֱלֹהִים אֱלֹהֵינוּ: יְבָרְכֵנוּ אֱלֹהִים וְיִירְאוּ אֹתוֹ כָּל־אַפְסֵי־אָרֶץ:

ערבית לימות החול ולמוצאי שבת

When מעריב is said בזמנו, the following verses are said before והוא רחום

שִׁיר הַמַּעֲלוֹת הִנֵּה בָּרְכוּ אֶת יְיָ כָּל עַבְדֵי יְיָ הָעוֹמְדִים בְּבֵית יְיָ בַּלֵּילוֹת: שְׂאוּ יְדֵכֶם קֹדֶשׁ וּבָרְכוּ אֶת יְיָ: יְבָרֶכְךָ יְיָ מִצִּיּוֹן עֹשֵׂה שָׁמַיִם וָאָרֶץ:

יְיָ צְבָאוֹת עִמָּנוּ מִשְׂגָּב לָנוּ אֱלֹהֵי יַעֲקֹב סֶלָה: ג״פ

יְיָ צְבָאוֹת אַשְׁרֵי אָדָם בֹּטֵחַ בָּךְ:   ג״פ

יְיָ הוֹשִׁיעָה הַמֶּלֶךְ יַעֲנֵנוּ בְיוֹם קָרְאֵנוּ:   ה׳ק   ג״פ

וְהוּא רַחוּם יְכַפֵּר עָוֹן וְלֹא יַשְׁחִית וְהִרְבָּה לְהָשִׁיב אַפּוֹ וְלֹא יָעִיר כָּל חֲמָתוֹ: יְיָ הוֹשִׁיעָה הַמֶּלֶךְ יַעֲנֵנוּ בְיוֹם קָרְאֵנוּ:

to You; I will sing to You upon a psaltery of ten strings. He Who gives victory to kings; He will free David, his servant, from the evil sword. Rescue me and deliver me from the tyranny of the sons of the stranger, whose mouth utters deceit and whose right hand is a right hand of falsehood, so that our sons may be as nurtured plants, reared to manliness in their youth; our daughters as nooks carved after the fashion of a palace. Our garners are full, overflowing with all manner of food; our sheep increase by the thousands, growing by the tens of thousands in our open fields. Our leaders are greatly burdened; there is no wantonness, no loose woman, no outcry in our streets. To salvation strides that nation with whom it is so. To salvation that nation whose God is *God!*

To Him who grants victory through the power of music. A Psalm. A Song. May God favor us and bless us, and make His face to shine among us ! To make known Your way on earth, Your salvation among all the nations. So that the nations shall render You homage, O God, all the nations shall render You homage one day. The nations will be glad and rejoice, for You will range the peoples in order, and will lead the nations upon earth! — Then the peoples shall render homage to God; the peoples shall all render homage to You. Then the earth shall have yielded its produce and *God,* our own God, shall bless us henceforth. God shall bless us, and all the ends of the earth shall fear Him.

EVENING PRAYER FOR WEEKDAYS AND FOR THE CONCLUSION OF THE SABBATH

And He, being compassionate, forgives iniquity, and does not allow destruction to set in, and many a time takes back His anger, and never lets all His wrath be stirred.

ערבית לימות החול ולמוצאי שבת

הוא רחום When, at night, which for us marks the start of a new day, we look back in retrospect upon what we have done during the day that has just passed, we are filled with a crushing sense of inadequacy, and only the thought of God's compassion in which He has so often granted us atonement

Simultaneously, the congregation says:

The חזן *calls out:*

חֹ בָּרְכוּ אֶת־יְיָ הַמְבֹרָךְ:

ק' יִתְבָּרַךְ וְיִשְׁתַּבַּח וְיִתְפָּאַר וְיִתְרוֹמַם
וְיִתְנַשֵּׂא שְׁמוֹ שֶׁל מֶלֶךְ מַלְכֵי הַמְּלָכִים
הַקָּדוֹשׁ בָּרוּךְ הוּא שֶׁהוּא רִאשׁוֹן וְהוּא
אַחֲרוֹן וּמִבַּלְעָדָיו אֵין אֱלֹהִים: סֹלוּ לָרֹכֵב
בָּעֲרָבוֹת בְּיָהּ שְׁמוֹ וְעִלְזוּ לְפָנָיו: וּשְׁמוֹ
מְרוֹמָם עַל־כָּל־בְּרָכָה וּתְהִלָּה:

קו"ח בָּרוּךְ יְיָ הַמְבֹרָךְ לְעוֹלָם וָעֶד:

בָּרוּךְ אַתָּה יְיָ אֱלֹהֵינוּ
מֶלֶךְ הָעוֹלָם אֲשֶׁר
בִּדְבָרוֹ מַעֲרִיב עֲרָבִים

בָּרוּךְ שֵׁם כְּבוֹד מַלְכוּתוֹ לְעוֹלָם וָעֶד:

יְהִי שֵׁם יְיָ מְבֹרָךְ מֵעַתָּה וְעַד עוֹלָם:

בְּחָכְמָה פּוֹתֵחַ שְׁעָרִים
וּבִתְבוּנָה מְשַׁנֶּה עִתִּים וּמַחֲלִיף אֶת־הַזְּמַנִּים וּמְסַדֵּר
אֶת־הַכּוֹכָבִים בְּמִשְׁמְרוֹתֵיהֶם בָּרָקִיעַ כִּרְצוֹנוֹ בּוֹרֵא
יוֹם וָלַיְלָה גּוֹלֵל אוֹר מִפְּנֵי־חֹשֶׁךְ וְחֹשֶׁךְ מִפְּנֵי־אוֹר ·
וּמַעֲבִיר יוֹם וּמֵבִיא לָיְלָה וּמַבְדִּיל בֵּין יוֹם וּבֵין לָיְלָה
יְיָ צְבָאוֹת שְׁמוֹ · אֵל חַי וְקַיָּם תָּמִיד יִמְלוֹךְ עָלֵינוּ
לְעוֹלָם וָעֶד · בָּרוּךְ אַתָּה יְיָ הַמַּעֲרִיב עֲרָבִים:

אַהֲבַת עוֹלָם בֵּית יִשְׂרָאֵל עַמְּךָ אָהָבְתָּ תּוֹרָה
וּמִצְוֹת חֻקִּים וּמִשְׁפָּטִים אוֹתָנוּ לִמַּדְתָּ עַל כֵּן יְיָ
אֱלֹהֵינוּ בְּשָׁכְבֵנוּ וּבְקוּמֵנוּ נָשִׂיחַ בְּחֻקֶּיךָ, וְנִשְׂמַח בְּדִבְרֵי

in the past can sustain us. It is solely this remembrance of God's former
mercies that impels us to dare voice the plea for help and salvation for the
future that is now to come. But we ourselves counter our own call with the
warning that we can hope for an answer from God to our cry for help only
if, from the very beginning, we will render Him homage as our King and
pledge Him our obedience. It is only if we, for our part, heed God's summons,
that we can hope to receive an answer from God to our own call.

For the translations of the prayers immediately following see p. 257 ff.

תוֹרָתְךָ וּבְמִצְוֹתֶיךָ לְעוֹלָם וָעֶד ・ כִּי הֵם חַיֵּינוּ וְאֹרֶךְ
יָמֵינוּ וּבָהֶם נֶהְגֶּה יוֹמָם וָלָיְלָה ・ וְאַהֲבָתְךָ אַל־תָּסִיר
מִמֶּנּוּ לְעוֹלָמִים ・ בָּרוּךְ אַתָּה יְיָ אוֹהֵב עַמּוֹ יִשְׂרָאֵל:

יחיד אומר אל מלך נאמן ・

דברים ו' ג'

שְׁמַע יִשְׂרָאֵל יְהֹוָה אֱלֹהֵינוּ יְהֹוָה ׀ אֶחָד:

בלחש בָּרוּךְ שֵׁם כְּבוֹד מַלְכוּתוֹ לְעוֹלָם וָעֶד:

וְאָהַבְתָּ אֵת יְהֹוָה אֱלֹהֶיךָ בְּכָל־לְבָבְךָ וּבְכָל־נַפְשְׁךָ
וּבְכָל־מְאֹדֶךָ: וְהָיוּ הַדְּבָרִים הָאֵלֶּה אֲשֶׁר אָנֹכִי מְצַוְּךָ
הַיּוֹם עַל־לְבָבֶךָ: וְשִׁנַּנְתָּם לְבָנֶיךָ וְדִבַּרְתָּ בָּם בְּשִׁבְתְּךָ
בְּבֵיתֶךָ וּבְלֶכְתְּךָ בַדֶּרֶךְ וּבְשָׁכְבְּךָ וּבְקוּמֶךָ: וּקְשַׁרְתָּם
לְאוֹת עַל־יָדֶךָ וְהָיוּ לְטֹטָפֹת בֵּין עֵינֶיךָ:
וּכְתַבְתָּם עַל־מְזֻזוֹת בֵּיתֶךָ וּבִשְׁעָרֶיךָ:

דברים יא י'ג וְהָיָה אִם־שָׁמֹעַ תִּשְׁמְעוּ אֶל־מִצְוֹתַי אֲשֶׁר אָנֹכִי
מְצַוֶּה אֶתְכֶם הַיּוֹם לְאַהֲבָה אֶת־יְהֹוָה אֱלֹהֵיכֶם וּלְעָבְדוֹ
בְּכָל־לְבַבְכֶם וּבְכָל־נַפְשְׁכֶם: וְנָתַתִּי מְטַר־אַרְצְכֶם
בְּעִתּוֹ יוֹרֶה וּמַלְקוֹשׁ וְאָסַפְתָּ דְגָנֶךָ וְתִירֹשְׁךָ וְיִצְהָרֶךָ:
וְנָתַתִּי עֵשֶׂב בְּשָׂדְךָ לִבְהֶמְתֶּךָ וְאָכַלְתָּ וְשָׂבָעְתָּ:
הִשָּׁמְרוּ לָכֶם פֶּן־יִפְתֶּה לְבַבְכֶם וְסַרְתֶּם וַעֲבַדְתֶּם
אֱלֹהִים אֲחֵרִים וְהִשְׁתַּחֲוִיתֶם לָהֶם: וְחָרָה אַף־יְהֹוָה
בָּכֶם וְעָצַר אֶת־הַשָּׁמַיִם וְלֹא־יִהְיֶה מָטָר וְהָאֲדָמָה לֹא

תִּתֵּן אֶת־יְבוּלָהּ וַאֲבַדְתֶּם מְהֵרָה מֵעַל הָאָרֶץ הַטֹּבָה
אֲשֶׁר יְהֹוָה נֹתֵן לָכֶם: וְשַׂמְתֶּם אֶת־דְּבָרַי אֵלֶּה עַל־
לְבַבְכֶם וְעַל־נַפְשְׁכֶם וּקְשַׁרְתֶּם אֹתָם לְאוֹת עַל־יֶדְכֶם
וְהָיוּ לְטוֹטָפֹת בֵּין עֵינֵיכֶם: וְלִמַּדְתֶּם אֹתָם אֶת־בְּנֵיכֶם
לְדַבֵּר בָּם בְּשִׁבְתְּךָ בְּבֵיתֶךָ וּבְלֶכְתְּךָ בַדֶּרֶךְ וּבְשָׁכְבְּךָ
וּבְקוּמֶךָ: וּכְתַבְתָּם עַל־מְזוּזוֹת בֵּיתֶךָ וּבִשְׁעָרֶיךָ: לְמַעַן
יִרְבּוּ יְמֵיכֶם וִימֵי בְנֵיכֶם עַל הָאֲדָמָה אֲשֶׁר נִשְׁבַּע
יְהֹוָה לַאֲבֹתֵיכֶם לָתֵת לָהֶם כִּימֵי הַשָּׁמַיִם עַל־הָאָרֶץ:

במדבר
ט"ו ל"ז
וַיֹּאמֶר יְהֹוָה אֶל־מֹשֶׁה לֵּאמֹר: דַּבֵּר אֶל־בְּנֵי
יִשְׂרָאֵל וְאָמַרְתָּ אֲלֵהֶם וְעָשׂוּ לָהֶם צִיצִת עַל־כַּנְפֵי
בִגְדֵיהֶם לְדֹרֹתָם וְנָתְנוּ עַל־צִיצִת הַכָּנָף פְּתִיל תְּכֵלֶת:
וְהָיָה לָכֶם לְצִיצִת וּרְאִיתֶם אֹתוֹ וּזְכַרְתֶּם אֶת־כָּל־
מִצְוֹת יְהֹוָה וַעֲשִׂיתֶם אֹתָם וְלֹא תָתוּרוּ אַחֲרֵי לְבַבְכֶם
וְאַחֲרֵי עֵינֵיכֶם אֲשֶׁר־אַתֶּם זֹנִים אַחֲרֵיהֶם: לְמַעַן
תִּזְכְּרוּ וַעֲשִׂיתֶם אֶת־כָּל־מִצְוֹתָי וִהְיִיתֶם קְדֹשִׁים
לֵאלֹהֵיכֶם: אֲנִי יְהֹוָה אֱלֹהֵיכֶם אֲשֶׁר הוֹצֵאתִי אֶתְכֶם
מֵאֶרֶץ מִצְרַיִם לִהְיוֹת לָכֶם לֵאלֹהִים אֲנִי יְהֹוָה
אֱלֹהֵיכֶם: יֹ לֹגֹרֹף אלהיכם לאמת.

אֱמֶת וֶאֱמוּנָה כָּל־זֹאת וְקַיָּם עָלֵינוּ כִּי הוּא יְיָ אֱלֹהֵינוּ וְאֵין

זוּלָתוֹ וַאֲנַחְנוּ יִשְׂרָאֵל עַמּוֹ הַפְּדֵנוּ מִיַּד מְלָכִים מַלְכֵּנוּ הַגּוֹאֲלֵנוּ
מִכַּף כָּל־הֶעָרִיצִים הָאֵל הַנִּפְרָע לָנוּ מִצָּרֵינוּ וְהַמְשַׁלֵּם גְּמוּל
לְכָל־אוֹיְבֵי נַפְשֵׁנוּ הָעוֹשֶׂה גְדוֹלוֹת עַד אֵין חֵקֶר וְנִפְלָאוֹת עַד־אֵין
מִסְפָּר · הַשָּׂם נַפְשֵׁנוּ בַּחַיִּים וְלֹא־נָתַן לַמּוֹט רַגְלֵנוּ הַמַּדְרִיכֵנוּ
עַל־בָּמוֹת אוֹיְבֵינוּ וַיָּרֶם קַרְנֵנוּ עַל כָּל־שׂוֹנְאֵינוּ · הָעוֹשֶׂה לָנוּ
נִסִּים וּנְקָמָה בְּפַרְעֹה אוֹתוֹת וּמוֹפְתִים בְּאַדְמַת בְּנֵי חָם · הַמַּכֶּה
בְּעֶבְרָתוֹ כָּל־בְּכוֹרֵי מִצְרָיִם וַיּוֹצֵא אֶת־עַמּוֹ יִשְׂרָאֵל מִתּוֹכָם
לְחֵרוּת עוֹלָם · הַמַּעֲבִיר בָּנָיו בֵּין גִּזְרֵי יַם־סוּף אֶת־רוֹדְפֵיהֶם
וְאֶת־שׂוֹנְאֵיהֶם בִּתְהוֹמוֹת טִבַּע : וְרָאוּ בָנָיו גְּבוּרָתוֹ שִׁבְּחוּ וְהוֹדוּ
לִשְׁמוֹ וּמַלְכוּתוֹ בְּרָצוֹן קִבְּלוּ עֲלֵיהֶם, מֹשֶׁה וּבְנֵי יִשְׂרָאֵל לְךָ עָנוּ
שִׁירָה בְּשִׂמְחָה רַבָּה וְאָמְרוּ כֻלָּם :

מִי־כָמֹכָה בָּאֵלִם יְהוָֹה מִי כָּמֹכָה נֶאְדָּר בַּקֹּדֶשׁ נוֹרָא תְהִלֹּת
עֹשֵׂה פֶלֶא : מַלְכוּתְךָ רָאוּ בָנֶיךָ בּוֹקֵעַ יָם לִפְנֵי מֹשֶׁה זֶה אֵלִי עָנוּ
וְאָמְרוּ :

יְהוָֹה · יִמְלֹךְ לְעוֹלָם וָעֶד :

וְנֶאֱמַר כִּי־פָדָה יְיָ אֶת־יַעֲקֹב וּגְאָלוֹ מִיַּד חָזָק מִמֶּנּוּ · בָּרוּךְ
אַתָּה יְיָ גָּאַל יִשְׂרָאֵל :

הַשְׁכִּיבֵנוּ יְיָ אֱלֹהֵינוּ לְשָׁלוֹם וְהַעֲמִידֵנוּ מַלְכֵּנוּ לְחַיִּים וּפְרוֹשׂ
עָלֵינוּ סֻכַּת שְׁלוֹמֶךָ וְתַקְּנֵנוּ בְּעֵצָה טוֹבָה מִלְּפָנֶיךָ וְהוֹשִׁיעֵנוּ
לְמַעַן שְׁמֶךָ וְהָגֵן בַּעֲדֵנוּ וְהָסֵר מֵעָלֵינוּ אוֹיֵב דֶּבֶר וְחֶרֶב וְרָעָב
וְיָגוֹן וְהָסֵר שָׂטָן מִלְּפָנֵינוּ וּמֵאַחֲרֵינוּ וּבְצֵל כְּנָפֶיךָ תַּסְתִּירֵנוּ כִּי אֵל

שׁוֹמְרֵנוּ וּמַצִּילֵנוּ אַתָּה כִּי אֵל מֶלֶךְ חַנּוּן וְרַחוּם אָתָּה וּשְׁמוֹר
צֵאתֵנוּ וּבוֹאֵנוּ לְחַיִּים וּלְשָׁלוֹם מֵעַתָּה וְעַד עוֹלָם: בָּרוּךְ אַתָּה
יְיָ שׁוֹמֵר עַמּוֹ יִשְׂרָאֵל לָעַד:

בָּרוּךְ יְיָ לְעוֹלָם אָמֵן וְאָמֵן: בָּרוּךְ יְיָ מִצִּיּוֹן שֹׁכֵן יְרוּשָׁלָ͏ִם
הַלְלוּיָהּ: בָּרוּךְ יְיָ אֱלֹהִים אֱלֹהֵי יִשְׂרָאֵל עֹשֵׂה נִפְלָאוֹת לְבַדּוֹ:
וּבָרוּךְ שֵׁם כְּבוֹדוֹ לְעוֹלָם וְיִמָּלֵא כְבוֹדוֹ אֶת־כָּל־הָאָרֶץ אָמֵן וְאָמֵן:
יְהִי כְבוֹד יְיָ לְעוֹלָם יִשְׂמַח יְיָ בְּמַעֲשָׂיו: יְהִי שֵׁם יְיָ מְבֹרָךְ מֵעַתָּה
וְעַד־עוֹלָם: כִּי לֹא־יִטֹּשׁ יְיָ אֶת־עַמּוֹ בַּעֲבוּר שְׁמוֹ הַגָּדוֹל כִּי הוֹאִיל
יְיָ לַעֲשׂוֹת אֶתְכֶם לוֹ לְעָם: וַיַּרְא כָּל־הָעָם וַיִּפְּלוּ עַל־פְּנֵיהֶם
וַיֹּאמְרוּ יְיָ הוּא הָאֱלֹהִים יְיָ הוּא הָאֱלֹהִים: וְהָיָה יְיָ לְמֶלֶךְ עַל־
כָּל־הָאָרֶץ בַּיּוֹם הַהוּא יִהְיֶה יְיָ אֶחָד וּשְׁמוֹ אֶחָד: יְהִי חַסְדְּךָ יְיָ
עָלֵינוּ כַּאֲשֶׁר יִחַלְנוּ לָךְ: הוֹשִׁיעֵנוּ יְיָ אֱלֹהֵינוּ וְקַבְּצֵנוּ מִן־הַגּוֹיִם
לְהוֹדוֹת לְשֵׁם קָדְשֶׁךָ לְהִשְׁתַּבֵּחַ בִּתְהִלָּתֶךָ: כָּל גּוֹיִם אֲשֶׁר עָשִׂיתָ
יָבוֹאוּ וְיִשְׁתַּחֲווּ לְפָנֶיךָ אֲדֹנָי וִיכַבְּדוּ לִשְׁמֶךָ: כִּי־גָדוֹל
אַתָּה וְעֹשֵׂה נִפְלָאוֹת אַתָּה אֱלֹהִים לְבַדֶּךָ: וַאֲנַחְנוּ עַמְּךָ וְצֹאן
מַרְעִיתֶךָ נוֹדֶה לְּךָ לְעוֹלָם לְדוֹר וָדוֹר נְסַפֵּר תְּהִלָּתֶךָ: בָּרוּךְ יְיָ
בַּיּוֹם· בָּרוּךְ יְיָ בַּלַּיְלָה· בָּרוּךְ יְיָ בְּשָׁכְבֵּנוּ· בָּרוּךְ יְיָ בְּקוּמֵנוּ: כִּי
בְיָדְךָ נַפְשׁוֹת הַחַיִּים וְהַמֵּתִים אֲשֶׁר בְּיָדוֹ נֶפֶשׁ כָּל־חָי וְרוּחַ כָּל־
בְּשַׂר אִישׁ: בְּיָדְךָ אַפְקִיד רוּחִי פָּדִיתָה אוֹתִי יְיָ אֵל אֱמֶת:
אֱלֹהֵינוּ שֶׁבַּשָּׁמַיִם יַחֵד שִׁמְךָ וְקַיֵּם מַלְכוּתְךָ תָּמִיד וּמְלוֹךְ עָלֵינוּ
לְעוֹלָם וָעֶד:

בָּרוּךְ ה' לְעוֹלָם אָמֵן וְאָמֵן As we have already noted in connection with
בְּרָכָה אַחַת מֵעֵין שֶׁבַע, p. 281, this paragraph that is inserted into the weekday
evening service is motivated by feelings of brotherly consideration for late-

Blessed be *God* forever, Amen and Amen! Blessed be *God* from out of Tzion, Who causes His Presence to dwell in Yerushalayim, Halaluyah. Blessed be *God,* God, the God of Yisrael, Who alone does wondrous things; blessed be the Name of His glory forever, and let His glory fill the entire earth. Amen and Amen. Let the glory of *God* be forever, and let *God* rejoice in His works; let the name of *God* be blessed from now and forever. For *God* will not abandon His people for His great Name's sake for *God* has begun to make you His people. All the people saw it and they fell upon their faces and said, "*God,* He is God, *God,* He is God!" And one day *God* will be King over all the earth; on that day shall *God* be One and His Name One." Let Your loving-kindness, O *God,* be upon us, even as we have waited for You. Save us, O *God* our God, and gather us from among the nations, so that we may render homage to Your holy Name and that we may glory in the praise of Your mighty acts. All the nations which You have made shall come one day and prostrate themselves before You, O my Lord, and shall give honor to Your Name. For You are great, and do wondrous things; You alone are God, But we, Your people and flock of Your pasture, we shall render You homage forever; we shall tell the fame of Your mighty acts to generation after generation. Blessed be *God* by day; blessed be *God* by night; blessed be *God* when we lie down; blessed be *God* when we rise up. For in Your hand are the souls of the living and the dead, in Whose hand is the soul of every living thing and the spirit of every human body. Into Your hand I commit my spirit for You have redeemed me, O *God* the God of truth. O our God in Heaven, create the Unity of Your Name, preserve Your kingdom forever and reign over us in all eternity.

---

comers in the House of God (Tosaphoth Berachoth 4b) (See above ibid.). Here, reminiscent of the eighteen *berachoth* of the *Shemone Esrei,* the Tetragrammaton occurs eighteen times. But even as the preceding *berachah* ended with the words שומר עמו ישראל לעד, these sentences, too, continue to speak in terms of the entire Jewish national community.

ברוך "May the will of God be done—and it will be done—throughout all times to come"—this is the eternal basis of all our vows and our convictions. Zion may be in ruins and we may be far away from Yerushalayim. Nevertheless, the place in Zion that was hallowed as the eternal Abode of God's

יִרְאוּ עֵינֵינוּ וְיִשְׂמַח לִבֵּנוּ וְתָגֵל נַפְשֵׁנוּ בִּישׁוּעָתְךָ בֶּאֱמֶת בֶּאֱמֹר
לְצִיּוֹן מָלַךְ אֱלֹהָיִךְ · יְיָ מֶלֶךְ, יְיָ מָלָךְ, יְיָ יִמְלֹךְ לְעוֹלָם וָעֶד : כִּי
הַמַּלְכוּת שֶׁלְּךָ הִיא וּלְעוֹלְמֵי עַד תִּמְלוֹךְ בְּכָבוֹד כִּי אֵין לָנוּ מֶלֶךְ
אֶלָּא אָתָּה : בָּרוּךְ אַתָּה יְיָ הַמֶּלֶךְ בִּכְבוֹדוֹ, תָּמִיד יִמְלֹךְ עָלֵינוּ
לְעוֹלָם וָעֶד וְעַל כָּל מַעֲשָׂיו :

הש"ץ אומר ה"ק, ואח"כ מתפללין תפלה בלחש, והש"ץ חזו חוזר.

אֲדֹנָי שְׂפָתַי תִּפְתָּח וּפִי יַגִּיד תְּהִלָּתֶךָ:

בָּרוּךְ אַתָּה יְיָ אֱלֹהֵינוּ וֵאלֹהֵי אֲבוֹתֵינוּ אֱלֹהֵי אַבְרָהָם
אֱלֹהֵי יִצְחָק וֵאלֹהֵי יַעֲקֹב הָאֵל הַגָּדוֹל הַגִּבּוֹר וְהַנּוֹרָא
אֵל עֶלְיוֹן גּוֹמֵל חֲסָדִים טוֹבִים וְקוֹנֵה הַכֹּל וְזוֹכֵר חַסְדֵי
אָבוֹת וּמֵבִיא גוֹאֵל לִבְנֵי בְנֵיהֶם לְמַעַן שְׁמוֹ בְּאַהֲבָה ·

During the ten days of תשובה, זכרנו is inserted here:

זָכְרֵנוּ לְחַיִּים מֶלֶךְ חָפֵץ בַּחַיִּים · וְכָתְבֵנוּ בְּסֵפֶר הַחַיִּים
לְמַעַנְךָ אֱלֹהִים חַיִּים :

מֶלֶךְ עוֹזֵר וּמוֹשִׁיעַ וּמָגֵן · בָּרוּךְ אַתָּה יְיָ מָגֵן אַבְרָהָם :
אַתָּה גִּבּוֹר לְעוֹלָם אֲדֹנָי מְחַיֵּה מֵתִים אַתָּה רַב
לְהוֹשִׁיעַ ·

From מוצאי סכות until פסח the following is inserted here:

מַשִּׁיב הָרוּחַ וּמוֹרִיד הַגָּשֶׁם :

מְכַלְכֵּל חַיִּים בְּחֶסֶד מְחַיֵּה מֵתִים בְּרַחֲמִים רַבִּים
סוֹמֵךְ נוֹפְלִים וְרוֹפֵא חוֹלִים וּמַתִּיר אֲסוּרִים וּמְקַיֵּם
אֱמוּנָתוֹ לִישֵׁנֵי עָפָר · מִי כָמוֹךָ בַּעַל גְּבוּרוֹת וּמִי דּוֹמֶה
לָּךְ מֶלֶךְ מֵמִית וּמְחַיֶּה וּמַצְמִיחַ יְשׁוּעָה ·

May our eyes behold, may our heart rejoice and our soul exult at Your salvation in truth when it will be said to Tzion, "Your God is now acknowledged as King." *God* is King, *God* was King, *God* will reign as King in all eternity. For the kingdom is Yours and in all eternity will You reign in glory, for we have no King beside You. Blessed be You, *God,* King in His glory; He will reign over us forever in all eternity, and over all His works.

Law, and Yerushalayim, which ever awaits His Presence, always remain the starting point of our relationship with our God, and it will be from Yerushalayim and Zion that the worship of Him will one day spread over all the world. כי לא יטוש For even though we are in exile, God's relationship with us has never been broken. Long ago God appointed us to be His people, the bearers of His Name before the eyes of all the peoples of the world. Therefore He will not abandon us even now, but, rather, train us until such time as we will be fully worthy of our destiny and capable of fulfilling it. In the days of Elijah the entire people of Israel seemed about to embrace the cult of Baal, but the prophet inspired the people anew, lifting them up to the level of pure recognition of the One God, of the worship of the One Sole God. And one day that wondrous event of long ago will come to pass once again. Only this time it will not be a fleeting fancy which speedily passes away, but a permanent resolve, leading to the eventual everlasting worship of God alone over all the earth. יהי חסדך: May the love of God be demonstrated in our case even as we have ever waited for it. May our ingathering from dispersion throughout the lands of the world come to pass as a miracle of world-wide import, revealing the greatness of God to all, and may it thus cause all the other nations, too, to assemble in universal homage to the One God.

ואנחנו But as for us, it remains our task to be the people of His Law and the sheep of His pasture, and to the fulfillment of this task we dedicate ourselves both day and night. בידך I commit my spirit to God with full confidence each night, for I know from past experience that my deliverance has always come from God, and that God will never change the ways of His Providence or the word of His promise.

אתה חוננתנו At the conclusion of Sabbaths and festivals אתה חוננתנו is inserted into the prayer for knowledge and understanding, *Attah chonen,* which actually is the first weekday prayer to be recited after the end of the holiday. There we are reminded of our duty to value and employ the intellectual talents granted us by God in order to gain a better knowledge of His Law. At the same time, the occurrence at this point of a portion of our regular weekday service is intended to teach us to understand and appreciate the dividing line drawn by the Law between the Sabbath or holiday on one hand and the ordinary working day on the other.

During the ten days of תשובה, מִי כָמוֹךָ is inserted here:

מִי כָמוֹךָ אַב הָרַחֲמִים זוֹכֵר יְצוּרָיו לְחַיִּים בְּרַחֲמִים:

וְנֶאֱמָן אַתָּה לְהַחֲיוֹת מֵתִים · בָּרוּךְ אַתָּה יְיָ מְחַיֵּה הַמֵּתִים:

אַתָּה קָדוֹשׁ וְשִׁמְךָ קָדוֹשׁ וּקְדוֹשִׁים בְּכָל־יוֹם יְהַלְלוּךָ סֶּלָה · בָּרוּךְ אַתָּה יְיָ הָאֵל (בעו״ת הַמֶּלֶךְ) הַקָּדוֹשׁ:

אַתָּה חוֹנֵן לְאָדָם דַּעַת וּמְלַמֵּד לֶאֱנוֹשׁ בִּינָה

On מוֹצָאֵי שַׁבָּת the following is added:

אַתָּה חוֹנַנְתָּנוּ לְמַדַּע תּוֹרָתֶךָ · וַתְּלַמְּדֵנוּ לַעֲשׂוֹת בָּהֶם חֻקֵּי רְצוֹנֶךָ וַתַּבְדֵּל יְיָ אֱלֹהֵינוּ בֵּין קֹדֶשׁ לְחוֹל בֵּין אוֹר לְחשֶׁךְ בֵּין יִשְׂרָאֵל לָעַמִּים בֵּין יוֹם הַשְּׁבִיעִי לְשֵׁשֶׁת יְמֵי הַמַּעֲשֶׂה אָבִינוּ מַלְכֵּנוּ הָחֵל עָלֵינוּ הַיָּמִים הַבָּאִים לִקְרָאתֵנוּ לְשָׁלוֹם חֲשׂוּכִים מִכָּל־חֵטְא וּמְנֻקִּים מִכָּל־עָוֹן וּמְדֻבָּקִים בְּיִרְאָתֶךָ:

(ו) חָנֵּנוּ מֵאִתְּךָ דֵּעָה בִּינָה וְהַשְׂכֵּל · בָּרוּךְ אַתָּה יְיָ חוֹנֵן הַדָּעַת:

הֲשִׁיבֵנוּ אָבִינוּ לְתוֹרָתֶךָ וְקָרְבֵנוּ מַלְכֵּנוּ לַעֲבוֹדָתֶךָ וְהַחֲזִירֵנוּ בִּתְשׁוּבָה שְׁלֵמָה לְפָנֶיךָ · בָּרוּךְ אַתָּה יְיָ הָרוֹצֶה בִּתְשׁוּבָה:

סְלַח־לָנוּ אָבִינוּ כִּי חָטָאנוּ מְחַל־לָנוּ מַלְכֵּנוּ כִּי פָשָׁעְנוּ כִּי מוֹחֵל וְסוֹלֵחַ אָתָּה · בָּרוּךְ אַתָּה יְיָ חַנּוּן הַמַּרְבֶּה לִסְלוֹחַ:

רְאֵה בְעָנְיֵנוּ וְרִיבָה רִיבֵנוּ וּגְאָלֵנוּ מְהֵרָה לְמַעַן שְׁמֶךָ כִּי גוֹאֵל חָזָק אָתָּה · בָּרוּךְ אַתָּה יְיָ גּוֹאֵל יִשְׂרָאֵל:

You have favored us so that we might acquire the knowledge of Your Torah and taught us through them to fulfill the statutes of Your will. You have made a distinction, O *God* our God, between the holy and the profane, between light and darkness, between Yisrael and the nations, between the Seventh Day and the six days of work. Our Father, our King, let the approaching days begin for us in peace, removed from all sin, cleansed of all iniquity, and devoted to the fear of You, and favor us with knowledge, insight and wisdom from You. Blessed be You, *God,* gracious Giver of knowledge.

The original text of this prayer seems to have been אתה חוננתנו למדע וכו׳ ותלמדנו לעשות בהם וכו׳. The substitution of מדע for למדע, as well as the elimination of בהם seem to be unnecessary. These changes might have been based upon the other version of the service which has also been discussed (Levush), according to which, on *Motzaei Shabbath,* the portion beginning with אתה חונן וכו׳ is omitted, and we are to start the prayer with *Attah Chonantanu.* But in view of our own custom not to omit the sentence beginning with *Attah chonen,* the original reading seems to us entirely appropriate and correct. As we have already noted repeatedly, *chonen* in itself denotes the granting of intellectual talents, and can have reference also to *da'ath* and *binah.* In other words, the thought expressed here would be "You have favored us with intellectual gifts" or "You have favored us with knowledge and insight *for* (or "that we might acquire") the knowledge of Law." In like manner, *bahem* refers to *da'ath* and *binah* found in the preceding sentence. God has favored us with gifts of the intellect so that we may know His Law, and we are to employ these Divinely-granted faculties also for the fulfillment of His statutes. ותבדל: The partition between the Sabbath and the working day is noted here together with the distinction drawn between holy and profane, light and darkness, and Yisrael and the rest of the nations of the world. This is to teach us a lesson of profound significance. The holy is set apart from the profane only to show that it is from the holy that the spirit of sanctity and sanctification should go out to permeate all the other phases of human life. That which is shut off from the light is so separated only that, under the cover of darkness, it may gather new strength in order then, suffused with light, to be awakened to new life and vigor. Yisrael, too, is set apart from the other nations only so that, through Yisrael, the rest of the nations may be won over to an ever-increasing extent to the truths it has revealed. The same analogy, we are told here, is applicable also to the distinction that has been made by God between the Sabbath and the working days of the week. The Sabbath was set apart from the six other days of the week only so that the truths which are symbolized by the Sabbath and which we are to take to our hearts anew each Sabbath Day may also accompany us into the workday life of the week to guide and to hallow us there.

רְפָאֵנוּ יְיָ וְנֵרָפֵא הוֹשִׁיעֵנוּ וְנִוָּשֵׁעָה כִּי תְהִלָּתֵנוּ
אָתָּה · וְהַעֲלֵה רְפוּאָה שְׁלֵמָה לְכָל־מַכּוֹתֵינוּ כִּי אֵל
מֶלֶךְ רוֹפֵא נֶאֱמָן וְרַחֲמָן אָתָּה · בָּרוּךְ אַתָּה יְיָ
רוֹפֵא חוֹלֵי עַמּוֹ יִשְׂרָאֵל:

בָּרֵךְ עָלֵינוּ יְיָ אֱלֹהֵינוּ אֶת־הַשָּׁנָה הַזֹּאת וְאֶת־כָּל־
מִינֵי תְבוּאָתָהּ לְטוֹבָה וְתֵן (טַל וּמָטָר לְ) בְּרָכָה עַל
פְּנֵי הָאֲדָמָה וְשַׂבְּעֵנוּ מִטּוּבֶךָ וּבָרֵךְ שְׁנָתֵנוּ כַּשָּׁנִים
הַטּוֹבוֹת · בָּרוּךְ אַתָּה יְיָ מְבָרֵךְ הַשָּׁנִים:

תְּקַע בְּשׁוֹפָר גָּדוֹל לְחֵרוּתֵנוּ וְשָׂא נֵס לְקַבֵּץ
גָּלֻיּוֹתֵינוּ וְקַבְּצֵנוּ יַחַד מֵאַרְבַּע כַּנְפוֹת הָאָרֶץ · בָּרוּךְ
אַתָּה יְיָ מְקַבֵּץ נִדְחֵי עַמּוֹ יִשְׂרָאֵל:

הָשִׁיבָה שׁוֹפְטֵינוּ כְּבָרִאשֹׁנָה וְיוֹעֲצֵינוּ כְּבַתְּחִלָּה
וְהָסֵר מִמֶּנּוּ יָגוֹן וַאֲנָחָה וּמְלֹךְ עָלֵינוּ אַתָּה יְיָ לְבַדְּךָ
בְּחֶסֶד וּבְרַחֲמִים וְצַדְּקֵנוּ בַּמִּשְׁפָּט · בָּרוּךְ אַתָּה יְיָ
מֶלֶךְ אוֹהֵב צְדָקָה וּמִשְׁפָּט:

(בעשי״ת הַמֶּלֶךְ הַמִּשְׁפָּט, וְאִם לֹא אָמְרוּ, דַעַת רוֹב הַפּוֹסְקִים שֶׁאֵין צָרִיךְ לַחֲזֹר.)

וְלַמַּלְשִׁינִים אַל־תְּהִי תִקְוָה וְכָל־עוֹשֵׂי רִשְׁעָה כְּרֶגַע
יֹאבֵדוּ וְכֻלָּם מְהֵרָה יִכָּרֵתוּ וְהַזֵּדִים מְהֵרָה תְעַקֵּר
וּתְשַׁבֵּר וּתְמַגֵּר וְתַכְנִיעַ בִּמְהֵרָה בְיָמֵינוּ · בָּרוּךְ אַתָּה
יְיָ שֹׁבֵר אוֹיְבִים וּמַכְנִיעַ זֵדִים:

עַל־הַצַּדִּיקִים וְעַל־הַחֲסִידִים וְעַל־זִקְנֵי עַמְּךָ בֵּית
יִשְׂרָאֵל וְעַל פְּלֵיטַת סוֹפְרֵיהֶם וְעַל גֵּרֵי הַצֶּדֶק וְעָלֵינוּ

יֶהֱמוּ רַחֲמֶיךָ יְיָ אֱלֹהֵינוּ וְתֵן שָׂכָר טוֹב לְכָל הַבּוֹטְחִים
בְּשִׁמְךָ בֶּאֱמֶת וְשִׂים חֶלְקֵנוּ עִמָּהֶם לְעוֹלָם וְלֹא נֵבוֹשׁ
כִּי־בְךָ בָּטָחְנוּ · בָּרוּךְ אַתָּה יְיָ מִשְׁעָן וּמִבְטָח לַצַּדִּיקִים:

וְלִירוּשָׁלַיִם עִירְךָ בְּרַחֲמִים תָּשׁוּב וְתִשְׁכּוֹן בְּתוֹכָהּ
כַּאֲשֶׁר דִּבַּרְתָּ וּבְנֵה אוֹתָהּ בְּקָרוֹב בְּיָמֵינוּ בִּנְיַן עוֹלָם
וְכִסֵּא דָוִד מְהֵרָה לְתוֹכָהּ תָּכִין · בָּרוּךְ אַתָּה יְיָ
בּוֹנֵה יְרוּשָׁלָיִם:

אֶת־צֶמַח דָּוִד עַבְדְּךָ מְהֵרָה תַצְמִיחַ וְקַרְנוֹ תָּרוּם
בִּישׁוּעָתֶךָ כִּי לִישׁוּעָתְךָ קִוִּינוּ כָּל־הַיּוֹם · בָּרוּךְ אַתָּה
יְיָ מַצְמִיחַ קֶרֶן יְשׁוּעָה:

שְׁמַע קוֹלֵנוּ יְיָ אֱלֹהֵינוּ חוּס וְרַחֵם עָלֵינוּ וְקַבֵּל
בְּרַחֲמִים וּבְרָצוֹן אֶת־תְּפִלָּתֵנוּ כִּי אֵל שׁוֹמֵעַ תְּפִלּוֹת
וְתַחֲנוּנִים אָתָּה · וּמִלְּפָנֶיךָ מַלְכֵּנוּ רֵיקָם אַל־תְּשִׁיבֵנוּ
כִּי אַתָּה שׁוֹמֵעַ תְּפִלַּת עַמְּךָ יִשְׂרָאֵל בְּרַחֲמִים · בָּרוּךְ
אַתָּה יְיָ שׁוֹמֵעַ תְּפִלָּה:

רְצֵה יְיָ אֱלֹהֵינוּ בְּעַמְּךָ יִשְׂרָאֵל וּבִתְפִלָּתָם · וְהָשֵׁב
אֶת־הָעֲבוֹדָה לִדְבִיר בֵּיתֶךָ וְאִשֵּׁי יִשְׂרָאֵל וּתְפִלָּתָם
בְּאַהֲבָה תְקַבֵּל בְּרָצוֹן וּתְהִי לְרָצוֹן תָּמִיד עֲבוֹדַת
יִשְׂרָאֵל עַמֶּךָ ·

On ר"ח and המועד חול *the following is inserted here:*

אֱלֹהֵינוּ וֵאלֹהֵי אֲבוֹתֵינוּ · יַעֲלֶה וְיָבֹא וְיַגִּיעַ וְיֵרָאֶה וְיֵרָצֶה וְיִשָּׁמַע
וְיִפָּקֵד וְיִזָּכֵר זִכְרוֹנֵנוּ וּפִקְדוֹנֵנוּ וְזִכְרוֹן אֲבוֹתֵינוּ · וְזִכְרוֹן מָשִׁיחַ בֶּן

דָּוִד עַבְדֶּךָ · וְזִכְרוֹן יְרוּשָׁלַיִם עִיר קָדְשֶׁךָ · וְזִכְרוֹן כָּל עַמְּךָ בֵּית
יִשְׂרָאֵל לְפָנֶיךָ · לִפְלֵיטָה וּלְטוֹבָה וּלְחֵן וּלְחֶסֶד וּלְרַחֲמִים וּלְחַיִּים
וּלְשָׁלוֹם בְּיוֹם לר״ח רֹאשׁ הַחֹדֶשׁ ׀ לפסח חַג הַמַּצּוֹת ׀ לסכות חַג הַסֻּכּוֹת
הַזֶּה · זָכְרֵנוּ יְיָ אֱלֹהֵינוּ בּוֹ לְטוֹבָה וּפָקְדֵנוּ בוֹ לִבְרָכָה וְהוֹשִׁיעֵנוּ בוֹ
לְחַיִּים · וּבִדְבַר יְשׁוּעָה וְרַחֲמִים · חוּס וְחָנֵּנוּ וְרַחֵם עָלֵינוּ
וְהוֹשִׁיעֵנוּ · כִּי אֵלֶיךָ עֵינֵינוּ · כִּי אֵל מֶלֶךְ חַנּוּן וְרַחוּם אָתָּה :

וְתֶחֱזֶינָה עֵינֵינוּ בְּשׁוּבְךָ לְצִיּוֹן בְּרַחֲמִים · בָּרוּךְ
אַתָּה יְיָ הַמַּחֲזִיר שְׁכִינָתוֹ לְצִיּוֹן :

מוֹדִים אֲנַחְנוּ לָךְ שָׁאַתָּה הוּא יְיָ אֱלֹהֵינוּ וֵאלֹהֵי אֲבוֹתֵינוּ
לְעוֹלָם וָעֶד · צוּר חַיֵּינוּ מָגֵן יִשְׁעֵנוּ אַתָּה הוּא לְדוֹר וָדוֹר · נוֹדֶה
לְךָ וּנְסַפֵּר תְּהִלָּתֶךָ עַל חַיֵּינוּ הַמְּסוּרִים בְּיָדֶךָ וְעַל נִשְׁמוֹתֵינוּ
הַפְּקוּדוֹת לָךְ וְעַל נִסֶּיךָ שֶׁבְּכָל יוֹם עִמָּנוּ וְעַל נִפְלְאוֹתֶיךָ וְטוֹבוֹתֶיךָ
שֶׁבְּכָל עֵת · עֶרֶב וָבֹקֶר וְצָהֳרָיִם · הַטּוֹב כִּי לֹא כָלוּ רַחֲמֶיךָ
וְהַמְרַחֵם כִּי לֹא תַמּוּ חֲסָדֶיךָ מֵעוֹלָם קִוִּינוּ לָךְ :

בחנוכה יאמרים על הנסים ; See p. 150

וְעַל־כֻּלָּם יִתְבָּרַךְ וְיִתְרוֹמַם שִׁמְךָ מַלְכֵּנוּ תָּמִיד
לְעוֹלָם וָעֶד :

בעשי״ת: וּכְתוֹב לְחַיִּים טוֹבִים כָּל־בְּנֵי בְרִיתֶךָ :

וְכֹל הַחַיִּים יוֹדוּךָ סֶּלָה וִיהַלְלוּ אֶת־שִׁמְךָ בֶּאֱמֶת
הָאֵל יְשׁוּעָתֵנוּ וְעֶזְרָתֵנוּ סֶלָה · בָּרוּךְ אַתָּה יְיָ הַטּוֹב
שִׁמְךָ וּלְךָ נָאֶה לְהוֹדוֹת :

שָׁלוֹם רָב עַל־יִשְׂרָאֵל עַמְּךָ תָּשִׂים לְעוֹלָם כִּי אַתָּה הוּא מֶלֶךְ
אָדוֹן לְכָל הַשָּׁלוֹם · וְטוֹב בְּעֵינֶיךָ לְבָרֵךְ אֶת־עַמְּךָ יִשְׂרָאֵל בְּכָל־
עֵת וּבְכָל שָׁעָה בִּשְׁלוֹמֶךָ ·

בעשי"ת

בְּסֵפֶר חַיִּים בְּרָכָה וְשָׁלוֹם וּפַרְנָסָה טוֹבָה נִזָּכֵר וְנִכָּתֵב לְפָנֶיךָ
אֲנַחְנוּ וְכָל עַמְּךָ בֵּית יִשְׂרָאֵל לְחַיִּים טוֹבִים וּלְשָׁלוֹם · בָּרוּךְ אַתָּה
יְיָ עוֹשֶׂה הַשָּׁלוֹם:

בָּרוּךְ אַתָּה יְיָ הַמְבָרֵךְ אֶת־עַמּוֹ יִשְׂרָאֵל בַּשָּׁלוֹם:

אֱלֹהַי · נְצוֹר לְשׁוֹנִי מֵרָע וּשְׂפָתַי מִדַּבֵּר מִרְמָה וְלִמְקַלְלַי נַפְשִׁי
תִדּוֹם וְנַפְשִׁי כֶּעָפָר לַכֹּל תִּהְיֶה: פְּתַח לִבִּי בְּתוֹרָתֶךָ וּבְמִצְוֹתֶיךָ
תִּרְדּוֹף נַפְשִׁי · וְכָל הַחוֹשְׁבִים עָלַי רָעָה מְהֵרָה הָפֵר עֲצָתָם וְקַלְקֵל
מַחֲשַׁבְתָּם · עֲשֵׂה לְמַעַן שְׁמֶךָ · עֲשֵׂה לְמַעַן יְמִינֶךָ · עֲשֵׂה לְמַעַן
קְדֻשָּׁתֶךָ · עֲשֵׂה לְמַעַן תּוֹרָתֶךָ · לְמַעַן יֵחָלְצוּן יְדִידֶיךָ הוֹשִׁיעָה
יְמִינְךָ וַעֲנֵנִי: יִהְיוּ לְרָצוֹן אִמְרֵי־פִי וְהֶגְיוֹן לִבִּי לְפָנֶיךָ יְיָ צוּרִי
וְגוֹאֲלִי: עֹשֶׂה שָׁלוֹם בִּמְרוֹמָיו הוּא יַעֲשֶׂה שָׁלוֹם עָלֵינוּ וְעַל כָּל
יִשְׂרָאֵל וְאִמְרוּ אָמֵן:

יְהִי רָצוֹן מִלְּפָנֶיךָ יְיָ אֱלֹהֵינוּ וֵאלֹהֵי אֲבוֹתֵינוּ שֶׁיִּבָּנֶה
בֵּית הַמִּקְדָּשׁ בִּמְהֵרָה בְיָמֵינוּ וְתֵן חֶלְקֵנוּ בְּתוֹרָתֶךָ:
וְשָׁם נַעֲבָדְךָ בְּיִרְאָה כִּימֵי עוֹלָם וּכְשָׁנִים קַדְמוֹנִיּוֹת:
וְעָרְבָה לַיְיָ מִנְחַת יְהוּדָה וִירוּשָׁלָיִם כִּימֵי עוֹלָם וּכְשָׁנִים קַדְמוֹנִיּוֹת:

If a יו"ט *falls on one of the six ensuing weekdays,* ויהי נועם *and* ואתה קדוש
are not said, it is also omitted on ט' באב.

half מוצאי שבת on ;עלינו and קדיש תתקבל is followed by מעריב *On weekdays,*
etc. ויהי נועם is followed by *Kaddish*

וִיהִי נֹעַם אֲדֹנָי אֱלֹהֵינוּ עָלֵינוּ וּמַעֲשֵׂה
יָדֵינוּ כּוֹנְנָה עָלֵינוּ וּמַעֲשֵׂה יָדֵינוּ כּוֹנְנֵהוּ:

יֹשֵׁב בְּסֵתֶר עֶלְיוֹן בְּצֵל שַׁדַּי יִתְלוֹנָן: אֹמַר לַיָי מַחְסִי וּמְצוּדָתִי
אֱלֹהַי אֶבְטַח־בּוֹ: כִּי הוּא יַצִּילְךָ מִפַּח יָקוּשׁ מִדֶּבֶר הַוּוֹת: בְּאֶבְרָתוֹ
יָסֶךְ לָךְ וְתַחַת כְּנָפָיו תֶּחְסֶה צִנָּה וְסֹחֵרָה אֲמִתּוֹ: לֹא־תִירָא
מִפַּחַד לָיְלָה מֵחֵץ יָעוּף יוֹמָם: מִדֶּבֶר בָּאֹפֶל יַהֲלֹךְ מִקֶּטֶב יָשׁוּד
צָהֳרָיִם: יִפֹּל מִצִּדְּךָ אֶלֶף וּרְבָבָה מִימִינֶךָ אֵלֶיךָ לֹא יִגָּשׁ: רַק
בְּעֵינֶיךָ תַבִּיט וְשִׁלֻּמַת רְשָׁעִים תִּרְאֶה: כִּי־אַתָּה יְיָ מַחְסִי עֶלְיוֹן
שַׂמְתָּ מְעוֹנֶךָ: לֹא־תְאֻנֶּה אֵלֶיךָ רָעָה וְנֶגַע לֹא־יִקְרַב בְּאָהֳלֶךָ: כִּי
מַלְאָכָיו יְצַוֶּה־לָּךְ לִשְׁמָרְךָ בְּכָל־דְּרָכֶיךָ: עַל־כַּפַּיִם יִשָּׂאוּנְךָ פֶּן
תִּגֹּף בָּאֶבֶן רַגְלֶךָ: עַל־שַׁחַל וָפֶתֶן תִּדְרֹךְ תִּרְמֹס כְּפִיר וְתַנִּין: כִּי
בִי חָשַׁק וַאֲפַלְּטֵהוּ אֲשַׂגְּבֵהוּ כִּי־יָדַע שְׁמִי: יִקְרָאֵנִי וְאֶעֱנֵהוּ עִמּוֹ
אָנֹכִי בְצָרָה אֲחַלְּצֵהוּ וַאֲכַבְּדֵהוּ: אֹרֶךְ יָמִים אַשְׂבִּיעֵהוּ וְאַרְאֵהוּ
בִּישׁוּעָתִי: ארך ימים וגו'.

וְאַתָּה קָדוֹשׁ יוֹשֵׁב תְּהִלּוֹת יִשְׂרָאֵל:
וְקָרָא זֶה אֶל־זֶה וְאָמַר קָדוֹשׁ· קָדוֹשׁ קָדוֹשׁ יְיָ צְבָאוֹת מְלֹא כָל־הָאָרֶץ

ויהי נועם. ואתה קדוש: After the introduction, we begin the actual transition from the Sabbath to the new week with selections and quotations from
the Holy Scriptures which are most appropriate not only to put us into the
proper frame of mind for the fulfillment of the tasks that await us, but also
to instill into us the spirit of calm, strength and serene trust in the help of
God for all our endeavors. We are to know that we may be quite certain
of His aid if only we will do what is right and pleasing in His eyes. It is
significant that the portion of the service should begin with *Vihi no'am* (Ps.
90:17) with which Moshe expresses as the basis for all of our endeavors as
Jews the wish that whatever is pleasant may come to us from God alone;

May pleasantness come to us, O Lord our God; establish upon us the work of our hands; and the work of our hands *You* establish it.

He dwelt in secret as *Elyon* and He wished still to dwell in the shadow us *Shaddai*. But I will say of *God*, Who is my Refuge, my Fortress, my God, in Whom I trust, that He will deliver you from the snare that is laid, from deadly pestilence. He will cover you with His pinions and you will take refuge beneath His wings; His truth is a barbed shield and an armor. You need not fear the terror of night, nor the arrow which flies by day, the pestilence that prowls in the dark, nor the death that rages at noon. A thousand may fall at your left and ten thousand at your right hand; it shall not come near to you. Only with your eyes shall you behold it, and witness the recompense of the lawless. For you have made *God*, [Who is] my Refuge, the Most High, the Support of your life. No trouble shall be sent to you nor shall the finger of God come near your tent. For He will give His angels charge over you, to keep you in all your ways. They will carry you upon their hands, lest you hurt your foot upon a stone. You will tread upon the jackal and the asp; you will trample the young lion and the serpent. "For he clings to Me with yearning; therefore I shall deliver him. I will set him on high, because he knows My Name. If he calls upon Me, then I shall answer him. I will be with him in distress, and I shall bring him to honor. I will satisfy him with length of days and let him behold my salvation."

And You O holy One, are still enthroned upon Yisrael's songs of praise. And one calls to the other and says, "Holy, holy, holy is *God Tzevaoth,* the fullness of all the earth is His glory." They re-

---

in other words, that we may be able to act independently, free and independent of our fellow-men, and guide our conduct solely by the eternal standard which we have received from the hands of God Himself. Freedom and law—these are the blessed pillars of all our endeavors as Jews. This thought is then logically followed by Psalm 91 *Yoshev besether* in which Moshe, in close connection with the preceding psalm, tells of the protection and of the historic immortality which his people will find under the direct guidance of God. Then we recite *Veattah kadosh,* the *Kedusha desidra* which pictures Israel's eternal survival and its position as the spiritual herald to the rest of mankind as our everlasting gifts, and the nearness of God and the hallowing of His

כְּבוֹדוֹ: וּמְקַבְּלִין דֵּין מִן דֵּין וְאָמְרִין קַדִּישׁ בִּשְׁמֵי מְרוֹמָא עִלָּאָה בֵּית

שְׁכִינְתֵּהּ, קַדִּישׁ עַל אַרְעָא עוֹבַד גְּבוּרְתֵּהּ, קַדִּישׁ לְעָלַם וּלְעָלְמֵי

עָלְמַיָּא· יְיָ צְבָאוֹת מַלְיָא כָל־אַרְעָא זִיו יְקָרֵהּ: וַתִּשָּׂאֵנִי רוּחַ

וָאֶשְׁמַע אַחֲרַי קוֹל רַעַשׁ גָּדוֹל בָּרוּךְ כְּבוֹד־יְיָ מִמְּקוֹמוֹ: וּנְטָלַתְנִי

רוּחָא וְשָׁמְעֵת בַּתְרַי קָל זִיעַ סַגִּיא דִּמְשַׁבְּחִין וְאָמְרִין בְּרִיךְ

יְקָרָא דַיְיָ מֵאֲתַר בֵּית שְׁכִינְתֵּהּ: יְיָ·יִמְלֹךְ לְעוֹלָם וָעֶד: יְיָ

מַלְכוּתֵהּ קָאֵם לְעָלַם וּלְעָלְמֵי עָלְמַיָּא: יְיָ אֱלֹהֵי אַבְרָהָם יִצְחָק

וְיִשְׂרָאֵל אֲבוֹתֵינוּ שָׁמְרָה־זֹּאת לְעוֹלָם לְיֵצֶר מַחְשְׁבוֹת לְבַב עַמֶּךָ

וְהָכֵן לְבָבָם אֵלֶיךָ: וְהוּא רַחוּם יְכַפֵּר עָוֹן וְלֹא יַשְׁחִית וְהִרְבָּה

לְהָשִׁיב אַפּוֹ וְלֹא יָעִיר כָּל־חֲמָתוֹ: כִּי־אַתָּה אֲדֹנָי טוֹב וְסַלָּח וְרַב־

חֶסֶד לְכָל־קֹרְאֶיךָ: צִדְקָתְךָ צֶדֶק לְעוֹלָם וְתוֹרָתְךָ אֱמֶת: תִּתֵּן

אֱמֶת לְיַעֲקֹב חֶסֶד לְאַבְרָהָם אֲשֶׁר־נִשְׁבַּעְתָּ לַאֲבֹתֵינוּ מִימֵי קֶדֶם:

בָּרוּךְ אֲדֹנָי יוֹם·יוֹם יַעֲמָס־לָנוּ הָאֵל יְשׁוּעָתֵנוּ סֶלָה: יְיָ צְבָאוֹת

עִמָּנוּ מִשְׂגָּב לָנוּ אֱלֹהֵי יַעֲקֹב סֶלָה: יְיָ צְבָאוֹת אַשְׁרֵי אָדָם

בֹּטֵחַ בָּךְ: יְיָ הוֹשִׁיעָה· הַמֶּלֶךְ יַעֲנֵנוּ בְיוֹם־קָרְאֵנוּ: בָּרוּךְ הוּא

אֱלֹהֵינוּ שֶׁבְּרָאָנוּ לִכְבוֹדוֹ וְהִבְדִּילָנוּ מִן־הַתּוֹעִים וְנָתַן לָנוּ תּוֹרַת

אֱמֶת וְחַיֵּי עוֹלָם נָטַע בְּתוֹכֵנוּ· הוּא יִפְתַּח לִבֵּנוּ בְּתוֹרָתוֹ וְיָשֵׂם

בְּלִבֵּנוּ אַהֲבָתוֹ וְיִרְאָתוֹ וְלַעֲשׂוֹת רְצוֹנוֹ וּלְעָבְדוֹ בְּלֵבָב שָׁלֵם לְמַעַן

Name as the goals of the "order" of the endeavors and activities of ordinary, everyday Jewish living. *Vihi no'am* and *Veattah kadosh* are recited only if the coming workday week will not be interrupted by a holiday.

ceive it from one another and say, "Holy in the highest heights of Heaven, the Abode of His Presence, holy on earth, the creation of His almighty power, holy forever and for all the eternities of eternity, is *God Tzevaoth;* the whole earth is filled with the radiance of His glory." When the spirit lifted me up, I heard behind me the voice of a great rushing, "Blessed be the glory of *God* from His Abode." And the spirit lifted me up, and I heard behind me the noise of a great movement of those who praised and spoke, "Blessed be the glory of *God* from the Abode of His Presence." "*God* shall reign forever and ever." *God,* His kingship remains forever and for all eternities of eternity. O *God,* God of Abraham, Yitzchak, and Yisrael, our fathers, keep this forever as the purpose in the thoughts of the hearts of Your people and turn their minds to You. But He being full of compassion forgives iniquity and does not destroy, and many a time repents of His anger and never stirs up all His wrath. For You, O my Lord, are good and forgiving and great in loving kindness for all those that call upon You. The righteousness You have taught is eternal righteousness and Your teaching is truth. Grant to Yaakov the truth and to Abraham the loving-kindness which You have sworn to our fathers from the days of old. Blessed be my Lord day by day; may He give us [a burden] to bear. Even the same God is also our salvation! *God Tzevaoth* is with us; the God of Yaakov is our high tower!— *God Tzevaoth,* forward forever strides the man that trusts in You!—May *God* grant salvation. As the King will He answer us on the day on which we call upon Him. Blessed be He, our God, Who created us for His glory and set us apart from those who go astray and Who has given us the Torah of truth and implanted life eternal into us. May He open our heart to His Torah, and put the love and fear of Him into our hearts, to do His will and to serve Him with a whole heart, so that we may not labor in vain nor bring forth for dismay. May it be Your will, O *God* our God and

לֹא נִיגַע לָרִיק וְלֹא נֵלֵד לַבֶּהָלָה: יְהִי רָצוֹן מִלְּפָנֶיךָ יְיָ אֱלֹהֵינוּ
וֵאלֹהֵי אֲבוֹתֵינוּ שֶׁנִּשְׁמוֹר חֻקֶּיךָ בָּעוֹלָם הַזֶּה וְנִזְכֶּה וְנִחְיֶה וְנִרְאֶה
וְנִירַשׁ טוֹבָה וּבְרָכָה לִשְׁנֵי יְמוֹת הַמָּשִׁיחַ וּלְחַיֵּי הָעוֹלָם הַבָּא:
לְמַעַן יְזַמֶּרְךָ כָבוֹד וְלֹא יִדֹּם · יְיָ אֱלֹהַי לְעוֹלָם אוֹדֶךָּ: בָּרוּךְ
הַגֶּבֶר אֲשֶׁר יִבְטַח בַּייָ וְהָיָה יְיָ מִבְטַחוֹ: בִּטְחוּ בַייָ עֲדֵי־עַד כִּי
בְּיָהּ יְיָ צוּר עוֹלָמִים: וְיִבְטְחוּ בְךָ יוֹדְעֵי שְׁמֶךָ כִּי לֹא־עָזַבְתָּ דֹרְשֶׁיךָ
יְיָ: יְיָ חָפֵץ לְמַעַן צִדְקוֹ יַגְדִּיל תּוֹרָה וְיַאְדִּיר: ק״ת

During the Omer time, the Omer is counted before ויתן לך. *On Chanukah the*
חזן *kindles the Chanukah lights before* ויתן לך.

וְיִתֶּן־לְךָ הָאֱלֹהִים מִטַּל הַשָּׁמַיִם וּמִשְׁמַנֵּי הָאָרֶץ
וְרֹב דָּגָן וְתִירֹשׁ: יַעַבְדוּךָ עַמִּים וְיִשְׁתַּחֲווּ לְךָ לְאֻמִּים
הֱוֵה גְבִיר לְאַחֶיךָ וְיִשְׁתַּחֲווּ לְךָ בְּנֵי אִמֶּךָ אֹרְרֶיךָ
אָרוּר וּמְבָרְכֶיךָ בָּרוּךְ: וְאֵל שַׁדַּי יְבָרֵךְ אֹתְךָ וְיַפְרְךָ
וְיַרְבֶּךָ וְהָיִיתָ לִקְהַל עַמִּים: וְיִתֶּן־לְךָ אֶת־בִּרְכַּת
אַבְרָהָם לְךָ וּלְזַרְעֲךָ אִתָּךְ לְרִשְׁתְּךָ אֶת־אֶרֶץ מְגֻרֶיךָ

ויתן לך **These verses, selected from the blessings of Yitzchak, Yaakov**
and Moshe are most appropriately part of this service, for they instil confidence in God's help and blessing into those who now enter upon the unknown that the new week is to bring. "May *God* give you"...Unlike Esau,
who, like yourself, was promised an abundance of material wealth, but who
was forced to rely upon himself, upon his own strength and prowess, you,
Yisrael, are to look to God alone for your happiness and prosperity on earth.

והיית לקהל עמים. ואל שדי וכו׳ **:** This is an excerpt from the blessing which
Yitzchak gave to Yaakov. Yitzchak said to his son: "God, Whose help alone
is sufficient for all things, will give you the wherewithal to establish a home
of your own, and then He will give you the strength to beget children and
to raise them in your own spirit so that they will be duplicates of yourself.

God of our fathers, that we may keep Your statutes in this world and thus become worthy of living, of seeing and inheriting happiness and blessings in the years of the days of the Messiah and in the life of the world to come. So that all that is glorious shall ceaselessly sing to You. O *God*, my God, I will do You homage forever. Blessed is the man who trusts in *God,* and to whom *God* is also the the source of His trust. Trust in *God* until the end of days, for in God, *God,* rests the Rock of All Time. And those who know Your Name shall trust in You, for You have never forsaken those who seek You, O *God*. *God* was pleased, because of His righteousness, to render the Torah increasingly great and glorious.

"May God give you of the dew of heaven and of the fatness of the soil, and an abundance of grain and wine. Peoples shall serve you and nations bow down before you, but become a man for your brothers, so that your mother's sons may bow down before you. Then he who curses you will be cursed and he who blesses you will be blessed." "And God, the All-Sufficient, will bless you and make you fruitful and multiply you, so that you may become a gathering of peoples; He will give you the blessing of Abraham, to you and to your seed with you, so that you may inherit the land to which you

---

Each of your children will have a distinct personality; they will be the ancestors of the future tribes of Yisrael, each with its own tribal peculiarities, *amim,* and yet they will all constitute one *kahal,* one single, unified gathering of peoples."

ברכת אביך וגו׳ מאל אביך וגו is taken from the blessing which Yaakov imparted to Yoseph. If a father in his extreme old age may have the joy of blessing his children, he owes this happy privilege solely to the blessing which he himself had received from his own father; he owes it to the *zechuth* of the purity of his parents at the moment of his conception. Note that the text reads *horai* and *not avothai.*

ואהבך The portion beginning with *Vaahevecha* is taken from the messages of Moshe to his people. The primary outgrowth of loyal obedience to God's Law, Moshe told the children of Israel, is that *Vaahevecha.* "*God* will deem you a faithful servant and He will therefore love you even as a master loves a faithful servant. Then *berachecha,* He will cause you to flourish and to prosper because you will promote only that which is in accordance with His

אֲשֶׁר־נָתַן אֱלֹהִים לְאַבְרָהָם: מֵאֵל אָבִיךָ וְיַעְזְרֶךָ
וְאֵת שַׁדַּי וִיבָרְכֶךָּ בִּרְכֹת שָׁמַיִם מֵעָל בִּרְכֹת תְּהוֹם
רֹבֶצֶת תָּחַת בִּרְכֹת שָׁדַיִם וָרָחַם: בִּרְכֹת אָבִיךָ גָּבְרוּ
עַל־בִּרְכֹת הוֹרַי עַד־תַּאֲוַת גִּבְעֹת עוֹלָם תִּהְיֶיןָ
לְרֹאשׁ יוֹסֵף וּלְקָדְקֹד נְזִיר אֶחָיו: וַאֲהֵבְךָ וּבֵרַכְךָ
וְהִרְבֶּךָ וּבֵרַךְ פְּרִי־בִטְנְךָ וּפְרִי־אַדְמָתֶךָ דְּגָנְךָ וְתִירֹשְׁךָ
וְיִצְהָרֶךָ שְׁגַר־אֲלָפֶיךָ וְעַשְׁתְּרֹת צֹאנֶךָ עַל הָאֲדָמָה
אֲשֶׁר־נִשְׁבַּע לַאֲבֹתֶיךָ לָתֶת לָךְ: בָּרוּךְ תִּהְיֶה מִכָּל־
הָעַמִּים לֹא־יִהְיֶה בְךָ עָקָר וַעֲקָרָה וּבִבְהֶמְתֶּךָ: וְהֵסִיר
יְיָ מִמְּךָ כָּל־חֹלִי וְכָל־מַדְוֵי מִצְרַיִם הָרָעִים אֲשֶׁר
יָדַעְתָּ לֹא יְשִׂימָם בָּךְ וּנְתָנָם בְּכָל־שֹׂנְאֶיךָ:

In אשכנז, המלאך *is not said here:*

נוֹפְלִין
מוֹסִיקִין
הַמַּלְאָךְ הַגֹּאֵל אֹתִי מִכָּל־רָע יְבָרֵךְ אֶת־הַנְּעָרִים וְיִקָּרֵא בָהֶם
שְׁמִי וְשֵׁם אֲבֹתַי אַבְרָהָם וְיִצְחָק וְיִדְגּוּ לָרֹב בְּקֶרֶב הָאָרֶץ: יְיָ
אֱלֹהֵיכֶם הִרְבָּה אֶתְכֶם וְהִנְּכֶם הַיּוֹם כְּכוֹכְבֵי הַשָּׁמַיִם לָרֹב: יְיָ
אֱלֹהֵי אֲבוֹתֵכֶם יֹסֵף עֲלֵיכֶם כָּכֶם אֶלֶף פְּעָמִים וִיבָרֵךְ אֶתְכֶם כַּאֲשֶׁר
דִּבֶּר לָכֶם:

---

will, and hence, if you will prosper, His own cause on earth will be advanced
as well. *Vehirbecha:* And you will be 'multiplied' through your children who
will emulate only your own spirit, your own attitude and your own loyalty
which you yourself have demonstrated to them in your daily living."

המלאך: This is an excerpt from the blessing which Yaakov gave Yoseph
for the latter's children. It was Yaakov's prayerful hope that God would

had been a stranger, which God had given to Abraham." "This is
from the God of your father, Who will help you, and, [as for] you,
remain with the All-Sufficient; He will bless you with blessings from
Heaven above, with blessings of the deep that couches below, with
blessings of breast and womb. Only through the blessings of my
progenitors have the blessings of your father ascended up to the
goal after which the mountains of all time do strive. They become
the portion of the head of Yoseph, the portion of the crown of the
head of the most abstemious of his brothers." "He will love you
and bless you and multiply you; He will bless the fruit of your body
and the fruit of your soil, your grain, your wine and your oil, the
offspring of your cattle and the abundance of your sheep, upon the
land which He swore to your fathers to give to you. You shall be
blessed more than all the peoples; there shall not be a barren male or
a barren female among you or among your cattle. And *God* will keep
far from you all illness, and all the evil sufferings of Mitzrayim,
which you know, He will not inflict upon you, but will inflict them
upon all those who hate you."

May the angel who redeemed me from all evil bless the lads
so that my name and the names of my fathers, Abraham and Yitzchak,
be carried on in them and that they may grow into a multitude, like
fish in the midst of the earth. *God* your God has multiplied you and
now you are like the stars of Heaven as to multitude. May *God*,
the God of your fathers, increase you yet a thousandfold, and bless
you even as He has promised you.

---

bless his grandchildren through the same *malach* through whom He had also
delivered Yaakov many years before. It is the prayer of Yaakov, too, that his
grandsons carry on that same destiny within which, and through which, God
had permitted him, Yaakov, to find both life and prosperity. Unlike Esau,
the descendants of Yaakov are not to live by their own hand and sword, but
instead, they are to seek and find protection and safekeeping only through
God, even as their ancestor Yaakov did during his own lifetime. In this manner
ויקרא וגו' Yaakov and his fathers will live on in their descendants. וידגו,
"like fish"; that is, in a separate habitat in depths beyond the range of the
human eye. In other words, the children of Yaakov will live quiet, happy
lives in the midst of mankind, but set apart as if in a separate habitat to
which those around them cannot follow them and the significance of which
the others cannot surmise.

בָּרוּךְ אַתָּה בָּעִיר וּבָרוּךְ אַתָּה בַּשָּׂדֶה: בָּרוּךְ אַתָּה
בְּבֹאֶךָ וּבָרוּךְ אַתָּה בְּצֵאתֶךָ: בָּרוּךְ טַנְאֲךָ וּמִשְׁאַרְתֶּךָ:
בָּרוּךְ פְּרִי־בִטְנְךָ וּפְרִי־אַדְמָתְךָ וּפְרִי בְהֶמְתֶּךָ שְׁגַר
אֲלָפֶיךָ וְעַשְׁתְּרוֹת צֹאנֶךָ: יְצַו יְיָ אִתְּךָ אֶת־הַבְּרָכָה
בַּאֲסָמֶיךָ וּבְכֹל מִשְׁלַח יָדֶךָ וּבֵרַכְךָ בָּאָרֶץ אֲשֶׁר־יְיָ
אֱלֹהֶיךָ נֹתֵן לָךְ: יִפְתַּח יְיָ לְךָ אֶת־אוֹצָרוֹ הַטּוֹב אֶת־
הַשָּׁמַיִם לָתֵת מְטַר־אַרְצְךָ בְּעִתּוֹ וּלְבָרֵךְ אֵת כָּל־
מַעֲשֵׂה יָדֶךָ וְהִלְוִיתָ גּוֹיִם רַבִּים וְאַתָּה לֹא תִלְוֶה: כִּי־
יְהוָה אֱלֹהֶיךָ בֵּרַכְךָ כַּאֲשֶׁר דִּבֶּר־לָךְ וְהַעֲבַטְתָּ גּוֹיִם
רַבִּים וְאַתָּה לֹא תַעֲבֹט וּמָשַׁלְתָּ בְּגוֹיִם רַבִּים וּבְךָ לֹא
יִמְשֹׁלוּ: אַשְׁרֶיךָ יִשְׂרָאֵל מִי כָמוֹךָ עַם נוֹשַׁע בַּיְיָ מָגֵן
עֶזְרֶךָ וַאֲשֶׁר־חֶרֶב גַּאֲוָתֶךָ וְיִכָּחֲשׁוּ אֹיְבֶיךָ לָךְ וְאַתָּה
עַל־בָּמוֹתֵימוֹ תִדְרֹךְ:

In אשכנז, מחיתי is not said here:

מָחִיתִי כָעָב פְּשָׁעֶיךָ וְכֶעָנָן חַטֹּאותֶיךָ שׁוּבָה אֵלַי כִּי גְאַלְתִּיךָ:

ברוך These are excerpts from the blessing of Moshe to his people. But
these four sentences, each beginning with *baruch*, are arranged here in an
order different from that in which they appear in the original Biblical text.
The two sentences beginning with *baruch attah* are put together to give special
emphasis to the thought that there must be personal blessing before there
can be any material blessing, and that material prosperity can come only as
a result of personal well-being. It is only because ברוך אתה בשדה וגו' ברוך אתה
בעיר וגו' that ברוך פרי בטנך וגו' ברוך טנאך וגו'. The prospering of your communal life (*ba'ir*) is not attributable to the fertility of your fields. It is only
because your life in the city has been worthy of being blessed that God has
caused your fields to flourish. In like manner, *boacha* must be blessed before

Blessed shall you be in the city, and blessed shall you be in the field. Blessed shall you be at your coming in, and blessed shall you be at your going out. Blessed shall be your basket and your trough. Blessed shall be the fruit of your body and the fruit of your soil and the fruit of your livestock, the offspring of your cattle and the abundance of your sheep. May *God* command the blessing [to go] with you in your larders and in every endeavor to which you put your hand, and may He bless you in the land which *God* your God gives you. May *God* open the heaven, His good treasury for you, to give you the rain of your land in its season and to bless all the work of your hand. May you lend to many nations, but may you not borrow from them. When *God* your God will have blessed you even as He has promised it to you, you will make many nations beholden to you, but you will not be beholden [to any], you will rule over many nations but they shall not rule over you. You stride forward forever, O Yisrael! who is like you, a nation, saved by *God,* the Shield of your Help, Who is the sword of your majesty. Your enemies will disavow [their past] before you, and you shall tread upon their high places.

I have blotted out your crimes as a mist. and your sins like a cloud; return to Me, for I have redeemed you. Jubilate, O heavens,

---

tsetecha can prosper. טנאך is "your basket", into which you place the fruit as you pluck it from your field. משארתך is the "kneading trough" in which you prepare the bread for your family. ברוך פרי בטנך It is because your children, by virtue of the manner of their conception and by virtue of their rearing, have become worthy of blessing, your fields and to your herds will be blessed also. יצו ה' אתך את הברכה God will command His blessing to accompany you wherever you will go. Everything that you do will prosper and flourish because you have undertaken it. באסמיך : God will bestow His blessing even upon that gain which you have already reaped and stored up. אשריך וגו' is the final message which Moshe delivered to the people of Israel. Moshe tells the Children of Yisrael that ואשר חרב וגו' "God will give you an exalted position among the nation such as other nations can attain and maintain only by means of the sword." ויכחשו The time will come when the light of the principles which you, O Yisrael, now champion, will shine forth victoriously so that those who formerly opposed you will disavow their past hostile attitude, and you will be able to ascend to the lofty goals of all human endeavor which they had vainly tried to attain by other means."

מחיתי : This is an excerpt from the Book of Isaiah (44:22—23; 47:4).

רָנּוּ שָׁמַיִם כִּי־עָשָׂה יְיָ הָרִיעוּ תַּחְתִּיּוֹת אָרֶץ פִּצְחוּ הָרִים רִנָּה
יַעַר וְכָל־עֵץ בּוֹ כִּי־גָאַל יְיָ יַעֲקֹב וּבְיִשְׂרָאֵל יִתְפָּאָר: גְּאָלֵנוּ יְיָ
צְבָאוֹת שְׁמוֹ קְדוֹשׁ יִשְׂרָאֵל:

יִשְׂרָאֵל נוֹשַׁע בַּיְיָ תְּשׁוּעַת עוֹלָמִים לֹא־תֵבֹשׁוּ וְלֹא־
תִכָּלְמוּ עַד־עוֹלְמֵי עַד: וַאֲכַלְתֶּם אָכוֹל וְשָׂבוֹעַ
וְהִלַּלְתֶּם אֶת־שֵׁם יְיָ אֱלֹהֵיכֶם אֲשֶׁר־עָשָׂה עִמָּכֶם
לְהַפְלִיא וְלֹא־יֵבֹשׁוּ עַמִּי לְעוֹלָם: וִידַעְתֶּם כִּי בְקֶרֶב
יִשְׂרָאֵל אָנִי וַאֲנִי יְיָ אֱלֹהֵיכֶם וְאֵין עוֹד וְלֹא־יֵבֹשׁוּ
עַמִּי לְעוֹלָם: כִּי־בְשִׂמְחָה תֵצֵאוּ וּבְשָׁלוֹם תּוּבָלוּן
הֶהָרִים וְהַגְּבָעוֹת יִפְצְחוּ לִפְנֵיכֶם רִנָּה וְכָל־עֲצֵי
הַשָּׂדֶה יִמְחֲאוּ־כָף: הִנֵּה אֵל יְשׁוּעָתִי אֶבְטַח וְלֹא
אֶפְחָד כִּי עָזִּי וְזִמְרָת יָהּ יְיָ וַיְהִי־לִי לִישׁוּעָה:
וּשְׁאַבְתֶּם־מַיִם בְּשָׂשׂוֹן מִמַּעַיְנֵי הַיְשׁוּעָה: וַאֲמַרְתֶּם
בַּיּוֹם הַהוּא הוֹדוּ לַיְיָ קִרְאוּ בִשְׁמוֹ הוֹדִיעוּ בָעַמִּים
עֲלִילֹתָיו הַזְכִּירוּ כִּי נִשְׂגָּב שְׁמוֹ: זַמְּרוּ יְיָ כִּי גֵאוּת
עָשָׂה מוּדַעַת זֹאת בְּכָל־הָאָרֶץ: צַהֲלִי וָרֹנִּי יוֹשֶׁבֶת
צִיּוֹן כִּי־גָדוֹל בְּקִרְבֵּךְ קְדוֹשׁ יִשְׂרָאֵל: וְאָמַר בַּיּוֹם

God says to Yisrael: כי גאלתיך "Now there is no longer any obstacle that should keep you from dedicating yourself wholeheartedly and unreservedly to My Service." רנו שמים See above p. 50 קדוש ישראל, He Whom Yisrael

for *God* has done it; exult, depths of the earth, break forth into joy, O mountains, forests and all trees therein, for *God* has redeemed Yaakov and will glory in Yisrael. Our Redeemer, *God Tzevaoth* is His Name, the Holy One of Yisrael.

Yisrael is saved by *God* for eternal victory; never again shall you be deceived or blush with shame. You shall eat in plenty and be satisfied, and you will proclaim the praise of *God* your God Who has dealt wondrously with you. and my people shall never be deceived. "You shall know that I am in the midst of Yisrael, and that I am your God, and there is none beside Him; and My people shall never be ashamed. For with joy shall you go forth, and in peace shall you be brought home; the mountains and hills will break forth into joy before you and all the trees of the field will clap their hands. Behold, *God* is my salvation; I will trust and shall not be afraid, for *God* is my victory and song, *God,* and this has been my salvation. Therefore draw water joyously from the wellsprings of salvation, and say on that day, "Avow thanks to *God,* proclaim His Name, make His ways known among the peoples; let it be remembered that His Name is exalted. Sing to *God* that He has done great things; this is known throughout the earth. Exult and jubilate, O dweller in Tzion, for great is the Holy One of Israel in your midst." On that day it shall be said,

---

worships as "The Holy One", as the sole true Holy Being, Whose sanctity is the source of all that which aspires to holiness and actually attains a portion thereof on earth.

ישראל נושע: Only from God can we receive such salvation as will not again end in disillusionment. תצאו: "shall you go forth"; i.e. from the Galuth. תובלון "shall you be brought home"; i.e. into the ancient Homeland. עזי is "my strength which helped me withstand all the onslaughts of trouble, and the song declaring that I have preserved the unbroken vigor of spirit to be able to soar up to a song of praise, beholding the ways of God. Both these, the 'strength' and the 'song', are gifts of God, and this was my salvation." ושאבתם Therefore, let all the generations that will follow our own draw from the same well-springs of salvation, that strength and inspiration which sustained our fathers in their wanderings through the wilderness of the ages. הזכירו Make it known to mankind and constantly remind all men of it. ואמר refers to the generation which will experience this Divine deliverance.

הַהוּא הִנֵּה אֱלֹהֵינוּ זֶה קִוִּינוּ לוֹ וְיוֹשִׁיעֵנוּ זֶה יְיָ קִוִּינוּ
לוֹ נָגִילָה וְנִשְׂמְחָה בִּישׁוּעָתוֹ:

בֵּית יעקב, אשכנז is not said here:

בְּמָקוֹם בֵּית יַעֲקֹב לְכוּ וְנֵלְכָה בְּאוֹר יְיָ: וְהָיָה אֱמוּנַת עִתֶּיךָ חֹסֶן
מוֹסִיפִין
יְשׁוּעֹת חָכְמַת וָדָעַת יִרְאַת יְיָ הִיא אוֹצָרוֹ: וַיְהִי דָוִד לְכָל־דְּרָכָיו
מַשְׂכִּיל וַיְיָ עִמּוֹ: פָּדָה בְשָׁלוֹם נַפְשִׁי מִקְּרָב־לִי כִּי־בְרַבִּים הָיוּ
עִמָּדִי: וַיֹּאמֶר הָעָם אֶל־שָׁאוּל הֲיוֹנָתָן יָמוּת אֲשֶׁר עָשָׂה הַיְשׁוּעָה
הַגְּדוֹלָה הַזֹּאת בְּיִשְׂרָאֵל חָלִילָה חַי־יְיָ אִם־יִפֹּל מִשַּׂעֲרַת רֹאשׁוֹ
אַרְצָה כִּי־עִם־אֱלֹהִים עָשָׂה הַיּוֹם הַזֶּה וַיִּפְדּוּ הָעָם אֶת־יוֹנָתָן
וְלֹא־מֵת: וּפְדוּיֵי יְיָ יְשֻׁבוּן וּבָאוּ צִיּוֹן בְּרִנָּה וְשִׂמְחַת עוֹלָם עַל־
רֹאשָׁם שָׂשׂוֹן וְשִׂמְחָה יַשִּׂיגוּ וְנָסוּ יָגוֹן וַאֲנָחָה: הָפַכְתָּ מִסְפְּדִי
לְמָחוֹל לִי פִּתַּחְתָּ שַׂקִּי וַתְּאַזְּרֵנִי שִׂמְחָה: וְלֹא־אָבָה יְיָ אֱלֹהֶיךָ
לִשְׁמֹעַ אֶל־בִּלְעָם וַיַּהֲפֹךְ יְיָ אֱלֹהֶיךָ לְּךָ אֶת־הַקְּלָלָה לִבְרָכָה כִּי
אֲהֵבְךָ יְיָ אֱלֹהֶיךָ: אָז תִּשְׂמַח בְּתוּלָה בְּמָחוֹל וּבַחֻרִים וּזְקֵנִים יַחְדָּו
וְהָפַכְתִּי אֶבְלָם לְשָׂשׂוֹן וְנִחַמְתִּים וְשִׂמַּחְתִּים מִיגוֹנָם: (* דרכיו קרי

The sentence beginning with בית is taken from the Book Isaiah. It is the
call of the nations to the House of Yaakov to walk before them to show them
the way in the light of God. והיה: the trust of all destinies and the strength
of all salvation attained is based upon that wisdom and that knowledge which
originate from the "treasure chamber" of the fear of God. ויהי: It was such
reason that David demonstrated in all of his ways; or, rather, he applied
such reason to all that he did. He saw to it that his ways would be the right
ones, and therefore God was with him. פדה: For David frankly acknowledged

"Behold. this is our *God* in Whom we have hoped that He should save us; this is *God*, in Whom we have placed our hope; let us exult and rejoice in His salvation."

O House of Yaakov, go forth, let us walk in the light of *God*. And the trust of your destinies, the strength of all salvation shall be wisdom and knowledge, whose treasury is the fear of *God*. David applied reason in all his ways; therefore *God* was with him. He has delivered my soul in peace from the battle that threatened me, even though those at my side were many indeed. The people said to Shaul: "Shall Yonathan die, who has wrought this great salvation in Yisrael? Far be it! As *God* lives, not a hair of his head shall fall to the ground, for with *God* has he wrought it today." So the people set Yonathan free and he did not die. Those set free by *God* will return and come to Tzion with jubilation, and everlasting joy shall be upon their heads; bliss and joy shall they attain, and sorrow and sighing shall flee away. You turned for me my mourning into dancing, you loosened my sackcloth and girded me with joy. *God* your God would not hearken to Balaam; instead, *God* your God turned the curse into a blessing for you, because *God* your God loved you. Then the maiden shall rejoice in dancing, young men and the old together; I will turn their mourning into bliss and I will comfort them and lift them up in rejoicing from their sorrow.

---

that even when masses of men stood at his side to help him it was to God alone that he owed every day unmarred by strife and peril. This verse, together with the eight verses that follow (ואמרתם וגו׳ until ואמרתם וגו׳ וכל שלום לך אשר) פדה בשלום וגו׳ is a composite (given in Berachoth 55b) of שלש הפכות שלש פדיות ושלש שלומות which should give every spirit that faces the future with dread the assurance that will sustain it and inspire it with confidence; namely, that, under God, we may expect with certainty that even the sadness of abject despair will ultimately be transfigured into its very opposite; deliverance from all evil, and peace and prosperity in every phase of our lives.

בּוֹרֵא נִיב שְׂפָתָיִם שָׁלוֹם ׀ שָׁלוֹם לָרָחוֹק וְלַקָּרוֹב אָמַר

יְיָ וּרְפָאתִיו: וְרוּחַ לָבְשָׁה אֶת־עֲמָשַׂי רֹאשׁ הַשָּׁלִישִׁים

לְךָ דָוִיד וְעִמְּךָ בֶן־יִשַׁי שָׁלוֹם ׀ שָׁלוֹם לְךָ וְשָׁלוֹם לְעֹזְרֶךָ

כִּי עֲזָרְךָ אֱלֹהֶיךָ וַיְקַבְּלֵם דָּוִיד וַיִּתְּנֵם בְּרָאשֵׁי הַגְּדוּד:

וַאֲמַרְתֶּם כֹּה לֶחָי וְאַתָּה שָׁלוֹם וּבֵיתְךָ שָׁלוֹם וְכֹל אֲשֶׁר־

לְךָ שָׁלוֹם: יְיָ עֹז לְעַמּוֹ יִתֵּן יְיָ יְבָרֵךְ אֶת־עַמּוֹ בַשָּׁלוֹם:

In אמר רבי, אשכנז is not said here:

כּפוּלין
מוסיף } אָמַר רַבִּי יוֹחָנָן בְּכָל־מָקוֹם שֶׁאַתָּה מוֹצֵא גְדֻלָּתוֹ שֶׁל־הַקָּדוֹשׁ

בָּרוּךְ הוּא שָׁם אַתָּה מוֹצֵא עַנְוְתָנוּתוֹ ׀ דָּבָר זֶה כָּתוּב בַּתּוֹרָה ׀

וְשָׁנוּי בַּנְּבִיאִים ׀ וּמְשֻׁלָּשׁ בַּכְּתוּבִים: כָּתוּב בַּתּוֹרָה כִּי יְיָ אֱלֹהֵיכֶם

הוּא אֱלֹהֵי הָאֱלֹהִים וַאֲדֹנֵי הָאֲדֹנִים הָאֵל הַגָּדֹל הַגִּבֹּר וְהַנּוֹרָא

אֲשֶׁר לֹא־יִשָּׂא פָנִים וְלֹא יִקַּח שֹׁחַד: וּכְתִיב בַּתְרֵהּ עֹשֶׂה מִשְׁפַּט

יָתוֹם וְאַלְמָנָה וְאֹהֵב גֵּר לָתֶת לוֹ לֶחֶם וְשִׂמְלָה: שָׁנוּי בַּנְּבִיאִים

אמר ר' יוחנן **:** Judaism is concerned not only with teaching its adherents of the all surpassing grandeur, power and greatness of God, but also, and quite particularly, with making all those on earth who are in need of His help aware of His immediate presence and nearness. This is one of the most striking features of Jewish ideology. This truth is contained in the very first verses of our Hallel hymns: מי כה׳ אלהינו המגביהי לשבת המשפילי etc. רם על גוים ה׳. לראות וגו׳ The fact that there exists one God Who reigns supreme over all the other forces of the Universe is not entirely new to the non-Jewish world. It was the particular mission of the Jewish people, however, to teach the world that God, though infinitely exalted, is very much present among men and near to every human being. Accordingly, Rabbi Yochanan points out (Megillah 31a) that in every Holy Book of the Word of God the proclamations of the majesty of God are coupled with references to His loving presence

"I create that which blossoms upon the lips; peace, peace to him who is far away and to him who is near," says *God,* "and I will heal him." The spirit came upon Amasai, who was chief of the captains: "To you, O David, and with you, O son of Yishai, peace! Peace to you, peace to all who help you, for God is your help." David received them and made them chiefs of the group. And thus you shall say, "Thus let it be with the living; may peace be with you, peace with your house, and peace with all that is yours." To His people, *God* will grant power to be victorious over all; *God* will bless His people with peace.

Rabbi Yochanan said: Wherever you will find the greatness of the Holy One, blessed be He, there will you find also His humility. This is written in the Torah, reiterated in the Prophets and stated a third time in the Holy Writings. It is written in the Torah: "For *God* your God is the God of Gods and the Lord of Lords, the great, mighty and awesome God Who has no regard for person and will not take a bribe." And immediately following it is written: "[It is] He Who executes the judgment of the orphan and the widow, and loves the stranger, giving him food and clothing." It is repeated in

---

which gently descends to those who are weak and in need of help. This is a truth which the Jew should never cease to remember for even one moment; it should be part of our every breath, and it is therefore only fitting that we be made aware of it once again as we enter into the struggle and strife of weekday living.

יהי ה' אלהינו עמנו: This is the wish with which King Solomon dismissed his people to return to their homes after the public ceremony in which the Temple was consecrated. ואתם הדבקים: These are the words which Moshe addressed to that generation which had emerged unscathed from all the trials and perils of the wilderness and which he now saw standing before him as he was about to depart from earthly life. With these farewell words he bade his people realize the glorious reward which their proven faithfulness had brought them, and to rejoice in this knowledge. כי נחם These are the words of Divine consolation uttered by the Prophet Isaiah. We are told that when

דִּכְתִיב כִּי כֹה אָמַר רָם וְנִשָּׂא שֹׁכֵן עַד וְקָדוֹשׁ שְׁמוֹ מָרוֹם וְקָדוֹשׁ
אֶשְׁכּוֹן וְאֶת־דַּכָּא וּשְׁפַל־רוּחַ לְהַחֲיוֹת רוּחַ שְׁפָלִים וּלְהַחֲיוֹת לֵב
נִדְכָּאִים: מְשֻׁלָּשׁ בַּכְּתוּבִים דִּכְתִיב שִׁירוּ ׀ לֵאלֹהִים זַמְּרוּ שְׁמוֹ
סֹלּוּ לָרֹכֵב בָּעֲרָבוֹת בְּיָהּ שְׁמוֹ וְעִלְזוּ לְפָנָיו: וּכְתִיב בַּתְרֵהּ אֲבִי
יְתוֹמִים וְדַיַּן אַלְמָנוֹת אֱלֹהִים בִּמְעוֹן קָדְשׁוֹ: יְהִי יְיָ אֱלֹהֵינוּ עִמָּנוּ
כַּאֲשֶׁר הָיָה עִם־אֲבוֹתֵינוּ אַל־יַעַזְבֵנוּ וְאַל־יִטְּשֵׁנוּ: וְאַתֶּם הַדְּבֵקִים בַּיְיָ
אֱלֹהֵיכֶם חַיִּים כֻּלְּכֶם הַיּוֹם: כִּי־נִחַם יְיָ צִיּוֹן נִחַם כָּל־חָרְבֹתֶיהָ
וַיָּשֶׂם מִדְבָּרָהּ כְּעֵדֶן וְעַרְבָתָהּ כְּגַן־יְיָ שָׂשׂוֹן וְשִׂמְחָה יִמָּצֵא בָהּ תּוֹדָה
וְקוֹל זִמְרָה: יְיָ חָפֵץ לְמַעַן צִדְקוֹ יַגְדִּיל תּוֹרָה וְיַאְדִּיר:

הַשַּׁ"ץ מַגְדִּיל בְּבֵי"כ, וְכֵן בְּמ"ש חֲנֻכָּה.

קכח שִׁיר הַמַּעֲלוֹת אַשְׁרֵי כָּל־יְרֵא יְהוָה הַהֹלֵךְ בִּדְרָכָיו: יְגִיעַ
כַּפֶּיךָ כִּי תֹאכֵל אַשְׁרֶיךָ וְטוֹב לָךְ: אֶשְׁתְּךָ ׀ כְּגֶפֶן פֹּרִיָּה בְּיַרְכְּתֵי
בֵיתֶךָ בָּנֶיךָ כִּשְׁתִלֵי זֵיתִים סָבִיב לְשֻׁלְחָנֶךָ: הִנֵּה כִי־כֵן יְבֹרַךְ
גָּבֶר יְרֵא יְהוָה: יְבָרֶכְךָ יְהוָה מִצִּיּוֹן וּרְאֵה בְּטוּב יְרוּשָׁלָ͏ִם כֹּל יְמֵי
חַיֶּיךָ: וּרְאֵה־בָנִים לְבָנֶיךָ שָׁלוֹם עַל־יִשְׂרָאֵל: עָלֵינוּ, קַדִּישׁ יָתוֹם·

בִּרְכַּת הַלְּבָנָה—738 page

The children are also blessed on מוֹצָאֵי שַׁבָּת

קוֹדֶם הַבְדָּלָה בְּמוֹצָאֵי שַׁבָּת מְנַגְּנִים פִּיּוּט זֶה.

אֵלִיָּהוּ הַנָּבִיא אֵלִיָּהוּ הַתִּשְׁבִּי אֵלִיָּהוּ הַגִּלְעָדִי בִּמְהֵרָה יָבֹא
אֵלֵינוּ עִם מָשִׁיחַ בֶּן־דָּוִד: אִישׁ אֲשֶׁר קִנֵּא לְשֵׁם הָאֵל · אִישׁ בִּשַּׂר
שָׁלוֹם עַל־יַד יְקוּתִיאֵל · אִישׁ גָּשׁ וַיְכַפֵּר עַל־בְּנֵי יִשְׂרָאֵל: אִישׁ · דּ'
דּוֹרוֹת שְׁנֵים־עָשָׂר רָאוּ עֵינָיו · אִישׁ הַנִּקְרָא בַּעַל שֵׂעָר בְּסִמָּנָיו · אִישׁ

the Prophets where it is written, "Thus says the High and Exalted One Who is enthroned in eternity and Whose Name is holy, I am enthroned in the high and holy place, but yet I am also with the contrite and those whose spirits are bowed down, to revive the spirit of the humble and to revive the heart of those that are contrite." And a third time it is written in the Holy Writings: "Sing to God, sing praises to His Name, soar up to Him Who guides worlds through barrenness by His Name *Yah* and exult greatly before His countenance." And immediately following it is written: "A Father of the orphans, a Defender of the widows is God in the Abode of His Sanctuary." May *God* our God be with us even as He was with our fathers; may He not leave us or forsake us. And you who have held fast to *God* your God, are all alive today. For *God* has comforted Tzion; He has comforted all of her ruins. He has made her wilderness like Eden and her desolate places like a garden of *God.* Bliss and joy shall be found there, thanksgiving and the voice of song. *God* was pleased, because of His righteousness, to render the Torah increasingly great and glorious.

A Song of Ascents. Forward strides each one who fears *God,* Who walks in His ways. The labor of your hands, when you eat of it, then you will stride forward and the good will be yours. Your wife is a fruitful vine in the innermost parts of your house, your children are like olive shoots around your table. Behold, if this is so, then the man who fears *God* is blessed. May *God* bless you out of Tzion, and [may you] look upon the good of Yerushalayim all the days of your life, and [may you] see children of your children. Peace upon Yisrael.

---

redemption will come, we will see that all the days of ruin and desolation which have gone before have been only preliminary episodes preparing us for the joy and gladness that will ultimately be our portion. ‏ה' חפץ וגו'‏. Finally, we have the assurance, which has meaning at all times, with regard to the ultimate era of the Divine kingdom on earth; namely, that, at all times and in every age, God will cause His Torah to become increasingly great and glorious.

וְאֵזוֹר עוֹר אָזוּר בְּמָתְנָיו · איהו אִישׁ זָעַף עַל עוֹבְדֵי חַמָּנִים · אִישׁ
חָשׁ וְנִשְׁבַּע מֵחֵזוֹת גִּשְׁמֵי מְעוֹנִים · אִישׁ טַל וּמָטָר עָצַר שָׁלוֹשׁ
שָׁנִים : איהו אִישׁ יָצָא לִמְצוֹא לְנַפְשׁוֹ נַחַת · אִישׁ כִּלְכְּלוּהוּ הָעֹרְבִים
וְלֹא מֵת לַשַּׁחַת · אִישׁ לְמַעֲנוֹ נִתְבָּרְכוּ כַּד וְצַפַּחַת : איהו אִישׁ
מוֹסָרָיו הִקְשִׁיבוּ כְמֵהִים · אִישׁ גֶּעֱנָה בָאֵשׁ מִשְּׁמֵי גְבוֹהִים · אִישׁ
סָחוּ אַחֲרָיו יְיָ הוּא הָאֱלֹהִים : איהו אִישׁ עָתִיד לְהִשְׁתַּלַּח מִשְּׁמֵי
עֲרָבוֹת · אִישׁ פָּקִיד עַל כָּל־בְּשׂוֹרוֹת טוֹבוֹת · אִישׁ צִיר נֶאֱמָן
לְהָשִׁיב לֵב בָּנִים עַל־אָבוֹת : איהו אִישׁ קָרָא קַנֹּא קִנֵּאתִי לַיְיָ
בְּתִפְאָרָה · אִישׁ רָכַב עַל־סוּסֵי אֵשׁ בַּסְּעָרָה · אִישׁ שֶׁלֹּא טָעַם טַעַם
מִיתָה וּקְבוּרָה : איהו אִישׁ תִּשְׁבִּי עַל־שְׁמוֹ נִקְרָא · תַּצְלִיחֵנוּ עַל־
יָדוֹ בַּתּוֹרָה · תַּשְׁמִיעֵנוּ מִפִּיו בְּשׂוֹרָה טוֹבָה בִּמְהֵרָה · וּתוֹצִיאֵנוּ
מֵאֲפֵלָה לְאוֹרָה : איהו אִישׁ תִּשְׁבִּי תַּצִּילֵנוּ מִפִּי אֲרָיוֹת · תְּבַשְּׂרֵנוּ
בְּשׂוֹרוֹת טוֹבוֹת · תְּשַׂמְּחֵנוּ בָּנִים עַל־אָבוֹת בְּמוֹצָאֵי שַׁבָּתוֹת : י·
כַּכָּתוּב · הִנֵּה אָנֹכִי שֹׁלֵחַ לָכֶם אֵת אֵלִיָּה הַנָּבִיא לִפְנֵי בּוֹא יוֹם
יְיָ הַגָּדוֹל וְהַנּוֹרָא · וְהֵשִׁיב לֵב־אָבוֹת עַל־בָּנִים וְלֵב בָּנִים עַל־אֲבוֹתָם :
איהו אַשְׁרֵי מִי שֶׁרָאָה פָנָיו בַּחֲלוֹם · אַשְׁרֵי מִי שֶׁנָּתַן לוֹ שָׁלוֹם
וְהֶחֱזִיר לוֹ שָׁלוֹם · יְיָ יְבָרֵךְ אֶת־עַמּוֹ בַשָּׁלוֹם ·

סֵדֶר הַבְדָּלָה

The cup is taken in the hand and the following is said:

הִנֵּה אֵל יְשׁוּעָתִי אֶבְטַח וְלֹא אֶפְחָד כִּי עָזִּי וְזִמְרָת יָהּ
יְיָ וַיְהִי־לִי לִישׁוּעָה : וּשְׁאַבְתֶּם מַיִם בְּשָׂשׂוֹן מִמַּעַיְנֵי
הַיְשׁוּעָה : לַיְיָ הַיְשׁוּעָה עַל־עַמְּךָ בִרְכָתֶךָ סֶּלָה : יְיָ

Behold, God is my salvation; I will trust and shall not be afraid,
for *God* is my victory and song, *God,* and this has been my salvation.
Therefore draw water joyously from the wellsprings of salvation, but
help rests with *God,* Your blessing upon Your people! — *God* Tzevaoth

---

הנה: Both in the Scriptures and in the mitzvoth of Jewish living the
term *kos,* "cup" always symbolizes a destiny or decree, a "portion" meted
out to us by God. Thus, when the Sabbath enters into our midst, we usher
it in by reciting the Kiddush over a cup, thus marking the Sabbath as an
institution appointed by Divine decree for our sanctification. In the same
manner, when we are about to return to the workday week, we remind ourselves of the meaning of the week to come by reciting the Havdalah over a
cup, thus symbolically indicating that the workday week, no less than the
Sabbath, is also ordained by God Himself, a period set aside for the fulfillment
of specific tasks that He has set us. Moreover, as we chant the Havdalah
service we remember that the workday week to come is set apart from the
Sabbath only so that the holiness won on the Sabbath may come to be demonstrated in our lives during all the six days that are to follow. That which
is set apart from other things as "holy" is so distinguished only in order that
it may imbue with holiness and consecration also every phase of life taking
place beyond its confines. Light is set apart from darkness only so that it may
give life and growth to the forces and materials that have gathered in the
darkness, and the people of Israel, too, was singled out from among all the
other nations to follow its own path through history only so that it may
serve to teach and enlighten the rest of mankind. In the same manner the
Seventh Day was set apart from the six working days only so that its Sabbath
spirit might permeate all of weekday life. By our conscientious endeavors
during the week in the service of our God we must demonstrate how well
we have learned from the Sabbath to subordinate all of our endeavors and
achievements beneath the rule of God, and how well we can put into practice
what the Sabbath has taught us. Our high resolve to strive during the week
to come only for that which will be pleasing in the sight of God should afford
us the gladsome and fearless trust that God will aid us in all our endeavors
and achievements. This our confidence we declare in the Havdalah by
הנה אל ישועתי.

In addition to the *kos,* however, the Havdalah ceremony has two other
symbols; namely, the *besamim* and the *ner* over which we recite blessings
before we utter the actual *birkath havdalah.* Since it is obvious that the term
ריח has some relationship to רוח, "pleasant fragrances" are construed to
refer to that kind of enjoyment affecting the physical senses which, at the
same time, has a direct, refreshing and invigorating effect on mind and spirit.

צְבָאוֹת עִמָּנוּ מִשְׂגָּב לָנוּ אֱלֹהֵי יַעֲקֹב סֶלָה׃ לַיְּהוּדִים
הָיְתָה אוֹרָה וְשִׂמְחָה וְשָׂשׂוֹן וִיקָר׃ כֵּן תִּהְיֶה לָנוּ׃ כּוֹס
יְשׁוּעוֹת אֶשָּׂא וּבְשֵׁם יְיָ אֶקְרָא׃

*Then, with the cup of wine, spices and a burning candle, the following Bracha
is said:*

בָּרוּךְ אַתָּה יְיָ, אֱלֹהֵינוּ מֶלֶךְ הָעוֹלָם, בּוֹרֵא פְּרִי הַגָּפֶן׃

*The cup is put down, the spices are taken up, and the following is said before
smelling the odor:*

בָּרוּךְ אַתָּה יְיָ, אֱלֹהֵינוּ מֶלֶךְ הָעוֹלָם, בּוֹרֵא מִינֵי בְשָׂמִים׃

The hand is brought close to the flame and the following is said:

בָּרוּךְ אַתָּה יְיָ, אֱלֹהֵינוּ מֶלֶךְ הָעוֹלָם, בּוֹרֵא מְאוֹרֵי הָאֵשׁ׃

The cup is taken back in the hand and the following is said:

בָּרוּךְ אַתָּה יְיָ, אֱלֹהֵינוּ מֶלֶךְ הָעוֹלָם, הַמַּבְדִּיל בֵּין קֹדֶשׁ לְחוֹל
בֵּין אוֹר לְחֹשֶׁךְ בֵּין יִשְׂרָאֵל לָעַמִּים׃ בֵּין יוֹם הַשְּׁבִיעִי לְשֵׁשֶׁת יְמֵי
הַמַּעֲשֶׂה׃ בָּרוּךְ אַתָּה יְיָ, הַמַּבְדִּיל בֵּין קֹדֶשׁ לְחוֹל׃

וְיוֹשֵׁב וְשׁוֹתֶה הַכּוֹס, וְיֵזִיר ט מֵעַט־יִין וְיַשְׁפִּיךְ עַל הַשֻׁלְחָן וּמְכַבֶּה ט בּ׳ וּלְאַחַר הַבְדָּלָה
אוֹמְרִים פִּיוּט הַמַּבְדִּיל יְכֹ׳ וְהַתְחָנָה רִבּוֹן הָעוֹלָמִים וְכוּ׳׃

הַמַּבְדִּיל בֵּין קֹדֶשׁ לְחוֹל׃ חַטֹּאתֵינוּ יִמְחוֹל׃ זַרְעֵנוּ
וְכַסְפֵּנוּ יַרְבֶּה כַחוֹל׃ וְכַכּוֹכָבִים בַּלַּיְלָה׃ יוֹם פָּנָה כְּצֵל
תֹּמֶר׃ אֶקְרָא לָאֵל עָלַי גוֹמֵר׃ אָמַר שׁוֹמֵר׃ אָתָא בֹקֶר
וְגַם־לָיְלָה׃ צִדְקָתְךָ כְּהַר־תָּבוֹר׃ עַל חֲטָאַי עָבוֹר
תַּעֲבוֹר׃ כְּיוֹם אֶתְמוֹל כִּי יַעֲבוֹר׃ וְאַשְׁמוּרָה בַלַּיְלָה׃
חָלְפָה עוֹנַת מִנְחָתִי׃ מִי יִתֵּן מְנוּחָתִי׃ יָגַעְתִּי בְּאַנְחָתִי
אַשְׂחֶה בְכָל־לָיְלָה׃ קוֹלִי בַל יֻנְטָל׃ פְּתַח לִי שַׁעַר

is with us; the God of Yaakov is our high tower! — The Jews had light and joy, bliss and dignity. So be it with us. I shall raise the cup of the many forms of salvation and call in the Name of *God*.

Blessed be You, *God* our God, King of the Universe, Creator of the fruit of the vine.

Blessed be You, *God* our God, King of the Universe, Creator of the various kinds of spices.

Blessed be You, *God* our God, King of the Universe, Creator of the flames of the fire.

Blessed be You, *God* our God, King of the Universe, Who has made a distinction between holy and profane, between light and darkness, between Yisrael and the nations, between the Seventh Day and the six days of work. Blessed be You, *God,* Who has made a distinction between holy and profane.

Thus the symbol of *besamim* at the conclusion of our Sabbath should remind us to take with us into weekday life the higher spiritual quickening and exaltation which we have won through our observance of the Sabbath, and to keep these spiritual values intact even in the midst of the toil and strife of the workday week.

מאורי האש: Fire, produced by human skill, with which we brighten our nights, is the foremost, indeed the one indispensable creative tool which the mind of man can employ to adapt earth's resources for his service. It is the most conspicuous symbol of man's dominion over all the earthly world. In accordance with God's command, as a sign of our homage and subordination to Him as the sole true Creator and Ruler of the Universe, we refrain from employing the power of fire on the Sabbath Day and resume the use of this mighty creative force only when the workday week begins again. Therefore it is certainly an ordinance of profound wisdom that bids us take the torch of fire in hand as we enter anew into the everyday life of the working week and that teaches us to look up and bless Him Who created the element of fire that lies dormant within earthly matter so that man, by his skill, may bring it forth from there to serve him in his dominion over the earth.

הַמַּנְטָל · שֶׁרֹאשִׁי נִמְלָא טָל · קְוֻצּוֹתַי רְסִיסֵי לָיְלָה:
הֵעָתֵר נוֹרָא וְאָיוֹם · אֲשַׁוֵּעַ תְּנָה פִּדְיוֹם · בְּנֶשֶׁף בְּעֶרֶב
יוֹם · בְּאִישׁוֹן לָיְלָה: קְרָאתִיךָ יָהּ הוֹשִׁיעֵנִי · אֹרַח
חַיִּים תּוֹדִיעֵנִי · מִדַּלָּה תְבַצְּעֵנִי · מִיּוֹם עַד לָיְלָה: טַהֵר
טִנּוּף מַעֲשַׂי · פֶּן יֹאמְרוּ מַכְעִיסַי · אַיֵּה אֱלוֹהַּ עוֹשָׂי · נֹתֵן
זְמִרוֹת בַּלָּיְלָה: נַחְנוּ בְיָדְךָ כַּחֹמֶר · סְלַח נָא עַל קַל
וָחֹמֶר · יוֹם לְיוֹם יַבִּיעַ אֹמֶר · וְלַיְלָה לְלָיְלָה: הַמַּבְדִּיל·

זה הרנון היכירוהו רז"ל בירושלמי פרק אין עומדין.

רִבּוֹן הָעוֹלָמִים אַב הָרַחֲמִים וְהַסְּלִיחוֹת, בְּסִמָּן טוֹב וּבְמַזָּל טוֹב
הָחֵל עָלֵינוּ אֶת־(שֵׁשֶׁת) יְמֵי הַמַּעֲשֶׂה הַבָּאִים לִקְרָאתֵנוּ לְשָׁלוֹם,
חֲשׂוּכִים מִכָּל־חֵטְא וָפֶשַׁע וּמְנֻקִּים מִכָּל־עָוֹן וְאַשְׁמָה וָרֶשַׁע,
וּמְדֻבָּקִים בְּתַלְמוּד תּוֹרָה וּבְמַעֲשִׂים טוֹבִים וַחֲנוּנִים דֵּעָה בִּינָה
וְהַשְׂכֵּל מֵאִתְּךָ, וְתַשְׁמִיעֵנוּ בָּהֶם שָׂשׂוֹן וְשִׂמְחָה וְלֹא תַעֲלֶה
קִנְאָתֵנוּ עַל־לֵב אָדָם וְלֹא קִנְאַת אָדָם תַּעֲלֶה עַל־לִבֵּנוּ· מַלְכֵּנוּ
אֱלֹהֵינוּ הָאָב הָרַחֲמָן, שִׂים בְּרָכָה וּרְוָחָה וְהַצְלָחָה בְּכָל־מַעֲשֵׂה
יָדֵינוּ, וְכָל־הַיּוֹעֵץ עָלֵינוּ וְעַל־עַמְּךָ בֵּית יִשְׂרָאֵל עֵצָה טוֹבָה
וּמַחֲשָׁבָה טוֹבָה אַמְּצוֹ וּבָרְכוֹ גַּדְּלוֹ וְקַיְּמוֹ קַיֵּם עֲצָתוֹ, כַּדָּבָר שֶׁנֶּאֱמַר
יִתֶּן־לְךָ כִלְבָבֶךָ וְכָל־עֲצָתְךָ יְמַלֵּא· וְנֶאֱמַר· וְתִגְזַר־אֹמֶר וְיָקָם־לָךְ
וְעַל־דְּרָכֶיךָ נָגַהּ אוֹר: וְכָל־הַיּוֹעֵץ עָלֵינוּ וְעַל־עַמְּךָ בֵּית יִשְׂרָאֵל
עֵצָה שֶׁאֵינָהּ טוֹבָה תּוֹפַר עֲצָתוֹ, כַּדָּבָר שֶׁנֶּאֱמַר יְיָ הֵפִיר עֲצַת
גּוֹיִם הֵנִיא מַחְשְׁבוֹת עַמִּים· וְנֶאֱמַר עֻצוּ עֵצָה וְתֻפָר וְחָפֵר דַּבְּרוּ דָבָר
וְלֹא יָקוּם כִּי עִמָּנוּ אֵל: וּפְתַח לָנוּ יְיָ אֱלֹהֵינוּ אַב הָרַחֲמִים אֲדוֹן
הַסְּלִיחוֹת בָּזֶה הַשָּׁבוּעַ וּבְכָל־שָׁבוּעַ, שַׁעֲרֵי אוֹרָה שַׁעֲרֵי אֹרֶךְ יָמִים

וְשָׁנִים שַׁעֲרֵי אֲרִיכַת אַפַּיִם, שַׁעֲרֵי בְרָכָה שַׁעֲרֵי בִינָה, שַׁעֲרֵי
גִּילָה שַׁעֲרֵי גְדֻלָּה שַׁעֲרֵי גְאֻלָּה שַׁעֲרֵי גְבוּרָה, שַׁעֲרֵי דִיצָה שַׁעֲרֵי
דֵעָה, שַׁעֲרֵי הוֹד שַׁעֲרֵי הָדָר שַׁעֲרֵי הַצְלָחָה שַׁעֲרֵי הַרְוָחָה, שַׁעֲרֵי
וַעַד טוֹב, שַׁעֲרֵי זְרִיזוּת שַׁעֲרֵי זִמְרָה שַׁעֲרֵי זְכֻיּוֹת שַׁעֲרֵי זִיו שַׁעֲרֵי
זֹהַר תּוֹרָה שַׁעֲרֵי זֹהַר חָכְמָה שַׁעֲרֵי זֹהַר בִּינָה שַׁעֲרֵי זֹהַר הַדַּעַת,
שַׁעֲרֵי חֶדְוָה שַׁעֲרֵי חֶמְלָה שַׁעֲרֵי חֵן וָחֶסֶד שַׁעֲרֵי חַיִּים טוֹבִים
שַׁעֲרֵי חָכְמָה, שַׁעֲרֵי טוֹבָה שַׁעֲרֵי טֹהַר, שַׁעֲרֵי יְשׁוּעָה שַׁעֲרֵי יֹשֶׁר,
שַׁעֲרֵי כַפָּרָה שַׁעֲרֵי כַלְכָּלָה שַׁעֲרֵי כָבוֹד, שַׁעֲרֵי לִמּוּד, שַׁעֲרֵי
מָזוֹן שַׁעֲרֵי מְנוּחוֹת שַׁעֲרֵי מְחִילוֹת שַׁעֲרֵי מַדָּע, שַׁעֲרֵי נֶחָמָה
שַׁעֲרֵי נְקִיּוּת, שַׁעֲרֵי סְלִיחָה שַׁעֲרֵי סַיַּעְתָּא דִּי־שְׁמַיָּא, שַׁעֲרֵי עֶזְרָה,
שַׁעֲרֵי פְדוּת שַׁעֲרֵי פַרְנָסָה טוֹבָה, שַׁעֲרֵי צְדָקָה שַׁעֲרֵי צָהֳלָה,
שַׁעֲרֵי קְדֻשָּׁה שַׁעֲרֵי קוֹמְמִיּוּת, שַׁעֲרֵי רַחֲמִים שַׁעֲרֵי רָצוֹן שַׁעֲרֵי
רְפוּאָה שְׁלֵמָה, שַׁעֲרֵי שָׁלוֹם שַׁעֲרֵי שִׂמְחָה שַׁעֲרֵי שְׁמוּעוֹת טוֹבוֹת
שַׁעֲרֵי שַׁלְוָה, שַׁעֲרֵי תוֹרָה שַׁעֲרֵי תְּפִלָּה שַׁעֲרֵי תְּשׁוּבָה שַׁעֲרֵי
תְּשׁוּעָה כְּמוֹ שֶׁכָּתוּב וּתְשׁוּעַת צַדִּיקִים מֵיְיָ מָעוּזָּם בְּעֵת צָרָה:
וַיַּעְזְרֵם יְיָ וַיְפַלְּטֵם יְפַלְּטֵם מֵרְשָׁעִים וְיוֹשִׁיעֵם כִּי חָסוּ בוֹ: וְנֶאֱמַר
חָשַׂף יְיָ אֶת זְרוֹעַ קָדְשׁוֹ לְעֵינֵי כָל־הַגּוֹיִם וְרָאוּ כָּל־אַפְסֵי־אָרֶץ
אֵת יְשׁוּעַת אֱלֹהֵינוּ: וְנֶאֱמַר קוֹל צֹפַיִךְ נָשְׂאוּ קוֹל יַחְדָּו יְרַנֵּנוּ כִּי
עַיִן בְּעַיִן יִרְאוּ בְּשׁוּב יְיָ צִיּוֹן: וְקַיֵּם לָנוּ יְיָ אֱלֹהֵינוּ מִקְרָא שֶׁכָּתוּב
מַה־נָּאווּ עַל־הֶהָרִים רַגְלֵי מְבַשֵּׂר מַשְׁמִיעַ שָׁלוֹם מְבַשֵּׂר טוֹב
מַשְׁמִיעַ יְשׁוּעָה אֹמֵר לְצִיּוֹן מָלַךְ אֱלֹהָיִךְ: רִאשׁוֹן לְצִיּוֹן הִנֵּה
הִנָּם וְלִירוּשָׁלַיִם מְבַשֵּׂר אֶתֵּן · אָמֵן סֶלָה:

On Passover, Shavuoth and Succoth, as well as on Rosh Chodesh and
Chanukkah, the Hallel is recited immediately after the Shemone Esrei of the
Morning Prayer. סדר נטילת לולב—page 612

בָּרוּךְ אַתָּה יְיָ אֱלֹהֵינוּ מֶלֶךְ הָעוֹלָם אֲשֶׁר
קִדְּשָׁנוּ בְּמִצְוֹתָיו וְצִוָּנוּ לִקְרוֹא אֶת־הַהַלֵּל:

קי״ג הַלְלוּיָהּ הַלְלוּ עַבְדֵי יְיָ הַלְלוּ אֶת־שֵׁם יְיָ: יְהִי שֵׁם
יְיָ מְבֹרָךְ מֵעַתָּה וְעַד־עוֹלָם: מִמִּזְרַח־שֶׁמֶשׁ עַד־מְבוֹאוֹ
מְהֻלָּל שֵׁם יְיָ: רָם עַל־כָּל־גּוֹיִם יְיָ עַל־הַשָּׁמַיִם כְּבוֹדוֹ:
מִי כַּיְיָ אֱלֹהֵינוּ הַמַּגְבִּיהִי לָשָׁבֶת: הַמַּשְׁפִּילִי לִרְאוֹת
בַּשָּׁמַיִם וּבָאָרֶץ: מְקִימִי מֵעָפָר דָּל מֵאַשְׁפֹּת יָרִים
אֶבְיוֹן: לְהוֹשִׁיבִי עִם־נְדִיבִים עִם נְדִיבֵי עַמּוֹ: מוֹשִׁיבִי
עֲקֶרֶת הַבַּיִת אֵם־הַבָּנִים שְׂמֵחָה הַלְלוּיָהּ:

קי״ד בְּצֵאת יִשְׂרָאֵל מִמִּצְרָיִם בֵּית יַעֲקֹב מֵעַם לֹעֵז:
הָיְתָה יְהוּדָה לְקָדְשׁוֹ יִשְׂרָאֵל מַמְשְׁלוֹתָיו: הַיָּם רָאָה
וַיָּנֹס הַיַּרְדֵּן יִסֹּב לְאָחוֹר: הֶהָרִים רָקְדוּ כְאֵילִים
גְּבָעוֹת כִּבְנֵי־צֹאן: מַה־לְּךָ הַיָּם כִּי תָנוּס הַיַּרְדֵּן תִּסֹּב
לְאָחוֹר: הֶהָרִים תִּרְקְדוּ כְאֵילִים גְּבָעוֹת כִּבְנֵי־צֹאן:
מִלִּפְנֵי אָדוֹן חוּלִי אָרֶץ מִלִּפְנֵי אֱלֽוֹהַּ יַעֲקֹב: הַהֹפְכִי
הַצּוּר אֲגַם־מָיִם חַלָּמִישׁ לְמַעְיְנוֹ־מָיִם:

הלל: Originally the reading of the *Hallel* had been intended only for
days commemorating the major instances of miraculous deliverance in our
history; namely, Passover, Shavuoth, Succoth and Chanukkah (Pesachim 17a,
Taanith 28b). On Purim the Reading of the Megillah takes the place of the
recital of Hallel. (Megillah 14a; Maimonides: *Hilchoth Megillah* 3:6). As
time went on, however, even the mere survival of the people of Yisrael in

On Passover, Shavuoth and Succoth, as well as on Rosh Chodesh and Chanukkah, the Hallel is recited immediately after the Shemone Esrei of the Morning Prayer.

Blessed be You, O *God* our God, King of the Universe, Who has sanctified us by His commandments and commanded us to read the *Hallel*.

Halaluyah! Praise, O servants of *God*, laud *God* in praise of His mighty acts. Blessed be the Name of *God* from this time forth and into eternity. Indeed, from the rising of the sun until its setting, the Name of *God* is lauded in praises of His mighty acts. [For] *God* is high above all nations; His glory is beyond the heavens. But who is like *God* our God, Who, though [He is] enthroned on high, looks down so deeply, into the heavens and upon the earth? He raises out of the dust him who has sunk low and lifts the defenseless up from the dunghill to set him next to princes, next to the princes of His people. He causes the barren woman of the house to sit as a joyous mother of children; Halaluyah!

When Yisrael went forth from Mitzrayim, the House of Yaakov forth from a people of alien tongue, Yehudah became His sanctuary, Yisrael His sphere of dominion. The sea saw it and fled, the Jordan sought to turn backward. The mountains skipped like rams, the hills like young sheep. What ails you, O sea, that you flee; O Jordan, that you turn backward; O mountains, that you skip like rams; O hills, like young sheep? Tremble, O earth, before the Master, before the God of Yaakov, Who turns the rock into a pool of water, pebbles into a fountain of water.

---

exile came to be considered one single, constant miracle of Divine deliverance. Even the Men of the Great Assembly already considered Yisrael's persevering survival in exile as no less a demonstration of God's omnipotence and majesty than any of the extroardinary, miraculous acts of God that are part of the history of the founding of Israel as a nation (Yoma 69b). Originally, the leaders in Yisrael had kept a list of all the days commemorating the deliverance of the Jewish people from major perils, anniversaries which were then declared as holidays on which *ta'anith vehesped* fasting and eulogies were forbidden. That list is still preserved for us to this day under the title of *Megillath Ta'anith*. As the Galuth continued, however, the dangers that beset the people of Yisrael became so numerous, and the instances of Divine rescue

On Rosh Chodesh and on the last six days of Passover, omit לֹא לָנוּ

קְטוֹ לֹא לָנוּ יְהוָֹה לֹא לָנוּ כִּי לְשִׁמְךָ תֵּן כָּבוֹד עַל־חַסְדְּךָ עַל־
אֲמִתֶּךָ: לָמָה יֹאמְרוּ הַגּוֹיִם אַיֵּה־נָא אֱלֹהֵיהֶם: וֵאלֹהֵינוּ בַשָּׁמָיִם
כֹּל אֲשֶׁר־חָפֵץ עָשָׂה: עֲצַבֵּיהֶם כֶּסֶף וְזָהָב מַעֲשֵׂה יְדֵי אָדָם: פֶּה
לָהֶם וְלֹא יְדַבֵּרוּ עֵינַיִם לָהֶם וְלֹא יִרְאוּ: אָזְנַיִם לָהֶם וְלֹא יִשְׁמָעוּ
אַף לָהֶם וְלֹא יְרִיחוּן: יְדֵיהֶם וְלֹא יְמִישׁוּן רַגְלֵיהֶם וְלֹא יְהַלֵּכוּ
לֹא־יֶהְגּוּ בִּגְרוֹנָם: כְּמוֹהֶם יִהְיוּ עֹשֵׂיהֶם כֹּל אֲשֶׁר־בֹּטֵחַ בָּהֶם:
יִשְׂרָאֵל בְּטַח בַּיהוָֹה עֶזְרָם וּמָגִנָּם הוּא: בֵּית אַהֲרֹן בִּטְחוּ בַיהוָֹה
עֶזְרָם וּמָגִנָּם הוּא: יִרְאֵי יְהוָֹה בִּטְחוּ בַיהוָֹה עֶזְרָם וּמָגִנָּם הוּא:

יְיָ זְכָרָנוּ יְבָרֵךְ יְבָרֵךְ אֶת־בֵּית יִשְׂרָאֵל יְבָרֵךְ אֶת־בֵּית
אַהֲרֹן: יְבָרֵךְ יִרְאֵי יְיָ הַקְּטַנִּים עִם־הַגְּדֹלִים: יֹסֵף
יְיָ עֲלֵיכֶם וְעַל־בְּנֵיכֶם: בְּרוּכִים אַתֶּם לַיְיָ עֹשֵׂה
שָׁמַיִם וָאָרֶץ: הַשָּׁמַיִם שָׁמַיִם לַיְיָ וְהָאָרֶץ נָתַן לִבְנֵי־
אָדָם: לֹא־הַמֵּתִים יְהַלְלוּ־יָהּ וְלֹא כָּל־יֹרְדֵי דוּמָה:
וַאֲנַחְנוּ נְבָרֵךְ יָהּ מֵעַתָּה וְעַד־עוֹלָם הַלְלוּיָהּ:

---

so manifold that, had the record of such anniversaries been continued, it
would have become necessary to declare nearly every day of the Jewish year
as a holiday. On the other hand, the authorities realized that danger and
deliverance had become so much a part of the very air which the people of
Yisrael breathed that many such instances could have come to pass by un-
noted. It is by no means improbable that the custom to read the *Hallel* on
every Rosh Chodesh had its origins in those days and was motivated by the
above considerations. For the institution of the reading of the Hallel on Rosh
Chodesh is not a *takkanath chazal,* but a *minhag* which has developed of
itself from out of our own life as a nation. However, it seems most appropriate
as a service of praise and thanksgiving, to keep us aware of the almighty rule
of God which keeps watch over us at all times and which is visibly demonstrated by the very fact of our survival even in Galuth. The Feast of the

On Rosh Chodesh and on the last six days of Passover, omit the following paragraph.

Not to us, *God* not to us, but to Your own Name give honor, for the sake of Your loving-kindness, for the sake of Your truth. Wherefore shall the nations say: "Where now is their God?" But our God is in the heavens, everything is as He has willed to bring it about. Their idols of silver and gold are the work of human hands; they have a mouth, but they do not speak; they have eyes, but they do not see; they have ears, but they do not hear; they have noses, but they do not smell; [they have] their hands, but they cannot touch with them; [they have] their feet, but they do not walk; they can breathe no sound with their throat. They who make them shall become like them; indeed, everyone who trusts in them. O Yisrael, trust in *God;* He is their help and their shield. O house of Aharon, trust in *God;* He is their help and their shield. O you who fear *God;* trust in *God,* He is their help and their shield.

God, Who has been mindful of us, He will bless. He will bless the House of Yisrael; He will bless the House of Aharon; He will bless those who fear *God* small and great alike; *God* will give you increase, to you and to your children. Blessed are you for *God,* the Maker of heaven and earth. The heavens are the heavens of *God,* but He has given the earth to the children of men. It is not the dead that proclaim God's might, and not all those who go down in silence. But as for us, we will bless the mighty *God* from this time forth and forever. Halaluyah!

New Moon is that *Mo'ed* institution which is fundamental to all the other *Mo'adim.* It represents the basis of our Jewish consciousness, a guarantee of the deliverance from sin which can be attained at any time through reunion with our God, and its symbol is the perpetual rejuvenation of the moon as it breaks forth from the cover of darkness to strive after the light. Like the moon, Yisrael, too, shall never be lost even when it walks in utter darkness. Yisrael is forever assured the possibility of a return to the light, if only it will not stray from the paths which have been assigned it by the Word of God. This thought is expressed in the blessing which we are to recite each month on beholding the New Moon.

We tone down the joy of the festival by shortening the Hallel on Rosh Chodesh and on the last six days of Pesach, days which commemorate the final downfall of the Egyptians and the deliverance of Israel from its enemies.

On Rosh Chodesh and on the last six days of Passover omit אהבתי

קטז אָהַבְתִּי כִּי יִשְׁמַע יְיָ אֶת־קוֹלִי תַּחֲנוּנָי: כִּי־הִטָּה אָזְנוֹ לִי
וּבְיָמַי אֶקְרָא: אֲפָפוּנִי חֶבְלֵי־מָוֶת וּמְצָרֵי שְׁאוֹל מְצָאוּנִי צָרָה
וְיָגוֹן אֶמְצָא: וּבְשֵׁם־יְיָ אֶקְרָא אָנָּה יְיָ מַלְּטָה נַפְשִׁי: חַנּוּן יְיָ וְצַדִּיק
וֵאלֹהֵינוּ מְרַחֵם: שֹׁמֵר פְּתָאיִם יְיָ דַּלּוֹתִי וְלִי יְהוֹשִׁיעַ: שׁוּבִי נַפְשִׁי
לִמְנוּחָיְכִי כִּי יְיָ גָּמַל עָלָיְכִי: כִּי חִלַּצְתָּ נַפְשִׁי מִמָּוֶת אֶת־עֵינִי מִן
דִּמְעָה אֶת־רַגְלִי מִדֶּחִי: אֶתְהַלֵּךְ לִפְנֵי יְיָ בְּאַרְצוֹת הַחַיִּים:
הֶאֱמַנְתִּי כִּי אֲדַבֵּר אֲנִי עָנִיתִי מְאֹד: אֲנִי אָמַרְתִּי בְחָפְזִי כָּל־
הָאָדָם כֹּזֵב:

מָה־אָשִׁיב לַיְיָ כָּל־תַּגְמוּלוֹהִי עָלָי: כּוֹס־יְשׁוּעוֹת
אֶשָּׂא וּבְשֵׁם יְיָ אֶקְרָא: נְדָרַי לַיְיָ אֲשַׁלֵּם נֶגְדָה־נָּא לְכָל
עַמּוֹ: יָקָר בְּעֵינֵי יְיָ הַמָּוְתָה לַחֲסִידָיו: אָנָּה יְיָ כִּי־אֲנִי
עַבְדֶּךָ אֲנִי עַבְדְּךָ בֶּן־אֲמָתֶךָ פִּתַּחְתָּ לְמוֹסֵרָי: לְךָ
אֶזְבַּח זֶבַח תּוֹדָה וּבְשֵׁם יְיָ אֶקְרָא: נְדָרַי לַיְיָ אֲשַׁלֵּם
נֶגְדָה־נָּא לְכָל־עַמּוֹ: בְּחַצְרוֹת בֵּית יְיָ בְּתוֹכֵכִי
יְרוּשָׁלָ͏ִם הַלְלוּיָהּ:

קיז הַלְלוּ אֶת־יְיָ כָּל־גּוֹיִם שַׁבְּחוּהוּ כָּל־הָאֻמִּים:
כִּי גָבַר עָלֵינוּ חַסְדּוֹ וֶאֱמֶת־יְיָ לְעוֹלָם הַלְלוּיָהּ:

Psalm 113 emphasizes the difference of the concept of God cherished
by the Jewish people from that held by the rest of the world. Psalm 114 deals
with the historic election and destiny of Israel . Psalm 115 discusses the ideas
and ideals which our obvious differences from the other nations must stir
up within us even while we dwell in their midst. Psalm 116 proclaims the
unshakeable trust which we should derive for the present and for all times to
come from the recollection of all the dangers we have experienced and overcome only through the help of God. This unalterable trust should serve to
sustain us constantly, regardless of the perils that the future may bring. At

On Rosh Chodesh and on the last six days of Passover omit the following paragraph.

I love my voice, indeed, my supplications, for *God* will hear. For He has inclined His ear to me in the past, and I will call [upon Him] in my fateful days. [When] the pains of death oppressed me, when the straits of the grave gained hold of me, when I faced trouble and sorrow, [when] I call upon the Name of God: "I beseech You, O *God,* deliver my soul," then *God* deals graciously [with me] and is just, and our God takes pity. *God* protects the unaware; I had been brought low, but He grants me new life. Return again and again, O my soul, to your resting places, for it is *God* Who has caused to ripen that which has come over you. But when You have delivered my soul from death, my eye from tears and my foot from stumbling, I shall walk before *God* in the lands of the living. So firmly convinced was I that I said it; I, who was so greatly afflicted. I said it during my hasty flight: "All mankind is deluded."

But what shall I do for *God* in return, once all His bounties, ripened, will have come over me? I shall raise the cup of salvation's many forms and call in the Name of *God.* I will fulfill my vows to *God;* O would that it were in the presence of all His people. Precious in the sight of *God* is even the ebb of life that has come to his devoted ones. If, O *God,* I am Your servant, I am Your servant only as the son of Your handmaid, O You Who has now loosened my bonds. I will bring You offerings to acknowledge my debt of gratitude, and call in the Name of *God.* I will fulfill my vows to *God;* O would that it were in the presence of all His people, in the courts of the House of *God,* in your midst, O Yerushalayim. Halaluyah!

O declare the praise of God's mighty acts, all you nations; laud Him, all you tribes of mankind. For His loving-kindness was mighty over us, and the faithfulness of *God* endures forever. Halaluyah!

---

the same time we are reminded that our miraculous survival qualifies us and obliges us to an ever growing degree to discharge our ordained task; namely, as the messengers of God, to call upon men and nations to recognize God and to worship Him. Such a call to all the nations is contained in the two verses that comprise Psalm 117. To this is joined Psalm 118, calling upon all men who thus return to God to join the Jewish nation in its homage

הוֹדוּ לַיְיָ כִּי־טוֹב   כִּי לְעוֹלָם חַסְדּוֹ: קְ הוֹדוּ ‏עיחה‎

יֹאמַר־נָא יִשְׂרָאֵל   כִּי לְעוֹלָם חַסְדּוֹ: קְ הוֹדוּ ‏חֹ‎

יֹאמְרוּ נָא בֵית־אַהֲרֹן   כִּי לְעוֹלָם חַסְדּוֹ: קְ הוֹדוּ ‏חֹ‎

יֹאמְרוּ נָא יִרְאֵי יְיָ   כִּי לְעוֹלָם חַסְדּוֹ: קְ הוֹדוּ ‏חֹ‎

מִן־הַמֵּצַר קָרָאתִי יָהּ עָנָנִי בַמֶּרְחַבְיָהּ: יְיָ לִי לֹא אִירָא
מַה־יַּעֲשֶׂה לִי אָדָם: יְיָ לִי בְּעֹזְרָי וַאֲנִי אֶרְאֶה בְשֹׂנְאָי:
טוֹב לַחֲסוֹת בַּיְיָ מִבְּטֹחַ בָּאָדָם: טוֹב לַחֲסוֹת בַּיְיָ מִבְּטֹחַ
בִּנְדִיבִים: כָּל־גּוֹיִם סְבָבוּנִי בְּשֵׁם יְיָ כִּי אֲמִילַם: סַבּוּנִי
גַם־סְבָבוּנִי בְּשֵׁם יְיָ כִּי אֲמִילַם: סַבּוּנִי כִדְבֹרִים דֹּעֲכוּ
כְּאֵשׁ קוֹצִים בְּשֵׁם יְיָ כִּי אֲמִילַם: דָּחֹה דְחִיתַנִי לִנְפֹּל וַיְיָ
עֲזָרָנִי: עָזִּי וְזִמְרָת יָהּ וַיְהִי־לִי לִישׁוּעָה: קוֹל רִנָּה
וִישׁוּעָה בְּאָהֳלֵי צַדִּיקִים יְמִין יְיָ עֹשָׂה חָיִל: יְמִין יְיָ
רוֹמֵמָה יְמִין יְיָ עֹשָׂה חָיִל: לֹא־אָמוּת כִּי אֶחְיֶה
וַאֲסַפֵּר מַעֲשֵׂי־יָהּ: יַסֹּר יִסְּרַנִּי יָּהּ וְלַמָּוֶת לֹא נְתָנָנִי:
פִּתְחוּ־לִי שַׁעֲרֵי־צֶדֶק אָבֹא בָם אוֹדֶה יָהּ: זֶה־הַשַּׁעַר
לַיְיָ צַדִּיקִים יָבֹאוּ בוֹ: אוֹדְךָ כִּי עֲנִיתָנִי וַתְּהִי־לִי
לִישׁוּעָה: אֶבֶן מָאֲסוּ הַבּוֹנִים הָיְתָה לְרֹאשׁ
פִּנָּה: אֶבֶן מָאֲסוּ הַבּוֹנִים הָיְתָה וֹּאת הִיא נִפְלָאת בְּעֵינֵינוּ:
מֵאֵת יְיָ הָיְתָה זֹּאת הִיא נִפְלָאת בְּעֵינֵינוּ:
מֵאֵת זֶה הַיּוֹם עָשָׂה יְיָ נָגִילָה וְנִשְׂמְחָה בוֹ: זֶה

החזן חוזר ומגן אנא והקל עונה.

אָנָּא יְיָ הוֹשִׁיעָה נָּא ‏אֲדֹנָי‎   אָנָּא יְיָ הוֹשִׁיעָה נָּא ‏אֲ‎

אָנָּא יְיָ הַצְלִיחָה נָּא ‏אֲדֹנָי‎   אָנָּא יְיָ הַצְלִיחָה נָּא: ‏אֲ‎

בָּרוּךְ הַבָּא בְּשֵׁם יְיָ בֵּרַכְנוּכֶם מִבֵּית יְיָ: בָּרוּךְ אֵל

Avow it to *God*, that He is good, that His loving-kindness
endures forever. So let Yisrael say it now, that His loving-kindness
endures forever. So let the House of Aharon say it now, that His
loving-kindness endures forever. So let those that fear *God* say it
now, that His loving-kindness endures forever. From out of straits
I called upon *God;* He answered me through the breadth of God.
God was for me; therefore I did not fear; what can man do to me?
If *God* is for me in my helpers, I shall calmly look upon those who
hate me. It is better to rely on *God* than to trust in man. It is better
to rely on *God* than to trust in princes. All the nations surrounded
me; it was with the Name of *God* that I faced them. They surrounded me; indeed, they closed in about me; it was with the Name of
God that I faced them. They surrounded me like ·bees; they were
put out as the fire of thorns; it was with the Name of *God* that
I faced them. True, you have struck me again and again that I might
fall, but *God* helped me. *God* was my strength and my song, and
this has become my salvation. Therefore let the voice of rejoicing
and salvation be in the tents of the righteous: "The right hand of
God does valiantly. The right hand of *God* has ever proven exalted.
The right hand of *God* does valiantly still." I shall not die, but I
shall live and recount the works of *God*. God has chastised me heavily, but He has not turned me over to death. Open for me the
gates of righteousness; I will enter into them and avow [my debt to]
God. This gate is God's, the righteous shall enter into it. I will avow
[my debt to] You, for You have answered me and have become my
salvation. The stone which the builders despised has become the
cornerstone. This is God's doing; it is marvelous in our own
eyes. *God* has made this day; we will rejoice in Him with our voices
and in our hearts.

"We beseech You, O *God*, grant new life;
we beseech You, O *God*, causes us to prosper."
"Let him who comes be blessed with the Name of *God*. We have

---

to Him, and, contemplating the events of Jewish history now taking place
before their very eyes, to adopt those convictions regarding the rule of God
and the calling of mankind which summon all men to enter into the gates
of the Jewish Sanctuary and to worship as "their God" that God Whose Law
is taught there.

יְיָ וַיָּאֶר לָנוּ אִסְרוּ־חַג בַּעֲבֹתִים עַד קַרְנוֹת הַמִּזְבֵּחַ: ٤
אֵלִי אַתָּה וְאוֹדֶךָּ אֱלֹהַי אֲרוֹמְמֶךָּ: ٤ הוֹדוּ לַיְיָ כִּי־
טוֹב כִּי לְעוֹלָם חַסְדּוֹ: הודו

יְהַלְלוּךָ יְיָ אֱלֹהֵינוּ (עַל) כָּל מַעֲשֶׂיךָ· וַחֲסִידֶיךָ צַדִּיקִים עוֹשֵׂי רְצוֹנֶךָ
וְכָל עַמְּךָ בֵּית יִשְׂרָאֵל בְּרִנָּה יוֹדוּ וִיבָרְכוּ וִישַׁבְּחוּ וִיפָאֲרוּ וִירוֹמְמוּ
וְיַעֲרִיצוּ וְיַקְדִּישׁוּ וְיַמְלִיכוּ אֶת שִׁמְךָ מַלְכֵּנוּ כִּי לְךָ טוֹב לְהוֹדוֹת
וּלְשִׁמְךָ נָאֶה לְזַמֵּר כִּי מֵעֹלָם וְעַד עֹלָם אַתָּה אֵל· בָּרוּךְ אַתָּה
יְיָ מֶלֶךְ מְהֻלָּל בַּתִּשְׁבָּחוֹת:

*The Reader recites the Kaddish; this is followed by the Reading from the
Torah. For the prayers before and after the Reading from the Torah for
Sabbaths and Holidays see p. 336; in the Weekday Prayer see p. 180*

blessed you out of the House of *God.*" "*God* is God when He has
given us light. Keep the festival offering bound with cords until you
reach the high corners of the altar." "You are my God; I shall acknowledge You; O my God, I will exalt You." Avow it to *God,* that He is
good, that His mercy endures forever.

All Your works shall proclaim Your praise, O *God* our God,
and let Your devoted ones, the righteous who do Your will, and
all Your people, the House of Yisrael, render homage with jubilation and bless and laud and extol and exalt, praise and sanctify and
glorify Your Name, O our King. For it is good to render You homage
and it is pleasant to sing to Your Name, for from eternity to eternity
You are God. Blessed be You, O *God,* King Whose praise is to be
proclaimed with hymns of praise.

אֲדֹנָי שְׂפָתַי תִּפְתָּח וּפִי יַגִּיד תְּהִלָּתֶךָ:

בָּרוּךְ אַתָּה יְיָ אֱלֹהֵינוּ וֵאלֹהֵי אֲבוֹתֵינוּ אֱלֹהֵי אַבְרָהָם אֱלֹהֵי יִצְחָק
וֵאלֹהֵי יַעֲקֹב הָאֵל הַגָּדוֹל הַגִּבּוֹר וְהַנּוֹרָא אֵל עֶלְיוֹן גּוֹמֵל חֲסָדִים
טוֹבִים וְקֹנֶה הַכֹּל וְזוֹכֵר חַסְדֵי אָבוֹת וּמֵבִיא גוֹאֵל לִבְנֵי בְנֵיהֶם
לְמַעַן שְׁמוֹ בְּאַהֲבָה · מֶלֶךְ עוֹזֵר וּמוֹשִׁיעַ וּמָגֵן · בָּרוּךְ אַתָּה יְיָ
מָגֵן אַבְרָהָם:

אַתָּה גִבּוֹר לְעוֹלָם אֲדֹנָי מְחַיֵּה מֵתִים אַתָּה רַב לְהוֹשִׁיעַ ·

From ר"ח חשון *until* ר"ח ניסן (inclusive) *the following is added:*
מַשִּׁיב הָרוּחַ וּמוֹרִיד הַגָּשֶׁם:

מְכַלְכֵּל חַיִּים בְּחֶסֶד מְחַיֵּה מֵתִים בְּרַחֲמִים רַבִּים סוֹמֵךְ נוֹפְלִים
וְרוֹפֵא חוֹלִים וּמַתִּיר אֲסוּרִים וּמְקַיֵּם אֱמוּנָתוֹ לִישֵׁנֵי עָפָר · מִי
כָמוֹךָ בַּעַל גְּבוּרוֹת וּמִי דּוֹמֶה לָּךְ מֶלֶךְ מֵמִית וּמְחַיֶּה וּמַצְמִיחַ
יְשׁוּעָה · וְנֶאֱמָן אַתָּה לְהַחֲיוֹת מֵתִים · בָּרוּךְ אַתָּה יְיָ מְחַיֵּה הַמֵּתִים:

הש"ץ אוֹמֵר קְדוּשַׁת נְקְדֵּשׁ זֵיטע 136.

אַתָּה קָדוֹשׁ וְשִׁמְךָ קָדוֹשׁ וּקְדוֹשִׁים בְּכָל יוֹם יְהַלְלוּךָ סֶּלָה ·
בָּרוּךְ אַתָּה יְיָ הָאֵל הַקָּדוֹשׁ:

תפלת מוסף לראש חדש בחול

זְמַן כַּפָּרָה. רָאשֵׁי חֳדָשִׁים: The renascence of the moon at the beginning
of our months has become the symbol of our own rebirth and of the redemption from sin and evil after which it is our task to strive. The renewal of the
moon is a symbol of the *kapparah*, of the elimination to be effected by our
own efforts, of all the dark stains that cloud our lives both material and
spiritual, as a result of our past transgressions. This rebirth and atonement

רָאשֵׁי חֳדָשִׁים לְעַמְּךָ נָתַתָּ זְמַן כַּפָּרָה לְכָל־תּוֹלְדוֹתָם · בִּהְיוֹתָם מַקְרִיבִים לְפָנֶיךָ זִבְחֵי רָצוֹן וּשְׂעִירֵי חַטָּאת לְכַפֵּר בַּעֲדָם · זִכָּרוֹן לְכֻלָּם יִהְיוּ · וּתְשׁוּעַת נַפְשָׁם מִיַּד שׂוֹנֵא: מִזְבֵּחַ חָדָשׁ בְּצִיּוֹן תָּכִין · וְעוֹלַת רֹאשׁ חֹדֶשׁ נַעֲלֶה עָלָיו וּשְׂעִירֵי עִזִּים נַעֲשֶׂה בְרָצוֹן · וּבַעֲבוֹדַת בֵּית הַמִּקְדָּשׁ נִשְׂמַח כֻּלָּנוּ · וּבְשִׁירֵי דָוִד עַבְדְּךָ הַנִּשְׁמָעִים בְּעִירֶךָ · הָאֲמוּרִים לִפְנֵי מִזְבְּחֶךָ: אַהֲבַת עוֹלָם תָּבִיא לָהֶם וּבְרִית אָבוֹת לַבָּנִים תִּזְכּוֹר: וַהֲבִיאֵנוּ לְצִיּוֹן עִירְךָ בְּרִנָּה וְלִירוּשָׁלַיִם בֵּית מִקְדָּשְׁךָ בְּשִׂמְחַת עוֹלָם · וְשָׁם נַעֲשֶׂה לְפָנֶיךָ אֶת קָרְבְּנוֹת חוֹבוֹתֵינוּ תְּמִידִים כְּסִדְרָם וּמוּסָפִים כְּהִלְכָתָם: וְאֶת מוּסַף יוֹם רֹאשׁ הַחֹדֶשׁ הַזֶּה נַעֲשֶׂה וְנַקְרִיב לְפָנֶיךָ בְּאַהֲבָה כְּמִצְוַת רְצוֹנֶךָ כְּמוֹ שֶׁכָּתַבְתָּ עָלֵינוּ בְּתוֹרָתֶךָ עַל־יְדֵי מֹשֶׁה עַבְדֶּךָ מִפִּי כְבוֹדֶךָ כָּאָמוּר:

וּבְרָאשֵׁי חָדְשֵׁיכֶם תַּקְרִיבוּ עֹלָה לַיְיָ פָּרִים בְּנֵי־בָקָר שְׁנַיִם וְאַיִל אֶחָד כְּבָשִׂים בְּנֵי־שָׁנָה שִׁבְעָה תְּמִימִם · וּמִנְחָתָם וְנִסְכֵּיהֶם

---

were expressed in symbolic terms by the New Moon offering. זבחי רצון are the *oloth*, the elevating-offerings, which are a free-will expression of our resolve ever to strive upward as it were, after the lofty goals set us by God. *Oloth* are the symbolic expression of our upward striving toward a new, rejuvenated future. שעירי חטאת symbolize atonement for a past clouded by sin, an atonement to be attained through the solemn pledge henceforth to persevere on the lofty plane of loyal fulfillment of our every duty. זכרון לכלם: the *korbenoth tzibbur* were purchased from a fund consisting of individual donations of half a shekel each that had to be made annually by every member of the House of Yisrael. Therefore these offerings served as a memorial representing *all* the contributors. Even in Exodus 30:16 we are already told of the half-shekel contributions that paid for the erection of the *adanim*, the base of the Sanctuary, that והיה לבני ישראל לזכרון לפני ה׳ לכפר על נפשותיכם. Through these contributions, a memorial before' God had been founded in behalf of every single member of the community of Yisrael so that atonement, too, would be granted for each and every Jewish individual. It is a זכרון לפני אלקינו the significance of which was stressed by the blowing of the *chatzo-*

The New Moons have You given to Your people, a season for atonement for all their generations, when they brought You free-will offerings and he-goats as sin offerings in order to obtain atonement for themselves. They were to be a memorial for them all, and a salvation of their soul from the hand of the enemy. A new altar will You set up in Tzion, and upon it we shall bring the elevating offering for the New Moon and prepare he-goats [symbolizing] the surrender of our own will. We shall all rejoice in the service of the Sanctuary and in the songs of David, Your servant, which were heard in Your city and uttered before Your altar. Love eternal will You bring them and You will remember the covenant of the fathers for the children. Bring us home with jubilation to Tzion Your city and to Yerushalayim, the abode of Your Sanctuary with joy everlasting. There we shall bring before You our obligatory offerings, the regular offerings according to their order, and the additional orders according to their rule. There we shall prepare the additional offering of this New Moon with love in accordance with the commandment of Your will, even as You have prescribed it as incumbent upon us in Your Torah through Moshe Your servant, by the sentence of Your glory, as it is said:

"And at the beginnings of your months you shall offer to *God* an elevating-offering: two young bullocks and one ram, yearling lambs seven in number, without blemish. And their gift of tribute

---

tzeroth when the *korbenoth tzibbur* were offered (Num. 10:9). (See Notes to *Ya'aleh veyavo* p. 146 above.)   שונא נפשנו refers to lust and wild passions which undermine the purity of our souls and our happiness even here on earth. ברצון : The offering of שעירי עזים which we bring on the New Moons should not be a routine act, performed without thought. The *sa'ir* is intended to be only a symbolic expression of our steadfast resistance to all evil which we should demonstrate by the surrender of our own will. אהבת עולם : Through these symbolic expressions of high resolve we ourselves should become worthy of God's love and thus benefit by the covenant which He made with our fathers. ובראשי חדשיכם· see p. 27 above.

לטובה. או״א חדש עלינו וגו׳ in order that we may receive that which is conducive to our "good" or our welfare. ולברכה : So that whatever we may have received may advance our salvation. ששון is jubilation evoked by extraordinary occurrences. שמחה is the gladness and joy that can be ours at all times.

כְּמִדְבָּר שְׁלֹשָׁה עֶשְׂרוֹנִים לַפָּר וּשְׁנֵי עֶשְׂרוֹנִים לָאַיִל וְעִשָּׂרוֹן לַכֶּבֶשׂ
וַיַּיִן כְּנִסְכּוֹ וְשָׂעִיר לְכַפֵּר וּשְׁנֵי תְמִידִים כְּהִלְכָתָם:

אֱלֹהֵינוּ וֵאלֹהֵי אֲבוֹתֵינוּ חַדֵּשׁ עָלֵינוּ אֶת־הַחֹדֶשׁ
הַזֶּה · לְטוֹבָה וְלִבְרָכָה · לְשָׂשׂוֹן וּלְשִׂמְחָה · לִישׁוּעָה
וּלְנֶחָמָה · לְפַרְנָסָה וּלְכַלְכָּלָה לְחַיִּים וּלְשָׁלוֹם ·
לִמְחִילַת חֵטְא וְלִסְלִיחַת עָוֹן (וּלְכַפָּרַת פָּשַׁע·) **In a leap year**
ר״ח אדר **until**
כִּי־בְעַמְּךָ יִשְׂרָאֵל בָּחַרְתָּ מִכָּל־הָאֻמּוֹת · וְחֻקֵּי רָאשֵׁי
חֳדָשִׁים לָהֶם קָבָעְתָּ · בָּרוּךְ אַתָּה יְיָ מְקַדֵּשׁ יִשְׂרָאֵל
וְרָאשֵׁי חֳדָשִׁים:

רְצֵה יְיָ אֱלֹהֵינוּ בְּעַמְּךָ יִשְׂרָאֵל וּבִתְפִלָּתָם · וְהָשֵׁב אֶת הָעֲבוֹדָה
לִדְבִיר בֵּיתֶךָ וְאִשֵּׁי יִשְׂרָאֵל וּתְפִלָּתָם בְּאַהֲבָה תְקַבֵּל בְּרָצוֹן וּתְהִי
לְרָצוֹן תָּמִיד עֲבוֹדַת יִשְׂרָאֵל עַמֶּךָ ·

וְתֶחֱזֶינָה עֵינֵינוּ בְּשׁוּבְךָ לְצִיּוֹן בְּרַחֲמִים · בָּרוּךְ אַתָּה יְיָ הַמַּחֲזִיר
שְׁכִינָתוֹ לְצִיּוֹן:

---

and their drink offerings as declared: three tenths for each bullock,
two tenths for the ram, and one tenth for each lamb, and wine like
its drink offering and one he-goat for atonement and two regular
offerings according to their rule.

Our God and God of our fathers, renew for us this month for
good and for blessing, for bliss and for joy, for salvation and consolation, for sustenance and maintenance, for life and for peace, for
the pardon of sin and the forgiveness of iniquity (and for the atonement of transgression). For You have chosen Your people Yisrael
from all nations, and instituted for them the statutes pertaining to
the beginnings of the months. Blessed be You, O *God,* Who hallows
Yisrael and the beginnings of the months.

מוֹדִים אֲנַחְנוּ לָךְ שָׁאַתָּה הוּא יְיָ אֱלֹהֵינוּ וֵאלֹהֵי אֲבוֹתֵינוּ
לְעוֹלָם וָעֶד· צוּר חַיֵּינוּ מָגֵן יִשְׁעֵנוּ אַתָּה הוּא לְדוֹר וָדוֹר· נוֹדֶה
לְּךָ וּנְסַפֵּר תְּהִלָּתֶךָ עַל חַיֵּינוּ הַמְּסוּרִים בְּיָדֶךָ וְעַל נִשְׁמוֹתֵינוּ
הַפְּקוּדוֹת לָךְ וְעַל נִסֶּיךָ שֶׁבְּכָל יוֹם עִמָּנוּ וְעַל נִפְלְאוֹתֶיךָ וְטוֹבוֹתֶיךָ
שֶׁבְּכָל עֵת· עֶרֶב וָבֹקֶר וְצָהֳרָיִם· הַטּוֹב כִּי לֹא כָלוּ רַחֲמֶיךָ
וְהַמְרַחֵם כִּי לֹא תַמּוּ חֲסָדֶיךָ מֵעוֹלָם קִוִּינוּ לָךְ:

On Chanukah על הנסים (*p. 150*) *is here inserted:*

וְעַל־כֻּלָּם יִתְבָּרַךְ וְיִתְרוֹמַם שִׁמְךָ מַלְכֵּנוּ תָּמִיד
לְעוֹלָם וָעֶד: וְכֹל הַחַיִּים יוֹדוּךָ סֶּלָה וִיהַלְלוּ אֶת־
שִׁמְךָ בֶּאֱמֶת הָאֵל יְשׁוּעָתֵנוּ וְעֶזְרָתֵנוּ סֶלָה· בָּרוּךְ
אַתָּה יְיָ הַטּוֹב שִׁמְךָ וּלְךָ נָאֶה לְהוֹדוֹת:

The חזן *adds this at the repetition of the* ש״ע:

אֱלֹהֵינוּ וֵאלֹהֵי אֲבוֹתֵינוּ בָּרְכֵנוּ בַּבְּרָכָה הַמְשֻׁלֶּשֶׁת בַּתּוֹרָה
הַכְּתוּבָה עַל יְדֵי מֹשֶׁה עַבְדֶּךָ הָאֲמוּרָה מִפִּי אַהֲרֹן וּבָנָיו
כֹּהֲנִים עַם קְדוֹשֶׁךָ כָּאָמוּר: יְבָרֶכְךָ יְיָ וְיִשְׁמְרֶךָ: יָאֵר יְיָ פָּנָיו
אֵלֶיךָ וִיחֻנֶּךָּ: יִשָּׂא יְיָ פָּנָיו אֵלֶיךָ וְיָשֵׂם לְךָ שָׁלוֹם:

שִׂים שָׁלוֹם טוֹבָה וּבְרָכָה חֵן וָחֶסֶד וְרַחֲמִים עָלֵינוּ וְעַל כָּל־
יִשְׂרָאֵל עַמֶּךָ בָּרְכֵנוּ אָבִינוּ כֻּלָּנוּ כְּאֶחָד בְּאוֹר פָּנֶיךָ כִּי בְאוֹר
פָּנֶיךָ נָתַתָּ לָּנוּ יְיָ אֱלֹהֵינוּ תּוֹרַת חַיִּים וְאַהֲבַת חֶסֶד וּצְדָקָה וּבְרָכָה
וְרַחֲמִים וְחַיִּים וְשָׁלוֹם וְטוֹב בְּעֵינֶיךָ לְבָרֵךְ אֶת־עַמְּךָ יִשְׂרָאֵל
בְּכָל־עֵת וּבְכָל־שָׁעָה בִּשְׁלוֹמֶךָ· בָּרוּךְ אַתָּה יְיָ הַמְבָרֵךְ אֶת־
עַמּוֹ יִשְׂרָאֵל בַּשָּׁלוֹם:

אֱלֹהַי· נְצוֹר לְשׁוֹנִי מֵרָע וּשְׂפָתַי מִדַּבֵּר מִרְמָה· וְלִמְקַלְלַי נַפְשִׁי
תִדּוֹם וְנַפְשִׁי כֶּעָפָר לַכֹּל תִּהְיֶה· פְּתַח לִבִּי בְּתוֹרָתֶךָ וּבְמִצְוֹתֶיךָ
תִּרְדּוֹף נַפְשִׁי· וְכָל הַחוֹשְׁבִים עָלַי רָעָה מְהֵרָה הָפֵר עֲצָתָם

וְקַלְקֵל מַחֲשַׁבְתָּם · עֲשֵׂה לְמַעַן שְׁמֶךָ עֲשֵׂה לְמַעַן יְמִינֶךָ עֲשֵׂה

לְמַעַן קְדֻשָּׁתֶךָ עֲשֵׂה לְמַעַן תּוֹרָתֶךָ · לְמַעַן יֵחָלְצוּן יְדִידֶיךָ

הוֹשִׁיעָה יְמִינְךָ וַעֲנֵנִי: יִהְיוּ לְרָצוֹן אִמְרֵי פִי וְהֶגְיוֹן לִבִּי לְפָנֶיךָ יְיָ

צוּרִי וְגֹאֲלִי: עֹשֶׂה שָׁלוֹם בִּמְרוֹמָיו הוּא יַעֲשֶׂה שָׁלוֹם עָלֵינוּ וְעַל

כָּל יִשְׂרָאֵל וְאִמְרוּ אָמֵן:

יְהִי רָצוֹן מִלְּפָנֶיךָ יְיָ אֱלֹהֵינוּ וֵאלֹהֵי אֲבוֹתֵינוּ שֶׁיִּבָּנֶה

בֵּית הַמִּקְדָּשׁ בִּמְהֵרָה בְיָמֵינוּ וְתֵן חֶלְקֵנוּ בְּתוֹרָתֶךָ:

וְשָׁם נַעֲבָדְךָ בְּיִרְאָה כִּימֵי עוֹלָם וּכְשָׁנִים קַדְמֹנִיּוֹת:

וְעָרְבָה לַיְיָ מִנְחַת יְהוּדָה וִירוּשָׁלָיִם כִּימֵי עוֹלָם וּכְשָׁנִים קַדְמֹנִיּוֹת:

תפלת מוסף של ר"ח שחל בשבת page 362

עֵרוּב תַּבְשִׁילִין

If the first day of a festival falls on Thursday or Friday, a special dish is prepared on ערב יו"ט so that one may cook enough on יו"ט to last for שבת. Bread is taken with some of the food which was cooked on ערב יו"ט (usually meat or fish) and the following Bracha is said:

בָּרוּךְ אַתָּה יְיָ, אֱלֹהֵינוּ מֶלֶךְ הָעוֹלָם, אֲשֶׁר

קִדְּשָׁנוּ בְּמִצְוֹתָיו וְצִוָּנוּ עַל מִצְוַת עֵרוּב:

בְּדֵן עֵרוּבָא יְהֵא שְׁרֵא לָנָא לְמֵיפָא וּלְבַשָּׁלָא וּלְאַטְמָנָא

וּלְאַדְלָקָא שְׁרָגָא וּלְמֶעְבַּד כָּל־צָרְכָּנָא מִיּוֹמָא טָבָא

לְשַׁבְּתָא לָנוּ וּלְכָל־הַדָּרִים בָּעִיר הַזֹּאת:

Blessed be You, O *God* our God, King of the Universe, Who has sanctified us by Your commandments and commanded us concerning the commandment of the *Eruv*.

By means of this *Eruv* may we be permitted to bake, cook, keep food warm, kindle lights and prepare on the Holiday all that we require for the Sabbath, we and all the inhabitants of this city.

עירוב תבשילין On Yom Tov we are permitted to prepare only those meals that are to be eaten on the holiday itself. We must not prepare any food that is meant to be consumed only after the holiday. Even if the day following the festival is a Sabbath, the food intended to be eaten on that Sabbath may be prepared on the holiday only if such preparation was begun before the onset of the festival. Thus we are to be reminded that we must not begin the preparation of food on Yom Tov, not even for the Sabbath, to say nothing of the stern prohibition against the preparation, on a holiday, of food for a regular working day. The symbolic dish which is prepared before a holiday followed immediately by a Sabbath in order to safeguard the sanctity of the Yom Tov is called *Eruv*. This designation is a carry-over from the term עירובי חצרות which denotes a symbolic dish employed to safeguard the sanctity of the Sabbath. It is only in the sense of this latter term that the word *Eruv* is acually employed in its literal connotation; i.e. that of "mingling':' or "commingling". For the *Eruv* symbolically effects the setting aside of boundaries between *reshuyoth,* territories, thus "commingling" two separate areas, making them one single zone.

סדר התפלה לרגלים
תפלת ערבית ושחרית ומנחה.
אֲדֹנָי שְׂפָתַי תִּפְתָּח וּפִי יַגִּיד תְּהִלָּתֶךָ:

בָּרוּךְ אַתָּה יְיָ אֱלֹהֵינוּ וֵאלֹהֵי אֲבוֹתֵינוּ אֱלֹהֵי אַבְרָהָם אֱלֹהֵי יִצְחָק וֵאלֹהֵי יַעֲקֹב הָאֵל הַגָּדוֹל הַגִּבּוֹר וְהַנּוֹרָא אֵל עֶלְיוֹן גּוֹמֵל חֲסָדִים טוֹבִים וְקוֹנֵה הַכֹּל וְזוֹכֵר חַסְדֵי אָבוֹת וּמֵבִיא גוֹאֵל לִבְנֵי בְנֵיהֶם לְמַעַן שְׁמוֹ בְּאַהֲבָה · מֶלֶךְ עוֹזֵר וּמוֹשִׁיעַ וּמָגֵן · בָּרוּךְ אַתָּה יְיָ מָגֵן אַבְרָהָם:

אַתָּה גִבּוֹר לְעוֹלָם אֲדֹנָי מְחַיֵּה מֵתִים אַתָּה רַב לְהוֹשִׁיעַ ·

פסח. of the first day of מוסף is inserted until מוסף שמיני עצרת, משיב הרוח מוסף
מַשִּׁיב הָרוּחַ וּמוֹרִיד הַגָּשֶׁם:

מְכַלְכֵּל חַיִּים בְּחֶסֶד מְחַיֶּה מֵתִים בְּרַחֲמִים רַבִּים סוֹמֵךְ נוֹפְלִים
וְרוֹפֵא חוֹלִים וּמַתִּיר אֲסוּרִים וּמְקַיֵּם אֱמוּנָתוֹ לִישֵׁנֵי עָפָר · מִי
כָמוֹךָ בַּעַל גְּבוּרוֹת וּמִי דּוֹמֶה לָּךְ מֶלֶךְ מֵמִית וּמְחַיֶּה וּמַצְמִיחַ
יְשׁוּעָה · וְנֶאֱמָן אַתָּה לְהַחֲיוֹת מֵתִים · בָּרוּךְ אַתָּה יְיָ מְחַיֵּה הַמֵּתִים:

בְּשַׁחֲרִית וּבְמִנְחָה הַשַּׁ"ץ אוֹמֵר קְדֻשַּׁת נִקְדַּשׁ P. 324

אַתָּה קָדוֹשׁ וְשִׁמְךָ קָדוֹשׁ וּקְדוֹשִׁים בְּכָל יוֹם יְהַלְלוּךָ סֶּלָה · בָּרוּךְ
אַתָּה יְיָ הָאֵל הַקָּדוֹשׁ:

אַתָּה בְחַרְתָּנוּ מִכָּל הָעַמִּים · אָהַבְתָּ אוֹתָנוּ · וְרָצִיתָ
בָּנוּ · וְרוֹמַמְתָּנוּ מִכָּל הַלְּשׁוֹנוֹת · וְקִדַּשְׁתָּנוּ בְּמִצְוֹתֶיךָ ·
וְקֵרַבְתָּנוּ מַלְכֵּנוּ לַעֲבוֹדָתֶךָ · וְשִׁמְךָ הַגָּדוֹל וְהַקָּדוֹשׁ
עָלֵינוּ קָרָאתָ:

At the Conclusion of the Sabbath

וַתּוֹדִיעֵנוּ יְיָ אֱלֹהֵינוּ אֶת מִשְׁפְּטֵי צִדְקֶךָ וַתְּלַמְּדֵנוּ לַעֲשׂוֹת חֻקֵּי
רְצוֹנֶךָ וַתִּתֶּן לָנוּ יְיָ אֱלֹהֵינוּ מִשְׁפָּטִים יְשָׁרִים וְתוֹרוֹת אֱמֶת חֻקִּים
וּמִצְוֹת טוֹבִים וַתַּנְחִילֵנוּ זְמַנֵּי שָׂשׂוֹן וּמוֹעֲדֵי קֹדֶשׁ וְחַגֵּי נְדָבָה ·
וַתּוֹרִישֵׁנוּ קְדֻשַּׁת שַׁבָּת וּכְבוֹד מוֹעֵד וַחֲגִיגַת הָרֶגֶל · וַתַּבְדֵּל יְיָ

תפלה לרגלים

אתה בחרתנו You have designated us for a specific task and destiny. **אהבת:**
You have found our character not entirely in contradiction with the sanctity
of Your own Being. **רצית:** You have deemed us a fit instrument for the
fulfillment of Your will. **ורוממתנו:** Among all the languages of mankind, it
is our tongue that You have chosen as the best suited vehicle for the revelation
of Your Torah and the message of Your prophets. **וקדשתנו:** And You have
constantly furthered the ennoblement of the spiritual and moral aspects of
our nature through the influence of Your commandments which we are to
fulfill. **וקרבתנו:** By giving us Your Law, You have become our King and so
have permitted us to draw near to You as Your loyal servants. **ושמך הגדול:**
By shaping all of our life's relationships and by Your evident guidance of
our destinies, You have made us the bearers of Your Name.

You have chosen us from among all peoples; You have loved us and taken pleasure in us. You have exalted us above all tongues and have sanctified us by Your commandments. You O our King, have drawn us near to Your service, and have called Your great and holy Name upon us.

At the Conclusion of the Sabbath

You, O *God* our God, have made known to us the ordinances of Your righteousness and taught us to perform the statutes of Your will. You, O *God* our God, have give us upright ordinances and teachings of truth, statutes and good commandments. You have caused us to inherit seasons of joy, holy festivals of assembly and rallying feasts for offerings of consecration. You gave us the holiness of the Sabbath as a heritage, the glory of festivals of assembly and the rallying feasts of the Pilgrim Festivals. And You, O *God* our God, have made a distinction between holy and profane, light and darkness,

---

ותודיענו : The Havdalah marks our passage from the sanctity of the Sabbath back to the working days of the week. In like manner, we must also recite a Havdalah to mark our transition from the holiness of the Sabbath to the lesser sanctity of the holiday. משפטי צדקך and חקי רצונך : Taken in a broader sense, all the commandments of God are *mishpatim* and *chukkim,* for they all teach us how to cope with every situation and how to fulfill our destiny, and they all work out for us the orbit within which we are to confine our own desires in accordance with the will of God. מצות, חקים, תורות, משפטים are the various categories of God's Law for the fulfillment of which the observance of our Sabbaths and Festivals should equip us, by renewing in our hearts the required understanding and attitudes. ותנחילנו : We are to observe our Sabbath and Festivals in such a manner as to be able to pass them on also to our descendants as their heritage. חגי נדבה, מעדי קדש, זמני ששון are all designations for the *regalim,* characterizing the various aspects of these Festivals. Each of the *regalim* has a dual significance, seasonal and historical. Viewed as "festive seasons", they are *zemanei sasson* seasons of great joy. Passover is the festival of spring; Shavuoth is that of the first fruits of the summer, and Succoth celebrates the rich autumn harvest. Historically speaking, the *regalim* are *mo'adei kodesh,* times appointed by God for us to meet with Him. Passover commemorates our liberation, Shavuoth celebrates the giving of the Law and Succoth recalls the tabernacles which the Children of Yisrael built in the wilderness. These are holidays through which, by means of the remembrance of the mighty acts of God at the time of the founding of our

אֱלֹהֵינוּ בֵּין קֹדֶשׁ לְחוֹל בֵּין אוֹר לְחֹשֶׁךְ בֵּין יִשְׂרָאֵל לָעַמִּים בֵּין
יוֹם הַשְּׁבִיעִי לְשֵׁשֶׁת יְמֵי הַמַּעֲשֶׂה בֵּין קְדֻשַּׁת שַׁבָּת לִקְדֻשַּׁת יוֹם
טוֹב הִבְדַּלְתָּ וְאֶת־יוֹם הַשְּׁבִיעִי מִשֵּׁשֶׁת יְמֵי הַמַּעֲשֶׂה קִדַּשְׁתָּ•
הִבְדַּלְתָּ וְקִדַּשְׁתָּ אֶת־עַמְּךָ יִשְׂרָאֵל בִּקְדֻשָּׁתֶךָ:

וַתִּתֶּן־לָנוּ יְיָ אֱלֹהֵינוּ בְּאַהֲבָה שַׁבָּתוֹת לִמְנוּחָה וּמוֹעֲדִים
לְשִׂמְחָה חַגִּים וּזְמַנִּים לְשָׂשׂוֹן אֶת־יוֹם הַשַּׁבָּת הַזֶּה וְאֶת יוֹם

לשמיני ועצרת ולש"ת.	לסכות	לשבועות	לבכח
הַשְּׁמִינִי חַג	חַג הַסֻּכּוֹת	חַג הַשָּׁבֻעוֹת	חַג הַמַּצּוֹת
הָעֲצֶרֶת הַזֶּה•	הַזֶּה• זְמַן	הַזֶּה• זְמַן	הַזֶּה• זְמַן
זְמַן שִׂמְחָתֵנוּ	שִׂמְחָתֵנוּ	מַתַּן תּוֹרָתֵנוּ	חֵרוּתֵנוּ

בְּאַהֲבָה מִקְרָא קֹדֶשׁ זֵכֶר לִיצִיאַת מִצְרָיִם:

---

nation, we always derive a new awareness of God's intimate relationship with us and of our own relationship with Him which requires of us that we sanctify all our lives. Seen from the vantage point of the gathering of our people around God and His Sanctuary, the *regalim* are *chagei nedavah* seasons when the entire nation rallies as in a circle, around its common focal point. They are symbolically expressed not only by the obligatory festival offerings of עולות ראיה and שלמי חגיגה, but also by the נדרים ונדבות, the free-will offerings of consecration, which, according to the precept in Lev. 23:28, had to be brought on *chol hamo'ed*. These symbolic acts were to make every individual son of Yisrael realize that even with respect to his most personal inner passions and emotions, he always had to regard himself a part of the whole and of the common Sanctuary. וחורישני: The sanctification of the Sabbath, the fitting tribute paid the *mo'ed* by the fulfillment of all the laws pertaining to it, and the *chaggigah* the festival offering by means of which we join the circle of the nation on the Pilgrim Festivals, are all a *Yerushah*, a blissful heritage which God granted us through the tradition of our fathers. Our holidays bear three designations; רגל, מועד, and חג. The term *mo'ed* implies the purpose of the Festival to renew our close relationship with God; *regel* implies our duty on these Festivals to make a pilgrimage to the Sanctuary of His Law; and *chag* indicates the reunion, thus renewed, of every individual with the "circle" of his national community. Thus the purpose of the Festivals is our renewed reunion with God, with His Law and finally with the nation.

Yisrael and the nations, between the Seventh Day and the six days of work. You have made a distinction between the sanctity of the Sabbath and the sanctity of Holiday, and You have sanctified the Seventh Day above the six working days; You have set apart Your people Yisrael and sanctified it by Your holiness.

And You have given us, O *God* our God, in love, (Sabbaths for rest and) festivals of assembly for rejoicing, festivals for rallying and seasons for delight, (this Sabbath day and) the day of

this Festival of Unleavened Bread, the season of our Freedom,

this Festival of Weeks, the season of the Giving of our Torah,

this Festival of Tabernacles, the season of our Rejoicing,

the Eighth Day, the Festival of Retaining, the season of our Rejoicing, (in love), a convocation to the Sanctuary, a remembrance of the Exodus from Mitzrayim.

Accordingly, we have three different types of offerings to symbolize each aspect of the holidays. *Shalmei simchah* express the purpose of the *mo'ed*, *oloth reiyah* that of the *regel*, and *chaggigah* that of the *chag.* ותבדל See above p. 549. בין קדושת שבת וכו': The sanctification of the Seventh Day should serve to impart holiness also to all our workday activities during the six days of the week to follow. In like manner, the greater sanctity of the Sabbath should be the source from which the holidays derive their holiness, for all the sanctity of the Festivals is based on the holiness of the Sabbath, as shown by the fact that the legislation in the twenty-third chapter of Leviticus which deals with the observance of the Festivals is preceded and introduced by the law pertaining to the observance of the Sabbath (Verse 3).

שבתות למנוחה: The *menuchah* of the Sabbath denotes not only the mandatory cessation from all weekday labor but also the inner peace which is to be derived directly through such subordination of all of the active and creative phases of our lives to the dominion of God.

ותתן לנו, On Sabbaths we repeatedly insert into our prayers the qualification *beahavah;* e.g. באהבה מקרא קודש. This does not refer to the "love" which *God* has shown *us* by giving us the Sabbath Day, for we also say ותתן לנו באהבה with reference to holidays. Instead, it denotes the love with which *we* celebrate the Sabbath. This may have a dual motive. The Festivals are dedicated to the remembrance of the giving of such national values as freedom, the Law, and the blessed harvest in which we rejoice. On the Sabbath, however, we celebrate solely our own pure relationship with God and our devotion to Him is then neither communicated, nor lessened, by any other consideration. It is the purest form of *ahavah* that fills our hearts on the Sabbath and that we demonstrate on that hallowed day. At the

אֱלֹהֵינוּ וֵאלֹהֵי אֲבוֹתֵינוּ · יַעֲלֶה וְיָבֹא וְיַגִּיעַ וְיֵרָאֶה וְיֵרָצֶה וְיִשָּׁמַע
וְיִפָּקֵד וְיִזָּכֵר זִכְרוֹנֵנוּ וּפִקְדוֹנֵנוּ וְזִכְרוֹן אֲבוֹתֵינוּ · וְזִכְרוֹן מָשִׁיחַ בֶּן
דָּוִד עַבְדֶּךָ · וְזִכְרוֹן יְרוּשָׁלַיִם עִיר קָדְשֶׁךָ · וְזִכְרוֹן כָּל־עַמְּךָ בֵּית
יִשְׂרָאֵל לְפָנֶיךָ · לִפְלֵיטָה וּלְטוֹבָה וּלְחֵן וּלְחֶסֶד וּלְרַחֲמִים וּלְחַיִּים
וּלְשָׁלוֹם בְּיוֹם לפסח חַג הַמַּצּוֹת · לשבועת חַג הַשָּׁבֻעוֹת · לסוכות חַג הַסֻּכּוֹת
לשמיני עצרת ולש״ת הַשְּׁמִינִי חַג הָעֲצֶרֶת הַזֶּה · זָכְרֵנוּ יְיָ אֱלֹהֵינוּ בּוֹ לְטוֹבָה,
וּפָקְדֵנוּ בוֹ לִבְרָכָה, וְהוֹשִׁיעֵנוּ בוֹ לְחַיִּים · וּבִדְבַר יְשׁוּעָה וְרַחֲמִים
חוּס וְחָנֵּנוּ וְרַחֵם עָלֵינוּ וְהוֹשִׁיעֵנוּ · כִּי אֵלֶיךָ עֵינֵינוּ · כִּי אֵל מֶלֶךְ
חַנּוּן וְרַחוּם אָתָּה:

וְהַשִּׂיאֵנוּ יְיָ אֱלֹהֵינוּ אֶת־בִּרְכַּת מוֹעֲדֶיךָ לְחַיִּים
וּלְשָׁלוֹם לְשִׂמְחָה וּלְשָׂשׂוֹן כַּאֲשֶׁר רָצִיתָ וְאָמַרְתָּ
לְבָרְכֵנוּ : לשבת אֱלֹהֵינוּ וֵאלֹהֵי אֲבוֹתֵינוּ רְצֵה בִמְנוּחָתֵנוּ קַדְּשֵׁנוּ
בְּמִצְוֹתֶיךָ וְתֵן חֶלְקֵנוּ בְּתוֹרָתֶךָ, שַׂבְּעֵנוּ מִטּוּבֶךָ
וְשַׂמְּחֵנוּ בִּישׁוּעָתֶךָ, וְטַהֵר לִבֵּנוּ לְעָבְדְּךָ בֶּאֱמֶת,
וְהַנְחִילֵנוּ יְיָ אֱלֹהֵינוּ בְּאַהֲבָה וּבְרָצוֹן בְּשִׂמְחָה וּבְשָׂשׂוֹן
שבת וּמוֹעֲדֵי קָדְשֶׁךָ, וְיִשְׂמְחוּ בְךָ יִשְׂרָאֵל מְקַדְּשֵׁי
שְׁמֶךָ · בָּרוּךְ אַתָּה יְיָ, מְקַדֵּשׁ השבת וְיִשְׂרָאֵל וְהַזְּמַנִּים:

---

same time, the Sabbath, by virtue of the cessation thereon of every workday
activity with which man may wield dominion over the physical world, betokens the most complete negation of all selfish arrogance. The obedience
which we render to this Sabbath Day is not grudgingly given. Instead, this
our obedience is in itself the expression of our perfect love of God, and we
rejoice at the opportunity of being able to demonstrate our feelings toward
Him by the most devoted fulfillment of His will. יעלה ויבא See above p. 146.

שמיני חג העצרת the Eighth Day of the Festival of Tabernacles, is a
separate festival in itself, רגל בפני עצמו. Its designation, atzereth, is derived
from the word atzor, meaning "to retain," or "to cause to remain." This
designation implies the entire purpose of the holiday; namely, to cause us
to "retain" all the impressions gained from the preceding seven days of the

Our God and God of our fathers, may our remembrance and the consideration of us and the remembrance of our fathers, the remembrance of Messiah the son of David Your servant, the remembrance of Yerushalayim, Your holy City, and the remembrance of all Your people, the House of Yisrael, rise and come, reach You and be seen, be accepted and heard, considered and remembered for deliverance and for well-being, for favor and loving-kindness, for compassion, for life and for peace on this day of — The Festival of Unleavened Bread — The Festival of Weeks — The Festival of Tabernacles. Remember us this day, O *God* our God, for good, be mindful of us for blessing, and save us for life; and in the promise of salvation and compassion spare us and favor us, for our eyes look up to You; for You, O God, are a gracious and compassionate King.

Cause us, O *God* our God, to take with us the blessing of Your festivals of assembly, for life and for peace, for joy and for bliss, even as You willed it, and did promise to bless us. (*On Sabbath, add:* Our God and God of our fathers, take pleasure in our rest) hallow us by Your commandments and grant our portion in Your Torah. Satisfy us from Your good, gladden us with Your salvation, purify our hearts to serve You in truth, and give us as an inheritance O *God* our God, (in love and favor), in joy and delight (the Sabbath and) Your holy festivals of assembly, so that Yisrael, Who sanctify Your Name, may rejoice in You. Blessed be You, O *God*, Who hallows (the Sabbath and) Yisrael and the seasons.

Festival, or better still, from the entire month of holidays that has gone before, so that we may take these impressions with us and apply them to our life of creative labor which we now resume, and so that they may not fade from our consciousness as a result of the manifold influences that await us in the workday world which we now re-enter after the end of our festive season.

והשיאנו: "Give us not only the blessings of Your festivals, but also cause us to take these blessings with us, out into our daily lives, so that *chayim*, and *shalom*, *simchah* and *sasson* may accrue to us thereby." By our reunion with God which takes place on the *Mo'adim* our strength for true and genuine living is renewed and intensified. At the same time this reunion helps us find a common ground for unity with all our brethren who, like ourselves, rally around God and His truth. It affords us the serenity which none can disturb and, at moments of special import, a heightened sense of that joy of living which, in the final analysis, can be found only with God, in

רְצֵה יְיָ אֱלֹהֵינוּ בְּעַמְּךָ יִשְׂרָאֵל וּבִתְפִלָּתָם · וְהָשֵׁב אֶת־הָעֲבוֹדָה
לִדְבִיר בֵּיתֶךָ, וְאִשֵּׁי יִשְׂרָאֵל וּתְפִלָּתָם בְּאַהֲבָה תְקַבֵּל בְּרָצוֹן
וּתְהִי לְרָצוֹן תָּמִיד עֲבוֹדַת יִשְׂרָאֵל עַמֶּךָ ·

וְתֶחֱזֶינָה עֵינֵינוּ בְּשׁוּבְךָ לְצִיּוֹן בְּרַחֲמִים · בָּרוּךְ אַתָּה יְיָ,
הַמַּחֲזִיר שְׁכִינָתוֹ לְצִיּוֹן:

מוֹדִים אֲנַחְנוּ לָךְ שָׁאַתָּה הוּא יְיָ אֱלֹהֵינוּ וֵאלֹהֵי אֲבוֹתֵינוּ לְעוֹלָם
וָעֶד · צוּר חַיֵּינוּ מָגֵן יִשְׁעֵנוּ אַתָּה הוּא לְדוֹר וָדוֹר · נוֹדֶה לְךָ וּנְסַפֵּר
תְּהִלָּתֶךָ עַל חַיֵּינוּ הַמְּסוּרִים בְּיָדֶךָ וְעַל נִשְׁמוֹתֵינוּ הַפְּקוּדוֹת לָךְ וְעַל
נִסֶּיךָ שֶׁבְּכָל יוֹם עִמָּנוּ וְעַל נִפְלְאוֹתֶיךָ וְטוֹבוֹתֶיךָ שֶׁבְּכָל עֵת, עֶרֶב
וָבֹקֶר וְצָהֳרָיִם · הַטּוֹב כִּי לֹא כָלוּ רַחֲמֶיךָ וְהַמְרַחֵם כִּי לֹא־תַמּוּ
חֲסָדֶיךָ מֵעוֹלָם קִוִּינוּ לָךְ:

וְעַל כֻּלָּם יִתְבָּרַךְ וְיִתְרוֹמַם שִׁמְךָ מַלְכֵּנוּ תָּמִיד לְעוֹלָם וָעֶד: וְכָל
הַחַיִּים יוֹדוּךָ סֶּלָה וִיהַלְלוּ אֶת שִׁמְךָ בֶּאֱמֶת הָאֵל יְשׁוּעָתֵנוּ
וְעֶזְרָתֵנוּ סֶלָה · בָּרוּךְ אַתָּה יְיָ הַטּוֹב שִׁמְךָ וּלְךָ נָאֶה לְהוֹדוֹת:

The חזן adds this when repeating the ש״ע:

אֱלֹהֵינוּ וֵאלֹהֵי אֲבוֹתֵינוּ בָּרְכֵנוּ בַּבְּרָכָה הַמְשֻׁלֶּשֶׁת בַּתּוֹרָה
הַכְּתוּבָה עַל יְדֵי מֹשֶׁה עַבְדֶּךָ הָאֲמוּרָה מִפִּי אַהֲרֹן וּבָנָיו כֹּהֲנִים
עַם קְדוֹשֶׁךָ כָּאָמוּר: יְבָרֶכְךָ יְיָ וְיִשְׁמְרֶךָ: יָאֵר יְיָ פָּנָיו אֵלֶיךָ
וִיחֻנֶּךָּ: יִשָּׂא יְיָ פָּנָיו אֵלֶיךָ וְיָשֵׂם לְךָ שָׁלוֹם:

בְּשַׁחֲרִית אוֹמְרִים זֶה.

שִׂים שָׁלוֹם טוֹבָה וּבְרָכָה חֵן וָחֶסֶד
וְרַחֲמִים עָלֵינוּ וְעַל כָּל יִשְׂרָאֵל עַמֶּךָ בָּרְכֵנוּ
אָבִינוּ כֻּלָּנוּ כְּאֶחָד בְּאוֹר פָּנֶיךָ כִּי בְאוֹר
פָּנֶיךָ נָתַתָּ לָּנוּ יְיָ אֱלֹהֵינוּ תּוֹרַת חַיִּים וְאַהֲבַת
חֶסֶד וּצְדָקָה וּבְרָכָה וְרַחֲמִים וְחַיִּים וְשָׁלוֹם
וְטוֹב בְּעֵינֶיךָ לְבָרֵךְ אֶת־עַמְּךָ יִשְׂרָאֵל
בְּכָל־עֵת וּבְכָל־שָׁעָה בִּשְׁלוֹמֶךָ:
בָּרוּךְ אַתָּה יְיָ הַמְבָרֵךְ אֶת־עַמּוֹ יִשְׂרָאֵל בַּשָּׁלוֹם:

בְּמִנְחָה וּבְעַרְבִית אוֹמְרִין זֶה:

שָׁלוֹם רָב עַל יִשְׂרָאֵל
עַמְּךָ תָּשִׂים לְעוֹלָם כִּי
אַתָּה הוּא מֶלֶךְ אָדוֹן
לְכָל הַשָּׁלוֹם וְטוֹב
בְּעֵינֶיךָ לְבָרֵךְ אֶת־עַמְּךָ
יִשְׂרָאֵל בְּכָל־עֵת וּבְכָל
שָׁעָה בִּשְׁלוֹמֶךָ:

אֱלֹהַי · נְצוֹר לְשׁוֹנִי מֵרָע וּשְׂפָתַי מִדַּבֵּר מִרְמָה וְלִמְקַלְלַי נַפְשִׁי
תִדּוֹם וְנַפְשִׁי כֶּעָפָר לַכֹּל תִּהְיֶה · פְּתַח לִבִּי בְּתוֹרָתֶךָ וּבְמִצְוֹתֶיךָ
תִּרְדּוֹף נַפְשִׁי וְכָל הַחוֹשְׁבִים עָלַי רָעָה מְהֵרָה הָפֵר עֲצָתָם וְקַלְקֵל
מַחֲשַׁבְתָּם · עֲשֵׂה לְמַעַן שְׁמֶךָ · עֲשֵׂה לְמַעַן יְמִינֶךָ · עֲשֵׂה לְמַעַן
קְדֻשָּׁתֶךָ · עֲשֵׂה לְמַעַן תּוֹרָתֶךָ · לְמַעַן יֵחָלְצוּן יְדִידֶיךָ הוֹשִׁיעָה
יְמִינְךָ וַעֲנֵנִי: יִהְיוּ לְרָצוֹן אִמְרֵי פִי וְהֶגְיוֹן לִבִּי לְפָנֶיךָ יְיָ צוּרִי
וְגֹאֲלִי: עֹשֶׂה שָׁלוֹם בִּמְרוֹמָיו הוּא יַעֲשֶׂה שָׁלוֹם עָלֵינוּ וְעַל כָּל
יִשְׂרָאֵל וְאִמְרוּ אָמֵן:

יְהִי רָצוֹן מִלְּפָנֶיךָ יְיָ אֱלֹהֵינוּ וֵאלֹהֵי אֲבוֹתֵינוּ שֶׁיִּבָּנֶה
בֵּית הַמִּקְדָּשׁ בִּמְהֵרָה בְיָמֵינוּ וְתֵן חֶלְקֵנוּ בְּתוֹרָתֶךָ:
וְשָׁם נַעֲבָדְךָ בְּיִרְאָה כִּימֵי עוֹלָם וּכְשָׁנִים קַדְמֹנִיּוֹת:
וְעָרְבָה לַיְיָ מִנְחַת יְהוּדָה וִירוּשָׁלָיִם כִּימֵי עוֹלָם וּכְשָׁנִים קַדְמֹנִיּוֹת:

God and through God alone. מקדש השבת וישראל והזמנים: All the festive seasons have had their origin in the history of Yisrael's founding, and their
purpose is to help in effecting the fulfillment of the task which has been
set the people of Yisrael. It is only through the existence of Yisrael, then,
that these festivals came into being, and it is for the sake of Yisrael that they
continue to exist. The *kedushah* of Israel preceded that of the *zemanim*. The
kedushah of the festive seasons stems from the *kedushah* of Yisrael itself;
the very fixing of their dates each year is dependent upon the *ibbur shanah*
and the *kiddush hachodesh* which must be performed by the highest authority
in the Jewish nation. But the relationship of the Sabbath with Yisrael is
quite different. It is Yisrael that had its origins in the Sabbath. The institution
of the Sabbath was originally intended to conserve among all of mankind the
truths about God and man's relationship to Him. However, mankind had
forfeited it. Hence Yisrael was chosen to reestablish this sacred institution,
and to restore and spread among men the views of God and man's relationship to Him that are afforded us by the observance of the Sabbath. Thus
Yisrael actually came into being because of the Sabbath, and it is for the sake
of the Sabbath that Yisrael has survived. Hence the *kedushah* of the Sabbath
preceded that of Yisrael. Moreover, the appointment of the Sabbath, as
opposed to that of the Festivals, is not dependent upon Yisrael; the Sabbath
has been fixed and appointed by God Himself once and for all times to come.
Therefore, on holidays that occur on weekdays, the blessing ends with
מקדש ישראל והזמנים, but when the Festival is also a Sabbath the blessing we
say reads מקדש השבת וישראל והזמנים, for the sanctity of Israel is derived only
from the sanctity of the Sabbath.

אֲדֹנָי שְׂפָתַי תִּפְתָּח וּפִי יַגִּיד תְּהִלָּתֶךָ:

בָּרוּךְ אַתָּה יְיָ אֱלֹהֵינוּ וֵאלֹהֵי אֲבוֹתֵינוּ אֱלֹהֵי אַבְרָהָם אֱלֹהֵי יִצְחָק
וֵאלֹהֵי יַעֲקֹב הָאֵל הַגָּדוֹל הַגִּבּוֹר וְהַנּוֹרָא אֵל עֶלְיוֹן גּוֹמֵל חֲסָדִים
טוֹבִים וְקֹנֵה הַכֹּל וְזוֹכֵר חַסְדֵי אָבוֹת וּמֵבִיא גוֹאֵל לִבְנֵי בְנֵיהֶם
לְמַעַן שְׁמוֹ בְּאַהֲבָה· מֶלֶךְ עוֹזֵר וּמוֹשִׁיעַ וּמָגֵן· בָּרוּךְ אַתָּה יְיָ
מָגֵן אַבְרָהָם:

אַתָּה גִּבּוֹר לְעוֹלָם אֲדֹנָי מְחַיֵּה מֵתִים אַתָּה רַב לְהוֹשִׁיעַ·

<small>לשמיני עצרת וש״ת</small> מַשִּׁיב הָרוּחַ וּמוֹרִיד הַגָּשֶׁם:

מְכַלְכֵּל חַיִּים בְּחֶסֶד מְחַיֵּה מֵתִים בְּרַחֲמִים רַבִּים סוֹמֵךְ נוֹפְלִים
וְרוֹפֵא חוֹלִים וּמַתִּיר אֲסוּרִים וּמְקַיֵּם אֱמוּנָתוֹ לִישֵׁנֵי עָפָר· מִי
כָמוֹךָ בַּעַל גְּבוּרוֹת וּמִי דּוֹמֶה לָּךְ מֶלֶךְ מֵמִית וּמְחַיֶּה וּמַצְמִיחַ
יְשׁוּעָה· וְנֶאֱמָן אַתָּה לְהַחֲיוֹת מֵתִים· בָּרוּךְ אַתָּה יְיָ מְחַיֵּה הַמֵּתִים:
אַתָּה קָדוֹשׁ וְשִׁמְךָ קָדוֹשׁ וּקְדוֹשִׁים בְּכָל־יוֹם יְהַלְלוּךָ סֶּלָה·
בָּרוּךְ אַתָּה יְיָ הָאֵל הַקָּדוֹשׁ: <small>הש״ץ אומר קדושת נעריצך</small> page 358

אַתָּה בְחַרְתָּנוּ מִכָּל־הָעַמִּים· אָהַבְתָּ אוֹתָנוּ· וְרָצִיתָ בָּנוּ·
וְרוֹמַמְתָּנוּ מִכָּל הַלְּשׁוֹנוֹת· וְקִדַּשְׁתָּנוּ בְּמִצְוֹתֶיךָ· וְקֵרַבְתָּנוּ מַלְכֵּנוּ
לַעֲבוֹדָתֶךָ· וְשִׁמְךָ הַגָּדוֹל וְהַקָּדוֹשׁ עָלֵינוּ קָרָאתָ:

וַתִּתֶּן לָנוּ יְיָ אֱלֹהֵינוּ בְּאַהֲבָה <small>שבתות למנוחה ו</small> מוֹעֲדִים לְשִׂמְחָה
חַגִּים וּזְמַנִּים לְשָׂשׂוֹן· אֶת יוֹם <small>השבת הזה ואת יום</small>

<small>לפסח</small>	<small>לשבועות</small>	<small>לסכות</small>	<small>לשמיני עצרת ולש״ת</small>
חַג הַמַּצּוֹת	חַג הַשָּׁבֻעוֹת	חַג הַסֻּכּוֹת	הַשְּׁמִינִי חַג
הַזֶּה· זְמַן	הַזֶּה· זְמַן	הַזֶּה· זְמַן	הָעֲצֶרֶת הַזֶּה
חֵרוּתֵנוּ	מַתַּן תּוֹרָתֵנוּ	שִׂמְחָתֵנוּ	זְמַן שִׂמְחָתֵנוּ

בְּאַהֲבָה מִקְרָא קֹדֶשׁ זֵכֶר לִיצִיאַת מִצְרָיִם:

וּמִפְּנֵי חֲטָאֵינוּ גָּלִינוּ מֵאַרְצֵנוּ וְנִתְרַחַקְנוּ מֵעַל אַדְמָתֵנוּ וְאֵין אֲנַחְנוּ
יְכוֹלִים לַעֲלוֹת וְלֵרָאוֹת וּלְהִשְׁתַּחֲווֹת לְפָנֶיךָ וְלַעֲשׂוֹת חוֹבוֹתֵינוּ בְּבֵית
בְּחִירָתֶךָ בַּבַּיִת הַגָּדוֹל וְהַקָּדוֹשׁ שֶׁנִּקְרָא שִׁמְךָ עָלָיו מִפְּנֵי הַיָּד

You have chosen us from among all peoples; You have loved us and taken pleasure in us. You have exalted us above all tongues and have sanctified us by Your commandments. You O our King, have drawn us near to Your service, and have called Your great and holy Name upon us.

And You have given us, O *God* our God, in love, (Sabbaths for rest and) festivals of assembly for rejoicing, festivals for rallying and seasons for delight, (this Sabbath day and) the day of
this Festival of Unleavened Bread, the season of our Freedom,
this Festival of Weeks, the season of the Giving of our Torah,
this Festival of Tabernacles, the season of our Rejoicing,
the Eighth Day, the Festival of Retaining, the season of our Rejoicing,
(in love), a convocation to the Sanctuary, a remembrance of the Exodus from Mitzrayim.

But as a result of our sins we were exiled from our land and removed from our soil, and we cannot now go up in order to appear and to prostrate ourselves before You and to perform our obligatory offerings in the House of Your choice, in the great and holy House over which Your Name is proclaimed, because of the

---

מארצנו. ומפני חטאינו i.e. from the *land* which embraced us all as one national entity. מאדמתנו, from the *soil* which bore us so that we might fulfill our task. לעלות implies the mandatory "Ascent" to the Temple from all the parts of the land. לראות denotes the mandatory personal appearance at the Temple. חובותינו are the obligatory offerings, the *temidim* and the *musaphim* as *korbenoth tzibbur*, and the *oloth reiyah, shalmei chaggigah* and *shalmei simchah* which are to be brought separately by every individual. פזורינו are those "separated" from one another. נפוצותינו are those dispersed to places far away.

שֶׁנִּשְׁתַּלַּחְתָּ, בְּמִקְדָּשֶׁךָ: יְהִי רָצוֹן מִלְּפָנֶיךָ יְיָ אֱלֹהֵינוּ וֵאלֹהֵי
אֲבוֹתֵינוּ מֶלֶךְ רַחֲמָן, שֶׁתָּשׁוּב וּתְרַחֵם עָלֵינוּ וְעַל מִקְדָּשְׁךָ בְּרַחֲמֶיךָ
הָרַבִּים וְתִבְנֵהוּ מְהֵרָה וּתְגַדֵּל כְּבוֹדוֹ: אָבִינוּ מַלְכֵּנוּ, גַּלֵּה כְּבוֹד
מַלְכוּתְךָ עָלֵינוּ מְהֵרָה וְהוֹפַע וְהִנָּשֵׂא עָלֵינוּ לְעֵינֵי כָּל־חָי, וְקָרֵב
פְזוּרֵינוּ מִבֵּין הַגּוֹיִם וּנְפוּצוֹתֵינוּ כַּנֵּס מִיַּרְכְּתֵי אָרֶץ, וַהֲבִיאֵנוּ לְצִיּוֹן
עִירְךָ בְּרִנָּה וְלִירוּשָׁלַיִם בֵּית מִקְדָּשְׁךָ בְּשִׂמְחַת עוֹלָם · וְשָׁם
נַעֲשֶׂה לְפָנֶיךָ אֶת קָרְבְּנוֹת חוֹבוֹתֵינוּ תְּמִידִים כְּסִדְרָם וּמוּסָפִים
כְּהִלְכָתָם: וְאֶת־מוּסַף יוֹם הַשַּׁבָּת הַזֶּה וְאֶת מוּסַף יוֹם

| לפסח | לשבועות | לסכות | לשמיני עצרת ולשמחת תורה |

חַג הַמַּצּוֹת | חַג הַשָּׁבֻעוֹת | חַג הַסֻּכּוֹת | הַשְּׁמִינִי חַג הָעֲצֶרֶת
הַזֶּה · נַעֲשֶׂה וְנַקְרִיב לְפָנֶיךָ בְּאַהֲבָה כְּמִצְוַת רְצוֹנֶךָ כְּמוֹ שֶׁכָּתַבְתָּ
עָלֵינוּ בְּתוֹרָתֶךָ עַל־יְדֵי מֹשֶׁה עַבְדְּךָ מִפִּי כְבוֹדֶךָ כָּאָמוּר:

לשבת וּבְיוֹם הַשַּׁבָּת שְׁנֵי־כְבָשִׂים בְּנֵי־שָׁנָה תְּמִימִם
וּשְׁנֵי עֶשְׂרֹנִים סֹלֶת מִנְחָה בְּלוּלָה בַשֶּׁמֶן וְנִסְכּוֹ:
עֹלַת שַׁבַּת בְּשַׁבַּתּוֹ עַל־עֹלַת הַתָּמִיד וְנִסְכָּהּ:

וביום השבת. In our notes to the portions of the Torah and Mishna which
deal with the sacrifices and which are read prior to the *Tefillath Shacharith.*
See p. 26 ff. We have already discussed, on the basis of our Commentary
to the Pentateuch, the significance of the Musaph sacrifices on Sabbath and
Festivals. The Musaph of Rosh Chodesh which is mentioned there constituted
the basic order for the Musaph offerings for all Festivals. They all serve to
express the ideal of the historic character of the Jewish people and of the
magnitude of its destiny, as well as the solemn resolve on the part of the
worshipper to become equal to this destiny and to remain on the lofty plane
of whatever degree of fulfillment he might already have attained. All the
offerings involve identical species of animals, and only some of those offerings
differ from one another with regard to quantity. Thus, on Rosh Chodesh,
Pesach, Shavuoth and Succoth two bullocks are to be offered, while on Rosh
Hashanah, Yom Kippur and Shemini Atzereth only one bullock is sacrificed.

violence that was done to Your Sanctuary. May it be Your will, O *God* our God and God of our fathers, compassionate King, in Your great compassion, to have compassion once more upon us and upon Your Sanctuary, to rebuild it soon and to cause its glory to be great. Our Father, our King, speedily reveal the glory of Your kingdom over us, appear and be exalted above us before the eyes of all things living, and unite our scattered [members] from their separation among the nations, and gather our dispersed from the ends of the earth, and bring us home to Tzion, Your city, in jubilation, and to Yerushalayim, the site of Your Sanctuary, with joy everlasting. There we shall bring before You our obligatory offerings, the regular offerings according to their order, and the additional offerings according to their rule. The additional offering of (this Sabbath and) — this Festival of Unleavened Bread — this Festival of Weeks — this Festival of Tabernacles — this Eighth Day, the Festival of Retaining — will we prepare and bring near to You with love in accordance with the commandment of Your will, even as You have prescribed it as incumbent upon us in Your Torah through Moshe Your servant, by the sentence of Your glory, as it is said:

On Sabbath: "And on the Sabbath Day two yearling lambs without blemish; two-tenths parts of fine flour as a gift of tribute mixed with oil, along with its drink offering. This is the elevating-offering of the Sabbath on every Sabbath, in addition to the regular elevating-offering and the drink offering thereof."

On Rosh Ha-Shanah and Yom Kippur we are to bring to the altar only *one* bullock. We are not yet ready to sacrifice two bullocks, because such an of-fering would be a symbolic claim that every single Jew has already fulfilled his own task and destiny in the service of God. Hence, on those two solemn occasions, we come into the Presence of our God with only one bullock, which symbolizes the ideal set for the nation as a whole to the level of which the individual has yet to find his way by his own efforts at self-refinement on Rosh Hashanah and Yom Kippur. In the same spirit, on the day of Shemini Atzereth, before we enter into the reality that often is so harsh and filled with trials, we bid one last farewell to the festival season with offerings which symbolically give proof of our awareness that all of us, together, belong to God and that we belong together, as regards both our fate and our life's work, on behalf of God's Law. On that day we offer at the altar *par echad* to show that we are *one* united working force, tilling the acre of the future

ביום א' וב' של סוכות.	לשבועות.	ביום א' וב' של פסח.

ביום א' וב' של פסח:

וּבַחֹדֶשׁ הָרִאשׁוֹן בְּאַרְבָּעָה עָשָׂר יוֹם לַחֹדֶשׁ פֶּסַח לַיהוָה: וּבַחֲמִשָּׁה עָשָׂר יוֹם לַחֹדֶשׁ הַזֶּה חָג שִׁבְעַת יָמִים מַצּוֹת יֵאָכֵל: בַּיּוֹם הָרִאשׁוֹן מִקְרָא קֹדֶשׁ כָּל־מְלָאכֶת עֲבֹדָה לֹא תַעֲשׂוּ:

מיום א' דחה"מ ואילך לומרין לבד והקרבתם.

וְהִקְרַבְתֶּם אִשֶּׁה עֹלָה לַיהוָה פָּרִים בְּנֵי־בָקָר שְׁנַיִם וְאַיִל אֶחָד וְשִׁבְעָה כְבָשִׂים בְּנֵי שָׁנָה תְּמִימִם יִהְיוּ לָכֶם:

לשבועות:

וּבְיוֹם הַבִּכּוּרִים בְּהַקְרִיבְכֶם מִנְחָה חֲדָשָׁה לַיהוָה בְּשָׁבֻעֹתֵיכֶם מִקְרָא־קֹדֶשׁ יִהְיֶה לָכֶם כָּל־מְלָאכֶת עֲבֹדָה לֹא תַעֲשׂוּ: וְהִקְרַבְתֶּם עוֹלָה לְרֵיחַ נִיחֹחַ לַיהוָה פָּרִים בְּנֵי־בָקָר שְׁנַיִם אַיִל אֶחָד שִׁבְעָה כְבָשִׂים בְּנֵי שָׁנָה:

ביום א' וב' של סוכות:

וּבַחֲמִשָּׁה עָשָׂר יוֹם לַחֹדֶשׁ הַשְּׁבִיעִי מִקְרָא קֹדֶשׁ יִהְיֶה לָכֶם כָּל־מְלָאכֶת עֲבֹדָה לֹא תַעֲשׂוּ וְחַגֹּתֶם חַג לַיהוָה שִׁבְעַת יָמִים: וְהִקְרַבְתֶּם עֹלָה אִשֵּׁה רֵיחַ נִיחֹחַ לַיהוָה פָּרִים בְּנֵי־בָקָר שְׁלֹשָׁה עָשָׂר אֵילִם שְׁנַיִם כְּבָשִׂים בְּנֵי־שָׁנָה אַרְבָּעָה עָשָׂר תְּמִימִם יִהְיוּ:

of all mankind; *ayil echad* to demonstrate the fact that we are a united nation, leading and guiding all the other nations, which are His flock, as it were, and *shiv'ah kevasim* to denote our position as the nation of the Covenant which, by virtue of our own fate, is to reveal the nature of the sovereignty of God.

The Musaph sacrifices pertaining to the Festival of Tabernacles require special study and explanation. Throughout the holiday the offering consists of the same types of animals, but their quantities vary in accordance with definite specifications. On other Mo'adim, the Musaph offering consists of one or two bullocks, one ram and seven lambs. On the first day of Succoth, however, our Musaph offering is to consist of *thirteen* bullocks, *two* rams and *fourteen* lambs. The number of rams and lambs to be offered remains constant throughout the seven days of the festival; i.e. two rams and fourteen lambs. But the number of bullocks to be sacrificed decreases by one each day so that the Musaph offering to be brought on the seventh day of Succoth consists

On the First Two Days of Passover

And in the first month, on the fourteenth day of the month, is the Passover dedicated to *God*. And on the fifteenth day of the month there shall be a festival, for seven days shall unleavened bread be eaten. On the first day there shall be a convocation to the Sanctuary; you shall do no servile work.

During all Eight Days of Passover

And you shall bring to *God* a fire offering as an elevating offering: two young bullocks, one ram and seven yearling lambs; they shall be to you without blemish.

On Shavuoth

And on the Day of the First Fruits, when you bring to *God* a new tribute offering, on your Festival of Weeks, you shall have a convocation to the Sanctuary; you shall do no servile work. And you shall bring to *God* as an elevating offering for His pleasure: two young bullocks, one ram, seven yearling lambs.

On the First Two Days of Succoth

And on the fifteenth day of the seventh month, you shall have a convocation to the Sanctuary; you shall do no servile work, and you shall keep a festival to *God* for seven days. And you shall bring to *God* an elevating-offering, a fire offering for His pleasure: thirteen young bullocks, two rams, fourteen yearling lambs; they shall be without blemish.

---

of only *seven* bullocks in addition to the two rams and the fourteen lambs. The fact that the Musaph offering on Succoth consists of *two* rams and *fourteen* lambs as compared to the *one* ram and the *seven* lambs which are required on the other Festivals indicates that the Musaph offering of Succoth is a double offering, so that the thirteen bullocks which are to be offered at the altar on the first day of the Festival should also be regarded not as one entity, but as the sum of *two* groups, one of seven and one of six. The symbolic significance of these quantities is as follows: On the most important festival celebrating Yisrael's awareness, as a nation, of its God, Yisrael comes into His presence with two groups of elevating-offerings; that is, one group consisting of seven lambs, one ram and seven bullocks, and another composed of seven lambs, one ram but only *six* bullocks. These two groups of animal offerings are the symbolic expression for two distinct entities in mankind. These two groups are equal to one another as regards the qualities represented by the lambs and the ram; in other words, both are equal in the relationship

וּמִנְחָתָם וְנִסְכֵּיהֶם כִּמְדֻבָּר ׳ שְׁלֹשָׁה עֶשְׂרֹנִים לַפָּר ׳

וּשְׁנֵי עֶשְׂרֹנִים לָאָיִל ׳ וְעִשָּׂרוֹן לַכֶּבֶשׂ וְיַיִן כְּנִסְכּוֹ ׳

וְשָׂעִיר לְכַפֵּר ׳ וּשְׁנֵי תְמִידִים כְּהִלְכָתָם׃

On the First Intermediate Day of Succoth

וּבַיּוֹם הַשֵּׁנִי פָּרִים בְּנֵי־בָקָר שְׁנֵים עָשָׂר אֵילִם

שְׁנָיִם כְּבָשִׂים בְּנֵי־שָׁנָה אַרְבָּעָה עָשָׂר תְּמִימִם׃

וּמִנְחָתָם וְנִסְכֵּיהֶם כִּמְדֻבָּר ׳ שְׁלֹשָׁה עֶשְׂרֹנִים לַפָּר ׳ וּשְׁנֵי עֶשְׂרֹנִים לָאָיִל ׳

וְעִשָּׂרוֹן לַכֶּבֶשׂ וְיַיִן כְּנִסְכּוֹ ׳ וְשָׂעִיר לְכַפֵּר ׳ וּשְׁנֵי תְמִידִים כְּהִלְכָתָם׃

וּבַיּוֹם הַשְּׁלִישִׁי פָּרִים עַשְׁתֵּי־עָשָׂר אֵילִם שְׁנָיִם כְּבָשִׂים

בְּנֵי־שָׁנָה אַרְבָּעָה עָשָׂר תְּמִימִם׃ וּמִנְחָתָם וְכוּ׳ אֵילִ״ם וכו׳.

On the Second Intermediate Day of Succoth

וּבַיּוֹם הַשְּׁלִישִׁי פָּרִים עַשְׁתֵּי־עָשָׂר אֵלִם שְׁנָיִם

כְּבָשִׂים בְּנֵי־שָׁנָה אַרְבָּעָה עָשָׂר תְּמִימִם׃

וּמִנְחָתָם וְנִסְכֵּיהֶם כִּמְדֻבָּר ׳ שְׁלֹשָׁה עֶשְׂרֹנִים לַפָּר ׳ וּשְׁנֵי עֶשְׂרֹנִים לָאָיִל ׳

וְעִשָּׂרוֹן לַכֶּבֶשׂ וְיַיִן כְּנִסְכּוֹ ׳ וְשָׂעִיר לְכַפֵּר ׳ וּשְׁנֵי תְמִידִים כְּהִלְכָתָם׃

וּבַיּוֹם הָרְבִיעִי פָּרִים עֲשָׂרָה אֵילִם שְׁנָיִם כְּבָשִׂים

בְּנֵי־שָׁנָה אַרְבָּעָה עָשָׂר תְּמִימִם׃ וּמִנְחָתָם וְכוּ׳ אֵילִ״ם וכו׳.

---

of their march through history to the one "Shepherd" of mankind *(keves)*,
and in the significance of their progress which is blessed with abundant vigor
(ayil). However, the two entities are not alike as regards the nature of their
task and *function* on earth (which are symbolized by the bullocks). The first
entity is not only a complete "seven" as regards its march through the ages
(kevasim). It is united with God by a covenant. Over and beyond the fact
that its course through history is a revelation of the One Invisible God Who
guides the Universe, it represents a perfect unit of "seven" also with regard
to the quality symbolized by the bullocks; that is, its every endeavor, its very

And their tribute offering and their drink offerings as prescribed: three tenths for every bullock, two tenths for the ram and one tenth for each lamb, and wine even as its drink offering, and one he-goat for atonement and two regular offerings in accordance with their rule.

On the First Intermediate Day of Succoth

And on the second day: twelve young bullocks, two rams, fourteen yearling lambs without blemish. And their tribute offering etc.

And on the third day: eleven bullocks, two rams, fourteen yearling lambs without blemish. And their tribute offering etc.

On the Second Intermediate Day of Succoth

And on the third day: eleven bullocks, two rams, fourteen yearling lambs without blemish. And their tribute offering, etc.

And on the fourth day: ten bullocks, two rams, fourteen yearling lambs without blemish. And their tribute offering, etc.

---

function on earth represents a complete "seven" as well. Every facet of its conduct is a revelation of the One God, to Whose laws this national entity has freely subordinated itself, and whatever the members of this group do is in itself a testimony to His will. Not so the other group. True, this second entity, too, is near God in its destinies; its history, its woe and weal, even as those of the first group, constitute a revelation of God, but not so its conduct. This second entity, even as the first, belongs to God, but only passively so. Unlike the first group, this unit does not actively, of its own initiative, demonstrate by its every action that it is His. It is therefore "seven" as regards its march through the ages (as shown by the seven lambs), but with respect to its conduct, (symbolized by the bullocks) it is only an incomplete "six". Its conduct is not shaped by the dictates of the will of its Lord and Creator. The origin of its history is Divine, but that of its conduct is not. Hence it is symbolically represented, in the second group of offerings, by the full seven lambs, but by only *six* bullocks.

On the Third Intermediate Day of Succoth

וּבַיּוֹם הָרְבִיעִי פָרִים עֲשָׂרָה אֵילִם שְׁנַיִם
כְּבָשִׂים בְּנֵי־שָׁנָה אַרְבָּעָה עָשָׂר תְּמִימִם:

וּמִנְחָתָם וְנִסְכֵּיהֶם כְּמְדֻבָּר. שְׁלֹשָׁה עֶשְׂרֹנִים לַפָּר. וּשְׁנֵי עֶשְׂרֹנִים לָאָיִל.
וְעִשָּׂרוֹן לַכֶּבֶשׂ וָיָיִן כְּנִסְכּוֹ. וְשָׂעִיר לְכַפֵּר. וּשְׁנֵי תְמִידִים כְּהִלְכָתָם:

וּבַיּוֹם הַחֲמִישִׁי פָרִים תִּשְׁעָה אֵילִם שְׁנַיִם כְּבָשִׂים
בְּנֵי־שָׁנָה אַרְבָּעָה עָשָׂר תְּמִימִם: וּמנחתם וכו' א''ו''א וכו'.

On the Fourth Intermediate Day of Succoth

וּבַיּוֹם הַחֲמִישִׁי פָרִים תִּשְׁעָה אֵילִם שְׁנַיִם
כְּבָשִׂים בְּנֵי־שָׁנָה אַרְבָּעָה עָשָׂר תְּמִימִם:

וּמִנְחָתָם וְנִסְכֵּיהֶם כְּמְדֻבָּר. שְׁלֹשָׁה עֶשְׂרֹנִים לַפָּר. וּשְׁנֵי עֶשְׂרֹנִים לָאָיִל
וְעִשָּׂרוֹן לַכֶּבֶשׂ וָיָיִן כְּנִסְכּוֹ. וְשָׂעִיר לְכַפֵּר. וּשְׁנֵי תְמִידִים כְּהִלְכָתָם:

וּבַיּוֹם הַשִּׁשִּׁי פָרִים שְׁמֹנָה אֵילִם שְׁנַיִם כְּבָשִׂים
בְּנֵי־שָׁנָה אַרְבָּעָה עָשָׂר תְּמִימִם: וּמנחתם וכו' א''ו''א וכו'.

להושענא רבא.

וּבַיּוֹם הַשִּׁשִּׁי פָרִים שְׁמֹנָה אֵילִם שְׁנַיִם
כְּבָשִׂים בְּנֵי־שָׁנָה אַרְבָּעָה עָשָׂר תְּמִימִם:

וּמִנְחָתָם וְנִסְכֵּיהֶם כְּמְדֻבָּר. שְׁלֹשָׁה עֶשְׂרֹנִים לַפָּר. וּשְׁנֵי עֶשְׂרֹנִים לָאָיִל
וְעִשָּׂרוֹן לַכֶּבֶשׂ וָיָיִן כְּנִסְכּוֹ. וְשָׂעִיר לְכַפֵּר. וּשְׁנֵי תְמִידִים כְּהִלְכָתָם:

וּבַיּוֹם הַשְּׁבִיעִי פָרִים שִׁבְעָה אֵילִם שְׁנַיִם כְּבָשִׂים
בְּנֵי־שָׁנָה אַרְבָּעָה עָשָׂר תְּמִימִם: וּמנחתם וכו' א''ו''א וכו'.

לשמיני עצרת ולשמחת תורה.

בַּיּוֹם הַשְּׁמִינִי עֲצֶרֶת תִּהְיֶה לָכֶם כָּל־מְלֶאכֶת עֲבֹדָה לֹא תַעֲשׂוּ:
וְהִקְרַבְתֶּם עֹלָה אִשֵּׁה רֵיחַ נִיחֹחַ לַיהֹוָה פַּר אֶחָד אַיִל אֶחָד
כְּבָשִׂים בְּנֵי־שָׁנָה שִׁבְעָה תְּמִימִם:

וּמִנְחָתָם וְנִסְכֵּיהֶם כְּמְדֻבָּר. שְׁלֹשָׁה עֶשְׂרֹנִים לַפָּר. וּשְׁנֵי עֶשְׂרֹנִים לָאָיִל
וְעִשָּׂרוֹן לַכֶּבֶשׂ וָיָיִן כְּנִסְכּוֹ. וְשָׂעִיר לְכַפֵּר. וּשְׁנֵי תְמִידִים כְּהִלְכָתָם:

On the Third Intermediate Day of Succoth

And on the fourth day: ten bullocks, two rams, fourteen yearling lambs without blemish. And their tribute offering, etc.

And on the fifth day: nine bullocks, two rams, fourteen yearling lambs without blemish. And their tribute offering, etc.

On the Fourth Intermediate Day of Succoth

And on the fifth day: nine bullocks, two rams, fourteen yearling lambs without blemish. And their tribute offering, etc.

And on the sixth day: eight bullocks, two rams, fourteen yearling lambs without blemish. And their tribute offering, etc.

On Hoshana Rabbah

And on the sixth day: eight bullocks, two rams, fourteen yearling lambs without blemish. And their tribute offering, etc.

And on the seventh day: seven bullocks, two rams, fourteen yearling lambs without blemish. And their tribute offering, etc.

On Shemini Atzereth and Simchath Torah

On the Eighth day you shall have a Festival of Retaining; you shall do no servile work, and you shall bring to *God* an elevating offering, a fire offering for His pleasure, one bullock, one ram, seven yearling lambs without blemish. And their tribute offering and their drink offerings, as prescribed; three tenths for every bullock, two tenths for the ram and one tenth for each lamb, and wine even as its drink offering and one he-goat for atonement and two regular offerings in accordance with their rule.

It is obvious that the first group represents the people of Yisrael and the second the rest of the nations. The contrast between these two entities is gradually disappearing, and finally, on the "seventh" day, the goal of all of mankind's development and of the mission of Yisrael for this purpose, Yisrael will stand united with the rest of mankind in homage to God and in loyal service to Him with all of life, then together, Yisrael and the nations will be seven bullocks. Yet, in keeping with their separate historical development and the differing nature of their qualifications for the fulfillment of the destiny of mankind, Yisrael and the nations will still remain two separate entities. Both are equally near to God in dignity and worth, and both stride forward in equal measure toward the attainment of the goals of all mankind; nevertheless they will remain two separate entities, separately represented by a unit of seven lambs and one ram each. (See Commentary to Num. Chap. 29.)

On the Sabbath, add:

לשבת יִשְׂמְחוּ בְמַלְכוּתְךָ שׁוֹמְרֵי שַׁבָּת וְקוֹרְאֵי עֹנֶג עַם מְקַדְּשֵׁי שְׁבִיעִי ·
כֻּלָם יִשְׂבְּעוּ וְיִתְעַנְּגוּ מִטּוּבֶךָ · וְהַשְּׁבִיעִי רָצִיתָ בּוֹ וְקִדַּשְׁתּוֹ חֶמְדַּת
יָמִים אֹתוֹ קָרָאתָ זֵכֶר לְמַעֲשֵׂה בְרֵאשִׁית:

אֱלֹהֵינוּ וֵאלֹהֵי אֲבוֹתֵינוּ מֶלֶךְ רַחֲמָן רַחֵם עָלֵינוּ טוֹב וּמֵטִיב
הִדָּרֶשׁ־לָנוּ שׁוּבָה אֵלֵינוּ בַּהֲמוֹן רַחֲמֶיךָ בִּגְלַל אָבוֹת שֶׁעָשׂוּ רְצוֹנֶךָ ·
בְּנֵה בֵיתְךָ כְּבַתְּחִלָּה וְכוֹנֵן מִקְדָּשְׁךָ עַל מְכוֹנוֹ וְהַרְאֵנוּ בְּבִנְיָנוֹ
וְשַׂמְּחֵנוּ בְּתִקּוּנוֹ וְהָשֵׁב כֹּהֲנִים לַעֲבוֹדָתָם וּלְוִיִּם לְשִׁירָם וּלְזִמְרָם
וְהָשֵׁב יִשְׂרָאֵל לִנְוֵיהֶם · וְשָׁם נַעֲלֶה וְנֵרָאֶה וְנִשְׁתַּחֲוֶה לְפָנֶיךָ
בְּשָׁלֹשׁ פַּעֲמֵי רְגָלֵינוּ. כַּכָּתוּב בְּתוֹרָתֶךָ · שָׁלֹשׁ פְּעָמִים · בַּשָּׁנָה
יֵרָאֶה כָל־זְכוּרְךָ אֶת־פְּנֵי · יְהֹוָה אֱלֹהֶיךָ בַּמָּקוֹם אֲשֶׁר יִבְחָר בְּחַג
הַמַּצּוֹת וּבְחַג הַשָּׁבֻעוֹת וּבְחַג הַסֻּכּוֹת וְלֹא יֵרָאֶה אֶת־פְּנֵי יְהֹוָה
רֵיקָם: אִישׁ כְּמַתְּנַת יָדוֹ כְּבִרְכַּת יְהֹוָה אֱלֹהֶיךָ אֲשֶׁר נָתַן לָךְ:
וְהַשִּׂיאֵנוּ יְיָ אֱלֹהֵינוּ אֶת בִּרְכַּת מוֹעֲדֶיךָ לְחַיִּים וּלְשָׁלוֹם לְשִׂמְחָה
וּלְשָׂשׂוֹן כַּאֲשֶׁר רָצִיתָ וְאָמַרְתָּ לְבָרְכֵנוּ: בשבת אלהינו ואלהי אבותינו

ישמחו : See above p. 367.

או״א. מלך רחמן Since He is the Ruler of the Universe, He has the power
to deliver us, and because He is *rachaman*, it is His will to do so. Our state
of exile, whatever form it may take, is always pitiable. Far away from the
soil of God's Law and distant from the Sanctuary, we are always in exile,
and the constantly recurring repudiations of justice and humanity on the part
of the nations provide never-ceasing justification for our appeal to God's
compassion. רחמים denotes the love, inalienable and always to be regained,
which a father bears for his child and a Creator for His works. הדרש לנו
see Ezekiel 37:37. המון derived from המה, see המון מעיך ורחמיך ; המון רחמיך
(Isa. 63:15). בגלל אבות "All that we can do now is appeal to Your compassion; only the merits of our fathers, who did Your will in faithful obedience

On the Sabbath, add: Those who keep the Sabbath and call it a delight shall rejoice in Your kingdom; the nation which sanctifies the Seventh Day shall all be satisfied and shall delight in Your good. You took pleasure in the Seventh Day and hallowed it; the [most] desirable of days did You proclaim as the memorial to the work of the world's beginning.

Our God and God of our fathers, compassionate King, have compassion upon us, cause us to find You a good and beneficent Being; return to us in the impulse of Your compassion, for the sake of the Fathers who did Your will, build Your House as at the beginning; establish Your Sanctuary upon its site. Let us behold its rebuilding and gladden us by its restoration. Restore the Priests to their service, the Levites to their song and their psalm, and lead Yisrael back to their dwelling places. There we shall ascend and appear and cast ourselves down before You at the three seasons of our pilgrimage, as it is written in Your Torah: "Three times a year shall all your males be seen directly before the countenance of *God* your God at that place which He shall select; on the Festival of Unleavened Bread, on Festival of Weeks and on the Festival of Tabernacles, and they shall not be seen empty-handed before the countenance of *God* Every one [shall bring offerings] according to the gift of his hand, in accordance with the blessing that *God* your God has given you.

---

in the past, can stand by our side in the present day." ביתך is "the House of which You O God, have said, ונועדתי לך שם that You would find us worthy there of Your nearness and that we are to find You there." מקדשך is "the place consecrated by You in which we are to sanctify ourselves by devoting all of our own being and subordinating all of our own desires to the fulfillment of Your Law." First בנה ביתך, and only thereafter והשב ישראל לנויהם. First we ask for the restoration of the Beth Hamikdash as the one central point which will hallow us and unite us round the Law of God that is the precious heritage of us all. Only after this do we pray that we be redistributed throughout our own homeland into our original homes that constitute the environs of the Sanctuary so that, on each of the three appointed Pilgrim Festivals, we may ascend to the Temple and know that we are united, gathering together about God's Sanctuary in common devotion to Him and to His Law. It is only such a restoration of the Sanctuary and such a return of our people to its homeland that will be conducive to the future salvation after which we are to strive. ולא יראו פני ריקם "And when you come before Me," says God, "you are not

רְצֵה בִמְנוּחָתֵנוּ קַדְּשֵׁנוּ בְּמִצְוֹתֶיךָ וְתֵן חֶלְקֵנוּ בְּתוֹרָתֶךָ שַׂבְּעֵנוּ מִטּוּבֶךָ
וְשַׂמְּחֵנוּ בִּישׁוּעָתֶךָ וְטַהֵר לִבֵּנוּ לְעָבְדְּךָ בֶּאֱמֶת וְהַנְחִילֵנוּ יְיָ אֱלֹהֵינוּ
בְּאַהֲבָה וּבְרָצוֹן בְּשִׂמְחָה וּבְשָׂשׂוֹן שבת ו מוֹעֲדֵי קָדְשֶׁךָ · וְיִשְׂמְחוּ
בְךָ יִשְׂרָאֵל מְקַדְּשֵׁי שְׁמֶךָ · בָּרוּךְ אַתָּה יְיָ מְקַדֵּשׁ השבת ו יִשְׂרָאֵל
וְהַזְּמַנִּים :

סדר נשיאת כפים—page 746

רְצֵה יְיָ אֱלֹהֵינוּ בְּעַמְּךָ יִשְׂרָאֵל וּבִתְפִלָּתָם · וְהָשֵׁב אֶת־הָעֲבוֹדָה
לִדְבִיר בֵּיתֶךָ וְאִשֵּׁי יִשְׂרָאֵל וּתְפִלָּתָם בְּאַהֲבָה תְקַבֵּל בְּרָצוֹן וּתְהִי
לְרָצוֹן תָּמִיד עֲבוֹדַת יִשְׂרָאֵל עַמֶּךָ ·

וְתֶחֱזֶינָה עֵינֵינוּ בְּשׁוּבְךָ לְצִיּוֹן בְּרַחֲמִים · בָּרוּךְ אַתָּה יְיָ
הַמַּחֲזִיר שְׁכִינָתוֹ לְצִיּוֹן:

---

to come empty-handed. When you leave your homes in order to show yourselves before My countenance, you are not to labor under the delusion that
the Temple is a thing apart from your home, that, while Heaven and the
things of the spirit belong to the Temple, the earth and the material wealth
of life are the exclusive property of the home alone." Nothing could be more
wrong than such an attitude. When we come before our God, we are to
come into His presence *together* with all of our possessions. As symbolized
by *olah uminchah zevach unesachim*, we are to place at His command all of
our personalities, together with all our tangible wealth of sustenance (*soleth*),
bodily vigor (*shemen*) and joy (*yayin*), and make them all part of the
consecration to be attained in the Temple. The three festival offerings that
are mandatory for every individual to bring are each dedicated to one of
the three main features that make our Festivals. The *oloth reiyah* are dedicated
to *regel*, the personal appearance of every Jew in the Sanctuary of the Law;
shalmei chaggigah to *chag*, the "reunion" with all of our fellow-Jews, and
shalmei simchah to *mo'ed*, our "meeting" with God. The last-named offering
symbolizes our joyous awareness of God's presence in the midst of our families,
which elevates the home to the status of a sanctuary, which makes our family
board an altar and all the members of our household priests and priestesses
devoted to the service, with all their lives, of the sacred task set them by God.
איש כמתנת ידו : Man's status before God, in His Sanctuary and among His
people is determined not by how much he actually *has*, but solely by how
much of the good which he has received from God he is *willing* to give as
a *gift* for purposes pleasing to God.

מוֹדִים אֲנַחְנוּ לָךְ שָׁאַתָּה הוּא יְיָ אֱלֹהֵינוּ וֵאלֹהֵי אֲבוֹתֵינוּ לְעוֹלָם
וָעֶד · צוּר חַיֵּינוּ מָגֵן יִשְׁעֵנוּ אַתָּה הוּא לְדוֹר וָדוֹר · נוֹדֶה לְךָ וּנְסַפֵּר
תְּהִלָּתֶךָ עַל חַיֵּינוּ הַמְּסוּרִים בְּיָדֶךָ וְעַל נִשְׁמוֹתֵינוּ הַפְּקוּדוֹת לָךְ
וְעַל נִסֶּיךָ שֶׁבְּכָל יוֹם עִמָּנוּ וְעַל נִפְלְאוֹתֶיךָ וְטוֹבוֹתֶיךָ שֶׁבְּכָל עֵת,
עֶרֶב וָבֹקֶר וְצָהֳרָיִם · הַטּוֹב כִּי לֹא כָלוּ רַחֲמֶיךָ וְהַמְרַחֵם כִּי לֹא
תַמּוּ חֲסָדֶיךָ מֵעוֹלָם קִוִּינוּ לָךְ:

וְעַל כֻּלָּם יִתְבָּרַךְ וְיִתְרוֹמַם שִׁמְךָ מַלְכֵּנוּ תָּמִיד לְעוֹלָם וָעֶד:
וְכֹל הַחַיִּים יוֹדוּךָ סֶּלָה וִיהַלְלוּ אֶת שִׁמְךָ בֶּאֱמֶת הָאֵל יְשׁוּעָתֵנוּ
וְעֶזְרָתֵנוּ סֶלָה · בָּרוּךְ אַתָּה יְיָ הַטּוֹב שִׁמְךָ וּלְךָ נָאֶה לְהוֹדוֹת:

The חזן adds this when repeating the ש״ע:

אֱלֹהֵינוּ וֵאלֹהֵי אֲבוֹתֵינוּ בָּרְכֵנוּ בַּבְּרָכָה הַמְשֻׁלֶּשֶׁת בַּתּוֹרָה
הַכְּתוּבָה עַל־יְדֵי מֹשֶׁה עַבְדֶּךָ הָאֲמוּרָה מִפִּי אַהֲרֹן וּבָנָיו כֹּהֲנִים
עַם קְדוֹשֶׁךָ כָּאָמוּר: יְבָרֶכְךָ יְיָ וְיִשְׁמְרֶךָ: יָאֵר יְיָ · פָּנָיו אֵלֶיךָ
וִיחֻנֶּךָ: יִשָּׂא יְיָ · פָּנָיו אֵלֶיךָ וְיָשֵׂם לְךָ שָׁלוֹם:

שִׂים שָׁלוֹם טוֹבָה וּבְרָכָה חֵן וָחֶסֶד וְרַחֲמִים עָלֵינוּ וְעַל כָּל־
יִשְׂרָאֵל עַמֶּךָ · בָּרְכֵנוּ אָבִינוּ כֻּלָּנוּ כְּאֶחָד בְּאוֹר פָּנֶיךָ · כִּי בְאוֹר
פָּנֶיךָ נָתַתָּ לָּנוּ יְיָ אֱלֹהֵינוּ תּוֹרַת חַיִּים וְאַהֲבַת חֶסֶד וּצְדָקָה וּבְרָכָה
וְרַחֲמִים וְחַיִּים וְשָׁלוֹם · וְטוֹב בְּעֵינֶיךָ לְבָרֵךְ אֶת־עַמְּךָ יִשְׂרָאֵל
בְּכָל־עֵת וּבְכָל־שָׁעָה בִּשְׁלוֹמֶךָ · בָּרוּךְ אַתָּה יְיָ הַמְבָרֵךְ אֶת־
עַמּוֹ יִשְׂרָאֵל בַּשָּׁלוֹם:

אֱלֹהַי · נְצוֹר לְשׁוֹנִי מֵרָע וּשְׂפָתַי מִדַּבֵּר מִרְמָה וְלִמְקַלְלַי נַפְשִׁי
תִדֹּם וְנַפְשִׁי כֶּעָפָר לַכֹּל תִּהְיֶה: פְּתַח לִבִּי בְּתוֹרָתֶךָ וּבְמִצְוֹתֶךָ
תִּרְדּוֹף נַפְשִׁי וְכָל הַחוֹשְׁבִים עָלַי רָעָה מְהֵרָה הָפֵר עֲצָתָם וְקַלְקֵל

מַחֲשַׁבְתָּם · עֲשֵׂה לְמַעַן שְׁמֶךָ · עֲשֵׂה לְמַעַן יְמִינֶךָ · עֲשֵׂה לְמַעַן

קְדֻשָּׁתֶךָ · עֲשֵׂה לְמַעַן תּוֹרָתֶךָ · לְמַעַן יֵחָלְצוּן יְדִידֶיךָ הוֹשִׁיעָה

יְמִינְךָ וַעֲנֵנִי: יִהְיוּ לְרָצוֹן אִמְרֵי־פִי וְהֶגְיוֹן לִבִּי לְפָנֶיךָ יְיָ צוּרִי

וְגֹאֲלִי: עֹשֶׂה שָׁלוֹם בִּמְרוֹמָיו הוּא יַעֲשֶׂה שָׁלוֹם עָלֵינוּ וְעַל כָּל

יִשְׂרָאֵל וְאִמְרוּ אָמֵן :

יְהִי רָצוֹן מִלְּפָנֶיךָ יְיָ אֱלֹהֵינוּ וֵאלֹהֵי אֲבוֹתֵינוּ שֶׁיִּבָּנֶה

בֵּית הַמִּקְדָּשׁ בִּמְהֵרָה בְיָמֵינוּ וְתֵן חֶלְקֵנוּ בְּתוֹרָתֶךָ:

וְשָׁם נַעֲבָדְךָ בְּיִרְאָה כִּימֵי עוֹלָם וּכְשָׁנִים קַדְמֹנִיּוֹת:

וְעָרְבָה לַיְיָ מִנְחַת יְהוּדָה וִירוּשָׁלָיִם כִּימֵי עוֹלָם וּכְשָׁנִים קַדְמֹנִיּוֹת:

סֵדֶר קִדּוּשׁ לֵיל שָׁלֹשׁ רְגָלִים

On שבת the following is preceded by יום הששי (P. 292):

בָּרוּךְ אַתָּה יְיָ אֱלֹהֵינוּ מֶלֶךְ הָעוֹלָם בּוֹרֵא פְּרִי הַגָּפֶן :

בָּרוּךְ אַתָּה יְיָ אֱלֹהֵינוּ מֶלֶךְ הָעוֹלָם אֲשֶׁר בָּחַר־בָּנוּ מִכָּל־עָם

וְרוֹמְמָנוּ מִכָּל לָשׁוֹן וְקִדְּשָׁנוּ בְּמִצְוֹתָיו · וַתִּתֶּן־לָנוּ יְיָ אֱלֹהֵינוּ בְּאַהֲבָה

שַׁבָּתוֹת לִמְנוּחָה וּ מוֹעֲדִים לְשִׂמְחָה חַגִּים וּזְמַנִּים לְשָׂשׂוֹן אֶת־יוֹם

הַשַּׁבָּת הַזֶּה וְאֶת יוֹם

שמיני עצרת ושׂ״ת	לסוכות	לשבועות	לפסח
הַשְּׁמִינִי חַג	חַג הַסֻּכּוֹת	חַג הַשָּׁבֻעוֹת	חַג הַמַּצּוֹת
הָעֲצֶרֶת הַזֶּה ·	זְמַן ·	הַזֶּה · זְמַן	הַזֶּה · זְמַן ·
זְמַן שִׂמְחָתֵנוּ	שִׂמְחָתֵנוּ	מַתַּן תּוֹרָתֵנוּ	חֵרוּתֵנוּ

בְּאַהֲבָה מִקְרָא קֹדֶשׁ זֵכֶר לִיצִיאַת מִצְרָיִם: כִּי בָנוּ בָחַרְתָּ וְאוֹתָנוּ

קִדַּשְׁתָּ מִכָּל־הָעַמִּים ושבת וּ מוֹעֲדֵי קָדְשֶׁךָ באהבה וברצון בְּשִׂמְחָה

וּבְשָׂשׂוֹן הִנְחַלְתָּנוּ: בָּרוּךְ אַתָּה יְיָ מְקַדֵּשׁ השבת וְיִשְׂרָאֵל וְהַזְּמַנִּים:

On מוצאי שבת the following is inserted:

בָּרוּךְ אַתָּה יְיָ אֱלֹהֵינוּ מֶלֶךְ הָעוֹלָם בּוֹרֵא מְאוֹרֵי הָאֵשׁ: בָּרוּךְ אַתָּה יְיָ אֱלֹהֵינוּ

On Sabbath begin with יום הששי

Blessed be You, O *God* our God, King of the Universe, Who creates the fruit of the vine.

Blessed be You, O *God* our God, King of the Universe, Who has chosen us from among all peoples, exalted us above all tongues and has sanctified us by His commandments. And You have given us, O *God* our God, in love, (Sabbaths for rest and) festivals of assembly for rejoicing, feasts of rallying and seasons for delight, (this Sabbath day and) the day of

this Festival of Unleavened Bread, the season of our Freedom,

this Festival of Weeks, the season of the Giving of our Torah,

this Festival of Tabernacles, the season of our Rejoicing,

the Eighth Day, the Festival of Retaining, the season of our Rejoicing,

(in love), a convocation to the Sanctuary, a remembrance of the Exodus from Mitzrayim. For You have chosen us; You have sanctified us from among all peoples, and the Sabbath and Your holy festivals of assembly (in love and in favor) in joy and delight You have given us as an inheritance. Blessed be You *God,* Who sanctifies (the Sabbath), Yisrael and the [festive] seasons.

At the Conclusion of the Sabbath add the following:

Blessed be You *God* our God, King of the Universe, Creator of the flames of fire. Blessed be You, *God* our God, King of the Universe, Who has made a distinction between holy and profane, between light and darkness, between Yisrael and the nations, between the Seventh Day and the six days of work. You have made a distinction between the sanctity of the Sabbath and the sanctity of the holiday, and You have sanctified the Seventh Day above the six working days; You have set apart Your people Yisrael and sanctified it by Your holiness. Blessed be You, O *God,* Who has made a distinction between holy and holy.

קדוש לרגלים : See Kiddush for Sabbath above.

אשר בחר : See אתה בחרתנו above.

בורא מאורי האש : See הבדלה and ותודיענו above.

שהחינו : "Who has given us the length of days," וקימנו and Who did not permit this length of life to be shortened by untoward accidents or circumstances.

מֶלֶךְ הָעוֹלָם הַמַּבְדִּיל בֵּין קֹדֶשׁ לְחוֹל בֵּין אוֹר לְחֹשֶׁךְ בֵּין יִשְׂרָאֵל לָעַמִּים· בֵּין

יוֹם הַשְּׁבִיעִי לְשֵׁשֶׁת יְמֵי הַמַּעֲשֶׂה· בֵּין קְדֻשַּׁת שַׁבָּת לִקְדֻשַּׁת יוֹם טוֹב הִבְדַּלְתָּ·

וְאֶת יוֹם הַשְּׁבִיעִי מִשֵּׁשֶׁת יְמֵי הַמַּעֲשֶׂה קִדַּשְׁתָּ· הִבְדַּלְתָּ וְקִדַּשְׁתָּ אֶת עַמְּךָ יִשְׂרָאֵל

בִּקְדֻשָּׁתֶךָ· בָּרוּךְ אַתָּה יְיָ הַמַּבְדִּיל בֵּין קֹדֶשׁ לְקֹדֶשׁ:

On the first night of Succoth this Beracha is said before שהחיינו ; on the second
night it is said afterwards.

בָּא"יְ אֱמֶ"הָ אֲשֶׁר קִדְּשָׁנוּ בְּמִצְוֹתָיו וְצִוָּנוּ לֵישֵׁב בַּסֻּכָּה:

On the seventh and eighth night of פסח, שהחיינו is not said:

בָּרוּךְ אַתָּה יְיָ אֱלֹהֵינוּ מֶלֶךְ הָעוֹלָם
שֶׁהֶחֱיָנוּ וְקִיְּמָנוּ וְהִגִּיעָנוּ לַזְּמַן הַזֶּה:

On the three רגלים, שחרית is said until תפלת לחש as on every שבת; when יו"ט
does not fall on שבת, המאיר לארץ is said instead of הכל יודוך. The תפלה
of יו"ט replaces the תפלת לחש of שבת (P. 593); then follows Hallel:

סדר נטילת לולב

יְהִי רָצוֹן מִלְּפָנֶךָ יְיָ אֱלֹהַי וֵאלֹהֵי אֲבוֹתַי בִּפְרִי עֵץ הָדָר וְכַפּוֹת תְּמָרִים וַעֲנַף

עֵץ עָבוֹת וְעַרְבֵי נָחַל אוֹתִיוֹת שִׁמְךָ הַמְיֻחָד תְּקָרֵב אֶחָד אֶל־אֶחָד וְהָיוּ לַאֲחָדִים

בְּיָדִי· וְלֵדַע אֵיךְ שִׁמְךָ נִקְרָא עָלַי וְיִירְאוּ מִגֶּשֶׁת אֵלָי· וּבְנַעֲנוּעִי אוֹתָם תַּשְׁפִּיעַ

When in the Succah, say:

Blessed be You, O *God* our God, King of the Universe, Who
has sanctified us by His commandments and commanded us to dwell
in the Succah.

On the last two evenings of Passover the following is omitted

Blessed be You, O *God* our God, King of the Universe, Who
has kept us alive and preserved us, and enabled us to attain this
season.

שֶׁפַע בְּרָכוֹת מִדַּעַת עֶלְיוֹן לְגַוֵּהּ אַפַּרְיוֹן לְמְכוֹן בֵּית אֱלֹהֵינוּ. וִיהֵא חָשׁוּב לְפָנֶיךָ
מִצְוַת אַרְבָּעָה מִינִים כְּאִלּוּ קִיַּמְתִּיהָ בְּכָל־פְּרָטֶיהָ וְשָׁרָשֶׁיהָ וְתַרְיַ״ג מִצְוֹת הַתְּלוּיִם
בָּהּ. כִּי כַוָּנָתִי לְיַחֲדָא שְׁמָא דְקוּדְשָׁא בְּרִיךְ הוּא וּשְׁכִינְתֵּהּ בִּדְחִילוּ וּרְחִימוּ לְיַחֵד
שֵׁם י״ה בו״ה בְּיַחוּדָא שְׁלִים בְּשֵׁם כָּל־יִשְׂרָאֵל אָמֵן. בָּרוּךְ יְיָ לְעוֹלָם אָמֵן וְאָמֵן:

The לולב *and the* אתרוג *are taken in the hand and the following Bracha is said:*

בָּרוּךְ אַתָּה יְיָ, אֱלֹהֵינוּ מֶלֶךְ הָעוֹלָם, אֲשֶׁר קִדְּשָׁנוּ בְּמִצְוֹתָיו וְצִוָּנוּ עַל־נְטִילַת לוּלָב:

On the first day of סכות, שההיינו *is added; it is said on the second day if the first day falls on* שבת.

בָּרוּךְ אַתָּה יְיָ, אֱלֹהֵינוּ מֶלֶךְ הָעוֹלָם שֶׁהֶחֱיָנוּ וְקִיְּמָנוּ וְהִגִּיעָנוּ לַזְּמַן הַזֶּה:

Upon leaving the Succah on שמיני עצרת *the following is said:*

יְהִי רָצוֹן לְפָנֶיךָ יְיָ אֱלֹהֵינוּ וֵאלֹהֵי אֲבוֹתֵינוּ כְּשֵׁם שֶׁקִּיַּמְתִּי וְיָשַׁבְתִּי בְּסֻכָּה זוֹ כֵּן אֶזְכֶּה (לַשָּׁנָה הַבָּאָה) לֵישֵׁב בְּסֻכַּת עוֹר שֶׁל לִוְיָתָן:

בתפלת מנחה של שלש רגלים אומרין אשרי ונל״ג ח״ק (ובשבת מוסיפין ואכי תפלתי ויקרין) תפלה בלחש (בנ״ע וש״ת מזכירין משיב הרוח) והש״ץ חוזר התפלה. קדיש תתקבל, עלינו, (ק״י.)

בערבית לשמחת התורה מתפללין כבל סדר ערבית שמיני עצרת, ואומרין משיב הרוח וגו׳ ומקדשין ואומרין יין.

תפלת ראש השנה
לערבית ושחרית ומנחה

אֲדֹנָי שְׂפָתַי תִּפְתָּח וּפִי יַגִּיד תְּהִלָּתֶךָ:

בָּרוּךְ אַתָּה יְיָ אֱלֹהֵינוּ וֵאלֹהֵי אֲבוֹתֵינוּ אֱלֹהֵי אַבְרָהָם אֱלֹהֵי יִצְחָק וֵאלֹהֵי יַעֲקֹב הָאֵל הַגָּדוֹל הַגִּבּוֹר וְהַנּוֹרָא אֵל עֶלְיוֹן גּוֹמֵל

חֲסָדִים טוֹבִים וְקֹנֵה הַכֹּל וְזוֹכֵר חַסְדֵי אָבוֹת וּמֵבִיא גוֹאֵל לִבְנֵי בְנֵיהֶם לְמַעַן שְׁמוֹ בְּאַהֲבָה:

זָכְרֵנוּ לְחַיִּים · מֶלֶךְ חָפֵץ בַּחַיִּים · וְכָתְבֵנוּ בְּסֵפֶר הַחַיִּים · לְמַעַנְךָ אֱלֹהִים חַיִּים · מֶלֶךְ עוֹזֵר וּמוֹשִׁיעַ וּמָגֵן · בָּרוּךְ אַתָּה יְיָ מָגֵן אַבְרָהָם:

אַתָּה גִבּוֹר לְעוֹלָם אֲדֹנָי מְחַיֵּה מֵתִים אַתָּה רַב לְהוֹשִׁיעַ ·

מְכַלְכֵּל חַיִּים בְּחֶסֶד מְחַיֵּה מֵתִים בְּרַחֲמִים רַבִּים סוֹמֵךְ נוֹפְלִים וְרוֹפֵא חוֹלִים וּמַתִּיר אֲסוּרִים וּמְקַיֵּם אֱמוּנָתוֹ לִישֵׁנֵי עָפָר · מִי כָמוֹךָ בַּעַל גְּבוּרוֹת וּמִי דוֹמֶה לָךְ מֶלֶךְ מֵמִית וּמְחַיֶּה וּמַצְמִיחַ יְשׁוּעָה: מִי כָמוֹךָ אַב הָרַחֲמִים · זוֹכֵר יְצוּרָיו לְחַיִּים בְּרַחֲמִים · וְנֶאֱמָן אַתָּה לְהַחֲיוֹת מֵתִים · בָּרוּךְ אַתָּה יְיָ מְחַיֵּה הַמֵּתִים:

אַתָּה קָדוֹשׁ וְשִׁמְךָ קָדוֹשׁ וּקְדוֹשִׁים בְּכָל יוֹם יְהַלְלוּךָ סֶּלָה:

וּבְכֵן תֵּן פַּחְדְּךָ יְיָ אֱלֹהֵינוּ עַל כָּל־מַעֲשֶׂיךָ וְאֵימָתְךָ עַל כָּל־מַה־שֶׁבָּרָאתָ וְיִירָאוּךָ כָּל־הַמַּעֲשִׂים וְיִשְׁתַּחֲווּ לְפָנֶיךָ כָּל־הַבְּרוּאִים וְיֵעָשׂוּ כֻלָּם אֲגֻדָּה אַחַת לַעֲשׂוֹת רְצוֹנְךָ בְּלֵבָב שָׁלֵם כְּמוֹ שֶׁיָּדַעְנוּ יְיָ אֱלֹהֵינוּ שֶׁהַשִּׁלְטָן לְפָנֶיךָ עֹז בְּיָדְךָ וּגְבוּרָה בִּימִינֶךָ וְשִׁמְךָ נוֹרָא עַל כָּל־מַה־שֶׁבָּרָאתָ:

וּבְכֵן תֵּן כָּבוֹד יְיָ לְעַמֶּךָ תְּהִלָּה לִירֵאֶיךָ וְתִקְוָה לְדוֹרְשֶׁיךָ וּפִתְחוֹן פֶּה לַמְיַחֲלִים לָךְ שִׂמְחָה לְאַרְצֶךָ וְשָׂשׂוֹן לְעִירֶךָ וּצְמִיחַת קֶרֶן לְדָוִד עַבְדֶּךָ וַעֲרִיכַת נֵר לְבֶן יִשַׁי מְשִׁיחֶךָ בִּמְהֵרָה בְיָמֵינוּ:

תפלת ראש השנה

ובכן תן פחדך : In keeping with the significance of Rosh Hashanah, the paragraph beginning with ובכן תן פחדך is a logical sequel to the preceding paragraph ending with וקדושים בכל יום יהללוך סלה. There we declared that only the holy ones may praise the Lord; in other words, the permission to sing

Now, therefore, impose Your awe, O *God,* our God, upon all Your works, and Your dread over all that You have created, so that all Your works may fear You and all [Your] creatures may cast themselves down before You and they all may form one single band to do Your will with all their heart, even as we know, O *God* our God, that dominion is before Your countenance, strength is in Your left hand, power in Your right hand, and that Your Name is feared above all that which You have created.

And then, O *God,* give honor to Your people, praise to those who fear You, hope to those who seek You, and freedom of speech to those who wait for You, joy to Your land, delight to Your city, exaltation to the horn of Your servant David and ready light to the son of Yishai, Your Anointed, speedily in our days.

His praises is granted only to those who submit to the will of God, and who, in all their thoughts, endeavors and achievements permit only that to prevail which is good and holy and in accordance with the will of God. To praise God while behaving at direct variance with His commandments is gross blasphemy. For He is *nora tehilloth,* as our fathers realized and proclaimed immediately upon their deliverance from peril. The entire period of *teshuvah* which is introduced by the *yom teru'ah* serves to remind us of this most basic truth of all of Jewish ideology. This solemn season recalls to our minds that all our future is dependent upon whether or not every living thing that breathes and works on earth becomes aware of the full import of the dread dominion of God, and whether or not, overwhelmed by the impact of this realization, all creatures that live and breathe will unite to form one single brotherhood on earth dedicated solely and unreservedly to the endeavor to do the will of God. These are the profound thoughts which the Shofar's call of *Malchuyoth* is to stir up within our hearts.

וּבְכֵן תֵּן כָּבוֹד: It is only once we shall have transformed our own personalities through complete obedience to God that our lot, too, will be changed for the better. Then loyalty to God will attain its proper place of honor; the fear of God will be praiseworthy in the eyes of all men. Men will no longer think it ridiculous to seek God, and those who wait upon Him will be permitted to voice their convictions freely. And the truly Jewish outgrowth of this transformation of ourselves will be the restoration of our people to the land that is part of its destiny, and the fulfillment of our people's purpose there, under the scepter of kings dedicated to the realization of these ends.

וּבְכֵן צַדִּיקִים יִרְאוּ וְיִשְׂמָחוּ וִישָׁרִים יַעֲלֹזוּ וַחֲסִידִים בְּרִנָּה
יָגִילוּ וְעוֹלָתָה תִּקְפָּץ־פִּיהָ · וְכָל־הָרִשְׁעָה כֻּלָּהּ כְּעָשָׁן תִּכְלֶה כִּי
תַעֲבִיר מֶמְשֶׁלֶת זָדוֹן מִן־הָאָרֶץ:

וְתִמְלֹךְ אַתָּה יְיָ לְבַדֶּךָ עַל כָּל־מַעֲשֶׂיךָ בְּהַר צִיּוֹן מִשְׁכַּן כְּבוֹדֶךָ
וּבִירוּשָׁלַיִם עִיר קָדְשֶׁךָ כַּכָּתוּב בְּדִבְרֵי קָדְשֶׁךָ יִמְלֹךְ יְיָ לְעוֹלָם
אֱלֹהַיִךְ צִיּוֹן לְדֹר וָדֹר הַלְלוּיָהּ:

קָדוֹשׁ אַתָּה וְנוֹרָא שְׁמֶךָ וְאֵין אֱלֹהַּ מִבַּלְעָדֶיךָ כַּכָּתוּב וַיִּגְבַּהּ יְיָ
צְבָאוֹת בַּמִּשְׁפָּט וְהָאֵל הַקָּדוֹשׁ נִקְדַּשׁ בִּצְדָקָה: בָּרוּךְ אַתָּה יְיָ
הַמֶּלֶךְ הַקָּדוֹשׁ:

אַתָּה בְחַרְתָּנוּ מִכָּל הָעַמִּים · אָהַבְתָּ אוֹתָנוּ · וְרָצִיתָ בָּנוּ ·
וְרוֹמַמְתָּנוּ מִכָּל הַלְּשׁוֹנוֹת · וְקִדַּשְׁתָּנוּ בְּמִצְוֹתֶיךָ וְקֵרַבְתָּנוּ מַלְכֵּנוּ
לַעֲבוֹדָתֶךָ · וְשִׁמְךָ הַגָּדוֹל וְהַקָּדוֹשׁ עָלֵינוּ קָרָאתָ:

On מוצאי שבת the following is inserted:

וַתּוֹדִיעֵנוּ יְיָ אֱלֹהֵינוּ אֶת־מִשְׁפְּטֵי צִדְקֶךָ וַתְּלַמְּדֵנוּ לַעֲשׂוֹת חֻקֵּי
רְצוֹנֶךָ וַתִּתֶּן־לָנוּ יְיָ אֱלֹהֵינוּ מִשְׁפָּטִים יְשָׁרִים וְתוֹרוֹת אֱמֶת חֻקִּים
וּמִצְוֹת טוֹבִים וַתַּנְחִילֵנוּ זְמַנֵּי שָׂשׂוֹן וּמוֹעֲדֵי קֹדֶשׁ וְחַגֵּי נְדָבָה ·
וַתּוֹרִישֵׁנוּ קְדֻשַּׁת שַׁבָּת וּכְבוֹד מוֹעֵד וַחֲגִיגַת הָרֶגֶל · וַתַּבְדֵּל יְיָ

וובכן צדיקים: Hand in hand with our own transformation, with the re-institution of our own national life under God and with the restoration of the dynasty anointed by Him in our own midst, will go a change for the better in all the rest of mankind as well. All that is just, upright and worthy of human dignity on earth will flourish, and all violence, lawlessness and tyranny will vanish from the world.

ותמלוך: And thus will begin the kingdom of God on earth, which is the ultimate goal of all man's development through the ages, and which centers forever in Jerusalem and Zion.

And then the righteous shall see and rejoice, and the upright exult, and the devoted jubilate triumphantly, and violence will close its mouth and all lawlessness shall vanish like smoke, when You will remove the dominion of tyranny from the earth.

And then You, O *God*, will reign alone over all Your works on Mount Tzion, the Abode of Your glory, and in Yerushalayim, the city of Your Sanctuary, even as it is written in Your holy words: *"God* will reign forever, your God, O Tzion, from generation to generation. Halaluyah!"

Holy are You and feared is Your Name, and there is no God beside You, even as it written: "Since *God Tzevaoth* has shown Himself exalted in judgement, and the holy God has sanctified Himself by clemency." Blessed be You, O *God*, the holy King.

פחד is the fear of danger to come; אימה denotes the dread of peril that is already present. מעשי ה׳ signifies God's creatures in terms of their God-given *form* and *structure;* every one of God's works is specifically built and designed for the *work* and *function* that has been assigned it as its own particular task. ברואי ה׳ denotes the works of Divine creation in terms of the very *life* and *existence* that was granted them by their Maker. We now pray that the fear of the danger that may threaten them should they misuse their God-given abilities may restrain *ma'asei Hashem* from abusing the faculties with which they were endowed at the time of their formation. Thus, may every living thing that God has made, filled with the realization of God's overwhelming might that should pervade every fiber of its very being, cast itself down before Him. צמיחת קרן refers to the restoration of the power of the reigning House of David. The metaphorical term עריכת נר refers to the cultivation of mind and spirit by the House of David, as symbolized in the Sanctuary by the *menorah,* the "Tree of Light", even as it is written יערוך את הנרות לפני ה׳ תמיד (Lev. 24:4). *Keren* and *ner* are represented in the Sanctuary by *shulchan* and *menorah.* ויגבה etc. The guiding principle in the ordering of men's relationships, צבאות, with one another, must be משפט, for Divine exercise of special clemency toward one man would work hardship upon his brother. In His own direct relationship with the individual human being and in His judgment of the sin which the individual may commit against Him directly, God, being אל הקדוש, permits צדקה, clemency, to prevail.

יום הזכרון יום תרועה: In Lev. 23:24 we are told concerning Rosh Ha-shanah: יהיה לכם שבתון זכרון תרועה. There both *zikkaron* and *teru'ah* are explained as acts which we ourselves are to perform. It is the review to which we are commanded to subject all of our past lives, and a logical out-

אֱלֹהֵינוּ בֵּין קֹדֶשׁ לְחֹל בֵּין אוֹר לְחֹשֶׁךְ בֵּין יִשְׂרָאֵל לָעַמִּים בֵּין
יוֹם הַשְּׁבִיעִי לְשֵׁשֶׁת יְמֵי הַמַּעֲשֶׂה· בֵּין קְדֻשַּׁת שַׁבָּת לִקְדֻשַּׁת יוֹם
טוֹב הִבְדַּלְתָּ וְאֶת־יוֹם הַשְּׁבִיעִי מִשֵּׁשֶׁת יְמֵי הַמַּעֲשֶׂה קִדַּשְׁתָּ·
הִבְדַּלְתָּ וְקִדַּשְׁתָּ אֶת־עַמְּךָ יִשְׂרָאֵל בִּקְדֻשָּׁתֶךָ:

וַתִּתֶּן־לָנוּ יְיָ אֱלֹהֵינוּ בְּאַהֲבָה אֶת־יוֹם הַשבת הזה ואת יום הַזִּכָּרוֹן
הַזֶּה· יוֹם זכרון תְּרוּעָה באהבה מִקְרָא קֹדֶשׁ זֵכֶר לִיצִיאַת מִצְרָיִם:

אֱלֹהֵינוּ וֵאלֹהֵי אֲבוֹתֵינוּ· יַעֲלֶה וְיָבֹא וְיַגִּיעַ וְיֵרָאֶה וְיֵרָצֶה וְיִשָּׁמַע
וְיִפָּקֵד וְיִזָּכֵר זִכְרוֹנֵנוּ וּפִקְדוֹנֵנוּ וְזִכְרוֹן אֲבוֹתֵינוּ· וְזִכְרוֹן מָשִׁיחַ בֶּן
דָּוִד עַבְדֶּךָ· וְזִכְרוֹן יְרוּשָׁלַיִם עִיר קָדְשֶׁךָ· וְזִכְרוֹן כָּל עַמְּךָ בֵּית
יִשְׂרָאֵל לְפָנֶיךָ· לִפְלֵיטָה וּלְטוֹבָה וּלְחֵן וּלְחֶסֶד וּלְרַחֲמִים וּלְחַיִּים
וּלְשָׁלוֹם בְּיוֹם הַזִּכָּרוֹן הַזֶּה· זָכְרֵנוּ יְיָ אֱלֹהֵינוּ בּוֹ לְטוֹבָה· וּפָקְדֵנוּ
בוֹ לִבְרָכָה· וְהוֹשִׁיעֵנוּ בוֹ לְחַיִּים· וּבִדְבַר יְשׁוּעָה וְרַחֲמִים חוּס
וְחָנֵּנוּ וְרַחֵם עָלֵינוּ וְהוֹשִׁיעֵנוּ· כִּי אֵלֶיךָ עֵינֵינוּ· כִּי אֵל מֶלֶךְ חַנּוּן
וְרַחוּם אָתָּה:

אֱלֹהֵינוּ וֵאלֹהֵי אֲבוֹתֵינוּ מְלוֹךְ עַל כָּל הָעוֹלָם כֻּלּוֹ בִּכְבוֹדֶךָ
וְהִנָּשֵׂא עַל כָּל־הָאָרֶץ בִּיקָרֶךָ· וְהוֹפַע בַּהֲדַר גְּאוֹן עֻזֶּךָ עַל כָּל־
יוֹשְׁבֵי תֵבֵל אַרְצֶךָ· וְיֵדַע כָּל־פָּעוּל כִּי אַתָּה פְעַלְתּוֹ וְיָבִין כָּל־
יְצוּר כִּי אַתָּה יְצַרְתּוֹ וְיֹאמַר כֹּל אֲשֶׁר נְשָׁמָה בְּאַפּוֹ יְיָ אֱלֹהֵי
יִשְׂרָאֵל מֶלֶךְ וּמַלְכוּתוֹ בַּכֹּל מָשָׁלָה: לשבת אלהינו ואלהי אבותינו רצה
בִמנוחתנו קַדְּשֵׁנוּ בְּמִצְוֹתֶיךָ וְתֵן חֶלְקֵנוּ בְּתוֹרָתֶךָ שַׂבְּעֵנוּ מִטּוּבֶךָ
וְשַׂמְּחֵנוּ בִּישׁוּעָתֶךָ· לשבת והנחילנו יי אלהינו באהבה וברצון שבת קדשך
וי' וינוחו בה ישראל מקדשי שמך· וְטַהֵר לִבֵּנוּ לְעָבְדְּךָ בֶּאֱמֶת כִּי אַתָּה
אֱלֹהִים אֱמֶת וּדְבָרְךָ אֱמֶת וְקַיָּם לָעַד· בָּרוּךְ אַתָּה יְיָ מֶלֶךְ עַל
כָּל־הָאָרֶץ מְקַדֵּשׁ השבת וְיִשְׂרָאֵל וְיוֹם הַזִּכָּרוֹן:

Our God and God of our fathers, reign over all the Universe in Your glory, and be exalted over all the earth in Your grandeur, shine forth in the brilliance of Your majestic might over all inhabitants of man's world on Your earth, so that every creature may recognize that You have made it, and so that whatsoever You have made may see that You have formed it, and that everything that has breath in its nostrils may say, "*God*, the God of Yisrael, is King and His kingdom rules over all things." (*On the Sabbath, add*: Our God and God of our fathers, take pleasure in our rest), hallow us by Your commandments and grant our portion in Your Torah. Satisfy us from Your good, gladden us with Your salvation, (*On the Sabbath, add*: and give us, O *God*, our God, in love and favor Your holy Sabbath so that Yisrael, who sanctify Your Name, may rest thereon), and purify our hearts to serve You in truth, for You are God in truth and Your word is truth and enduring forever. Blessed be You, O *God*, King over all the earth, Who hallows (the Sabbath and) Yisrael and the Day of Remembrance.

---

growth of this review is the act of *teru'ah*, the signal to be given ourselves in the name of God by the blast of the Shofar, summoning us to break with all our past errors and to abandon everything in our lives that does not meet with God's favor. However, the *teru'ah* addressed to us in the name of God to call upon us to mend our ways indicates that God, too, examines our past lives and pronounces judgment over them. Thus Rosh Hashanah is a *Yom hazikkaron* not only for the Jew, but also for God, a day on which God remembers us as He examines our past conduct even as we ourselves should stop and thoughtfully reexamine the paths we have followed. Hence Rosh Hashanah is a day of remembrance not only for ourselves but also for God.

או״א מלוך: Of the triad consisting of שופרות and זכרונות, מלכיות which constitutes the truths taught us by Rosh Hashanah, the concept of *malchuyoth* signifying as it does the recognition and homage of God as the world's sole King, Ruler and Master, is the ideal most forcibly impressed upon us on Rosh Hashanah. *Zichronoth*, the realization that God examines and sits in judgment over all our past conduct is the thought which should dominate the entire week of *teshuvah* that follows, as we earnestly endeavor to mend our ways in accordance with Divine command. Finally, the *shofaroth*, the call of the Shofar which symbolizes our liberation from the shackles of past error and which guides us on to a purer, untroubled future, is the parting gift that is left us by Yom Kippur. In view of the foregoing, it is the concept

רְצֵה יְיָ אֱלֹהֵינוּ בְּעַמְּךָ יִשְׂרָאֵל וּבִתְפִלָּתָם · וְהָשֵׁב אֶת הָעֲבוֹדָה
לִדְבִיר בֵּיתֶךָ · וְאִשֵּׁי יִשְׂרָאֵל וּתְפִלָּתָם בְּאַהֲבָה תְקַבֵּל בְּרָצוֹן וּתְהִי
לְרָצוֹן תָּמִיד עֲבוֹדַת יִשְׂרָאֵל עַמֶּךָ ·

וְתֶחֱזֶינָה עֵינֵינוּ בְּשׁוּבְךָ לְצִיּוֹן בְּרַחֲמִים · בָּרוּךְ אַתָּה יְיָ הַמַּחֲזִיר
שְׁכִינָתוֹ לְצִיּוֹן :

מוֹדִים אֲנַחְנוּ לָךְ שָׁאַתָּה הוּא יְיָ אֱלֹהֵינוּ וֵאלֹהֵי אֲבוֹתֵינוּ
לְעוֹלָם וָעֶד · צוּר חַיֵּינוּ מָגֵן יִשְׁעֵנוּ אַתָּה הוּא לְדוֹר וָדוֹר · נוֹדֶה
לְּךָ וּנְסַפֵּר תְּהִלָּתֶךָ עַל חַיֵּינוּ הַמְּסוּרִים בְּיָדֶךָ וְעַל נִשְׁמוֹתֵינוּ
הַפְּקוּדוֹת לָךְ וְעַל נִסֶּיךָ שֶׁבְּכָל יוֹם עִמָּנוּ וְעַל נִפְלְאוֹתֶיךָ וְטוֹבוֹתֶיךָ
שֶׁבְּכָל עֵת · עֶרֶב וָבֹקֶר וְצָהֳרָיִם · הַטּוֹב כִּי לֹא כָלוּ רַחֲמֶיךָ
וְהַמְרַחֵם כִּי לֹא תַמּוּ חֲסָדֶיךָ מֵעוֹלָם קִוִּינוּ לָךְ :

וְעַל כֻּלָּם יִתְבָּרַךְ וְיִתְרוֹמַם שִׁמְךָ מַלְכֵּנוּ תָּמִיד לְעוֹלָם וָעֶד :

וּכְתוֹב לְחַיִּים טוֹבִים כָּל־בְּנֵי בְרִיתֶךָ ·

וְכֹל הַחַיִּים יוֹדוּךָ סֶּלָה וִיהַלְלוּ אֶת שִׁמְךָ בֶּאֱמֶת הָאֵל יְשׁוּעָתֵנוּ
וְעֶזְרָתֵנוּ סֶלָה · בָּרוּךְ אַתָּה יְיָ הַטּוֹב שִׁמְךָ וּלְךָ נָאֶה לְהוֹדוֹת :

---

of the *malchuyoth* that, more than either of the other two concepts, constitutes
the theme of our Rosh Hashanah prayers. מלך : מלוך means not only to "rule"
or "reign", but also "to begin a reign", as in מלך אדוניה ; מלך אבשלום (II Sam.
15:10, I Kings 1:11). But logically, the plea מלוך וכו' here can mean only,
"Let Your rule become evident in all the abundance of Your glory." For we
know that God has reigned supreme at all times; it is only man who, until
now, has failed to recognize God's rule and to render it homage, and we now
pray that man at long last may come to know God's universal sovereignty
and pay it the tribute of unreserved obedience. וטהר לבנו וכו' Even as God
Himself is forever *emeth* in unchanging truth, and even as His Word, the
Law and the promise revealed to us are truth eternal and unalterable, so
our own devoted service to Him, doing His will, should also come to be
emeth unswerving and constant. But for this purpose we must first have
טהרת לב. We must cleanse and purify our hearts of every passion and impulse
that might tempt us to transgress the Law or that might stand in the way
of our doing what is right.

בשחרית אומרין זה.

במנחה ובערבית אומרין זה:

שִׂים שָׁלוֹם טוֹבָה וּבְרָכָה חֵן וָחֶסֶד
וְרַחֲמִים עָלֵינוּ וְעַל כָּל יִשְׂרָאֵל עַמֶּךָ· בָּרְכֵנוּ
אָבִינוּ כֻּלָּנוּ כְּאֶחָד בְּאוֹר פָּנֶיךָ· כִּי בְאוֹר
פָּנֶיךָ נָתַתָּ לָּנוּ יְיָ אֱלֹהֵינוּ תּוֹרַת חַיִּים וְאַהֲבַת
חֶסֶד וּצְדָקָה וּבְרָכָה וְרַחֲמִים וְחַיִּים וְשָׁלוֹם
וְטוֹב בְּעֵינֶיךָ לְבָרֵךְ אֶת עַמְּךָ יִשְׂרָאֵל
בְּכָל עֵת וּבְכָל שָׁעָה בִּשְׁלוֹמֶךָ:

שָׁלוֹם רָב עַל יִשְׂרָאֵל
עַמְּךָ תָּשִׂים לְעוֹלָם כִּי
אַתָּה הוּא מֶלֶךְ אָדוֹן
לְכָל הַשָּׁלוֹם וְטוֹב
בְּעֵינֶיךָ לְבָרֵךְ אֶת עַמְּךָ
יִשְׂרָאֵל בְּכָל עֵת וּבְכָל
שָׁעָה בִּשְׁלוֹמֶךָ:

בְּסֵפֶר חַיִּים בְּרָכָה וְשָׁלוֹם וּפַרְנָסָה טוֹבָה נִזָּכֵר וְנִכָּתֵב לְפָנֶיךָ
אֲנַחְנוּ וְכָל עַמְּךָ בֵּית יִשְׂרָאֵל לְחַיִּים טוֹבִים וּלְשָׁלוֹם· בָּרוּךְ אַתָּה
יְיָ עוֹשֵׂה הַשָּׁלוֹם:

אֱלֹהַי· נְצוֹר לְשׁוֹנִי מֵרָע וּשְׂפָתַי מִדַּבֵּר מִרְמָה וְלִמְקַלְלַי נַפְשִׁי
תִדּוֹם וְנַפְשִׁי כֶּעָפָר לַכֹּל תִּהְיֶה: פְּתַח לִבִּי בְּתוֹרָתֶךָ וּבְמִצְוֹתֶךָ
תִּרְדּוֹף נַפְשִׁי וְכָל הַחוֹשְׁבִים עָלַי רָעָה מְהֵרָה הָפֵר עֲצָתָם וְקַלְקֵל
מַחֲשַׁבְתָּם· עֲשֵׂה לְמַעַן שְׁמֶךָ· עֲשֵׂה לְמַעַן יְמִינֶךָ· עֲשֵׂה לְמַעַן
קְדֻשָּׁתֶךָ· עֲשֵׂה לְמַעַן תּוֹרָתֶךָ· לְמַעַן יֵחָלְצוּן יְדִידֶיךָ הוֹשִׁיעָה
יְמִינְךָ וַעֲנֵנִי: יִהְיוּ לְרָצוֹן אִמְרֵי פִי וְהֶגְיוֹן לִבִּי לְפָנֶיךָ יְיָ צוּרִי
וְגֹאֲלִי: עֹשֶׂה שָׁלוֹם בִּמְרוֹמָיו הוּא יַעֲשֶׂה שָׁלוֹם עָלֵינוּ וְעַל כָּל
יִשְׂרָאֵל וְאִמְרוּ אָמֵן:

יְהִי רָצוֹן מִלְּפָנֶיךָ יְיָ אֱלֹהֵינוּ וֵאלֹהֵי אֲבוֹתֵינוּ שֶׁיִּבָּנֶה
בֵּית הַמִּקְדָּשׁ בִּמְהֵרָה בְיָמֵינוּ וְתֵן חֶלְקֵנוּ בְּתוֹרָתֶךָ:
וְשָׁם נַעֲבָדְךָ בְּיִרְאָה כִּימֵי עוֹלָם וּבְשָׁנִים קַדְמוֹנִיּוֹת:
וְעָרְבָה לַיְיָ מִנְחַת יְהוּדָה וִירוּשָׁלָםִ כִּימֵי עוֹלָם וּבְשָׁנִים קַדְמוֹנִיּוֹת:

The following greeting is exchanged on the eve of ר"ה:

ליחיד לְשָׁנָה טוֹבָה תִּכָּתֵב: לרבים לְשָׁנָה טוֹבָה תִּכָּתֵבוּ:

לנקבה לְשָׁנָה טוֹבָה תִּכָּתֵבִי: לרבות לְשָׁנָה טוֹבָה תִּכָּתֵבְנָה:

On שבת the following is preceded by יום הששי (P. 292):

סַבְרִי מָרָנָן וְרַבָּנָן וְרַבּוֹתַי

בָּרוּךְ אַתָּה יְיָ אֱלֹהֵינוּ מֶלֶךְ הָעוֹלָם בּוֹרֵא פְּרִי הַגָּפֶן:

בָּרוּךְ אַתָּה יְיָ אֱלֹהֵינוּ מֶלֶךְ הָעוֹלָם אֲשֶׁר בָּחַר בָּנוּ מִכָּל־עָם
וְרוֹמְמָנוּ מִכָּל־לָשׁוֹן וְקִדְּשָׁנוּ בְּמִצְוֹתָיו · וַתִּתֶּן לָנוּ יְיָ אֱלֹהֵינוּ בְּאַהֲבָה
אֶת יום השבת הזה ואת יום הַזִּכָּרוֹן הַזֶּה יוֹם זִכְרוֹן תְּרוּעָה באהבה
מִקְרָא קֹדֶשׁ זֵכֶר לִיצִיאַת מִצְרָיִם · כִּי בָנוּ בָחַרְתָּ וְאוֹתָנוּ קִדַּשְׁתָּ
מִכָּל־הָעַמִּים · וּדְבָרְךָ אֱמֶת וְקַיָּם לָעַד · בָּרוּךְ אַתָּה יְיָ מֶלֶךְ עַל
כָּל־הָאָרֶץ מְקַדֵּשׁ השבת ו יִשְׂרָאֵל וְיוֹם הַזִּכָּרוֹן:

On מוצאי שבת the following is inserted:

בָּרוּךְ אַתָּה יְיָ אֱלֹהֵינוּ מֶלֶךְ הָעוֹלָם בּוֹרֵא מְאוֹרֵי הָאֵשׁ: בָּרוּךְ אַתָּה יְיָ אֱלֹהֵינוּ
מֶלֶךְ הָעוֹלָם הַמַּבְדִּיל בֵּין קֹדֶשׁ לְחוֹל בֵּין אוֹר לְחשֶׁךְ בֵּין יִשְׂרָאֵל לָעַמִּים · בֵּין
יוֹם הַשְּׁבִיעִי לְשֵׁשֶׁת יְמֵי הַמַּעֲשֶׂה · בֵּין קְדֻשַּׁת שַׁבָּת לִקְדֻשַּׁת יוֹם טוֹב הִבְדַּלְתָּ ·
וְאֶת יוֹם הַשְּׁבִיעִי מִשֵּׁשֶׁת יְמֵי הַמַּעֲשֶׂה קִדַּשְׁתָּ · הִבְדַּלְתָּ וְקִדַּשְׁתָּ אֶת עַמְּךָ יִשְׂרָאֵל
בִּקְדֻשָּׁתֶךָ · בָּרוּךְ אַתָּה יְיָ הַמַּבְדִּיל בֵּין קֹדֶשׁ לְקֹדֶשׁ:

שהחיינו is said on both nights:

בָּרוּךְ אַתָּה יְיָ אֱלֹהֵינוּ מֶלֶךְ הָעוֹלָם שֶׁהֶחֱיָנוּ וְקִיְּמָנוּ וְהִגִּיעָנוּ לַזְּמַן הַזֶּה:

After the קדוש at the meal the המוציא is recited over the two breads; then a
piece of sweet apple is dipped into honey and this Bracha is said:

בָּרוּךְ אַתָּה יְיָ אֱלֹהֵינוּ מֶלֶךְ הָעוֹלָם בּוֹרֵא פְּרִי הָעֵץ:

The piece of apple is taken and the following is said:

יְהִי רָצוֹן מִלְּפָנֶיךָ יְיָ אֱלֹהֵינוּ וֵאלֹהֵי אֲבוֹתֵינוּ שֶׁתְּחַדֵּשׁ עָלֵינוּ שָׁנָה טוֹבָה וּמְתוּקָה:

סדר אבינו מלכנו

אבינו מלכנו is said at Shacharith and Minchah from Rosh Hashana to
Yom Kippur. It is omitted on the Sabbath and at Minchah on Friday and on
Erev Yom Kippur. However, if Yom Kippur falls upon a Sabbath, אבינו מלכנו
is recited at Shacharith on Erev Yom Kippur.

אָבִינוּ מַלְכֵּנוּ חָטָאנוּ לְפָנֶיךָ:
אָבִינוּ מַלְכֵּנוּ אֵין לָנוּ מֶלֶךְ אֶלָּא אָתָּה:
אָבִינוּ מַלְכֵּנוּ עֲשֵׂה עִמָּנוּ לְמַעַן שְׁמֶךָ:
אָבִינוּ מַלְכֵּנוּ חַדֵּשׁ עָלֵינוּ שָׁנָה טוֹבָה:
אָבִינוּ מַלְכֵּנוּ בַּטֵּל מֵעָלֵינוּ כָּל־גְּזֵרוֹת קָשׁוֹת:

623 · סדר אבינו מלכנו

אבינו מלכנו *is said at Shacharith and Minchah from Rosh Hashana to Yom Kippur. It is omitted on the Sabbath and at Minchah on Friday and on Erev Yom Kippur. However, if Yom Kippur falls upon a Sabbath,* אבינו מלכנו *is recited at Shacharith on Erev Yom Kippur.*

Our Father, our King, we have sinned before You.

Our Father, our King, we have no King beside You.

Our Father, our King, deal with us in accordance with Your Name.

Our Father, our King, renew for us a good year.

Our Father, our King, annul every harsh decree concerning us.

אבינו מלכנו: God is our Father and our King. Fatherlike, He never withholds His compassion from us; like a King He commands over our destinies and requires of us that we obey Him. This is the thought which, during the ten days of our "return" to Him, guides us forth again and again from our errors, back to the feet of our God as His servants and His children. חטאנו לפניך Our past errors which have persisted into the present and which we have not yet managed to overcome are the cause and reason for our persisting exile which is to end in redemption. אין לנו מלך אלא אתה: And yet, despite this physical banishment and spiritual estrangement we still have none other than God to guide our lives and to shape our destinies. Therefore, עשה עמנו למען שמך, we also wait on none other but God to shape our future and we appeal to that abundance of loving-kindness which is guaranteed us by His very Name that implies His eternal readiness to grant us a new future. The term *shanah tovah* summarizes all our hopes and inmost yearnings for the future. Now we enumerate them, one by one, the hopes and wishes which we cherish in our hearts for the year that is to come. Naturally, the first of these is the plea for the removal of גזרות קשות, all those troubles that inhibit the growth of all that is good. It is most significantly in keeping with our exiled state that this is immediately followed by כלה, הפר, בטל (and in some communities also by סתום) prayers for protection and help in the perils prepared for us by the hostile peoples in whose midst we live. Unfortunately our present sad experiences are ample proof that these pleas are more than justified even today, and that it is only the part of rash thoughtlessness to demand the elimination of these verses from the prayer book because "they are no longer timely." It is only after this that we add כלה, מנע, and שלח, asking that we be spared from all physical pain and also from those social evils which are not necessarily the result of hostility directed specifically against the Jewish people (משחית, שבי, חרב). It is significant that the prayers for deliverance from physical suffering and social evils should take precedence over החזירנו בתשובה, the prayer for Divine aid in our efforts at selfcorrection. We would have been justified in expecting this last plea to come first, preceding all the others, for there can be no doubt that the improvement in our

אָבִינוּ מַלְכֵּנוּ בַּטֵּל מַחְשְׁבוֹת שׂוֹנְאֵינוּ:

אָבִינוּ מַלְכֵּנוּ הָפֵר עֲצַת אוֹיְבֵינוּ:

אָבִינוּ מַלְכֵּנוּ כַּלֵּה כָּל־צָר וּמַשְׂטִין מֵעָלֵינוּ:

אָבִינוּ מַלְכֵּנוּ סְתוֹם פִּיוֹת מַשְׂטִינֵינוּ וּמְקַטְרִגֵינוּ:

אָבִינוּ מַלְכֵּנוּ כַּלֵּה דֶּבֶר וְחֶרֶב וְרָעָב וּשְׁבִי וּמַשְׁחִית וּמַגֵּפָה

מִבְּנֵי בְרִיתֶךָ:

אָבִינוּ מַלְכֵּנוּ מְנַע מַגֵּפָה מִנַּחֲלָתֶךָ:

אָבִינוּ מַלְכֵּנוּ שְׁלַח רְפוּאָה שְׁלֵמָה לְחוֹלֵי עַמֶּךָ:

אָבִינוּ מַלְכֵּנוּ הַחֲזִירֵנוּ בִּתְשׁוּבָה שְׁלֵמָה לְפָנֶיךָ:

אָבִינוּ מַלְכֵּנוּ סְלַח וּמְחַל לְכָל־עֲוֹנוֹתֵינוּ:

אָבִינוּ מַלְכֵּנוּ מְחֵה וְהַעֲבֵר פְּשָׁעֵינוּ (וְחַטֹּאתֵינוּ) מִנֶּגֶד עֵינֶיךָ:

אָבִינוּ מַלְכֵּנוּ קְרַע רוֹעַ גְּזַר דִּינֵנוּ:

אָבִינוּ מַלְכֵּנוּ מָחוֹק בְּרַחֲמֶיךָ הָרַבִּים כָּל־שִׁטְרֵי חוֹבוֹתֵינוּ:

אָבִינוּ מַלְכֵּנוּ זְכוֹר כִּי־עָפָר אֲנָחְנוּ:

אָבִינוּ מַלְכֵּנוּ זָכְרֵנוּ בְּזִכָּרוֹן טוֹב לְפָנֶיךָ:

---

lot is dependent upon the extent to which we better our ways. Unfortunately, history has shown that ameliorations in our material status have frequently resulted in our spiritual retrogression. It has been proven repeatedly that יאי עניותא לישראל oppression actually benefits the people of Yisrael, and serves as a challenge to our people to muster all its spiritual and moral grandeur. It was in the midst of the sufferings of exile that we truly proved our constancy, and it has been mostly in times of economic disaster and social catastrophe that we have resolved to sin no more. All too frequently prosperity has caused our nation to waver in its loyalty, and any improvement in our lot, either social or economic, all too often helped relegate to oblivion all our solemn resolves to turn over a new leaf. It may well be that this prayer for perfect *teshuvah* was deliberately put after rather than before the plea for the betterment of our situation, both material and spiritual, in order to warn us to rid ourselves, at long last, of the moral weakness which deprived us of the ability to cope with happiness and prosperity and which has been the cause of all our troubles. כתבנו בספר : Statements in the Holy Scriptures

Our Father, our King, annul the designs of those who hate us.

Our Father, our King, thwart the plans of our enemies.

Our Father, our King, destroy every oppressor and adversary from us.

(Our Father, our King, close the mouths of our adversaries and
                accusers.)

Our Father, our King, remove pestilence, sword, famine, captivity,
           destruction and plague from the sons of Your covenant.

Our Father, our King, keep away the plague from Your inheritance.

Our Father, our King, send perfect healing to the sick of Your
           people.

Our Father, our King, cause us to return to You in perfect repent-
           ance.

Our Father, our King, forgive and pardon all our sins.

Our Father, our King, blot out and remove our transgressions from
           before Your eyes.

Our Father, our King, rend asunder the evil sentence of our judgment.

Our Father, our King, erase in Your great compassion all the records
           of our guilt.

Our Father, our King, remember that we are dust.

Our Father, our King, remember us with a good remembrance before
           You.

(Exod. 32:32, 33), מחני נא מספרך אשר כתבת, מי אשר חטא לי אמחנו מספרי   such as
Psalm 69:29, 56:9 and Malachi 3:16 all indicate this thought: Since all there
is was brought into being by the "Word" of God, and since all that which
is yet to be will come about also only at His "Word", all the works and ways
of His sovereignty together may be construed and taken as the content of one
single "Book" of God, and כתבנו בספר חיים טובים etc. actually means, "Number
us among those who, through Your Providence, will be allotted a good life."
נקום לעינינו. Throughout its long existence, the people of Yisrael, sorely-tried
like no other nation in history, has borne again and again the most outrageous
atrocities, maltreatments and cruelties without ever raising an avenging hand
against its foes and oppressors and without ever attempting to work retribution upon the peoples and rulers who had unleashed upon it their excesses
of fanatical inhumanity. The one motive which, more than anything else,
has protected Israel from the base impulses of vengefulness, is represented by
the recital of those portions of our prayer book which teach us that we must
commit to none other but God all vengeance and retribution for the hurt
we may sustain at the hands of others. Our regular perusal of the statements
in our sacred literature with reference to the promise and reassurance that

During Ne'ilah
substitute חתמנו
for כתבנו.

אָבִינוּ מַלְכֵּנוּ כָּתְבֵנוּ בְּסֵפֶר חַיִּים טוֹבִים:

אָבִינוּ מַלְכֵּנוּ כָּתְבֵנוּ בְּסֵפֶר זְכִיּוֹת:

אָבִינוּ מַלְכֵּנוּ כָּתְבֵנוּ בְּסֵפֶר פַּרְנָסָה וְכַלְכָּלָה:

אָבִינוּ מַלְכֵּנוּ כָּתְבֵנוּ בְּסֵפֶר גְּאֻלָּה וִישׁוּעָה:

אָבִינוּ מַלְכֵּנוּ כָּתְבֵנוּ בְּסֵפֶר סְלִיחָה וּמְחִילָה:

אָבִינוּ מַלְכֵּנוּ הַצְמַח לָנוּ יְשׁוּעָה בְּקָרוֹב:

אָבִינוּ מַלְכֵּנוּ הָרֵם קֶרֶן יִשְׂרָאֵל עַמֶּךָ:

אָבִינוּ מַלְכֵּנוּ הָרֵם קֶרֶן מְשִׁיחֶךָ:

אָבִינוּ מַלְכֵּנוּ מַלֵּא יָדֵינוּ מִבִּרְכוֹתֶיךָ: אָבִינוּ מַלְכֵּנוּ מַלֵּא אֲסָמֵינוּ שָׂבָע:

אָבִינוּ מַלְכֵּנוּ שְׁמַע קוֹלֵנוּ חוּס וְרַחֵם עָלֵינוּ:

אָבִינוּ מַלְכֵּנוּ קַבֵּל בְּרַחֲמִים וּבְרָצוֹן אֶת־תְּפִלָּתֵנוּ:

אָבִינוּ מַלְכֵּנוּ פְּתַח שַׁעֲרֵי שָׁמַיִם לִתְפִלָּתֵנוּ:

אָבִינוּ מַלְכֵּנוּ נָא אַל תְּשִׁיבֵנוּ רֵיקָם מִלְּפָנֶיךָ:

אָבִינוּ מַלְכֵּנוּ תְּהִי הַשָּׁעָה הַזֹּאת שְׁעַת רַחֲמִים וְעֵת רָצוֹן מִלְּפָנֶיךָ:

אָבִינוּ מַלְכֵּנוּ חֲמוֹל עָלֵינוּ וְעַל־עוֹלָלֵינוּ וְטַפֵּנוּ:

אָבִינוּ מַלְכֵּנוּ עֲשֵׂה לְמַעַן הֲרוּגִים עַל־שֵׁם קָדְשֶׁךָ:

אָבִינוּ מַלְכֵּנוּ עֲשֵׂה לְמַעַן טְבוּחִים עַל יִחוּדֶךָ:

אָבִינוּ מַלְכֵּנוּ עֲשֵׂה לְמַעַן בָּאֵי בָאֵשׁ וּבַמַּיִם עַל־קִדּוּשׁ שְׁמֶךָ:

אָבִינוּ מַלְכֵּנוּ נְקוֹם לְעֵינֵינוּ נִקְמַת דַּם־עֲבָדֶיךָ הַשָּׁפוּךְ:

God sees all that we must bear, and reserves for Himself the right to exact
retribution for every hurt that we have suffered at the hands of our foes,
has kept us free of the lust for vengeance. It is due only to our trust in the
truth of these promises that we have found the strength to submit to murder
without ever becoming murderers ourselves, to bear strangling without ever
becoming hangmen ourselves, and to tolerate robbery at the hands of our
foes without ever robbing in return. It was only through these our prayers
that, in the midst of a populace that derided, hated and mistreated us we
could remain loyal to the rulers of the lands to which we have been dispersed
and keep alive within our hearts sentiments of human sympathy for their

Our Father, our King, inscribe_* us in the Book of the Good Life.

Our Father, our King, inscribe us in the Book of Merits.

Our Father, our King, inscribe us in the Book of Sustenance and Maintenance.

Our Father, our King, inscribe us in the Book of Redemption and Salvation.

Our Father, our King, inscribe us in the Book of Forgiveness and Pardon.

Our Father, our King, cause salvation speedily to spring forth for us.

Our Father, our King, exalt the horn of Your people Yisrael.

Our Father, our King, exalt the horn of Your anointed.

(Our Father, our King, fill our hands with Your blessings.)

(Our Father, our King, fill our larders with plenty.)

Our Father, our King, hear our voice, spare us and have compassion upon us.

Our Father, our King, accept our prayer with compassion and favor.

(Our Father, our King, open the portals of Heaven to our prayer.)

Our Father, our King, turn us not back empty from Your presence.

(Our Father, our King, let this hour be an hour of compassion and a time of favor before You.)

(Our Father, our King, have compassion upon us, and upon our children and infants.)

Our Father, our King, do it for the sake of those who were slain for Your holy Name.

Our Father, our King, do it for the sake of those who were slaughtered for Your Unity.

Our Father, our King, do it for the sake of those who went through fire and water for the sanctification of Your Name.

Our Father, our King, avenge before our eyes the blood of Your servants that has been shed.

---

*   *During Ne'ilah services on Yom Kippur, say "seal us".*

---

peoples, so that our relationships with the nations in whose midst we have lived have always been marked by kindness and humanity on our part. These appeals to God have helped us remain human and kind in the midst of all the inhumanity round about us.

אָבִינוּ מַלְכֵּנוּ עֲשֵׂה לְמַעַנְךָ אִם־לֹא־לְמַעֲנֵנוּ:

אָבִינוּ מַלְכֵּנוּ עֲשֵׂה לְמַעַנְךָ וְהוֹשִׁיעֵנוּ:

אָבִינוּ מַלְכֵּנוּ עֲשֵׂה לְמַעַן רַחֲמֶיךָ הָרַבִּים:

אָבִינוּ מַלְכֵּנוּ עֲשֵׂה לְמַעַן שְׁמְךָ הַגָּדוֹל הַגִּבּוֹר וְהַנּוֹרָא שֶׁנִּקְרָא
עָלֵינוּ:

אָבִינוּ מַלְכֵּנוּ חָנֵּנוּ וַעֲנֵנוּ כִּי אֵין בָּנוּ מַעֲשִׂים עֲשֵׂה עִמָּנוּ צְדָקָה וָחֶסֶד וְהוֹשִׁיעֵנוּ:

אֲדֹנָי שְׂפָתַי תִּפְתָּח וּפִי יַגִּיד תְּהִלָּתֶךָ:

בָּרוּךְ אַתָּה יְיָ אֱלֹהֵינוּ וֵאלֹהֵי אֲבוֹתֵינוּ אֱלֹהֵי אַבְרָהָם אֱלֹהֵי
יִצְחָק וֵאלֹהֵי יַעֲקֹב הָאֵל הַגָּדוֹל הַגִּבּוֹר וְהַנּוֹרָא אֵל עֶלְיוֹן גּוֹמֵל
חֲסָדִים טוֹבִים וְקֹנֵה הַכֹּל וְזוֹכֵר חַסְדֵי אָבוֹת וּמֵבִיא גוֹאֵל לִבְנֵי
בְנֵיהֶם לְמַעַן שְׁמוֹ בְּאַהֲבָה •

זָכְרֵנוּ לְחַיִּים • מֶלֶךְ חָפֵץ בַּחַיִּים • וְכָתְבֵנוּ בְּסֵפֶר הַחַיִּים • לְמַעַנְךָ
אֱלֹהִים חַיִּים • מֶלֶךְ עוֹזֵר וּמוֹשִׁיעַ וּמָגֵן • בָּרוּךְ אַתָּה יְיָ מָגֵן אַבְרָהָם:

אַתָּה גִּבּוֹר לְעוֹלָם אֲדֹנָי מְחַיֵּה מֵתִים אַתָּה רַב לְהוֹשִׁיעַ •

מְכַלְכֵּל חַיִּים בְּחֶסֶד מְחַיֵּה מֵתִים בְּרַחֲמִים רַבִּים סוֹמֵךְ נוֹפְלִים
וְרוֹפֵא חוֹלִים וּמַתִּיר אֲסוּרִים וּמְקַיֵּם אֱמוּנָתוֹ לִישֵׁנֵי עָפָר • מִי
כָמוֹךָ בַּעַל גְּבוּרוֹת וּמִי דּוֹמֶה לָּךְ מֶלֶךְ מֵמִית וּמְחַיֶּה וּמַצְמִיחַ יְשׁוּעָה:

מִי כָמוֹךָ אַב הָרַחֲמִים • זוֹכֵר יְצוּרָיו לְחַיִּים בְּרַחֲמִים • וְנֶאֱמָן
אַתָּה לְהַחֲיוֹת מֵתִים • בָּרוּךְ אַתָּה יְיָ מְחַיֵּה הַמֵּתִים:

Our Father, our King, do it for Your sake, if not for our sake.

Our Father, our King, do it for Your sake and save us.

Our Father, our King, do it for the sake of Your great compassion.

Our Father, our King, do it for the sake of the great, mighty and
awesome Name which is proclaimed over us.

Our Father, our King, favor us and answer us, for we have no
[good] works; deal with us in clemency and
loving-kindness and save us.

אַתָּה קָדוֹשׁ וְשִׁמְךָ קָדוֹשׁ וּקְדוֹשִׁים בְּכָל יוֹם יְהַלְלוּךָ פֶּלָה:

וּבְכֵן תֵּן פַּחְדְּךָ יְיָ אֱלֹהֵינוּ עַל כָּל מַעֲשֶׂיךָ וְאֵימָתְךָ עַל כָּל מַה
שֶּׁבָּרָאתָ וְיִירָאוּךָ כָּל הַמַּעֲשִׂים וְיִשְׁתַּחֲווּ לְפָנֶיךָ כָּל הַבְּרוּאִים
וְיֵעָשׂוּ כֻלָּם אֲגֻדָּה אֶחָת לַעֲשׂוֹת רְצוֹנְךָ בְּלֵבָב שָׁלֵם כְּמוֹ שֶׁיָּדַעְנוּ
יְיָ אֱלֹהֵינוּ שֶׁהַשָּׁלְטָן לְפָנֶיךָ עֹז בְּיָדְךָ וּגְבוּרָה בִּימִינֶךָ וְשִׁמְךָ
נוֹרָא עַל כָּל מַה שֶּׁבָּרָאתָ:

וּבְכֵן תֵּן כָּבוֹד יְיָ לְעַמֶּךָ תְּהִלָּה לִירֵאֶיךָ וְתִקְוָה לְדוֹרְשֶׁיךָ וּפִתְחוֹן
פֶּה לַמְיַחֲלִים לָךְ שִׂמְחָה לְאַרְצֶךָ וְשָׂשׂוֹן לְעִירֶךָ וּצְמִיחַת קֶרֶן
לְדָוִד עַבְדֶּךָ וַעֲרִיכַת גֵר לְבֶן יִשַׁי מְשִׁיחֶךָ בִּמְהֵרָה בְּיָמֵינוּ:

וּבְכֵן צַדִּיקִים יִרְאוּ וְיִשְׂמָחוּ וִישָׁרִים יַעֲלֹזוּ וַחֲסִידִים בְּרִנָּה
יָגִילוּ וְעוֹלָתָה תִּקְפָּץ פִּיהָ וְכָל הָרִשְׁעָה כֻּלָּהּ כְּעָשָׁן תִּכְלֶה כִּי
תַעֲבִיר מֶמְשֶׁלֶת זָדוֹן מִן הָאָרֶץ:

וְתִמְלוֹךְ אַתָּה יְיָ לְבַדֶּךָ עַל כָּל מַעֲשֶׂיךָ בְּהַר צִיּוֹן מִשְׁכַּן
כְּבוֹדֶךָ וּבִירוּשָׁלַיִם עִיר קָדְשֶׁךָ כַּכָּתוּב בְּדִבְרֵי קָדְשֶׁךָ יִמְלֹךְ יְיָ
לְעוֹלָם אֱלֹהַיִךְ צִיּוֹן לְדֹר וָדֹר הַלְלוּיָהּ:

קָדוֹשׁ אַתָּה וְנוֹרָא שְׁמֶךָ וְאֵין אֱלוֹהַּ מִבַּלְעָדֶיךָ כַּכָּתוּב וַיִּגְבַּהּ יְיָ
צְבָאוֹת בַּמִּשְׁפָּט וְהָאֵל הַקָּדוֹשׁ נִקְדַּשׁ בִּצְדָקָה: בָּרוּךְ אַתָּה יְיָ
הַמֶּלֶךְ הַקָּדוֹשׁ:

אַתָּה בְחַרְתָּנוּ מִכָּל הָעַמִּים · אָהַבְתָּ אוֹתָנוּ · וְרָצִיתָ בָּנוּ ·
וְרוֹמַמְתָּנוּ מִכָּל הַלְּשׁוֹנוֹת · וְקִדַּשְׁתָּנוּ בְּמִצְוֹתֶיךָ · וְקֵרַבְתָּנוּ מַלְכֵּנוּ
לַעֲבוֹדָתֶךָ · וְשִׁמְךָ הַגָּדוֹל וְהַקָּדוֹשׁ עָלֵינוּ קָרָאתָ:

וַתִּתֶּן לָנוּ יְיָ אֱלֹהֵינוּ בְּאַהֲבָה אֶת יוֹם הַשַּׁבָּת הַזֶּה וְאֶת יוֹם
הַזִּכָּרוֹן הַזֶּה · יוֹם זִכְרוֹן תְּרוּעָה בְּאַהֲבָה מִקְרָא קֹדֶשׁ זֵכֶר
לִיצִיאַת מִצְרָיִם:

ומפני חטאינו גלינו מארצנו ונתרחקנו מעל אדמתנו ואין
אנחנו יכולים לעשות חובותינו בבית בחירתך בבית הגדול
והקדוש שנקרא שמך עליו מפני היד שנשתלחה במקדשך:
יהי רצון מלפניך יי אלהינו ואלהי אבותינו מלך רחמן שתשוב
ותרחם עלינו ועל מקדשך ברחמיך הרבים ותבנהו מהרה
ותגדל כבודו: אבינו מלכנו גלה כבוד מלכותך עלינו מהרה
והופע והנשא עלינו לעיני כל חי וקרב פזורינו מבין הגוים
ונפוצותינו כנס מירכתי ארץ והביאנו לציון עירך ברנה
ולירושלים בית מקדשך בשמחת עולם ושם נעשה לפניך את
קרבנות חובותינו תמידים כסדרם ומוספים כהלכתם: ואת
מוספי יום (השבת הזה ויום) הזכרון הזה נעשה ונקריב לפניך
באהבה כמצות רצונך כמו שכתבת עלינו בתורתך על ידי
משה עבדך מפי כבודך כאמור:

וביום השבת שני כבשים בני שנה תמימם
ושני עשרנים סלת מנחה בלולה בשמן ונסכו:
עלת שבת בשבתו על עלת התמיד ונסכה:

ובחדש השביעי באחד לחדש מקרא קדש יהיה
לכם כל מלאכת עבדה לא תעשו יום תרועה יהיה
לכם: ועשיתם עלה לריח ניחח ליי פר בן בקר אחד
איל אחד כבשים בני שנה שבעה תמימם:

וּבַחדֶשׁ הַשְּׁבִיעִי Note the difference in wording: instead of *vehikravtem*
which appears in the sacrificial regulations pertaining to the other *Mo'adim*,
we are told here וַעֲשִׂיתֶם. The thought implicit in this change in wording is as

And in the seventh month, on the first day of the month, you shall have a convocation to the Sanctuary; you shall do no servile work; it shall be to you a day of stirring sound. And you shall prepare for *God* as an elevating-offering as an expression of your obedience one bullock, one ram, seven yearling lambs without blemish. And

---

follows: "You dare not yet come into the presence of God with a symbolic expression of the ideal of your destiny, still less with two bullocks which would imply claim that every single individual in Yisrael has already fulfilled his destiny in the service of God." Instead, we are told here, *va'asitem*: "For the present, you are to give only a general indication of the symbolic expression of your destiny. You are to offer one bullock symbolically portraying your nation in its entirety as an efficient working force in the service of God." This is the common destiny through which every individual must find his way back to the service of God as the Shofar sounds its call. (See notes above to the Musaph of the Pilgrim Festivals p. 604).

עלינו : The thoughts expressed by שופרות, זכרונות, מלכיות ; namely, that God *reigns,* that He *remembers* and that He now *calls upon us* to follow Him into a new future which He guides, are the basic truths which we are given to take to heart anew each time we stand upon the threshold of a new year. They are impressed upon us in the Musaph service by means of detailed references to appropriate quotations from the Bible. For each of these three cardinal truths we are given ten different Biblical quotations, three from the Torah, then three from the Kethuvim, and three from the Nevi'im. The last quotation is again from the Torah; for it is the Torah that is the exclusive basic source of all of Jewish truth, and neither Neviim nor Kethuvim contain any thought that has not, in fact, been propounded in some form in the Torah. Accordingly, these series of references both begin and end with quotations from the Pentateuch. In keeping with the principle מעלין בקדש ולא מורידין ; to go ever upward and forward, and never backward and downward with respect to things holy, the quotations from the Kethuvim precede those from the Neviim; for while the Kethuvim are only the outpourings of sacred inspiration borne by the *ruach hakodesh,* the words of the Neviim are actual, direct, Divine revelation. It should not be made to appear as if that which was already verified through *divrei nevuah* were still in need of confirmation by Kethuvim. Rather, that which is written in the Kethuvim is confirmed by the Neviim and sealed by the Torah. Each Biblical documentation of these three basic truths is preceded by a preface which first introduces the thought; i.e. עלינו, אתה זוכר, אתה נגלית and closes with a blessing declaring an inference from the truth just discussed, in terms of the future for which we hope and pray; i.e. או"א מלוך, או"א זכרנו, או"א תקע. As we have already noted repeatedly,

וּמִנְחָתָם וְנִסְכֵּיהֶם כִּמְדֻבָּר שְׁלֹשָׁה עֶשְׂרֹנִים לַפָּר

וּשְׁנֵי עֶשְׂרֹנִים לָאַיִל וְעִשָּׂרוֹן לַכֶּבֶשׂ וְיַיִן כְּנִסְכּוֹ

וּשְׁנֵי שְׂעִירִים לְכַפֵּר ·

וּשְׁנֵי תְמִידִים כְּהִלְכָתָם: מִלְּבַד

עֹלַת הַחֹדֶשׁ וּמִנְחָתָהּ · וְעֹלַת

הַתָּמִיד וּמִנְחָתָהּ · וְנִסְכֵּיהֶם

כְּמִשְׁפָּטָם לְרֵיחַ נִיחֹחַ אִשֶּׁה לַיְיָ:

וְשָׂעִיר לְכַפֵּר מִלְּבַד עֹלַת
הַחֹדֶשׁ וּמִנְחָתָהּ וְשָׂעִיר
לְחַטָּאת וְנִסְכֵּיהֶם
כְּמִשְׁפָּטָם וּשְׁנֵי תְמִידִים
כְּהִלְכָתָם :

בק"ק פפ"דם ובכותי' אומרי'

יִשְׂמְחוּ בְמַלְכוּתְךָ שׁוֹמְרֵי שַׁבָּת וְקוֹרְאֵי עֹנֶג עַם מְקַדְּשֵׁי שְׁבִיעִי

כֻּלָּם יִשְׂבְּעוּ וְיִתְעַנְּגוּ מִטּוּבֶךָ · וּבַשְּׁבִיעִי רָצִיתָ בּוֹ וְקִדַּשְׁתּוֹ חֶמְדַּת

יָמִים אוֹתוֹ קָרָאתָ זֵכֶר לְמַעֲשֵׂה בְרֵאשִׁית:

מלכיות

עָלֵינוּ לְשַׁבֵּחַ לַאֲדוֹן הַכֹּל לָתֵת גְּדֻלָּה לְיוֹצֵר בְּרֵאשִׁית שֶׁלֹּא

עָשָׂנוּ כְּגוֹיֵי הָאֲרָצוֹת וְלֹא שָׂמָנוּ כְּמִשְׁפְּחוֹת הָאֲדָמָה שֶׁלֹּא שָׂם

חֶלְקֵנוּ כָּהֶם וְגֹרָלֵנוּ כְּכָל־הֲמוֹנָם* וַאֲנַחְנוּ כֹּרְעִים וּמִשְׁתַּחֲוִים

וּמוֹדִים לִפְנֵי מֶלֶךְ מַלְכֵי הַמְּלָכִים הַקָּדוֹשׁ בָּרוּךְ הוּא שֶׁהוּא

נוֹטֶה שָׁמַיִם וְיֹסֵד אָרֶץ וּמוֹשַׁב* יְקָרוֹ בַּשָּׁמַיִם מִמַּעַל וּשְׁכִינַת

עֻזּוֹ בְּגָבְהֵי מְרוֹמִים: הוּא אֱלֹהֵינוּ אֵין עוֹד · אֱמֶת מַלְכֵּנוּ אֶפֶס

זוּלָתוֹ · כַּכָּתוּב בְּתוֹרָתוֹ · וְיָדַעְתָּ הַיּוֹם וַהֲשֵׁבֹתָ אֶל־לְבָבֶךָ כִּי יְיָ

הוּא הָאֱלֹהִים בַּשָּׁמַיִם מִמַּעַל וְעַל־הָאָרֶץ מִתָּחַת אֵין עוֹד:

* שֶׁהֵם מִשְׁתַּחֲוִים לְהֶבֶל וָרִיק וּמִתְפַּלְּלִים אֶל אֵל לֹא יוֹשִׁיעַ.

נ"א וְכִסֵּא כְּבוֹדוֹ נ"א אֵין אַחֵר.

---

on Rosh Hashanah the thought of *Malchuyoth* comes to the fore as particularly in keeping with the character of that sacred Festival, and therefore
Malchuyoth is inserted into the blessing of *kedushath hayom* אתה בחרתנו
down to מקדש ישראל ויום הזכרון.

עלינו (see above p. 208) here serves as an introduction to the *Malchuyoth*
First it sets forth the clear cut contrast between our own ideas and those of

their offering of tribute and their drink offerings as prescribed; three tenths for the bullock, two-tenths for the ram and one tenth for each lamb, and wine even as its drink offering, and two he-goats for atonement and two regular offerings in accordance with their rule. This is in addition to the elevating-offering of the New Moon and its offering of tribute and regular elevating-offering and its gift of tribute, and their drink offerings according to their rule as an expression of obedience, a fire offering to *God*.

It is incumbent upon us to praise the Lord of All Things, to ascribe greatness to Him Who still continues to shape the work of the Beginning, Who has not made us like the peoples of the lands, and not given us a position like the families of the earth, since He did not let our portion be like theirs, nor our lot like that of all their multitudes. For we bend the knee and cast ourselves down and avow it before the Supreme King of Kings, the Holy One, blessed be He, that it is He Who stretches forth the heavens and establishes the earth, that the seat of His glory is in Heaven above, and the presence of His invincible might is in the loftiest heights. He is our God, none beside Him. He is our King in truth; there is none beside Him, even as it is written in His Torah: "You shall know it this day, and repeatedly lay it upon your heart, that *God* alone is God, in Heaven above and on earth below; there is none beside Him."

---

the rest of mankind concerning God and man's relation with and position before Him. Then on the basis of this concept of God, it proclaims, in equally clear-cut terms, the eventual complete return of all men to the homage of the One God, and their devotion to the exclusive service of Him.

לא הביט : The non-Jewish seer [Balaam] who was called to curse but was compelled to bless, said, "*God* saw no cause to decree disaster for His people." For God does not foresee that the people of Yisrael would make wrongful use of the power which He, God, might confer upon it. Much rather, God will be with Yisrael because the homage of Him as King is a living force within the soul of that people. ויהי, "God"—or rather, more in accordance with the context,—"The Law of God" was King in Jeshurun. It was the sole ruling, commanding and governing power in Yisrael, and it was only through common homage to God and to His Law that the tribes of Israel were welded into one united nation. Other national entities are linked by common ownership of a piece of territory, but Yisrael is united only through common homage to God and to His Law. כי לה׳ : One day all men will render Him homage, and even today every development in the history of the nations

עַל־כֵּן נְקַוֶּה לְּךָ יְיָ אֱלֹהֵינוּ לִרְאוֹת מְהֵרָה בְּתִפְאֶרֶת עֻזֶּךָ לְהַעֲבִיר
גִּלּוּלִים מִן־הָאָרֶץ וְהָאֱלִילִים כָּרוֹת יִכָּרֵתוּן · לְתַקֵּן עוֹלָם בְּמַלְכוּת
שַׁדַּי וְכָל־בְּנֵי בָשָׂר יִקְרְאוּ בִשְׁמֶךָ · לְהַפְנוֹת אֵלֶיךָ כָּל־רִשְׁעֵי
אָרֶץ · יַכִּירוּ וְיֵדְעוּ כָּל־יוֹשְׁבֵי תֵבֵל כִּי לְךָ תִּכְרַע כָּל־בֶּרֶךְ תִּשָּׁבַע
כָּל־לָשׁוֹן: לְפָנֶיךָ יְיָ אֱלֹהֵינוּ יִכְרְעוּ וְיִפֹּלוּ · וְלִכְבוֹד שִׁמְךָ יְקָר
יִתֵּנוּ · וִיקַבְּלוּ כֻלָּם אֶת־עֹל מַלְכוּתֶךָ · וְתִמְלוֹךְ עֲלֵיהֶם מְהֵרָה
לְעוֹלָם וָעֶד · כִּי הַמַּלְכוּת שֶׁלְּךָ הִיא וּלְעוֹלְמֵי עַד תִּמְלוֹךְ בְּכָבוֹד:
כַּכָּתוּב בְּתוֹרָתֶךָ יְיָ יִמְלֹךְ לְעֹלָם וָעֶד:

וְנֶאֱמַר לֹא־הִבִּיט אָוֶן בְּיַעֲקֹב וְלֹא־רָאָה עָמָל בְּיִשְׂרָאֵל יְיָ
אֱלֹהָיו עִמּוֹ וּתְרוּעַת מֶלֶךְ בּוֹ: וְנֶאֱמַר וַיְהִי בִישֻׁרוּן מֶלֶךְ בְּהִתְאַסֵּף
רָאשֵׁי עָם יַחַד שִׁבְטֵי יִשְׂרָאֵל: וּבְדִבְרֵי קָדְשְׁךָ כָּתוּב לֵאמֹר
כִּי לַיְיָ הַמְּלוּכָה וּמֹשֵׁל בַּגּוֹיִם: וְנֶאֱמַר יְיָ מָלָךְ גֵּאוּת לָבֵשׁ לָבֵשׁ
יְיָ עֹז הִתְאַזָּר אַף תִּכּוֹן תֵּבֵל בַּל תִּמּוֹט: וְנֶאֱמַר שְׂאוּ שְׁעָרִים
רָאשֵׁיכֶם וְהִנָּשְׂאוּ פִּתְחֵי עוֹלָם וְיָבוֹא מֶלֶךְ הַכָּבוֹד: מִי זֶה מֶלֶךְ
הַכָּבוֹד · יְיָ עִזּוּז וְגִבּוֹר יְיָ גִּבּוֹר מִלְחָמָה: שְׂאוּ שְׁעָרִים רָאשֵׁיכֶם
וּשְׂאוּ פִּתְחֵי עוֹלָם וְיָבֹא מֶלֶךְ הַכָּבוֹד: מִי הוּא זֶה מֶלֶךְ הַכָּבוֹד ·
יְיָ צְבָאוֹת הוּא מֶלֶךְ הַכָּבוֹד סֶלָה: וְעַל־יְדֵי עֲבָדֶיךָ הַנְּבִיאִים
כָּתוּב לֵאמֹר כֹּה אָמַר יְיָ מֶלֶךְ־יִשְׂרָאֵל וְגֹאֲלוֹ יְיָ צְבָאוֹת אֲנִי
רִאשׁוֹן וַאֲנִי אַחֲרוֹן וּמִבַּלְעָדַי אֵין אֱלֹהִים: וְנֶאֱמַר וְעָלוּ מוֹשִׁעִים
בְּהַר צִיּוֹן לִשְׁפֹּט אֶת־הַר עֵשָׂו וְהָיְתָה לַיְיָ הַמְּלוּכָה: וְנֶאֱמַר
וְהָיָה יְיָ לְמֶלֶךְ עַל־כָּל־הָאָרֶץ בַּיּוֹם הַהוּא יִהְיֶה יְיָ אֶחָד וּשְׁמוֹ
אֶחָד: וּבְתוֹרָתְךָ כָּתוּב לֵאמֹר שְׁמַע יִשְׂרָאֵל יְיָ אֱלֹהֵינוּ יְיָ אֶחָד:

אֱלֹהֵינוּ וֵאלֹהֵי אֲבוֹתֵינוּ · מְלוֹךְ עַל כָּל־הָעוֹלָם כֻּלּוֹ בִּכְבוֹדֶךָ
וְהִנָּשֵׂא עַל כָּל־הָאָרֶץ בִּיקָרֶךָ וְהוֹפַע בַּהֲדַר גְּאוֹן עֻזֶּךָ עַל כָּל־
יוֹשְׁבֵי תֵבֵל אַרְצֶךָ · וְיֵדַע כָּל־פָּעוּל כִּי אַתָּה פְעַלְתּוֹ וְיָבִין כָּל־
יְצוּר כִּי אַתָּה יְצַרְתּוֹ וְיֹאמַר כֹּל אֲשֶׁר נְשָׁמָה בְאַפּוֹ יְיָ אֱלֹהֵי

We therefore put our hope in You, O *God* our God, that we may soon behold the glorification of Your invincible might, to banish the idols from the earth so that the [false] gods will vanish entirely, that the world will be perfected through the reign of the All-Sufficient, so that all mortals will call upon Your Name, to turn all the lawless of the earth to You, so that all the inhabitants of the world of men may realize and know that to You every knee must bend, every tongue must swear allegiance. Before You, O *God*, our God, they will bend the knee and cast themselves down; they will give honor to the glory of Your Name and they will all accept the yoke of Your kingdom. Thus may You soon reign over them forever, for the kingdom is Yours, and to all eternity will You reign in glory, even as is written in Your Torah: "*God* shall reign in all eternity," and it is said: "Then *God* will be King over all the earth; on that day shall *God* be One and His Name One."

And it is said: "He beheld no abuse of power in Yaakov; therefore He saw no trouble in Yisrael, *God,* his God was with him and homage to the King was with him." And it is said, "He was King in Yeshurun. Since the heads of the people rallied round Him, the tribes of Yisrael were united all together." And in Your holy words it is written: "For the dominion will be *God's* and He rules among the nations." And it is said: "*God* has begun his reign; he has clothed Himself in majesty; *God* has clothed Himself, He has girded Himself with invincibility; now the world of men, too, will be firmly established and be moved no more." And it is said: "Lift up your heads, O gates, be lifted up to become portals of the future, so that the King of Glory may come in. 'Who is the King of Glory?' '*God,* invincible and strong, *God,* the Mighty One in battle.' Lift up your heads again, O gates, lift them up to become portals of the future, so that the King of Glory may come in.' 'Who, then, is this King of Glory?' '*God Tzevaoth;* He is the King of Glory!' " And by Your servants, the Prophets, it is written, "Thus said *God,* the King and Redeemer of Yisrael, *God Tzevaoth*: 'I am the First and I am the Last, and there is no God beside Me.' " And it is said, "They ascend as bringers of salvation upon Mount Tzion to judge the Mountain of Esau, and the Kingdom shall be *God's*." And in Your Torah it is written: "Hear Yisrael, *God* our God, is *God* the only One!"

יִשְׂרָאֵל מֶלֶךְ וּמַלְכוּתוֹ בַּכֹּל מָשָׁלָה: לשבת אלהינו ואלהי אבותינו רצה
בִמְנוּחָתֵנוּ קַדְּשֵׁנוּ בְּמִצְוֹתֶיךָ וְתֵן חֶלְקֵנוּ בְּתוֹרָתֶךָ, שַׂבְּעֵנוּ מִטּוּבֶךָ
וְשַׂמְּחֵנוּ בִּישׁוּעָתֶךָ. לשבת והנחילנו יי אלהינו באהבה וברצון שבת קדשך
ויגוחו־בה ישראל מקדשי שמך · וְטַהֵר לִבֵּנוּ לְעָבְדְּךָ בֶּאֱמֶת·כִּי אַתָּה
אֱלֹהִים אֱמֶת וּדְבָרְךָ אֱמֶת וְקַיָּם לָעַד·בָּרוּךְ אַתָּה יְיָ, מֶלֶךְ עַל
כָּל־הָאָרֶץ מְקַדֵּשׁ השבת וְיִשְׂרָאֵל וְיוֹם הַזִּכָּרוֹן:

זכרונות
אַתָּה זוֹכֵר מַעֲשֵׂה עוֹלָם וּפוֹקֵד כָּל יְצוּרֵי קֶדֶם·לְפָנֶיךָ נִגְלוּ
כָל־תַּעֲלוּמוֹת וַהֲמוֹן נִסְתָּרוֹת שֶׁמִּבְּרֵאשִׁית·כִּי אֵין שִׁכְחָה לִפְנֵי
כִסֵּא כְבוֹדֶךָ·וְאֵין נִסְתָּר מִנֶּגֶד עֵינֶיךָ: אַתָּה זוֹכֵר אֶת־כָּל־
הַמִּפְעָל·וְגַם כָּל־הַיְצוּר לֹא נִכְחָד מִמֶּךָּ·הַכֹּל גָּלוּי וְיָדוּעַ לְפָנֶיךָ
יְיָ אֱלֹהֵינוּ·צוֹפֶה וּמַבִּיט עַד־סוֹף כָּל הַדּוֹרוֹת·כִּי תָבִיא חֹק
זִכָּרוֹן לְהִפָּקֵד כָּל־רוּחַ וָנָפֶשׁ·לְהִזָּכֵר מַעֲשִׂים רַבִּים וַהֲמוֹן בְּרִיּוֹת
לְאֵין תַּכְלִית·מֵרֵאשִׁית כָּזֹאת הוֹדַעְתָּ·וּמִלְּפָנִים אוֹתָהּ גִּלִּיתָ·
זֶה הַיּוֹם תְּחִלַּת מַעֲשֶׂיךָ זִכָּרוֹן לְיוֹם רִאשׁוֹן·כִּי חֹק לְיִשְׂרָאֵל
הוּא מִשְׁפָּט לֵאלֹהֵי יַעֲקֹב: וְעַל הַמְּדִינוֹת בּוֹ יֵאָמֵר אֵי־זוֹ לַחֶרֶב

---

stands beneath His Providence which is to lead all of mankind to this ultimate goal. ה' מלך see p. 76 שאו שערים see p. 193 אני ראשון: "All things
have come from Me, and all things shall eventually lead to Me," says God.
ועלו מושיעים It is not as "the ones that were saved" but as the "bringers of
salvation to all of mankind" that those who, until now, have been despised
as far west as France and Spain as "Palestinian traders" will go up once
more to their ancient homeland. And then the Kingdom will be God's alone
(See Obad. 1:20, 21). שמע ישראל: This is the final documentation from the
Torah for *Malchuyoth*.

או"א מלוך והופע והנשא: Let Your Providence be so evident that they will
all recognize You and render You homage.

You remember that which has come to pass from eternity and You are mindful of all that which has been formed in past. Before You are revealed all secrets and the abundance of hidden things from the world's beginning. For nothing is forgotten before the Throne of Your glory, and nothing is hidden from Your eyes. You remember all that which has been wrought, and all that which is formed is not concealed from You. All things are revealed and known before You, O *God* our God; You see and behold until the end of all generations. For You will set an appointed memorial when every spirit and every soul will be considered, when many deeds and an infinite number of creatures will be remembered. You have made this known from the beginning and revealed it from antiquity. This day, the beginning of Your works, is a memorial of the First Day, for there is a statute for Yisrael; the God of Yaakov sits in judgment. And thereon [a sentence] is uttered over the lands, which of them shall be destined for the sword and which for peace, which for famine

---

אתה זוכר : Not only that which happens now and which came to pass recently is present before you at every moment of Your sovereignty; You are mindful, too, at all times of all that man has ever striven for and achieved in even the remotest past. For in every instant of the present, and in every instant that is yet to be, You cause to ripen upon the field of the future the good and the evil from those seeds which men of both past and present have sown with their deeds. מראשית : The very first man was doomed to death because he had transgressed Your interdiction, but You, in Your great compassion, opened for him the portals of a future renewed and restored. Ever since then, You have appointed that first day of man's existence on earth, which was the first day also of Your judgment and Your grace to mankind, as a day upon which, every year, judgment will be passed on all of humanity." מעשה איש וכו' : Many considerations enter into the determining of a man's future fate. God weighs all of his past conduct and the course of all his past life; the consequences of his every act, the fruits, good or evil, that have remained of all his previous conduct; his thoughts and plans; the things he wished to do but could not carry out, either because he was prevented from doing so or because he lacked the needed firmness of resolve, and finally, the motives that impelled his behavior. For it is by the standard of all these considerations that the moral worth of a man's past stands or falls, and this, too, determines the expectations he may properly have of the future, and the sum total of these factors goes to make up the fate that is to be decreed for him.

וְאֵינוֹ לַשָּׁלוֹם· אֵינוֹ לָרָעָב· וְאֵינוֹ לָשָּׂבַע· וּבְרִיּוֹת בּוֹ יִפָּקֵדוּ·
לְהַזְכִּירָם לַחַיִּים וְלַמָּוֶת: מִי לֹא נִפְקַד כְּהַיּוֹם הַזֶּה· כִּי זֵכֶר
כָּל־הַיָּצוּר לְפָנֶיךָ בָּא· מַעֲשֵׂה אִישׁ וּפְקֻדָּתוֹ· וַעֲלִילוֹת מִצְעֲדֵי
גָבֶר· מַחְשְׁבוֹת אָדָם וְתַחְבּוּלוֹתָיו וְיִצְרֵי מַעַלְלֵי אִישׁ: אַשְׁרֵי אִישׁ
שֶׁלֹּא יִשְׁכָּחֶךָּ· וּבֶן־אָדָם יִתְאַמֶּץ־בָּךְ· כִּי דוֹרְשֶׁיךָ לְעוֹלָם לֹא
יִכָּשֵׁלוּ· וְלֹא יִכָּלְמוּ לָנֶצַח כָּל־הַחוֹסִים בָּךְ: כִּי זֵכֶר כָּל־הַמַּעֲשִׂים
לְפָנֶיךָ בָּא· וְאַתָּה דוֹרֵשׁ מַעֲשֵׂה כֻלָּם: וְגַם אֶת־נֹחַ בְּאַהֲבָה
זָכַרְתָּ· וַתִּפְקְדֵהוּ בִּדְבַר יְשׁוּעָה וְרַחֲמִים· בַּהֲבִיאֲךָ אֶת־מֵי הַמַּבּוּל
לְשַׁחֵת כָּל־בָּשָׂר מִפְּנֵי רֹעַ מַעַלְלֵיהֶם· עַל־כֵּן זִכְרוֹנוֹ בָּא לְפָנֶיךָ
יְיָ אֱלֹהֵינוּ לְהַרְבּוֹת זַרְעוֹ כְּעַפְרוֹת תֵּבֵל· וְצֶאֱצָאָיו כְּחוֹל הַיָּם:
כַּכָּתוּב בְּתוֹרָתֶךָ, וַיִּזְכֹּר אֱלֹהִים אֶת־נֹחַ וְאֵת־כָּל־הַחַיָּה וְאֵת־כָּל־
הַבְּהֵמָה אֲשֶׁר אִתּוֹ בַּתֵּבָה וַיַּעֲבֵר אֱלֹהִים רוּחַ עַל־הָאָרֶץ וַיָּשֹׁכּוּ
הַמָּיִם: וְנֶאֱמַר, וַיִּשְׁמַע אֱלֹהִים אֶת־נַאֲקָתָם וַיִּזְכֹּר אֱלֹהִים אֶת־
בְּרִיתוֹ אֶת־אַבְרָהָם אֶת־יִצְחָק וְאֶת־יַעֲקֹב: וְנֶאֱמַר, וְזָכַרְתִּי אֶת־

אשרי: Happy is he who remembers God in the same degree as God
remembers him, and who thus makes himself worthy of finding with God,
Who now judges him, the strength and support for moral regeneration and
for the attainment of a new future. וגם את נח באהבה: Although His sentence
doomed all of mankind to perish because of its moral corruption, God knew
how to seek out and find the sole man who had remained worthy of His
love, and saved him from the universal destruction so that he might father
a new generation of mankind. את בריתי אברהם We read here *not*: "My covenant *with* Abraham", etc. but "My covenant *Abraham*" etc.; i.e. "My covenant named 'Abraham', My covenant named 'Yitzchak' and My covenant
named 'Yaakob'." Each of our patriarchs has his own unique position in our
history. Abraham was a *nesi Elokim*, a prince in the midst of the nations
and they honored him. The position of Yitzchak was an isolated individual,
troubled by the envy of the nations. The lot of his son Yaakov was one of
suffering servitude. And yet all three were equally great in their close relationship with God and in their importance in history, and hence all three

and which for plenty. And on it, creatures will be remembered, and recorded for life or for death. Who is it that is not considered today? For the remembrance of all that is formed comes before You, the conduct of man and his fate, and the results of the footsteps of each man, man's thoughts and his schemes and the motives of the deeds of each man. Happy is the man who does not forget You, the son of man who strengthens himself in You. For those who seek You shall never stumble, and all those who put their trust in You shall never be put to shame. For the remembrance of all creatures comes before You and You inquire into all their conduct. Noach, too, You remembered with love and decreed over him with a promise of salvation and compassion, when You brought to pass the life-destroying waters to eradicate all flesh because of the wickedness of their deeds. Therefore his memory came before You, O *God* our God, to multiply his seed as the dust particles of the world and his descendants like the sand of the sea. Even as it is written in Your Torah; "And then God remembered Noach and all the animals and all the cattle which were with him in the Ark, and God caused a wind to pass over the earth, and the waters grew calm." And it is said: "God heard their cry of terror, then God remembered His covenant with Abraham, with Yitzchak and with Yaakov." And it is said: "And then I shall

---

served as models for all of their descendants whose destinies have also been varied and changing but who, whatever their lot may be, must at all times discharge the task set them by God and be sure to retain for themselves the preserving nearness of God and His covenant. The names of the Patriarchs are given in reverse order; that is, not "Avraham, Yitzchak and Yaakov", but "Yaakov, Yitzchak and Avraham." For the Divine promise speaks first of our descent into the abject depths of Galuth and then of our eventual resurrection to a new life. First we must prove our worth by bearing with dignity a state of Galuth similar to that of our forefather Yaakov. Only when, thereafter, even in envied wealth such as was Yitzchak's, we will still prove our complete loyalty to God and our worthiness of His covenant, then will the "covenant *Abraham*" prove its efficacy in our history as well, and we will shine forth before all the other nations as נשיאי אלקים, a people ennobled by God.

זכר עשה: Even as God remembers us in and through all the ways of His Providence, so He wants us and all the generations to come, in turn, to remain mindful of His wondrous ways, and for this purpose He instituted memorial days which recur each year. טרף: The very fact that, in a world

בְּרִיתִי יַעֲקוֹב וְאַף אֶת־בְּרִיתִי יִצְחָק וְאַף אֶת־בְּרִיתִי אַבְרָהָם
אֶזְכֹּר וְהָאָרֶץ אֶזְכֹּר: וּבְדִבְרֵי קָדְשְׁךָ כָּתוּב לֵאמֹר, זֵכֶר עָשָׂה
לְנִפְלְאֹתָיו חַנּוּן וְרַחוּם יְיָ: וְנֶאֱמַר, טֶרֶף נָתַן לִירֵאָיו יִזְכֹּר לְעוֹלָם
בְּרִיתוֹ: וְנֶאֱמַר וַיִּזְכֹּר לָהֶם בְּרִיתוֹ וַיִּנָּחֵם כְּרֹב חֲסָדָיו: וְעַל־יְדֵי
עֲבָדֶיךָ הַנְּבִיאִים כָּתוּב לֵאמֹר, הָלֹךְ וְקָרָאתָ בְאָזְנֵי יְרוּשָׁלַם
לֵאמֹר כֹּה אָמַר יְיָ זָכַרְתִּי לָךְ חֶסֶד נְעוּרַיִךְ אַהֲבַת כְּלוּלֹתָיִךְ
לֶכְתֵּךְ אַחֲרַי בַּמִּדְבָּר בְּאֶרֶץ לֹא זְרוּעָה: וְנֶאֱמַר, וְזָכַרְתִּי אֲנִי אֶת־
בְּרִיתִי אוֹתָךְ בִּימֵי נְעוּרָיִךְ וַהֲקִימוֹתִי לָךְ בְּרִית עוֹלָם: וְנֶאֱמַר,
הֲבֵן יַקִּיר לִי אֶפְרַיִם אִם יֶלֶד שַׁעֲשׁוּעִים כִּי־מִדֵּי דַבְּרִי בּוֹ זָכֹר
אֶזְכְּרֶנּוּ עוֹד עַל־כֵּן הָמוּ מֵעַי לוֹ רַחֵם אֲרַחֲמֶנּוּ נְאֻם־יְיָ:

אֱלֹהֵינוּ וֵאלֹהֵי אֲבוֹתֵינוּ · זָכְרֵנוּ בְּזִכָּרוֹן טוֹב לְפָנֶיךָ וּפָקְדֵנוּ
בִּפְקֻדַּת יְשׁוּעָה וְרַחֲמִים מִשְּׁמֵי שְׁמֵי קֶדֶם וּזְכָר־לָנוּ יְיָ אֱלֹהֵינוּ
אֶת־הַבְּרִית וְאֶת־הַחֶסֶד וְאֶת־הַשְּׁבוּעָה אֲשֶׁר נִשְׁבַּעְתָּ לְאַבְרָהָם
אָבִינוּ בְּהַר הַמּוֹרִיָּה וְתֵרָאֶה לְפָנֶיךָ עֲקֵדָה שֶׁעָקַד אַבְרָהָם אָבִינוּ
אֶת־יִצְחָק בְּנוֹ עַל גַּב הַמִּזְבֵּחַ וְכָבַשׁ רַחֲמָיו לַעֲשׂוֹת רְצוֹנְךָ בְּלֵבָב
שָׁלֵם · כֵּן יִכְבְּשׁוּ רַחֲמֶיךָ אֶת־כַּעַסְךָ מֵעָלֵינוּ וּבְטוּבְךָ הַגָּדוֹל
יָשׁוּב חֲרוֹן אַפְּךָ מֵעַמְּךָ וּמֵעִירְךָ וּמִנַּחֲלָתֶךָ · וְקַיֶּם־לָנוּ יְיָ אֱלֹהֵינוּ
אֶת־הַדָּבָר שֶׁהִבְטַחְתָּנוּ בְּתוֹרָתֶךָ עַל־יְדֵי מֹשֶׁה עַבְדְּךָ מִפִּי
כְבוֹדֶךָ כָּאָמוּר: וְזָכַרְתִּי לָהֶם בְּרִית רִאשֹׁנִים אֲשֶׁר הוֹצֵאתִי
אֹתָם מֵאֶרֶץ מִצְרַיִם לְעֵינֵי הַגּוֹיִם לִהְיוֹת לָהֶם לֵאלֹהִים אֲנִי יְדֹנָה:
כִּי זוֹכֵר כָּל הַנִּשְׁכָּחוֹת אַתָּה הוּא מֵעוֹלָם וְאֵין שִׁכְחָה לִפְנֵי כִסֵּא

remember my covenant *Yaakov,* and also my covenant *Yitzchak* and also my covenant *Abraham,* and I shall remember the Land." And in Your holy words it is written: "He has made a memorial for His miracles, that *God* is gracious and full of compassion." And: "[Once] He has given food to those who fear Him, He will remember His covenant forever." And it is said: "He remembered His covenant For them; He let Himself be moved to repent according to the fullness of His acts of loving-kindness." And by Your servants, the Prophets, it is written: "Go and proclaim it to the ears of Yerushalayim: Thus said *God,* 'I remember for you the devotion of your youth, the love of your bridal state, how you followed Me into the wilderness, into a land that was not sown.' " And it is said; "I shall remember My covenant with you in the days of your youth and I shall preserve for you an eternal covenant." And it is said: "Is Ephraim to Me a precious son or a child that holds My thoughts? For as often as I have spoken against him, I yet remember him constantly; therefore My inmost being rushes out to him; I shall surely have compassion upon him, says *God.*"

Our God and God of our fathers, remember us with a good remembrance before You, and consider us with a decree of salvation and compassion from the Heavens of Heavens of antiquity, and remember for us, O *God* our God, the covenant and the loving-kindness and the vow which You have sworn to our father Abraham on Mount Moriah, and cause to appear before You the binding with which our father Abraham bound his son Yitzchak atop the altar, and how he prevailed over his compassion to do Your will with his whole heart. Even thus may Your own compassion prevail over Your wrath for us, and, in Your great goodness, may the blazing of Your anger turn aside from Your people and Your City and from Your inheritance. And fulfill for us, O *God* our God, the promise of which You have assured us in Your Torah through Moshe Your servant, from the

---

of little conscience, the God-fearing attain as "a gift of God" the livelihood which others gain by *teref,* by means of inhuman "robbery", shows that God is eternally mindful of His covenant. שעשועים denotes constant thought, mental occupation. *Yeled sha'ashu'im* is a child to whom our thoughts constantly turn, a child who holds our thoughts. עקדה is not the actual act of offering up, but the binding, the preparation of the offering for the rite of sacrifice.

כְּבוֹדֶךָ · וַעֲקֵבַת יִצְחָק לְזַרְעוֹ (שֶׁל יַעֲקֹב) הַיּוֹם בְּרַחֲמִים תִּזְכּוֹר ·
בָּרוּךְ אַתָּה יְיָ, זוֹכֵר הַבְּרִית:

אַתָּה נִגְלֵיתָ בַּעֲנַן כְּבוֹדֶךָ עַל עַם קָדְשֶׁךָ לְדַבֵּר עִמָּם · מִן הַשָּׁמַיִם
הִשְׁמַעְתָּם קוֹלֶךָ וְנִגְלֵיתָ עֲלֵיהֶם בְּעַרְפְלֵי טֹהַר · גַּם (כָּל) הָעוֹלָם כֻּלּוֹ
חָל מִפָּנֶיךָ וּבְרִיּוֹת בְּרֵאשִׁית חָרְדוּ מִמֶּךָּ בְּהִגָּלוֹתְךָ מַלְכֵּנוּ עַל־
הַר סִינַי לְלַמֵּד לְעַמְּךָ תּוֹרָה וּמִצְוֹת · וַתַּשְׁמִיעֵם אֶת־הוֹד קוֹלֶךָ
וְדִבְּרוֹת קָדְשְׁךָ מִלַּהֲבוֹת אֵשׁ, בְּקוֹלוֹת וּבְרָקִים עֲלֵיהֶם נִגְלֵיתָ
וּבְקוֹל שׁוֹפָר עֲלֵיהֶם הוֹפָעְתָּ: כַּכָּתוּב בְּתוֹרָתֶךָ, וַיְהִי בַיּוֹם הַשְּׁלִישִׁי
בִּהְיֹת הַבֹּקֶר וַיְהִי קֹלֹת וּבְרָקִים וְעָנָן כָּבֵד עַל־הָהָר וְקֹל שֹׁפָר
חָזָק מְאֹד וַיֶּחֱרַד כָּל־הָעָם אֲשֶׁר בַּמַּחֲנֶה: וַיֹּאמַר, וַיְהִי קוֹל הַשֹּׁפָר

בריות בראשית ,אתה נגלית are those works that came into being as a direct
result of God's command, such as the sun, the moon and the stars that have
existed since the Creation, as distinguished from those phenomena which come
about and pass away in the course of nature as ordained by God for all time
to come. קול שופר was the call that went out to Yisrael at the time of the
Giving of the Law, summoning the people to draw near to God and to do
His will.

עלה אלהים בתרועה : When, in response to the *teru'ah*, God will have received the homage rightly due His majesty, He will reveal Himself in His
attribute of 'ה, leading men and nations in loving-kindness to their salvation.
Then the *teru'ah* will turn into *teki'ah*, and, *bekol shofar,* with the sustained,
unbroken sound of the Shofar, God will call us to Him as a loving Father.
בחצוצרות וקול שופר : *chatzotzroth* is the instrument which men use to summon
other men, and God as well, for help and support. By means of the Shofar
it is God Who calls upon man, or man, in behalf of God, calls upon himself
and his fellow-men, to draw near to God and to obey His will. Our *chatzotzroth* before God must always be joined by *kol shofar;* if God is to answer
our call, we must heed His summons first; If He is to be our Helper, He
must first become our King.

תקעו see above, p. 268 הלולים see above p. 91 שוכני ארץ refers to those
who live outside the urban communities of man. האובדים בארץ אשור denotes the
Ten Tribes who were led away in captivity by Assyria and who are lost to
us until that day when redemption will come.

mouth of Your glory, as it is said, "I shall remember for them the covenant of the forefathers, whom I had brought out of the land of Mitzrayim before the eyes of the nations, to be to them a God, I *God*." For You have ever remembered all that was forgotten, and there is no forgetting before the throne of Your glory, and may You remember today with compassion the binding of Yitzchak for his seed. Blessed be You, O *God,* Who remembers the covenant.

In the mist of Your glory You were revealed above Your holy people to speak with them; You made them hear Your voice from Heaven above and were revealed to them in pure clouds. The whole world, too, went into travail before You, and the creatures of the world's beginning trembled at Your presence, when You, O our King, revealed Yourself on Mount Sinai, to teach Your people the Torah and the commandments. You caused them to hear the majesty of Your voice and the utterances of Your holiness from flames of fire, amidst thunder and lightning were You revealed over them, and with the sound of the Shofar You appeared to them. Even as it is written in Your Torah: "And it was on the third day, when it was morning, and there were thunders and lightnings, a heavy mist upon the mountain and an exceedingly loud sound of the Shofar. And all the people that were in the camp trembled." And it is said: "And while the

---

נפוצותינו ,פזורינו ,גלויותינו ,או"א תקע זכו' · We have been taken away from our homeland. Separated from one another, we have been absorbed by the peoples among whom we live and we are scattered all over the earth.

וביום שמחתכם. All *temidim* and *musaphim* were accompanied by the sounding of the *chatzotzeroth,* and to these was joined the sound of the Shofar, as we have noted above in connection with בחצוצרות וקול שופר. We are not certain whether *yom simchah* denotes the Sabbath and *mo'adim* refers to *tamid,* or whether, instead, *mo'adim* refers to Sabbath and *yom simchah* to *tamid.* See Commentary to Num. 10:10. כי אתה שומע, "For when we sound the Shofar in accordance with Your command in order to summon ourselves to come to You and to obey Your will, You hear it, and when we sound the blast of the *teru'ah* to call upon ourselves to abandon all that which is not pleasing to You, You perceive it." ואין דומה לך : "And there is none beside You. You are unique in Your unrivaled majesty, and unique, at the same time, in Your unequalled nearness to all men, and You give compassionate consideration even to the mere fact that we sound the *teru'ah,* the *call* to a return to loyalty and to moral rebirth."

הוֹלֵךְ וְחָזֵק מְאֹד מֹשֶׁה יְדַבֵּר וְהָאֱלֹהִים יַעֲנֶנּוּ בְקוֹל: וְנֶאֱמַר, וְכָל־
הָעָם רֹאִים אֶת־הַקּוֹלֹת וְאֶת־הַלַּפִּידִם וְאֵת קוֹל הַשֹּׁפָר וְאֶת־הָהָר
עָשֵׁן וַיַּרְא הָעָם וַיָּנֻעוּ וַיַּעַמְדוּ מֵרָחֹק: וּבְדִבְרֵי קָדְשְׁךָ כָּתוּב
לֵאמֹר, עָלָה אֱלֹהִים בִּתְרוּעָה יְיָ בְּקוֹל שׁוֹפָר: וְנֶאֱמַר, בַּחֲצֹצְרוֹת
וְקוֹל שׁוֹפָר הָרִיעוּ לִפְנֵי הַמֶּלֶךְ יְיָ: וְנֶאֱמַר, תִּקְעוּ בַחֹדֶשׁ שׁוֹפָר
בַּכֶּסֶה לְיוֹם חַגֵּנוּ: כִּי חֹק לְיִשְׂרָאֵל הוּא מִשְׁפָּט לֵאלֹהֵי יַעֲקֹב:
וְנֶאֱמַר, הַלְלוּיָהּ הַלְלוּ אֵל בְּקָדְשׁוֹ הַלְלוּהוּ בִּרְקִיעַ עֻזּוֹ: הַלְלוּהוּ
בִגְבוּרֹתָיו הַלְלוּהוּ כְּרֹב גֻּדְלוֹ: הַלְלוּהוּ בְּתֵקַע שׁוֹפָר הַלְלוּהוּ
בְּנֵבֶל וְכִנּוֹר: הַלְלוּהוּ בְתֹף וּמָחוֹל הַלְלוּהוּ בְּמִנִּים וְעֻגָב: הַלְלוּהוּ
בְּצִלְצְלֵי־שָׁמַע הַלְלוּהוּ בְּצִלְצְלֵי תְרוּעָה: כֹּל הַנְּשָׁמָה תְּהַלֵּל
יָהּ, הַלְלוּיָהּ: וְעַל־יְדֵי עֲבָדֶיךָ הַנְּבִיאִים כָּתוּב לֵאמֹר, כָּל־יֹשְׁבֵי
תֵבֵל וְשֹׁכְנֵי אָרֶץ כִּנְשֹׂא־נֵס הָרִים תִּרְאוּ וְכִתְקֹעַ שׁוֹפָר תִּשְׁמָעוּ:
וְנֶאֱמַר, וְהָיָה בַּיּוֹם הַהוּא יִתָּקַע בְּשׁוֹפָר גָּדוֹל וּבָאוּ הָאֹבְדִים
בְּאֶרֶץ אַשּׁוּר וְהַנִּדָּחִים בְּאֶרֶץ מִצְרָיִם וְהִשְׁתַּחֲווּ לַיְיָ בְּהַר הַקֹּדֶשׁ
בִּירוּשָׁלָיִם: וְנֶאֱמַר, וַיְיָ עֲלֵיהֶם יֵרָאֶה וְיָצָא כַבָּרָק חִצּוֹ וַאדֹנָי
יֱהוִֹה בַּשּׁוֹפָר יִתְקָע וְהָלַךְ בְּסַעֲרוֹת תֵּימָן: יְיָ צְבָאוֹת יָגֵן עֲלֵיהֶם:
כֵּן תָּגֵן עַל עַמְּךָ יִשְׂרָאֵל בִּשְׁלוֹמֶךָ:

אֱלֹהֵינוּ וֵאלֹהֵי אֲבוֹתֵינוּ· תְּקַע בְּשׁוֹפָר גָּדוֹל לְחֵרוּתֵנוּ וְשָׂא נֵס
לְקַבֵּץ גָּלֻיּוֹתֵינוּ וְקָרֵב פְּזוּרֵינוּ מִבֵּין הַגּוֹיִם וּנְפוּצוֹתֵינוּ כַּנֵּס מִיַּרְכְּתֵי
אָרֶץ וַהֲבִיאֵנוּ לְצִיּוֹן עִירְךָ בְּרִנָּה וְלִירוּשָׁלַיִם בֵּית מִקְדָּשְׁךָ בְּשִׂמְחַת
עוֹלָם· וְשָׁם נַעֲשֶׂה לְפָנֶיךָ (אֶת־קָרְבְּנוֹת חוֹבוֹתֵינוּ) כְּמִצְוָּה (כ"ז
כִּמְצֻוֶּה) עָלֵינוּ בְּתוֹרָתֶךָ עַל יְדֵי מֹשֶׁה עַבְדְּךָ מִפִּי כְבוֹדֶךָ כָּאָמוּר:
וּבְיוֹם שִׂמְחַתְכֶם וּבְמוֹעֲדֵיכֶם וּבְרָאשֵׁי חָדְשֵׁכֶם וּתְקַעְתֶּם בַּחֲצֹצְרוֹת

sound of the Shofar continued and grew stronger and stronger, Moshe spoke and God answered him aloud." And it is said: "And the entire people perceived the sounds and the flames, and the sound of the Shofar, and the mountain smoking; the people saw and trembled, and stood afar off." And in Your holy words it is written: "Once God [of justice] has gone up in the homage of *teru'ah,* He appears as *God* of loving-kindness, with the call of the Shofar." And it is said: "With trumpets and call of the Shofar waken homage to *God,* the King." And it is said; "But blow the Shofar on the New Moon; on the day of the veiling of the moon for the day of our feast. For there is one law for Yisrael, the God of Yaakov sits in judgement." And it is said: "Halaluyah! proclaim the praise of God in His Sanctuary; proclaim Him in the firmament of His invincible power. Proclaim His praise from His mighty acts; proclaim His praise according to the abundance of His greatness. Proclaim His praise with the call of the Shofar; proclaim His praise with the psalter and harp. Proclaim His praise with the timbrel and the dance; proclaim His praise with stringed instruments and the flute. Proclaim His praise with the loud-sounding cymbals; proclaim His praise with the stirring cymbals. Let every breath of life proclaim the Lord's praise: Halaluyah." And by Your servants, the Prophets, it is written: "All you inhabitants of the world of man and you dwellers on earth, you will see it when the ensign will be raised on the mountain, and you will hear it when the Shofar will be sounded." And it is said, "And it will come to pass, on that day the great Shofar will be sounded, and those who were lost in the land of Ashur and those who were outcasts in the land of Mitzrayim will come and cast themselves down before *God* on the holy mountain in Yerushalayim." And it is said; "And *God* appears over them and His arrow goes forth like lightning and my Lord, *God* Who shows loving-kindness even in justice, will sound the Shofar and go forward in the tempests of the South. *God* Tzevaoth will shield them." So may You be a shield for Your people Yisrael with Your peace.

Our God and God of our fathers, sound the great Shofar for our freedom and raise aloft a banner to bring near our scattered [remnants] from their intermingling among the nations, and gather our dispersed from the ends of the earth, and bring us home to Tzion,

עַל עֹלֹתֵיכֶם וְעַל זִבְחֵי שַׁלְמֵיכֶם וְהָיוּ לָכֶם לְזִכָּרוֹן לִפְנֵי אֱלֹהֵיכֶם
אֲנִי יְיָ אֱלֹהֵיכֶם: כִּי אַתָּה שׁוֹמֵעַ קוֹל שׁוֹפָר וּמַאֲזִין תְּרוּעָה וְאֵין
דּוֹמֶה לָּךְ · בָּרוּךְ אַתָּה יְיָ שׁוֹמֵעַ קוֹל תְּרוּעַת עַמּוֹ יִשְׂרָאֵל בְּרַחֲמִים:

סדר נשיאת כפים—page 746

רְצֵה יְיָ אֱלֹהֵינוּ בְּעַמְּךָ יִשְׂרָאֵל וּבִתְפִלָּתָם · וְהָשֵׁב אֶת הָעֲבוֹדָה
לִדְבִיר בֵּיתֶךָ וְאִשֵּׁי יִשְׂרָאֵל וּתְפִלָּתָם בְּאַהֲבָה תְקַבֵּל בְּרָצוֹן
וּתְהִי לְרָצוֹן תָּמִיד עֲבוֹדַת יִשְׂרָאֵל עַמֶּךָ ·

וְתֶחֱזֶינָה עֵינֵינוּ בְּשׁוּבְךָ לְצִיּוֹן בְּרַחֲמִים · בָּרוּךְ אַתָּה יְיָ הַמַּחֲזִיר
שְׁכִינָתוֹ לְצִיּוֹן:

מוֹדִים אֲנַחְנוּ לָךְ שָׁאַתָּה הוּא יְיָ אֱלֹהֵינוּ וֵאלֹהֵי אֲבוֹתֵינוּ לְעוֹלָם
וָעֶד · צוּר חַיֵּינוּ מָגֵן יִשְׁעֵנוּ אַתָּה הוּא לְדוֹר וָדוֹר · נוֹדֶה לְּךָ
וּנְסַפֵּר תְּהִלָּתֶךָ · עַל חַיֵּינוּ הַמְּסוּרִים בְּיָדֶךָ וְעַל נִשְׁמוֹתֵינוּ הַפְּקוּדוֹת
לָךְ וְעַל נִסֶּיךָ שֶׁבְּכָל יוֹם עִמָּנוּ וְעַל נִפְלְאוֹתֶיךָ וְטוֹבוֹתֶיךָ שֶׁבְּכָל־
עֵת · עֶרֶב וָבֹקֶר וְצָהֳרָיִם · הַטּוֹב כִּי לֹא־כָלוּ רַחֲמֶיךָ וְהַמְרַחֵם כִּי
לֹא־תַמּוּ חֲסָדֶיךָ מֵעוֹלָם קִוִּינוּ לָךְ:

וְעַל כֻּלָּם יִתְבָּרַךְ וְיִתְרוֹמַם שִׁמְךָ מַלְכֵּנוּ תָּמִיד לְעוֹלָם וָעֶד:

וּכְתוֹב לְחַיִּים טוֹבִים כָּל־בְּנֵי בְרִיתֶךָ:

Your City, in jubilation, and to Yerushalayim, the site of Your Sanctuary, with joy everlasting. There we shall bring before You our
obligatory offerings, even as was enjoined upon us by Your Torah
through Moshe Your servant from the mouth of Your glory, as is
said: "On a day of your rejoicing and upon your festive seasons and
on the beginnings of your months you shall sound the trumpets at
your elevating-offerings and at your peace meal offerings, and they
shall be to you as a memorial before your God, I, *God,* your God."
For You hear the sound of the Shofar and incline Your ear to the
teru'ah, and there is none like You. Blessed be You, O *God,* Who
hears the teru'ah blast of His people Yisrael.

וְכָל הַחַיִּים יוֹדוּךָ פֶּלָה וִיהַלְלוּ אֶת שִׁמְךָ בֶּאֱמֶת הָאֵל יְשׁוּעָתֵנוּ
וְעֶזְרָתֵנוּ סֶלָה· בָּרוּךְ אַתָּה יְיָ הַטּוֹב שִׁמְךָ וּלְךָ נָאֶה לְהוֹדוֹת:

שִׂים שָׁלוֹם טוֹבָה וּבְרָכָה חֵן וָחֶסֶד וְרַחֲמִים עָלֵינוּ וְעַל כָּל־
יִשְׂרָאֵל עַמֶּךָ בָּרְכֵנוּ אָבִינוּ כֻּלָּנוּ כְּאֶחָד בְּאוֹר פָּנֶיךָ כִּי בְאוֹר
פָּנֶיךָ נָתַתָּ לָנוּ יְיָ אֱלֹהֵינוּ תּוֹרַת חַיִּים וְאַהֲבַת חֶסֶד וּצְדָקָה וּבְרָכָה
וְרַחֲמִים וְחַיִּים וְשָׁלוֹם וְטוֹב בְּעֵינֶיךָ לְבָרֵךְ אֶת־עַמְּךָ יִשְׂרָאֵל
בְּכָל עֵת וּבְכָל שָׁעָה בִּשְׁלוֹמֶךָ·

בְּסֵפֶר חַיִּים בְּרָכָה וְשָׁלוֹם וּפַרְנָסָה טוֹבָה נִזָּכֵר וְנִכָּתֵב לְפָנֶיךָ
אֲנַחְנוּ וְכָל עַמְּךָ בֵּית יִשְׂרָאֵל לְחַיִּים טוֹבִים וּלְשָׁלוֹם· בָּרוּךְ אַתָּה
יְיָ עוֹשֵׂה הַשָּׁלוֹם:

אֱלֹהַי· נְצוֹר לְשׁוֹנִי מֵרָע וּשְׂפָתַי מִדַּבֵּר מִרְמָה וְלִמְקַלְלַי נַפְשִׁי
תִדּוֹם וְנַפְשִׁי כֶּעָפָר לַכֹּל תִּהְיֶה: פְּתַח לִבִּי בְּתוֹרָתֶךָ וּבְמִצְוֹתֶיךָ
תִּרְדּוֹף נַפְשִׁי· וְכָל הַחוֹשְׁבִים עָלַי רָעָה מְהֵרָה הָפֵר עֲצָתָם וְקַלְקֵל
מַחֲשַׁבְתָּם· עֲשֵׂה לְמַעַן שְׁמֶךָ· עֲשֵׂה לְמַעַן יְמִינֶךָ· עֲשֵׂה לְמַעַן
קְדֻשָּׁתֶךָ· עֲשֵׂה לְמַעַן תּוֹרָתֶךָ· לְמַעַן יֵחָלְצוּן יְדִידֶיךָ הוֹשִׁיעָה
יְמִינְךָ וַעֲנֵנִי: יִהְיוּ לְרָצוֹן אִמְרֵי־פִי וְהֶגְיוֹן לִבִּי לְפָנֶיךָ יְיָ צוּרִי
וְגֹאֲלִי: עֹשֶׂה שָׁלוֹם בִּמְרוֹמָיו הוּא יַעֲשֶׂה שָׁלוֹם עָלֵינוּ וְעַל
כָּל יִשְׂרָאֵל וְאִמְרוּ אָמֵן:

יְהִי רָצוֹן מִלְּפָנֶיךָ יְיָ אֱלֹהֵינוּ וֵאלֹהֵי אֲבוֹתֵינוּ שֶׁיִּבָּנֶה
בֵּית הַמִּקְדָּשׁ בִּמְהֵרָה בְיָמֵינוּ וְתֵן חֶלְקֵנוּ בְּתוֹרָתֶךָ:
וְשָׁם נַעֲבָדְךָ בְּיִרְאָה כִּימֵי עוֹלָם וּכְשָׁנִים קַדְמוֹנִיּוֹת:
וְעָרְבָה לַיְיָ מִנְחַת יְהוּדָה וִירוּשָׁלָיִם כִּימֵי עוֹלָם וּכְשָׁנִים קַדְמוֹנִיּוֹת:

On the first day of ר"ה after מנחה before sundown one goes to a body of water
which contains fish and says the following verses; if the first day falls on שבת,
this is done on the second day:

מִי אֵל כָּמוֹךָ נֹשֵׂא עָוֹן וְעֹבֵר עַל־פֶּשַׁע לִשְׁאֵרִית נַחֲלָתוֹ לֹא־
הֶחֱזִיק לָעַד אַפּוֹ כִּי חָפֵץ חֶסֶד הוּא: יָשׁוּב יְרַחֲמֵנוּ יִכְבֹּשׁ עֲוֹנֹתֵינוּ
וְתַשְׁלִיךְ בִּמְצֻלוֹת יָם כָּל־חַטֹּאתָם: וְכָל־חַטֹּאת עַמְּךָ בֵּית יִשְׂרָאֵל
תַּשְׁלִיךְ בִּמְקוֹם אֲשֶׁר לֹא־יִזָּכְרוּ וְלֹא־יִפָּקְדוּ וְלֹא־יַעֲלוּ עַל־לֵב לְעוֹלָם:
תִּתֵּן אֱמֶת לְיַעֲקֹב חֶסֶד לְאַבְרָהָם אֲשֶׁר־נִשְׁבַּעְתָּ לַאֲבֹתֵינוּ מִימֵי קֶדֶם:

סדר הכפרות לערב יום כפור

The כפרה is taken in the right hand and the following is said:

בְּנֵי אָדָם יֹשְׁבֵי חֹשֶׁךְ וְצַלְמָוֶת אֲסִירֵי עֳנִי וּבַרְזֶל: יוֹצִיאֵם מֵחֹשֶׁךְ וְצַלְמָוֶת
וּמוֹסְרוֹתֵיהֶם יְנַתֵּק: אֱוִילִים מִדֶּרֶךְ פִּשְׁעָם וּמֵעֲוֹנֹתֵיהֶם יִתְעַנּוּ: כָּל־אֹכֶל תְּתַעֵב
נַפְשָׁם וַיַּגִּיעוּ עַד־שַׁעֲרֵי מָוֶת: וַיִּזְעֲקוּ אֶל־יְיָ בַּצַּר לָהֶם מִמְּצֻקוֹתֵיהֶם יוֹשִׁיעֵם: יִשְׁלַח
דְּבָרוֹ וְיִרְפָּאֵם וִימַלֵּט מִשְּׁחִיתוֹתָם: יוֹדוּ לַיְיָ חַסְדּוֹ וְנִפְלְאוֹתָיו לִבְנֵי אָדָם: אִם־יֵשׁ
עָלָיו מַלְאָךְ מֵלִיץ אֶחָד מִנִּי־אָלֶף לְהַגִּיד לְאָדָם יָשְׁרוֹ: וַיְחֻנֶּנּוּ וַיֹּאמֶר פְּדָעֵהוּ
מֵרֶדֶת שַׁחַת מָצָאתִי כֹפֶר:

When administering the כפרה to oneself: וּמִסְבֵּב סָבִיב רֹאשׁוֹ וְאוֹמֵר

זֶה חֲלִיפָתִי זֶה תְּמוּרָתִי זֶה כַּפָּרָתִי זֶה הַתַּרְנְגוֹל יֵלֵךְ לְמִיתָה וַאֲנִי אֶכָּנֵס
וְאֵלֵךְ לְחַיִּים טוֹבִים אֲרֻכִּים וּלְשָׁלוֹם:

וְחוֹזֵר וְקוֹרֵא בְּנֵי אָדָם וְגו' וְכֵן עוֹשֶׂה ג' פְּעָמִים, וְאַחַ"כ שׁוֹחֵט מִיָּד סָמוּךְ לִסְמִיכָה.

When administering the כפרה to oneself and to another: הַמְסַבֵּב לְעַצְמוֹ וּלְאַחֵר עִמּוֹ

זֶה חֲלִיפָתֵנוּ זֶה תְּמוּרָתֵנוּ זֶה כַּפָּרָתֵנוּ זֶה הַתַּרְנְגוֹל יֵלֵךְ לְמִיתָה וַאֲנַחְנוּ נִכָּנֵס
וְנֵלֵךְ לְחַיִּים טוֹבִים אֲרֻכִּים וּלְשָׁלוֹם:

When administering the כפרה to a man: הַמְסַבֵּב לְיַחִיד אוֹמֵר

זֶה חֲלִיפָתְךָ זֶה תְּמוּרָתְךָ זֶה כַּפָּרָתְךָ זֶה הַתַּרְנְגוֹל יֵלֵךְ לְמִיתָה וְאַתָּה תִּכָּנֵס
וְתֵלֵךְ לְחַיִּים טוֹבִים אֲרֻכִּים וּלְשָׁלוֹם:

לרבים בתרנגול אחד   When administering the כפרה to several men:

זֶה חֲלִיפַתְכֶם זֶה תְּמוּרַתְכֶם זֶה כַּפָּרַתְכֶם זֶה הַתַּרְנְגוֹל יֵלֵךְ לְמִיתָה וְאַתֶּם תִּכָּנְסוּ וְתֵלְכוּ לְחַיִּים טוֹבִים אֲרֵכִים וּלְשָׁלוֹם:

המסנב לנקנה   When administering the כפרה to a woman:

זֹאת חֲלִיפָתֵךְ זֹאת תְּמוּרָתֵךְ זֹאת כַּפָּרָתֵךְ זֹאת הַתַּרְנְגוֹלֶת תֵּלֵךְ לְמִיתָה וְאַתְּ תִּכָּנְסִי וְתֵלְכִי לְחַיִּים טוֹבִים אֲרֵכִים וּלְשָׁלוֹם:

המסנב לנקנות נאחת   When administering the כפרה to several women:

זֹאת חֲלִיפַתְכֶן זֹאת תְּמוּרַתְכֶן זֹאת כַּפָּרַתְכֶן זֹאת הַתַּרְנְגוֹלֶת תֵּלֵךְ לְמִיתָה וְאַתֶּן תִּכָּנַסְנָה וְתֵלַכְנָה לְחַיִּים טוֹבִים אֲרֵכִים וּלְשָׁלוֹם:

המסנב לרבים ברבים, וכן לזעזברת   When administering several כפרות to several persons:

אֵלּוּ חֲלִיפוֹתֵיכֶם אֵלּוּ תְּמוּרוֹתֵיכֶם אֵלּוּ כַּפָּרוֹתֵיכֶם אֵלּוּ הַתַּרְנְ וֹלִים יֵלְכוּ לְמִיתָה וְאַתֶּם תִּכָּנְסוּ וְתֵלְכוּ לְחַיִּים טוֹבִים אֲרֵכִים וּלְשָׁלוֹם:

<h1 dir="rtl" align="center">תפלת יום כפור</h1>
לערבית ושחרית ומנחה.

אֲדֹנָי שְׂפָתַי תִּפְתָּח וּפִי יַגִּיד תְּהִלָּתֶךָ:

בָּרוּךְ אַתָּה יְיָ אֱלֹהֵינוּ וֵאלֹהֵי אֲבוֹתֵינוּ אֱלֹהֵי אַבְרָהָם אֱלֹהֵי יִצְחָק וֵאלֹהֵי יַעֲקֹב הָאֵל הַגָּדוֹל הַגִּבּוֹר וְהַנּוֹרָא אֵל עֶלְיוֹן גּוֹמֵל חֲסָדִים טוֹבִים וְקֹנֵה הַכֹּל וְזוֹכֵר חַסְדֵּי אָבוֹת וּמֵבִיא גוֹאֵל לִבְנֵי בְנֵיהֶם לְמַעַן שְׁמוֹ בְּאַהֲבָה:

זָכְרֵנוּ לְחַיִּים · מֶלֶךְ חָפֵץ בַּחַיִּים · וְכָתְבֵנוּ בְּסֵפֶר הַחַיִּים · לְמַעַנְךָ אֱלֹהִים חַיִּים· מֶלֶךְ עוֹזֵר וּמוֹשִׁיעַ וּמָגֵן· בָּרוּךְ אַתָּה יְיָ מָגֵן אַבְרָהָם:

אַתָּה גִבּוֹר לְעוֹלָם אֲדֹנָי מְחַיֵּה מֵתִים אַתָּה רַב לְהוֹשִׁיעַ· מְכַלְכֵּל חַיִּים בְּחֶסֶד מְחַיֵּה מֵתִים בְּרַחֲמִים רַבִּים סוֹמֵךְ נוֹפְלִים וְרוֹפֵא חוֹלִים וּמַתִּיר אֲסוּרִים וּמְקַיֵּם אֱמוּנָתוֹ לִישֵׁנֵי עָפָר · מִי כָמוֹךָ בַּעַל גְּבוּרוֹת וּמִי דּוֹמֶה לָּךְ מֶלֶךְ מֵמִית וּמְחַיֶּה וּמַצְמִיחַ יְשׁוּעָה:

מִי כָמוֹךָ אַב הָרַחֲמִים · זוֹכֵר יְצוּרָיו לְחַיִּים בְּרַחֲמִים · וְנֶאֱמָן
אַתָּה לְהַחֲיוֹת מֵתִים · בָּרוּךְ אַתָּה יְיָ מְחַיֶּה הַמֵּתִים:

אַתָּה קָדוֹשׁ וְשִׁמְךָ קָדוֹשׁ וּקְדוֹשִׁים בְּכָל יוֹם יְהַלְלוּךָ סֶּלָה:

וּבְכֵן תֵּן פַּחְדְּךָ יְיָ אֱלֹהֵינוּ עַל כָּל מַעֲשֶׂיךָ וְאֵימָתְךָ עַל כָּל מַה
שֶּׁבָּרָאתָ וְיִירָאוּךָ כָּל הַמַּעֲשִׂים וְיִשְׁתַּחֲווּ לְפָנֶיךָ כָּל הַבְּרוּאִים
וְיֵעָשׂוּ כֻלָּם אֲגֻדָּה אֶחָת לַעֲשׂוֹת רְצוֹנְךָ בְּלֵבָב שָׁלֵם כְּמוֹ שֶׁיָּדַעְנוּ
יְיָ אֱלֹהֵינוּ שֶׁהַשָּׁלְטָן לְפָנֶיךָ עֹז בְּיָדְךָ וּגְבוּרָה בִּימִינֶךָ וְשִׁמְךָ
נוֹרָא עַל כָּל מַה שֶּׁבָּרָאתָ:

וּבְכֵן תֵּן כָּבוֹד יְיָ לְעַמֶּךָ תְּהִלָּה לִירֵאֶיךָ וְתִקְוָה לְדוֹרְשֶׁיךָ וּפִתְחוֹן
פֶּה לַמְיַחֲלִים לָךְ שִׂמְחָה לְאַרְצֶךָ וְשָׂשׂוֹן לְעִירֶךָ וּצְמִיחַת קֶרֶן
לְדָוִד עַבְדֶּךָ וַעֲרִיכַת נֵר לְבֶן יִשַׁי מְשִׁיחֶךָ בִּמְהֵרָה בְיָמֵינוּ:

וּבְכֵן צַדִּיקִים יִרְאוּ וְיִשְׂמָחוּ וִישָׁרִים יַעֲלֹזוּ וַחֲסִידִים בְּרִנָּה
יָגִילוּ וְעוֹלָתָה תִּקְפָּץ פִּיהָ · וְכָל הָרִשְׁעָה כֻּלָּהּ בֶּעָשָׁן תִּכְלֶה כִּי
תַעֲבִיר מֶמְשֶׁלֶת זָדוֹן מִן הָאָרֶץ:

וְתִמְלוֹךְ אַתָּה יְיָ לְבַדֶּךָ עַל כָּל מַעֲשֶׂיךָ בְּהַר צִיּוֹן מִשְׁכַּן
כְּבוֹדֶךָ וּבִירוּשָׁלַיִם עִיר קָדְשֶׁךָ כַּכָּתוּב בְּדִבְרֵי קָדְשֶׁךָ יִמְלֹךְ יְיָ
לְעוֹלָם אֱלֹהַיִךְ צִיּוֹן לְדֹר וָדֹר הַלְלוּיָהּ:

קָדוֹשׁ אַתָּה וְנוֹרָא שְׁמֶךָ וְאֵין אֱלֹוהַּ מִבַּלְעָדֶיךָ כַּכָּתוּב וַיִּגְבַּהּ יְיָ
צְבָאוֹת בַּמִּשְׁפָּט וְהָאֵל הַקָּדוֹשׁ נִקְדַּשׁ בִּצְדָקָה: בָּרוּךְ אַתָּה יְיָ
הַמֶּלֶךְ הַקָּדוֹשׁ:

אַתָּה בְחַרְתָּנוּ מִכָּל הָעַמִּים · אָהַבְתָּ אוֹתָנוּ · וְרָצִיתָ בָּנוּ ·
וְרוֹמַמְתָּנוּ מִכָּל הַלְּשׁוֹנוֹת · וְקִדַּשְׁתָּנוּ בְּמִצְוֹתֶיךָ · וְקֵרַבְתָּנוּ מַלְכֵּנוּ
לַעֲבוֹדָתֶךָ · וְשִׁמְךָ הַגָּדוֹל וְהַקָּדוֹשׁ עָלֵינוּ קָרָאתָ:

וַתִּתֶּן־לָנוּ יְיָ אֱלֹהֵינוּ בְּאַהֲבָה אֶת־יוֹם הַשַּׁבָּת הַזֶּה לִקְדוּשָׁה וְלִמְנוּחָה

וְאֶת יוֹם הַכִּפֻּרִים הַזֶּה לִמְחִילָה וְלִסְלִיחָה וּלְכַפָּרָה וְלִמְחָל־בּוֹ אֶת־

כָּל־עֲוֹנוֹתֵינוּ בְּאַהֲבָה מִקְרָא קֹדֶשׁ זֵכֶר לִיצִיאַת מִצְרָיִם:

אֱלֹהֵינוּ וֵאלֹהֵי אֲבוֹתֵינוּ · יַעֲלֶה וְיָבֹא וְיַגִּיעַ וְיֵרָאֶה וְיֵרָצֶה וְיִשָּׁמַע

וְיִפָּקֵד וְיִזָּכֵר זִכְרוֹנֵנוּ וּפִקְדוֹנֵנוּ וְזִכְרוֹן אֲבוֹתֵינוּ · וְזִכְרוֹן מָשִׁיחַ בֶּן

דָּוִד עַבְדֶּךָ · וְזִכְרוֹן יְרוּשָׁלַיִם עִיר קָדְשֶׁךָ · וְזִכְרוֹן כָּל עַמְּךָ בֵּית

יִשְׂרָאֵל לְפָנֶיךָ · לִפְלֵיטָה וּלְטוֹבָה וּלְחֵן וּלְחֶסֶד וּלְרַחֲמִים וּלְחַיִּים

וּלְשָׁלוֹם בְּיוֹם הַכִּפֻּרִים הַזֶּה · זָכְרֵנוּ יְיָ אֱלֹהֵינוּ בּוֹ לְטוֹבָה · וּפָקְדֵנוּ

בוֹ לִבְרָכָה · וְהוֹשִׁיעֵנוּ בוֹ לְחַיִּים · וּבִדְבַר יְשׁוּעָה וְרַחֲמִים חוּס

וְחָנֵּנוּ וְרַחֵם עָלֵינוּ וְהוֹשִׁיעֵנוּ · כִּי אֵלֶיךָ עֵינֵינוּ · כִּי אֵל מֶלֶךְ

חַנּוּן וְרַחוּם אָתָּה:

אֱלֹהֵינוּ וֵאלֹהֵי אֲבוֹתֵינוּ מְחַל לַעֲוֹנוֹתֵינוּ בְּיוֹם הַשַּׁבָּת הַזֶּה וּבְיוֹם

הַכִּפֻּרִים הַזֶּה · מְחֵה וְהַעֲבֵר פְּשָׁעֵינוּ (וְחַטֹּאתֵינוּ) מִנֶּגֶד עֵינֶיךָ ·

And You have given us, O *God* our God, in love, (this Sabbath
Day for sanctification and for rest and) this Day of Atonements for
pardon and forgiveness and atonement (in love) to obtain pardon
thereon for all our sins, a convocation to the Sanctuary, a remembrance
of the exodus from Mitzrayim.

Our God and God of our fathers, forgive our sins on this (Sabbath day and this) Day of Atonements; blot out and remove our transgressions and our errors from before Your eyes, even as it is said:

מחילה is "pardon"; i.e. a waiver of the punishment due the guilty party.
סליחה is "forgiveness"; to "forgive" is to bring it to pass that the relationship
of the wrongdoer to the forgiver should not be marred by the wrong or injustice
perpetrated by the sinner. כפרה is "atonement"; i.e. the complete remission of
the consequences of our wrongful acts in our inner and outer lives alike. Were
it not for the intervention of the wondrous power of God's grace, our moral

כָּאמוּר אָנֹכִי אָנֹכִי הוּא מֹחֶה פְשָׁעֶיךָ לְמַעֲנִי וְחַטֹּאתֶיךָ לֹא אֶזְכֹּר:

וְנֶאֱמַר מָחִיתִי כָעָב פְּשָׁעֶיךָ וְכֶעָנָן חַטֹּאותֶיךָ שׁוּבָה אֵלַי כִּי גְאַלְתִּיךָ:

וְנֶאֱמַר כִּי בַיּוֹם הַזֶּה יְכַפֵּר עֲלֵיכֶם לְטַהֵר אֶתְכֶם מִכֹּל חַטֹּאתֵיכֶם

לִפְנֵי יְיָ תִּטְהָרוּ: (אלהינו ואלהי אבותינו רצה במנוחתנו) קַדְּשֵׁנוּ

בְּמִצְוֹתֶיךָ וְתֵן חֶלְקֵנוּ בְּתוֹרָתֶךָ ׳ שַׂבְּעֵנוּ מִטּוּבֶךָ וְשַׂמְּחֵנוּ בִּישׁוּעָתֶךָ ׳

(והנחילנו יי אלהינו באהבה וברצון שבת קדשך וינוחו בה ישראל מקדשי שמך)

וְטַהֵר לִבֵּנוּ לְעָבְדְּךָ בֶּאֱמֶת ׳ כִּי אַתָּה סָלְחָן לְיִשְׂרָאֵל וּמָחֳלָן

לְשִׁבְטֵי יְשֻׁרוּן בְּכָל דּוֹר וָדוֹר וּמִבַּלְעָדֶיךָ אֵין לָנוּ מֶלֶךְ מוֹחֵל

וְסוֹלֵחַ ׳ בָּרוּךְ אַתָּה יְיָ מֶלֶךְ מוֹחֵל וְסוֹלֵחַ לַעֲוֹנוֹתֵינוּ וְלַעֲוֹנוֹת

עַמּוֹ בֵּית יִשְׂרָאֵל ׳ וּמַעֲבִיר אַשְׁמוֹתֵינוּ בְּכָל שָׁנָה וְשָׁנָה ׳ מֶלֶךְ עַל

כָּל הָאָרֶץ מְקַדֵּשׁ השבת וְיִשְׂרָאֵל וְיוֹם הַכִּפֻּרִים:

---

strength and our physical and social welfare would have been forfeit long ago as a consequence of our transgressions. This would be our fate in accordance with the law of cause and effect which functions in God's world according to His will. It is only God Himself, He Who originally ordained that law of causality Who, in the omnipotence of His will, can also suspend that law. Only He can cause the wrong which was done to become as if it had never occurred. Only God can uproot in their entirety the curses which the wrong that was perpetrated may have sown into the field of our future. This wondrous power of His grace He has assured to every person who observes Yom Kippur by true *teshuvah*. יום כפורים, not יום כפרה; Stress is thus put upon the infinite number and kinds of transgressions and errors of a lifetime for which the Day of Atonement can afford us *kapparah*.

למעני "for My own sake"; i.e. "for the sake of the favor and loving-kindness which is in keeping with My nature and which is in accordance with the purpose of My sovereignty." מחיתי: "I have ever been to you a God Who forgives and pardons; return to Me now, too, for you could have perished long ago in sin and evil, but I have delivered you from both." כענן, כעב Once God will have delivered us from our iniquities then, through His grace, our transgressions will become like clouds and our sins like a mist. Even as both rain and thunder leave only blessings in their wake once they have passed away, so, too, our sins, once we have overcome them, benefit the development of our future moral loyalty, for, according to our Sages, sinners who have been cleansed of their transgressions attain a lofty level which

"I, even I, am He Who blots out your transgressions for My own sake, and I shall not remember your sins." And it is said, "I have blotted out your transgressions as a cloud and your sins as a mist; return to Me, for I have redeemed you." And it is said: "For on this day He shall make atonement for you, to cleanse you; you shall become cleansed of all your sins before *God*." (*On the Sabbath, add*: Our God and God of our fathers, take pleasure in our rest), sanctify us by Your commandments and grant our portion in Your Torah, satisfy us from Your good and gladden us by Your salvation (*On the Sabbath, add*: and give us, O *God* our God, in love and favor Your holy Sabbath as an inheritance, that Yisrael, who hallow Your Name, may rest thereon), and purify our hearts to serve You in truth, for You are Forgiver of Yisrael and the Pardoner of the tribes of Yeshurun in every generation, and beside You we have no King, Who pardons and forgives. Blessed be You, O *God*, King Who pardons and forgives our iniquities and the iniquities of His people, the House of Yisrael, and Who removes our trespasses from year to year, King over all the earth, Who sanctifies (the Sabbath and) Yisrael and the Day of Atonements.

---

those who have never sinned in their lives can never reach. במקום שבעלי תשובה "For on this day." In the Torah, כי ביום הזה ,עומדים אין צדיקים גמורים יכולין לעמוד this sentence refers to the commandment given in that portion which enjoins fasting and the cessation of all work on the Tenth Day of the Seventh Month, *inui* and *issur melachah*. The Tenth Day of Tishri was the day on which a new set of tablets, upon which the old law was inscribed, was given as surety for the *kapparah* for the *egel* incident, the gravest sin ever to have been committed by the people of Yisrael. For this reason the Tenth Day of Tishri has remained forever that day which, with its every recurrence, is to bring us, from the almighty, wondrous grace of God, *kapparah* as well as *taharah*, a rebirth that is to preserve us from the consequences, both tangible and intangible, of our past transgressions. We are therefore to observe this day by *inui* and *issur melachah*. By *inui*, abstaining from every physical enjoyment, we are to demonstrate our awareness of the fact that, by our sinful surrender to lust and temptation, we have forfeited the moral purity of our inner being. *Issur melachah*, the cessation on our part of every workday activity which would represent our dominion over the world about us, symbolizes our admission that, by our transgressions against the world around us and by our misuse of our Divinely-ordained position in nature and sociey, we have forfeited not only our right to this position, but also to any Divine assistance

רְצֵה יְיָ אֱלֹהֵינוּ בְּעַמְּךָ יִשְׂרָאֵל וּבִתְפִלָּתָם · וְהָשֵׁב אֶת־הָעֲבוֹדָה
לִדְבִיר בֵּיתֶךָ · וְאִשֵּׁי יִשְׂרָאֵל וּתְפִלָּתָם בְּאַהֲבָה תְקַבֵּל בְּרָצוֹן וּתְהִי
לְרָצוֹן תָּמִיד עֲבוֹדַת יִשְׂרָאֵל עַמֶּךָ ·

וְתֶחֱזֶינָה עֵינֵינוּ בְּשׁוּבְךָ לְצִיּוֹן בְּרַחֲמִים · בָּרוּךְ אַתָּה יְיָ
הַמַּחֲזִיר שְׁכִינָתוֹ לְצִיּוֹן:

מוֹדִים אֲנַחְנוּ לָךְ שָׁאַתָּה הוּא יְיָ אֱלֹהֵינוּ וֵאלֹהֵי אֲבוֹתֵינוּ לְעוֹלָם
וָעֶד · צוּר חַיֵּינוּ מָגֵן יִשְׁעֵנוּ אַתָּה הוּא לְדוֹר וָדוֹר · נוֹדֶה לְּךָ וּנְסַפֵּר
תְּהִלָּתֶךָ עַל חַיֵּינוּ הַמְּסוּרִים בְּיָדֶךָ וְעַל נִשְׁמוֹתֵינוּ הַפְּקוּדוֹת לָךְ
וְעַל נִסֶּיךָ שֶׁבְּכָל יוֹם עִמָּנוּ וְעַל נִפְלְאוֹתֶיךָ וְטוֹבוֹתֶיךָ שֶׁבְּכָל עֵת,
עֶרֶב וָבֹקֶר וְצָהֳרָיִם · הַטּוֹב כִּי לֹא כָלוּ רַחֲמֶיךָ וְהַמְרַחֵם כִּי לֹא
תַמּוּ חֲסָדֶיךָ מֵעוֹלָם קִוִּינוּ לָךְ:

וְעַל כֻּלָּם יִתְבָּרַךְ וְיִתְרוֹמַם שִׁמְךָ מַלְכֵּנוּ תָּמִיד לְעוֹלָם וָעֶד:

וּכְתוֹב לְחַיִּים טוֹבִים כָּל־בְּנֵי בְרִיתֶךָ:

וְכֹל הַחַיִּים יוֹדוּךָ סֶּלָה וִיהַלְלוּ אֶת שִׁמְךָ בֶּאֱמֶת הָאֵל יְשׁוּעָתֵנוּ
וְעֶזְרָתֵנוּ סֶלָה · בָּרוּךְ אַתָּה יְיָ הַטּוֹב שִׁמְךָ וּלְךָ נָאֶה לְהוֹדוֹת:

<table>
<tr><td>בְּעַרְבִית אוֹמְרִין זֶה:</td><td>בְּשַׁחֲרִית וּבְמִנְחָה אוֹמְרִין זֶה.</td></tr>
</table>

בְּעַרְבִית אוֹמְרִין זֶה:	בְּשַׁחֲרִית וּבְמִנְחָה אוֹמְרִין זֶה.
שָׁלוֹם רָב עַל יִשְׂרָאֵל	שִׂים שָׁלוֹם טוֹבָה וּבְרָכָה חֵן וָחֶסֶד
עַמְּךָ תָּשִׂים לְעוֹלָם כִּי	וְרַחֲמִים עָלֵינוּ וְעַל כָּל יִשְׂרָאֵל עַמֶּךָ · בָּרְכֵנוּ
אַתָּה הוּא מֶלֶךְ אָדוֹן	אָבִינוּ כֻּלָּנוּ כְּאֶחָד בְּאוֹר פָּנֶיךָ · כִּי בְאוֹר
לְכָל הַשָּׁלוֹם וְטוֹב	פָּנֶיךָ נָתַתָּ לָּנוּ יְיָ אֱלֹהֵינוּ תּוֹרַת חַיִּים וְאַהֲבַת
בְּעֵינֶיךָ לְבָרֵךְ אֶת־עַמְּךָ	חֶסֶד וּצְדָקָה וּבְרָכָה וְרַחֲמִים וְחַיִּים וְשָׁלוֹם
יִשְׂרָאֵל בְּכָל־עֵת וּבְכָל	וְטוֹב בְּעֵינֶיךָ לְבָרֵךְ אֶת־עַמְּךָ יִשְׂרָאֵל
שָׁעָה בִּשְׁלוֹמֶךָ:	בְּכָל־עֵת וּבְכָל־שָׁעָה בִּשְׁלוֹמֶךָ:

בְּסֵפֶר חַיִּים בְּרָכָה וְשָׁלוֹם וּפַרְנָסָה טוֹבָה, נִזָּכֵר וְנִכָּתֵב לְפָנֶיךָ
אֲנַחְנוּ וְכָל עַמְּךָ בֵּית יִשְׂרָאֵל לְחַיִּים טוֹבִים וּלְשָׁלוֹם · בָּרוּךְ אַתָּה
יְיָ עוֹשֶׂה הַשָּׁלוֹם:

אֱלֹהֵינוּ וֵאלֹהֵי אֲבוֹתֵינוּ ·

תָּבֹא לְפָנֶיךָ תְּפִלָּתֵנוּ, וְאַל תִּתְעַלַּם מִתְּחִנָּתֵנוּ · שֶׁאֵין אֲנַחְנוּ עַזֵּי

פָנִים וּקְשֵׁי עֹרֶף לוֹמַר לְפָנֶיךָ יְיָ אֱלֹהֵינוּ וֵאלֹהֵי אֲבוֹתֵינוּ צַדִּיקִים

אֲנַחְנוּ וְלֹא חָטָאנוּ אֲבָל אֲנַחְנוּ חָטָאנוּ :

Our God and God of our fathers, may our prayer come before
You and withdraw not from our supplication, for we are not impudent
and stubborn that we should say before You, O *God* our God and God
of our fathers; "We are righteous and have not sinned." Truly, we
have sinned.

---

in and for the maintenance of this our exalted station. Our future existence
is now dependent upon *tahara,* an inner rebirth, and upon *kapparah* a visible
outer renascence in which the pernicious consequences of our past sins will
be "buried". Both *taharah* and *kapparah* are gifts which we can find only
before the countenance of God, Who shows His great loving-kindness in the
almighty power of His wondrous favor. מֶלֶךְ עַל כָּל הָאָרֶץ מְקַדֵּשׁ, מֶלֶךְ מוֹחֵל וְסוֹלֵחַ
יִשְׂרָאֵל וְיוֹם הַכִּפּוּרִים : God is the King Who is the almighty Ruler over the Universe, and the supreme revelation of His might is Yom Kippur, that day
which He made holy and on which He performs for us the greatest miracle
of all—the obliteration of what has occurred in the past, and the remission
of what otherwise would have been the consequences of previous sin.

אֱו״א : The first step of *teshuvah,* which is the most essential and at the
same time the most difficult, is וִידּוּי, the *confession,* or, rather הַתוֹדָה, the
admission to oneself that one has sinned. It is not God Who needs an avowal
or confession from us, for He knows us through and through, in fact, much
better than we know ourselves. But we ourselves are very much in need of
such honest and unreserved confession. It is to our own selves that we must
admit that we have done wrong, for without such confession to ourselves
we can never become better. It is a difficult admission indeed for a man to
make. There is within each and every one of us a small defender who is ready
at all times to deny outright that we have done wrong at all, or at least to
make excuses, to mitigate and to cloak our transgression. In this manner our
defender veils from our sight the true picture of ourselves as we really are,

אָשַׁמְנוּ · בָּגַדְנוּ · גָּזַלְנוּ · דִּבַּרְנוּ דְפִי · הֶעֱוֵינוּ ·
וְהִרְשַׁעְנוּ · זַדְנוּ · חָמַסְנוּ · טָפַלְנוּ שֶׁקֶר · יָעַצְנוּ רָע ·
כִּזַּבְנוּ · לַצְנוּ · מָרַדְנוּ נִאַצְנוּ · סָרַרְנוּ · עָוִינוּ · פָּשַׁעְנוּ ·
צָרַרְנוּ · קִשִּׁינוּ עֹרֶף · רָשַׁעְנוּ · שִׁחַתְנוּ · תִּעַבְנוּ ·
תָּעִינוּ · תִּעְתָּעְנוּ ·

סַרְנוּ מִמִּצְוֹתֶיךָ וּמִמִּשְׁפָּטֶיךָ הַטּוֹבִים וְלֹא שָׁוָה לָנוּ: וְאַתָּה צַדִּיק
עַל כָּל־הַבָּא עָלֵינוּ · כִּי אֱמֶת עָשִׂיתָ וַאֲנַחְנוּ הִרְשָׁעְנוּ:

מַה נֹּאמַר לְפָנֶיךָ יוֹשֵׁב מָרוֹם, וּמַה נְּסַפֵּר לְפָנֶיךָ שׁוֹכֵן שְׁחָקִים ·
הֲלֹא כָּל־הַנִּסְתָּרוֹת וְהַנִּגְלוֹת אַתָּה יוֹדֵעַ:

אַתָּה יוֹדֵעַ רָזֵי עוֹלָם · וְתַעֲלוּמוֹת סִתְרֵי כָל־חָי ·
אַתָּה חוֹפֵשׂ כָּל חַדְרֵי בָטֶן וּבוֹחֵן כְּלָיוֹת וָלֵב: אֵין דָּבָר
נֶעְלָם מִמֶּךָּ · וְאֵין נִסְתָּר מִנֶּגֶד עֵינֶיךָ:

וּבְכֵן יְהִי רָצוֹן מִלְּפָנֶיךָ יְיָ אֱלֹהֵינוּ וֵאלֹהֵי אֲבוֹתֵינוּ ·
שֶׁתִּסְלַח לָנוּ עַל כָּל חַטֹּאתֵינוּ · וְתִמְחַל־לָנוּ עַל כָּל
עֲוֹנוֹתֵינוּ · וּתְכַפֶּר־לָנוּ עַל כָּל פְּשָׁעֵינוּ:

---

but by so doing, also very effectively blocks the path to our betterment. Therefore אבל אנחנו חטאנו is the first, most essential and indispensable part of the
confession that we must make to ourselves. "Truly, we have sinned."

The confession of sins which now follows is an enumeration of all the
many sins and errors known to mankind. It is entirely in the plural form. For
these are sins which certainly will not be lacking in the collective life of the
community of Yisrael as such. Moreover, in keeping with the principle
כל ישראל ערבין זה לזה that all Israelites are responsible for one another, even
he who is not aware of having been guilty of such a sin himself should seriously consider whether he himself had not sinned by neglecting to do anything
in his power that might have kept his fellow-Jew from committing the transgression. For, according to our Sages שהיה בידם למחות ולא מחו : ז"ל (Avodah
Zarah 4a, Sabbath 55a) all those who, though by no means sure that such

We have done wrong, we have been faithless, we have robbed, we have uttered blasphemy, we have been perverse, and we have per-petrated acts of lawlessness, we have been willful, we have done violence, we have forged lies; we have counseled evil, we have deceived, we have scoffed, we have rebelled, we have been scornful, we have been disobedient, we have succumbed to perversity, we have transgressed, we have persecuted, we have been stubborn; we have been lawless, we have corrupted, we have committed abomination, we have gone astray and we have led astray.

We have strayed from Your commandments and from Your good ordinances, and it has brought us no profit, and You are righteous in all that has come upon us, for You have acted faithfully, but we were lawless.

What shall we say before You, O You Who dwells on high; what shall we recount before You Who abides in the Heavens? Do You not know all things, both hidden and revealed? You know the secrets of the world and the most hidden mysteries of all the living. You search into the inmost recesses, and try passions and heart. Nothing is concealed from You and nothing is hidden from before Your eyes.

Therefore may it be Your will, O *God* our God and God of our fathers, to grant us forgiveness for all our sins, and to grant us pardon for all our iniquities, and to grant us remission for all our transgressions,

---

attempts on their part would have ended in failure, have not even tried to restrain their brother from wrongdoing by warning and exhortation, share in their brother's sin.

אשמנו refers to a wrongful act for which we would be deserving of שממה "desolation", the total loss of all joy and happiness. בגדנו denotes a "breach of faith" with either man or God. העוינו: Whatever God has commanded us is the sole "straight" way of life, the only type of conduct entirely worthy of ourselves as well as appropriate to the other people and circumstances to which we must relate. It also is the goal that was set for us by God, a goal after which we are to strive without deviation. It is the only "straight" course and every deviation from it is "crookedness" or "perversity". הרשענו The term הרשיע means to have one's course of action guided not by the Law but only by one's own whims. זדנו implies an act committed with the full know-ledge that it is wrong, as opposed to *shegagah* which denotes unintentional

עַל חֵטְא שֶׁחָטָאנוּ לְפָנֶיךָ בְּאֹנֶס וּבְרָצוֹן:

וְעַל חֵטְא שֶׁחָטָאנוּ לְפָנֶיךָ בְּאִמּוּץ הַלֵּב:

עַל חֵטְא שֶׁחָטָאנוּ לְפָנֶיךָ בִּבְלִי דָעַת:

וְעַל חֵטְא שֶׁחָטָאנוּ לְפָנֶיךָ בְּבִטּוּי שְׂפָתָיִם:

עַל חֵטְא שֶׁחָטָאנוּ לְפָנֶיךָ בְּגָלוּי וּבַסָּתֶר:

וְעַל חֵטְא שֶׁחָטָאנוּ לְפָנֶיךָ בְּגִלּוּי עֲרָיוֹת:

עַל חֵטְא שֶׁחָטָאנוּ לְפָנֶיךָ בְּדִבּוּר פֶּה:

וְעַל חֵטְא שֶׁחָטָאנוּ לְפָנֶיךָ בְּדַעַת וּבְמִרְמָה:

עַל חֵטְא שֶׁחָטָאנוּ לְפָנֶיךָ בְּהַרְהוֹר הַלֵּב:

וְעַל חֵטְא שֶׁחָטָאנוּ לְפָנֶיךָ בְּהוֹנָאַת רֵעַ:

עַל חֵטְא שֶׁחָטָאנוּ לְפָנֶיךָ בְּוִדּוּי פֶּה:

וְעַל חֵטְא שֶׁחָטָאנוּ לְפָנֶיךָ בִּוְעִידַת זְנוּת:

עַל חֵטְא שֶׁחָטָאנוּ לְפָנֶיךָ בְּזָדוֹן וּבִשְׁגָגָה:

---

error. טפלנו שקר may mean either "we have cast the slur of falsehood upon others" (as in Ps. 119:69) or "we have clung to falsehood." עוינו, as distinguished from העוינו, means, "our very character had lost its 'straightness', it had utterly succumbed to crookedness (or perversity)." פשענו. פשע is the extreme type of transgression. It refers to cases in which the sinner does the wrong not *even though* God has forbidden it, but out of spite, *for the very reason* that it displeases God. It is a purposeful, deliberate transgression against the Law of God. רשענו as distinguished from הרשענו, means "we were lawless altogether; we have withheld our obedience from the Law." תעלומות סתרי refers to that which man would prefer to keep concealed and the exposure of which he dreads.

תסלח על חטאתינו: "May You not allow the evil which we have done in error to disturb Your relationship with us; תמחול על עונותינו may You not inflict upon us the punishment which we would deserve for that evil which we have done knowingly, תכפר על פשעינו and may You not visit upon us the destruction which we would deserve because of our acts of deliberate, purposeful rebellion against You."

for the sin which we have committed before You under compulsion or in wilfulness;

and for the sin which we have committed before You in the hardening of the heart;

for the sin which we have committed before You unwittingly;

and for the sin which we have committed before You by the rashness of the lips;

for the sin which we have committed before You openly and in secret;

and for the sin which we have committed before You by unchastity;

for the sin which we have committed before You by the speech of the mouth;

and for the sin which we have committed before You with full knowledge and with deceit;

for the sin which we have committed before You by the meditation of the heart;

and for the sin which we have committed before You by wronging our neighbor;

for the sin which we have committed before You by confession with the mouth;

and for the sin which we have committed before You by association with impurity;

for the sin which we have committed before You in presumption or in error;

אמוץ הלב. על חטא as in Deut. 15:7; "by forcibly suppressing any nobler emotions that might have stirred within our hearts." בודוי פה: by having framed a confession with our lips, without, however, taking appropriate action as well. טומאת שפתים denotes obscene speech. ביודעים ובלא יודעים may imply also "with or without the knowledge *of those against whom we have sinned*" (Yaavetz).

בכפת שחד as in מתן בסתר יכפה אף (Prov. 21:14) (Yaavetz). It can refer either to the giver or to the receiver of the bribe.

לשון הרע includes any aspersion, even if it be justified, cast upon the character of another, or upon his way of life.

במשא ובמתן, "in taking and giving", denotes any business transaction.

בנטית גרון, "by the stretched-forth neck", is an expression for "arrogance".

וְעַל חֵטְא שֶׁחָטָאנוּ לְפָנֶיךָ בְּזִלְזוּל הוֹרִים וּמוֹרִים:

עַל חֵטְא שֶׁחָטָאנוּ לְפָנֶיךָ בְּחוֹזֶק יָד:

וְעַל חֵטְא שֶׁחָטָאנוּ לְפָנֶיךָ בְּחִלּוּל הַשֵּׁם:

עַל חֵטְא שֶׁחָטָאנוּ לְפָנֶיךָ בְּטִפְשׁוּת פֶּה:

וְעַל חֵטְא שֶׁחָטָאנוּ לְפָנֶיךָ בְּטֻמְאַת שְׂפָתָיִם:

עַל חֵטְא שֶׁחָטָאנוּ לְפָנֶיךָ בְּיֵצֶר הָרָע:

וְעַל חֵטְא שֶׁחָטָאנוּ לְפָנֶיךָ בְּיוֹדְעִים וּבְלֹא יוֹדְעִים:

וְעַל כֻּלָּם אֱלוֹהַּ סְלִיחוֹת סְלַח־לָנוּ • מְחַל־לָנוּ • כַּפֶּר־לָנוּ:

עַל חֵטְא שֶׁחָטָאנוּ לְפָנֶיךָ בְּכַפַּת שֹׁחַד:

וְעַל חֵטְא שֶׁחָטָאנוּ לְפָנֶיךָ בְּכַחַשׁ וּבְכָזָב:

עַל חֵטְא שֶׁחָטָאנוּ לְפָנֶיךָ בְּלָשׁוֹן הָרָע:

וְעַל חֵטְא שֶׁחָטָאנוּ לְפָנֶיךָ בְּלָצוֹן:

עַל חֵטְא שֶׁחָטָאנוּ לְפָנֶיךָ בְּמַשָּׂא וּבְמַתָּן:

וְעַל חֵטְא שֶׁחָטָאנוּ לְפָנֶיךָ בְּמַאֲכָל וּבְמִשְׁתֶּה:

עַל חֵטְא שֶׁחָטָאנוּ לְפָנֶיךָ בְּנֶשֶׁךְ וּבְמַרְבִּית:

וְעַל חֵטְא שֶׁחָטָאנוּ לְפָנֶיךָ בִּנְטִיַּת גָּרוֹן:

עַל חֵטְא שֶׁחָטָאנוּ לְפָנֶיךָ בְּשִׂקּוּר עָיִן:

וְעַל חֵטְא שֶׁחָטָאנוּ לְפָנֶיךָ בְּשִׂיחַ שִׂפְתוֹתֵינוּ:

עַל חֵטְא שֶׁחָטָאנוּ לְפָנֶיךָ בְּעֵינַיִם רָמוֹת:

וְעַל חֵטְא שֶׁחָטָאנוּ לְפָנֶיךָ בְּעַזּוּת מֵצַח:

רכיל, רכילות, is the "talebearer", the newsmonger who spreads news concerning his neighbor's affairs from house to house without considering whether or not it would please or benefit his victim to have his affairs thus made known.

and for the sin which we have committed before You by contempt for parents and teachers;

for the sin which we have committed before You by violence;

and for the sin which we have committed before You by the profanation of the Divine Name;

for the sin which we have committed before You by the folly of the mouth;

and for the sin which we have committed before You by the impurity of the lips;

for the sin which we have committed before You by the evil impulse;

and for the sin which we have committed before You knowingly or unknowingly.

For all these, O God of forgiveness, forgive us, pardon us, grant us remission.

For the sin which we have committed before You by taking bribes;

and for the sin which we have committed before You by denying and lying;

for the sin which we have committed before You by slander;

and for the sin which we have committed before You by scoffing;

for the sin which we have committed before You in taking and giving;

and for the sin which we have committed before You in eating and drinking;

for the sin which we have committed before You by usury and interest;

and for the sin which we have committed before You by the neck stretched forth [in arrogance];

for the sin which we have committed before You with wanton looks;

and for the sin which we have committed before You by the gossip of our lips;

for the sin which we have committed before You with haughty eyes;

and for the sin which we have committed before You by effron-tery.

וְעַל כֻּלָּם אֱלוֹהַ סְלִיחוֹת סְלַח־לָנוּ · מְחַל־לָנוּ · כַּפֶּר־לָנוּ:

עַל חֵטְא שֶׁחָטָאנוּ לְפָנֶיךָ בִּפְרִיקַת עֹל:

וְעַל חֵטְא שֶׁחָטָאנוּ לְפָנֶיךָ בִּפְלִילוּת:

עַל חֵטְא שֶׁחָטָאנוּ לְפָנֶיךָ בִּצְדִיַּת רֵעַ:

וְעַל חֵטְא שֶׁחָטָאנוּ לְפָנֶיךָ בְּצָרוּת עָיִן:

עַל חֵטְא שֶׁחָטָאנוּ לְפָנֶיךָ בְּקַלּוּת רֹאשׁ:

וְעַל חֵטְא שֶׁחָטָאנוּ לְפָנֶיךָ בְּקַשְׁיוּת עֹרֶף:

עַל חֵטְא שֶׁחָטָאנוּ לְפָנֶיךָ בְּרִיצַת רַגְלַיִם לְהָרַע:

וְעַל חֵטְא שֶׁחָטָאנוּ לְפָנֶיךָ בִּרְכִילוּת:

עַל חֵטְא שֶׁחָטָאנוּ לְפָנֶיךָ בִּשְׁבוּעַת שָׁוְא:

וְעַל חֵטְא שֶׁחָטָאנוּ לְפָנֶיךָ בְּשִׂנְאַת חִנָּם:

עַל חֵטְא שֶׁחָטָאנוּ לְפָנֶיךָ בִּתְשׂוּמֶת יָד:

וְעַל חֵטְא שֶׁחָטָאנוּ לְפָנֶיךָ בְּתִמְהוֹן לֵבָב:

וְעַל כֻּלָּם אֱלוֹהַ סְלִיחוֹת סְלַח־לָנוּ · מְחַל־לָנוּ · כַּפֶּר־לָנוּ:

וְעַל חֲטָאִים שֶׁאָנוּ חַיָּבִים עֲלֵיהֶם עוֹלָה:

וְעַל חֲטָאִים שֶׁאָנוּ חַיָּבִים עֲלֵיהֶם חַטָּאת:

וְעַל חֲטָאִים שֶׁאָנוּ חַיָּבִים עֲלֵיהֶם קָרְבָּן עוֹלֶה וְיוֹרֵד:

וְעַל חֲטָאִים שֶׁאָנוּ חַיָּבִים עֲלֵיהֶם אָשָׁם וַדַּי וְתָלוּי:

וְעַל חֲטָאִים שֶׁאָנוּ חַיָּבִים עֲלֵיהֶם מַכַּת מַרְדּוּת:

וְעַל חֲטָאִים שֶׁאָנוּ חַיָּבִים עֲלֵיהֶם מַלְקוּת אַרְבָּעִים:

וְעַל חֲטָאִים שֶׁאָנוּ חַיָּבִים עֲלֵיהֶם מִיתָה בִּידֵי שָׁמָיִם:

מכפר על עשה ועל עולה is the offering to atone for neglect of one's duty: is
לא תעשה הניתק לעשה.
חטאת is the offering to atone for such transgressions as were committed
in error, שגגה, and which, had they been perpetrated on purpose במזיד, would
incur the penalty of כרת.

For all these, O God of forgivenesses, forgive us, pardon us, grant us remission.

For the sin which we have committed before You by breaking off the yoke [of Your Law];

and for the sin which we have commited before You in passing judgment;

for the sin which we have committed before You by setting snares for our neighbor;

and for the sin which we have commited before You by envy;

for the sin which we have committed before You by frivolity;

and for the sin which we have committed before You by stubbornness;

for the sin which we have committed before You by running to evil;

and for the sin which we have committed before You by talebearing;

for the sin which we have committed before You by vain oaths;

and for the sin which we have committed before You by causeless hatred;

for the sin which we have committed before You with money entrusted to our care;

and for the sin which we have committed before You with confusion of mind.

For all these, O God of forgiveness, forgive us, pardon us, grant us remission.

And for the sins for which we owe an elevating-offering;

and for the sins for which we owe a sin offering;

and for the sins for which we owe an offering of varying degree;

and for the sins for which we owe an offering, whether for certain or for doubtful trespass;

and for the sins for which we are liable to the penalty of chastisement for insubordination;

and for the sins for which we are liable to the penalty of forty stripes;

and for the sins for which we are liable to death by the hand of Heaven;

וְעַל חֲטָאִים שֶׁאָנוּ חַיָּבִים עֲלֵיהֶם כָּרֵת וַעֲרִירִי (כ"י וַעֲרִירוֹת) :

וְעַל כֻּלָּם אֱלֹוֹהַ סְלִיחוֹת סְלַח־לָנוּ · מְחַל־לָנוּ · כַּפֶּר־לָנוּ :

וְעַל חֲטָאִים שֶׁ"ח עֲלֵיהֶם אַרְבַּע מִיתוֹת בֵּית דִּין ·
סְקִילָה · שְׂרֵפָה · הֶרֶג · וְחֶנֶק · עַל מִצְוַת עֲשֵׂה וְעַל מִצְוַת
לֹא תַעֲשֶׂה · בֵּין שֶׁיֵּשׁ בָּהּ קוּם עֲשֵׂה · וּבֵין שֶׁאֵין בָּהּ קוּם
עֲשֵׂה · אֶת־הַגְּלוּיִים לָנוּ וְאֶת־שֶׁאֵינָם גְּלוּיִים לָנוּ · אֶת־
הַגְּלוּיִים לָנוּ כְּבָר אֲמַרְנוּם לְפָנֶיךָ וְהוֹדִינוּ לְךָ עֲלֵיהֶם ·
וְאֶת־שֶׁאֵינָם גְּלוּיִים לָנוּ לְפָנֶיךָ הֵם גְּלוּיִים וִידוּעִים ·
כַּדָּבָר שֶׁנֶּאֱמַר הַנִּסְתָּרֹת לַיְיָ אֱלֹהֵינוּ · וְהַנִּגְלֹת לָנוּ
וּלְבָנֵינוּ עַד־עוֹלָם · לַעֲשׂוֹת אֶת־כָּל־דִּבְרֵי הַתּוֹרָה
הַזֹּאת : כִּי אַתָּה סָלְחָן לְיִשְׂרָאֵל וּמָחֳלָן לְשִׁבְטֵי יְשֻׁרוּן
בְּכָל דּוֹר וָדוֹר וּמִבַּלְעָדֶיךָ אֵין לָנוּ מֶלֶךְ מוֹחֵל
וְסוֹלֵחַ (אֶלָּא אַתָּה) :

אֱלֹהַי · עַד שֶׁלֹּא נוֹצַרְתִּי אֵינִי כְדַי · וְעַכְשָׁו שֶׁנּוֹצַרְתִּי כְּאִלּוּ לֹא
נוֹצַרְתִּי · עָפָר אֲנִי בְּחַיָּי · קַל וָחֹמֶר בְּמִיתָתִי · הֲרֵי אֲנִי לְפָנֶיךָ כִּכְלִי
מָלֵא בוּשָׁה וּכְלִמָּה · יְהִי רָצוֹן מִלְּפָנֶיךָ יְיָ אֱלֹהַי וֵאלֹהֵי אֲבוֹתַי שֶׁלֹּא
אֶחֱטָא עוֹד · וּמַה שֶּׁחָטָאתִי לְפָנֶיךָ מָרֵק בְּרַחֲמֶיךָ הָרַבִּים · אֲבָל
לֹא עַל יְדֵי יִסּוּרִים וָחֳלָיִם רָעִים :

עולה ויורד are offerings ordained in the Fifth Chapter of Leviticus, the
quantities of which vary depending upon the material wealth of the person
who must give the offering.

אשם ודאי, discussed in Lev. 5:14–16, 20–26, serves to atone for transgressions involving the wrongful aggrandizement of one's own wealth at the
expense of another. Before this offering can be brought, however, proper
restitution first must have been made by the transgressor to the injured party.

and for the sins for which we are liable to the penalty of being cut off and of childlessness;

For all these, O God of forgiveness, forgive us, pardon us, grant us remission.

And also for the sins for which we are liable to any of the four death penalties executed by the Court of Justice — stoning, burning, execution and strangling, for [the violation of] positive commandments or prohibitions, [regardless of] whether or not such violation can be rectified by the subsequent fulfillment of a positive commandment, for sins, whether they be manifest to us or not. Those sins that are manifest to us we have already declared before You and we have admitted them; as for those that are not manifest to us; they are revealed and known before You, even as has been said: "The hidden things belong to *God* our God; but the revealed things belong to us and to our children forever, that we may fulfill all the words of this Torah." For You are the Forgiver of Yisrael and the Pardoner of the tribes of Yeshurun in every generation, and beside You we have no King Who pardons and forgives.

O my God, before I was created, I was of no worth, and now that I have been created, I am as if I had not been created. Dust I am in life, how much more so in death. I am here before You like a vessel filled with shame and confusion. May it be Your will, O *God,* my God and God of my fathers, that I may sin no more, and as to the sins that I have committed before You, blot them out in Your abundant compassion, but not by means of affliction and evil diseases.

אשם תלוי is brought in cases of uncertainty with regard to transgressions which, if perpetrated on purpose, would be punishable by *kareth,* and if committed unintentionally, must be atoned for by *chatath.*

מכת מרדות applies in cases involving violations of Rabbinic prohibitions.

מלקות ארבעים applies in cases involving violations of Biblical prohibitions.

הרג denotes execution by the sword.

בין שיש בו קום עשה. In Torath Kohanim to Lev. 1:4 and also in Makkoth 17a, the Mishna explains לא תעשה שיש בו קום עשה as being a לאו הניתק לעשה a prohibition the violation of which could be rectified by the subsequent performance of a positive commandment; e.g. לא תגזול and והשיב את הגזילה. Accordingly, בין שיש בו וכו׳ here, too, seems to be an apposition to the preceding מצות לא תעשה.

אֱלֹהַי· נְצוֹר לְשׁוֹנִי מֵרָע וּשְׂפָתַי מִדַּבֵּר מִרְמָה וְלִמְקַלְלַי נַפְשִׁי
תִדּוֹם וְנַפְשִׁי כֶּעָפָר לַכֹּל תִּהְיֶה: פְּתַח לִבִּי בְּתוֹרָתֶךָ וּבְמִצְוֹתֶיךָ
תִּרְדּוֹף נַפְשִׁי וְכָל הַחוֹשְׁבִים עָלַי רָעָה מְהֵרָה הָפֵר עֲצָתָם וְקַלְקֵל
מַחֲשַׁבְתָּם· עֲשֵׂה לְמַעַן שְׁמֶךָ· עֲשֵׂה לְמַעַן יְמִינֶךָ· עֲשֵׂה לְמַעַן
קְדֻשָּׁתֶךָ· עֲשֵׂה לְמַעַן תּוֹרָתֶךָ· לְמַעַן יֵחָלְצוּן יְדִידֶיךָ הוֹשִׁיעָה
יְמִינְךָ וַעֲנֵנִי: יִהְיוּ לְרָצוֹן אִמְרֵי־פִי וְהֶגְיוֹן לִבִּי לְפָנֶיךָ יְיָ צוּרִי
וְגֹאֲלִי: עֹשֶׂה שָׁלוֹם בִּמְרוֹמָיו הוּא יַעֲשֶׂה שָׁלוֹם עָלֵינוּ וְעַל כָּל
יִשְׂרָאֵל וְאִמְרוּ אָמֵן :

יְהִי רָצוֹן מִלְּפָנֶיךָ יְיָ אֱלֹהֵינוּ וֵאלֹהֵי אֲבוֹתֵינוּ שֶׁיִּבָּנֶה
בֵּית הַמִּקְדָּשׁ בִּמְהֵרָה בְיָמֵינוּ וְתֵן חֶלְקֵנוּ בְּתוֹרָתֶךָ:
וְשָׁם נַעֲבָדְךָ בְּיִרְאָה כִּימֵי עוֹלָם וּכְשָׁנִים קַדְמֹנִיּוֹת:
וְעָרְבָה לַיְיָ מִנְחַת יְהוּדָה וִירוּשָׁלָיִם כִּימֵי עוֹלָם וּכְשָׁנִים קַדְמֹנִיּוֹת:

תְּפִלַּת מוּסָף לְיוֹם כִּפּוּר

אֲדֹנָי שְׂפָתַי תִּפְתָּח וּפִי יַגִּיד תְּהִלָּתֶךָ:

בָּרוּךְ אַתָּה יְיָ אֱלֹהֵינוּ וֵאלֹהֵי אֲבוֹתֵינוּ אֱלֹהֵי אַבְרָהָם אֱלֹהֵי יִצְחָק
וֵאלֹהֵי יַעֲקֹב הָאֵל הַגָּדוֹל הַגִּבּוֹר וְהַנּוֹרָא אֵל עֶלְיוֹן גּוֹמֵל חֲסָדִים
טוֹבִים וְקֹנֵה הַכֹּל וְזוֹכֵר חַסְדֵי אָבוֹת וּמֵבִיא גוֹאֵל לִבְנֵי בְנֵיהֶם
לְמַעַן שְׁמוֹ בְּאַהֲבָה·

זָכְרֵנוּ לְחַיִּים מֶלֶךְ חָפֵץ בַּחַיִּים· וְכָתְבֵנוּ בְּסֵפֶר הַחַיִּים
לְמַעַנְךָ אֱלֹהִים חַיִּים: מֶלֶךְ עוֹזֵר וּמוֹשִׁיעַ וּמָגֵן· בָּרוּךְ אַתָּה
יְיָ מָגֵן אַבְרָהָם:

אַתָּה גִּבּוֹר לְעוֹלָם אֲדֹנָי מְחַיֶּה מֵתִים אַתָּה רַב
לְהוֹשִׁיעַ·

מְכַלְכֵּל חַיִּים בְּחֶסֶד מְחַיֶּה מֵתִים בְּרַחֲמִים רַבִּים סוֹמֵךְ נוֹפְלִים
וְרוֹפֵא חוֹלִים וּמַתִּיר אֲסוּרִים וּמְקַיֵּם אֱמוּנָתוֹ לִישֵׁנֵי עָפָר · מִי
כָמְוֹךָ בַּעַל גְּבוּרוֹת וּמִי דְּוֹמֶה לָּךְ מֶלֶךְ מֵמִית וּמְחַיֶּה וּמַצְמִיחַ יְשׁוּעָה:
מִי כָמְוֹךָ אַב הָרַחֲמִים · זוֹכֵר יְצוּרָיו לְחַיִּים בְּרַחֲמִים · וְנֶאֱמָן
אַתָּה לְהַחֲיוֹת מֵתִים · בָּרוּךְ אַתָּה יְיָ מְחַיֶּה הַמֵּתִים:

אַתָּה קָדוֹשׁ וְשִׁמְךָ קָדוֹשׁ וּקְדוֹשִׁים בְּכָל יוֹם יְהַלְלוּךָ סֶּלָה:

וּבְכֵן תֵּן פַּחְדְּךָ יְיָ אֱלֹהֵינוּ עַל כָּל־מַעֲשֶׂיךָ וְאֵימָתְךָ עַל כָּל־מַה
שֶּׁבָּרָאתָ וְיִירָאוּךָ כָּל־הַמַּעֲשִׂים וְיִשְׁתַּחֲווּ לְפָנֶיךָ כָּל־הַבְּרוּאִים
וְיֵעָשׂוּ כֻלָּם אֲגֻדָּה אַחַת לַעֲשׂוֹת רְצוֹנְךָ בְּלֵבָב שָׁלֵם כְּמוֹ שֶׁיָּדַעְנוּ
יְיָ אֱלֹהֵינוּ שֶׁהַשָּׁלְטָן לְפָנֶיךָ עֹז בְּיָדְךָ וּגְבוּרָה בִּימִינֶךָ וְשִׁמְךָ
נוֹרָא עַל כָּל־מַה־שֶּׁבָּרָאתָ:

וּבְכֵן תֵּן כָּבוֹד יְיָ לְעַמֶּךָ תְּהִלָּה לִירֵאֶיךָ וְתִקְוָה לְדוֹרְשֶׁיךָ וּפִתְחוֹן
פֶּה לַמְיַחֲלִים לָךְ שִׂמְחָה לְאַרְצֶךָ וְשָׂשׂוֹן לְעִירֶךָ וּצְמִיחַת קֶרֶן
לְדָוִד עַבְדֶּךָ וַעֲרִיכַת נֵר לְבֶן יִשַׁי מְשִׁיחֶךָ בִּמְהֵרָה בְּיָמֵינוּ:

וּבְכֵן צַדִּיקִים יִרְאוּ וְיִשְׂמָחוּ וִישָׁרִים יַעֲלְזוּ וַחֲסִידִים בְּרִנָּה
יָגִילוּ וְעוֹלָתָה תִּקְפָּץ־פִּיהָ · וְכָל־הָרִשְׁעָה כָּלָּהּ כֶּעָשָׁן תִּכְלֶה כִּי
תַעֲבִיר מֶמְשֶׁלֶת זָדוֹן מִן־הָאָרֶץ:

וְתִמְלֹךְ אַתָּה יְיָ לְבַדֶּךָ עַל כָּל־מַעֲשֶׂיךָ בְּהַר צִיּוֹן מִשְׁכַּן
כְּבוֹדֶךָ וּבִירוּשָׁלַיִם עִיר קָדְשֶׁךָ כַּכָּתוּב בְּדִבְרֵי קָדְשֶׁךָ יִמְלֹךְ יְיָ
לְעוֹלָם אֱלֹהַיִךְ צִיּוֹן לְדֹר וָדֹר הַלְלוּיָהּ:

קָדוֹשׁ אַתָּה וְנוֹרָא שְׁמֶךָ וְאֵין אֱלוֹהַּ מִבַּלְעָדֶיךָ כַּכָּתוּב וַיִּגְבַּהּ יְיָ
צְבָאוֹת בַּמִּשְׁפָּט וְהָאֵל הַקָּדוֹשׁ נִקְדַּשׁ בִּצְדָקָה: בָּרוּךְ אַתָּה יְיָ
הַמֶּלֶךְ הַקָּדוֹשׁ:

אַתָּה בְחַרְתָּנוּ מִכָּל־הָעַמִּים · אָהַבְתָּ אוֹתָנוּ · וְרָצִיתָ בָּנוּ · וְרוֹמַמְתָּנוּ מִכָּל הַלְּשׁוֹנוֹת · וְקִדַּשְׁתָּנוּ בְּמִצְוֹתֶיךָ · וְקֵרַבְתָּנוּ מַלְכֵּנוּ לַעֲבוֹדָתֶךָ · וְשִׁמְךָ הַגָּדוֹל וְהַקָּדוֹשׁ עָלֵינוּ קָרָאתָ:

וַתִּתֶּן לָנוּ יְיָ אֱלֹהֵינוּ בְּאַהֲבָה אֶת־יוֹם השבת הזה לקדושה ולמנוחה ואת יום הַכִּפֻּרִים הַזֶּה לִמְחִילָה וְלִסְלִיחָה וּלְכַפָּרָה וְלִמְחָל־בּוֹ אֶת־ כָּל־עֲוֹנֹתֵינוּ באהבה מִקְרָא קֹדֶשׁ זֵכֶר לִיצִיאַת מִצְרָיִם:

וּמִפְּנֵי חֲטָאֵינוּ גָּלִינוּ מֵאַרְצֵנוּ וְנִתְרַחַקְנוּ מֵעַל אַדְמָתֵנוּ וְאֵין אֲנַחְנוּ יְכוֹלִים לַעֲשׂוֹת חוֹבוֹתֵינוּ בְּבֵית בְּחִירָתֶךָ בַּבַּיִת הַגָּדוֹל וְהַקָּדוֹשׁ שֶׁנִּקְרָא שִׁמְךָ עָלָיו מִפְּנֵי הַיָּד שֶׁנִּשְׁתַּלְּחָה בְּמִקְדָּשֶׁךָ:

יְהִי רָצוֹן מִלְּפָנֶיךָ יְיָ אֱלֹהֵינוּ וֵאלֹהֵי אֲבוֹתֵינוּ מֶלֶךְ רַחֲמָן שֶׁתָּשׁוּב וּתְרַחֵם עָלֵינוּ וְעַל מִקְדָּשְׁךָ בְּרַחֲמֶיךָ הָרַבִּים וְתִבְנֵהוּ מְהֵרָה וּתְגַדֵּל כְּבוֹדוֹ: אָבִינוּ מַלְכֵּנוּ, גַּלֵּה כְּבוֹד מַלְכוּתְךָ עָלֵינוּ מְהֵרָה וְהוֹפַע וְהִנָּשֵׂא עָלֵינוּ לְעֵינֵי כָּל־חָי · וְקָרֵב פְּזוּרֵינוּ מִבֵּין הַגּוֹיִם וּנְפוּצוֹתֵינוּ כַּנֵּס מִיַּרְכְּתֵי־אָרֶץ · וַהֲבִיאֵנוּ לְצִיּוֹן עִירְךָ בְּרִנָּה וְלִירוּשָׁלַיִם בֵּית מִקְדָּשְׁךָ בְּשִׂמְחַת עוֹלָם וְשָׁם נַעֲשֶׂה לְפָנֶיךָ אֶת קָרְבְּנוֹת חוֹבוֹתֵינוּ תְּמִידִים כְּסִדְרָם וּמוּסָפִים כְּהִלְכָתָם: וְאֵת מוּסַף יוֹם השבת הזה וְאֵת מוּסַף יוֹם הַכִּפֻּרִים הַזֶּה · נַעֲשֶׂה וְנַקְרִיב לְפָנֶיךָ בְּאַהֲבָה כְּמִצְוַת רְצוֹנֶךָ כְּמוֹ שֶׁכָּתַבְתָּ עָלֵינוּ בְּתוֹרָתֶךָ עַל יְדֵי מֹשֶׁה עַבְדֶּךָ מִפִּי כְבוֹדֶךָ כָּאָמוּר:

לשבת וּבְיוֹם הַשַּׁבָּת שְׁנֵי־כְבָשִׂים בְּנֵי־שָׁנָה תְּמִימִם

וּשְׁנֵי עֶשְׂרֹנִים סֹלֶת מִנְחָה בְּלוּלָה בַשֶּׁמֶן וְנִסְכּוֹ:

עֹלַת שַׁבַּת בְּשַׁבַּתּוֹ עַל־עֹלַת הַתָּמִיד וְנִסְכָּהּ:

וּבֶעָשׂוֹר לַחֹדֶשׁ הַשְּׁבִיעִי הַזֶּה מִקְרָא־קֹדֶשׁ יִהְיֶה לָכֶם וְעִנִּיתֶם אֶת־נַפְשֹׁתֵיכֶם כָּל־מְלָאכָה לֹא תַעֲשׂוּ:

And on the tenth day of this seventh month you shall have a convocation to the Sanctuary and you shall afflict your souls. You may do no manner of work. And you shall bring to God as an elevating-offering as an expression of compliance: one young bullock, one ram, seven yearling lambs; they shall be to you without blemish.

And their tribute offering and their drink offerings as declared: three tenths for the bullock, two-tenths for the ram, one tenth for each lamb, and wine in accordance with its drink offering, and two he-goats for atonement and two regular elevating-offerings according to their rule.

מוסף ליום הכפורים

ובעשור: In the Sanctuary of the Law a series of uniquely solemn acts of *Avodah* prescribed in the Sixteenth Chapter of the Book of Leviticus is to symbolize the renewal of our bond with the new Tablets of the Law which we received on the first Yom Kippur and which were enshrined beneath the wings of Cherubim beside the original broken Tablets. While these rites are performed in the Sanctuary, we are commanded to proceed as follows: "You, who have been summoned to God and who await your rebirth at His hands are to observe this day by עַנּוּי and שביתה מכל מלאכה, by abstaining from all the enjoyments of life and by refraining from all creative work, so that you may remember that, without the gift of Divine grace, the future of all your life and work on earth would have been forfeit and you would have been doomed to total destruction as the result of your sins. Then, *vehikravtem*, in gladsome confidence in the promise of your future restored, you are to come near to God with the elevating-offering, symbolizing the ideal of your destiny. You pledge to be His "bullock", His faithful worker on the acre of His harvest for mankind; you solemnly promise to go forward as a "ram", a "model" leading the nations, which are all His "herd". The seven lambs symbolize your vow to follow in eternal youthful vigor His Providence and guidance which reveals His might. You solemnly promise to be *temimim* in all these things, to devote all of your personality without reservations to these ends, and to view all the riches and pleasures that aid you in such endeavors, such conduct and in leading such a life, (*nesachim* and *menachoth*) as gifts of God received solely for the furtherance of these endeavors, and of this way of life, and for the fulfillment of your destiny. And finally, you vow, with *sa'ir*-like steadfastness, to maintain yourselves on the high level of this your destiny."

ושני שעירים לכפר. The one *sa'ir* is the *chattath* which is part of the *Mo'ed* group to be offered on Yom Kippur. The other *sa'ir* is the שעיר לה׳ which is offered as part of the *Avodah* of the High Priest; its blood was sprinkled שבע למטה לפני הכפרת and אחת למעלה על הכפרת in the Holy of Holies.

וְהִקְרַבְתֶּם עֹלָה לַיְיָ רֵיחַ נִיחֹחַ פַּר בֶּן־בָּקָר אֶחָד אַיִל
אֶחָד כְּבָשִׂים בְּנֵי־שָׁנָה שִׁבְעָה תְּמִימִם יִהְיוּ לָכֶם:
וּמִנְחָתָם וְנִסְכֵּיהֶם כִּמְדֻבָּר שְׁלֹשָׁה עֶשְׂרֹנִים לַפָּר
שְׁנֵי עֶשְׂרֹנִים לָאַיִל • וְעִשָּׂרוֹן לַכֶּבֶשׂ • וְיַיִן כְּנִסְכּוֹ וּשְׁנֵי
שְׂעִירִים לְכַפֵּר • (כ״א וְשָׂעִיר לְכַפֵּר מִלְּבַד חַטַּאת הַכִּפּוּרִים)
וּשְׁנֵי תְמִידִים כְּהִלְכָתָם:

לשבת יִשְׂמְחוּ בְמַלְכוּתְךָ שׁוֹמְרֵי שַׁבָּת וְקוֹרְאֵי עֹנֶג עַם מְקַדְּשֵׁי שְׁבִיעִי
כֻּלָּם יִשְׂבְּעוּ וְיִתְעַנְּגוּ מִטּוּבֶךָ • וּבַשְּׁבִיעִי רָצִיתָ בּוֹ וְקִדַּשְׁתּוֹ חֶמְדַּת
יָמִים אוֹתוֹ קָרָאתָ זֵכֶר לְמַעֲשֵׂה בְרֵאשִׁית:

אֱלֹהֵינוּ וֵאלֹהֵי אֲבוֹתֵינוּ • מְחַל לַעֲוֹנוֹתֵינוּ בְּיוֹם הַשַּׁבָּת הַזֶּה וּבְיוֹם
הַכִּפּוּרִים הַזֶּה • מְחֵה וְהַעֲבֵר פְּשָׁעֵינוּ (וְחַטֹּאתֵינוּ) מִנֶּגֶד עֵינֶיךָ •
כָּאָמוּר אָנֹכִי אָנֹכִי הוּא מֹחֶה פְשָׁעֶיךָ לְמַעֲנִי וְחַטֹּאתֶיךָ לֹא־אֶזְכֹּר:
וְנֶאֱמַר מָחִיתִי כָעָב פְּשָׁעֶיךָ וְכֶעָנָן חַטֹּאתֶיךָ שׁוּבָה אֵלַי כִּי גְאַלְתִּיךָ:
וְנֶאֱמַר כִּי־בַיּוֹם הַזֶּה יְכַפֵּר עֲלֵיכֶם לְטַהֵר אֶתְכֶם מִכֹּל חַטֹּאתֵיכֶם
לִפְנֵי יְיָ תִּטְהָרוּ: (אֱלֹהֵינוּ וֵאלֹהֵי אֲבוֹתֵינוּ רְצֵה בִמְנוּחָתֵנוּ) קַדְּשֵׁנוּ
בְּמִצְוֹתֶיךָ וְתֵן חֶלְקֵנוּ בְּתוֹרָתֶךָ • שַׂבְּעֵנוּ מִטּוּבֶךָ וְשַׂמְּחֵנוּ בִּישׁוּעָתֶךָ •
(וְהַנְחִילֵנוּ יְיָ אֱלֹהֵינוּ בְּאַהֲבָה וּבְרָצוֹן שַׁבַּת קָדְשֶׁךָ וְיָנוּחוּ בָהּ יִשְׂרָאֵל מְקַדְּשֵׁי שְׁמֶךָ)
וְטַהֵר לִבֵּנוּ לְעָבְדְּךָ בֶּאֱמֶת • כִּי אַתָּה סָלְחָן לְיִשְׂרָאֵל וּמָחֳלָן
לְשִׁבְטֵי יְשֻׁרוּן בְּכָל־דּוֹר וָדוֹר וּמִבַּלְעָדֶיךָ אֵין לָנוּ מֶלֶךְ מוֹחֵל
וְסוֹלֵחַ (אֶלָּא אַתָּה)• בָּרוּךְ אַתָּה יְיָ, מֶלֶךְ מוֹחֵל וְסוֹלֵחַ לַעֲוֹנוֹתֵינוּ
וְלַעֲוֹנוֹת עַמּוֹ בֵּית יִשְׂרָאֵל, וּמַעֲבִיר אַשְׁמוֹתֵינוּ בְּכָל־שָׁנָה וְשָׁנָה •
מֶלֶךְ עַל כָּל־הָאָרֶץ מְקַדֵּשׁ הַשַּׁבָּת וְיִשְׂרָאֵל וְיוֹם הַכִּפּוּרִים:

רְצֵה יְיָ אֱלֹהֵינוּ בְּעַמְּךָ יִשְׂרָאֵל וּבִתְפִלָּתָם · וְהָשֵׁב אֶת־הָעֲבוֹדָה לִדְבִיר בֵּיתֶךָ וְאִשֵּׁי יִשְׂרָאֵל וּתְפִלָּתָם בְּאַהֲבָה תְקַבֵּל בְּרָצוֹן וּתְהִי לְרָצוֹן תָּמִיד עֲבוֹדַת יִשְׂרָאֵל עַמֶּךָ ·

סדר נשיאת כפים—page 746

וְתֶחֱזֶינָה עֵינֵינוּ בְּשׁוּבְךָ לְצִיּוֹן בְּרַחֲמִים · בָּרוּךְ אַתָּה יְיָ הַמַּחֲזִיר שְׁכִינָתוֹ לְצִיּוֹן:

מוֹדִים אֲנַחְנוּ לָךְ שָׁאַתָּה הוּא יְיָ אֱלֹהֵינוּ וֵאלֹהֵי אֲבוֹתֵינוּ לְעוֹלָם וָעֶד · צוּר חַיֵּינוּ מָגֵן יִשְׁעֵנוּ אַתָּה הוּא לְדוֹר וָדוֹר · נוֹדֶה לְךָ וּנְסַפֵּר תְּהִלָּתֶךָ עַל חַיֵּינוּ הַמְּסוּרִים בְּיָדֶךָ וְעַל נִשְׁמוֹתֵינוּ הַפְּקוּדוֹת לָךְ וְעַל נִסֶּיךָ שֶׁבְּכָל יוֹם עִמָּנוּ וְעַל נִפְלְאוֹתֶיךָ וְטוֹבוֹתֶיךָ שֶׁבְּכָל עֵת, עֶרֶב וָבֹקֶר וְצָהֳרָיִם · הַטּוֹב כִּי לֹא כָלוּ רַחֲמֶיךָ וְהַמְרַחֵם כִּי לֹא תַמּוּ חֲסָדֶיךָ מֵעוֹלָם קִוִּינוּ לָךְ:

וְעַל־כֻּלָּם יִתְבָּרַךְ וְיִתְרוֹמַם שִׁמְךָ מַלְכֵּנוּ תָּמִיד לְעוֹלָם וָעֶד:

וּכְתוֹב לְחַיִּים טוֹבִים כָּל־בְּנֵי בְרִיתֶךָ:

וְכֹל הַחַיִּים יוֹדוּךָ סֶּלָה וִיהַלְלוּ אֶת־שִׁמְךָ בֶּאֱמֶת הָאֵל יְשׁוּעָתֵנוּ וְעֶזְרָתֵנוּ סֶלָה · בָּרוּךְ אַתָּה יְיָ הַטּוֹב שִׁמְךָ וּלְךָ נָאֶה לְהוֹדוֹת:

שִׂים שָׁלוֹם טוֹבָה וּבְרָכָה חֵן וָחֶסֶד וְרַחֲמִים עָלֵינוּ וְעַל כָּל־ יִשְׂרָאֵל עַמֶּךָ בָּרְכֵנוּ אָבִינוּ כֻּלָּנוּ כְּאֶחָד בְּאוֹר פָּנֶיךָ כִּי בְאוֹר פָּנֶיךָ נָתַתָּ לָּנוּ יְיָ אֱלֹהֵינוּ תּוֹרַת חַיִּים וְאַהֲבַת חֶסֶד וּצְדָקָה וּבְרָכָה וְרַחֲמִים וְחַיִּים וְשָׁלוֹם וְטוֹב בְּעֵינֶיךָ לְבָרֵךְ אֶת־עַמְּךָ יִשְׂרָאֵל

בְּכָל־עֵת וּבְכָל־שָׁעָה בִּשְׁלוֹמֶךָ ּ בְּסֵפֶר חַיִּים בְּרָכָה וְשָׁלוֹם
וּפַרְנָסָה טוֹבָה נִזָּכֵר וְנִכָּתֵב לְפָנֶיךָ אֲנַחְנוּ וְכָל עַמְּךָ בֵּית
יִשְׂרָאֵל לְחַיִּים טוֹבִים וּלְשָׁלוֹם ּ בָּרוּךְ אַתָּה יְיָ עוֹשֵׂה הַשָּׁלוֹם:

אֱלֹהֵינוּ וֵאלֹהֵי אֲבוֹתֵינוּ ּ

תָּבֹא לְפָנֶיךָ תְּפִלָּתֵנוּ ּ וְאַל תִּתְעַלַּם מִתְּחִנָּתֵנוּ ּ שֶׁאֵין אֲנַחְנוּ עַזֵּי
פָנִים וּקְשֵׁי עֹרֶף לוֹמַר לְפָנֶיךָ יְיָ אֱלֹהֵינוּ וֵאלֹהֵי אֲבוֹתֵינוּ צַדִּיקִים
אֲנַחְנוּ וְלֹא חָטָאנוּ אֲבָל אֲנַחְנוּ חָטָאנוּ:

אָשַׁמְנוּ ּ בָּגַדְנוּ ּ גָּזַלְנוּ ּ דִּבַּרְנוּ דְפִי ּ הֶעֱוִינוּ ּ
וְהִרְשַׁעְנוּ ּ זַדְנוּ ּ חָמַסְנוּ ּ טָפַלְנוּ שֶׁקֶר ּ יָעַצְנוּ רָע ּ
כִּזַּבְנוּ ּ לַצְנוּ ּ מָרַדְנוּ ּ נִאַצְנוּ ּ סָרַרְנוּ ּ עָוִינוּ ּ פָּשַׁעְנוּ ּ
צָרַרְנוּ ּ קִשִּׁינוּ עֹרֶף ּ רָשַׁעְנוּ ּ שִׁחַתְנוּ ּ תִּעַבְנוּ ּ
תָּעִינוּ ּ תִּעְתָּעְנוּ ּ

סַרְנוּ מִמִּצְוֹתֶיךָ וּמִמִּשְׁפָּטֶיךָ הַטּוֹבִים וְלֹא שָׁוָה לָנוּ: וְאַתָּה צַדִּיק
עַל כָּל־הַבָּא עָלֵינוּ ּ כִּי אֱמֶת עָשִׂיתָ וַאֲנַחְנוּ הִרְשָׁעְנוּ:

מַה נֹּאמַר לְפָנֶיךָ יוֹשֵׁב מָרוֹם, וּמַה נְּסַפֵּר לְפָנֶיךָ שׁוֹכֵן שְׁחָקִים ּ
הֲלֹא כָּל־הַנִּסְתָּרוֹת וְהַנִּגְלוֹת אַתָּה יוֹדֵעַ:

אַתָּה יוֹדֵעַ רָזֵי עוֹלָם ּ וְתַעֲלוּמוֹת סִתְרֵי כָל־חָי:
אַתָּה חוֹפֵשׂ כָּל־חַדְרֵי בָטֶן וּבוֹחֵן כְּלָיוֹת וָלֵב: אֵין דָּבָר
נֶעְלָם מִמֶּךָּ ּ וְאֵין נִסְתָּר מִנֶּגֶד עֵינֶיךָ:

וּבְכֵן יְהִי רָצוֹן מִלְּפָנֶיךָ יְיָ אֱלֹהֵינוּ וֵאלֹהֵי אֲבוֹתֵינוּ ּ
שֶׁתִּסְלַח לָנוּ עַל כָּל חַטֹּאתֵינוּ ּ וְתִמְחָל־לָנוּ עַל כָּל
עֲוֹנוֹתֵינוּ ּ וּתְכַפֶּר־לָנוּ עַל כָּל פְּשָׁעֵינוּ:

עַל חֵטְא שֶׁחָטָאנוּ לְפָנֶיךָ בְּאֹנֶס וּבְרָצוֹן:

וְעַל חֵטְא שֶׁחָטָאנוּ לְפָנֶיךָ בְּאִמּוּץ הַלֵּב:

עַל חֵטְא שֶׁחָטָאנוּ לְפָנֶיךָ בִּבְלִי דָעַת:

וְעַל חֵטְא שֶׁחָטָאנוּ לְפָנֶיךָ בְּבִטּוּי שְׂפָתָיִם:

עַל חֵטְא שֶׁחָטָאנוּ לְפָנֶיךָ בְּגָלוּי וּבַסָּתֶר:

וְעַל חֵטְא שֶׁחָטָאנוּ לְפָנֶיךָ בְּגִלּוּי עֲרָיוֹת:

עַל חֵטְא שֶׁחָטָאנוּ לְפָנֶיךָ בְּדִבּוּר פֶּה:

וְעַל חֵטְא שֶׁחָטָאנוּ לְפָנֶיךָ בְּדַעַת וּבְמִרְמָה:

עַל חֵטְא שֶׁחָטָאנוּ לְפָנֶיךָ בְּהַרְהוֹר הַלֵּב:

וְעַל חֵטְא שֶׁחָטָאנוּ לְפָנֶיךָ בְּהוֹנָאַת רֵעַ:

עַל חֵטְא שֶׁחָטָאנוּ לְפָנֶיךָ בְּוִדּוּי פֶּה:

וְעַל חֵטְא שֶׁחָטָאנוּ לְפָנֶיךָ בְּוְעִידַת זְנוּת:

עַל חֵטְא שֶׁחָטָאנוּ לְפָנֶיךָ בְּזָדוֹן וּבִשְׁגָגָה:

וְעַל חֵטְא שֶׁחָטָאנוּ לְפָנֶיךָ בְּזִלְזוּל הוֹרִים וּמוֹרִים:

עַל חֵטְא שֶׁחָטָאנוּ לְפָנֶיךָ בְּחֹזֶק יָד:

וְעַל חֵטְא שֶׁחָטָאנוּ לְפָנֶיךָ בְּחִלּוּל הַשֵּׁם:

עַל חֵטְא שֶׁחָטָאנוּ לְפָנֶיךָ בְּטִפְשׁוּת פֶּה:

וְעַל חֵטְא שֶׁחָטָאנוּ לְפָנֶיךָ בְּטֻמְאַת שְׂפָתָיִם:

עַל חֵטְא שֶׁחָטָאנוּ לְפָנֶיךָ בְּיֵצֶר הָרָע:

וְעַל חֵטְא שֶׁחָטָאנוּ לְפָנֶיךָ בְּיוֹדְעִים וּבְלֹא יוֹדְעִים:

וְעַל כֻּלָּם אֱלוֹהַּ סְלִיחוֹת סְלַח־לָנוּ · מְחַל־לָנוּ · כַּפֶּר־לָנוּ:

עַל חֵטְא שֶׁחָטָאנוּ לְפָנֶיךָ בְּכַפַּת שֹׁחַד:

וְעַל חֵטְא שֶׁחָטָאנוּ לְפָנֶיךָ בְּכַחַשׁ וּבְכָזָב:

עַל חֵטְא שֶׁחָטָאנוּ לְפָנֶיךָ בִּלְשׁוֹן הָרָע:

וְעַל חֵטְא שֶׁחָטָאנוּ לְפָנֶיךָ בְּלָצוֹן:

עַל חֵטְא שֶׁחָטָאנוּ לְפָנֶיךָ בְּמַשָּׂא וּבְמַתָּן:

וְעַל חֵטְא שֶׁחָטָאנוּ לְפָנֶיךָ בְּמַאֲכָל וּבְמִשְׁתֶּה:

עַל חֵטְא שֶׁחָטָאנוּ לְפָנֶיךָ בְּנֶשֶׁךְ וּבְמַרְבִּית:

וְעַל חֵטְא שֶׁחָטָאנוּ לְפָנֶיךָ בִּנְטִיַּת גָּרוֹן:

עַל חֵטְא שֶׁחָטָאנוּ לְפָנֶיךָ בְּשִׁקּוּר עָיִן:

וְעַל חֵטְא שֶׁחָטָאנוּ לְפָנֶיךָ בְּשִׂיחַ שִׂפְתוֹתֵינוּ:

עַל חֵטְא שֶׁחָטָאנוּ לְפָנֶיךָ בְּעֵינַיִם רָמוֹת:

וְעַל חֵטְא שֶׁחָטָאנוּ לְפָנֶיךָ בְּעַזּוּת מֶצַח:

וְעַל כֻּלָּם אֱלוֹהַּ סְלִיחוֹת סְלַח־לָנוּ· מְחַל־לָנוּ· כַּפֶּר־לָנוּ:

עַל חֵטְא שֶׁחָטָאנוּ לְפָנֶיךָ בִּפְרִיקַת עֹל:

וְעַל חֵטְא שֶׁחָטָאנוּ לְפָנֶיךָ בִּפְלִילוּת:

עַל חֵטְא שֶׁחָטָאנוּ לְפָנֶיךָ בִּצְדִיַּת רֵעַ:

וְעַל חֵטְא שֶׁחָטָאנוּ לְפָנֶיךָ בְּצָרוּת עָיִן:

עַל חֵטְא שֶׁחָטָאנוּ לְפָנֶיךָ בְּקַלּוּת רֹאשׁ:

וְעַל חֵטְא שֶׁחָטָאנוּ לְפָנֶיךָ בְּקַשְׁיוּת עֹרֶף:

עַל חֵטְא שֶׁחָטָאנוּ לְפָנֶיךָ בְּרִיצַת רַגְלַיִם לְהָרַע:

וְעַל חֵטְא שֶׁחָטָאנוּ לְפָנֶיךָ בִּרְכִילוּת:

עַל חֵטְא שֶׁחָטָאנוּ לְפָנֶיךָ בִּשְׁבוּעַת שָׁוְא:

וְעַל חֵטְא שֶׁחָטָאנוּ לְפָנֶיךָ בְּשִׂנְאַת חִנָּם:

עַל חֵטְא שֶׁחָטָאנוּ לְפָנֶיךָ בִּתְשׂוּמֶת יָד:

וְעַל חֵטְא שֶׁחָטָאנוּ לְפָנֶיךָ בְּתִמְהוֹן לֵבָב:

וְעַל כֻּלָּם אֱלוֹהַּ סְלִיחוֹת סְלַח־לָנוּ· מְחַל־לָנוּ· כַּפֶּר־לָנוּ:

וְעַל חֲטָאִים שֶׁאָנוּ חַיָּבִים עֲלֵיהֶם עוֹלָה:

וְעַל חֲטָאִים שֶׁאָנוּ חַיָּבִים עֲלֵיהֶם חַטָּאת:

וְעַל חֲטָאִים שֶׁאָנוּ חַיָּבִים עֲלֵיהֶם קָרְבָּן עוֹלֶה וְיוֹרֵד:

According to the minhag of most congregations:

וְעַל חֲטָאִים שֶׁאָנוּ חַיָּבִים עֲלֵיהֶם אָשָׁם וַדַּי וְתָלוּי:

וְעַל חֲטָאִים שֶׁאָנוּ חַיָּבִים עֲלֵיהֶם מַכַּת מַרְדּוּת:

וְעַל חֲטָאִים שֶׁאָנוּ חַיָּבִים עֲלֵיהֶם מַלְקוּת אַרְבָּעִים:

וְעַל חֲטָאִים שֶׁאָנוּ חַיָּבִים עֲלֵיהֶם מִיתָה בִּידֵי שָׁמָיִם:

וְעַל חֲטָאִים שֶׁאָנוּ חַיָּבִים עֲלֵיהֶם כָּרֵת וַעֲרִירִי (נ״א וַעֲרִירוּת):

וְעַל כֻּלָּם אֱלוֹהַּ סְלִיחוֹת סְלַח־לָנוּ · מְחַל־לָנוּ · כַּפֶּר־לָנוּ:

וְעַל חֲטָאִים שֶׁ״ח עֲלֵיהֶם אַרְבַּע מִיתוֹת בֵּית דִּין ·
סְקִילָה · שְׂרֵפָה · הֶרֶג · וְחֶנֶק · עַל מִצְוַת עֲשֵׂה וְעַל מִצְוַת
לֹא תַעֲשֶׂה · בֵּין שֶׁיֵּשׁ בָּהּ קוּם עֲשֵׂה · וּבֵין שֶׁאֵין בָּהּ קוּם
עֲשֵׂה · אֶת־הַגְּלוּיִם לָנוּ וְאֶת־שֶׁאֵינָם גְּלוּיִם לָנוּ · אֶת־
הַגְּלוּיִם לָנוּ כְּבָר אֲמַרְנוּם לְפָנֶיךָ וְהוֹדִינוּ לְךָ עֲלֵיהֶם ·
וְאֶת־שֶׁאֵינָם גְּלוּיִם לָנוּ לְפָנֶיךָ הֵם גְּלוּיִם וִידוּעִים ·
כַּדָּבָר שֶׁנֶּאֱמַר הַנִּסְתָּרֹת לַייָ אֱלֹהֵינוּ · וְהַנִּגְלֹת לָנוּ

According to the Frankfurt Minhag and that of several other congregations,

וְעַל חֲטָאִים שֶׁאָנוּ חַיָּבִים עֲלֵיהֶם אָשָׁם:

וְעַל חֲטָאִים שֶׁאָנוּ חַיָּבִים עֲלֵיהֶם אָשָׁם תָּלוּי:

וְעַל חֲטָאִים שֶׁאָנוּ חַיָּבִים עֲלֵיהֶם כָּרֵת:

וְעַל חֲטָאִים שֶׁאָנוּ חַיָּבִים עֲלֵיהֶם מִיתָה בִּידֵי שָׁמָיִם:

וְעַל חֲטָאִים שֶׁאָנוּ חַיָּבִים עֲלֵיהֶם מַלְקוּת אַרְבָּעִים:

וְעַל חֲטָאִים שֶׁאָנוּ חַיָּבִים עֲלֵיהֶם מַכַּת מַרְדּוּת: ועל כלם וכו׳·

וּרְבָנֵינוּ עַד־עוֹלָם · לַעֲשׂוֹת אֶת־כָּל־דִּבְרֵי הַתּוֹרָה
הַזֹּאת: כִּי אַתָּה סָלְחָן לְיִשְׂרָאֵל וּמָחֳלָן לְשִׁבְטֵי יְשֻׁרוּן
בְּכָל־ דּוֹר וָדוֹר · וּמִבַּלְעָדֶיךָ אֵין לָנוּ מֶלֶךְ מוֹחֵל
וְסוֹלֵחַ (אלא אתה):

אֱלֹהַי, עַד שֶׁלֹּא נוֹצַרְתִּי אֵינִי כְדַי · וְעַכְשָׁו שֶׁנּוֹצַרְתִּי כְּאִלּוּ לֹא
נוֹצַרְתִּי · עָפָר אֲנִי בְּחַיָּי · קַל וָחֹמֶר בְּמִיתָתִי · הֲרֵי אֲנִי לְפָנֶיךָ כִּכְלִי
מָלֵא בוּשָׁה וּכְלִמָּה · יְהִי רָצוֹן מִלְּפָנֶיךָ יְיָ אֱלֹהַי וֵאלֹהֵי אֲבוֹתַי שֶׁלֹּא
אֶחֱטָא עוֹד · וּמַה שֶּׁחָטָאתִי לְפָנֶיךָ מָרֵק בְּרַחֲמֶיךָ הָרַבִּים · אֲבָל
לֹא עַל יְדֵי יִסּוּרִים וָחֳלָיִם רָעִים:

אֱלֹהַי · נְצוֹר לְשׁוֹנִי מֵרָע וּשְׂפָתַי מִדַּבֵּר מִרְמָה, וְלִמְקַלְלַי נַפְשִׁי
תִדּוֹם וְנַפְשִׁי כֶּעָפָר לַכֹּל תִּהְיֶה, פְּתַח לִבִּי בְּתוֹרָתֶךָ וּבְמִצְוֹתֶיךָ
תִּרְדּוֹף נַפְשִׁי, וְכָל הַחוֹשְׁבִים עָלַי רָעָה מְהֵרָה הָפֵר עֲצָתָם
וְקַלְקֵל מַחֲשַׁבְתָּם · עֲשֵׂה לְמַעַן שְׁמֶךָ עֲשֵׂה לְמַעַן יְמִינֶךָ עֲשֵׂה
לְמַעַן קְדֻשָּׁתֶךָ עֲשֵׂה לְמַעַן תּוֹרָתֶךָ · לְמַעַן יֵחָלְצוּן יְדִידֶיךָ
הוֹשִׁיעָה יְמִינְךָ וַעֲנֵנִי: יִהְיוּ לְרָצוֹן אִמְרֵי פִי וְהֶגְיוֹן לִבִּי לְפָנֶיךָ יְיָ
צוּרִי וְגֹאֲלִי · עֹשֶׂה שָׁלוֹם בִּמְרוֹמָיו הוּא יַעֲשֶׂה שָׁלוֹם עָלֵינוּ וְעַל
כָּל יִשְׂרָאֵל וְאִמְרוּ אָמֵן:

יְהִי רָצוֹן לְפָנֶיךָ יְיָ אֱלֹהֵינוּ וֵאלֹהֵי אֲבוֹתֵינוּ שֶׁיִּבָּנֶה
בֵּית הַמִּקְדָּשׁ בִּמְהֵרָה בְיָמֵינוּ וְתֵן חֶלְקֵנוּ בְּתוֹרָתֶךָ:
וְשָׁם נַעֲבָדְךָ בְּיִרְאָה כִּימֵי עוֹלָם וּכְשָׁנִים קַדְמוֹנִיּוֹת:
וְעָרְבָה לַיְיָ מִנְחַת יְהוּדָה וִירוּשָׁלָיִם כִּימֵי עוֹלָם וּכְשָׁנִים קַדְמוֹנִיּוֹת:

אֲדֹנָי שְׂפָתַי תִּפְתָּח וּפִי יַגִּיד תְּהִלָּתֶךָ:

בָּרוּךְ אַתָּה יְיָ אֱלֹהֵינוּ וֵאלֹהֵי אֲבוֹתֵינוּ אֱלֹהֵי אַבְרָהָם אֱלֹהֵי
יִצְחָק וֵאלֹהֵי יַעֲקֹב הָאֵל הַגָּדוֹל הַגִּבּוֹר וְהַנּוֹרָא אֵל עֶלְיוֹן גּוֹמֵל
חֲסָדִים טוֹבִים וְקֹנֵה הַכֹּל וְזוֹכֵר חַסְדֵי אָבוֹת וּמֵבִיא גוֹאֵל לִבְנֵי
בְנֵיהֶם לְמַעַן שְׁמוֹ בְּאַהֲבָה:

זָכְרֵנוּ לְחַיִּים· מֶלֶךְ חָפֵץ בַּחַיִּים· וְחָתְמֵנוּ בְּסֵפֶר הַחַיִּים· לְמַעַנְךָ
אֱלֹהִים חַיִּים· מֶלֶךְ עוֹזֵר וּמוֹשִׁיעַ וּמָגֵן· בָּרוּךְ אַתָּה יְיָ מָגֵן אַבְרָהָם:

אַתָּה גִבּוֹר לְעוֹלָם אֲדֹנָי מְחַיֶּה מֵתִים אַתָּה רַב לְהוֹשִׁיעַ·

מְכַלְכֵּל חַיִּים בְּחֶסֶד מְחַיֶּה מֵתִים בְּרַחֲמִים רַבִּים סוֹמֵךְ נוֹפְלִים
וְרוֹפֵא חוֹלִים וּמַתִּיר אֲסוּרִים וּמְקַיֵּם אֱמוּנָתוֹ לִישֵׁנֵי עָפָר· מִי
כָמוֹךָ בַּעַל גְּבוּרוֹת וּמִי דּוֹמֶה לָּךְ מֶלֶךְ מֵמִית וּמְחַיֶּה וּמַצְמִיחַ יְשׁוּעָה:
מִי כָמוֹךָ אַב הָרַחֲמִים· זוֹכֵר יְצוּרָיו לְחַיִּים בְּרַחֲמִים· וְנֶאֱמָן
אַתָּה לְהַחֲיוֹת מֵתִים· בָּרוּךְ אַתָּה יְיָ מְחַיֶּה הַמֵּתִים:

אַתָּה קָדוֹשׁ וְשִׁמְךָ קָדוֹשׁ וּקְדוֹשִׁים בְּכָל יוֹם יְהַלְלוּךָ סֶּלָה:

וּבְכֵן תֵּן פַּחְדְּךָ יְיָ אֱלֹהֵינוּ עַל כָּל־מַעֲשֶׂיךָ וְאֵימָתְךָ עַל כָּל־
מַה־שֶּׁבָּרָאתָ וְיִירָאוּךָ כָּל־הַמַּעֲשִׂים וְיִשְׁתַּחֲווּ לְפָנֶיךָ כָּל־הַבְּרוּאִים
וְיֵעָשׂוּ כֻלָּם אֲגֻדָּה אַחַת לַעֲשׂוֹת רְצוֹנְךָ בְּלֵבָב שָׁלֵם כְּמוֹ שֶׁיָּדַעְנוּ
יְיָ אֱלֹהֵינוּ שֶׁהַשָּׁלְטָן לְפָנֶיךָ עֹז בְּיָדְךָ וּגְבוּרָה בִּימִינֶךָ וְשִׁמְךָ
נוֹרָא עַל כָּל־מַה־שֶּׁבָּרָאתָ:

וּבְכֵן תֵּן כָּבוֹד יְיָ לְעַמֶּךָ תְּהִלָּה לִירֵאֶיךָ וְתִקְוָה לְדוֹרְשֶׁיךָ וּפִתְחוֹן
פֶּה לַמְיַחֲלִים לָךְ שִׂמְחָה לְאַרְצֶךָ וְשָׂשׂוֹן לְעִירֶךָ וּצְמִיחַת קֶרֶן
לְדָוִד עַבְדֶּךָ וַעֲרִיכַת נֵר לְבֶן יִשַׁי מְשִׁיחֶךָ בִּמְהֵרָה בְיָמֵינוּ:

וּבְכֵן צַדִּיקִים יִרְאוּ וְיִשְׂמָחוּ וִישָׁרִים יַעֲלֹזוּ וַחֲסִידִים בְּרִנָּה יָגִילוּ וְעוֹלָתָה תִּקְפָּץ־פִּיהָ ׃ וְכָל־הָרִשְׁעָה כֻּלָּהּ כְּעָשָׁן תִּכְלֶה כִּי תַעֲבִיר מֶמְשֶׁלֶת זָדוֹן מִן־הָאָרֶץ ׃

וְתִמְלֹךְ אַתָּה יְיָ לְבַדֶּךָ עַל כָּל־מַעֲשֶׂיךָ בְּהַר צִיּוֹן מִשְׁכַּן כְּבוֹדֶךָ וּבִירוּשָׁלַיִם עִיר קָדְשֶׁךָ כַּכָּתוּב בְּדִבְרֵי קָדְשֶׁךָ יִמְלֹךְ יְיָ לְעוֹלָם אֱלֹהַיִךְ צִיּוֹן לְדֹר וָדֹר הַלְלוּיָהּ ׃

קָדוֹשׁ אַתָּה וְנוֹרָא שְׁמֶךָ וְאֵין אֱלוֹהַּ מִבַּלְעָדֶיךָ כַּכָּתוּב וַיִּגְבַּהּ יְיָ צְבָאוֹת בַּמִּשְׁפָּט וְהָאֵל הַקָּדוֹשׁ נִקְדַּשׁ בִּצְדָקָה ׃ בָּרוּךְ אַתָּה יְיָ הַמֶּלֶךְ הַקָּדוֹשׁ ׃

אַתָּה בְחַרְתָּנוּ מִכָּל־הָעַמִּים ׃ **אָהַבְתָּ** אוֹתָנוּ ׃ וְרָצִיתָ בָּנוּ ׃ וְרוֹמַמְתָּנוּ מִכָּל הַלְּשׁוֹנוֹת ׃ וְקִדַּשְׁתָּנוּ בְּמִצְוֹתֶיךָ ׃ וְקֵרַבְתָּנוּ מַלְכֵּנוּ לַעֲבֹדָתֶךָ ׃ וְשִׁמְךָ הַגָּדוֹל וְהַקָּדוֹשׁ עָלֵינוּ קָרָאתָ ׃

וַתִּתֶּן־לָנוּ יְיָ אֱלֹהֵינוּ בְּאַהֲבָה אֶת־יוֹם השבת הזה לקדושה ולמנוחה ואת יום הַכִּפֻּרִים הַזֶּה לִמְחִילָה וְלִסְלִיחָה וּלְכַפָּרָה וְלִמְחָל־בּוֹ אֶת־ כָּל־עֲוֹנוֹתֵינוּ באהבה מִקְרָא קֹדֶשׁ זֵכֶר לִיצִיאַת מִצְרָיִם ׃

אֱלֹהֵינוּ וֵאלֹהֵי אֲבוֹתֵינוּ ׃ יַעֲלֶה וְיָבֹא וְיַגִּיעַ וְיֵרָאֶה וְיֵרָצֶה וְיִשָּׁמַע וְיִפָּקֵד וְיִזָּכֵר זִכְרוֹנֵנוּ וּפִקְדוֹנֵנוּ וְזִכְרוֹן אֲבוֹתֵינוּ ׃ וְזִכְרוֹן מָשִׁיחַ בֶּן דָּוִד עַבְדֶּךָ ׃ וְזִכְרוֹן יְרוּשָׁלַיִם עִיר קָדְשֶׁךָ ׃ וְזִכְרוֹן כָּל עַמְּךָ בֵּית יִשְׂרָאֵל לְפָנֶיךָ ׃ לִפְלֵיטָה וּלְטוֹבָה וּלְחֵן וּלְחֶסֶד וּלְרַחֲמִים וּלְחַיִּים וּלְשָׁלוֹם בְּיוֹם הַכִּפֻּרִים הַזֶּה ׃ זָכְרֵנוּ יְיָ אֱלֹהֵינוּ בּוֹ לְטוֹבָה ׃ וּפָקְדֵנוּ בוֹ לִבְרָכָה ׃ וְהוֹשִׁיעֵנוּ בוֹ לְחַיִּים ׃ וּבִדְבַר יְשׁוּעָה וְרַחֲמִים חוּס וְחָנֵּנוּ וְרַחֵם עָלֵינוּ וְהוֹשִׁיעֵנוּ ׃ כִּי אֵלֶיךָ עֵינֵינוּ ׃ כִּי אֵל מֶלֶךְ חַנּוּן וְרַחוּם אָתָּה ׃

אֱלֹהֵינוּ וֵאלֹהֵי אֲבוֹתֵינוּ ׃ מְחַל לַעֲוֹנוֹתֵינוּ בְּיוֹם השבת הזה ובּיום הַכִּפֻּרִים הַזֶּה ׃ מְחֵה וְהַעֲבֵר פְּשָׁעֵינוּ (וְחַטֹּאתֵינוּ) מִנֶּגֶד עֵינֶיךָ ׃ כָּאָמוּר אָנֹכִי אָנֹכִי הוּא מֹחֶה פְשָׁעֶיךָ לְמַעֲנִי וְחַטֹּאתֶיךָ לֹא־אֶזְכֹּר ׃ וְנֶאֱמַר מָחִיתִי כָעָב פְּשָׁעֶיךָ וְכֶעָנָן חַטֹּאתֶיךָ שׁוּבָה אֵלַי כִּי גְאַלְתִּיךָ ׃

וְנֶאֱמַר כִּי בַיּוֹם הַזֶּה יְכַפֵּר עֲלֵיכֶם לְטַהֵר אֶתְכֶם מִכֹּל חַטֹּאתֵיכֶם לִפְנֵי יְיָ תִּטְהָרוּ: (אֱלֹהֵינוּ וֵאלֹהֵי אֲבוֹתֵינוּ רְצֵה בִמְנוּחָתֵנוּ) קַדְּשֵׁנוּ בְּמִצְוֹתֶיךָ וְתֵן חֶלְקֵנוּ בְּתוֹרָתֶךָ · שַׂבְּעֵנוּ מִטּוּבֶךָ וְשַׂמְּחֵנוּ בִּישׁוּעָתֶךָ · (וְהַנְחִילֵנוּ יְיָ אֱלֹהֵינוּ בְּאַהֲבָה וּבְרָצוֹן שַׁבַּת קָדְשֶׁךָ וְיָנוּחוּ בָה יִשְׂרָאֵל מְקַדְּשֵׁי שְׁמֶךָ) וְטַהֵר לִבֵּנוּ לְעָבְדְּךָ בֶּאֱמֶת · כִּי אַתָּה סָלְחָן לְיִשְׂרָאֵל וּמָחֳלָן לְשִׁבְטֵי יְשֻׁרוּן בְּכָל דּוֹר וָדוֹר וּמִבַּלְעָדֶיךָ אֵין לָנוּ מֶלֶךְ מוֹחֵל וְסוֹלֵחַ (אֶלָּא אַתָּה) · בָּרוּךְ אַתָּה יְיָ · מֶלֶךְ מוֹחֵל וְסוֹלֵחַ לַעֲוֹנוֹתֵינוּ וְלַעֲוֹנוֹת עַמּוֹ בֵּית יִשְׂרָאֵל · וּמַעֲבִיר אַשְׁמוֹתֵינוּ בְּכָל שָׁנָה וְשָׁנָה · מֶלֶךְ עַל כָּל־הָאָרֶץ מְקַדֵּשׁ הַשַּׁבָּת וְיִשְׂרָאֵל וְיוֹם הַכִּפּוּרִים :

רְצֵה יְיָ אֱלֹהֵינוּ בְּעַמְּךָ יִשְׂרָאֵל וּבִתְפִלָּתָם · וְהָשֵׁב אֶת־הָעֲבוֹדָה לִדְבִיר בֵּיתֶךָ, וְאִשֵּׁי יִשְׂרָאֵל וּתְפִלָּתָם בְּאַהֲבָה תְקַבֵּל בְּרָצוֹן, וּתְהִי לְרָצוֹן תָּמִיד עֲבוֹדַת יִשְׂרָאֵל עַמֶּךָ ·

וְתֶחֱזֶינָה עֵינֵינוּ בְּשׁוּבְךָ לְצִיּוֹן בְּרַחֲמִים · בָּרוּךְ אַתָּה יְיָ, הַמַּחֲזִיר שְׁכִינָתוֹ לְצִיּוֹן :

מוֹדִים אֲנַחְנוּ לָךְ שָׁאַתָּה הוּא יְיָ אֱלֹהֵינוּ וֵאלֹהֵי אֲבוֹתֵינוּ לְעוֹלָם וָעֶד · צוּר חַיֵּינוּ מָגֵן יִשְׁעֵנוּ אַתָּה הוּא לְדוֹר וָדוֹר · נוֹדֶה לְּךָ וּנְסַפֵּר תְּהִלָּתֶךָ עַל חַיֵּינוּ הַמְּסוּרִים בְּיָדֶךָ וְעַל נִשְׁמוֹתֵינוּ הַפְּקוּדוֹת לָךְ וְעַל נִסֶּיךָ שֶׁבְּכָל יוֹם עִמָּנוּ וְעַל נִפְלְאוֹתֶיךָ וְטוֹבוֹתֶיךָ שֶׁבְּכָל עֵת, עֶרֶב וָבֹקֶר וְצָהֳרָיִם · הַטּוֹב כִּי לֹא כָלוּ רַחֲמֶיךָ וְהַמְרַחֵם כִּי לֹא־תַמּוּ חֲסָדֶיךָ מֵעוֹלָם קִוִּינוּ לָךְ :

וְעַל כֻּלָּם יִתְבָּרַךְ וְיִתְרוֹמַם שִׁמְךָ מַלְכֵּנוּ תָּמִיד לְעוֹלָם וָעֶד : וַחֲתוֹם לְחַיִּים טוֹבִים כָּל־בְּנֵי בְרִיתֶךָ :

וְכֹל הַחַיִּים יוֹדוּךָ סֶּלָה וִיהַלְלוּ אֶת שִׁמְךָ בֶּאֱמֶת הָאֵל יְשׁוּעָתֵנוּ וְעֶזְרָתֵנוּ סֶלָה · בָּרוּךְ אַתָּה יְיָ הַטּוֹב שִׁמְךָ וּלְךָ נָאֶה לְהוֹדוֹת:

שִׂים שָׁלוֹם טוֹבָה וּבְרָכָה חֵן וָחֶסֶד וְרַחֲמִים עָלֵינוּ וְעַל כָּל־ יִשְׂרָאֵל עַמֶּךָ · בָּרְכֵנוּ אָבִינוּ כֻּלָּנוּ כְּאֶחָד בְּאוֹר פָּנֶיךָ · כִּי בְאוֹר פָּנֶיךָ נָתַתָּ לָּנוּ יְיָ אֱלֹהֵינוּ תּוֹרַת חַיִּים וְאַהֲבַת חֶסֶד וּצְדָקָה וּבְרָכָה וְרַחֲמִים וְחַיִּים וְשָׁלוֹם · וְטוֹב בְּעֵינֶיךָ לְבָרֵךְ אֶת־עַמְּךָ יִשְׂרָאֵל בְּכָל־עֵת וּבְכָל־שָׁעָה בִּשְׁלוֹמֶךָ · בְּסֵפֶר חַיִּים בְּרָכָה וְשָׁלוֹם

וּפַרְנָסָה טוֹבָה נִזָּכֵר וְנִכָּתֵב לְפָנֶיךָ אֲנַחְנוּ וְכָל עַמְּךָ בֵּית
יִשְׂרָאֵל לְחַיִּים טוֹבִים וּלְשָׁלוֹם ּ בָּרוּךְ אַתָּה יְיָ עוֹשֵׂה הַשָּׁלוֹם:

אֱלֹהֵינוּ וֵאלֹהֵי אֲבוֹתֵינוּ ּ

תָּבֹא לְפָנֶיךָ תְּפִלָּתֵנוּ, וְאַל תִּתְעַלַּם מִתְּחִנָּתֵנוּ שֶׁאֵין אֲנַחְנוּ עַזֵּי
פָנִים וּקְשֵׁי עֹרֶף לוֹמַר לְפָנֶיךָ יְיָ אֱלֹהֵינוּ וֵאלֹהֵי אֲבוֹתֵינוּ צַדִּיקִים
אֲנַחְנוּ וְלֹא חָטָאנוּ אֲבָל אֲנַחְנוּ חָטָאנוּ:

אָשַׁמְנוּ ּ בָּגַדְנוּ ּ גָּזַלְנוּ ּ דִּבַּרְנוּ דֹפִי ּ הֶעֱוִינוּ ּ
וְהִרְשַׁעְנוּ ּ זַדְנוּ ּ חָמַסְנוּ ּ טָפַלְנוּ שֶׁקֶר ּ יָעַצְנוּ רָע ּ
כִּזַּבְנוּ ּ לַצְנוּ ּ מָרַדְנוּ ּ נִאַצְנוּ ּ סָרַרְנוּ ּ עָוִינוּ ּ פָּשַׁעְנוּ ּ
צָרַרְנוּ ּ קִשִּׁינוּ עֹרֶף ּ רָשַׁעְנוּ ּ שִׁחַתְנוּ ּ תִּעַבְנוּ ּ
תָּעִינוּ ּ תִּעְתָּעְנוּ ּ

סַרְנוּ מִמִּצְוֹתֶיךָ וּמִמִּשְׁפָּטֶיךָ הַטּוֹבִים וְלֹא שָׁוָה לָנוּ: וְאַתָּה צַדִּיק
עַל כָּל הַבָּא עָלֵינוּ ּ כִּי אֱמֶת עָשִׂיתָ וַאֲנַחְנוּ הִרְשָׁעְנוּ:

מַה נֹּאמַר לְפָנֶיךָ יוֹשֵׁב מָרוֹם ּ וּמַה נְּסַפֵּר לְפָנֶיךָ שׁוֹכֵן
שְׁחָקִים ּ הֲלֹא כָּל־הַנִּסְתָּרוֹת וְהַנִּגְלוֹת אַתָּה יוֹדֵעַ:

אַתָּה נוֹתֵן יָד לְפוֹשְׁעִים וִימִינְךָ פְּשׁוּטָה לְקַבֵּל שָׁבִים ּ וַתְּלַמְּדֵנוּ
יְיָ אֱלֹהֵינוּ לְהִתְוַדּוֹת לְפָנֶיךָ עַל כָּל־עֲוֹנוֹתֵינוּ לְמַעַן נֶחְדַּל מֵעשֶׁק
יָדֵינוּ וּתְקַבְּלֵנוּ בִּתְשׁוּבָה שְׁלֵמָה לְפָנֶיךָ כָּאִשִּׁים וּכְנִיחוֹחִים לְמַעַן
דְּבָרֶיךָ אֲשֶׁר אָמָרְתָּ: אֵין קֵץ לְאִשֵּׁי חוֹבוֹתֵינוּ וְאֵין מִסְפָּר לְנִיחֹחֵי
אַשְׁמוֹתֵינוּ ּ וְאַתָּה יוֹדֵעַ שֶׁאַחֲרִיתֵנוּ רִמָּה וְתוֹלֵעָה לְפִיכָךְ הִרְבֵּיתָ
סְלִיחָתֵנוּ ּ מָה אֲנַחְנוּ מֶה חַיֵּינוּ מֶה חַסְדֵּנוּ מַה־צִּדְקֵנוּ מַה יְּשְׁעֵנוּ
מַה כֹּחֵנוּ מַה גְּבוּרָתֵנוּ מַה נֹּאמַר לְפָנֶיךָ יְיָ אֱלֹהֵינוּ וֵאלֹהֵי
אֲבוֹתֵינוּ הֲלֹא כָּל־הַגִּבּוֹרִים כְּאַיִן לְפָנֶיךָ וְאַנְשֵׁי הַשֵּׁם כְּלֹא הָיוּ

You give hand to transgressors, and Your right hand is stretched out to accept those who return [to You], and You have taught us, O *God* our God, to admit all our iniquities to ourselves before You so that we may desist from the injustice of our hands; and may You accept us in Your presence in a perfect return [to You] even as fire offerings and expressions of compliance, for the sake of Your words which You have spoken. There would be no end to the fire offerings required, and the expressions of compliance of our sins offerings would be numberless. But You know that our end is the worm and the moth. Therefore You have granted us much forgiveness. What are we? What is our life? What is our loving-kindness? What is our righteousness? What our salvation? What our strength? What our might? What shall we say before You, O *God* our God and God of our fathers? For are not all heroes as naught before You, and men of renown as if they had never been, wise men as if they were without

---

נעילה ליום הכפורים

אתה נותן יד "You are willing to meet even those who deliberately transgressed Your Law. You give them the call and the opportunity to return to You and You are ready at all times to receive those who do return. Let no one, therefore, say, 'It is too late.' " להתודות לפניך is the specific expression for the confession of sins. The literal meaning of this expression is that we "admit *to ourselves*" that we have been sinners before God. This is the essential prerequisite for our moral betterment; we must admit to ourselves, freely and without disguise, that we have done wrong. כאשים : By the acts of sacrifice upon the fires of the altar we symbolically express our pledge to immerse all of our being into the fire of God's Law so that we may be cleansed, enlightened and revived thereby. We express in the symbolic terms of ריח ניחוח לה' the pledge that henceforth we shall live solely and entirely for the fulfillment of His will. "Even so," we pray, "may You now accept this same vow and this same high resolve as we express it in words today." אין קץ All of our lives would not be sufficient to make amends for the burden of guilt which we bear as the result of past sin. But You know the brevity of our lives and our frailty, and You have covered our bareness of merit with Your abundance of forgiveness."

וַחֲכָמִים כִּבְלִי מַדָּע וּנְבוֹנִים כִּבְלִי הַשְׂכֵּל כִּי רֹב מַעֲשֵׂיהֶם תֹּהוּ
וִימֵי חַיֵּיהֶם הֶבֶל לְפָנֶיךָ וּמוֹתַר הָאָדָם מִן הַבְּהֵמָה אָיִן כִּי הַכֹּל
הָבֶל:

אַתָּה הִבְדַּלְתָּ אֱנוֹשׁ מֵרֹאשׁ וַתַּכִּירֵהוּ לַעֲמוֹד לְפָנֶיךָ: כִּי מִי
יֹאמַר לְךָ מַה תִּפְעָל וְאִם־יִצְדַּק מַה־יִּתֶּן־לָךְ: וַתִּתֶּן־לָנוּ יְיָ
אֱלֹהֵינוּ בְּאַהֲבָה אֶת־יוֹם (*הַשַּׁבָּת הַזֶּה וְאֶת יוֹם) (צוֹם) הַכִּפֻּרִים הַזֶּה
קֵץ וּמְחִילָה וּסְלִיחָה עַל כָּל־עֲוֹנוֹתֵינוּ לְמַעַן נֶחְדַּל מֵעֹשֶׁק יָדֵינוּ
וְנָשׁוּב אֵלֶיךָ לַעֲשׂוֹת חֻקֵּי רְצוֹנְךָ בְּלֵבָב שָׁלֵם: וְאַתָּה בְּרַחֲמֶיךָ
הָרַבִּים רַחֵם עָלֵינוּ כִּי לֹא תַחְפּוֹץ בְּהַשְׁחָתַת עוֹלָם • שֶׁנֶּאֱמַר
דִּרְשׁוּ יְיָ בְּהִמָּצְאוֹ קְרָאֻהוּ בִּהְיוֹתוֹ קָרוֹב: וְנֶאֱמַר יַעֲזֹב רָשָׁע דַּרְכּוֹ
וְאִישׁ אָוֶן מַחְשְׁבֹתָיו וְיָשֹׁב אֶל־יְיָ וִירַחֲמֵהוּ וְאֶל־אֱלֹהֵינוּ כִּי־יַרְבֶּה
לִסְלוֹחַ: וְאַתָּה אֱלוֹהַּ סְלִיחוֹת חַנּוּן וְרַחוּם אֶרֶךְ־אַפַּיִם וְרַב־
חֶסֶד וּמַרְבֶּה לְהֵיטִיב וְרוֹצֶה אַתָּה בִּתְשׁוּבַת רְשָׁעִים וְאֵין אַתָּה
חָפֵץ בְּמִיתָתָם • שֶׁנֶּאֱמַר אֱמֹר אֲלֵיהֶם חַי־אָנִי נְאֻם אֲדֹנָי יֱהֹוִה
אִם־אֶחְפֹּץ בְּמוֹת הָרָשָׁע כִּי אִם־בְּשׁוּב רָשָׁע מִדַּרְכּוֹ וְחָיָה •

(* הַיָּחִיד אֵינוֹ מַזְכִּיר שֶׁל שַׁבָּת •

אתה הבדלת "Notwithstanding his physical, spiritual and moral inadequacy, You have given to man a position high above that of all the other
creatures. You are not accountable to any one for Your acts, and if You have
so distinguished such an undependable creature as man, You did not do it
for Your own advantage. For even if man were perfect in righteousness he
could render You nothing in return. It was for our sake and for our sake
alone that You opened for us a path to moral regeneration and to increasingly
complete loyalty to our duty. It is Your wish, by means of Yom Kippur, to

knowledge, and men of insight as if they were without understanding? For the mass of their deeds is void, the days of their lives are null before You, and the distinction of man from the beast is no more, For all is vanity.

You have set mortal man apart from the very beginning and given him the privilege to stand before You. For who shall tell You what You shall do? And if he is righteous, what can he give to You? And You have given us, O *God* our God, in love (this Sabbath day and) this (Fast) Day of Atonements to be the end, pardon and forgiveness for all our sins, so that we may cease from the injustice of our hands and return to You to fulfill the laws of Your will with a whole heart. And You, in Your abundant compassion, have compassion upon us! For You do not desire the destruction of the world, for it is said: "Seek *God* where He is to be found; call upon Him when He is near." And it is said: "Let the lawless abandon his way and the man of violence his thoughts and let him return to *God,* and He will have compassion upon him; and to our God, for He will abundantly forgive." And You, O God of forgiveness, gracious and compassionate, slow to anger and great in love and abundant in kindness, You take pleasure in the return of the lawless and do not desire their death. For it is said: "Say to them, 'As truly as I live,' says the Lord, *God* Who shows His loving-kindness even in judgment, 'I take no pleasure in the death of the lawless but only in that the lawless man

---

obliterate all our past sins and to guide us toward a new and purer future. ואתה : Without Your compassion and Your willingness to grant us remission, man and all of his world would have perished long ago because of his sins and the consequences thereof which would seem inevitable." דרשו ה' Your search for God is not in vain. He can be found, and He waits for you to seek Him and to call upon Him, particularly on those days which He has specifically appointed for your return. השיב, והשיבו is "to make restitution", "to make amends" for one's error or transgression.

שׁוּבוּ שׁוּבוּ מִדַּרְכֵיכֶם הָרָעִים וְלָמָּה תָמוּתוּ בֵּית יִשְׂרָאֵל: וְנֶאֱמַר
הֶחָפֹץ אֶחְפֹּץ מוֹת רָשָׁע נְאֻם אֲדֹנָי יְהוִה הֲלֹא בְּשׁוּבוֹ מִדְּרָכָיו
וְחָיָה: וְנֶאֱמַר כִּי לֹא אֶחְפֹּץ בְּמוֹת הַמֵּת נְאֻם אֲדֹנָי יְהוִה·
וְהָשִׁיבוּ וִחְיוּ: כִּי אַתָּה סָלְחָן לְיִשְׂרָאֵל וּמָחֳלָן לְשִׁבְטֵי יְשֻׁרוּן
בְּכָל־דּוֹר וָדוֹר וּמִבַּלְעָדֶיךָ אֵין לָנוּ מֶלֶךְ מוֹחֵל וְסוֹלֵחַ (אֶלָּא אָתָּה):

אֱלֹהַי· עַד שֶׁלֹּא נוֹצַרְתִּי אֵינִי כְדַאי· וְעַכְשָׁו שֶׁנּוֹצַרְתִּי כְּאִלּוּ
לֹא נוֹצַרְתִּי· עָפָר אֲנִי בְּחַיָּי· קַל וָחֹמֶר בְּמִיתָתִי· הֲרֵי אֲנִי לְפָנֶיךָ
כִּכְלִי מָלֵא בּוּשָׁה וּכְלִמָּה· יְהִי רָצוֹן מִלְּפָנֶיךָ יְיָ אֱלֹהַי וֵאלֹהֵי
אֲבוֹתַי שֶׁלֹּא אֶחֱטָא עוֹד· וּמַה־שֶּׁחָטָאתִי לְפָנֶיךָ מָרֵק בְּרַחֲמֶיךָ
הָרַבִּים· אֲבָל לֹא עַל־יְדֵי יִסּוּרִים וָחֳלָיִם רָעִים:

אֱלֹהַי· נְצוֹר לְשׁוֹנִי מֵרָע וּשְׂפָתַי מִדַּבֵּר מִרְמָה וְלִמְקַלְלַי נַפְשִׁי
תִדּוֹם וְנַפְשִׁי כֶּעָפָר לַכֹּל תִּהְיֶה: פְּתַח לִבִּי בְּתוֹרָתֶךָ וּבְמִצְוֹתֶיךָ
תִּרְדּוֹף נַפְשִׁי· וְכָל הַחוֹשְׁבִים עָלַי רָעָה מְהֵרָה הָפֵר עֲצָתָם וְקַלְקֵל
מַחֲשַׁבְתָּם· עֲשֵׂה לְמַעַן שְׁמֶךָ· עֲשֵׂה לְמַעַן יְמִינֶךָ· עֲשֵׂה לְמַעַן
קְדֻשָּׁתֶךָ· עֲשֵׂה לְמַעַן תּוֹרָתֶךָ· לְמַעַן יֵחָלְצוּן יְדִידֶיךָ הוֹשִׁיעָה
יְמִינְךָ וַעֲנֵנִי: יִהְיוּ לְרָצוֹן אִמְרֵי־פִי וְהֶגְיוֹן לִבִּי לְפָנֶיךָ יְיָ צוּרִי
וְגֹאֲלִי: עֹשֶׂה שָׁלוֹם בִּמְרוֹמָיו הוּא יַעֲשֶׂה שָׁלוֹם עָלֵינוּ וְעַל כָּל
יִשְׂרָאֵל וְאִמְרוּ אָמֵן:

יְהִי רָצוֹן לְפָנֶיךָ יְיָ אֱלֹהֵינוּ וֵאלֹהֵי אֲבוֹתֵינוּ שֶׁיִּבָּנֶה
בֵּית הַמִּקְדָּשׁ בִּמְהֵרָה בְּיָמֵינוּ וְתֵן חֶלְקֵנוּ בְּתוֹרָתֶךָ:
וְשָׁם נַעֲבָדְךָ בְּיִרְאָה כִּימֵי עוֹלָם וּכְשָׁנִים קַדְמֹנִיּוֹת:
וְעָרְבָה לַיְיָ מִנְחַת יְהוּדָה וִירוּשָׁלָיִם כִּימֵי עוֹלָם וּכְשָׁנִים קַדְמֹנִיּוֹת:

turn aside from his path and live.'" Return, O return from your evil ways, why will you die, O House of Yisraël? And it is said: "Do I indeed desire the death of the lawless man, says my Lord, God Who shows His loving-kindness even in judgment, truly, if he will turn aside from his paths, he will live." And it is said: "For I desire not the death of him who dies, says the Lord, *God,* Who shows His loving-kindness even in judgment; make amends, and live." For You are the Forgiver of Yisrael and the Pardoner of the tribes of Yeshurun in every generation, and beside You we have no King Who pardons and forgives.

סדר חנוכה

Before kindling the Chanukkah lights the following blessings are said

בָּרוּךְ אַתָּה יְיָ אֱלֹהֵינוּ מֶלֶךְ הָעוֹלָם, אֲשֶׁר קִדְּשָׁנוּ בְּמִצְוֹתָיו וְצִוָּנוּ לְהַדְלִיק נֵר שֶׁלַּחֲנֻכָּה:

Blessed be You, O *God* our God, King of the Universe, Who has sanctified us by His commandments and commanded us to kindle the Chanukkah lights.

חנכה

חנכה : What we commemorate each year at this time is not the anniversary of the dedication of a new Temple edifice. It is not the *dedication,* but the *re-dedication* of the Temple that we celebrate each Chanukkah. For the Temple edifice as such had not sustained any kind of physical damage, and therefore was not in need of physical restoration. It was the *soul* of the Temple that had departed. What was lacking was the congregation that had made up the Temple, those men who, with their heart's blood, with their loyalty to the Law, and with their enthusiastic fulfillment of life's duty, should have represented the true, living Temple of God. The living congregation, of which the Temple of stone and wood should have been only the image and model,

בָּרוּךְ אַתָּה יְיָ אֱלֹהֵינוּ מֶלֶךְ הָעוֹלָם, שֶׁעָשָׂה
נִסִּים לַאֲבוֹתֵינוּ בַּיָּמִים הָהֵם בַּזְּמַן הַזֶּה:

On the first night of Chanukkah add

בָּרוּךְ אַתָּה יְיָ אֱלֹהֵינוּ מֶלֶךְ הָעוֹלָם,
שֶׁהֶחֱיָנוּ וְקִיְּמָנוּ וְהִגִּיעָנוּ לַזְּמַן הַזֶּה:

While the lights are kindled the following is recited

הַנֵּרוֹת הַלָּלוּ אֲנַחְנוּ מַדְלִיקִים עַל הַנִּסִּים וְעַל הַתְּשׁוּעוֹת
וְעַל הַנִּפְלָאוֹת שֶׁעָשִׂיתָ לַאֲבוֹתֵינוּ עַל־יְדֵי כֹּהֲנֶיךָ הַקְּדוֹשִׁים,
וְכָל־שְׁמֹנַת יְמֵי חֲנֻכָּה הַנֵּרוֹת הַלָּלוּ קֹדֶשׁ וְאֵין לָנוּ רְשׁוּת לְהִשְׁתַּמֵּשׁ
בָּהֶם, אֶלָּא לִרְאוֹתָם בִּלְבָד, כְּדֵי לְהוֹדוֹת לִשְׁמֶךָ עַל־נִסֶּיךָ וְעַל־
יְשׁוּעָתֶךָ וְעַל־נִפְלְאוֹתֶיךָ: כך היא גירסת אבודרהם והטור.

After the kindling of the lights the following hymn is sung

מָעוֹז צוּר יְשׁוּעָתִי, לְךָ נָאֶה לְשַׁבֵּחַ•

תִּכּוֹן בֵּית תְּפִלָּתִי, וְשָׁם תּוֹדָה נְזַבֵּחַ,

לְעֵת תָּכִין מַטְבֵּחַ, מִצָּר הַמְנַבֵּחַ,

אָז אֶגְמוֹר, בְּשִׁיר מִזְמוֹר, חֲנֻכַּת הַמִּזְבֵּחַ:

---

had succumbed to the sly seduction of the high and mighty and of the priests, and to the fanaticism of the Greeks which these tempters had stirred up. First these, the Torah-true congregation of God, had to be won back: ‎וּאחר כן‎, and only thereafter ‎באו לדביר ביתך‎ did they come to the Abode of His Word in the Sanctuary, remove from it all the physical trappings of idolatry and cleanse the Sanctuary of all that was profane. And then they kindled lights in praise and thanksgiving to God not in the Temple itself but in the courts surrounding the Temple. For our future welfare, even as did our deliverance in the past, does not depend on the light that shines in the lamp in the Temple, but on the lights that burn in the homes of the people who constitute the true environs of the House of God.

‎הן במחנה אל פני מנורה יאירו‎: ‎הן במחנה‎: We read in our Chanukkah piyut that they shone in the *camp* of Yisrael, facing the direction of the Temple lamp. ‎נר איש וביתו‎: Every individual was directly responsible primarily for

Blessed be You, O *God* our God, King of the Universe, Who performed miracles for our fathers in those days, at this season.

On the first night of Chanukkah add

Blessed be You, O *God* our God, King of the Universe, Who has kept us in life and sustained us and enabled us to reach this season.

While the lights are kindled the following is recited

We kindle these lights on account of the miracles, the victories and the wonders which You wrought for our fathers through Your holy Priests. During all the eight days of Chanukkah these lights are sacred, and we are not permitted to make use of them, but only to look upon them in order to give thanks to Your Name for Your miracles and Your salvation and Your wonders.

After the kindling of the lights the following hymn is sung

O Stronghold, Rock of my salvation; seemly it is to praise You. You will establish the House of my prayer, and there we shall offer You thanksgivings. When You will prepare judgment, deliverance from the raging foe, I shall complete, with song and psalm, the dedication of the Altar.

---

the kindling of the lights in his own home. But המהדרין those who seek to discharge their task more fully, we are told, will not be content merely to see that their home as such is illuminated with the light of the Law of the Lord. נר לכל אחד ואחד: They will strive to win every single member of their household, in accordance with his individual personality, for the light of this Law. והמהדרין מן המהדרין: Those who have a thorough understanding of their task, יום ראשון מדליק אחת מכאן ואלך מוסיף והולך begin by kindling only one light, and then increase the number of lights by one each day. In their eyes their task becomes greater כנגד הימים היוצאים in direct proportion to the time they have spent on it, and the principle that guides them in their conduct is מעלין בקדש ולא מורידין, not to slacken, but to make steadily growing progress in all things holy.

אקב"ו: Even though the law pertaining to *ner Chanukkah* is only a Rabbinic ordinance, we nevertheless say *vetzivanu* because the Law (Deut. 17:10, 11) that enjoins us conscientiously to fulfill all the precepts set forth by the Rabbinic authorities is of Divine origin.

נסים. הנרות denotes the great acts of God, describing them as "signposts" and symbols that stand out as "standards" or "banners" to teach and to guide

רְעוֹת שָׂבְעָה נַפְשִׁי,   בְּיָגוֹן כֹּחִי כָּלָה ·

חַיַּי מֵרְרוּ בְקֹשִׁי,   בְּשִׁעְבּוּד מַלְכוּת עֶגְלָה ·

וּבְיָדוֹ הַגְּדֹלָה,   הוֹצִיא אֶת־הַסְּגֻלָּה,

חֵיל פַּרְעֹה, וְכָל־זַרְעוֹ, יָרְדוּ כְּאֶבֶן מְצוּלָה:

דְּבִיר קָדְשׁוֹ הֱבִיאַנִי,   וְגַם שָׁם לֹא שָׁקַטְתִּי ·

וּבָא נוֹגֵשׂ וְהִגְלַנִי,   כִּי זָרִים עָבַדְתִּי ·

וְיֵין רַעַל מָסַכְתִּי,   כִּמְעַט שֶׁעָבַרְתִּי,

קֵץ בָּבֶל, זְרֻבָּבֶל, לְקֵץ שִׁבְעִים נוֹשָׁעְתִּי:

כְּרוֹת קוֹמַת בְּרוֹשׁ בִּקֵּשׁ   אֲגָגִי בֶּן־הַמְּדָתָא ·

וְנִהְיָתָה לּוֹ לְמוֹקֵשׁ,   וְגַאֲוָתוֹ נִשְׁבָּתָה ·

רֹאשׁ יְמִינִי נִשֵּׂאתָ,   וְאוֹיֵב שְׁמוֹ מָחִיתָ,

רֹב בָּנָיו, וְקִנְיָנָיו, עַל הָעֵץ תָּלִיתָ:

יְוָנִים נִקְבְּצוּ עָלַי,   אֲזַי בִּימֵי חַשְׁמַנִּים ·

וּפָרְצוּ חוֹמוֹת מִגְדָּלַי,   וְטִמְּאוּ כָּל־הַשְּׁמָנִים ·

וּמִנּוֹתַר קַנְקַנִּים,   נַעֲשָׂה נֵס לַשּׁוֹשַׁנִּים,

בְּנֵי בִינָה, יְמֵי שְׁמֹנָה, קָבְעוּ שִׁיר וּרְנָנִים:

---

us. The expression נפלאות describes these extraordinary occurrences in terms of their independence from the regular order of things. להודות: We give thanks to God's "Name"; i.e. by recognizing and acknowledging the miracles wrought in our history by the "knowledge" which lives within us, of God, of His nature and of His reign. Thus we also read in the *Hallel*: בשם ה' כי אמילם.

בית תפלתי, מעוז is the Temple in Yerushalayim, as in כי ביתי בית תפלתי (Isa. 56:7). מלכות עגלה. In Jeremiah 46:20 we find עגלה יפהפיה יקרא לכל העמים likening the Kingdom of Egypt in full flower to a young and beautiful heifer. ידו הגדלה: His power, which is the epitome of greatness. יין רעל מסכתי. The literal translation of *masachti* is "I mixed." To "mix" wine means to prepare

Sated was my soul with troubles, my strength spent with sorrow; they had embittered my life with hardship, enslaved by the kingdom of the heifer. But with His great power He led forth His chosen, while Pharaoh's hosts and all of his seed sank like a stone into the shadowy deep.

To the holy Abode of His word He brought me, but even there I found no rest; the captor came and led me captive, because I had served alien gods and had prepared for myself heady wine. But hardly had I gone away, Zerubbabel came, Babel's end, and, after seventy years, I was saved.

The Aggagite, son of Hamedatha, sought to cut down the lofty pine. But it became his own snare, and his arrogance was broken. The head of the Binyaminite You did raise, but the name of the foe You blotted out, of his sons and of the abundance of his wealth; and him You hanged upon the gallows.

The Greeks had gathered against me in the days of the Hasmoneans; they had broken down the walls of my towers and defiled all the oils. And from one remnant in the flasks a miracle was wrought for the roses, and, blessed with insight, they appointed eight days for song and jubilation.

---

wine for drinking. In other words, "the wine of the pagans was so heady that it could not be drunk without an admixture of water." "I prepared heady wine for myself"; this means "I was dazed and intoxicated with the heady wine of error and delusion." עברתי : "I had gone away"; "I had been taken away from my homeland and led captive to Babylonia." (Cf. ואת העם העביר אתו לערים Gen. 47:21.) על העץ תלית. רוב בניו וקנייניו could hardly refer to *kinyanav* hence it is most probable that רוב בניו וקנייניו is the object [not of *talitha* but] of *machitha*. לשושנים : In many places in the Holy Scriptures the term "rose" is employed with reference to the people of Yisrael. Yisrael is a rose protected by thorns, which no impudent hand may violate with impunity.

On the 13th day of Adar (in a leap year in Adar II) is the fast day תענית אסתר
on which עננו is inserted in the ש״ע at מנחה (at שחרית it is said only by the
חזן at the repetition of the ש״ע); at שחרית and at מנחה the Torah portion of
ויחל is read; if Purim falls on Sunday the fastday is advanced to the preceding
Thursday.

Purim is on the 14th of Adar (in a leap year in Adar II); neither, קל ארך אפים,
בימי מרדכי וגו') is inserted על הנסים the ש״ע In. is said למנצח יענך nor תחנון
(ועל כלם ;at grace before) ועל הכל before

of ש״ע of קדיש תתקבל is read twice on Purim· in the evening after מגלת אסתר
(בשלח end of) פרשת ויבא עמלק and in the morning after the reading of מעריב
and the return of the ספר תורה to the ארון הקדש.

Before the Reading of the מגלה the Reader recites the following

בָּרוּךְ אַתָּה יְיָ אֱלֹהֵינוּ מֶלֶךְ הָעוֹלָם· אֲשֶׁר
קִדְּשָׁנוּ בְּמִצְוֹתָיו וְצִוָּנוּ עַל מִקְרָא מְגִלָּה:
בָּרוּךְ אַתָּה יְיָ אֱלֹהֵינוּ מֶלֶךְ הָעוֹלָם· שֶׁעָשָׂה
נִסִּים לַאֲבוֹתֵינוּ בַּיָּמִים הָהֵם בַּזְּמַן הַזֶּה:

In many congregations שהחיינו is recited only on the Eve of Purim

בָּרוּךְ אַתָּה יְיָ אֱלֹהֵינוּ מֶלֶךְ הָעוֹלָם·
שֶׁהֶחֱיָנוּ וְקִיְּמָנוּ וְהִגִּיעָנוּ לַזְּמַן הַזֶּה:

After the Reading of the Megillah say

בָּרוּךְ אַתָּה יְיָ אֱלֹהֵינוּ מֶלֶךְ הָעוֹלָם· הָאֵל הָרָב אֶת
רִיבֵנוּ וְהַדָּן אֶת דִּינֵנוּ וְהַנּוֹקֵם אֶת נִקְמָתֵנוּ וְהַמְשַׁלֵּם
גְּמוּל לְכָל אוֹיְבֵי נַפְשֵׁנוּ וְהַנִּפְרָע לָנוּ מִצָּרֵינוּ: בָּרוּךְ
אַתָּה יְיָ הַנִּפְרָע לְעַמּוֹ יִשְׂרָאֵל מִכָּל צָרֵיהֶם· הָאֵל
הַמּוֹשִׁיעַ:

פורים

מגלה is derived from the verb גלל, and denotes a parchment "roll", in
other words, a "manuscript". In the Book of Esther itself, the Megillath Esther
is often referred to as *Iggereth, Iggereth Purim,* "the Letter", "The Letter

Before the Reading of the מגלה *the Reader recites the following three blessings.*

Blessed be You, O *God* our God, King of the Universe, Who has sanctified us by His commandments and commanded us concerning the Reading of the Megillah.

Blessed be You, O *God* our God, King of the Universe, Who performed miracles for our fathers in those days, at this season.

In many congregations שהחינו *is recited only on the Eve of Purim*

Blessed be You, O *God* our God, King of the Universe, Who has kept us in life and sustained us and enabled us to reach this season.

After the Reading of the Megillah say

Blessed be You, O *God* our God, King of the Universe, the God Who pleads our cause, judges our right, avenges our wrong and renders retribution to all the enemies of our soul, and Who exacts payment for us from our oppressors. Blessed be You, O *God,* Who exacts payment in behalf of Your people Yisrael from all their oppressors, God, Who saves.

Concerning Purim". It is a "circular" written at the time of the miraculous event which Purim commemorates and is addressed to all the generations to come, telling them of the miracle which the feast of Purim celebrates. It is a message of exhortation, comfort, hope and trust intended to sustain future generations of the Jewish people through the trials which might befall them during the centuries of exile to come. It is as such and in this spirit that we are to read the Megillah. On Purim we do not recite the *Hallel;* its place is taken by the Megillah, which may be called a "Hallel of Exile" because it celebrates not a deliverance *from,* but only a deliverance amidst exile (Megillah 14a).

ברוך **האל הרב** וכו' : With this blessing we renounce every thought of vengeance and every independent effort at effecting retribution from our enemies, acknowledging, instead, that God is the sole true, genuine and all-sufficient Champion of our destinies against all of our foes.

In the Morning Prayer the following paragraph is omitted

אֲשֶׁר הֵנִיא עֲצַת גּוֹיִם וַיָּפֶר מַחְשְׁבוֹת עֲרוּמִים: בְּקוּם עָלֵינוּ
אָדָם רָשָׁע, נֵצֶר זָדוֹן מִזֶּרַע עֲמָלֵק: גָּאָה בְעָשְׁרוֹ וְכָרָה לוֹ בּוֹר
וּגְדֻלָּתוֹ יָקְשָׁה לּוֹ לָכֶד: דִּמָּה בְנַפְשׁוֹ לִלְכּוֹד וְנִלְכָּד, בִּקֵּשׁ לְהַשְׁמִיד
וְנִשְׁמַד מְהֵרָה: הָמָן הוֹדִיעַ אֵיבַת אֲבוֹתָיו וְעוֹרֵר שִׂנְאַת אַחִים
לְבָנִים: וְלֹא־זָכַר רַחֲמֵי שָׁאוּל כִּי־בְחֶמְלָתוֹ עַל־אֲגָג נוֹלַד אוֹיֵב:
זָמַם רָשָׁע לְהַכְרִית צַדִּיק, וְנִלְכַּד טָמֵא בִּידֵי טָהוֹר: חֶסֶד גָּבַר
עַל־שִׁגְגַת אָב וְרָשָׁע הוֹסִיף חֵטְא עַל־חֲטָאָיו: טָמַן בְּלִבּוֹ מַחְשְׁבוֹת
עֲרוּמָיו וַיִּתְמַכֵּר לַעֲשׂוֹת רָעָה: יָדוֹ שָׁלַח בִּקְדוֹשֵׁי אֵל, כַּסְפּוֹ נָתַן
לְהַכְרִית זִכְרָם: כִּרְאוֹת מָרְדְּכַי כִּי־יָצָא קֶצֶף וְדָתֵי הָמָן נִתְּנוּ
בְשׁוּשָׁן, לָבַשׁ שַׂק וְקָשַׁר מִסְפֵּד וְגָזַר צוֹם וַיֵּשֶׁב עַל־הָאֵפֶר: מִי
זֶה יַעֲמוֹד לְכַפֵּר שְׁגָגָה וְלִמְחוֹל חַטַּאת עֲוֹן אֲבוֹתֵינוּ: נֵץ פָּרַח
מִלּוּלָב, הֵן הֲדַסָּה עָמְדָה לְעוֹרֵר יְשֵׁנִים: סָרִיסֶיהָ הִבְהִילוּ לְהָמָן
לְהַשְׁקוֹתוֹ יֵין חֲמַת תַּנִּינִים: עָמַד בְּעָשְׁרוֹ וְנָפַל בְּרִשְׁעוֹ, עָשָׂה לּוֹ
עֵץ וְנִתְלָה עָלָיו: פִּיהֶם פָּתְחוּ כָּל־יוֹשְׁבֵי תֵבֵל כִּי פוּר הָמָן נֶהְפַּךְ
לְפוּרֵנוּ: צַדִּיק נֶחֱלַץ מִיַּד רָשָׁע, אוֹיֵב נִתַּן תַּחַת נַפְשׁוֹ: קִיְּמוּ
עֲלֵיהֶם לַעֲשׂוֹת פּוּרִים וְלִשְׂמוֹחַ בְּכָל־שָׁנָה וְשָׁנָה: רָאִיתָ אֶת־
תְּפִלַּת מָרְדְּכַי וְאֶסְתֵּר, הָמָן וּבָנָיו עַל־הָעֵץ תָּלִיתָ:

שנאת אחים .אשר הניא refers to Amalek, the ancestor of Haman. איבת אבותיו
i.e. the hatred of Esau for the descendants of his brother Jacob. רחמי שאול:
It was to Shaul's pity upon Agag that Haman owed the very fact of his birth.
חסד גבר : Mordechai was a descendant of King Shaul and, by virtue of his
piety, Mordechai atoned for the error of his ancestor while Haman piled still
more sins upon the wrong already done by Amalek, his forebear. The expression קשר מספד is incorrect. In II Samuel, 3:31 we read חגרו שקים וספדו.
It would appear that the expression קשר שק מספד was derived from that
Biblical verse and that, in this case, the word שק is to be implied from what
goes before. לכפר שגגה refers to the sin involved in partaking of the royal

In the Morning Prayer the following paragraph is omitted

O You Who brought to naught the counsel of the nations and
thwarted the plans of the crafty, when a lawless man rose up against
us, a wicked offshoot of the seed of Amalek. He was proud of his
wealth, and it dug him a pit, and his greatness became his snare. In
his soul he sought to entrap, but was himself entrapped; he sought to
destroy, but was himself speedily destroyed. Haman displayed the
hatred of his parents and worked the hatred of the brothers upon the
children, and did not remember the compassion of Shaul, because of
whose compassion for Agag he, the enemy, was born. The lawless
man plotted to cut off the righteous, and the unclean was caught in
the hands of the pure. Piety prevailed over the error of the ancestor,
but the lawless man piled sin upon his sins. In his heart he hid his
crafty plans and gave himself entirely to doing evil. He stretched
forth his hand against those sanctified by God; he had given his
money to wipe out their memory. When Mordechai saw that wrath
had gone forth and Haman's decree had been given in Shushan, he
put on sackcloth, girded himself with the girdle of mourning, ordained a fast and sat upon ashes. Who will rise up to atone for error, to
obtain pardon for the sin and iniquity of our fathers? A branch
sprouted forth from the palm; Hadassah arose to awaken the sleeping;
her servants drove Haman to make him drink the wine of snake poison.
He rose by his wealth but fell by his wickedness; he had built a
gallows for his purpose and was himself hanged upon it. All the
inhabitants of the world proclaimed it loudly that Haman's lot had
been turned to be our lot; the righteous was freed from the hand
of the lawless; and the enemy was put in his stead. Then they ordained
it for themselves to observe Purim and to rejoice thereon every year.
You looked upon the prayer of Mordechai and Esther; Haman and
his sons You hanged upon the gallows.

---

banquet, a transgression that had incurred us the fate which now threatened
us. נץ פרח : In Midrash Shir Hashirim to the verse זאת קומתך דמתה לתמר
the period of Mordechai and Esther is compared to a palm tree. לעורר ישנים
may mean either "to awaken her contemporaries (who were 'sleeping', as it
were) to do *teshuvah*" or "to awaken those who were sleeping in the dust
to plead with God in behalf of the Jews."

In the morning one begins here after הקל המושיע:

שׁוֹשַׁנַּת יַעֲקֹב צָהֲלָה וְשָׂמֵחָה בִּרְאוֹתָם יַחַד תְּכֵלֶת
מָרְדֳּכָי: תְּשׁוּעָתָם הָיִיתָ לָנֶצַח וְתִקְוָתָם בְּכָל־דּוֹר
וָדוֹר: לְהוֹדִיעַ שֶׁכָּל־קֹוֶיךָ לֹא יֵבֹשׁוּ וְלֹא יִכָּלְמוּ לָנֶצַח
כָּל־הַחוֹסִים בָּךְ: אָרוּר הָמָן אֲשֶׁר בִּקֵּשׁ לְאַבְּדִי בָּרוּךְ
מָרְדֳּכַי הַיְּהוּדִי אֲרוּרָה זֶרֶשׁ אֵשֶׁת מַפְחִידִי בְּרוּכָה
אֶסְתֵּר מְגִנָּה בַּעֲדִי וְגַם חַרְבוֹנָה זָכוּר לְטוֹב:

קדיש (P. 548), ואתה קדוש *this is followed by* מוצאי שבת) *In the evening (except*
without תתקבל *and* עלינו (P. 208). On מוצאי שבת *the regular* ויהי נעם *is said,*
followed by הבדלה, ויתן לך, ואתה קדוש (P. 548). *In the morning, after the*
Megillah reading עלינו *and* ק"ש, ובא לציון, אשרי *are said:*

The Rose of Yaakov rejoiced and was glad when they all beheld
the purple robe of Mordechai. You have ever been their salvation
and their hope in every generation, to make known that all those who
hope in You shall not be deceived, and all those who put their trust
in You shall never blush with shame. Accursed is Haman, who sought
to destroy me; blessed is Mordechai, the Jew; Accursed is Zeresh, the
wife of my menace; blessed is Esther, who shielded me, and Charbonah, too, shall be remembered for good.

וגם חרבנה: Charbonah was the man who, at the right time, before the
wrath of the vacillating king could die down, reminded the King that the
gallows which Haman had originally erected at his home to hang Mordechai
was ready to receive its builder instead.

סדר סעודה וברכותיה

Hands are washed before the meal; while drying them, the following Bracha
is said: בָּרוּךְ אַתָּה יְיָ אֱלֹהֵינוּ מֶלֶךְ
הָעוֹלָם אֲשֶׁר קִדְּשָׁנוּ בְּמִצְוֹתָיו וְצִוָּנוּ עַל נְטִילַת יָדָיִם:

Before the meal, the following Bracha is said over the bread:
בָּרוּךְ אַתָּה יְיָ אֱלֹהֵינוּ מֶלֶךְ הָעוֹלָם הַמּוֹצִיא לֶחֶם מִן הָאָרֶץ:

If there is wine at the meal ברכת המוציא *is preceded by the following*
over a full cup of wine: ברכה בָּרוּךְ אַתָּה יְיָ אֱלֹהֵינוּ מֶלֶךְ
הָעוֹלָם בּוֹרֵא פְּרִי הַגָּפֶן *and one drinks from it.*

After the meal, before saying grace על נהרות בבל *is said; however, on days
when no* תחנון *is said* שיר המעלות *takes the place of* על נהרות.

עַל־נַהֲרוֹת בָּבֶל שָׁם יָשַׁבְנוּ גַּם־
בָּכִינוּ בְּזָכְרֵנוּ אֶת־צִיּוֹן: עַל־עֲרָבִים
בְּתוֹכָהּ תָּלִינוּ כִּנֹּרוֹתֵינוּ: כִּי שָׁם
שְׁאֵלוּנוּ שׁוֹבֵינוּ דִּבְרֵי־שִׁיר וְתוֹלָלֵינוּ
שִׂמְחָה שִׁירוּ לָנוּ מִשִּׁיר צִיּוֹן: אֵיךְ
נָשִׁיר אֶת־שִׁיר יְיָ עַל אַדְמַת נֵכָר:
אִם־אֶשְׁכָּחֵךְ יְרוּשָׁלָ͏ִם תִּשְׁכַּח יְמִינִי:
תִּדְבַּק לְשׁוֹנִי לְחִכִּי אִם־לֹא אֶזְכְּרֵכִי
אִם־לֹא אַעֲלֶה אֶת־יְרוּשָׁלַ͏ִם עַל־רֹאשׁ
שִׂמְחָתִי: זְכֹר יְהוָה לִבְנֵי אֱדוֹם אֵת
יוֹם יְרוּשָׁלָ͏ִם הָאֹמְרִים עָרוּ עָרוּ
עַד הַיְסוֹד בָּהּ: בַּת בָּבֶל הַשְּׁדוּדָה
אַשְׁרֵי שֶׁיְשַׁלֶּם־לָךְ אֶת־גְּמוּלֵךְ שֶׁגָּמַלְתְּ
לָנוּ: אַשְׁרֵי שֶׁיֹּאחֵז וְנִפֵּץ אֶת־עֹלָלַיִךְ
אֶל־הַסָּלַע:

שִׁיר הַמַּעֲלוֹת · בְּשׁוּב יְיָ
אֶת־שִׁיבַת צִיּוֹן הָיִינוּ
כְּחֹלְמִים: אָז יִמָּלֵא שְׂחֹק
פִּינוּ וּלְשׁוֹנֵנוּ רִנָּה אָז
יֹאמְרוּ בַגּוֹיִם הִגְדִּיל יְיָ
לַעֲשׂוֹת עִם־אֵלֶּה: הִגְדִּיל
יְיָ לַעֲשׂוֹת עִמָּנוּ הָיִינוּ
שְׂמֵחִים: שׁוּבָה יְיָ אֶת
שְׁבִיתֵנוּ כַּאֲפִיקִים בַּנֶּגֶב:
הַזֹּרְעִים בְּדִמְעָה בְּרִנָּה
יִקְצֹרוּ:   הָלוֹךְ   יֵלֵךְ
וּבָכֹה נֹשֵׂא מֶשֶׁךְ־הַזָּרַע
בֹּא־יָבֹא   בְרִנָּה   נֹשֵׂא
אֲלֻמֹּתָיו:

If there is wine at the meal כּוֹס יְשׁוּעוֹת אֶשָּׂא וּבְשֵׁם ה' יִקְרָא *is spoken over a full
cup of wine which one keeps holding while saying grace:*

*If three or more males who have attained the 13th year ate together, they say
grace together* (זמון)*. One leader recites the grace aloud while the others say it
quietly responding to the* ברכות *with* אמן*. The leader begins:*

רַבּוֹתַי הַב לָן וּנְבָרֵךְ ! מָדער: רַבּוֹתַי וויר וואָלֶּן בּענטשען!

the others respond יְהִי שֵׁם־יְיָ מְבֹרָךְ מֵעַתָּה וְעַד עוֹלָם. *then he says*

בִּרְשׁוּת = = = נְבָרֵךְ) שֶׁאָכַלְנוּ מִשֶּׁלּוֹ: *if there are ten men, he adds* (אֱלֹהֵינוּ

the others respond בָּרוּךְ) *if ten* (אֱלֹהֵינוּ שֶׁאָכַלְנוּ מִשֶּׁלּוֹ וּבְטוּבוֹ

חָיִינוּ: *others who have not eaten with them say:*) בָּרוּךְ וּמְבֹרָךְ

the leader says: שְׁמוֹ תָּמִיד לְעוֹלָם וָעֶד) בָּרוּךְ) *if ten*

אֱלֹהֵינוּ) שֶׁאָכַלְנוּ מִשֶּׁלּוֹ וּבְטוּבוֹ חָיִינוּ: בָּרוּךְ הוּא וּבָרוּךְ שְׁמוֹ:

When saying grace alone, begin here:

בָּרוּךְ אַתָּה יְיָ אֱלֹהֵינוּ מֶלֶךְ הָעוֹלָם, הַזָּן אֶת־הָעוֹלָם,
כֻּלּוֹ בְּטוּבוֹ בְּחֵן בְּחֶסֶד וּבְרַחֲמִים הוּא נוֹתֵן לֶחֶם לְכָל־
בָּשָׂר, כִּי לְעוֹלָם חַסְדּוֹ: וּבְטוּבוֹ הַגָּדוֹל תָּמִיד לֹא־
חָסַר לָנוּ וְאַל יֶחְסַר־לָנוּ מָזוֹן לְעוֹלָם וָעֶד בַּעֲבוּר
שְׁמוֹ הַגָּדוֹל: כִּי הוּא זָן וּמְפַרְנֵס לַכֹּל וּמֵטִיב לַכֹּל
וּמֵכִין מָזוֹן לְכָל־בְּרִיּוֹתָיו אֲשֶׁר בָּרָא · בָּרוּךְ אַתָּה יְיָ
הַזָּן אֶת־הַכֹּל:

נוֹדֶה לְךָ יְיָ אֱלֹהֵינוּ עַל שֶׁהִנְחַלְתָּ לַאֲבוֹתֵינוּ אֶרֶץ
חֶמְדָּה טוֹבָה וּרְחָבָה וְעַל שֶׁהוֹצֵאתָנוּ יְיָ אֱלֹהֵינוּ
מֵאֶרֶץ מִצְרַיִם וּפְדִיתָנוּ מִבֵּית עֲבָדִים וְעַל בְּרִיתְךָ
שֶׁחָתַמְתָּ בִּבְשָׂרֵנוּ וְעַל תּוֹרָתְךָ שֶׁלִּמַּדְתָּנוּ וְעַל חֻקֶּיךָ
שֶׁהוֹדַעְתָּנוּ וְעַל חַיִּים חֵן וָחֶסֶד שֶׁחוֹנַנְתָּנוּ וְעַל אֲכִילַת
מָזוֹן שָׁאַתָּה זָן וּמְפַרְנֵס אוֹתָנוּ תָּמִיד בְּכָל־יוֹם וּבְכָל־
עֵת וּבְכָל־שָׁעָה:

On Chanukkah and Purim add עַל הַנִּסִים *see p. 150*

ברכת המזון

In Deuteronomy 8:1 we are told that the one condition for the fulfillment
of God's promise of life and prosperity for His people and the preservation
of the land upon which Yisrael was to live and grow, was that the people
of Yisrael, in turn, faithfully fulfill His Divine Law: כל המצוה וגו׳ למען תחיון וגו׳.
We are asked to remember our journey through the wilderness that was so
replete with trials and lessons for the future; we are bidden to recall at all
times God's direct care and concern, as visibly demonstrated by the wondrous
Mannah, and by our miraculous survival throughout our wanderings until
we entered the fertile and fruitful Promised Land: וזכרת את כל הדרך וגו׳.
Immediately thereafter we are told ואכלת ושבעת וברכת את ה׳ אלקיך על הארץ הטובה
אשר נתן לך. "And then, when you have eaten and are satisfied, bless God,

Blessed be You, O *God,* our God, King of the Universe, Who nourishes the whole world with His goodness, with favor, loving-kindness and compassion. He gives food to all flesh because His loving-kindness endures forever. And through His great goodness we have never wanted for food, nor shall we ever want for it, for His great Name's sake. For He feeds and sustains all beings, does good to all and prepares food for all His creatures which He has created. Blessed be You, O *God,* Who gives food to all.

We thank You, O *God* our God, because You have given as a heritage to our fathers a desirable, good and spacious land, and because You brought us forth, O *God* our God, from the land of Mitzrayim and delivered us from the house of bondage, as well as for Your covenant which You have sealed in our flesh, and for Your Torah which You have taught us, for Your statutes which You have made known to us, and for the life, favor and loving-kindness which You have bestowed upon us, and for the food, for You feed and sustain us constantly every day, in every season and at every hour.

On Chanukkah and Purim add   על הנסים   see p. 150

---

your God, for the good land which He has given you." This Biblical commandment is the basis for the *Birkat Hamazon,* the grace to be recited after partaking of bread. Even in the midst of everyday circumstances, after an ordinary meal, we are to preserve and nurture in our hearts the conviction which the miracle of the gift of the heavenly Mannah has instilled into us in the wilderness; namely, that each and every home and soul on earth is favored by God's direct, immediate care and concern. Hence we are to look even upon every piece of plain bread as no less a direct gift of God than the Mannah which was sent down from Heaven to our fathers long ago when they journeyed through the wilderness. The Halachah deduces this commandment from *lechem* mentioned immediately before; i.e. ארץ אשר לא במסכנות תאכל בה לחם and commands us to recite the *Birkat Hamazon* after partaking of bread prepared from any of the following five species of grain: wheat, barley, spelt, oats and rye.

Our *Birkat Hamazon* consists of four *berachoth*: ברכת הארץ ,ברכת הזן, בונה ירושלים, and הטוב והמטיב.

1. ברכת הזן is a verbal expression of the conviction that *"God"* and His Name both imply the "gift of a new future" for every human soul. He gives careful, individual attention to every single soul and to its needs for its future existence. Hence we should view every piece of bread that we eat

If one forgot to say על הנסים *and remembers it before finishing* ועל הכל
(even before אתה *and* 'ה*)*, *it may be added here followed by* ועל הכל; *if one
has already said* 'ברוך אתה ה, *it may be added before* הרחמן הוא יזכנו *by insert-*
ing the הרחמן הוא יעשה *mentioned there:*

וְעַל הַכֹּל יְיָ אֱלֹהֵינוּ אֲנַחְנוּ מוֹדִים לָךְ וּמְבָרְכִים
אוֹתָךְ יִתְבָּרַךְ שִׁמְךָ בְּפִי כָּל־חַי תָּמִיד לְעוֹלָם וָעֶד:
כַּכָּתוּב וְאָכַלְתָּ וְשָׂבָעְתָּ וּבֵרַכְתָּ אֶת־יְיָ אֱלֹהֶיךָ עַל־
הָאָרֶץ הַטֹּבָה אֲשֶׁר נָתַן־לָךְ · בָּרוּךְ אַתָּה יְיָ עַל־
הָאָרֶץ וְעַל־הַמָּזוֹן:

רַחֵם יְיָ אֱלֹהֵינוּ עַל־יִשְׂרָאֵל עַמֶּךָ וְעַל יְרוּשָׁלַיִם עִירֶךָ
וְעַל צִיּוֹן מִשְׁכַּן כְּבוֹדֶךָ וְעַל מַלְכוּת בֵּית דָּוִד מְשִׁיחֶךָ
וְעַל הַבַּיִת הַגָּדוֹל וְהַקָּדוֹשׁ שֶׁנִּקְרָא שִׁמְךָ עָלָיו:
אֱלֹהֵינוּ אָבִינוּ רְעֵנוּ זוּנֵנוּ פַּרְנְסֵנוּ וְכַלְכְּלֵנוּ וְהַרְוִיחֵנוּ
וְהַרְוַח־לָנוּ יְיָ אֱלֹהֵינוּ מְהֵרָה מִכָּל־צָרוֹתֵינוּ וְנָא אַל־
תַּצְרִיכֵנוּ יְיָ אֱלֹהֵינוּ לֹא לִידֵי מַתְּנַת בָּשָׂר וָדָם וְלֹא
לִידֵי הַלְוָאָתָם כִּי אִם־לְיָדְךָ הַמְּלֵאָה הַפְּתוּחָה הַקְּדוֹשָׁה
וְהָרְחָבָה שֶׁלֹּא נֵבוֹשׁ וְלֹא נִכָּלֵם לְעוֹלָם וָעֶד:

and every moment of continued existence afforded us by this food as gifts of
His "goodness", סובו which, depending upon the merits of the receiver, may
take the form of grace and favor (חן) loving-kindness (חסד) or of that compassion that is the inalienable gift bestowed upon every human being (רחמים).
When we recite the blessing ברוך אתה ה' הזן את הכל we pledge that we will
consecrate all of our lives to the service of Him Who has gives us life and
Who feeds and sustains all living things.

2. ברכת הארץ : By virtue of their special destiny, the Jewish individual
and the Jewish people, enjoy an exceptional relationship with the all-sustaining

For all this, O *God*, our God, we thank You and bless You;
blessed be your Name by the mouth of all living things constantly
and forever, even as it is written, "When you have eaten and are
satisfied, you shall bless *God*, your God, for the good land which He
has given you." Blessed be You, O *God*, for the land and for the
food.

Have compassion, O *God*, our God, upon Yisrael Your people,
upon Yerushalayim Your City, upon Tzion, the Abode of Your glory,
upon the Kingdom of the House of David, Your Anointed, and upon
the great and the holy House over which Your Name was proclaimed,
O our Father, tend us, feed us, sustain us, nourish us, relieve us, and
speedily grant us relief, O *God* our God, from all our troubles. And
O *God* our God, let us not be in need of the gifts of human hands,
or of their loans, but only of Your hand, which is full, open, holy and
ample, so that we may not be ashamed nor blush with shame forever
and ever.

Providence of God. He demonstrated to the people of Yisrael His extraordinary concern for them at the very beginning of their history; first, by the
promise which He gave to our patriarch concerning the Land of Yisrael, and
then by the fulfillment of this promise, once Yisrael, in Egypt, had grown
into a nation and through its redemption had become ready and mature for
freedom and independence. However, the promise concerning the Holy Land
(Gen. Chap. 17) was preceded by a covenant between God and His people,
the covenant of *Milah*, which was to be preserved by Abraham and his descendants for all times and by means of which Abraham and all the generations to follow were to recognize and acknowledge God forever as *their* God,
the sole ruler of their destinies and the sole guide for their conduct. להיות לך
ולזרעך אחריך לאלקים. ארץ Thus the basic condition for our possession of the
Promised Land is the ברית, and our continued possession of the Land is dependent upon whether or not we fulfill the purpose for which we were given
it; namely, the observance of the Torah, even as it is written in Psalm 105:44,
ויתן להם ארצות גוים ועמל לאמים יירשו בעבור ישמרו חוקיו ותורותיו ינצורו 45 When we broke faith
with this purpose, we met with the fate which had been predicted to us also,
early in our history; we were exiled from our own homeland, and we are
told that, once exiled, we may hope for a restoration of our homeland only
if we ourselves will loyally return to our destiny: ושבת עד ה' אלקיך ושמעת בקולו
ככל אשר אנכי מצוך היום אתה ובניך בכל לבבך ובכל נפשך ושב ה' אלקיך את שבותך וגו'
אם יהיה נדחך וגו' והביאך ה' אלקיך אל הארץ אשר ירשו אבותיך וירשתה וגו' (Deut. 30:2).

On Sabbath add רצה

רְצֵה וְהַחֲלִיצֵנוּ יְיָ אֱלֹהֵינוּ בְּמִצְוֹתֶיךָ וּבְמִצְוַת יוֹם הַשְּׁבִיעִי הַשַּׁבָּת הַגָּדוֹל וְהַקָּדוֹשׁ הַזֶּה כִּי יוֹם זֶה גָּדוֹל וְקָדוֹשׁ הוּא לְפָנֶיךָ לִשְׁבָּת־בּוֹ וְלָנוּחַ בּוֹ בְּאַהֲבָה כְּמִצְוַת רְצוֹנֶךָ · בִּרְצוֹנְךָ הָנִיחַ לָנוּ יְיָ אֱלֹהֵינוּ שֶׁלֹּא תְהִי צָרָה וְיָגוֹן וַאֲנָחָה בְּיוֹם מְנוּחָתֵנוּ וְהַרְאֵנוּ יְיָ אֱלֹהֵינוּ בְּנֶחָמַת צִיּוֹן עִירֶךָ וּבְבִנְיַן יְרוּשָׁלַםִ עִיר קָדְשֶׁךָ כִּי אַתָּה הוּא בַּעַל הַיְשׁוּעוֹת וּבַעַל הַנֶּחָמוֹת׃

On Rosh Chodesh and Yom Tov add יעלה ויבא

אֱלֹהֵינוּ וֵאלֹהֵי אֲבוֹתֵינוּ · יַעֲלֶה וְיָבֹא וְיַגִּיעַ וְיֵרָאֶה וְיֵרָצֶה וְיִשָּׁמַע וְיִפָּקֵד וְיִזָּכֵר זִכְרוֹנֵנוּ וּפִקְדוֹנֵנוּ וְזִכְרוֹן אֲבוֹתֵינוּ · וְזִכְרוֹן מָשִׁיחַ בֶּן דָּוִד עַבְדֶּךָ · וְזִכְרוֹן יְרוּשָׁלַםִ עִיר קָדְשֶׁךָ · וְזִכְרוֹן כָּל־עַמְּךָ בֵּית יִשְׂרָאֵל לְפָנֶיךָ · לִפְלֵיטָה וּלְטוֹבָה וּלְחֵן וּלְחֶסֶד וּלְרַחֲמִים וּלְחַיִּים וּלְשָׁלוֹם בְּיוֹם לר"ח רֹאשׁ הַחֹדֶשׁ · לר"ה הַזִּכָּרוֹן · לסוכ חַג הַסֻּכּוֹת הַשְּׁמִינִי חַג הָעֲצֶרֶת | לפסח חַג הַמַּצּוֹת | לשבועות חַג הַשָּׁבֻעוֹת לשמ"ע ושמ"ת הַזֶּה · זָכְרֵנוּ יְיָ אֱלֹהֵינוּ בּוֹ לְטוֹבָה וּפָקְדֵנוּ בּוֹ לִבְרָכָה וְהוֹשִׁיעֵנוּ בּוֹ לְחַיִּים· וּבִדְבַר יְשׁוּעָה וְרַחֲמִים חוּס וְחָנֵּנוּ וְרַחֵם עָלֵינוּ וְהוֹשִׁיעֵנוּ· כִּי אֵלֶיךָ עֵינֵינוּ · כִּי אֵל (מֶלֶךְ) חַנּוּן וְרַחוּם אָתָּה׃

וּבְנֵה יְרוּשָׁלַםִ עִיר הַקֹּדֶשׁ בִּמְהֵרָה בְיָמֵינוּ בָּרוּךְ אַתָּה יְיָ, בֹּנֵה בְרַחֲמָיו יְרוּשָׁלָםִ· אָמֵן׃

Hence this land, both in flower and in desolation, is to us a permanent memorial of the Divine Providence which keeps watch particularly over the Jewish people. At the same time, it is eternal testimony to that truth which we are to take to our hearts for all times to come; namely, that all we need do to become worthy of God's preserving and sustaining care at all times and at

(*On Sabbath add*): Be pleased, O *God* our God, to fortify us by Your commandments, and by the commandment pertaining to the Seventh Day, this great and holy Sabbath; for this day is great and holy before You, that we may refrain thereon from every manner of work, and rest upon it in love in accordance with the commandment of Your will. In Your favor, O *God* our God, grant us rest so that there be no distress, no grief or sighing on the day of our rest, and let us, O *God* our God, behold the consolation of Tzion, Your City, and the rebuilding of Yerushalayim, the city of Your Sanctuary, for You are the Lord of all salvation and the Lord of all consolation.

(*On Rosh Chodesh and Yom Tov add* יעלה ויבא *for transl. see p.* 147)

And rebuild Yerushalayim, the holy city, speedily in our days. Blessed be You, O *God,* Who in His compassion rebuilds Yerushalayim Amen.

---

every moment is to remain faithful to the duty assigned us by Him through *Berith Abraham* and Torah. It is to the remembrance of this memorial and of this truth that the second *berachah* of the Grace after Meals, the *Birkath Haaretz* is dedicated.

3. בונה ירושלים : The Law which sums up our purpose as a Jewish nation was given an eternal dwelling place in the holy Temple in Yerushalayim and Tzion, and the Dynasty of David was instituted to act as the bearer and preserver of our national community for the fulfillment of this purpose. It was David who fought to obtain political independence for his people and who by the strains of his lyre bequeathed to us eternal inspiration for our destiny as a nation. It is only in association with a prayer for our collective welfare as a nation that the Jew may plead with God for himself as an individual. Hence, while our nation was in full flower, the prayers for our welfare as individuals were always said only in conjunction with corresponding petitions for the preservation of the Temple and of the Dynasty of David. Now that we are in exile our prayers for ourselves are closely linked with supplications for the restoration of these two Divinely-appointed institutions. It is this permanent association of our own welfare as individuals with that of our entire nation that is indicated by the content of the third Blessing in our Grace after Meals.

*)בָּרוּךְ אַתָּה יְיָ, אֱלֹהֵינוּ מֶלֶךְ הָעוֹלָם, הָאֵל אָבִינוּ
מַלְכֵּנוּ אַדִּירֵנוּ בּוֹרְאֵנוּ גּוֹאֲלֵנוּ יוֹצְרֵנוּ קְדוֹשֵׁנוּ קְדוֹשׁ
יַעֲקֹב רוֹעֵנוּ רוֹעֵה יִשְׂרָאֵל הַמֶּלֶךְ הַטּוֹב וְהַמֵּטִיב לַכֹּל
שֶׁבְּכָל־יוֹם וָיוֹם הוּא הֵטִיב הוּא מֵטִיב הוּא יֵטִיב לָנוּ:
הוּא גְמָלָנוּ הוּא גוֹמְלֵנוּ הוּא יִגְמְלֵנוּ לָעַד לְחֵן לְחֶסֶד
וּלְרַחֲמִים וּלְרֶוַח הַצָּלָה וְהַצְלָחָה בְּרָכָה וִישׁוּעָה
נֶחָמָה פַּרְנָסָה וְכַלְכָּלָה וְרַחֲמִים וְחַיִּים וְשָׁלוֹם וְכָל־
טוֹב, וּמִכָּל־טוּב אַל־יְחַסְּרֵנוּ:

If one forgot to say שבת *on* רצה, *the following is inserted here:*
בָּרוּךְ אַתָּה יְיָ אֱלֹהֵינוּ מֶלֶךְ הָעוֹלָם אֲשֶׁר נָתַן שַׁבָּתוֹת לִמְנוּחָה לְעַמּוֹ יִשְׂרָאֵל
בְּאַהֲבָה לְאוֹת וְלִבְרִית, בָּרוּךְ אַתָּה יְיָ מְקַדֵּשׁ הַשַּׁבָּת:

If one forgot to say יעלה ויבא *on* ר"ח, *the following is inserted here:*
בָּ"אַ"יְ אֱ"מֶ"הָ אֲשֶׁר נָתַן רָאשֵׁי חֳדָשִׁים לְעַמּוֹ יִשְׂרָאֵל לְזִכָּרוֹן:

If ר"ח *falls on* שבת *and one forgot to say* רצה *and* יעלה ויבא:
בָּרוּךְ אַתָּה יְיָ אֱלֹהֵינוּ מֶלֶךְ הָעוֹלָם אֲשֶׁר נָתַן שַׁבָּתוֹת לִמְנוּחָה לְעַמּוֹ יִשְׂרָאֵל בְּאַהֲבָה
לְאוֹת וְלִבְרִית וְרָאשֵׁי חֳדָשִׁים לְזִכָּרוֹן בָּ"אַ"יְ מְקַדֵּשׁ הַשַּׁבָּת וְיִשְׂרָאֵל וְרָאשֵׁי חֳדָשִׁים:

If one forgot to say יעלה ויבא *on* יו"ט, *the following is inserted here:*
בָּ"אַ"יְ אֱלֹהֵינוּ מֶלֶךְ הָעוֹלָם אֲשֶׁר נָתַן יָמִים טוֹבִים לְעַמּוֹ יִשְׂרָאֵל לְשָׂשׂוֹן
וּלְשִׂמְחָה אֶת־יוֹם חַג [פלוני] הַזֶּה, בָּרוּךְ אַתָּה יְיָ מְקַדֵּשׁ יִשְׂרָאֵל וְהַזְּמַנִּים:

If יו"ט *falls on* שבת *and one forgot to say* רצה *and* יעלה ויבא:
בָּרוּךְ אַתָּה יְיָ אֱלֹהֵינוּ מֶלֶךְ הָעֹלָם אֲשֶׁר נָתַן שַׁבָּתוֹת לִמְנוּחָה לְעַמּוֹ יִשְׂרָאֵל
בְּאַהֲבָה לְאוֹת וְלִבְרִית וְיָמִים טוֹבִים לְשָׂשׂוֹן וּלְשִׂמְחָה אֶת־יוֹם חַג [פלוני] הַזֶּה,
בָּרוּךְ אַתָּה יְיָ מְקַדֵּשׁ הַשַּׁבָּת וְיִשְׂרָאֵל וְהַזְּמַנִּים:

If one forgot to say יעלה ויבא *on* ר"ה, *the following is inserted here:*
בָּ"אַ"יְ אֱ"מֶ"הָ אֲשֶׁר נָתַן יָמִים טוֹבִים לְעַמּוֹ יִשְׂרָאֵל אֶת־יוֹם הַזִּכָּרוֹן הַזֶּה:

If ר"ה *falls on* שבת *and one forgot to say* רצה *and* יעלה ויבא:
בָּרוּךְ אַתָּה אֱלֹהֵינוּ מֶלֶךְ הָעוֹלָם אֲשֶׁר נָתַן שַׁבָּתוֹת לִמְנוּחָה לְעַמּוֹ יִשְׂרָאֵל
בְּאַהֲבָה לְאוֹת וְלִבְרִית וְיָמִים טוֹבִים לְיִשְׂרָאֵל אֶת־יוֹם הַזִּכָּרוֹן הַזֶּה, בָּרוּךְ אַתָּה
יְיָ מְקַדֵּשׁ הַשַּׁבָּת וְיִשְׂרָאֵל וְיוֹם הַזִּכָּרוֹן:

Blessed be You, O *God* our God, King of the Universe, O God, our Father, our King, our Mighty One, our Creator, our Redeemer, our Maker, our Holy One, the Holy One of Yaakov, our Shepherd, the Shepherd of Yisrael, O King, Who is kind and Who does good to all! He alone has done good to us day after day; it is He alone who does good, and it is He alone who will do good to us in the future, He alone has caused our destiny to bear ripe fruit; it is He alone Who causes it thus to ripen, and He alone, too, will continue to cause it thus to ripen, for favor, for loving-kindness and compassion, for relief, rescue and success, for blessing and salvation, for consolation, sustenance and nourishment, and for compassion, for life, for peace and all good. And with all the good may He not cause us to become wanting.

---

4. הטוב והמטיב: The three blessings preceding this paragraph cover all the motives which, according to Biblical Law, should be recalled in the *Birkat-Hamazon*. However, when, during the reign of Hadrian, the uprising led by Bar Kochba proved a disastrous error, it became essential that the Jewish people be reminded for all times of another important fact; namely, that Yisrael must never again attempt to restore its national independence by its own power; it was to entrust its future as a nation solely to Divine Providence. Therefore when the nation, crushed by this new blow, had recovered its breath and hailed even the permission to give a decent burial to the hundreds of thousands who had fallen about Betar as the dawn of a better day the sages who met at Yavneh added yet another blessing to the prayer for the restoration of Yerushalayim. This fourth Blessing is an acknowledgement that it has always been God and God alone Who has given us, and still gives us to this very day, that good in which we have had cause to rejoice and that for future good, too, we may look to none other but God, and none beside Him. הוא הטיב הוא מטיב הוא ייטיב לנו וכו׳, הוא יגמלנו וגו׳, הוא ימלוך הוא ישבור זכו׳.

On Chanukkah and Purim the second Blessing, the avowal of thanks for the acts of Divine Providence that made us an independent nation is augmented by *Al Hanisim*, a prayer of thanksgiving for the miraculous rescues which we commemorate on Chanukkah and Purim. On Sabbaths, Rosh Chodesh and Yom Tov the third Blessing, the general prayer for the preservation of our well-being and restoration of our national independence is supplemented by special supplications in keeping with the significance of

הָרַחֲמָן · הוּא יִמְלוֹךְ עָלֵינוּ לְעוֹלָם וָעֶד:

הָרַחֲמָן · הוּא יִתְבָּרַךְ בַּשָּׁמַיִם וּבָאָרֶץ:

הָרַחֲמָן · הוּא יִשְׁתַּבַּח לְדוֹר דּוֹרִים וְיִתְפָּאַר בָּנוּ
לָנֶצַח נְצָחִים וְיִתְהַדַּר בָּנוּ לָעַד וּלְעוֹלְמֵי עוֹלָמִים:

הָרַחֲמָן · הוּא יְפַרְנְסֵנוּ בְּכָבוֹד: הָרַחֲמָן · הוּא יִשְׁבּוֹר
עֻלֵּנוּ מֵעַל צַוָּארֵנוּ וְהוּא יוֹלִיכֵנוּ קוֹמְמִיּוּת לְאַרְצֵנוּ:

הָרַחֲמָן · הוּא יִשְׁלַח בְּרָכָה מְרֻבָּה בַּבַּיִת הַזֶּה וְעַל
שֻׁלְחָן זֶה שֶׁאָכַלְנוּ עָלָיו: הָרַחֲמָן · הוּא יִשְׁלַח לָנוּ אֶת־
אֵלִיָּה הַנָּבִיא זָכוּר לַטּוֹב וִיבַשֶּׂר־לָנוּ בְּשׂוֹרוֹת טוֹבוֹת
יְשׁוּעוֹת וְנֶחָמוֹת: הָרַחֲמָן הוּא יְבָרֵךְ אֶת (אָבִי) מוֹרִי
בַּעַל הַבַּיִת הַזֶּה, וְאֶת (אִמִּי) מוֹרָתִי בַּעֲלַת הַבַּיִת הַזֶּה,
אוֹתָם וְאֶת בֵּיתָם וְאֶת זַרְעָם וְאֶת כָּל־אֲשֶׁר לָהֶם אוֹתָנוּ
וְאֶת כָּל־אֲשֶׁר לָנוּ כְּמוֹ שֶׁנִּתְבָּרְכוּ אֲבוֹתֵינוּ אַבְרָהָם
יִצְחָק וְיַעֲקֹב בַּכֹּל מִכֹּל כֹּל · כֵּן יְבָרֵךְ אוֹתָנוּ כֻּלָּנוּ
יַחַד בִּבְרָכָה שְׁלֵמָה · וְנֹאמַר אָמֵן:

---

the day, for the specific blessings to be afforded us by the Sabbath or holiday.
On Sabbaths we recite *Retzeh;* on holidays, *Ya'aleh Veyavo.*

No other craving is so apt to turn man into a self-centered creature
viewing every other human being only as a rival on the path to happiness

May the Compassionate One reign over us to all eternity. Let the Compassionate One be blessed in heaven and on earth. Let the Compassionate One be praised from generation to generation, glorified among us to all eternity, and garbed in majesty in our midst for everlasting. May the Compassionate One grant us an honorable livelihood. May the Compassionate One break our yoke from off our neck and lead us upright into our land. May the Compassionate One send abundant blessing into this house, and upon this table at which we have eaten. May the Compassionate One send us Elijah the Prophet (may he be remembered for good) to bring us good news of salvation and consolation. May the Compassionate One bless (my father, my teacher) the master of this house, and (my mother, my teacher), the mistress of this house, them, their household, their children and all that belongs to them, also us and all that is ours, even as our fathers, Abraham, Yitzchak and Yaakov were blessed in everything, by everything and with everything, so may He bless all of us together with a perfect blessing, and let us say, Amen.

---

than the urge to satisfy the hunger for food. It is most probably for this reason that our Sages, seeking as they did to educate and discipline us by their ordinances, put such stress upon the communal element in the act of eating. When three or more persons have broken bread together, we are commanded to have one of the company call upon the rest of those assembled to recite *Birkat Hamazon* together. In this manner we are to proclaim and recall the truth that it is the One God (and when ten are gathered round the table, that it is אלקינו the One God Who is the common God of all the Jewish people) of Whose bounty we have all partaken, and Whose goodness has enabled us all to live and to remain alive. This communal act of homage to God as the sole Father, Preserver and Sustainer Who is equally near to all of us should blot out any and all feelings of jealous rivalry from our hearts and implant in their place sentiments of kinship for all of our brethren under the common Fatherhood of God. We are not to regard our brother's prosperity as prejudicial to our own welfare; instead, we are to know that He Who is the Father of us all is sufficiently rich and kind to give to every human soul at all times that which is good and beneficial for it.

בַּמָּרוֹם יְלַמְּדוּ עֲלֵיהֶם וְעָלֵינוּ זְכוּת שֶׁתְּהִי לְמִשְׁמֶרֶת
שָׁלוֹם · וְנִשָּׂא בְרָכָה מֵאֵת יְיָ וּצְדָקָה מֵאֱלֹהֵי יִשְׁעֵנוּ ·
וְנִמְצָא־חֵן וְשֵׂכֶל טוֹב בְּעֵינֵי אֱלֹהִים וְאָדָם:

לשבת הָרַחֲמָן הוּא יַנְחִילֵנוּ יוֹם שֶׁכֻּלּוֹ שַׁבָּת וּמְנוּחָה לְחַיֵּי הָעוֹלָמִים:

לר״ח הָרַחֲמָן הוּא יְחַדֵּשׁ עָלֵינוּ אֶת־הַחֹדֶשׁ הַזֶּה לְטוֹבָה וְלִבְרָכָה:

ליו״ט הָרַחֲמָן הוּא יַנְחִילֵנוּ יוֹם שֶׁכֻּלּוֹ טוֹב:

לר״ה הָרַחֲמָן הוּא יְחַדֵּשׁ עָלֵינוּ אֶת־הַשָּׁנָה הַזֹּאת לְטוֹבָה וְלִבְרָכָה:

לחה״מ וסוכות הָרַחֲמָן הוּא יָקִים לָנוּ אֶת־סֻכַּת דָּוִד הַנֹּפֶלֶת:

הָרַחֲמָן הוּא יְזַכֵּנוּ לִימוֹת הַמָּשִׁיחַ וּלְחַיֵּי הָעוֹלָם
הַבָּא · מַגְדִּיל (בר״ח ושבת וי״ט וחה״מ אומרים מִגְדּוֹל) יְשׁוּעוֹת מַלְכּוֹ
וְעֹשֶׂה חֶסֶד לִמְשִׁיחוֹ לְדָוִד וּלְזַרְעוֹ עַד־עוֹלָם: עֹשֶׂה
שָׁלוֹם בִּמְרוֹמָיו הוּא יַעֲשֶׂה שָׁלוֹם עָלֵינוּ וְעַל כָּל־
יִשְׂרָאֵל · וְאִמְרוּ אָמֵן:

יְראוּ אֶת־יְיָ קְדֹשָׁיו כִּי אֵין מַחְסוֹר לִירֵאָיו: כְּפִירִים רָשׁוּ
וְרָעֵבוּ וְדֹרְשֵׁי יְיָ לֹא־יַחְסְרוּ כָל־טוֹב: הוֹדוּ לַייָ כִּי־טוֹב כִּי לְעוֹלָם
חַסְדּוֹ: פּוֹתֵחַ אֶת־יָדֶךָ וּמַשְׂבִּיעַ לְכָל־חַי רָצוֹן: בָּרוּךְ הַגֶּבֶר אֲשֶׁר
יִבְטַח בַּייָ וְהָיָה יְיָ מִבְטַחוֹ: נַעַר הָיִיתִי גַּם־זָקַנְתִּי וְלֹא־רָאִיתִי צַדִּיק נֶעֱזָב וְזַרְעוֹ מְבַקֶּשׁ־לָחֶם:
יְיָ עֹז לְעַמּוֹ יִתֵּן יְיָ יְבָרֵךְ אֶת־עַמּוֹ בַשָּׁלוֹם:

If one forgot to interpolate על הנסים *before* ועל הכל, *it may be inserted here
and the following is said before* הרחמן הוא יזכנו

הָרַחֲמָן הוּא יַעֲשֶׂה לָנוּ נִסִּים וְנִפְלָאוֹת כְּמוֹ שֶׁעָשָׂה לַאֲבוֹתֵינוּ בַּיָּמִים הָהֵם
בַּזְּמַן הַזֶּה · בִּימֵי וכו׳. (*see p. 150*)

May those on high plead for them and for all of us so that it may contribute to enduring peace, and that we may receive a blessing from *God* and kindness from the God of our salvation, and we become worthy of favor and obtain good understanding in the sight of God and man.

On Sabbath: May the Compassionate One let us inherit that day which shall be all Sabbath and rest for life everlasting.

On Rosh Chodesh: May the Compassionate One renew this month for us for good and for blessing.

On Festivals: May the Compassionate One let us inherit that day which is altogether good.

On Rosh Hashanah: May the Compassionate One renew this year for us for good and for blessing.

On the Intermediate Days of Succoth: May the Compassionate One restore for us the falling Tabernacle of David.

May the Compassionate One make us worthy of reaching the days of the Messiah and life everlasting; He Who makes great the salvation of His King (*on Sabbath, Rosh Chodesh, Chol Hamoed and Yom Tov say*: He Who is a tower of salvation to his King) and shows loving-kindness to His Anointed, to David and his descendants forever. May He Who makes peace in His High places. make peace for us and for all of Yisrael, and let us say, Amen.

O fear *God*, you who are sanctified to Him, for there is no want for them that fear Him. Young lions have always become poor and suffered hunger, but they who seek *God* shall never want for any good thing. Avow it to *God* that He is good, that his love endures forever. Yea, You open Your hand and satisfy the desire of every living thing. Blessed is the man who trusts in *God*, and to whom God is the source of His trust.

I was young and I have grown old, but I have never seen a righteous man, forsaken, whose progeny was forced to beg for bread.

May *God* grant to His people the power to be victorious over all; may *God* bless His people with peace.

The statement וברכת את ה' אלקיך by which the Law of God commanded us to recite a *Birkath Hamazon* after meals has become the model and fundamental for that great institution of *"berachoth"* which our Sages have woven into the fabric of our lives in order to educate and discipline the spirit of the Jewish people. The Law of God makes our enjoyment of the fruit of the land an occasion for turning our thoughts away from the fruit itself and to remember the One Who gave us both the fruit and the Land, and thus impels us to frame solemn resolves for our future life and conduct — these are the ideals which the Law summarizes in the concept of the *berachah*. In the same manner, the Sages, in their wisdom, have viewed also all of our lives and all the phases of life as teachings and guideposts to remind us of God and of our debt to Him, and they have taught us, over and over again, to turn our eyes upward to God and, through the pledge of ברוך אתה וכו' ever to renew our vow to Him to serve Him with all of our lives. Every type of pleasure, every important phenomenon of nature, every memorable event in the changing course of life, and every opportunity afforded us for the performance of *mitzvoth*, ברכות הנהנין, ברכות הראיה והשמיעה, ברכות המצות, all serve as occasions for reciting the pledge, and help us find, in and for every circumstance, the right relationship to God, *our* God. It is significant that, in our *berachoth*, the concept of מלך העולם: מלכות is added to that of ד' אלקיך: ישם i. e. ד' אלקינו which was given us in the Torah, and the Halachah teaches us that כל ברכה שאין בה שם ומלכות אינה ברכה. It is the purpose of all the *berachoth* to turn our thoughts from moments that affect us individually "in the temporal world" to the "Timeless Ruler," so that we may recognize Him as ה' אלקינו to Whom we render homage as such by consecrating all of our being and dedicating all of our endeavors to Him.

ברכות הנהנין
Blessings to be recited in connection with the partaking of food

כל הנהנה מן העולם הזה בלא ברכה: In Berachoth 35a we are taught that he who enjoys any of the pleasures of this world without reciting a *berachah*, a "blessing," *ma'al*, violates a sacred thing; כאלו נהנה מקדשי שמים it is as if he had unlawfully partaken of treasures consecrated to God, for לה' הארץ ומלואה, the earth and its fullness are God's and only the recital of the *berachah*, the pledge to use the strength gained from the pleasure we have had in the service of God to do His will, confers upon us the privilege of enjoying anything on God's earth even as it is written: השמים שמים לה' והארץ נתן לבני אדם. "It is only לה', in their position as 'the property of *God*', guided and governed by Him, that the heavens are truly 'heavens', that the heavens give to the earth that which helps the earth grow and prosper, and it is God, too, Who gave the earth to mankind." Until such time as we have recited the *berachah*, before we have pledged to employ the benefits gained by our pleasure only in His service to do His will, לה' הארץ ומלואה the earth and all that fills it belong to God. It is only after man has uttered the pledge of the *berachah* that הארץ נתן לבני אדם he will receive the earth from God and thus acquire the privilege of partaking of its riches. We are further told: כל הנהנה מן העולם הזה בלא ברכה כאלו גוזל להק׳ב׳ה׳ וכנסת ישראל שנאמר גוזל אביו ואמו ואומר אין פשע חבר הוא לאיש משחית ואין אביו אלא הק׳ב׳ה׳ שנאמר הלא הוא אביך קנך ואין אמו אלא כנסת ישראל שנאמר שמע בני מוסר אביך ואל תטוש תורת אמך. He who partakes of any of the pleasures of this world without reciting a *berachah* actually commits a theft. He has stolen from God and from the Jewish community, even as it is said, "He who steals from his father and mother and says that he has committed no crime, by virtue of this statement has already become the accomplice of a man who works destruction." God is our Father and *Knesseth Yisrael,* the Jewish community' is our Mother, since it has given birth to us for God and trained us to do His will. It is the welfare of this our "Mother" that God has made the goal and purpose of all of His commandments, to the fulfillment of which we are bound anew each time He grants us sustenance or pleasure. We are told that a son who robs his father and mother and asserts that he has actually committed no crime, claiming that his parents would always permit him to benefit by their property and eventually would leave it all to him anyhow, and that he has not injured a third party by his deed, is an evil man. For with such an attitude he is already well on the way to becoming a harmful element among his fellow men. It is with this in mind that the Torah so harshly condemns the *ben sorer umoreh* even if he is only an adolescent. Given the facts above concerning our "Father" and "Mother," we can readily see why he who enjoys any part of God's world under the false assumption that he has the full rights of ownership thereto, without reciting a *berachah* before, is wicked. He who partakes of the pleasures of earth without reminding himself that God is the sole true Owner of that of which he has partaken; who fails to consider that God has given first claim to these treasures to his community and who thus is not aware that he is obligated and indebted to God and community alike, is a dangerous individual. For such a thoughtless man who has so completely forgotten God, the world about him, and his duty to both, has sunk to that base level of egotism which paves the way to a future life of evil and crime.

Before partaking of bread:

בָּרוּךְ אַתָּה יְיָ אֱלֹהֵינוּ מֶלֶךְ הָעוֹלָם הַמּוֹצִיא לֶחֶם מִן הָאָרֶץ:

Blessed be You, O *God* our God, King of the Universe, Who causes bread to grow forth from the earth.

המוציא: We have already noted above that the term *lechem*, "bread," as understood here, includes only that which is prepared from the following five species of grain; wheat, barley, spelt, oats and rye. The washing of the

Before partaking of any food other than bread that is prepared from the five species of grain:

בָּרוּךְ אַתָּה יְיָ, אֱלֹהֵינוּ מֶלֶךְ הָעוֹלָם, בּוֹרֵא מִינֵי מְזוֹנוֹת:

Before drinking wine:

בָּרוּךְ אַתָּה יְיָ, אֱלֹהֵינוּ מֶלֶךְ הָעוֹלָם, בּוֹרֵא פְּרִי הַגָּפֶן:

After partaking of any food. other than bread, prepared from the five species of grain, after drinking wine, or after eating grapes, figs. pomegranates, olives or dates:

בָּרוּךְ אַתָּה יְיָ, אֱלֹהֵינוּ מֶלֶךְ הָעוֹלָם, עַל

After wine together with foods prepared from the above-named five species of grain:	*After one of the five kinds of fruit*	*After wine:*	*After foods prepared from the five species of grain:*
הַמִּחְיָה וְעַל	הָעֵץ וְעַל	הַמִּחְיָה וְעַל הַכַּלְכָּלָה	
הַכַּלְכָּלָה	פְּרִי הָעֵץ	עַל הַגֶּפֶן וְעַל פְּרִי הַגֶּפֶן	הַגֶּפֶן וְעַל פְּרִי הַגֶּפֶן

עַל תְּנוּבַת הַשָּׂדֶה וְעַל אֶרֶץ חֶמְדָּה טוֹבָה וּרְחָבָה שֶׁרָצִיתָ
וְהִנְחַלְתָּ לַאֲבוֹתֵינוּ לֶאֱכֹל מִפִּרְיָהּ וְלִשְׂבֹּעַ מִטּוּבָהּ ∙ רַחֵם יְיָ אֱלֹהֵינוּ
וְעַל יִשְׂרָאֵל עַמֶּךָ וְעַל יְרוּשָׁלַיִם עִירֶךָ וְעַל צִיּוֹן מִשְׁכַּן כְּבוֹדֶךָ

---

hands, נטילת ידים, (literally "the lifting up of the hands" see p. 6 which is performed before we eat bread, has some connection with the ceremonial washing of the hands prescribed for the Priests in the Temple before they partook of their *terumah*, מפני סרך תרומה,-Chulin 106a) and also with the commandment והתקדשתם, "sanctify yourselves" (Lev. 11 : 44, Berachoth 53b). Thus, quite in keeping with the literal meaning of *netilath*, it is a priestly consecration of the hand, signifying the elevation of the physical enjoyment of food to the character of a moral act, and a sanctification of the bodily life that was preserved and strengthened by the physical enjoyment.

בורא מיני מזונות : All foods which are prepared from the five species of grain, including those which do not come under the classification of "bread," are regarded as *mazon*, as "nourishing food" (זון).

בורא פרי הגפן : On partaking of any other fruit or even of the grape in its natural state, we recite the blessing בורא פרי העץ : But the drinking of wine, the noblest produce of all the trees, המשמח אלקים ואנשים, is accompanied by a distinct blessing of its own. Wine is considered the sole true "fruit of the vine" for the extraction of which the vine was planted. We have already noted above that we have been commanded, (Deut. 8 : 10) to recite a *berachah*

*Before partaking of any food other than bread that is prepared from
the five species of grain:*

Blessed be You, O *God* our God, King of the Universe, Who
creates various kinds of food.

Before drinking wine:

Blessed be You, O *God* our God, King of the Universe, Who
creates the fruit of the vine.

*After partaking of any food, other than bread, prepared from the
five species of grain, after drinking wine, or after eating grapes, figs,
pomegranates, olives or dates:*

Blessed be You, O *God* our God, King of the Universe, for the

After foods prepared from the five species of grain:

sustenance and the nourishment;

After wine:

the vine and the fruit of the vine;

After one of the five kinds of fruit mentioned above:

the tree and the fruit of the tree;

*After having partaken of wine together with any foods (other than
bread) prepared from the above-named five species of grain:*

the sustenance and the nourishment, for the vine and the fruit
of the vine;

for the produce of the field and for the desirable, good and spacious
land which You have given to our fathers as an inheritance in favor,
that they might eat of its fruit and be satisfied with its goodness.
Have compassion, O *God* our God, upon Your people Yisrael, upon
Yerushalayim, Your City and upon Tzion, the Abode of Your glory,

---

after eating, thus vowing to God that we will dedicate all of our lives to
His service. It is not quite certain whether this Biblical commandment is
applicable only to the eating of bread as mentioned in Verse 9, immediately
preceding the precept (this would correspond to our present-day *Birkat
Hamazon*) or whether the reciting of such a *berachah* upon partaking of any
of the seven species of fruit named in Verse 8 of the Biblical injuction is
also a commandment directly ordained by the Torah. It is most commonly
assumed that only the *Birkat Hamazon* to be recited after the eating of bread
is actually a Torah commandment, and that the reciting of a blessing also
after the eating of the seven kinds of fruit enumerated in Verse 8 was an
ordinance derived by the Sages from the Biblical commandment. This blessing

וְעַל מִזְבַּחֶךָ וְעַל הֵיכָלֶךָ וּבְנֵה יְרוּשָׁלַיִם עִיר הַקֹּדֶשׁ בִּמְהֵרָה

בְיָמֵינוּ וְהַעֲלֵנוּ לְתוֹכָהּ וְשַׂמְּחֵנוּ בְּבִנְיָנָהּ, וְנֹאכַל מִפִּרְיָהּ וְנִשְׂבַּע

מִטּוּבָהּ וּנְבָרֶכְךָ עָלֶיהָ בִּקְדֻשָּׁה וּבְטָהֳרָה:

בשבת   וּרְצֵה וְהַחֲלִיצֵנוּ בְּיוֹם הַשַּׁבָּת הַזֶּה:

בר"ח   וְזָכְרֵנוּ לְטוֹבָה בְּיוֹם רֹאשׁ הַחֹדֶשׁ הַזֶּה:

ביו"ט   וְשַׂמְּחֵנוּ בְּיוֹם חַג (פלוני) הַזֶּה:

בר"ה   וְזָכְרֵנוּ לְטוֹבָה בְּיוֹם הַזִּכָּרוֹן הַזֶּה:

כִּי־אַתָּה יְיָ טוֹב וּמֵטִיב לַכֹּל, וְנוֹדֶה לְךָ עַל הָאָרֶץ

וְעַל הַמִּחְיָה וְעַל	וְעַל הַפֵּרוֹת ·	וְעַל פְּרִי הַגָּפֶן ·	וְעַל הַמִּחְיָה ·
פְּרִי הַגֶּפֶן כָּא"י, עַל	בָּרוּךְ אַתָּה	בָּרוּךְ אַתָּה יְיָ,	בָּרוּךְ אַתָּה
הָאָרֶץ וְעַל הַמִּחְיָה	יְיָ, עַל הָאָרֶץ	יְיָ, עַל וְעַל הָאָרֶץ	יְיָ, עַל הָאָרֶץ וְעַל
וְעַל פְּרִי הַגֶּפֶן:	וְעַל הַפֵּרוֹת:	פְּרִי הַגָּפֶן:	הַמִּחְיָה:

On eating fruit of the trees: על פרי העץ

בָּרוּךְ אַתָּה יְיָ, אֱלֹהֵינוּ מֶלֶךְ הָעוֹלָם, בּוֹרֵא פְּרִי הָעֵץ:

On eating fruit of the ground: על פרי האדמה

בָּרוּךְ אַתָּה יְיָ, אֱלֹהֵינוּ מֶלֶךְ הָעוֹלָם, בּוֹרֵא פְּרִי הָאֲדָמָה:

על המחיה ועל הכלכלה etc. is an abridged version of the *Birkat Hamazon* and is therefore referred to as ברכה אחת מעין שלש, one single blessing summarizing the contents of all the three *berachoth* of the *Birkat Hamazon*. Thus על המחיה ועל הכלכלה in the abridged version would correspond to the ברכת הזן in the regular רחם ה' אלקינו to the ועל ארץ חמדה טובה; ברכת המזון to the ברכת הארץ; and הטוב והמטיב which was added to the *Birkat Hamazon* much later, is parallelled in the abridged version by the phrase על העץ ועל פרי העץ, על הגפן ועל פרי הגפן. We give thanks כי אתה ה' טוב ומטיב to God not only "for the vine" but also *"for the fruit* of the vine"; not only for the tree but also *for the fruit* of the tree. It would seem that this wording for the blessings expresses a profound thought; namely, that, once the tree

upon Your altar and upon Your Temple, and rebuild Yerushalayim, the City of Your Sanctuary, speedily in our days; lead us up there and make us rejoice in its rebuilding. May we eat of its fruit and be satisfied with its goodness so that we may bless You for it in holiness and purity.

On Sabbath add: And be pleased to fortify us on this Sabbath Day,
On Rosh Chodesh, add: And remember us for good on this New Moon day,
On Festivals, add: And gladden us on this ——————— Day,
On Rosh Hashanah, add: And remember us for good on this Day of Remembrance,

for You O *God*, are good and do good to all. To You we give thanks for the land,

After foods prepared from the five species of grain:
and for the sustenance. Blessed be You, O *God*, for the land and for the sustenance.

After wine:
and for the fruit of the vine. Blessed be You, O *God*, for the land and for the fruit of the vine.

After one of the five kinds of fruit mentioned above:
and for the fruits. Blessed be You, O *God*, for the land and for the fruits.

After having partaken of wine together with any foods (other than bread) prepared from the above-named five species of grain:
and for the sustenance and the fruit of the vine. Blessed be You, O *God*, for the land, for the sustenance and for the fruit of the vine.

On eating fruit of the trees:

Blessed be You, O *God* our God, King of the Universe, Who has created the fruit of the tree.

On eating fruit of the ground:

Blessed be You, O *God* our God, King of the Universe, Who has created the fruit of the earth.

---

has yielded its fruit, we must not look upon the fruit as a natural and inevitable outgrowth of the strength given the tree at its creation, but as a second gift of God, separate from the tree, an additional manifestation of

On partaking of any other food:

בָּרוּךְ אַתָּה יְיָ, אֱלֹהֵינוּ מֶלֶךְ הָעוֹלָם שֶׁהַכֹּל נִהְיֶה בִּדְבָרוֹ:

After eating any foods other than those prepared from the above-named five species of grain, after any fruit growing on trees (other than the five fruits mentioned above), after any herbs or vegetables, and after any beverage excepting wine:

בָּא"י, אֱ"מֶ"ה, בּוֹרֵא נְפָשׁוֹת רַבּוֹת וְחֶסְרוֹנָן עַל כָּל־מַה־שֶּׁבָּרָאתָ לְהַחֲיוֹת (בָּהֶם) נֶפֶשׁ כָּל־חָי, בָּרוּךְ חֵי הָעוֹלָמִים:

Blessings to be recited on smelling various fragrances: ברכות הריח

On smelling fragrant woods or barks: על ריח עץ בושם

בָּרוּךְ אַתָּה יְיָ, אֱלֹהֵינוּ מֶלֶךְ הָעוֹלָם, בּוֹרֵא עֲצֵי בְשָׂמִים:

On smelling fragrant herbs or plants: על ריח עשב ריח

בָּרוּךְ אַתָּה יְיָ, אֱלֹהֵינוּ מֶלֶךְ הָעוֹלָם, בּוֹרֵא עִשְׂבוֹת בְשָׂמִים:

On smelling fragrant fruit: על ריח פרי טוב

בָּרוּךְ אַתָּה יְיָ, אֱלֹהֵינוּ מֶלֶךְ הָעוֹלָם, הַנּוֹתֵן רֵיחַ טוֹב בַּפֵּרוֹת:

On smelling fragrant oils: על שמן אפרסמון

בָּרוּךְ אַתָּה יְיָ, אֱלֹהֵינוּ מֶלֶךְ הָעוֹלָם, בּוֹרֵא שֶׁמֶן עָרֵב:

On smelling any other fragrance: על ריח בשמים

בָּרוּךְ אַתָּה יְיָ, אֱלֹהֵינוּ מֶלֶךְ הָעוֹלָם, בּוֹרֵא מִינֵי בְשָׂמִים:

ברכות הראיה והשמיעה

On seeing lightning. shooting stars, sheet-lightning, great deserts or high mountains, or on witnessing a sunrise:

הרואה ברקים וכוכבים המעופפים ומדבריות גדולים וכן הרואה החמה בראש מחזור הגדול בתקופת ניסן בל' בבוקר מברך:

בָּרוּךְ אַתָּה יְיָ, אֱלֹהֵינוּ מֶלֶךְ הָעוֹלָם, עֹשֶׂה מַעֲשֵׂה בְרֵאשִׁית:

His almighty rule. For the tree could grow but never bring forth blossoms; or the tree could blossom but never bear fruit, and therefore we must thank God not only for having created the tree, but also for having made it possible for us to enjoy its fruit.

חֵי הָעוֹלָמִים: God is the Prime Source of all life and the One living Being that endures through all the ages. Every spark of life that glows within any living thing in this Universe is derived directly from Him. And even as He was the One Who called all living things into being, so He is also the One Who has provided them with all they need in order to go on living.

On partaking of any other food:

Blessed be You, O *God* our God, King of the Universe, by whose word all things come into being.

After eating any foods other than those prepared from the above-named five species of grain, after any fruit growing on trees (other than the five fruits mentioned above), after any herbs or vegetables, and after any beverage excepting wine:

Blessed be You, O *God* our God, King of the Universe, Who has created many things and their needs. For all the things that You have created, to sustain the souls of all living things, be blessed, O You, the Living Force of all Times.

Blessings to be recited on smelling various fragrances:

On smelling fragrant woods or barks:

Blesse l be You, O *God* our God, King of the Universe, Who has created fragrant woods.

On smelling fragrant herbs or plants:

Blessed be You, O *God* our God, King of the Universe, Who has created fragrant herbs.

On smelling fragrant fruit:

Blessed be You, O *God* our God, King of the Universe, Who has given a pleasant scent to fruits.

On smelling fragrant oils:

Blessed be You, O *God* our God, King of the Universe, Who has created fragrant oil.

On smelling any other fragrance:

Blessed be You, O *God* our God, King of the Universe, Who has created various kinds of spices.

Blessings to be recited on witnessing natural phenomena or unusual sights, and on various occasions and events:

On seeing lightning. shooting stars, sheet-lightning, great deserts or high mountains, or on witnessing a sunrise:

Blessed be You, O *God* our God, King of the Universe, Who created the work of the Beginning.

ברכות הראיה והשמיעה

No other institution reveals the greatness of our Sages as the fathers, teachers and disciplinarians of their people through the ages down to the

On hearing thunder, or upon witnessing a storm or earth-quake:

בָּרוּךְ אַתָּה יְיָ, אֱלֹהֵינוּ מֶלֶךְ הָעוֹלָם, שֶׁכֹּחוֹ וּגְבוּרָתוֹ מָלֵא עוֹלָם:

On seeing a rainbow: הרואה הקשת בענן:

בָּא"יְ, אֱמֶ"הָ, זוֹכֵר הַבְּרִית וְנֶאֱמָן בִּבְרִיתוֹ וְקַיָּם בְּמַאֲמָרוֹ:

On seeing trees blooming   הרואה אילנות בעת פריחת
for the first time in the year: כלנס מכרך נראה הראשונה:

בָּרוּךְ אַתָּה יְיָ, אֱמֶ"הָ, שֶׁלֹּא חִסַּר בְּעוֹלָמוֹ דָבָר וּבָרָא בוֹ בְּרִיּוֹת
טוֹבוֹת וְאִילָנוֹת טוֹבִים לְהַנּוֹת בָּהֶם בְּנֵי אָדָם:

On seeing the ocean: הרואה ים האוקינוס:

בָּרוּךְ אַתָּה יְיָ, אֱלֹהֵינוּ מֶלֶךְ הָעוֹלָם, שֶׁעָשָׂה אֶת־הַיָּם הַגָּדוֹל:

On seeing trees or   הרואה אילנות טובים
creatures of unusual beauty: ובריות כאות מנרך:

בָּרוּךְ אַתָּה יְיָ, אֱלֹהֵינוּ מֶלֶךְ הָעוֹלָם, שֶׁכָּכָה לוֹ בְּעוֹלָמוֹ:

On seeing a person of abnormal appearance: הרואה אדם משונה:

בָּרוּךְ אַתָּה יְיָ, אֱלֹהֵינוּ מֶלֶךְ הָעוֹלָם, מְשַׁנֶּה הַבְּרִיּוֹת:

*On taking possession of a new home. on acquiring new clothing or
household effects, or on tasting any fruit for the first time in the
season:*

בָּא"יְ, אֱלֹהֵינוּ מֶלֶךְ הָעוֹלָם, שֶׁהֶחֱיָנוּ וְקִיְּמָנוּ וְהִגִּיעָנוּ לַזְּמַן הַזֶּה:

On putting on a new garment: הלובש מלבוש חדש:

בָּרוּךְ אַתָּה יְיָ, אֱלֹהֵינוּ מֶלֶךְ הָעוֹלָם, מַלְבִּישׁ עֲרֻמִּים:

On hearing good news affecting, the recipient only:

בָּא"יְ, אֱלֹהֵינוּ מֶלֶךְ הָעוֹלָם, שֶׁהֶחֱיָנוּ וְקִיְּמָנוּ וְהִגִּיעָנוּ לַזְּמַן הַזֶּה:

---

present day so clearly as does the institution of these *berachoth*. It is these
berachoth that have trained the Jew not to meander through the world un-
thinkingly and unfeelingly. Hence he does not need secluded recesses in houses
of worship to remove him from crude materialism and to elevate him to a
higher plane; rather, the *berachoth* have taught the Jew to view the entire
physical and material world with all of its change and its infinite variety of
events and phenomena, as a Temple in which to glorify his God and as a
lectern from which he hears his duty and calling taught and expounded. Thus
even as the Jew deals with the affairs of this world, he communes with his
God. He perceives the voice of God not only in the bread and the food which
preserve and enhance his physical life, but also in all the bright and shining

On hearing thunder, or upon witnessing a storm or earth-quake:

Blessed be You, O *God* our God, King of the Universe, Whose strength and might fill the world.

On seeing a rainbow:

Blessed be You, O *God* our God, King of the Universe, Who remembers the covenant and Who is faithful to His covenant and keeps His promise.

On seeing trees blooming for the first time in the year:

Blessed be You, O *God* our God, King of the Universe, Who has withheld nothing from His world and has created beautiful creatures and beautiful trees in it, so that men may delight in them.

On seeing the ocean:

Blessed be You, O *God* our God, King of the Universe, Who has made the great sea.

On seeing trees or creatures of unusual beauty:

Blessed be You, O *God* our God, King of the Universe, Who has such as these in Your world.

On seeing a person of abnormal appearance:

Blessed be You, O *God* our God, King of the Universe, Who varies the appearance of men.

Blessings to be recited on various occasions:

On taking possession of a new home. on acquiring new clothing or household effects, or on tasting any fruit for the first time in the season:

Blessed be You, O *God* our God, King of the Universe, Who has kept us in life and sustained us and enabled us to reach this season.

On putting on a new garment:

Blessed be You, O *God* our God, King of the Universe, Who clothes the naked.

On hearing good news affecting the recipient only:

Blessed be You, O *God* our God, King of the Universe, Who has kept us in life, and sustained us and enabled us to reach this season.

---

meteors of Heaven and earth, in every great masterpiece of Creation that overawes his spirit, in every new blossom that heralds to him the return of spring, and in every form of great beauty or bizarre grotesqueness at which

On hearing good news that concern
others in addition to the recipient: עַל שְׁמוּעוֹת טוֹבוֹת לוֹ וְלַאֲחֵרִים:

בָּרוּךְ אַתָּה יְיָ, אֱלֹהֵינוּ מֶלֶךְ הָעוֹלָם, הַטּוֹב וְהַמֵּטִיב:

On hearing sad news: עַל שְׁמוּעוֹת רָעוֹת:

בָּרוּךְ אַתָּה יְיָ, אֱלֹהֵינוּ מֶלֶךְ הָעוֹלָם, דַּיַּן הָאֱמֶת:

On seeing a friend for the first time הָרוֹאֶה אֶת חֲבֵרוֹ שֶׁנִּתְרַפֵּא מֵחָלְיוֹ:
after his recovery from serious

בָּרוּךְ רַחֲמָנָא מַלְכָּא דְּעָלְמָא דִּי יַהֲבָךְ לָן וְלֹא יַהֲבָךְ לְעַפְרָא:

On seeing a friend after a separation הָרוֹאֶה אֶת חֲבֵרוֹ הֶחָבִיב
of a year or more: לוֹ אַחַר י"ב חֳדָשִׁים:

בָּרוּךְ אַתָּה יְיָ, אֱלֹהֵינוּ מֶלֶךְ הָעוֹלָם, מְחַיֵּה מֵתִים:

On seeing a sage distinguished for his knowledge of the Torah:

בָּרוּךְ אַתָּה יְיָ, אֱלֹהֵינוּ מֶלֶךְ הָעוֹלָם שֶׁחָלַק מֵחָכְמָתוֹ לִירֵאָיו:

On seeing a learned non-Jew: הָרוֹאֶה חָכָם בְּחָכְמַת הָעוֹלָם:

בָּרוּךְ אַתָּה יְיָ, אֱלֹהֵינוּ מֶלֶךְ הָעוֹלָם, שֶׁנָּתַן מֵחָכְמָתוֹ לְבָשָׂר וָדָם:

On seeing a ruler and his court: הָרוֹאֶה מֶלֶךְ
עִם חֵילָיו:

בָּרוּךְ אַתָּה יְיָ, אֱלֹהֵינוּ מֶלֶךְ הָעוֹלָם, שֶׁנָּתַן מִכְּבוֹדוֹ לְבָשָׂר וָדָם:

On seeing synagogues that have הָרוֹאֶה בָּתֵּי כְנֵסִיּוֹת שֶׁנִּתְיַשְּׁבוּ
been rebuilt: מֵחָרְבָּנָן יֹאמַר:

בָּרוּךְ אַתָּה יְיָ, אֱלֹהֵינוּ מֶלֶךְ הָעוֹלָם, מַצִּיב גְּבוּל אַלְמָנָה:

On returning to a place where one has experienced הָרוֹאֶה מָקוֹם שֶׁנַּ
a miraculous rescue from great peril: נַעֲשָׂה לוֹ בּוֹ נֵס מְבָרֵךְ:

בָּא יְיָ, אֱלֹהֵינוּ מֶלֶךְ הָעוֹלָם, שֶׁעָשָׂה לִי נֵס בַּמָּקוֹם הַזֶּה:

On affixing a Mezuzah to a doorpost: הַקּוֹבֵעַ מְזוּזָה מְבָרֵךְ:

בָּא"יָ, אֱ"מֶ"הָ, אֲשֶׁר קִדְּשָׁנוּ בְּמִצְוֹתָיו וְצִוָּנוּ לִקְבּוֹעַ מְזוּזָה:

On erecting a railing or other protective barrier around a well, a flat
roof or other dangerous place:

בָּא"יָ, אֱ"מֶ הָעוֹלָם, אֲשֶׁר קִדְּשָׁנוּ בְּמִצְוֹתָיו וְצִוָּנוּ לַעֲשׂוֹת מַעֲקֶה:

---

he gazes in amazement. All these phenomena of nature reveal to the Jew the power, wisdom and goodness of the Creator Who rules and maintains all living things even to this very day, and they remind him to live for his duty in God's world as a child and servant of God, even as he has pledged to do by reciting the appropriate blessings, of which each begins with the same high resolve: בָּרוּךְ אַתָּה ה' וכו'.

On hearing good news that concern others in addition to the recipient:

Blessed be You, O *God* our God, King of the Universe, Who is good and does good.

On hearing sad news:

Blessed be You, O *God* our God, King of the Universe, the true Judge.

On seeing a friend for the first time after his recovery from serious illness:

Blessed be the Compassionate King of the world Who restored you to us and did not deliver you up to the dust.

On seeing a friend after a separation of a year or more:

Blessed be You, O *God* our God, King of the Universe, Who revives the dead.

On seeing a sage distinguished for his knowledge of the Torah:

Blessed be You, O *God* our God, King of the Universe, Who has imparted of His wisdom to those that fear Him.

On seeing a learned non-Jew; or any person of profound secular learning:

Blessed be You, O *God* our God, King of the Universe, Who has given of His wisdom to flesh and blood.

On seeing a ruler and his court:

Blessed be You, O *God* our God, King of the Universe, Who has given of His glory to flesh and blood.

On seeing synagogues that have been rebuilt:

Blessed be You, O *God* our God, King of the Universe, Who restores the borders of the widow [of Tzion].

On returning to a place where one has experienced a miraculous rescue from great peril:

Blessed be You, O *God* our God, King of the Universe, Who performed a miracle for me at this place.

On affixing a Mezuzah to a doorpost:

Blessed be You, O *God* our God, King of the Universe, Who has sanctified us by His commandments and commanded us to affix a *Mezuzah.*

On erecting a railing or other protective barrier around a well, a flat roof or other dangerous place:

Blessed be You, O *God* our God, King of the Universe, Who

has sanctified us by His commandments and commanded us to erect a protective barrier.

Before redeeming one's vineyard in the fourth year: הפודה כרם רבעי שלו מברך:

בָּא"י, אֱ"מֶ"הָ, אֲשֶׁר קִדְּשָׁנוּ בְּמִצְוֹתָיו וְצִוָּנוּ עַל־פִּדְיוֹן כֶּרֶם רְבָעִי:

Blessed be You, O *God* our God, King of the Universe, Who has sanctified us by His commandments and commanded us concerning the redemption of the produce of the vineyard in the fourth year.

Before the טבילה *of glass or metal dishes:*　　　כלים של זכוכית או של
מתכת כשטובילם יברך:

בָּרוּךְ אַתָּה יְיָ, אֱלֹהֵינוּ מֶלֶךְ הָעוֹלָם, אֲשֶׁר קִדְּשָׁנוּ בְּמִצְוֹתָיו וְצִוָּנוּ עַל־טְבִילַת כֶּלִי (ואם הם רבים יאמר כֵּלִים):

Blessed be You, O *God* our God, King of the Universe, Who has sanctified us by His commandments and commanded us concerning the immersion of kitchen utensils.

Before the kneading of a dough containing app. three pounds of flour with water and before the taking of חלה *the following Bracha is said (after which the* חלה *is burned):*

בָּרוּךְ אַתָּה יְיָ אֱלֹהֵינוּ מֶלֶךְ הָעוֹלָם אֲשֶׁר קִדְּשָׁנוּ בְּמִצְוֹתָיו וְצִוָּנוּ לְהַפְרִישׁ חַלָּה מִן־הָעִסָּה:

Blessed be You, O *God* our God, King of the Universe, Who has sanctified us by His commandments and commanded us to separate the *challah* from the dough.

More keenly still do we perceive the hand of God in every aspect of life in this terrestrial world when we are faced with the variety of events, both joyous and sad, that are part of human living, when life makes us aware of *hashgachah peratith* the love and righteousness of God's rule in which He ordains the destinies of every individual. The events and happenings, joyous and sad that affect us or those close to us, the high position that certain individuals occupy in the society of man and the talents of mind and spirit that elevate gifted mortals above their brethren, all make us aware of the wisdom and insight with which God distributes His gifts among men. We are thus summoned solemnly to resolve in turn to employ our own fate and our own station in life with all that life has given us as well as with what we have been denied, for the discharge of our life's task, in the unshakeable certainty that granting and denying, giving as well as taking are all ways of the same hand of God, loving and disciplining, all for the same purpose; namely, to guide us on to the one lofty goal of our destiny, the nearness of His Presence in this life. By reciting ברוך אתה ה' וכו', we renew

תְּפִלַּת הַדֶּרֶךְ

Before undertaking a trip, the following is said (no more than once a day):

יְהִי רָצוֹן מִלְּפָנֶיךָ יְיָ אֱלֹהֵינוּ שֶׁתּוֹלִיכֵנוּ לְשָׁלוֹם וְתַצְעִידֵנוּ לְשָׁלוֹם וְתִסְמְכֵנוּ וְתַנְחֵנוּ אֶל מְחוֹז חֶפְצֵנוּ לְחַיִּים וּלְשִׂמְחָה וּלְשָׁלוֹם (וְתַחֲזִירֵנוּ לְבֵיתֵנוּ לְשָׁלוֹם) · וְתַצִּילֵנוּ מִכַּף כָּל־אוֹיֵב וְאוֹרֵב בַּדֶּרֶךְ וּמִכָּל־מִינֵי פֻּרְעָנִיּוֹת הַמִּתְרַגְּשׁוֹת לָבוֹא לָעוֹלָם · וְתִשְׁלַח בְּרָכָה בְּמַעֲשֵׂה יָדֵינוּ וְתִתְּנֵנוּ לְחֵן וּלְחֶסֶד וּלְרַחֲמִים בְּעֵינֶיךָ וּבְעֵינֵי כָל־רוֹאֵינוּ · וְתִשְׁמַע קוֹל תַּחֲנוּנֵינוּ כִּי אֵל שׁוֹמֵעַ תְּפִלָּה וְתַחֲנוּן אָתָּה · בָּרוּךְ אַתָּה יְיָ שׁוֹמֵעַ תְּפִלָּה:

וְאוֹמֵר ג׳פ׳ וְיַעֲקֹב הָלַךְ לְדַרְכּוֹ וַיִּפְגְּעוּ בוֹ מַלְאֲכֵי אֱלֹהִים: וַיֹּאמֶר יַעֲקֹב כַּאֲשֶׁר
***
רָאָם מַחֲנֵה אֱלֹהִים זֶה וַיִּקְרָא שֵׁם הַמָּקוֹם הַהוּא מַחֲנָיִם:

לִישׁוּעָתְךָ קִוִּיתִי יְיָ: קִוִּיתִי יְיָ לִישׁוּעָתְךָ· יְיָ לִישׁוּעָתְךָ קִוִּיתִי:

---

our solemn pledge to follow both in joy and in affliction, in unchanging constancy, His Presence, the awareness of which is a source of ever growing bliss.

הטוב והמטיב is said only on the occasion of an event that brings happiness to others in addition to ourselves. When the happy event affects only the individual himself he recites שהחיינו. This is a thought of profound significance. He whose emotions have not been ennobled by the spirit of the teachings of Judaism, regards his happiness as doubly great if he is the only one who has cause to rejoice in it. But he who is possessed of a truly Jewish heart and a Jewish spirit finds genuine joy in his happiness and gives thanks to God as the Beneficent One Who is good and does good, only if others, too, have cause to rejoice in the happiness with which God has blessed him.

שחלק מחכמתו ליראיו : The *chochmah* of the *yirei Hashem* consists in the knowledge and fulfillment of the Torah. And the Torah, in turn, is part of the *chochmath Hashem,* the wisdom of Him Who has set down in it the truths and ordinances of His own wisdom which man is to fulfill in both practice and spirit.

בָּרוּךְ אַתָּה יְיָ אֱלֹהֵינוּ מֶלֶךְ הָעוֹלָם הַמַּפִּיל חֶבְלֵי
שֵׁנָה עַל־עֵינַי וּתְנוּמָה עַל־עַפְעַפָּי: וִיהִי רָצוֹן מִלְּפָנֶיךָ
יְיָ אֱלֹהַי וֵאלֹהֵי אֲבוֹתַי שֶׁתַּשְׁכִּיבֵנִי לְשָׁלוֹם וְתַעֲמִידֵנִי
לְשָׁלוֹם וְאַל יְבַהֲלוּנִי רַעְיוֹנַי וַחֲלוֹמוֹת רָעִים וְהִרְהוּרִים
רָעִים וּתְהִי מִטָּתִי שְׁלֵמָה לְפָנֶיךָ וְהָאֵר עֵינַי פֶּן־אִישַׁן
הַמָּוֶת כִּי אַתָּה הַמֵּאִיר לְאִישׁוֹן בַּת־עָיִן. בָּרוּךְ אַתָּה
יְיָ, הַמֵּאִיר לְעוֹלָם כֻּלּוֹ בִּכְבוֹדוֹ:

אל מלך נאמן.

דברים ו'

שְׁמַע יִשְׂרָאֵל יְהֹוָה אֱלֹהֵינוּ יְהֹוָה ׀ אֶחָד:
בלחש בָּרוּךְ שֵׁם כְּבוֹד מַלְכוּתוֹ לְעוֹלָם וָעֶד:
וְאָהַבְתָּ אֵת יְהֹוָה אֱלֹהֶיךָ בְּכָל־לְבָבְךָ וּבְכָל־נַפְשְׁךָ
וּבְכָל־מְאֹדֶךָ: וְהָיוּ הַדְּבָרִים הָאֵלֶּה אֲשֶׁר אָנֹכִי מְצַוְּךָ
הַיּוֹם עַל־לְבָבֶךָ: וְשִׁנַּנְתָּם לְבָנֶיךָ וְדִבַּרְתָּ בָּם בְּשִׁבְתְּךָ
בְּבֵיתֶךָ וּבְלֶכְתְּךָ בַדֶּרֶךְ וּבְשָׁכְבְּךָ וּבְקוּמֶךָ: וּקְשַׁרְתָּם
לְאוֹת עַל־יָדֶךָ וְהָיוּ לְטֹטָפֹת בֵּין עֵינֶיךָ:
וּכְתַבְתָּם עַל־מְזֻזוֹת בֵּיתֶךָ וּבִשְׁעָרֶיךָ:

וִיהִי ׀ נֹעַם אֲדֹנָי אֱלֹהֵינוּ עָלֵינוּ וּמַעֲשֵׂה
יָדֵינוּ כּוֹנְנָה עָלֵינוּ וּמַעֲשֵׂה יָדֵינוּ כּוֹנְנֵהוּ:

יֹשֵׁב בְּסֵתֶר עֶלְיוֹן בְּצֵל שַׁדַּי יִתְלוֹנָן: אֹמַר לַיָי מַחְסִי וּמְצוּדָתִי
אֱלֹהַי אֶבְטַח־בּוֹ: כִּי הוּא יַצִּילְךָ מִפַּח יָקוּשׁ מִדֶּבֶר הַוּוֹת: בְּאֶבְרָתוֹ

יָסֶךְ לָךְ וְתַחַת כְּנָפָיו תֶּחְסֶה צִנָּה וְסֹחֵרָה אֲמִתּוֹ: לֹא־תִירָא
מִפַּחַד לָיְלָה מֵחֵץ יָעוּף יוֹמָם: מִדֶּבֶר בָּאֹפֶל יַהֲלֹךְ מִקֶּטֶב יָשׁוּד
צָהֳרָיִם: יִפֹּל מִצִּדְּךָ ׀ אֶלֶף וּרְבָבָה מִימִינֶךָ אֵלֶיךָ לֹא יִגָּשׁ: רַק
בְּעֵינֶיךָ תַבִּיט וְשִׁלֻּמַת רְשָׁעִים תִּרְאֶה: כִּי־אַתָּה יְיָ מַחְסִי עֶלְיוֹן
שַׂמְתָּ מְעוֹנֶךָ: לֹא־תְאֻנֶּה אֵלֶיךָ רָעָה וְנֶגַע לֹא־יִקְרַב בְּאָהֳלֶךָ: כִּי
מַלְאָכָיו יְצַוֶּה־לָּךְ לִשְׁמָרְךָ בְּכָל־דְּרָכֶיךָ: עַל־כַּפַּיִם יִשָּׂאוּנְךָ פֶּן
תִּגֹּף בָּאֶבֶן רַגְלֶךָ: עַל־שַׁחַל וָפֶתֶן תִּדְרֹךְ תִּרְמֹס כְּפִיר וְתַנִּין: כִּי
בִי חָשַׁק וַאֲפַלְּטֵהוּ אֲשַׂגְּבֵהוּ כִּי־יָדַע שְׁמִי: יִקְרָאֵנִי וְאֶעֱנֵהוּ עִמּוֹ
אָנֹכִי בְצָרָה אֲחַלְּצֵהוּ וַאֲכַבְּדֵהוּ: אֹרֶךְ יָמִים אַשְׂבִּיעֵהוּ וְאַרְאֵהוּ
בִּישׁוּעָתִי: ארך ימים וגו׳.

כרוך ·Blessed be You, O *God* our God, King of the Universe, Who
makes the bands of sleep to fall upon my eyes and slumber upon
my eyelashes. May it be Your will, O *God* my God and God of my
fathers, to grant that I lie down in peace and that I may rise again
in peace, and let not my thoughts frighten me, nor evil dreams, nor
evil fancies, but let my bed be undisturbed before You, and grant
light to my eyes, lest I sleep the sleep of death. For it is You Who
grants light to the dark of the eyelid. Blessed be You, O *God*, Who
grants light to the whole world in His glory.

שתשכיבני לשלום : is "to lie down in peace," reconciled with all that with which
we had to contend during the day that has passed, and untroubled by anything that could disturb our sleep. ותעמידני לשלום "to rise up in peace;" that
is, may we not take any of the unkind thoughts and moods of the past into
the new life upon which we will enter when we awaken the next morning,
and may we rise on the next day unencumbered by those influences that would
be inimical to our life and endeavors during our waking hours on the day to
come. God, Who calls us to sleep and summons us to awaken, has it within
His power also to grant us peace in and for both sleeping and waking. רעיוני
"Our" thoughts, which we entertained and formulated during our waking
hours give rise to the dreams and imaginings of our sleep. אישון is "the dark,"
as in אישון לילה (Prov. 7:9), בת עין, as in בבת עין, is the "portal of the eye,"
i.e. "the eyelid."

יְיָ מָה־רַבּוּ צָרָי רַבִּים קָמִים עָלָי: רַבִּים אוֹמְרִים לְנַפְשִׁי אֵין
יְשׁוּעָתָה לּוֹ בֵאלֹהִים סֶלָה: וְאַתָּה יְיָ מָגֵן בַּעֲדִי כְּבוֹדִי וּמֵרִים
רֹאשִׁי: קוֹלִי אֶל־יְיָ אֶקְרָא וַיַּעֲנֵנִי מֵהַר קָדְשׁוֹ סֶלָה: אֲנִי שָׁכַבְתִּי
וָאִישָׁנָה הֱקִיצוֹתִי כִּי יְיָ יִסְמְכֵנִי: לֹא־אִירָא מֵרִבְבוֹת עָם אֲשֶׁר
סָבִיב שָׁתוּ עָלָי: קוּמָה יְיָ הוֹשִׁיעֵנִי אֱלֹהַי כִּי הִכִּיתָ אֶת־כָּל־אֹיְבַי
לֶחִי שִׁנֵּי רְשָׁעִים שִׁבַּרְתָּ: לַיְיָ הַיְשׁוּעָה עַל־עַמְּךָ בִרְכָתֶךָ סֶּלָה:

הַשְׁכִּיבֵנוּ יְיָ אֱלֹהֵינוּ לְשָׁלוֹם וְהַעֲמִידֵנוּ מַלְכֵּנוּ לְחַיִּים וּפְרוֹשׂ
עָלֵינוּ סֻכַּת שְׁלוֹמֶךָ וְתַקְּנֵנוּ בְּעֵצָה טוֹבָה מִלְּפָנֶיךָ וְהוֹשִׁיעֵנוּ
לְמַעַן שְׁמֶךָ וְהָגֵן בַּעֲדֵנוּ וְהָסֵר מֵעָלֵינוּ אוֹיֵב דֶּבֶר וְחֶרֶב וְרָעָב
וְיָגוֹן וְהָסֵר שָׂטָן מִלְּפָנֵינוּ וּמֵאַחֲרֵינוּ וּבְצֵל כְּנָפֶיךָ תַּסְתִּירֵנוּ כִּי אֵל
שׁוֹמְרֵנוּ וּמַצִּילֵנוּ אָתָּה כִּי אֵל מֶלֶךְ חַנּוּן וְרַחוּם אָתָּה וּשְׁמוֹר
צֵאתֵנוּ וּבוֹאֵנוּ לְחַיִּים וּלְשָׁלוֹם מֵעַתָּה וְעַד עוֹלָם:

בָּרוּךְ יְיָ בַּיּוֹם· בָּרוּךְ יְיָ בַּלָּיְלָה· בָּרוּךְ יְיָ בְּשָׁכְבֵנוּ· בָּרוּךְ יְיָ בְּקוּמֵנוּ
כִּי בְיָדְךָ נַפְשׁוֹת הַחַיִּים וְהַמֵּתִים אֲשֶׁר בְּיָדוֹ נֶפֶשׁ כָּל־חָי וְרוּחַ כָּל־
בְּשַׂר אִישׁ: בְּיָדְךָ· אַפְקִיד רוּחִי פָּדִיתָה אוֹתִי יְיָ אֵל אֱמֶת:
אֱלֹהֵינוּ שֶׁבַּשָּׁמַיִם יַחֵד שִׁמְךָ וְקַיֵּם מַלְכוּתְךָ תָּמִיד וּמְלוֹךְ עָלֵינוּ
לְעוֹלָם וָעֶד:

יִרְאוּ עֵינֵינוּ וְיִשְׂמַח לִבֵּנוּ וְתָגֵל נַפְשֵׁנוּ בִּישׁוּעָתְךָ בֶּאֱמֶת בֶּאֱמֹר
לְצִיּוֹן מָלַךְ אֱלֹהָיִךְ· יְיָ מֶלֶךְ· יְיָ מָלָךְ· יְיָ יִמְלֹךְ לְעוֹלָם וָעֶד: כִּי
הַמַּלְכוּת שֶׁלְּךָ הִיא וּלְעוֹלְמֵי עַד תִּמְלוֹךְ בְּכָבוֹד כִּי אֵין לָנוּ מֶלֶךְ
אֶלָּא אָתָּה:

הַמַּלְאָךְ הַגּוֹאֵל אֹתִי מִכָּל־רָע יְבָרֵךְ אֶת־הַנְּעָרִים וְיִקָּרֵא בָהֶם

O, how many are my oppressors; many are they who rise up against me; many are there that say of my soul: "There is no more help for him from God, the Judge!" But You remain *God*, a shield about me, yea, my glory, and even now You raise my head! When I weep, I call to *God*, and He has already heard me from the mountain of His Sanctuary! — I have lain down — and I slept — and I awoke, because *God* sustains me! Therefore I do not fear the tens of thousands who have set themselves against me round about. Arise, *God*, help me, my God, for You have struck all my foes upon the cheek; You have broken the teeth of the lawless. But help rests with *God*, Your blessing upon Your people!

השכבינו translation see p. 267.

יראו, ברוך see p. 539

The angel who redeemed me from all evil bless the lads so that my name and the names of my fathers, Abraham and Yitzchak, be

---

ה׳ מה רבו: (Ps. 3) This Psalm is most appropriate to save from despair him who is crushed by the burden of grievous guilt and suffering and to raise him up to new life and strength. Carried away by base passion, David, the King, has broken the moral law and destroyed the domestic felicity of one of his subjects. Now he must atone for his sin; he is compelled to flee from his own son who has deprived him of both his throne and his home. Rebellion and the reproach and judgment of his people deliver him up to hopeless despair. Yet, in the simple fact that he has lain down, slept and awakened once more, he finds the assurance that God has not forsaken him after all. Thus he joyously brings comfort and new courage to the hearts of all those bowed down by guilt and misery, by calling out to them: "By the very act of permitting you to awaken to a new day, God assures you that He will help you regain the lost purity and serenity of your life."

ואתה ה׳: "Even though You exercise Your sovereignty over me at this very moment as a Judge, *Elokim*, You will still remain *Hashem*. Your judgment is only a form of love that will lead me from aberration and its consequences to a new, pure life."

קולי: "If my voice is heard, then it is to God to Whom I call.'

הר קדשו: is the place of *teshuvah* and *kapparah*.

המלאך: It was the hope and desire of Yaakob that God might ordain also for all of his descendants the same trials and sorrows, and in the end, the same answer to their prayers, that he, Yaakob, himself had experienced in his own long life. Yaakob felt that a life such as he himself had lived would be best suited to help his children become and remain capable and

שְׁמִי וְשֵׁם אֲבֹתַי אַבְרָהָם וְיִצְחָק וְיִדְגּוּ לָרֹב בְּקֶרֶב הָאָרֶץ: וַיֹּאמֶר
אִם־שָׁמוֹעַ תִּשְׁמַע לְקוֹל יְיָ אֱלֹהֶיךָ וְהַיָּשָׁר בְּעֵינָיו תַּעֲשֶׂה וְהַאֲזַנְתָּ
לְמִצְוֹתָיו וְשָׁמַרְתָּ כָּל־חֻקָּיו כָּל־הַמַּחֲלָה אֲשֶׁר שַׂמְתִּי בְמִצְרַיִם
לֹא־אָשִׂים עָלֶיךָ כִּי אֲנִי יְיָ רֹפְאֶךָ: וַיֹּאמֶר יְיָ אֶל־הַשָּׂטָן יִגְעַר יְיָ
בְּךָ הַשָּׂטָן וְיִגְעַר יְיָ בְּךָ הַבֹּחֵר בִּירוּשָׁלִָם הֲלוֹא זֶה אוּד מֻצָּל מֵאֵשׁ:
הִנֵּה מִטָּתוֹ שֶׁלִּשְׁלֹמֹה שִׁשִּׁים גִּבֹּרִים סָבִיב לָהּ מִגִּבֹּרֵי יִשְׂרָאֵל:
כֻּלָּם אֲחֻזֵי חֶרֶב מְלֻמְּדֵי מִלְחָמָה אִישׁ חַרְבּוֹ עַל־יְרֵכוֹ מִפַּחַד
בַּלֵּילוֹת: יְבָרֶכְךָ יְיָ וְיִשְׁמְרֶךָ: יָאֵר יְיָ׳פָּנָיו אֵלֶיךָ וִיחֻנֶּךָּ: יִשָּׂא
יְיָ׳פָּנָיו אֵלֶיךָ וְיָשֵׂם לְךָ שָׁלוֹם:

הִנֵּה לֹא יָנוּם וְלֹא יִישָׁן שׁוֹמֵר יִשְׂרָאֵל: ג״פ

לִישׁוּעָתְךָ קִוִּיתִי יְיָ׳ קִוִּיתִי יְיָ לִישׁוּעָתְךָ׳
יְיָ לִישׁוּעָתְךָ קִוִּיתִי: ג״פ

בְּשֵׁם יְיָ אֱלֹהֵי יִשְׂרָאֵל מִימִינִי מִיכָאֵל וּמִשְּׂמֹאלִי
גַבְרִיאֵל · וּמִלְּפָנַי אוּרִיאֵל · וּמֵאֲחֹרַי רְפָאֵל ·
וְעַל רֹאשִׁי שְׁכִינַת אֵל: ג״פ

worthy of preserving the heritage of their fathers and to find quiet, happiness
on earth such as the nations round about them could never know of or even
surmise. Even as the fish in the sea below us enjoy a quiet but happy and
cheerful existence of which the humans on the land above have no conception,
so the true sons of Yaakob, if only they remain humbly and quietly in their
own appointed sphere, will be able to attain a degree of serenity and happiness such as the people about them, who have but little understanding for
them, will never be able to comprehend. וידגו derived from דגה, the root of
דג.

ויאמר אם שמוע: This is the same truth which God put into the hands
of His nation as a guiding staff and compass when, redeemed from Egyptian
slavery, Yisrael began its arduous journey through the wilderness. ויאמר ה׳ אל
השטן. Centuries later, that people, through its own fault, lost the homeland

carried on in them and that they may grow into a multitude, like fish in the midst of the earth.

And he said: "If only you will listen earnestly to the voice of *God*, your God, and do that which is right in His eyes, and if you will give ear to His commandments and keep all of His statutes, then I will not inflict upon you all the ill which I decreed for Mitzrayim, for I, *God*, am your healer."

And *God* said to Satan: "*God* will rebuke you, O Satan, *God* will rebuke you, He Who has chosen Yerushalayim; for is this not a fire-brand snatched from the fire?"

Behold the bed of Shlomo! Sixty mighty men are about it, mighty men of Yisrael, all with their swords drawn, trained in warfare; each man his sword at his side, because of the fear in the nights.

May *God* bless you and keep you. May *God* light up His countenance for you and favor you. May *God* turn His countenance toward you and establish peace upon you.

Behold, the Guardian of Yisrael shall neither slumber nor sleep.

For Your salvation do I hope, O *God;* I hope, O *God*, for Your salvation; O *God*, for Your salvation do I hope.

In the Name of *God*, the God of Yisrael: may Michael be at my right hand, Gabriel at my left, Uriel before me, Raphael behind me, and above my head, the Presence of God.

---

to which it had thus journeyed, and when the exiles returned to the Holy Land once more, it was under circumstances not indicating the obvious, direct protection of God but demanding fierce hand-to hand struggle against hostile men. It was then that the leaders of Yisrael who were charged with the reestablishment of the nation and the rebuilding of the Temple under the most difficult conditions conceivable learned that, of course, in this world that has turned away from all that is good and right, "Satan" "hindrance," as a rule, appears at the "right hand:" עוֹמֵד עַל יְמִינוֹ לְשִׂטְנוֹ. He who elects to follow the "left side," the side turned away from the "right" will always find wide-open doors and smoothly paved paths in this world. It is only the good who must contend with obstacles and difficulties. But in the end God will push the obstacles aside and make way for the leader who will set an example in doing what is "good and right." For God views such a man as an instrument which, withstanding the fiery heat of opposing elements, is capable of maintaining itself intact and strong for His service.

Finally, the prayer which we recite before we retire for the night makes reference to the bedstead of King Shelomo. We are told: "Behold, Shelomo

שִׁיר הַמַּעֲלוֹת אַשְׁרֵי כָּל־יְרֵא יְיָ הַהֹלֵךְ בִּדְרָכָיו: יְגִיעַ כַּפֶּיךָ כִּי

תֹאכֵל אַשְׁרֶיךָ וְטוֹב לָךְ: אֶשְׁתְּךָ כְּגֶפֶן פֹּרִיָּה בְּיַרְכְּתֵי בֵיתֶךָ

בָּנֶיךָ כִּשְׁתִלֵי זֵיתִים סָבִיב לְשֻׁלְחָנֶךָ: הִנֵּה כִּי־כֵן יְבֹרַךְ גָּבֶר יְרֵא

יְיָ: יְבָרֶכְךָ יְיָ מִצִּיּוֹן וּרְאֵה בְּטוּב יְרוּשָׁלָ͏ִם כֹּל יְמֵי חַיֶּיךָ: וּרְאֵה

בָנִים לְבָנֶיךָ שָׁלוֹם עַל יִשְׂרָאֵל:

רִגְזוּ וְאַל־תֶּחֱטָאוּ אִמְרוּ בִלְבַבְכֶם עַל־מִשְׁכַּבְכֶם וְדֹמּוּ סֶלָה: ג"פ

אֲדוֹן עוֹלָם אֲשֶׁר מָלַךְ . בְּטֶרֶם כָּל־יְצִיר נִבְרָא :

לְעֵת נַעֲשָׂה בְחֶפְצוֹ כֹּל . אֲזַי מֶלֶךְ שְׁמוֹ נִקְרָא :

וְאַחֲרֵי כִּכְלוֹת הַכֹּל . לְבַדּוֹ יִמְלוֹךְ נוֹרָא :

וְהוּא הָיָה וְהוּא הֹוֶה . וְהוּא יִהְיֶה בְּתִפְאָרָה :

וְהוּא אֶחָד וְאֵין שֵׁנִי . לְהַמְשִׁיל לוֹ לְהַחְבִּירָה :

בְּלִי רֵאשִׁית בְּלִי תַכְלִית . וְלוֹ הָעֹז וְהַמִּשְׂרָה :

וְהוּא אֵלִי וְחַי גֹּאֲלִי . וְצוּר חֶבְלִי בְּעֵת צָרָה :

וְהוּא נִסִּי וּמָנוֹס לִי . מְנָת כּוֹסִי בְּיוֹם אֶקְרָא :

בְּיָדוֹ אַפְקִיד רוּחִי . בְּעֵת אִישָׁן וְאָעִירָה :

וְעִם־רוּחִי גְּוִיָּתִי . יְיָ לִי וְלֹא אִירָא :

שִׁוִּיתִי יְיָ לְנֶגְדִּי תָמִיד כִּי מִימִינִי בַּל־אֶמּוֹט. שָׁמְרֵנִי אֵל כִּי חָסִיתִי בָךְ:

בְּיָדְךָ אַפְקִיד רוּחִי פָּדִיתָ אוֹתִי יְיָ אֵל אֱמֶת:

was the wealthiest, mightiest and greatest of kings, and yet, at a time when he had grown morally weak and had erred, sixty warriors, trained in the art of battle, had to stand about him with swords drawn in order to guard him from the terrors of the night." (Here Shir Hashirim Rabbah comments as follows: תני עד שלא יחטא אדם נותנין לו אימה ויראה והבריות מתפחדין ממנו כיון שהוא חוטא נותנין עליו אימה ויראה, ומתפחד הוא מאחרים "When a man hasn't yet sinned, his fellow-beings on earth stand in awe of him, but once he has sinned, he himself is overcome by fear and dread of others,חטא שלא עד וכו' שכן לך הדע שלמה היה רודה בשרים ובשרות וכו' ותענוגות בני האדם שדה ושדות וכו' (קהלת ב' ח') כיון שחטא מינה לו ששים גבורים מגבורי ישראל והעמידן לשמור לו את מטתו הדא הוא דכתיב הנה מטתו וכו' כולם אחוזי חרב שהיה מתפחד מן הרוחות "But as for you," we are told, "who are neither kings, nor mighty, nor even wealthy, you will need no armed warriors to guard you from the terrors of the night, if only you will be good. If you will lead a good life, God will be your Protector. He will bless you; He will give you light and favor you. His everwaking Presence will ever be near to you and He will give you peace." הנה "You will be able to sleep in peace for He Who never slumbers nor sleeps will watch over you."

לישועתך: It is for the salvation of God alone, and none other, that you hope; even though you still do not behold it yourself, you hope for His salvation, and it is in 'ה, Who is ever ready to grant new life, that you place all of your hopes.

בשם ה': It is "in the Name of God," at His command, that His angels surround you; Michael, performing His unique miracles; Gabriel, the messenger of His almighty power; Uriel, who bears the light of God before you; Raphael, who brings you healing from Him; and above your head, you have the Presence of God Himself.

שיר המעלות: When night brings rest from daily work and opens the heart to hopes and yearnings, this Psalm depicts for us true happiness as it may be found in a Jewish home, a happiness which is inherent in that ideal, that "good" and that prosperity to which all our desires and our endeavors may and should be consecrated. The sources of this kind of happiness are "the fear of God" and "labor;" its components are a man's wife and children, an interest in all the material and spiritual concerns of his people, in the future of his own family and in that of all Yisrael. אשרי The fear of God and honest adherence to His ways are in themselves sufficient to secure "happiness" as such. But if, in addition to this happy fear of God, man's labor is crowned with visible success, then he has indeed reached the pinnacle of all the "good" that can be attained on earth. He has then attained that sweet bliss which is entirely unknown to him who, without any effort of his own, has been given the material wealth of a life free of want, and who has never had to "work" to provide for his wife and children.

רגזו: The only concern, the only fear which we may have is the fear of sin. Let your high resolve to shun all sin be the quiet and solemn pledge, to be heard by God alone, which you make as you lie upon your bed.

Those who have not visited the Cemetery for thirty days, recite the following prayer as they enter the burial ground:

בָּרוּךְ אַתָּה יְיָ אֱלֹהֵינוּ מֶלֶךְ הָעוֹלָם, אֲשֶׁר יָצַר אֶתְכֶם בַּדִּין,
וְזָן וְכִלְכֵּל אֶתְכֶם בַּדִּין, וְהֵמִית אֶתְכֶם בַּדִּין, וְיוֹדֵעַ מִסְפַּר כֻּלְכֶם
בַּדִּין, וְעָתִיד לְהַחֲזִיר וּלְהַחֲיוֹתְכֶם בַּדִּין: בָּרוּךְ אַתָּה יְיָ מְחַיֵּה הַמֵּתִים:

צִדּוּק הדין : The destinies of man, the ordinary happenings of everyday life as well as the extraordinary occurrences, take one of two outward forms –– granting and preservation, or withholding and bereavement. At first glance, these two aspects of human destiny would seem opposites, and they are known, too, by different designations: *middath hadin* and *middath harachamim*. But the thinking mind will realize that, actually, the two differing forms that our destinies may take are not opposites at all. Even deprivation and withholding by the hand of God is only another form of Divine loving-kindness; God denies us and takes from us only that which would not be conducive to our welfare were it granted us. Furthermore, even while He withholds or takes from us what we most desire, He always allows the quality of love to prevail, and never permits the measure of loss or withholding to be greater than the person so stricken could bear. At the same time His loving-kindness as demonstrated by His gifts is always modified by justice, and in this it differs from much of human kindness, which all too often is motivated not by feelings of thoughtful consideration for another, but by a gush of weak sentimentality, and thus is an act of egocentric self gratification on the part of the giver rather than a favor bestowed solely with the purpose of advancing the welfare of the receiver.

Of all the acts of Divine withholding and deprivation, it is death that has the most shattering impact on man. Death seems to deprive him of all physical existence on earth and to take from him all of the terrestrial world; in dying, man parts with all things, and all things depart from him. Death, more than any other event in human life, would seem an obvious manifestation of *din*, the withholding and bereaving aspect of God's reign. Now the sense of grief at the loss of the departed must be clarified and refined so that those left behind may come to accept and value even the *din* that is so manifest in the Divine decree of death, as *tzedek*, as another dictate of that Divine justice which forms the basis of all the ways of God, even when He grants and preserves. Such is the purpose of the *Tzidduk Hadin*, (the declaration that God's ways are just and righteous altogether) as the burial service is referred to in Jewish living.

ברוך : This blessing, which is to be recited upon viewing the graves of our dead is extraordinary and unique in that in one and the same paragraph God and the departed (who are portrayed as the objects of His rule as He

Those who have not visited the Cemetery for thirty days, recite the
following prayer as they enter the burial ground:

Blessed be You, O *God* our God, King of the Universe, Who
has fashioned you in judgment, Who fed and nourished you in
judgment, Who brought death to you in judgment, Who knows the
number of you all in justice, and will hereafter restore you to life
in judgment. Blessed be You, O *God,* Who revives the dead.

---

creates and preserves, causes death and restores life) are both addressed in
the second person. Instead of "Blessed be You, God, ... Who has
fashioned *them* in judgment" we read "Blessed be You, O *God* . . . .
Who has fashioned *you* . . . ." Perhaps we would not be too far from
correct in assuming that this conspicously ungrammatical and awkward form
for the blessing was chosen deliberately in order to remind us all the more
forcefully as we stand at the gravesides of our departed that their spirits, even
though we cannot see them, are still very much present there, and that, for
this reason, we must employ terms of direct address rather than speak of
them in the third person, as if they were absent.

אשר יצר אתכם בדין : If the term *din* is employed here even in connection
with the creation and the fashioning of a human being, then the term *din* must
be interpreted in a broader sense than simply as the kind of "judgment" in
which sentence is passed concerning a man's guilt or innocence. For when man
first enters this life he has neither guit nor merit. Rather, *din,* here, as it does
throughout this berachah, denotes that aspect of Divine Providence which
considers every individual human being within the context of the society and
circumstances in which he had his origins, and of the people and things that
relate to him both actively and passively, of those that exert an influence on
him and those that he influences in his turn. A consideration of what would
be "rightfully due" to all these human relationships, it would seem, would
have some part in the determining of the decree which Divine justice ordains
for that individual. Particularly the sin or merit of parents and ancestors is
a major factor taken into consideration by Divine providence as the individual
is fashioned and brought into the world at birth. In keeping with the fact
that He is פוקד עון אבות, God may make the path of the mortal about to be
born a steep trail, beset with trials and affliction and then, in His creative love,
endow that man with distinctive abilities and moral strength to equip him for
the journey along the arduous road ordained for him. On the other hand, if
God sees fit to demonstrate His attribute of עושה חסד לאלפים and a smooth
lane of happiness beckons to the human about to be born, this even path is
no less filled with trials and challenges, and here, too, the newly-born individual
may be geared by his Maker with the faculties and the moral fiber required

אַתָּה גִבּוֹר לְעוֹלָם אֲדֹנָי מְחַיֶּה מֵתִים אַתָּה רַב לְהוֹשִׁיעַ ·
מְכַלְכֵּל חַיִּים בְּחֶסֶד מְחַיֶּה מֵתִים בְּרַחֲמִים רַבִּים סוֹמֵךְ נוֹפְלִים
וְרוֹפֵא חוֹלִים וּמַתִּיר אֲסוּרִים וּמְקַיֵּם אֱמוּנָתוֹ לִישֵׁנֵי עָפָר · מִי
כָמוֹךָ בַּעַל גְּבוּרוֹת וּמִי דוֹמֶה לָךְ מֶלֶךְ מֵמִית וּמְחַיֶּה וּמַצְמִיחַ
יְשׁוּעָה · וְנֶאֱמָן אַתָּה לְהַחֲיוֹת מֵתִים ·

After arriving with the מת at the בית חיים, הצור תמים is said; it is not spoken
on days when no תחנון is said; neither is it said on ערב שבת or ערב יו"ט after
חצות:

הַצּוּר תָּמִים פָּעֳלוֹ כִּי כָל־דְּרָכָיו מִשְׁפָּט · אֵל אֱמוּנָה וְאֵין עָוֶל
צַדִּיק וְיָשָׁר הוּא : הַצּוּר תָּמִים בְּכָל־פָּעַל · מִי יֹאמַר לוֹ מַה תִּפְעָל·
הַשַּׁלִּיט בְּמַטָּה וּבְמַעַל · מֵמִית וּמְחַיֶּה מוֹרִיד שְׁאוֹל וַיָּעַל : הַצּוּר
תָּמִים בְּכָל־מַעֲשֶׂה · מִי יֹאמַר לוֹ מַה תַּעֲשֶׂה · הָאוֹמֵר וְעֹשֶׂה ·
חֶסֶד חִנָּם לָנוּ תַעֲשֶׂה · וּבִזְכוּת הַנֶּעֱקַד כְּשֶׂה · הַקְשִׁיבָה וַעֲשֵׂה :

---

to meet the tests that await him upon the way he has been given to walk.
At any rate, the above would be a plausible explanation for יצירה בדין,
ויודע מספר כלכם בדין. זן וכלכל והמית בדין Even after death every single soul
remains the object of God's particular concern, with careful consideration
given to that which would be its rightful due. ועתיד להחזיר וכו' : Even at
the time of the Resurrection of the Dead, every individual will stand in *din*
before Him, each in and according to his own worth.

אתה גבור see p. 131 ff.

צור, הצור, the unchangeable One, the צור and צייר Who is firm and
fashions and conquers all things (see Comm. to Deut. 32:4) — His work is תמים,
perfect altogether. To the purblind human eye His ways may seem in conflict
with His goals; yet, at every instant of His reign, as it marches on, His work
is perfect, regardless of whether the one who is called away be an old man or
a child. His work is perfect and complete always; it cannot be more or less
than it is nor may it come sooner or later than it came, for at the moment

You, O my Lord, are all-powerful forever. You are the One Who revives the dead; You are abundantly strong to save. He sustains the living with loving-kindness, revives the dead with great compassion, supports the falling, heals the sick, unchains the bound, and keeps His faith with the slumberers in the dust. Who is like You, O Master of mighty acts, and Who is like You, a King Who kills and restores life and causes salvation to grow? And You are faithful to revive the dead.

The Rock, His work is perfect, for all His ways are judgment; a God of faithfulness and no iniquity, just and upright is He. The Rock, perfect in all His work: who could say to Him "What are You working?" He rules on earth and on high; He causes death and restores to life; He brings down to the grave and raises up again. The Rock, perfect in every deed: who could say to Him "What are You doing?" O You Who promises and fulfills, show us loving-kindness undeserved, and for the sake of him who was bound like a lamb [to be sacrificed] hear us and act. Just in all Your ways, O

---

that it comes to pass it accomplishes that which is meet and proper for that very moment and for the persons and circumstances thus affected; for כל דרכיו משפט the purpose of all the ways and aspects of His Providence is solely to translate the demands of justice and righteousness into living reality. אל אמונה Let every living thing entrust itself unreservedly to His care and providence, for He does violence and injustice to none; justice and righteousness are the stamp of all His ways.

בזכות הנעקד כשה : Even as Yitzchak was fully prepared to submit to a Divine decree of death on the sacrificial altar, unwavering and without a murmur, so may we, too, prove to be true sons of Yitzchak and may we, too, benefit by his merits.

צדיק בכל דרכיו : But He Who is just and righteous in all His ways is also slow to anger and of great compassion, and He will let us behold His judgment and righteousness in the form of forbearance and compassion if only we will make ourselves worthy of experiencing these Divine qualities.

צַדִּיק בְּכָל־דְּרָכָיו הַצּוּר תָּמִים · אֶרֶךְ אַפַּיִם וּמָלֵא רַחֲמִים ·
חֲמָל־נָא וְחוּס נָא עַל אָבוֹת וּבָנִים · כִּי לְךָ אָדוֹן הַסְּלִיחוֹת
וְהָרַחֲמִים: צַדִּיק אַתָּה יְיָ לְהָמִית וּלְהַחֲיוֹת · אֲשֶׁר בְּיָדְךָ פִּקְדוֹן
כָּל־רוּחוֹת · חָלִילָה לְךָ זִכְרוֹנֵנוּ לִמְחוֹת · וְיִהְיוּ נָא עֵינֶיךָ בְּרַחֲמִים
עָלֵינוּ פְקֻחוֹת · כִּי לְךָ אָדוֹן הָרַחֲמִים וְהַסְּלִיחוֹת: אָדָם אִם בֶּן־
שָׁנָה יִהְיֶה · אוֹ אֶלֶף שָׁנִים יִחְיֶה · מַה־יִּתְרוֹן לוֹ, כְּלֹא הָיָה יִהְיֶה ·
בָּרוּךְ דַּיַּן הָאֱמֶת מֵמִית וּמְחַיֶּה: בָּרוּךְ הוּא · כִּי אֱמֶת דִּינוֹ ·
וּמְשׁוֹטֵט הַכֹּל בְּעֵינוֹ · וּמְשַׁלֵּם לְאָדָם חֶשְׁבּוֹנוֹ וְדִינוֹ · וְהַכֹּל לִשְׁמוֹ
הוֹדָיָה יִתֵּנוּ: יָדַעְנוּ יְיָ כִּי צֶדֶק מִשְׁפָּטֶךָ · תִּצְדַּק בְּדָבְרֶךָ · וְתִזְכֶּה
בְשָׁפְטֶךָ · וְאֵין לְהַרְהֵר אַחַר מִדַּת שָׁפְטֶךָ · צַדִּיק אַתָּה יְיָ וְיָשָׁר
מִשְׁפָּטֶיךָ: דַּיַּן אֱמֶת · שׁוֹפֵט צֶדֶק וֶאֱמֶת: בָּרוּךְ דַּיַּן הָאֱמֶת ·
שֶׁכָּל־מִשְׁפָּטָיו צֶדֶק וֶאֱמֶת: נֶפֶשׁ כָּל־חַי בְּיָדֶךָ · צֶדֶק מָלְאָה
יְמִינְךָ וְיָדֶךָ · רַחֵם עַל פְּלֵטַת צֹאן יָדֶךָ · וְתֹאמַר לַמַּלְאָךְ הֶרֶף
יָדֶךָ: גְּדֹל הָעֵצָה וְרַב הָעֲלִילִיָּה · אֲשֶׁר עֵינֶיךָ פְקֻחוֹת עַל־כָּל־
דַּרְכֵי בְּנֵי אָדָם · לָתֵת לְאִישׁ כִּדְרָכָיו וְכִפְרִי מַעֲלָלָיו: לְהַגִּיד כִּי יָשָׁר
יְיָ צוּרִי וְלֹא עַוְלָתָה בּוֹ: יְיָ נָתַן וַיְיָ לָקָח · יְהִי שֵׁם יְיָ מְבֹרָךְ: וְהוּא
רַחוּם יְכַפֵּר עָוֹן וְלֹא יַשְׁחִית · וְהִרְבָּה לְהָשִׁיב אַפּוֹ וְלֹא יָעִיר
כָּל־חֲמָתוֹ:

After the קבורה *the* יתומים *recite this* קדיש *and* קהל *joins In until* :ויקרה

יִתְגַּדַּל וְיִתְקַדַּשׁ שְׁמֵהּ רַבָּא בְּעָלְמָא דִּי הוּא עָתִיד לְאִתְחַדָּתָא
וּלְאַחֲיָאָה מֵתַיָּא וּלְאַסָּקָא יָתְהוֹן לְחַיֵּי עָלְמָא וּלְמִבְנֵא קַרְתָּא דִּי־

יתגדל: Of the phenomena of life on earth, death is the mightiest of all
natural forces. None can withstand it; death casts down even the mightiest
of men, lost beyond rescue, and puts an ends to every power and authority.
But it was revealed to us that, by the will, the power and the decree of the
Almighty, the One God, even death itself is overcome, that even death is only

perfect Rock, slow to anger and full of compassion, spare and have pity upon parents and children, for Yours, O Lord, is forgiveness and compassion. Just are You, O *God,* in causing death and restoring to life; in Your hand is the keeping of all spirits. Far is it from You to blot out our memory; O let Your eyes therefore be upon us in compassion, for Yours, O Lord, are compassion and forgiveness. Whether a man live one year or a thousand years, what does he gain? He will be as though he had never been. Blessed be He, the true Judge, Who causes death and restores to life. Blessed be He, for His judgment is true, He discerns all things with His eye and renders man his recompense and his rightful due, and all must render acknowledgement to His Name. We know, O *God,* that Your judgment is just; You are just in Your speech, pure in Your judgment, and it is not ours to brood over the standard of Your judgment. You are just, O *God,* and Your judgments are right. O You true Judge, You judge in truth and right! Blessed be You, O true Judge, Whose judgments are all truth and right; the soul of every living thing is in Your hand; full of justice is Your saving right hand and Your chastising left hand, have compassion upon the remnant of the flock of Your hand and say to the angel, "Stay your hand." You are great in counsel and mighty in action; Your eyes are open upon all the ways of the children of men, to give to each according to his ways and in keeping with the fruit of his doings, to declare that *God* is upright, my Rock, in whom there is no injustice. *God* has given; *God* has taken; blessed be the Name of *God!* And He, being full of compassion, forgives iniquity and does not destroy, and many a time He repents of His anger and never stirs up all His wrath.

His great Name will be recognized in all its greatness and holiness in the world which is to be created anew, when He will revive the dead and raise them to life eternal, when He will rebuild the city

---

a transient state, and that those who now slumber in their graves await only a call from the Almighty in order to awaken them, to burst their graves asunder and to cause them to rise from the dust to a new life. It is from our firm confidence that this will indeed come to pass, that we derive also the unshakeable trust in the eventual resurrection and rejuvenation of all those

יְרוּשָׁלֵם וּלְשַׁכְלְלָא הֵיכְלֵהּ בְּגַוַּהּ וּלְמֶעֱקַר וּלְמֵעְקַר פָּלְחָנָא נֻכְרָאָה מִן־
אַרְעָא וְלַאֲתָבָה פָּלְחָנָא דִי־שְׁמַיָּא לְאַתְרֵהּ וְיַמְלִיךְ קֻדְשָׁא בְּרִיךְ
הוּא בְּמַלְכוּתֵהּ וִיקָרֵהּ בְּחַיֵּיכוֹן וּבְיוֹמֵיכוֹן וּבְחַיֵּי דְכָל בֵּית יִשְׂרָאֵל
בַּעֲגָלָא וּבִזְמַן קָרִיב, וְאִמְרוּ יכו'.

Before leaving the בית חיים, *those present form two rows* (שורה) *through which the* אבל *passes; they say to him:*

הַמָּקוֹם יְנַחֵם אוֹתְךָ (אֶתְכֶם) בְּתוֹךְ שְׁאָר אֲבֵלֵי צִיּוֹן וִירוּשָׁלָיִם:

Grass is torn out, thrown behind the back, and the following is said:

וְיָצִיצוּ מֵעִיר כְּעֵשֶׂב הָאָרֶץ: (מייגנע זוסגען) זָכוּר כִּי עָפָר אֲנָחְנוּ:

After leaving the בית חיים, *one washes the hands and says:*

בִּלַּע הַמָּוֶת לָנֶצַח וּמָחָה אֲדֹנָי יְהוִֹה דִּמְעָה מֵעַל כָּל־
פָּנִים וְחֶרְפַּת עַמּוֹ יָסִיר מֵעַל כָּל־הָאָרֶץ כִּי יְיָ דִּבֵּר:

Here follows ויהי נועם:

———◦⟨◦⟩◦———

persons and things whose death according to God's promise, is a temporary phase only, after which they will rise again to flourish anew and to live forever. Moreover, God has promised us through His prophets (Isa. 11:65, 66 etc.) that there will be a new heaven and a new earth, and that nature and mankind will be restored to that state of perfect bliss of Paradise which they had forfeited only because of the errors of men. Our trust in this Divine assurance includes also the implicit trust that, hand in hand with the fulfillment of this promise, God's Jewish State and His Jewish Sanctuary will also be restored, and that finally, the Kingdom of God will reign supreme everywhere on earth. Hence, it is to this resurrection of all that has gone down to the grave in the sad present that we look with renewed confidence, and it is in this resurrection that we reaffirm our unchanging trust whenever we have laid one of our dead into his earthly grave.

המקום: It is the purpose of all our prayers to cultivate in our hearts a sense of selfless solidarity with our brethren. If we yearn for blessings and prosperity of which others, too, are in need, we are to hope and pray for these Divine gifts not for ourselves alone but only in conjunction with hopes and prayers for the welfare of all of our brethren. So, too, when we seek to comfort the mourners at a burial service, our words of sympathy are couched in terms of the wish that the mourners at this funeral be comforted "together with all the others who are in need of consolation." If may be that אבלי ציון וירושלים refers also to "those who mourn *for* Tzion and Yerushalayim;" in other

of Yerushalayim and complete His Temple therein; He will remove all alien worship from the earth and restore in its place the service of Heaven, and the Holy One, blessed be He, will reign in His sovereignty and in His glory. May it come to pass during your life-time and during your days and during the days of all the House of Yisrael, speedily and soon, and let us say, Amen. etc.

May God comfort you together with all the other mourners of Tzion and Yerushalayim.

May they blossom out of the city like the grass of the earth.

He shall make death vanish forever, and my Lord, Who is merciful even in stern justice, shall wipe away the tears from all faces, and He shall remove the insult against His people from all the earth, for *God* has said it.

---

words, we voice the hope that the consolation which we seek for the mourners at this burial service may come also to those who mourn *for* Yerushalayim and Tzion; that is, hand in hand with that consolation which Tzion and Yeru-shalayim have long awaited.

ויציצו : This, the sixteenth verse of Psalm 72, concludes the portrayal given in that Psalm of the happy and blessed life of individuals and a nation flourishing under the wise leadership of a ruler inspired by the spirit of God. Even as the motherly earth contains all the elements that grass requires in order to grow and thrive as originally intended, so human relationships, shaped by the influence of God, should provide for men and nations that element which they need in order to flourish and to prosper as originally ordained in the Divine plan. It is with this heartening thought that we turn away from the graves in the open field and prepare to go back to the city and to the living.

בלע : The contemplation of death and decay is not the thought that Judaism would have us take with us through life. The custom of washing our hands after a funeral is intended, symbolically, to free our vigorous, active lives, which we are to put to creative use, from any mood of depression tainted by thoughts of death and the grave. In keeping with this idea, we now recite the verse from the Book of Isaiah (25:8) which heralds the eventual disappearance of death and of human tears that will ultimately come hand in hand with the cessation from the earth of all insults against the people of God.

הַלְלוּיָהּ הַלְלוּ אֶת־יְהוָה מִן־הַשָּׁמַיִם הַלְלוּהוּ בַּמְּרוֹמִים: הַלְלוּהוּ
כָל־מַלְאָכָיו הַלְלוּהוּ כָּל־צְבָאָיו: הַלְלוּהוּ שֶׁמֶשׁ וְיָרֵחַ הַלְלוּהוּ
כָּל־כּוֹכְבֵי אוֹר: הַלְלוּהוּ שְׁמֵי הַשָּׁמָיִם וְהַמַּיִם אֲשֶׁר מֵעַל הַשָּׁמָיִם
יְהַלְלוּ אֶת־שֵׁם יְהוָה כִּי הוּא צִוָּה וְנִבְרָאוּ: וַיַּעֲמִידֵם לָעַד לְעוֹלָם
חָק־נָתַן וְלֹא יַעֲבוֹר:

כִּי־אֶרְאֶה שָׁמֶיךָ מַעֲשֵׂה אֶצְבְּעֹתֶיךָ יָרֵחַ וְכוֹכָבִים אֲשֶׁר כּוֹנָנְתָּה:
מָה־אֱנוֹשׁ כִּי־תִזְכְּרֶנּוּ וּבֶן־אָדָם כִּי תִפְקְדֶנּוּ:

בָּרוּךְ אַתָּה יְיָ אֱלֹהֵינוּ מֶלֶךְ הָעוֹלָם· אֲשֶׁר בְּמַאֲמָרוֹ
בָּרָא שְׁחָקִים· וּבְרוּחַ פִּיו כָּל־צְבָאָם· חֹק וּזְמַן נָתַן
לָהֶם· שֶׁלֹּא יְשַׁנּוּ אֶת תַּפְקִידָם: שָׂשִׂים וּשְׂמֵחִים
לַעֲשׂוֹת רְצוֹן קוֹנָם· פּוֹעֵל אֱמֶת שֶׁפְּעֻלָּתוֹ אֱמֶת·
וְלַלְּבָנָה אָמַר שֶׁתִּתְחַדֵּשׁ עֲטֶרֶת תִּפְאֶרֶת לַעֲמוּסֵי
בָטֶן· הָעֲתִידִים לְהִתְחַדֵּשׁ כְּמוֹתָהּ· וּלְפָאֵר לְיוֹצְרָם
עַל שֵׁם כְּבוֹד מַלְכוּתוֹ· בָּרוּךְ אַתָּה יְיָ מְחַדֵּשׁ חֳדָשִׁים:

ברוך : The constancy in change, the regularity of the alternating aspects of the moon constitutes the clearest, brightest revelation of the Creator, Ruler and Lawgiver of the Universe. Therefore, at the beginning of every month, when we behold the moon as it reappears and its light grows stronger, we step out to view it and to utter the pledge, the *berachah*, of homage to God. We bless Him Whose word of creation and law shines upon the starry sky and Who, through the heavenly bodies which, joyously obedient. never deviate from their assigned orbits, has shown us a model of what our own attitude should be; namely, that we, too, are to complete our round of service in life on earth in serene and loyal obedience within those paths that we have been assigned by God.

Blessed be You, O *God* our God, King of the Universe, Who created the heavens by His command, and all their host by the breath of His mouth. You gave them a fixed statute and season so that they should not alter their appointed charge. They are glad and rejoice to do the will of their Owner. The Worker of truth Whose work is true. He bade the moon renew itself, O a crown of glory to those burdened from birth, who likewise are destined to renew themselves and to glorify their Creator because of the glory of His kingdom. Blessed be You, O *God,* Who renews the months.

אשר במאמרו : (see Commentary to Gen. 1:22.) חק, (derived from חקק, related to חגג, "to move in a circle" or "to run a course") refers to the "Law" which assigns a fixed course or orbit to each heavenly body and makes it keep within the limits of this prescribed course. זמן refers to the fixed "season" within which each heavenly body completes its orbit. תפקידם is the charge fulfilled in time and space. קונם With regard to both their existence and their function they are the property of God, their Owner, Who made them and rules over them.

פועל אמת : As opposed to the inconstancy that characterizes the terrestrial world, the heavenly phenomena are marked by stability and continuity, and it is possible even for mortal man, by observation and calculation, to predict the occurrence and recurrence of these phenomena in advance. This continuity which is always predictable in advance is the picture of *emeth,* a picture of truth, constant and unchanging, which is the creation of the unalterable, almighty will of God the Creator, Who is *po'el emeth,* and therefore *pe'ulatho emeth.*

At the same time, the moon serves as a sign for the Nation of God which, like the moon, moves on through continuous change across the horizon of the history of the nations. When the Jewish people first entered the orbit of world history, its God said to it: החדש הזה לכם. With these words He promised that it would be Yisrael's inalienable destiny to emerge again and again out of the darkness of its fate into light, and He also assigned to Yisrael the eternal task ever to struggle from out of the darkness of error into the light of truth. עמוסי בטן : From the very beginning of its existence as a nation, Yisrael has been charged (or "burdened") with a definite task and destiny. Continually renewed and reborn, like the moon, they are to serve as an instrument in the hand of God for His glory and for the establishment of His Kingdom on earth by virtue of their path which they follow across the horizon of the nations.

ג״פ בָּרוּךְ יוֹצְרֵךְ *בָּרוּךְ עוֹשֵׂךְ· בָּרוּךְ קוֹנֵךְ· בָּרוּךְ בּוֹרְאֵךְ:

ורוקק כנגד הלבנה ואומר ג״פ. (ויזהר שלא ירכע בנרכיו רק זוקף בחלצעותיו).

ג״פ כְּשֵׁם שֶׁאֲנִי רוֹקֵד כְּנֶגְדֵּךְ· וְאֵינִי יָכוֹל לִנְגַּע

בָּךְ· כָּךְ לֹא יוּכְלוּ כָּל־אוֹיְבַי לִנְגַּע בִּי לְרָעָה:

ג״פ תִּפֹּל עֲלֵיהֶם אֵימָתָה וָפַחַד בִּגְדֹל זְרוֹעֲךָ יִדְּמוּ כָּאָבֶן:

כָּאָבֶן יִדְּמוּ זְרוֹעֲךָ בִּגְדֹל וָפַחַד אֵימָתָה עֲלֵיהֶם תִּפֹּל:

דָּוִד מֶלֶךְ יִשְׂרָאֵל חַי וְקַיָּם:

ושואל לחברו ג״פ שָׁלוֹם עֲלֵיכֶם: וחברו משיב ג״פ עֲלֵיכֶם שָׁלוֹם:

ג״פ סִמָּן טוֹב וּמַזָּל טוֹב יְהִי לָנוּ וּלְכָל יִשְׂרָאֵל אָמֵן:

קוֹל דּוֹדִי הִנֵּה זֶה בָּא· מְדַלֵּג עַל הֶהָרִים· מְקַפֵּץ עַל הַגְּבָעוֹת:

דּוֹמֶה דוֹדִי לִצְבִי אוֹ לְעֹפֶר הָאַיָּלִים· הִנֵּה זֶה עוֹמֵד אַחַר כָּתְלֵנוּ·

מַשְׁגִּיחַ מִן הַחַלֹּנוֹת מֵצִיץ מִן הַחֲרַכִּים:

ברוך : As we look upon the moon, we remember God Who formed and shaped it, Who, as its Owner, makes the moon serve His purposes in nature and among mankind, and Who created it solely for this form, for this shape and for this service. We remember Him now so that we may render Him homage as our Creator and Master, the Being Who made and fashioned us, too. Allusion to this thought is made by the arrangement of the words בוראך, קונך, עושך, יוצרך in such succession that their initials form the name of יעקב, implying that the Creator and Leader of nature and mankind had given to our forefather Yaakob a place in the history of nations comparable to that of the moon upon the horizon.

כשם : At the same time we gain the confidence that even as our efforts to touch the moon by attempting to raise our bodies from the earth will always be in vain, so, too, no foe will be able to reach us to disturb the orbit and course of our life's duty if only we ourselves, like the moon, will remain in unswerving constancy upon the path assigned us by our Maker.

תפול : (Exod. 15:16) Even as our fathers marched through the sea and journeyed through the wilderness at God's command, and God spread the Shield of His dread about them, so, too, His rule and guidance will become evident and will protect us even now in our own wanderings through the surging swells and the desolate wastelands of the history of the nations.

דוד : According to Rosh Hashanah 25a this was the code message by which Rabbi Yehudah Ha-nasi had asked Rabbi Chiya to notify him that he had fulfilled the Kiddush Hachodesh with which he had been charged. For

Blessed be He Who fashioned you; blessed be He Who made you; blessed be your Owner; blessed be your Creator.

Even as I raise myself up to you but cannot touch you, so may my foes be unable to touch me with evil intent.

May fear and dread overtake them; since Your arm is mighty may they be stricken dumb as stone.

David, the King of Yisrael, lives and remains forever.

Peace be unto you; unto you be peace.

May there be a good sign and good fortune for us and for all of Yisrael.

The voice of my beloved! Behold, he comes, leaping over mountains, bounding over the hills. My beloved is like a hart or a young deer. Behold, He stands behind our wall; He sees through the windows; He looks through the lattice.

In the school of Rabbi Yishmael it was taught: Had Yisrael no other privilege but to appear once a month before the countenance of their Father in Heaven to do Him homage, it would be sufficient for them. Therefore Abbaya said that it had to be recited standing.

---

of David it was said כירח יכון עולם ועד בשחק נאמן סלה (Ps. 89:38) that, even though the course of David's life, like the course of the moon, would be a process of constant change and that at times, like the moon, he might even seem to vanish from sight, David even as the moon, which is eternal, nevertheless shall live and remain for all time. And even as the moon will always bear faithful testimony to God's almighty power in the skies above, so, David, too, will ever remain a constant, loyal witness for God's rule and man's goal and destiny upon the horizon of the nations.

סמן טוב, שלום : The confidence with which we await the Divinely-promised renewal and rebirth of our own prosperity, a trust that is reawakened within our hearts each month as our eyes behold the light of the New Moon, also makes us aware that all of our brethren have the same hopes and aspirations that we ourselves cherish, and impels us to include all of our fellow humans in the future covenant of peace.

קול דודי : (Cant. 2:8,9). The vindication of our confidence in the eventual fulfillment of God's promise is not a thing of the far-away future. However many the mountains and hills of time that may yet stand between our present, and that distant future, some sound from that far-off day has found its way to us even now and teaches us of God's nearness which only the heart and the spirit can perceive, but which is very much present in our homes, and of His kindly eye which looks upon and watches over even the most quiet and modest aspects of our lives.

תָּנָא דְּבֵי רַבִּי יִשְׁמָעֵאל: אִלְמָלֵא לֹא זָכוּ יִשְׂרָאֵל אֶלָּא לְהַקְבִּיל פְּנֵי אֲבִיהֶם
שֶׁבַּשָּׁמַיִם פַּעַם אַחַת בַּחֹדֶשׁ דַּיָּם: אָמַר אַבַּיֵי הִלְכָּךְ צָרֵךְ לְמֵימְרָא מְעֻמָּד:

מִי זֹאת עֹלָה מִן הַמִּדְבָּר מִתְרַפֶּקֶת עַל דּוֹדָהּ:

וִיהִי רָצוֹן מִלְּפָנֶיךָ יְיָ אֱלֹהַי וֵאלֹהֵי אֲבוֹתַי לְמַלֹּאות פְּגִימַת
הַלְּבָנָה. וְלֹא יִהְיֶה שׁוּם מִעוּט. וִיהִי אוֹר הַלְּבָנָה כְּאוֹר הַחַמָּה.
וּכְאוֹר שִׁבְעַת יְמֵי בְרֵאשִׁית: כְּמוֹ שֶׁהָיְתָה קֹדֶם מִעוּטָהּ. שֶׁנֶּאֱמַר
אֶת־שְׁנֵי הַמְּאֹרוֹת הַגְּדֹלִים. וְיִתְקַיֵּם מִקְרָא שֶׁכָּתוּב וּבִקְשׁוּ אֶת־
יְיָ אֱלֹהֵיהֶם וְאֵת דָּוִד מַלְכָּם אָמֵן:

שִׁיר לַמַּעֲלוֹת אֶשָּׂא עֵינַי אֶל־הֶהָרִים מֵאַיִן יָבֹא עֶזְרִי: עֶזְרִי מֵעִם
יְהֹוָה עֹשֵׂה שָׁמַיִם וָאָרֶץ: אַל־יִתֵּן לַמּוֹט רַגְלֶךָ אַל־יָנוּם שֹׁמְרֶךָ:
הִנֵּה לֹא־יָנוּם וְלֹא יִישָׁן שׁוֹמֵר יִשְׂרָאֵל: יְהֹוָה שֹׁמְרֶךָ יְהֹוָה צִלְּךָ
עַל־יַד יְמִינֶךָ: יוֹמָם הַשֶּׁמֶשׁ לֹא־יַכֶּכָּה וְיָרֵחַ בַּלָּיְלָה: יְהֹוָה
יִשְׁמָרְךָ מִכָּל־רָע יִשְׁמֹר אֶת־נַפְשֶׁךָ: יְהֹוָה יִשְׁמָר־צֵאתְךָ וּבוֹאֶךָ
מֵעַתָּה וְעַד־עוֹלָם:

הַלְלוּיָהּ. הַלְלוּ־אֵל בְּקָדְשׁוֹ הַלְלוּהוּ בִּרְקִיעַ עֻזּוֹ: הַלְלוּהוּ
בִגְבוּרֹתָיו הַלְלוּהוּ כְּרֹב גֻּדְלוֹ: הַלְלוּהוּ בְּתֵקַע שׁוֹפָר הַלְלוּהוּ
בְּנֵבֶל וְכִנּוֹר: הַלְלוּהוּ בְּתֹף וּמָחוֹל הַלְלוּהוּ בְּמִנִּים וְעֻגָב: הַלְלוּהוּ
בְצִלְצְלֵי־שָׁמַע הַלְלוּהוּ בְּצִלְצְלֵי תְרוּעָה: כֹּל הַנְּשָׁמָה תְּהַלֵּל
יָהּ הַלְלוּיָהּ: וְנוֹהֲגִים לֹאמַר מִזְמוֹר ס״ז, לַמְנַצֵּחַ בִּנְגִינֹת וְכוּ׳.

שיר היחוד ליום השבת

בָּרוֹב הַקְּהִלּוֹת וַאֲפִילוּ בְּאוֹתָן בְּאוֹתָן שֶׁאֵין נוֹהֲגִין לֵאמַר **שִׁיר הַיִּחוּד** כָּל יְמוֹת הַחֹל, מ״מ
בְּשַׁבָּת נוֹהֲגִין לֵאמַר **שִׁיר הַיִּחוּד** לַשַּׁבָּת וְלֹאחַר אָנְעִים זְמִירוֹת.

אָז בַּיּוֹם הַשְּׁבִיעִי נַחְתָּ. יוֹם הַשַּׁבָּת עַל כֵּן בֵּרַכְתָּ:

וְעַל כָּל פֹּעַל תְּהִלָּה עֲרוּכָה. חֲסָדֶיךָ בְּכָל עֵת וְיִבְרְכוּכָה:

בָּרוּךְ יְיָ יוֹצֵר כֻּלָּם · אֱלֹהִים חַיִּים וּמֶלֶךְ עוֹלָם :

כִּי מֵעוֹלָם עַל עֲבָדֶיךָ · רַב רַחֲמֶיךָ וַחֲסָדֶיךָ :

וּבְמִצְרַיִם הַחִלּוֹתָ · לְהוֹדִיעַ כִּי מְאֹד נַעֲלֵיתָ ·

עַל כָּל אֱלֹהִים · בַּעֲשׂוֹת כָּהֶם שְׁפָטִים גְּדוֹלִים וּבֵאלֹהֵיהֶם :

בְּבִקְעֲךָ יָם סוּף עַמְּךָ רָאוּ · הַיָּד הַגְּדוֹלָה · וַיִּירָאוּ ·

נִבְהֲגָתָ עַמְּךָ לַעֲשׂוֹת לָךְ · שֵׁם תִּפְאֶרֶת לְהֵרָאוֹת גָּדְלָךְ :

וְדִבַּרְתָּ עִמָּם מִן הַשָּׁמַיִם · וְגַם הֶעָבִים נָטְפוּ מָיִם :

יָדַעְתָּ לֶכְתָּם הַמִּדְבָּר · בְּאֶרֶץ צִיָּה אִישׁ לֹא עָבָר :

חִּתָּה לְעָמְךָ דָּגָן שָׁמָיִם · וְבֶעָפָר שְׂאֵר וּמְצוּר מָיִם :

תְּגָרֵשׁ גּוֹיִם רַבִּים עֲמָמִים · יִירְשׁוּ אַרְצָם וַעֲמַל לְאֻמִּים :

בַּעֲבוּר יִשְׁמְרוּ חֻקִּים וְהוֹרוֹת · אִמְרוֹת יְיָ אֲמָרוֹת טְהוֹרוֹת :

וַיִּתְעַדְּנוּ בְּמִרְעֶה שָׁמֵן · וּמֵחַלְמִישׁ צוּר פַּלְגֵי שָׁמֶן :

בְּנוֹחָם בָּנוּ עִיר קָדְשֶׁךָ · וַיְפָאֲרוּ בֵּית מִקְדָּשֶׁךָ :

וַתֹּאמֶר פֹּה אֵשֵׁב לְאֹרֶךְ יָמִים · צֵידָהּ בָּרֵךְ אַבָּרֵךְ :

כִּי שָׁם יִזְבְּחוּ זִבְחֵי צֶדֶק · אַף כֹּהֲנֶיךָ יִלְבְּשׁוּ צֶדֶק :

וּבֵית הַלֵּוִי נְעִימוֹת יְזַמֵּרוּ · לָךְ יִתְרוֹעֲעוּ אַף יָשִׁירוּ :

בֵּית יִשְׂרָאֵל וִירְאֵי יְיָ · יְכַבְּדוּ וְיוֹדוּ שִׁמְךָ יְיָ :

הֲטִיבוֹת מְאֹד לָרִאשׁוֹנִים · כֵּן תֵּיטִיב גַּם לָאַחֲרוֹנִים :

יְיָ תָּשִׁישׁ נָא עָלֵינוּ · כַּאֲשֶׁר שַׂשְׂתָּ עַל אֲבוֹתֵינוּ ·

אוֹתָנוּ לְהַרְבּוֹת וּלְהֵיטִיב · וְנוֹדֶה לְךָ לְעוֹלָם כִּי תֵיטִיב :

יְיָ תִּבְנֶה עִירְךָ מְהֵרָה · כִּי עָלֶיהָ שִׁמְךָ נִקְרָא :

וְקֶרֶן דָּוִד תַּצְמִיחַ בָּהּ · וְתִשְׁכֹּן לְעוֹלָם יְיָ בְּקִרְבָּהּ :

וְזִבְחֵי צֶדֶק שָׁמָּה נִזְבָּחָה · וְכִימֵי קֶדֶם תֶּעֱרַב מִנְחָה :

וּבָרֵךְ עַמְּךָ בְּאוֹר פָּנֶיךָ · כִּי חֲפֵצִים לַעֲשׂוֹת רְצוֹנֶךָ :

וּבִרְצוֹנְךָ תַּעֲשֶׂה חֶפְצֵנוּ · הַבֶּט־נָא עַמְּךָ כֻּלָּנוּ :

בְּחַרְתָּנוּ הֱיוֹת לְךָ לְעַם סְגֻלָּה · עַל עַמְּךָ בִרְכָתְךָ סֶּלָה :

וְתָמִיד נְסַפֵּר תְּהִלָּתֶךָ · וּנְהַלֵּל לְשֵׁם תִּפְאַרְתֶּךָ :

וּמִבִּרְכָתְךָ עַמְּךָ יְבֹרָךְ · כִּי אֵת כָּל אֲשֶׁר תְּבָרֵךְ מְבֹרָךְ :

אֲנִי בְעֶדִי אֲחַלֶּה בּוֹרְאִי · וַאֲבָרְכֵהוּ כָּל יְמֵי צְבָאִי :

יְהִי שֵׁם יְיָ מְבֹרָךְ לְעוֹלָם · מִן הָעוֹלָם וְעַד הָעוֹלָם :

כַּכָּתוּב בָּרוּךְ יְיָ אֱלֹהֵי יִשְׂרָאֵל מִן הָעוֹלָם וְעַד הָעוֹלָם · וַיֹּאמְרוּ כָל הָעָם אָמֵן
וְהַלֵּל לַיְיָ: עָנָה דָנִיֵּאל וְאָמַר לֶהֱוֵא שְׁמֵהּ דִּי אֱלָהָא מְבָרַךְ מִן עָלְמָא וְעַד עָלְמָא
דִּי חָכְמְתָא וּגְבוּרְתָּא דִּי לֵהּ הִיא : וְנֶאֱמַר וַיֹּאמְרוּ הַלְוִיִּם יֵשׁוּעַ וְקַדְמִיאֵל בָּנִי חֲשַׁבְנְיָה
שֵׁרֵבְיָה הוֹדִיָּה שְׁבַנְיָה פְּתַחְיָה קוּמוּ בָּרֲכוּ אֶת יְיָ אֱלֹהֵיכֶם מִן הָעוֹלָם עַד הָעוֹלָם
וִיבָרְכוּ שֵׁם כְּבוֹדֶךָ וּמְרוֹמַם עַל כָּל בְּרָכָה וּתְהִלָּה : וְנֶאֱמַר בָּרוּךְ יְיָ אֱלֹהֵי יִשְׂרָאֵל
מִן הָעוֹלָם וְעַד הָעוֹלָם וְאָמַר כָּל הָעָם אָמֵן הַלְלוּיָהּ : וְנֶאֱמַר וַיְבָרֶךְ דָּוִיד אֶת יְיָ לְעֵינֵי
כָּל הַקָּהָל וַיֹּאמֶר דָּוִיד · בָּרוּךְ אַתָּה יְיָ אֱלֹהֵי יִשְׂרָאֵל אָבִינוּ מֵעוֹלָם וְעַד עוֹלָם :

שיר הכבוד

כשפותחין ארון הקדש לאנעים זמירות יש לומר ל' פסוקים אלו.

שְׂאוּ שְׁעָרִים רָאשֵׁיכֶם וְהִנָּשְׂאוּ פִּתְחֵי עוֹלָם וְיָבוֹא מֶלֶךְ הַכָּבוֹד :
מִי זֶה מֶלֶךְ הַכָּבוֹד יְיָ עִזּוּז וְגִבּוֹר יְיָ גִּבּוֹר מִלְחָמָה :
שְׂאוּ שְׁעָרִים רָאשֵׁיכֶם וּשְׂאוּ פִּתְחֵי עוֹלָם וְיָבֹא מֶלֶךְ הַכָּבוֹד :
מִי הוּא זֶה מֶלֶךְ הַכָּבוֹד יְיָ צְבָאוֹת הוּא מֶלֶךְ הַכָּבוֹד סֶלָה :

אַנְעִים זְמִירוֹת וְשִׁירִים אֶאֱרוֹג · כִּי אֵלֶיךָ נַפְשִׁי תַעֲרוֹג :

נַפְשִׁי חִמְּדָה בְּצֵל יָדֶךָ לָדַעַת כָּל רָז סוֹדֶךָ :

מִדֵּי דַבְּרִי בִּכְבוֹדֶךָ הוֹמֶה לִבִּי אֶל דּוֹדֶיךָ :

עַל כֵּן אֲדַבֵּר בְּךָ נִכְבָּדוֹת · וְשִׁמְךָ אֲכַבֵּד בְּשִׁירֵי יְדִידוֹת :

יכ"ס א"ב.

אֲסַפְּרָה כְבוֹדְךָ וְלֹא רְאִיתִיךָ · אֲדַמְּךָ אֲכַנְּךָ וְלֹא יְדַעְתִּיךָ :

בְּיַד נְבִיאֶיךָ בְּסוֹד עֲבָדֶיךָ · דִּמִּיתָ הֲדַר כְּבוֹד הוֹדֶךָ :

גְּדֻלָּתְךָ וּגְבוּרָתֶךָ · כִּנּוּ לְתֹקֶף פְּעֻלָּתֶךָ :

דִּמּוּ אוֹתְךָ וְלֹא כְפִי יֶשְׁךָ · וַיְשַׁוּוּךָ לְפִי מַעֲשֶׂיךָ :

הַמְשִׁילְךָ בְּרוֹב חֶזְיוֹנוֹת · הִנְּךָ אֶחָד בְּכָל דִּמְיוֹנוֹת:

יֶחֱזוּ בְךָ זִקְנָה וּבַחֲרוּת · וּשְׂעַר רֹאשְׁךָ בְּשֵׂיבָה וְשַׁחֲרוּת:

זִקְנָה בְּיוֹם דִּין וּבַחֲרוּת בְּיוֹם קְרָב · כְּאִישׁ מִלְחָמוֹת יָדָיו לוֹ רָב:

חָבַשׁ כּוֹבַע יְשׁוּעָה בְּרֹאשׁוֹ · הוֹשִׁיעָה לּוֹ יְמִינוֹ וּזְרוֹעַ קָדְשׁוֹ:

טַלְלֵי אוֹרוֹת רֹאשׁוֹ נִמְלָא · וּקְוֻצּוֹתָיו רְסִיסֵי לָיְלָה:

יִתְפָּאֵר בִּי כִּי חָפֵץ בִּי · וְהוּא יִהְיֶה לִּי לַעֲטֶרֶת צְבִי:

כֶּתֶם טָהוֹר פָּז דְּמוּת רֹאשׁוֹ · וְחַק עַל מֵצַח כְּבוֹד שֵׁם קָדְשׁוֹ:

לְחֵן וּלְכָבוֹד צְבִי תִפְאָרָה · אֻמָּתוֹ לוֹ עִטְּרָה עֲטָרָה:

מַחְלְפוֹת רֹאשׁוֹ כְּבִימֵי בְחוּרוֹת · קְוֻצּוֹתָיו תַּלְתַּלִּים שְׁחוֹרוֹת:

נְוֵה הַצֶּדֶק צְבִי תִפְאַרְתּוֹ · יַעֲלֶה נָּא עַל רֹאשׁ שִׂמְחָתוֹ:

סְגֻלָּתוֹ תְּהִי בְיָדוֹ עֲטֶרֶת · וּצְנִיף מְלוּכָה צְבִי תִפְאֶרֶת:

עֲמוּסִים נְשָׂאָם עֲטֶרֶת עִנְּדָם · מֵאֲשֶׁר יָקְרוּ בְעֵינָיו כִּבְּדָם:

פְּאֵרוֹ עָלַי וּפְאֵרִי עָלָיו · וְקָרוֹב אֵלַי בְּקָרְאִי אֵלָיו:

צַח וְאָדוֹם לִלְבוּשׁוֹ אָדֹם · פּוּרָה בְּדָרְכוֹ בְּבוֹאוֹ מֵאֱדוֹם:

קֶשֶׁר תְּפִלִּין הֶרְאָה לֶעָנָיו · תְּמוּנַת יְיָ לְנֶגֶד עֵינָיו:

רוֹצֶה בְעַמּוֹ עֲנָוִים יְפָאֵר · יוֹשֵׁב תְּהִלּוֹת בָּם לְהִתְפָּאֵר:

רֹאשׁ דְּבָרְךָ אֱמֶת קוֹרֵא מֵרֹאשׁ · דּוֹר וָדוֹר עַם דּוֹרֶשְׁךָ דְּרוֹשׁ:

שִׁית הֲמוֹן שִׁירַי נָא עָלֶיךָ · וְרִנָּתִי תִּקְרַב אֵלֶיךָ:

תְּהִלָּתִי תְּהִי לְרֹאשְׁךָ עֲטֶרֶת · וּתְפִלָּתִי תִּכּוֹן קְטֹרֶת:

תִּיקַר שִׁירַת רָשׁ בְּעֵינֶיךָ · כַּשִּׁיר יוּשַׁר עַל קָרְבָּנֶיךָ:

בִּרְכָתִי תַעֲלֶה לְרֹאשׁ מַשְׁבִּר · מְחוֹלֵל וּמוֹלִיד צַדִּיק כַּבִּיר:

וּבְבִרְכָתִי תְנַעֲנַע לִי רֹאשׁ · וְאוֹתָהּ קַח לְךָ כִּבְשָׂמִים רֹאשׁ:

יֶעֱרַב נָא שִׂיחִי עָלֶיךָ · כִּי נַפְשִׁי תַעֲרוֹג אֵלֶיךָ:

לז״ן רְצֵה יְיָ אֱלֹהֵינוּ בְּעַמְּךָ יִשְׂרָאֵל וּבִתְפִלָּתָם · וְהָשֵׁב אֶת הָעֲבוֹדָה
לִדְבִיר בֵּיתֶךָ · וְאִשֵּׁי יִשְׂרָאֵל וּתְפִלָּתָם בְּאַהֲבָה תְקַבֵּל בְּרָצוֹן · וּתְהִי
לְרָצוֹן תָּמִיד עֲבוֹדַת יִשְׂרָאֵל עַמֶּךָ :

וְתֶעֱרַב עָלֶיךָ עֲתִירָתֵנוּ כְּעוֹלָה וּכְקָרְבָּן · אָנָּא רַחוּם בְּרַחֲמֶיךָ הָרַבִּים
הָשֵׁב שְׁכִינָתְךָ לְצִיּוֹן וְסֵדֶר הָעֲבוֹדָה לִירוּשָׁלָיִם · וְתֶחֱזֶינָה עֵינֵינוּ
בְּשׁוּבְךָ לְצִיּוֹן בְּרַחֲמִים · וְשָׁם נַעֲבָדְךָ בְּיִרְאָה כִּימֵי עוֹלָם וּכְשָׁנִים
קַדְמוֹנִיּוֹת : הש״ץ מסיים בָּרוּךְ אַתָּה יְיָ שֶׁאוֹתְךָ לְבַדְּךָ בְּיִרְאָה נַעֲבֹד :

מוֹדִים דרבנן

מוֹדִים אֲנַחְנוּ לָךְ שָׁאַתָּה הוּא
יְיָ אֱלֹהֵינוּ וֵאלֹהֵי אֲבוֹתֵינוּ לְעוֹלָם
וָעֶד · צוּר חַיֵּינוּ מָגֵן יִשְׁעֵנוּ אַתָּה
הוּא לְדוֹר וָדוֹר · נוֹדֶה לְּךָ וּנְסַפֵּר
תְּהִלָּתֶךָ עַל חַיֵּינוּ הַמְּסוּרִים
בְּיָדֶךָ וְעַל נִשְׁמוֹתֵינוּ הַפְּקוּדוֹת
לָךְ וְעַל נִסֶּיךָ שֶׁבְּכָל יוֹם עִמָּנוּ
וְעַל נִפְלְאוֹתֶיךָ וְטוֹבוֹתֶיךָ שֶׁבְּכָל עֵת. עֶרֶב וָבֹקֶר וְצָהֳרָיִם · הַטּוֹב כִּי
לֹא כָלוּ רַחֲמֶיךָ וְהַמְרַחֵם כִּי לֹא תַמּוּ חֲסָדֶיךָ מֵעוֹלָם קִוִּינוּ לָךְ :

מוֹדִים אֲנַחְנוּ לָךְ שָׁאַתָּה הוּא
יְיָ אֱלֹהֵינוּ וֵאלֹהֵי אֲבוֹתֵינוּ אֱלֹהֵי כָל בָּשָׂר יוֹצְרֵנוּ
יוֹצֵר בְּרֵאשִׁית בְּרָכוֹת וְהוֹדָאוֹת לְשִׁמְךָ
הַגָּדוֹל וְהַקָּדוֹשׁ עַל שֶׁהֶחֱיִיתָנוּ וְקִיַּמְתָּנוּ
כֵּן תְּחַיֵּנוּ וּתְקַיְּמֵנוּ וְתֶאֱסוֹף גָּלֻיּוֹתֵינוּ
לְחַצְרוֹת קָדְשֶׁיךָ לִשְׁמוֹר חֻקֶּיךָ וְלַעֲשׂוֹת
רְצוֹנֶךָ וּלְעָבְדְּךָ בְּלֵבָב שָׁלֵם עַל שֶׁאֲנַחְנוּ
מוֹדִים לָךְ · בָּרוּךְ אֵל הַהוֹדָאוֹת :

וְעַל כֻּלָּם יִתְבָּרַךְ וְיִתְרוֹמַם שִׁמְךָ מַלְכֵּנוּ תָּמִיד לְעוֹלָם וָעֶד :

נל״ה וי״כ וּכְתוֹב לְחַיִּים טוֹבִים כָּל־בְּנֵי בְרִיתֶךָ :

וְכֹל הַחַיִּים יוֹדוּךָ סֶּלָה וִיהַלְלוּ אֶת שִׁמְךָ בֶּאֱמֶת הָאֵל יְשׁוּעָתֵנוּ
וְעֶזְרָתֵנוּ סֶלָה · בָּרוּךְ אַתָּה יְיָ הַטּוֹב שִׁמְךָ וּלְךָ נָאֶה לְהוֹדוֹת :

אֱלֹהֵינוּ וֵאלֹהֵי אֲבוֹתֵינוּ בָּרְכֵנוּ בַבְּרָכָה הַמְשֻׁלֶּשֶׁת בַּתּוֹרָה
הַכְּתוּבָה עַל־יְדֵי מֹשֶׁה עַבְדֶּךָ הָאֲמוּרָה מִפִּי אַהֲרֹן וּבָנָיו
הש״ץ בקול כֹּהֲנִים עַם קְדוֹשֶׁךָ כָּאָמוּר :

והכהנים מברכין בָּרוּךְ אַתָּה יְיָ אֱלֹהֵינוּ מֶלֶךְ הָעוֹלָם אֲשֶׁר קִדְּשָׁנוּ
בִּקְדֻשָׁתוֹ שֶׁל אַהֲרֹן וְצִוָּנוּ לְבָרֵךְ אֶת עַמּוֹ יִשְׂרָאֵל בְּאַהֲבָה :

הש״ץ מקרא. הקהל עומד.

יְבָרֶכְךָ יְבָרֶכְךָ יְיָ מִצִּיּוֹן עֹשֵׂה שָׁמַיִם וָאָרֶץ :

יְיָ יְיָ אֲדֹנֵינוּ מָה אַדִּיר שִׁמְךָ בְּכָל הָאָרֶץ :

וְיִשְׁמְרֶֽךָ שְׁמָרֵֽנִי אֵל כִּי חָסִֽיתִי בָךְ: כשהכהנים מנגני' וישמרך אומרים זה:

While the כהנים *sing during the words* וִיחֻנֶּֽךָ *and* וְיִשְׁמְרֶךָ, *the following is said:*

רִבּֽוֹנוֹ שֶׁל עוֹלָם אֲנִי שֶׁלָּךְ וַחֲלוֹמוֹתַי שֶׁלָּךְ חֲלוֹם חָלָֽמְתִּי וְאֵינִי יוֹדֵֽעַ מַה הוּא וִיהִי רָצוֹן מִלְּפָנֶֽיךָ יְיָ אֱלֹהַי וֵאלֹהֵי אֲבוֹתַי שֶׁיִּהְיוּ כָּל חֲלוֹמוֹתַי עָלַי וְעַל כָּל יִשְׂרָאֵל לְטוֹבָה בֵּין שֶׁחָלַֽמְתִּי עַל עַצְמִי וּבֵין שֶׁחָלַֽמְתִּי עַל אֲחֵרִים וּבֵין שֶׁחָלְמוּ אֲחֵרִים עָלַי אִם טוֹבִים הֵם חַזְּקֵם וְאַמְּצֵם וְיִתְקַיְּמוּ בִי וּבָהֶם כַּחֲלוֹמוֹת יוֹסֵף הַצַּדִּיק. וְאִם צְרִיכִים רְפוּאָה רְפָאֵם כְּחִזְקִיָּֽהוּ מֶֽלֶךְ יְהוּדָה מֵחָלְיוֹ וּכְמִרְיָם הַנְּבִיאָה מִצָּרַעְתָּהּ וּכְנַעֲמָן מִצָּרַעְתּוֹ וּכְמֵי מָרָה עַל יְדֵי מֹשֶׁה רַבֵּֽינוּ וּכְמֵי יְרִיחוֹ עַל יְדֵי אֱלִישָׁע. וּכְשֵׁם שֶׁהָפַֽכְתָּ אֶת קִלְלַת בִּלְעָם הָרָשָׁע מִקְּלָלָה לִבְרָכָה כֵּן תַּהֲפֹךְ כָּל חֲלוֹמוֹתַי עָלַי וְעַל כָּל יִשְׂרָאֵל לְטוֹבָה וְתִשְׁמְרֵֽנִי וּתְחָנֵּֽנִי וְתִרְצֵֽנִי: אָמֵן.

יָאֵר   אֱלֹהִים יְחָנֵּֽנוּ וִיבָרְכֵֽנוּ יָאֵר פָּנָיו אִתָּֽנוּ סֶֽלָה:

יְיָ   יְיָ יְיָ אֵל רַחוּם וְחַנּוּן אֶֽרֶךְ אַפַּֽיִם וְרַב חֶֽסֶד וֶאֱמֶת:

פָּנָיו   פְּנֵה אֵלַי וְחָנֵּֽנִי כִּי יָחִיד וְעָנִי אָֽנִי:

אֵלֶֽיךָ   אֵלֶֽיךָ יְיָ נַפְשִׁי אֶשָּׂא:

וִיחֻנֶּֽךָ   הִנֵּה כְעֵינֵי עֲבָדִים אֶל יַד אֲדוֹנֵיהֶם כְּעֵינֵי שִׁפְחָה אֶל יַד גְּבִרְתָּהּ כֵּן עֵינֵֽינוּ אֶל יְיָ אֱלֹהֵֽינוּ עַד שֶׁיְּחָנֵּֽנוּ: רבש״ע. אָמֵן:

יִשָּׂא   יִשָּׂא בְרָכָה מֵאֵת יְיָ וּצְדָקָה מֵאֱלֹהֵי יִשְׁעוֹ: (וּמְצָא־חֵן וְשֵֽׂכֶל טוֹב בְּעֵינֵי אֱלֹהִים וְאָדָם:

יְיָ   יְיָ חָנֵּֽנוּ לְךָ קִוִּֽינוּ הֱיֵה זְרֹעָם לַבְּקָרִים אַף־יְשׁוּעָתֵֽנוּ בְּעֵת צָרָה:

פָּנָיו   אַל־תַּסְתֵּר פָּנֶֽיךָ מִמֶּֽנִּי בְּיוֹם צַר לִי הַטֵּה־אֵלַי אָזְנֶֽךָ בְּיוֹם אֶקְרָא מַהֵר עֲנֵֽנִי:

אֵלֶֽיךָ   אֵלֶֽיךָ נָשָֽׂאתִי אֶת־עֵינַי הַיֹּשְׁבִי בַּשָּׁמָֽיִם:

וְיָשֵׂם   וְשָׂמוּ אֶת־שְׁמִי עַל־בְּנֵי יִשְׂרָאֵל וַאֲנִי אֲבָרְכֵם:

לְךָ   לְךָ יְיָ הַגְּדֻלָּה וְהַגְּבוּרָה וְהַתִּפְאֶֽרֶת וְהַנֵּֽצַח וְהַהוֹד כִּי־כֹל בַּשָּׁמַֽיִם וּבָאָֽרֶץ לְךָ יְיָ הַמַּמְלָכָה וְהַמִּתְנַשֵּׂא לְכֹל לְרֹאשׁ:

שָׁלוֹם   שָׁלוֹם. שָׁלוֹם לָרָחוֹק וְלַקָּרוֹב אָמַר יְיָ וּרְפָאתִיו:

While the כהנים *sing during the word* שלום, *the following is said:*

יְהִי רָצוֹן מִלְּפָנֶֽיךָ יְיָ אֱלֹהַי וֵאלֹהֵי אֲבוֹתַי שֶׁתַּעֲשֶׂה לְמַֽעַן קְדֻשַּׁת חֲסָדֶֽיךָ וְגֹֽדֶל

רַחֲמֶיךָ הַפְּשׁוּטִים וּלְמַעַן טָהֳרַת שִׁמְךָ הַגָּדוֹל הַגִּבּוֹר וְהַנּוֹרָא בֶּן־עֶשְׂרִים וּשְׁתַּיִם

אוֹתִיּוֹת הַיּוֹצֵא מִפְּסוּקִים שֶׁל־בִּרְכַּת כֹּהֲנִים הָאֲמוּרָה מִפִּי אַהֲרֹן וּבָנָיו עַם קָדְשֶׁךָ

שֶׁתִּהְיֶה קְרוֹב לִי בְּקָרְאִי לָךְ וְתִשְׁמַע תְּפִלָּתִי וְאַנְקָתִי תָּמִיד כְּשֵׁם שֶׁשָּׁמַעְתָּ אֶנְקַת

יַעֲקֹב תְּמִימֶךָ הַנִּקְרָא אִישׁ תָּם. וְתִתֶּן־לִי וּלְכָל־נַפְשׁוֹת בֵּיתִי מְזוֹנוֹתֵינוּ וּפַרְנָסָתֵנוּ

בְּרֶוַח וְלֹא בְצִמְצוּם בְּהֶתֵּר וְלֹא בְאִסוּר בְּנַחַת וְלֹא בְצַעַר מִתַּחַת יָדְךָ הָרְחָבָה

כְּשֵׁם שֶׁנָּתַתָּ פַּת לֶחֶם לֶאֱכֹל וּבֶגֶד לִלְבּוֹשׁ לְיַעֲקֹב אָבִינוּ הַנִּקְרָא אִישׁ תָּם ·

וְתִתְּנֵנִי לְאַהֲבָה וּלְחֵן וּלְחֶסֶד בְּעֵינֶיךָ וּבְעֵינֵי כָל־רוֹאֵינוּ · וְיִהְיוּ דְבָרַי נִשְׁמָעִים

לַעֲבוֹדָתֶךָ · כְּשֵׁם שֶׁנָּתַתָּ אֶת־יוֹסֵף צַדִּיקֶךָ בְּשָׁעָה שֶׁהִלְבִּישׁוֹ אָבִיו כְּתֹנֶת פַּסִּים

לְחֵן וּלְחֶסֶד וּלְרַחֲמִים בְּעֵינֶיךָ וּבְעֵינֵי כָל־רוֹאָיו · וְתַעֲשֶׂה עִמִּי נִפְלָאוֹת וְנִסִּים

וּלְטוֹבָה אוֹת, וְתַצְלִיחֵנִי בִּדְרָכַי, וְתֵן בְּלִבִּי בִּינָה לְהָבִין וּלְהַשְׂכִּיל וּלְקַיֵּם אֶת

כָּל־דִּבְרֵי תַלְמוּד תּוֹרָתֶךָ וְסוֹדוֹתֶיהָ · וְתַצִּילֵנִי מִשְּׁגִיאוֹת וּתְטַהֵר רַעְיוֹנַי וְלִבִּי

לַעֲבוֹדָתֶךָ · וְתַאֲרִיךְ יָמַי   (וִימֵי אִשְׁתִּי, וּבָנַי, וּבְנוֹתַי)   (וִימֵי אָבִי וְאִמִּי)

בְּטוֹב וּבַנְעִימוֹת בְּרֹב עֹז וְשָׁלוֹם ·   אָמֵן סֶלָה:

After the כהנים *have completed the blessing, the congregation says* אמן *and then the following:*

אַדִּיר בַּמָּרוֹם שׁוֹכֵן בִּגְבוּרָה · אַתָּה שָׁלוֹם וְשִׁמְךָ שָׁלוֹם · יְהִי רָצוֹן

שֶׁתָּשִׂים עָלֵינוּ וְעַל עַמְּךָ בֵּית יִשְׂרָאֵל חַיִּים וּבְרָכָה לְמִשְׁמֶרֶת שָׁלוֹם:

וְהַכֹּהֲנִים מַחֲזִירִים פְּנֵיהֶם כְּלַפֵּי הַהֵיכָל וְאוֹמְרִים:

רִבּוֹן הָעוֹלָם, עָשִׂינוּ מַה שֶּׁגָּזַרְתָּ עָלֵינוּ אַף אַתָּה עֲשֵׂה עִמָּנוּ כְּאֲשֶׁר

הִבְטַחְתָּנוּ · הַשְׁקִיפָה מִמְּעוֹן קָדְשְׁךָ מִן הַשָּׁמַיִם וּבָרֵךְ אֶת־עַמְּךָ

אֶת־יִשְׂרָאֵל וְאֵת הָאֲדָמָה אֲשֶׁר נָתַתָּה לָנוּ כַּאֲשֶׁר נִשְׁבַּעְתָּ

לַאֲבוֹתֵינוּ אֶרֶץ זָבַת חָלָב וּדְבָשׁ : חזן שִׂים שָׁלוֹם וכו'.

סדר ספירת העומר

לְשֵׁם יְחוּד קוּדְשָׁא בְּרִיךְ הוּא וּשְׁכִינְתֵּיהּ בִּדְחִילוּ וּרְחִימוּ לְיַחֵד שֵׁם י"ה בו"ה
בְּיִחוּדָא שְׁלִים בְּשֵׁם כָּל יִשְׂרָאֵל: הִנְנִי מְקַיֵּם מִצְוַת עֲשֵׂה שֶׁל סְפִירַת הָעוֹמֶר
כְּמוֹ שֶׁכָּתוּב בַּתּוֹרָה, וּסְפַרְתֶּם לָכֶם מִמָּחֳרַת הַשַּׁבָּת וכו' תִּסְפְּרוּ חֲמִשִּׁים יוֹם.

בָּרוּךְ אַתָּה יְיָ, אֱלֹהֵינוּ מֶלֶךְ הָעוֹלָם, אֲשֶׁר

קִדְּשָׁנוּ בְּמִצְוֹתָיו וְצִוָּנוּ עַל־סְפִירַת הָעוֹמֶר:

בליל ג' של פסח **הַיּוֹם יוֹם אֶחָד לָעֹמֶר:**

הָרַחֲמָן יַחֲזִיר עֲבוֹדַת בֵּית הַמִּקְדָּשׁ לִמְקוֹמָהּ:

יְהִי רָצוֹן לְפָנֶיךָ יְיָ אֱלֹהֵינוּ וֵאלֹהֵי אֲבוֹתֵינוּ שֶׁיִּבָּנֶה בֵּית
הַמִּקְדָּשׁ בִּמְהֵרָה בְיָמֵינוּ וְתֵן חֶלְקֵנוּ בְּתוֹרָתֶךָ: וְשָׁם
נַעֲבָדְךָ בְּיִרְאָה כִּימֵי עוֹלָם וּכְשָׁנִים קַדְמֹנִיּוֹת:

לַמְנַצֵּחַ בִּנְגִינֹת מִזְמוֹר שִׁיר: אֱלֹהִים יְחָנֵּנוּ יכו'. אָנָּא בכח וכו'.

בליל י"ו ניסן: הַיּוֹם שְׁנֵי יָמִים לָעֹמֶר:

בליל י"ח ניסן: הַיּוֹם שְׁלֹשָׁה יָמִים לָעֹמֶר:

בליל י"ט ניסן: הַיּוֹם אַרְבָּעָה יָמִים לָעֹמֶר:

בליל כ' ניסן: הַיּוֹם חֲמִשָּׁה יָמִים לָעֹמֶר:

בליל כ"א ניסן: הַיּוֹם שִׁשָּׁה יָמִים לָעֹמֶר:

וּבְכֵן בְּאֹפֶן הַלֵּילוֹת יִסְפֹּר יֵשׁ יוֹתֵר עַד ל' סִיוָן שֶׁנִּשְׁלְמוּ ז' שָׁבוּעוֹת.

הַיּוֹם שִׁבְעָה יָמִים שֶׁהֵם שָׁבוּעַ אֶחָד לָעֹמֶר:

הַיּוֹם שְׁמוֹנָה יָמִים שֶׁהֵם שָׁבוּעַ אֶחָד וְיוֹם אֶחָד לָעֹמֶר:

הַיּוֹם תִּשְׁעָה יָמִים שֶׁהֵם שָׁבוּעַ אֶחָד וּשְׁנֵי יָמִים לָעֹמֶר:

הַיּוֹם עֲשָׂרָה יָמִים שֶׁהֵם שָׁבוּעַ אֶחָד וּשְׁלֹשָׁה יָמִים לָעֹמֶר:

הַיּוֹם אַחַד עָשָׂר יוֹם שֶׁהֵם שָׁבוּעַ אֶחָד וְאַרְבָּעָה יָמִים לָעֹמֶר:

הַיּוֹם שְׁנֵים עָשָׂר יוֹם שֶׁהֵם שָׁבוּעַ אֶחָד וַחֲמִשָּׁה יָמִים לָעֹמֶר:

הַיּוֹם שְׁלֹשָׁה עָשָׂר יוֹם שֶׁהֵם שָׁבוּעַ אֶחָד וְשִׁשָּׁה יָמִים לָעֹמֶר:

הַיּוֹם אַרְבָּעָה עָשָׂר יוֹם שֶׁהֵם שְׁנֵי שָׁבוּעוֹת לָעֹמֶר:

הַיּוֹם חֲמִשָּׁה עָשָׂר יוֹם שֶׁהֵם שְׁנֵי שָׁבוּעוֹת וְיוֹם אֶחָד לָעֹמֶר:

הַיּוֹם שִׁשָּׁה עָשָׂר יוֹם שֶׁהֵם שְׁנֵי שָׁבוּעוֹת וּשְׁנֵי יָמִים לָעֹמֶר:

הַיּוֹם שִׁבְעָה עָשָׂר יוֹם שֶׁהֵם שְׁנֵי שָׁבוּעוֹת וּשְׁלֹשָׁה יָמִים לָעֹמֶר:

הַיּוֹם שְׁמֹנָה עָשָׂר יוֹם שֶׁהֵם שְׁנֵי שָׁבוּעוֹת וְאַרְבָּעָה יָמִים לָעֹמֶר:

הַיּוֹם תִּשְׁעָה עָשָׂר יוֹם שֶׁהֵם שְׁנֵי שָׁבוּעוֹת וַחֲמִשָּׁה יָמִים לָעֹמֶר:

הַיּוֹם עֶשְׂרִים יוֹם שֶׁהֵם שְׁנֵי שָׁבוּעוֹת וְשִׁשָּׁה יָמִים לָעֹמֶר:

הַיּוֹם אֶחָד וְעֶשְׂרִים יוֹם שֶׁהֵם שְׁלֹשָׁה שָׁבוּעוֹת לָעֹמֶר:

הַיּוֹם שְׁנַיִם וְעֶשְׂרִים יוֹם שֶׁהֵם שְׁלֹשָׁה שָׁבוּעוֹת וְיוֹם אֶחָד לָעֹמֶר:

הַיּוֹם שְׁלֹשָׁה וְעֶשְׂרִים יוֹם שֶׁהֵם שְׁלֹשָׁה שָׁבוּעוֹת וּשְׁנֵי יָמִים לָעֹמֶר:

הַיּוֹם אַרְבָּעָה וְעֶשְׂרִים יוֹם שֶׁהֵם שְׁלֹשָׁה שָׁבוּעוֹת וּשְׁלֹשָׁה יָמִים לָעֹמֶר:

הַיּוֹם חֲמִשָּׁה וְעֶשְׂרִים יוֹם שֶׁהֵם שְׁלֹשָׁה שָׁבוּעוֹת וְאַרְבָּעָה יָמִים לָעֹמֶר:

הַיּוֹם שִׁשָּׁה וְעֶשְׂרִים יוֹם שֶׁהֵם שְׁלֹשָׁה שָׁבוּעוֹת וַחֲמִשָּׁה יָמִים לָעֹמֶר:

הַיּוֹם שִׁבְעָה וְעֶשְׂרִים יוֹם שֶׁהֵם שְׁלֹשָׁה שָׁבוּעוֹת וְשִׁשָּׁה יָמִים לָעֹמֶר:

הַיּוֹם שְׁמֹנָה וְעֶשְׂרִים יוֹם שֶׁהֵם אַרְבָּעָה שָׁבוּעוֹת לָעֹמֶר:

הַיּוֹם תִּשְׁעָה וְעֶשְׂרִים יוֹם שֶׁהֵם אַרְבָּעָה שָׁבוּעוֹת וְיוֹם אֶחָד לָעֹמֶר:

הַיּוֹם שְׁלֹשִׁים יוֹם שֶׁהֵם אַרְבָּעָה שָׁבוּעוֹת וּשְׁנֵי יָמִים לָעֹמֶר:

הַיּוֹם אֶחָד וּשְׁלֹשִׁים יוֹם שֶׁהֵם אַרְבָּעָה שָׁבוּעוֹת וּשְׁלֹשָׁה יָמִים לָעֹמֶר:

הַיּוֹם שְׁנַיִם וּשְׁלֹשִׁים יוֹם שֶׁהֵם אַרְבָּעָה שָׁבוּעוֹת וְאַרְבָּעָה יָמִים לָעֹמֶר:

הַיּוֹם שְׁלֹשָׁה וּשְׁלֹשִׁים יוֹם שֶׁהֵם אַרְבָּעָה שָׁבוּעוֹת וַחֲמִשָּׁה יָמִים לָעֹמֶר:

הַיּוֹם אַרְבָּעָה וּשְׁלֹשִׁים יוֹם שֶׁהֵם אַרְבָּעָה שָׁבוּעוֹת וְשִׁשָּׁה יָמִים לָעֹמֶר:

הַיּוֹם חֲמִשָּׁה וּשְׁלֹשִׁים יוֹם שֶׁהֵם חֲמִשָּׁה שָׁבוּעוֹת לָעֹמֶר:

הַיּוֹם שִׁשָּׁה וּשְׁלֹשִׁים יוֹם שֶׁהֵם חֲמִשָּׁה שָׁבוּעוֹת וְיוֹם אֶחָד לָעֹמֶר:

הַיּוֹם שִׁבְעָה וּשְׁלֹשִׁים יוֹם שֶׁהֵם חֲמִשָּׁה שָׁבוּעוֹת וּשְׁנֵי יָמִים לָעֹמֶר:

הַיּוֹם שְׁמֹנָה וּשְׁלֹשִׁים יוֹם שֶׁהֵם חֲמִשָּׁה שָׁבוּעוֹת וּשְׁלֹשָׁה יָמִים לָעֹמֶר:

הַיּוֹם תִּשְׁעָה וּשְׁלֹשִׁים יוֹם שֶׁהֵם אַרְבָּעָה שָׁבוּעוֹת וְאַרְבָּעָה יָמִים לָעֹמֶר:

הַיּוֹם אַרְבָּעִים יוֹם שֶׁהֵם חֲמִשָּׁה שָׁבוּעוֹת וַחֲמִשָּׁה יָמִים לָעֹמֶר:

הַיּוֹם אֶחָד וְאַרְבָּעִים יוֹם שֶׁהֵם חֲמִשָּׁה שָׁבוּעוֹת וְשִׁשָּׁה יָמִים לָעֹמֶר:

הַיּוֹם שְׁנַיִם וְאַרְבָּעִים יוֹם שֶׁהֵם שִׁשָּׁה שָׁבוּעוֹת לָעֹמֶר:

הַיּוֹם שְׁלֹשָׁה וְאַרְבָּעִים יוֹם שֶׁהֵם שִׁשָּׁה שָׁבוּעוֹת וְיוֹם אֶחָד לָעֹמֶר:

הַיּוֹם אַרְבָּעָה וְאַרְבָּעִים יוֹם שֶׁהֵם שִׁשָּׁה שָׁבוּעוֹת וּשְׁנֵי יָמִים לָעֹמֶר:

הַיּוֹם חֲמִשָּׁה וְאַרְבָּעִים יוֹם שֶׁהֵם שִׁשָּׁה שָׁבוּעוֹת וּשְׁלֹשָׁה יָמִים לָעֹמֶר:

הַיּוֹם שִׁשָּׁה וְאַרְבָּעִים יוֹם שֶׁהֵם שִׁשָּׁה שָׁבוּעוֹת וְאַרְבָּעָה יָמִים לָעֹמֶר:

הַיּוֹם שִׁבְעָה וְאַרְבָּעִים יוֹם שֶׁהֵם שִׁשָּׁה שָׁבוּעוֹת וַחֲמִשָּׁה יָמִים לָעֹמֶר:

הַיּוֹם שְׁמֹנָה וְאַרְבָּעִים יוֹם שֶׁהֵם שִׁשָּׁה שָׁבוּעוֹת וְשִׁשָּׁה יָמִים לָעֹמֶר:

הַיּוֹם תִּשְׁעָה וְאַרְבָּעִים יוֹם שֶׁהֵם שִׁבְעָה שָׁבוּעוֹת לָעֹמֶר:

כשמביאין התינוק לביהכ"נ כל צריכין לקום מפניו, וגם נאה שעוסקים במצות הברית מייגין כל העם להיות בעמידה כמ"ש ויעמוד העם בברית. ונהגו אומרים כל הקהל בקול רם

בָּרוּךְ הַבָּא

אח"כ יקח המוהל את הנער מן המביא אותו ויאמר בשמחה.

אמר הקב"ה לאברהם אבינו התהלך לפני והיה המים:

הַנְנִי מוּכָן וּמְזוּמָן לְקַיֵּים מִצְוַת עֲשֵׂה שֶׁצִּוָנוּ הַבּוֹרֵא יִתְבָּרֵךְ לָמוּל.

וכשהאב של את בנו יאמר שצונו למול את בני:

לְשֵׁם יְחוּד קוּדְשָׁא בְּרִיךְ הוּא וּשְׁכִינְתֵּיהּ בִּדְחִילוּ וּרְחִימוּ:

ויטס את התינוק על הכסא אשר הכין לאליהו ויאמר:

זֶה הַכִּסֵּא שֶׁל אֵלִיָּהוּ זָכוּר לַטּוֹב: לִישׁוּעָתְךָ קִוִּיתִי יְיָ:

שִׁבַּרְתִּי לִישׁוּעָתְךָ יְיָ. וּמִצְוֹתֶיךָ עָשִׂיתִי: אֵלִיָּהוּ מַלְאַךְ הַבְּרִית־

הִנֵּה שֶׁלְּךָ לְפָנֶיךָ: עֲמוֹד עַל יְמִינִי וְסָמְכֵנִי: שִׁבַּרְתִּי לִישׁוּעָתְךָ

יְיָ: שָׂשׂ אָנֹכִי עַל אִמְרָתֶךָ. כְּמוֹצֵא שָׁלָל רָב: שָׁלוֹם רָב לְאֹהֲבֵי

תוֹרָתֶךָ. וְאֵין לָמוֹ מִכְשׁוֹל: אַשְׁרֵי תִּבְחַר וּתְקָרֵב יִשְׁכֹּן חֲצֵרֶיךָ:

והקהל עונין נִשְׂבְּעָה בְּטוּב בֵּיתֶךָ קְדוֹשׁ הֵיכָלֶךָ:

ויקח המוהל את הנער מכסאו של אליהו ויניחו על ברכי
הסנדק ותופס עור הערלה בין חלצעותיו ומברך בקול רם.

בָּרוּךְ אַתָּה יְיָ, אֱלֹהֵינוּ מֶלֶךְ הָעוֹלָם, אֲשֶׁר קִדְּשָׁנוּ בְּמִצְוֹתָיו וְצִוָּנוּ עַל הַמִּילָה:

The father of the child says:

בָּרוּךְ אַתָּה יְיָ, אֱלֹהֵינוּ מֶלֶךְ הָעוֹלָם, אֲשֶׁר קִדְּשָׁנוּ בְּמִצְוֹתָיו וְצִוָּנוּ לְהַכְנִיסוֹ בִּבְרִיתוֹ שֶׁל־אַבְרָהָם אָבִינוּ:

Those present respond here:

כְּשֵׁם שֶׁנִּכְנַס לַבְּרִית. כֵּן יִכָּנֵס לַתּוֹרָה וּלְחֻפָּה וּלְמַעֲשִׂים טוֹבִים:

ואחר שנעשה החתוך כראוי יחזור לעשות הפריעה. והמליזה ונוטל את הכוס בידו ומברך
בורא פרי הגפן, ואשר קדש ידיד וכו'.

It is the duty of the father to redeem his wife's first-born son after he has reached the age of 30 days. The redemption ceremony takes place on the 31st day. If this days falls on שבת or יו״ט, the ceremony is postponed until the first ensuing weekday. If the father is a כהן or לוי, or if the mother is a כוהנת or לויה no redemption is required for their child. The ceremony proceeds as follows: the father places the redemption fee before the כהן. Then he presents his son to the כהן and says:

ישראל שנולד לו בן זכר והוא בכור לאמו, אע״פ שאינו בכור לאביו, חייב לפדותו אחר שעברו עליו שלשים יום, וביום שלשים ואחד יפדנו מיד. כהן ולוי פטור מפדיון בנו, וכן אם האם היא כהנת או לויה פטור מפדיון בנו. המנהג לעשות סעודה בפדיון, ואחר ברכת המוציא פודין. וזה סדר הפדיון. האב יקח כסף חמשה סלעים (הם י״ד אונקן למנהג אשכנז או ה' זילבעררובעל [רוסוכאנד] ויסים לפני הכהן, או יסים לפניו כל דבר השוה ה' סלעים, חוץ מקרקעות ושטרות ואם פדה בהם אינו פדוי. אחר זה יקח את בנו ויתן אותו לכהן ויאמר:

אִשְׁתִּי זֶה יָלְדָה לִי בֵן זָכָר זֶה פֶּטֶר רֶחֶם:

The כהן asks the father:

אֵיזֶה תִּרְצֶה יוֹתֵר, בִּנְךָ בְּכוֹרְךָ זֶה, אוֹ חֲמִשָּׁה סְלָעִים שֶׁנִּתְחַיַּבְתָּ בְּפִדְיוֹנוֹ?

The father takes the money and answers:

אֶת־בְּנִי בְכוֹרִי אֲנִי רוֹצֶה יוֹתֵר, וְהֵא לְךָ חֲמִשָּׁה סְלָעִים בְּפִדְיוֹנוֹ:

The father says the following Bracha:

בָּרוּךְ אַתָּה יְיָ, אֱלֹהֵינוּ מֶלֶךְ הָעוֹלָם, אֲשֶׁר קִדְּשָׁנוּ בְּמִצְוֹתָיו, וְצִוָּנוּ עַל־פִּדְיוֹן הַבֵּן:

בָּרוּךְ אַיְיָ, אֱלֹהֵינוּ מֶלֶךְ הָעוֹלָם, שֶׁהֶחֱיָנוּ וְקִיְּמָנוּ וְהִגִּיעָנוּ לַזְמַן הַזֶּה:

He gives the money to the כהן and takes his child back; the כהן says:

בִּנְךָ פָּדוּי · בִּנְךָ פָּדוּי · בִּנְךָ פָּדוּי:

The כהן blesses the child as follows:

יְשִׂמְךָ אֱלֹהִים כְּאֶפְרַיִם וְכִמְנַשֶּׁה: יְבָרֶכְךָ יְיָ וְיִשְׁמְרֶךָ: יָאֵר יְיָ פָּנָיו אֵלֶיךָ וִיחֻנֶּךָּ: יִשָּׂא יְיָ | פָּנָיו אֵלֶיךָ וְיָשֵׂם לְךָ שָׁלוֹם: יְיָ שֹׁמְרֶךָ יְיָ צִלְּךָ עַל־יַד יְמִינֶךָ: כִּי אֹרֶךְ יָמִים וּשְׁנוֹת חַיִּים וְשָׁלוֹם יוֹסִיפוּ לָךְ: יְיָ יִשְׁמָרְךָ מִכָּל־רָע יִשְׁמֹר אֶת־נַפְשֶׁךָ· אָמֵן. יתח״כ חיכלים ושותיס ושפחיס.

יִתְגַּדַּל וְיִתְקַדַּשׁ שְׁמֵהּ רַבָּא בְּעָלְמָא דִּי־בְרָא כִרְעוּתֵהּ וְיַמְלִיךְ
מַלְכוּתֵהּ בְּחַיֵּיכוֹן וּבְיוֹמֵיכוֹן וּבְחַיֵּי דְכָל־בֵּית יִשְׂרָאֵל בַּעֲגָלָא וּבִזְמַן
קָרִיב, וְאִמְרוּ אָמֵן ·

יְהֵא שְׁמֵהּ רַבָּא מְבָרַךְ לְעָלַם וּלְעָלְמֵי עָלְמַיָּא:

יִתְבָּרַךְ וְיִשְׁתַּבַּח וְיִתְפָּאַר וְיִתְרוֹמַם וְיִתְנַשֵּׂא וְיִתְהַדָּר וְיִתְעַלֶּה
וְיִתְהַלָּל שְׁמֵהּ דְּקֻדְשָׁא בְּרִיךְ הוּא לְעֵלָּא מִן־כָּל־בִּרְכָתָא וְשִׁירָתָא
תֻּשְׁבְּחָתָא וְנֶחֱמָתָא דַּאֲמִירָן בְּעָלְמָא, וְאִמְרוּ אָמֵן:

עַל יִשְׂרָאֵל וְעַל רַבָּנָן וְעַל תַּלְמִידֵיהוֹן וְעַל כָּל־תַּלְמִידֵי
תַלְמִידֵיהוֹן וְעַל כָּל־מָן דְּעָסְקִין בְּאוֹרַיְתָא דִּי בְּאַתְרָא הָדֵן וְדִי
בְכָל־אֲתַר וַאֲתַר יְהֵא לְהוֹן (ולכו) שְׁלָמָא רַבָּא חִנָּא וְחִסְדָּא
וְרַחֲמִין וְחַיִּין אֲרִיכִין וּמְזוֹנָא רְוִיחָא וּפֻרְקָנָא מִן־קֳדָם אֲבוּהוֹן דִּי
בִשְׁמַיָּא, וְאִמְרוּ אָמֵן:

יְהֵא שְׁלָמָא רַבָּא מִן־שְׁמַיָּא וְחַיִּים עָלֵינוּ וְעַל־כָּל־יִשְׂרָאֵל,
וְאִמְרוּ אָמֵן:

עֹשֶׂה שָׁלוֹם בִּמְרוֹמָיו הוּא יַעֲשֶׂה שָׁלוֹם עָלֵינוּ וְעַל־כָּל־יִשְׂרָאֵל,
וְאִמְרוּ אָמֵן:

The translation and commentary to the Kaddish *is on page 206.*

The translation and commentary to the Kaddish is on page 206.

על ישראל **על ישראל** The paragraph beginning with is inserted into the
Kaddish which is said after studying the [orally] transmitted Law recorded
in the *Mishnah* and of the teachings of the *Aggadah* based on these transmitted
laws. Here we pray for the peace and welfare of all the teachers and disciples
of the Law so that they may be enabled to dedicate themselves undisturbed to
the study and the dissemination of the Law and so that, in this manner, all
that which is good and upon which our own welfare as a people depends may
be nurtured and preserved in our midst. Therefore we pray for the welfare
of the people of Yisrael, and, for the sake of Yisrael, also for that of the
hanan.